Business Ethics

Case Studies and Selected Readings

SEVENTH EDITION

MARIANNE MOODY JENNINGS

Arizona State University

SOUTH-WESTERN
CENGAGE Learning

Australia • Brazil • Japan • Korea • Mexico • Singapore • Spain • United Kingdom • United States

SOUTH-WESTERN
CENGAGE Learning

Business Ethics: Case Studies and Selected Readings, Seventh Edition International Edition
Marianne M.Jennings

Vice President of Editorial, Business: Jack W. Calhoun

Editor-in-Chief: Rob Dewey

Acquisitions Editor: Vicky True-Baker

Senior Developmental Editor: Laura Bofinger Ansara

Editorial Assistant: Patrick Ian Clark

Marketing Manager: Laura-Aurora Stopa

Senior Content Project Manager: Colleen A. Farmer

Media Editor: Kristen Meere

Senior Frontlist Buyer, Manufacturing: Kevin Kluck

Senior Marketing Communications Manager: Sarah Greber

Production Service: MPS Limited, a Macmillan Company

Senior Art Director: Michelle Kunkler

Internal Designer: Juli Cook/Plan-It-Publishing, Inc.

Cover Designer: Tin Box Studios

Cover Image:
  color image: Shutterstock Images/ Junial Enterprises; b/w image: David Buffington/Getty Images

Library of Congress Control Number: 2010938756

International Edition:

ISBN-13: 978-0-538-47354-5

ISBN-10: 0-538-47354-1

Cengage Learning International Offices

Asia
www.cengageasia.com
tel: (65) 6410 1200

Australia/New Zealand
www.cengage.com.au
tel: (61) 3 9685 4111

Brazil
www.cengage.com.br
tel: (011) 3665 9900

India
www.cengage.co.in
tel: (91) 11 30484837/38

Latin America
www.cengage.com.mx
tel: +52 (55) 1500 6000

UK/Europe/Middle East/Africa
www.cengage.co.uk
tel: (44) 207 067 2500

Represented in Canada by Nelson Education, Ltd.
www.nelson.com
tel: (416) 752 9100 / (800) 668 0671

Cengage Learning is a leading provider of customized learning solutions with office locations around the globe, including Singapore, the United Kingdom, Australia, Mexico, Brazil, and Japan. Locate your local office at: **www.cengage.com/global**

For product information: **www.cengage.com/international**
Visit your local office: **www.cengage.com/global**
Visit our corporate website: **www.cengage.com**

AVAILABILITY OF RESOURCES MAY DIFFER BY REGION. Check with your local Cengage Learning representative for details.

Printed in the United States of America
1 2 3 4 5 6 7 14 13 12 11

Brief Contents

Preface   xiii
Acknowledgments   xxviii

UNIT 1   **Ethical Theory, Philosophical Foundations, Our Reasoning Flaws, and Types of Ethical Dilemmas**   1

SECTION A   *Defining Ethics   3*
SECTION B   *Resolving Ethical Dilemmas   29*

UNIT 2   **Solving Ethical Dilemmas and Personal Introspection**   45

SECTION A   *Business and Ethics: How Do They Work Together?   47*
SECTION B   *What Gets in the Way of Ethical Decisions in Business?   59*
SECTION C   *Resolving Ethical Dilemmas in Business   71*

UNIT 3   **Business, Stakeholders, Social Responsibility, and Sustainability**   89

SECTION A   *Business and Society: The Tough Issues of Economics, Social Responsibility, and Business   91*
SECTION B   *Applying Social Responsibility and Stakeholder Theory   132*
SECTION C   *Social Responsibility and Sustainability   149*

UNIT 4   **Ethics and Company Culture**   157

SECTION A   *Temptation at Work for Individual Gain and That Credo   159*
SECTION B   *The Organizational Behavior Factors   164*
SECTION C   *The Structural Factors: Governance, Example, and Leadership   212*
SECTION D   *The Industry Practices and Legal Factors   257*
SECTION E   *The Fear-and-Silence Factors   279*

UNIT 5   **Ethics in International Business**   313

SECTION A   *Conflicts Between the Corporation's Ethics and Business Practices in Foreign Countries   315*
SECTION B   *Bribes, Grease Payments, and When in Rome . . .   340*

iii

UNIT 6   Ethics, Business Operations, and Rights   351

SECTION A   *Workplace Safety*   353
SECTION B   *Workplace Loyalty*   356
SECTION C   *Workplace Conflicts*   361
SECTION D   *Workplace Diversity and Atmosphere*   373
SECTION E   *Workplace Privacy and Personal Lives*   385
SECTION F   *Workplace Confrontation*   395
SECTION G   *Workplace and the Environment*   405

UNIT 7   Ethics and Products   423

SECTION A   *Advertising Content*   425
SECTION B   *Product Safety*   441
SECTION C   *Product Sales*   464
SECTION D   *Contracts*   478
SECTION E   *Products and Social Issues*   487

UNIT 8   Ethics and Competition   493

SECTION A   *Covenants Not to Compete*   495
SECTION B   *All's Fair, or Is It?*   505
SECTION C   *Intellectual Property and Ethics*   514

UNIT 9   Ethics and Government   523

SECTION A   *Government Employees*   525
SECTION B   *Government Contracts*   542
SECTION C   *Government Responsibilities*   551

UNIT 10   Ethics and Nonprofits   557

SECTION A   *Nonprofits and Fraud*   559
SECTION B   *Nonprofits and Management*   565

Alphabetical Index   571
Business Discipline Index   575
Product/Company/Individuals/Subject Index   582
Topic Index   603

Contents

Preface xiii
Acknowledgments xxviii

1

UNIT   Ethical Theory, Philosophical Foundations, Our Reasoning
Flaws, and Types of Ethical Dilemmas

SECTION A

Defining Ethics   3
Reading 1.1   You, Your Values, and a Credo   3
Reading 1.2   The Parable of the Sadhu   4
Reading 1.3   What Are Ethics? From Line-Cutting to Kant   10
Reading 1.4   The Types of Ethical Dilemmas: From Truth to Honesty to Conflicts   17
Reading 1.5   On Rationalizing and Labeling: The Things We Do That Make
                 Us Uncomfortable, but We Do Them Anyway   22
Reading 1.6   The Slippery Slope, the Blurred Lines, and How We Never Do Just
                 One Thing   26
Case 1.7   Hank Greenberg and AIG   27

SECTION B

Resolving Ethical Dilemmas   29
Reading 1.8   Some Simple Tests for Resolving Ethical Dilemmas   29
Reading 1.9   Some Steps for Analyzing Ethical Dilemmas   34
Case 1.10   The Little Teacher Who Could: Piper, Kansas, and Term Papers   34
Case 1.11   The Movie Ticket   37
Case 1.12   Puffing Your Résumé   37
Case 1.13   Dad, the Actuary, and the Stats Class   39
Reading 1.14   On Plagiarism   40
Case 1.15   Wi-Fi Piggybacking   41
Case 1.16   The Ethics Officer and First Class for TSA   41
Case 1.17   Speeding on the Job: Obeying the Rules: Why We Do and Don't   42
Case 1.18   The Pack of Gum   43

2

UNIT   Solving Ethical Dilemmas and Personal Introspection

SECTION A

Business and Ethics: How Do They Work Together?   47
Reading 2.1   What's Different about Business Ethics?   47
Reading 2.2   The Ethics of Responsibility   48
Reading 2.3   Is Business Bluffing Ethical?   49

SECTION B

What Gets in the Way of Ethical Decisions in Business?   59

Reading 2.4   How Leaders Lose Their Way: What Price Hubris?   59
Reading 2.5   Moral Relativism and the Either/or Conundrum   61
Reading 2.6   P=ƒ(x) The Probability of an Ethical Outcome Is a Function of the Amount
         of Money Involved: Pressure   62
Case 2.7   Martha Stewart: Not Such a Good Thing   63
Case 2.8   On Leaving to Spend More Time with Family   69

SECTION C

Resolving Ethical Dilemmas in Business   71

Reading 2.9   The Areas of Ethical Challenges in Business   71
Reading 2.10   A Structured Approach for Solving Ethical Dilemmas and Trying Out Your
         Ethical Skills on Some Business Cases   72
Case 2.11   What Was Up with Wall Street? The Goldman Standard and
         Shades of Gray   73
Case 2.12   What Happens in Boulder Stays in Boulder: Cell Phone Alibis   84
Case 2.13   Travel Expenses: A Chance for Extra Income   84
Case 2.14   Do Cheaters Prosper?   85
Case 2.15   The Rigged Election   86
Case 2.16   West Virginia University and the Governor's Daughter   86

3
UNIT   Business, Stakeholders, Social Responsibility, and Sustainability

SECTION A

Business and Society: The Tough Issues of Economics,
Social Responsibility, and Business   91

Reading 3.1   The Social Responsibility of Business Is to Increase Its Profits   91
Reading 3.2   A Stakeholder Theory of the Modern Corporation   96
Reading 3.3   Business with a Soul: A Reexamination of What Counts in
         Business Ethics   101
Reading 3.4   Appeasing Stakeholders with Public Relations   104
Reading 3.5   Michael Novak on Capitalism and the Corporation   105
Reading 3.6   Marjorie Kelly and the Divine Right of Capital   108
Reading 3.7   Schools of Thought on Social Responsibility   111
Case 3.8   Adelphia: Good Works via a Hand in the Till   113
Reading 3.9   The Regulatory Cycle, Social Responsibility, Business Strategy,
         and Equilibrium   117
Case 3.10   Fannie, Freddie, Wall Street, Main Street, and the Subprime Mortgage Market:
         Of Moral Hazards   121

SECTION B

Applying Social Responsibility and Stakeholder Theory   132

Case 3.11   Whole Foods, John Mackey, and Health Care Debates   132
Case 3.12   Ice-T, the *Body Count* Album, and Shareholder Uprisings   133
Case 3.13   Baseball and Steroids   138
Case 3.14   Michael Vick, Dogs, Rush Limbaugh, and the NFL   145
Case 3.15   Dayton-Hudson's Contributions to Planned Parenthood, and Target and the
         Bell Ringers   146

SECTION C

Social Responsibility and Sustainability 149

Reading 3.16 The New Environmentalism 149
Case 3.17 Herman Miller and Its Rain Forest Chairs 151
Case 3.18 The Death of the Great Disposable Diaper Debate 153

4 UNIT Ethics and Company Culture

SECTION A

Temptation at Work for Individual Gain and That Credo 159

Reading 4.1 The Moving Line 159
Reading 4.2 Not All Employees Are Equal When It Comes to Moral Development 160

SECTION B

The Organizational Behavior Factors 164

Reading 4.3 Why Corporations Can't Control Chicanery 164
Reading 4.4 The Effects of Compensation Systems: Incentives, Bonuses, Pay, and Ethics 172
Reading 4.5 The Subprime Saga: Bear Stearns, Lehman, Merrill, and CDOs 176
Case 4.6 HealthSouth: The Scrushy Way 183
Case 4.7 Jett and Kidder, Leeson and Barings, Kerviel and Société Générale: Compensation-Fueled Dishonesty 192
Case 4.8 Royal Dutch and the Reserves 199
Reading 4.9 Stock Options, Backdating, and Disclosure Options: What Happened Here? 200
Case 4.10 FINOVA and the Loan Write-Off 206

SECTION C

The Structural Factors: Governance, Example, and Leadership 212

Reading 4.11 A Primer on Sarbanes–Oxley 212
Case 4.12 Bank of America: The Merrill Takeover, the Disclosures, and the Board 216
Case 4.13 Dennis Kozlowski: Tyco and the $6,000 Shower Curtain 218
Case 4.14 Bausch & Lomb and Krispy Kreme: Channel Stuffing and Cannibalism 228
Case 4.15 Enron: The CFO, Conflicts, and Cooking the Books with Natural Gas and Electricity 233
Case 4.16 Arthur Andersen: A Fallen Giant 246
Reading 4.17 The New Shareholder: Taking Over to Change the Culture 253

SECTION D

The Industry Practices and Legal Factors 257

Reading 4.18 If It's Legal, It's Ethical; and Besides, Everyone Does It 257
Reading 4.19 A Primer on Accounting Issues and Ethics and Earnings Management 262
Case 4.20 The Ethics of Bankruptcy 272
Case 4.21 The Ethics of Walking Away 275

SECTION E

The Fear-and-Silence Factors 279

Reading 4.22 The Options for Whistle-Blowers 279
Case 4.23 Beech-Nut and the No-Apple-Juice Apple Juice 280
Case 4.24 NASA and the Space Shuttle Booster Rockets 285

Case 4.25   Westland/Hallmark Meat Packing Company and the Cattle Standers   288
Reading 4.26   Getting Information from Employees Who Know to Those Who Can
               and Will Respond   289
Case 4.27   WorldCom: The Little Company That Couldn't After All   293
Case 4.28   Bernie Madoff: Just Stay Away from the 17th Floor   311

5

UNIT   Ethics in International Business

SECTION A

*Conflicts Between the Corporation's Ethics and Business Practices
in Foreign Countries*   315

Reading 5.1   Why an International Code of Ethics Would Be Good for Business   315
Case 5.2   Chiquita Banana and Mercenary Protection   319
Case 5.3   Transnational Shipping and the Pirates   322
Case 5.4   The Former Soviet Union: A Study of Three Companies: PwC,
               Ikea, and AES   323
Case 5.5   Product Dumping   325
Case 5.6   On Sweatshops, Nike, and Kathie Lee   326
Case 5.7   Bhopal: When Safety Standards Differ   333
Case 5.8   Nestlé: When Products Translate Differently   335
Case 5.9   Google, Yahoo, and Human Rights in China   337

SECTION B

Bribes, Grease Payments, and When in Rome . . .   340

Reading 5.10   A Primer on the FCPA   340
Case 5.11   Siemens and Bribery, Everywhere   342
Case 5.12   Salt Lake City, the Olympics, and Bribery   344

6

UNIT   Ethics, Business Operations, and Rights

SECTION A

Workplace Safety   353

Reading 6.1   Two Sets of Books on Safety   353
Case 6.2   Sleeping on the Job and on the Way Home   353
Case 6.3   Cintas and OSHA   354

SECTION B

Workplace Loyalty   356

Case 6.4   Aaron Feuerstein and Malden Mills   356
Case 6.5   Plant Closings, Downsizings, Company Closings,
               Government Takeovers, Bankruptcies, and Pensions   358

SECTION C

Workplace Conflicts   361

Case 6.6   JCPenney and Its Wealthy Buyer   361
Case 6.7   The Trading Desk, Perks, and "Dwarf Tossing"   362
Case 6.8   Docs, Pharmas, Medical Journals, Funded Research, and Pizza   363
Case 6.9   The Analyst Who Needed a Preschool   367
Case 6.10   Julie Roehm: The Walmart Ad Exec with Expensive Tastes   370

SECTION D

Workplace Diversity and Atmosphere   373

Case 6.11   English-Only Employer Policies   373
Case 6.12   On-the-Job Fetal Injuries   374
Reading 6.13   The Benefits of Diversity: Remarks of Doug Daft, Former
        CEO of Coca-Cola   376
Case 6.14   *Seinfeld* in the Workplace   380
Case 6.15   Toyota, the CEO, the Assistant, and Inaction   381
Case 6.16   Arizona Senate Bill 1070: Immigration Laws, Employers, Enforcement,
        and Emotion   382

SECTION E

Workplace Privacy and Personal Lives   385

Case 6.17   Facebook MySpace, and YouTube Screening of Employees   385
Case 6.18   Bloggers, Chat Rooms, and E-Mail: Your Employer Is Watching   386
Case 6.19   Jack Welch and the Harvard Interview   387
Reading 6.20   Is It None of Our Business?   390

SECTION F

Workplace Confrontation   395

Reading 6.21   The Glowing Recommendation   395
Reading 6.22   The Ethics of Confrontation   396
Case 6.23   Ann Hopkins and Price Waterhouse   399

SECTION G

Workplace and the Environment   405

Case 6.24   Exxon and Alaska   405
Case 6.25   BP: Pipeline, Refinery, and Offshore-Drilling Safety   411

7
UNIT   Ethics and Products

SECTION A

Advertising Content   425

Case 7.1   Joe Camel: The Cartoon Character Who Sold Cigarettes and Nearly
        Felled an Industry   425
Case 7.2   Spring Break, Beer, and Alcohol on Campus   430
Case 7.3   Cheerios and Cholesterol and Rice Krispies and Immunity   432
Case 7.4   Subprime Loans—The Under-the-Radar Loans That Felled a Market   434
Case 7.5   Hollywood Ads   438
Case 7.6   Kraft, Barney Rubble, and Shrek   438
Case 7.7   Craigslist and Ad Screening   439

SECTION B

Product Safety   441

Reading 7.8   A Primer on Product Liability   441
Case 7.9   Tylenol: Decades of Dilemmas   444
Case 7.10   Merck and Vioxx   447
Case 7.11   Ford and Its Pinto and GM and Its Malibu: The Repeating Exploding Gas
        Tank Problem   452

Case 7.12   Toyota: Sudden Acceleration or Bad Drivers or Pesky Floor Mats?   458
Case 7.13   *E. coli,* Jack-in-the-Box, and Cooking Temperatures   461
Case 7.14   Peanut Corporation of America and Salmonella   462

SECTION C

Product Sales   464
Case 7.15   Pfizer and the $2.3 Billion Fine for Sales Tactics   464
Case 7.16   The Mess at Marsh McLennan   465
Case 7.17   Frozen Coke and Burger King and the Richmond Rigging   468
Case 7.18   Slotting: Facilitation, Costs, or Bribery?   472

SECTION D

Contracts   478
Case 7.19   Intel and the Chips: When You Have Made a Mistake   478
Case 7.20   Sears and High-Cost Auto Repairs   481

SECTION E

Products and Social Issues   487
Case 7.21   The Mommy Doll   487
Case 7.22   Stem-Cell Research   487
Case 7.23   Toro and Its Product Liability Program   489
Case 7.24   Fast Food Liability   490

8 UNIT   Ethics and Competition

SECTION A

Covenants Not to Compete   495
Reading 8.1   A Primer on Covenants Not to Compete: Are They Valid?   495
Case 8.2   Boeing, Lockheed, and the Documents   496
Case 8.3   Starwood, Hilton, and the Suspiciously Similar New Hotel Designs   501

SECTION B

All's Fair, or Is It?   505
Reading 8.4   Adam Smith: An Excerpt from *The Theory of Moral Sentiments*   505
Case 8.5   The Coke Employee Who Offered Inside Information to Pepsi   506
Case 8.6   The Compliance Officer Who Strayed   508
Case 8.7   Jonathan Lebed: The Middle School Tycoon   510
Case 8.8   Simmons, Mervyn's, and the Private Equity Firms That Bankrupt Them   511

SECTION C

Intellectual Property and Ethics   514
Case 8.9   Tiffany, Louis Vuitton, eBay, Landlords, and Knock-Offs   514
Case 8.10   Copyright, Songs, and Charities   518
Case 8.11   Microsoft vs. Google and "Snippets" of Books   519
Case 8.12   The Little Intermittent Windshield Wiper and Its Little Inventor   520

9

UNIT Ethics and Government

SECTION A

Government Employees 525

Reading 9.1   The Fish Bowl Existence of Government   525
Case 9.2   The Minerals Management Service: The Arms-Length Affairs with
                Oil Executives   527
Case 9.3   Kodak, the Appraiser, and the Assessor: Lots of Back Scratching
                on Valuation   531
Case 9.4   The Governor and a Senate Seat Vacated by a President   532
Case 9.5   The Man Who Writes the Internal Revenue Code Has Tax Issues: The Rangel
                Round-Up   534
Case 9.6   "I Was Just Following Orders": The CIA, Interrogations, and the Role of Legal
                Opinions in the Conduct of Organizations   536
Case 9.7   Paul Wolfowitz and the World Bank   538
Case 9.8   Hiding the Slip-Up on Oil Lease Accounting: Interior Motives   540
Case 9.9   Joe the Plumber, Child Support Records, and the Public
                Official's Disclosure   540

SECTION B

Government Contracts 542

Case 9.10   Stanford University and Government Overhead Payments   542
Case 9.11   Yale University and the Compensation of Professors for
                Government Research: Double-Dipping or Confusion?   545
Case 9.12   Minority-Owned Businesses and Reality   545
Case 9.13   The My Tai Concession and the County Supervisor   546
Case 9.14   Government Pricing and Finding a Way Around It   546
Case 9.15   Taser and Stunning Behavior   547
Case 9.16   Boeing and the Recruiting of the Government Purchasing Agent   548

SECTION C

Government Responsibilities 551

Case 9.17   The Prosecutors Who Withheld Evidence: The Senator's Trial   551
Case 9.18   The Duke Lacrosse Team and the Prosecutor   551
Case 9.19   FEMA, Hurricane Katrina, and the Dilemmas of
                Regulation versus Human Life   554

10

UNIT Ethics and Nonprofits

SECTION A

Nonprofits and Fraud 559

Case 10.1   New Era: If It Sounds Too Good to Be True, It Is Too Good to Be True   559
Case 10.2   The Baptist Foundation: Funds of the Faithful   562

SECTION B

Nonprofits and Management   565
Case 10.3   ACORN: Community Organizers, Undercover Videos, and Advice   565
Case 10.4   Giving and Spending the United Way   566
Case 10.5   The Red Cross, New York, and Ground Zero   568
Case 10.6   The Cornell Researchers Funded by the Foundation   569

Alphabetical Index 571
Business Discipline Index 575
Product/Company/Individuals/Subject Index. 582
Topic Index 603

Preface

The Josephson Institute released its data for 2008 on cheating in high school and found that 64 percent of the students surveyed say that they have cheated on an exam in the past year, and 82 percent say that they have lied to a teacher in the past year. When asked if they had copied another's homework, 82 percent said that they had but did not consider it cheating. "Team work" was their label for this practice. The Center for Academic Integrity at Clemson University and Professor Donald McCabe of Rutgers report that college cheating has grown from 11 percent in 1963 to 49 percent in 1993 to 75 percent in 2006.[1] Professor McCabe also found that MBAs have the highest rate of self-reported academic dishonesty (57 percent) of all graduate disciplines. Longitudinally, it would seem we have a decline. Many argue that there is no decline; rather, they offer, we are simply more honest about our ethical breaches. There is little comfort in this reassurance that we're more honest about our cheating. And there remains a disconnect between this conduct and an understanding of what ethics is. The Josephson Institute also found that the high school students who report that they cheat feel very comfortable about their behavior, with 92 percent saying they are satisfied with their character and ethics and 83 percent believing that they would be listed by their friends as one of the most ethical people they know. Perhaps we are more honest about our cheating. But perhaps that honesty results from our belief that cheating is not an ethical issue.

Research indicates that if students cheat in high school, they will bring the practices into college. And if they cheat in college, they will bring those practices into the workplace. A look at some of the events in business since the publication of the sixth edition of this book tells us that we are not quite there yet in terms of helping businesspeople understand when they are in the midst of an ethical dilemma and how those dilemmas should be resolved. The following list indicates that we did not make it 5 years from the time of the post-Enron Sarbanes–Oxley fundamental changes in the way we were doing business to another crisis that demands even more reforms:

- Beginning in 2007, a financial crisis that nearly felled the stock market began as we realized that the housing boom may have been fueled partially by mortgages given to those who were probably not qualified, who falsified their applications, and who benefited from inflated property appraisals. Based on those mortgages, secondary bundled financial instruments made their way into investment banks' portfolios and ours. When those mortgage-backed instruments had to be written down, asset values plummeted, stock portfolios tanked, and Wall Street teetered so much that the federal government had to provide a bail-out to banks and insurers. As more of the story unfolds, we realize that bankers, analysts, and others were aware of what was a house of cards but rode the financial wave while it lasted. Sadly, evidence has emerged that some of the banks may have been betting against their own clients and stacking the mortgage instrument deck against them. Siemens paid the largest fine in the history of the Foreign Corrupt Practices Act for what was an international practice of bribery to at least 10 nations over a 4-year period. Bernie Madoff was able to pull over a $50-billion Ponzi scheme for 18 years; even Steven Spielberg and Kevin Bacon lost money to Bernie as he escaped detection despite three Securities and Exchange Commission investigations into his operations. Craig's List made its way into the headlines because of a murder that resulted from the racy portions of its online classified advertising. The fines companies have paid for ethical and legal lapses continue to hover at the $1 billion mark as a matter of course:

---

[1]The Center for Academic Integrity study has been conducted by Professor Donald McCabe on a regular basis over the years. This survey had 4,500 student respondents. For more information on Professor McCabe and his work on academic integrity and the Center for Academic Integrity, go to http://www.cai.org.

- Pfizer paid a $2.3 billion fine for its sales reps crossing the line on how drugs can be marketed
- Siemens paid a $5.8 billion fine for bribery
- Citigroup set aside $5.8 billion for losses on mortgage-backed securities
- Merrill Lynch set aside $10 billion for losses

And then there are those events that fall short of criminal conduct or civil fines misconduct. These are the day-to-day ethical breaches that capture media headlines and cause continuing concerns about the ethical culture of business. There are the employees who left Starwood Hotels for Hilton Hotels, along with documents, plans, and strategies that found their way into Hilton's plans for a new hotel chain. Toyota recalled millions of cars over a yet-to-be-solved phenomenon of sudden acceleration in its cars. We all debated the issues of waterboarding and interrogation techniques by government employees and whether following orders was ethical. The world of sports brought us questions about how sports teams should deal with a player such as Michael Vick, who pleaded guilty to federal charges in a dog-fighting enterprise. BP's spill from the Deepwater Horizon rig off the coast of Louisiana resulted in a $20-billion down payment by the company on damages, and the questions raised about BP in the sixth edition are the same issues we see in its latest accident—did keeping costs low trump decisions about risk and company practices? From analysts to the factory workers producing peanut base for cookies and crackers, pressure often got in the way of moral clarity in business decisions. Those pressures then translated into ethical lapses that involve everything from pushing the envelope on truth to earnings management that crosses over into cooking the books and fraud. Weak product designs and products' defects often produce a chain of memos or e-mails in the company that reflect employee concerns about product safety. College sports, baseball, and politics all have their ethical issues. The cycles between major ethical and financial collapses seem to be growing shorter. Businesses do exist to make a profit, but business ethics exists to set parameters for earning that profit. Business ethics is also a key element of business decision processes and strategies because the cases in this book teach us that the long-term perspective, not the sort-term fix, serves businesses better in that profit role. This book of readings and cases explores those parameters and their importance. This book teaches, through detailed study of the people and companies, that business conducted without ethics is a nonsustainable competitive model. Ethical shortcuts translate into a short-term existence. Initially, these shortcuts produce a phenomenon such as those seen with Lehman Brothers, Merrill Lynch, and Peanut Corporation of America. These companies are no longer viable entities because they crossed ethical lines. For a time, they were at the top of their game—flummoxing their competitors on how they were able to do what they were doing, and so profitably. But then that magnificent force of truth finds its way to the surface, and the company that does not factor in the ethics of its decisions and conduct finds itself falling to the earth like a meteor's flash. Long-term personal and business success demand ethics. This edition takes a look at everything from the subprime lending market, a market that brought easy pickings in terms of profit so long as real-estate values held firm, to the world of sports and the downfall of so many. This book connects the moral sentiments of markets with the wealth of nations. Business without ethics is self-destructive.

New to This Edition

A Slightly New Structure and Approach to Address the Chronic Repetition of the Ethical Lapses

We've been down this road before, and the historic patterns are now emerging for study and insight. In 1986, before Ivan Boesky was a household name and Michael Douglas was Gordon Gekko in *Wall Street,* I began teaching a business ethics course in the

MBA program in the College of Business at Arizona State University. The course was an elective. I had trouble making the minimum enrollments. However, two things changed: my enrollments and my fate. First, the American Association of Collegiate Schools of Business (AACSB) changed the curriculum for graduate and undergraduate business degree programs and required the coverage of ethics. The other event actually was a series of events. Indictments, convictions, and guilty pleas by major companies and their officers—from E.F. Hutton to Union Carbide to Beech-Nut to Exxon—brought national attention to the need to incorporate values in American businesses and instill them in business leaders.

Whether out of fear, curiosity, or the need for reaccreditation, business schools and students began to embrace the concept of studying business ethics. My course went from a little-known elective to the final required course in the MBA program. In the years since, the interest in business ethics has only increased. Following junk bonds and insider trading, we rolled into the savings and loan collapses; and once we had that straightened out, we rolled into Enron, WorldCom, HealthSouth, Tyco, and Adelphia, and we even lost Martha Stewart along the way. We were quite sure, what with all the Sarbanes–Oxley changes and demands on boards, CEO, CFOs, and auditors that we were through with that level of misconduct. We were, however, wrong. New Century Financial, one of the first of the subprime lenders to collapse, found one angry bankruptcy trustee. The trustee's report concluded that he found the acquiescence of the auditor to the client's refusal to write down the bad loans astonishing in what he called "the post-Enron era." The Lehman Brothers bankruptcy trustee found a letter from a risk officer at the investment banker who tried to warn the CEO and CFO that the firm's financial reports violated its code of ethics. The trustee also found that the risk officer was fired.

Three decades plus after Boesky we have the Galleon hedge fund insider trading web emerge in 2009 with a staggering repetitiveness that finds us wondering, "Do they not see the ethical and legal issues? Do they just not know that they are crossing these line? Do they see the patterns from business history?" The good thing about repetitive patterns is that we gain insight into the paths, the reasoning, and the pressures of those involved. The key is to bring out those patterns and train our new business leaders to recognize them and, most importantly, to stop the train of self-destruction those patterns set off. This edition is reorganized to offer greater insights, knowledge, and perspective on these patterns for a new generation of leaders. Today, nearly 100 percent of the Fortune 500 companies have a code of ethics. We are up to over 75 percent of companies having some form of ethics training. But, we are not quite there until our business leaders grasp the perspective of ethics and its relationship to economics, organizational behavior, company culture, reputation, and financial performance. This edition is structured to walk us through all aspects and types of ethical dilemmas and how we can cope with the pressures that often deprive us of good ethical analysis.

Unit 1: Our Ethics

Unit 1 addresses the questions of: What is this ethics thing? How do I manage to work philosophy into my decision processes? How do I find solutions to ethical dilemmas? How do I know when I am really analyzing as opposed to rationalizing or succumbing to pressure? A change to this unit is a right-out-of-the-blocks focus on developing a credo—a way of helping us to think about ethical issues in advance and decide what we would and would not do in a situation. If we think about issues in advance, then when the pressure hits we at least have the cognitive dissonance of realizing that we did see the issues differently when we were not under so much pressure.

Unit 2: Business and Ethics

Once we have focused on ourselves and our ethical standards, we move into analysis of ethical issues in business. This unit offers the introspection of this question: Are my personal ethical standards different when I am at work? Should they be? Why are they different? Further, the magnitude of the mistakes that business-people continued to make, despite all the warnings from ongoing debacles, did not indicate that these were close calls. Something had gone awry in their ethics training in business school for them to drift so far from virtue. I continue to emphasize in teaching, consulting, and writing that helping students and businesspeople see that personal ethics and business ethics are one and the same is critical to making virtue a part of business culture. Virtue is the goal for most of us in all aspects of our lives. Whether we commit to fidelity in a personal relationship or take the laundry detergent back into the store to pay because we forgot it was on the bottom of our grocery cart, we show virtue. Ethics in business is no different, and we need not behave differently at work than we do in that grocery store parking lot as we make the decision to be honest and fair with the store owner. Substitute a shareholder and the disclosure of option dates and true costs, and we have our laundry detergent example with a stock market twist.

New to this unit is a focus on the patterns that interfere with good ethical analysis in business such as pressure, hubris, and a singular focus on moral relativism as opposed to a deeper look at the consequences of reliance on that model. In this unit, there is evidence of a change in overall structure. Rather than having a large grouping of cases focused on financial issues, the cases are spread throughout the units to show that the issues and patterns in financial cases are no different from those in product liability or employee rights cases. Instructors and students tended to skim over the financial cases because, "They are covered in other courses," or "We are not really comfortable with finance." We study these cases in ethics for the patterns of culture, hubris, and poor ethical analysis. So, Martha Stewart is in this unit along with Goldman Sachs. The financial markets issues are not front and center as we focus on the psychology of their decision processes rather than on the substance of the underlying transactions. This unit also includes the overarching theme of the book over all of its editions: plenty of real-life examples from newspapers, business journals, and my experiences as a consultant and board member. Knowing that other instructors and students were in need of examples, I have turned my experiences into cases and coupled them with the most memorable readings in the field to provide a training and thought-provoking experience on business ethics.

Unit 3: Social Responsibility and Ethics

Unit 3 offers us the bigger perspective—once we slog through the decision processes of fraud, embezzlement, puffing resumes, and cheating on our travel expenses, we move to discussion and understanding of the role of business in society. The cases in this unit are broken into an introduction to business and society, the obligations of business toward our moral ecology, and the issues of the environment and sustainability.

Unit 4: Company Culture, Individual Pressures, and Ethics

Unit 4 is the psychology section that tackles companies' ethical lapses, with the realization that beyond individual ethical lapses (as with one bad apple), there are barrel factors that must be addressed to prevent ethical lapses. This section, through the finance cases and the weaving in of corporate governance, explores those barrel factors with the recognition that beyond individual lapses there are company, industry, and societal norms that do cause companies and individuals to move that line away from ethical standards to "everybody does it" here at the company, in our industry, and in society. The cases here explore how business incentives, organizational behavior practices and processes, reporting mechanisms, industry practices, and societal norms contribute to poor ethical analysis, decisions, and that self-destructive behavior. Recognizing and addressing those barrel issues is the theme of Unit 4.

Unit 5: International Business and Ethics

Unit 5 is new to this edition, with a call-out of international issues. This unit helps students to understand the need for better and deeper ethical analysis of the issues in international business and the importance of analyzing the countries and their ethical standards prior to doing business there. The section addresses the risks and costs of ethical lapses and succumbing to local standards as opposed to establishing company standards prior to those pressure points that occur in international competition.

Unit 6: Employment Issues and Ethics

Unit 6 is a combination unit that draws together cases from units in the sixth edition to bring together all the workplace issues that affect employees and managers, from safety to conflicts, to privacy, to the lost art of confrontation about employee conduct, this section is the one for understanding how ethics bumps shoulders with technology, profits, and privacy.

Unit 7: Products and Ethics

Unit 7 is yet another newly combined unit that addresses all the issues related to product development, sales, safety, and advertising. From recalls to racy dolls to advertising to the contracts themselves, this section focuses on the ethical issues that involved the how, what, and where of sales of products.

Unit 8: Competition and Ethics

Unit 8 has the luxury of focusing entirely on competition. With the contracts issues grouped in Unit 7 on products, this unit has expanded coverage of the ever-growing concerns about covenants not to compete and employee breaches of those covenants. The societal issues of infringement are emphasized as students analyze cases that illustrate the costs of not honoring intellectual property rights.

Unit 9: Government and Ethics

Unit 9 is a slightly expanded government ethics unit because, well, there have been so many fascinating ethical issues involving and affecting government agencies and employees. From the CIA waterboarding to the behavior of the Minerals Management Services with oil company executives, this unit carries a great deal of drama, but also some terrific teaching moments on the parallels between behaviors in business and government.

Unit 10: Nonprofits and Ethics

Unit 10 on nonprofits includes two new cases on research funding disclosures as well as a case on an undercover investigation of ACORN that is an excellent case for weighing the violation of the law in the interest of exposing an ethical breach by an organization.

For more on organization of a course using the new structure, refer to the following discussion of Ethical Common Denominators.

And, for the seventh edition, we have more and new cases in the government and nonprofit sections. As it turns out, the patterns in culture and misconduct are the same across organizations. These updated and expanded sections prepare students for interaction in organizations that have different accounting processes but still face the same pressures employees feel in business. Their pressures are not those of profit, but of deadlines, fundraising, rankings, and even just hubris, the classic component in the Greek tragedies by which heroes fall.

The seventh edition continues the features students and instructors embraced in the first six editions, including both short and long cases, discussion questions, hypothetical situations, and up-to-the-moment current, ongoing, and real ethical dilemmas. Some of the long-standing favorites are back by popular demand—such as the Nestlé infant formula experience and Union Carbide in Bhopal, with their long-standing lessons in doing the right thing. There are so many "oldies but goodies" when it comes to ethics cases, but length constraints do not allow me to continue to include in this book all the oldies along with the new cases that promise to be oldies but goodies. Check out the availability of custom options noted at the end of this section. Now there are further opportunities to integrate cases from previous editions into your course.

The seventh edition continues the new training tool introduced in the previous edition to help businesspeople who are working their way through an ethical dilemma. In the discussion questions for many of the cases the "Compare and Contrast" questions continue. These are questions that provide an example of a company that made a decision different from the one made by management in the case at hand. For example, in the Tylenol case (Case 7.9—an oldie but goodie that has been updated for this edition), the students will find a question that highlights this company's past conduct in comparison with its conduct in a current situation in which the FDA has accused the company of surreptitiously buying up tainted product in order to avoid a recall. There is a contrast between its recall of the 1980s, which was so rapid and received so much acclaim, and its behavior in this event. Why do some companies choose one path while others succumb to pressure? What was different about their decision-making processes? What did they see that the other companies and their leaders did not take into account? This feature is a response to those who worry that students are not given examples of "good companies." The problem with touting goodness is that it is impossible to know everything a company is or is not doing. For example, Fannie Mae was named the most ethical company in America for 2 years running. Yet it had to do a $7-billion restatement of earnings and is now defunct as a shored-up government entity. BP was an environmental darling for nearly a decade for its responsible environmental programs. However, recent events cast doubt on how much environmental and safety dedication the company had. There is a risk in learning of goodness if that goodness is superficial or limited. Studying individual scenarios of contrasting behavior is the learning tool, not the touting of a single company that can always have a lapse. There are no saints in this journey and keeping the text credible requires a recognition of that limitation but uses it to emphasize the vigilance we all need, as individuals and in business, to avoid lapses and progress in moral development.

Finding and Studying the Cases and Readings

The seventh edition continues the classic readings in business ethics that provide insight into the importance of ethics in business and how to resolve ethical dilemmas. The seventh edition also continues the presence of integrated readings throughout the book to provide substantive thoughts on the particular areas covered in each section. The organizational structure and indexes, continued from the sixth edition, make material, companies, people, and products easy to locate. A case can be located using the table of contents, the alphabetical index, the topical index, the people index, or the product index, which lists both products and companies by name. An index for business disciplines groups the cases by accounting, management, and the other disciplines in colleges of business.

How to Use the "Ethical Common Denominators across Business Topics Chart"

New to this edition is the Ethical Common Denominators across Business Topics chart, or simply, the ECD chart. This chart addresses that slight discomfort some instructors have with the financial cases and helps students understand that underlying every ethical dilemma are the common patterns of psychology and pressure as well as the need for solid ethical analysis. The facts change, but the issues and analysis do not. The ECD chart provides various ways for instruction, according to instructor preference, needs, and time constraints. The chart groups the cases by the usual business and ethics topics. If, for example, you wanted to cover the environmental cases all in one fell swoop, you could do so by focusing on the cases listed under the Business, Social Responsibility, and Sustainability Unit (3), focusing on Section C, Social Responsibility and Sustainability. However, the reading in that section, "The New Environmentalism" is a terrific one for teaching students about leadership, the regulatory cycle, and how businesses really compete more effectively if they address societal concerns *before* a crisis or demands for regulation. Adam Smith and his theories on markets appears in Section 8, but there is no reason he could not be shifted back to the coverage of the philosophical foundations. An instructor can mix in all the sections on ethical analysis. Note that there is a case from each unit there because you can pick and choose what topics to cover as you teach how to analyze. The ECD chart allows you to introduce that broad exposure to the pervasiveness of ethical issues early in your course, or you can simply use the cases in that unit and go on to topical areas. The ECD chart allows you to break up the finance cases into areas of discussion on psychology, culture, organizational behavior, hubris, and pressure. You need not focus on the structure of CDOs and secondary instruments markets to understand the culture at Lehman and how its culture led its sales force and managers down a path that proved to be self-destructive. Likewise, you can mix in a Ponzi scheme in a nonprofit with Bernie Madoff to help students understand how similar the cases are in the issues missed as they pursued a business model that could not be sustained over time. The case on the undercover investigation of ACORN is a great nonprofit case, but it would fit well in Unit 1 as you ask students to deal with whether breaking the law would be justified to expose illegal conduct. The ECD chart allows a mix-and-match approach or a straight topical approach—both of which allow us to see that the facts change but good ethical analysis applies, always.

The EDC Chart—Ethical Common Denominators across Business Topics

	Description	Subcategories	Cases	Readings
OVERALL	**THEME**	**AREAS**		
Philosophical foundations	Case/reading affords opportunity for exploring ethical theories	Utilitarianism; moral relativism; egoism; divine command; rights; justice; virtue ethics	Case 1.7 Case 3.8 Case 3.10 Case 5.6 Case 5.8 Case 5.9 Case 6.12 Case 6.16 Case 7.22 Case 8.8 Case 9.6	Reading 1.1 Reading 1.2 Reading 1.3 Reading 2.2 Reading 2.3 Reading 3.1 Reading 3.2 Reading 3.3 Reading 3.4 Reading 3.5 Reading 3.6 Reading 3.7 Reading 4.5 Reading 4.18 Reading 8.4

(Continued)

	Description	Subcategories	Cases	Readings
OVERALL	**THEME**	**AREAS**		
Ethical analysis	Case/reading provides opportunity for logical walk-through of ethical dilemmas and their resolution	Either/or conundrum; models for decision-making	Case 1.7 Case 1.10 Case 1.11 Case 1.12 Case 1.13 Case 1.15 Case 1.16 Case 4.21 Case 5.3 Case 5.4 Case 5.12 Case 6.5 Case 7.22 Case 7.24 Case 8.8 Case 9.6 Case 10.3	Reading 1.4 Reading 1.8 Reading 1.9 Reading 1.14 Reading 2.1 Reading 2.2 Reading 2.3 Reading 2.10 Reading 4.18 Reading 6.21
Psychology of decision-making	Case/reading provides insight into psychological factors that overpower ethical reasoning	Pressure; financial constraints; hubris; rationalizations; drivers; enablers	Case 3.10 Case 4.8 Case 4.10 Case 4.24 Case 4.28 Case 5.2 Case 6.9 Case 7.14 Case 8.2 Case 8.3 Case 8.5 Case 9.16 Case 9.17 Case 10.1 Case 10.2	Reading 1.5 Reading 2.3 Reading 3.9 Reading 4.1
Culture/organizational behavior	Case/reading provides insight into how the organization and culture overpower ethical reasoning; the bad apple vs. bad barrel syndrome	Compensation systems; enforcement; confrontation; raising ethical issues; fear and silence in organizations	Case 3.8 Case 4.6 Case 4.8 Case 4.10 Case 4.16 Case 4.23 Case 4.24 Case 4.25 Case 4.27 Case 4.28 Case 5.11 Case 6.3 Case 6.10 Case 6.14 Case 6.25 Case 7.10 Case 7.12 Case 8.2 Case 8.3 Case 9.2 Case 9.4 Case 9.8 Case 10.1 Case 10.2	Reading 2.4 Reading 2.6 Reading 4.3 Reading 4.4 Reading 4.26 Reading 6.1 Reading 6.21 Reading 6.22 Reading 6.23

	Description	Subcategories	Cases	Readings
OVERALL	**THEME**	**AREAS**		
Economic theory	Case/reading provides backdrop for discussion of relationship between ethics and economics	Fair trade; living wage; downsizing; property rights; laissez-faire; moral hazard; nature of markets; effects of demand and supply	Case 1.15 Case 2.11 Case 4.20 Case 4.21 Case 5.6 Case 6.4 Case 6.5 Case 7.16 Case 7.18 Case 7.24 Case 8.8 Case 9.14	Reading 3.1 Reading 3.9 Reading 4.5 Reading 5.1 Reading 8.1 Reading 8.4
Personal introspection; credo	Case/reading provides an opportunity for students to put themselves in the position of those facing the dilemmas; developing tools for resisting pressure	Personal ethics vs. business ethics; the lines you would never cross to get a job, to keep a job, to earn a bonus, to meet goals	Case 1.10 Case 1.17 Case 2.7 Case 2.12 Case 4.7 Case 4.21 Case 6.4 Case 7.16 Case 7.17 Case 8.2 Case 8.6 Case 8.7 Case 9.6 Case 9.16 Case 10.4	Reading 1.1 Reading 1.2 Reading 1.3 Reading 1.6 Reading 3.3 Reading 4.1 Reading 4.2
Social responsibility	Case/reading provides opportunity for discussion of the role of business in society	Pension between profits and impact on society; the role of philanthropy by business; tension between short-term gains and long-term impacts; balancing social and public policy issues with business activities	Case 3.8 Case 3.10 Case 3.11 Case 3.12 Case 3.13 Case 3.14 Case 3.15 Case 3.16 Case 3.17 Case 5.2 Case 5.3 Case 5.5 Case 5.7 Case 5.8 Case 5.9 Case 6.4 Case 6.24 Case 6.25 Case 7.1 Case 7.2 Case 7.6 Case 7.7 Case 7.21 Case 7.22 Case 7.24 Case 8.8 Case 9.15 Case 10.3	Reading 3.1 Reading 3.2 Reading 3.3 Reading 3.4 Reading 3.5 Reading 3.6 Reading 3.7 Reading 4.17 Reading 6.21

(Continued)

	Description	Subcategories	Cases	Readings
OVERALL	**THEME**	**AREAS**		
Stakeholder theory	Case/reading provides opportunity for learning how to list stakeholders and examine their perspectives on an ethical dilemma	Systemic effects; who is affected by decision and/or action; implications if everyone chose your course of behavior	Case 1.11 Case 1.17 Case 2.12 Case 3.17 Case 3.18 Case 5.8 Case 5.9 Case 6.4 Case 6.5 Case 6.24 Case 6.25 Case 7.4 Case 7.21 Case 7.23 Case 7.24 Case 7.21 Case 7.24 Case 8.8 Case 9.10 Case 9.13 Case 9.17 Case 10.4 Case 10.5	Reading 3.2 Reading 3.3 Reading 3.4 Reading 3.7 Reading 3.16 Reading 4.17 Reading 6.21 Reading 6.22
Moral ecology	Case/reading provides an opportunity for analyzing effect of business conduct on fabric of society	Health harms from business activity; tension between freedom of speech and impact of speech; personal conduct of business leaders	Case 3.12 Case 3.13 Case 3.14 Case 5.6 Case 5.9 Case 6.19 Case 7.21 Case 8.2 Case 9.4 Case 10.4	Reading 3.5 Reading 6.20
Leadership	Case/reading provides an opportunity for understanding the role of managers in company culture and decisions	Tone-at-the-top; example; conduct of managers and supervisors; manager's responses to employee concerns	Case 2.11 Case 3.8 Case 3.10 Case 3.13 Case 4.8 Case 4.25 Case 6.25 Case 7.9 Case 7.23 Case 8.2 Case 9.5 Case 9.7 Case 9.9 Case 9.10 Case 9.18 Case 10.4	Reading 2.3 Reading 2.4 Reading 3.2 Reading 3.5 Reading 3.16 Reading 4.9 Reading 4.26 Reading 6.20 Reading 6.21 Reading 6.22
Governance	Case/reading provides an opportunity for examining the role of the board and corporate processes on culture and ethical analysis and decision-making	Compensation systems; compliance; internal controls	Case 3.10 Case 4.12 Case 4.13 Case 4.15 Case 4.27 Case 5.4 Case 6.15 Case 7.19	Reading 4.4 Reading 4.9 Reading 4.11 Reading 4.17 Reading 4.26

	Description	Subcategories	Cases	Readings
OVERALL	**THEME**	**AREAS**		
			Case 8.2 Case 9.5 Case 9.7 Case 9.10 Case 10.4	
Whistle-blowing	Case/reading examines individual actions in dealing with ethical issues	Speaking up; approaches to raising issues	Case 3.10 Case 4.6 Case 4.12 Case 4.23 Case 4.24 Case 6.25 Case 7.10 Case 7.11 Case 7.15 Case 7.17 Case 8.2 Case 9.2 Case 9.14 Case 10.2	Reading 4.2 Reading 4.26
The gray area	Case/reading focuses on law vs. ethics—can vs. should. The loophole	Regulatory cycle; industry behaviors; slippery slope; gray area	Case 1.7 Case 1.12 Case 2.11 Case 4.20 Case 4.21 Case 7.5 Case 7.15 Case 9.6 Case 9.11 Case 9.14 Case 10.6	Reading 1.5 Reading 4.1 Reading 4.18 Reading 4.19 Reading 6.1
Categories of ethical dilemmas	Case/reading helps to illustrate where ethical dilemmas exist	Honesty; false impression; balancing ethical issues; conflicts of interest; taking unfair advantage	Case 1.12 Case 2.11 Case 3.11 Case 4.28 Case 5.3 Case 5.4 Case 5.8 Case 6.8 Case 6.25 Case 7.4 Case 7.5 Case 7.17 Case 8.5 Case 8.9 Case 9.3 Case 9.4 Case 9.13 Case 9.15 Case 10.5 Case 10.6	Reading 1.4 Reading 2.6 Reading 4.5 Reading 4.18 Reading 6.1

(Continued)

	Description	Subcategories	Cases	Readings
THE BUSINESS	**TOPIC**	**AREAS**		
Financial reporting/ accounting	Case/reading involves FASB, GAAP issues, and interpretation of rules	Red flags; materiality; EBITDA; loading dock behaviors; cookie-jar reserves; spring-loading	Case 2.11 Case 3.8 Case 3.10 Case 4.6 Case 4.27 Case 4.28 Case 5.11 Case 6.19 Case 7.16 Case 9.8 Case 10.2	Reading 4.3 Reading 4.9 Reading 4.11
Product liability	Case/reading involves decision on product quality/ safety	Design defects; recalls; product dumping; risk tolerance; low-probability events	Case 4.23 Case 5.5 Case 5.8 Case 7.9 Case 7.10 Case 7.11 Case 7.12 Case 7.13 Case 7.14 Case 7.23 Case 7.24	Reading 7.8
Technology	Case/reading involves ethical dilemmas that arise due to new technologies	Privacy of individuals; privacy of employees; social networking; theft; screening; testing	Case 1.15 Case 2.12 Case 4.7 Case 4.27 Case 6.17 Case 6.18 Case 7.22 Case 8.7	
Supply chain	Case/reading involves issues in contracts, relationships with vendors, purchasing managers	Conflicts of interest; commercial bribery; contracts	Case 3.17 Case 3.18 Case 4.14 Case 5.2 Case 5.6 Case 5.7 Case 6.6 Case 6.7 Case 6.8 Case 6.9 Case 6.10 Case 6.25 Case 7.12 Case 7.13 Case 7.14 Case 7.18	Reading 3.16 Reading 5.1
Marketing and sales	Case/reading involves ethical issues in advertising, pricing, product distribution	Antitrust issues; PR; framing issues; psychological tools of marketing; services marketing	Case 2.11 Case 3.18 Case 4.28 Case 5.8 Case 6.7 Case 6.8 Case 7.1 Case 7.2 Case 7.3 Case 7.5 Case 7.6 Case 7.7	Reading 3.3 Reading 7.8

	Description	Subcategories	Cases	Readings
THE BUSINESS	**TOPIC**	**AREAS**		
Marketing and sales *(continued)*			Case 7.15 Case 7.16 Case 7.17 Case 7.18 Case 7.20 Case 8.5 Case 10.5	
Government activities	Case/reading involves business relationships with and within government	Bribery, conflicts of interest, public issues and debate; PACs; government contracting	Case 3.10 Case 5.4 Case 7.4 Case 7.22 Case 9.2 Case 9.3 Case 9.4 Case 9.5 Case 9.6 Case 9.7 Case 9.8 Case 9.9 Case 9.13 Case 9.16 Case 9.17 Case 9.18	Reading 3.9 Reading 4.1 Reading 9.1
Sustainability	Case/reading involves business relationship with environment	Climate issues; pollution; carbon footprints	Case 3.17 Case 3.18 Case 5.7 Case 6.24 Case 6.25 Case 9.2	Reading 3.16
Discrimination	Case/reading deals with issues in equal opportunity	Affirmative action; sexual harassment; diversity in the workforce; HR policies	Case 6.11 Case 6.12 Case 6.14 Case 6.15 Case 6.16 Case 6.23 Case 9.12	Reading 6.13
Intellectual property	Case/reading deals with ownership of property and competitors' access	Copyrights; trademarks; reverse engineering; anti-compete clauses; downloading; software copies	Case 1.10 Case 8.2 Case 8.3 Case 8.5 Case 8.9 Case 8.10 Case 8.11 Case 8.12 Case 9.12	
International business	Case/reading covers ethical issues in operating multi-nationally	FCPA; bribery; product dumping, living wage, factory conditions, geopolitical issues; fair trade; human rights violations; mercenary issues	Case 5.2 Case 5.3 Case 5.4 Case 5.5 Case 5.6 Case 5.7 Case 5.8 Case 5.9 Case 5.11 Case 6.25 Case 9.7	Reading 2.4 Reading 5.1 Reading 5.10

(Continued)

	Description	Subcategories	Cases	Readings
THE BUSINESS	**TOPIC**	**AREAS**		
Financial markets	Case/reading focuses on issues in the capital markets	Insider trading, short sales, risk; disclosure; hedge funds	Case 2.11 Case 3.10 Case 2.7 Case 4.12 Case 6.7 Case 6.9 Case 8.6 Case 8.7 Case 8.8	Reading 3.9 Reading 4.11 Reading 4.19
Employee rights and responsibilities	Case/reading focuses on employee work and employer supervision	Employee privacy; employee productivity; personal activity (net-surfing); employer monitoring; employer use of social networks	Case 2.8 Case 2.13 Case 5.9 Case 6.2 Case 6.3 Case 6.4 Case 6.5 Case 6.17 Case 6.18 Case 6.19 Case 6.23 Case 6.24 Case 8.2 Case 8.3 Case 9.8 Case 9.9 Case 10.2	Reading 2.9 Reading 6.20 Reading 8.1
Operations	Case/reading focuses on production	Safety; regulatory compliance; training; work conditions	Case 3.17 Case 5.6 Case 5.7 Case 6.2 Case 6.3 Case 6.25 Case 7.13 Case 7.14 Case 8.6	Reading 6.1
Information systems	Case/reading focuses on data: development, use, access	Stats and interpretation; role of data processing in decision-making	Case 4.7 Case 4.28 Case 6.17 Case 6.18 Case 7.13 Case 7.21 Case 8.6 Case 9.8	
Contract obligations and performance	Case/reading focuses on legal and ethical obligations under contracts	Performance; damages; breach; interpretation	Case 1.18 Case 3.14 Case 4.5 Case 4.20 Case 4.21 Case 6.10 Case 7.19 Case 7.20 Case 8.3 Case 9.10 Case 9.11	

	Description	Subcategories	Cases	Readings
THE BUSINESS	**TOPIC**	**AREAS**		
Nonprofit organizations	Unique character of nonprofits	Good intentions vs. good actions	Case 10.1 Case 10.2 Case 10.3 Case 10.4 Case 10.5 Case 10.6	

Supplements

Access to Companion Site Resources

To access additional course materials and companion resources, please visit www.cengagebrain.com. At the CengageBrain.com home page, search for this book's ISBN (found on the back cover of your book) using the search box at the top of the page. This will take you to this book's product page, where free companion resources can be found. Instructors must go to login.cengage.com for access to instructor materials.

Instructor's Manual with Test Bank

The instructor's manual with Test Bank is updated with more sample test objective- and essay-answer questions of varying lengths and structures. The questions have been coded for topic and even some for case-specific questions so that exams can be created by subject area. The PowerPoint package, which includes illustrative charts to assist instructors in walking classes through the more complex cases, has been updated and expanded. Instructors can access the Instructor's Manual with Test Bank at login.cengage.com.

PowerPoint Slides

Developed by the author, Microsoft PowerPoint slides are available for use by students as an aid to note-taking, and by instructors for enhancing their lectures. Instructors can access PowerPoint files at login.cengage.com.

Business Law Digital Video Library

This dynamic video library features more that sixty video clips that spark class discussion and clarify core legal principles. The library is organized into five series: Legal Conflicts in Business (includes specific modern business and e-commerce scenarios); Ask the Instructor (presents straightforward explanations of concepts for student review); Drama of the Law (features classic business scenarios that spark classroom participation); Real World Legal (explores conflicts that arise in a variety of business environments), and LawFlix (contains clips from many popular films). Access for students is provided via a code when bundled with a new textbook, or it can be purchased at www.cengagebrain.com.

Customized Selections of Case Studies and Readings

Instructors always have the option to customize your choice of cases and readings. Case studies and readings from both the fifth and sixth editions of Jennings's *Business Ethics* can be found by visiting www.textchoice.com/collections. Select the Business Ethics option. This collection includes intuitive browse and search features, allowing you to quickly and easily find the content you need. Selections can be used to create an affordable course companion or to integrate material into your customized textbook. Now you have choices and a rich resource to tap into so that you can tailor topics and depth of coverage for your own course needs.

Acknowledgments

This book is not mine. It is the result of the efforts and sacrifices of many. I am grateful to the reviewers for their comments and insights. Their patience, expertise, and service are remarkable. I have many colleagues around the world who continue to provide me with insights, input, and improvements, but my colleagues listed below provided the time and effort of a page-by-page review.

John W. Baker, Jr.
Northwest Missouri State University

Cheryl L. Bernier
Central New Mexico Community College

Jeff Cohu
Rochester College

Jeffrey Douglas Penley
Catawba Valley Community College

Teressa Elliott
Northern Kentucky University

Charlene Y. Fitzwater
Immaculata University

Andy Garcia
Bowling Green State University

Glenn M. Greenfield
Lawrence Technological University

Steven P. Gunning
Curry College, Milton, MA

Thomas L. Jackson
Benedictine University at Springfield

Steven Jordan
Walsh College

Gene R. Laczniak
Marquette University

Joseph W. Leonard
Miami University

William A. Morehead
Delta State University

Thomas Oxenreider
Montreat College

Rod Thirion
Pikes Peak Community College

Gary J. Valcana
Athens State University

Miriam Weismann
Suffolk University

Teri Whilden
Northwest Nazarene University

Jason K. Wolins
Humphreys College, Stockton, CA

I am grateful for the students and professors who continue to help me with ideas for new cases, corrections (those typos!), and insights that help me as I work on each edition.

I am fortunate to have Laura Bofinger Ansara continuing as my developmental editor for this edition. She has a tall order, this one of reining in an author who would have a 700-page book if she could. I am grateful for the time she takes to understand the cases and all my pedagogical goals. She continues to come back with those important e-mails that say, "But what about this? Could we do it this way? Would this be better?" I daresay she is right when she does so. I am grateful to Vicky True-Baker and Rob Dewey for their continuing support of all my work. I continue to love editors. Where I see only deadlines, they see both the big picture of the book and its details: They have vision. I am grateful for their vision in supporting this book at a time when ethics was not on the tip of everyone's SOXs and tongues. They trusted me and understood the role of ethics in business and supported a project that was novel and risky.

I am grateful to my parents for the values they inculcated in me. Their ethical perspective has been an inspiration, a comfort, and, in many cases, the final say in my decision-making processes. I am especially grateful to my father for his continual research on and quest for examples of ethical and not-so-ethical behavior in action in the world of business. I am grateful for my family's understanding and support. I am most grateful for the reminder their very presence gives me of what is truly important. In a world that measures success by "stuff" acquired, they have given me the peace that comes from devotion, decisions, and actions grounded in a personal credo of "others first." This road less taken offers so many rich intangibles that we can, with that treasure trove, take or leave "the stuff." My hope is that those who use this book gain and use the same perspective on "stuff."

Marianne M.Jennings
Professor of Legal and Ethical Studies in Business
W.P. Carey School of Business
Arizona State University
marianne.jennings@asu.edu

Ethical Theory, Philosophical Foundations, Our Reasoning Flaws, and Types of Ethical Dilemmas

UNIT ONE

Before we begin the study of business ethics, we should do some introspection: what does ethics mean to me personally? The purpose of this unit is to provide you with an introspective look at you and your views on ethics before we bring the business component to you and ethics.

This unit explains three things: what ethics are, why we should care about ethics, and how to resolve ethical dilemmas. The materials in this unit serve as the foundation for the study of issues in business ethics. We begin with a personal look at ethics, discuss why it matters, and then decide how to resolve ethical dilemmas.

Defining Ethics

Reading 1.1

You, Your Values, and a Credo

We have a tendency to look at folks who get into ethical and legal trouble and say, "I know I would never behave like that." You probably would not, but you are only seeing them at their last step. You did not see the tiny steps that led to their eventual downfall. Study how and why they made the decisions they made. The idea is to try to avoid feeling superior to those who have made mistakes; real learning comes with understanding the flaws in their analyses and reasoning processes as well as the types of pressures that caused them to do what they did. Your goal is to develop a process for analysis and reasoning, one that finds you looking at ethical issues more deeply, instead of through the prism of emotions, desires, and pressures. You are not just studying ethics, you are studying business history. But, you are also studying you. Try to relate your vulnerabilities to theirs. Remember as you read these cases that you are reading about bright, capable, and educated individuals who made mistakes. The mistakes often seem clear when you study them in hindsight. But their ethical analyses at the time they were making these decisions was flawed, whether through poor perspective, pressure, or sometimes, the stuff of Greek tragedies: hubris.

One of the goals of this text is to help you avoid the traps and pitfalls that consume some people in business. As you study the cases in this unit and the others that follow try not to be too hard on the human subjects. Learn from them and try to discover the flaws in their ethical analyses.

One step that can give us greater clarity when we face ethical dilemmas is a credo. A credo is different from a code of ethics and does not consist of the virtues that companies usually list in a code of ethics, such as: we are always honest; we follow the laws. The credo demands more because it sets the parameters for those virtues. A credo is virtue in action. A credo defines you and your ethical boundaries.

You get your personal credo with introspection on two areas of questions:

1. Who are you? Many people define themselves by the trappings of success, such as how much money they have or make, the type of cars they drive, their clothes, and all things tangible and material. A credo grounds you and means that you need to find a way to describe yourself in terms or qualities that are part of you no matter what happens to you financially, professionally, or in your career. For example, one good answer to "Who are you?" might be that you have a talent and ability for art or writing. Another may be that you are kind, showing those Solomon-like virtues in Reading 1.1 to others around you. List those qualities you could have and keep regardless of all the outer trappings.

2. The second part of your credo consists of answering this question: What are the things that you would never do to get a job? To keep a job? To earn a bonus? The answer to this question results in a list, one that you should be keeping as you read the cases and study the individual businesspeople who made mistakes. Perhaps the title of your list could be "Things I Would Never Do to Be Successful," "Things I Would Never Do to Be Promoted," or even "Things

I Would Never Do to Make Money." One scientist reflected on the most important line that he would never cross, and after you have studied a few of the product liability cases you will come to understand why this boundary was important to him, "I would never change the results of a study to get funding or promise anyone favorable results in exchange for funding." A worker at a refinery wrote this as his credo, "I would never compromise safety to stay on schedule or get my bonus." An auditor in a state auditor general's office wrote, "I would never sign a document that I know contains false information." The credo is a detailed list, gleaned from reading about the experiences of others, that puts the meat on Polonius's immortal advice to his son, Laertes, in Shakespeare's *Hamlet,* "To thine own self be true" (*Hamlet,* Act I, Scene III). We quote Polonius without really asking, "What does that mean?" The credo takes us from eloquent advice to daily action. The credo is a personal application of the lessons in the cases. You will spot the lack of definitive lines in these case studies and begin to understand how their decision processes were so shortsighted. The goal is to help you think more carefully, more deeply, and more fully about ethical issues.

As you think about your credo, especially who you are, keep the following thought from Jimmy Dunne III in mind. Mr. Dunne was the only partner who survived the near destruction of his financial firm, Sandler O'Neill, when the World Trade Center collapsed on September 11, 2001. Only 17 of Sandler O'Neill's 83 employees survived the tower's collapse. Mr. Dunne has been tireless in raising money for the families of the employees who lost their lives that day. When asked by *Forbes* magazine why he works so hard, Mr. Dunne responded, "Fifteen years from now, my son will meet the son or daughter of one of our people who died that day, and I will be judged on what that kid tells my son about what Sandler O'Neill did for his family." His personal credo focuses on both the long-term reputation of his firm and the impact his choices can have on his children's reputations.

Discussion Question

Explain the role "How do I want to be remembered?" plays in your credo?

Reading 1.2 The Parable of the Sadhu

Pressure, Small Windows of Opportunity, and Temptation[1]

Bowen H. McCoy

[In 1982], as the first participant in the new six-month sabbatical program that Morgan Stanley has adopted, I enjoyed a rare opportunity to collect my thoughts as well as do some traveling. I spent the first three months in Nepal, walking 600 miles through 200 villages in the Himalayas and climbing some 120,000 vertical feet. On the trip my sole Western companion was an anthropologist who shed light on the cultural patterns of the villages we passed through.

During the Nepal hike, something occurred that has had a powerful impact on my thinking about corporate ethics. Although some might argue that the experience has no relevance to business, it was a situation in which a basic ethical dilemma suddenly intruded into the lives of a group of individuals. How the group responded I think holds a lesson for all organizations no matter how defined.

The Sadhu

The Nepal experience was more rugged and adventuresome than I had anticipated. Most commercial treks last two or three weeks and cover a quarter of the distance we traveled.

---

[1]Reprinted by permission of *Harvard Business Review.* From "The Parable of the Sadhu," by Bowen H. McCoy, *Harvard Business Review* 61 (September/October 1983), 103–108. Copyright © 1983 by the Harvard Business School Publishing Corporation; all rights reserved.

My friend Stephen, the anthropologist, and I were halfway through the 60-day Himalayan part of the trip when we reached the high point, an 18,000-foot pass over a crest that we'd have to traverse to reach the village of Muklinath [*sic*], an ancient holy place for pilgrims.

Six years earlier I had suffered pulmonary edema, an acute form of altitude sickness, at 16,500 feet in the vicinity of Everest base camp, so we were understandably concerned about what would happen at 18,000 feet. Moreover, the Himalayas were having their wettest spring in 20 years; hip-deep powder and ice had already driven us off one ridge. If we failed to cross the pass, I feared that the last half of our "once in a lifetime" trip would be ruined.

The night before we would try the pass, we camped at a hut at 14,500 feet. In the photos taken at that camp, my face appears wan. The last village we'd passed through was a sturdy two-day walk below us, and I was tired.

During the late afternoon, four backpackers from New Zealand joined us, and we spent most of the night awake, anticipating the climb. Below we could see the fires of two other parties, which turned out to be two Swiss couples and a Japanese hiking club.

To get over the steep part of the climb before the sun melted the steps cut in the ice, we departed at 3:30 A.M. The New Zealanders left first, followed by Stephen and myself, our porters and Sherpas, and then the Swiss. The Japanese lingered in their camp. The sky was clear, and we were confident that no spring storm would erupt that day to close the pass.

At 15,500 feet, it looked to me as if Stephen were shuffling and staggering a bit, which are symptoms of altitude sickness. (The initial stage of altitude sickness brings a headache and nausea. As the condition worsens, a climber may encounter difficult breathing, disorientation, aphasia, and paralysis.) I felt strong, my adrenaline was flowing, but I was very concerned about my ultimate ability to get across. A couple of our porters were also suffering from the height, and Pasang, our Sherpa sirdar (leader), was worried.

Just after daybreak, while we rested at 15,500 feet, one of the New Zealanders, who had gone ahead, came staggering down toward us with a body slung across his shoulders. He dumped the almost naked, barefoot body of an Indian holy man—a sadhu—at my feet. He had found the pilgrim lying on the ice, shivering and suffering from hypothermia. I cradled the sadhu's head and laid him out on the rocks. The New Zealander was angry. He wanted to get across the pass before the bright sun melted the snow. He said, "Look, I've done what I can. You have porters and Sherpa guides. You care for him. We're going on!" He turned and went back up the mountain to join his friends.

I took a carotid pulse and found that the sadhu was still alive. We figured he had probably visited the holy shrines at Muklinath [*sic*] and was on his way home. It was fruitless to question why he had chosen this desperately high route instead of the safe, heavily traveled caravan route through the Kali Gandaki Gorge. Or why he was almost naked and with no shoes, or how long he had been lying in the pass. The answers weren't going to solve our problem.

Stephen and the four Swiss began stripping off outer clothing and opening their packs. The sadhu was soon clothed from head to foot. He was not able to walk, but he was very much alive. I looked down the mountain and spotted below the Japanese climbers marching up with a horse.

Without a great deal of thought, I told Stephen and Pasang that I was concerned about withstanding the heights to come and wanted to get over the pass. I took off after several of our porters who had gone ahead.

On the steep part of the ascent where, if the ice steps had given way, I would have slid down about 3,000 feet, I felt vertigo. I stopped for a breather, allowing the Swiss to catch up with me. I inquired about the sadhu and Stephen. They said that the sadhu was fine and that Stephen was just behind. I set off again for the summit.

Stephen arrived at the summit an hour after I did. Still exhilarated by victory, I ran down the snow slope to congratulate him. He was suffering from altitude sickness, walking fifteen steps, then stopping, walking fifteen steps, then stopping, walking fifteen steps, then stopping. When I reached them, Stephen glared at me and said: "How do you feel about contributing to the death of a fellow man?"

I did not fully comprehend what he meant.

"Is the sadhu dead?" I inquired.

"No," replied Stephen, "but he surely will be!"

After I had gone, and the Swiss had departed not long after, Stephen had remained with the sadhu. When the Japanese had arrived, Stephen had asked to use their horse to transport the sadhu down to the hut. They had refused. He had then asked Pasang to have a group of our porters carry the sadhu. Pasang had resisted the idea, saying that the porters would have to exert all their energy to get themselves over the pass. He had thought they could not carry a man down 1,000 feet to the hut, reclimb the slope, and get across safely before the snow melted. Pasang had pressed Stephen not to delay any longer.

The Sherpas had carried the sadhu down to a rock in the sun at about 15,000 feet and had pointed out the hut another 500 feet below. The Japanese had given him food and drink. When they had last seen him he was listlessly throwing rocks at the Japanese party's dog, which had frightened him.

We do not know if the sadhu lived or died.

For many of the following days and evenings Stephen and I discussed and debated our behavior toward the sadhu. Stephen is a committed Quaker with deep moral vision. He said, "I feel that what happened with the sadhu is a good example of the breakdown between the individual ethic and the corporate ethic. No one person was willing to assume ultimate responsibility for the sadhu. Each was willing to do his bit just so long as it was not too inconvenient. When it got to be a bother, everyone just passed the buck to someone else and took off. Jesus was relevant to a more individualist stage of society, and how do we interpret his teaching today in a world filled with large, impersonal organizations and groups?"

I defended the larger group, saying, "Look, we all cared. We all stopped and gave aid and comfort. Everyone did his bit. The New Zealander carried him down below the snow line. I took his pulse and suggested we treat him for hypothermia. You and the Swiss gave him clothing and got him warmed up. The Japanese gave him food and water. The Sherpas carried him down to the sun and pointed out the easy trail toward the hut. He was well enough to throw rocks at a dog. What more could we do?"

"You have just described the typical affluent Westerner's response to a problem. Throwing money—in this case food and sweaters—at it, but not solving the fundamentals!" Stephen retorted.

"What would satisfy you?" I said. "Here we are, a group of New Zealanders, Swiss, Americans, and Japanese who have never met before and who are at the apex of one of the most powerful experiences of our lives. Some years the pass is so bad no one gets over it. What right does an almost naked pilgrim who chooses the wrong trail have to disrupt our lives? Even the Sherpas had no interest in risking the trip to help him beyond a certain point."

Stephen calmly rebutted, "I wonder what the Sherpas would have done if the sadhu had been a well-dressed Nepali, or what the Japanese would have done if the sadhu had been a well-dressed Asian, or what you would have done, Buzz, if the sadhu had been a well-dressed Western woman?"

"Where, in your opinion," I asked instead, "is the limit of our responsibility in a situation like this? We had our own well-being to worry about. Our Sherpa guides were unwilling to jeopardize us or the porters for the sadhu. No one else on the mountain was willing to commit himself beyond certain self-imposed limits."

Stephen said, "As individual Christians or people with a Western ethical tradition, we can fulfill our obligations in such a situation only if (1) the sadhu dies in our care, (2) the sadhu demonstrates to us that he could undertake the two-day walk down to the village, or (3) we carry the sadhu for two days down to the village and convince someone there to take care of him."

"Leaving the sadhu in the sun with food and clothing, while he demonstrated hand-eye coordination by throwing a rock at a dog, comes close to fulfilling items one and two," I answered. "And it wouldn't have made sense to take him to the village where the people appeared to be far less caring than the Sherpas, so the third condition is impractical. Are you really saying that, no matter what the implications, we should, at the drop of a hat, have changed our entire plan?"

The Individual vs. the Group Ethic

Despite my arguments, I felt and continue to feel guilt about the sadhu. I had literally walked through a classic moral dilemma without fully thinking through the consequences. My excuses for my actions include a high adrenaline flow, a superordinate goal, and a once-in-a-lifetime opportunity—factors in the usual corporate situation, especially when one is under stress.

Real moral dilemmas are ambiguous, and many of us hike right through them, unaware that they exist. When, usually after the fact, someone makes an issue of them, we tend to resent his or her bringing it up. Often, when the full import of what we have done (or not done) falls on us, we dig into a defensive position from which it is very difficult to emerge. In rare circumstances we may contemplate what we have done from inside a prison.

Had we mountaineers been free of physical and mental stress caused by the effort and the high altitude, we might have treated the sadhu differently. Yet isn't stress the real test of personal and corporate values? The instant decisions executives make under pressure reveal the most about personal and corporate character.

Among the many questions that occur to me when pondering my experience are: What are the practical limits of moral imagination and vision? Is there a collective or institutional ethic beyond the ethics of the individual? At what level of effort or commitment can one discharge one's ethical responsibilities?

Not every ethical dilemma has a right solution. Reasonable people often disagree; otherwise there would be no dilemma. In a business context, however, it is essential that managers agree on a process for dealing with dilemmas.

The sadhu experience offers an interesting parallel to business situations. An immediate response was mandatory. Failure to act was a decision in itself. Up on the mountain we could not resign and submit our résumé to a headhunter. In contrast to philosophy, business involves action and implementation—getting things done. Managers must come up with answers to problems based on what they see and what they allow to influence their decision-making processes. On the mountain, none of us but Stephen realized the true dimensions of the situation we were facing.

One of our problems was that as a group we had no process for developing a consensus. We had no sense of purpose or plan. The difficulties of dealing with the sadhu were so complex that no one person could handle it. Because it did not have a set of preconditions that could guide its action to an acceptable resolution, the group reacted instinctively as individuals. The cross-cultural nature of the group added a further layer of complexity. We had no leader with whom we could all identify and in whose purpose we believed. Only Stephen was willing to take charge, but he could not gain adequate support to care for the sadhu.

Some organizations do have a value system that transcends the personal values of the managers. Such values, which go beyond profitability, are usually revealed when the organization is under stress. People throughout the organization generally accept its values, which, because they are not presented as a rigid list of commandments, may be somewhat ambiguous. The stories people tell, rather than printed materials, transmit these conceptions of what is proper behavior.

For twenty years I have been exposed at senior levels to a variety of corporations and organizations. It is amazing how quickly an outsider can sense the tone and style of an organization and the degree of tolerated openness and freedom to challenge management.

Organizations that do not have a heritage of mutually accepted, shared values tend to become unhinged during stress, with each individual bailing out for himself. In the great takeover battles we have witnessed during past years, companies that had strong cultures drew the wagons around them and fought it out, while other companies saw executives, supported by their golden parachutes, bail out of the struggles.

Because corporations and their members are interdependent, for the corporation to be strong the members need to share a preconceived notion of what is correct behavior, a "business ethic," and think of it as a positive force, not a constraint.

As an investment banker I am continually warned by well-meaning lawyers, clients, and associates to be wary of conflicts of interest. Yet if I were to run away from every difficult situation, I wouldn't be an effective investment banker. I have to feel my way through conflicts. An effective manager can't run from risk either; he or she has to confront and deal with risk. To feel "safe" in doing this, managers need the guidelines of an agreed-on process and set of values within the organization.

After my three months in Nepal, I spent three months as an executive-in-residence at both Stanford Business School and the Center for Ethics and Social Policy at the Graduate Theological Union at Berkeley. These six months away from my job gave me time to assimilate twenty years of business experience. My thoughts turned often to the meaning of the leadership role in any large organization. Students at the seminary thought of themselves as antibusiness. But when I questioned them they agreed that they distrusted all large organizations, including the church. They perceived all large organizations as impersonal and opposed to individual values and needs. Yet we all know of organizations where people's values and beliefs are respected and their expressions encouraged. What makes the difference? Can we identify the difference and, as a result, manage more effectively?

The word "ethics" turns off many and confuses more. Yet the notions of shared values and an agreed-on process for dealing with adversity and change—what many people mean when they talk about corporate culture—seem to be at the heart of the ethical issue. People who are in touch with their own core beliefs and the beliefs of others and are sustained by them can be more comfortable living on the cutting edge. At times, taking a tough line or a decisive stand in a muddle of ambiguity is the only ethical thing to do. If a manager is indecisive and spends time trying to figure out the "good" thing to do, the enterprise may be lost.

Business ethics, then, has to do with the authenticity and integrity of the enterprise. To be ethical is to follow the business as well as the cultural goals of the corporation, its owners, its employees, and its customers. Those who cannot serve the corporate vision are not authentic business people and, therefore, are not ethical in the business sense.

At this stage of my own business experience I have a strong interest in organizational behavior. Sociologists are keenly studying what they call corporate stories, legends, and heroes as a way organizations have of transmitting the value system. Corporations such as Arco have even hired consultants to perform an audit of their corporate culture. In a company, the leader is the person who understands, interprets, and manages the corporate value system. Effective managers are then action-oriented people who resolve conflict, are tolerant of ambiguity, stress, and change, and have a strong sense of purpose for themselves and their organizations.

If all this is true, I wonder about the role of the professional manager who moves from company to company. How can he or she quickly absorb the values and culture of different organizations? Or is there, indeed, an art of management that is totally transportable? Assuming such fungible managers do exist, is it proper for them to manipulate the values of others?

What would have happened had Stephen and I carried the sadhu for two days back to the village and become involved with the villagers in his care? In four trips to Nepal my most interesting experiences occurred in 1975 when I lived in a Sherpa home in the Khumbu for five days recovering from altitude sickness. The high point of Stephen's trip was an invitation to participate in a family funeral ceremony in Manang. Neither experience had to do with climbing the high passes of the Himalayas. Why were we so reluctant to try the lower path, the ambiguous trail? Perhaps because we did not have a leader who could reveal the greater purpose of the trip to us.

Why didn't Stephen with his moral vision opt to take the sadhu under his personal care? The answer is because, in part, Stephen was hard-stressed physically himself, and because, in part, without some support system that involved our involuntary and episodic community on the mountain, it was beyond his individual capacity to do so.

I see the current interest in corporate culture and corporate value systems as a positive response to Stephen's pessimism about the decline of the role of the individual in large organizations. Individuals who operate from a thoughtful set of personal values provide the foundation of a corporate culture. A corporate tradition that encourages freedom of inquiry, supports personal values, and reinforces a focused sense of direction can fulfill the need for individuality along with the prosperity and success of the group. Without such corporate support, the individual is lost.

That is the lesson of the sadhu. In a complex corporate situation, the individual requires or deserves the support of the group. If people cannot find such support from their organization, they don't know how to act. If such support is forthcoming, a person has a stake in the success of the group, and can add much to the process of establishing and maintaining a corporate culture. It is management's challenge to be sensitive to individual needs, to shape them, and to direct and focus them for the benefit of the group as a whole.

For each of us the sadhu lives. Should we stop what we are doing and comfort him; or should we keep trudging up toward the high pass? Should I pause to help the derelict I pass on the street each night as I walk by the Yale Club en route to Grand Central Station? Am I his brother? What is the nature of our responsibility if we consider ourselves to be ethical persons? Perhaps it is to change the values of the group so that it can, with all its resources, take the other road.

Discussion Questions

1. In 2006, the Bowen McCoy phenomenon repeated itself. Forty climbers passed by Briton David Sharp as he lay by the side of the path on an Everest trek. David Sharp died on the mountain. However, the following week, American guide Dan Mazur stayed with Australian Lincoln Hall until help could arrive. Mr. Hall survived, but Mr. Mazur had to forgo his climb and the resulting financial losses from not being able to lead his group to the summit. What questions and analysis might affect the decision processes in these two situations? Some gripping information to think about as you consider the issues: since Sir Edmund Hillary's initial conquest of Everest in 1953, some 3,000 climbers have made it to the top and 200 have died trying; and the cost of a climb is $60,000. Do you have some thoughts on your

credo based on Mr. McCoy's and Mr. Mazur's experiences and actions?

2. Why do you think no one made sure the sadhu was going to be fine? What would they have had to do to be sure that the sadhu would live?

3. Are the rules of the mountain different from the rules of our day-to-day lives? Is it survival of the fittest on the mountain?

4. Why do you think Mr. McCoy wrote about his experience?

Reading 1.3

What Are Ethics? From Line-Cutting to Kant

The temptation is remarkable. The run is long. The body screams, "No more!" So, when some runners in the New York City Marathon hit the Queensboro Bridge temptation sets in and, rather than finishing the last 10 miles through Harlem and the Bronx, they hop a ride on the subway and head toward the finish line at Central Park. A total of 46 runners used the subway solution to finish the race in the 2008 New York City Marathon. We look at this conduct and react, "That is REALLY unfair." Others, particularly the 46, respond, "So I skipped a few boroughs. I didn't do anything illegal." That's where ethics come in; ethics apply where there are no laws but our universal reaction is, "It just doesn't seem right."

We all don't run marathons (or run partial marathons), but we do see ethical issues and lapses each day. When the revelations about golf superstar Tiger Woods's marital infidelity slowly and painfully dribbled out in the media, the result was not an arrest but our reaction of dismay for the unfairness of his conduct and the false impression his public/endorsement persona left that was inconsistent with his private behavior. We feel something's not right, but there is not always a criminal wrong or even a punishment. Phoebe Prince, an Irish immigrant attending South Hadley High School in Massachusetts, committed suicide on January 14, 2010, after a lengthy period of bullying by a clique of five popular students. The district attorney has cobbled together some criminal charges against the five taunters but the criminal case is much more difficult to make than the ethical case against the five for interpersonal abuse. We look at the tragedy and wonder why the five did not curb their own conduct? That idea of self-policing, of stopping ourselves when we are hurting others, even though our conduct does not violate a law, is the self-restraint that ethics brings.

We are probably unanimous in our conclusion that those in the examples cited all behaved unethically. We may not be able to zero in on what bothers us about their conduct, but we know an ethics violation, or an ethical breach, when we see one.

But what is ethics? What do we mean when we say that someone has acted unethically? Ethical standards are not the standards of the law. In fact, they are a higher standard. A great many philosophers have gone round and round trying to define ethics and debated the great ethical dilemmas of their time and ours. They have debated everything from the sources of authority on what is right and what is wrong to finding the answers to ethical dilemmas. An understanding of their language and views might help you to explain what exactly you are studying and can also provide you with insights as you study the cases about personal and business ethics. Ethical theories have been described and evolved as a means for applying logic and analysis to ethical dilemmas. The theories provide us with ways of looking at issues so that we are not limited to concluding, "I think. . . ." The theories provide the means for you to approach a dilemma to determine why you think as you do, whether you have missed some issues and facts in reaching your conclusion, and if there are others with different views who have points that require further analysis.

Normative Standards as Ethics

Sometimes referred to as *normative standards* in philosophy, ethical standards are the generally accepted rules of conduct that govern society. Ethical rules are both standards and expectations for behavior, and we have developed them for nearly all aspects of life. For example, no statute in any state makes it a crime for someone to cut in line in order to save the waiting time involved by going to the end of the line. But we all view those who "take cuts in line" with disdain. We sneer at those cars that sneak along the side of the road to get around a line of traffic as we sit and wait our turn. We resent those who tromp up to the cash register in front of us, ignoring the fact that we were there first and that our time is valuable too.

If you have ever resented a line-cutter, then you understand ethics and have applied ethical standards in life. Waiting your turn in line is an expectation society has. "Waiting your turn" is not an ordinance, a statute, or even a federal regulation. "Waiting your turn" is an age-old principle developed because it was fair to proceed with the first person in line being the first to be served. "Waiting your turn" exists because when there are large groups waiting for the same road, theater tickets, or fast food at noon in a busy downtown area, we found that lines ensured order and that waiting your turn was a just way of allocating the limited space and time allotted for the movie tickets, the traffic, or the food. "Waiting your turn" is an expected but unwritten behavior that plays a critical role in an orderly society.

So it is with ethics. Ethics consists of those unwritten rules we have developed for our interactions with each other. These unwritten rules govern us when we are sharing resources or honoring contracts. "Waiting your turn" is a higher standard than the laws that are passed to maintain order. Those laws apply when physical force or threats are used to push to the front of the line. Assault, battery, and threats are forms of criminal conduct for which the offender can be prosecuted. But these laws do not address the high school taunters who make life miserable for the less popular. In fact, trying to make a crime out of these too-cruel interactions in the teen years often finds the courts ruling that the statute is too vague. But ethical standards do come in to fill that gap. The stealthy line-cutter who simply sneaks to the front, perhaps using a friend and a conversation as a decoy for edging into the front, breaks no laws but does offend our notions of fairness and justice. One individual put him or herself above others and took advantage of their time and too-good natures.

Because line-cutters violate the basic procedures and unwritten rules for line formation and order, they have committed an ethical breach. Ethics consists of standards and norms for behavior that are beyond laws and legal rights. We don't put line-cutters in jail, but we do refer to them as unethical. There are other examples of unethical behavior that carry no legal penalty. If a married person commits adultery, no one has committed a crime, but the adulterer has broken a trust with his or her spouse. We do not put adulterers in jail, but we do label their conduct with adjectives such as *unfaithful* and even use a lay term to describe adultery: *cheating*.

Speaking of cheating, looking at someone else's paper during an exam is not a criminal violation. You may be sanctioned by your professor and there may be penalties imposed by your college, but you will not be prosecuted by the county attorney for cheating. Your conduct was unethical because you did not earn your standing and grade under the same set of rules applied to the other students. Just like the line-cutter, your conduct is not fair to those who spent their time studying. Your cheating is unjust because you are getting ahead using someone else's work.

In these examples of line-cutters, adulterers, and exam cheaters, there are certain common adjectives that come to our minds: "That's *unfair*!" "That was *dishonest*!" and "That was *unjust*!" You have just defined ethics for yourself. Ethics is more than just common, or normative, standards of behavior. Ethics is honesty, fairness, and justice. The principles of ethics, when honored, ensure that the playing field is level, that we win by using our own work and ideas, and that we are honest and fair in our interactions with each other, whether personally or in business. However, there are other ways of defining ethical standards beyond just the normative tests of what most people "feel" is the right thing to do.

Divine Command Theory

The Divine Command Theory is one in which the resolution of dilemmas is based upon religious beliefs. Ethical dilemmas are resolved according to tenets of a faith, such as the Ten Commandments for the Jewish and Christian faiths. Central to this theory is that decisions in ethical dilemmas are made on the basis of guidance from a divine being. In some countries the Divine Command Theory has influenced the law, as in some Muslim nations in which adultery is not only unethical but also illegal and sometimes punishable by death. In other countries, the concept of natural law runs in parallel with the Divine Command Theory. Natural law proposes that there are certain rights and conduct controlled by God, and that no matter what a society does, it should not drift from those tenets. For example, in the United States, the Declaration of Independence relied on the notion of natural law, stating that we had rights because they were given to us by our Creator.

Ethical Egoism Theory: Ayn Rand and Atlas

Ethical Egoism holds that we all act in our own self-interest and that all of us should limit our judgment to our own ethical egos and not interfere with the exercise of ethical egoism by others. This view holds that everything is determined by self-interest. We act as we do and decide to behave as we do because we have determined that it is in our own self-interest.

One philosopher who believed in ethical egoism was the novelist Ayn Rand, who wrote books about business and business leaders' decisions in ethical dilemmas, such as *The Fountainhead* and *Atlas Shrugged*. These two famous books made Ms. Rand's point about ethical dilemmas: the world would be better if we did not feel so guilty about the choices we make in ethical dilemmas and just acknowledged that it is all self-interest. Ms. Rand, as an ethical egoist, would maintain order by putting in place the necessary legal protections so that we did not harm each other.

"Hobbesian" Self-Interest and Government

Ms. Rand subscribed to the school of thought of philosopher Thomas Hobbes, who also believed that ethical egoism was the central factor in human decisions. Hobbes also warned that there would be chaos because of ethical egoism if we did not have laws in place to control that terrible drive of self-interest. Hobbes felt we needed great power in government to control ethical egoism.

Adam Smith, Self-Interest, and Moral Sentiments

Although he too believed that humans act in their own self-interest, and so was a bit of an ethical egoist, Adam Smith, a philosopher and an economist, also maintained that humans define self-interest differently from the selfishness theory that Hobbes and Rand feared would consume the world if not checked by legal safeguards. Adam Smith wrote, in *The Theory of the Moral Sentiments,* that humans are rational and understand that, for example fraud is in no one's self-interest—not even that of the perpetrator, who does benefit temporarily until, as in the case of so many executives today, federal and state officials come calling with subpoenas and indictments. (For an excerpt from Adam Smith's *Moral Sentiments,* see Reading 8.4.) That is, many believe that they can lie in business transactions and get ahead. Adam Smith argues that although many can and do lie to close a deal or get ahead, they cannot continue that pattern of selfish behavior because just one or two times of treating others this way results in a business community spreading the word: don't do business with them because they cannot be trusted. The result is that they are shunned from doing business at least for a time, if not forever. In other words, Smith believed that there was some force of long-term self-interest that keeps businesses running ethically and that chaos only results in limited markets for limited periods as one or two rotten apples use their Ethical Egoism in a selfish, rather than self-interest, sense to their own temporary advantage.

The Utilitarian Theory: Bentham and Mill

Philosophers Jeremy Bentham and John Stuart Mill moved to the opposite end of ethical egoism and argued that resolution of ethical dilemmas requires a balancing effort in which we minimize the harms that result from a decision even as we maximize the benefits. Mill is known for his *greatest happiness principle,* which provides that we should resolve ethical dilemmas by bringing the greatest good to the greatest number of people. There will always be a few disgruntled souls in every ethical dilemma solution, so we just do the most good that we can.

Some of the issues to which we have applied utilitarianism include those that involve some form of rationing of resources in order to provide for all, such as with providing universal health care even though some individuals may not be able to obtain advanced treatments in the interest of providing some health care for all. There is a constant balancing of the interests of the most good for the greatest number when the interests of protecting the environment are weighed against the need for electricity, cars, and factories. Utilitarianism is a theory of balancing that requires us to look at the impact of our proposed solutions to ethical dilemmas from the viewpoints of all those who are affected and try to do the greatest good for the greatest number.

The Categorical Imperative and Immanuel Kant

Philosopher Immanuel Kant's theories are complex, but he is a respecter of persons. That is, Kant does not allow any resolution of an ethical dilemma in which human beings are used as a means by which others obtain benefits. That might sound confusing, so Kant's theory reduced to simplest terms is that you cannot use others in a way that gives you a one-sided benefit. Everyone must operate under the same usage rules. In Kant's words, "One ought only to act such that the principle of one's act could become a universal law of human action in a world in which one would hope to live." Ask yourself this question: If you hit a car in a parking lot and damaged it but you could be guaranteed that no one saw you do it, would you leave a note on the other car with contact information? If you answered, "No, because that's happened to me 12 times before and no one left me a note," then you are unhappy with universal behaviors but are unwilling to commit to universal standards of honesty and disclosure to remedy those behaviors.

Philosophers are not the easiest folks to reason along with, so an illustration will help us grasp their deep thoughts. For example, there are those who find it unethical to have workers in developing nations labor in garment sweatshops for pennies per hour. The pennies-per-hour wage seems unjust to them. However, suppose the company was operating under one of its universal principles: Always pay a fair wage to those who work for it. A "fair wage" in that country might be pennies, and the company owner could argue, "I would work for that wage if I lived in that country." The company owner could also argue, "But, if I lived in the United States, I would not work for that wage, would require a much higher wage, and would want benefits, and we do provide that to all of our U.S. workers." The employer applies the same standard, but the wages are different.

The company has developed its own ethical standard that is universally applicable, and those who own the company could live with it if it were applied to them, but context is everything under the categorical imperative. The basic question is, are you comfortable living in a world operating under the standards you have established, or would you deem them unfair or unjust?

There is one more part to Kant's theory: you not only have to be fair but also have to want to do it for all the right reasons. Self-interest was not a big seller with Kant, and he wants universal principles adopted with all goodwill and pureness of heart. So, to not engage in fraud in business because you don't want to get caught is not a sufficient basis for a rule against fraud. Kant wants you to adopt and accept these ethical standards because you don't want to use other people as a means to your enrichment at their expense.

The Contractarians and Justice

Blame philosophers John Locke and John Rawls for this theory, sometimes called the *theory of justice* and sometimes referred to as the *social contract*. Kant's flaw, according to this one modern and one not-so-modern philosopher (Rawls is from the twentieth century, and Locke from the seventeenth), is that he assumed we could all have a meeting of the minds on what were the good rules for society. Locke and Rawls preferred just putting the rules into place via a social contract that is created under circumstances in which we reflect and imagine what it would be like if we had no rules or law at all. If we started with a blank slate, or *tabula rasa* as these philosophers would say, rational people would agree—perhaps in their own self-interest, or perhaps to be fair—that certain universal rules must apply. Rational people, thinking through the results and consequences if there were not rules, would develop rules such as "Don't take my property without my permission" and "I would like the same type of court proceeding that rich people have even if I am not so rich."

Locke and Rawls have their grounding in other schools of thought, such as natural law and utilitarianism, but their solution is provided by having those in the midst of a dilemma work to imagine not only that there are no existing rules but also that they don't know how they will be affected by the outcome of the decision, that is, which side they are on in the dilemma. With those constraints, Locke and Rawls argue, we would always choose the fairest and most equitable resolution of the dilemma. The idea of Locke and Rawls is to have us step back from the emotion of the moment and make universal principles that will survive the test of time.

Rights Theory

The Rights Theory is also known as an *Entitlement Theory* and is one of the more modern theories of ethics, as philosophical theories go. Robert Nozick is the key modern-day philosopher on this theory, which has two big elements: (1) everyone has a set of rights, and (2) it's up to the governments to protect those rights. Under this big umbrella of ethical theory, we have the protection of human rights that covers issues such as sweatshops, abortion, slavery, property ownership and use, justice (as in court processes), animal rights, privacy, and euthanasia. Nozick's school of thought faces head-on all the controversial and emotional issues of ethics including everything from human dignity in suffering to third-trimester abortions. Nozick hits the issues head-on, but not always with resolutions because governments protecting those rights are put into place by Egoists, Kantians, and Divine Command Theory followers.

A utilitarian would resolve an ethical dilemma differently from a Nozick follower. Think about the following example. The FBI has just arrested a terrorist who is clearly a leader in a movement that plans to plant bombs in the nation's trains, subways, and airports. This individual has significant information about upcoming planned attacks but refuses to speak. A utilitarian would want the greatest good for the greatest number and would feel that harsh interrogation methods would be justified to save thousands of lives. However, Nozick might balk at such a proposal because the captured terrorist's human rights are violated. These ideological differences enhance our ability to see issues from a 360-degree perspective as we analyze them.

Moral Relativists

Moral relativists believe in time-and-place ethics. Arson is not always wrong in their book. If you live in a neighborhood in which drug dealers are operating a crystal meth lab or crack house, committing arson to drive away the drug dealers is ethically justified. If you are a parent and your child is starving, stealing a loaf of bread is ethically correct. The proper resolution to ethical dilemmas is based upon weighing the competing factors at the moment and then making a determination to take the lesser of the evils as the resolution. Moral Relativists do not believe in absolute rules, virtue ethics, or even the social contract. Their beliefs center on the pressure of the moment and whether the pressure justifies the action taken. Former Enron Chief Financial Officer Andrew Fastow, in his testimony against his former bosses at their criminal trial for fraud, said, "I thought I was being a hero for Enron. At the time, I thought I was helping myself and helping Enron to make its numbers" (Andrew Fastow, trial testimony, March 7, 2006). In classic moral relativist mode, a little fraud to help the company survive was not ethically problematic at the time for Mr. Fastow. In hindsight, Mr. Fastow would also comment, "I lost my moral compass."

Back to Plato and Aristotle: Virtue Ethics

Although it seems odd that Aristotle and Plato are last in the list of theorists, there is reason to this ethical madness. Aristotle and Plato taught that solving ethical dilemmas requires training, that individuals solve ethical dilemmas when they develop and nurture a set of virtues. Aristotle cultivated virtue in his students and encouraged them to solve ethical dilemmas using those virtues that he had integrated into their thoughts. One of the purposes of this book is to help you develop a set of virtues that can serve as a guide in making both personal and business decisions. Think of your credo as the foundation for those virtues.

Solomon's Virtues

Some modern philosophers have embraced this notion of virtue ethics and have developed lists of what constitutes a virtuous businessperson. The following list of virtue ethics was developed by the late Professor Robert Solomon:

Virtue Standard	Definition
Ability	Being dependable and competent
Acceptance	Making the best of a bad situation
Amiability	Fostering agreeable social contexts

Virtue Standard	Definition
Articulateness	Ability to make and defend one's case
Attentiveness	Listening and understanding
Autonomy	Having a personal identity
Caring	Worrying about the well-being of others despite power
Charisma	Inspiring others
Compassion	Sympathetic
Coolheadedness	Retaining control and reasonableness in heated situations
Courage	Doing the right thing despite the cost
Determination	Seeing a task through to completion
Fairness	Giving others their due; creating harmony
Generosity	Sharing; enhancing others' well-being
Graciousness	Establishing a congenial environment
Gratitude	Giving proper credit
Heroism	Doing the right thing despite the consequences
Honesty	Telling the truth; not lying
Humility	Giving proper credit
Humor	Bringing relief; making the world better
Independence	Getting things done despite bureaucracy
Integrity	Being a model of trustworthiness
Justice	Treating others fairly
Loyalty	Working for the well-being of an organization
Pride	Being admired by others
Prudence	Minimizing company and personal losses
Responsibility	Doing what it takes to do the right thing
Saintliness	Approaching the ideal in behavior
Shame (capable of)	Regaining acceptance after wrong behavior
Spirit	Appreciating a larger picture in situations
Toughness	Maintaining one's position
Trust	Dependable
Trustworthiness	Fulfilling one's responsibilities
Wittiness	Lightening the conversation when warranted
Zeal	Getting the job done right; enthusiasm[1]

[1]From *A Better Way to Think About Business* by Robert Solomon, copyright © 1999 by Robert Solomon, p. 18. Used by permission of Oxford University Press. See also Kevin J. Shanahan and Michael R. Hyman, "The Development of a Virtue Ethics Scale," 42 *Journal of Business Ethics*, 2002, pp. 197, 200.

The list offers a tall order because these are difficult traits to develop and keep. But, as you study the companies, issues, and cases, you will begin to understand the mighty role that these virtues play in seeing the ethical issues, discussing them from all viewpoints, and finding a resolution that enable businesses to survive over the long term.

Discussion Questions

1. Your friend, spouse, child, or parent needs a specialized medical treatment. Without the specialized treatment, they cannot survive. You are able to get that treatment for them, but the cost is $6,800. You don't have $6,800, but you hold a job in the Department of Motor Vehicles. As part of your duties there, you process the checks, money orders, and other forms of payment sent in for vehicle registration. You could endorse these items, cash them, and have those funds. You feel that because you open the mail with the checks and money orders, no one will be able to discover the true amounts of funds coming in, and you can credit the vehicle owners' accounts so that their registrations are renewed. Under the various schools of thought on ethics, evaluate whether the embezzlement would be justified.

2. What is the difference between virtue ethics and utilitarianism?

3. In the movie *Changing Lanes,* Ben Affleck plays a young lawyer who is anxious to become a senior partner in a law firm in which one of the senior partners is his father-in-law, played by the late Sidney Pollack. Affleck discovers that his father-in-law has embezzled from clients, forged documents, and committed perjury, all felonies and all certainly grounds for disbarment. Affleck finally confronts Pollack and asks, "How do you live with yourself?" Pollack responds that he did indeed forge, embezzle, and perjure himself, but with the money that he made he is one of the city's greatest philanthropists. "At the end of the day, if I've done more good over here than bad in making the money, I'm happy." Under which ethical theories would you place Affleck and Pollack's ethical posture?

4. Could businesses use moral relativism to justify false financial reports? For example, suppose that the CFO says, "I did fudge on some of the numbers in our financial reports, but that kept 6,000 employees from losing their jobs." What problems do you see with moral relativism in this situation?

Reading 1.4

The Types of Ethical Dilemmas: From Truth to Honesty to Conflicts

The following twelve categories were developed and listed in *Exchange,* the magazine of the Brigham Young University School of Business.

Taking Things That Don't Belong to You

Everything from the unauthorized use of the Pitney Bowes postage meter at your office for mailing personal letters to exaggerations on travel expenses belongs in this category of ethical violations. Using the copy machine at work for your personal copies is another simple example of the type of conduct that fits into this category. Regardless of size or motivation, unauthorized use of someone else's property or taking property under false pretenses still means taking something that does not belong to you. A chief financial officer of a large electric utility reported that after taking a cab from LaGuardia International Airport to his midtown Manhattan hotel, he asked for a receipt. The cab driver handed him a full book of blank receipts and drove away. Apparently the problem of accurately reporting travel expenses involves more than just employees.

Saying Things You Know Are Not True

This category deals with the virtue of honesty. Assume you are trying to sell your car, one in which you had an accident, but which you have repaired. If the potential buyer asks if the car has been in an accident and you reply, "No," then you have given false information. If you take credit for someone else's idea or work, then you have, by your conduct, said something that is not true. If you do not give credit to others who have given you ideas or helped with a project, then you have not been forthright. If, in evaluating your team members on a school project, you certify that all carried their workload when, in fact, one of your team members was a real slacker, you have said something that was not true. If you do not disclose an accident that you had in the last year on an insurance application, you have not told the truth. If you state that you have a college degree on your résumé, but have not yet graduated, you have committed an ethical breach. If, in filling out a credit application, you put the salary you have when your employer announced a 25% pay cut beginning next quarter, you have not told the truth.

Giving or Allowing False Impressions

This category of ethical breach is the legal technicality category. What you have said is technically the truth, but it does mislead the other side. For example, if your professor asks you, "Did you have a chance to read the assigned ethics cases?" Even if you had not read the cases, you could answer a "Yes!" and be technically correct. You had "a chance" to read the cases; but you did not read them. The answer is not a falsehood, because you may have had plenty of chances to read the cases, but you didn't read the cases.

If you were to stand by silently while a coworker was blamed for something you did, you would leave a false impression. You haven't lied, but you allowed an impression of false blame to continue. Many offers that you receive in the mail have envelopes that make them seem as if they came from the Social Security Administration or another federal agency. The desired effect is to mislead those who receive the envelopes into trusting the company or providing information. That effect works, as attorneys general verify through their cases of fraud brought on behalf of senior citizens who have been misled by this false impression method.

A landscaping company that places decorative rocks in a drawing and bid for a customer contract proposal has created the impression that the rocks are included in the bid. If, after the customer signs the contract the landscaper reveals that the rocks require additional payment, the customer has been misled with a false impression that came from the drawing including the rocks.

Buying Influence or Engaging in Conflict of Interest

This category finds someone in the position of conflicting loyalties. An officer of a corporation should not be entering into contracts between his company and a company that he has created as part of a sideline of work. The officer is conflicted between his duty to negotiate the best contract and price for his corporation and his interest as a business owner in maximizing his profits. In his role as an officer, he wants the most he can get at the lowest price. In his role as a business owner, he wants the highest price he can get with the fewest demands. The interests are in conflict, and this category of ethical breach dictates that those conflicts be resolved or avoided.

Conflicts of interest need not be as direct as self-dealing by an officer of the company. For example, there would be a conflict of interest if a company awarded a construction contract to a firm owned by the father of the state attorney general while the state attorney general's office is investigating that company. A county administrator has a conflict of interest by accepting paid travel from contractors who are interested in bidding on the stadium project. Certainly, it is a good idea for the administrator to see the stadiums around the country and get an idea of the contractors' quality of work. But, the county should pay for those site visits, not the contractors. The administrator's job as a county employee is to hire the most qualified contractor at the best price. However, the benefits of paid travel would and could vary and contractors could use those site visits and travel perks to influence the decision on the award of the county contract for the stadium. Their interests in obtaining the contract are at odds with the county's interest in seeking the best stadium, not the best travel perks for the administrator. The administrator's loyalties to the county and the accommodating contractors are in conflict.

Those who are involved in this conflict-of-interest situations often protest, "But I would never allow that to influence me." The ethical violation is the conflict. Whether the conflict can or will influence those it touches is not the issue, for neither party can prove conclusively that a *quid pro quo* was not intended. The possibility exists, and it creates suspicion. Conflicts of interest are not difficult. They are managed in one of two ways: don't do it, or disclose it.

Hiding or Divulging Information

Taking your firm's product development or trade secrets to a new place of employment is the ethical breach of divulging proprietary information. Failing to disclose the results of medical studies that indicate your firm's new drug has significant side effects is the ethical breach of hiding information that the product could be harmful to purchasers. A bank that sells financial and marketing information about its customers without their knowledge or permission has divulged information that should be kept confidential.

Taking Unfair Advantage

Many consumer protection laws exist because so many businesses took unfair advantage of those who were not educated or were unable to discern the nuances of complex contracts. Credit disclosure requirements, truth-in-lending provisions, and new regulations on auto leasing all resulted because businesses misled consumers who could not easily follow the jargon of long and complex agreements. *USA Today* illustrated the fairness issues with a riddle. Suppose you have no cash and need to buy $100 worth of groceries. Which would cost you more?

  a. Taking out a payday loan with a 450 percent APR
  b. Overdrawing your debit card and paying the $27 fee

The answer is b because the $27 fee on your debit card would be equal to a 704 percent interest rate. (Assuming a 14-day repayment period and an average $17.25 fee per $100 for a payday loan).[2] Disclosures of the real costs of debt have been on a steady increase since 1970 as lenders and credit card companies found ways to charge fees that were not always clear from the lending and card agreements. Late fees often exceeded the unpaid card balance. While these fees were increasing, companies were also shortening the billing cycle so that customers had less time to pay. Cutoff times for payment at 9:00 AM were not disclosed as 9 AM, which meant that the customer had to pay a day earlier because mail does not arrive by 9 AM. These fees and practices were, for nearly a decade, an ethical issue of taking unfair advantage. Because credit card companies did not take care of the issues of unfairness, these practices are now prohibited or regulated. Under the Credit Card Accountability and Disclosure Act of 2010 (CARD), all of these practices are now regulated by law.

[2]Kathy Chu, "Anger at Overdraft Fees Gets Hotter, Bigger and Louder," *USA Today*, September 29, 2009, p. 1B.

Committing Acts of Personal Decadence

Although many argue about the ethical notion of an employee's right to privacy, it has become increasingly clear that personal conduct outside the job can influence performance and company reputation. Personal indiscretions by Tiger Woods affected the brand and reputation of his sponsors, from Accenture to Gatorade. Conduct in our personal lives does have an impact on how well we perform our jobs, including whether we can perform our jobs safely. For example, a company driver must abstain from substance abuse because with alcohol or drugs in his blood, he creates both safety and liability issues for his employer. Even the traditional company Christmas party and picnic have come under scrutiny, as the behavior of employees at, and following, these events has brought harm to others in the form of alcohol-related accidents.

Perpetrating Interpersonal Abuse

A manager who keeps asking an employee for a date not only violates the laws against sexual harassment but also has committed the ethical breach of interpersonal abuse. Interpersonal abuse consists of conduct that is demeaning, unfair, or hostile or involves others so that privacy issues arise. A manager who is verbally abusive to an employee falls into this category. The former CEO of HealthSouth, Richard Scrushy, held what his employees called the "Monday morning beatings." These were meetings during which managers who had not met their numbers goals were upbraided in front of others and subjected to humiliating criticism. A Merrill Lynch executive who dreaded the chastisement when Merrill did not match Goldman Sachs' earnings complained, "It got to the point where you didn't want to be in the office on Goldman earnings days."[3] A manager correcting an employee's conduct in front of a customer has not violated any laws, but has humiliated the employee and involved outsiders who have no reason to know of any employee issues. In some cases in this category, there are laws to protect employees from this type of conduct, but we are able to look at this conduct and see the ethical issue as we sum up with, "It's not fair," or, "It's not right."

Permitting Organizational Abuse

This category covers the way companies treat employees. Many U.S. firms with operations overseas, such as Nike, Levi Strauss, The Gap, and Esprit, have faced questions related to organizational abuse, including the treatment of workers in these companies' international operations and plants. Child labor, low wages, and overly long work hours all present ethical issues even though the laws of other countries are not violated by these practices. Although a business cannot change the culture of another country, it can perpetuate—or alleviate—organizational abuse through its respect of human rights in its international operations (see Case 5.6).

Violating Rules

Many rules, particularly when the size of an organization leads to bureaucracy and lines of authority, seem burdensome to employees trying to do their jobs. Stanford University experienced difficulties in this area of ethics when it used funds from federal grants for miscellaneous university purposes (see Case 9.10). Questions arose about the propriety of the expenditures, which quite possibly could have been legal under federal regulations in place at the time, but were not within the standards, policies, and guidelines on what were considered appropriate research expenditures. The results were some rather extravagant expenses billed to the federal government as research expenditures. Claiming

---

[3]Randall Smith, "O'Neal Out as Merrill Reels from Loss," *Wall Street Journal*, October 29, 2007, pp. A1, A16.

expenses beyond the rules and policies, although not a violation of the law at the time, was an ethical violation that damaged Stanford's reputation. Although rules can be revised and studied because of problems they create, they should be honored by employees until those changes are made.

Condoning Unethical Actions

In this category, the wrong is actually a failure to report an ethical breach in any of the other categories. What if you witnessed a fellow employee embezzling company funds by forging her signature on a check that was to be voided? Would you report that violation? What if you knew that an officer of your company was giving false testimony in a deposition? Would you speak up and let the court or lawyers know that the testimony is false? Recent studies indicate that over 80 percent of students who see a fellow student cheating would not report the cheating. A winking tolerance of others' unethical behavior is an ethical breach. Suppose that as a product designer you were aware of a fundamental flaw in your company's new product—a product predicted to catapult your firm to record earnings. Would you pursue the problem to the point of halting the distribution of the product? Would you disclose what you know to the public if you could not get your company to act?

Balancing Ethical Dilemmas

In these types of situations, there are no right or wrong answers; rather, there are dilemmas to be resolved. For example, Google continues to struggle with its decision to do business in the People's Republic of China because of known human rights violations by the government there and the government's censorship of its search engine. Decades earlier, other companies debated doing business in South Africa when that country's government followed a policy of apartheid. In some respects, the presence of these companies would help by advancing human rights by just affording those who had previously been unable the chance to work or attend school and, certainly, by improving the standard of living for at least some international operations workers. On the other hand, their ability to recruit businesses could help such governments sustain themselves by enabling them to point to economic successes despite human rights violations.

These twelve categories are resources for you to use as you analyze the cases in this book. As you read, think through the twelve categories and determine what ethical breaches have occurred. These categories help you in spotting the ethical issues in each of the cases.

Discussion Questions

1. Why do we have these categories of ethical dilemmas? How is it helpful to have this list?
2. Consider the following situations and determine which of the twelve categories each issue fits into.

   a. PGA golfer Phil Mickelson was scheduled to play in the 2009 Masters Tournament when he learned that his wife Amy had cancer. Mr. Mickelson had sponsors for his participation but felt that he needed to be with his wife and children. He withdrew from the tournament. As you categorize this dilemma be sure to think about the aftermath. Mr. Mickelson did play the 2010 Masters, where his wife Amy made her first public appearance on the 13th hole of the last round. Mr. Mickelson described his win that followed that year as being "for Amy." Discuss any lessons you can glean about balancing from this experience.

   b. A manager at a bank branch requires those employees who arrive late for work to clean the restrooms at the bank. The branch does have a janitorial service, but the manager's motto is "If you're late, the bathrooms must look great." An employee finds the work of cleaning the bathrooms in her professional clothes demeaning. Which category applies?

c. Jack Walls is the purchasing manager for a small manufacturer. He has decided to award a contract for office supplies to Office Mart. No one knows of Jack's decision yet, but Office Mart is anxious for the business and offers Jack a three-day ski vacation in Telluride, Colorado. Jack would love to take the trip but can't decide if there is an ethics question. Help Jack decide if there is.

3. In November 2008, golfer J. P. Hayes was participating in the PGA Tour's Qualifying Tournament, often called Q-School. Mr. Hayes, then 42, discovered after the second round of play that he had used a Titleist prototype ball for play that day, a ball not approved for PGA play. After his discovery, Mr. Hayes called a PGA official to let him know what had happened. As he suspected, Mr. Hayes was disqualified from Q-School. Achievement at this tournament means a type of automatic right to participate in the PGA's tournaments for the year. Without Q-school status, golfers do not qualify automatically for tournament play and have to hope for getting into tournaments by other means. The difference in earnings for the year for the golfer who does not qualify at Q-School versus the golfer who does is millions. Mr. Hayes said, "I'm kind of at a point in my career where if I have a light year, it might be a good thing. I'm looking forward to playing less and spending more time with my family. It's not the end of the world. It will be fine. It is fine."[4] Classify Mr. Hayes under the ethical schools of thought. Describe his credo.

Reading 1.5

On Rationalizing and Labeling: The Things We Do That Make Us Uncomfortable, but We Do Them Anyway

We often see ethical issues around us, and we understand ethics are important. But we are often reluctant to raise ethical issues, or, sometimes, we use strategies to avoid facing ethical issues. These strategies help salve our consciences. This section covers the strategies: rationalizations and avoidance techniques we use to avoid facing ethical issues.

Call It by a Different Name: "Way Harsh" Labels vs. Warm Language

If we can attach a lovely label to what we are doing, we won't have to face the ethical issue. For example, some people, including U.S. Justice Department lawyers, refer to the downloading of music from the Internet as *copyright infringement*. However, many who download music assure us that it is really just the lovely practice of *peer-to-peer file sharing*. How can something that sounds so generous be an ethical issue? Yet there is an ethical issue because copying copyrighted music without permission is taking something that does not belong to you or taking unfair advantage.

When baseball star Roger Clemens was confronted with lying about steroid use, he denied it and said that he did not lie but rather, "I misremembered." When Connecticut Attorney General Richard Blumenthal was confronted with the fact that he had overstated his military service as being in Vietnam when he served in the Marine Reserves only in the United States, he said, "I misspoke."

The financial practice of juggling numbers in financial statements, sometimes referred to as *smoothing earnings, financing engineering,* or sometimes just *aggressive accounting,* is less eloquently known as *cooking the books*. The latter description helps us to see that we have an ethical issue in the category of telling the truth or not leaving a false impression. But if we call what we are doing *earnings management,* then we never have to face

---

[4]"Hayes Turns Himself In for Using Wrong Ball, DQ'd from PGA Qualifier," espn.com news. November 23, 2008, http://sports.espn.go.com/golf/news/story?id=3712372. Accessed April 28, 2010.

the ethical issue because we are doing something that is finance strategy, not an ethics issue. One investor, when asked what he thought about earnings management, said, "I don't call it earnings management. I call it lying." Referring back to the categories helps us to be sure we are facing the issue and not skirting it with a different name.

Rationalizing Dilemmas Away: "Everybody Else Does It"

We can feel very comfortable and not have to face an ethical issue if we simply assure ourselves, "Everybody else does it." We use majority vote as our standard for ethics. A good day-to-day example is "Everybody speeds, and so I speed." There remains the problem that speeding is still a breach of one of the ethical categories: following the rules. Although you may feel the speed limit is too low or unnecessary, your ethical obligation is to follow those speed limits unless and until you successfully persuade others to change the laws because of your valid points about speed limits. One tool that helps us to overcome the easy slip into this rationalization is to define the set of *everybody*. Sometimes if we just ask for a list of "everybody," our reasoning flaw becomes obvious. "There's no list," we might hear as a response; "We just know everyone does it." With the speeding example, defining the set finds you in a group with some of the FBI's most wanted criminals, such as Timothy McVeigh, the executed Oklahoma City bomber; Ted Bundy, the executed serial murderer; and Warren Jeffs, the polygamist convicted of being an accessory to rape, all of whom ran afoul of traffic laws while they were at large and were caught because they were stopped for what we do as well: minor traffic offenses.

Rationalizing Dilemmas Away: "If We Don't Do It, Someone Else Will"

This rationalization is one businesspeople use as they face tough competition. They are saying, "Someone will do it anyway and make money, so why shouldn't it be us?" For Halloween 1994, there were O. J. Simpson masks and plastic knives and Nicole Brown Simpson masks and costumes complete with slashes and bloodstains. When Nicole Simpson's family objected to this violation of the basic standard of decency, a costume shop owner commented that if he didn't sell the items, someone down the street would. Nothing about the marketing of the costumes was illegal, but the ethical issues surrounding profiting from the brutal murder of a young mother abound.

Rationalizing Dilemmas Away: "That's the Way It Has Always Been Done"

When we hear, "That's the way it's always been done," our innovation feelers as well as our ethical radar should be up. We should be asking, "Is there a better way to do this?" Just as "Everybody does it" is not ethical analysis, neither is relying on the past and its standards a process of ethical reasoning. Business practices are not always sound. For example, the field of corporate governance within business ethics has taught for years that a good board for a company has independent directors, that is, directors who are not employed by the company, under consulting contracts with the company, or related to officers of the company. Independent boards were good ethical practice, but many companies resisted because their boards had always been structured a certain way and they would stick to that, saying, "This is the way our board has always looked." With the collapses of Enron, Adelphia, WorldCom, and HealthSouth and the scandal of substantial officer loans at Tyco, both Congress through the Sarbanes–Oxley (SOX) Act of 2002 and the Securities and Exchange Commission (SEC) through follow-up regulations now mandate an independent corporate board (see Reading 4.11 for a summary of the SOX changes). When board members performed consulting services for their companies, there was a conflict of interest. But everybody was doing it, and it was the way corporations had always been governed. This typical and prevailing practice resulted in lax corporate boards and company collapses. Unquestioning adherence to a pattern or practice of behavior often indicates an underlying ethical dilemma.

Rationalizing Dilemmas Away: "We'll Wait until the Lawyers Tell Us It's Wrong"

Many people rely only on the law as their ethical standard, but that reliance means that they have resolved only the legal issue, not the ethical one. Lawyers are trained to provide only the parameters of the law. In many situations, they offer an opinion that is correct in that a company's conduct does not violate the law. Whether the conduct they have passed judgment on as legal is ethical is a different question. For example, a team of White House lawyers concluded in a memo in March 2003 that international law did not ban torture of prisoners in Iraq because they were technically not prisoners of war. However, when pictures of prisoner abuse at the Abu Ghraib prison in Iraq emerged, the reaction of the public and the world was very different. The ethical analysis, which went beyond interpretation of the law, was that the torture and abuse were wrong, regardless of its compliance with treaty standards. Following the abuse scandal, the U.S. government adopted new standards for interrogation of prisoners. Although the lawyers were perfectly correct in their legal analysis, that legal analysis did not cover the ethical breaches of interpersonal and organizational abuse.

Rationalizing Dilemmas Away: "It Doesn't Really Hurt Anyone"

We often think that our ethical missteps are just small ones that don't really affect anyone else. We are not thinking through the consequences of our actions when we rationalize rather than analyze ethical issues in this manner. For example, it is probably true that one person who misrepresents her income on a mortgage application is not going to undermine the real estate market. However, if everyone who believes his or her misrepresentation on a mortgage application is singular and isolated, we end up with a great many mortgages in default, a glut of foreclosures, and a collapsed housing market. We lived through these systemic effects beginning in 2007 as the mortgage market collapsed. In analyzing ethical issues, we turn to Kant and other schools of thought and ask, "What if everyone behaved this way? What would the world be like?" Good ethical analysis requires a look at the impact of collective individual behaviors on the system.

When we are the sole rubberneckers on the freeway, traffic remains unaffected. But if everyone rubbernecks, we have a traffic jam. All of us making poor ethical choices would cause significant harm. A man interviewed after he was arrested for defrauding insurance companies through staged auto accidents remarked, "It didn't really hurt anyone. Insurance companies can afford it." The second part of his statement is accurate. The insurance companies can afford it—but not without cost to someone else. Such fraud harms all of us because we must pay higher premiums to allow insurers to absorb the costs of investigating and paying for fraudulent claims.

Rationalizing Dilemmas Away: "The System Is Unfair"

Somehow an ethical breach doesn't seem as bad if we feel we are doing it because we have been given an unfair hand. The professor is unreasonable and demanding, so why not buy a term paper from the Internet? Often touted by students as a justification for cheating on exams, this rationalization eases our consciences by telling us we are cheating only to make up for deficiencies in the system. Yet just one person cheating can send ripples through an entire system. The credibility of grades and the institution come into question as students obtain grades through means beyond the system's standards. If all students cheat, then the grading system is meaningless. We have no way to determine which students truly have the knowledge base and skills and which ones simply cheated to attain their standing.

Rationalizing Dilemmas Away: "It's a Gray Area"

One of the most popular rationalizations of recent years has been to claim, "Well, business doesn't have black and white. There's a great deal of gray." Sometimes the extent of ethical analysis in a business situation is to merely state, "It's a gray area," and the response from the group holding the discussion is "Fine! So long as we're in the gray area, we're moving on." In an interview with *Sports Illustrated,* racecar driver Danica Patrick was asked, "If you could take a performance-enhancing drug and not get caught, would you do it if it allowed you to win Indy?" She responded, "Yeah, it would be like finding a gray area. In motorsports we work in the gray areas a lot. You're trying to find where the holes are in the rule book.[5]

However, would those involved in their gray areas change their actions and decisions with the benefit of hindsight or even just more analysis of the issue? There will always be a gray area, but it may be a short-lived strategy. The sophisticated securities that were based on pools of mortgages were easily created, sold, and resold in an unregulated area of the market. But when the mortgages went south, so also did these investments and the companies that had based their strategies for growth on these gray areas (Lehman Brothers and Bear Stearns), and some are struggling to recover (Citigroup). Ethical analysis demands more than being satisfied with, "It's a gray area." Does everyone believe it is gray? Why do I want it to be gray? What if the gray area ends?

Rationalizing Dilemmas Away: "I Was Just Following Orders"

In many criminal trials and disputes over responsibility and liability, many managers will disclaim their responsibility by stating, "I was just following orders." In fact, when Lehman Brothers collapsed in 2008 because of its substantial holdings in high-risk mortgage pool instruments, many of its fund managers, who were aware of the risks, said, "I have blood on my hands." But then they explained the reason they kept selling the toxic securities even though they were aware of the problems—'They made me do it; I don't have to examine what I did."[6] Following orders does not excuse us from responsibility, both legally and ethically, for the financial harm to those who purchased those toxic securities.

Judges who preside over the criminal trials of war criminals often remind defendants that an order is not necessarily legal or moral. Good ethical analysis requires us to question or depart from orders when others will be harmed or wronged.

Rationalizing Dilemmas Away: "We All Don't Share the Same Ethics"

This rationalization is used quite frequently in companies with international operations. We often hear, "Well, this is culturally acceptable in other countries." We need a bit more depth and a great deal more analysis if this rationalization creeps into our discussions. Name one culture where individuals are known to claim, "There is nothing I like better than having a good old-fashioned fraud perpetrated against me," or, "I really enjoy being physically abused at work." This rationalization is a failure to acknowledge that there are some common values that demand universal application and consideration as we grapple with our decisions and behaviors around the world. You will never hear anyone, regardless of cultural differences, who says, 'Well, we here in _____ readily accept

---

[5]http://sportsillustrated.cnn.com/2009/racing/06/02/Danica_PED/index.html, June 2, 2009. Accessed July 8, 2010. Ms. Patrick has subsequently said she was only kidding in her response.

[6]Louise Story and Thomas Landon, Jr., "Life After Lehman: Workers Move On," *New York Times,* September 14, 2009, p. BU 1.

being swindled." This rationalization does not take a hard look at the conduct and whether there are indeed some universal values.

Discussion Questions

1. A recent *USA Today* survey found that 64 percent of patients in hospitals took towels, linens, and other items home with them.[7] Give a list of rationalizations these patients and their families might use that give them comfort in taking the items.

2. One former Lehman Brothers employee whose sales efforts and structuring of securities investments helped lead to the demise of the bank he loved and to an economic unraveling worldwide confessed, "I have blood on my hands."[8] Many individuals lost their life savings and others lost their retirement funds, but the employee explained that he did what he did because he was ordered to do so. Give some examples from history of how the ratio-

nalization of following orders resulted in horrific harm to many.

3. A man has developed a license plate that cannot be photographed by the red light and speeding cameras. When asked how he felt about facilitating drivers in breaking the law, he replied, "I am not the one with my foot to the gas pedal. They are. I make a product they can use." What rationalization(s) is he using?

4. A parent has instructed his young son to not mention his Uncle Ted's odd shoes and clothing: "If Uncle Ted asks you how you like his clothes or shoes, just tell him they are very nice." His son said, "But that's not the truth, Dad." The father's response was, "It's a white lie and it doesn't really hurt anyone." Evaluate the father's ethical posture.

Reading 1.6

The Slippery Slope, the Blurred Lines, and How We Never Do Just One Thing

In Scott Smith's book, *A Simple Plan,* the lead character Hank, his brother Jacob, and a friend Lou come upon a small plane buried in the rural snowdrifts of Ohio. Upon opening the plane's door they find the decomposing body of the pilot and a duffel bag full of $100 bills in ten-thousand-dollar packets—$3 million total. Initially, Hank tells his brother and Lou not to touch the money so that the police can conduct a proper investigation, but then a plan is hatched. Lou and Jacob want to keep one packet of the money and ask Hank what's wrong with doing that. Hank scolds them and says, "For starters, it's stealing." Hank reminds them that with that much money someone would be looking for it and would know that they had taken a packet. Hank also reminds them that even if he didn't take a packet he would be an accomplice if Jacob and Lou did.

Lou then proposes a solution: take it all. Hank wisely warns the two they could not spend it because everyone in their small town would know. So, Lou proposes a "simple plan." They will sit on the money for awhile and when the investigation is over and things have cooled down, they can move away and live on their shares of the money. Again, Hank reminds them that it is stealing. But Jacob calls it by a different name: lost treasure. Hank succumbs. Such an easy thing, simple plan.

But the initial decision was flawed. Whatever its soft label, their decision to walk away with the duffel bag was indeed taking something that did not belong to them. From there, the characters begin a game of whack-a-mole. With each twist and turn they

[7] "Theft a Problem at Hospitals," *USA Today*, March 5, 2010, p. 1A.
[8] Louise Story and Landon Thomas, Jr. "Tales from Lehman's Crypt," *New York Times*, Sept. 12, 2009, p. SB1.

have to cross another line to cover up their seizure of the duffel bag. There is a lie to the sheriff and the problem of a neighbor seeing them near the plane, and more problems come at them each day. Each new problem requires a resolution that involves more dastardly choices. The characters keep slipping, eventually committing murder.

Once you step outside those ethical norms, you do keep going. The proverbial slope becomes more slippery. Professor Dan Ariely of Duke University found that folks who knowingly wore fake designer sunglasses were more than twice as likely to cheat on an unrelated task given to them than those who were not wearing the fake sunglasses.[9] Once we have made peace with trademark infringement, we are willing to cross other lines. We just get comfortable with each step.

Discussion Questions

1. Marilee Jones, the former dean of admissions of the Massachusetts Institute of Technology (MIT), resigned after twenty-eight years as an administrator in the admissions office. The dean for undergraduate education received information questioning Ms. Jones's academic credentials. Her résumé, used when she was hired by MIT, indicated that she had degrees from Albany Medical College, Union College, and Rensselaer Polytechnic Institute. In fact, she had no degrees from any of these schools or from anywhere else. She had attended Rensselaer Polytechnic as a part-time nonmatriculated student during the 1974–75 school year, but the other institutions had no record of any attendance at their schools.

   When Ms. Jones arrived at MIT for her entry-level position in 1979, a degree was probably not required. However, she did progress through the ranks of the admissions office, and, in 1997, she was appointed dean of admissions. She explained that she wanted to disclose her lack of degrees at that point but that she had gone on for so long that she did not know how to come clean with the truth. Point to the initial decision, why it was flawed, why Ms. Jones made that decision, and what had to be done after that as a result of that choice.

2. Can you list some lines for your credo that you can glean from *A Simple Plan* and Ms. Jones's experience?

Case 1.7

Hank Greenberg and AIG

Hank Greenberg was the formidable CEO of AIG, the largest insurer in the United States. Mr. Greenberg was removed from his position when the SEC raised issues regarding the company's accounting practices and the accuracy of its financial statements. AIG eventually released financial statements that reduced its profits by $4.4 billion and, by 2008, had to be bailed out by the federal government in order to preserve the financial markets. Mr. Greenberg maintained then and maintains now that he did nothing wrong.

A story from his youth offers some insight into his ethical philosophy. When he was stationed in London during World War II, the United States and its military command were concerned about the conduct of U.S. soldiers and the impressions they left. They also recognized the need for the soldiers to have some recreation. The commanding officers gave the soldiers extra leave days if they used them for cultural events. The commanding officers had the theater, the symphony, and the ballet in mind as culture, not the usual activities for leave, such as drinking and chasing women (and, all too often, catching the women). The only requirement for the extra leave day was that the soldiers had to bring back a playbill or program from whatever cultural event they had attended.

---

[9]Dan Ariely home page, http://web.mit.edu/ariely/www/MIT. Accessed July, 20, 2010.

Mr. Greenberg would buy a ticket to the theater, go in, collect the playbill, and then head out the side exit to spend the time on other activities, the types of activities the commanders were trying to have the soldiers avoid, to wit, carousing. Mr. Greenberg had his proof of cultural activities, but he also had his usual fun.

Discussion Questions

1. Did Mr. Greenberg violate any rules as a soldier? Isn't the lack of clarity on the part of the commanding officers what caused the problem? What's wrong with using a loophole in the system?

2. Apply the various schools of thought, and see if you can fit Mr. Greenberg into one or more. As you do, think about the following excerpt from an editorial Mr. Greenberg wrote for the *Wall Street Journal:* "So, in order to stay out of the crosshairs of government regulators, com-panies are avoiding risks they might otherwise take to innovate or grow their businesses: 'Keep your head down.'"[10]

3. Do you believe that a pattern established in youth surfaced as he was running AIG?

4. In a 2006 AP survey of adults, 33 percent said it is "okay" to lie about your age, although only to make yourself younger, not for purposes of underage drinking. What rationalization(s) are the 33 percent using?

[10]Maurice R. Greenberg, "Regulation, Yes. Strangulation, No," *The Wall Street Journal,* August 21, 2006, p. A10.

Resolving Ethical Dilemmas

Reading 1.8
Some Simple Tests for Resolving Ethical Dilemmas

Nearly every business professor and philosopher has weighed in with models and tests that can be used for resolving ethical issues. The following sections offer summaries of the thoughts and models of others in the field of ethics.

Management Guru: Dr. Peter Drucker

An internationally known management expert, Dr. Peter Drucker offers the following as an overview for all ethical dilemmas: *primum non nocere,* which in translation means, "Above all do no harm." Adapted from the motto of the medical profession, Dr. Drucker's simple ethical test in a short phrase encourages us to make decisions that do not harm others. This test would keep us from releasing a product that had a defect that could cause injury. This test would have us be fair and decent in the working conditions we provide for workers in other countries. This test would also prevent us from not disclosing relevant information during contract negotiations. Johnson & Johnson has used Dr. Drucker's simple approach as the core of its business credo. (see Case 7.9)

Laura Nash: Harvard Divinity School Meets Business

Ethicist Laura Nash, of the Harvard Divinity School, has one of the more detailed decision-making models, with twelve questions to be asked in evaluating an ethical dilemma:

1. **Have you defined the problem accurately?** For example, often philosophical questions are phrased as follows: would you steal a loaf of bread if you were starving? The problem might be better defined by asking, "Is there a way other than stealing to take care of my hunger?" The rephrasing of the question helps us think in terms of honoring our values rather than rationalizing to justify taking property from another.

2. **How would you define the problem if you stood on the other side of the fence?** This question asks us to live by the same rules that we apply to others. For example, Donald Trump recently explained that when his employees develop a construction proposal for a customer for a price of $75 million, he simply adds on $50 to $60 million to the price and tells the customer the price is $125 million. Trump's firm then builds it for $100 million and is praised by the client for bringing the project in under price. Mr. Trump explains that the customer thinks he did a great job when he really did not. If Trump were on the other side, would he feel the same way about this method he uses for "managing customer expectations"? And note the use of the soft label here. This question forces us to look at our standards in a more universal way.

3. **How did this situation occur in the first place?** This question helps us in the future. We use it to avoid being placed in the same predicament again. For example, suppose that an employee has asked his supervisor for a letter of recommendation for a new job the employee may get if the references are good. The supervisor has always had difficulty with the employee, but found him to be

tolerable, kept him on at the company, and never really discussed any of his performance issues with him or even put those concerns in his annual evaluation. Does he make things up for the letter? Does he refuse to write the letter? Does he say innocuous things in the letter such as "He was always on time for work." This reluctant supervisor is in this situation because he has never been honest and candid with the employee. The employee is not aware that the supervisor had any problems or issues with him because the fact that he has asked for the reference shows that there has not been forthright communication.

4. **To whom and what do you give your loyalties as a person and as a member of the corporation?** Suppose that you know that your manager has submitted false travel invoices to the company. The expenses are false, padded, and unnecessary. No one in the accounting or audit department has caught his scheme. Saying something means you are loyal to your company (the corporation), but you have sacrificed your loyalty to your manager.

5. **What is your intention in making this decision?** Often we offer a different public reason for what we are doing as a means of avoiding examination of the real issue. An officer of a company may say that liberal accounting interpretations help the company, smooth out earnings, and keep the share price stable. But her real intention may be to reach the financial and numbers goals that allow her to earn her bonus.

6. **How does this intention compare with the likely results?** Continuing with the previous example, the stated intention of increasing or maintaining shareholder value may work for a time, but, eventually, the officer and the company will need to face the truth about the company's real financial picture. And the officer's real intention will be foiled as well because under Sarbanes–Oxley, officers who earn bonuses based on false financial statements must repay those bonuses and face criminal penalties as well.

7. **Whom could your decision or action injure?** Under this question, think of not only the direct harm that can result from a poor ethical choice but all the ripple effects as well. For example, in the case of the marathoners who took the subway during the New York City race, the real winners in three age categories were affected because they were not given their trophies or the rankings they deserved for nearly one year. Those who sponsor marathons now have to implement physical and electronic monitors to police runners. Those who enter the race must pay additional costs to cover this monitoring. And, of course, there is the cost of the post-race investigations. Not only do we never do just one thing; there is never just one person affected when we choose to bend the rules just a bit.

8. **Can you engage the affected parties in a discussion of the problem before you make your decision?** If you are considering "cheating" on a spouse or significant other, you face an ethical dilemma. The fact that you could not discuss what you are about to do with a person who has been very close to you and who you would betray indicates that your secret decision and action cross an ethical line.

9. **Are you confident that your position will be as valid over a long period of time as it seems now?** Sometimes cheating on an exam or purchasing a paper on the Internet seems to be an expedient way of solving time pressures, financial worries about going to school, and even just the concerns about finishing a semester or a degree. However, this question asks you to think about this small decision over the time frame of your life. When you look back, how will you feel about this decision? Or, what if your friend, roommate, or even someone who happens to see you cheat carries that knowledge of your ethical indiscretion with him or her? You always have the worry that he or she will know of your misstep and perhaps would be involved in your future in such a way that this knowledge could affect your potential. For example, what if someone who knows that you cheated works for a company you very much want to work for? Suppose further that the person interviewing you sees that you went to the same school as their employee. One question to that employee might be "Say, I see you went to school at Western U. I interviewed a Josh Blake from Western U. He wants to work with us. Do you know him? And what do you think of him?" Think ahead to their response: "Yes, I knew him at school. He cheated." Interestingly, this feedback is what happened to Joseph Jett, a Wall Street investment banker who was at the heart of a trading scandal at Kidder Peabody (see Case 4.7 for more details). When his credentials of a Harvard MBA were reported, someone from the school emerged to let the world know that although he had finished his course work at Harvard, he did not have his degree because he had not paid some fees. The fees might have been unpaid parking tickets. The fees may

have been library fines. What seemed like expedient budget decisions at the time he was a graduate student turned out to be something that harmed Mr. Jett's credibility when he was most in need of a good reputation. Over the long term your decision might not seem as expedient as it did during the pressure crunch of college.

10. **Could you disclose without qualms your decision or action to your boss, your CEO, the board of directors, your family, or society as a whole?** This question asks you to evaluate your conduct as if it were being reviewed by those who run your company. If you are thinking of padding your expense account, realize that you could not talk about your actions with these people because you are betraying their trust. This question also has a second part to it: could you tell your family? Sometimes we rationalize our way through business conduct or personal conduct, but know that if we had to face our families, we would realize we landed on the wrong side of the ethical decision. In the movie *While You Were Sleeping,* Peter is a wealthy lawyer who has fallen away from his parents' simple values. When his mother learns that Peter is engaged to marry an already married woman, she exclaims, "You proposed to a married woman?" Peter looks very sheepish. What seemed to be a fine decision in the confines of his social life suddenly looked different when his family was told.

11. **What is the symbolic potential of your action if understood? If misunderstood?** A good illustration for application of this question is in conflict-of-interest questions. For example, Barbara Walters, prior to her retirement from regular network news reporter for ABC News, was a cohost of the ABC prime-time news show *20/20.* In December 1996, Ms. Walters interviewed British composer Andrew Lloyd Webber (now Sir Andrew Lloyd Webber), and the flattering interview aired the same month as a segment on *20/20,* just prior to the opening of Sir Webber's Broadway production of *Sunset Boulevard.*

    Two months after the interview aired, a report in the *New York Post* revealed that Ms. Walters had invested $100,000 in Sir Webber's just-premiered *Sunset Boulevard.* ABC News responded that had it known of the investment, it would have disclosed it before the interview aired. ABC does have a policy on conflicts that permits correspondents to cover "businesses in which they have a minority interest."

    Sir Webber's *Sunset* cost $10 million to produce and investors received back 85 percent of their initial investment. Ms. Walters' interest in Sunset was 1 percent.

    Applying this question, even if everyone understands Ms. Walters' good intentions, the appearance is that of a conflict between her role as an investor in Webber's production and that of her role as an objective reporter, and regardless of its size the public is likely to perceive that the favorable journalism piece was done to pump up the production and, hence, ensure a return on her investment.

12. **Under what conditions would you allow exceptions to your stand?** You may have a strong value of always being on time for class, events, meetings, and appointments. You have adopted an absolute value on not being tardy. However, sometimes other values conflict. For example, suppose that your friend became ill and needed someone to drive her to the hospital, making you late for a meeting. You would be comfortable with that variance because your exceptions relate to the well-being of others. Likewise, you would drive more slowly and carefully in a storm to get to your meeting, something that will make you late. But, again, your exception is the safety and well-being of others. You won't be late because you stopped to talk or you didn't leave your apartment on time, but you are comfortable being late, an exception to your rule on punctuality, when safety and well-being are at stake.

These questions help us gain perspective and various views on the issue before us, and at least two of the questions focus on the past—what brought us to the dilemma and how we might avoid such dilemmas when we have caused them to arise.

A Minister and a One-Minute Manager Do Ethics: Blanchard and Peale

The late Dr. Norman Vincent Peale, an internationally known minister, and management expert Kenneth Blanchard, author of *The One Minute Manager,* offer three questions that managers should ponder in resolving ethical dilemmas: Is it legal? Is it balanced? How does it make me feel?

If the answer to the first question, "Is it legal?" is no, you might want to stop there. Although conscientious objectors are certainly needed in the world, trying out those philosophical battles with the SEC and Internal Revenue Service (IRS) might not be as effective as the results achieved by Dr. Martin Luther King Jr. or Mahatma Gandhi. There is a place for these moral battles, but your role as an agent of a business might not be an optimum place to exercise the Divine Command Theory. In early 2010, four individuals from the company Wise Guys, Inc., were indicted for wire fraud as well as gaining unauthorized access to computers for their cornering of the ticket markets for the 2006 Rose Bowl, the 2007 MLB playoffs, the play *Wicked*, and concerts for Bruce Springsteen and Hannah Montana.[11] The four had hired Bulgarian programmers to circumvent the controls placed on ticket sites to require entry of data prior to being able to purchase tickets. The result was that the four cornered the primary and, consequently, secondary ticket markets and prices, for the events noted. Regardless of how strongly we may feel about having access to tickets, the four are accused of violating the laws by circumventing computer access controls.

Answering the second Blanchard and Peale question, "Is it balanced?" requires a manager to step back and view a problem from other perspectives—those of other parties, owners, shareholders, or the community. For example, an M&M/Mars cacao buyer was able to secure a very low price on cacao for his company because of pending government takeovers and political disruption. M&M/Mars officers decided to pay more for the cacao than the negotiated figure. Their reason was that some day their company would not have the upper hand, and then they would want to be treated fairly when the price became the seller's choice.

Answering "How does it make me feel?" requires a manager to do a self-examination of his or her comfort level with a decision. Some decisions, though they may be legal and may appear balanced, can still make a manager uncomfortable. For example, many managers feel uncomfortable about the "management" of earnings when inventory and shipments are controlled to maximize bonuses or to produce a particularly good result for a quarter. Although they've done nothing illegal, managers who engage in such practices often suffer such physical effects as insomnia and appetite problems.

The Oracle of Omaha: Warren Buffett's Front-Page-of-the-Newspaper Test

This very simple ethical model requires only that a decision maker envision how a reporter would describe a decision or action on the front page of a local or national newspaper. For example, with regard to the NBC News report on the sidesaddle gas tanks in GM pickup trucks, the *USA Today* headline read, "GM Suit Attacks NBC Report: Says Show Faked Fiery Truck Crash." Would NBC have made the same decisions about its staging of the truck crash if that headline had been foreseen?

When Salomon Brothers' illegal cornering of the U.S. government's bond market was revealed, the *BusinessWeek* headline read, "How Bad Will It Get?"; nearly two years later, a follow-up story on Salomon's crisis strategy was headlined, "The Bomb Shelter That Salomon Built." During the aftermath of the bond market scandal, the interim chairman of Salomon, Warren Buffett, told employees, "Contemplating any business act, an employee should ask himself whether he would be willing to see it immediately described by an informed and critical reporter on the front page of his local paper, there to be read by his spouse, children, and friends. At Salomon we simply want no part of any activities that pass legal tests but that we, as citizens, would find offensive."

---

[11]Joel Stonington, "Four Charged in Bid to Buy, Resell Tickets," *The Wall Street Journal*, March 2, 2010, http://online .wsj.com/article/SB10001424052748703943504575095622582020594.html.

The Jennings National Enquirer Test

The purpose of this test is to have you step back from the business setting in which decisions are made and view the issue and choices from the perspective of an objective outsider. A modification of this test, named for its author, is the *National Enquirer* test: "Make up the worst possible headline you can think of and then re-evaluate your decision. In late 2007, when several large investment banking firms had to take multibillion-dollar losses for their excesses in the subprime lending market, the cover of *Fortune* magazine read, "What Were They Smoking?" Such a candid headline turns our heads a bit and forces us to see issues differently because of its metaphorical punch to the gut. Their views and perceptions can be quite different because they are not subject to the same pressures and biases. The purpose of this test is to help managers envision how their actions and decisions look to the outside world.

The *Wall Street Journal* Model

The *Wall Street Journal* model for resolution of ethical dilemmas consists of three components: (1) Am I in compliance with the law? (2) What contribution does this choice of action make to the company, the shareholders, the community, and others? And (3) what are the short- and long-term consequences of this decision? Like the Blanchard–Peale model, any proposed conduct must first be in compliance with the law. The next step requires an evaluation of a decision's contributions to the shareholders, the employees, the community, and the customers. For example, furniture manufacturer Herman Miller decided both to invest in equipment that would exceed the requirements for compliance with the 1990 Clean Air Act and to refrain from using rain forest woods in producing its signature Eames chair. The decision was costly to the shareholders at first, but ultimately they, the community, and customers enjoyed the benefits of a reputation for environmental responsibility as well as good working relationships with regulators, who found the company to be forthright and credible in its management of environmental regulatory compliance.

Finally, managers are asked to envision the consequences of a decision, such as whether headlines that are unfavorable to the firm may result. Sometimes the opposite is true. A decision that seems costly actually provides long-term benefit for the company. The initial consequences for Herman Miller's decisions were a reduction in profits because of the costs of the sustainability changes it made in its products and operations. However, the long-term consequences were the respect of environmental regulators, a responsive public committed to rain forest preservation, and Miller's recognition by *BusinessWeek* as an outstanding firm for 1992. The impact of Delta CEO Gerald Grinstein's decision to not accept his bonus for bringing the airline through a massive and successful Chapter 11 restructuring had profound effects on both the stock price and the morale of company employees. A decision to accept the perfectly legal bonus could have had adverse consequences that he avoided with his thoughtful decision to forgo a $10 million payment.

Other Models

Of course, there are much simpler models for making ethical business decisions. One stems from Immanuel Kant's categorical imperative (see pp. 13–14), loosely similar to the Golden Rule of the Bible: "Do unto others as you would have them do unto you." Treating others or others' money as we would want to be treated is a powerful evaluation technique in ethical dilemmas. Another way of looking at issues is to apply your standards in all situations and think about whether you would be comfortable. In other words, if the world lived by your personal ethical standards, would you be comfortable or would you be nervous?

Discussion Questions

1. Take the various models and offer a chart or diagram to show the common elements in each.
2. After viewing the chart, make a list of the kinds of things all those who have developed the models want us to think about as we resolve ethical dilemmas. Remember, you are working to develop a 360-degree perspective on issues. Stopping at legality is not enough if you are going to think through all the consequences of decisions. Just because something is legal does not mean it is ethical.

Reading 1.9

Some Steps for Analyzing Ethical Dilemmas

Although you now have a list of the categories of ethical breaches and many different models for resolution, you may still be apprehensive about bringing it all together in an analysis. Here are some steps to help you get at the cases, issues, and dilemmas from all perspectives.

Steps for Analyzing Ethical Dilemmas and Case Studies in Business

1. Make sure you have a grasp of all of the facts available. Be sure you are familiar with all the facts.
2. List any information you would like to have but don't and what assumptions you would have to make, if any, in resolving the dilemma.
3. Take each person involved in the dilemma and list the concerns they face or might have. Be sure to consider the impact on those not specifically mentioned in the case. For example, product safety issues don't involve just engineers' careers and company profits; shareholders, customers, customers' families, and even communities supported by the business are affected by a business decision on what to do about a product and its safety issue.
4. Develop a list of resolutions for the problem. Apply the various models for reaching this resolution. You may also find that as you apply the various models to the dilemma, you find additional insights for questions 1, 2, and 3. If the breach has already occurred, consider the possible remedies and develop systemic changes so that such breaches do not occur in the future.
5. Evaluate the resolutions for costs, legalities, and impact. Try to determine how each of the parties will react to and will be affected by each of the resolutions you have proposed.
6. Make a recommendation on the actions that should be taken.

In some of the cases you will be evaluating the ethics of conduct after the fact. In those situations, your recommendations and resolutions will center on reforms and perhaps recompense for the parties affected.

Each case in this book requires you to examine different perspectives and analyze the impact that the resolution of a dilemma has on the parties involved. Return to these models to question the propriety of the actions taken in each case. Examine the origins of the ethical dilemmas and explore possible solutions. As you work through the cases, you will find yourself developing a new awareness of values and their importance in making business decisions. Try your hand at a few before proceeding to the following sections. The following diverse cases offer an opportunity for application of the materials from this section and give you the chance to hone your skills for ethical resolutions.

Case 1.10

The Little Teacher Who Could: Piper, Kansas, and Term Papers

Piper High School is in Piper, Kansas, a town located about twenty miles west of Kansas City, Missouri. Christine Pelton was a high school science teacher there. Ms. Pelton, twenty-six, had a degree in education from the University of Kansas and had been at

Piper for two years. She was teaching a botany class for sophomores, a course that included an extensive project as part of the course requirements. The project, which included a lengthy paper and creative exhibits and illustrations, had been part of the curriculum and Piper High School tradition for ten years. Students were required to collect twenty different leaves, write one or two paragraphs about the leaves, and then do an oral presentation on their projects.

When Ms. Pelton was describing the writing portion of the project and its requirements to her students, she warned them not to use papers posted on the Internet for their projects. She had her students sign contracts that indicated they would receive a "0" grade if they turned in others' work as their own. The paper counted for 50 percent of their grade in the course. When the projects were turned in, Ms. Pelton noticed that some of the students' writing in portions of their papers was well above their usual quality and ability. Using an online service called Turn It In (http://www.turnitin.com), she found that 28 of her 118 students had taken substantial portions of their papers from the Internet.[12] She gave the students a "0" grade on their term paper projects. The result was that many of the students would fail the semester in the course.

The students' parents protested, and both her principal, Michael Adams, and the school district superintendent, Michael Rooney, backed her decision. However, the parents appealed to the school board, and the board ordered Ms. Pelton to raise the grades. Mr. Rooney, acting at the board's direction, told Ms. Pelton that the decision of the board was that the leaf project's weight should be changed from 50 percent to 30 percent of the course's total semester grade, and that the 28 students should have only 600 points deducted from their grade rather than the full 1,800 points the project was originally worth.

Ms. Pelton said, "I was really shocked at what their decision was. They didn't even talk to me or ask my side."[13] The result was that 27 of the 28 students avoided receiving an "F" grade in the course, but the changed weight also meant that 20 of the students who had not plagiarized their papers got a lower grade as a result. She resigned in protest on the day following the board's decision. She received twenty-four job offers from around the country following her resignation. Mr. Adams, the principal, and one teacher resigned at the end of the year to protest the lack of support for Ms. Pelton. Mr. Adams cited personal reasons for his resignation, but he added, "You can read between the lines."[14] At the time of Ms. Pelton's experience, 50 percent of the teachers had indicated they would resign. The superintendent, Michael Rooney, remained and said he stood by the teacher, but did not think that the school board was wrong: "I take orders as does everyone else, and the Board of Education is empowered with making the final decisions in the school district."[15]

The board debated the case in executive session and refused to release information, citing the privacy rights of the students. The local district attorney for Wyandotte County, Nick A. Tomasik, filed suit against the board for violating open meetings laws. The board members were deposed as part of his civil action. Citizens of Piper began a recall action against several of the school board members. The local chapter of the National Education Association, representing the eighty-five teachers in the district, was brought into settlement negotiations on the suit because of its concerns that action that affects teachers can be taken without input and without understanding the nature of the issues and concerns.

---

[12] Another program that can be used is http://www.mydropbox.com.

[13] "School Board Undoes Teacher's F's," *Wichita (Kans.) Eagle,* January 31, 2002, http://www.kansas.com/mld.

[14] Andrew Trotter, "Plagiarism Controversy Engulfs Kansas School," *Education Week,* April 3, 2003, http://www.edweek.org/ew/newstory.cfm?slug=29piper.h21.

[15] *Id.*

The fallout for Piper has been national. *Education Week* reported the following as results of the actions of the students and the school board:

> All twelve deans of Kansas State University signed a letter to the Piper school board that included the statement "We will expect Piper students . . . to buy into [the university's honor code] as a part of our culture."

> Angered, Piper school board member James Swanson—who is one of the targets of the recall drive—wrote the university to note that the implication that Piper students might be subject to greater scrutiny because of one controversial incident involving only 28 students was unfair. He received an apology from university officials.

> More troubling to the community, Piper students have also been mocked. At an interscholastic sporting event involving Piper, signs appeared among the spectators that read "Plagiarists."

> Students have reported that their academic awards, such as scholarships, have been derided by others. And one girl, wearing a Piper High sweatshirt while taking a college entrance exam, was told pointedly by the proctor, "There will be no cheating."[16]

Several of the parents pointed to the fact that there was no explanation in the Piper High School handbook on plagiarism. They also said that the students were unclear on what could be used, when they had to reword, and when quotations marks are necessary. Other parents complained about Ms. Pelton's inexperience. One teacher said, "I would have given them a chance to rewrite the paper."

Both the school board and the principal asked Ms. Pelton to stay, but she explained, "I just couldn't. I went to my class and tried to teach the kids, but they were whooping and hollering and saying, 'We don't have to listen to you any more.'"[17] Ms. Pelton began operating a day care center out of her home.

The annual Rutgers University survey on academic cheating reveals that 15 percent of college papers turned in for grades are completely copied from the Internet. In a look at Internet papers, the New Jersey Bar Foundation found the following:

> A Rutgers University survey of nearly 4,500 high school students revealed that only 46 percent of the students surveyed thought that cutting and pasting text directly from a Web site without attributing the information was cheating, while only 74 percent of those surveyed thought that copying an entire paper was cheating. Donald McCabe, the Rutgers University researcher that conducted the survey told USA Today, "In the students' minds what is on the Internet is public knowledge."[18]

A senior from the Piper, Kansas, school told CBS News, "It probably sounds twisted, but I would say that in this day and age, cheating is almost not wrong."[19]

Almost one year later the school board adopted guidelines on plagiarism for use in the district's school as policy. The Center for Academic Integrity gave its Champion of Integrity Award for 2002 to Ms. Pelton and Mr. Adams.

---

[16]Andrew Trotter, "Plagiarism Controversy Engulfs School," *Education Week*, April 3, 2002, http://www.edweek.org/ew/newstory.cfm?slug_29piper.h21.

[17]*Id.*

[18]New Jersey State Bar Foundation, http://www.njsbf.com/njsbf/student/eagle/winter03-2.cfm. Accessed July 20, 2010.

[19]Leonard Pitts, Jr., "Your Kid's Going to Pay for Cheating—Eventually," June 21, 2002. http://www.jewishworldreview.com/0602/pitts062102.asp. Accessed July 20, 2010.

The center's criteria for this award are that the teacher or administrator took:

1. an action, speech, or demonstration that draws attention to a violation of academic integrity
2. an action that, in an attempt to promote or uphold academic integrity, may subject the nominee to reprisal or ridicule
3. an action motivated by commitment to and conviction about the importance of academic integrity and not by public acclaim or monetary gains[20]

Discussion Questions

1. Do you believe the students understood that what they did was wrong? Why is this information important in your analysis?
2. Was the penalty appropriate?
3. What do you think of the grading modifications the board required? Be sure to list who was affected when you answer this question.
4. What did the parents miss in their decisions to intervene?
5. Evaluate the statement of the senior that cheating is no longer wrong.
6. What were the consequences for Piper and the students?

For More Information

Jodi Wilgoren, "School Cheating Scandal Tests a Town's Values," *New York Times,* February 14, 2002, pp. A1, A28.

Case 1.11

The Movie Ticket

You and your friend have purchased movie tickets to see *Avatar*. After seeing the movie, you realize as you are walking down the multiplex hallway that no theater employees are there and that you could slip into *The Hurt Locker* and see that at absolutely no cost. Your friend says, "Why not? Who's to know? Besides, it doesn't hurt anyone. Look at the price of a movie these days. These people are making money!"

You find that you hesitate just a bit. Should you take in the extra movie for free?

Discussion Questions

1. Be sure to apply the questions from the model. Consider systemic effects.
2. Offer your final decision on the second free movie and your explanation for your decision.

Case 1.12

Puffing Your Résumé

The résumé is a door opener for a job seeker. What's on it can get you in the door or cause the door to be slammed in your face. With that type of pressure, it is not surprising to learn that one 2006 study by a group of executive search firms showed that 43 percent of all résumés contain material misstatements.[21] A 2008 CareerBuilder.com survey of HR managers found that 49 percent of résumés had materially false information.[22] A *Wall Street Journal* analysis of the credentials of 358 executive and board members at

[20]http://www.academicintegrity.org/cai_champ.asp. Accessed July 20, 2010.

[21]Dan Barry, "Cheating Hearts and Lying Résumés," *New York Times,* December 14, 1997, pp. WK1, WK4.

[22]Don Macsai, "And I Invented Velcro," *BusinessWeek,* August 4, 2008, p. 15.

fifty-three publicly traded companies found discrepancies in seven of the executives'/
board members' claims about their background and experience and reality, most dealing
with them claiming to hold MBAs when they did not.[23]

Ed Andler, an expert in credential verification, says that one-third of all résumés contain some level of "creative writing." Mr. Andler notes that assembly-line workers don't
mention misdemeanor convictions and middle managers embellish their educational
background. One reference-checking firm looked into the background of a security guard
applicant and found he was wanted for manslaughter in another state.

Vericon Resources, Inc., a background check firm, has found that 2 percent of the
applicants they investigate are hiding a criminal past. Vericon also notes, however, that
potential employers can easily discover whether job candidates are lying about previous
employment by requesting W-2s from previous employers.

In one résumé-"puffing" case, according to Michael Oliver, a former executive re-
cruiter who is presently director of staffing for Dial Corporation, a strong candidate for
a senior marketing management position said he had an MBA from Harvard and four
years' experience at a previous company, where he had been a vice president of marketing. Actually, Harvard had never heard of him, he had worked for the firm for only two
years, and he had been a senior product manager, not a vice president.

In 1997, Dianna Green, a senior vice president at Duquesne Light, left her position at
that utility. The memo from the CEO described her departure as one that would allow
Ms. Green to pursue "other career interests she has had for many years." Despite the memo's
expression of sadness at her departure, Ms. Green was fired for lying on her résumé by stating that she had an administration MBA when, in fact, she did not.[24]

Ms. Green had worked her way up through the company and had been responsible
for handling the human resources issues in Duquesne's nine years of downsizing. At
the time of her termination, she was a director at Pennsylvania's largest bank and known
widely for her community service.

On the day following her termination, Ms. Green was found dead of a self-inflicted
gunshot wound.[25]

Discussion Questions

1. What do you learn from the tragedy of Ms. Green? Peter Crist, a background check expert, said, "You can't live in my world and cover stuff up. At some point in time, you will be found out if you don't come clean. It doesn't matter if it was 2 days ago or 20 years ago." As you think through these examples, can you develop some important principles that could be important for your credo?[26] Was the tragedy of Ms. Green avoidable? Was Duquesne Light justified in terminating her?

2. George O'Leary was hired by Notre Dame University as its head football coach in December 2001. However, just five days after Notre Dame announced Mr. O'Leary's appointment, Mr. O'Leary resigned. Mr. O'Leary's résumé indicated that he had a master's degree in education from New York University (NYU) and that he played college football for three years. O'Leary had been a student at NYU, but he never received a degree from the institution. O'Leary went to college in New Hampshire, but never played in a

[23]Keith J. Winstein, "Inflated Credentials Surface in Executive Suite," *Wall Street Journal*, November 13, 2008, p. B1.

[24]The information was revealed after Ms. Green was deposed in a suit by a former subordinate for termination. Because Ms. Green hesitated in giving a year for her degree, the plaintiff's lawyer checked and found no degree and notified Duquesne officials. Duquesne officials then negotiated a severance package.

[25]It should be noted that Ms. Green was suffering from diabetes to such an extent that she could no longer see well enough to drive. Also, during the year before her termination, her mother had died of a stroke and her youngest brother also had died. Carol Hymowitz and Raju Narisetti, "A Promising Career Comes to a Tragic End, and a City Asks Why," *Wall Street Journal*, May 9, 1997, pp. A1, A8.

[26]JoAnn S. Lublin, "No Easy Solution for Lies on a Résumé," *Wall Street Journal*, April 27, 2007, p. B2.

football game at his college and never received a letter as he claimed. When Notre Dame announced the resignation, Mr. O'Leary issued the following statement, "Due to a selfish and thoughtless act many years ago, I have personally embarrassed Notre Dame, its alumni and fans." Why did the misrepresentations, which had been part of his résumé for many years, go undetected? Evaluate the risk associated with the passage of time and a résumé inaccuracy. Would it be wrong to engage in résumé puffing and then disclose the actual facts in an interview? Be sure to apply the models.

3. Suppose that you had earned but, due to a hold on your academic record because of unpaid debts, had never been formally awarded a college degree. Would you state on your résumé that you had a college degree?

4. Suppose that, in an otherwise good career track, you were laid off because of an economic downturn and remained unemployed for thirteen months. Would you attempt to conceal the thirteen-month lapse in your résumé?

5. Is puffing a short-term solution in a tight job market?

6. James Joseph Minder was appointed to the board of gun manufacturer Smith & Wesson,

headquartered in Scottsdale, Arizona, in 2001. In early 2004, he assumed the position of chairman of the board. One month later, he resigned as chair of the board because the local newspaper, the *Arizona Republic,* reported that Mr. Minder had completed a 3.5- to 10-year prison sentence for a series of armed robberies and an escape from prison. He had carried a sawed-off shotgun during the string of robberies, committed while he was a student at the University of Michigan. Mr. Minder indicated that he had never tried to hide his past. In 1969, when he was released from prison, he finished his degree and earned a master's degree from the University of Michigan. He spent twenty years running a successful nonprofit center for inner-city youth until his retirement in 1997, when he moved to Arizona. Mr. Minder's position is that the subject of his troubled youth and criminal past never came up, so he never disclosed it.[27] Evaluate Mr. Minder's position and silence. What do you think of Smith & Wesson's press release indicating that Mr. Minder "had led an exemplary life for 35 years"? Mr. Minder remains on the board. Why did the public react so negatively to his past and position?

7. Is there something for your credo that you learn from all of these résumé experiences?

Case 1.13

Dad, the Actuary, and the Stats Class

Joe, a student taking a statistics course, was injured by a hit-and-run driver. The injuries were serious, and Joe was on a ventilator. Although Joe did recover, he required therapy for restoring his cognitive skills. He asked for more time to complete his course work, but the professor denied the request. Joe would have to reimburse his employer for the tuition if he did not complete the course with a passing grade. Joe's father works with stats a great deal. Joe's father went and took the course final for Joe, and Joe earned an "A" in the course.

Discussion Questions

1. What school of ethical thought does Joe's father follow?

2. Was Joe's father justified in helping Joe, an innocent victim in an accident? Does your answer change if you learn that Joe's father is an actuary?

3. List those who are affected by Joe's father's actions.

4. Can you think of alternatives to Joe's father's solution?

5. Evaluate the systemic effects if everyone behaved as Joe's father did.

---

[27]http://money.cnn.com/2004/02/27/news/smith_wesson/?cnn=yes. Accessed July 20, 2010.

Reading 1.14

On Plagiarism

Clarify the distinctions between *plagiarism, paraphrasing, and direct citation.*

Consider the following source and three ways that a student might be tempted to make use of it:

Source: The joker in the European pack was Italy. For a time hopes were entertained of her as a force against Germany, but these disappeared under Mussolini. In 1935 Italy made a belated attempt to participate in the scramble for Africa by invading Ethiopia. It was clearly a breach of the covenant of the League of Nations for one of its members to attack another. France and Great Britain, as great powers, Mediterranean powers, and African colonial powers, were bound to take the lead against Italy at the league. But they did so feebly and halfheartedly because they did not want to alienate a possible ally against Germany. The result was the worst possible: the league failed to check aggression, Ethiopia lost her independence, and Italy was alienated after all.[28]

Version A: Italy, one might say, was the joker in the European deck. When she invaded Ethiopia, it was clearly a breach of the covenant of the League of Nations; yet the efforts of England and France to take the lead against her were feeble and halfhearted. It appears that those great powers had no wish to alienate a possible ally against Hitler's rearmed Germany.

Comment: Clearly plagiarism. Though the facts cited are public knowledge, the stolen phrases aren't. Note that the writer's interweaving of his own words with the source's does not render him innocent of plagiarism.

Version B: Italy was the joker in the European deck. Under Mussolini in 1935, she made a belated attempt to participate in the scramble for Africa by invading Ethiopia. As J. M. Roberts points out, this violated the covenant of the League of Nations (J. M. Roberts, *History of the World* [New York: Knopf, 1976], p. 845). But France and Britain, not wanting to alienate a possible ally against Germany, put up only feeble and halfhearted opposition to the Ethiopian adventure. The outcome, as Roberts observes, was "the worst possible: the league failed to check aggression, Ethiopia lost her independence, and Italy was alienated after all" (Roberts, p. 845).

Comment: Still plagiarism. The two correct citations of Roberts serve as a kind of alibi for the appropriating of other, unacknowledged phrases. But the alibi has no force: some of Roberts's words are again being presented as the writer's.

Version C: Much has been written about German rearmament and militarism in the period 1933–1939. But Germany's dominance in Europe was by no means a foregone conclusion. The fact is that the balance of power might have been tipped against Hitler if one or two things had turned out differently. Take Italy's gravitation toward an alliance with Germany, for example. That alliance seemed so very far from inevitable that Britain and France actually muted their criticism of the Ethiopian invasion in the hope of remaining friends with Italy. They opposed the Italians in the League of Nations, as J. M. Roberts observes, "feebly and halfheartedly because they did not want to alienate a possible ally against Germany" (J. M. Roberts, *History of the World* [New York: Knopf, 1976], p. 845). Suppose Italy, France, and Britain had retained a certain common interest. Would Hitler have been able to get away with his remarkable bluffing and bullying in the later 1930s?

Comment: No plagiarism. The writer has been influenced by the public facts mentioned by Roberts, but he hasn't tried to pass off Roberts's conclusions as his own. The one clear borrowing is properly acknowledged.

Quoted from Frederick Crews, *The Random House Handbook*, 6th ed. (New York: McGraw-Hill, 1992), 181–83.

---

[28] J. M. Roberts, *History of the World* [New York: Knopf, 1976], p. 845.

Discussion Questions

1. List the important tools you have learned from this reading that will help you during your education.
2. Are there some additions you could make to your credo based on this instruction?

3. Make a list of what students gain through plagiarism. Make a list of the risks. Make a list of what students forgo when they engage in plagiarism.

Case 1.15

Wi-Fi Piggybacking

A new issue, which involves technology, is developing and might require legal steps. Internet users are piggybacking onto their neighbors' wireless service providers. The original subscriber pays a monthly fee for the service, but, without security, those located in the area are able to tap into the wireless network. They bog down the speed of the service. *Piggybacking* is the term applied to the unauthorized tapping into someone else's wireless Internet connection. Once limited to geeks and hackers, the practice is now common among the ordinary folk who just want free Internet service.

One college student said, "I don't think it's stealing. I always find people out there who aren't protecting their connection, so I just feel free to go ahead and use it." According to a recent survey, only about 30 percent of the 4,500 wireless networks onto which the surveyors logged were encrypted.

Another apartment dweller said she leaves her connection wide open because "I'm sticking it to the man. I open up my network, leave it wide open for anyone to jump on." One of the users of another's wireless network said, "I feel sort of bad about it, but I do it anyway. It just seems harmless." She said that if she gets caught, "I'm a grandmother. They're not going to yell at an old lady. I'll just play the dumb card."

Some neighbors ask those with wireless service if they could pay them in exchange for their occasional use rather than paying a wireless company for full-blown service. But the original subscribers do not really want to run their own Internet service.

Discussion Questions

1. What do you think of the statements of the users?
2. Apply Kant's theory to this situation and determine what his rule would be.

3. What will happen if enough neighbors piggyback on their neighbors' wireless access?

Compare & Contrast

Compare this conduct to cuts in line. What's different about piggybacking from cutting in line? What similarities are there between the explanations the piggybackers give and those offered by the employees who pad their expense accounts? What role does "sticking it to the man" play in ethical analysis? What does that phrase do for piggybackers and expense account padders?

Case 1.16

The Ethics Officer and First Class for TSA

Joan Drake is an ethics officer with a major U.S. corporation. At the airport, as she is trying to leave on a business trip, she is faced with very long lines at the security checkpoint. In an effort to maximize use of personnel and equipment, a TSA official asks Joan to go over to the first-class line where no one is waiting and go through that security line. Joan heeds the TSA official's instruction and sails through security.

Following this first-class upgrade experience via TSA, Joan noticed that the TSA officials really did not look closely at the boarding passes of passengers to determine whether they were first class. As a result, Joan, a dyed-in-the-wool coach flyer, began using the first-class line all the time with her coach boarding passes. "It saves everyone time and helps TSA look more efficient. I don't think there is anything wrong with using your brain to figure out a loophole like this."

Discussion Questions

1. Is Joan just getting ahead by using her head?
2. Evaluate Joan's statement that she is really helping everyone by her conduct.
3. Do you see any category of ethical breach here?
4. What would happen if everyone behaved as Joan does?

Compare & Contrast

Decide whether the following situation is different from Joan's. At some airports, there are several security checkpoints located at different gate wings. For example, there are checkpoints at the A gates, the B gates, the C gates, and so on. Once you are through the security checkpoint, you can access any of the A, B, or C gates, but if you go through the A checkpoint, you will have a hefty hike to the C gates if that's where your plane departs. Would there be any problem with going through Gate A when the lines are shorter there than they are at Gate C and then walking from the Gate A checkpoint to the Gate C checkpoint? Is this situation different from or the same as Joan's?

Case 1.17

Speeding on the Job: Obeying the Rules: Why We Do and Don't

Two police officers were caught on photo radar traveling (in their police cars, but not with sirens on) at 72 and 76 mph. The two officers were issued tickets. The policy of the police department was to require the officers to pay their own tickets when caught speeding on the job (when the sirens are not on, obviously) and to disclose the citations and officers' names to the public. When the media confronted the officers about speeding on the job, one responded, "We thought the speed limit was 65 mph." The speed limit was 65 mph normally in the photo-radar segment of the freeway, but construction work had it reduced to a 55 mph rate.

Discussion Questions

1. Why is compliance with employer rules important?
2. Why did the officers believe they were not speeding at 72 and 76 mph? A motto of the North Carolina State Troopers is, "Nine you're fine. Ten you're mine." What do the troopers mean? Relate their conduct to normative standards and discuss its effect on our conduct.
3. As you think about this simple example of speeding, ask yourself whether in your business or personal life there might be other areas where you are speeding but the normative standards have shifted.
4. Consider these thoughts from a former student:

   You briefly cited an example of following the traffic laws, and the members of the class took it quite out of proportion, and indeed the general reaction turned out to be one of rationalizing. But something about what you said really caused me to consider that subject and within those five minutes of discussion form a resolve. You see, I had always been an exceedingly excessive speeder, to the point where, if caught, I could get in BIG trouble. This always surprised people to find out about me, but I think it developed in my first year at ASU when I had an hour commute to campus. Regardless, I terrified everyone but myself. But when you said of speeding, "Is it ethical?" it really took me aback. I looked at the fact of it itself: it is a law to follow the speed regulations, which are in place for safety and order. I looked at myself: someone who wants to be able to be ethical in all things and for all of her life. I realized that if I give room for allowances on what *I know* is wrong, then how can I know that those *allowances* won't grow? I could not allow it. And in those five minutes, when the class was going on about photo radar, I grasped an understanding of my speeding that had previously escaped me: it's just not ethical.

It has now been five months from that day, and I can report that for five months I have not exceeded the posted speed limit. It is something of which I am constantly aware, and though I often rely on my cruise control, I have seen that choosing to be ethical, has given me strength to overcome other questions and situations. There have also been moments, as simple as that of peacefully coming to a stop at a red light, where I have been impressed with the thoughts, "That could have been a dangerous situation, but because you chose to follow the standards you are safe." I also notice that, though I may be running late or excited to get somewhere, I just have no desire to speed, and things, occurrences on the road, or actions by other drivers that may have previously upset me have no effect on me, maybe aside from chuckling at a reaction I may have seen myself having before. So I say thank you for your words and lessons, for I have seen a change in myself and a change in my life.

What message does this student have for you?

Case 1.18

The Pack of Gum

You have just purchased $130 of groceries. Upon returning home you discover that you did not pay for a pack of gum you picked up from the assortment of gums and mints at the checkout belt at the grocery store. You have the gum, but it is not on your receipt.

Discussion Questions

1. Would you take the gum back?
2. Should you take the gum back?

Solving Ethical Dilemmas and Personal Introspection

"Ability may get you to the top, but it takes character to keep you there."

—The late John Wooden, former basketball coach, UCLA

"A person with an ethical mind asks, 'If all workers in my profession . . . did what I do, what would the world be like?'"

—Professor Howard Gardner, Harvard University

The study of business ethics is not the study of what is legal but of the application of ethics to business decisions. For example, regardless of legislative and regulatory requirements, most of us are committed to safety and fairness for employees in the workplace. But what happens when there are conflicting ethical demands?

Employees also have certain moral standards, such as following instructions, doing an honest day's work for a day's pay, and being loyal to their employers. But what happens when their employers are producing products that, because of inadequate testing, will be harmful to users? To whom do employees turn if employers reject them and their concerns about the products?

Businesses, consumers, and employees too often subscribe to the "What's good for GM is good for the country" theory of business ethics. Jeff Dachis, the founder and former CEO of Razorfish, once said when he was questioned about the lack of independence on his board, "My partner and I control 10 percent of the company. What's good for me is good for all shareholders. Management isn't screwing up. We've created enormous shareholder value."[1] He spoke when his stock was worth $56 in June 1999. In May 2001, when he added three independent directors to his board and resigned as CEO, Razorfish stock was trading at $1.11 per share. No one at Razorfish did anything illegal, but it is the presence of perspective in a company through its board and also through the analytical framework of ethics that may save a company from its hubris. Businesses have now begun to realize that, even though Sir Alfred Coke alleges that a corporation has no conscience, the corporation must develop one. That conscience develops as firms and the individuals within them develop perspective on and guidelines for their respective conduct.

How does a business behave when the law does not dictate its conduct or the law permits conduct that might benefit shareholders but is harmful to others? And what do businesspeople do when their personal values conflict with what's in the best interest of their companies? An individual may think that lobbyists are antithetical to democracy but knows that without lobbyists his business and industry will not be represented in legislative matters. This unit deals with the overlapping ethical issues—those that affect us personally and in our business lives. From Novak to Carr to Drucker you have the opportunity to explore what some of the best minds in the field of business and society have offered in thinking about ethics and business. This unit has three parts. Section A defines business ethics and offers some insights into how business and personal ethics work together. Section B delves into the psychological factors that affect us as we work in a business setting: What gets in the way of effective ethical analysis in business? Section B also provides an important discussion of the reality of pressure at work: What gets in the way of ethics in business? Section C gives you the chance to understand a structured approach for analyzing ethical dilemmas. Section C also includes cases to help you apply all that you have learned in analysis, categories, rationalizations, and the reality of pressures in business.

---

[1] Erick Schonfeld, "Doing Business the Dot-Com Way," *Fortune*, March 20, 2000, 116.

Business and Ethics: How Do They Work Together?

Reading 2.1

What's Different about Business Ethics?

Based on your readings in Unit 1, you understand that society recognizes the value of ethics. The cases in Unit 1 focused on your individual conduct. But businesses are groups of individuals, and those individuals' ethical standards may not translate into a group setting. In addition, businesses are accountable to shareholders, creditors, and others who may be affected but are not always part of the business's decision processes and ethical analysis.

Businesses and managers also need a framework and process for ethical analysis. Some businesses simply adopt an ethical standard of following the law. If it's legal, then it's ethical is their standard. However, many actions well within the law still raise ethical issues. For example, the federal standard for slaughtering cows is that they must be "standers," i.e., able to stand up as they enter the pens. If they are "downers," they cannot be put into the meat supply and must be euthanized. However, the employees at Hallmark/Westland Meat Packing Co., motivated to not lose those sunk costs in lost cattle, used water hoses, electric prods, and forklifts to get the cattle to their feet so that they could be slaughtered for meat. A Humane Society undercover video documented this interpretation of the "stander" regulation. The result was the largest recall of beef in the United States. The company was following a legal standard and not looking at the intent of the regulation or beyond the present cost savings of getting more cattle into the meat supply. Its analysis did not take into account the risk of diseased meat making its way into the meat supply. Just the discovery of Hallmark/Westland's operations resulted in a shutdown of the company's operations. The plant has reopened under new ownership and is now called American Beef Packers. (See Case 4.25 for more information.) The defense of compliance with the law ignores the underlying ethical issues and the resulting risk. In other words the company was not walking through the categories, rationalizations, and analytical steps you studied in Unit 1.

Ethical decisions require businesses to look beyond compliance. There will always be a loophole, as you studied in the discussion of "It's a gray area" in Unit 1. But, as you will see throughout the remainder of this unit and the book, those loopholes are temporary and risky. A standard of legal compliance is akin to a pilot shaving the treetops of legal boundaries. As military pilots advise, "You can only tie the record for low-altitude flying." Asking whether conduct is legally and regulatory compliant is but one part of an ethical analysis.

But businesses have other factors at play in ethical dilemmas, beyond just the personal introspection you studied in Unit 1. There are organizational behavior factors such as performance and incentive plans. For example, at Hallmark/Westland, the manager of the cattle pens told police that he had to meet a quota of 500 cattle per day for slaughter.[2] Those performance pressures have to be factored in as you are making your business decisions. The issue would be clear to us in the laboratory setting of the classroom because our job, bonus, retention, or promotion is not on the line. Business decisions are

---

[2]David Kesmodel, "Oversight Flaw Led to Meat Recall," *Wall Street Journal*, March 11, 2008, p. B1.

made in the midst of economic pressures that must be studied and understood in order to analyze an ethical issue completely.

Discussion Questions

1. Think of something that you did at work in the past year that still bothers you. For example, one manager wrote, "I disagreed with a performance evaluation of an employee but I didn't speak up." Another wrote, "I let someone else take the blame for something I did." Fit these actions and your own example into one of the categories of ethical dilemmas in Unit 1. Then think through the reasons that you and these managers did what was bothersome.

2. Now think of something you did in your personal life in the past year that still bothers you. For example, one student wrote, "I lied to relatives on the phone so that they wouldn't come and visit," and another wrote, "I filled out an insurance form for a friend who had his bike stolen. I had sold it to him for $150 and he asked me to put down that I had sold it to him for $250 so that they insurance company would pay him enough to get a new bike to replace it." Again, think through the categories that apply as well as the reasons for doing these things.

3. As you think through your bothersome business and personal actions, decide whether ethics in our personal lives and business lives are really different.

Reading 2.2

The Ethics of Responsibility[3]

Peter Drucker

Countless sermons have been preached and printed on the ethics of business or the ethics of the businessman. Most have nothing to do with business and little to do with ethics.

One main topic is plain, everyday honesty. Businessmen, we are told solemnly, should not cheat, steal, lie, bribe, or take bribes. But nor should anyone else. Men and women do not acquire exemption from ordinary rules of personal behavior because of their work or job. Nor, however, do they cease to be human beings when appointed vice-president, city manager, or college dean. And there has always been a number of people who cheat, steal, lie, bribe, or take bribes. The problem is one of moral values and moral education, of the individual, of the family, of the school. But there neither is a separate ethics of business, nor is one needed.

All that is needed is to mete out stiff punishments to those—whether business executives or others—who yield to temptation. In England a magistrate still tends to hand down a harsher punishment in a drunken-driving case if the accused has gone to one of the well-known public schools or to Oxford or Cambridge. And the conviction still rates a headline in the evening paper: "Eton graduate convicted of drunken driving." No one expects an Eton education to produce temperance leaders. But it is still a badge of distinction, if not privilege. And not to treat a wearer of such a badge more harshly than an ordinary workingman who has had one too many would offend the community's sense of justice. But no one considers this a problem of the "ethics of the Eton graduate."

The other common theme in the discussion of ethics in business has nothing to do with ethics.

Such things as the employment of call girls to entertain customers are not matters of ethics but matters of esthetics. "Do I want to see a pimp when I look at myself in the mirror while shaving?" is the real question.

---

[3]From Peter F. Drucker, *Management: Tasks, Responsibilities, Practices* (New York: Harper & Row, 1974), 366–367. Copyright © 1973, 1974 by Peter F. Drucker. Reprinted by permission of HarperCollins Publishers Inc.

The first responsibility of a professional was spelled out clearly 2,500 years ago, in the Hippocratic oath of the Greek physician: *Primum non nocere:* "Above all, not knowingly to do harm."

No professional, be he doctor, lawyer, or manager, can promise that he will indeed do good for his client. All he can do is try. But he can promise that he will not knowingly do harm.

Discussion Questions

1. Does Dr. Drucker believe personal ethics and business ethics can be separated?

2. What is the Drucker test for ethics for business managers?

Reading 2.3
Is Business Bluffing Ethical?[4]

Albert Z. Carr

In the following classic reading, Albert Carr compares business to poker and offers a justification for business bluffing. Mr. Carr provides a different perspective from the previous discussion with its various models and categories geared more toward absolutes.

A respected businessman with whom I discussed the theme of this article remarked with some heat, "You mean to say you're going to encourage men to bluff? Why, bluffing is nothing more than a form of lying! You're advising them to lie!"

I agreed that the basis of private morality is a respect for truth and that the closer a businessman comes to the truth, the more he deserves respect. At the same time, I suggested that most bluffing in business might be regarded simply as game strategy—much like bluffing in poker, which does not reflect on the morality of the bluffer.

I quoted Henry Taylor, the British statesman who pointed out that "falsehood ceases to be falsehood when it is understood on all sides that the truth is not expected to be spoken"—an exact description of bluffing in poker, diplomacy, and business. I cited the analogy of the criminal court, where the criminal is not expected to tell the truth when he pleads "not guilty." Everyone from the judge down takes it for granted that the job of the defendant's attorney is to get his client off, not to reveal the truth; and this is considered ethical practice. I mentioned Representative Omar Burleson, the Democrat from Texas, who was quoted as saying, in regard to the ethics of Congress, "Ethics is a barrel of worms"[5]—a pungent summing up of the problem of deciding who is ethical in politics.

I reminded my friend that millions of businessmen feel constrained every day to say *yes* to their bosses when they secretly believe *no* and that this is generally accepted as permissible strategy when the alternative might be the loss of a job. The essential point, I said, is that the ethics of business are games ethics, different from the ethics of religion.

He remained unconvinced. Referring to the company of which he is president, he declared: "Maybe that's good enough for some businessmen, but I can tell you that we pride ourselves on our ethics. In thirty years not one customer has ever questioned my word or asked to check our figures. We're loyal to our customers and fair to our suppliers. I regard my handshake on a deal as a contract. I've never entered into price-fixing schemes with my competitors. I've never allowed my salesmen to spread injurious rumors about other companies. Our union contract is the best in our industry. And, if I do say so myself, our ethical standards are of the highest!"

He really was saying, without realizing it, that he was living up to the ethical standards of the business game—which are a far cry from those of private life. Like a gentlemanly poker player, he did not play in cahoots with others at the table, try to smear their reputations, or hold back chips he owed them.

But this same fine man, at that very time, was allowing one of his products to be advertised in a way that made it sound a great deal better than it actually was. Another item in his product line was notorious among dealers for its "built-in-obsolescence." He was holding back from the market a much-improved product because he did not want it to interfere with sales of the inferior item it would have replaced. He had joined with certain of his competitors in hiring a lobbyist to push a state legislature, by methods that he preferred not to know too much about, into amending a bill then being enacted.

In his view these things had nothing to do with ethics; they were merely normal business practice. He himself undoubtedly avoided outright falsehoods—never lied in so many words. But the entire organization that he ruled was deeply involved in numerous strategies of deception.

Pressure to Deceive

Most executives from time to time are almost compelled, in the interest of their companies or themselves, to practice some form of deception when negotiating with customers, dealers, labor unions, government officials or even other department[s] of their companies. By conscious misstatements, concealment of pertinent facts, or exaggeration—in short, by bluffing—they seek to persuade others to agree with them. I think it is fair to say that if the individual executive refuses to bluff from time to time—if he feels obligated to tell the truth, the whole truth, and nothing but the truth—he is ignoring opportunities permitted under the rules and is at a heavy disadvantage in his business dealings.

But here and there a businessman is unable to reconcile himself to the bluff in which he plays a part. His conscience, perhaps spurred by religious idealism, troubles him. He feels guilty; he may develop an ulcer or a nervous tic. Before any executive can make profitable use of the strategy of the bluff, he needs to make sure that in bluffing he will not lose self-respect or become emotionally disturbed. If he is to reconcile personal integrity and high standards of honesty with the practical requirements of business, he must feel that his bluffs are ethically justified. The justification rests on the fact that business, as practiced by individuals as well as by corporations, has the impersonal character of a game—a game that demands both special strategy and an understanding of its special ethics.

The game is played at all levels of corporate life, from the highest to the lowest. At the very instant that a man decides to enter business, he may be forced into a game situation, as is shown by the recent experience of a Cornell honor graduate who applied for a job with a large company.

This applicant was given a psychological test which included the statement, "Of the following magazines, check any that you have read either regularly or from time to time, and double-check those which interest you most. *Reader's Digest, Time, Fortune, Saturday Evening Post, The New Republic, Life, Look, Ramparts, Newsweek, Business Week, U.S. News & World Report, The Nation, Playboy, Esquire, Harper's, Sports Illustrated.*"

His tastes in reading were broad, and at one time or another he had read almost all of these magazines. He was a subscriber to *The New Republic,* an enthusiast for *Ramparts,* and an avid student of the pictures in *Playboy.* He was not sure whether his interest in *Playboy* would be held against him, but he had a shrewd suspicion that if he confessed to an interest in *Ramparts* and *The New Republic,* he would be thought a liberal, a radical, or at least an intellectual, and his chances of getting the job, which he needed, would greatly diminish. He therefore checked five of the more conservative magazines. Apparently it was a sound decision, for he got the job.

He had made a game player's decision, consistent with business ethics.

A similar case is that of a magazine space salesman who, owing to a merger, suddenly found himself out of a job:

This man was 58, and, in spite of a good record, his chance of getting a job elsewhere in a business where youth is favored in hiring practice was not good. He was a vigorous, healthy man, and only a considerable amount of gray in his hair suggested his age. Before beginning his job search he touched up his hair with a black dye to confine the gray to his temples. He knew that the truth about his age might well come out in time, but he calculated that he could deal with that situation when it arose. He and his wife decided that he could easily pass for 45, and he so stated his age on his résumé.

This was a lie, yet within the accepted rules of the business game, no moral culpability attaches to it.

The Poker Analogy

We can learn a good deal about the nature of business by comparing it with poker. While both have a large element of chance, in the long run the winner is the man who plays with steady skill. In both games ultimate victory requires intimate knowledge of the rules, insight into the psychology of the other players, a bold front, a considerable amount of self-discipline, and the ability to respond swiftly and effectively to opportunities provided by chance.

No one expects poker to be played on the ethical principles preached in churches. In poker it is right and proper to bluff a friend out of the rewards of being dealt a good hand. A player feels no more than a slight twinge of sympathy, if that, when—with nothing better than a single ace in his hand—he strips a heavy loser, who holds a pair, of the rest of his chips. It was up to the other fellow to protect himself. In the words of an excellent poker player, former President Harry Truman, "If you can't stand the heat, stay out of the kitchen." If one shows mercy to a loser in poker, it is a personal gesture, divorced from the rules of the game.

Poker has its special ethics, and here I am not referring to rules against cheating. The man who keeps an ace up his sleeve or who marks the cards is more than unethical; he is a crook, and can be punished as such—kicked out of the game or, in the Old West, shot.

In contrast to the cheat, the unethical poker player is one who, while abiding by the letter of the rules, finds ways to put the other players at an unfair disadvantage. Perhaps he unnerves them with loud talk. Or he tries to get them drunk. Or he plays in cahoots with someone else at the table. Ethical poker players frown on such tactics.

Poker's own brand of ethics is different from the ethical ideals of civilized human relationships. The game calls for distrust of the other fellow. It ignores the claim of friendship. Cunning deception and concealment of one's strength and intentions, not kindness and openheartedness, are vital in poker. No one thinks any the worse of poker on that account. And no one should think any the worse of the game of business because its standards of right and wrong differ from the prevailing traditions of morality in our society.

Discard the Golden Rule

This view of business is especially worrisome to people without much business experience. A minister of my acquaintance once protested that business cannot possibly function in our society unless it is based on the Judeo-Christian system of ethics. He told me:

"I know some businessmen have supplied call girls to customers, but there are always a few rotten apples in every barrel. That doesn't mean the rest of the fruit isn't

sound. Surely the vast majority of businessmen are ethical. I myself am acquainted with many who adhere to strict codes of ethics based fundamentally on religious teachings. They contribute to good causes. They participate in community activities. They cooperate with other companies to improve working conditions in their industries. Certainly they are not indifferent to ethics."

That most businessmen are not indifferent to ethics in their private lives, everyone will agree. My point is that in their office lives they cease to be private citizens; they become game players who must be guided by a somewhat different set of ethical standards.

The point was forcefully made to me by a Midwestern executive who has given a good deal of thought to the question:

"So long as a businessman complies with the laws of the land and avoids telling malicious lies, he's ethical. If the law as written gives a man a wide-open chance to make a killing, he'd be a fool not to take advantage of it. If he doesn't, somebody else will. There's no obligation on him to stop and consider who is going to get hurt. If the law says he can do it, that's all the justification he needs. There's nothing unethical about that. It's just plain business sense."

This executive (call him Robbins) took the stand that even industrial espionage, which is frowned on by some businessmen, ought not to be considered unethical. He recalled a recent meeting of the National Industrial Conference Board where an authority on marketing made a speech in which he deplored the employment of spies by business organizations. More and more companies, he pointed out, find it cheaper to penetrate the secrets of competitors with concealed cameras and microphones or by bribing employees than to set up costly research and design departments of their own. A whole branch of the electronics industry has grown up with this trend, he continued, providing equipment to make industrial espionage easier.

Disturbing? The marketing expert found it so. But when it came to a remedy, he could only appeal to "respect for the golden rule." Robbins thought this a confession of defeat, believing that the golden rule, for all its value as an ideal for society, is simply not feasible as a guide for business. A good part of the time the businessman is trying to do unto others as he hopes others will not do unto him.[6] Robbins continued:

"Espionage of one kind or another has become so common in business that it's like taking a drink during Prohibition—it's not considered sinful. And we don't even have Prohibition where espionage is concerned; the law is very tolerant in this area. There's no more shame for a business that uses a secret agent than there is for a nation. Bear in mind that there already is at least one large corporation— you can buy its stock over the counter—that makes millions by providing counterespionage service to industrial firms. Espionage in business is not an ethical problem; it's an established technique of business competition."

"We Don't Make the Laws."

Wherever we turn in business, we can perceive the sharp distinction between its ethical standards and those of the churches. Newspapers abound with sensational stories growing out of this distinction:

- We read one day that Senator Philip A. Hart of Michigan has attacked food processors for deceptive packaging of numerous products.[7]

---

[6]See Bruce D. Henderson, "Brinkmanship in Business," *Harvard Business Review,* March–April 1967, 49.

[7]*The New York Times,* November 21, 1966.

- The next day there is a congressional to-do over Ralph Nader's book, *Unsafe At Any Speed,* which demonstrates that automobile companies for years have neglected the safety of car-owning families.[8]
- Then another Senator, Lee Metcalf of Montana, and journalist Vic Reinemer show in their book, *Overcharge,* the methods by which utility companies elude regulating government bodies to extract unduly large payments from users of electricity.[9]

These are merely dramatic instances of a prevailing condition; there is hardly a major industry at which a similar attack could not be aimed. Critics of business regard such behavior as unethical, but the companies concerned know that they are merely playing the business game.

Among the most respected of our business institutions are the insurance companies. A group of insurance executives meeting recently in New England was startled when their guest speaker, social critic Daniel Patrick Moynihan, roundly berated them for "unethical" practices. They had been guilty, Moynihan alleged, of using outdated actuarial tables to obtain unfairly high premiums. They habitually delayed the hearings of lawsuits against them in order to tire out the plaintiffs and win cheap settlements. In their employment policies they used ingenious devices to discriminate against certain minority groups.[10]

It was difficult for the audience to deny the validity of these charges. But these men were business game players. Their reaction to Moynihan's attack was much the same as that of the automobile manufacturers to Nader, of the utilities to Senator Metcalf, and of the food processors to Senator Hart. If the laws governing their businesses change, or if public opinion becomes clamorous, they will make the necessary adjustments. But morally they have, in their view, done nothing wrong. As long as they comply with the letter of the law, they are within their rights to operate their businesses as they see fit.

The small business is in the same position as the great corporation in this respect. For example:

In 1967 a key manufacturer was accused of providing master keys for automobiles to mail-order customers, although it was obvious that some of the purchasers might be automobile thieves. His defense was plain and straightforward. If there was nothing in the law to prevent him from selling his keys to anyone who ordered them, it was not up to him to inquire as to his customers' motives. Why was it any worse, he insisted, for him to sell car keys by mail, than for mail-order houses to sell guns that might be used for murder? Until the law was changed, the key manufacturer could regard himself as being just as ethical as any other businessman by the rules of the business game.[11]

Violations of the ethical ideals of society are common in business, but they are not necessarily violations of business principles. Each year the Federal Trade Commission orders hundreds of companies, many of them of the first magnitude, to "cease and desist" from practices which, judged by ordinary standards, are of questionable morality but which are stoutly defended by the companies concerned.

In one case, a firm manufacturing a well-known mouth-wash was accused of using a cheap form of alcohol possibly deleterious to health. The company's chief executive, after testifying in Washington, made this comment privately:

We broke no law. We're in a highly competitive industry. If we're going to stay in business, we have to look for profit wherever the law permits. We don't make the

---

[8]Ralph Nader, *Unsafe at Any Speed: The Designed-in Dangers of the American Automobile* (New York: Grossman Publishers, Inc., 1965).

[9]U.S. Senator Lee Metcalf and Vic Reinemer, *Overcharge: How Electric Utilities Exploit and Mislead the Public, and What You Can Do About It* (New York: David McKay Company, Inc., 1967).

[10]*The New York Times,* January 17, 1967.

[11]Cited by Ralph Nader in "Business Crime," *The New Republic,* July 1, 1967, 7.

laws. We obey them. Then why do we have to put up with this "holier than thou" talk about ethics? It's sheer hypocrisy. We're not in business to promote ethics. Look at the cigarette companies, for God's sake! If the ethics aren't embodied in the laws by the men who made them, you can't expect businessmen to fill the lack. Why, a sudden submission to Christian ethics by businessmen would bring about the greatest economic upheaval in history!

It may be noted that the government failed to prove its case against him.

Cast Illusions Aside

Talk about ethics by businessmen is often a thin decorative coating over the hard realities of the game:

Once I listened to a speech by a young executive who pointed to a new industry code as proof that his company and its competitors were deeply aware of their responsibilities to society. It was a code of ethics, he said. The industry was going to police itself, to dissuade constituent companies from wrongdoing. His eyes shone with conviction and enthusiasm.

The same day there was a meeting in a hotel room where the industry's top executives met with the "czar" who was to administer the new code, a man of high repute. No one who was present could doubt their common attitude. In their eyes the code was designed primarily to forestall a move by the federal government to impose stern restrictions on the industry. They felt that the code would hamper them a good deal less than new federal laws would. It was, in other words, conceived as a protection for the industry, not for the public.

The young executive accepted the surface explanation of the code; these leaders, all experienced game players, did not deceive themselves for a moment about its purpose.

The illusion that business can afford to be guided by ethics as conceived in private life is often fostered by speeches and articles containing such phrases as, "It pays to be ethical," or, "Sound ethics is good business." Actually this is not an ethical position at all; it is a self-serving calculation in disguise. The speaker is really saying that in the long run a company can make more money if it does not antagonize competitors, suppliers, employees, and customers by squeezing them too hard. He is saying that oversharp policies reduce ultimate gains. That is true, but it has nothing to do with ethics. The underlying attitude is much like that in the familiar story of the shopkeeper who finds an extra twenty-dollar bill in the cash register, debates with himself the ethical problem—should he tell his partner?—and finally decides to share the money because the gesture will give him an edge over the s.o.b. the next time they quarrel.

I think it is fair to sum up the prevailing attitude of businessmen on ethics as follows:

We live in what is probably the most competitive of the world's civilized societies. Our customs encourage a high degree of aggression in the individuals striving for success. Business is our main area of competition, and it has been ritualized into a game of strategy. The basic rules of the game have been set by the government, which attempts to detect and punish business frauds. But as long as a company does not transgress the rules of the game set by law, it has the legal right to shape its strategy without reference to anything but its profits. If it takes a long-term view of its profits, it will preserve amicable relations, so far as possible, with those with whom it deals. A wise businessman will not seek advantage to the point where he generates dangerous hostility among employees, competitors, customers, government, or the public at large. But decisions in this area are, in the final test, decisions of strategy, not of ethics.

The Individual and the Game

An individual within a company often finds it difficult to adjust to the requirements of the business game. He tries to preserve his private ethical standards in situations that call for game strategy. When he is obliged to carry out company policies that challenge his conception of himself as an ethical man, he suffers.

It disturbs him when he is ordered, for instance, to deny a raise to a man who deserves it, to fire an employee of long standing, to prepare advertising that he believes to be misleading, to conceal facts that he feels customers are entitled to know, to cheapen the quality of materials used in the manufacture of an established product, to sell as new a product that he knows to be rebuilt, to exaggerate the curative powers of a medicinal preparation, or to coerce dealers.

There are some fortunate executives who, by the nature of their work and circumstances, never have to face problems of this kind. But in one form or another the ethical dilemma is felt sooner or later by most businessmen. Possibly the dilemma is most painful not when the company forces the action on the executive but when he originates it himself—that is, when he has taken or is contemplating a step which is in his own interest but which runs counter to his early moral conditioning. To illustrate:

- The manager of an export department, eager to show rising sales, is pressed by a big customer to provide invoices which, while containing no overt falsehood that would violate a U.S. law, are so worded that the customer may be able to evade certain taxes in his homeland.
- A company president finds that an aging executive, within a few years of retirement and his pension, is not as productive as formerly. Should he be kept on?
- The produce manager of a supermarket debates with himself whether to get rid of a lot of half-rotten tomatoes by including one, with its good side exposed, in every tomato six-pack.
- An accountant discovers that he has taken an improper deduction on his company's tax return and fears the consequences if he calls the matter to the president's attention, though he himself has done nothing illegal. Perhaps if he says nothing, no one will notice the error.
- A chief executive officer is asked by his directors to comment on a rumor that he owns stock in another company with which he has placed large orders. He could deny it, for the stock is in the name of his son-in-law and he has earlier formally instructed his son-in-law to sell the holding.

Temptations of this kind constantly arise in business. If an executive allows himself to be torn between a decision based on business considerations and one based on his private ethical code, he exposes himself to a grave psychological strain.

This is not to say that sound business strategy necessarily runs counter to ethical ideals. They may frequently coincide; and when they do, everyone is gratified. But the major tests of every move in business, as in all games of strategy, are legality and profit. A man who intends to be a winner in the business game must have a game player's attitude.

The business strategist's decisions must be as impersonal as those of a surgeon performing an operation—concentrating on objective and technique, and subordinating personal feelings. If the chief executive admits that his son-in-law owns the stock, it is because he stands to lose more if the fact comes out later than if he states it boldly and at once. If the supermarket manager orders the rotten tomatoes to be discarded, he does so to avoid an increase in consumer complaints and a loss of goodwill. The company president decides not to fire the elderly executive in the belief that the negative reaction of other employees would in the long run cost the company more than it would lose in keeping him and paying his pension.

All sensible businessmen prefer to be truthful, but they seldom feel inclined to tell the *whole* truth. In the business game truth-telling usually has to be kept within narrow limits if trouble is to be avoided. The point was neatly made a long time ago (in 1888) by one of John D. Rockefeller's associates, Paul Babcock, to Standard Oil Company executives who were about to testify before a government investigating committee: "Parry every question with answers which, while perfectly truthful, are evasive of bottom facts."[12]

This was, is, and probably always will be regarded as wise and permissible business strategy.

For Office Use Only

An executive's family life can easily be dislocated if he fails to make a sharp distinction between the ethical systems of the home and the office—or if his wife does not grasp that distinction. Many a businessman who has remarked to his wife, "I had to let Jones go today" or "I had to admit to the boss that Jim has been goofing off lately," has been met with an indignant protest. "How could you do a thing like that? You know Jones is over 50 and will have a lot of trouble getting another job." Or, "You did that to Jim? With his wife ill and the all the worry she's been having with the kids?"

If the executive insists that he had no choice because the profits of the company and his own security were involved, he may see a certain cool and ominous reappraisal in his wife's eyes. Many wives are not prepared to accept the fact that business operates with a special code of ethics. An illuminating illustration of this comes from a Southern sales executive who related a conversation he had had with his wife at a time when a hotly contested political campaign was being waged in their state:

> "I made the mistake of telling her that I had had lunch with Colby, who gives me about half my business. Colby mentioned that his company had a stake in the election. Then he said, 'By the way, I'm treasurer of the citizens' committee for Lang. I'm collecting contributions. Can I count on you for a hundred dollars?'

> "Well, there I was. I was opposed to Lang, but I knew Colby. If he withdrew his business, I could be in a bad spot. So I just smiled and wrote out a check then and there. He thanked me, and we started to talk about his next order. Maybe he thought I shared his political views. If so, I wasn't going to lose any sleep over it.

> "I should have had sense enough not to tell Mary about it. She hit the ceiling. She said she was disappointed in me. She said I hadn't acted like a man, that I should have stood up to Colby.

> "I said, 'Look, it was an either-or situation. I had to do it or risk losing the business.'

> "She came back at me with, 'I don't believe it. You could have been honest with him. You could have said that you didn't feel you ought to contribute to a campaign for a man you weren't going to vote for. I'm sure he would have understood.'

> "I said, 'Mary, you're a wonderful woman, but you're way off the track. Do you know what would have happened if I had said that? Colby would have smiled and

---

[12]Babcock in a memorandum to Rockefeller (Rockefeller Archives).

said, "Oh, I didn't realize. Forget it." But in his eyes from that moment I would be an oddball, maybe a bit of a radical. He would have listened to me talk about his order and would have promised to give it consideration. After that I wouldn't hear from him for a week. Then I would telephone and learn from his secretary that he wasn't yet ready to place the order. And in about a month I would hear through the grapevine that he was giving his business to another company. A month after that I'd be out of a job.'

"She was silent for a while. Then she said, 'Tom, something is wrong with business when a man is forced to choose between his family's security and his moral obligation to himself. It's easy for me to say you should have stood up to him—but if you had, you might have felt you were betraying me and the kids. I'm sorry that you did it, Tom, but I can't blame you. Something is wrong with business!'"

This wife saw the problem in terms of moral obligation as conceived in private life; her husband saw it as a matter of game strategy. As a player in a weak position, he felt that he could not afford to indulge an ethical sentiment that might have cost him his seat at the table.

Playing to Win

Some men might challenge the Colbys of business—might accept serious setbacks to their business careers rather than risk a feeling of moral cowardice. They merit our respect—but as private individuals, not businessmen. When the skillful player of the business game is compelled to submit to unfair pressure, he does not castigate himself for moral weakness. Instead, he strives to put himself into a strong position where he can defend himself against such pressures in the future without loss.

If a man plans to take a seat in the business game, he owes it to himself to master the principles by which the game is played, including its special ethical outlook. He can then hardly fail to recognize that an occasional bluff may well be justified in terms of the game's ethics and warranted in terms of economic necessity. Once he clears his mind on this point, he is in a good position to match his strategy against that of the other players. He can then determine objectively whether a bluff in a given situation has a good chance of succeeding and can decide when and how to bluff, without a feeling of ethical transgression.

To be a winner, a man must play to win. This does not mean that he must be ruthless, cruel, harsh, or treacherous. On the contrary, the better his reputation for integrity, honesty, and decency, the better his chances of victory will be in the long run. But from time to time every businessman, like every poker player, is offered a choice between certain loss and bluffing within the legal rules of the game. If he is not resigned to losing, if he wants to rise in his company and industry, then in such a crisis he will bluff—and bluff hard.

Every now and then one meets a successful businessman who has conveniently forgotten the small or large deceptions that he practiced on his way to fortune. "God gave me my money," old John D. Rockefeller once piously told a Sunday school class. It would be a rare tycoon in our time who would risk the horse laugh with which such a remark would be greeted.

In the last third of the twentieth century even children are aware that if a man has become prosperous in business, he has sometimes departed from the strict truth in order to overcome obstacles or has practiced the more subtle deceptions of the half-truth or the misleading omission. Whatever the form of the bluff, it is an integral part of the game, and the executive who does not master its techniques is not likely to accumulate much money or power.

Discussion Questions

1. Do you agree or disagree with Carr's premise?
2. Does everyone operate at the same level of bluffing?
3. How is the phrase "Sound ethics is good business" characterized?

Compare & Contrast

Carr notes that espionage has become so common that it is no longer considered an ethical issue but an effective means of competition. Compare this comment with the list of rationalizations and apply them to the statement. What are the key differences in the two scholars' views on ethics in business? Then compare Dr. Drucker's simple means of analysis with Carr's views. Can Dr. Drucker's views help in Carr's complex situations?

What Gets in the Way of Ethical Decisions in Business?

Reading 2.4

How Leaders Lose Their Way: What Price Hubris?[13]

Companies such as Enron, WorldCom, Adelphia, Lehman, New Century Financial, Fannie Mae, and Countrywide (companies you will study) engaged in outrageous behaviors, but their journeys into the hinterlands of huckstering was one of a gradual sort. They descended gradually to their ethical and, eventually, financial collapses.

No one in these companies sat together in the initial stages of either their success or the beginning of their declines, numbers difficulties, or inability to meet the quarterlies, and plotted, "You know what would be great! A gigantic fraud that we perpetuate on the shareholders, the creditors, and analysts. It will make us more money than we ever dreamed of. Fraud—that's the answer."

There is a tendency to create the comforting image in our minds that somehow those who engaged in these outrageous behaviors were misled, duped victims, or were so corrupt that they are part of only a limited number of souls who would dare tread in areas where the landmines of lies explode and the traps of fraud ensnare. We want to believe that they are so ethically different from the rest of us, cut from a different ethical fabric altogether and hence more susceptible to the temptations of fraud. A piece in the *Wall Street Journal*, following the collapses of Enron and WorldCom was entitled, "How Could They Have Done It?", the essence of which was the exploration of the two questions all observers posed as they watched, mouths agape, when these $9 billion frauds dribbled out: Where were their minds when they made these decisions? What on earth were they thinking?[14]

Following Martha Stewart's indictment, a reporter called to inquire, "What is the difference between us and a Martha Stewart? Or us and a Dennis Kozlowski?" My response was very simple, "Not much." They begin as entrepreneurs with novel ideas, willing to work hard work to enjoy success. They end with much of their success lost and tarnished reputations from criminal trials. How do intelligent and capable people find themselves reduced to the behaviors that find them in felony trials?

Arthur Andersen, the accounting firm that met its demise because of its certification of the fraudulent financial statements of Enron, has a history peppered with examples of the firm's absolute ethical standards that went well beyond the accounting rules. In 1915, Andersen was certifying the financial statements for a steamship company, one of its biggest clients. The financial statements were for the period through December 31, 1914. However, in February 1915, as the statements were being finalized, the company lost one of its ships in a storm. Arthur Andersen refused to certify the 1914 statements without disclosing the loss of the ship, a loss that would have a fundamental impact on income, despite the fact that it was in the next year.[15] In the 1980s, when the savings and

---

[13]Adapted from Marianne M. Jennings, "The Disconnect Between and Among Legal Ethics, Business Ethics, Law, and Virtue: Learning Not to Make Ethics So Complex," *University of St. Thomas Law Journal* 1:995, 2004.

[14]Holman W. Jenkins Jr., "How Could They Have Done It?" *Wall Street Journal*, August 28, 2001, A15.

[15]Susan E. Squires, Cynthia J. Smith, Lorna McDougall, and William R. Yeack, *Inside Arthur Andersen: Shifting Values, Unexpected Consequences* (2003), 32.

loan industry collapsed, all of the then–Big 8 accounting firms, except for Andersen, experienced heavy losses because of their liability for audit work on the collapsed financial institutions. Andersen professionals did not think that the S&L accounting practice of including the value of deferred taxes in earnings was sound. When its S&L clients refused to change their accounting, under the guise of "everybody does it," Andersen resigned all of its S&L accounts rather than put its imprimatur to financial statements it believed contained improper accounting.[16] Yet, just a little over a decade later, Andersen, through David Duncan, was authorizing thousands of off-the-book-entities at Enron in order to hang on to a valuable audit and consulting client.

Apart from the organizational incentive systems and culture shifts that can affect reliance on absolute standards, there are individual lapses. The literature in ethical decision-making indicates that the decline in ethical standards begins gradually and can consume those with tremendous ability and track records of success precisely because they have enjoyed so much success to that point.[17] These are the individuals to whom everyone turns for problem resolution, outstanding work effort, and results. Success has been the reward for their ability. They are the "go-to" people in an organization who have always been able to find resolutions for problems and ways to remove obstacles that stand in the way of achievement and success. Hubris consumes them when they find that eventual setback or obstacle they cannot conquer. Unwilling to admit that there may not always be a legal or ethical fix, they seek ways to avoid disclosure of a downturn or that they have hit a wall. They cannot get the product out on time and still guarantee its safety. They cannot complete the job on time and still meet quality standards. They are faced with the harsh reality of their human limitations. Releasing financial statements that are something less then projections when you have been on an earnings roll is difficult because you have been on a pedestal for so long.

Yet, like the figures in Greek tragedies, we all have our walls that we hit that require an admission that the fix will take a while and we may need a little help. Every successful lawyer must face that trial when no one can pull a win from the hat. Every athlete has that game or race when victory is not theirs. How do they face this setback? Too often with steroids, falsified financials, and withheld evidence. It is not always greed that drives ruthless ambition; both fiction and biography teach that hubris spawns deceit. Pride, that inability to face the wall, as the saying teaches, goeth before a fall. Even if no money were involved, it is difficult for them to step down, even if just for a time, while at the top of their go-to game.

From the Greek tragedies to Shakespeare's nobles, literature teaches us what newspapers bear out: the rise, fall and costs of hubris. Erroneous confidence and an exaggerated sense of control emerge, in fiction and nonfiction alike, in Greek mythology and in the Napoleonic wars, do drive poor ethical choices in high-pressure situations.

How do leaders know when they are losing their ways? What do the classics teach us? What have we learned from the case studies in business ethics? There are common characteristics of business people who lose their ways:

a. They become increasingly isolated because they are unwilling to tolerate dissent. They have but one perspective, a trait that is antithetical to good ethical analysis, something that requires a 360-degree perspective to remedy.
b. They fancy themselves as being above the rules, different from the "average person," who must follow the mundane rules of the world. Like a teenager, they believe the rules do not apply to them.

---

[16]Barbara Ley Toffler, Final Accounting: Ambition, Greed and the Fall of Arthur Andersen (2004) p. 19.

[17]David M. Messick and Max H. Bazerman, "Ethical Leadership and the Psychology of Decision Making," *Sloan Management Review* 37:9, 1996.

c. They have defined themselves by the trappings of their success: their salaries, bonuses, cars, houses, and material possessions. The possibility of losing their material possessions and social status becomes the driving force of their decisions and leadership. They are no longer pursuing leadership for the sake of helping society with their products or services or employees by helping them advance. Their leadership is for their personal status.

d. They have a sense of invincibility—that they can solve any problem because they have been so successful for so long. That invincibility finds them taking larger risks with the hope of staying on top.

e. They have lost a good purpose in being a leader in business. Initially their leadership role sprang from their desire to help others or improve the world. They had a good new product or they had a way of working with people that propelled them to success. When they switch from that purpose of their leadership to one of more, more, more, they lose the self-confidence and inner purpose that gave them perspective on their decisions, including the perspective of their ethical values.

Discussion Questions

1. What would the role of adherence to your credo play in preventing you from losing your way?

2. Looking at the list of how leaders lose their way, develop a list of actions that would stop these problems from taking hold.

3. Drawing on Unit 1 and "The Parable of the Sadhu," describe how Buzz McCoy lost his way as a leader on the mountain.

Compare & Contrast

William Wilberforce was a member of the British Parliament who is credited with obtaining passage of the Slavery Abolition Act of 1833 in England. Mr. Wilberforce has been credited for the persistent leadership he provided to see the act to its passage. Mr. Wilberforce was also a philanthropist and a founder of the Society for the Prevention of Cruelty to Animals. Mr. Wilberforce died just 3 days after the Abolition Act was passed. What distinguishing characteristics do you see in Mr. Wilberforce that are different from the characteristics that indicate a leader is losing his or her way?

Reading 2.5

Moral Relativism and the Either/or Conundrum

A typical form of flawed reasoning that businesses fall into is the either/or conundrum. This flawed analysis finds us reaching a decision because the pressure is great, the consequences even greater, and the justification compelling. Defining dilemmas in the either/or conundrum produces artificial choices that somehow ignore the ethics and values we brought with us before we run into the pressure of the moment. Buzz McCoy in "The Parable of the Sadhu" fell into this trap when, in the midst of his challenge, he framed his situation as, "Either I let the sadhu go and make the climb or help him and once again miss my goal." McCoy then gives us some insight on how the either/or conundrum cuts effective analysis short. At the end of his article he adds that his most memorable experience of his time in Nepal was not reaching the pinnacle, but, rather, those moments he spent in the village at base camp when he had altitude sickness. The immersion in culture, the weddings experienced, and the kindness of the villagers were the true rich experiences of his climbs, not the conquest of the summit. In defining the issue by achievement of a predetermined goal, we fall victim to the either/or conundrum.

However, analyzing a decision by values rephrases the question from, "Does our present need justify my departure from my values?" to "Is there a way to solve this problem that is consistent with my values?" For example, in 2000, Ikea, the Swedish retailer, was on the eve of the grand opening of its flagship store in Moscow. Government officials who run the public utility came requesting their personal payoffs for providing the retail store with its electricity. One part of Ikea's code of ethics, indeed, its credo, is that it does not pay bribes anywhere it does business. On the other hand, Ikea did have commitments to vendors, creditors, and employees for the opening of the store. If Ikea phrases the ethical issue as, "To bribe or not to bribe, that is the question," it will fall into the either/or conundrum. If, however, it phrases the question as, "Is there a way to get the store open without compromising our values?" it will begin exploring alternatives rather than accepting the compromise of its ethics as the only solution. Ikea did come up with a solution; it rented generators to provide power for the store. Indeed, that approach to electricity has become its business model in Russia. Avoiding the either/or trap removes the blinders that moral relativism often imposes as we try to analyze an issue.

Discussion Questions

1. Describe a time when you have fallen into an either/or trap.
2. Ikea, in 2009, discovered that the Russian executive it had hired to manage its generator contracts was accepting kickbacks from the companies that wanted to do business with Ikea.[18] What lessons should Ikea and other companies learn from this experience.

Reading 2.6

P = f(x) The Probability of an Ethical Outcome Is a Function of the Amount of Money Involved: Pressure

A forthcoming article in the *Academy of Management Journal* presents research that high-performing companies are more likely to break the law. The CFA Institute (Certified Financial Analysts) has a saying, $P = f(x)$. For you non-mathers out there, the translation is that the probability of an ethical outcome is a direct function of the amount of money involved. The more money involved, the less likely as ethical outcome. So, the slope of the line is negative.

There is the hubris, the pedestal effect, the inability to accept a setback, and the failure to understand that we all hit a wall once in a while. Sometimes we have to take a loss. Sometimes we need to step off the pedestal. This new study demonstrates that when managers at high-performing companies succumb to these pressures they do go ethically nuts.

Professor Yuri Mishina from Michigan State and his coauthor colleagues Professors Dykes, Block, and Pollock in "Why 'Good' Firms Do Bad Things: The Effects of High Aspirations, High Expectations and Prominence on the Incidence of Corporate Illegality" conclude that there is something about being on an earnings roll that clouds judgment. In addition to the cyclone of hubris, managers are trying to grapple with the pressures of sunk-cost avoidance, investor relations, and the sandbox mentality of just "making those numbers," even when they are not real.

But, again, business managers face pressures similar to those we encounter in our personal lives. A friend rented a truck to help his aunt move from the large home she had enjoyed with her husband of many years who had just passed away to a more easily managed apartment. He did not take the insurance coverage for the truck because, as he said, "I know how to drive!" Safety tip for renting moving trucks: Your auto insurance

---

[18]Ikea terminated the executive. Andrew E. Kramer, "Ikea Tries to Build Public Case Against Corruption," *New York Times*, September 12, 2009, p. B1.

probably doesn't cover you! The large truck proved to be a challenge, and my friend scraped the back top of the truck on some eaves as he turned a corner rather inartfully. There were two thoughts that came to his mind: (1) That's gonna be expensive; and (2) Should I try and hide this from the rental guy? Oh, that second thought! There is that little part in all of us that doesn't want to ante up and another little part that believes we can actually dupe the other guy so that we need not pay for something that really is our responsibility. But my friend drove into the U-Haul rental center and pointed out the hole, the scratch, and the damage in all of its uninsured glory. The initial response from the rental guy was, "Wow! That's bad!" Then he paused and said, "I'm not going to worry about it."

My friend wonders how different the ending might have been had he not 'fessed up. How different this generous soul of a rental manager might have been had he discovered the damage after my friend skedaddled and/or skulked out of there. There is that simple but powerful and decisive model from Unit I, "If I were the U-Haul manager, how would I feel if someone tried to hide damage from me?" The fog and pressures that interfere with good ethical decisions can be managed with the simple recall of those questions.

Discussion Questions

1. Think of an example of a situation in which you resisted pressure to act unethically.
2. Refer to the Goldman case in Case 2.11. Make a list of the pressures Tourre felt.
3. How could your credo help in resisting pressure?

Case 2.7

Martha Stewart: Not Such a Good Thing

Martha Helen Kostyra was born in 1941 in Jersey City, New Jersey, and worked her way through Barnard College with the money she earned working as both a fashion model and a maid. She was married to Andy Stewart, a graduate of Yale Law School, in 1961, during her sophomore year. As Andy became a Manhattan lawyer, Martha completed her degree in art history at Barnard. In 1965, she had her only child, a daughter, Alexis.

In 1968, she became a licensed securities broker and a member of the New York Stock Exchange. She had a successful five-year stint on Wall Street until she and Andy purchased a home in Westport, Connecticut, a home that would become known as Turkey Hill. Martha left Wall Street to become a full-time mother and homemaker in the quintessential suburban haven.

During this time, Martha became well-known for her skills as a hostess, and friends began to ask her to handle their parties and receptions. Martha began a catering business, A Catered Affair, that continued to expand and grow. By the time she published her first book in the early 1980s, her now-diverse business, known as Martha Stewart, Inc., included a retail store with prepared foods, and a catering business. She continued to diversify the companies holdings through endorsements such as the one for a line of products at Kmart.

In 1991, Martha ventured into both magazine publishing and television. *Martha Stewart Living* became a highly successful monthly magazine, and she had one of the most successful syndicated television shows. Martha took her company public on the New York Stock Exchange in 1999, and it was one of the hottest IPOs of the decade. The value of her interest in her company doubled in just the opening minutes as the shares sold.

By 2001, she had four magazines, thirty-four books, a newspaper column, a radio show, a catalogue sales company, and a weekly spot on *CBS This Morning*. A business icon, she was elected to the board of the New York Stock Exchange in June 2001. There seemed to be no end to the talent and success of Ms. Stewart. Everything she touched brought returns. Some speculated that association with her name enabled Kmart to survive bankruptcy.

However, it was Ms. Stewart's investment in a friend's biotech company that would cause her empire to crash. Ms. Stewart's troubles began with her ownership of 5,000 ImClone shares.[19] ImClone Systems, Inc., a pharmaceutical company, was poised in December 2001 to market Erbitux, an anticancer drug, pending FDA approval. Oddly, Erbitux was developed at the Anderson Cancer Research Institute in Houston, Texas, headed by Dr. John Mendelsohn, who served on the Enron board and its audit committee.[20] Enron and its chair, the late Kenneth Lay, were significant donors to the center. Dr. Mendelsohn also served on ImClone's board.[21] (See Case 4.15.)

Ms. Stewart was a friend of Dr. Samuel D. Waksal, the CEO of ImClone. She had invested in ImClone based upon his recommendation.[22] However, there were rumblings during the fall of 2001 that FDA approval might not be forthcoming. There were some indications during this period that both Dr. Waksal and Ms. Stewart were becoming anxious about their investment. Dr. Waksal owned 79,797 shares of ImClone stock, but, like so many other CEOs of the era, he had pledged the shares as collateral for loans, and he was deeply in debt.

When Bristol-Myers Squibb made a tender offer for ImClone shares in October 2001, at a price of $70 per share, Ms. Stewart had instructed her broker at Merrill Lynch, Peter Bacanovic, and his assistant, Douglas Faneuil, to accept the tender offer.[23] However, so many shareholders took the offer that Ms. Stewart was able to sell only about 1,000 of her shares. Her remaining interest was 3,928 shares, and the rumblings about ImClone and FDA approval only continued.

Employees at ImClone were aware, by early December 2001, that FDA approval for Erbitux was not likely. In fact, there was an internal memo outlining the issues and suggesting that FDA approval would not be forthcoming.[24] Harlan Waksal, Sam's brother, and also an officer of ImClone, sold $50 million worth of ImClone shares shortly after the memo was written.[25]

The share price for ImClone was over $70 in December 2001, but by December 26, 2001, the executive team at ImClone was "99 percent certain" that FDA approval would not be forthcoming. Their plan was to announce what would be the inevitable denial of approval on December 28, 2001, a Friday, after the markets had closed.[26] Dr. Waksal

[19]Alessandra Stanley and Constance L. Hays, "Martha Stewart's To-Do List May Include Image Polishing," *New York Times*, June 23, 2003, pp. A1, A24.

[20]Andrew Pollack and David Cay Johnston, "Former Chief of ImClone Systems Is Charged with Insider Trading," *New York Times*, June 13, 2002, pp. B1, B6; and Jerry Markon, "Active Inquiry Is Underway on Ms. Stewart," *Wall Street Journal*, June 14, 2002, pp. C1, C10.

[21]Jo Thomas and Reed Abelson, "How a Top Medical Researcher Became Entangled with Enron," *New York Times*, January 28, 2002, pp. C1, C2.

[22]Andrew Pollack and David Cay Johnston, "Former Chief of ImClone Systems Is Charged with Insider Trading," *New York Times*, June 13, 2002, pp. C1, C6; Constance L. Hays, "Prosecutor Says Martha Stewart Spun Web of Lies about Shares," *New York Times*, January 28, 2004, pp. C1, C11; and Leslie Eaton, "The Ghost of Waksal Past Hovers over the Stewart Trial," *New York Times*, February 17, 2004, pp. C1, C6.

[23]Constance L. Hays and Patrick McGeehan, "A Closer Look at Martha Stewart's Trade," *New York Times*, Monday, July 15, 2002, pp. C1, C9.

[24]Hays and McGeehan, "A Closer Look at Martha Stewart's Trade," pp. C1, C9.

[25]*Id.*; and Andrew Pollack, "ImClone's Cancer Drug Is Back, and U.S. Approval Is Expected," *New York Times*, February 11, 2004, pp. C1, C2.

[26]Riva D. Atlas, "ImClone Sues Former Chief to Recover $7 Million," *New York Times*, Thursday, August 15, 2002, p. C3.

returned from a Caribbean vacation to sell his shares and also tipped family members to do the same. Using the same broker, Mr. Bacanovic, Dr. Waksal tried to sell his shares but was told that he would need approval from ImClone's general counsel to do so. Dr. Waksal then transferred his shares to his daughter and tried the sale through Bank of America, but was given the same requirement. Dr. Waksal forged the approval of the ImClone general counsel and the shares were sold, but Dr. Waksal eventually entered a guilty plea to bank fraud and conspiracy and just completed serving seven years in federal prison.[27] Dr. Waksal's daughters were also attempting to sell their 40,000 shares of ImClone.[28]

Mr. Faneuil became concerned when Dr. Waksal was trying to transfer shares to his daughter in order to sell them, so he sought approval from a Merrill Lynch accountant, who indicated it was illegal.[29] At that point, Mr. Faneuil contacted Mr. Bacanovic, who was on vacation in Florida, and explained the rapid series of trading by the Waksal family. Mr. Bacanovic responded, "Oh my God, get Martha on the phone."[30] When Mr. Faneuil questioned whether telling Ms. Stewart was legal, Mr. Bacanovic responded, "Of course. You must. You've got to. That's the whole point."[31] Mr. Faneuil eventually reached Martha, who was on her way to a vacation in San Jose del Cabo, Mexico, and who called from the Houston airport. The conversation was as follows:

Ms. Stewart:	Hi, This is Martha.
Mr. Faneuil:	Peter thought you'd like to act on the information that Sam is selling all his shares.
Ms. Stewart:	All of his shares?
Mr. Faneuil:	What he does have here, he's trying to sell.
Ms. Stewart **(later in the call):**	I want to sell.

The 3,928 shares were sold at approximately $58 per share on December 27, 2001, for a total of $229,002. If Ms. Stewart had waited until the next day, December 28, 2001, when ImClone made the announcement about the FDA's lack of approval, she could have sold the shares for a total of $189,495. The savings: $39,507.

When Dr. Waksal's illegal sales were uncovered and he entered his guilty plea, the federal government turned its attention to sales of the stock by others, including Ms. Stewart. Ms. Stewart was questioned by agents and attorneys and was ultimately charged not with stock fraud but with lying to federal investigators. When Mr. Bacanovic and Mr. Faneuil were confronted initially by an in-house investigation at Merrill with questions about Mr. Waksal's and Ms. Stewart's sale of ImClone stock, they offered their first explanation: "It was a tax-loss selling."[32] Mr. Faneuil told SEC investigators that Ms. Stewart had called for the price of the stock and then indicated to him to go ahead and sell it.

[27]Andrew Pollack and David Cay Johnston, "Former Chief of ImClone Systems Is Charged with Insider Trading," *New York Times*, June 13, 2002, pp. C1, C6; and Pollack, "ImClone's Cancer Drug Is Back, and U.S. Approval Is Expected," pp. C1, C2.

[28]Constance L. Hays, "Setback for Prosecutors in Martha Stewart Trial," *New York Times*, January 30, 2004, pp. C1, C4.

[29]Greg Farrell, "Faneuil Describes ImClone Stock Sales," *USA Today*, February 4, 2004, p. 1B.

[30]Matthew Rose and Kara Scannell, "Stewart Trial Hears Key Witness," *Wall Street Journal*, February 4, 2004, pp. C1, C2

[31]*Id.*

[32]Greg Farrell, "Faneuil: Broker Changed Stories," *USA Today*, February 5, 2004, p. 1B.

In early January 2002, one of Ms. Stewart's employees called Mr. Faneuil to complain that the sale of the ImClone stock "completely screws up our tax-loss selling plan."[33]

At that point, Mr. Bacanovic and Mr. Faneuil changed their story on the tax-planning sale: they were following orders on a $60 stop-loss agreement that Ms. Stewart already had in place. The court described the events in early January, when Bacanovic returned from vacation as follows:

> He (Bacanovic) recounted the $60 per share stop-loss order story to the SEC in a telephone interview later that day (January 7, 2002), explaining that on December 27 he advised Stewart that ImClone had dropped below $60, and she told him to sell it.

> After speaking to the SEC, Bacanovic took Faneuil out for coffee and a talk. Bacanovic explained Stewart's integral role in advancing his career and stressed his loyalty to her. Faneuil brought up the events of December 27 and reminded Bacanovic that he knew what really transpired, at which point Bacanovic asserted that Faneuil did not know what was going on that day and admonished Faneuil for being selfish.

> When Faneuil returned from a week's vacation in mid-January, Bacanovic told him that he had met recently with Stewart and discussed the events of December 27 with her. Stewart's calendar, which Armstrong maintained, reflected a breakfast meeting with Bacanovic on January 16. According to Faneuil, Bacanovic said to him, "Everyone's telling the same story. This was a $60 stop-loss order. That was the reason for her sale. We're all on the same page, and it's the truth. It's the true story. Everyone's telling the same story."[34]

However, paperwork was not on the same page as the parties and their story. If a stop-loss order existed, it dated from October 2001 and related to Omnimedia's holdings of stock, not Ms. Stewart's personal holdings. The worksheet that Mr. Bacanovic produced also told a different story. The sheet detailed Ms. Stewart's stock holdings and had the notation "@ 60" next to ImClone, written in what prosecution evidence showed was "scientifically distinguishable ink" compared with all the other notes on the worksheet.[35] The jury found the different ink to be proof of the charges of obstruction and conspiracy to obstruct the government's investigation.[36] As a result the second story, on the stop-loss order, did not fly. They were then all faced with not just one false story, but two false stories among them. As even Martha Stewart's lawyer noted, with the hope that the brokers would be blamed and not his client, "[Their] cover story has as many holes in it as a Swiss cheese."[37]

In June 2002, Faneuil admitted to Merrill Lynch and to the government investigators that he had lied twice to the SEC about the content of his December 27 phone conversation with Stewart. Faneuil said that the lies and subsequent cover-up became too much to bear. He entered into a cooperation agreement with the government, pleading guilty to a misdemeanor of receiving things of value (New York Knicks tickets) as a consideration for not disclosing a violation of the law.[38]

---

[33]*Id.*

[34]*U.S. v. Stewart*, 433 F.3d 272, 284-285 (2d Cir. 2005).

[35]Kara Scannell and Matthew Rose, "Worksheet's Importance Grows in Stewart Case," *Wall Street Journal*, February 17, 2004, pp. C1, C2.

[36]Kara Scannell and Matthew Rose, "In Stewart Case, Reluctant Jurors Found Guilt after Foolish Mistake," *Wall Street Journal*, March 8, 2004, pp. A1, A6.

[37]Constance L. Hays and Jonathan D. Glater, "More Tactics than Theatrics at the Stewart Trial," *New York Times*, February 10, 2004, pp. A1, C9.

[38]*U.S. v. Stewart*, 433 F.2d at 287.

On March 5, 2004, a Manhattan jury found Martha Stewart guilty of four felony counts, including conspiracy, obstruction of an investigation, and two counts of making false statements to federal investigators. Meg Crane, a graphic designer, one of the jurors in the case, summed up the feelings of her fellow panelists after the verdicts were announced: "We all felt terrible about it at the end. It felt like such a foolish mistake that was increased as it went along."[39] The foreperson of the jury, Rosemary McMahon, a schoolteacher, cried and lost sleep before the jury rendered its verdict, and she noted, "We thought of everything to try to find them not guilty of these charges. We just couldn't."[40] Mr. Bacanovic was also convicted along with Ms. Stewart.

Because of the criminal conviction, Mr. Bacanovic has been banned from the security industry. He describes his life since being released from prison (a sentence served largely in the federal prison in Nevada) as follows: "I am chronically sick and chronically unemployed and without any specific plan about how to proceed next."[41]

Ms. Stewart was a billionaire at the time she sold the ImClone shares. The amount she saved seems insignificant, immaterial, and irrelevant in the grand scheme of her investment portfolio, including substantial holdings of stock in her own company, Martha Stewart Omnimedia, Inc., which was selling for $70 per share on December 27, 2001. On December 19, 2003, just weeks before the start of her trial, Omnimedia was at $9.11. Trading in Omnimedia had to be halted when the Stewart verdict was announced on March 12, 2004 was $10.13, and it would fall to $7.10 in the week following. For every $1 drop in the price of Omnimedia shares, Ms. Stewart has lost $30 million.[42]

Following revelations about the investigation into the sale of the ImClone stock, Ms. Stewart resigned from her position on the board of the New York Stock Exchange as well as from her position as chair of the board of Omnimedia. Following her conviction, she resigned from her position on the board of Revlon, a position she had held for eight years. The New York Times Syndication services dropped her "Ask Martha" column, a loss of 200 papers. Westwood One, the radio syndicator for the "Ask Martha" audio segments, lost affiliates immediately upon her conviction. Viacom pulled *Martha Stewart Living* from its CBS and UPN stations, and the show is now sold individually to independent stations.[43] Ad revenues for her publications, the single largest source of revenue for Omnimedia, began a steady decline when the investigation of the sale of the shares became public.[44] From 2002 to 2003, ad revenues dropped 25.6 percent.[45] Ms. Stewart was forced to resign as CEO of the company she had built from her home in Connecticut.

On July 16, 2004, Ms. Stewart was sentenced to five months in federal prison and five months of house arrest, something she would complete at her 150-acre Bedford, New York, farm. On October 8, 2004, Ms. Stewart reported to a minimum security prison in West Virginia to serve her five-month sentence. She stated that she was abandoning the appeal of her case because "closure" was important, and she wanted to complete her sentence in time to plant her spring garden. The appellate court later ruled that there had been no reversible error and affirmed her conviction.[46] Others felt that she wanted to be

---

[39]Scannell and Rose, "In Stewart Case, Reluctant Jurors Found Guilt after Foolish Mistake," pp. A1, A6.

[40]*Id.*

[41]Landon Thomas Jr., "The Broker Who Fell to Earth," *New York Times*, October 13, 2006, C1, C4.

[42]Karla Scannell and Matthew Rose, "Stewart Trial Gets under Way," *New York Times*, January 28, 2004, pp. C1, C5.

[43]Theresa Howard, "Business Partners Shy from Stewart," *USA Today*, March 9, 2004, p. 1B.

[44]Gregory Zuckerman, "Martha: The Doyenne of Dilemmas," *Wall Street Journal*, March 8, 2004, pp. C1, C2.

[45]Suzanne Vranica, Matthew Rose, and Janet Adamy, "Living—without Martha," *Wall Street Journal*, March 8, 2004, pp. B1, B11.

[46]*U.S. v. Stewart*, 433 F.3d 273 (2d Cir. 2005).

free by March because filming for the fall season of her television show would begin in March 2005.[47] When Ms. Stewart was released to house arrest, she encountered some difficulties with her time limits for being away from her home. She was also quoted as saying about her ankle monitor, "I know how to get it off. I watched them put it on. It's on the Internet. I looked it up."[48]

The price of her company's stock when she reported to prison was $12.03. The price of ImClone stock on that same day was $54.10 per share. ImClone would climb as high as $90 per share. Since Martha's indictment, Martha Stewart Omnimedia climbed to a high of $42 per share, but between 2006 and 2008 sank to between $17 and $24 per share despite a booming market. Following the 2008 market crash, the stock dipped to as low as $1.93. Following the market's upturn in 2010, the stock price averaged at about $7.00.

Discussion Questions

1. What issues did Stewart, Bacanovic, and Faneuil miss in making their decisions about selling the ImClone stock and in their conduct following the sales? Apply the models and make a list of suggested questions they could have asked that might have affected their decisions.

2. Was selling the shares illegal? If selling the shares was not illegal, was it unethical?

3. What do we learn about long-term consequences from Ms. Stewart's conduct and case?

4. What advice can you offer someone who has engaged in trading similar to Ms. Stewart's? Make a list of all the costs of Ms. Stewart's sale of the stock and compare it with the losses she avoided by selling the day before the public announcement.

Compare & Contrast

Consider Mr. Faneuil's statement that he could not live with the lies. Also, reflect on Mr. Bacanovic's experiences after prison and the following additional information.

Mr. Bacanovic had been so close to Ms. Stewart that he spent Christmases with her at her Connecticut home. They shared the bond of fathers with East European heritages, "fierce personal ambition," and "a keen appreciation for the rewards that high society can bring."[49]

He remained loyal to Ms. Stewart because he said he did not want to be a Diana Brooks, the former CEO of Sotheby's who turned against her chairman, with the result being his conviction and her light sentence of house arrest. He asked Ms. Stewart's daughter, Alexis, for help with his legal fees but was told that no one felt he was owed anything. The result was a fine of $75,000 as well as a prison sentence.

He served his sentence in Las Vegas and was known as "the Broker" to his fellow inmates. He said that no one knew his name; he was identified only as "Martha Stewart's broker." *Slate* magazine covered both the Bacanovic and Stewart trials and observed that even following the trials no one is really quite sure who said what to whom because the only two people who knew what was really said, Mr. Bacanovic and Ms. Stewart, never took the stand. Their convictions were based on jury perceptions. What can you take away for your credo from their experiences?

When Dr. Waksal was interviewed for his presentencing report he told the probation officer that he was a "social drinker" and had, perhaps five glasses of wine per week. However, a federal program permits federal felons to shave up to 12 months from their sentences if they complete a drug-rehab/counseling program. One month after the interview

---

[47]Patricia Sellers, "Why Martha Really Chose Jail," *Fortune*, October 4, 2004, p. 34.

[48]"They Said It," *People*, December 31, 2005, p. 89.

[49]*Id.*

with the probation officer, Waksal's lawyers informed a federal judge that Waksal now had a "dependence on alcohol" and requested approval for Waksal's entry into a prison rehab program. Dr. Waksal shaved 9 months off his sentence.

Make a list of lessons. Compare and contrast Martha's postconviction life with Bacanovic's and Waksal's. Any take-aways from the contrast?

Case 2.8

On Leaving to Spend More Time with Family

PR experts say that when a high-ranking executive leaves a company there are two standard phrases used, "spending more time with family" and "pursuing other interests." However, neither phrase proves to be true, and, indeed, may be a temporary face-saving measure for an executive or company in trouble. For example, Jeffrey Skilling, the now-convicted former CEO of Enron, left the company just months before its collapse with the first phrase of "spending more time with his family." The termination agreements are required by regulators and must give a reason, but one PR expert notes, "Who are they kidding?"[50]

The following are examples and consequences:

Name	Title	Company	Reason	Fate
Tara Poseley	CEO	Design Within Reach	"Spend more time with family and pursue other interests."	Named President Disney Retail Stores just 5 months later
Beryl B. Raff	CEO	Zales	"Well, this afternoon I'm going to be driving the carpool. And my son's very excited about that."	Named Senior VP JCPenney 3 months later
John N. Ford	state senator	Tennessee	"To spend the rest of my time with my family clearing my name."	Convicted on one count of bribery for taking $55,000 in bribes from contractors; other federal charges on bribery are pending; sentenced to 66 months in prison
Brenda C. Barnes	CEO	Pepsi NA	"To devote more time to her three young children." (1997)	Interim president Starwood Hotels (1997); took board positions (1997); CEO Sara Lee (2004)
Afshin Mohebbi	Pres COO	Qwest	"Spend more time with family." (2002)	42-count indictment (2004) immunity for testimony
Daniel P. Burnham	CEO Chairman	Raytheon	"Spend more time with family, teach, and join corporate boards." (2003)	2006 SEC filed complaint on accounting improprieties by Burnham and others; returned bonuses

(Continued)

---

[50]Katie Hafner, "Canned Phrases for Making an Exit," *New York Times*, December 23, 2006, pp. B1, B7.

Name	Title	Company	Reason	Fate
Carly Fiorina	CEO	Hewlett-Packard	She felt she had been fired and refused a generic family statement because, "No, that's not the truth. Telling the truth is about what's right and wrong. It's pretty basic."[51]	Best-selling book; Running for U.S. Senate in California (2010)
Stephen Collins	CEO	Double Click	"Spend more time with family."	Still spending time with family

Discussion Questions

1. Is it dishonest to use the family/other interests reason when it is not true?
2. Is there a securities law violation?
3. Give some rationalizations that companies and individuals could offer for the explanations.
4. Does the "spending more time with family" explanation help to preserve dignity? Does it help prevent a drop in the company's stock price?
5. At a time when serious questions about the federal budget figures and deficits were swirling, White House Budget Director Peter Orzag announced his resignation with only a few weeks' notice. The reason given was that Mr. Orzag was "going to spend more time with his family." Mr. Orzag had raised some eyebrows because of his divorce followed by an engagement that occurred at the time a child he had fathered was being born. A reporter quipped, "You mean to spend more time with his families?" Are the ethical issues for government officials' resignations the same as for those in business? What does the reporter's comment reveal about personal conduct and professional lives?

Compare & Contrast

What is different about Ms. Fiorina's response? Why did she refuse the family statement? What in her explanation gives you an idea for your credo and some insight into hers? HP was not under any cloud of suspicion about its financial issues, whereas most of the other companies were or had performance problems when the executives resigned. Why did the circumstances of the company make a difference in the type of explanation for a departure?

[51] Id.

Resolving Ethical Dilemmas in Business

SECTION 2C

Reading 2.9

The Areas of Ethical Challenges in Business[52]

The remaining pages of this book present more readings and cases that are grouped by topical areas. The cases are divided into categories based on The Conference Board's groupings of ethical dilemmas in business. (The Conference Board is a private research and information group that focuses on corporate and business issues.) Each category represents a grouping of the types of ethical dilemmas that were ranked most important by CEOs in ongoing surveys conducted by the Ethics Resource Center. As you work through business ethics dilemmas, you will be applying what you learned in Unit 1 to these topic areas in business.

Individual Values and the Business Organization

    Employee Conflicts of Interest

    Inappropriate Gifts

    Security of Company Records

    Personal Honesty

Individual Rights and the Business Organization

    Corporate Due Process

    Employee Screening

    Employee Privacy

    Sexual Harassment

    Affirmative Action/Equal Employment Opportunity

    Employment at Will

    Whistle-Blowing

    Employee Rights

    Comparable Worth

Business Operations

    Financial and Cash Management Procedures

    Conflicts between the Corporation's Ethical Code and Accepted Business

    Practices in Foreign Countries

    Unauthorized Payments to Foreign Officials

    Workplace Safety

    Plant Closures and Downsizing

    Environmental Issues

    Purchasing: Conflicts and Bribery

---

[52]Used by permission of The Conference Board.

Business and Its Competition

    Advertising Content

    Appropriation of Others' Ideas

    Product Pricing

Business and Its Product

    Contract Relations

    Product Safety

    Product Quality

    Customer Privacy

Business and Its Stakeholders

    Shareholders' Interests

    Executive Salaries

    Corporate Contributions

    Social Issues

Business and Government

    Government Employees

    Government Contracts

    Government Responsibilities

Discussion Questions

Place the following issues and topics in the appropriate categories.

1. A credit card company selling purchasing information about its customers to various marketing firms
2. A former employee taking proprietary customer lists to his new employer
3. A company offering employment to a government official who is in a position to award contracts to that company
4. Paying a bribe to a government official in another country
5. An employee purchasing her retail employer's gift cards using her employee discount and then selling those cards on the Internet
6. Failure to pay income taxes because you are paid in cash

Reading 2.10

A Structured Approach for Solving Ethical Dilemmas and Trying Out Your Ethical Skills on Some Business Cases

The facts in business cases may change from movie theater tickets and Wi-Fi piggybacking to issues of bribery, insider trading, and capitalization of ordinary expenses, but the issues and nature of ethical dilemmas still harken back to the same questions and format (after-the-fact vs. in-the-midst-of) you learned in Unit 1.

However, because you will be a businessperson evaluating an ethical issue, add a few additional questions to the format in Reading 1.9.

1. Do your numbers. Think about the costs of your decision, both long- and short-term. For example, not disclosing information about the company's financial performance buys you time and prevents a drop in the company's share price. But if things do not improve you will be grappling with two problems: the drop in the share price and the company's loss of trust and credibility for not disclosing the information sooner. Just as ethical analysis requires you to gain a 360-degree perspective, a look at the numbers considers all costs. Will we lose customers? Will our cost of capital

increase if we do have a major accident or an unsafe product? What happens if we cut the maintenance budget too much? We save money temporarily but will the lack of maintenance affect safety?

2. Recall the categories from Reading 1.4 and be sure that you have considered all the ethical issues.

3. Make sure that you have applied all the questions that are used under the various models in Reading 1.8 to verify that you have really thought through the issue, such as whether what you want to do is even legal.

4. Check for those warm language labels and rationalizations that may find you overlooking an issue as you find comfort in avoiding real analysis.

5. Be sure to consider other cases you have or will study and whether those historical precedents might be of help in analyzing your present situation and dilemma.

6. Bring in the other areas of business to be sure you are looking at the ethical issue fully. For example, consider any strategic advantages in your decision. Be sure to apply economic principles to proposed actions. Think through the organizational behavior implications of your decision. In other words, integrate what you know about business as you analyze from an ethical perspective.

Try your hand at a few business-type cases before proceeding to the following sections. These rather short cases offer an opportunity for application of the materials from this section and give you the chance to hone your skills for ethical resolutions.

Case 2.11

What Was Up with Wall Street? The Goldman Standard and Shades of Gray

Humble Roots

Goldman Sachs was founded in 1869 with the humble purpose of being both an originator and a clearinghouse for commercial paper. Marcus Goldman, a German immigrant, founded the company along with his son-in-law, Samuel Sachs. The company's strategy was to provide loans for small businesses and then create a market for the loans through the sale of commercial paper. But the stodgy negotiable instruments market proved insufficient to attracting new talent so the firm began a gradual drift from its founders' influence and its basic roots in tangible one-on-one business loans. In the late 1920s, Goldman undertook an investment strategy that would contribute to the 1929 market crash. Goldman launched the investment trust, a vehicle by which anyone could invest small or large amounts of money and hold shares in the trust, which then purchased a portfolio of stocks. The trust income then came from the returns on the stocks in the portfolio.

Investment Strategy

The 1920s and Layering

Even in its initial foray into the layered investment strategies that would still be in play a century later, Goldman was using its own customers to make money. The layering strategy, formulated in the late 1920s, works like this: Goldman creates an investment company and buys 90 percent of the shares in that company with its own money. Because the shares have sold so well, the public (not realizing that Goldman itself had purchased the shares and driven the price up) wants a piece of the company. So, the shares that Goldman initially bought for, say, $100, it is able to turn around and sell to the public for $110. But, Goldman would continue to buy shares on the secondary market, and the price would climb to $120 and then $150 and so on. With the money Goldman made on this initial corporation, it would create a new corporation and use the same strategy to drive up the price, moving on to another new corporation with more demand and higher share prices. However, all the layers in the chain are completely dependent upon the market continuing to grow and the solvency of Goldman because, as one writer has described it: Goldman invests $1.00 and borrows $9 (through the sales to the public); Goldman then takes the $1 investment and the $9 borrowed (for a total of $10) and borrows $90 with an investment of only $10 and from there moves onto $100 and $900.[53] Diagrammatically, the leveraged deals are shown below.

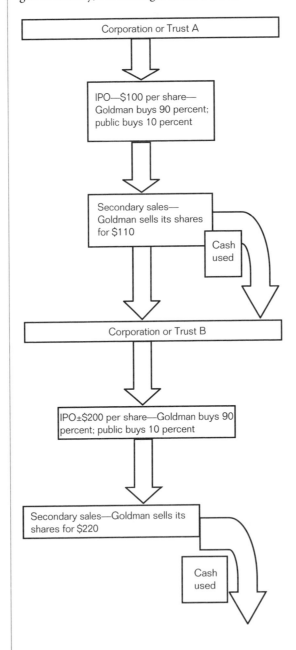

[53]Matt Taibbi, "The Great American Bubble Machine," *Rolling Stone,* July 9–23, 2010, p. 54.

Leverage extraordinaire was the theme that began in the late 1920s with this layering and continued through to the subprime mortgage secondary instrument market that resulted in the market crash of 2008. In the 1920s, the public was investing in stock portfolios. Goldman nearly collapsed when the stock market crashed in 1929.

The 1990s and Internet IPOs

The Goldman business strategies bring to mind the classic description of all market bubbles: they were "selling air." The Holland tulip market in the 1630s has been described as follows:

> *The story of the founding and growth of the Holland tulip market is a remarkably similar one. When the tulip was developed, people were enamored of it. They began buying tulips, fields of tulips and developing tulips. When tulips were no longer available, they began buying tulip bulbs because they would have a tulip at some time in the future. When there were no bulbs left, they created a market for tulip bulb futures. At the height of the market, one tulip bulb future cost $10,000 in present-day dollars. There was a market of air with complete dependence on the creation of bulbs in the future; these were investments in air completely dependent upon the honor of those selling these derivative tulip instruments.*
>
> *Eventually investors realized that those who sold the futures could not possibly deliver all that they had sold, and the market collapsed. The impact on the Holland economy was centuries in length.*[54]

And "selling air" took on a double entendre in the 1990s when Goldman became the Wall Street giant on taking Internet companies public. In 1999, the same year Goldman itself went public, Goldman underwrote 47 companies. What was not clear to investors in this round of phenomenal market growth, just as the nature of the layers of trusts and corporations was not clear to investors in the 1920s, was that the standard underwriting practice of requiring that a company show three years of profitability before being taken public was no longer enforced. That profitability standard had been slowly eased back to one year and then to one quarter. In fact, some Internet IPOs that Goldman underwrote had not yet seen any profits, and their business plans indicated that profits were not on the immediate horizon.

It was also during the go-go Internet 1990s that Goldman began a practice it would carry forward to future transactions, a practice that does affect its clients. Goldman engaged in laddering, which is an agreement between Goldman and its best clients for the allocation of a certain portion of the IPO at a preestablished price. However, under a laddering arrangement, those clients also had to agree to purchase a certain number of shares later during the IPO rollout at price $10 to $15 higher. To get some of the IPO, the clients had to agree to participate through laddering. Laddering is a trick, a sort of insider scam by the underwriter and its favored clients. The underwriter locks precommitted buyers at a price above the initial price and the shares of the IPO are guaranteed to rise. Goldman knows the fixed hand, but those in the market who are evaluating the IPO do not know that the increase is price is not due to legitimate demand for the company's shares. There was no transparency to the preestablished agreements for later purchase, known as "aftermarket purchases." The market demand, spurred by the predetermined secondary pricing, is synthetic, a result of Goldman's manufactured demand. For example, in 2000, Goldman was the underwriter for eToys, whose stock was

---

[54]Marianne M. Jennings, "A Contrarian's View: New Wine in Old Bottles: New Economy and Old Ethics, Can It Work?," chapter in *Ethics and Technology*, as retold from Mike Dash, *Tulipomania: The Story of the World's Most Coveted Flower & the Extraordinary Passions It Arose* (1999).

priced for the IPO at $20. Goldman had laddered the shares, and the price climbed to $75 per share by the end of the first day. By March 2001, eToys was in bankruptcy. Then Goldman Chairman Hank Paulson condemned the practice when the firms received its SEC Wells notice for laddering but denied any charges of securities fraud. Goldman settled the SEC charges on laddering by agreeing to pay a $40-million fine.[55]

The 2000s and CDOs

Prior to its becoming a publicly traded company at the time of the dot-com bubble, Goldman had been known for giving clients back their money if there was risk to reputation or relationship. In the 2000s, however, something shifted as the market for mortgage-backed securities such as collateralized debt obligations, or CDOs, grew exponentially. When Goldman entered this burgeoning market for financial instruments, it developed a different posture of a combination of defiance as well as "toes to the line" on legal issues. Goldman's October 2007 10Q reflected a shift for the firm from investment in CDOs to short sales, a bet against the mortgage-backed securities it continued to sell to its clients. "During most of 2007, we maintained a net short subprime (mortgage) position and therefore stood to benefit from declining prices in the mortgage market."[56] Nobel laureate economist Joseph Stiglitz compares Goldman's business model to gambling and concludes, "Goldman's activity is of negative social value. Its recent profits came from trading, which basically amounts to profiting from insider information at the expense of others."[57]

In 2008, Goldman changed its status from investment bank to bank holding company, a change that brought it under the regulatory arm of the Federal Reserve Bank. At the time, Goldman indicated that it made the move because investors had lost faith in the ability of the SEC to regulate investment banks. However, the change did make Federal Reserve funds available to Goldman, the types of loans that carry zero-percent interest and terms that carry no time limits. The easy availability of those funds allowed for substantial leveraging and even more expansion into the mortgage securitization market.

Diagrammatically, the structure of the CDO investment vehicles looks the same as the original 1920s model. The distinction was in the type of instrument. The financial model illustrated has not changed, nor has the risk. Because Goldman was at the foundation of all the corporations in the investment chain, any market or company misstep would cause the ripple effect a market crash. In the 2008 stock market crash, Goldman received $10 billion in government funds in order to survive.[58] The CDO market is described in more detail in the "'Toes-to-theLine' Activities" section.

Goldman: Its Culture and Philosophies

The company has had several management mantras. One is "long-term greedy," which Goldman executives translate to mean "don't kill the marketplace."[59] The other mantra is "Filthy rich by forty," which served as the motivational slogan for young people recruited into the firm for the long hours and demands for financial creativity in structuring offerings.[60] Somewhere in the 1990s, the two slogans were at war. Some have

---

[55]*SEC v. Goldman Sachs,* http://www.sec.gov/litigation/complaints/comp19051.pdf. January 25, 2005. Settlement at http://www.sec.gov/litigation/litreleases/lr19051.htm. Accessed July 20, 2010.

[56]http://www.sec.gov/Archives/edgar/data/. Accessed July 20, 2010.

[57]Gogoi, "Goldman's Big Rebound Raises Some Eyebrows," pp. 1B, 2B.

[58]David Lynch, "Goldman Hearings Strike a Defiant Note," *USA Today,* April 28, 2010, p. 1B.

[59]*Id.* at 56.

[60]John Arlidge, "I'm Doing God's Work. Meet Mr. Goldman," *London Times Interview, The Sunday Times,* November 8, 2009, p. 1.

attributed the change to the fact that the company went public in 1999. Without the partners personally liable for company losses, many believe the investment strategies changed dramatically.

Rolling Stone magazine has described the company as "a great vampire squid wrapped around the face of humanity, relentlessly jamming its blood funnel into anything that smells like money."[61] Goldman has launched the wealth and careers of business moguls and political powerhouses alike. Henry Paulson and Robert Rubin, both Goldman alums, served as Secretary of the Treasury. Former New Jersey Governor Jon Corzine made his legendary fortune at Goldman. Jim Cramer, the very noisy MSNBC analyst; John Thain, former CEO at Merrill; and Robert Steel, former Wachovia CEO, cut their financial-world teeth at Goldman. Goldman remains politically well connected, with Mr. Blankfein attending two White House events between January 2009 and April 2010. Mr. Blankfein was a presidential guest at the Kennedy Center for a 2010 event. Goldman employees contributed $1 million to the Obama presidential campaign and former White House Counsel, Gregory Craig, who left the Obama administration in January 2010 after one year of service, is serving on the Goldman defense team for the 2009 SEC charges. When asked whether he was violating the Obama administration rules on conflicts that prohibited former administration officials from working for companies as lobbyists for two years, Mr. Craig responded, "I am a lawyer, not a lobbyist."[62]

By the end of 2009, Goldman became the first large investment bank to be charged civilly for its conduct with investors and customers in that risky mortgage market. Goldman was initially defiant when the charges were announced, as it pronounced to business publications that it is, "Not Guilty, Not One Little Bit."[63] Indeed, Goldman CEO Lloyd Blankfein explained Goldman's critical role in society, "We help companies to grow by helping them to raise capital. Companies that grow create wealth. This, in turn, allows people to have jobs that create more growth and more wealth. It's a virtuous cycle. We have a social purpose."[64]

Mr. Blankfein says he has never forgotten his roots, which included living in a government housing project in Brooklyn. Although he attended Harvard on a scholarship at age 16, he was part of a one-income family and his father at one point lost his job as a truck driver. During that time, Mr. Blankfein, at age 13, sold peanuts and popcorn in Yankee Stadium to help the family make ends meet. Eventually his father landed a job as a mail sorter with the U.S. Post Office.[65] "I went to a fancy school. . . . But I grew up in a position to understand the stresses and strains of the real economy."[66]

Goldman's "Toes-to-the-Line" Activities and Issues

Stock Tips

The SEC prohibits an analyst from issuing reports on securities that run contrary to the analysts' true beliefs about the securities. The SEC also requires investment firms to engage in "fair dealing with its customers."[67] Whether those two requirements were met at the investment firms continues to be the subject of debate. Goldman held what were known as "trading huddles." The huddles found analysts and traders meeting to

[61]Matt Taibbi, "The Great American Bubble Machine," p. 52.

[62]Peter Baker, "Ex-Adviser to Obama Now Lawyer for Goldman," *New York Times,* April 21, 2010, p. B11.

[63]Robert Farzad and Paula Dwyer, "Not Guilty. Not One Little Bit," *Bloomberg BusinessWeek,* April 12, 2010, p. 31.

[64]Arlidge, "I'm Doing God's Work," p. 2.

[65]Pallavi Gogoi, "Goldman's Big Rebound Raises Some Eyebrows," *USA Today,* September 16, 2009, pp. 1B, 2B.

[66]*Id.*

[67]Susanne Craig, "Goldman's Trading Trips Reward Its Biggest Clients," *Wall Street Journal,* August 24, 2009, p. A1.

determine short and long investments on particular shares. The conclusions of the huddles were then shared with Goldman's traders and a selected few of Goldman's thousands of clients; and those conclusions were often different from the Goldman analysts' reports and recommendations that were issued publicly. Other firms such as Morgan Stanley also have huddles in addition to their published research recommendations, but their conclusions from the weekly meetings are then sent out in an e-mail blast to all clients.

One distinction between Goldman's huddles and those of other investment firms was that Goldman's huddles did not involve equity research analysts, the analysts who are subject to the SEC rules. Rather, those who participated in the huddle were from Goldman's "Fundamental Strategies Group," a group that would be exempt from the SEC rules.[68]

The complaint from market participants and other firms was that Goldman was giving an edge to certain investors and not distributing information completely. However, Goldman is not privy to inside information about the stocks. Rather its weekly updates, it claims, are just that—updates based on new market developments. Eric Danallo, a former deputy New York Attorney General, argues that the spirit of the law should control the conduct, not a strained interpretation, "Analysts should give consistent advice to all their customers, be they small investors or big trading clients."[69]

The Auction-Rate Markets

Wall Street firms were able to profit from their participation in what was known as the auction-rate markets. These securities were touted as mutual-fund grade with a higher yield. Their clients would bid on securities being sold through a once-per-month auction that the investment firms were selling. What their clients did not know is that their own investment advisers were bidding up the value of the instruments. The prices were reset weekly based on the demand, but the investment firms were creating that demand through their bids, bids that they never intended to execute because their clients would always bid more. The investment firms were setting a market floor for the market they were running even as they were encouraging their clients to get in on what appeared to be a thriving market. When Goldman, the fifth largest underwriter of the market, pulled out, there was no longer a market for the securities. Clients were left holding $40 billion in securities they were told were as good as cash. Arthur Levitt, the former chairman of the SEC, responded to the problem, "Very few issues have shaken public confidence in the integrity of our markets as much as this."[70]

Through legal action brought by New York Attorney General Andrew Cuomo, Merrill Lynch, Citigroup, UBS, Goldman, and others agreed to buy back their clients' auction-rate securities. However, Goldman only agreed to buy back its smaller investors' auction-rate securities. Goldman left its larger investors holding the unsellable securities.[71]

Betting against the Clients: Abacus, the Fabulous Fab, and CDOs

In a frank and stunning memo written to its clients in January 2010, Goldman Sachs admitted that it often made recommendations to clients that it had already positioned itself to profit from. For example, Goldman made recommendations to clients to purchase collateralized debt obligations (CDOs), the mortgage-backed debt instruments, as it was pushing to have the instruments rated high even as it was positioning itself short

---

[68]Andrew Ross Sorkin, "At Goldman, E-Mail Message Lays Bare Conflicts in Trading," *New York Times,* January 13, 2010, p. B1.

[69]*Id.,* p. A10.

[70]Liz Rappaport, "Goldman Balks at Helping Rich Clients Recover from 'Auction Rate' Securities," *Wall Street Journal,* August 14, 2008, p. C1.

[71]*Id.*

on the instruments. Positioning short means that Goldman stood to make money when the value of the CDOs declined. Internal e-mails at Goldman found the investment banker referring to CDO securities as "junk," "s_____," or "crappy."[72] When Goldman executives were asked about their internal negative characterizations of securities it was touting and selling to its clients, a Goldman executive, David Viniar responded, "I think that's very unfortunate to have on email." When his response elicited laughter in the hearing room, Mr. Viniar changed his answer to, "It's very unfortunate to have said that in any form."[73] The following diagram is adapted from an article on the Goldman strategy.[74]

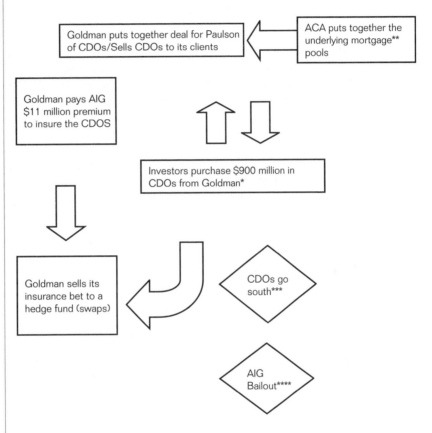

*Investors believe they are investing in mutual-fund grade securities and will receive returns on their purchase.

**SEC alleges Paulson had input on quality of mortgages in the pool.

***Investors lose their $900 million, which is then used by hedge funds to pay Goldman, and AIG must pay for those losses it insured.

****Federal government bails out AIG.

The SEC filed a civil action in April 2010 against Goldman for its conduct in a CDO deal known as ABACUS. According to the complaint, 31-year-old Goldman employee Fabrice Tourre put together a deal of CDOs with the mortgage pool handpicked by

[72]Michael M. Phillips, "Senators Seek, Fail to Get an 'I'm Sorry,'" *Wall Street Journal*, April 28, 2010, pp. A3, A5.

[73]*Id.* at A5.

[74]Gretchen Morgenson and Louise Story, "Banks Bundled Debt, Bet Against It and Won," *New York Times*, December 4, 2009, pp. A1, B4.

John Paulson, a financial wizard who planned to position himself short on the securities Goldman would sell to its clients. The SEC complaint alleges that Paulson chose mortgage pools that were dogs, i.e., "crappy." Those mortgages were chosen because having these securities "tank" was important to Goldman and Paulson because of their positions on the mortgage instrument markets. However, Mr. Tourre and Goldman had a third party, ACA Management, actually structure the deal so that they were distanced from choosing the mortgage pools for the instruments.

ACA folks were curious about their role and sent e-mails to Goldman inquiring as to why Paulson would exclude Wells Fargo mortgages from the pool because Wells was known for "quality" subprime mortgages. ACA (not charged with any violations) comes across in the complaint as a firm that was asking all the right questions over and over again. It was seeking reassurance, and received it from Goldman's team. The complaint tells a story of Goldman using a trusting firm, one that was relying on Goldman's reputation, to distance itself from Paulson and what amounted to a transaction/security offering that was set up from the beginning to allow Paulson and Goldman to profit from their short positions on the CDO market.

The issue that Goldman contested initially with the charges was whether it knowingly failed to disclose its position and strategies to investors. Goldman maintained that its clients were "qualified" and/or "sophisticated" investors to whom the firm was not required to provide the detailed information that is mandated under general public offerings. Goldman's position initially was that the clients who purchased the instruments were in a position and had a level of knowledge of markets to understand and process the risk and realize that all investment bankers are positioned in the market according to their theories on risk.

Goldman also pointed out that its memo read in part, "We may trade, and have existing positions, based on trading ideas before we have discussed those ideas with you."[75] The disclosure of the Goldman client-contra positions had appeared in the fine print in Goldman's marketing materials, but the memo represented the first time that Goldman had discussed it openly with its clients.

Experts indicate that Goldman was disclosing its conflict as a way of managing client relationships and trading positions. One expert has noted that the way the markets have evolved, client and investment firm relationships are "laden with conflicts of interest."[76]

On the eve of the congressional hearings into Goldman's role as an investment banker in the collapse of the CDO market, Goldman released a series of e-mails from Tourre that served to place him in a bad light. One of the e-mails, to his girlfriend in London, contained the following:

> *Darling you should take a look at this article. . . . Very insightful. . . . More and more leverage in the system, l'edifice entier risque de s'effondrer a tout moment. . . . Seul survivant potentiel, the fabulous Fab (as Mitch would kindly call me, even though there is nothing fabulous about me, just kindness, altruism and deep love for some gorgeous and super-smart French girl in London), standing in the middle of all these complex, highly levered, exotic trades he created without necessarily understanding all the implications of those monstruosities[sic]!!! Anyway, not feeling too guilty about this, the real purpose of my job is to make capital markets more efficient and ultimately provide the US consumer with more efficient ways to leverage and finance himself, so there is a humble, noble and ethical reason for my job ;) amazing how good I am in convincing myself!!!*

---

[75]Sorkin, "At Goldman, E-Mail Message Lays Bare Conflicts in Trading," p.B1.
[76]*Id.*

Sweetheart, I am now going to try to get away from ABX and other ethical questions, and immediately plunge into Freakonomics. . . . I feel blessed to be with you, to be able to learn and share special things with you. I love when you advise me on books I should be reading. I feel like we share a lot of things in common, a lot of values, topics we are interested in and intrigued by. . . . I just love you!!![77]

Goldman's activities in deals such as this have been described as "Heads Goldman wins, tails you lose."[78] Professor William K. Black at the University of Missouri at Kansas City has written, "Every game has a sucker, and in this case, the sucker was not so much AIG as it was the U.S. government and the taxpayer."[79] Mr. Blankfein defended his firm's conduct in November 2009 in an interview with the *London Times* by stating that he was just a banker "doing God's work."[80]

Executive Compensation and Shareholder Say on Pay

In 2008, Goldman received $10 billion from the U.S. government as part of the national bailout of financial firms. Goldman paid no bonuses in 2008. By the end of 2009, Goldman had a record year for its profits. As a result of the earnings record, the firm's compensation and bonus plans meant that its bonus pool totaled $20 billion.

When the earnings were announced, Great Britain's Chancellor of Exchequer, Alistair Darling, announced a 50 percent tax on bonuses paid to bankers. Just a few days later President Barack Obama gave a speech in which he referred disparagingly to "fat-cat bankers."[81]

However, after a week of internal meetings, Goldman CEO Lloyd Blankfein, acknowledging that "people are pissed off, mad, and bent out of shape" at bankers, issued a statement indicating that the firm's top thirty executives would not be receiving cash bonuses for 2009.[82] Mr. Blankfein and the top four executives received $9 million in stock as their bonuses, an amount that was about one-half of the bonuses paid to Jamie Dimon, the CEO of JPMorgan Chase and just a fraction of Mr. Blankfein's 2007 bonus of $65 million.[83] The bonuses for other Wall Street CEOs were: James Gorman (Morgan Stanley): $8.1 million; Brian Moynihan (Bank of America): $800,000; and Vikram Pandit (Citigroup): $1.00.

The decision did not affect the company's 31,000 other employees (at that time) and consultants who will benefit from the bonus pool, with a resulting amount of $800,000 per employee.[84]

In meeting with shareholders, the company also released information about new pay practices:

- Bonuses for 2009 would be paid in stock' with the stock being "Shares at Risk," which means that employees cannot touch the shares for five years.
- In future years, bonuses would be paid 70 percent in "Shares at Risk" and 30 percent cash.
- All shares are subject to a claw-back provision, which means the bonus can be lost if the employee was involved in any type of securities fraud or malfeasance.
- Shareholders will have a "say on pay" in future years, with the right to cast a nonbinding vote on the company's proposed compensation plans.[85]

---

[77]*SEC v. Goldman Sachs and Fabrice Tourre*, 10 Civ. 3229 (BJ) (S.D.N.Y. filed April 16, 2010). www.sec.gov. Accessed July 20, 2010.

[78]Farzad and Dwyer, "Not Guilty, Not One Little Bit," p. 31.

[79]*Id., p.* 32.

[80]Arlidge, "I'm Doing God's Work.," p. 1.

[81]Ian Katz and Christine Harper, "The 'Fat Cats' Try to Look Slimmer," *BusinessWeek,* December 28, 2009, and January 4, 2010, p. 26.

[82]Arlidge, "I'm Doing God's Work," p. 1.

[83]Susanne Craig and Matthias Rieker, "Goldman CEO Bows on Pay," *Wall Street Journal,* February 6–7, 2010, p. A1.

[84]Susanne Craig, "Goldman Blinks on Bonuses," *Wall Street Journal,* December 11, 2009, p. A1.

[85]Louise Story, "Goldman Sachs Bars Cash Bonuses for Top Officers," *New York Times,* December 11, 2009, p. A1.

TIAA-CREF, a teachers' pension plan that holds $1 billion in Goldman shares, praised the new provisions, indicating that Goldman had set a "high standard" for Wall Street firms.[86]

In addition, Goldman is weighing the adoption of a requirement that its executives give a percentage of their bonuses to charity. If adopted, the requirement would mirror one that existed at Bear Stearns, which was that executives had to give 4 percent of their income to charity. Bear Stearns then verified the contribution by requiring executives to submit their income tax returns for review.[87]

The Bailout for the Cash-Short Executives

Jon Winkelried, Goldman's co–chief operating officer, and Gregory K. Palm, its general counsel, two of the company's largest shareholders, were short on cash. Mr. Winkelried was paid $19.7 million for about 30 percent of his holdings and Mr. Palm was paid $38.3 million for 25 percent of his holdings.[88] Goldman feared that if the two sold their interests in the market that there would result in market turmoil from rattled investors. Another executive pledged 500,000 of his shares in exchange for a loan from Goldman.

Under Sarbanes–Oxley, publicly traded companies are prohibited from making loans to executives. Goldman indicates the transactions were not loans but stock purchases from the executives.

Goldman Settles Up and the Future

The SEC charges had an impact on Goldman, because of their serious nature and their focus on client trust and also because Goldman did not disclose in two 10Q filings that followed that it had received a Wells notice from the SEC on the possible charges.[89] Its market cap fell by $12.4 billion when the SEC charges were announced in April 2010, a loss of $21 billion. Its share price dropped from $190 to $145 within the two months following.

Goldman's initial defiance was tempered and on July 16, 2010, the SEC announced a settlement with the company. Goldman agreed to pay $550 million in penalties and client reimbursements. Clients' losses have been estimated at $1 billion.

As of May 2010, Goldman had assets of over $1 trillion. Its annual revenues for 2009 topped $13 billion, with first-quarter earnings for 2010 of $3.2 billion, showing it on track for a repeat. The company has 32,000 employees worldwide and takes no new clients unless they have a minimum of $10 million to invest. As of July 20, 2010, Goldman's stock price was at $148.50, an uptick from the low point of $129.50 in July 2010, just days before the settlement announcement.

Discussion Questions

1. Go back through the case and make a list of each action or practice that could be called a gray area.
2. Evaluate each of the actions or practices using ethical analysis models other than the question, "Is it legal?"
3. List all of those who were affected by the Goldman gray areas you have found. Describe the impact of Goldman's strategies and products up and down the economic chain.
4. What factors in the Goldman culture influenced the decisions of the employees, executives, traders, and advisers?
5. During the April 2010 hearings on Goldman's CDO transactions, Senator Claire McCaskill said to Mr. Blankfein as he testified before

---

[86]*Id.*

[87]Louise Story, "Goldman Weighs Requirement for Charity," *New York Times*, January 11, 2010, p. B1.

[88]Louise Story, "Goldman Bailed Out 2 Executives," *New York Times*, March 28, 2009, p. B1.

[89]"Silence Was Goldman; Will a Price Be Paid?" *Wall Street Journal*, April 19, 2010, p. C8. A Wells notice is an advance notification from the SEC to a target in an investigation.

Congress, "It feels like you guys are betting on the game you're playing," and securities law expert, Professor John Coffee said, "I think we're seeing another one of those periodic eruptions because we see this story of investment bankers who seem to be playing both sides against the middle, and the investor looks like a sucker."[90] The SEC complaint on the Goldman CDOs paints a picture of a company playing both sides of a deal even as it knew the hands both sides were playing. Senator John Ensign, a senator from Nevada was offended when other senators referred to Goldman's operations as akin to running a Las Vegas casino because he said it was an insult to the casinos. Continuing the metaphor, Senator Ensign explained that Goldman was running the casino and using an eye-in-the-sky to figure out any hand played by its patrons. Gambling math does give the house a leg or two up anyway, but the SEC complaint paints a picture of investors never having a chance because the other side not only knew the hand they played but the other side, Goldman, was setting up the cards to be dealt and the nature of the deck before the game began.

Think back to the Albert Carr reading on ethics in business (Reading 2.3) and apply it to what happened in the CDO market. Was Goldman just bluffing or did it have cards up its sleeve? Evaluate Mr. Blankfein's statement that Goldman does not have disclosure responsibilities to those who are "qualified" or "sophisticated" investors under SEC rules.

6. Howard Chen, a banking analyst, issued these observations on the Goldman settlement: (1) He observed that there would be no management changes at Goldman; and, (2) "We do not anticipate any material long-term impact to the firm's client franchise."[91] What concerns do you have about these perhaps very accurate observations about the settlement?

Compare & Contrast

Senator Susan Collins of Maine posed a question to several Goldman executives during the April 2010 congressional hearings, "I understand that you do not have a legal fiduciary obligation. But did the firm expect you to act in the best interests of your clients as opposed to acting in the best interests of the firm? Could you give me a yes or no to whether or not you considered yourself to have a duty to act in the best interests of your clients?"[92] Fabrice Tourre responded only with, "I believe we have a duty to serve our clients well."[93] Mr. Blankfein responded with the following, "While we strongly disagree with the SEC's complaint, I also recognize how such a complicated transaction may look to many people. To them, it is confirmation of how out of control they believe Wall Street has become, no matter how sophisticated the parties or what disclosures were made. We have to do a better job of striking the balance between what an informed client believes is important to his or her investing goals and what the public believes is overly complex and risky."[94] Other Goldman executives provided the following responses to Senator Collins, "It's our responsibility. . . in helping them transact at levels that are fair market prices and help meet their needs," and "Conceptually it seems like an interesting idea."[95]

Investment advisers are not considered fiduciaries under federal or state law. Without that legally imposed fiduciary duty, the advisers can legally engage in transactions that may not be in the best interests of their clients. That is, they are free to sell, sell, sell

---

[90]David Lynch, "Goldman Hearings Strike a Defiant Note," *USA Today,* April 28, 2010, p. 1B, at 2B.

[91]http://pulse.alacra.com/analyst-comments/Howard_Chen-A1904. Accessed July 20, 2010.

[92]Wall Street and the Financial Crisis: The Role of Investment Banks, Hearings of the Permanent Subcommittee on Investigations, April 27, 2010, http://hsgac.senate.gov/public/index.cfm?FuseAction=Hearings.Hearing&Hearing_ID=-f07ef2bf-914c-494c-aa66-27129f8e6282. Accessed July 20, 2010.

[93]*Id.*

[94]*Id.*

[95]*Id.*

products from their firms that make more money for their firms but may not be in the best interests of the client, as was done with the CDOs. In another e-mail, Mr. Tourre wrote, "I'm [*sic*] managed to sell a few abacus bonds to widows and orphans that I ran into at the airport, apparently these Belgians adore synthetic abs cdo2." (June 17, 2007).[96]

What is Senator Collins asking of the Goldman executives in terms of what you have learned about stakeholders and ethical analysis? Evaluate Mr. Tourre's and Mr. Blankfein's postures and those of the other Goldman executives on the role of business in society.

Case 2.12

What Happens in Boulder Stays in Boulder: Cell Phone Alibis

The *New York Times* ran an article entitled, "For Liars and Loafers, Cell Phones Offer an Alibi."[97] The article explains, among other things, that 20-year-old Kenny Hall wished to spend a weekend in Boulder, Colorado, with a woman other than his girlfriend. Mr. Hall sent out text messages seeking help from a network of individuals who help each other miss dates, get out of obligations, cancel blind dates, ditch work and school, and generally provide alibis to each other. Mr. Hall's text message yielded a response from someone at the University of Colorado, Boulder, who offered to call Mr. Hall's girlfriend, posing as the soccer coach from that university and indicate that Mr. Hall needed to be there for a tryout. The area code from the young volunteer's cell phone matched that of the university.

The article points out that there are even freelance deceivers who will make these types of calls for $2.99 each. One of the owners of such a freelance company indicates, "It lets you control your environment." An owner of a European alibi club shut his business down after he got a new girlfriend: "She thought it was immoral. Imagine that!"

Discussion Questions

1. Are these alibi clubs immoral?

2. Would you participate in an alibi cell phone club? Explain your decision using the models you have applied.

Compare & Contrast

Why do you think the new European girlfriend felt so differently from others and felt so strongly about these alibi services? Be sure to think of the role of a credo in developing your answer.

Case 2.13

Travel Expenses: A Chance for Extra Income

The *New York Times Magazine* profiled the problems with employees' submissions for travel and entertainment expenses reimbursement. American Express reported that employees spend $156 billion annually on travel and entertainment related to business. Internal auditors at companies listed types of expenses for which employees have sought reimbursement: hairdresser, traffic tickets, and kennel fees.

Although the IRS raised the amount allowable for undocumented expenses to $75, most companies keep their limit for employees at $25. One company auditor commented that all taxi cab rides now cost $24.97 and if the company went with the IRS limit, the cab fares would climb to $74.65.

---

[96]John D. McKinnon and Susanne Craig, "Investigators Interview Tourre," *Wall Street Journal,* April 26, 2010, p. B5.

[97]Matt Richtel, "For Liars and Loafers, Cell Phones Offer an Alibi," *The New York Times,* June 26, 2004, pp. B1, B14.

Some of the horror stories submitted by auditors on travel and entertainment expenses submitted by employees:

- One employee submitted a bill for $12 for a tin of cookies. When questioned, he could not explain how it had been used but asked for reimbursement anyway because all he would have to do is "make up" a couple of taxi rides to get it back anyway;
- $225 for three hockey tickets, except that the names on the tickets were the employee's family members;
- $625 for wallpapering. The employee had included it with her other travel expenses and even had the wallpaper receipt written in a different language in order to throw off any questions; and
- $275 sports jacket submitted as a restaurant bill. The travel office called the number listed on the receipt and asked if food was sold there. The response was, "No, we're a men's clothing store."[98]

Discussion Questions

1. The auditors noted that employees who are confronted often respond with similar justifications:
   "The company owes it to me."
   "It doesn't really hurt anyone."
   "Everybody does this."
   Are these justifications or rationalizations?
2. Why do employees risk questionable expenses?
3. Who is harmed by dishonest expense submissions?

4. There is a book called "How to Pad Your Expense Report . . . and Get Away with It!" by Employee X. Employee X says that he offers these suggestions because of the "obscene salaries" of executives. Employee X also notes that he has been cheating on his expenses for so long that he doesn't even think about it anymore. Can you see any of the rationalizations in Employee X's views? What critical point do you discern from habit and ethics working together?

Case 2.14

Do Cheaters Prosper?

In a book entitled *Cheaters Always Prosper: 50 Ways to Beat the System without Being Caught,*[99] James Brazil (a pen name), a college student from the University of California, Santa Barbara, has provided fifty ways to obtain a "free lunch." One suggestion is to place shards of glass in your dessert at a fancy restaurant and then "raise hell." The manager or owner will then come running with certificates for free meals and probably waive your bill.

Another suggestion is, rather than spend $400 on new tires for your car, rent a car for a day for $35 and switch the rental car tires with your tires. So long as your car tires are not bald, the rental car company employees will not notice, and you will have your new tires for a mere $35.

Discussion Questions

1. Are these suggestions ethical?
2. Was publishing the book with the suggestions ethical?

3. Do any of these suggestions cost anyone any money?

---

[98]Paul Burnham Finney, "Hey, It's on the Company!" *The New York Times Magazine*, March 8, 1998, pp. 99–100.

[99]*Citadel Press*, October 1996.

Case 2.15

The Rigged Election

The Finance Club at Harvard University is a prestigious organization for Harvard MBA students. The student members have the opportunity to interact with public officials like Senator William Proxmire and business executives such as Bruce Wasserstein. The Finance Club also serves as a network for job hunting.

Each spring, the club holds elections for its officers, including two co-presidents. In the spring of 1992, after initial balloting, there was a tie between two teams of two co-presidents. Murry Gunty was one member of one of the teams and busily recruited students to vote in a runoff election. Two of the votes Mr. Gunty recruited were from students who were not members of the club but who had used someone else's name to vote; they voted under names of absentee members of the Finance Club. The new votes gave Mr. Gunty his victory.[100]

After an anonymous tip, the elections were set aside and the runners-up installed as co-presidents. Mr. Gunty was required to write a paper on ethics.[101]

Discussion Questions

1. In the words of the school newspaper publisher, "Why would anyone do this? It's just a club." Why did they do it?
2. Was anyone really hurt by the conduct?
3. Would you have reported the conduct anonymously or disclosed it publicly?
4. Is there a principle for your credo in this case study involving students?
5. Mr. Gunty is now the managing partner of Blackstreet Capital, a firm he founded eighteen years ago. You can Google Mr. Gunty's name and pull up the ballot-stuffing issue as well as a number of blogs on Mr. Gunty and his conduct. What are the long-term implications of this graduate school conduct for Mr. Gunty?

Case 2.16

West Virginia University and the Governor's Daughter

Heather Bresch is the daughter of West Virginia governor, Joe Manchin III. She is also a friend and former business associate of Mike Garrison, the president (until September 2008) of West Virginia University. Ms. Bresch was named the chief operating officer (now CEO) at Mylan, Inc., the third-largest manufacturer of generic drugs in the world. Mylan is headed by chairman, Milan Puskar, who is a major campaign contributor to Mr. Manchin and the largest donor to West Virginia University ($20 million given in 2003).

> *When Ms. Bresch was named to the position of COO, the press release indicated that she had received her MBA from West Virginia University. A reporter for the Pittsburgh Post-Gazette discovered when he called to verify Ms. Bresch's credentials that she had completed only 22 credit hours of the 48 credit hours required for the MBA degree. Provost Gerald E. Lang and business school dean, R. Stephen Sears had awarded Ms. Bresch the degree retroactively. An investigation revealed that Ms. Bresch and others (the original total was 70) may have been given their degrees despite not having completed the necessary courses.*

---

[100]Gilbert Fuchsberg, "Harvard Has Some Crimson Faces over a Lesson in Practical Politics," *The Wall Street Journal,* April 9, 1992, p. B1.

[101]"Harvard Student Rigging Election Must Write Paper," *The Wall Street Journal,* April 24, 1992, p. A3.

University president Mike Garrison would not denounce the award of the degrees and, because of student protests during graduation ("Garrison Must Resign" written on their hats), was forced to resign. In 2008, a special panel reviewed the University's degrees and conducted an audit. The panel concluded that some degrees should have been awarded and that others were not justifiably awarded. Ms. Bresch's degree was one the panel concluded was not awarded properly. Ms. Bresch then wrote to the Board of Governors of West Virginia University and asked them to explain the disparity in treatment between her case and the other 288 degrees that were permitted to stand. Shortly after her request, Ms. Bresch was named CEO at Mylan.

Discussion Questions

1. What did the university president miss in making his decision about the retroactive degree?

2. Why did he make the decision?

3. Make a list of who is affected by the decision about the degree.

Business, Stakeholders, Social Responsibility, and Sustainability

UNIT THREE

Still another level of ethics is the responsibility of the corporation to its community—what contributions and efforts should corporations make to others beyond their shareholders? A company that manufactures athletic shoes finds cheap labor in developing nations. The company pays minimum wage for that country, but those wages wouldn't bring enough in one month to allow the workers to buy a pair of the company's shoes. Call centers in India have young people working round-the-clock on shifts that result in the loss of their personal and family time. Factory conditions meet that nation's standards but violate nearly all U.S. minimum standards. Without the cheap labor, the shoe manufacturer believes it can't compete. Without the jobs, the nation can't develop, but children are working 50-hour weeks in these third-world countries. Fair and just treatment in the workplace is an issue the company must face in making a decision for foreign outsourcing of labor. But there are compelling points even the workers in those countries and the parents of the children make about the use of cheap labor as a benefit to them and their countries' economic development.

And how do corporations best contribute to communities and societies? Through boycotts or through economic development? These are difficult questions that have brought some of the past century's greatest minds in search of answers. This unit provides you with their depth of thought on the social responsibility of corporations.

Business and Society: The Tough Issues of Economics, Social Responsibility, and Business

SECTION 3A

In the following readings, the late Dr. Milton Friedman, a Nobel laureate, and Professor Edward Freeman present different views on the role of ethics in business as well as the role of business in society. But you also have the views of Michael Novak, Ronald Coase, Jon Entine, and Marjorie Kelly as you study the depth of these difficult questions related to the role of business in society. You can now add to your steps for resolving dilemmas the additional factor of your position and the position of the company and those individuals involved as to the role of business in society.

Reading 3.1

The Social Responsibility of Business Is to Increase Its Profits[1]

Milton Friedman

When I hear businessmen speak eloquently about the "social responsibilities of business in a free-enterprise system," I am reminded of the wonderful line about the Frenchman who discovered at the age of 70 that he had been speaking prose all his life. The businessmen believe that they are defending free enterprise when they declaim that business is not concerned "merely" with profit but also with promoting desirable "social" ends; that business has a "social conscience" and takes seriously its responsibilities for providing employment, eliminating discrimination, avoiding pollution, and whatever else may be the catchwords of the contemporary crop of reformers. In fact they are—or would be if they or anyone else took them seriously—preaching pure and unadulterated socialism. Businessmen who talk this way are unwitting puppets of the intellectual forces that have been undermining the basis of a free society these past decades.

The discussions of the "social responsibilities of business" are notable for their analytical looseness and lack of rigor. What does it mean to say that "business" has responsibilities? Only people can have responsibilities. A corporation is an artificial person and in this sense may have artificial responsibilities, but "business" as a whole cannot be said to have responsibilities, even in this vague sense. The first step toward clarity in examining the doctrine of the social responsibility of business is to ask precisely what it implies for whom.

Presumably, the individuals who are to be responsible are businessmen, which means individual proprietors or corporate executives. Most of the discussion of social responsibility is directed at corporations, so in what follows I shall mostly neglect the individual proprietor and speak of corporate executives.

In a free-enterprise, private-property system, a corporate executive is an employee of the owners of the business. He has direct responsibility to his employers. That responsibility is to conduct the business in accordance with their desires, which generally will be to make as much money as possible while conforming to the basic rules of the society, both those embodied in law and those embodied in ethical custom. Of course, in some cases his employers may have a different objective. A group of persons might establish a corporation for an eleemosynary purpose—for example, a hospital or a school. The

manager of such a corporation will not have money profit as his objective but the rendering of certain services.

In either case, the key point is that, in his capacity as a corporate executive, the manager is the agent of the individuals who own the corporation or establish the eleemosynary institution, and his primary responsibility is to them.

Needless to say, this does not mean that it is easy to judge how well he is performing his task. But at least the criterion of performance is straightforward, and the persons among whom a voluntary contractual arrangement exists are clearly defined.

Of course, the corporate executive is also a person in his own right. As a person, he may have many other responsibilities that he recognizes or assumes voluntarily—to his family, his conscience, his feelings of charity, his church, his clubs, his city, his country. He may feel impelled by these responsibilities to devote part of his income to causes he regards as worthy, to refuse to work for particular corporations, even to leave his job, for example, to join his country's armed forces. If we wish, we may refer to some of these responsibilities as "social responsibilities." But in these respects he is acting as a principal, not an agent; he is spending his own money or time or energy, not the money of his employers or the time or energy he had contracted to devote to their purposes. If these are "social responsibilities," they are the social responsibilities of individuals, not of business.

What does it mean to say that the corporate executive has a "social responsibility" in his capacity as businessman? If this statement is not pure rhetoric, it must mean that he is to act in some way that is not in the interest of his employers. For example, that he is to refrain from increasing the price of the product in order to contribute to the social objective of preventing inflation, even though a price increase would be in the best interests of the corporation. Or that he is to make expenditures on reducing pollution beyond the amount that is in the best interests of the corporation or that is required by law in order to contribute to the social objective of improving the environment. Or that, at the expense of corporate profits, he is to hire "hard-core" unemployed instead of better-qualified available workmen to contribute to the social objective of reducing poverty.

In each of these cases, the corporate executive would be spending someone else's money for a general social interest. Insofar as his actions in accord with his "social responsibility" reduce returns to stockholders, he is spending their money. Insofar as his actions raise the price to customers, he is spending the customers' money. Insofar as his actions lower the wages of some employees, he is spending their money.

The stockholders or the customers or the employees could separately spend their own money on the particular action if they wished to do so. The executive is exercising a distinct "social responsibility," rather than serving as an agent of the stockholders or the customers or the employees, only if he spends the money in a different way than they would have spent it.

But if he does this, he is in effect imposing taxes, on the one hand, and deciding how the tax proceeds shall be spent, on the other.

This process raises political questions on two levels: principle and consequences. On the level of political principle, the imposition of taxes and the expenditure of tax proceeds are governmental functions. We have established elaborate constitutional, parliamentary, and judicial provisions to control these functions, to assure that taxes are imposed so far as possible in accordance with the preferences and desires of the public—after all, "taxation without representation" was one of the battle cries of the American Revolution. We have a system of checks and balances to separate the legislative function of imposing taxes and enacting expenditures from the executive function of collecting taxes and administering expenditure programs and from the judicial function of mediating disputes and interpreting the law.

Here the businessman—self-selected or appointed directly or indirectly by stockholders—is to be simultaneously legislator, executive, and jurist. He is to decide whom to tax by how much and for what purpose, and he is to spend the proceeds—all this guided only by general exhortations from on high to restrain inflation, improve the environment, fight poverty, and so on and on.

The whole justification for permitting the corporate executive to be selected by the stockholders is that the executive is an agent serving the interests of his principal. This justification disappears when the corporate executive imposes taxes and spends the proceeds for "social" purposes. He becomes in effect a public employee, a civil servant, even though he remains in name an employee of a private enterprise. On grounds of political principle, it is intolerable that such civil servants—insofar as their actions in the name of social responsibility are real and not just window-dressing—should be selected as they are now. If they are to be civil servants, then they must be selected through a political process. If they are to impose taxes and make expenditures to foster "social" objectives, then political machinery must be set up to guide the assessment of taxes and to determine through a political process the objectives to be served.

This is the basic reason why the doctrine of "social responsibility" involves the acceptance of the socialist view that political mechanisms, not market mechanisms, are the appropriate way to determine the allocation of scarce resources to alternative uses.

On the grounds of consequences, can the corporate executive in fact discharge his alleged "social responsibilities"? On the one hand, suppose he could get away with spending the stockholders' or customers' or employees' money. How is he to know how to spend it? He is told that he must contribute to fighting inflation. How is he to know what action of his will contribute to that end? He is presumably an expert in running his company—in producing a product or selling it or financing it. But nothing about his selection makes him an expert on inflation. Will his holding down the price of his product reduce inflationary pressure? Or, by leaving more spending power in the hands of his customers, simply divert it elsewhere? Or, by forcing him to produce less because of the lower price, will it simply contribute to shortages? Even if he could answer these questions, how much cost is he justified in imposing on his stockholders, customers, and employees for this social purpose? What is his appropriate share and what is the appropriate share of others?

And, whether he wants to or not, can he get away with spending his stockholders', customers', or employees' money? Will not the stockholders fire him? (Either the present ones or those who take over when his actions in the name of social responsibility have reduced the corporation's profits and the price of its stock.) His customers and his employees can desert him for other producers and employers less scrupulous in exercising their social responsibilities.

This facet of "social responsibility" doctrine is brought into sharp relief when the doctrine is used to justify wage restraint by trade unions. The conflict of interest is naked and clear when union officials are asked to subordinate the interest of their members to some more general social purpose. If the union officials try to enforce wage restraint, the consequence is likely to be wildcat strikes, rank-and-file revolts and the emergence of strong competitors for their jobs. We thus have the ironic phenomenon that union leaders—at least in the U.S.—have objected to government interference with the market far more consistently and courageously than have business leaders.

The difficulty of exercising "social responsibility" illustrates, of course, the great virtue of private competitive enterprise—it forces people to be responsible for their own actions and makes it difficult for them to "exploit" other people for either selfish or unselfish purposes. They can do good—but only at their own expense.

Many a reader who has followed the argument this far may be tempted to remonstrate that it is well and good to speak of government's having the responsibility to impose taxes and determine expenditures for such "social" purposes as controlling pollution or training the hard-core unemployed, but that the problems are too urgent to wait on the slow course of political processes, that the exercise of social responsibility by businessmen is a quicker and surer way to solve pressing current problems.

Aside from the question of fact—I share Adam Smith's skepticism about the benefits that can be expected from "those who affected to trade for the public good"—this argument must be rejected on grounds of principle. What it amounts to is an assertion that those who favor the taxes and expenditures in question have failed to persuade a majority of their fellow citizens to be of like mind and that they are seeking to attain by undemocratic procedures what they cannot attain by democratic procedures. In a free society, it is hard for "good" people to do "good," but that is a small price to pay for making it hard for "evil" people to do "evil," especially since one man's good is another's evil.

I have, for simplicity, concentrated on the special case of the corporate executive, except only for the brief digression on trade unions. But precisely the same argument applies to the newer phenomenon of calling upon stockholders to require corporations to exercise social responsibility (the recent GM crusade, for example). In most of these cases, what is in effect involved is some stockholders trying to get other stockholders (or customers or employees) to contribute against their will to "social" causes favored by the activists. Insofar as they succeed, they are again imposing taxes and spending the proceeds.

The situation of the individual proprietor is somewhat different. If he acts to reduce the returns of his enterprise in order to exercise his "social responsibility," he is spending his own money, not someone else's. If he wishes to spend his money on such purposes, that is his right, and I cannot see that there is any objection to his doing so. In the process, he, too, may impose costs on employees and customers. However, because he is far less likely than a large corporation or union to have monopolistic power, any such side effects will tend to be minor.

Of course, in practice the doctrine of social responsibility is frequently a cloak for actions that are justified on other grounds rather than a reason for those actions.

To illustrate, it may well be in the long-run interest of a corporation that is a major employer in a small community to devote resources to providing amenities to that community or to improving its government. That may make it easier to attract desirable employees, [or] it may reduce the wage bill or lessen losses from pilferage and sabotage or have other worthwhile effects. Or it may be that, given the laws about the deductibility of corporate charitable contributions, the stockholders can contribute more to charities they favor by having the corporation make the gift than by doing it themselves, since they can in that way contribute an amount that would otherwise have been paid as corporate taxes.

In each of these—and many similar—cases, there is a strong temptation to rationalize these actions as an exercise of "social responsibility." In the present climate of opinion, with its widespread aversion to "capitalism," "profits," the "soulless corporation" and so on, this is one way for a corporation to generate goodwill as a by-product of expenditures that are entirely justified in its own self-interest.

It would be inconsistent of me to call on corporate executives to refrain from this hypocritical window-dressing because it harms the foundations of a free society. That would be to call on them to exercise a "social responsibility"! If our institutions, and the attitudes of the public, make it in their self-interest to cloak their actions in this way, I cannot summon much indignation to denounce them. At the same time, I can express admiration for those individual proprietors or owners of closely held corporations or stockholders of more broadly held corporations who disdain such tactics as approaching fraud.

Whether blameworthy or not, the use of the cloak of social responsibility, and the nonsense spoken in its name by influential and prestigious businessmen, does clearly harm the foundations of a free society. I have been impressed time and again by the schizophrenic character of many businessmen. They are capable of being extremely far-sighted and clear-headed in matters that are internal to their businesses. They are incredibly short-sighted and muddle-headed in matters that are outside their businesses but affect the possible survival of business in general. This short-sightedness is strikingly exemplified in the calls from many businessmen for wage and price guidelines or controls or incomes policies. There is nothing that could do more in a brief period to destroy a market system and replace it by a centrally controlled system than effective governmental control of prices and wages.

The short-sightedness is also exemplified in speeches by businessmen on social responsibility. This may gain them kudos in the short run. But it helps to strengthen the already too prevalent view that the pursuit of profits is wicked and immoral and must be curbed and controlled by external forces. Once this view is adopted, the external forces that curb the market will not be the social consciences, however highly developed, of the pontificating executives; it will be the iron fist of government bureaucrats. Here, as with price and wage controls, businessmen seem to me to reveal a suicidal impulse.

The political principle that underlies the market mechanism is unanimity. In an ideal free market resting on private property, no individual can coerce any other, all cooperation is voluntary, all parties to such cooperation benefit or they need not participate. There are no "social" values, no "social" responsibilities in any sense other than the shared values and responsibilities of individuals. Society is a collection of individuals and of the various groups they voluntarily form.

The political principle that underlies the political mechanism is conformity. The individual must serve a more general social interest—whether that be determined by a church or a dictator or a majority. The individual may have a vote and a say in what is to be done, but if he is overruled, he must conform. It is appropriate for some to require others to contribute to a general social purpose whether they wish to or not. Unfortunately, unanimity is not always feasible. There are some respects in which conformity appears unavoidable, so I do not see how one can avoid the use of the political mechanism altogether.

But the doctrine of "social responsibility" taken seriously would extend the scope of the political mechanism to every human activity. It does not differ in philosophy from the most explicitly collectivist doctrine. It differs only by professing to believe that collectivist ends can be attained without collectivist means. That is why, in my book *Capitalism and Freedom,* I have called it a "fundamentally subversive doctrine" in a free society, and have said that in such a society, "there is one and only one social responsibility of business—to use its resources and engage in activities designed to increase its profits so long as it stays within the rules of the game, which is to say, engages in open and free competition without deception or fraud."

Discussion Questions

1. How does Dr. Friedman characterize discussions on the "social responsibilities of business"? Why?

2. What is the role of a corporate executive selected by stockholders?

3. What analogy does Dr. Friedman draw between trade union wages and corporations' decisions based on social responsibilities?

Compare & Contrast

Would Dr. Friedman ever support voluntary actions on the part of a corporation (e.g., conduct not prohibited specifically or mandated by law)? For example, Dr. Friedman has made use of the Gary, Indiana, example. At one point, Gary experienced intense air pollution from the operation of steel mills there. The emissions from the mills were legal at that time. Dr. Friedman has noted that if an executive could show that reducing emissions voluntarily would save the company money on health costs and enhance its ability to recruit employees and managers, then such voluntary and socially responsible actions would be consistent with the corporation's role in society. How does his position in this situation compare and contrast with his position on corporate philanthropy? Can he make the same argument for donations in a community?

Reading 3.2

A Stakeholder Theory of the Modern Corporation[2]

R. Edward Freeman

Corporations have ceased to be merely legal devices through which the private business transactions of individuals may be carried on. Though still much used for this purpose, the corporate form has acquired a larger significance. The corporation has, in fact, become both a method of property tenure and a means of organizing economic life. Grown to tremendous proportions, there may be said to have evolved a "corporate system"—which has attracted to itself a combination of attributes and powers, and has attained a degree of prominence entitling it to be dealt with as a major social institution.[3]

Despite these prophetic words of Berle and Means (1932), scholars and managers alike continue to hold sacred the view that managers bear a special relationship to the stockholders in the firm. Since stockholders own shares in the firm, they have certain rights and privileges, which must be granted to them by management, as well as by others. Sanctions, in the form of "the law of corporations" and other protective mechanisms in the form of social custom, accepted management practice, myth, and ritual, are thought to reinforce the assumption of the primacy of the stockholder.

The purpose of this paper is to pose several challenges to this assumption, from within the framework of managerial capitalism, and to suggest the bare bones of an alternative theory, *a stakeholder theory of the modern corporation.* I do not seek the demise of the modern corporation, either intellectually or in fact. Rather, I seek its transformation. In the words of Neurath, we shall attempt to "rebuild the ship, plank by plank, while it remains afloat."[4]

My thesis is that I can revitalize the concept of managerial capitalism by replacing the notion that managers have a duty to stockholders with the notion that managers bear a fiduciary duty to stakeholders. Stakeholders are those groups who have a stake or claim in the firm. Specifically I include suppliers, customers, employees, stockholders, and the local community, as well as management in its role as an agent for these groups. I argue that the legal, economic, political, and moral challenges to the currently received theory

---

[2]From William R. Evan and R. Edward Freeman, "A Stakeholder Theory of the Modern Corporation: Kantian Capitalism," and R. Edward Freeman, "The Politics of Stakeholder Theory," *Business Ethics Quarterly* 4 (1994): Commerce Clearing House, 409-21.

[3]A. Berle and G. Means, *The Modern Corporation and Private Property* (New York: 1932), 1.

[4]The metaphor of rebuilding the ship while afloat is attributed to Neurath by W. Quine, *Word and Object* (Cambridge, Mass.: Harvard University Press, 1960). The point is that to keep the ship afloat during repairs, we must replace a plank with one that will do a better job. Our argument is that stakeholder capitalism can so replace the current version of managerial capitalism.

of the firm, as a nexus of contracts among the owners of the factors of production and customers, require us to revise this concept. That is, each of these stakeholder groups has a right not to be treated as a means to some end, and therefore must participate in determining the future direction of the firm in which they have a stake.

The crux of my argument is that we must reconceptualize the firm around the following question: For whose benefit and at whose expense should the firm be managed? I shall set forth such a reconceptualization in the form of a *stakeholder theory of the firm*. I shall then critically examine the stakeholder view and its implications for the future of the capitalistic system.

The Attack on Managerial Capitalism

The Legal Argument

The basic idea of managerial capitalism is that in return for controlling the firm, management vigorously pursues the interests of the stockholders. Central to the managerial view of the firm is the idea that management can pursue market transactions with suppliers and customers in an unconstrained manner.

The law of corporations gives a less clear-cut answer to the question: In whose interest and for whose benefit should the modern corporation be governed? While it says that the corporations should be run primarily in the interests of the stockholders in the firm, it further says that the corporation exists "in contemplation of the law" and has personality as a "legal person," limited liability for its actions, and immortality, since its existence transcends that of its members. Therefore, directors and other officers of the firm have a fiduciary obligation to stockholders in the sense that the "affairs of the corporation" must be conducted in the interest of the stockholders. And stockholders can theoretically bring suit against those directors and managers for doing otherwise. But since the corporation is a legal person, existing in contemplation of the law, managers of the corporation are constrained by law.

Until recently, there was no constraint at all. In this century, however, the law has evolved to effectively constrain the pursuit of stockholder interests at the expense of other claimants of the firm. It has, in effect, required that the claims of customers, suppliers, local communities, and employees be taken into consideration, though in general they are subordinated to the claims of the stockholders.

For instance, the doctrine of "privity of contract," as articulated in *Winterbottom v. Wright* in 1842, has been eroded by recent development in product liability law.. . . Caveat emptor has been replaced, in large part, with *caveat venditor* (let the seller beware).

The same argument is applicable to management's dealings with employees. The National Labor Relations Act gave employees the right to unionize and bargain in good faith. It set up the National Labor Relations Board to enforce these rights with management. The Equal Pay Act of 1963 and Title VII of the Civil Rights Act of 1964 constrain management from discrimination in hiring practices; these have been followed with the Age Discrimination in Employment Act of 1967.

The law has also protected the interests of local communities. The Clean Air Act and Clean Water Act have constrained management from "spoiling the commons."

I have argued that the result of such changes in the legal system can be viewed as giving some rights to those groups that have a claim on the firm, for example, customers, suppliers, employees, local communities, stockholders, and management. It raises the question, at the core of the theory of the firm: In whose interest and for whose benefit should the firm be managed? The answer proposed by managerial capitalism is clearly "the stockholders," but I have argued that the law has been progressively circumscribing the answer.

The Economic Argument

In its pure ideological form managerial capitalism seeks to maximize the interests of stockholders. In its perennial criticism of government regulation, management espouses the "invisible hand" doctrine. It contends that it creates the greatest good for the greatest number, and therefore government need not intervene. However, we know that externalities, moral hazards, and monopoly power exist in fact, whether or not they exist in theory. Further, some of the legal apparatus mentioned above has evolved to deal with just these issues.

The problem of the "tragedy of the commons" or the free-rider problem pervades the concept of public goods such as water and air. No one has incentive to incur the cost of clean-up or the cost of nonpollution since the marginal gain of one firm's action is small. Every firm reasons this way, and the result is pollution of water and air. Since the industrial revolution, firms have sought to internalize the benefits and externalize the costs of their actions. The cost must be borne by all, through taxation and regulation; hence we have the emergence of the environmental regulations of the 1970s.

Similarly, moral hazards arise when the purchaser of a good or service can pass along the cost of that good. There is not incentive to economize, on the part of either the producer or the consumer, and there is excessive use of the resources involved. The institutionalized practice of third-party payment in health care is a prime example.

Finally, we see the avoidance of competitive behavior on the part of firms, each seeking to monopolize a small portion of the market and not compete with one another. In a number of industries, oligopolies have merged, and while there is questionable evidence that oligopolies are not the most efficient corporate form in some industries, suffice it to say that the potential for abuse of market power has again led to regulation of managerial activity. In the classic case, AT&T, arguably one of the great technological and managerial achievements of the century, was broken up into eight separate companies to prevent its abuse of monopoly power.

Externalities, moral hazards, and monopoly power have led to more external control on managerial capitalism. There are de facto constraints, due to these economic facts of life, on the ability of management to act in the interests of the stockholders.

A Stakeholder Theory of the Firm

The Stakeholder Concept

Corporations have stakeholders, that is, groups and individuals who benefit from or are harmed by, and whose rights are violated or respected by, corporate actions. The concept of stakeholders is a generalization of the notion of stockholders, who themselves have some special claim on the firm. Just as stockholders have a right to demand certain actions by management, so do other stakeholders have a right to make claims. The exact nature of these claims is a difficult question that I shall address, but the logic is identical to that of the stockholder theory. Stakes require action of a certain sort, and conflicting stakes require methods of resolution.

Freeman and Reed (1983)[5] distinguish two senses of *stakeholder*. The "narrow definition" includes those groups who are vital to the survival and success of the corporation. The "wide definition" includes any group or individual who can affect or is affected by the corporation. I shall begin with a modest aim: to articulate a stakeholder theory using the narrow definition.

---

[5]E. Freeman and D. Reed, "Stockholders and Stakeholders: A New Perspective on Corporate Governance," in *Corporate Governance: A Definitive Exploration of the Issues*, ed. C. Huizinga, (University of California, Los Angeles, Extension Press, 1983).

Stakeholders of the Modern Corporation

Figure 3.1 depicts the stakeholders in a typical corporation. The stakes of each are reciprocal, since each can affect the other in terms of harms and benefits as well as rights and duties. The stakes of each are not univocal and would vary by particular corporation. I merely set forth some general notions that seem to be common to many large firms.

Owners have financial stake[s] in the corporations in the form of stocks, bonds, and so on, and they expect some kind of financial return from them. Either they have given money directly to the firm, or they have some historical claim made through a series of morally justified exchanges. The firm affects their livelihood or, if a substantial portion of their retirement income is in stocks or bonds, their ability to care for themselves when they can no longer work. Of course, the stakes of owners will differ by type of owner, preferences for money, moral preferences, and so on, as well as by type of firm. The owners of AT&T are quite different from the owners of Ford Motor Company, with stock of the former company being widely dispersed among 3 million stockholders and that of the latter being held by a small family group as well as by a large group of public stockholders.

Employees have their jobs and usually their livelihood at stake; they often have specialized skills for which there is usually no perfectly elastic market. In return for their labor, they expect security, wages, benefits, and meaningful work. In return for their loyalty, the corporation is expected to provide for them and carry them through difficult times. Employees are expected to follow the instructions of management most of the time, to speak favorably about the company, and to be responsible citizens in the local Communities in which the company operates. Where they are used as a means to an end, they must participate in decisions affecting such use. The evidence that such policies and values as described here lead to productive company–employee relationships is compelling. It is equally compelling to realize that the opportunities for "bad faith" on the part of both management and employees are tremendous. "Mock participation" in quality circles, singing the company song, and wearing the company uniform solely to please management all lead to distrust and unproductive work.

Suppliers, interpreted in a stakeholder sense, are vital to the success of the firm, for raw materials will determine the final product's quality and price. In turn the firm is a customer of the supplier and is therefore vital to the success and survival of the supplier. When the firm treats the supplier as a valued member of the stakeholder network, rather than as simply a source of materials, the supplier will respond when the firm is in need. Chrysler traditionally had very close ties to its suppliers, even to the extent that led some to suspect the transfer of illegal payments. And when Chrysler was on the brink of disaster, the suppliers responded with price cuts, accepting late payments, financing, and so on. Supplier and company can rise and fall together. Of course, again, the particular supplier relationships will depend on a number of variables such as the number of suppliers and whether the supplies are finished goods or raw materials.

Stakeholders in a Typical Corporation

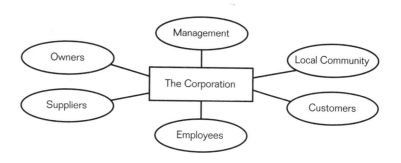

Customers exchange resources for the products of the firm and in return receive the benefits of the products. Customers provide the lifeblood of the firm in the form of revenue. Given the level of reinvestment of earnings in large corporations, customers indirectly pay for the development of new products and services. Peters and Waterman (1982)[6] have argued that being close to the customer leads to success with other stakeholders and that a distinguishing characteristic of some companies that have performed well is their emphasis on the customer. By paying attention to customers' needs, management automatically addresses the needs of suppliers and owners. Moreover, it seems that the ethics of customer service carries over to the community. Almost without fail the "excellent companies" in Peters and Waterman's study have good reputations in the community. I would argue that Peters and Waterman have found multiple applications of Kant's dictum, "Treat persons as ends unto themselves," and it should come as no surprise that persons respond to such respectful treatment, be they customers, suppliers, owners, employees, or members of the local community. The real surprise is the novelty of the application of Kant's rule in a theory of good management practice.

The local community grants the firm the right to build facilities and, in turn, benefits from the tax base and economic and social contribution of the firm. In return for the provision of local services, the firm is expected to be a good citizen, as is any person, either "natural or artificial." The firm cannot expose the community to unreasonable hazards in the form of pollution, toxic waste, and so on. If for some reason the firm must leave a community, it is expected to work with local leaders to make the transition as smoothly as possible. Of course, the firm does not have perfect knowledge, but when it discovers some danger or runs afoul of new competition, it is expected to inform the local community and to work with the community to overcome any problem. When the firm mismanages its relationship with the local community, it is in the same position as a citizen who commits a crime. It has violated the implicit social contract with the community and should expect to be distrusted and ostracized. It should not be surprised when punitive measures are invoked.

I have not included "competitors" as stakeholders in the narrow sense, since strictly speaking they are not necessary for the survival and success of the firm; the stakeholder theory works equally well in monopoly contexts. However, competitors and government would be the first to be included in an extension of this basic theory. It is simply not true that the interests of competitors in an industry are always in conflict. There is no reason why trade associations and other multi-organizational groups cannot band together to solve common problems that have little to do with how to restrain trade. Implementation of stakeholder management principles, in the long run, mitigates the need for industrial policy and an increasing role for government intervention and regulation.

The Role of Management

Management plays a special role, for it too has a stake in the modern corporation. On the one hand, management's stake is like that of employees, with some kind of explicit or implicit employment contract. But, on the other hand, management has a duty of safeguarding the welfare of the abstract entity that is the corporation. In short, management, especially top management, must look after the health of the corporation, and this involves balancing the multiple claims of conflicting stakeholders. Owners want higher financial returns, while customers want more money spent on research and development. Employees want higher wages and better benefits, while the local community wants better parks and day-care facilities.

The task of management in today's corporation is akin to that of King Solomon. The stakeholder theory does not give primacy to one stakeholder group over another, though

---

[6]T. Peters and R. Waterman, *In Search of Excellence* (New York: Harper and Row, 1982).

surely there will be times when one group will benefit at the expense of others. In general, however, management must keep the relationships among stakeholders in balance. When these relationships become imbalanced, the survival of the firm is in jeopardy.

When wages are too high and product quality is too low, customers leave, suppliers suffer, and owners sell their stocks and bonds, depressing the stock price and making it difficult to raise new capital at favorable rates. Note, however, that the reason for paying returns to owners is not that they "own" the firm, but that their support is necessary for the survival of the firm, and that they have a legitimate claim on the firm. Similar reasoning applies in turn to each stakeholder group.

A stakeholder theory of the firm must redefine the purpose of the firm. The stockholder theory claims that the purpose of the firm is to maximize the welfare of the stockholders, perhaps subject to some moral or social constraints, either because such maximization leads to the greatest good or because of property rights. The purpose of the firm is quite different in my view.

Discussion Questions

1. What problems does Freeman see with having government regulation control the operation of corporations?
2. List the stakeholders of a corporation. Are government and competitors included? Why or why not?
3. Explain the references to Kant and King Solomon.
4. The City of Phoenix, because of its rapid growth, has reached a point where its airport is not large enough to accommodate all incoming and outgoing air traffic. Managers for the city indicate the airport needs two new runways as well as additional flight paths over the city in order to meet the growing demands of commercial airlines for use of Phoenix as an international hub. List all who will be affected by and/or benefit from the expansion of the airport.
5. Suppose that there are objections to the airport expansion. List categories of those you believe might object. Are they stakeholders of commercial airlines? Should they have a say in whether the airlines expand service to Phoenix? Should they have a say in whether the airlines pay for the expansion of the Phoenix Airport?

Compare & Contrast

What problems does Freeman see with having the free market control the operation of corporations? How would Dr. Friedman answer Dr. Freeman's point that there are great costs and only marginal benefits associated with voluntary or socially responsible actions by companies? Explain how stakeholder priorities would be established. For example, the construction of a mosque at Ground Zero would bring the economic benefits of revitalizing the area as the property is rebuilt as well as the construction jobs. However, the families of the 9-11-01 World Trade Center attacks object to its construction on sensitivity grounds. Others support First Amendment rights for the mosque builders. Who gets priority as a stakeholder?

Reading 3.3

Business with a Soul: A Reexamination of What Counts in Business Ethics[7]

Jon Entine Marianne M. Jennings

"Rain-forest chic" is a label coined in the popular business press for the increasingly popular corporate branding strategy of capitalizing on consumer use of environmental issues as a screen for buying decisions. Companies have parleyed this market strategy

---

[7]From Jon Entine and Marianne M. Jennings, "Business with a Soul: A Reexamination of What Counts in Business Ethics," *Hamline Journal of Law & Public Policy* 20:1 (1998).

into product successes. Shampoo bottles, powder blush and toothpaste carry labels that read "no animal testing." Star-Kist markets that its tuna is netted "Dolphin-Free." Rainforest chic marketing provides a compelling two-for-one sale: buy hair conditioner or ice cream made with nuts from the rainforest and get social justice for free.

Corporate social responsibility has caught the attention of academic researchers. The icons of corporate social responsibility (CSR) are familiar brand names: The Body Shop International cosmetics; Ben & Jerry's Homemade ice cream; Starbucks coffee, Tom's of Maine toothpaste, Working Assets long distance company, Celestial Seasonings teas, and a collection of clothing and sneaker retailers including Esprit, Patagonia and, until the sweatshop controversy is over, Nike. These companies, all of which have engaged in marketing campaigns to promote their social consciousness, represent a coterie of '60s entrepreneurial companies with charismatic founders who have grown niche businesses into multi-national corporations. Their companies and products are associated with the labels "green" and "socially responsible."

These socially responsible companies promote themselves in contrast to companies who are caricatured as corporate desperados such as: Gillette, Dow Chemical, Exxon, every tobacco company, defense contractors, the entire chemical industry and all energy providers (unless perhaps they are a solar company or a wind-power start-up).

Such a simplistic equation of social responsibility obscures the reality that business ethicists have failed to examine closely either what constitutes business ethics or whether these particular firms would qualify as ethical by standards other than those measured by political issues or self-defined parameters. Business and business ethics are much more complex than the breeziness of social responsibility. Understanding the corporate soul requires far more than the shallow categories of the CSR. The soul of a company is more complex than that of an individual.

The consequences of using these trendy standards as a basis for philosophical applications or as a measure for firms' ethics are substantial for the credibility of the academy. Relevant business data [are] ignored; close examination of operations and products is foreclosed in the name of social consciousness. Larger firms whose forward strides have had a greater social, economic or environmental impact are ignored or demonized in the name of this new brand ethics. Companies with a culture of ethics but without tendencies toward self-aggrandizement are sometimes trampled in the marketplace and denigrated in the CSR movement.

*****

Despite Friedman's adherence to the agency theory, he does, however, outline scenarios in which he believes that social involvement is not only acceptable but also required. Friedman isolates instances when managers should step beyond the constraints of their agency relationship and what the law requires if they can demonstrate that involvement in social issues benefits shareholders. He cites "green marketing" as an example. Friedman once described oil company television ads as "turning his stomach" for they made it seem that the purpose of energy companies was to preserve the environment. However, Friedman adds that he would probably sue oil company executives if they didn't engage in such "nonsense" because oil companies must profess social responsibility to appeal to the public-at-large, remain competitive and ensure profits.

Extending the same reasoning, Friedman supports "green practices" as well as green marketing in limited situations. Ordinarily, Friedman's notion of social responsibility provides that if it is cheaper to pay a fine for releasing effluent into the water surrounding a plant than it is not to pollute or to clean it up, then releasing the effluent is the most responsible action. Friedman advocates the use of taxes or government regulation to control behavior (positive law). However, if an executive can demonstrate that the controversy surrounding the release of the effluents (a) makes it difficult to recruit and retain employees; or (b) offers the prospect of adverse publicity or litigation that diminishes its ability to compete, then voluntary reduction of the effluent, or voluntary clean-up is an appropriate extension of agency authority. If an energy company could mitigate these adverse consequences by modifying environmental practices, then it is compelled to act in its shareholders' best interest by doing so.

Conservative theorist Michael Novak acknowledges that investors have a right to a "reasonable return" but adds new corporate responsibilities, such as to "create new wealth" and "new jobs," guarantee "upward mobility" fairly reward "hard work and talent," promote "progress in the arts and useful sciences" and "diversify the interests of the public." He then adds seven "external responsibilities" including promoting "community" and "dignity," and "protecting the moral ecology of freedom," all of which he believes are crucial to the health of civil society. Novak views business as a moral calling as opposed to being merely a profession.

The notions built into the continuum about business ethics present a Hobbesian choice between a faddish concept of social responsibility such as an opposition to animal testing and classic stakeholder concepts such as responsiveness to investors, customers and employees. For instance, helping the homeless is a noble cause, and certainly one that would place a company at the top of the social responsibility continuum. Few would suggest that a small grocery store with thin profit margins should be judged by whether it feeds the homeless in the town in which it operates. The owners and employees of that store depend upon profit for their livelihood, its customers depend on the store being open, and the community prospers if the store becomes more profitable and expands. By devoting its resources to feeding the homeless, such a grocery store would possibly exacerbate the homeless problem as its employees are no longer employed because the business would become extinct.

[Misinformation clouds the social responsibility measures.]. . . For years after its introduction in 1990, "Rainforest Crunch" ice cream, the flagship product of Ben & Jerry's, was touted as a successful experiment in the partnering of American business with Amazon preservationists. According to company materials, "Rainforest Crunch" was created in part to help indigenous peoples find an alternative to selling their timber rights to mining and forestry industrialists. [It was a noble impulse but turned out to be little more than a brilliant marketing gimmick. For years, Ben & Jerry's purchased no nuts for its ice cream from rainforest aboriginals; more than 95% of the Brazil nuts it sourced were purchased off commercial exchanges supplied by businesses, not indigenous peoples, in Latin America that now dominate the Brazil nut market].

Moreover, many anthropologists maintain that the harvest has actually contributed to falling nut prices and an increase in the selling off of land rights to industrialists to compensate for the economic short-fall. The Ben & Jerry's program actually exacerbated the very problem it was purported to address. In early 1995, Ben & Jerry's pulled the claims on its Rainforest Crunch label. Although the disastrous details of the harvest are widely known in the activist media and SR business community, Ben & Jerry's has been given a relative pass on the disastrous consequences.

Body Shop International ("BSI") has long been touted as the premier socially responsible business. By its own estimates, BSI was averaging 10,000 positive media mentions a year until 1994. In September of 1994, investigative work by Jon Entine, co-author of this article, and numerous journalists and social researchers, revealed a huge ethical gap between BSI's marketing image and its actual practices. This deception—conscious or not—is pervasive: Roddick stole The Body Shop name and marketing concept, fabricated key elements of the company myth, misrepresented its charitable contributions and fair trade programs and has been beset by employee morale and franchise problems. Moreover, its "natural" products are filled with petrochemical colorings, fragrances, preservatives and base ingredients such as mineral oil and petrolatum. Its cosmetics are considered "low-end products at a premium price" according to a recent article in *Women's Wear Daily* and numerous reviews by cosmetic product experts.

*****

Can a shareholder or customer trust a firm simply because it has adopted a posture of social responsibility? Can a shareholder or customer assume that a firm is less honorable if it states that it is accountable first and foremost to its shareholders? The answer to both questions is "no."

No company is ethically perfect. No company, just as no individual, is without sin or exempt from mistakes. Consequently, the obsession to anoint icons of CSR only interferes with candid evaluations of the soul of a company.

Determining the soul of a company requires those conducting the examination to look beyond ever-changing political issues. CSR has come to promote narrow and contradictory social agendas as opposed to universal measures of integrity. For example, honesty in business dealings is a universal measure of a company's soul. Looking beyond facile symbolism opens up an examination of ethics. There are eight questions that should be answered about a company to determine the character of its soul.

1. Does the company comply with the law?
2. Does the company have a sense of propriety?
3. How honestly do product claims match with reality?
4. How forthcoming is the company with information?
5. How does the company treat its employees?
6. How does the company handle third-party ethics issues?
7. How charitable is the company?
8. How does the company react when faced with negative disclosures?

With this modest proposal is the basis for an objective look at companies.

Discussion Questions

1. Contrast the authors' views with those of Friedman and Freeman.
2. What is the difference between the authors' eight questions and traditional measures of social responsibility?
3. Would the model mean that a tobacco company could be labeled an "honest" company?

Reading 3.4

Appeasing Stakeholders with Public Relations[8]

This reading provides a different perspective on the stakeholder versus shareholder debate. The author questions its wisdom and precision.

Robert Halfon

The problem in today's era of corporate pseudo-ethics is that the pendulum has shifted too far. From genuine philanthropy "corporate responsibility" has mutated into a dangerous form of political correctness. The enlightened, entrepreneurial philanthropy of old has, through activist agitation, become the burden of today's so-called "corporate responsibility." At least four distinct trends are in evidence here: the rise of single-issue activist groups; the targeting of companies with dealings in specific countries or specific

---

[8]From Robert Halfon, *Corporate Irresponsibility: Is Business Appeasing Anti-business Activists?* (London: The Social Affair Unit, 1998), 7.

industries; a rise in public sympathy for such actions; and a seal of approval guaranteed by many Western governments today.

Corporations have an obligation to anticipate and deal with these threats. This can be done in a number of ways. First, every important commercial activity should be rigorously assessed for its political risk. This means the risks or threats a business may face (from pressure groups, governments, *et al.*) in undertaking a particular activity. Business needs to inform itself at the highest level of the political environment in which it operates. As one commentator on these matters argues without hesitation:

> *The lessons that need to be understood are simple. It does not matter where you are, or how big you are, if you are not prepared, pressure groups have the ability to make your company a member of the endangered species. You cannot respond effectively in six minutes to a campaign that has probably taken six months to organize. . . . Our first option is to ignore the increasing threat of pressure groups and lose everything. Our second option is to fight back, challenge and probably win. We have the opportunity to deliver results by promoting morality; challenging credibility; setting policy and practices; offering solutions and advice.*[9]

Once the political risks are evaluated, then two actions are required: first, for businesses to mount an efficient public relations campaign, arguing the case for corporate capitalism and stressing how their activities are benefiting the national—or global— economy in which they operate. All businesses, forewarned, should be proactive, not reactive. They must be prepared to fight fire with fire and, if necessary, should be prepared to take their case all the way to the courts. Secondly, companies across the spectrum must band together and act in unison to limit the unaccountable, undemocratic and often extra-legal activities of the activist groups they are up against.

Discussion Questions

1. What does Halfon see as the proper tools for handling stakeholder objections?
2. Can you describe a situation in which his tool may not be effective? What are the costs to the company if his tools fail to halt the opposition of stakeholders to a proposed corporate action?

Reading 3.5
Michael Novak on Capitalism and the Corporation[10]

Michael Novak

Business corporations—either independent of the state or commissioned by the state (the latter at first more common)—were designed to continue beyond the life of the founding generation, began to provide goods and services on a scale theretofore unseen, and needed vast amounts of human and financial capital. These voluntary associations had to prove themselves, often against quite entrenched opposition from the social classes they threatened (the landed aristocracy for example). And yet, as Karl Marx noted, they transformed the world. They were indispensable to making it free and prosperous. Yet from the beginning, long before Marx appeared on the scene, business corporations had enemies.

For centuries, men of commerce had been ill thought of by farmers and fishermen, landowners, aristocrats, churchmen, poets, and philosophers—seen as pursuers of mammon,

---

[9]Tony Meehan, "The Art of Media Manipulation," *The Herald*, May 10, 1997.

[10]From "Michael Novak on Capitalism and the Corporation" from *The Fire of Invention: Civil Society and the Future of the Corporation* (1997), p. 32.

middlemen who bought cheap and sold dear, sophisticates and cheats, hucksters, admirers not of the noble but the merely useful, men with souls of slaves, cosmopolitans without loyalties. The counts against them are as old as portions of the Bible, Plato and Aristotle, Horace and Cicero. Aristocrats most businessmen certainly were not. It is a curious but also crucial fact that men of business have been morally assaulted for, many generations now, both by the aristocratic and the humanistic Right and by the modern Socialist, social democratic, and merely progovernmental Left. Elites on both sides denounce them, chiefly on moral (but also on aesthetic) grounds. When critics reluctantly discover that most of what businessmen do is legal and moral, and even useful, they retreat to thinking it unlovely. Anticapitalism is a far, far darker dye than socialism, and harder to remove.

While it is true that business leaders have few pretensions of being aristocrats or literary intellectuals or social reformers—not, at least, through their work in business—it is important to say that business is a morally serious calling. Through business you can do great good or great evil, and all the variations on the scale. But if you do good, you have the advantage that it is the design of business as a practice and as an institution that you do so; whereas if you do evil, it is because you have twisted a good thing to your own evil purposes and have no one to blame but yourself. The market may make or break you, favor your new product or leave it on the shelf—the market does not smile on everyone alike—but in moral matters one is never in a position to say, "The market made me do it." You did it. You are the agent in the market; the market is no agent.

In the early Middle Ages, in sum, the corporation began as burial societies, then monasteries and towns and universities. Implicitly rooted in rights of association, the corporation was "an instrument of privilege and a kind of exclusive body, tightly controlled by the state for reasons of its own." But, as Oscar Handlin points out, in the infant United States there was great resistance to dependence on royal charters from far across the ocean and a great desire among citizens to form corporations on their own to meet innumerable needs. The citizens of Massachusetts, for example, as early as 1636 made up a charter of incorporation for Harvard University, much to the shock of violated royal prerogative on the other side of the Atlantic. Thus, by 1750, while England still had but two universities, the American colonies had six. By 1880, there were more universities in the state of Ohio than in all of Europe combined. Similarly, the railroad had been invented in England, but ten years later there were more miles of railroad in the United States than in all of Britain—and all of Europe—combined. When American lawyers did not even know how to write up proper incorporation papers, they nonetheless did so, and business corporations multiplied up and down the Eastern seaboard.

Thus, in the United States, the business corporation came into its independent own. Here were born the very first manufacturing corporations in the world. Here corporations ceased being based on state privilege, monopoly, trust, or grant and became inventions of civil society and independent citizens. The state retained a right to *approve of* applications and to register them, for good legal order, but it did not create a right or convey its own power to the corporation or guarantee the latter's survival. The corporation, to survive, could no longer depend on its privileges; it could survive only if it met the needs of its customers and the purposes of its investors. It brought civil society not only independence from the state but also unparalleled social flexibility and a zest for risk and dare.

From the point of view of civil society, the business enterprise is an important social good for four reasons. First, it creates jobs. Second, it provides desirable goods and services. Third, through its profits it creates wealth that did not exist before. And fourth, it is a private social instrument, independent of the state, for the moral and material support of other activities of society.

Moreover, sources of private capital and private wealth, independent of the state, are crucial to the survival of liberty. The alternative is dependence on government, the opposite of liberty. The chief funder of the many works of civil society, from hospitals and research institutions to museums, the opera, orchestras, and universities is the business corporation. The corporation today is even a major funder of public television. Absent the financial resources of major corporations, civil society would be a poor thing indeed.

Finally, it should be observed that the ownership of publicly owned companies extends through more than half the American adult population. The largest holders of stocks and bonds are the pension plans of workers, in the public sector as well as the private sector.

The word stakeholder has two senses. The term derives from the time of the Homestead Act, when Americans heading West could take out a claim on a parcel of land and be guaranteed the ownership thereof by the protection of the state. The federal government sponsored this act for two reasons: first, to make sure that the West developed as free states, not slave states, and second, to reap the benefits of a regime of private ownership and private practical intelligence. At that time, Americans believed (in lessons derived from the experience of ancient Rome and Greece as well as from medieval Europe and Britain) that the common good is better served by a regime of private property than by common ownership or state ownership. They further believed that more intelligence springs from a multitude of practical owners of their own property than from a prestigious body of planners, however, brilliant.

In this context, *stakeholder* means *owner* and private *risk taker*. The purpose of an arrangement of society into many private stakeholders is to secure the *general* welfare and the larger *public* interest. The stakeholder society in this sense is the very foundation of the free society. Maintaining it entails investment, hard work, responsibility, risk, and earned reward or, often enough, personal failure. Freedom is tied to risk and responsibility.

The social democratic sense of the term *stakeholder* is quite different. Stakeholders are all those who deem themselves entitled to make demands on the system and to receive from it. A Britain, for example, imagined as a "stakeholder society" is one in which each citizen is entitled to make claims on others according to his or her needs. These needs are infinitely expansive, however, so perpetual dissatisfaction is guaranteed. No conceivable amount of security or health care can satisfy human beings; our longings are infinite, beyond all earthly satisfaction. If today's ten most dangerous diseases are conquered, the next ten will rise to cause new anxiety. A stakeholder society is bound to be like the nest of open-mouthed chicks. The length between the desire to receive and personal responsibility never forms.

The social democratic dream has many of the characteristics of a religion. It is, in particular, the dream of a united national community, conferring on all a sense of belonging and participation and being cared for. In practice, of course, things work out quite differently. Its schemes of social belonging usually end up with populations far too accustomed to receiving and demanding. Those most skilled at mobilizing demands fare best. While social democracy speaks the language of community and compassion and caring, the reality is original sin, that is, socialized self-interest. Social democratic societies are not notably happy or contented societies.

The paradox of socialism is that it actually results in the opposite of its hopes: an unparalleled isolation of individuals from the bonds of personal responsibility and social cooperation. . . . Eight score years ago Tocqueville also foresaw this effect:

> I am trying to imagine under what novel features despotism may appear in the world. In the first place, I see an innumerable multitude of men, alike and equal, constantly circling around in pursuit of the petty and banal pleasures with which they glut their souls. . . . Over this kind of men stands an immense, protective power which is alone responsible for securing their enjoyment and watching over their fate. That power is absolute, thoughtful of detail, orderly, provident, and gentle. It would resemble parental authority, if, father like, it tried to

prepare its charges for a man's life, but on the contrary, it only tries to keep them in perpetual childhood. . . . It gladly works for their happiness but wants to be sole agent and judge of it. It provides for their security, foresees and supplies their necessities, facilitates their pleasures, manages their principal concerns, directs their industry, makes rules for their testaments, and divides their inheritances. Why should it not entirely relieve them from the trouble of thinking and all the cares of living?

—Alexis de Tocquevile, DEMOCRACY IN AMERICA (1966), at pp. 691–692

That is not a stakeholding society. That is serfdom.

It is time, then for public enemy number one, the business corporation, to take account of its own identity, its essential role in the future of self-governing republics, and its central position in the building of the chief alternative to government: civil society. The corporation is what it is and does what it does; but it is an invention of free people, not a cold meteor fallen from the skies. It has changed often in history and, by its very self-discipline, inventiveness, and creativity, has surmounted even greater threats than it faces today. Now, however, it will need a greater degree of philosophical and public policy self-consciousness than ever before. The corporation has some serious external enemies and some serious internal flaws—for example, in the procedures that lead to excessive compensation at the top, to excessive insecurity at all levels, to anomalies of self-governance, to turmoil about patents. The business corporation is once again in a fight for its life, and the sooner the dangers than menace it are exactly discerned the better.

Discussion Questions

1. How long has the corporation existed?
2. What is the difference between the British and European corporation and the U.S. corporation? What does Dr. Novak feel is the result of the difference?
3. What are the two definitions of *stakeholders*?
4. Describe the effects of social democracy. What is the danger of perpetual demand without responsibility?
5. What does Dr. Novak mean when he says the corporation is "not a cold meteor fallen from the sky"?

Compare & Contrast

This reading from Dr. Novak targets the stakeholder model. What historical perspective does Dr. Novak give to the term *stakeholder* that makes his notion different from Dr. Freeman's? Why does Dr. Novak use the term *serfdom*? How does this term relate to Dr. Friedman's view that stakeholder theory is socialism?

Reading 3.6
Marjorie Kelly and the Divine Right of Capital[11]

Marjorie Kelly

What do shareholders contribute, to justify the extraordinary allegiance they receive? They take risk, we're told. They put their money on the line, so corporations might grow and prosper. Let's test the truth of this with a little quiz:
Stockholders fund major public corporations—true or false?
False. Or, actually, a tiny bit true—but for the most part, massively false. In fact, most "investment" dollars don't go to corporations but to other speculators. Equity investments

[11]From Marjorie Kelly, *The Divine Right of Capital: Dethroning the Corporate Aristocracy* (San Francisco: Berrett-Koehler, 2001).

reach a public corporation only when new common stock is sold—which for major corporations is a rare event. Among the Dow Jones industrials, only a handful have sold any new common stock in thirty years. Many have sold none in fifty years.

The stock market works like a used car market, as former accounting professor Ralph Estes observes in *Tyranny of the Bottom Line*. When you buy a 1997 Ford Escort, the money goes not to Ford but to the previous owner of the car. Ford gets the buyer's money only when it sells a new car. Similarly, companies get stockholders' money only when they sell new common stock.

So, what do stockholders contribute to justify the extraordinary allegiance they receive? Very little. Yet this tiny contribution allows them essentially to install a pipeline and dictate that the corporation's sole purpose is to funnel wealth into it.

It's odd. And it's connected to a second oddity—that we believe stockholders *are* the corporation. When we say that a corporation did well, we mean that its shareholders did well. The company's local community might be devastated by plant closings. Employees might be shouldering a crushing workload. Still we will say, "The corporation did well."

One does not see rising employee incomes as a measure of corporate success. Indeed, gains to employees are losses to the corporation. And this betrays an unconscious bias: that employees are not really part of the corporation. They have no claim on the wealth they create, no say in governance, and no vote for the board of directors. They're not citizens of corporate society, but subjects.

We think of this as the natural law of the market. It's more accurately the result of the corporate governance structure, which violates market principles. In real markets, everyone scrambles to get what they can, and they keep what they earn. In the construct of the corporation, one group gets what another earns.

The oddity of it all is veiled by the incantation of a single magical word: *ownership*. Because we say stockholders own corporations, they are permitted to contribute very little, and take quite a lot.

What an extraordinary word. One is tempted to recall the comment that Lycophron, an ancient Greek philosopher, made during an early Athenian slave uprising against the aristocracy. "The splendor of noble birth is imaginary and its [prerogatives] are based upon mere word."

The problem is not the free market, but the design of the corporation. It's important to separate these two concepts we have been schooled to equate. In truth, the market is a relatively innocent notion. It's about buyers and sellers bargaining on equal footing to set prices. It might be said that a free market means an unregulated one, but in today's scheme it means a market with one primary form of regulation: that of property rights.

Shareholder primacy is a form of entitlement. And entitlement has no place in a market economy. It is a form of privilege. And privilege accruing to property ownership is a remnant of the aristocratic past. That more people own stock today has not changed the market's essential aristocratic bias. Of the total gain in marketable wealth from 1983 to 1998, more than half went to the richest 1 percent. Others of us may have gotten a few crumbs from this feast, but in their pursuit we have too often been led to work against our own interests. Physicians applaud when their portfolios rise in value, yet wonder why insurance companies are ruthlessly holding down medical payments. Employees cheer when their 401(k) plans post gains, yet wonder why layoffs are decimating their firms. Their own portfolios hold the answer.

How do we begin to change such an entrenched and ancient system of discrimination? We begin by seeing it for what it is, and naming it as illegitimate. For doing so allows us to reclaim our economic sovereignty—which means remembering that corporations are creations of the law, that they exist only because we the people allow them to exist, and that we create the parameters of their existence.

In tracing the roots of this myth, [I] venture into what French philosopher Michel Foucalt would call an *archaeology of knowledge:* a foundation dig, examining the ancient conceptual structures on which aristocratic bias is built.

1. **Worldview:** In the worldview of corporate financial statements, the aim is to pay property holders as much as possible, and employees as little as possible.
2. **Privilege:** Stockholders claim wealth they do little to create, much as nobles claimed privilege they did not earn.
3. **Property:** Like a feudal estate, a corporation is considered a piece of property—not a human community—so it can be owned and sold by the propertied class.
4. **Governance:** Corporations function with an aristocratic governance structure where members of the propertied class alone may vote.
5. **Liberty:** Corporate capitalism embraces a predemocratic concept of liberty reserved for property holders, which thrives by restricting the liberty of employees and the community.
6. **Sovereignty:** Corporations assert that they are private and the free market will self-regulate, much as feudal barons asserted a sovereignty independent of the Crown.

Myths take many forms. In essence, they are stories we tell ourselves, like the story that discrimination based on property ownership is permissible, even mandatory.

Stockholder privilege rests on the notion that corporations are not human communities, but pieces of property, which means they can be owned and sold by the propertied class. This to some extent mirrors the ancient beliefs that wives belonged to their husbands, and vassals belonged to feudal lords.

In the predemocratic mindset, persons without property were not permitted to vote. And so it is with employees today, for stockholders alone govern the corporation. The public corporation is a kind of inverted monarchy, with representatives of the share-owning aristocracy hiring and firing the CEO-king. It is a structure reminiscent of England after the Glorious Revolution of 1688, in which Parliament—which represented the landed class, first asserted power over the monarch.

Articulating an ideology for economic democracy. . . draws on varied efforts to reform corporations, but its aim is also to focus those efforts more effectively, by grounding them in the larger project of democracy—the great project of the Enlightenment, the historical project of moving society from monarchy to democracy, Because economic democracy will take different forms from political democracy, this venture draws on market principles. . . . I suggest six principles for economic democracy, mirroring the six principles of economic aristocracy:

1. **Enlightenment:** Because all persons are created equal, the economic rights of employees and the community are equal to those of the capital owners.
2. **Quality:** Under market principles, wealth does not legitimately belong only to stockholders. Corporate wealth belongs to those who create it, and community wealth belongs to all.
3. **Public good:** As semipublic governments, public corporations are more than pieces of private property on private contracts. They have a responsibility to the public good.
4. **Democracy:** The corporation is a human community, and like the larger community of which it is a part, it is best governed democratically.
5. **Justice:** In keeping with equal treatment of persons before the law, wealthy persons may not claim greater rights than others, and corporations may not claim the rights of persons.
6. **(r)Evolution:** As it is the right of the people to alter or abolish government, it is the right of the people to alter or abolish the corporations that now govern the world.

. . . As Michel Foucault observed, ideas are mechanisms of power. "A stupid despot may constrain his slaves with iron chains, but a true politician binds them even more strongly by the chain of their own ideas."

Nobel Prize-winning economist Milton Friedman famously wrote that the only social responsibility of the corporation is to make a profit.

In corporate society, good is what in the interest of stockholders. That is the primary criterion of morality. It means the corporation has the right to do financial violence to its employees or the environment (conducting massive layoffs, clear-cutting forests), or to attack other corporations (brutal competition, hostile takeovers), if that increases the well-being of the ruling tribe, the stockholders.

Haitian contract workers sewing Disney garments might be paid starvation-level wages (28 cents an hour), but this isn't considered a corporate problem—unless it erupts as a public relations problem, which threatens earnings (that is, stockholders' interests). And this is so, even when paying a living wage would have a negligible effect on earnings. But no matter, Worker income must be minimized.

Shareholder primacy is the wrench in the gears of evolution. It is shareholder primacy that thwarts corporations from their natural movement toward wider economic sovereignty for all.

We should recall Kant's imperative when we as reformers find ourselves telling corporations, "Treat employees well because then stockholders will prosper." Or when we find ourselves saying, "Practice environmental stewardship, because then profits will increase."

These, unfortunately, are the arguments often made by social investing professional, and my own publication, *Business Ethics,* is as guilty as any other. But this argument in a sense is self-defeating, for it implies that stockholder gain is the only measure that matters. Ultimately, we must assert that other measures of prosperity matter too—like wage increases, or well-funded schools, or a healthy environment. Until we begin asserting this, we will not have fully claimed our power.

Corporations today are governments of the propertied class, exercising power over Americans that is greater than the power once exercised by kings. They are governments that have become destructive of our inalienable [*sic*] rights as people. We end their illegitimate reign and institute a new economic government, laying its foundation on such principles as seem most likely to effect our safety and happiness.

Discussion Questions

1. List the differences in perceptions between Novak and Kelly about corporations.
2. What distinction does Kelly make about the role of corporations?
3. How do the two authors differ on happiness?
4. Does Kelly propose a social democracy?

Compare & Contrast

How would Novak address the principles of aristocracy? Refer back to the Novak reading, Reading 3.5. How do the seven external and internal responsibilities of corporations address some of the concerns Kelly raises, for example, about the wages Disney contractors pay to Haitian workers?

Reading 3.7
Schools of Thought on Social Responsibility[12]

The following excerpt deals with the various schools of thought on social responsibility. These postures can be found across industries and can be used as a framework for analysis of dilemmas.

---

[12]From *Business: Its Legal, Ethical and Global Environment*, 9th ed., by Marianne M. Jennings, 48–50. Copyright © 2011. Reprinted with permission of South-Western, a division of Cengage Learning.

Ethical Postures, Social Responsibility, and Business Practice

The ethical perspective of a business often sets the tone for its operations and employees' choices. Historically, the philosophical debate over the role of business in society has evolved into four schools of thought on ethical behavior based on the responses to two questions: (1) Whose interest should a corporation serve? and (2) To whom should a corporation be responsive in order to best serve that interest? There are only two answers to these questions—"shareholders only" and "the larger society"—and the combination of those answers defines the school of thought.

Inherence

According to the inherence school of thought, managers answer only to shareholders and act only with shareholders' interests in mind. This type of manager would not become involved in any political or social issues unless it was in the shareholders' best interests to do so, and provided the involvement did not backfire and cost the firm sales. Milton Friedman's philosophy, as previously expressed, is an example of inherence. To illustrate how a business following the inherence school of thought would behave, consider the issue of a proposed increase in residential property taxes for school-funding purposes. A business that subscribes to the inherence school would support a school-tax increase only if the educational issue affected the company's performance and only if such a position did not offend those who opposed the tax increase.

Enlightened Self-Interest

According to this school of thought, the manager is responsible to the shareholders but serves them best by being responsive to the larger society. Enlightened self-interest is based on the view that, in the long run, business value is enhanced if business is responsive to the needs of society. In this school, managers are free to speak out on societal issues without the constraint of offending someone, as in inherence. Businesses would anticipate social changes and needs and be early advocates for change. For example, many corporations today have instituted job sharing, child-care facilities, and sick-child care in response to the changing structure of the American family and workforce. This responsiveness to the needs of the larger society should also be beneficial to shareholders, because it enables the business to retain a quality workforce.

The Invisible Hand

The invisible hand school of thought is the opposite of enlightened self-interest. According to this philosophy, business ought to serve the larger society and it does this best when it serves the shareholders only. Such businesses allow government to set the standards and boundaries for appropriate behavior and simply adhere to these governmental constraints as a way of maximizing benefits to their shareholders. They become involved in issues of social responsibility or in political issues only when society lacks sufficient information on an issue to make a decision. Even then, their involvement is limited to presenting data and does not extend to advocating a particular viewpoint or position. This school of thought holds that it is best for society to guide itself and that businesses work best when they serve shareholders within those constraints.

Social Responsibility

In the social responsibility school of thought, the role of business is to serve the larger society, and that is best accomplished by being responsive to the larger society. This view is simply a reflection of the idea that businesses profit by being responsive to society and its needs. A business following this school of thought would advocate full disclosure of product information to consumers in its advertising and would encourage political activism on the part of its managers and employees on all issues, not just those that affect the corporation. These businesses believe that their sense of social responsibility contributes to their long-term success.

Discussion Question

Does Friedman's position blend across categories?

Case 3.8

Adelphia: Good Works via a Hand in the Till

John Rigas opened his first business in 1952 in Coudersport, Pennsylvania, an old-fashioned movie theater, something he still would own at the time he would be indicted for fraud and other felonies in running Adelphia, the giant cable firm that would spring from this small beginning in media entertainment.

His foray into cable began when he and his brother bought a cable franchise for $300, also in 1952. They chose the name "Adelphia" for their new company, a name which is Greek for "brothers."[13] Early in the 1980s, John bought out his brother's interest in Adelphia and began bringing his now-grown sons into the business. By 2002, Adelphia was operating cable companies in 32 states and had 5.7 million subscribers. At its peak, Adelphia was the sixth largest cable company in the United States. Adelphia claimed that its aggressive marketing was partially responsible for its amazing growth and earnings.[14] Adelphia's annual reports also touted its "clustering strategy," something others in the cable industry did not really understand.[15] Many doubted the existence of such a strategy and questioned Adelphia's performance, but when it went public, its stock skyrocketed.

The Rigas family was respected, indeed revered, in Coudersport. John Rigas was often called "a Greek god" by the locals for his stunning looks as well as his generosity with everyone from employees to the needy. However, subsequent investigations would show that the Rigases had "borrowed" over $3 billion from the corporation for personal investments in hockey teams, golf courses, and even the independent film company created by daughter Ellen Rigas Venetis (married to Peter Venetis, who was also an officer of Adelphia).[16]

There were also webs of transactions between the Rigas family and Adelphia. For example, John Rigas owned a furniture store from which Adelphia purchased all of its office furniture. However, Adelphia then gave the furniture store free ads on its cable and Internet services. A seasoned federal investigator was quite taken aback by what the Justice Department's review of corporate records uncovered, "We've never seen anything like this. The level of self-dealing is quite serious."[17] Mrs. John Rigas, Doris, was paid $12.8 million for her work as a designer and decorator for Adelphia offices. The Rigas family farm, billed as a honey farm in local literature, really just provided landscaping,

[13]Eric Dash, "Sorrow Mixed with Disbelief for Patrons of a Community," *New York Times,* July 9, 2004, pp. A1, A5.

[14]www.adelphia.com/investorsrelations. Accessed April 28, 2010. Because the company no longer exists, this source used originally is no longer available. The 10K reports can be found at www.sec.gov using the EDGAR data base.

[15]www.adelphia.com/relations/1999. Accessed April 28, 2010. Because the company no longer exists, this information is not available at the site used originally. The company's 10k's can still be found at www.sec.gov. Use the EDGAR data base.

[16]Robert Frank and Deborah Solomon, "Adelphia and Rigas Family Had a Vast Network of Business Ties," *Wall Street Journal,* May 24, 2002, pp. A1, A5.

[17]*Id.*

maintenance and snow removal services to Adelphia, for a fee.[18] Adelphia invested $3 million in "Songcatcher," a film produced by Ellen Rigas Venetis.[19]

The family managed to conceal the self-dealing quite well from its auditors. When the financial statements were finally restated, cash flow had to be reduced by about $50 million per quarter. In total, the Rigases had concealed $3 billion of takings from the company from its external auditor, Deloitte Touche.[20] Timothy Werth, who was Adelphia's director of accounting, entered a guilty plea to fraud, securities fraud, wire fraud, conspiracy, and other crimes related to the concealment as well as the falsification of earnings.[21] In his statement of facts for his guilty plea, Mr. Werth said that he had been cooking the books from the time he first joined Adelphia when he was 30 years old, some ten years.

The Rigases owned 20 percent of Adelphia stock, and, as a result, held 60 percent of the voting shares of the company. Because of their share control, the board consisted of 60 percent Rigas family affiliates, including John Rigas, sons Michael, James, and Timothy, and son-in-law, Peter Venetis.[22] The family also did business with Adelphia in other ways, and the transactions always seemed to net a nice profit for the Rigases. For example, Adelphia paid $25 million for the timber rights to a piece of property that it then sold to the Rigas family for $500,000.[23] There were substantial loans made to members of the Rigas family by the corporation, some used for business investments and some used to keep them from selling Adelphia shares to satisfy personal investment responsibilities. There were also conflicts galore among officers, board members, and the Rigas family with the officers and board members actually competing with Adelphia for the purchase of cable systems and, with something that takes the term chutzpah to a new level, the company providing the credit, collateral, and financing for the family members to make the purchases for themselves. The total amount of the loans to the Rigas family was $2.3 billion, much of that amount concealed from the board and auditors through off-the-book entities.[24] It was when a financial analyst uncovered at least $1 billion in off-the-book debts, that the board filed an 8-K disclosure statement and investigators came calling.[25]

The Rigases also owned finance companies that purchased cable services and then those finance companies entered into contracts to sell cable services to Adelphia.[26] Adelphia was required to purchase the cable services at full retail prices from the Rigas firms. Nell Minow, a renowned corporate governance expert and head of The Corporate Library said the following about these arrangements, "Even the existence of a credit line that allows the family to buy cable systems raises conflict-of-interest questions because the company was actually funding the family's ability to compete for properties."[27]

One accounting and financial expert said the conduct by the Rigases at Adelphia was just "plain-vanilla-old-fashioned self-dealing."[28] Many referred to the Rigases' conduct as

---

[18]Susan Pulliam and Deborah Solomon, "Adelphia Faces Irate Shareholders," *Wall Street Journal*, April 4, 2002, pp. C1, C2; and Geraldine Fabrikant, "A Family Affair at Adelphia Communications," *New York Times*, April 4, 2002, p. C1.

[19]Fabrikant, "A Family Affair at Adelphia Communications," p. C1; and Geraldine Fabrikant, "New Questions on Auditors for Adelphia," *New York Times*, May 25, 2002, p. B1, at B4.

[20]Christine Nuzum, "Adelphia's 'Accounting Magic' Fooled Auditors, Witness Says," *Wall Street Journal*, May 5, 2004, p. C5.

[21]"Former Adelphia Executive Enters a Guilty Plea," *New York Times*, November 3, 2003, p. B3.

[22]This information was taken from the proxy for Adelphia for 2001.

[23]Nuzum, *Id.*

[24]www.sec.gov/edgar. March 27, 2002, 8-K filing. Accessed September 11, 2010.

[25]Geraldine Fabrikant, "Adelphia Fails to Make Note Payment," *New York Times*, May 17, 2002, p. C1.

[26]Geraldine Fabrikant, "New Questions on Auditors for Adelphia," *New York Times*, May 25, 2002, pp. B1, B4.

[27]*Id.*

[28]*Id.*

not clever and nothing more than a classic "personal piggy bank" case.[29] The lines between the Rigases' activities and ownership and Adelphia's ownership were so blurred that local tax records showed that Adelphia paid the real estate taxes for all of the Rigas families and their twelve homes with one check.[30] Adelphia also fronted $12.8 million for the construction of a golf course owned by the Rigas family.[31]

Wayne Carlin, the regional director for the SEC's northeast division said, "The thing that makes this case stand out is the scope and magnitude of the looting of the company on the part of the Rigas family. In terms of brazenness and the sheer amount of dollars yanked out of this public company and yanked out of the pockets of investors, it's really quite stunning. It's even stunning to someone like me who is in the business of unraveling these kinds of schemes."[32]

Adelphia was, however, a godsend, as it were, to Pennsylvania.[33] Suffering from declines in the coal and steel industries, the Pennsylvania economy was greatly depressed during Adelphia's rise. Because it was a company in a growing industry, nearly everyone in Coudersport would work directly for Adelphia or would benefit indirectly as their businesses picked up because of the company's growth. Rigas was so respected and beloved in the small central Pennsylvania town that it would often take him one hour to walk one block along Main Street because so many people stopped to talk with him, and mostly to thank him for what he had done with the company as well as for them personally.[34] The Rigas family also benefited local business because of their profligate spending on homes, events, help, and decorating.[35] At least 20 Adelphia employees worked personally for the Rigas family. One of those employees served as a chef for the Rigas family.[36] Country folklore holds that the local drycleaner had the following exchange with Mr. Rigas about his wife, Doris, and her spending, "That woman is costing you millions." To which Mr. Rigas replied, "Well, sometimes it's worth it. Because when she's bothering [the contractors], she's not bothering me."[37]

The Rigas family was very generous with the people of Coudersport. Mr. Rigas donated to the Coudersport Fire Department and paid $50,000 so that the veterans' monument in the town could have the worn-away names of the veterans restored. He gave the necessary funds to McDonald's and Subway so that they could change the outward appearances of their businesses to look more like the Main Street USA image that the Rigases wanted to preserve in Coudersport.[38] The Rigas family threw the Coudersport Christmas party. Doris decorated two large Christmas trees for the party with 16,000 lights each.[39] Mr. Rigas used the original theater that began his business career to allow more people to attend the movies. The prices at the Rigas Coudersport theater: Adelphia employees admitted for free; others for $4; candy for 60 cents and popcorn in a tub for $2.25.[40]

---

[29]*Id.*

[30]Devin Leonard, "Adelphia," *Fortune*, August 12, 2002, pp. 137, 146.

[31]Jerry Markon and Robert Frank, "Five Adelphia Officials Arrested on Fraud Charges," *Wall Street Journal*, July 25, 2002, p. A3.

[32]*Id.*; and David Lieberman, "Adelphia's Woes 'a Total Shock' to Many," *USA Today*, April 5, 2002, p. 3B.

[33]Markon and Frank, "Five Adelphia Officials Arrested on Fraud Charges," p. A3; and Lieberman, "Adelphia's Woes 'a Total Shock' to Many," *USA Today*, April 5, 2002, p. 3B.

[34]Deborah Solomon and Robert Frank, "Adelphia Story: Founding Family Retreats in Crisis," *Wall Street Journal*, April 5, 2002, pp. B1, B4.

[35]Leonard, "Adelphia," p. 137.

[36]Geraldine Fabrikant, "Adelphia Said to Inflate Customers and Cash Flow," *New York Times*, June 8, 2002, pp. B1, B3.

[37]Leonard, "Adelphia," p. 137.

[38]John Schwartz, "In Hometown of Adelphia, Pride, but Worry About the Future, Too," *New York Times*, May 28, 2002, p. C1

[39]Leonard, "Adelphia," p. 137.

[40]Schwartz, "In Hometown of Adelphia, Pride, But Worry About the Future, Too," p. C1.

Adelphia's philanthropic program was called, "Because we're concerned," and donations went to Boy Scouts and Girl Scouts of America, the March of Dimes, Ronald McDonald House, YMWC, YWCA, Habitat for Humanity, Leukemia Society of America, Lupus Foundation of America, Meals on Wheels, and Toys for Tots.[41] The Tennessee Titans' stadium was named "Adelphia Field." (The stadium is now LP Field.)

But Rigas philanthropy went beyond these large public actions and donations. When John Rigas read a story in the local paper about someone experiencing financial difficulties, he would send them a check and a note that read, "I read your story in the newspaper."[42] Mr. Rigas offered the company jet to employees and family members who needed to go out of state for medical care. Mr. Rigas would even follow up with personal phone calls to these beneficiaries of the corporate jet by calling to see how the treatment had gone.[43] Mr. Rigas was inducted into the Cable Television Hall of Fame for his good works in Coudersport and the other communities served by Adelphia.[44]

The reaction in Coudersport to the Adelphia collapse and all of the indictments of the Rigas family was one of utter shock and disbelief. One Adelphia officer said that he "hasn't heard Rigas utter a slur or profanity in 32 years. The whole story isn't known. That's part of the problem."[45] One town member explained, "Whatever has to be done to make it right, they'll do. People don't know the real John Rigas."[46]

John Rigas and his son, Timothy, were convicted of bank fraud, securities fraud, and conspiracy. Michael Rigas was acquitted of conspiracy and wire fraud, but there was a hung jury on securities and bank fraud. The judge declared a mistrial.[47] John Rigas was originally sentenced to 15 years, but with an intervening U.S. Supreme Court decision on the proper application of the sentencing guidelines, Mr. Rigas was resentenced in 2007. However, his sentence remained at 15 years because the federal judge noted that were it not for Mr. Rigas's age and failing health, he would have imposed a longer sentence. Because he was 82 at the time of the sentencing, Mr. Rigas will spend his life in prison unless he is able to show through a doctor's report that he is within six months of death. He will be released if and when that medical certification can be made. The judge also said he would review the sentence again when and if Mr. Rigas has served two years.

Discussion Questions

1. Does using money for good deeds excuse violations of the law or accounting principles? Is John Rigas a Robin Hood?

2. Why do you think the officers got comfortable with the conflicts and mixing together of personal and company business interests? Did the philanthropy and good for Pennsylvania provide their justification?

Compare & Contrast

1. What principles of social responsibility do you develop from this case? Are virtue ethics different from the issues raised in social responsibility? Was the Rigas family socially responsible? Were they ethical? Was Adelphia a socially responsible company? Was its conduct fair to its shareholders?

---

[41]www.adelphia.com/investors—annual reports for 1999 and 2000. Because the company no longer exists, this source used originally is no longer available. The 10K reports can be found at www.sec.gov using the EDGAR data base.

[42]Leonard, "Adelphia," pp. 137, 146.

[43]Schwartz, "In Hometown of Adelphia, Pride, But Worry About the Future, Too," p. C1.

[44]Id.

[45]David Lieberman, "Adelphia's Woes 'a Total Shock' to Many," *USA Today*, April 5, 2002, p. 3B.

[46]Id.

[47]Barry Meier, "Michael Rigas Is Free for Now after Mistrial Declared," *New York Times*, July 16, 2004, p. B1.

2. When he was indicted, Mr. Rigas issued the following statement: "We did nothing wrong; My conscience is clear about that."[48] He also attributed all of the government indictments as well as the shareholders' litigation against him as "a big P.R. effort on the part of the outside directors and their lawyers to shift responsibility."[49] Given Mr. Rigas's convictions, why did he remain so defiant and unwilling to acknowledge the misconduct? As you study other cases in the book, note how many other convicted CEOs express the same sentiments. Offer some reasons they might feel so diametrically different from those who have prosecuted them, convicted them, or sought recovery for their losses.

Reading 3.9

The Regulatory Cycle, Social Responsibility, Business Strategy, and Equilibrium[50]

Introduction

Some years ago, when he was serving as the CEO for Motorola, before going on to become Kodak's CEO, George Fisher spoke to a group of our masters students from both engineering and business. One of the questions the students asked after he had given his thoughts on success in life and business was, "How do you become a leader in business?" His response was that those in business should take an evolving problem in their business unit, their company, their industry, or their community and fix it before the problem was regulated or litigated. He assured the students that business people who voluntarily undertake self-correction are always ahead of the game.

There is a diagram I use to teach students this Fisher principle of leadership that shows how its best execution is found in focusing on ethics. That diagram, based on the political science model developed by Professor James Frierson, appears below.

FIGURE 3.2

Leadership and Ethics: Making Choices before Liability

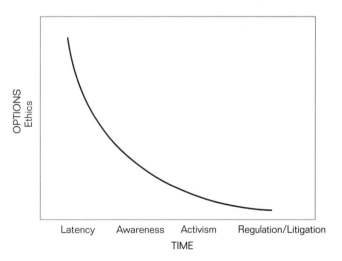

Adapted from James Frierson's "Public Policy Forecasting: A New Approach," *SAM Advanced Management Journal*, Spring 1985, pp. 18–23.

---

[48]From *Business: Its Legal, Ethical and Global Environment*, 9th ed., by Marianne Jennings, 60. Copyright © 2011. Reprinted with permission by South-Western, a division of Cengage Learning.

[49]Andrew Ross Sorkin, "Fallen Founder of Adelphia Tries to Explain," *New York Times*, April 7, 2003, p. C1.

[50]Marianne Jennings. "How Ethics Trump Market Inefficiencies and Thwart the Need for Regulation," *Corporate Finance Review* 10(5):36–41 (2006).

Understanding this cycle, what it represents, what moves it, and how companies and industries should respond is a critical part of the study of ethics in business. The phenomenon of a rapidly moving regulatory force drives home the reality that businesses and industries are always better off self-regulating than waiting for government regulations. A historical study of the cycle phenomenon reveals that regulators, as bureaucratic as they are, can move far more quickly than market forces to solve market frauds, abuses, and other perversions that occur when the moral sentiments of markets do not prevail as Adam Smith intended in his assumptions about economic efficiencies.

Every market, consumer, or industry issue that is subject to regulation or litigation began as an ethical issue. Because the law and regulations afforded businesses wide latitude in a particular area, some seized the moment a bit too aggressively. That aggressive seizure of a loophole, without the checks and balances of ethics and market morality, puts companies, industries and individuals at a disadvantage when the inevitable regulation arrives because their practices have been so foreign to the now mandated morality. The X axis of the diagram represents time and the Y axis represents options for self-regulation. The longer companies and industries wait prior to taking self-corrective action, the less likely their self-correction will be allowed and the more likely regulators are to impose regulation with often unintended consequences, including additional costs, as illustrated below with the addition of a second curve that depicts costs. The Figure 3.3 diagram depicts the regulatory cycle with an additional line to illustrate the fact that the firm's costs increase the longer the time period for addressing the evolving issues.

FIGURE 3.3

Leadership and Ethics: Making Choices before Liability

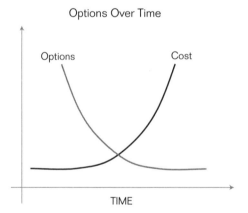

Understanding and applying the regulatory cycle is a means of exercising company and industry leadership. Examining issues in light of the cycle provides firms with the opportunity for self-regulation, often a cheaper and more efficient means of curbing the misdeeds that too often occupy loophole areas of markets and industries.

The Stages and Activities of the Regulatory Cycle

Every area that is now the subject of regulation or litigation began at the left side of the regulatory cycle, in the latency stage, with plenty of options for how to handle a gray area. During this phase of the cycle only those in the industry and perhaps academics and researchers are aware of the evolving issue. For example, the issue of under-funding pensions has been an evolving concern for the past 15 years. Companies, researchers, and corporate governance experts expressed concerns about the funding, investments, and reporting on pension plans. But the issue remained one of interest only to those in the financial field. It failed to gain traction in daily newspapers such as *USA Today* or in weekly news magazine publications. However, the bankruptcy of United Airlines and its bankruptcy court ruling excusing it from its pension obligations have moved the issue from the latency stage through the public awareness stage to activism, or the demand for reform of pension funding, and, shortly, new mandates for companies on pension funding. Suddenly the issue of pensions and sudden losses was the cover story for *Time* and *Newsweek*. Consumers and employees were demanding to know, "How safe is my pension?"[51]

Companies had been able to capitalize on a rather large loophole in pension reporting requirements. When United Airlines (UA) declared bankruptcy, the Federal Pension Benefit Guaranty Corporation discovered that UA's pension was under funded by 50%. The shortage the federal agency will need to supply in order to provide UA employees with their pension benefits is estimated at $8.4 to $10 billion. UA did nothing that violated the law in its pension funding and reporting.[52]

Under a federal pension law enacted in 1974, companies found quite a loophole that enabled them to report better financial results because they were not required to report any pension shortfalls to the Federal Pension Benefit Guaranty Corporation unless their pension funding fell below 50% of requirements. The 50% figure was, however, a guide for reporting a "state of emergency" in the pension plan and its funding. Under interpretations of the law, most companies declared their plans fully funded so long as they did not dip below 50%. United reported a shortfall in 2004 of about $74 million.

The SEC [Securities and Exchange Commission] requires companies to report pension funding shortfalls in their annual reports when pension funding falls below 90%. Of the 100 largest pension funds examined by a Department of Labor study in 2003, only six of the plans were truly at the 90% funding level and those six companies had their SEC reports consistent with their Federal Pension Benefit Guaranty Corporation. The audit estimates the shortfall in total private pension plan funding at $450 billion. The Federal Pension Benefit Guarantee Corporation's deficit from paying pensions is now $23.5 billion. With that level of shortfall and media attention, massive reforms came with the passage of the Pension Protection Act of 2006.

The pattern in the regulatory cycle is always the same. Someone finds a loophole in the law and those in the industry take advantage of that loophole as a strategy for maximizing their returns. History repeats itself when it comes to the regulatory cycle. For example, prior to the savings and loan crisis and collapse of the late 1980s and early 1990s, appraisers were not regulated. The qualifications for an appraiser were limited and issues such as conflicts of interest (where the appraisers stood to benefit in a transaction if the land value came in at an appropriate level) were not controlled. In an area in which there are few legal guidelines, leeway translates into licentiousness and then abuses that often graduate into fraud. The firms begin by crossing those ethical lines of conflicts of interest or only asking whether something can be done (such as the pension funding and reporting issues), and not whether it *should* be done.

Those basic ethical violations, centering on basic values such as fairness in real estate transactions or honoring the pension commitment made to employees, cause emotional reactions and outrage. Courts and/or legislatures step in to legislate ethics.

---

[51]Marilyn Adams, "'Fundamentally Broken' Pension System In 'Need of a Fix,'" *USA Today*, November 15, 2005, pp. 1B, 2B.

[52]Mary Williams Walsh, "Pension Loopholes Helped United Hide its Troubles," *New York Times*, June 7, 2005, pp. C1, C3.

What is perhaps so difficult for executives to grasp about the regulatory cycle is that it moves, not by data or logic, but rather by emotion and by public perception. Public perception changes through examples and anecdotes.

The U.S. tax deductibility limits on CEO pay, as ill-defined and designed as they were, resulted from public emotion and outcry over executive compensation. There are continuing demands for reforms. Stock option grants are a gently percolating issue to watch as continuing attention and outrage build.[53]

Presently, companies are grappling with the expensive and intense mandates of Sarbanes-Oxley regulations. The statutorily imposed mandates on board structure, conflicts, financial reporting, and certification of processes and reports have found many firms with delayed filings and restatements.

Still, one of the benefits of anticipating issues in the latency stage is that a company is then prepared for implementation and may enjoy a period of competitive advantage because it is not distracted by complex regulations and their implementation. Their practices found them in compliance before the law and regulatory mandates existed. Some firms have taken Sarbanes-Oxley [SOX] in stride and found that its provision even provide them with some efficiencies.

How To Seize the Moment and Manage the Cycle

There are businesses that do seize the latency moment. There is little question that the electric utility industry would look a great deal different today if it had not handled the issue of EMF (electromagnetic fields) as effectively and openly as it did.

As we look back over the art of financial reporting, we see a host of ethical issues that went on unmanaged until SOX was passed and mandated. The audit firms themselves are now fully regulated for their complicity in the frauds at WorldCom, Enron, Adelphia and others. The federal government must authorize them to conduct audits and the role of the accounting profession in setting ethical standards has been usurped by the government—federal laws now determine what constitutes a conflict of interest on the part of an auditor because the profession had not defined a conflict broadly enough to cover the clearly conflicting interests auditors had with their clients. Officers are now required to pay back bonuses earned because of inflated earnings reports. Ethically there was no other answer but that the company be repaid those bonuses, but too few executives saw the issue and SOX requires that the officers restore their bonus payments to the company if the numbers have been inflated.

How can a director who is not independent be an effective member of the board audit or compensation committee? The conflict is overwhelming and even the disclosure of a director's dual role does not cure the conflict. The result of too many abuses of conflicting relationships by too many directors is that federal law now requires independent directors only on the audit and compensation committees of the board. How could the issue have evolved to the point of federal mandates? It got to the point because there were ethical breaches, the result was a wild ride in terms of both compensation and inaccurate financial reports. When the degree of abuses unfolded, the public became emotional and demanded action. That action came in the form of strict requirements for board structure.

There are ethical issues that are now in the latency stage—that stage where the public is not aware of a problem and no one is filing suit or demanding regulation. What follows is a list of questions to help anticipate the cycle:

- What is the topic of discussion in the industry?
- What concerns are academics and others expressing about your product, your production, and the future?

---
[53]The result was SEC investigation of over 250 companies for backdating in their options grants.

- Are you capitalizing on a loophole in the law?
- Have you disclosed what loophole you are using?
- If you have not disclosed the loophole, what are your reasons for keeping it close to the vest?
- Are your actions fair or do they put someone at risk?
- Are others in your industry doing the same thing?

Discussion Questions

1. Name some issues that you have seen or are seeing moving through the regulatory cycle.

2. How should a business respond when the public is emotionally charged about its practices, its products, or operations?

Case 3.10

Fannie, Freddie, Wall Street, Main Street, and the Subprime Mortgage Market: Of Moral Hazards

Background on Fannie Mae

Fannie Mae was created as a different sort of business entity, a shareholder-owned corporation with a federal charter. The federal government created Fannie Mae in 1938 during the Roosevelt administration to increase affordable housing availability and to attract investment into the housing market. The charge to Fannie Mae was to be sure that there was a stable mortgage market with consistent availability of mortgage funds for consumers to purchase homes. Initially, Fannie Mae was federally funded, but in 1968, it was rechartered as a shareholder-owned corporation with the responsibility of obtaining all of its capital from the private market, not the federal government. On its website, Fannie Mae describes its commitment and mission as follows:

- Expand access to homeownership for first-time home buyers and help raise the minority homeownership rate with the ultimate goal of closing the homeownership gap entirely;
- Make homeownership and rental housing a success for families at risk of losing their homes;
- Expand the supply of affordable housing where it is needed most, which includes initiatives for workforce housing and supportive housing for the chronically homeless; and
- Transform targeted communities, including urban, rural, and Native American, by channeling all the company's tools and resources and aligning efforts with partners in these areas.

A Model Corporate Citizen

In 2004, *Business Ethics* magazine named Fannie Mae the most ethical company in the United States. It had been in the top ten corporate citizens for several years (number 9 in 2000 and number 3 in 2001 and 2002).[54] Marjorie Kelly, the editor-in-chief of the magazine (see Reading 3.6), described the standards for the award, which was created in 1996, as follows:

> *Just what does it mean to be a good corporate citizen today? To our minds, it means simply this: treating a mix of stakeholders well. And by stakeholders, we mean those who have a "stake" in the firm—because they have risked financial, social, human, and knowledge capital in the corporation, or because they are impacted by its activities. While lists of stakeholders can be long, we focus on four groups: employees, customers, stockholders, and the community. Being a good citizen means attending to the company's impact on all these groups.*[55]

---

[54]In 2003, Fannie Mae was number 12. *Business Ethics*, March/April 2003.

[55]*Business Ethics*, May/June 2000.

In 2001, the magazine explained why Fannie Mae was one of the country's top corporate citizens:

Fannie Mae scores high in the areas of community and diversity, and has been ranked near the top of everyone's "best" list, including Fortune's "Best Companies for Minorities," Working Mother's "Best Companies for Working Mothers," and The American Benefactor's "America's Most Generous Companies." Franklin D. Raines, an African American, is CEO, and there are two women and two minorities among the companies eight senior line executives.[56]

In 2002, *Business Ethics* described third-ranked Fannie Mae as follows:

The purpose of Fannie Mae, a private company with an unusual federal charter, is to spread home ownership among Americans. Its ten-year, $2 trillion program—the American Dream Commitment—aims to increase home ownership rates for minorities, new immigrants, young families, and those in low-income communities.

In 2001, over 51 percent of Fannie Mae's financing went to low- and moderate-income households. "A great deal of our work serves populations that are underserved, typically, and we've shown that it's an imminently bankable proposition," said Barry Zigas, senior vice president in Fannie Mae's National Community Lending Center. "It is our goal to keep expanding our reach to impaired borrowers and to help lower their costs."

"That represents a striking contrast to other financial firms, many of which prey upon rather than help low-income borrowers. To aid the victims of predatory lenders, Fannie Mae allows additional flexibility in underwriting new loans for people trapped in abusive loans, if they could have initially qualified for conventional financing. In January the company committed $31 million to purchasing these type of loans."[57]

The Community Reinvestment Act (CRA) is a federal statute that established a government program to get people who would otherwise not qualify (i.e., no credit history and no down payment) into homes with the goals of helping these folks and thereby revitalizing blighted areas. Banks and lenders were evaluated for their commitment to these loans, and no bank or lender wanted a bad rating.

Simultaneously, the federal government anticipated push-back from lenders who would point out that these were high-risk loans and required greater returns. However, lenders were evaluated for their CRA commitment, which included their creativity in granting the loans. In addition, lenders faced prosecution by the Justice Department for discrimination in lending if their loan portfolios did not include a sufficient number of CRA loans. All the while, Fannie Mae served as the purchaser for these loans, eventually packaging them and selling them as securitized mortgage pools. The CRA loans had borrowers with less equity, higher default rates, and more foreclosures. There was also an exacerbating effect of this false sense of security on the part of the high-risk borrowers about their mortgages. Because these risky borrowers were not really anteing up the actual cost of their homes (and remember, these were folks who had never had a mortgage before, had bad credit histories, and may not have had much in the way of financial literacy), they overextended and overspent in other areas. In short, they were maxed out in all areas because they were lulled into a false sense of financial security with such a low mortgage payment. Because Fannie Mae owned or guaranteed half of the $12 trillion mortgage debt in the United States, any problems with those mortgages could and did

---

[56]*Business Ethics*, May/June 2001.

[57]*Business Ethics*, May/June 2002.

lead to a financial crisis for Fannie, the U.S. stock market, and the economy. [58] Then–Federal Reserve Chairman Alan Greenspan warned of the looming problems at Fannie Mae in 2005. He testified before Congress, "The Federal Reserve Board has been unable to find any credible purpose for the huge balance sheets built by Fannie and Freddie other than profit."[59] Others, including the St. Louis Federal Reserve chairman, William Poole, warned that the huge debt load rendered Fannie and Freddie insolvent.

The Darker Side of Corporate Citizen Fannie

Even as the mortgage issues were evolving under the radar and Fannie was being recognized for its corporate citizenship, there were issues in Fannie's operations that went undetected for nearly a decade.

Fannie Mae: The Super-Achiever with an EPS Goal

Fannie Mae was a company driven to earnings targets through a compensation system tied to those results. And Fannie Mae had a phenomenal run based on those incentives in terms of its financial performance:

- For more than a decade, Fannie Mae achieved consistent, double-digit growth in earnings.[60]
- In that same decade, Fannie Mae's mortgage portfolio grew by five times to $895 billion.[61]
- From 2001 to 2004, its profits totaled $24 billion.[62]
- Through 2004, Fannie Mae's shares were trading at over $80.[63]

Fannie Mae was able to smooth earnings through decisions on the recording of interest costs, and used questionable discretion in determining the accounting treatment for buying and selling its mortgage assets. Those decisions allowed executives at the company to smooth earnings growth with a resulting guaranteed payout to them under the incentive plans.[64]

Those incentive plans were based on earnings per share targets (EPS) that had to be reached in order for the officers to earn their annual bonuses. The incentive plans began in 1995, with a kick-up in 1998 as Franklin Raines, then chairman and CEO, set a goal of doubling the company's earnings per share (EPS) from $3.23 to $6.46 in five years.[65] Raines, the former budget director for the Clinton administration, was able to make the EPS goal a part of Fannie Mae's culture. Mr. Raines said, "The future is so bright that I am willing to set a goal that our EPS will double over the next five years."[66] Sampath Rajappa, Fannie Mae's senior vice president of operations risk (akin to the Office of Auditing), gave the following pep talk to his team in 2000, as the EPS goals continued:

By now every one of you must have a 6.46 branded in your brains. You must be able to say it in your sleep, you must be able to recite it forwards and backwards, you must have a raging fire in your belly that burns away all doubts, you must live, breathe and

---

[58]Julie Creswell, "Long Protected by Washington, Fannie and Freddie Ballooned," *New York Times*, July 13, 2008, p. A7.

[59]*Id.*, p. A18.

[60]James R. Hagerty and John D. McKinnon, "Fannie Mae Board Agrees to Changes it Long Resisted," *Wall Street Journal*, July 28, 2004, p. A1.

[61]*Id.*

[62]Alex Berenson, "Assessing What Will Happen to Fannie Mae," *New York Times*, December 17, 2004, p. C1.

[63]Paul Dwyer, Amy Borrus, and Mara Hovanesian, "Fannie Mae: What's the Damage?" *Fortune*, October 11, 2004, p. 45.

[64]Office of Federal Housing Enterprise Oversight , report, November 15, 2005. Report found at http://www.fhfa.gov/Default.aspx?Page=4. Accessed July 20, 2010. The OFHEO was merged into the federal Finance Housing Agency in 2009 following Fannie Mae's collapse.

[65]Bethany McLean, "The Fall of Fannie Mae," *Fortune*, January 25, 2005, pp. 123, 128.

[66]*Id.*

dream 6.46, you must be obsessed on 6.46. . . . After all, thanks to Frank, we all have a lot of money riding on it. . . . We must do this with a fiery determination, not on some days, not on most days but day in and day out, give it your best, not 50%, not 75%, not 100%, but 150%. Remember Frank has given us an opportunity to earn not just our salaries, benefits, raises . . . but substantially over and above if we make 6.46.

So it is our moral obligation to give well above our 100% and if we do this, we would have made tangible contributions toward Frank's goals.[67]

For 1998, the size of the annual bonus payout pool was linked to specific EPS targets:

- Earnings Per Share (EPS) Range for 1998 AIP Corporate Goals
- $3.13 minimum payout $3.18 target payout $3.23 maximum payout[68]

For Fannie Mae to pay out the maximum amount in incentives in 1998, EPS would have to come in at $3.23. If EPS was below the $3.13 minimum, there would be no incentive payout. The 1998 EPS was $3.2309. The maximum payout goal was met, as the OFHEO report noted, "right down to the penny." The final OFHEO report concluded that the executive team at Fannie Mae determined what number it needed to get to the maximum EPS level and then worked backwards to achieve that result. One series of e-mails finds the executives agreeing on what number they were comfortable with as using for the "volatility adjustment."[69]

The following table shows the difference between salary (what would have been paid if the minimum target were not met) and the award under the Incentive Plan (AIP).

1998 Salary and Bonus of Senior Fannie Mae Executives

Officer	Title	Salary	AIP Award/ Bonus
James A. Johnson	Chairman and CEO	$966,000	$1,932,000
Franklin D. Raines	Chairman and CEO designate	$526,154	$1,109,589
Lawrence M. Small	President and COO	$783,839	$1,108,259
Jamie Gorelick	Vice chairman	$567,000	$779,625
J. Timothy Howard	Executive vice president (EVP) and CFO	$395,000	$493,750
Robert J. Levin	EVP, housing and community development	$395,000	$493,750

"Right down to the penny" was not a serendipitous achievement. For example, Fannie Mae's gains and losses on risky derivatives were kept off the books by treating them as hedges, a decision that was made without determining whether such treatment qualified under the accounting rules for exemptions from earnings statements. These losses were eventually brought back into earnings with a multibillion impact when these types of improprieties were uncovered in 2005.[70]

---

[67]Office of Federal Housing Enterprise Oversight (OFHEO), *Final Report of the Special Examination of Fannie Mae*, May 2006 (Washington, DC: OFHEO), p. 50 (hereinafter referred to as *OFHEO Final Report*).

[68]OFHEO, Office of Compliance, *Report of Findings to Date: Special Examination of Fannie Mae*, September 17, 2004 (Washington, DC: OFHEO), pp. vii, 149 (hereinafter referred to as *OFHEO Interim Report*).

[69]*OFHEO Final Report*, p. 51.

[70]*Id.*, p. 45

Fannie Mae and Volatility

Fannie Mae's policies on amortization, a critical accounting area for a company buying and holding mortgage loans, were developed by the chief financial officer (CFO) with no input from the company's controller. Fannie Mae's amortization policies were not in compliance with GAAP (Generally Accepted Accounting Principles).[71] The amortization policies relied on a computer model that would shorten the amortization of the life of a loan in order to peak earnings performance with higher yields. Fascinatingly, the amortization policies were developed because of a mantra within the company of "no more surprises."[72] The philosophy was that in order to attract funding for the mortgage market, there needed to be stability that would attract investors. The officers at the company reasoned that "volatility" was a barrier to accomplishing its goals of a stable and available source of mortgage funds for homes. When the computer model was developed, the officers reasoned that they were simply adjusting for what was "arbitrary volatility." However, "arbitrary volatility" turned out to be a difficult-to-grasp concept for those outside Fannie Mae.[73] Further, the volatility measures and adjustments appeared to have a direct correlation with the EPS goals that resulted in the awards to the officers. Even those within Fannie Mae struggled to explain to investigators what was really happening with their adjustments.

In the OFHEO report, an investigator asked Janet Pennewell, Fannie Mae's vice president of resource and planning, "What is arbitrary volatility in earnings?" Ms. Pennewell responded,

> *Arbitrary volatility, in our view, was introduced when—I can give you an example of what would cause, in our view, arbitrary volatility. If your constant effective yield was dramatically different between one quarter and the next quarter because of an arbitrary decision you had or view—changing your view of long-term interest rates that caused a dramatic change in the constant effective yield that you were reporting, you could therefore be in a position where you might be booking 300 million of income in one quarter and 200 million of expense in the next quarter, introduced merely by what your assumption about future interest rates was. And to us that was arbitrary volatility because it really just literally because of your view, your expectation of interest rate and the way that you were modeling your premium and discount constant effective yield, you would introduce something into your financial statements that, again, wasn't very reflective of how you really expect that mortgage to perform over its entire expected life, and was not very representative of the fundamental financial performance of the company."[74]*

The operative words "to us" appeared to have fueled accounting decisions. But, there was an overriding problem with Fannie Mae's reliance on arbitrary volatility. Fannie Mae had fixed-rate mortgages in its portfolio. Market fluctuations on interest rates were irrelevant for most of its portfolio.[75]

---

[71]Fannie Mae's "Purchase Premium and Discount Amortization Policy," its internal policies on accounting and financial reporting on its loan portfolio, did not comply with GAAP. *OFHEO Interim Report*, pp. vii and 149. The final report was issued in February 2006, with no new surprises or altered conclusions beyond what appeared in this interim report. Greg Farrell, "No New Problems in Report on Fannie, *USA Today*, February 24, 2006, p. 1B.

[72]*OFHEO Interim Report*, p. v.

[73]*Id.*

[74]*OFHEO Final Report*, p. 6.

[75]This portion of the discussion was adapted from Marianne M. Jennings, "Fraud Is the Moving Target, Not Corporate Securities Attorneys: The Market Relevance of Firing before Being Fired upon and Not Being 'Shocked, Shocked' That Fraud Is Going On," 46 *Washburn L.J.* 27 (2006).

Fannie Mae's Accounting

The accounting practices of Fannie Mae were so aggressive that when Raines, lawyers, and others met with the SEC to discuss the agency's demand for a restatement in 2005, the SEC told Raines that Fannie's financial reports were inaccurate in "material respects." When pressed for specifics, Donald Nicolaisen, head of the SEC's accounting division, held up a piece of paper that represented the four corners of what was permissible under GAAP and told Raines, "You weren't even on the page."[76] The OFHEO report on Fannie Mae's accounting practices "paints an ugly picture of a company tottering under the weight of baleful misdeeds that have marked the corporate scandals of the past three years: dishonest accounting, lax internal controls, insufficient capital, and me-first managers who only care that earnings are high enough to get fat bonuses and stock options."[77]

When Franklin Raines and Fannie Mae CFO J. Timothy Howard were removed by the board at the end of 2005, Daniel H. Mudd, the former chief operating officer during the time frame in which the accounting issues arose, was appointed CEO.[78] When congressional hearings were held following the OFHEO report, Mudd testified that he was "as shocked as anyone" about the accounting scandals at the company at which he had served as a senior officer.[79] He added, "I was shocked and stunned," when Senator Chuck Hagel confronted Mudd with "I'm astounded that you would stay with this institution."[80]

There were other issues that exacerbated the accounting decisions at Fannie Mae. Mr. Howard, as CFO, had two functions: to set the targets for Fannie's financial performance and make the calls on the financial reports that determined whether those targets (and hence his incentive pay and bonuses) would be met.[81] In effect, the function of targets and determination of how to meet those targets rested with one officer in the company. The internal control structure at Fannie Mae was weak even by the most lax internal control standards.[82]

In 1998, when Fannie Mae CEO Raines set the EPS goals, the charge spread throughout the company, and the OFHEO report concluded that the result was a culture that "improperly stressed stable earnings growth."[83] Also in 1998, Armando Falcone of the OFHEO issued a warning report that challenged Fannie Mae's accounting and stunning lack of internal controls. The report was buried until the 2004 report, readily dismissed by Fannie Mae executives and members of Congress who were enamored of Fannie's financial performance, as the work of "pencil brains" who did not understand a model that was working.[84]

The Unraveling of the Fannie Mae Mystique

Employees within Fannie Mae did begin to raise questions. In November 2003, a full year before Fannie Mae's issues would become public, Roger Barnes, then an employee in the Controller's Office at the company, left Fannie Mae because of his frustration with

[76]McLean, "The Fall of Fannie Mae," pp. 123, 138.

[77]*Id.*, p. 45.

[78]Stephen Labaton, "Chief Is Ousted at Fannie Mae under Pressure," *New York Times*, December 22, 2004, p. A1.

[79]David S. Hilzenrath and Annys Shin, "Senators Grill Fannie Mae Chief," *Washington Post*, June 16, 2006, p. D2.

[80]Marcie Gordon, "Fannie Mae Execs Face Intense Questioning from Senators," *USA Today*, June 16, 2006, p. 4B.

[81] *Id.*

[82]*Id.*

[83]Stephen Labaton and Rick Dash, "New Report Criticizes Big Lender," *New York Times*, February 24, 2006, pp. C1, C6.

[84]*Id.*, p. 128.

the lack of response from the Office of Auditing at Fannie. He had provided a detailed concern about the company's accounting policy that internal audit did not investigate in an appropriate manner.[85] No one at Fannie Mae took any steps to investigate Barnes's warnings about the flaws in the computer models for amortization. Worse, in one instance, Mr. Barnes notified the head of the Office of Auditing that at least one on-top adjustment had been made in order to make Fannie's results meet those that had been forecasted.[86] At the time Barnes raised his concern, Fannie Mae had an Ethics and Compliance Office, but it was housed within the company's litigation division and was headed by a lawyer whose primary responsibility was defending the company against allegations and suits by employees.

When those in charge of the Office of Auditing (Mr. Rajappa, of EPS 6.46 pep talk fame, was the person who handled the allegations and investigation) investigated Barnes's allegations, they were not given access to the necessary information and the investigation was dropped.[87] Many of the officers at Fannie disclosed in interviews that they were aware of the Barnes allegation of an intentional act related to financial reporting, but none of them followed up on the issue or required an investigation.[88] Barnes was correct, but was ignored, and he left Fannie Mae. He would later be vindicated by the OFHEO report, but the report was not issued until after he had left Fannie Mae.[89] Fannie Mae settled with Barnes before any suit for wrongful termination was filed. In 2002, at about the same time Barnes was raising his concerns internally, the *Wall Street Journal* began raising questions about Fannie Mae's accounting practices.[90] Those concerns were reported and editorialized in that newspaper for two years. No action was taken, however, until the OFEHO interim report was released.

The final OFHEO report noted that Fannie Mae's then CEO, Daniel Mudd, listened in 2003 as employees expressed concerns about the company's accounting policies. However, Mr. Mudd took no steps to follow up on either the questions or concerns that the employees had raised in the meeting that also subsequently turned out to accurately reflect the financial reporting missteps and misdeeds at Fannie Mae.[91] The special report done for Fannie Mae's board indicates that the Legal Department at Fannie Mae was aware of the Barnes allegations, but it deferred to internal audit for making any decisions about the merits of the allegations.[92]

Then–New York Attorney General Eliot Spitzer's (Mr. Spitzer became governor in 2007 and resigned in 2008 because of a sex scandal) investigation into insurance companies added an aside to the Fannie Mae scandal and revealed yet another red flag from a Fannie Mae employee. In 2002, Fannie Mae bought a finite-risk policy from Radian Insurance to shift $40 million in income from 2003 to 2004. Radian booked the transaction as a loan, but Fannie called it an insurance policy on its books. In a January 9, 2002, e-mail, Louis Hoyes, Fannie Mae's chief for residential mortgages, wrote about the Radian deal, "I would like to express an extremely strong no vote. . . . Should we be exposing Fannie Mae to this type of political risk to 'move' $40 million of income? I believe

---

[85] *OFHEO Interim Report*, p. iv.

[86] *OFHEO Interim Report*, p. 75.

[87] *Id.*, p. 78.

[88] *Id.* However, the OFHEO investigation reveals inconsistencies in the Office of Auditing's take on the Barnes allegations. *Id.*, p. 76.

[89] Paul Reiss, Wifkund, et al., *A Report to the Special Review Committee of the Board of Directors of Fannie Mae*, February 23, 2006, p. 25 (hereinafter referred to as *Board Report*).

[90] "Systemic Political Risk," *Wall Street Journal*, September 30, 2005, p. A10.

[91] Eric Dash, *Regulators Denounce Fannie Mae, New York Times*, May 24, 2006, p. C1. Mr. Mudd said, "I absolutely wish I had handled it differently"; *Id.*

[92] *Board Report*, p. 28.

not."[93] No further action was taken on the question raised; the deal went through as planned, and the income was shifted to another year.

The Fallout at Fannie Mae

Fannie Mae paid a $125 million fine to OFHEO for its accounting improprieties.[94] As part of that settlement, Fannie Mae's board agreed to new officers, new systems of internal control, and the presence of outside consultants to monitor the company's progress. The agency concluded that it would take years for Fannie Mae to work through all of the accounting issues and corrective actions needed to prevent similar accounting missteps in the future.[95] Fannie Mae settled charges of accounting issues with the SEC for $400 million.[96] Investigations into the role of third parties and their relationships to Fannie Mae and "actions and inactions" with them are pending.[97] Former head of the SEC Harvey Pitt commented, "When a company has engaged in wrongful conduct, the inquiry [inevitably turns to] who knew about it, who could have prevented it, who facilitated it."[98]

The head of the OFHEO, upon release of the Fannie Mae report, said of the company's operations, "More than any other case I've seen, it's all there."[99]

When he was serving as the CEO of Fannie Mae as well as the chair of the Business Roundtable, Franklin Raines testified before Congress in March 2002 in favor of passage of Sarbanes–Oxley. The following are excerpts from his testimony, which began with a reference to the tone at the top:

> The success of the American free enterprise system obtains from the merger of corporate responsibility with individual responsibility, and The Business Roundtable believes that responsibility starts at the top.

> We understand why the American people are stunned and outraged by the failure of corporate leadership and governance at Enron. It is wholly irresponsible and unacceptable for corporate leaders to say they did not know—or suggest it was not their duty to know—about the operations and activities of their company, particularly when it comes to risks that threaten the fundamental viability of their company.

> First, the paramount duty of the board of directors of a public corporation is to select and oversee competent and ethical management to run the company on a day-to-day basis.

> Second, it is the responsibility of management to operate the company in a competent and ethical manner. Senior management is expected to know how the company earns its income and what risks the company is undertaking in the course of carrying out its business. Management should never put personal interests ahead of or in conflict with the interests of the company.[100]

[93]Dawn Kopecki, "It Looks Like Fannie Had Some Help," *BusinessWeek*, June 12, 2006, pp. 36, 38. Radian's general counsel had this comment on the deal: "We have not done anything improper or illegal in this particular case or in any other case"; *Id.* Odd to get that kind of a wide swath from general counsel.

[94]Edward Iwata, "Celebrated CEO Faces Critics," *USA Today*, October 6, 2004, pp. 1B, 2B.

[95]"Fannie Mae Overhaul May Take Years," *New York Times*, June 16, 2006, p. C3.

[96]Elliott Blair Smith, "Fannie Mae to Pay $400 Million Fine," *USA Today*, May 24, 2006, p. 1B.

[97]Kopecki, "It Looks Like Fannie Had Some Help," p. 36.

[98]*Id.*

[99]Dwyer, Borrus, and Hovanesian, "Fannie Mae: What's the Damage?" pp. 45, 48.

[100]Statement by Franklin D. Raines, chairman, Corporate Governance Task Force of the Business Roundtable, before the U.S. House Committee on Financial Services, Washington, DC, March 20, 2002.

The final Fannie Mae report was issued in May 2006 with no new surprises or altered conclusions beyond what appeared in the interim report.[101]

Fannie Mae concluded the financial statement questions and issues with, among other things, a $6.3 billion restatement of revenue for the period from 1998 through 2004. Mr. Raines earned $90 million in bonuses for this period. The report also concluded that management had created an "unethical and arrogant culture" with bonus targets that were achieved through the use of cookie jar reserves that "manipulated earnings."[102] OFHEO filed 101 civil charges against Mr. Raines, former Fannie Mae CFO J. Timothy Howard, and former Controller Leanne G. Spencer. The suits asked for the return of $115 million in incentive plan payouts to the three.[103] The suit also asked for $100 million in penalties. The three settled the case by agreeing to pay $31.4 million. Mr. Raines issued the following statement when the case was settled, "While I long ago accepted managerial accountability for any errors committed by subordinates while I was CEO, it is a very different matter to suggest that I was legally culpable in any way," Raines said in a statement. "I was not. This settlement is not an acknowledgment of wrongdoing on my part, because I did not break any laws or rules while leading Fannie Mae. At most, this is an agreement to disagree."[104]

The Evolving Financial Meltdown and the Conflicts

Once the restatement was completed, Fannie Mae returned to increasing its mortgage portfolio. But, Fannie also built relationships. Through its foundation, the Fannie Mae Foundation, Fannie (subsequently investigated by the IRS for violating the use of a charitable foundation for political purposes) made donations to charities on the basis of the political contacts they were able to list on their applications for funding.[105] Bruce Marks, the CEO of Neighborhood Assistance Corporation, a recipient of Fannie Foundation funds explained, "Many institutions rely on Fannie Mae and understand that those funds are contingent on public support for its policies. Fannie Mae has intimidated virtually all of them into remaining silent."[106] Donations went to those groups that supported CRA loans, including the annual fundraisers for several congressional groups. In exchange, when regulatory or legislative action was pending that was unfavorable to Fannie, those members of Congress would come out in support of Fannie, what one member of Congress called, "a gorilla that has outgrown its cage."[107] When the SEC wanted to push to have Fannie Mae register its securities as other companies did, at least six members of Congress wrote letters of support for Fannie and the SEC backed down from its demand.

Fannie's board members also stood to benefit from continuing Fannie's growth and mortgage policies. Lenders, seeking to curry favor with Fannie in having it purchase their mortgages, offered special loan terms to Fannie executives and board members, as well as to members of Congress. The following chart lists those loans that were given by Countrywide under a special program that was nicknamed, "FOA," for "Friends of Angelo."[108] Angelo Mozilo was the CEO of Countrywide, a company that

---

[101]Greg Farrell, "No New Problems in Report on Fannie," *USA Today*, February 24, 2006, p. 1B.

[102]OFHEO, "Report of Findings to Date, Special Examination of Fannie Mae," September 17, 2004, http://www.ofheo .gov. Accessed June 19, 2010.

[103]Eric Dash, "Fannie Mae Ex-Officers Sued by U.S.," *New York Times*, December 19, 2006, pp. C1, C9.

[104]James R. Hagerty, "Fannie Mae Settlement Proves Anticlimactic," *Wall Street Journal*, April 21, 2008, p. A3.

[105]Dawn Kopecki, "Philanthropy, Fannie Mae Style," *BusinessWeek*, April 2, 2007, p. 36.

[106]*Id.*

[107]Julie Creswell, "Long Protected by Washington, Fannie and Freddie Ballooned," *New York Times*, July 13, 2008, p. A7

[108]Paul Gigot, "The Fannie Mae Gang," *Wall Street Journal*, July 23, 2008, p. A17.

collapsed under the weight of its subprime mortgages, nearly all of which were purchased by Fannie Mae.

FOAs at Countrywide			
Name/Title	**Amount**	**Rate**	**Years**
Franklin Raines	$982,253	5.125%	10
Former CEO	$986,340	4.125%	10
Fannie Mae			
Jamie Gorelick	$960,149	5.00%	10
Vice Chair			
Fannie Mae			
James Johnson	$971,650	3.875%	3
Former CEO			
Fannie Mae			
Daniel Mudd	$2,965,000	4.250%	7
COO/CEO			
Fannie Mae			

Between 2005 and 2008, Fannie Mae guaranteed $270 billion in risky loans, an amount that was three times the amount of risky loans it had guaranteed in all of its existence (since 1938, when it was created during the Roosevelt administration). The mortgage loans were risky because the income of the borrowers had not been verified, the borrowers had little or no equity in the property, the real level of payments that would be due under the loans did not take effect until three to five years after, and most of the borrowers had little or a poor credit history.

When employees expressed concerns that there were too many mortgages being evaluated, that the computer system was not effective in determining risk, and that Fannie's exposure was too great, Mr. Mudd, then-CEO, instructed them, "Get aggressive on risk-taking or get out of the company."[109] During the years from 2004 to 2006, the company operated without a permanent chief risk officer. When a permanent risk officer was hired in 2006, he advised Mr. Mudd to scale back on risk. Mr. Mudd rebuffed the suggestion because he explained that Congress and shareholders wanted him to take more risks. In September 2008, the federal government had to pay $200 billion in order to restore Fannie to solvency and prevent the quake that would have shaken other firms if Fannie had defaulted on its guarantees.

Discussion Questions

1. Consider the ethics recognition that Fannie Mae received and the reasons given for those awards. Then consider that Fannie Mae was rated by Standard & Poor's on its corporate

---

[109]Charles Duhigg, "Pressured to Take More Risks, Fannie Reached Tipping Point," *New York Times*, October 5, 2008, p. A1.

governance scoring system as being a 9, with 10 being the maximum CGS score. Fannie Mae received a 9.3 for its board structure and process.[110] What issues do you see with regard to these outside evaluations of companies that relate to governance and ethics? Is there a difference between social responsibility and ethics? Is there a connection between good governance practices and ethics?

2. List the signals that were missed in Fannie Mae's devolution. Were they missed or ignored? Evaluate the actions of Mr. Barnes and Fannie Mae's response to him.[111]

3. What observations can you make about incentive plans and earnings management? Incentive plans and internal controls?

4. Why was dealing with the volatility not the issue? Why were the changes in the numbers necessary?

5. Evaluate the pep talk of the vice president of risk operations and its effect on Fannie Mae's culture. Are there some ideas for your credo that stem from the conduct and responses of various executives at Fannie Mae? Did Mr. Mudd carry that culture forward in his positions on risk?

6. The theory of moral hazard holds that failure is a necessary part of an economic system. Where would this theory have applied in preventing the demise of Fannie Mae? Be sure to look at all aspects of the case in providing your answer.

---

[110]Standard & Poor's, "Setting the Standard," http://www.standardandpoors.com. January 30, 2003. Accessed April 28, 2010.

[111]Mr. Barnes now travels and addresses ethics, audit, accounting, financial reporting, and internal control issues. Mr. Barnes has been particularly active in working with college students in helping them to sort through the ethical issues in these areas.

Applying Social Responsibility and Stakeholder Theory

Issues of social responsibility can dominate the press coverage of a corporation and infiltrate its annual meeting through shareholder proposals on social responsibility issues. Now that you have both the decision models for ethical analysis, ethical theory, and the schools of thought on social responsibility, you are ready for analysis. This section provides you with practice in the analysis of ethical issues.

Case 3.11

Whole Foods, John Mackey, and Health Care Debates

John Mackey, the CEO of Whole Foods, wrote an op-ed piece that appeared in the *Wall Street Journal* on August 12, 2009.[112] Mr. Mackey's piece was about the proposed legislation to reform health care, a piece that focused on "less government control and more individual empowerment." Mr. Mackey included in his piece several suggestions for reform that were largely contrary to the House bill pending:

- Remove legal obstacles to allowing high-deductible plans.
- Equalize tax laws so that employer-provided health insurance and individually owned health insurance have the same tax benefits.
- Repeal all laws that prohibit insurance companies from competing across state lines.
- Repeal government mandates on what insurers must cover.
- Enact tort reform.
- Make costs transparent.
- Enact Medicare reform.
- Revise tax laws to provide deductions for those who want to contribute to help others obtain health insurance.

In the same piece, Mr. Mackey also admonished Americans to eat healthier food, lose weight, and, as a result, be healthier. Of course, Mr. Mackey's chain focuses on a theme of healthy eating, a theme that distinguishes the chain in its marketing and merchandise.

Mr. Mackey allows his employees to vote on the types of health benefits they want and noted that his Canadian and British employees opt for supplemental health care coverage so that they can purchase better care than their governments provide.

Mr. Mackey does provide health care coverage for all of his employees and is known as a model CEO for his willingness to accept a salary of $1, instead relying on the increase in value of the company's stock for his compensation. Mr. Mackey is also well known and respected in the social-responsibility community and CSR investment funds. He has been singled out by many groups for his ethical business practices.

However, as a result of his op-ed piece, there were both online and on-site boycotts of his stores by those who favor the government option in health care reform. The backlash was strong, with longtime Whole Foods customers halting their patronage of the store. On the other hand, Mr. Mackey has gained customers from those who favor his types of reforms.

---

[112]Mr. Mackey was known for his sock puppeting before for his foray into health care issues. Andrew Martin, "CEO of Whole Foods Extolled His Stock Online," *New York Times*, July 13, 2007, p. C4.

Discussion Questions

1. How would Milton Friedman respond to Mr. Mackey's actions in writing the editorial?
2. Is there a socially responsible approach to health care? Is it the government option? How does that option compare with Mr. Mackey's proposals?
3. Is it ethical for customers to boycott?
4. Is there a risk for businesses and executives when they become involved in social and political issues? Evaluate the constitutional law issue in this situation: the flaws in the "free speech" responses to the boycotts of Whole Foods.

For More Information

John Mackey, "The Whole Foods Alternative to ObamaCare," *Wall Street Journal,* August 12, 2009, p. A15.

Case 3.12

Ice-T, the Body Count *Album, and Shareholder Uprisings*

Ice-T (Tracy Morrow), a black rap artist signed under the Time Warner label, released an album called *Body Count* in 1992 that contained a controversial song, "Cop Killer." The lyrics included, "I've got my twelve-gauge sawed-off. . . . I'm 'bout to dust some cops off. . . . die, pig, die."

The song set off a storm of protest from law enforcement groups. At the annual meeting of Time Warner at the Beverly Wilshire Hotel, 1,100 shareholders, as well as police representatives and their spokesman, Charlton Heston, denounced Time Warner executives in a five-hour session on the album and its content. Heston noted that the compact disc had been shipped to radio stations in small replicas of body bags. One police officer said the company had "lost its moral compass, or never had it." Others said that Time Warner seemed to cultivate these types of artists. One shareholder claimed that Time Warner was always "pushing the envelope" with its artists, such as Madonna with her *Sex* book, and its products, such as the film *The Last Temptation of Christ,* which drew large protests from religious groups. Another shareholder pointed out that Gerald Levin, then–Time Warner president, promised a stuttering-awareness group that the cartoon character Porky Pig would be changed after they made far fewer vocal protests.

Levin responded that the album would not be pulled. He defended it as "depicting the despair and anger that hang in the air of every American inner city, not advocating attacks on police." Levin announced Time Warner would sponsor a TV forum for artists, law enforcement officials, and others to discuss such topics as racism and free speech. At the meeting, Levin also announced a four-for-one stock split and a 12 percent increase in Time Warner's dividend.

The protests continued after the meeting. Philadelphia's municipal pension fund decided to sell $1.6 million in Time Warner holdings to protest the Ice-T song. Said Louis J. Campione, a police officer and member of the city's Board of Pensions and Retirement, "It's fine that somebody would express their opinions, but we don't have to support it."

Several CEOs responded to Levin's and Time Warner's support of the song.[113] Roger Salquist, then-CEO of Calgene, Inc., who went on to be a controversial technology liaison at UC Davis, noted,

---

[113] *The Wall Street Journal.* Eastern ed. (Staff Produced Copy Only) by Wall Street Journal News Round Up. Copyright 1992 by Dow Jones & Co. Inc. Reproduced with permission of Dow Jones & Co. Inc. in the format textbook via Copyright Clearance Center.

I'm outraged. I think the concept of free speech has been perverted. It's anti-American, it's anti-humanity, and there is no excuse for it.

I hope it kills them. It's certainly not something I tolerate, and I find their behavior offensive as a corporation.

If you can increase sales with controversy without harming people, that's one thing. [But Time Warner's decision to support Ice-T] is outside the bounds of what I consider acceptable behavior and decency in this country.

David Geffen, chairman of Geffen Records (now a co-owner with Steven Spielberg and Jeffrey Katzenberg of DreamWorks, the film production company), who refused to release Geto Boys records because of lyrics, said,

The question is not about business, it is about responsibility. Should someone make money by advocating the murder of policemen? To say that this whole issue is not about profit is silly. It certainly is not about artistic freedom.

If the album were about language, sex, or drugs, there are people on both sides of these issues. But when it comes down to murder, I don't think there is any part of society that approves of it. . . . I wish [Time Warner] would show some sensitivity by donating the profits to a fund for wounded policemen.

Jerry Greenfield, cofounder of Ben & Jerry's Homemade, Inc., responded that "songs like 'Cop Killer' aren't constructive, but we as a society need to look at what we've created. I don't condone cop killing. [But] to reach a more just and equitable society everyone's voice must be heard."

Neal Fox, then-CEO of A. Sulka & Company (an apparel retailer owned by Luxco Investments), said,

As a businessperson, my inclination is to say that Time Warner management has to be consistent. Once you've decided to get behind this product and support it, you can't express feelings of censorship. They didn't have recourse.

Also, they are defending flag and country for the industry. If they bend to pressures regarding the material, it opens a Pandora's box for all creative work being done in the entertainment industry.

On a personal basis, I abhor the concept, but on a corporate basis, I understand their reasoning.

John W. Hatsopoulos, then–executive vice president of Thermo Electron Corporation (now president and CEO), had this to say:

I think the fact that a major U.S. corporation would almost encourage kids to attack the police force is horrible. Time Warner is a huge corporation. That they would encourage something like this for a few bucks. . . . You know about yelling fire in a crowded theater.

I was so upset I was looking at [Thermo Electron's] pension plan to see if we owned any Time Warner stock [in order to sell it]. But we don't own any.

Bud Konheim, longstanding CEO of Nicole Miller, Ltd., weighed in with the following:

I don't think that people in the media can say that advertising influences consumers to buy cars or shirts, and then argue that violence on television or in music has no

impact. The idea of media is to influence people's minds, and if you are inciting people to riot, it's very dangerous.

It's also disappointing that they chose to defend themselves. It was a knee-jerk reaction instead of seizing the role to assert moral leadership. They had a great opportunity. Unfortunately, I don't think they will pay for this decision because there is already so much dust in people's eyes.

George Sanborn, then-CEO of Sanborn, Inc., said, "Would you release the album if it said, 'Kill a Jew or bash a fag'? I think we all know what the answer would be. They're doing it to make money."

Marc B. Nathanson, CEO of Falcon Cable Systems Company, and a member of the board of directors for the Hollywood Bowl, responded, "If you aren't happy with the product, you don't have to buy it. I might not like what [someone like Ice-T] has to say, but I would vigorously defend his right to express his viewpoint."

Stoney M. Stubbs Jr. chairman of Frozen Food Express Industries, Inc., commented, "The more attention these types of things get, the better the products sell. I don't particularly approve of the way they play on people's emotions, but from a business standpoint [Time Warner is] probably going to make some money off it. They're protecting the people that make them the money. . . . the artists."[114]

Despite the flap over the album, sales were less than spectacular. It reached number 32 on the Billboard Top 200 album chart and sold 300,000 copies.[115]

Levin had defended Time Warner's position:

Time Warner is determined to be a global force for encouraging the confrontation of ideas. We know that profits are the source of our strength and independence, of our ability to produce and distribute the work of our artists and writers, but we won't retreat in the face of threats of boycotts or political grandstanding. In the short run, cutting and running would be the surest and safest way to put this controversy behind us and get on with our business. But in the long run, it would be a destructive precedent. It would be a signal to all the artists and journalists inside and outside Time Warner that if they wish to be heard, then they must tailor their minds and souls to fit the reigning orthodoxies.

In the weeks and months ahead, Time Warner intends to use the debate engendered by the uproar over this one song to create a forum in which we can bring together the different sides in this controversy. We will invest in fostering the open discussion of the violent tensions that Ice-T's music has exposed.

We're under no illusions. We know all the wounds can't be healed by such a process or all the bitterness—on both sides—talked out of existence. But we believe that the future of our country—indeed, of our world—is contained in the commitment to truth and free expression, in the refusal to run away.[116]

By August 1992, protests against the song had grown and sales suffered. Ice-T made the decision himself to withdraw "Cop Killer" from the *Body Count* album. Time Warner

---

[114]"Time Warner's Ice-T Defense Is Assailed," *The Wall Street Journal*, July 23, 1992, pp. B1, B8.

[115]Mark Landler, "Time Warner Seeks a Delicate Balance in Rap Music Furor," *The New York Times*, June 5, 1995, p. 1B.

[116]*The Wall Street Journal.* Eastern ed. (Staff Produced Copy Only) by Holman W. Jenkins, Jr. Copyright 1996 by Dow Jones & Co. Inc. Reproduced with permission of Dow Jones & Co. Inc. in the format textbook via Copyright Clearance Center.

asked music stores to exchange the *Body Count* CDs for ones without "Cop Killer." Some store owners refused, saying there were much worse records. Former Geto Boys member Willie D said Ice-T's free speech rights were violated. "We're living in a communist country and everyone's afraid to say it," he said.

Following the flap over the song, the Time Warner board met to establish general company policies to bar distribution of music deemed inappropriate. By February 1993, Time Warner and Ice-T agreed that Ice-T would leave the Time Warner label because of "creative differences." The split came after Time Warner executives objected to Ice-T's proposed cover for his new album, which showed black men attacking whites. In an ironic twist, Ice-T is now a co-star on the NBC television series *Law and Order: Special Victims Unit* as Detective Odafin "Fin" Tutuola, partner of Richard Belzer's character, Detective John Munch.[117]

In 2004, Ice-T introduced his own line of clothing, a trend among rap music stars. He had been on a six-year hiatus from music because of the death of two of his group members. The drummer, Beatmaster V, died of leukemia, and Mooseman, the bass player, was killed in South Central Los Angeles. Ice-T commented that Mooseman's death was the kind of thing "I rap about every day."[118] The album that followed *Body Count—Violent Demise, Last Days*—was barely heard and rarely sold. Living in New Jersey, the man credited with founding gangsta rap is preparing for a *Body Count II* album, and has offered the following perspective on the first *Body Count* album and where the country is at:

I wasn't trying to start all that drama with that [Body Count] album. On the song "Cop Killer" I was just being honest. I never really reached for controversy. I just said what was on my mind, like I'm saying now.[119]

Since Clinton was in the White House, everybody became very complacent, everybody kicked back. He had sex in the White House, what's there to worry about? But now we got Bush—or son of a Bush—in there, and he's out to control the world. He's trying to be Julius Caesar and so it's time for more music about things. It's time for Body Count.

Following the Ice-T issue, Time Warner's board undertook a strategy of steering the company into more family-oriented entertainment. It began its transition with the 1993 release of such movies as *Dennis the Menace, Free Willy,* and *The Secret Garden.*

However, Time Warner's reputation would continue to be a social and political lightning rod. In June 1995, presidential candidate Senator Robert Dole pointed to Time Warner's rap albums and movies as societal problems. Public outcry against Time Warner resulted.

In June 1995, C. DeLores Tucker, then 67 years old, and head of the National Political Congress of Black Women, handed Time Warner Chairman Michael J. Fuchs the following lyrics from a Time Warner label recording:

Her body's beautiful,
so I'm thinkin' rape.
Grabbed the bitch by her mouth,
slam her down on the couch.
She begged in a low voice:
"Please don't kill me."

[117]http://www.nbc.com/lawandorder. Accessed July 12, 2010.

[118]http://www.vh1.com/artists/news/1459713/01272003/ice_t.jhtml. Accessed October 21, 2004.

[119]http://www.vh1.com/artists/news/1459713/01272003/ice_t.jhtml (accessed October 21, 2004).

I slit her throat
and watch her shake like on TV.

—GETO BOYS, "MIND OF A LUNATIC"

and told Mr. Fuchs: "Read this out loud. I'll give you $100 to read it." Mr. Fuchs declined.

Mrs. Tucker was joined by William Bennett, a GOP activist and former secretary of education. Mrs. Tucker believes Time Warner is "pimping pornography to children for the almighty dollar. Corporations need to understand: What does it profit a corporation to gain the world but lose its soul? That's the real bottom line."

In June 1995, following Mrs. Tucker's national campaign, Time Warner fired Doug Morris, the chairman of domestic music operations. By July, Morris and Time Warner were in litigation. Morris had been a defender of gangsta rap music and had acquired the Interscope label that produced albums for the late Tupac Shakur and Snoop Doggy Dogg. Mr. Fuchs said the termination had nothing to do with the rap controversy.

Rap music grew in popularity for about 12 years, but from 2005 to 2006 dropped 21 percent in sales. In 2006, no rap album made it into the top ten albums for the year. Rap is back to its level of a decade ago, which is about 10 percent of total sales in the record industry. About 50 percent of Americans believe that rap/hip-hop is a negative influence in society. Some retail chains, including Walmart, have refused even during the upswing in popularity of rap/hip-hop to carry the gangsta rap albums, and some radio stations have declined to play the songs. The songs cited included the following:

I'd rather use my gun 'cause I get the money quicker. . . . got them in the frame—Bang! Bang! . . . blowing [expletive] to the moon.

—TUPAC SHAKUR, "STRUGGLIN"

These lyrics contain slang expressions for using an AK-47 machine gun to murder a police officer:

It's 1-8-7 on a [expletive] cop. . . . so what the [expletive] does a nigger like you gotta say? Got to take trip to the MIA and serve your ass with a [expletive] AK.

—SNOOP DOGGY DOGG, "THA' SHIZNIT"

Discussion Questions

1. Was Ice-T's song an exercise of artistic freedom or sensationalism for profit?
2. Would you have taken Levin's position?
3. Evaluate the First Amendment argument.
4. Would shareholder objections influence your response to such a controversy?
5. What was Time Warner's purpose in firing Morris? By November 1995, Time Warner's Levin fired Michael Fuchs. What message is there for executives in controversial products?
6. Offer your thoughts on Ice-T's new career and role as a police officer.
7. Rapper Lil Wayne used lyrics from the Rolling Stones' 1965 song, "Playing With Fire," in his "Playing With Fire" song that was part of his "The Carter III" CD. Abkco Music filed an infringement suit against Lil Wayne for using the lyrics after it had denied him permission. Abkco was going to grant permission to Lil until it read all of the song's lyrics, described as "explicit, sexist, and offensive." The suit was settled in an interesting manner. Abkco, under the terms of the settlement, has required Lil Wayne to remove the song from the CD and from iTunes. The Rolling Stones didn't want the money—they didn't want to be associated with Lil Wayne. Are the Rolling Stones controlling artistic expression? Is this the same right exercised by Time Warner but the other way?

For More Information

Ethan Smith, "Rapper to Pull Song in Copyright Fight," *Wall Street Journal*, January 30, 2009, p. B8.

Compare & Contrast

What are the values in conflict in this case? Why are some CEOs so opposed to Time Warner releasing the CD, and why do some see the controversy as an opportunity? How does Michael Novak's point about a company contributing to the moral ecology relate to this case study?

Case 3.13

Baseball and Steroids

On March 17, 2005, former and current major league baseball players and Commissioner Bud Selig testified before the U.S. House of Representatives Government Reform Committee, along with the parents of young baseball players who had taken their own lives after taking steroids. The House held hearings to determine whether government regulation of Major League Baseball's drug-testing policies to prevent and detect use in the sport is necessary.

The committee issued subpoenas for the hearing to seven current or former major league players: Jose Canseco, Jason Giambi, Mark McGwire, Rafael Palmeiro, Curt Schilling, Sammy Sosa, and Frank Thomas. Subpoenas were also issued to four baseball officials: Robert Manfred, executive vice president and labor counsel, Major League Baseball; Don Fehr, executive director and general counsel, Major League Baseball Players Association; Sandy Alderson, former general manager of the Oakland Athletics and current MLB executive vice president of baseball operations; and Kevin Towers, general manager of the San Diego Padres. Only Jose Canseco, Don Fehr, and Rob Manfred had already agreed to appear voluntarily, according to a release by the committee chair.[120]

Committee Chair Tom Davis made an opening statement that offered the background on the issues related to steroid use that had led to the congressional investigation and this hearing[121]:

Fourteen years ago, anabolic steroids were added to the Controlled Substance Act as a Schedule III drug, making it illegal to possess or sell them without a valid prescription. Today, however, evidence strongly suggests that steroid use among teenagers— especially aspiring athletes—is a large and growing problem. There is an absolute correlation between the culture of steroids in high schools and the culture of steroids in major league clubhouses. Kids get the message when it appears that it's okay for professional athletes to use steroids. If the pros do it, college athletes will, too. And if it's an edge in college, high school students will want the edge, too.

There is a pyramid of steroid use in society. And today, our investigation starts where it should: with the owners and players at the top of the pyramid.

Congress first investigated drugs and professional sports, including steroids over 30 years ago. I think perhaps the only two people in the room who will remember this are me and Commissioner Selig, because I believe he became an owner in 1970.

---

[120]http://www.commondreams.org/news2005/0309-22.htm. Accessed April 28, 2010.

[121]House Committee on Government Reform press release, March 9, 2005, "Government Reform Committee Statement on Issuance of Subpoena to Major League Baseball Executives and Players," CommonDreams.org News Center, http://www.commondreams.org/news2005/0309-22.htm. Accessed December 12, 2007.

In 1973, the year I first ran for Congress, the House Committee on Interstate and Foreign Commerce concluded a year-long investigation that found—and I quote—"drug use exists . . . in all sports and levels of competition. . . . In some instances, the degree of improper drug use—primarily amphetamines and anabolic steroids—can only be described as alarming."

The Committee's chairman—Harley Staggers—was concerned that making those findings public in a hearing would garner excessive attention and might actually encourage teenagers to use steroids. Instead, he quietly met with the commissioners of the major sports, and they assured him the problem would be taken care of.

Chairman Staggers urged Baseball Commissioner Bowie Kuhn to consider instituting tough penalties and testing. And he trusted Commissioner Kuhn to do that. In fact, in a press release in May 1973, Chairman Staggers said—and again I quote—"Based on the constructive responses and assurances I have received from these gentlemen, I think self-regulation will be intensified, and will be effective."

But as we now know from 30 years of history, baseball failed to regulate itself.

Let's fast forward to 1988. Jose Canseco was widely suspected of using steroids. Fans in opposing parks even chanted the phrase "steroids" when he came to bat. But according to Mr. Canseco, no one in major league baseball talked with him or asked him any questions about steroids. He was never asked to submit to a drug test. Instead, he was voted the American League's Most Valuable Player.

In 1991, Fay Vincent, then baseball's commissioner, finally took unilateral action and released a Commissioner's Policy that said "the possession, sale, or use of any illegal drug or controlled substance by Major League players and personnel is strictly prohibited. . . . This prohibition applies to all illegal drugs and controlled substances, including steroids." This policy didn't give Major League Baseball the right to demand that players take mandatory drug tests, but it was a step in the right direction and demonstrated the league's authority to act on its own to respond to allegations of steroid use.

In 1992, Bud Selig was appointed commissioner and replaced Mr. Vincent. One year later, in 1993, the Centers for Disease Control reported that 1 in 45 teenagers had used illegal steroids.

In 1995, the first of a series of detailed investigative reports about steroid use in baseball was published. The Los Angeles Times *quoted one major league general manager who said: "We all know there's steroid use, and it's definitely become more prevalent. . . . I think 10% to 20%." Another general manager estimated that steroid use was closer to 30%.*

In response to that story, Commissioner Selig said, "If baseball has a problem, I must say candidly that we were not aware of it. But should we concern ourselves as an industry? I don't know."

In 1996, Ken Caminiti, who was using steroids, won the Most Valuable Player Award. That same year, Pat Courtney, a major league spokesman, commented on steroids and said, "I don't think the concern is there that it's being used."

In 1997, the Denver Post *investigated the issue, reporting that as many as 20% of big league ballplayers used illegal steroids.*

In 1998, baseball hit the height of its post-baseball strike resurgence, as Sammy Sosa and Mark McGwire both shattered Roger Maris's home run record.

In 1999, the Centers for Disease Control reported that 1 in 27 teenagers had used illegal steroids.

In July 2000, a Boston Red Sox infielder had steroids seized from his car. Three months later, the New York Times published a front-page story on the rampant use of steroids by professional baseball players. And here's what a major league spokesman said the very same year: "steroids have never been much of an issue."

In June 2002, Sports Illustrated *put steroids on its cover and reported that baseball "had become a pharmacological trade show." One major league player estimated that 40% to 50% of major league players used steroids.*

After that Sports Illustrated *article, Major League Baseball and the players' union finally agreed to a steroid testing regimen. Independent experts strongly criticized the program as weak and limited in scope. But in 2003, when the first results were disclosed, Rob Manfred, baseball's Vice President for labor relations, said, "A positive rate of 5% is hardly a sign that you have rampant use of anything."*

The same year, the Centers for Disease Control reported that 1 in 16 high school students had used illegal steroids.

The allegations and revelations about steroid use in baseball have only intensified in recent months. We have learned that Jason Giambi, a former most valuable player, Gary Sheffield, and Barry Bonds, who has won the most valuable player award seven times, testified before a federal grand jury in San Francisco about their steroid use.

The Centers for Disease Control and Prevention tells us that more than 500,000 high school students have tried steroids, nearly triple the number just ten years ago. A second national survey, conducted in 2004 by the National Institute on Drug Abuse and the University of Michigan, found that over 40 percent of 12th graders described steroids as "fairly easy" or "very easy" to get, and the perception among high school students that steroids are harmful has dropped from 71 percent in 1992 to 56% in 2004.

This is but a snapshot of the startling data we face. Today we take the committee's first steps toward understanding how we got here, and how we begin turning those numbers around. Down the road, we need to look at whether and how Congress should exercise its legislative powers to further restrict the use and distribution of these substances.

Our specific purpose today is to consider MLB's recently negotiated drug policy; how the testing policy will be implemented; how it will effectively address the use of prohibited drugs by players; and, most importantly, the larger societal and public health ramifications of steroid use.

Yesterday, USA Today *reported that 79% of players surveyed believe steroids played a role in record-breaking performances by some high-profile players. While our focus is not on the impact of steroids on MLB records, the survey does underscore the importance of our inquiry.*

A majority of players think steroids are influencing individual achievements—that's exactly our point. We need to recognize the dangerous vicious cycle that perception creates.

Too many college athletes believe they have to consider steroids if they're going to make it to the pros; high school athletes, in turn, think steroids might be the key to getting a scholarship. It's time to break that cycle, and it needs to happen from the top down.

When I go to Little League opening games these days, kids aren't just talking about their favorite teams' chances in the pennant race; they're talking about which pro players are on the juice.

After the 1994 MLB players strike, rumors and allegations of steroid use in the league began to surface. Since then, long standing records were broken. Along with these broken records came allegations of steroid use among MLB's star players. Despite the circulating rumors of illegal drug use, MLB and the Players Association did not respond with a collective bargaining agreement to ban the use of steroids until 2002. The result was an almost decade long question mark as to, not only the validity of the new MLB records, but also the credibility of the game itself.

In February of this year, former MLB All-Star Jose Canseco released a book that not only alleges steroid use by well known MLB players, but also discusses the prevalence of steroids in baseball during his 17-year career. After hearing Commissioner Bud Selig's public statements that MLB would not launch an investigation into Mr. Canseco's allegations, my Ranking Member Henry Waxman wrote me asking for a Committee hearing to, quote, "find out what really happened and to get to the bottom of this growing scandal." End quote. Furthermore, today's hearing will not be the end of our inquiry. Far from it. Nor will Major League Baseball be our sole or even primary focus. We're in the first inning of what could be an extra inning ballgame.

This is the beginning, not the end. We believe this hearing will give us good information about the prevalence of steroids in professional baseball, shine light on the sometimes tragic results of steroid use by high school and college athletes, and provide leads as to where to take our investigation next.

Leads from Senator Bunning about how to restore integrity to the game.

Leads from medical experts about how to better educate all Americans about the very real dangers of steroid use.

Leads from parents whose stories today will poignantly illustrate that, like it or not, professional athletes are role models, and their actions can lead to tragic imitation.

We are grateful to the players who have joined us today to share their perspectives on the role and prevalence of performance enhancing drugs in baseball. Some have been vocal about the need for baseball to address its steroid problem; I applaud them for accepting this calling.

Others have an opportunity today to either clear their name or take public responsibility for their actions, and perhaps offer cautionary tales to our youth. In total, we think the six current and former players offer a broad perspective on the issue of steroids and baseball, and we're looking forward to hearing from all of them.

Finally, we are fortunate to have with us a final panel of witnesses representing MLB, the Players' Association, and front office management. This panel is, quite frankly, where the rubber will meet the road. If the players are cogs, this is the machine. If the players have been silent, these are the enforcers and promoters of the code.

Ultimately, it is MLB, the union, and team executives that will determine the strength of the game's testing policy. Ultimately, it is MLB and the union that will or will not determine accountability and punishment. Ultimately, it is MLB and the union that can remove the cloud over baseball, and maybe save some lives in the process.

Oh, somewhere in this favored land the sun is shining bright;

The band is playing somewhere, and somewhere hearts are light;

And somewhere men are laughing, and somewhere children shout;

But there is no joy in Mudville—until the truth comes out.[122]

Following are excerpts from the players' and former players' testimony:

Jose Canseco, whose book, *Juiced*, alleges that he, Sammy Sosa, and Mark McGwire, all used steroids:

The book that I wrote was meant to convey one message. The preface makes my position very clear. I do not condone or encourage the use of any particular drugs, medicine, or illegal substances in any aspect of life. I did not write my book to single out any one individual or player. I am saddened that the media and others have chosen to focus on the names in the book and not on the real culprit behind the issue.

Because of my truthful revelations I have had to endure attacks on my credibility. I have had to relive parts of my life that I thought had been long since buried and gone. All of these attacks have been spurred on by an organization that holds itself above the law. An organization that chose to exploit its players for the increased revenue that lines its pockets and then sacrifice those same players to protect the web of secrecy that was hidden for so many years. The time has come to end this secrecy and to confront those who refuse to acknowledge their role in encouraging the behavior we are gathered to discuss.

The pressure associated with winning games, pleasing fans, and getting the big contract, led me, and others, to engage in behavior that would produce immediate results.

Why did I take steroids? The answer is simple. Because, myself and others had no choice if we wanted to continue playing. Because MLB did nothing to take it out of the sport.

Baseball owners and the players union have been very much aware of the undeniable that as a nation we will do anything to win. They turned a blind eye to the clear evidence of steroid use in baseball. Why? Because it sold tickets and resurrected a game that had recently suffered a black eye from a player strike.

In answer to a question, Mr. Canseco said,

It was as acceptable in the late '80s and the mid-'90s as a cup of coffee.[123]

Mark McGwire, now retired, and a record holder:

Asking me, or any other player, to answer questions about who took steroids in front of television cameras, will not solve this problem. If a player answers "no," he simply will not be believed. If he answers "yes," he risks public scorn and endless government investigations. My lawyers have advised me that I cannot answer these

---

[122]http://reform.house.gov/GovReform/Hearings/EventSingle.aspx?EventID=1637. Accessed April 28, 2010.

[123]http://reform.house.gov/GovReform/Hearings/EventSingle.aspx?EventID=1637. Accessed April 28, 2010.

questions without jeopardizing my friends, my family or myself. I intend to follow their advice.[124]

Curt Schilling, a Boston Red Sox player, also made a statement that included the following:

First, I hope the Committee recognizes the danger of possibly glorifying the so-called author scheduled to testify today or by indirectly assisting him to sell more books through his claims that what he is doing is somehow good for this country or the game of baseball. A book which devotes hundreds of pages to glorifying steroid usage and which contends that steroid usage is justified and will be the norm in this country in several years is a disgrace, was written irresponsibly and sends exactly the opposite message that needs to be sent to kids. The allegations made in that book, the attempts to smear the names of players, both past and present, having been made by one who for years vehemently denied steroid use should be seen for what they are, an attempt to make money at the expense of others. I hope we come out of this proceeding aware of what we are dealing with when we talk about that so-called author and that we not create a buzz that results in young athletes buying the book and being misled on the issues and dangers of steroids.[125]

Rafael Palmeiro, a Baltimore Oriole at the time of the hearing, and former Texas Ranger, testified, "I have never used steroids. Period. I don't know how to say it any more clearly than that. Never. The reference to me in Mr. Canseco's book is absolutely false." By August 2005, Mr. Palmeiro would be the first big-name player to be suspended under the tougher policies that Commissioner Selig described at the congressional hearings. By the time of the Palmeiro suspension, there had been six other players suspended for testing positive. Mr. Palmeiro was suspended for 10 days following a drug test that was positive for the presence of steroids.[126] Several people associated with MLB said that the league was aware of the positive test about one month before the suspension was announced but allowed Mr. Palmeiro to hit, as it were, the milestone of 3,000 hits before suspending him. MLB took out a full-page ad in major newspapers to congratulate Mr. Palmeiro on his achievement, only one of four players in the history of the game to reach 3,000 hits and 500 home runs. He was then suspended. Congress also investigated Mr. Palmeiro for perjury but concluded it could bring no charges because there was too much time elapsed from when he testified and when he tested positive for steroids. There was no way to establish that he had used steroids prior to the hearing.

The regulatory process was stalled, but the Justice Department and local prosecutors continued their pursuit of the players. The battle over the use of the drug-testing results began when the Major League Baseball Players' Association—the union representing athletes who play for Major League Baseball filed a motion to quash the subpoenas that had been issued to the labs. The federal government then obtained warrants and conducted the searches at several labs. The documents the government obtained in those searches included a twenty-five-page master list of all MLB players tested during the 2003 season and a thirty-four-page list of positive drug testing results for thirty-four players.

However, federal district courts dealt the prosecution efforts a blow when federal judges ordered the government to return evidence agents had seized from private labs, including the names of drug tests results of over 100 Major League Baseball players. The evidence, and the names included, had been seized as part of an investigation into

---

[124]http://reform.house.gov/GovReform/Hearings/EventSingle.aspx?EventID=1637 Click on Mark McGwire. Accessed April 28, 2010.

[125]http://reform.house.gov/GovReform/Hearings/EventSingle.aspx?EventID=1637. Accessed April 28, 2010.

[126]Bill Pennington, "Baseball Bans Longtime Star for Steroid Use," *New York Times*, August 2, 2005, p. A1.

possible perjury charges against some of the players. The federal prosecutors appealed to the Ninth Circuit Court of Appeals and in a 2-1 decision the federal appellate court ruled that the federal government's raid of testing labs in California and Nevada that yielded positive test results was a constitutional search and seizure and that the information could be used for prosecution of the players. San Francisco player Barry Bonds was indicted in November 2007 on federal charges of perjury before a grand jury as a result of this investigation that included evidence seized from Balco, Bay Area Lab Cooperative, one of the alleged suppliers of steroids to the baseball players.

As the government's case proceeded, MLB hired former Senator George Mitchell in March 2006 to conduct an investigation into the steroid issue in baseball as well as determine whether the MLB's policies were working. However, there was resistance to the choice because Mr. Mitchell serves on the board of directors for the Boston Red Sox. Undaunted, former Senator Mitchell began an investigation that hit a roadblock when players refused to talk with him. Faced with litigation, Jason Giambi of the New York Yankees agreed to cooperate with Mitchell.[127] Mitchell pursued Giambi because he testified before a grand jury in 2003 that he had used steroids and in an interview with *USA Today* said, "What we should have done a long time ago was stand up, players, ownership, everybody, and say, 'We made a mistake.'"[128]

Congress has continued its involvement and oversight with Rep. Henry Waxman of California, the chair of the committee that conducted the 2005 hearings, who said, "Federal legislation may be needed to restore confidence in the integrity of the game."[129]

In 2006, two reporters published *Game of Shadows,* a book in which steroid use by Barry Bonds and other players was not only obvious but had been testified about at the grand jury. Commentators have noted that Mark Fainaru-Wada and Lance Williams did the research and asked the tough questions that MLB should have, and the result was a damning book that has resulted in Bonds being booed by baseball fans in every stadium he enters. Tommy Lasorda said that if there were any celebrations for Bonds upon breaking the record, he would not join in, "For me, records were meant to be broken, but you don't do it by cheating. When you're stealing signs, that's all part of the game. But when you cheat to that degree, it's not good at all."[130]

On December 13, 2007, former Senator George Mitchell released his report on steroid use in major league baseball to Commissioner Bud Selig. The full report and the executive summary can be found at mlb.com.

Mr. McGwire, Alex Rodriguez, and others have confessed to steroid use. Roger Clemens was indicted in 2010 for lying to Congress under oath about his steroid use. Mr. Bonds and Mr. Rodriguez both passed the 600 mark on home runs.

Discussion Questions

1. What is the responsibility of MLB with regard to the steroid issue? Be sure to apply some of the ethical analysis models you have studied. Couldn't MLB argue that it is not an enforcement agent, and it has no way of determining whether every player is using steroids at any given time? Does this argument excuse any responsibility on the part of MLB?

2. Do you see any rationalizations for the steroid use or the lack of an effective policy on its use in MLB?

---

[127]Bob Nightengale, "Giambi Set to Cooperate with Mitchell," *USA Today,* June 22, 2007, p. 1C.

[128]*Id.*

[129]Howard Fendrich, "Congress: Not Enough Evidence Against Palmeiro for Perjury Charges," *AP wire report,* November 10, 2005.

[130]Bob Nightengale, "Lasorda to Pass on Any Festivities for Bonds," *USA Today,* May 12, 2006, p. 1C.

3. What is the responsibility of MLB and the players to the young people who are using steroids?

4. Discuss the Canseco allegations that MLB just wanted revenue and turned a blind eye to steroid use. Apply the various social responsibility theories to this point and discuss the flaws in this competitive model. How does its conduct with Mr. Palmeiro affect your discussion of this question?

5. Commissioner Selig offered the following in his testimony, "I should also say a word about our players. For some time now the majority of our great and talented athletes have deeply —and rightly—resented two things. They have resented being put at a competitive disadvantage by their refusal to jeopardize their health and the integrity of the game by using illegal and dangerous substances. And they have deeply—and rightly—resented the fact that they live under a cloud of suspicion that taints their achievements on the field." Using his statement, explain how unethical behavior hurts those who comply with the rules. Apply these same principles to academic dishonesty.

6. When he was inducted into Baseball's Hall of Fame in 2005, Ryne Sandberg said, "I didn't play the game right because I saw a reward at the end of the tunnel. I played the game right because that's what you're supposed to do."[131]

   Mark McGwire was eligible for the Hall of Fame in 2007. Barry Bonds broke Hank Aaron's home-run record in 2007, but did so before he was indicted for perjury. The debate over their induction into the Hall of Fame continues. *Sports Illustrated* has noted that Barry Bonds could end up "in baseball purgatory with Pete Rose."[132] What lessons about ethics do the McGwire and Bonds outcomes and controversy provide?

7. As of 2010, the criminal investigations were still pending as federal courts grappled with the issue of whether to admit laboratory records as evidence in the criminal prosecutions of baseball players. Mr. Clemens filed suit against Brian McNamee, his former trainer, for defamation because his trainer testified that Mr. Clemens had used steroids. The suit, however, was dismissed because of Mr. McNamee's privilege for testifying under oath as well as the publication of a body of evidence in the book *American Icon: The Fall of Roger Clemens and the Rise of Steroids in America's Pastime*, which included the following quote:

   > Clemens was determined to prove he wasn't fading, and McNamee, having just arrived at the Show, was committed to staying there. So there would be other injections, but with the first one the two men crossed a stark line into territory they would never escape. Clemens became a cheater, and McNamee became his enabler.[133]

   Are there any lessons about a credo here? What is the role of pressure in our ethical analysis?

Case 3.14

Michael Vick, Dogs, Rush Limbaugh, and the NFL

The NFL has been under increasing public criticism because of its failure to take definitive action when its players are involved in criminal conduct. For example, former Atlanta Falcons quarterback Michael Vick signed a contract with the Philadelphia Eagles after being released from federal prison, having served an 18-month sentence for pleading guilty to dog-fighting and conspiracy charges. The contract with the Eagles is a two-year contract, with $1.6 million for the first year and an option on the second year for $5.2 million.

The NFL, however, retained some control over the contract. Mr. Vick was at first permitted only to practice with the team and not permitted to play until the third preseason game. Also, both Mr. Vick's NFL play approval and his contract with the Eagles have a so-called morals clause. That is, if Mr. Vick violates any of the terms of his probation,

---

[131]"Sandberg, Boggs Relish Hall of Fame Induction Day," *USA Today*, August 1, 2005, p. 1C.

[132]Tom Verducci, "The Consequences," *Sports Illustrated*, March 13, 2006, p. 53.

[133]Teri Thompson, Nathaniel Vinton, Michael O'Keeffe, and Christian Red (2009).

which would include any arrests or charges, he would be suspended again and he would also be in breach of contract. This morals clause is more stringent and well defined than those in other contracts because of the ongoing probation supervision. Violations of his probation could include possession of a weapon, the failure to meet his probation officer as required, the failure to meet the terms of community service requirements, and travel outside the country without prior approval.

On his 30th birthday celebration in April 2010 in Virginia Beach, Mr. Vick was keeping company with one of the co-defendants from his federal dog-fighting case and the celebration somehow reached a point of exchanging gunfire. Mr. Vick's role remains unclear but, as *Sports Illustrated* noted, the video and Vick's side of the tale of birthday-parties-gone-bad do not match.[134] An ex-con on probation with the Feds and the NFL in a gun-themed party in a bar with a former co-defendant does not seem to live up to the morals clause. The NFL and the Eagles issued tepid statements about Mr. Vick's future, but he has played in the 2010 preseason games as well as the Eagles' opener. Mr. Vick has been attending church and has also performed his community service requirements.

Discussion Questions

1. What would happen if the Eagles allowed Mr. Vick to continue with his contract if the Feds find that there has been a probation violation by his birthday celebration?
2. Are there social responsibility issues in allowing Mr. Vick to play once again because of the nature of the underlying charges, i.e., dog fighting? What if he is permitted to continue after the birthday party?
3. As the Michael Vick issues with his conviction and prison term were being debated, radio talk host Rush Limbaugh was asked to withdraw from his involvement in a financial group that was in the process of buying the Los Angeles Rams. Both the player's union and other team owners objected to Mr. Limbaugh as an NFL owner because of the views he expresses during his nationally syndicated radio program. Discuss the Ice-T case in relation to this boycott of Mr. Limbaugh. Do the same censorship arguments apply here? Why or why not?

For More Information

Nate Davis, "Vick Finds Taker, Signs with Eagles," *USA Today*, August 14, 2009, p. 1C.

Case 3.15

Dayton-Hudson's Contributions to Planned Parenthood, and Target and the Bell Ringers

Dayton-Hudson Corporation is a multistate department store chain. In 1990, its charitable foundation gave $18,000 to Planned Parenthood and other contributions to the Children's Home Society, the Association for the Advancement of Young Women, and the Young Women's Christian Association. It had contributed to Planned Parenthood for twenty-two years.

Pro-life groups have vocally criticized corporate foundations that support Planned Parenthood and have persuaded JCPenney Company and American Telephone and Telegraph (AT&T) to stop their contributions to the organization. After Pioneer Hi-Bred International's foundation gave $25,000 to Planned Parenthood of Greater Iowa for rural clinics that did not perform abortions, Midwestern farmers began circulating a flyer headlined, "Is Pioneer Hi-Bred Pro-Abortion?" CEO Thomas Urban canceled the

---

[134]Damon Huck, "The Final Act," *Sports Illustrated*, July 12, 2010, p. 16.

donation, saying, "We were blackmailed, but you can't put the core business at risk."[135] When pro-life groups raised their objections with the Dayton-Hudson foundation, the foundation's board decided to halt its contributions to Planned Parenthood.

Pro-choice supporters responded strongly by boycotting Dayton-Hudson stores, writing letters to newspaper editors, and closing charge accounts. Pickets appeared outside Dayton-Hudson stores, and picketers cut up their charge cards for media cameras.

A trustee for the New York City Employees Retirement System, which owned 438,290 Dayton shares, commented, "By antagonizing consumers, they've threatened the value of our investment."[136]

Dayton-Hudson decided to resume its funding of Planned Parenthood, even though pro-life groups announced plans to boycott the company's stores.[137] The Dayton-Hudson experience was a foreshadowing of the rock-and-a-hard-place dilemmas retailers face on emotionally charged issues. Target, the nation's second largest discount retailer after WalMart, made a decision in December 2004 to ban the red pots and bell ringers of the Salvation Army from outside its stores. In years past, the discount stores had made an exception to its "no solicitation" policy by allowing the Salvation Army a presence there. Central management for the store indicated that it had so many requests that it could no longer handle them all and that its formal policy would now be an absolute prohibition, including against those seeking petition signatures.

The impact to the Salvation Army was a loss of about 10 percent of its bell-ringer donations. Each year the Salvation Army raises $90 million through the Christmas program, and Target's 1,200 stores were responsible for $9 million of that amount. WalMart announced at the time of the Target announcement that it would continue to allow the bell ringers outside its stores.

Fueled by talk-radio backlash and pundit outreach, Target was inundated with complaints from customers and was the target, as it were, of several groups' efforts to have customers refuse to spend their Christmas dollars at the Target stores. The backlash was so strong that on Sunday, January 9, 2005, Target had a full-color three-page foldout (front and back print) insert in major newspapers around the country. The foldout emphasized Target's commitment to the community and philanthropy, and described the types of efforts in which it is involved and to which it donates its funds. Target donates $2 million per week to various charities and has a volunteer program for its employees that results in hundreds of thousands of hours of community service by Target employees.

Discussion Questions

1. Is there any way for a corporation to meet all demands in formulating policies on philanthropic giving?

2. Should contributions be considered simply an extension of marketing and made accordingly?

Compare & Contrast

1. Is giving in to objections to certain donations by special interest groups ethical? Is this an issue of social responsibility? Does Target's policy seem reasonable? Why was there the backlash? Did Wal Mart capitalize on the Target decision? Did the decision cost Target customers? Did it gain

---

[135]Richard Gibson, "Boycott Drive against Pioneer Hi-Bred Shows Perils of Corporate Philanthropy," *The Wall Street Journal*, June 10, 1992, p. B1.

[136]Kevin Kelly, "Dayton-Hudson Finds There's No Graceful Way to Flip-Flop," *Business Week*, September 24, 1990, p. 50.

[137]Fern Portnoy, "Corporate Giving Creates Tough Decisions, Fragile Balances," *Denver Business Journal*, November 15, 1991, p. 15.

customers? What makes companies take such different postures? Is it the action of their managers/executives? Are there customer demographic differences?

2. Currently, companies that have indicated an interest in conducting, or taken steps to conduct, embryonic stem-cell research have had shareholder proposals objecting to such projects or requesting that the company adopt a policy in advance of shunning such research. The proposals, such as one for the Merck 2004 annual meeting, are often submitted by religious groups that own shares in the company. Do these companies face a different dilemma from that of Dayton-Hudson? What makes companies take such different postures? Is it the action of their managers/executives? Are there customer demographic differences?

3. Some pharmacists have refused to fill prescriptions for RU-486 (the morning-after pill) because of their religious and moral convictions. Some pharmacies have refused to stock RU-486 because of the moral convictions of their staff. How do these companies resolve their postures on right to life, abortion, and choice? What makes some companies shun RU-486 while others agree to sell it? Why do some companies terminate pharmacists who refuse to dispense RU-486, and why do other companies accommodate those pharmacists?

Social Responsibility and Sustainability

Reading 3.16
The New Environmentalism[138]

Richard MacLean[139] and Marianne M. Jennings

Boston Harbor doesn't smell. Annual Earth Day celebrations seem hushed in comparison to the first in 1970. Love Canal is but a reference in Oliver Stone films. Could we have achieved a different kind of silent spring? If all is quiet on the environmental front, why did Generation Xers dressed as sea turtles link with labor unions and the eco-friendly from 42 nations to protest the WTO meeting in Seattle? That odd combination of Birkenstocks and Teamsters should give any CEO pause, but the sheer weirdness and senseless property damage make Seattle easy to dismiss. It is a mistake to do so. Environmental issues are afoot in the same quiet fashion as Rachel Carson's first efforts.

The environmental movement of 30 years ago got its legs because the public was galvanized into action when pollution was in their backyards. Today's environmental issues are not conspicuous. Greenpeace learns there is PVC in Barbie and its pressure on Mattel, Inc., turns her into vegetable-based plastic. While issues, like the fish population of the North Atlantic, may not be visible or even of concern to many, the activists have widened their sights and now have honed skills. The nature of international trade and the wonder of Internet communication for organizing movements makes the stakes on emerging environmental issues higher than they were when landfills and effluents were the causes du jour.

Today's environmental issues, such as genetically-altered food, over-fishing, economic equity, and population control, can pack an emotional punch. Former President Clinton, the master at throwing the feel-good left hook, played the environment big in the State of the Union address and at the post-WTO conference during his administration. President Obama has emphasized his so-called "Cap and Trade" program that would phase out carbon fuels. Most companies are not prepared to respond because their environmental efforts are outmoded. They remain myopically focused on regulatory compliance and fail to take this generation's environmental focus seriously. Further, environmental professionals have witnessed a decade of cutbacks and consolidations in their ranks after two decades of staff growth. Today's environmental managers face a tough job market, mounting family obligations, and a retirement looming on the horizon—if only they can make it. They concentrate on working the internal and external bureaucracies.

A "green arthritis" has infected the business world. Environmental managers who once put forward a "Save the Planet" mantra that comforted the general public, now use "Don't rock the boat" as a motto. These once creative leaders nowadays put a positive spin on company performance in an annual report on recycled paper and assure

---

[138]From "Green Arthritis: The Stagnation of Environmental Strategy," white paper. Reprinted with the permission of the authors.

[139]Richard MacLean is the owner of Competitive Environment, Inc., and a former corporate environmental manager with General Electric and Arizona Public Service.

their management that all necessary systems are in place and regulatory compliance is improving.

But beneath, there is a powerful undertow that requires the same aggressive management these specialists brought to the *Silent Spring* backlash. Fortunately, there is a cure for green arthritis.

CEOs, not the environmental staff, should lead the way in this new environmental frontier, recognizing that threats may actually be opportunities. CEOs can be lulled into a sense of false security on environmental issues. In fact, what may be under control are only the procedural, regulatory compliance, and public relations aspects of environmental matters, not the strategic ones. Reliance on environmental management systems such as ISO 14000 or traditional compliance audits rarely reveals anything new.

ISO 14000 illustrates both the best and worst of environmental management. At its best, the ISO standard is a step-by-step guide to environmental management. At its worse, it substitutes a bureaucratic, one-size-fits-all process for strategic thinking. The questions raised by executive management must go beyond "Did we get our facilities ISO registered?" to assurances that these processes provide the degree of environmental assurance stakeholders expect.

Additionally, companies have signed on to a number of voluntary government, industry, and NGO initiatives to improve their images as environmentally responsible. Are they true responses? Do they just buy time? Will they survive close scrutiny?

Companies would never dream of substituting a process devised by a standard-setting organization for their unique strategic-planning or market-forecasting methodology. Yet, their environmental vision consists of handing over their destiny to a bureaucratic stamp of approval. The challenge is to make these processes robust in order to address the protests while serving shareholders.

Such enlightened self-interest often requires unconventional voluntary actions to thwart costly controls and public relations disasters. DuPont faced one of the first global environmental issues and voluntarily phased out CFCs. It could have continued the fight in the courts. Instead, DuPont made a brilliant strategic choice that was also environmentally friendly—it moved into fluorochemicals, a market as rewarding as CFCs, but safer and all without the protests.

To assess emerging issues, companies must heed warning signs. Seattle was not just about turtles but supply chain issues and public opinion on moral limits to international trade. Did your staff place the issues raised there into a context that applies to your business? If they did not, your company experiences one of the symptoms of green arthritis—the information is not flowing. "Under control" is not an adequate response. These environmental issues must be managed, not handled with so-called green wash that costs companies credibility. For example, initial studies on EMFs indicating an association between overhead electrical wires and childhood leukemia presented an environmentalist's and trial lawyer's dream, complete with the Paul Brodeur series in the *New Yorker* on electric utilities killing small children. The electric utility industry could have handled the issue or managed the issue. Handling the issue means questioning the studies, sneering a bit, and doing the usual lobbying for liability exemptions. Managing the issue is sponsoring highly credible, peer-reviewed studies, educating the public about the issue, and placing overhead lines prudently while the data [are] being collected. The result of the management path has been the death of EMF fear and litigation. Had utilities handled this issue as Dow Corning handled silicone, a case in which a company was a victim of junk science, the industry would be in the process of settling class action lawsuits today.

There is also need for an overall strategy of managing information about the environment that goes far beyond the typical public relations responses. Gen Xers, out in full force in Seattle, bring their issues, those of the new environmental movement, straight from their schools. Michael Sanera's *Facts Not Fear* analyzed K-12 texts and found children learning well beyond global warming. They are taught the evils of capitalism and given unequivocal information that the world is overpopulated, that fossil fuel use is an imperialistic U.S. problem, and that any pesticide is a human killer. Teachers have students involved in letter-writing campaigns to CEOs on everything from animal testing to genetic engineering. Part of a comprehensive environmental strategy requires understanding this influential grass roots environmental educational movement.

Environmental issues remain a very powerful wild card. Vegetarian Barbie is but one small sign of what lies ahead, and the arthritically green will not be ready. The battles have become very political and very fierce.

In September 2005, the IRS began an audit of Greenpeace, an environmental group known for its passionate opposition to businesses it believes harm the environment. It has been known to steer its boats in the paths of oil tankers and whaling boats. The IRS audit was focused on whether Greenpeace was entitled to its charitable organization tax exemption or whether it had crossed the line into political activity.

The Public Interest Watch (PIW), a group that is self-described as a nonprofit watchdog group, sent a letter to the IRS requesting the IRS audit of Greenpeace and offering that the environmental group might be involved in money laundering and other illegal activity.

In its public filings, PIW disclosed that $120,000 of the $124,094 in donations that the group received from August 2003 to July 2004 were from Exxon-Mobil. Greenpeace has called Exxon-Mobil the "No. 1 climate criminal."[140] Greenpeace activists have chained themselves to fences at Exxon-Mobil headquarters and last year spilled red wine on all the tablecloths at a dinner at which the Exxon-Mobil CEO, Lee Raymond, was a guest of honor.

The Greenpeace IRS audit uncovered the illegal activity (chaining to the fence is trespassing) and found nine "deficiencies" in its audit, but did not revoke its tax-exempt status. Greenpeace received $24 million in tax-exempt donations in 2005. PIW has sent letters to the IRS on other nonprofit organizations as well.

PIW is tax-exempt, but donations to it are not tax deductible. It is run by a former lobbyist.

Discussion Questions

1. Who should be responsible for environmental issues and programs in a company, and why?
2. What is the difference between the environmental issues of thirty years ago and today's issues?
3. Explain the examples of proactive behavior given and why there was business benefit in those decisions and actions.
4. Evaluate the actions of Greenpeace and PIW. Can you assume that those dedicated to environmental causes will always be forthright? Is the use of the audit tool ethical?

Case 3.17

Herman Miller and Its Rain Forest Chairs

In March 1990, Bill Foley, research manager for Herman Miller, Inc., began a routine evaluation of new woods to use in the firm's signature piece—the $2,277 Eames chair. The Eames chair is a distinctive office chair with a rosewood exterior finish and a leather seat and was sold in the Sharper Image's stores and catalog.

---

[140]Steve Stecklow, "Did a Group Financed by Exxon Prompt IRS to Audit Greenpeace?" *Wall Street Journal*, March 21, 2006, pp. A1, A10.

At that time, the chair was made of two species of trees: rosewood and Honduran mahogany. Foley realized that Miller's use of the tropical hardwoods was helping destroy rain forests. Foley banned the use of the woods in the chairs once existing supplies were exhausted. The Eames chair would no longer have its traditional rosewood finish.

Foley's decision prompted former CEO Richard H. Ruch to react: "That's going to kill that [chair]."[141] Effects on sales could not be quantified.

Herman Miller, based in Zeeland, Michigan, and founded in 1923 by D. J. DePree, a devout Baptist, manufactures office furniture and partitions. The corporation follows a participatory-management tradition and takes environmentally friendly actions. The vice president of the Michigan Audubon Society noted that Miller has cut the trash it hauls to landfills by 90 percent since 1982: "Herman Miller has been doing a super job."[142]

Herman Miller built an $11 million waste-to-energy heating and cooling plant. The plant saves $750,000 per year in fuel and landfill costs. In 1991, the company found a buyer for the 800,000 pounds of scrap fabric it had been dumping in landfills. A North Carolina firm shreds it for insulation for automobile roof linings and dashboards. Selling the scrap fabric saves Miller $50,000 per year in dumping fees.

Herman Miller employees once used 800,000 styrofoam cups a year. But in 1991, the company passed out 5,000 mugs to its employees and banished styrofoam. The mugs carry the following admonition: "On spaceship earth there are no passengers . . . only crew." Styrofoam in packaging was also reduced 70 percent for a cost savings of $1.4 million.

Herman Miller also spent $800,000 for two incinerators that burn 98 percent of the toxic solvents that escape from booths where wood is stained and varnished. These furnaces exceeded the 1990 Clean Air Act requirements. It was likely that the incinerators would be obsolete within three years, when nontoxic products became available for staining and finishing wood, but having the furnaces was "ethically correct," former CEO Ruch said in response to questions from the board of directors.[143]

Herman Miller keeps pursuing environmentally safe processes, including finding a use for its sawdust by-product. However, for the fiscal year ended May 31, 1991, its net profit had fallen 70 percent from 1990 to $14 million on total sales of $878 million.

In 1992, Herman Miller's board hired J. Kermit Campbell as CEO. Mr. Campbell continued in the Ruch tradition and wrote essays for employees on risk taking and for managers on "staying out of the way." From 1992 to 1995, sales growth at Herman Miller was explosive, but as one analyst described it, "expenses exploded." Despite sales growth during this time, profits dropped 89 percent to a mere $4.3 million.

Miller's board, concerned about Campbell's lack of expedience, announced Campbell's resignation and began an aggressive program of downsizing. Between May and July 1995, 130 jobs were eliminated. Also in 1995, sales dropped from $879 to $804 million. The board promoted Michael Volkema, then thirty-nine and head of Miller's file cabinet division, to CEO.[144]

Volkema refocused Herman Miller's name with a line of well-made, lower-priced office furniture using a strategy and division called SQA (Simple, Quick, and Affordable). The dealers for SQA work with customers to configure office furniture plans, and Miller ships all the pieces ordered in less than two weeks.

---

[141]David Woodruff, "Herman Miller: How Green Is My Factory?" *Business Week*, September 16, 1991, pp. 54–55.

[142]*Id.*

[143]*Id.*

[144]Susan Chandler, "An Empty Chair at Herman Miller," *Business Week*, July 24, 1996, p. 44.

Revenues in 1997 were $200 million with record earnings of $78 million. In 1998, Miller acquired dealerships around the country and downsized from its then 1,500 employees.[145]

Volkema notes that staying too long with an "outdated strategy and marketing" nearly cost the company. By 1999, Herman Miller was giving Steelcase, the country's number one office furniture manufacturer, stiff competition, as it were, with its Aeron chair. The Aeron chair, which comes in hundreds of versions, has lumbar adjustments, varying types of arms, different upholstery colors, and a mesh back. Its price is $765 to $1,190, and it is said to be capitalizing on its "Austin Powers–like" look. The chair has thirty-five patents and is the result of $35 million in R&D expenditures and cooperation with researchers at Michigan State, the University of Vermont, and Cornell who specialize in ergonomics. The seat features a sort of spine imprimatur. That is, the chair almost conforms to its user's spine.[146]

Since 2002, Herman Miller has been named one of the "Sustainable Business 20," which is a list of the top twenty stocks of companies with strong environmental initiatives as well as good financial performance. The list is compiled by Progressive Investor, a publication of SustainableBusiness.com. In announcing the list, http://www.sustainablebusiness.com said, "Our goal is to create a list that showcases public companies that, over the past year, have made substantial progress in either greening their internal operations or growing a business based on an important green technology."[147]

For the fiscal year ended June 30, 2010, Herman Miller's earning had declined 19%. It is working to expand its product base to include home furnishing. The company consistently appears in CRO magazine's "100 Best Corporate Citizens" and was cited by *Fortune* magazine in 2010 as one of the U.S.'s "Most Admired" companies and was also named by the magazine as one of the "Top 100 Companies to Work For." One of its corporate goals is "0" pounds of waste by 2020. It was ranked as one of the 18 safest companies in the U.S. in 2008. Herman's Miller's NASDAQ listing finds its shares priced at $18, or about half its 2007 levels. Its expansion into home furnishings from its traditional limitations of office furniture has found a new market and fueled the increased sales.

Discussion Questions

1. Evaluate Foley's decision on changing the Eames chair woods. Consider the moral standards at issue for various stakeholders.

2. Is it troublesome that Miller's profits were off when Foley made the decision?

3. Is Herman Miller bluffing with "green marketing"? Would Albert Carr (Reading 2.3) support Herman Miller's actions for different reasons?

4. Why would Herman Miller decide to buy equipment that exceeded the 1990 Clean Air Act standards when it would not be needed in three years?

5. With sales and warnings down, should Herman Miller change its sustainability focus and cut costs by eliminating some of its green programs? Discuss the stakeholder issues in this question as well as the risks of a sustainability focus.

Case 3.18

The Death of the Great Disposable Diaper Debate

In the late 1980s, environmentalists raised concerns about the disposal of diapers in municipal landfills, space for which is scarce and becoming more so. The average infant uses 7,800 diapers in the first 130 weeks of life.

---

[145]Bruce Upjohn, "A Touch of Schizophrenia," *Forbes*, July 7, 1997, pp. 57–59.

[146]Terril Yue Jones, "Sit on It," *Forbes*, July 5, 1999, 53–54.

[147]"Sustainable Business 20," *Progressive Investor*, July 17, 2007, http://www.sustainablebusiness.com.

The debate over disposable diapers was complex. Disposable diapers account for just 2 percent of municipal solid waste. The time required for plastic to break down is 200 to 500 years. Eighteen billion disposable diapers go into landfills each year. An Arthur D. Little study comparing the environmental impact of cloth and disposable diapers over the products' lifetimes found cloth diapers consume more energy and water than disposables. Cloth diapers also cost more (not counting diaper-service fees) and create more air and water pollution through washing. Critics point out that the study was commissioned by Procter & Gamble, the largest maker of disposable diapers, with 50 percent of the market. However, the study was a sophisticated "life-cycle analysis" that used elaborate computer models, and Arthur D. Little, although now defunct, was considered an eminent research firm.[148]

In surveys in the early 1990s, four of five American parents preferred disposables. Most hospital staffs and day care centers favor using disposables, even though many personally use cloth diapers. Switching from disposable to cloth diapers costs about 2.5 percent more. The disposability of the diapers was also improving, with companies devoting significant R&D dollars to reducing the time for biodegradation. Procter & Gamble created advanced techniques for industrial composting of solid waste and spent $20 million to develop diapers that break down into humus.[149]

Environmentalists, however, were quite successful in obtaining regulation of disposables. Twenty states considered taxes or complete bans on disposables. Nebraska banned nonbio-degradable disposables, with a law that took effect in October 1993. Maine required day care centers to accept children who wear cloth diapers. New York considered requiring that new mothers be given information explaining the environmental threat of disposables. In 1990, the Wisconsin legislature barely defeated a measure to tax disposables.

Alternatives to disposables were being developed. R Med International distributes Tender Care, a disposable diaper that degrades in two to five years because its outer lining is made of cornstarch. However, the price of these diapers was substantially higher than that of other disposables and made mass market appeal impossible.

The great disposable diaper debate peaked on Earth Day in 1990. After the Little study appeared, parents' guilt about rain forests and landfills was relieved, and by 1997, 80 percent of all babies were wearing disposables. Many attribute the change in attitude as well as the halt in legislative and regulatory action to Procter & Gamble's effective public relations using the Little study results. Also, Allen Hershkowitz, a senior scientist at the Natural Resources Defense Council, said, "The pediatric dermatology clearly seemed to favor disposables, while the environmental issues were murky." Environmentalists referred to Mr. Hershkowitz as "the skipper of the *Exxon Valdez*."[150]

During the 1990s, all disposable diaper manufacturers were able to develop materials that were much thinner and lighter than their predecessors. Not only were the diapers decomposing faster, but they also took up less room in the landfills.

By 1997, the National Association of Diaper Services (NADS) reported its membership at an all-time low, with closings of cloth diaper services even in ecologically conscious Boston. There are no diaper services located in any of New York City's five boroughs. Their current marketing campaign emphasizes a two-year guarantee for potty-training with diapers free after that. Babies, the NADS says, can't feel the wetness in disposables.

[148]Arthur Little declared bankruptcy in January 2002. Jonathan D. Glater, "Arthur D. Little Plans Bankruptcy Filing," *New York Times*, February 6, 2002, p. C4.
[149]Zachary Schiller, "Turning Pampers into Plant Food?" *Business Week*, October 22, 1990, p. 38.
[150]Kathleen Deveny, "States Mull Rash of Diaper Regulations," *Wall Street Journal*, June 15, 1990, p. B1.

The Internet has created a new submarket for cloth diapers because the network of parents who prefer cloth diapers is so easily connected. The two national companies remain Mother-ease of New York and Kooshies Baby Products of Ontario, Canada, but there are several small companies, including Darla's Place, based in Imlay City, Michigan. Founded by Darla Sowders because of her frustration with the national brands, the company uses at-home mothers to sew its product, which captures the "brown market," or the market for used diapers. The diapers are sewn a certain way that customers say prevents leaks. The brand is regarded as the "champagne" of diapers and sells at a premium above other diapers in the submarket. Despite this activity, Kimberly-Clark indicates there is no change in the demand for cloth diapers or any reduction in the use of disposables.[151] P&G reports sagging diaper sales, as it were, and is competing with a new premium brand marketed as an item of clothing.[152]

Discussion Questions

1. Did Arthur D. Little have a conflict of interest with Procter & Gamble's sponsorship of its work?
2. Would it be a breach of duty to the hospital's patients and shareholders to adopt a position (that is, using cloth diapers) that increases costs?
3. Do people ignore environmental issues for the sake of convenience? Do your arguments depend on whether you must change diapers?
4. What lessons are learned from this case for applicability in other industries?
5. Did environmentalists exaggerate?

[151]Lisa Moricoli Latham, "The Diaper Rush of 1999: Cloth Makes a Comeback on the Net," *New York Times*, September 19, 1999, p. BU6.

[152]Emily Nelson, "Diaper Sales Sagging, P&G Thinks Young to Reposition Pampers," *Wall Street Journal*, December 27, 2001, pp. A1, A2.

Ethics and Company Culture

The conscience that is dark with shame for his own deeds or for another's, may well, indeed, feel harshness in your words;

Nevertheless, do not resort to lies, let what you write reveal all you have seen, and let those men who itch scratch where it hurts.

Though when your words are taken in at first they may taste bitter, but once well-digested they will become a vital nutrient.

—Dante, *Paradiso* XVII, 124–132

At times, individuals who have become part of a larger organization feel that their personal values are in conflict with those of the organization. The types of ethical dilemmas that arise between an individual and his or her company include conflicts of interests and issues of honesty, fairness, and loyalty. Rogue employees do happen, but it is possible that good apples turn rogue (rotten) in a bad barrel. Sometimes employees make poor ethical choices because their personal temptations are too great and they cross those lines established in personal and individual ethics in Units 1 and 2. Other ethical lapses happen because of company practices. Bonus and incentive plans will get results from employees, but those results may be achieved as a result of crossing a few ethical lines and violating the credo here and there. Then there are the industry practices. When your entire industry is engaged in subprime lending, are you not hurting your customers if you also do not write subprime loans despite the impact of those loans on the markets and the economy? This unit looks at all three of these sources of pressure that contribute to ethical missteps: personal, company, and industry.

Temptation at Work for Individual Gain and That Credo

No one wakes up one day and thinks, "You know what would be good? A gigantic fraud! I believe I will create a gigantic fraud and make money that way." They have to ease themselves into creating a fraud. No one wakes up one day and says, "I believe I will go to work and embezzle $100,000." They will begin by using the postage meter or copier for personal reasons and work their way up to the $100,000, perhaps even taking it in small increments in order to adjust their comfort level with their conduct. One of the tasks we have in studying, understanding, and living ethics in business is drawing lines for ourselves on what we will not do and then honoring the lines we have chosen. If we start moving the lines, we can find ourselves in complete violation of the standards and absolutes we have set for ourselves, and we got there incrementally. The following concise and insightful reading provides pithy insight into this process of moving the line.

Reading 4.1

The Moving Line

George Lefcoe

George Lefcoe, a renowned USC law professor and expert in real property, zoning, and development and, for a time, a commissioner of the Los Angeles County Regional Planning Commission, offered the following thoughts on his retirement and the seduction of public office[1]:

> *I really missed the cards from engineers I never met, the wine and cheese from development companies I never heard of, and the honey baked ham from, of all places, Forest Lawn Cemetery, even though the company was never an applicant before the commission when I was there.*
>
> *My first Christmas as a commissioner—when I received the ham—I tried to return it, though for the record, I did not, since no one at Forest Lawn seemed authorized to accept the ham, apparently not even for burial. My guess is that not one of the many public servants who received the ham had ever tried to return it.*
>
> *When I received another ham the next Christmas, I gave it to a worthy charity. The next year, some worthy friends were having a party so I gave it to them. The next year I had a party and we enjoyed the ham.*
>
> *In the fifth year, about the tenth of December, I began wondering, where is my ham?*

[1]From George Lefcoe, quoted in, "Notable, Quotable," *Wall Street Journal*, December 18, 1998, p. A14.

Discussion Questions

1. What was Professor Lefcoe's absolute line?
2. How did he cross it? As you review his gradual slippage, be sure to think about your credo and personal lines that Unit 1 encouraged you to develop. Think about this question: how did he go from an absolute standard of accepting nothing—indeed, returning the gifts—to expecting the gifts?
3. As you think about Professor Lefcoe, rely on this metaphor. When you buy a new car, think about your initial feelings on food and beverages in the car. Perhaps bottled water at first. Then you move into the brown beverages. Then food enters the new car. Then red punch, sundaes, and ketchup. How did we evolve to a position that is the exact opposite of our original absolute line? In answering this question about the line, consider the following reading.

Reading 4.2

Not All Employees Are Equal When It Comes to Moral Development[2]

The experts in organizational behavior tell us that when it comes to incentive plans not all employees are created equal. That is, their literature says to tailor those incentive plans individually because what motivates one employee may be a ho-hum for another. For example, those who have just entered the work force will probably jump at an extra $10,000 per year even though the promotion and salary bump will require longer hours. More seasoned employees or employees with family demands might respond, "No thanks. I'd rather have the time at home." Some employees want flexibility while others just want the cash. Some employees work for benefits while others just want the benefits of work. Good managers respond with appropriate incentives for these different types of employees.

So it is with employees and their moral development. They are not all created equal. Ethics training may be enough for one type. Ethics training for others may be water off a duck's back. The need to begin a process of evaluating employees for their moral development came to mind as the latest insider trading ring was made public in the final days of October 2009. The allegations are that Galleon, [at that time] one of the country's largest hedge funds, was a longstanding beneficiary of inside information from employees, traders, brokers, and others and that this inside information was then used to create the legendary and unusually consistent returns for which Galleon was famous. Identified in the Galleon-related indictments is the notorious "Tipper A." The tipper is the one providing the inside information, i.e., stock tips, to the tippees, the outsiders who use the inside information to position themselves for market gains in advance of the information's public disclosure.

Who is Tipper A? Well, the *Wall Street Journal* indicates she is Roomy Khan. Yes, right out of a Grisham novel comes a character named Roomy Khan, a former Intel employee who, ironically, was under house arrest for six months in 2002 for passing along proprietary inside information about Intel to those who then profited in the market. Mind you, Roomy Khan does not pass along inside info out of the goodness of her heart or a profound belief in the market's need for asymmetrical information. Roomy Khan had to pay back her gains as part of the 2002 case. One cannot help but wonder: Why would someone who has already experienced legal difficulties return to the same behaviors? More relevantly for ethics and compliance officers, why would a publicly traded company hire someone who has a history of passing along inside information? Most importantly, why would any company that hired Roomy Khan not keep a close watch

---

[2]Marianne M. Jennings, "Not All Employees Are Equal When It Comes to Moral Development," *New Perspectives: Journal of the Association of Healthcare Auditors*, March 2010, p. 19.

on her activities? And keeping an eye on any stock trades that seem to occur in advance of public announcements would also be a good idea. Ethics training will not have much effect on our Roomy Khans because there is a different psychology at work in her behavior. Understanding that different employees require different compliance techniques is a concept in its infancy stages of development and application. But there is a framework to consider.

Years of study and interaction with organizations and their employees have yielded the following categories of employees when it comes to moral development. Herewith is a list with a brief explanation and an example. Coming issues will examine what can and should be done about our merry moral categories

- Morally clueless. These folks do not seem to be aware of rules. They function in their own world and have little or no sensitivity to the impact of their conduct on others or even the impropriety of that conduct. The character George Costanza in the *Seinfeld* series was a classic example. In one episode, Mr. Costanza was caught in the act of having an affair with a member of the janitorial staff on the desk of a colleague. When caught his response was, "What? Is there something wrong with this? Who knew?"

- Morally superior/moral egotist. The moral egotist believes that the rules are for others who are less gifted. Rules were developed for the plodders, not the stars. During the era of the dot-com boom, we had many morally superior characters. For example, Sanjay Kumar, the former CEO of Computer Associates often explained his creative accounting on his company's results as follows, "Standard accounting rules [are] not the best way to measure [CA's] results because it had changed to a new business model offering its clients more flexibility."[3] Dullards follow rules. Moral egotists soar. At least until they run into the SEC. Mr. Kumar is doing 12 years for securities fraud. Computer Associates became known as the company whose earnings were reported on the basis of a new calendar innovation: the 35-day months. With super-star docs and researchers, we often see the moral egotist syndrome. They cannot be bothered with all the regulation and the concerns about conflicts of interest. Moral egotists believe it is impossible for them to experience a conflict of interest because they can process influences better than others who must follow such rules.

- Inherently moral. Ah, the ethics officer's dream. These are the folks who, if you put them in a room and said, "Don't move from this chair," would not move from the chair, with or without a surveillance camera observing them. They will always do the right thing because they have a strong moral code that they live. Mother Teresa comes to mind. In the secular world there is Ed Begley, Jr. He worries about the environment but everything from his house to his mode of transportation demonstrates commitment to his concerns. No hypocrisy among the inherently moral—only commitment to values and a life that reflects those values.

- Amoral technician. This character makes no determinations about right or wrong. The amoral technician does not violate rules. The amoral technician simply finds out what the rules are, what the law is, and then functions within those parameters, right down to the line/wire. They work, and often game, the system with personal feelings and ethics being irrelevant. Andrew Fastow was an amoral technician, brilliant in his use of FASB and accounting loopholes and absolutely unaffected by the impact this loophole approach had on those who had invested in his company.

- Moral schizophrenic. This type of moral development means that the employee has one set of ethics at work and another in personal life, and vice versa, one set of ethics in personal life and another at work. The NBA referee Tim Donaghey who was betting on NBA games even as he called them was known in his personal life for a phenomenal summer basketball camp for children with developmental disabilities and issues. The moral schizophrenic is capable of saying, "Okay, so I threw a few NBA games for gambling. But look what I did with the money!" Donaghey entered a guilty plea and did 15 months.

- Moral procrastinator/postponer. This category of employee is fully aware of ethical issues and the rules and laws but has made a conscious decision to worry about the "ethics stuff" and morality at

---

[3]Alex Berenson, "Computer Associates Officials Stand By Their Accounting Methods," *New York Times*, May 1, 2001, C1, C7.

some time in the future. That time in the future is after they have made enough money. Andrew Carnegie is the classic example. Mr. Carnegie made a fortune as an industrialist, an industrialist with some moments in labor management that saw fatalities. Mr. Carnegie gave his fortune away. If you have been in a public library in the United States you were a beneficiary of his noblesse oblige. But it was an oblige born of postponing ethics until a time when the income was not in jeopardy.

- Moral compartmentalizer or rationalizer. You hear these phrases from the moral compartmentalizer. "Everybody does this." "That's the way we have always done things." "I only do this in certain situations." "I would never allow my kids to do this." This is the Willy Loman syndrome: A man has to sell, sell, sell, no matter what. Ethics apply sometimes, but when you are involved in sales, those lines do have to bend just a bit.

- Morally desensitized. These are the souls who should provide the motivation for working on ethical culture. These employees were once keenly aware of ethical lines and issues but have been beaten down in their objections and have given up raising those concerns. They cope with the cognitive dissonance in their value system by no longer being affected by them. Indeed, they may just join in on the unethical festivities. During the Watergate scandal in the Nixon administration, Charles Colson was a classic example of a morally desensitized soul. He was an experienced and respected lawyer, but because no one was making any headway in stopping the cascading consequences of the Watergate burglary, he just joined in with the group and found himself in prison. Mr. Colson has taken the lessons of his experience and used them to help business people. However, he has also founded a program that focuses on teaching inmates about morality and faith.

- Morally detached. Herein is another group that should find us striving to improve organizational culture. The morally detached are still acutely aware of ethical issues but the rules of the sandbox have worn them down so that they simply go along in a depressed manner. They will not join in, but they do stop objecting. These folks are sometimes called the morally disengaged or the morally disillusioned. The former ethics officer and associate counsel at Hewlett-Packard at the time of the board's great pretexting plan (i.e., the company using private investigators to spy on board members) fell into this category. He was worried about the pretexting, asked security about the pretexting, and inquired as to whether they were crossing legal lines. However, he was unable to make any headway because the directive was coming from the very top of the company. He simply distanced himself from the activities. He did not participate, but he also did not leave nor report the conduct.

- Moral chameleon. This frightening character adapts to ethics of those he/she is working with at the time. One's ethics depend. Those ethics can change depending upon which industry you are in and which company has hired you. They adapt as high schoolers do with their cliques. If one group is making fun of the math club and they are in that group, they join in on the math ridicule. For example, in the Marsh McLennan collusion case, one broker was worried about the issue of price fixing. He prefaced his note expressing his concerns with, "I'm not some goody two-shoes. . . ." He wanted his colleagues to know he was one of them even though he was worried about their practices. A recent Ford truck ad was a moral chameleon's dream, if they are part of the pick-up driving group. The ad boasted about the trucks, "Made by the guys we used to cheat off in high school."

- Moral sycophant. Present far too often in organizations, this character adopts the ethics of those who are in charge. They will be whatever kind of sycophant the leaders want them to be. In October 2009, the *New York Times* ran a lengthy story about the former employees in Lehman and their involvement in the largely worthless mortgage instrument markets. "I was just following orders," was the common explanation. One brave broker also added, "I have blood on my hands."[4] But, as all sycophants explain, and ethical issues aside, he too was just following orders.

[4]Louise Story and Landon Thomas, Jr., "Tales From Lehman's Crypt," *New York Times*, September 9, 2009, SB, p. 1.

Discussion Questions

1. Are you able to place yourself in any of these categories? Why? Give the circumstances that led to your response and behavior.

2. Think of the individuals involved in the cases you have studied so far and develop a chart that categorizes their behavior according to these types of moral development.

Reading 4.3

Why Corporations Can't Control Chicanery[5]

Saul Gellerman

Recent corporate scandals prove that the lessons of previous scandals have not yet been learned. Management still blames rogue employees, and pundits still blame business schools. Most companies would rather not touch the real cause: pressures that push management to test the boundaries of the permissible. As a result, some executives are inevitably confronted with more temptation to do the wrong thing, and more opportunity to do it, than they can resist. Policies that assume everyone will nobly rise above that combination are unrealistic. The best defense lies in painful structural changes that minimize both the temptation and the opportunity to loot the company and defraud investors. It happens, on average, about every 12 years: Someone who works for a big company gets caught cooking the books. In a smaller company, the same offense might not be newsworthy. But if the company is well-known, the media—whose job, after all, is to sniff out headlines—react swiftly. Swarms of reporters descend on the company, with prosecutors and politicians not far behind. In a matter of hours, another of corporate America's household names is all over Page One, mired in a messy, potentially damaging scandal.

Management usually defines its predicament as being primarily a problem in public relations, and calls in the damage-control experts. And right there—in diagnosing the problem as a mere crisis in reputation, rather than the inevitable result of the way they do business—the seeds of yet another corporate disaster, due to sprout in about another 12 years, are sown. It will probably strike a different company, but that makes it all the more dangerous, because the next corporate victim will be blind to the lesson not learned by the first one. The next big scandal, in other words, could strike any big company.

Short-Term Effects

Next, top executives, taking their cue from the wily police chief played by Claude Raines in Casablanca, proclaim themselves to be "shocked, shocked!" at the unauthorized misconduct of a few rogue employees—who promptly become ex-employees. Public relations consultants then prescribe massive doses of good works, such as well-publicized sponsorships of socially beneficial programs (prenatal health care? adult literacy?), to associate the company's name in the public's mind with doing the right thing—conspicuously. Thanks to the public's notoriously short memory, the whole unpleasant episode is soon forgotten.

Today's horrendous scandal inevitably becomes tomorrow's stale news—unless, that is, the prosecutors or the regulators strike pay dirt during the discovery phase of their

[5]*Business Horizons*, May–June 2001, pp. 17–22.

investigation, and if the company's attorneys can't head them off. That could cause the company to implode, which is what happened to financial giants E.F. Hutton and Drexel Burnham about a dozen years ago. Their current counterparts include the once-mighty Arthur Andersen and WorldCom.

Convictions are, of course, the ultimate PR disaster. Firms do not want to do business with a demonstrably crooked company, if only because their own stockholders would surely question their sanity for even thinking of it. Avoiding corporate destruction is the best reason for companies to rein in the chicanery of their own employees. But as that continuing 12-year cycle indicates, their track record is not very good. There are three reasons for that. First, management is ambivalent about really clamping down on the kinds of mischief that can get a company into serious trouble. Second, when they do try to get a handle on it, they are likely to use ineffective methods. Third, they are likely to shrink from the kinds of drastic structural changes that could halt these abuses altogether.

Managerial Ambivalence

A corporation's executives are caught between avoiding the sanctions of the authorities and the displeasure of the stock market. They are forever in the gray zone between maximizing profits and risking the incursions of inquisitive reporters and ambitious prosecutors. (Rudy Giuliani, be it remembered, made his reputation by sending Michael Milken to jail.)

Executives are also in competition with those of other companies, whose profit performance becomes the standard by which their own is judged. They are thus constantly pushed toward the fuzzy, indistinct line that separates barely acceptable practices from those that are intolerable. It should not be surprising, then, that they send mixed messages to the middle managers who make the company's day-to-day, tactical decisions.

I once attended a management meeting of a company that had to walk a fine line between competitiveness and a looming antitrust injunction. A top executive, addressing an audience of middle managers, pounded the lectern for emphasis as he shouted at the top of his lungs, "We want our competitors to survive!" To which he added, in a clearly audible stage whisper, "barely." He was, I think, expressing the essence of the dilemma in which executives find themselves: to go as far as they dare in a lucrative but dangerous direction without ever quite going too far. You can bet that when the Enron scandal hit the headlines, many a corporation ordered an immediate review of its own accounting practices and put any questionable tactics on hold. How much document-shredding went on in companies that were not (at least not then) the targets of investigation is a fascinating but unanswerable question.

This much is certain: When executives send mixed messages, their subordinates are left to decipher their real meaning. The usual translation is: "If the rewards are not enough to motivate you, we don't need you. Just do whatever you have to do to make your numbers. And remember, anyone stupid enough to get caught will be hung out to dry."

Of course, hardly anyone is foolish enough to say such things for the record. But all that executives really have to do is hint to their subordinates that the race will be won by the most audacious among them, rather than by the most deliberate, and then leave them to draw the necessary inferences. So it should not be surprising when subordinates decide that lifting debts from the balance sheet and stashing them somewhere else, or masking ordinary expenses as long-term investments, is what their bosses really had in mind. Most executives are likely to welcome the results such tactics bring, and do not condemn them until someone outside the company finds out, or until an insider blows the whistle. For all these reasons, executives tend to approach internal reforms with mixed feelings. For many of them—perhaps most—the bottom line is their highest priority, especially if their own compensation is tied to it. That makes them reluctant to give up a tactic that has already worked to their advantage. But from a longer-range perspective, any given quarter's bottom line is a secondary goal. The primary goal, always, is corporate survival. In the long run, you can make a lot more money from a steadily profitable company that is still in business than from a spectacularly profitable company that lost the confidence of its customers and is now deservedly defunct.

Ineffective Methods I: Preaching Ethics

When executives undertake to prevent future scandals, they usually seek to prevent "misunderstandings" of their policy guidance. The most common way of doing this is to provide employees with a written "Code of Ethics," most of which states boldly, but imprecisely, that the highest standards of decency, honesty, and fairness are demanded of everyone at all times, and that deviations from those standards will not be tolerated. The main problem with these codes is that they are seldom referred to after the hoopla with which they are introduced has died down. For all practical purposes, they are forgotten after a few months simply for lack of emphasis.

Recognizing the inadequacy of trying to control behavior by merely distributing documents, many companies have gone one step further by bringing in consultants to provide ethics training. Usually these are academics with credentials in philosophy who have "majored," so to speak, in the study of ethics. Their objective is to arm employees with analytical methods that enable them to discern where a line can be drawn between right and wrong. These consultants illustrate their message with case examples of how easily one can be tempted, or deceived, into taking the wrong turn when making what appears on the surface to be an ordinary business decision. But these courses usually amount to little more than highly sophisticated Sunday School lessons.

There is no question but that an intelligent student will come out of them with an intellectual grasp of ethical principles and how they apply to on-the-job decision making. That such an understanding will beget ethical behavior on the job—especially when the actual challenge occurs long after the course has ended, under heavy pressure for results, in the presence of dangled temptation, and in a culture that stresses winning at all costs—is at best dubious.

Giving the right answer to an ethical problem in a classroom, and applying that same answer in the heat of battle, are two very different things. Unless a way can be found to make what are usually near-instantaneous, gut-level decisions in an atmosphere of classroom-like serenity, under the benign guidance of a professor who has your best interests at heart (as distinct from a demanding boss who will not take "no" for an answer), providing employees with formal training in ethics will be an exercise in futility.

Training does not get at the root of the problem, which is not a lack of ethical intent or ethical wisdom, but rather the circumstances in which most critical managerial decisions are made. Thus, a student may in fact be conversant with such advanced ethical concepts as the Categorical Imperative of Immanuel Kant, or the Utilitarianism of Jeremy Bentham, but will either completely forget them at the moment of decision or discard them as irrelevant when that decision must be made under fire. Knowing full well that what you contemplate doing is wrong is not, alas, an effective deterrent when the rewards of wrongdoing are extravagant, the risks of being found out seem remote, and the consequences of not doing what your superiors seem to want can be devastating to your career.

Ineffective Methods II: Excluding Unethical Employees

Another popular but equally ineffective method used by companies that want to avoid potentially dangerous scandals is to try to prevent unscrupulous people from getting into positions in which they could harm the company. Psychologists are brought in to try to weed out executive candidates who seem overly predisposed to cutting corners or bending rules. The psychologists attempt to peer, as it were, into the innermost psyches of candidates for high-level positions, usually by administering various tests, studying their life histories, and/or interviewing people who have known them well at various stages of their lives.

To authorize such screening requires a great deal more faith in the predictive powers of psychological methods than their record would justify. Many executives are aware of that but reason that in the event of another failure they can always say they did all they could to prevent it. Psychologists operate on the (correct) assumption that some people are more likely than others to simply brush rules aside and let the consequences be damned. If individuals carrying that trait can be screened out before they acquire the power to make fateful decisions, the company will be spared the disastrous consequences of their rashness. (The flip side of that screening is that you also eliminate people of uncommon initiative.) The psychologists survey candidates for jobs in which critical decisions can be made, hoping to ensure that only men and women of probity, wisdom, and self-restraint get to make the really big ones.

In practice, there are two severe problems with this approach, either of which is enough to invalidate it. The first concerns its feasibility: Can executive crooks actually be weeded out before they do irreparable harm? The second concerns the realism of its underlying premise: Is corporate misconduct actually the work of just a few "bad apples"—that is, a handful of incorrigibly unscrupulous executives? When you dig down into the details, the feasibility question turns out to be tougher than it may appear at first. There are not just one but two types of potential offenders whom the psychologists have to detect.

First, there are those for whom self-serving, irresponsible acts are a way of life. Clinically, these people are usually diagnosed as psychopaths. Fortunately for society, they are relatively rare. Fortunately for employers, most of them quickly acquire the kinds of records that human resource departments routinely screen out. But their very scarcity makes hunting for them among the employees of a big company rather like hunting for a few needles in an enormous haystack. There may not be any of them there in the first place; and if there are, their disdain for rules is likely to be blatantly obvious without tests. The second target for the psychologists are people whose morals are not especially rigid and who might not be above doing the wrong thing if they encountered sufficiently permissive conditions. This group is likely to be quite large. The practical problem they present is that excluding them from positions of power would probably make a majority of employees, virtually all of whom are innocent, the targets of discrimination. Many a capable, promising, and heretofore honorable employee would be ruled ineligible for higher-level posts if the absence of a stern, steely character were considered a disqualification. Among the remaining few—those whose characters were deemed "impervious" to temptation (the quotation marks are unavoidable)—it might be difficult to find those who were also sufficiently imaginative and decisive to handle executive responsibilities. The practical result is that management has little choice but to take its chances on executive candidates who might, under the wrong circumstances, present risks of wrongdoing. Then there is the question of whether psychologists can actually make all those distinctions accurately and reliably. The long answer requires at least a semester in a good psychology program, because of the inherent difficulty in trying to demonstrate such things incontrovertibly. The short answer is: Probably not.

The Origins of Unethical Conduct

The sad truth seems to be that when it pays to do the wrong thing, someone will. Singling out that "someone" in advance is, for the reasons just discussed, at best impractical and at worst improbable. Many employees—possibly even most—will resist the temptation, but in a large enough group, someone will give in. And it only takes one aggressive risk-taker, or a few, to ease a company onto the initially lucrative but inevitably slippery slope that leads, all too readily, to its own destruction. Why do they do it? What motivates people who usually have a lot to lose (in most cases, a career that was off to an excellent start) to risk everything on a fast buck? Every corporate scoundrel probably had his own set of motives. But the one common denominator that influenced all of them is that they did it because they could. The opportunity was there, and they seized it. Had there been no opportunity, they would still be what they were before the fatal temptation presented itself: highly regarded, promising employees with a great future and perfectly clean records.

In other words, whether one's behavior is going to be ethical or unethical is, to a large extent, situational. It is not the result of an inadequate understanding of ethics, or of fault lines within one's character, but of being in the wrong place at the wrong time. A wise sociologist once observed, "The main reason there aren't more affairs is that there aren't more opportunities." The same can be said of resorting to creative accounting, of bribing employees to put their own interests above those of clients, even of defrauding widows and orphans. Opportunity, not ignorance or inherent evil, is the culprit. If that thought strikes you as too cynical, answer this question for yourself: Suppose you are out of town, alone, in a city where you know no one and no one knows you. You enter a taxi cab, and as it rushes off toward your destination you notice beside you, on the back seat, the wallet of a previous passenger. It is stuffed with hundred-dollar bills. What will you do? Obviously, there will be some kind of identification in that wallet, so what you should do is contact its owner and arrange to return the wallet and its contents to him. But the question I am asking is not what you should do, but what you *would* do. If you returned the wallet, many would applaud your honesty. Yet many others would call you a fool. (After all, they might note, those would be tax-free dollars.) The only way to get a definitive answer to the question would be to put you in a taxi in a strange city, with no one but yourself in a position to see what actually happened. Absent that ultimate test, all of us have a right to be at least somewhat skeptical about what each of the rest of us would do. And if that is the case, it should not be surprising if circumstances that management deliberately creates, or knowingly tolerates, can lead people with previously unblemished records to reach for those fast bucks. Exalted ideas about human nature have no place in a realistic plan to control employee misconduct. To achieve that goal, you have to start with the following assumptions: that everyone (with no exceptions) is at least potentially dishonest; that temptation and opportunity are the two main contributors to potential dishonesty; and that the best way to keep everyone honest is to eliminate, or at least severely restrict, both of them.

Bad Apples or Bad Barrels?

An old saying has it that a few bad apples, if not removed, can spoil all the other apples in the barrel. That is the principle underlying the attempt to screen out unreliable managers before they rise too high in the hierarchy. But the attempt itself is probably futile. To pursue the analogy, the problem is not with the apples (that is, the individual executives themselves) but rather with the barrel (the system of constraints and licenses in which they operate). John C. Coffee, Jr., a professor at the Columbia Law School, dealt with exactly that problem in analyzing the reasons why auditors at Enron and elsewhere acquiesced in their clients' attempts at "earnings management." During the 1990s, he noted, the costs to auditors of doing that went down, while the benefits went up: The costs declined because in several decisions the Supreme Court made it harder to sue accountants, while Congress passed legislation that, among other things, reduced their maximum liability. . . . In any profession, but especially for custodians of the public trust, advocacy and objectivity cannot be safely combined. (Coffee 2002)

In other words, the government, not just greedy executives, had a hand in this. Constraints designed to dissuade accountants from colluding with clients to misrepresent their earnings, or at least to present them in an extremely optimistic light, had eroded because of decisions taken by both the judicial and legislative branches. Risks that had been thought foolish under prior rules now seemed worth thinking about. Inevitably, someone experimented with tactics that had previously been discouraged, just to see what would happen. And when nothing happened, others followed suit. Soon, methods that might once have been considered unthinkable became, instead, the norm.

The Need for Structural Change

Bigger fines and stricter enforcement of existing rules are not the answer. That is because so many minds are virtually programmed to seek ways around restrictions on personal freedom—especially when it pays to evade them. Ingenuity always wins out over regulation. Instead, the way to keep all those perfectly clean records as clean as ever lies in structural changes that remove either the incentive to misbehave or the opportunity to do so, or (preferably) both. Of course, such changes come with a price tag attached.

The solutions suggested here are hardly panaceas. They cannot make any of these problems disappear altogether, and they certainly are not painless. But the present sorry situation of American business demands challenges to the kinds of established thinking that got us into this mess. Four areas seem especially ripe for structural change: boards of directors, organization structure, executive pay, and the auditor-client relationship.

Boards of Directors

In theory, boards are the shareholder's (and the public's) last line of defense against managerial chicanery. In practice, they have been overly acquiescent and (in too many cases) insufficiently inquisitive about what is really going on in the companies they allegedly govern. For both reasons, boards have come under fire from critics who see them as too chummy with, and therefore too easily conned by, management.

Much has been written about the role of inside directors, whose service on the board of a company they also manage would appear to involve an inherent conflict of interest—not unlike that of a fox guarding a hen house. It is true that inside directors bring with them a detailed, expert knowledge of company operations to which outside directors often need access. On the other hand, there is no good reason why outside directors could not question any manager who had information they needed without having to give him a vote on the board's policy decisions. But another issue regarding board performance, though at least as important as the "inside vs. outside" question, has received less attention: the board's competence to carry out its duties. Some boards appear to have been asleep at the switch while great harm was being done to their companies. Enron's board, for example, got into an unseemly finger-pointing contest with management once the extent of the firm's accounting shenanigans began to emerge. Do boards consist chiefly of semi-informed, easily satisfied figureheads capable of presiding over a company but not actively steering it? I doubt that. But to the extent that there may be any truth at all in that stereotype, it is probably because directors are simply playing the role they have been given to play. Keeping their hands off, leaving the heavy lifting to management, and being satisfied with only a general overview of how the company is achieving its reported results is what is commonly expected of them. Nevertheless, we must ask whether it is indeed possible for anyone to bear the ultimate responsibility for a company's fortunes with such a loose grip on its reins.

Another issue that has not received enough attention is the fact that board members (with the frequent exception of the chairman) serve on only a part-time basis. Outside directors, of whom so much more is now expected than before, usually have full-time jobs elsewhere and necessarily treat their directorships as secondary responsibilities. If boards are to do what they are supposed to do—control their firms, rather than merely preside over them—they will have to become the antithesis of what they have been. And if we are to have active, hands-on, fully informed boards of directors, a majority of them will have to serve full-time. They will also have to be given the authority of a military inspector-general: the right to go anywhere, ask any question of anyone, and apply appropriate sanctions to whoever attempts to conceal information from them. Will management like this? Of course not. Will relationships between such a board and its management become tense and adversarial? Possibly. But are these prices worth paying to put the representatives of the owners actually in charge of their company? That is a question on which reasonable people may differ. For myself, I suggest that fewer scandals, and fewer bear markets prolonged and worsened by shareholder disgust, would make all that discomfort well worth it in the end.

Organization Structure

Organizations with built-in conflicts of interest have tried to enjoy the best of both worlds by erecting so-called "Chinese Walls" (prohibited contacts or discussions) in order to separate employees who could collaborate too easily in ways that could compromise the firm's integrity. The most striking recent example of an unsuccessful attempt to prevent corruption by merely forbidding it was Merrill Lynch.

Investment bankers realized that having securities analysts under the same roof with them could be a huge competitive advantage when seeking corporate underwriting accounts. So the "wall" was breeched by giving analysts a financial stake in obtaining underwriting business, simply by inducing them to add some undeserved luster to their evaluations of the prospective client's company.

Trying to repair the wall by punishing those who have breached it or by increasing the penalties for those who try it in the future are probably futile, simply because the incentive is still there. The problem at Merrill Lynch was not the villainy of a few investment bankers, or the willing collaboration of a few financial analysts, but rather the common corporate roof over both of them. Their ready access to each other made the deception of the company's brokerage clients possible, and perhaps even inevitable. The only way to eliminate both the incentive and the opportunity for this kind of gambit is to spin off one of the two units into a separately owned and managed company. Of course, that would also eliminate opportunities for perfectly legitimate synergy. Like the executive who wanted his competitors to survive (barely), brokerages that are also investment bankers have to walk a fine line between maximizing their profits and risking the loss of their reputation. It would be a hard choice, because in all probability the sum of the profits generated by two totally separated units would be less than those produced by those same units under a single but perpetually endangered corporate ownership.

Executive Pay

Some CEOs and other high-level executives have been grossly overpaid, at the ultimate expense of the companies' shareholders. During the stock market boom of the late 1990s, this attracted little comment because everyone else was prospering too. But when stock prices fell early in the new century, questions arose about whether the earnings of the 1990s that had pumped up those prices were real—and complacency over executive pay quickly changed to outrage. How much are top executives worth? In the real world, they are worth whatever a board of directors, conscious of its fiduciary responsibility to share-holders, sees fit to pay them. The real issue is not the pay package itself but the basis on which it is calculated, usually a fiscal year. But as we have learned to our sorrow, earn-ings often have to be recalculated long after they were first officially announced, and fiscal "skeletons" sometimes don't emerge from wherever they were buried until years afterward. In other words, the problem is not so much in the size of the pay package as in the payment schedule. The only way for the directors of a big company to be reason-ably certain that the performance on which an executive's pay is based has been accu-rately measured is to let enough time pass between its initial calculation and the actual transfer of funds. That means sequestering the incentive component of an executive's pay for several years, and then paying it out gradually over a period of several more years. Boards might even consider attaching strings to those payouts, in the form of mandatory reimbursement, in the event subsequent discoveries make those initial reports question-able. Until those initially reported earnings are no longer uncertain, these executives can live on their salaries (an arrangement that most non-executives would consider neither cruel nor unusual). Will CEOs and other beneficiaries of lucrative pay packages like this? Of course not. But it will give them an incentive to see to it that there are no hid-den accounting tricks, errors, or omissions in the reports they pass on to their boards. And if a board has to stiffen its spine to face down a CEO who finds these restrictions too onerous, that is exactly what their shareholders have a right to expect of them.

Auditors and the Audited

The incentive for external auditors to collaborate with a client's attempts to present its financial reports in the most favorable light is to keep the client's auditing business. In the past, there was often an even bigger incentive: to keep the client's consulting busi-ness. But even if—as now seems likely—auditing firms have to get out of the consulting business, the temptation for auditors to please the people they are paid to police will still be there.

The problem is not that corporate accountants (or their boss, the chief financial offi-cer) are inherently dishonest. Instead, the problem lies in the structure of their relation-ship with their auditors. The auditors are hirelings whom the company can dispense with as it pleases and simply replace with other auditors. The effect is that the company is expected to police itself, which places both the temptation and the opportunity to coerce the auditors squarely in the hands of the client's financial staff. It should not be surprising that some people on that staff, realizing how much power they have, decide to exercise it.

The solution is term limits for auditors. They should contract with their clients to prowl through their books for a fixed number of years, with no options for renewal. Since there is no point in trying to hold on to a client you are going to lose anyway, auditors would have no incentive to bend over backwards to please the client. They could then return to the at least quasi-adversarial relationship that their respective roles require of them. All of the changes prescribed here are strong medicine. They won't taste good, and they probably won't go down easily. But boards and management must recog-nize that the likely alternative is yet another round of scandals, possibly even worse than this one, perhaps a dozen or so years down the road. Sooner or later, the public and its elected representatives will declare that enough is enough and force changes like these (or even tougher ones) down the throats of both guilty and innocent companies. It would be much better for all concerned if companies undertook the necessary reforms by themselves, now, without waiting for that.

References and Selected Bibliography

Coffee, John C., Jr. 2002. Guarding the gatekeepers. *New York Times* (13 May): A17.

Discussion Questions

1. What relationships would need to be restructured in order to prevent some of the problems with financial reports? How should they be restructured?

2. Why does the author conclude that ethics training is not effective? Would it be dangerous to not have ethics training for employees?

3. How would the author restructure compensation packages?

4. Refer to Case 2.11 and discuss the compensation changes made at Goldman following the market collapse in 2008.

Reading 4.4

The Effects of Compensation Systems: Incentives, Bonuses, Pay, and Ethics[6]

How are the mighty fallen![7] As we watch financial firms and businesses fold in near domino fashion, we find ourselves wondering what we did or could now do differently that has or will serve to distinguish us from the fallen. Dropping international markets and collapsing businesses do wear on the nerves when the casualties continue over months-long periods. But in the dark of this financial storm, there are some very clear and simple perspectives and ideas that could serve us well. Amidst the fog of misdeeds and missteps, there are concepts of ethical culture and sound governance to be considered and applied. Threats that could cause further collapses continue to abound and the reality of additional and costly regulation looms, but there is still time for some self-correction. Herewith a few suggestions related to perception that could help to avert looming heavy handed regulatory and legislative controls that could impede our progress out of the economic slump.

Suspend Your Compensation Plans and Revisit Your Incentive and Compensation Formulas and Processes

American International Group (AIG), granted a bail-out from the U.S. government, had, as of the end of October 2008, $619 million in bonuses scheduled to be paid to its executives and former CEO. The year 2008 was not a good one for AIG; it was headed into bankruptcy until Treasury Secretary Henry Paulson agreed to provide a capital infusion. The attorney general of New York has extracted an agreement from the company to suspend those payments. The agreement provided that taxpayers had made an involuntary investment in AIG, the company clearly did not, by any measure, perform in a manner that warranted bonuses for its executives, and that there must be different compensation rules when taxpayers are in charge as involuntary stakeholders.

Companies tend to see these compensation packages as contracts between them and their executives and, despite any economic crunch or crash the company experiences,

---

[6]Adapted from an article by Marianne M. Jennings in *Corporate Finance Review* 13(4):37–40 (2009).

[7]2 Samuel 1:19, *The Holy Bible*, King James version.

those contracts must be honored. Board members maintain that by paying the compensation packages negotiated they are simply averting the litigation that would result if the executives' package were suspended. Keeping one's promise is a noble and normative thing to do, but those firms that are beneficiaries of government noblesse oblige should process the contract argument with the following nuances: (1) they have a new set of bosses/board members in the form of taxpayers; (2) if there had been no government support, their firms would not still be standing and, ergo, would be subject to pay recovery limitations of bankruptcy priorities on wages; and (3) there is a great deal of emotional micromanagement of all companies because of increasing job losses (i.e., no income). In short, exceptional times call for exceptions to those contractual bonds and perceived moral obligations on compensation packages.

For those companies not grappling with their new federal investment partners there are still unresolved compensation issues. Government mandated limitations on executive compensation have been floating about since the Clinton era limitation of tax deductibility of executive compensation over $1,000,000. The unintended consequences to that good-intentions limitation was the stock option compensation formula with the resulting abuses there that led to over 200 companies being investigated, the conviction of one CEO, a host of board compensation committee reforms, and new procedures limiting, eliminating, or controlling option grants. The level of executive compensation remains a lightening rod issue that now experiences heightened attention because of the economic turmoil. The U.S. House of Representatives' Committee on Oversight and Government Reform has issued document requests related to and held hearings on executive compensation.[8]

Companies have two choices on compensation packages: (1) they can opt to self-regulate; or (2) they can wait for new regulation to place limitations that could produce further unintended consequences as they add additional compliance costs. The reforms are already percolating to the surface in the form of shareholder proposals. For the shareholder season in 2007, about 10% of the shareholder proposals that required shareholder approval for executive compensation passed. Additional government reform is on the horizon, particularly with the change in the political climate in the United States.

There is one additional issue that has been addressed by about one-half of the S&P companies. That issue is disclosure of the full relationship between the company and the company's pay consultants. Many of the consulting firms providing companies opinions on the structure and soundness of the companies' executive pay structure are actually retained by those same companies to provide the frameworks for and elements of that pay structure. The House Committee found that 113 of the top Fortune 250 firms had pay consultants[9] that played dual roles for those companies. The average compensation for consulting services for the compensation firms for their work on structuring pay packages was $2.3 million; the average fees for the compensation firms' work on certifying the soundness of the formulas for the compensation and incentives was $220,000. The report also found that two-thirds of the companies with these extensive relationships with their pay consultants did not disclose the extent of those relationships.

In other words, pay consulting firms are doing what audit firms were doing pre-Enron. The same firms who are offering their imprimatur for the soundness of the companies' practices are the ones that designed those practices. Here, however, the disparity between the consulting services and the certification services is more along the lines of 10:1 vs. the audit firms which were about split evenly between consulting and audit fees.

---

[8]The hearings were held in December 2007. The full committee report on the hearing can be found at http://oversight.house.gov/documents.

[9]In July 2010, the Dodd-Frank Wall Street Reform and Consumer Protection Act took effect. It imposes new requirements on compensation committees and pay consultants.

We realized post-Enron that it takes a fairly strong-willed firm that designed a company's internal controls to turn around and say that those internal controls are no good. So it is with pay structure design and pay structure soundness. Those functions must now be performed by separate firms. Presently, the compensation conflicts are where the audit conflicts were pre-Enron. The law requires that companies disclose only the identity of the firm that provides the opinion on the soundness of the companies' compensation packages and formulas. The companies need not disclose the extent of their additional consulting relationships with the certifying firm.

If I were in charge at a company, I would work on the following areas of executive compensation:

1. Establish better relationships with shareholder groups that have reform proposals[10]:

    Disclose the extent of the company's relationships with pay consultants. There are questions as to whether the companies that do not disclose these consulting arrangements are in compliance with SEC rules on executive compensation consultant disclosures. The SEC rule provides that there must be disclosure of "any role of compensation consultants in determining or recommending the amount or form of executive and director compensation."[11] The SEC has also offered interpretive guidance that requires companies to disclose all consultants that played a role in determining pay.[12] The Conference Board offers the following suggestion:

    > When the compensation committee uses information and services from outside consultants, it must ensure that consultants are independent of management and provide objective, neutral advice to the committee. . . . The economics of the consultants' engagement for services is very important as an insight into independence. Any imbalance in fees generated by management versus fees generated on behalf of the committee should receive intense scrutiny[13];

2. Consider bifurcation of the design and certification functions of pay consultants;

3. Check with compensation consulting firms to see what checks and balances they have implemented internally to guard against potential conflicts and independence[14]; and

4. Consider bold reforms in compensation packages looking at issues such as upper limitations, pay relationship limitations (limits on pay of executives as compared to employee salaries),[15] kill clauses (events that mean there are no bonuses paid), and limits on or elimination of perks (see below).

There is goodwill out there for the taking for companies that undertake bold reforms in the area of executive compensation.

---

[10]Two activist groups that received an open forum in Congress were Institute for Policy Studies and United for a Fair Economy. Their research can be found at: Executive Excess 2007. The Staggering Social Cost of U.S. Business Leadership (August 2007). Also see faireconomy.com (accessed September, 2010).

[11]SEC, Final Rules on Executive Compensation and Related Party Disclosures, Items 402 (b) and 407 (e) of Regulation S-K (August 29, 2006).

[12]SEC, Staff Interpretation: Item 407 of Regulation S-K—Corporate Governance (March 13, 2007).

[13]The Conference Board, The Evolving Relationship Between Compensation Committees and Consultants, 6, 15 (January 2006). Also see http://www.conference-board.org/ectf (accessed September, 2010).

[14]Some of the executive compensation consulting firms have voluntarily implemented internal rotation and independence policies akin to those audit firms use, i.e., senior consultant must rotate out from account after five years and/or another senior consultant must review the work of the consultant that works with the company. On the other hand, some of the executive compensation firms have internal documents that reflect the desire of the firm to "cross-sell" companies on a wide variety of services the firms provide. Their goal is more business.

[15]This emotionally charged issue was highlighted in the congressional hearings and its reports and continues to be a draw in terms of attracting public attention as well as activism. Below is an excerpt from the report:

> Dramatic increases in executive compensation have widened the gulf between CEO pay and the pay of the average worker. In 1980, CEOs in the United States were paid 40 times the average worker. In 2006, the average Fortune 250 CEO was paid over 600 times the average worker. While CEO pay has soared, employees at the bottom of the pay scale have seen their real wages decline. In real terms, the value of the new federal minimum wage, $5.85 per hour, is 13% below its value a decade ago.

Check Your Perks and Retreats

In October 2008, AIG spent $443,000, including $23,000 for spa treatments, at a California St. Regis resort for a retreat for top-performers that was held within one week of the government's rescue loan of $85 billion to the mismanaged firm. This conduct is akin to that of the friend who orders steak and lobster just after borrowing rent money from you.

An insurance company clearly needs to reward those agents who sold, sold, sold. But, at a time when economic angst is at a peak, surpassed only by the level of anger in the picking-up-the-tab taxpayers, taking a pass on the annual spa extravaganza for the agents might be a good idea.

AIG was in the news in November when it hosted another retreat for independent advisors at a swank Arizona resort. The explanations to the press were that this event was educational; the advisors needed to know about AIG products. When the press attention continued, the company canceled the scheduled appearance of former Steelers player Terry Bradshaw. Some experts noted the costs to the company if the event is canceled and the loss of loyalty and goodwill that are built by such events. However, in these times of corporate resentment, companies cannot speak legalese to those who see extravagance. These are times for heightened sensitivity to anything that could be eliminated or curbed.

Now is the time for all good managers to come to the aid of their companies by issuing general edicts on perks. Once again, there is goodwill for the taking for companies that voluntarily cut back during this era of angst, cutbacks, job losses, and poor earnings results. The following suggestions would be a way to accomplish these self-restraints with full cooperation of employees who might be affected.

1. Bring employees into the loop and ask for their ideas on how to cut costs without cutting jobs;
2. Ask for ideas from all areas of the company and all employees. One company had employees suggest that in lieu of the company holiday party that they all employees simply participate in on a Saturday community clean-up event that was sponsored by a group that has been a part of one employee's life for nearly 20 years; and
3. Set the tone by cutting expenses at the top. Private jet travel, auto allowances, and private car services are a few of the executive expenses being voluntarily cut as a way of setting an example for employees.

Culture is symbolic. Companies are in need of cultures that reflect an economy that is struggling. These small steps can provide the credibility businesses need to steer through the regulatory hearings and mazes of proposed controls that have resulted from perceived excess in everything from pay to perks to risk. There are many free marketers and Friedman disciples among us who are able to make the intellectually sound argument that the market will remedy excesses and that pay decisions are best left to the companies with the oversight of shareholders who are free to participate through their votes or vote through their departure from the companies that are not performing but are rewarding managers nonetheless. In theory they are correct. However, economic theory must operate within the reality of human emotion. Human emotion is controlling the markets these days. Perception is everything. Taking control of those negative perceptions, even when logic supplies an explanation, creates goodwill and results in trust. These voluntary actions must be simple and symbolic, along the lines of those provided here. With trust restored, we may be able to find our way out of the teetering economy so susceptible to perceptions of breach.

Discussion Questions

1. Develop a chart that shows the distinctions between prevalent compensation packages and the new approaches suggested. Study the Dodd-Frank Wall Street Reform and Consumer Protection Act for mandates on compensation and the board's role.

2. Refer to Case 2.11 and discuss the changes Goldman has made in its compensation packages and why and what additional changes could help the company.

3. What does the piece discuss about Friedman vs. human emotion?

Reading 4.5

The Subprime Saga: Bear Stearns, Lehman, Merrill, and CDOs[16]

"What were they smoking?" The *Fortune* cover story featured those words in a 3.5-inch headline as well as photos of Chuck Prince, Citigroup ($9.8 billion loss), Jimmy Cayne, Bear Stearns ($450 million loss),[17] John Mack, Morgan Stanley ($3.7 billion loss), and Stan O'Neal, Merrill Lynch ($7.9 billion).[18] Their photos and losses were followed by the subtitle, "How the best minds on Wall Street lost millions."[19] We had just managed to get our minds around the options backdating problem with the comfort that came from knowing that such bad habits by executive and too-complicit board compensation committees could no longer occur because Sarbanes–Oxley had more timely reporting requirements. Sure, we were at $5.3 billion in total restatements for options, had one CEO convicted, and 3 out of 10 indicted general counsel pleading guilty, but we had caught the problem, installed statutory prevention tools, and were ready to gloss over this tempest-from-a-past-era-teapot. Like a water torture program, however, the subprime mess trickled forth. Beazer Homes admitted that it broke federal laws in helping buyers qualify for mortgages, but that was just one builder.[20] Countrywide Financial had its problems, but what would you expect in their subprime market? So, by August 2007, we had cut its stock value in half.[21] And we witnessed the default rate on home mortgages climbing, but attributing that problem to a downturn in the economy, which was due to oil prices, which was due to war, which was due to . . . , gave us comfort.[22] Unmistakably, the mortgage market was melting down, but a shoulder shrug and "so what if a few deadbeats lose their homes" were the responses. However, with collateralized debt obligations (CDOs), a mortgage market runs wider and deeper than even the best of the best on Wall Street contemplated. The banks were heavily invested in that subprime market, and the subprime mortgages had gone south. Once again, we found the classic scenario of companies, operating in a regulatory no-man's land, staying at the party a little too long and drinking too much. A few had even arrived late and still partook.

Not to pour too much salt on fresh wounds of 35 percent and 36 percent share price drops for Citigroup and Merrill, respectively, but we have been down this road of high

---

[16]Adapted from "The Lessons of the Subprime Lending Market," by Marianne M. Jennings in *Corporate Finance Review* 12(3):44-48 (2007)

[17]Bear Stearns has since announced a $1.2 billion write-down, and a resulting loss, the first loss in the firm's 84-year history. Jennifer Levitz and Kate Kelly, "Bear Faces First Loss, Fraud Complaint," *Wall Street Journal,* November 15, 2007, pp. C1, C2.

[18]The losses for the others have been changing daily, so the author surrenders in terms of how high the figures are or will be.

[19]*Fortune,* November 26, 2007 (cover).

[20]Floyd Norris, "Builder Said It Broke Federal Rules; Will Restate Earnings," *New York Times,* October 12, 2007, p. C3.

[21]James R. Hagerty and Karen Richardson, "Why Is Countrywide Sliding? It's Unclear, That's the Issue," *Wall Street Journal,* August 29, 2005, pp. C1, C4; Gretchen Morgenson, "Inside the Countrywide Lending Spree," *New York Times,* August 26, 2007, pp. SB-1, 8.

[22]Richard Beales, Alex Barker, and Saskia Scholtes, "Fraud Inquiry Goes to Roots of Debt Chaos," *Financial Times,* March 29, 2007, p. 21.

risk, overly optimistic bets, initial phenomenal returns, and collapses. Junk bonds, savings and loans and their property appraisals, and the high-tech/dot-com boom were of the same pattern from other eras. Different investment vehicles; same crash and burn. A look back at some other *Fortune* covers is an eerie reminder of lessons not learned. The cover of *Fortune* for May 14, 2001, just after that era's bubble burst, featured analyst Mary Meeker and the caption, "Can We Ever Trust Again?" How did they miss that one? How could the analysts have been so wrong? Still, one year later the cover of *Fortune* featured Sallie Krawcheck and the caption, "In Search of the Last Honest Analyst."[23] We were not confident the problem had been solved. Here we are today, with slightly more plebian phraseology asking the same question Judge Stanley Sporkin asked in 1990 when we had the S&L losses, "Where were these professionals . . . when these clearly improper transactions were being consummated? Why didn't any of them speak up or disassociate themselves from the transactions?"[24] Once again, we are stunned by the failure of financial wizards to catch these multi-billion dollar overvaluations.

However, there is something quite troublingly different about this meltdown from those of the junk bond, S&L, and dot-com eras: We have not managed to make it 10 years without a breach of trust. We were living with the assumption that these types of financial and ethical debacles would only arise once a decade as those new to the businesses affected by the last issue forgot the historical underpinnings of the market and their own institutional histories. Five years out from the promised transparency of Sarbanes–Oxley finds investors asking the same question: Can we trust these people? As the *Fortune* piece noted in its introduction,

> *Two things stand out about the credit crisis cascading through Wall Street: It is both totally shocking and utterly predictable. Shocking, because a pack of the highest-paid executives on the planet, lauded as the best minds in business and backed by cadres of math whizzes and computer geeks, managed to lose tens of billions of dollars on exotic instruments built on the shaky foundation of subprime mortgages.*[25]

The shocking part is incorrect. The utterly predictable part is indeed correct. Herewith some thoughts on those two thoughts through a discussion of the governance and ethics issues the best-of-the-best missed on the road to this breakdown in financial reporting and accountability.

Why We're Not "Shocked, Shocked" at the Losses[26]

Many of us, although unable to quantify the extent of the losses, have been expressing concerns about subprime loans in general, including the use of subprime loans as a foundation for financial instruments for the past two years. We were, as in the dot-com and Enron eras, pooh-poohed as being overly cautious and, again, overly focused on ethical issues. Yet, the ethical issues in the subprime lending market were compelling. The subprime market saw loans for 100 percent of purchase price, loans based on false information (the Beazer issue), and loans to those ill-equipped to handle credit generally and certainly incapable of managing ARM mortgages that would find their payments doubling when market rates kicked in on their loans. Of course opening up mortgages to the

[23]*Fortune*, June 10, 2002, and beneath the caption was the stinging phrase, "Her analysts are paid for research, not deals."

[24]*Lincoln Sav. & Loan Ass'n v Wall*, 743 F.Supp. 901, at 920 (D.C.Cir.1990). Judge Sporkin referred to both lawyers and accountants/auditors in his question.

[25]Shawn Tully, "Wall Street's Money Machine Breaks Down," *Fortune*, November 26, 2007, pp. 65, 66.

[26]*Casa Blanca* (Warner Brothers 1942); *See also*, Marianne M. Jennings, "Fraud Is the Moving Target, Not Corporate Securities Attorneys: The Market Relevance of Firing Before Being Fired Upon and Not Being 'Shocked, Shocked' That Fraud Is Going On," 46 *Washburn L. Rev.* 27 (2007)

ill-equipped with poor track records resulted in more mortgages, and the low hanging fruit of high credit risks found the mortgage brokers calling with creative packages. Even with a skill set for applying *caveat emptor,* these credit risks were no match for brokers who had tasted double-digit returns and driven Ferraris, whether leased or owned. Neither business models nor markets can have "taking advantage of those with lesser information or bargaining power" as a foundation. Whether the path is one of pyramid scheme, false advertising, or inherent bargaining disparity, all such roads lead to negative firm and market impact, with perhaps the greatest casualty being market trust as we cope with, "Not again!"

Perhaps a contra example of how the subprime market should have been handled makes a compelling case against the companies argument that they are "shocked, shocked" by their numbers. North Carolina has largely escaped the wrath of the subprime foreclosures and resulting market downturn because of tougher lending laws it enacted in 1999. Its so-called predatory lending law, passed in a state with some of the United State's largest financial institutions headquartered there, is one that has become the model for other states as well as for proposed reforms wending their way through Congress. The legislation, which helped consumers, lenders, and the North Carolina economy, is perhaps a case study in how staying ahead of evolving issues and placing restraints on nefarious activities can benefit business. That regulatory cycle emerges again: deal with the abuses in the regulatory no-man's land before they become a financial, regulatory, or litigation crisis.

North Carolina's predatory lending law includes the following protections, protections that surely would have been wise self-restraints by lenders during the real estate boom and certainly would have helped preserve the value and lower the risk in the CDO portfolios of the banks now forced to take the write-downs[27]:

- Limitations on the amount of interest that can be charged on residential mortgage loans in the amount of $300,000 or less as well as any additional fees lenders add on to the loans
- Limits on fees that may be charged in connection with a modification, renewal, extension, or amendment of any of the terms of a home loan, other than a high-cost home loan. The permitted fees are essentially the same as those allowed for the making of a new loan, with the exception of a loan application, origination, or commitment fee.
- Limits on fees to third parties involved with the processing of the loan
- Eliminates penalties for consumers who pay off their debts early
- Requires lenders to verify income of debtors
- Puts limits on fees brokers can collect for arranging mortgages

Martin Eakes, one of the business people (and a trained lawyer), who worked to get North Carolina's law in place said, "Subprime mortgages can be productive and fruitful. We just have to put boundaries in place."[28] Ah, there it is. There is nothing inherently evil about the subprime market; but those boundaries are important. North Carolina also provided the data for what harms can befall an economy when subprime loans go south. Studies by then attorney general Mike Easely (now North Carolina's governor) showed what foreclosures did in poorer neighborhoods. The impact on the general area as well as the real estate market was a bit of a foreshadowing of the much larger nationwide economic impact we have witnessed. The systemic effects of subprime loans were documented clearly in this state's reforms even before the real estate market experienced its boom. The impact of the foreclosed loans was the risk inherent in instruments tied to such loans.

The very basic notions of consumer law, fairness, disclosure, and risk were ignored or minimized in the sophisticated models used for structuring and evaluating the portfolios

---

[27]N.C.G.S.A. § 24-8.

[28]Nanette Byrnes, "These Tough Lending Laws Could Travel," *BusinessWeek*, November 5, 2007, pp. 70–71.

of companies such as Citigroup and Merrill Lynch. A model based on a flawed assumption about something as simple as the quality of the mortgages is still a flawed model. The question underpinning all the CDOs and related derivative investments should have been, "How high is the risk on the mortgages?" or "What's the credit quality of the borrower?" That basic question was either not evaluated or not answered realistically for both the investment decisions and the ongoing evaluations of value for purposes of financial reports.

"Utterly Predictable"

If the underlying question on the subprime/mortgage investment vehicles was such a basic finance question, how come so few with so much experience and so many tools at their disposal got it so wrong for so long? The answer to this question rests in the culture of the companies. These companies had many of the same traits that existed in other giants fallen through a lack of financial transparency and the eventual disclosure of a less-than-pretty picture. Think Enron with its off-the-books debt and mark-to-market accounting, WorldCom with its capitalization of ordinary expenses, Adelphia with its executive loans, and so on. We have a different set of companies in a different industry, but the traits that contribute to the lack of transparency and eventual losses are the same. High risk, little transparency, and iffy evaluation lead to what insiders claim to be surprise losses. However, as dissimilar as the companies are in industry and tactics, there are similarities in culture. There are seven cultural traits, that characterize companies that have ethical lapses, such as a lack of transparency in financial statements, with the resulting financial melt downs. The companies with the largest write-downs had at least four of those traits.

a. Iconic CEOs

These companies had Street legends at their helms. Chuck Prince was handpicked by Sandy Weill to head up Citigroup. Weill steered the ship during the rowdiness of Jack Grubman and the WorldCom unwavering support and Prince was his protégé. Who would question Prince? In fact, even when there were bizarre rumblings, we did not bat an eye. In early 2007, Prince had a mess on his hands as he terminated Todd S. Thomson, the head of global investment, with stories about Thomson's relationship with Maria S. Bartiromo, private jets, and conflicts with her role as a CNBC anchor floating about.[29] Known as "the money-honey mess," some outside the company predicted that the ouster, on what were called meager grounds, meant there was more Citigroup bad news on the horizon as Prince found scapegoats.[30] Thomson was a known dissenter when it came to Prince.

Stan O'Neal was an indefatigable "numbers guy" who was brought in to streamline Merrill Lynch. Mr. O'Neal initiated the relationship with Long-Term Capital Management, a hedge fund. O'Neal took Merrill from a safe, trading house to a leveraged player. Merrill weathered the storm from the infamous Enron barge deal with a judicial opinion that, while reversing the convictions of the Merrill employers, was not flattering. In a nut shell the court held that the Merrill employees could not be held criminally liable when the company itself (Enron) made the Enron executives do it and the Merrill folks were outsiders who could not be considered part of a fraud when the very officers of Enron were presenting the deal as good for Enron (if that makes any sense):

> *Here, the private and personal benefit, i.e. increased personal bonuses, that allegedly diverged from the corporate interest was itself a promise of the corporation.*

---

[29]Bill Carter, "As Citigroup Chief Totters, CNBC Reporter Is Having a Great Year," *New York Times,* November 5, 2007, pp. C1, C5.

[30]Barney Gimbel, "Deconstructing the Money-Honey Mess," *Fortune,* March 5, 2007, p. 14.

According to the Government, Enron itself created an incentive structure tying employee compensation to the attainment of corporate earnings targets. In other words, this case presents a situation in which the employer itself created among its employees an understanding of its interest that, however benighted that understanding, was thought to be furthered by a scheme involving a fiduciary breach; in essence, all were driven by the concern that Enron would suffer absent the scheme. Given that the only personal benefit or incentive originated with Enron itself—not from a third party as in the case of bribery or kickbacks, nor from one's own business affairs outside the fiduciary relationship as in the case of self-dealing—Enron's legitimate interests were not so clearly distinguishable from the corporate goals communicated to the Defendants (via their compensation incentives) that the Defendants should have recognized, based on the nature of our past case law, that the "employee services" taken to achieve those corporate goals constituted a criminal breach of duty to Enron. We therefore conclude that the scheme as alleged falls outside the scope of honest-services fraud.[31]

On the mortgage instrument front, O'Neal stated, just 3 months prior to the announcement of the multi-billion dollar write-downs, that Merrill's hit was not bad and all was under control. When he announced $5 billion in early October, the market concluded that the extent of the write-down meant the models were flawed.[32] Just three weeks later, the upping of the figure to $8 billion meant his resignation.

John Mack was brought back to Morgan Stanley after Phil Purcell retired under pressure that was unrelenting, from both internal and external sources. Mack had retired in 2001 after Purcell refused to yield in a power struggle. Such a triumphant return is bound to set an iconic tone, to wit, "Mack is back!"[33]

Jimmy Cayne's status and leadership approach emerged when the Bear Sterns losses did. He spent a good deal of time in recreational activities, something that made for derisive reports, but only from outsiders.[34] No one inside the company would question Cayne.

And there are others in the high-risk fold that were not highlighted on the cover. UBS, Wachovia, Bank of America, and Lehman have all had losses creeping up with trickle releases. Presently, the write-downs do not appear to be completed or accurate. Even Merrill may have to recognize more losses.

In the three companies with the surprising losses (either by scope or reputation), stars were at the helm and had been brought in to clean up some messiness. For a time, they were all very successful, providing returns to shareholders and premium yields on bonds. But their star quality, coupled with results, meant that few in their companies would either challenge them or be willing to be the bearers of bad news (see below). The write-down "surprises" are easily explained and do not reflect well on either their business models or the willingness of employees to talk with these leaders about emerging issues. In simplest terms, the problem was the mortgages backing the bonds had been assigned risk levels based on default rates in a primo market, not a declining one. In short, the default rates were faulty (and the risk levels incorrect) because of a failure to take full account of the subprime market and its inherent and higher risk. As noted earlier, this higher risk was not unknown information about subprimes, but no one seemed willing to discuss that issue with their leaders.

---

[31]*U.S. v Brown*, 495 F.3d 509 (5th Cir.2006).

[32]Randall Smith, "A Five Billion Bath At Merrill Bares Deeper Divisions," *Wall Street Journal*, October 6, 2007, p. A1.

[33]Ann Davis, "Morgan Stanley's Change in Focus," *Wall Street Journal*, June 27, 2005, pp. C1, C5.

[34]Cayne was golfing and on a bridge tournament trip during the critical time of the crisis. Kate Kelly, "Bear CEO's Handling of Crisis Raises Issues," *Wall Street Journal*, November 1, 2007, pp. A1, A16. Mr. Cayne spent 10 of July's 21 working days golfing or at the tournament.

b. Pressure to Meet Numbers

It was not that bright people in the companies did not see the problems or risk. The structure, the incentives, and the returns and rewards all contributed to a silence that belied common sense. One cannot, after all, wish his or her way into value.

One post-mortem analysis noted that at Merrill, "They lost more than others. Merrill tended to focus its efforts in the highest risk areas because that's where the rate of return was greatest."[35] And an executive commented after the $5 billion loss was announced, "We've seen this before."[36] O'Neal was, ironically, a numbers man who grilled his executives on results. One of his frequent tactics was comparisons between Merrill and Goldman, such as why Goldman had higher growth in bond profits, with one Merrill executive noting, "It got to the point where you didn't want to be in the office on Goldman earnings days."[37] Employees called operations meetings "staged" and always found O'Neal aloof. And there were a series of terminations in the last year that found three high-ranking Merrill executives summoned for five to fifteen-minute sessions in which they were shown the door for not reaching numbers goals. Those terminations were scuttlebutt throughout the company. And those interested in staying knew that results, not bad news, were the key to remaining employed. When you have forgotten the basic notion that higher returns mean higher risk, that pertinent information needs to percolate to the top and did not in the case of Merrill because it was afflicted with the same type of culture that allowed the Enron-era companies to go on for so long with so much wrong that was not factored into financials.

Prince had the Thomson termination, something that had a similar chilling effect as the Merrill terminations. Cayne's aloofness created a similar reticence on the parts of employees and executives who probably understood their exposure on CDOs.

The latest research shows that uncovering financial issues and fraud has its best shot in employees.[38] Neither regulators nor auditors are as likely to have information about financial report missteps as employees. The key is creating a culture in which the employees, who now tell us they were aware of the subprime issues and the need for write-downs, have the avenues and motivation for disclosure to those who will respond. Those companies now experiencing the lightest hits from the subprimes had cultures in which the numbers were questioned, from the top. Jamie Dimon at J.P. Morgan is known for his extensive involvement in operations there and his ability to hone in on numbers and ask the tough questions of employees. His approach is one that signals to employees not that the company wants only results, but that the results must be accurate and legitimate.[39] Compare the J.P. Morgan write down of $339 million with the other firms' billions. Likewise, Goldman and Lehman have small write-downs in comparison because of the hands-on operational experience and drilling techniques of officers who ask where the numbers came from, doing more than accepting numbers presented.

[35]Jenny Anderson, "A Big Loss at Merrill Stirs Worries About Risk Control," *New York Times*, October 6, 2007, pp. B1, B2.

[36]*Id.*

[37]Randall Smith, "O'Neal Out as Merrill Reels from Loss," *Wall Street Journal*, October 29, 2007, pp. A1, A16.

[38]Alexander Dyck, Adair Morse, & Luigi Zingales, "Who Blows the Whistle on Corporate Fraud?" *Financial Economics*, February 2007. The authors find that employees are the best source for detecting fraud and support financial incentives for gaining more information from them, e.g., more *qui tam* recovery.

[39]Randall Smith and Aaron Luchetti, "Merrill Taps Thain as CEO," *Wall Street Journal*, November 15, 2007, pp. A1, A21.

c. Innovation Like No Other

"The banks were in denial. They thought they were smarter than the market."[40] Somehow the companies examined here were able to convince themselves that showing phenomenal earnings for such a long stretch meant invincibility and an immunity from the basics of market risk, returns, and exposure. Fancying yourself above the fray means that the rules, whether of the market or accounting, do not apply to your business model. Ignoring those basic principles simply postpones the inevitable subjugation to those principles, and the longer the postponement, the greater the losses.

d. Weak Boards

All of the boards, including Citigroup, have credentialed members. Robert Rubin, the former treasury secretary, has stepped up as chairman at Citi, but how did he miss the problem? By Rubin's own admission he did not know what a liquidity put was until the summer of 2007. And in what should be a shocking interview for governance gurus everywhere (and a big help on shareholder litigation), Rubin noted, "I tried to help people as they thought their way through this. Myself, at that point, I had no familiarity at all with CDOs."[41] Those on the board of a bank have an obligation to understand the instruments that are a foundation of the bank's portfolio. Yet Rubin insists it was not his job to know, "The answer is simple. It did not go on under my nose. I am not senior management. I have this side role."[42]

Former AT&T CEO Michael Armstrong missing the signals is even more extraordinary because Armstrong was a survivor of the overvaluation era that characterized the telecoms. Yet, as chair of Citi's audit committee, he did not see the similar strains or was unwilling to raise the flag. There is an ugly history with Armstrong, Weill, and Jack Grubman. Weill leaned on Grubman for a favorable AT&T rating in exchange for Weill's influence in getting Grubman's twins into preschool.[43] And Armstrong then sided with Weill in the battle for control of Citi against his co-CEO, John Reed. Credentials do not make for a strong board, and Prince's departure alone cannot fix the lax supervision of numbers at Citi. A board shakeup could have benefited the company back in the Weill days and is necessary now as it moves forward and sheds the Weill and Prince shadows and styles. Indeed, all the boards may want to revisit the notion of expertise—why did no one on the boards question the risk, the numbers, the operations, or even, just three months prior to the announcements of the write-downs, whether the subprime meltdown would affect their companies' financials? An even more basic question is why did the board members not take the time to understand the definitions and risks of the instruments that were the cornerstone of the companies' portfolios?

"The Sage Advice Lost in the Computer Models"

Even without the common traits analysis, we have some simpler principles that would have helped the boards, the media, the analysts, and even the investors in these banks. That old adage, "If it sounds too good to be true, it is too good to be true." The kinds of returns that the banks and their investors were enjoying on investments based on subprime loans were too high to not have high risk associated with them. They simply had not been transparent about that risk.

---

[40]Shawn Tully, "Wall Street's Money Machine Breaks Down," *Fortune*, November 26, 2007, pp. 65, 78.

[41]Carol J. Loomis, "Robert Rubin on The Job He Never Wanted," *Fortune* , November 26, 2007, pp. 68–69.

[42]*Id.*

[43]Mara Der Hovanasian, "Can Citi Regroup?" *BusinessWeek*, November 19, 2007, pp. 31, 32. The history is found at Charles Gasparino, "Ghosts of E-Mails Continue to Haunt Wall Street," *Wall Street Journal*, November 18, 2002, pp. C1, C13, and Charles Gasparino, Anita Raghavan, and Rebecca Blumenstein, "Citigroup Now Has New Worry: What Grubman Will Say," *Wall Street Journal*, October 10, 2002, p. A1.

There is another simple lesson, which is that there is no substitute for learning not just what the numbers are but how staff got to those numbers. In looking at the companies that have had the least impact we find that, as noted earlier, there was a culture of, "How exactly did you get these numbers?," a natural and ongoing skepticism that signaled employees that the numbers had to be supportable, not just within range. The value of dissent in companies had been vastly underestimated and underutilized.

One final lesson was noted in the introduction. A sustainable competitive business model cannot be based on taking advantage of those with less information. A market works, not because of asymmetrical information, but because of transparency. That transparency was not there at the point of the subprime loan negotiations and the fog carried through to the risk evaluation as well as the valuations of the collateralized mortgage bonds themselves. Throughout the chain, the terms, the value, and the risk were not clear to the players. Such failure to disclose is neither the stuff of ethics nor of thriving markets. The subprime mess, when all is said and done, comes down to the basic ethical standard of forthrightness at all levels of companies and throughout the market.

Discussion Questions

1. Make a list of the cultural factors that ran across the companies that proved to be predictors of their ethical lapses and collapses.

2. How could the adage "if it sounds too good to be true" influence the structure of an investment portfolio?

3. What relationship does the article maintain between and among ethics, risk, and business decisions and strategies?

Case 4.6

HealthSouth: The Scrushy Way

HealthSouth, a chain of hospitals and rehabilitation centers, used its celebrity and sports figure patients as a means of marketing and distinction. Press releases touted sports figures' use of HealthSouth facilities, such as the press release when Lucio, the Brazilian World Cup soccer star, had surgery at a HealthSouth facility.[44]

HealthSouth touted its new hospitals as something others would emulate.[45] The language in their annual reports and brochures was "the hospital model for the future of health care."

HealthSouth's website listed celebrities who have "used HealthSouth facilities: Michael Jordan, Kobe Bryant, Tara Lipinski, Troy Aikman, Bo Jackson, Scottie Pippen, Shaq O'Neal, Terry Bradshaw and Roger Clemens."[46] Its service model, the four steps from diagnosis through surgery through inpatient rehabilitation and finally to outpatient rehabilitation, was also its mark of distinction from other health care providers. The four steps are still featured in a logo on the website as well as in its annual reports.

HealthSouth called its new hospitals "the hospitals of the future," and competitors began to copy those models.[47] From 1987 through 1997, HealthSouth's stock rose at a rate of 31 percent per year.[48] The stock had gone from $1 per share at the time of its initial public offering (IPO) in 1986 to $31 per share in 1998. In April 1998, CEO

---

[44]HealthSouth press release, December 12, 2002, http://www.healthsouth.com. Accessed June 23, 2003.

[45]Reed Abelson and Milt Freudenheim, "The Scrushy Mix: Strict and So Lenient," *New York Times*, April 20, 2003, pp. BU-1, 12.

[46]HealthSouth, http://www.healthsouth.com/investor, accessed June 23, 2003.

[47]Abelson and Freudenheim, "The Scrushy Mix," pp. BU-1, 12.

[48]John Helyar, "Insatiable King Richard," *Fortune*, July 7, 2002, pp. 76, 82.

Richard Scrushy told analysts that HealthSouth had matched or beat earnings estimates for forty-seven quarters in a row.[49] It became a billion-dollar company through acquisitions. HealthSouth profits were restated in 2002 and 2003 to reflect $2.5 billion less in earnings, for periods dating back to 1994, with $1.1 billion occurring during 1997 and 1998. Subsequent corrections reveal that HealthSouth's revenues were overstated by $2.5 billion, a figure 2500 percent higher than what was reported from 1997 through 2001.[50] The stock was trading on pink sheets at $0.165 per share in mid-April 2003, from a $31 high in 1998.[51]

The Corporate Culture

CEO Richard Scrushy held Monday morning meetings with his executives. When the company was not meeting the numbers and analysts' expectations, Mr. Scrushy's instructions to the officers were "Go figure it out."[52] At one meeting he announced, "I want each one of the [divisional] presidents to e-mail all of their people who miss their budget. I don't care whether it's by a dollar."[53]

One officer noted, "The corporate culture created the fraud, and the fraud created the corporate culture."[54] In an interview in the fall of 2002, Mr. Scrushy explained his management technique: "Shine a light on someone—it's funny how numbers improve."[55]

Monday morning management meetings with HealthSouth's then–CEO Richard Scrushy and his executive team in which they covered "the numbers" were referred to internally as the "Monday-morning beatings." Mr. Scrushy confronted employees not only with strategic issues, such as hospital performance, but also with the sizes of their cellular telephone bills: "Interviews with associates of Mr. Scrushy, government officials and former employees, as well as a review of the litigation history of HealthSouth, paint a picture of an executive who ruled by top-down fear, threatened critics with reprisals and paid his loyal subordinates well."[56]

One of the CFOs recorded conversations he had with Scrushy. For example, Richard Scrushy declared in a recorded conversation with William Owens, one of HealthSouth's CFOs,

[If you] fixed [financial statements] immediately, you'll get killed. But if you fix it over time, if you go quarter to quarter, you can fix it. Engineer your way out of what you engineered your way into. I don't know what to say. You need to do what you need to do.[57] We just need to get those numbers where we want them to be. You're my guy. You've got the technology and the know-how.[58]

In 1998, employees began posting notices on Yahoo message board about Health-South along with derogatory comments about Mr. Scrushy, using pseudonyms. Mr. Scrushy hired security to determine who was responsible for the postings and eventually shut down employee computer access to the message boards.[59]

Mr. Scrushy was known to place calls to his facility administrators from parking lots of HealthSouth facilities at 1 A.M. to notify them that he was standing in their parking

[49]Abelson and Freudenheim, "The Scrushy Mix," pp. BU-1, 12.

[50]Id., p. 84.

[51]Id., pp. BU-1, 12.

[52]Id., p. 84.

[53]Id., p. 86.

[54]Id., p. 84.

[55]Id., pp. BU-1, 12.

[56]Id., pp. BU1, 12.

[57]"Secret Recording Is Played at a HealthSouth Hearing," *New York Times*, April 11, 2003, p. C2.

[58]Greg Farrell, "Tape of Ex-HealthSouth CEP Revealed," *USA Today*, April 11, 2003, p. 1B.

[59]Helyar, "Insatiable King Richard," pp. 76, at 82.

lots and that he had found litter there. They were then forced to come to the facility immediately to fix the problem. He began arriving at work with security guards and kept them outside his door at all times.[60]

HealthSouth had a young officer team. For example, the vice president of reimbursements for the company, a critical position because of the importance of compliance in terms of bills submission under Medicare rules as well as the associated financial reporting issues regarding the revenues associated with reimbursement, was given to a twenty-seven year old.[61] HealthSouth had five CFOs from 1998 through 2003, and the final CFO prior to the collapse was just twenty-eight years old when Mr. Scrushy chose him for the ascent to that second-in-command position.[62] Mr. Scrushy did not favor hiring MBAs. He had none in his direct reports, but he did hire what he called "advance-them-up-from-nowhere Alabamians."[63]

Diana Henze, a HealthSouth employee, provided the following testimony at the congressional hearings on the company's collapse.

> My name is Diana Henze, and I live in Birmingham, Alabama. I am 39 years old, married with two children. I graduated from the University of Montevallo in 1985 with a B.S. degree in accounting. After a few accounting positions, I began working for a Birmingham-based healthcare company, ReLife, in 1994. In December of that year, ReLife was acquired by HealthSouth, and I began working in HealthSouth's accounting department. In 1995 and 1996, I helped install a standardized accounting software package for the accounting department. In 1997, I was promoted to Assistant Vice President of Finance, and in 1998, I was promoted to Vice President of Finance. My responsibilities were somewhat ad hoc, but included running the accounting computer system, preparing quarterly consolidations and assisting in the SEC filings.
>
> Sometime in 1998, after re-running several consolidation processes for one quarter end, I noticed that earnings and earnings per share jumped up. The amount and timing of those changes seemed odd to me so I approached my supervisor, Ken Livesay, who was the Assistant Controller. Ken told me that the increase in earnings was the result of the reversal of some over-reserves and over-accruals. At the time, Ken's explanation appeared to be reasonable and I did not pursue the matter further. I did notice a jump in earnings the next quarter, but I did not question Ken about it.
>
> In January of 1999, I went on maternity leave to have my second son, Douglas, and did not work on the year-end consolidation or the 10-K preparation for 1998. Shortly after returning to work in March, I assisted in preparing the first quarter consolidation and 10Q preparation for 1999. During that process, I noticed the numbers changing again, and I approached Ken Livesay a second time. I told him, "You can't tell me that we have enough reserves to reverse that would justify this type of swing in the numbers." When he told me that I was right, I informed him that I did not understand what was going on, but would have no part in any wrong-doing.
>
> Ken apparently went to Bill Owens, the Controller, with my suspicions because Bill called me in an attempt to justify what they were doing. Bill said that HealthSouth had to make its numbers or innocent people would lose their jobs and the company would suffer. I told Bill that I believed that whatever was going on to be fraudulent,

---

[60]*Id.*

[61]This information was gleaned from a review of HealthSouth's 10-Ks from 1994 through 2002. See Securities and Exchange Commission website, http://www.sec.gov/edgar, for these documents.

[62]*Id.*

[63]Helyar, "Insatiable King Richard," pp. 76, 84.

and I would not participate in it and wanted no part of it. I also asked him to stop whatever it was they were doing and told him that I was going to keep an eye on it.

The numbers continued to change in the second and third quarter of 1999. After the third quarter, I went to Ken and said "enough is enough," because the numbers still appeared to be moving with irregularities. I told him I was to going to report these suspicions to our Compliance Department because I suspected that fraud was being committed within the accounting department. Ken said to do what I needed to do.

In October or November of 1999, I went to our Corporate Compliance Department and made an official complaint to Kelly Cullison, who was Vice President of Corporate Compliance. I gave her information on my suspicions and where I thought some of the "entries" were being made. I also gave her information on how to write specific types of queries against the transactional tables within our system, which helped her look at the fluctuations that were being made and of which I was suspicious. I did not have access to the supporting documentation of the suspect journal entries, and therefore, could not give her that information. As it turns out, Kelly did not have access to the information necessary to investigate my complaint of suspected fraud.

Ken Livesay called me to ask if I had gone to the Compliance Department with my complaint because he had been called to Mike Martin's (Chief Financial Officer) office about it. I confirmed that I had gone to the Compliance Department and filed a complaint. In a follow-up discussion with Kelly Cullison, I told her that I stood by my complaint and would not withdraw it. I do not mean to imply in any way that Kelly tried to get me to withdraw my complaint because she did not do that.

Shortly after I filed the complaint, Ken Livesay was moved to the position of Chief Information Officer (CIO), and two others were promoted to his previous position of Assistant Controller. I felt that I had been overlooked for this position and I confronted Bill Owens about this. I was told by Bill that he could not put me in that position, because I would not do what "they wanted me to do."

Within a few days or weeks I requested a transfer from the accounting department and was transferred immediately to our ITG (Information Technology Group) Department. Soon after joining ITG, I began working on an internet project and ultimately moved to that department under the supervision of Scott Stone in January 2001. Under HealthSouth's new leadership, in May of 2003, I was promoted to Assistant Controller of the Corporate Division. I enjoy my work now, and believe HealthSouth is a good company which can be a profitable business if run properly.[64]

There was also a high level of turnover in the executive team, particularly among those executives age fifty and older. These executives disappeared rapidly from the slate of officers, and that age group was no longer represented after 1998. Those officers who were experienced were replaced by younger officers who were brought in by Mr. Scrushy. Their bonuses and salaries grew at exponential rates, particularly the longer they stayed.[65] HealthSouth had an extensive loan program for executives in order "to enhance equity ownership." The key executives owed significant amounts of money to the company that they borrowed in order to exercise their stock options.[66]

---

[64] "The Financial Collapse of HealthSouth," Subcommitee on Oversight and Investigations of the House Energy and Commerce Committee http://archives.energycommerce.house.gov/reparchives/108/Hearings/10162003hearing1110/Cohen1747.htm. (Accessed September 17, 2010).

[65] Id.

[66] Securities and Exchange Commission, http://www.sec.gov/edgar: see disclosures in proxy statements for 1995–2002.

HealthSouth's former head of internal audit offered the following testimony before Congress on the HealthSouth hearings:

My name is Teresa Sanders, and I currently live in Birmingham, Alabama. I am 39 years old. In 1986, I graduated from the University of Alabama with a degree in accounting. I received my master's degree in accounting in 1988.

I began working with Ernst & Young in August of 1988 as a staff auditor, and I was laid off in February of 1990. In March of that year (1990), I was hired by Health-South as the Internal Auditor. During my employment I received three promotions, and when I left my title became Group Vice President and Chief Auditing Officer. My immediate supervisor was Richard Scrushy, and I reported directly to him for over nine years. I left HealthSouth in November of 1999.

I was hired by HealthSouth to audit our field operations. When I started at Health-South, the company had thirty-five (35) field facilities, and by the time I left the number had grown to approximately two thousand (2000). I had complete access to the financial books of the field operations in order to do my audits. However, I did not have access to the corporate financial books. I did not need access to the corporate books to perform field audits. Ernst & Young performed the audit on the corporate books and any reports to the SEC.

As part of my duties as the Chief Auditing Officer, I had to make reports to the audit committee of the Board of Directors. All the meetings that I had with the audit committee were before the full Board except one time in either 1997 or 1998, when I met separately with the audit committee. However, that meeting was attended by Tony Tanner.

In 1996, Richard Scrushy approached me about establishing a fifty (50) point check-list which became known as the "Pristine Audit." After Mr. Scrushy asked me to develop the checklist, I sent him a memo expressing my opinion about the checklist. I have attached a copy of my memo. Mr. Scrushy did not appreciate my opinion on the matter and again instructed me to develop the checklist for his approval. Mr. Scrushy informed me the Pristine Audit was to be handled by Ernst & Young.

I developed the fifty (50) point checklist which Mr. Scrushy approved. I am attaching a copy of the checklist. As you can see, the Pristine Checklist has nothing to do with auditing the financial books of a field facility. The Pristine Audit was nothing more than a cosmetic, white glove, walk through of a facility. It was in the nature of quality control and had nothing to do with the financial viability of a particular facility.

By the time I left HealthSouth, I was having problems with Mike Martin. He turned off my computer access to the general ledgers of the field operations. I needed access to those ledgers to do my audits. I had to manually retrieve hard copies of those ledgers, if needed, which was very time consuming. I also did not like the way that Health-South handled an internal sexual harassment investigation. It was my opinion that the offending employee should have been terminated. Although I heard rumors that "they were playing with the books," I had no knowledge that anyone at HealthSouth was committing fraud. I ultimately left HealthSouth because I received a better job offer with Eastern Health Services Systems in the compliance department as the Compliance Officer. I was tired of traveling and my new job did not require any travel.[67]

[67] "The Financial Collapse of HealthSouth," Subcommittee on Oversight and Investigations of the House Energy and Commerce Committee http://archives.energycommerce.house.gov/reparchives/108/Hearings/10162003hearing1110/Cohen1747.htm. (Accessed September 17, 2010).

Scrushy: CEO

Mr. Scrushy was a flamboyant CEO who had Bo Jackson and Jason Hervey, the teenager from the TV series *The Wonder Years,* paid to accompany him to HealthSouth events. Mr. Scrushy had a weekly Birmingham radio show with Mr. Hervey that was sponsored by HealthSouth. Mr. Scrushy doled out the use of the company jet to politicians and athletes on a regular basis. But he also used the company jet himself for transporting his own rock band to various locations for concerts and company events. Mr. Scrushy was in the process of promoting a female rock trio when HealthSouth collapsed.[68]

Mr. Scrushy's personal assets included a mansion in Birmingham, a $3 million 14,000-square-foot lakefront home in Lake Martin, Alabama; a ninety-two-foot yacht; and thirty-four cars, including two Rolls-Royces and one Lamborghini.[69] He owned eleven businesses that he controlled through one operating company that also owned his wife's clothing company, Upseedaisies.[70] On his payroll were four housekeepers, two nannies, a ship captain, boat crew, and security personnel.[71]

Mr. Scrushy's companies did extensive business with HealthSouth. G.G. Enterprises, a company named for Mr. Scrushy's parents, sold computers to HealthSouth, a contract that eventually resulted in an investigation by the federal government for overcharging. Scrushy's personal accountant committed suicide in September 2002, and Scrushy filed a police report after the death accusing the deceased accountant of embezzling $500,000.

From the Junior Miss Pageant of Alabama to scholarships for his community college alma mater, Richard Scrushy, like Bernie Ebbers (see Case 4.27), was unusually generous with the organizations and people in the small-town atmosphere in which he had experienced his stunning rise to success. The Vestavia Hills Public Library was renamed the Richard M. Scrushy Public Library because of his generous donations.[72] There was the Richard M. Scrushy campus of Jefferson State Community College, from which he graduated, and the Richard M. Scrushy Parkway that ran through the center of town. The Scrushy charity activity was weekly, and he used his celebrity sports clients to draw attention to the events.[73]

The HealthSouth Board

Following the $2.5 billion in earnings restatements by HealthSouth, one of its directors, Joel C. Gordon, observed, "We [directors] really don't know a lot about what has been occurring at the company."[74] However, there were the following revelations about the structure and activities of board members:

- One director had earned $250,000 per year on a consulting contract with HealthSouth for a seven-year period.
- Another director had a joint investment venture with Mr. Scrushy on a $395,000 investment property.
- Another director was awarded a $5.6 million contract for his company to install glass at a hospital being built by HealthSouth.

---

[68]Helyar, "Insatiable King Richard," pp. 76, 84.

[69]Abelson and Freudenheim, "The Scrushy Mix," p. C1. During the hearing in which he was asking the federal court to release some of his assets (the judge had awarded him $15,000 per week living expenses previously), Mr. Scrushy could not remember what he owned and didn't own and took the Fifth Amendment against self-incrimination thirty times. "Ousted Chief of HealthSouth Resists Questions on His Assets," *New York Times,* April 10, 2003, p. C4. "I can't recall" and "I can't speak to the accuracy of this" were other responses.

[70]Greg Farrell, "Scrushy 'Was Set Up,' Says Lawyer," *USA Today,* April 15, 2003, p. 3B.

[71]Helyar, "Insatiable King Richard," pp. 76, 84.

[72]*Id.*, pp. 76, 80.

[73]*Id.*

[74]Joann S. Lublin and Ann Carrns, "Directors Had Lucrative Links at HealthSouth," *Wall Street Journal,* April 11, 2003, pp. B1, B3.

- Med Center Direct, a hospital supply company that operated online and did business with Health-South, was owned by Mr. Scrushy, six directors, and one of those director's wives.
- The audit committee and the compensation committee had consisted of the same three directors since 1986.
- Two of the directors had served on the board for eighteen years.
- One director received a $425,000 donation to his charity from HealthSouth just prior to his going on the board.[75]

A corporate governance expert has said the conduct of the HealthSouth board amounted to "gross negligence."[76] One Delaware judge has issued an opinion on one aspect of litigation against the board and noted, "The company, under Scrushy's managerial leadership, has been quite generous with a cause very important to Hanson (the director who accepted the donation to his College Football Hall of Fame). . . . compromising ties to the key officials who are suspected of malfeasance."[77]

Dr. Philip Watkins, a cardiologist, testified at congressional hearings on the Health-South collapse and stated the following:

I became involved with HealthSouth, a brand new company then known as Amcare, in 1983, after I first met Mr. Scrushy. Mr. Scrushy proposed a merger of my practice's cardiac rehabilitation facility with Amcare to form what is known as a "CORF"—Comprehensive Outpatient Rehabilitation Facility. The unique concept of a CORF was to combine outpatient surgery and rehabilitation facilities into one stand-alone medical complex in order to ease patient burden and expense, and ultimately provide for more successful patient recoveries.

In 1984, I was asked by Mr. Scrushy to join the Company's Board of Directors, two years before HealthSouth became a publicly traded company in 1986. As a physician and director, it was determined that I could add valuable insight by talking to physicians and helping to meet their needs in working with our facilities. Our ability to provide high quality, efficient, low cost patient care was the core of the Company's business.

Early on, I was appointed Chairman of the Board's Audit & Compensation Committee. At that time the Company was a startup with such a small board that these two functions were combined to form one committee. At that time, many companies followed this practice. Later, the committees were separated into two distinct committees.

As Chairman of the Audit & Compensation Committee, I worked with and relied upon the outside experts hired by our Board. For example, we hired Mercer Human Resource Consulting to assist the Committee as our compensation consultants. Mercer retains a reputation as one of the largest and most relied upon compensation consulting firms in the country. Mercer analyzed the compensation trends of similar firms in the healthcare industry and, along with other experts, advised the Compensation Committee. It was based upon this information and advice that we determined the compensation packages of HealthSouth's management team.

By all accounts, HealthSouth was growing at an exciting pace, and was singled out by numerous industry publications, including Forbes and Fortune, as an up and coming star in the field of outpatient surgery and rehabilitation. Since I joined the Health-South Board in 1984, I have seen HealthSouth grow from a company with two rehabilitation facilities—one in Little Rock and one in Birmingham—to become the largest outpatient surgery company, rehabilitation company and diagnostic services company

---

[75]Lublin and Carrns, "Directors Had Lucrative Links at HealthSouth," pp. B1, B3.
[76]Id.
[77]Id.

in the world with over 48,000 employees throughout the country. The compensation for HealthSouth senior executives, including Mr. Scrushy, was based upon this apparent outstanding performance, and the Committee was always assured by the independent analyses of experts such as Mercer that the Board's compensation philosophy was entirely in keeping with the best practices at the time. Specifically, we implemented a performance based incentive-compensation program, which included annual bonuses and stock option grants under a stockholder-approved option plan.

We now know the numbers we relied on and were certified by our outside accountants to calculate senior management compensation were fraudulent. If the Compensation Committee had known of the fraud, Mr. Scrushy and others would have been terminated immediately and would never have received these salaries, bonuses, and stock options.

I was as shocked and angry as the rest of the public when I learned that senior members of HealthSouth's management team had been perpetrating a fraud on HealthSouth's stockholders. The Board of Directors was similarly deceived. These criminal conspirators were able to fraudulently conceal or otherwise alter information and documents such that all of the experts including the accounting firm of Ernst & Young did not detect the fraud. As a corporate director, I relied on the accuracy of information provided to me by management and by outside experts such as Ernst & Young. It is now evident that because the truth had been so thoroughly concealed by certain former members of management, the probing questions and activism of this Board could not have discovered the existence of this accounting fraud.

In addition to questioning former management and outside experts, the Company had in place internal control systems designed, in part, to catch fraud. But every system of checks and balances is only as good as the people who are there and use them. Ms. Henze testified that she did use the compliance system we had set up to receive and act upon such information. That's how the compliance system was supposed to work. It is incomprehensible to me how designated compliance personnel could have received such apparently clear information and could not have told Ernst & Young, the Audit Committee or the Board.

Just to be clear, the fraud occurred at a corporate level. Ernst & Young conducted the corporate-wide audit. In contrast, internal audit conducted facility level audits. The Subcommittee heard testimony two weeks ago from Ms. Teresa Sanders and Mr. Greg Smith of HealthSouth's internal audit department. The Audit Committee did meet on a regular basis with Ms. Sanders and Mr. Smith and received their reports and questioned both of them. In fact, I had more internal auditors added to the internal audit staff after talking to Ms. Sanders. They never told us they had any suspicion of impropriety.

Let me conclude by saying that I am proud of my service to the HealthSouth Board. HealthSouth enabled me to combine my obligation as a medical doctor to patients with that as a director of the Company to the stockholders. Had I known of the hidden fraud being perpetrated on us all, I would have acted quickly and decisively, just as the current Board has in removing those responsible. HealthSouth is one of the great healthcare companies in America and I am confident that it will continue to be under the guidance of the new management team. I look forward to answering any questions you or any other members of the Subcommittee may have.[78]

---

[78]"The Financial Collapse of HealthSouth," Subcommitee on Oversight and Investigations of the House Energy and Commerce Committee http://archives.energycommerce.house.gov/reparchives/108/Hearings/10162003hearing1110/Cohen1747.htm. (Accessed September 17, 2010).

In 1996, eight of the fourteen board members were also company officers. The ratio of insiders did decrease after 1996.

Trials, Pleas, and Convictions

Fifteen of HealthSouth's executives entered guilty pleas to various federal charges. HealthSouth's former CFOs testified against Mr. Scrushy at his criminal trial and for the government. Only one CFO had no culpability. He left the company because of his concerns about the financial reporting. Scrushy had his going-away cake made for him. The cake read, "Eat _____." The other CFOs entered guilty pleas. The following chart provides a summary of the guilty pleas of the CFOs and other officers.

William Owens	CFO	Wire and securities fraud; falsifying financials; filing false certification on financial statements with the SEC
Weston Smith	CFO	Wire and securities fraud; falsifying financials; filing false certification on financial statements with the SEC
Michael Martin	CFO	Conspiracy to commit wire and securities fraud; falsifying financials
Malcolm McVay	CFO	Conspiracy to commit wire and securities fraud; falsifying financials
Aaron Beam	CFO	Bank fraud
Angela Ayers	VP, finance and accounting	Conspiracy to commit securities fraud
Cathy Edwards	VP, asset management	Conspiracy to commit securities fraud
Rebecca Kay Morgan	VP, accounting	Conspiracy to commit securities fraud
Virginia Valentine	Assistant VP	Conspiracy to commit securities fraud
Emery Harris	VP/assistant controller	Conspiracy to commit wire and securities fraud
Kenneth Livesay	Assistant controller/CIO	Conspiracy to commit wire and securities fraud
Richard Botts	Senior VP, tax	Conspiracy to commit securities fraud; falsifying financials; mail fraud[79]

Mr. Scrushy joined a church in his hometown just prior to the trial and made substantial contributions. The pastors of the church attended the Scrushy trial each day. Leslie Scrushy, Mr. Scrushy's second wife, attended the church regularly and often spoke in tongues from the pulpit. Mr. Scrushy's son had a daily television show on one of the local television stations that Mr. Scrushy owned. He provided daily coverage of the trial, complete with interviews of the pastors and others attending the trial. The show enjoyed very high ratings. Mr. Scrushy was acquitted of all thirty-six federal felony charges related to the HealthSouth collapse in June 2005, following long (twenty-one days) and intense deliberations by a jury that seemed to have doubts even after that verdict was returned. One sign held by a former HealthSouth employee who stood outside

[79]"HealthSouth Guilty Pleas," *USA Today*, May 20, 2005, p. 1B.

the court room read, "Still guilty in God's eyes."[80] In a postverdict interview, Scrushy said, "The truth has come to the surface."[81]

Mr. Scrushy was subsequently convicted of bribery of an Alabama official in federal district court. He was sentenced to six years and ten months in federal prison.[82] Because of a U.S. Supreme Court decision on the requirements for proof of "honest services fraud," Mr. Scrushy's conviction was reversed and his sentence will now be reviewed by a federal district court judge. Mr. Scrushy has asked for an early release from prison based on the reversal. As of July 2010, he was at the halfway mark on his seven-year sentence. There are a total of $2.28 billion in civil judgments against him. Both of his multimillion-dollar homes have been taken over by the judgment creditors.

Discussion Questions

1. What in the culture of HealthSouth made it difficult for employees to raise concerns about the company's practices and financial reporting?

2. Find the common factors in the companies in this Unit and others.

Compare & Contrast

What is the difference between the CFOs who left the company and officers who stayed, many of whom were promoted? Consider the congressional testimony of the various officers and others associated with HealthSouth. What made their view of the situation at the company different?

Case 4.7

Jett and Kidder, Leeson and Barings, Kerviel and Société Générale: Compensation-Fueled Dishonesty

There Is No Such Thing as a Rogue Trader[83]

There is no such thing as a rogue trader. So I wrote in these pages in 1996 in analyzing the Nick Leeson/Joseph Jett losses and characterizations. Joseph Jett was the then-32-year-old bond trader who found an accounting loophole/computer internal control flaw and was able to fabricate nearly one-half billion in sales for his bond division at the now defunct Kidder Peabody, with, of course, the accompanying bonuses for him.

Jett seemed to be part of a string of individual managers or traders who took their companies to the cleaners, all under the internal control, regulatory, and audit radar. Joseph Jett earned his Harvard master's degree in business administration in 1987.[84] Dismissed from his first post-degree job at CS First Boston, he then worked for Morgan Stanley but was laid off in the post-1980s Wall Street cutbacks. Despite his lack of experience in government securities, Jett was hired in 1991 by Kidder Peabody & Company to work in the government bonds section of its fixed-income department.

---

[80]Reed Abelson and Jonathan Glater, "A Style That Connects with Hometown Jurors," *New York Times*, June 29, 2005, pp. C1, C4.

[81]Greg Farrell, "Scrushy Acquitted of All 36 Charges," *USA Today*, June 29, 2005, p. 1A.

[82]Bob Johnson, "Scrushy Gets Nearly 7 Years in Prison," *USA Today*, June 29, 2007, p. 2B.

[83]Adapted from Marianne M. Jennings, "There's No Such Thing as a Rogue Trader," *Corporate Finance Review* 12(6): 40–46 (2008). Author of, most recently, *The Seven Signs of Ethical Collapse: How To Spot Moral Meltdowns in Companies Before It Is Too Late* (New York: St. Martin's Press, 2006).

[84]Because of a balance on his tuition bill, he did not receive his degree until 1994. In June 1994, he paid the balance due on his tuition, and Harvard processed his degree.

At the time Jett was hired, the Kidder fixed-income department was headed by Edward A. Cerullo, an exceptionally bright, hands-off manager who emphasized profits and was credited with turning Kidder around following the late-1980s insider trading scandals. Some fixed-income traders so feared telling Cerullo of losses that they under-reported their profits at certain times so that they would have reserves to cover any future losses.

At the time of Cerullo's tenure and Jett's employment, Kidder Peabody was owned by General Electric (GE), which had purchased it in 1986 for $602 million. To establish Kidder as a Wall Street force, GE poured $1 billion into the firm and had begun to see a return only from 1991 to 1994.

Jett's initial performance in the bonds section was poor: he lost money. Fellow traders recalled Jett's first months on the job as demonstrating his lack of knowledge; some questioned whether Jett should have been hired at all. Even when Jett began earning profits, his reputation remained mediocre. "I don't think he knew the market. He made mistakes a rookie would make," said a former Kidder trader who worked in the 750-member fixed-income section with Jett.

Hugh Bush, a trader at Kidder, raised questions when he examined Jett's trades. In April 1992, Bush accused Jett of "mismarking" or misrecording trading positions, an illegal practice. Bush's allegations were never investigated, and he was fired within a month.

In 1991, Linda LaPrade sued Kidder, claiming that she was terminated as a vice president when she brought illegal trading to the attention of Cerullo. She also claimed she was told to increase allotments from government agency security issuers by "any means necessary."

During this same period, Jett's profits bulged to 20 percent of the fixed-income group's total, and he was made head of the government bond department. Jett's profits, however, did not exist. Jett had taken advantage of an accounting loophole at Kidder that enabled him to earn a $9 million bonus for 1993 alone. The fictitious profits were posted through an accounting system that separated out the interest portion of the bond. Jett captured the profit on the "strip" (the interest portion of the bond) before it was reconstituted or turned back into the original bond. Kidder's system recognized profits on the date that the reconstituted bond was entered into the system. The result was that over two and one-half years, Jett generated $350 million in fictitious profits. When the scheme was uncovered by auditors in April 1994, GE had to take a $210 million write-off in its second quarter. On April 17, 1994, Jett was fired, his bonus and accounts were frozen, and the SEC began an investigation.

There was also Nick Leeson, the fund manager who, through his leveraged derivative investments, brought down Barings Bank, the bank that financed the Napoleonic wars. In 1995, Leeson racked up a $1.4 billion loss for Barings with a bad bet on the yen. The then-28-year-old Leeson did time in a German prison. About the same time, Robert Citron, a government funds manager in Orange County, had positioned the county in risky derivatives, and got it all wrong. Orange County would file bankruptcy. And we certainly can't forget Brian Hunter at Amaranth, Iguchi at Daiwa, and Hamanaka at Sumitomo. Big trades, big losses.

Now, enter Jérôme Kerviel, in 2008, at the ripe old age of 31. With this former Société Générale's racking up $7.09 billion in losses we are back to the same theory that emerges each time a trader defies internal controls and the brightest minds of the financial world. Rogues all, we say. Shame on them. But, is the fact that rogues exist the only lesson we can take away from all of these seemingly shameless high-risk souls?

No internal control system is infallible. No audit or auditor can detect all system flaws. Even with certification of internal controls and all manner of SOX 404 compliance, we still have breakthroughs. Kerviel did know a great deal about his bank's internal control processes, knowledge that allowed circumvention. In-depth employee knowledge of internal controls systems is an oversight easily fixed by more frequent system changes. As one expert noted, it's a little like becoming a thief after you have training as a locksmith. It is a tad easier to get into the place where the loot is located.[85] Quite simply, Kerviel knew when the bank did its nightly reconciliation, and he was able to post to cover his exposure whilst working around that time of reconciliation.[86] But, fix this lapse and there will be another breach by another bright mind with personal drive and ambition or a simple need for cash.

The story at Société Générale, a 144-year-old institution that was the second largest bank in France and one of the most respected, has emerged in the same way that it did at Kidder and Barings. At first announcement, the rogue acted alone. Then we begin to hear the rumblings of questions unanswered, signals unheeded, and inexplicable profits welcomed. There is a certain chutzpah in companies that act surprised given the number of flags and signals that unfold. Therein lie the real lessons of Jett, Leeson, Kerviel, and more. There is a glaring oversight in all internal control systems, one that no company or consultant has addressed competently. The systems fail to consider a touchy, feely, squishy element: humans perform jobs, and part of effective internal controls is human observation, a qualitative task that offers no Excel spreadsheet or statistical Six Sigma. As one French expert phrased it, we have the most sophisticated home security alarm systems possible, and then we are robbed because we forget to close the window. French Finance Minister Christine Lagarde said that Société Générale relied too extensively on computer risk models and failed to look at "the human factors."[87] So how do you get at those human factors? How do we accomplish the simple act of closing the window? There are patterns among the so-called rogues that give us some clues for prevention.

The Isolated Loner Who Seeks Attention

When the Kerviel, Jett, and Leeson misdeeds became public, there were the comments from those who knew them that run parallel to those we hear from neighbors of just-discovered serial cannibals, "He was a quiet man." Leeson was odd and withdrawn. Jett had the self-perceived isolation of his race and that feeling of inadequacy that came from his checkered work history. Kerviel was a loner who suffered from the insecurity of having taken his education at a lesser university.[88] He wanted to be noticed, to be someone. The description that appeared in the *New York Times* tugs at the heart strings for its sheer sadness of dashed dreams:

> He failed in a bid for town council in his 20s; he never rose higher than a green belt, a mid-level rank, after years of judo training—because of his bad knees; and he attended an average college where he earned respectable but unremarkable grades.[89]

Kerviel attended the University of Lyon, a school started by French banks for the very purpose of training just the ranks of middle managers that the banks need. A professor described Kerviel as a student just like all the others who did not distinguish himself.

[85]Doreen Carvajal and Caroline Brothers, "'Rogue Trader' Is Remembered as Mr. Average," *New York Times*, January 26, 2008, pp. A1, A6.

[86]Nelson D. Schwartz and Katrin Bennhold, "A Trader's Secret, a Bank's Missteps," *New York Times*, February 5, 2008, pp. C1, C8.

[87]Kara Scannell, David Gauthier-Villars, and Amir Efrati, "SEC Probes French Bank," *Wall Street Journal*, February 5, 2008, p. A3.

[88]John W. Miller, "Hometown Boys: Tiny French Ville Drawn into Scandal," *Wall Street Journal*, January 28, 2008, pp. A1, A12.

[89]Doreen Carvajal and Caroline Brothers, "'Rogue Trader' Is Remembered as Mr. Average," *New York Times*, Jan. 26, 2008, pp. A1, A6.

The lack of engagement and self-confidence fuel the loner's diabolical side. Embezzlement, fraud, and other financial tomfoolery that elude internal controls are easier when there's no face on the harm and no interaction for accountability. And that sense of entitlement for the injustices they've endured make the license with company funds that much easier with the rationalization of, "I'll show them!" Kerviel told prosecutors in his first interview with them, "I was held in lower regard than the others because of my educational and professional background."[90]

Misdeeds come, as they always have, from opportunity and need. Failed internal controls give the opportunity, and the quest for recognition, not the money itself, is the need. Indeed, Société Générale's assurance that Kerviel did not profit personally from the trades is verification and akin to the former Orange County Treasurer, Robert Citron. A government employee gains no percentage bonus from dumping public funds into high-risk derivatives. But he can become the toast of the community for a brilliant portfolio, at least until he bets wrong. Citron did, and, as a result, Orange County became one of the few counties in the United States to be forced into bankruptcy.

High Performance

There is a quasi-quantitative common factor that precedes a rogue's downfall. All rogues perform well beyond expectations initially. Leeson was bringing in dollars as no one at Barings ever had, and all without a college education. Jett had increased the revenues in the Kidder bond department from 7 percent to 27 percent from 1992 to 1993. Bond markets are simply not that volatile. Citron was recognized nationally for his brilliant portfolio management of public funds. And Kerviel's earnings and bonus seemed to defy the young trader's IT background. In short, these folks were making money that should have raised eyebrows, if not audit red flags. One of the challenges any company faces is learning to ask questions when the news is good. Here the news was too good to be true, but the question of, "How is this possible?" was not percolating up to the right levels for response or investigation. Blind concurrence is a root cause; "rogue trader" is the superficial and finger-pointing analysis. Rogues exist in fertile organizations that grant autonomy in exchange for performance. Kerviel told prosecutors, "As long as we were winning, and this wasn't too visible and suited everybody, nobody said anything."[91]

In all of the organizations that claim that they fell victim to rogues, there were some who were raising questions about the high performance. In Kerviel's case, an auditor raised a question about one of his posted trades because it was posted on a Saturday, a day the markets are not open, and an error that enters into the backdating and fixing a young person who is evading internal controls would use. The young auditor took Kerviel's assurances because the auditor did not want to seem pushy. Being pushy is an auditor's job, especially when a trader is showing trades posted on days the markets are closed. Société Générale's CEO has admitted that the bank's internal controls systems were going 80 mph whilst the trading was going at 130 mph.[92]

Young 'Uns

There is one more signal that emerges and reemerges in these cases. These three and other villains who spin debt or financial yarns, and/or churn accounts, reach their pinnacles of access and power between the ages of 28 and 35. Perhaps this is the age when frustration sets in. They have lived through elusive success and a lack of recognition and

---

[90]David Gauthier-Villars and Stacy Meichtry, "Kerviel Felt Out of His League," *Wall Street Journal*, Jan. 31, 2008, pp. C1 and C2.

[91]Carrick Mollenkamp and David Gauthier-Villars, "France Presses Bank to Dump Besieged Chief over Trading," *Wall Street Journal*, January 30, 2008, pp. A1, A14.

[92]Schwartz and Bennhold, "A Trader's Secret, A Bank's Missteps," pp. C1, C8.

accolades. "Enough!" they seem to shout out from that isolated existence. They appear to reach a point of doing whatever it takes to attain the financial success and attention that has been out of reach in their professional lives.

What lesson do companies take from this factor? Well, those in the 28 to 35 age bracket would be wise to exercise some introspection and self-control. Use caution on caution. For companies, watch your employees in that range. Watch them carefully. In fact, a mentor/shadow program during this era might not be a bad idea. And be careful how compensation systems motivate employees in this age group.

Those Odd Things That Too Often Fall to the Cutting Room Floor

As the Kerviel story has emerged, some information that was odd but ignored has also emerged. Kerviel had a cell phone bill that ran to 1,000 euros per month. He was once questioned as to why he had such a high cell phone bill when he was a trader who worked at his desk all day. Those responsible for company expenses could not understand why his bill would be so high. As later information revealed, Kerviel was having extensive conversations with Moussa Bakir, a 32-year-old broker, for purposes of sending trades to cover his trades at the bank. The bank's e-mail system uncovered messages between Kerviel and Bakir, one of which from Bakir read, "You have done nothing illegal in terms of the law."[93] Mr. Kerviel's trial ended on June 26, 2010, he was found guilty, and he was sentenced to three years. He was ordered to pay $7 billion (4.9 Euros) in restitution. To the end of the trial, Mr. Kerviel maintained that the bank was aware of what he was doing but took no action and he was simply doing his job.

Excess cell phone bills or e-mails are not the left side of an equation that has fraud as its right side. However, letting this type of information fall to the cutting room floor is a mistake. Alone, you may just have evidence of a chatty trader. Couple the bills with the other factors here and you have a qualitative case for a closer look. Those cutting room floor pieces of information often can be grouped to force us to ask, "What am I missing?" And the fact that an employee is low on the totem pole does not mean there are not issues. Kerviel was in the so-called dull area of trading. Some of the dismissiveness of a problem perhaps came from the snootiness about the dull Delta team.[94] Kerviel was even able to dupe auditors with fake e-mail confirmations of trades that he had produced, something easily confirmed if the auditors had cross-checked with the bank's e-mail system.[95]

The information emerging in the Kerviel matter also indicates the bank did not have a sense of urgency when questions emerged. Items fell to the cutting room floor temporarily as well. For example, the surveillance office at Eurex notified a Société Générale compliance officer that Kerviel had engaged in several transactions that raised a red flag at the exchange. Société Générale received the notification on November 7, 2007. It did not respond to Eurex until November 20, 2007, and simply mollified the exchange by saying that the after-hour trades were due to the volatility in U.S. and European markets.[96] Eurex even asked the bank if Kerviel's trades had been entered manually.[97] Kerviel told bank auditors that if he revealed all of his strategies to Eurex that the bank

[93]Nicola Clark and Katrin Bennhold, "2nd Trader Emerges in Inquiry in France," *New York Times*, February 9, 2008, pp. B1, B4. One does wonder how something is illegal but does not violate the law and vice versa.
[94]David Gauthier-Williams and Carrick Mollenkamp, "The Loss Where No One Looked," *Wall Street Journal*, January 28, 2008, pp. C1, C3.
[95]David Gauthier-Villars and Carrick Mollenkamp, "Société Générale Blew Chances to Nab Trader," *Wall Street Journal*, February 29, 2008, pp. A1, A13.
[96]Schwartz and Bennhold, "a Trader's Secrets, a Bank's Missteps," pp. C1, C8.
[97]*Id.*

would lose its advantage in trading over its competitors, a refusal the auditors accepted and passed along to Eurex.

When the exchange was not satisfied with the explanation, it asked for more information on November 26, 2007. Despite Kerviel's ongoing exceeding of trading limits, Société Générale got back to Eurex on December 10, 2007. From there, the bank's risk managers took no further action. By the time of Kerviel's $2 billion trade on January 18, 2008, it would be too late. The bank's losses were a foregone conclusion.

Part of the cutting room floor phenomenon is also suppression of information—keeping bad news at the lowest level. In Christine Lagarde's report on Kerviel's trades and the bank's missteps, Ms. Lagarde pointed to three causal factors: (1) moving Kerviel from internal controls to trading; (2) lax security in the bank's computer system; and (3) the failure of those in risk management to alert management about the inquiries from Eurex. Those at the trading level and internal controls area were aware of the concerns, but neither of the two inquires made their way to management.[98]

Invincibility—"Covert Arrogance"

When the Société Générale loss emerged, the largest loss ever by a single trader, stunned regulators, auditors, and markets wondered aloud, "How could this have happened without anyone knowing the exposure?" The questions were similar when we were hit with the magnitude of the Enron and WorldCom frauds and a number of others that reached only the $2 to $3 billion levels. Part of the explanation is that because the bank or companies and their executives involved have been so well regarded and have done so well, that both they and those who work there have a feeling of invincibility, an arrogance that finds them fancying themselves immune from failure. One CEO who has lived through major problems erupting with no signals has referred to the phenomenon as "covert arrogance" in officers and employees.

Once the organization and individual have had a taste of a $2 billion gain, the desire for a repeat sets in and self-control disappears. They have done so well that they believe the roll can keep going. Warren Buffett has described control of this repeat desire to be a key to long-term success in business, "Once you have ordinary intelligence, what you need is the temperament to control the urges that get other people into trouble in investing."[99]

When that run of success is threatened, the behavior that results is of a type that indicates nothing else matters. They are now hell bent on preserving their success, even if their methods are bizarre, illegal, highly risky, or destructive to the company. France's chief prosecutor in the Kerviel case said, "When you have been performing these operations for months without being discovered, there is a kind of spiral, where you ultimately think yourself much stronger than the rest of the world."[100]

The antidote for this unscientific factor in trading is an internal control system that checks for the wild trades, something that failed at Société Générale.

Turning a Blind Eye

A blind eye has allowed the rogues. The success they show, seemingly too good to be true, causes us to engage in the willing suspension of disbelief. William T. Esrey, the CEO of Sprint described the challenges his company faced as the supernatural earnings of WorldCom confounded them, "Our performance did not quite compare and we were blaming ourselves. We didn't understand what we were doing wrong. We were like,

---

[98]Katrin Bennhold and James Kanter, "France Said to Suggest New Controls for Its Bank," *New York Times,* February 4, 2008, pp. C1, C5.

[99]Jenny Anderson, "Craving the High That Risky Trading Can Bring," *New York Times,* February 7, 2008, pp. C1, C9.

[100]Doreen Carvajal and James Kanter, "A Quest for Glory and a Bonus Ends in Disgrace," *New York Times,* January 29, 2008, pp. C1, C10.

'What are we missing here?'"[101] There is nothing he was missing, but the rest of us were not asking the tough questions when the rogues defied basic economics. As one Société Générale executive phrased it, the traders who were making money "were untouchable. They had the power."[102]

Mr. Kerviel told prosecutors that bank officials did not want to intervene when he was making money, ". . . they didn't want to intervene. They know the machinery."[103] He also noted that the bank took no action despite his having raised one of the basic red flags for auditors: he took only four days of holiday during 2007, "It is one of the rules of internal controls; a trader who doesn't take holidays is a trader who doesn't want his books to be seen by others."[104] Kerviel also told prosecutors, "I cannot believe that my superiors did not realize the amount I was risking. It is impossible to generate such profit with small positions. That's what leads me to say that while I was [in the black], my supervisors closed their eyes on the methods I was using and the volumes I was trading."[105]

Yet we still emerge with childlike surprise from these multi-billion losses at the hands of rogues who led us down the primrose and supernatural path, always professing our, "Who knew?" We could have known if we focused less on systems and more on human nature, historical patterns, and our belief that rogues happen. Rogues do indeed happen, but not unless we turn a blind eye. Fool me once. . . .

Discussion Questions

1. When the logistics of the Jett fraud were explained, former GE Chairman John F. (Jack) Welch Jr. said, "It's a pity that this ever happened. Jett could have made $2 to 3 million honestly." Categorize Jett according to the categories of moral development. Were there organizational factors that influenced the conduct of the men in these three cases? As you answer this question, consider the findings of the SE in Jett's case:

    We find that Jett's purported trading strategy deceived Kidder about the profitability of his securities trading. Jett created and implemented a scheme that exploited an anomaly in Kidder's computer system. The scheme generated "profits" on the firm's books that transformed Jett's failed securities trading into an apparent success. As a result, Kidder doubled Jett's salary, promoted him, and paid him multi-million-dollar bonuses. These "profits" misrepresented Kidder's financial condition on firm books, records, and regulatory filings, and would have to be written off, at firm expense. When inventory constraints during the balance sheet reduction effort impinged on his scheme, Jett himself claims he adapted it by developing and implementing the idea of "offsetting" recons, which allowed him to continue to book illusory profits. This was a scheme devised and orchestrated by Jett for his benefit.

    Jett argues that he disclosed the facts about his "trading strategy" to Mullin, Cerullo, some of their subordinates, such as Bernstein, and an internal auditor, that they could have learned the facts from various firm documents or reports, and that they benefitted from the profits. Mr. Kerviel maintained throughout his case that his superiors were aware of what he was doing and benefited from his efforts. What can you learn from this part of these two individuals' experiences?

2. An executive noted that Wall Street firms "have become victims of compensation schemes resulting in outrageously high salaries

---

[101]Seth Schiesel, "Trying to Catch WorldCom's Mirage," *New York Times*, June 30, 2002, p. BU1.

[102]Schwartz and Bennhold, "A Trader's Secret, a Bank's Missteps," pp. C1, C8.

[103]*Id.*

[104]David Gauthier-Villars and Carrick Mollenkamp, "Portrait Emerges of Rogue Trader at French Bank," *Wall Street Journal*, February 2, 2008, pp. A1, A7.

[105]David Gauthier-Villars and Stacy Meichtry, "Kerviel Felt Out of His League," *Wall Street Journal*, January 31, 2008, pp. C1, C2.

and bonuses. It brings out the worst in people who have any worst in them." Are compensation schemes responsible for poor ethical choices? Does a firm establish an ethical tone or culture with its compensation system? Should the supervisors in the three companies have realized that "something was not right"?

Case 4.8

Royal Dutch and the Reserves[106]

The Royal Dutch/Shell Group was required to take a write-down on the amount of oil reserves it was carrying on its books. Chairman Sir Philip Watts placed tremendous numbers pressure on executives and managers in the company. Walter van de Vijver, the company's exploration chief, was given the directive to get the company's reserves where they needed to be for purposes of ensuring the company's AAA rating. Bonuses for a significant group of officers, in an amount of 2 percent, were tied to increases in reserves, Sir Philip's instructions were to "leave no stone unturned" in making sure that for every barrel of oil sold, there was another barrel added to the reported reserves.[107]

As a result of this focus on reserves, the culture at Royal Dutch was one that was quite different from the usual vision of geologists and scientists. Managers were required to write and appear in skits that were then performed for the officers and chairman with a focus on creativity and finding reserves. One manager ran on stage naked to draw attention to his aggressiveness. Another staged a "Jerry Springer" skit, and still another pledged to return to the Dutch oil fields and bring more from those declining wells.[108] Managers were forced to hold hands and share each others' intimate secrets. They were also asked to raise their arms in the air in an exercise whose purpose no one is quite sure of. Some theorized that it might have been a sort of barrel dance to bring the fertile oil fields to their door.

Van de Vijver first raised the issue of the possible overstatement of the company's reserves with Watts in early 2002, and then documented his concerns with a memo to his files.[109] Watts gave van de Vijver a negative evaluation because of increasing tension between the two over the reserves. In response, van de Vijver sent Watts an e-mail in November 2003 with the following complaint: "I am becoming sick and tired of lying about the extent of our reserves issues and the downward revisions that need to be done because of far too aggressive/optimistic bookings."[110] Despite this documented battle between two of the company's highest-ranking officials, months would pass before the company disclosed the overstatement of reserves and took the necessary accounting write-downs.

The bonuses for the management team for 2003 and 2004 were booked before the overstatement release was sent out and the accounting adjustments taken. Memos and e-mails show that a large group of top officers was aware of the reserves issues.[111] By the time the information was finally released to the public, following an SEC inquiry in

---

[106]Adapted from Marianne M. Jennings, "The Seven Signs of Ethical Collapse: How to Spot Moral Meltdowns in Companies before It's Too Late."(2006).

[107]Stephen Labaton and Heather Timmons, "Discord at Top Seen as Factor in Shell's Woes," *New York Times*, April 20, 2004, pp. A1, C7.

[108]Chip Cummins and Álmar Latour, "How Shell's Move to Revamp Culture Ended in Scandal," *Wall Street Journal*, November 2, 2004, p. A1.

[109]Chip Cummins, "Former Chairman of Shell Was Told of Reserves Issues," *Wall Street Journal*, March 8, 2004, p. A1.

[110]Labaton and Timmons, "Discord at Top Seen as Factor in Shell's Woes," p. C7.

[111]Chip Cummins and Alexei Barrionuevo, "Shell Ex-Officials Hid Troubles amid Clash over Disclosure," *Wall Street Journal*, April 4, 2004, pp. A1, A12.

February 2004, Royal Dutch had to take a 22 percent reduction in its reserves figure. As a result, earnings from 2000 to 2003 were revised downward by $100 million. The company's chief financial officer, Judy Boynton, appeared to be aware of the overstatement of reserves but took no action. The three are no longer working at Royal Dutch.[112]

The company's share price dropped dramatically, and the SEC as well as officials in Britain collected a total of $150 million in fines for the overstatements of the reserve numbers.[113]

Discussion Questions

1. List the elements in the Royal Dutch culture that contributed to the decisions to overstate reserves and to continue those overstatements.

2. What issues did the executives and Sir Philip miss in their decisions to just keep the AAA rating with sufficient reserve numbers?

3. What did the company have in common with HealthSouth?

Reading 4.9

Stock Options, Backdating, and Disclosure Options: What Happened Here?[114]

"The Bottom Line on Options"[115]

"UnitedHealth Option Grants Raise Questions"[116]

"Converse to Restate Results after Options Audit"[117]

"UnitedHealth Chief Seeks End to Options"[118]

"CEO Seeks to Halt Stock-Based Pay at UnitedHealth"[119]

"Cost of Options Worries Investors"[120]

"Stock Options at Wholesale"[121]

"Questions Raised on Still More Stock Options"[122]

"'Backdate' Suits Are in the Pipeline"[123]

"Monster Worldwide Gave Officials Options Ahead of Share Run-Ups"[124]

"Tech CEOs' Pay Falls as Firms Cut Out Options"[125]

"During 1990s, Microsoft Practiced Type of Stock-Options Backdating"[126]

---

[112]Laurie P. Cohen and James Bandler, "Shell Finance Chief Has Faced Critics Before," *Wall Street Journal*, March 26, 2004, p. C1.

[113]Heather Timmons, "Shell to Pay $150 Million in Settlements on Reserves," July 30, 2004, pp. C1, C7.

[114]Reprinted with permission, Marianne M. Jennings, "Stock Options: What Happened Here?," *Corporate Finance Review* 11, no. 2 (2006): 44–48.

[115]*BusinessWeek*, April 3, 2006, p. 32.

[116]*Wall Street Journal*, April 17, 2006, p. C1.

[117]*Wall Street Journal*, April 18, 2006, p. A3.

[118]*New York Times*, April 19, 2006, p. C9.

[119]*Wall Street Journal*, April 19, 2006, p. A1.

[120]*Wall Street Journal*, April 24, 2006, p. C1.

[121]*New York Times*, April 29, 2006, p. B1.

[122]*New York Times*, May 6, 2006, p. C1.

[123]*National Law Journal*, June 5, 2006, p. 1.

[124]*Wall Street Journal*, June 12, 2006, p. A1.

[125]*Wall Street Journal*, June 15, 2006, p. B1.

[126]*Wall Street Journal*, June 16, 2006, p. A1.

"Home Depot Is Latest to Find Options Problem"[127]

"Still Addicted to Options"[128]

"Options Timing Raises Concerns among Insurers"[129]

"Microsoft Defends Its Options Dating, Saying It Followed Accounting Rules"[130]

"Why '90s Audits Failed to Flag Suspect Options"[131]

"Another Dodgy Way to Dole Out Options"[132]

"Options Watch: Inquiries Stand at 40"[133]

"Timely Question: How to Undo Unfair Options"[134]

"Options Gone Wild!"[135]

"Apple Tells of Problems on Options"[136]

"CA Misses Report Deadline"[137]

The headlines tell the same story in the usual sequence. We discover a company that has used a questionable accounting or financial reporting practice. We confront that company, wag our fingers, cluck our tongues, and demand change. Then we realize that the company may well be just the tip of the iceberg. Other firms 'fess up to the same practice. In their defense we hear from the companies' spokespersons, "We followed GAAP," or, "Everybody did it this way." The regulators move in, restatements abound, and we are left scratching our heads and asking the same question that has been uttered far too often over the past decade, "How could this happen?"

Enron was not the only company using mark-to-market accounting. Enron went to extremes, but virtually every utility had increasing portions of their earnings from energy trading contracts that allowed a great deal of discretion on the when and how much to book. Likewise, WorldCom and Tyco were creative mergers-and-acquisitions-accounting writ large. But companies with far fewer acquisitions and mergers were using the same tools to push the accounting envelope on a smaller scale. There are always percolating practices and financial reporting trends. Some companies push the envelope farther on those practices than others. As a result, all of us will be swept up in the inevitable, "Wait a minute!" net that is cast when a less-than-transparent practice comes to the surface.

As we think about this repeating pattern, add one more headline: "Options Put Giants in a Jam." The headline sounds similar to all the others, but it is distinct. This headline is from *BusinessWeek* in 2001.[138] At that time, there were issues centered on company use and control of options. Had we paid heed then, we might have put tighter controls on the executive option grants practices that have been dogging us for most of 2006 and will continue as the SEC completes forty announced investigations of companies, their options practices, and the accounting related to those grants.

---

[127] *Wall Street Journal*, June 17–18, 2006, p. A3.

[128] *New York Times*, June 18, 2006, p. 3–1 (Sunday Business Section).

[129] *Wall Street Journal*, June 20, 2006, p. C1.

[130] *Wall Street Journal*, June 21, 2006, p. C1.

[131] *Wall Street Journal*, June 22, 2006, p. B1.

[132] *BusinessWeek*, June 26, 2006, p. 40.

[133] *BusinessWeek*, June 26, 2006, p. 32.

[134] *Wall Street Journal*, June 27, 2006, p. C1.

[135] *Fortune*, July 10, 2006, p. 86.

[136] *New York Times*, June 30, 2006, p. C1.

[137] *New York Times*, June 30, 2006, p. C1.

[138] Debra Sparks, "Options Put Giants in a Jam," *BusinessWeek*, January 15, 2001, p. 68.

The backdating of options strike prices is one in a long line of corporate finance practices that have followed the same evolutionary pattern. And with each of these accounting and financial reporting issues, there is a pattern, some common threads, along the steady decline to "We forgot to expense $1.6 billion in options" (as was the case with UnitedHealth) that might help us as we navigate the next evolving issues. As the common threads emerge, executives and boards should begin focusing on the next issue: what practice fits this pattern, and do we need to make changes?

Common Thread #1: What We Are Doing Complies with Accounting Rules and the Law and Is Ethical, Sort Of

William W. McGuire, UnitedHealth Group's CEO, had the classic explanation of his company's additional $1.6 billion in options expenses that were not booked: "I can say that, to my knowledge, every member of management in this company believes that, at the time, we collectively followed appropriate practices for those option grants which affected all of our employees, not simply selected executives, and that such activities were within guidelines and consistent with our stated program objectives."[139] Translation and qualifiers:

- There may be other facts that change my statement ("to my knowledge").
- Everybody here thought it was okay ("we collectively").
- It may not be right, but we thought it was ("every member of management believes that, at the time").
- Not just we executives got options; the employees were in on this too ("not simply selected executives").
- Not sure about propriety now, but they sure did meet our own goals and rules ("the activities were within guidelines and consistent with our stated program objectives").

The parsed legal statement is an indicator that even if there are not legal difficulties with whatever options practices UnitedHealth employed, there are ethical issues. The sheer defensiveness and highly qualified nature of the statement is indicative of a hand caught in the cookie jar marked "Accounting Rules and Regulatory Loopholes to Be Taken Advantage Of." What is perhaps most telling about the confidence in accounting, legal, and ethical propriety of the options practices is Mr. McGuire's nonresponse when asked whether the options grants were backdated: "We sleep with good conscience."[140]

Nearly thirty years of study and instruction in the fields of law and ethics have convinced me that businesspeople know when they have crossed a legal and/or ethical line. The challenge for them, and the temptation, is that crossing that line makes things so much easier, at least temporarily, for them, for their companies, and for their investors. Crossing that line does avoid pain, temporarily, and often has the added literal and figurative bonus for the executives who decide the line can move just a bit this once.

Options really do have some complexities in terms of both their timing and their award. And options do serve an important role in a start-up or a company that is looking to expand its employee talent base. The company may not have the cash to compensate the talent, but the talent can be attracted by options. The issue is the disclosure of that eventual compensation expense: how much it will be and when it will come due. And not all options are created equal. There are several practices on options that have become all lumped together, but were rationalized in various ways by executives, boards, and auditors:

[139]AP, "UnitedHealth Chief Seeks End to Options," *New York Times*, April 19, 2006, p. C9.
[140]*Id.*

- Backdating: The granting of a stock option is dated back to an earlier date, one that had a much lower price and allows an immediate return to the executive or employee. For example, suppose that ABC Company stock is worth $90 today. However, the stock was at $60 just a few months earlier. If the award date is backdated to that lower strike price, the option grantee has an immediate gain of $30 per share.
- Backdating with limitations: Microsoft has admitted some nuanced backdating in the 1990s, but it was only backdating for the past thirty days. The options were granted at a strike price that was the lowest price of the stock during the thirty-day period prior to the award.
- Spring-loading: Options are granted just prior to a major announcement by a company that sees its stock price jump. Once again, there is an immediate gain once the news is public.
- Downloading: Options are granted just following bad news announcements that drive the stock price down. Grantees thus have a very low share price and can wait until the stock climbs again and then realize a return on those options.

What makes it difficult to create a civil or criminal case against the company or executives is proving that the information (in the case of spring-loading or backdating) would have a material effect on the stock price. The options are dated in advance of the announcements and the resultant market effects, so part of the element of proof is knowledge that the information would affect the stock price, and in a positive way. Further, proof of that intent would almost require establishing that the company and its officers were aware that all other variables, such as market conditions and issues, would remain in equilibrium. These elements make both criminal and civil cases difficult to pursue.

However, it is precisely because of that difficulty in proving legal violations that the companies and executives that use these formulas for strike prices feel comfortable in a legal sense. As one expert noted, proving that the announcement would "juice the stock price" is a tall order, particularly when there is just a one-time grant that proved fortuitous. Jacob S. Frenkel, a former SEC enforcement lawyer has called it "a much grayer area."[141]

Further, not even the auditors picked up on the options dating issues by these companies. Options-tracking software was used from 1995 until today, but the programs kept track of the options grants and the resulting impact on the company's financials, and that information was then filed with the SEC. However, the software was not sophisticated enough to pick up changes in grant dates nor was there the audit infrastructure in place to review grant dates.[142] The Sarbanes–Oxley changes have also made it more difficult to change the grant dates because executive options must be disclosed within two days of the grant. Pre-Sarbanes–Oxley, the 8-K disclosures were done at the end of the month in which they were granted. Further, given that the rules on expensing options were not in effect (and have still not fully taken effect with all the exemptions), there was a bit of a financial black hole on what was really happening with the options and how much they were costing the company. Where there is insufficient oversight or regulation, there is room for interpretation and loopholes. The options grants fit perfectly in the classic regulatory cycle pattern of a latency stage issue that was well known in companies and financial circles but not understood or imagined by investors and regulators.

Common Thread #2: Everybody Does It

Just the headline introduction indicates the pervasiveness of the options questions and issues. In addition to the comfort of operating in a gray area, companies and executives had the conscience-easing factor that they were not alone in their practices. Indeed, the

---

[141]Jane Sasseen, "Another Dodgy Way to Dole Out Options," *BusinessWeek*, June 26, 2006, p. 40.

[142]George Anders, "Why '90s Audits Failed to Flag Suspect Options," *Wall Street Journal*, June 22, 2006, p. B1.

issue had floated around academic circles since the time that we realized the companies, such as Dell and Microsoft, were playing the puts and calls game with their own stock.[143] The legal and ethical issue that arose is whether executives, knowing what they were facing in terms of their position on the puts and calls, would control the flow of information in order to influence the share price. The thought seemed insidious and diabolical at the time, that executives would actually manipulate the release of information to influence stock price. The thought crossed over into the question of the award of options. Perhaps even the academic detachment was lost in the "everybody does it" shuffle that made such widespread manipulation difficult to comprehend as a reality. The "everybody does it" assurance, coupled with the inherent complexity of these types of grants, often blind us to the reality of how wrong the conduct is on a very simple level of "Is this fair?" (see discussion below).

The failure of the academic world to issue warnings was partly a function of data availability and partly a function of an unwillingness to attribute option date manipulation to executives and boards in the granting of options. As one academic noted, the initial idea papers on the timing of options grants were met with skepticism because "The whole idea seemed so sinister."[144] The initial studies in finance journals concluded that while there were abnormal returns before (low) and after (high) stock option grants, they were "statistically indistinguishable."[145] Other studies suggested there was significance, but additional studies proved difficult in terms of access to data.[146] The topic was dropped by the finance journals.[147] Professor Erik Lie, then of the College of William and Mary, who had written an idea paper that was met with shrugs, was undaunted. Collecting the data from companies was problematic because it involved individual company contact with company public relations officers and investment relations directors, who rebuffed his requests if they responded. When the data on the grants and daily tracking data became more easily accessible through databases, Professor Lie, by that time at the University of Iowa, had at it and found that "abnormal stock returns are negative before unscheduled executive option awards and positive afterward."[148] Interestingly, his results were not accepted into the finance journals but appeared in *Management Science*. The finance researcher who originally suggested the options problem credits Lie for his ability to see all possible explanations for the data and explore it fully.

Again, this academic debate fits the pattern. This line of research and debate was percolating even as the options practices increased and morphed. The pattern offers a signal to board members. It is not enough for them to understand accounting and financial reporting. They should be paying attention to the debates by academics who explore, and sometimes resist exploration, those areas where the law and regulation have not yet caught up with innovative, albeit ethically creative, practices.

Common Thread #3: The Line Keeps Getting Pushed Back Until the SEC Calls

Although Professor Lie deserves his due for his work and findings, his study was published in 2005, and the options issue did not heat up until the confluence of the accounting disclosures on options expenses with the realization of how much those options

[143]Sparks, "Options Put Giants in a Jam," pp. 68–69.

[144]Steve Stecklow, "Options Study Becomes Required Reading," *Wall Street Journal*, May 30, 2006, p. B1.

[145]David Aboody and Ron Kaznik, "Stock Options Awards and the Timing of Corporate Voluntary Disclosures," *Journal of Finance* 59 (2000), 1651.

[146]Kevin W. Chauvin and Catherine Shenoy, "Stock Price Decreases Prior to Executive Stock Options," *Journal of Corporate Finance* 7 (2001), 53.

[147]The topic had been floating about since 1997 in the *Journal of Finance*. David Yermack, "Good Timing: CEO Stock Option Awards and Company News Announcements," *Journal of Finance* 52 (1997), 449.

[148]Erik Lie, "On the Timing of CEO Stock Option Awards," *Management Science* 51 (2005), 802.

would really cost. Exploring the cost of the options then led to the next question of how so many executives could be doing so well with options. The study and economic reality collided, and the SEC is now on the scene conducting a full investigation. Perhaps the $1.6 billion options expense announced by UnitedHealth was the tipping point that caused pointed questions in boardrooms and the resulting flurry of company confessions. Even with the good professor's findings, companies were not stepping forward with accountability. Companies waited nearly a year after the study to see if questions would arise. Perhaps that year would have been longer had not the expenses that resulted from the implementation of the new accounting for options attracted so much attention and analysis. If there had been voluntary disclosures as a result of the suggestions of options backdating made in 1997, how different both the debate on options disclosures and practices on awards would have been. Perhaps most stunning about the revelation of the extent of the problem is that the practice continued post-Sarbanes–Oxley, let alone post-Enron. Transparency being the new goal of the regulations, hidden formulas for backdating options do carry a certain degree of chutzpah. But, the line was pushed gradually in terms of costs to the company. The extension of options to more executives and employees only increased the comfort level because the perception of fairness increased as the opportunities were available to more employees in the companies. With each push of the options envelope, there was some comfort in knowing that these practices had gone on for so long with no repercussions and that so many more people were benefiting. Still, when the eventual full public disclosure comes, there is a sheepishness that comes from the realization of how far they had slipped. The ubiquitous parsing begins. United Health's example was offered earlier. Microsoft's statement was that the practice of the lowest strike price in the thirty days prior was "no longer practiced," and the former manager for stock and retirement programs at the company said, "My experience working there was they operated the [option] plan with high levels of integrity."[149] The difficulty is that integrity does sometimes get away from us what with all the complexities of finance and options. But, we are left with the fourth and final common thread to address.

Common Thread #4: It's All about the Fairness

Once we get past the computer modeling and the graphic patterns on the issue of options, their grants, and the strike price, there is a fundamental truth that stares at us: the options timing issues is all about fairness. Those who benefited from a retroactive strike price or a strike price decided upon in advance of the release of company information that will move the stock price created a market in which executives and employees benefited from their creation of a market operating with asymmetrical information. They took advantage of a situation in which they had superior knowledge in order to gain maximum benefit from a compensation program paid for by their own investors. There is an inherent conflict of interest that those who benefit from stock options have when they have control over three things: the information the company releases and when; the accounting decisions for the company; and the financial reports that the company releases. Putting those powers together in the same people who hold personal interests in the timing of grants of stock options presents temptation that asks too much of even our corporate saints. Human nature is the reason conflicts of interest rules exist, and there are two way to manage a conflict of interest: do not engage in the conduct that creates a conflict or disclose the conflict to those who might be affected. The companies that were involved in awarding options based on strike prices that were backdated or

[149]Charles Forelle and James Bandler, "During 1990s, Microsoft Practiced Type of Stock-Options Backdating," *Wall Street Journal*, June 16, 2006, p. A1.

spring-loaded had created conflicts of interest that were neither managed nor disclosed. When all the complications of market fluctuations are analyzed and explanations offered, the issue of backdating options has gripped the market, discussions and the SEC because, regardless of legal violations, we are left with that gut reaction inherent in all ethical issues: it just was not fair. This simple test, along with checks for the first three common factors, could serve us well in all of the complicated questions of accounting, financial reporting, and, as we learned here, compensation. As they percolate, we should watch, evaluate, think through the pattern, and finally ask whether what we are doing is fair.

Discussion Questions

1. Give some tests from Units 1 and 2 that would help with answering the question "Is this fair?"
2. Consider the conduct of Dr. McGuire. Why do you think he believed and continues to believe that he did nothing unethical or illegal?
3. What credo ideas do you gain from the officers involved in these cases?
4. The criminal conviction of former Brocade CEO, Greg Reyes, was reversed because the prosecutor in the case made misleading statements and withheld evidence about who knew what at Brocade about the options. Mr. Reyes was the sole member of Brocade's board's compensation committee and, as such, had the authority to determine all compensation packages for executives, including himself and his options. Mr. Reyes also argued that he, as the compensation committee, awarded the options to himself and others with the full blessing of the finance folks at Brocade. Prosecutors in the case argued in their closing statement that the finance folks did not know and that Mr. Reyes had acted secretly and with criminal intent. However, the prosecutors had in their possession statements from those who were at the head of the finance department at Brocade. Those statements indicated that they did indeed know about the options. The appellate court found that this withheld evidence was critical. Does Mr. Reyes's acting as the sole authority for approving his options raise any ethical issues? What thoughts do you gain about the "gray area" from this situation and the era of options? Evaluate the ethics of the prosecutors in the case. Be sure to think about a possible credo component for a prosecutor.

Case 4.10

FINOVA and the Loan Write-Off

The FINOVA Group, Inc., was formed as a commercial finance firm in 1992. It was created as a spin-off from the Greyhound Financial Corporation (GFC). GFC underwent a complete restructuring at that time and other spin-offs included the Dial Corporation.

FINOVA, headquartered in Phoenix, Arizona, quickly became a Wall Street darling. Its growth was ferocious. By 1993, its loan portfolio was over $1 billion both through its own loans as well as the acquisition of U.S. Bancorp Financial, Ambassador Factors, and TriCon Capital. In 1994, FINOVA had a successful $226 million stock offering. By 1995, its loan portfolio was $4.3 billion. Standard & Poors rated the company's senior debt as *A,* and Duff & Phelps upgraded its rating to *A* in 1995 when FINOVA issued $115 million in convertible preferred shares and its portfolio reached $6 billion. FINOVA's income went from $30.3 million in 1991 to $117 million by 1996 to $13.12 billion in 1999. *Forbes* named FINOVA to its Platinum 400 list of the fastest-growing and most profitable companies in January 2000.

FINOVA was consistently named as one of the top companies to work for in the United States (it debuted as number 12 on the list published by *Fortune* magazine in 1998 and subsequent years). Its benefits included an on-site gym for employee workouts and tuition for the children of FINOVA employees (up to $3,000 per child) who attended any one of the three Arizona state universities under what FINOVA called the "Future Leaders Grant Program."[150] FINOVA also had generous bonus and incentive plans tied to the stock price of the company. *Fortune* magazine described the 500 stock options each employee is given when hired, the free on-site massages every Friday, concierge services, and unlimited time off with pay for volunteer work as a "breathtaking array of benefits."[151]

The name *FINOVA* was chosen as a combination of "financial" and "innovators." However, some with language training pointed out that FINOVA is a Celtic term that means "pig with lipstick." FINOVA took pride in its strategic distinction from other finance companies. It was able to borrow cheaply and then make loans to businesses at a premium. Its borrowers were those who were too small, too new, or too much in debt to qualify at banks.[152] Its 1997 annual report included the following language from FINOVA's CEO and chairman of the board, Sam Eichenfield:

FINOVA is, today, one of America's largest independent commercial finance companies. We concentrate on serving midsize business—companies with annual sales of $10 million to $300 million—with arguably the industry's broadest array of financing products and services. The goals we set forth in our first Annual Report were to:

- *grow our income by no less than 10% per year;*
- *provide our shareholders with an overall return greater than that of the S&P 500;*
- *preserve and enhance the quality of our loan portfolios;*
- *continue enjoying improved credit ratings*

We have met those goals and, because they remain equally valid today, we intend to continue meeting or surpassing them in the future. Many observers comment on FINOVA's thoughtfulness and discipline and, indeed, FINOVA prides itself on its focus.

FINOVA also had a reputation for its generous giving in the community. Again, from its 1997 annual report:

FINOVA believes that it has a responsibility to support the communities in which its people live and work. Only by doing so can we help guarantee the future health and vitality of our clients and prospects, and only by doing so can we assure ourselves of our continuing ability to attract the best people.

Over the years, not only have FINOVA and its people contributed monetarily to a broad range of charitable, educational and cultural causes, but FINOVA people have contributed their time and energy to a variety of volunteer efforts.

In 1996, FINOVA contributed more than $1.5 million and thousands of volunteer hours to educate and develop youth, house the homeless, feed the hungry, elevate the arts, and support many other deserving causes around the country.

FINOVA's ascent continued in the years following the 1997 report. Its stock price climbed above $50 per share, and management continued to emphasize reaching the income goals and the goals for portfolio growth. Throughout the company, many spoke of the unwritten goal of reaching a stock price of $60 per share. That climb in stock price was rewarded. The stock traded in the $50 range for most of 1998 and 1999, reaching a high of $54.50 in July 1999.

---

[150]Dawn Gilbertson, "Finova's Perks Winning Notice," *(Phoenix) Arizona Republic*, December 22, 1998, pp. E1, E9.

[151]"The 100 Best Companies to Work For," *Fortune*, January 11, 1999, p. 122.

[152]Riva D. Atlas, "Caught in a Credit Squeeze," *New York Times*, November 2, 2000, pp. C1, C21.

At the end of 1998, FINOVA reported that Mr. Eichenfield's compensation for the year was $6.5 million, the highest for any CEO of firms headquartered in Phoenix. More than half of the compensation consisted of bonuses. Mr. Eichenfield and his wife purchased a $3 million home in nearby Paradise Valley shortly following the year-end announcement in 1998 of his compensation.[153] Mr. Eichenfield was named the 1999 Fabulous Phoenician by *Phoenix Magazine,* which included the following description:

> *A true mensch in every sense of the word, Sam casually says, "I do what I can," referring to the community for which he has done so much. While he maintains a modest air on the outside, Sam admits, "I take a lot of pride in having created a lot of opportunity for a lot of people." As long as Sam is head of FINOVA and lives in this community, we're sure there will be many more people who will benefit from his kindness and his generosity.*[154]

It was sometime during the period from 1996 through 1998 that issues regarding financial reporting arose within the company. FINOVA had a decentralized management structure that created autonomous units. There were at least sixteen different finance divisions such as Commercial Equipment Finance, Commercial Real Estate Finance, Corporate Finance, Factoring Services, Franchise Finance, Government Finance, Healthcare Finance, Inventory Finance, Transportation Finance, and Rediscount Finance. Each of these units had its own manager, credit manager, and financial manager. In many cases, the failure of one unit to meet prescribed goals resulted in another unit making up for that shortcoming through some changes in that unit's numbers that they would report for the consolidated financial statements of FINOVA.

The Resort Finance division was a particularly high-risk segment of the company. Resort Finance was the term used to describe what were time-share interests that FINOVA was financing.[155] Time-share financing is a particularly risky form of financing because lenders are loaning money to borrowers who live in France for property located in the Bahamas that has been built by a company from the Netherlands and is managed by a firm with its headquarters in Britain. The confluence of laws, jurisdiction, and rights makes it nearly impossible to collect should the borrowers default. And the default rate is high because time-sharing interests are a luxury item that are the first payments to be dropped when households experience a drop in income because of illness or the loss of a job.

Resort Finance would prove to be a particularly weak spot in the company and an area in which questions about FINOVA's financial reporting would arise. For example, FINOVA had a time-share property loan for an RV park in Arkansas that had a golf course and restaurant. The idea, when first acted on in 1992, was that folks could pay for a place to park their RV in beautiful Arkansas for a week or two in a time-share RV resort. When the loan was made in 1992, the property had a book value of $800,000. At the time of the default in 1995, the property was worth $500,000. FINOVA took back the property but did not write down the loan. It did, however, continue to report the loan as an earning asset even as it capitalized the expenses it incurred to maintain the golf course and restaurant. By 1997, FINOVA was carrying the Arkansas time-share resort on its books as a $5.5 million earning asset. One manager remarked, "You couldn't sell all of Arkansas and get $5.5 million and we were carrying a bad loan at that amount."[156]

---

[153] "Finova Chief Splurges on $3 Million Mansion," *(Phoenix) Arizona Republic,* January 23, 1998, pp. E1, E7.

[154] *Phoenix Magazine,* 1999.

[155] Interviews with Jeff Dangemond, former finance/portfolio manager, FINOVA, 1996–2000.

[156] *Id.*

Because of its lending strategies, FINOVA had higher risk in virtually all of its lending divisions. For example, it was highly invested in high-tech companies because they fit the category of too new and too risky for banks.

However, FINOVA edged into the *Fortune* 1000 and built new company headquarters in Scottsdale, Arizona, as part of a revitalization project there. Its headquarters housed 380 employees, cost $50 million to construct, and was located just north of the tiny Scottsdale Fashion Square shopping mall. FINOVA had about 1,000 other employees at offices around the world.

In the first quarter of 1999, FINOVA again caught national attention for the cover of its annual report that would soon be released. The cover featured a robot, but the head of the robot had an underlying wheel that readers could rotate. There were six heads to the robot, all photos of FINOVA employees. The torso of the robot was a safe, and the arms and legs were made of symbols of the various industries in which FINOVA had lending interests. "When you have innovators in your name, you can't do a generic annual report," was the description from a FINOVA PR spokesman.[157]

However, the buzz over the annual report cover was small compared to what happened when the cover, printed ten weeks in advance of the content, was to be coupled with the numbers inside the report. FINOVA announced that its annual report would be delayed. It was unclear what was happening until its long-standing auditors, Deloitte and Touche, were fired. Mr. Eichenfield explained that FINOVA fired its auditors because they had waited so long to discuss their concerns and issues with management. He indicated that he felt they should have raised the issues much earlier than on the eve of the release of the numbers.[158]

FINOVA then hired Ernst & Young, but when the annual report was finally released the company also announced that it would be restating earnings for the year. The price of the company's stock began to decline. FINOVA worked diligently to restore credibility, with its officers noting that the auditors' disagreements with management's numbers were often because the company was too conservative in its accounting and that there were counterbalances for decisions on aggressive vs. conservative accounting practices.[159] However, with a shift in economic conditions and the end of the high-tech market run, the asset quality of FINOVA's portfolio was deteriorating. FINOVA's acquisition of the Fremont Financial Group of California for $765 million only increased investors' concerns about the direction of the company and the quality of its management. By the end of 1999, its stock price had dipped to $34 per share.

In early 2000, when it was again time for the release of the annual report, there was to be another announcement about FINOVA's financial position. FINOVA announced that it was writing down a $70 million loan to a California computer manufacturer. Ernst & Young refused to certify the financial statements until the write-off was taken and the resulting shake-up followed.[160] At the same time as the announcement of the write-off, the FINOVA board announced Sam Eichenfield's retirement with a compensation package of $10 million.[161]

FINOVA had to take an $80 million hit, or $0.74 per share, in one day to cover the loan write-off of $70 million plus the compensation package. FINOVA's stock, which had dipped to $32 per share when the 1998 issues on the annual report delay first surfaced, dropped to $19.88 in one day of heavy trading. The 38 percent dip in stock value

[157] "Cover of Finova's '98 Report Turns Heads," *(Phoenix) Arizona Republic*, April 9, 1999, p. E1.

[158] Dawn Gilbertson, "Finova Record Smudged," *(Phoenix) Arizona Republic*, April 18, 1999, pp. D1, D2.

[159] Max Jarman, "Finova Group's Stock Sinks," *(Phoenix) Arizona Republic*, December 10, 1999, pp. E1, E2.

[160] Anne Brady, "Shareholders Sue Finova Executives," *(Mesa, Ariz.) Tribune*, May 20, 2000, p. B1.

[161] Dawn Gilbertson, "Surprises at Finova," *(Phoenix) Arizona Republic*, March 28, 2000, pp. B1, B9.

was the largest for any stock that day on the New York Stock Exchange, March 27, 2000.[162] As analysts noted, there was a downward spiral because the trust had been breached in 1998; confidence was not regained, and this latest write-off and its delay served to shake investor confidence. Two rating agencies immediately lowered FINOVA's credit ratings, and the costs of its funds jumped dramatically.[163]

Shareholder lawsuits began in May 2000 with several alleging that the $70 million loan had been in default eight months earlier but that, because of bonus and compensation packages tied to the share price, the officers and managers opted not to write the loan off in order to maximize their compensation packages, which were computed at the end of December before the write-off was taken.

Also during May 2000, Credit Suisse First Boston, hired to aid the company strategically, announced that FINOVA had lost a $500 million line of credit from banks. Such a loss was seen as mandating the sale of the company because commercial loan companies must have $1 in a credit line as backup for every $1 in commercial paper. FINOVA's stock fell to $12.62 on May 9, 2000.[164] Analysts noted that FINOVA's aggressive growth strategy placed it in a particularly vulnerable situation because, as credit lines dried up, it had more exposure on its large loan portfolios. Further, the nature of those portfolios was such that its default rate was higher than other commercial lenders. Analysts valued its loan portfolio at $0.58 on the dollar.[165]

By early 2001, FINOVA was reporting that it had lost $1 billion for the year.[166] It declared Chapter 11 bankruptcy on March 7, 2001. Its default on its bond debt was the largest since the Great Depression. Its bankruptcy is the eighth largest in history, with Enron displacing it in fall 2001 (Case 4.15), and WorldCom then displacing Enron (see Case 4.27). Now ranking number one is Lehman Brothers (Case 4.5). Its stock price fell to $1.64 per share on April 2, 2001. The stock would fall to $0.88 per share until Warren Buffett's Berkshire Hathaway Company and Leucadia National Corporation made a buyout proposal for FINOVA, which caused the stock to jump to $2.13 in March 2001.[167] Berkshire Hathaway owns $1.4 billion of FINOVA's debt, including $300 million in bank debt and $1.1 billion in public bonds.

GE Capital and Goldman Sachs then countered the Buffett offer, but the bankruptcy court approved the Buffett offer.[168] However, pursuant to its rights under the agreement, the Buffett team backed out of the purchase. Berkshire Hathaway did purchase 25 percent of FINOVA's shares, and FINOVA was able to restructure itself in Chapter 11 bankruptcy. FINOVA emerged from Chapter 11 in 2001, but in November 2006, the company's board of directors voted to liquidate the company. The business was officially closed on December 4, 2006. The company's 10-K report for 2006 indicates that it will not be able to repay its note holders and that all of its assets have been pledged to existing creditors. All of the company offices, except one located in Scottsdale, Arizona, have been closed, with the resulting reduction in force of nearly all employees. The offices in Scottsdale have been moved from the opulent headquarters on Scottsdale Road, and the building FINOVA built is now occupied by a number of companies and professional offices. Its stock reached

[162]*Id.*

[163]Rhonda L. Rundle, "Finova Retains Credit Suisse Unit to Assess Operations," *Wall Street Journal*, May 10, 2000, p. A12.

[164]Donna Hogan, "Finova Finances May Force Sale," *(Mesa, Ariz.) Tribune*, May 9, 2000, pp. B1, B2.

[165]Atlas, "Caught in a Credit Squeeze," pp. C1, C21.

[166]Max Jarman, "Finova Posts $1 Billion Loss," *(Phoenix) Arizona Republic*, April 3, 2001, p. D1.

[167]Paul M. Sherer and Devon Spurgeon, "Finova Agrees to a Bailout by Berkshire and Leucadia," *Wall Street Journal*, February 28, 2001, pp. C1, C18.

[168]Edward Gately, "Bankruptcy Court OKs Finova Plan," *(Mesa, Ariz.) Tribune*, August 11, 2001, p. B1.

a high price of $0.12 per share during 2006, with a low price of $0.06. Its Chapter 11 bankruptcy ended in December 2009.

Discussion Questions

1. Why do you think the officers and managers waited until the auditors required it to write off the $70 million loan? Given FINOVA's fate and its freefall in stock price to a final price of $0.12, what issues did the executives miss in analyzing the decision to write down or not write down the loan? Whose interests were served by the decision?

2. Do you think the incentive plans had any effect on the reported earnings? Why or why not?

3. Was FINOVA so generous with its perks for employees that there was a resulting loyalty that was blinding the employees to the real financial condition of the company and the financial reporting issues? Would these perks have had an effect on you if you worked for FINOVA?

4. Was FINOVA forthcoming about the level of risk in its business?

Compare & Contrast

The FINOVA employees are gone or have been laid off. What impression do you think their time at FINOVA makes as prospective employers read their résumés? Do you see any lines for your credo in the experience of these young businesspeople at a young company?

The Structural Factors: Governance, Example, and Leadership

Reading 4.11

A Primer on Sarbanes–Oxley[169]

The Sarbanes–Oxley Act of 2002, with actual names of the Investor Confidence Act, the Public Accounting and Corporate Accountability Act, Public Company Accounting Reform and Investor Protection Act of 2002, and several others that focused on the purpose of the legislation, was passed to buoy up public confidence in the financial reports of public companies and increase transparency in those financial reports. The introduction to SOX, as it has come to be known, gives the following purpose: *an act to protect investors by improving the accuracy and reliability of corporate disclosures made pursuant to the securities laws, and for other purposes.*

The new portions of the law appear at 15 U.S.C. §7201. However, because many of the provisions amend the Securities Exchange Act of 1934, which begins at 78 U.S.C. §1 *et seq.,* many of the provisions can be found there.

Part I: The Creation of the Public Company Accounting Oversight Board

This section of SOX established a quasi-governmental entity called the Public Company Accounting Oversight Board (PCAOB, but called *Peek-a-Boo*), under the direction of the SEC, to (1) oversee the audit of public companies covered by the federal securities laws (the 1933 and 1934 Acts); (2) establish audit report standards and rules; and (3) investigate, inspect, and enforce compliance through both the registration and regulation of public accounting firms. An accounting firm and a non-profit organization challenged the constitutionality of the federal government delegating its enforcement authority to a quasi-government body such as PCAOB, but the U.S. Supreme Court upheld the board as a constitutional exercise of federal power over the regulation of the financial markets. However, the court struck down a provision that permitted the president to remove a PCAOB chair only for cause because such a limit interfered with the president's constitutional duty of enforcing the law.[170]

PCAOB was given the authority to require public accounting firms that conduct audits of companies that are covered under federal securities laws to register with PCAOB. This registration control gives PCAOB both the means and the authority to discipline public accounting firms, including the ability to impose sanctions such as prohibitions on conducting future audits. PCAOB's powers related to intentional conduct or repeated negligent conduct by audit firms when they have done company audits and financial certifications.

This portion of SOX also gives the SEC the authority to determine what are or are not "generally accepted" accounting principles for purposes of complying with securities laws. These so-called GAAP rules were once the province of the accounting profession, but that authority was transferred to regulators under SOX. The SEC was also directed to study and then adopt a system of principles-based accounting for purposes of

---

[169]Adapted from the House and Senate summary of the Sarbanes–Oxley Act of 2002 that appeared on the Senate website in August 2002.

[170]*Free Enterprise Fund v Public Company Accounting Oversight Board*, 130 S.Ct. 3138 (2010).

compliance with the securities law on registrations and required filings by publicly traded companies. The study of and movement toward principles-based accounting has been slow, with no major changes as of 2010.

Part II: Auditor Independence

This portion of SOX is a bit of a statutory code of ethics for public accounting firms. Accounting firms that audit publicly traded companies cannot also perform the following consulting services for the companies they audit:

1. Bookkeeping and other services related to the accounting records or financial statements of the audit client
2. Design and implementation of financial information systems
3. Appraisal and valuation services, fairness opinions, and contribution-in-kind reports
4. Actuarial services
5. Internal audit outsourcing services
6. Management functions and human resources
7. Broker or dealer, investment adviser, and investment banking services
8. Legal services and expert services unrelated to the audit

Any other consulting services that are not listed in this section cannot be performed without preapproval by PCAOB.

Another conflicts prohibition is that the audit firm cannot audit, for one year, a company that has one of its former employees as a member of senior management. For example, if a partner from PwC is hired by Xena Corporation as its controller or CFO, PwC cannot be the auditor (for SEC purposes) for Xena for one year. There must be at least one year between the hire date of the former partner and the start of the audit if PwC is to conduct the audit.

There are procedural requirements in this section such as the audit partner for the accounting firm must be rotated every five years. Also, the auditor must report directly to the audit committee of the company. A proposal to require rotation of the actual audit firm was debated but not passed.

This section encourages states to develop laws and regulations that are applicable to accounting firms that may not be involved with SEC work.

Part III: Corporate Responsibility

This section of SOX deals with the audit committees of publicly traded companies and makes these committees responsible for the hiring, compensation, and oversight of the public accounting firm responsible for conducting the company's audits and certifying its financial statements. All members of the audit committee must be members of the company's board of directors, and must be independent. *Independent* is defined by the SEC to require that the director be an outside board member (not an officer), not have been an officer for a period of time (if retired from the company), not have close relatives working in management in the company, and not have contractual or consulting ties to the company. The SEC and companies have developed complex checklists to help directors determine whether they meet the standards for independence for purposes of qualifying audit committee membership.

In addition to these structural changes in audit committees, this portion of SOX is also the officer certification section. The company's CEO and CFO are required to certify the financial statements the company files with the SEC as being fair in their representation of the company's financial condition and accurate "in all material respects." A bit of a penalty is associated with this section and the certification. CFOs and CEOs are now required to forfeit any bonuses and compensation that were received based on financial reports that subsequently had to be restated because they were not materially accurate or fair in their disclosures.

Under this section, the SEC is given the authority to ban those who violate securities laws from serving as an officer or director of a publicly traded company if the SEC can prove that they are unfit to serve. The standard under the statute is "substantial unfitness." For example, a director who has been involved in insider trading in the company's shares would be banned. Likewise, an officer who backdated stock options could be similarly banned. Since its enactment, the SEC has used this provision to ban officers and directors for life as well as for limited times, such as for five years.

One final section in Part III of SOX was passed in response to activity at Enron in the months leading up to its collapse. The officers of the company were selling off their stock even as employees were prohibited from selling theirs because of blackout periods on pension plans, those times when owners of the plans cannot trade in the company stock. Officers, such as Jeffrey Skilling and J. Clifford Baxter, walked away with the cash from selling at the stock's high point, whereas employees, because of the blackout period, were left to simply watch as Enron's stock lost virtually all of its value.

SOX now holds officers of the company subject to the blackout periods. The penalty for violating this prohibition on stock dealing is that the officers must return any profits from blackout period trading to the company. This requirement to return the profits exists even when the trading was not intentional.

Part IV: Enhanced Financial Disclosures

This section of SOX is the accounting section. Again, in direct response to the Enron issues, Congress directed the SEC to do something about accounting practices for off-balance sheet transactions, including special purpose entities (SPEs—see Case 4.15 for more background) and relationships that, although immaterial in amount, may have a material effect upon the financial status of the company. For example, a spin-off company that concealed $2 million in company debt is not a material amount. But if the spin-off company is involved in leveraged transactions (as was the case with Enron) and the company has agreed to serve as a guarantor to investors in the spin-off for those leveraged amounts, then the spin-off can have a material effect. Since the passage of SOX, the SEC has changed the rules for off-balance sheet transactions quite substantially.

Interestingly, the SEC is now investigating a similar issue in the collapse of Lehman Brothers. Lehman used a strategy known as Repo 105, which was a strategy for transferring its debt off the books. At one point, Lehman was able to hide $50 billion in debt from public disclosure using a strategy that resulted in the collapse of Enron and the elimination of SPE transfers. Lehman, however, found a means of spinning debt off the books using contracts, a bit of a loophole around the SPE provision, a loophole that will be closed now.

A second portion of Part IV gets right to the heart of pro forma and EBITDA. The result is, of course, as will be discussed in Reading 4.19, the requirement of using GAAP and non-GAAP side by side.

A third segment of Part IV deals again with officers. In direct response to the issues at WorldCom (Case 4.27), Adelphia (Reading 3.8), and others, corporations can no longer make personal loans to corporate executives. The only exception is when the company is in the business of making loans; that is, GE executives are permitted to use GE Capital so long as they have the same types of loans that are available to the general public. Another officer requirement shortens the time for them to disclose transactions in the company's shares. Prior to SOX, the executives simply had to disclose transactions within ten days from the end of the month in which the transactions occurred. The disclosure period now is within two business days of the transaction. Again, in all of the companies that experienced financial collapse and/or restatements, the executives were dealing in company stock at a fast clip, but shareholders, creditors, and other outsiders were not aware of the transactions for weeks after they occurred and well after the drop in value in the shares. As a result of the activities that led to these two major statutory revisions, this portion of SOX also requires companies to develop a separate code of ethics for senior financial officers, one that applies to the principal financial officer, comptroller, and/or principal accounting officer. Interestingly, Enron had just such a separate code of ethics. However, the board did waive its provisions to allow Mr. Fastow to have the off-the-book transactions.

Referred to fondly now as just *404*, this portion of SOX requires companies to include an internal control report and assessment as part of the 10-K annual reports. A public accounting firm that issues the audit report must also certify and report on the state of the company's internal controls.

Although the audit committee provisions are covered in a different section, Part IV does mandate that every audit committee have at least one member who is a financial expert. The SEC has already established rules for who qualifies as a financial expert, and companies' annual reports identify the financial expert and give the background.

Part V: Analyst Conflicts of Interest

The issue of analysts and their conflicts (see Cases 6.7 and 6.9) was one that contributed to the failure of the markets to heed the warning signals at Enron, WorldCom, and other companies. The SEC is still in the process of addressing conflicts of interest in the stock research industry, a function that was part of the investment banking and brokerage firms that stood to benefit if internal analysts continue to issue positive reports on their clients. The SEC has already promulgated or has in process rules that address the following specifics in analysts' relationships and activities:

1. Prepublication clearance or approval of research reports by investment bankers
2. Supervision, compensation, and evaluation of securities analysts by investment bankers
3. Retaliation against a securities analyst by an investment banker because of an unfavorable research report that may adversely affect an investment banker's relationship or a broker's or dealer's relationship with the company that is discussed in the report
4. Separating securities analysts from pressure or oversight by investment bankers in a way that might potentially create bias
5. Developing rules on disclosure by securities analysts and broker/dealers of specified conflicts of interest

Part VI: Corporate and Criminal Fraud Accountability

This section of SOX is the expansion, cleanup, and criminal law portion that created new crimes, increased penalties on existing crimes, and elaborated on the elements required to prove already existing crimes. Also known as the Corporate and Criminal Fraud Accountability Act of 2002, this SOX section makes the following changes:

a. Obstruction of justice: In updating the obstruction of justice crime to cover destruction of papers, e-mails, and other records, SOX makes it a crime to knowingly destroy, alter, conceal, or falsify records with the intent to obstruct or influence an investigation in a matter in federal jurisdiction or in bankruptcy. Also under this section, in direct response to the issues at Arthur Andersen (see Case 4.16), auditors must keep their audit and review work papers on their clients for a five-year period.

b. Federal bankruptcy law changed: This portion makes fines, profits, and penalties that result from violation of federal securities laws a non-dischargeable debt in bankruptcy. Also, if there has been common law fraud involved in the sale of securities, any judgment owed as a result of the fraud is also a nondischargeable bankruptcy debt.

  c. Extends the time for bringing a civil law suit for securities fraud: The change is that suits must be brought no later than the earlier of (1) five years after the date of the alleged violation; or (2) two years after its discovery.

  d. U.S. Sentencing Commission Changes: Directs the United States Sentencing Commission to review and amend federal sentencing guidelines to ensure that the sentences and penalties are sufficient to deter and punish violations involving (1) obstruction of justice, (2) record destruction, (3) fraud when the number of victims adversely involved is significantly greater than fifty or when it endangers the solvency or financial security of a substantial number of victims, and (4) organizational criminal misconduct.

  e. Employee protections: Prohibits retaliation against employees in publicly traded companies who assist in an investigation of possible federal violations or file or participate in a shareholder suit for fraud against the company. This section also imposes up-the-ladder reporting requirements. That is, both auditors and attorneys must take their concerns about fraud or 404 failures to the board. Auditors are required to make public disclosures if the board is non-responsive, but lawyers, because of the privilege, are not required to do so. This section was intended to provide cover for employees who made disclosures about their company's false financial reporting. However, the protection has not been particularly effective because the courts have narrowly interpreted the protection to include only those acts of whistle-blowing related to the financial statements. For example, an employee who reports a company's failure to disclose a product flaw (something that will affect financial performance eventually) is not entitled to SOX protection.

  f. Harsher sentences: Increases the fines and imprisonment periods for fraud by officers of publicly traded companies.

Part VII: White-Collar Crime Penalty Enhancements

Called the White-Collar Crime Penalty Enhancement Act of 2002, this portion of SOX ups the ante for fraud, wire fraud, conspiracy and the crimes usually charged when a company goes south financially.

  a. Criminal penalties for violation of Employee Retirement Income Security Act of 1974 (ERISA) are increased, again in response to the failed Enron pensions.

  b. Officers who certify financial statements either recklessly or knowingly face imprisonment of (1) ten years for willful violation, and (2) five years for reckless and knowing violation.

  c. Obstruction of justice penalties are increased to a maximum ten-year prison term.

  d. Allows the SEC to freeze bonus, incentive, and other payoffs to corporate officers when there is an ongoing investigation at the company for possible violations of federal securities laws.

  e. The SEC can prohibit someone who has used manipulative and deceptive devices or engaged in fraudulent interstate transactions from serving as officer or director of a publicly traded corporation (using the unfitness-to-serve standard).

Discussion Questions

1. List all of the issues and activities you see that are now covered by SOX that could, or should have been, handled as ethical issues and resolved voluntarily.

2. What additional costs do you see as a result of the new SOX requirements?

3. What list of governance practices would you give to a company so that it could be in compliance with SOX?

Case 4.12

Bank of America: The Merrill Takeover, the Disclosures, and the Board

Timothy J. Mayopoulos was the general counsel for Bank of America until just shortly before its merger/acquisition of Merrill Lynch was approved by the shareholders. Mr. Mayopoulos was escorted from the Bank of America building in Charlotte, North

Carolina, following the day he met with the board, a meeting at which the board was told that Merrill had heretofore undisclosed losses that had not been publicly disclosed to shareholders who would be asked to approve the planned merger. Mr. Mayopoulos had talked with B of A's CFO about the losses prior to his meeting with the board. He was escorted out by security personnel and was not permitted to return to his office and collect his belongings.

Mr. Mayopoulos has given testimony to New York Attorney General Andrew Cuomo, the official who has been investigating whether information about the scope of the losses was withheld from B of A shareholders prior to their vote on approval of the merger/acquisition. Mr. Mayopoulos, however, declined to disclose to Mr. Cuomo's office the content of the advice he gave to the bank, citing legal ethics rules.[171]

Mr. Cuomo asked B of A to waive "the privilege" because its refusal was hindering his office's ability to investigate what happened in the days leading up to the merger/acquisition.

B of A has also refused initially to waive its attorney–client privilege in the ongoing investigation of the merger/acquisition by the SEC. B of A and the SEC had reached a $33 million settlement in the investigation.[172] However, a federal judge blocked the settlement because he wanted more details on the role of Mr. Mayopoulos. The case was settled in 2010 for a fine of $150 million.[173] However, both Mr. Lewis and CFO Joe Price were charged with fraud by Mr. Cuomo.[174] Mr. Lewis resigned as CEO in October 2009.

B of A's CFO has given testimony to Mr. Cuomo that indicates he simply followed Mr. Mayopoulos's advice. Mr. Mayopoulos did testify in the Cuomo investigation that he had spoken with outside counsel about the merger/acquisition/disclosure issues. B of A's outside counsel is Wachtell, Lipton, Rosen & Katz.

B of A's CEO, Kenneth D. Lewis, testified that Mr. Mayopoulos was fired because B of A had more executives than it needed following the merger. Merrill Lynch executives have testified that they were in a meeting with Mr. Mayopoulos regarding the structure of the combined legal departments of the two companies when he was called from the meeting and dismissed from the company.

Mr. Mayopoulos is now general counsel for Fannie Mae, but, in an ironic note, Mr. Mayopoulos still resides in Charlotte, North Carolina, on the same street as Mr. Lewis. The neighborhood block parties during the summer of 2009 must have been tense.

Discussion Questions

1. What is the lawyer–client privilege and when does it apply? Does it apply to general counsel and to outside counsel? When is the privilege waived? What does SOX have to do with this case?

2. Why do you think Mr. Mayopoulos stood so firm on his refusal to answer questions about what happened in the days leading up to the merger and his termination prior to B of A's waiver of the privilege?

3. What impact would Mr. Mayopoulos's termination have on the culture of Bank of America?

---

[171]Louise Story, "Bank Firing of Counsel Is Examined," *New York Times*, September 9, 2009, p. C1.

[172]Dan Fitzpatrick, "New York Nears Charges on Merrill Deal," *Wall Street Journal*, September 9, 2009, p. C1.

[173]Louise Story, "Cuomo Sues Bank of America Even as It Settles with S.E.C.," *New York Times*, February 4, 2010, p. B1; and http://www.sec.gov/litigation/litreleases/2010/lr21407.htm. Accessed July 17, 2010.

[174]Kevin McCoy, "Bank of America Charged with Fraud," *USA Today*, February 4, 2010, p. 2B.

Case 4.13

Dennis Kozlowski: Tyco and the $6,000 Shower Curtain[175]

Tyco International began as a research laboratory, founded in 1960 by Arthur Rosenburg, with the idea of doing contract research work for the government. By 1962, Rosenburg had incorporated and begun doing work for companies in the areas of high-tech materials and energy conversion, with two divisions of the holding company, Tyco Semiconductor and Materials Research Laboratory. By 1964, the company went public and became primarily a manufacturer of products for commercial use. Today, Tyco is a conglomerate with a presence in over 100 countries and over 250,000 employees. Between 1991 and 2001, CEO Dennis Kozlowski took Tyco from $3 billion in annual sales to $36 billion in 2001 by paying $60 billion for more than 200 acquisitions.[176] Tyco's performance was phenomenal.

- From 1992 through 1999, Tyco's stock price grew fifteenfold.[177]
- Tyco's earnings grew by 25 percent each year during Kozlowski's era.[178]
- During 1999, Tyco's stock price rose 65 percent.[179]
- Tyco spent $50 billion on acquisitions in nine years.[180]
- The company's debt-to-equity ratio nearly doubled from 25 percent to 47 percent in one year (2001).[181]

In a move to reduce its U.S. tax bills, Tyco is based out of Bermuda, despite having its headquarters in Exeter, New Hampshire.[182] Tyco, with a stake in telecommunications as well, is the parent company to Grinnell Security Systems, health care products companies, and many other acquired firms, which has been its strategy for growth.[183] In fact, the troubles that Tyco experienced initially were often attributed to a skittish market reacting to the falls of Enron and WorldCom as well as problems with Global Crossing and Kmart.[184]

Shortly after Enron's bankruptcy, Tyco began to experience a decline in its share price. From December 2001 through the middle of January 2002, Tyco's shares lost 20 percent of their value.[185] In fact, following a conference in which then-CEO Dennis Kozlowski tried to reassure the public and analysts that Tyco's accounting was sound, the shares were the most heavily traded of the day (68 million on January 15, 2002), and the price dropped $4.45 to $47.95 per share.[186] However, at the same time as the

[175]Adapted from Marianne M. Jennings, "The Yeehaw Factor," *Wyoming Law Review* 3 (2003): 387–511.

[176]Daniel Eisenberg, "Dennis the Menace," *Time*, June 17, 2002, 47; and Mark Maremont, John Hechinger, Jerry Markon, and Gregory Zuckerman, "Kozlowski Quits under a Cloud, Worsening Worries about Tyco," *Wall Street Journal*, June 4, 2002, pp. A1, A10.

[177]Alex Berenson, "Ex-Tyco Chief, a Big Risk Taker, Now Confronts the Legal System," *New York Times*, June 10, 2002, p. B1.

[178]*BusinessWeek Online*, January 14, 2002, http://www.businessweek.com.

[179]*BusinessWeek Online*, January 11, 1999, http://www.businessweek.com.

[180]*BusinessWeek Online*, January 14, 2002, http://www.businessweek.com.

[181]*Id.*

[182]Information from Tyco, http://www.tyco.com; see "Investor Relations, Tyco History." See also Alex Berenson, "Tyco Shares Fall as Investors Show Concern on Accounting," *New York Times*, January 16, 2002, p. C1.

[183]*Id.* Tyco bought Grinnell, the security system and fire alarm company; Ludlow, the packaging company; and a host of others during its especially aggressive expansion period from 1973 to 1982.

[184]Kopin Tan, "Tyco's Options Soar, While Volatility Spikes on Concerns over U.S. Accounting Practices," *Wall Street Journal*, January 30, 2002, p. C14.

[185]Alex Berenson, "Tyco Shares Fall as Investors Show Concern on Accounting," *New York Times*, January 16, 2002, p. C1.

[186]*Id.*

loss of investor confidence in the accounting of public corporations came Tyco's announcement that its earnings had dropped 24 percent for fiscal year 2001.[187] By February, the share price had tumbled to $29.90, a drop of 50 percent from January 1, 2002.[188] Tyco was forced to borrow funds as it experienced what one analyst called a "crisis in confidence," noting, "The lack of confidence in the company by the capital markets to a degree becomes a self-fulfilling prophecy."[189]

Then there was another problem that emerged on January 28, 2002. Tyco announced that it had paid $20 million to one of its outside directors, Frank E. Walsh, and a charity of which he was the head, for him to broker a deal for one of Tyco's acquisitions.[190] The acquisition was CIT Group Finance, and Tyco acquired it for $9.5 billion.[191] Mr. Walsh, who would later plead guilty to a violation of a New York statute as well as a violation of federal securities laws, withheld information about the brokerage fee from the Tyco board and did not disclose the information as required in the company's SEC filings.[192] Once the SEC moved in to investigate, the company's stock continued its decline.[193] From January 2002 to August 2002, Tyco's stock price declined 80 percent.[194]

What Went Wrong: The Accounting Issues

Investors and markets are not always jittery for no reason. There were some Tyco accounting issues that centered on its acquisitions and its accounting for those acquisitions.[195] What caused investors to seize upon Tyco's financials was that it seemed to be heavily in debt despite the fact that it was reporting oodles of cash flow.[196] This financial picture resulted because of Tyco's accounting for its "goodwill."[197] When one company acquires another company, it must include the assets acquired in its balance sheet. The acquirer is in charge of establishing the value for the assets acquired. From 1998 to 2001, Tyco spent $30 billion on acquisitions and attributed $30 billion to goodwill.

The problem lies in the fact that the assets that are acquired are not carried on Tyco's books with any significant value. Assets, under accounting rules, lose their value over time. Goodwill stays the same in perpetuity. However, if Tyco turns around and sells the assets it has acquired and booked at virtually zero value, the profit that it makes is

---

[187]John Hechinger, "Tyco to Lay Off 44% of Its Workers at Telecom Unit," *Wall Street Journal*, February 8, 2002, p. A5.

[188]Alex Berenson and Andrew Ross Sorkin, "Tyco Shares Tumble on Growing Worries of a Cash Squeeze," *New York Times*, February 5, 2002, p. C1.

[189]*Id.*

[190]Kate Kelly and Gregory Zuckerman, "Tyco Worries Send Stock Prices Lower Again," *Wall Street Journal*, February 5, 2002, p. C1.

[191]Laurie P. Cohen and Mark Maremont, "Tyco Ex-Director Pleads Guilty," *Wall Street Journal*, December 18, 2002, p. C1.

[192]Andrew Ross Sorkin, "Tyco Figure Pays $22.5 Million in Guilty Plea," *New York Times*, December 18, 2002, pp. C1, C2; and E. S. Browning, "Stocks Slump in Late-Day Selloff on Round of Ugly Corporate News," *Wall Street Journal*, June 4, 2002, pp. A3, A8.

[193]Michael Schroeder and John Hechinger, "SEC Reopens Tyco Investigation," *Wall Street Journal*, June 13, 2002, p. A2.

[194]Kevin McCoy, "Authorities Widen Tyco Case, Look at Other Officials' Actions," *USA Today*, August 13, 2003, p. 1A.

[195]Floyd Norris, "Now Will Come the Sorting Out of the Chief Executive's Legacy," *New York Times*, June 4, 2002, pp. C1, C10.

[196]Mark Maremont, "Tyco Made $8 Billion of Acquisitions over 3 Years but Didn't Disclose Them," *Wall Street Journal*, February 4, 2002, p. A3.

[197]"Goodwill" is an asset under accounting rules that takes into account the sort of customer value a business has. For example, if you buy a dry-cleaning business, you are paying for not only the hangers and the pressers and racks but also for that dry cleaner's reputation in the community, the tendency of customers to return, and their willingness to bring their dry cleaning to this establishment—goodwill.

reflected in the income of the company. The only way an investor in Tyco would be able to tell what has really happened in the accounting for an acquisition would be for the investor to have access to the balance sheets of the acquired companies, so that he or she could see the value of the assets as they were carried on the books of the acquired company. The bump to earnings from the sale of the assets is lovely, but the bump to profits, with no offsetting costs, is tremendous.

There were additional accounting issues related to the Tyco acquisitions. One big one was that despite having made 700 acquisitions between 1998 and 2001 for about $8 billion, Tyco never disclosed the acquisitions to the public.[198] The eventual disclosure of the phenomenal number of acquisitions did explain the lack of cash, but it also deprived investors of the chance to determine how much of Tyco's growth was due to acquisitions versus running existing businesses.

The nondisclosure of the acquisitions also helped with another accounting strategy. When Tyco made acquisitions, its goal was always to make the company acquired look as much like a dog as possible. Tyco was a spring-loader extraordinaire. (See Reading 4.9 for a full explanation of spring-loading.) Spring-loading at Tyco involved having the company being acquired pay everything for which it has a bill, whether that bill was due or not. When Tyco acquired Raychem, its treasurer sent out the following e-mail:

> At Tyco's request, all major Raychem sites will pay all pending payables, whether they are due or not. . . . I understand from Ray [Raychem's CFO] that we have agreed to do this, even though we will be spending the money for no tangible benefit either to Raychem or Tyco.[199]

Tyco employees, when working with a company to be acquired, would also pump up the reserves, with one employee of Tyco asking an employee of an acquired firm, "How high can we get these things? How can we justify getting this higher?"[200] The final report of a team led by attorney David Boies (the lawyer who represented Napster, the U.S. government in its case against Microsoft, and also Al Gore in the Florida ballot dispute after the 2000 presidential election), retained by the Tyco board to determine what was going on with the company, indicates that Tyco executives used both incentives and pressure on executives in order to get them to push the envelope on accounting rules to maximize results.[201] Mr. Boies referred to the accounting practices of the executives as "financial engineering."

It was not, however, a case in which the accounting issues went unnoticed. The warnings, from the company's outside legal counsel, went unheeded. A May 25, 2000, e-mail from William McLucas of Wilmer Cutler to Mr. Mark Belnick, then–general counsel for Tyco, contains clear warnings about the questionable accounting treatments as well as the pressure those preparing the financial reports were experiencing, "We have found issues that will likely interest the SEC . . . creativeness is employed in hitting the forecasts. . . . There is also a bad letter from the Sigma people just before the acquisition confirming that they were asked to hold product shipment just before the closing."[202]

---

[198]Maremont, "Tyco Made $8 Billion of Acquisitions over 3 Years but Didn't Disclose Them," p. A3.

[199]Herb Greenberg, "Does Tyco Play Accounting Games?" *Fortune,* April 1, 2002, pp. 83, 86.

[200]*Id.*

[201]Kurt Eichenwald, "Pushing Accounting Rules to the Edge of the Envelope," *New York Times,* December 31, 2002, pp. C1, C2.

[202]Laurie P. Cohen and Mark Maremont, "E-Mails Show Tyco's Lawyers Had Concerns," *Wall Street Journal,* December 27, 2002, p. C1.

The lawyer concluded that Tyco's financial reports smelled of "something funny which is likely apparent if any decent accountant looks at this."[203]

What Went Wrong: A Profligate Spender as CEO

Tyco was graced with a CEO whose profligate spending cost the company dearly, in dollars and reputation, and whose tight fist with his own money got him indicted. Dennis Kozlowski was a scary CEO whose philosophy was "Money is the only way to keep score."[204] Mr. Kozlowski was one of the country's highest-paid CEOs. In 2001, his compensation package of $411.8 million put him at number two among the CEOs of the Fortune 500 companies."[205] Mr. Kozlowski was featured on the cover of *BusinessWeek* and called "the most aggressive dealmaker in Corporate America."[206] He was included in the magazine's top twenty-five managers of the year. Indeed, when Tyco's problems and accounting issues emerged, many of Wall Street's "superstar" money managers were stunned.[207]

In addition to his salary, Mr. Kozlowski was a spender. There were extensive personal expenses documented that began to percolate before problems at Tyco emerged. Tyco's outside legal counsel raised concerns about payments Tyco was making to Mr. Kozlowski's then-mistress (and now Kozlowski's second ex-wife), Karen Mayo, and advised that they be disclosed in SEC documents. Employees in Tyco refused to make the disclosures and continued making the payments.[208] The e-mail from partner Lewis Liman at Wilmer Cutler, sent March 23, 2000, to Tyco's general counsel, Mark Belnick, read, "There are payments to a woman whom the folks in finance describe as Dennis's girlfriend. I do not know Dennis's situation, but this is an embarrassing fact."[209]

Before Tyco took its dive, Mr. Kozlowski had accumulated three Harleys; a 130-foot sailing yacht; a private plane; and homes in New York City (including a thirteen-room Fifth Avenue apartment, purchased in 2000),[210] New Hampshire, Nantucket, and Boca Raton (15,000 square feet, purchased in 2001); and was a part owner of the New Jersey Nets and the New Jersey Devils.[211] His Fifth Avenue apartment cost $16.8 million to buy and $3 million in renovations, and he spent $11 million on furnishings.[212] The items were delineated in the press, and the following purchases for the apartment were charged to Tyco: $6,000 for a shower curtain, $15,000 for a dog umbrella stand; $6,300 for a sewing basket, $17,100 for a traveling toilette box, $2,200 for a gilt metal

[203]Mark Maremont and Laurie P. Cohen, "Tyco Probe Expands to Include Auditor PricewaterhouseCoopers," *Wall Street Journal*, September 30, 2002, p. A1.

[204]Eisenberg, "Dennis the Menace," 47.

[205]Jonathan D. Glater, "A Star Lawyer Finds Himself the Target of a Peer," *New York Times*, September 24, 2002, pp. C1, C8.

[206]*BusinessWeek Online*, January 14, 2002, http://www.businessweek.com.

[207]Gregory Zuckerman, "Heralded Investors Suffer Huge Losses with Tyco Meltdown," *Wall Street Journal*, June 10, 2002, p. C1.

[208]Cohen and Maremont, "E-Mails Show Tyco's Lawyers Had Concerns," p. C1.

[209]*Id.*

[210]Theresa Howard, "Tyco Puts Kozlowski's $16.8M NYC Digs on Market," *USA Today*, September 19, 2002, p. 3B.

[211]Laurie P. Cohen and Mark Maremont, "Tyco Relocations to Florida Are Probed," *Wall Street Journal*, June 10, 2002, p. A3; Alex Berenson and William K. Rashbaum, "Tyco Ex-Chief Is Said to Face Wider Inquiry into Finances," *New York Times*, June 7, 2002, p. C1; and Kris Maher, "Scandal and Excess Make It Hard to Sell Mr. Kozlowski's Boat," *New York Times*, September 23, 2002, p. A1.

[212]Andrew Ross Sorkin, "Tyco Details Lavish Lives of Executives," *New York Times*, September 19, 2002, p. C1. The New York City apartment was sold for $21.8 million in October 2004. William Neuman, "Tyco to Sell Ex-Chief's Apartment for $21 Million," *New York Times*, October 9, 2004, pp. B1, B4.

wastebasket, $2,900 for coat hangers, $5,960 for two sets of sheets, $1,650 for a notebook, and $445 for a pincushion.[213]

For his then-new wife Karen Mayo's fortieth birthday, Kozlowski flew Jimmy Buffett and dozens of Karen's friends to a villa outside Sardinia for a multiday birthday celebration.[214] A memo on the party was attached as an exhibit to Tyco's 8-K, filed on September 17, 2002. The process for receiving the guests and the party schedule are described in detail, right down to what type of music was playing and at what level. The waiters were dressed in Roman togas, and there was an ice sculpture of David through which the vodka flowed. The memo includes a guest list and space for the crew of the yacht that the Kozlowskis sailed to Sardinia.[215] The total cost for the party was $2.1 million.[216] Tyco also paid Mr. Kozlowski's American Express bill, which was $80,000 for one month. A later report uncovered a $110,000 bill Tyco paid for a thirteen-day stay by Mr. Kozlowski at a London hotel.[217] Ironically, Mr. Kozlowski told a *BusinessWeek* reporter in 2001, on a tour of Tyco's humble Exeter, New Hampshire, offices, "We don't believe in perks, not even executive parking spots."[218]

Mr. Kozlowski appeared to be financing the lifestyle through Tyco's Key Employee Corporate Loan Program ("the KELP") and relocation loan programs (see the following pages for details). According to SEC documents, Mr. Kozlowski borrowed more than $270 million from the KELP "but us[ed] only about $29 million to cover intended uses for the loans. He used the remaining $242 million of supposed KELP loans for personal expenses, including yachts, fine art, estate jewelry, luxury apartments and vacation estates, personal business ventures, and investments, all unrelated to Tyco."[219]

Mr. Kozlowski was on the board of the Whitney Museum of Art and had Tyco donate $4.5 million to the traveling museum shows that the Whitney sponsored.[220] He was an avid fundraiser for various philanthropic endeavors. In fact, he was at a fundraiser for the New York Botanical Garden when the news of his possible indictment (see the following pages) first spread.[221] Tyco donated $1.7 million for the construction of the Kozlowski Athletic Complex at the private school, Berwick Academy, which one of his daughters attended and where he served as trustee, and $5 million to Seton Hall, his alma mater, for a building that was called the Koz Plex.[222]

Mr. Kozlowski also donated personally, particularly to charities in the Boca Raton area, where he had retained a public relations executive and where he had been given a

[213]Kevin McCoy, "Directors' Firms on Payroll at Tyco," *USA Today*, September 18, 2002, p. 1B. These items are also listed in the 8-K for September 17, 2002.

[214]Don Halasy, "Why Tyco Boss Fell," New York Post, June 9, 2002, http://www.nypost.com; and Laurie P. Cohen, "Ex-Tyco CEO's Ex to Post $10 Million for His Bail Bond," *Wall Street Journal*, September 20, 2002, p. A5.

[215]Tyco 8-K filing, September 17, 2002, http://www.sec.gov/edgar.

[216]Mark Maremont and Laurie P. Cohen, "How Tyco's CEO Enriched Himself," *Wall Street Journal*, August 7, 2002, p. A1.

[217]Mark Maremont and Laurie P. Cohen, "Tyco's Internal Inquiry Concludes Questionable Accounting Was Used," *Wall Street Journal*, December 31, 2002, pp. A1, A4; and Alex Berenson, "Changing the Definition of Cash Flow Helped Tyco," *New York Times*, December 31, 2002, pp. C1, C2.

[218]Anthony Bianco, William Symonds, Nanette Byrnes, and David Polek, "The Rise and Fall of Dennis Kozlowski," *BusinessWeek Online*, December 23, 2002, http://www.businessweek.com.

[219]Securities and Exchange Commission, http://www.sec.gov/releases/litigation; and Kevin McCoy, "Directors' Firms on Payroll at Tyco," *USA Today*, September 18, 2002, p. 1B. These items are also listed in Tyco's 8-K filed on September 17, 2002; see http://www.sec.gov/edgar. See also Theresa Howard, "Tyco Puts Kozlowski's $16.8M NYC Digs on Market," *USA Today*, September 19, 2002, p. 3B; and Andrew Ross Sorkin, "Tyco Details Lavish Lives of Executives," *New York Times*, September 18, 2002, p. C1. And see Tyco's 8-K filed on September 17, 2002.

[220]Don Halasy, "Why Tyco Boss Fell," June 9, 2002, http://www.nypost.com.

[221]Id.; and Carol Vogel, "Kozlowski's Quest for Entrée into the Art World," *New York Times*, June 6, 2002, pp. C1, C5.

[222]Maremont and Cohen, "How Tyco's CEO Enriched Himself," p. A1; and John Byrne, "Seton Hall of Shame," *BusinessWeek Online*, September 20, 2002, http://www.businessweek.com.

fair amount of coverage in the *Palm Beach Post* for his contributions to local charities.[223] There is even some confusion about who was donating how much and from which tills. Kozlowski had pledged $106 million in Tyco funds to charity, but $43 million of that was given in his own name.[224] He had donated $1.3 million to the Nantucket Conservation Foundation in his own name with the express desire that the land next to his property there not be developed.[225] Tyco gave $3 million to a hospital in Boca Raton and $500,000 to an arts center there. United Way of America gave Mr. Kozlowski its "million-dollar giver" award.[226]

Mr. Kozlowski saw to it that friends were awarded contracts that Tyco paid. For example, Wendy Valliere was a personal friend of the Kozlowskis and was hired to decorate the New York City apartment. Her firm's bill was $7.5 million.[227] However, Ms. Valliere was not alone as a personal employee.[228] In 1996, Mr. Kozlowski also hired Michael Castania, a consultant who had helped him with his yacht, as an executive who was housed at Boca Raton. He was an Australian yachting expert who went on to lead Team Tyco, a corporate yachting racing team, to fourth place in the Volvo Challenge Race in June 2002.[229] Tyco also hired Ms. Mayo's personal trainer from the days when she was still married to her ex-husband and Mr. Kozlowski was still married to his ex-wife, but Mr. Kozlowski was supporting Ms. Mayo in a beach condo in Nantucket.[230]

Mr. Kozlowski was also an active player in Manhattan's art market. In June 2002 the *New York Times* reported that Mr. Kozlowski was being investigated by the district attorney's office in Manhattan for evasion of $1 million in sales tax on $13 million in art sales over a ten-month period.[231] Mr. Kozlowski resigned from Tyco immediately following the emergence of the report and before an indictment was handed down. A market that was already reeling from Enron and WorldCom dropped 215 points in one day, and Tyco's stock fell 27 percent that same day.[232] In fact, the indictment was handed down the following day.[233]

[223]*Id.*, p. A6. Barry Epstein, a Palm Beach PR executive, said, "I represented Dennis personally. I reported to him and guided him on community involvement." Mr. Epstein has conceded that most of the money was Tyco's, not Mr. Kozlowski's.

[224]Kevin McCoy and Gary Strauss, "Kozlowski, Others Accused of Using Tyco as 'Piggy Bank,'" *USA Today*, September 13, 2002, pp. 1B, 2B.

[225]Maremont and Cohen, "How Tyco's CEO Enriched Himself," pp. A1, A6.

[226]*Id.*

[227]*Id.*

[228]Mark Maremont and Laurie P. Cohen, "Interior Design on a Budget: The Tyco Way," *Wall Street Journal*, September 18, 2002, pp. B1–B5.

[229]Maremont and Cohen, "How Tyco's CEO Enriched Himself," pp. A1, A6.

[230]Anthony Bianco, William Symonds, Nanette Byrnes, and David Polek, "The Rise and Fall of Dennis Kozlowski," *BusinessWeek Online*, December 23, 2002, http://www.businessweek.com.

[231]Alex Berenson, "Investigation Is Said to Focus on Tyco Chief over Sales Tax," *New York Times*, June 3, 2002, p. C1; Laurie P. Cohen and Mark Maremont, "Expanding Tyco Inquiry Focuses on Firm's Spending on Executives," *Wall Street Journal*, June 7, 2002, pp. A1, A5; and Nanette Byrnes, "Online Extra: The Hunch That Led to Tyco's Tumble," *BusinessWeek Online*, December 23, 2002, http://www.businessweek.com.

[232]Mark Maremont, John Hechinger, Jerry Markon, and Gregory Zuckerman, "Kozlowski Quits under a Cloud, Worsening Worries about Tyco," *Wall Street Journal*, June 4, 2002, p. A1; and Adam Shell, "Markets Fall as Tyco CEO's Resignation Adds to Woes," *USA Today*, June 4, 2002, p. 1B.

[233]Thor Valdmanis, "Art Purchases Put Ex-Tyco Chief in Hot Water," *USA Today*, June 5, 2002, p. 1B; Mark Maremont and Jerry Markon, "Former Tyco Chief Is Indicted for Avoiding Sales Tax on Art," *Wall Street Journal*, June 5, 2002, p. A1; Alex Berenson and Carol Vogel, "Ex-Tyco Chief Is Indicted in Tax Case," *New York Times*, June 5, 2002, p. C1; David Cay Johnston, "A Tax That's Often Ignored Suddenly Attracts Attention," *New York Times*, June 5, 2002, p. C1; Brooks Barnes and Alexandra Peers, "Sales-Tax Probe Puts Art World in Harsh Light," *Wall Street Journal*, June 5, 2002, pp. B1, B3; Susan Saulny, "Tyco's Ex-Chief to Seek Dismissal of Indictments," August 15, 2002, p. C3; Mark Maremont and Laurie P. Cohen, "Former Tyco CEO Is Charged with Two New Felony Counts," *Wall Street Journal*, June 27, 2002, p. A3; and Andrew Ross Sorkin and Susan Saulny, "Former Tyco Chief Faces New Charges," *New York Times*, June 27, 2002, p. C1.

Tyco's Culture

Mr. Kozlowski had a strategy for getting the type of people he needed to succumb to the pressure for numbers achievement. He told *BusinessWeek* that he chooses managers from the "same model as himself. Smart, poor, and wants to be rich."[234] Meeting numbers meant bonuses; exceeding those numbers meant "the sky was the limit." The CEO of one of Tyco's subsidiaries had a salary of $625,000, but when he boosted sales by 62 percent, his bonus was $13 million.[235]

Mr. Kozlowski was known for being autocratic and prone to temper flare-ups.[236] When he was CEO of Tyco's Grinnell Fire Protection Systems Co., Mr. Kozlowski had an annual awards banquet where he presented awards to the best warehouse manager as well as the worst warehouse manager. The worst manager would have to walk to the front of the room in what other managers described as a "death sentence."[237]

The Loans

Tyco's Key Employee Corporate Loan Program (the "KELP") was established to encourage employees to own Tyco shares by offering dedicated loans to pay the taxes due when shares granted under Tyco's restricted share ownership plan became vested. There was no way to pay the taxes except to sell some of the shares for cash, and the loan program permitted the officers to pledge their shares in exchange for cash that was then used to pay the income tax that was due on this employee benefit.[238] Mr. Kozlowski made it clear that the loan program was available to all of his new hires, including Mark Swartz, the CFO, and Mark Belnick, Tyco's general counsel and executive vice president.[239]

The second loan program was a relocation program, which was established to help employees who had to move from New Hampshire to New York. The idea was to provide low-interest loans for employees who had to relocate from one set of company offices to another in order to lessen the impact of moving to a much costlier housing market.[240] One of the requirements of the relocation program was the employee's certification that he or she was indeed moving from New Hampshire to New York, or, in some cases, to Boca Raton.

Mr. Belnick has explained through his lawyer that he was entitled to the loans from the "relocation program" because he had such in writing from Mr. Kozlowski. Mr. Kozlowski offered this perk to Mr. Belnick despite the fact that Mr. Belnick was a partner in a New York City law firm and would be working in New York City for Tyco. He received the relocation fee for a difference of 25 miles between his home and Tyco's New York offices, and despite the fact that he had never lived in New Hampshire as the relocation loan program required. Although he actually didn't need to move, Mr. Belnick borrowed $4 million anyway and used it to buy and renovate an apartment in New York City. Later, he borrowed another $10 million to construct a home in Park City, Utah, because he was moving his family there and would divide his time between the

[234]William C. Symonds and Pamela L. Moore, "The Most Aggressive CEO," *BusinessWeek Online*, May 28, 2001, http://www.businessweek.com.

[235]*Id.*

[236]Bianco, Symonds, Byrnes, and Poleck, "The Rise and Fall of Dennis Kozlowski," http://www.businessweek.com.

[237]*Id.*

[238]This information was obtained from the press release that the SEC issued when it filed suit against Mark Swartz, Dennis Kozlowski, and Mark Belnick for the return of the loan amounts. http://www.sec.gov/releases/litigation.

[239]In an 8-K filed with the SEC on September 17, 2002, Tyco outlined the loans, the spending, and its plans for the future. The 8-K is available at http://www.sec.gov/edgar. A synopsis of the information filed in the 8-K is available at http://www.tyco.com under "Press Releases."

[240]The rate as disclosed in the 2002 proxy was 6.24 percent.

two locations and the extensive international travel his job required.[241] Mr. Belnick got Mr. Kozlowski's approval for both loans, but he didn't do the corporate paperwork for relocation.

Mr. Belnick told friends from the time that he began his work with Tyco that he was uncomfortable because he was not in the loop with information from either Mr. Kozlowski or the board. However, Mr. Kozlowski offered him more lucrative contracts and additional loans, and Mr. Belnick remained on board.[242] However, as noted in the case, there are e-mails from Tyco's outside counsel, the Wilmer Cutler firm, that indicate some information was seeping through to Mr. Belnick, and that outside counsel had concerns that were kept silent once transmitted to Mr. Belnick.

During the same period, CFO Swartz availed himself of $85 million of KELP loans. However, he used only $13 million for payment of taxes and spent the remaining $72 million for personal investments, business ventures, real estate holdings, and trusts.[243] Mr. Swartz used more than $32 million of interest-free relocation loans, and, according to SEC documents, used almost $9 million of those relocation loans for purposes not authorized under the program, including purchasing a yacht and investing in real estate.[244]

Patricia Prue, the vice president for HR at Tyco and the one responsible for processing the paperwork for the forgiveness of the officers' loans, and who had benefited from the loan forgiveness program herself, approached Mr. Kozlowski in September 2000 and asked for documentation that the board had indeed approved all the loan forgiveness for which she was doing the paperwork. Mr. Kozlowski, without ever producing board minutes, wrote a memo to Ms. Prue, "A decision has been made to forgive the relocation loans for those individuals whose efforts were instrumental to successfully completing the TyCom I.P.O."[245] Ms. Prue had received a loan of $748,309, had the loan forgiven, and then was given $521,087 to pay the taxes on the loan forgiveness.[246] Ms. Prue's bonuses totaled $13,534,523, and she was given $9,424,815 to pay the taxes on the bonuses.[247]

The issue of board approval on the loans remains a question, but compensation committee minutes from February 21, 2002, show that the committee was given a list of loans to officers and also approved Mr. Belnick's new compensation package. There was no public disclosure of these developments or the committee's review.[248] In grand jury testimony, Patricia Prue, who testified in exchange for immunity from prosecution, indicated that board member Joshua Berman pressured her in June 2002 to change the

---

[241]Nicholas Varchaver, "Fall from Grace," *Fortune,* October 28, 2002, 112, 115; Amy Borrus, Mike McNamee, Williams Symonds, Nanette Byrnes, and Andrew Park, "Reform: Business Gets Religion," *BusinessWeek Online,* February 3, 2003, http://www.businessweek.com; and Jonathan D. Glater, "A Star Lawyer Finds Himself the Target of a Peer," *New York Times,* September 24, 2002, p. C1.

[242]Glater, "A Star Lawyer Finds Himself the Target of a Peer," pp. C1, C8.

[243]Securities and Exchange Commission, http://www.sec.gov/releases/litigation. The SEC has also filed suit against Mr. Swartz, seeking the return of these funds. Mr. Swartz was also indicted by the State of New York and spent some time in jail as his family scrambled to post his bail.

[244]Securities and Exchange Commission, http://www.sec.gov/releases/litigation. These exhibits and lists are found in the 8-K for September 17, 2002, at http://www.sec.gov/edgar. Andrew Ross Sorkin and Jonathan D. Glater, "Tyco Planning to Disclose Making Loans to Employees," *New York Times,* September 16, 2002, p. C1; and "Ex-Chief of Tyco Posts $10 Million in Bail," *New York Times,* September 21, 2002, p. B14.

[245]*Id.;* and Kevin McCoy, "Kozlowski's Statement in Question," *USA Today,* January 9, 2002, p. 1B.

[246]Andrew Ross Sorkin, "Tyco Details Lavish Lives of Executives," *New York Times,* September 18, 2002, pp. C1, C6.

[247]"Helping Fatcats Dodge the Taxman," *BusinessWeek Online,* June 20, 2002. http://www.businessweek.com.

[248]Andrew Ross Sorkin and Jonathan D. Glater, "Some Tyco Board Members Knew of Pay Packages, Records Show," *New York Times,* September 23, 2002, p. A1. Mr. Belnick was fired before he was indicted on felony charges. Laurie P. Cohen, "Tyco Ex-Counsel Claims Auditors Knew of Loans," *Wall Street Journal,* October 22, 2002, p. A6.

minutes from that February compensation committee meeting.[249] Mr. Berman denies the allegation. However, Ms. Prue did send a memo on June 7, 2002, to John Fort, Mr. Swartz, and the board's governance committee with the following included: "As a result of the fact that I was recently pressured by Josh Berman to engage in conduct which I regarded as dishonest—and which I have refused to do—I will decline to have any personal contact with him in the future. In addition, I ask that Josh not go to my staff with any requests for information or directions."[250]

Mr. Kozlowski paid $56 million in bonuses to executives eligible for the KELP program, then gave them $39 million to pay the taxes on the bonuses, and then forgave the KELP loans given to pay taxes on the shares awarded in addition to the bonuses. A report commissioned by the Tyco board following the Kozlowski departure refers to the Tyco culture as one of greed and deception designed to ensure personal enrichment.[251]

The relocation loan program was a source of $46 million for Mr. Kozlowski, and SEC documents allege that he "used at least $28 million of those relocation loans to purchase, among other things, luxury properties in New Hampshire, Nantucket, and Connecticut as well as a $7 million Park Avenue apartment for his then (now former) wife."[252]

Mr. Kozlowski's officer team was small and obedient.[253] Tyco had only 400 employees at its central offices and Kozlowski only interacted with a few, a means of keeping information close to the vest.[254] Mark Swartz, Tyco's former CFO, was forty years old at the time of Tyco's fall and his indictment on thirty-eight counts of grand larceny, conspiracy, and falsifying business records.[255] Tyco hired him in 1991, away from Deloitte & Touche's due diligence team. By 1993, he was head of Tyco's acquisitions team, and by 1995, he was Tyco's CFO, at age thirty-three. Mr. Kozlowski nominated Mr. Swartz for a CFO award that year, and *CFO Magazine* honored Mr. Swartz with its 2000 Excellence Award.[256] Indeed, Mr. Kozlowski and Mr. Swartz were inextricably intertwined, with Mr. Swartz even serving as trustee for one of Mr. Kozlowski's trusts for holding title to real property.[257] Both men also used a loophole in securities law to sell millions of shares of Tyco stock even as they declared publicly that they were not selling their shares in the company.[258]

Tyco's Fall

Mr. Kozlowski and Mr. Swartz were indicted under New York State laws for stealing $170 million from the company and for profiting $430 million by selling off their shares while withholding information from the public about the true financial condition of Tyco.[259] The charges against the two were based on a state law that prohibits a criminal

---

[249] *Id.*, p. A22.

[250] *Id.*, p. A22. Both sides acknowledge the authenticity of the memo from Ms. Prue.

[251] Andrew Ross Sorkin, "Tyco Details Lavish Lives of Executives," *New York Times*, September 18, 2002, p. C1. These bonuses are from the year 2000. Kevin McCoy, "Tyco Spent Millions on Exec Perks, Records Say," *USA Today*, September 17, 2002, p. 1B.

[252] *Id.*; and Cohen, "Ex-Tyco CEO's Ex to Post $10 Million for His Bail Bond," p. A5.

[253] Alex Berenson, "Ex-Tyco Chief, a Big Risk Taker, Now Confronts the Legal System," *New York Times*, June 10, 2002, p. B1.

[254] Anthony Bianco, William Symonds, Nanette Byrnes, and David Polek, "The Rise and Fall of Dennis Kozlowski," *BusinessWeek Online*, December 23, 2002, http://www.businessweek.com.

[255] Nicholas Varchaver, "Fall from Grace," *Fortune*, October 28, 2002, 112, 114; and Andrew Ross Sorkin, "2 Top Tyco Executives Charged with $600 Million Fraud Scheme," *New York Times*, September 13, 2002, pp. A1, C3.

[256] *Id.*

[257] Alex Berenson, "From Dream Team at Tyco to a Refrain of Dennis Who?" *New York Times*, June 6, 2002, p. C1.

[258] *Id.*, pp. C1, C5.

[259] Andrew Ross Sorkin, "Ex-Tyco Chief, Free Spender, Going to Court," *New York Times*, September 29, 2003, pp. A1, A15.

enterprise, a type of crime generally associated with organized crime. Their joint trial began in October 2003 and ran until April 2004, when the case ended in a bizarre mistrial. When the jury began deliberations, one juror, Ruth Jordan, was labeled by some of her fellow jurors as a holdout who refused to deliberate the case. Some courtroom observers felt that Ms. Jordan had flashed an "OK" hand signal to the defendants and their counsel.[260] The judge urged the jurors to continue deliberating despite obvious rancor. Ms. Jordan came to be labeled "holdout granny" and "batty blueblood" in the media.[261] However, several media outlets published her name (one with a photo), and when she reported to the judge that she had received a threat, the judge declared a mistrial.[262] The thrust of the defense was that everything Mr. Kozlowski and Mr. Swartz did was in the open, with board approval, and therefore did not fit the requirements for a criminal enterprise.[263]

Mr. Belnick was also indicted and tried, and was acquitted of all charges.[264]

Mr. Kozlowski and Mr. Swartz were retried and convicted on the charges of embezzlement and fraud. The two were convicted on twenty-two of the twenty-three counts of larceny in their indictments. The total amount the prosecution proved was looted from the company was $150 million.

Mr. Kozlowski took the stand to testify, and the jurors indicated that he was simply not a credible witness. When asked why he did not report $25 million in income, he responded that he just wasn't thinking when he signed his tax return. Jurors found an oversight of $25 million difficult to believe.

One portion of the case focused on the use of Tyco funds to buy and redecorate Mr. Kozlowski's New York City apartment (at a cost of $18 million). He acknowledged that he did not oversee it as he should have and that some of the decorations purchased were expensive and "godawful." He told jurors that he later stuffed many of the items "into a closet."[265]

Mr. Kozlowski paid $21.2 million to settle charges related to sales tax evasion on his purchases and sales of his personal art collection. Mr. Kozlowski also settled federal income tax evasion charges. Mr. Swartz's trial for tax evasion was postponed in April 2010. The evasion charges related to the underreporting of the income gleaned from the larceny for which they were convicted.

Kozlowski and Swartz were both sentenced on the larceny convictions to between 8 1/3 and twenty-five years in New York State prison. Mr. Kozlowski was also ordered to pay $167 million in restitution and fines. Mr. Swartz was ordered to pay $72 million in fines and restitution. Both were handcuffed and immediately remanded to state prison following their sentences being imposed. The judge did not grant their motion to remain free while their appeals were pending.[266] The two men have exhausted their appeals and continue to serve their prison sentences in New York.

Tyco agreed to pay $3 billion to settle class action suits brought by its shareholders for fraud committed by Kozlowski and Swartz, the fourth largest shareholder settlement

---

[260]David Carr and Adam Liptak, "In Tyco Trial, an Apparent Gesture Has Many Meanings," *New York Times*, March 29, 2004, pp. C1, C6.

[261]*Id.*

[262]Andrew Ross Sorkin, "Judge Ends Trial When Tyco Juror Reports Threat," *New York Times*, April 3, 2004, pp. A1, B4; and "Mistrials and Tribulations," *Fortune*, April 19, 2004, 42.

[263]Jonathan D. Glater, "Tyco Case Shows Difficulty of Deciding Criminal Intent," *New York Times*, April 8, 2004, pp. C1, C4.

[264]"Ex-Tyco Official Says Actions Were Proper," *New York Times*, June 26, 2004, p. B14.

[265]Andrew Ross Sorkin, "Ex-Chief and Aide Guilty of Looting Millions at Tyco," *New York Times*, June 18, 2005, pp. A1, B4.

[266]Andrew Ross Sorkin, "Ex-Tyco Officers Get 8 to 25 Years," *New York Times*, September 20, 2005, pp. A1, C8; Kevin McCoy, "Ex-Tyco Chiefs Whisked Off to Prison," *USA Today*, September 20, 2005, p. 1B; and Mark Maremont, "Tyco Ex-Officials Get Jail Terms, Big Fines," *Wall Street Journal*, September 20, 2005, pp. C1, C4.

of the Enron era.[267] Tyco's share price dropped from $240 per share in 2002 to less than $25 by 2003. Since 2007, the share price has remained at below $50.

Discussion Questions

1. Recall your readings from Unit 2 on the relationship between ethics and economics. How did Tyco's initial problems establish this connection as a very real one for the U.S. markets? What made Tyco's stock price fall initially? Evaluate this comment from a market observer: "When a CEO steps down for (alleged) tax evasion, it sends the message that all of Corporate America is crooked."[268] "It makes you think, 'Why did he do it? Is there another shoe to drop?'"[269]

2. Warren Rudman, former U.S. senator and a member of the board at Raytheon, who knew and worked with Mark Belnick, was astonished at Mr. Belnick's indictment when it was issued. Mr. Rudman said, when told of Mr. Belnick's fall from grace: "I don't understand. Ethical, straight, cross the t's, dot the i's—that's my experience with Mark Belnick."[270] Mr. Belnick was acquitted of all charges after a jury trial in the summer of 2004. Does his acquittal mean that he acted ethically? What ethical breaches can you find in his behavior at Tyco? What provisions in a credo might have helped Mr. Belnick see the issues more clearly?

3. What do you think of the ethics of Ms. Prue?

4. How do you think the spending and the loans were able to go on for so long?

5. What questions could Mr. Kozlowski and Mr. Swartz have asked themselves to better evaluate their conduct?

6. Evaluate the e-mails from Wilmer Cutler to general counsel and others in the company. Why were these warnings signs unheeded?

7. Make a list of the lines Mr. Kozlowski crossed in his tenure as CEO. Can any of those items help you in developing your credo? Mr. Kozlowski said, when he was named CEO of the Year by *BusinessWeek,*

> Most of us made it to the chief executive position because of a particularly high degree [of] responsibility.... We are offended most by the perception that we would waste the resources of a company that is a major part of our life and livelihood, and that we would be happy with directors who would permit waste.... So as a CEO I want a strong, competent board.[271]

What was he not seeing in his conduct? Had he grown complacent? Is it difficult for us to see ethical breaches that we commit?

Case 4.14

Bausch & Lomb and Krispy Kreme: Channel Stuffing and Cannibalism

The Hong Kong division of Bausch & Lomb enjoyed double-digit growth during the 1980s and 1990s. In some years, earnings increased 25 percent; by 1993, the Hong Kong operation had total revenues of $100 million. Earnings on contact lenses sales seemed to be absolutely unbeatable, with sales increasing at a double-digit pace.

It was in 1994 that Bausch & Lomb's twelve continuous years of double-digit growth in both sales and earnings (excluding one-time events) came to a halt with a company announcement that excessive distributor inventories would result in a significant reduction in 1994 earnings. The final result was a decline of 54 percent in earnings to

---

[267]Floyd Norris, "Tyco to Pay $3 Billion in Settlement," *New York Times*, May 16, 2007, pp. C1, C14.

[268]*Id.*

[269]Adam Shell, "Markets Fall as Tyco CEO's Resignation Adds to Woes," *USA Today*, June 4, 2002, p. 1B.

[270]Glater, "A Star Lawyer Finds Himself the Target of a Peer," pp. C1, C8.

[271]"Match Game," *Fortune*, November 18, 2002, p. 34.

$88.5 million. Sales were down only slightly to $1.9 billion. The below table reflects the shortfalls.[272]

Division	**Millions of dollars**		
	1993	**Planned 1994**	**Actual 1994**
TOTAL BAUSCH & LOMB			
Sales	1872.2	2051.9	1850.6
Operating Earnings	300.9	344.7	168.8
US EYEWEAR			
Sales	190.1	200.0	153.5
Operating Earnings	42.3	48.6	19.7
US CONTACT LENS			
Sales	151.0	176.0	85.8
Operating Earnings	16.8	20.5	−61.7
ASIA-PACIFIC			
Sales	148.9	169.7	107.8
Operating Earnings	34.6	46.8	4.0
ORAL CARE			
Sales	68.8	73.0	50.8
Operating Earnings	2.6	4.2	−10.3
MIRACLE EAR*			
Sales	—	57.9	37.3
Operating Earnings	—	2.3	−12.9
CANADA AND LATIN AMERICA			
Sales	126.1	154.0	113.4
Operating Earnings	17.8	27.3	6.4
EUROPE, MIDDLE EAST, AFRICA			
Sales	246.5	249.0	240.6
Operating Earnings	60.7	60.3	53.0

* Acquired during 1993

An SEC investigation, as well as one by *BusinessWeek*, revealed some underlying problems in operations of Ray-Ban Sunglasses. For example, the Hong Kong unit was faking sales to real customers but then dumping the glasses at discount prices to gray markets. The contact lens division shipped products that were never ordered to doctors in order to boost sales. Some distributors had up to two years of unordered inventories. The U.S., Latin American, and Asian contact lens divisions also dumped lenses on the gray market, forcing Bausch & Lomb to compete with itself.

---

[272]Mark Maremont, "Blind Ambition," *BusinessWeek*, October 23, 1995, 78–92.

The SEC charged Bausch & Lomb with violation of federal securities law for overstatement of earnings. The company issued an earnings restatement that reduced revenues by $42.1 million and net profit by $13 million for 1993.[273] Bausch & Lomb settled the charges with the SEC in 1997. Without admitting or denying the allegations, Bausch & Lomb agreed to a cease and desist order and John Logan, a regional sales director for the contact lens division, agreed to pay a $10,000 fine. The cease and desist order also named the former president of Bausch & Lomb's contact lens division, the former controller, the vice president of finance, and the former director of distributor sales.[274]

Bausch & Lomb emphasized that the SEC found no evidence that top management knew of the overstatement of profits at the time it was made. However, the SEC's associate director of enforcement said, "That's precisely the point. Here is a company where there was tremendous pressure down the line to make the numbers. The commission's view is that senior management has to be especially vigilant where the pressure to make the numbers creates the risk of improper revenue recognition."[275]

Former employees testified they were given a target number each year by operating unit and no excuses were accepted. "Here's your number" was the common direction managers gave to sales personnel and even accountants within the company. When "the number" was not made, they were confronted with this question: "Do you want me to go back to the analysts and tell them we can't make the numbers?"[276] One division manager, expecting a shortfall, said he was told to make the numbers but "don't do anything stupid." The manager said, "I'd walk away saying, 'I'd be stupid not to make the numbers.'" Another manager said that in order to meet targets, they did 70 percent of their shipments in the last three days of the month.[277] Managers lived in fear of what they called "red ball day." *Red ball day* was the end of the calendar quarter, so named because a red sticky dot was placed on the calendar. As red ball day approached, credit was extended to customers who shouldn't have had credit, credit terms went beyond what was healthy and normal for receivables, and deep discounts abounded. One employee described panic-stricken managers doing whatever it takes to meet the number for red ball day.

The executive bonus plan was based on the following factors: 30 percent sales growth, 30 percent earnings growth, and 30 percent return on equity. The remaining 10 percent was customer satisfaction.[278]

Bausch & Lomb also settled a shareholder lawsuit over the overstatement of earnings for $42 million.[279] Following this settlement and with the SEC charges behind it, Bausch & Lomb began its climb back from its tarnished image. It has, as the analysts prone to make puns have noted, lost its focus and has had trouble seeing the vision of the future clearly and sharpening its image. Its overseas operations have been a drain because those sales account for $1.8 billion in sales, but the devaluation of other currencies has been costly.[280] It tried to enter the two-week contact lens market but found that Johnson & Johnson had beat it there and had it fairly cornered.[281]

---

[273]Mark Maremont, "Bausch & Lomb and Former Executives Settle SEC Accounting-Fraud Charges," *Wall Street Journal,* November 18, 1997, p. A6.

[274]Mark Maremont, "Judgment Day at Bausch & Lomb," *BusinessWeek,* December 25, 1995, 39; and Floyd Norris, "Bausch & Lomb and SEC Settle Dispute on '93 Profits," *New York Times,* November 18, 1997, p. C2.

[275]*Id.*

[276]Mark Maremont, "Blind Ambition," *BusinessWeek,* October 23, 1995, 78–92.

[277]Maremont, "Blind Ambition," pp. 78–92.

[278]*Id.*

[279]Mark Maremont, "Bausch & Lomb's Board Puts on Its Glasses," *BusinessWeek,* November 6, 1995, 41.

[280]"Bausch & Lomb to Introduce New Contacts," *Wall Street Journal,* March 18, 1999, pp. B1, B9.

[281]Claudia H. Deutsch, "New Chief Inherits a Bausch & Lomb That Is Listing Badly," *New York Times,* November 17, 2001, pp. C1, C2.

The 148-year-old company that was once synonymous with eye care and quality has had a rugged climb back up, and it had not yet reached its former levels of success in sales, revenues, or earnings by 2000.[282] However, once it began its recovery in 2002, it was hit with news from an internal probe that revealed accounting issues in its Brazilian operations. Bausch & Lomb self-reported those issues to the SEC. Also in 2002, the company was hit with a tip from an outsider that its new CEO, Ronald Zarrella,[283] did not have an MBA from NYU, as his résumé listed. The board demanded the correction and an apology, which Mr. Zarrella issued, but he remained as the CEO.[284] The directors noted that Mr. Zarrella was doing a great job of cleaning house and improving performance. The Bausch & Lomb director of communication indicated that "people make mistakes" and "It was his obligation to proofread his bio carefully."[285] One analyst indicated Mr. Zarrella should have resigned because "believability" was critical for Bausch & Lomb as it tried to recover from its long-lasting slump.

In 2003, the company had to recall one of its ReNu soft contact lens solutions (MoistureLoc) because of a connection between the product and fusarium fungus eye infections. When the eye infections began appearing in Asia, the company initially denied a connection, although 63 percent of the patients with the eye disease were using the MoistureLoc product. After several weeks of testing and new infections, the company recalled the product.[286] The product represented $100 million in annual sales for the company, but the company attributed the infections to a lot manufactured in South Carolina that was, therefore, limited in scope.

However, in 2005, Bausch & Lomb, acting more quickly than with the Asian MoistureLoc experience, issued yet another recall of MoistureLoc because of yet another link to eye disease. This time the recall was more generic because of the nature of the product's ingredients, not a flaw in production. Bausch & Lomb sales for 2006 were down by 78 percent as a result of the recall and loss of consumer confidence.[287]

Krispy Kreme: The Atkins Diet and Channel Stuffing

In 2004, Krispy Kreme donuts was under investigation by the SEC for its accounting practices. Upon announcement of the investigation, the company's stock, that had been at $49.74 in 2003, dropped to $15.71, its lowest for 2004.[288] The stock had already dropped earlier in the year because the company announced it would not meet earnings targets, blaming the decline on the low-carb diet craze.[289] CEO Scott Livengood explained, "This [low-carb] phenomenon has affected us most heavily in our off-premises sales channels, in particular sales of packaged doughnuts to grocery store customers."[290] However, suspicions arose as analysts pointed out that Dunkin' Donuts

---

[282]Zina Moukheiber, "Eye Strain," Forbes, October 4, 1999, 58–60; see also Erile Norton, "CEO Gill to Retire from Bausch & Lomb; Carpenter Is Seen as Possible Successor," *Wall Street Journal,* December 14, 1995, p. B3.

[283]Bausch and Lomb spells it with two "r" s but GM, where he was before he became CEO of Bausch spells it with one "r."

[284]William M. Buckeley, "Bausch & Lomb Now Says CEO Has No MBA," *Wall Street Journal,* October 21, 2002, p. A10.

[285]*Id.*

[286]Sylvia Pagán Westphal, "Bausch & Lomb Recalls Contact-Lens Solution," *Wall Street Journal,* May 16, 2003, p. A3.

[287]Jennifer Levitz, "Bausch & Lomb Slashes Forecast amid Signs of Consumer Backlash," *Wall Street Journal,* August 9, 2006, p. A2.

[288]Greg Farrell, "Investigation Dunks Krispy Kreme," *USA Today,* July 30, 2004, p.1B.

[289]Gretchen Morgenson, "Did Someone Say Doughnuts? Yes. The S.E.C.," *New York Times,* July 30, 2004, pp. C1, C6.

[290]Andrew Stein, "Diets Hurt Donuts," CNNMoney.com, May 7, 2004, http://money.cnn.com/2004/05/07/news/midcaps/krispy_kreme.

was not experiencing the same Atkins down-turn in sales. When an analyst pushed back and why the Atkins and South Beach diets would have such an impact when, traditionally, doughnuts have never been a part of any diet, Mr. Livengood responded, "our intention is to give you the facts as we know them. . . . This is not an unraveling. . . . The jury is out. This could be a new way of eating, even though it is not supported by nutritionists."[291]

There were, however, other issues. By the end of 2005, Krispy Kreme would restate its financial for 2004. Rather than the $48.6 million in profits it had reported, the company actually had losses of $198.3 million. The company also disclosed that it had found material weaknesses in its internal control system resulting in the shipment of goods in advance or without customer orders.[292] The report of the auditor concluded:

> In our judgment, Livengood as CEO and Tate as COO failed to establish a management tone and environment that demanded accurate accounting and financial reporting or to put in place controls, procedures and resources adequate for a business experiencing explosive growth. These failures led or contributed to accounting errors—substantially all of which had the effect of increasing EPS—at the same time that Livengood, Tate and others were profiting greatly from stock options, cash bonuses tied to EPS growth and generous perquisites.[293]

The audit report also gave examples of the accounting errors:

> The most egregious accounting errors we have uncovered involve (i) round-trip transactions in connection with each of the Dallas, Michigan and Northern California franchise acquisitions that resulted in the improper recognition of income or improper reduction of expense, and (ii) the improper recognition of revenue on certain shipments of equipment made months before the franchisees were ready to install the equipment in new stores. Most of these transactions occurred at the end of a fiscal period. Although the individual amounts involved in these transactions are relatively small in dollar amount, each had a material impact on the Company meeting or exceeding its EPS guidance for the particular period because $1 million of pre-tax income for KKD roughly equated to one penny of EPS. These errors raise serious questions about the integrity or competence of those involved and underscore the lack of appropriate accounting and legal controls at the Company.

> In the Dallas franchise acquisition, which closed on June 27, 2003, the Company sold doughnut-making equipment to the Dallas franchisee for approximately $700,000 and agreed at the same time to increase the purchase price for the franchise to cover the price of the equipment. The Company erroneously recorded the approximately $700,000 sales price as revenue rather than as an offset to the increased franchise purchase price. This error contributed approximately half a penny of earnings in the second quarter of fiscal 2004, a quarter in which the Company exceeded its EPS guidance by one penny. When later asked by a senior officer responsible for accounting whether the equipment sale was in the ordinary course, Tate did not disclose that the purchase price for the Dallas franchise had been increased to cover the cost of the equipment.

Livengood insisted on being at the center of all decision-making, yet he was viewed as unapproachable by his management team. Senior managers functioned in solitary silos

---

[291]*Id.*

[292]www.sec.gov. 10-Q filing, December 2005.

[293]www.sec.gov. 8-K filing, November 2005.

without access to all critical facts or an understanding of what others were doing. In addition to the problems with the management culture, the CFO position at Krispy Kreme turned over three times in four years.

The recommendations of the auditor focused on the company's compensation system and recommended an overhaul of the metrics as well as how its payouts are accounted for and reported to the board. The report recommended that the audit committee and the compensation committee review the bonuses that are paid out to employees.

Discussion Questions

1. What went wrong with the Bausch & Lomb culture? A study by Professor Yuri Mishina and others concludes that high-performing companies are more likely to break the law. What do you see at Bausch & Lomb and Krispy Kreme that supports their findings?

2. How were these companies affected? Financially? Competitively?

3. What changes or checks and balances would you put into a company to prevent these types of issues?

4. Why do you think Bausch & Lomb has struggled for so many years to make a recovery that seems to elude it?

5. Reviewing the unfortunate series of events in both companies, what credo moments do you see?

Case 4.15

Enron: The CFO, Conflicts, and Cooking the Books with Natural Gas and Electricity[294]

Introduction

Enron Corp. was an energy company that was incorporated in Oregon in 1985 with its principal executive offices located in Houston, Texas. By the end of 2001, Enron Corp. was the world's largest energy company, holding 25 percent of all of the world's energy trading contracts.[295] Enron's own public relations materials described it as "one of the world's leading electricity, natural gas, and communications companies" that "markets electricity and natural gas, delivers physical commodities and financial and risk management services to companies around the world, and has developed an intelligent network platform to facilitate online business."[296] Enron was also one of the world's most admired corporations, holding a consistent place in *Fortune* magazine's 100 best companies to work for. The sign in the lobby of Enron's headquarters read, WORLD'S LEADING COMPANY.[297] Employees at Enron's headquarters had access to an on-site health club, subsidized Starbucks coffee, concierge service that included massages, and car washes, all for free.[298] Those employees with Enron Broadband received free Palm Pilots, free cell phones, and free wireless laptops.[299]

In November 2001, a week following credit agencies' downgrading of its debt to "junk" grade, Enron filed for bankruptcy. At that time, it was the largest bankruptcy

---

[294]Adapted from Marianne M. Jennings, "A Primer on ENRON: Lessons from a Perfect Storm of Financial Reporting, Corporate Governance and Ethical Culture Failures," *California Western Law Review* 39 (2003):163–262.

[295]Noelle Knox, "Enron to Fire 4,000 from Headquarters," *USA Today*, December 4, 2001, p. 1B.

[296]From the class action complaint filed in the Southern District of Texas, *Kaufman v Enron.*

[297]Bethany McClean, "Why Enron Went Bust," *Fortune*, December 24, 2001, pp. 59–72.

[298]Alexei Barrionuevo, "Jobless in a Flash, Enron's Ex-Employees Are Stunned, Bitter, Ashamed," *Wall Street Journal,* December 11, 2001, pp. B1, B12.

[299]*Id.*

($62 billion) in the history of the United States.[300] Since then, it has dropped and is now just one of the ten largest bankruptcies in the history of the United States.

Background on Enron

Enron began as the merger of two gas pipelines, Houston Natural Gas and Internorth, orchestrated by Kenneth Lay, and emerged as an energy trading company. Poised to ride the wave of deregulation of electricity, Enron would be a power supplier to utilities. It would trade in energy and offer electricity for sale around the country by locking in supply contracts at fixed prices and then hedging on those contracts in other markets. There are few who dispute that its strategic plan at the beginning showed great foresight and that its timing for market entry was impeccable. It was the first mover in this market and it enjoyed phenomenal growth. It became the largest energy trader in the world, with $40 billion in revenue in 1998, $60 billion in 1999, and $101 billion in 2000. Its internal strategy was to grow revenue by 15 percent per year.[301]

When Enron rolled out its online trading of energy as a commodity, it was as if there had been a Wall Street created for energy contracts. Enron itself had 1,800 contracts in that online market. It had really created a market for weather futures so that utilities could be insulated by swings in the weather and the resulting impact on the prices of power. It virtually controlled the energy market in the United States. By December 2000 Enron's shares were selling for $85 each. Its employees had their 401(k)s heavily invested in Enron stock, and the company had a matching program in which it contributed additional shares of stock to savings and retirement plans when employees chose to fund them with Enron stock.

When competition began to heat up in energy trading, Enron began some diversification activities that proved to be disasters in terms of producing earnings. It acquired a water business that collapsed nearly instantaneously. It also had some international investments, particularly power plants in Brazil and India, that had gone south. Its $1 billion investment in a 2,184-megawatt power plant in India was in ongoing disputes as its political and regulatory relations in that country had deteriorated and the state utility stopped paying its bills for the power.[302]

In 1999, it announced its foray into fiber optics and the broadband market. Enron overanticipated the market in this area and experienced substantial losses related to the expansion of its broadband market. Like Corning and other companies that overbuilt, Enron began bleeding quickly from losses related to this diversification.[303]

The Financial Reporting Issues

Mark-to-Market Accounting

Enron followed the FASB's rules for energy traders, which permit such companies to include in current earnings those profits they expect to earn on energy contracts and related derivative estimates.[304] The result is that many energy companies had been

[300]Richard A. Oppel Jr. and Riva D. Atlas, "Hobbled Enron Tries to Stay on Its Feet," *New York Times*, December 4, 2001, pp. C1, C8.

[301]"Why John Olson Wasn't Bullish on Enron," http://knowledge.Wharton.upenn.edu/013002_ss3. Accessed July 28, 2010.

[302]Saritha Rai, "New Doubts on Enron's India Investment," *New York Times*, November 21, 2001, p. W1.

[303]Proposed complaint, class action litigation, November 2001, http://www.kaplanfox.com. Accessed July 28, 2010.

[304]Jonathan Weil, "After Enron, 'Mark to Market' Accounting Gets Scrutiny," *Wall Street Journal*, December 4, 2001, pp. C1, C2.

posting earnings, quite substantial, for noncash gains that they expect to realize some time in the future. Known as *mark-to-market accounting,* energy companies and other industries utilize a financial reporting tool intended to provide insight into the true value of the company through a matching of contracts to market price in commodities with price fluctuations. However, those mark-to-market earnings are based on assumptions. An example helps to illustrate the wild differences that might occur when values are placed on these energy contracts that are marked to the market price. Suppose that an energy company has a contract to sell gas for $2.00 per gallon, with the contract to begin in 2004 and run through 2014. If the price of gas in 2007 is $1.80 per gallon, then the value of that contract can be booked accordingly and handsomely, with a showing of a 20 percent profit margin. However, suppose that the price of gasoline then climbs to $ 2.20 per gallon during 2008. What is the manager's resolution and reconciliation in the financial statement of this change in price? The company has a ten-year commitment to sell gas at a price that will produce losses. Likewise, suppose that the price of gas declines further to $0.50 per gallon in 2008. How is this change reflected in the financial statements, or does the company leave the value as it was originally booked in 2007? And how much of the contract is booked into the present year? And what is its value presently?

The difficulty with mark-to-market accounting is that the numbers that the energy companies carry for earnings on these future contracts are subjective. The numbers they carry depend upon assumptions about market factors. Those assumptions used in computing future earnings booked in the present are not revealed in the financial reports and investors have no way of knowing the validity of those assumptions or even whether they are conservative or aggressive assumptions about energy market expectations. It becomes difficult for investors to cross-compare financial statements of energy companies because they are unable to compare what are apples and oranges in terms of earnings because of the futuristic nature of the income and the possibility that those figures may never come to fruition.

For example, the unrealized gains portion of Enron's pretax profit for 2000 was about 50 percent of the total $1.41 billion profit originally reported. That amount was one-third in 1999.

This practice of mark-to-market accounting proved to be particularly hazardous for Enron management because their bonuses and performance ratings were tied to meeting earnings goals. The result was that their judgment on the fair value of these energy contracts, some as long as twenty years into the future, was greatly biased in favor of present recognition of substantial value.[305] The value of these contracts is dependent upon assumptions and variables, which are not discussed in the financial statements, not readily available to investors and shareholders, and include wild cards such as the weather, the price of natural gas, and market conditions in general. One analyst has noted, "Whenever there's a considerable amount of discretion that companies have in reporting their earnings, one gets concerned that some companies may overstate those earnings in certain situations where they feel pressure to make earnings goals."[306] A FASB study showed that when a hypothetical example on energy contracts was given at a conference, the valuations by managers for the contracts ranged from $40 million to $153 million.[307]

Some analysts were concerned about this method of accounting because these are noncash earnings. Some noted that Enron's noncash earnings were over 50 percent of

---

[305]Susan Lee, "Enron's Success Story," *Wall Street Journal,* December 26, 2001, p. A11.

[306]*Id.*

[307]Weil, "After Enron, 'Mark to Market' Accounting Gets Scrutiny," p. C2.

its revenues. Others discovered the same issues when they noted that Enron's margins and cash flow did not match up with its phenomenal earnings records.[308] For example, Jim Chanos, of Kynikos Associates, commented that no one was really sure how Enron made money and that its operating margins were very low for the reported revenue. Mr. Chanos concluded that Enron was a "giant hedge fund sitting on top of a pipeline."[309] Mr. Chanos noted that Wall Street loved Enron because it consistently met targets, but he was skeptical because of off-the-balance sheet transactions (see below for more information).[310] Mr. Chanos and others who brought questions to Enron were readily dismissed. For example, *Fortune* reporter Bethany McClean experienced pressure in 2000 when she began asking questions about the revenues and margins. Then-Chairman, and now the late Ken Lay, called her editor to request that she be removed from the story. The Enron CEO at the time, Jeffrey Skilling, refused to answer her questions and labeled her line of inquiry as "unethical."[311] During an analysts' telephonic conference with Mr. Skilling in which Mr. Chanos asked why Enron had not provided a balance sheet, Mr. Skilling called Mr. Chanos an "a—h_____."[312] Mr. Chanos opted for selling Enron shares short and declined to disclose the amount of money he has made as a result of his position.

John Olson, presently an analyst with a Houston company, reflected that most analysts were unwilling to ask questions. When Mr. Olson asked Mr. Skilling questions about how Enron was making money, Mr. Skilling responded that Enron was part of the new economy and that Olson "didn't get it."[313] Mr. Olson advised his company's clients not to invest in Enron because, as he explained to them, "Never invest in something you can't understand."[314] Mr. Olson was fired by Merrill Lynch following the publication of his skeptical analysis about Enron. Merrill Lynch continues to deny that it fired Mr. Olson for that reason. Enron was a critical client for Merrill Lynch. In fact, Merrill would become known for its role in Andrew Fastow's infamous "Wanna buy a barge?" deal, in which Merrill purchased a barge temporarily from Enron. The purchase permitted Enron to meet its numbers goals, and even the general counsel at Merrill had expressed concern that Merrill might be participating in Enron's earnings management. Four former Merrill investment bankers were indicted and convicted for their roles in the "wanna buy a barge" Enron transaction.[315] All but one of the convictions were reversed on appeal because the investment bankers could not have known the extent of Fastow's frauds or the full scope and meaning of the transaction. The court held that the investment bankers were allowed to rely on the representations of a company's officer and could not be convicted of participating in fraud when an agent of the company arranged the transaction.

---

[308]McClean, "Why Enron Went Bust," pp. 62–63. Ms. McLean had written a story in the summer of 2001 entitled, "Is Enron Overpriced?" for *Fortune*. The lead line to the story was "How exactly does Enron make its money?" The story was buried. It enjoyed little coverage or attention until November 2001. Ms. McClean is now an analyst on the Enron case for NBC and has been featured on numerous news shows. Felicity Barringer, "10 Months Ago, Questions on Enron Came and Went with Little Notice," *New York Times*, January 28, 2002, p. A11. Ms. McClean wrote a book with Peter Elkind, *The Smartest Guys in the Room* (2003).

[309]*Id.*

[310]Cassell Bryan-Low and Suzanne McGee, "Enron Short Seller Detected Red Flags in Regulatory Filings," *Wall Street Journal*, November 5, 2001, pp. C1, C2.

[311]McClean, "Why Enron Went Bust," p. 60.

[312]Bryan-Low and McGee, "Enron Short Seller Detected Red Flags in Regulatory Filings," p. C2.

[313]"Why John Olson Wasn't Bullish on Enron," http://knowledge.Wharton.upenn.edu/013002_ss3. Accessed July 28, 2010.

[314]*Id.*

[315]Kurt Eichenwald, "Jury Convicts 5 Involved in Enron Deal with Merrill," *New York Times*, November 4, 2004, pp. C1, C4.

When *U.S. News & World Report* published Mr. Olson's analysis and advice, Kenneth Lay sent Mr. Olson's boss a handwritten note with the following:

John Olson has been wrong about Enron for over 10 years and is still wrong. But he is consistant [sic].

Upon reading the note sent to his boss, Mr. Olson responded, "You know that I'm old and I'm worthless, but at least I can spell *consistent*."[316]

Off-the-Books Entities

Not only did Enron's books suffer from the problem of mark-to-market accounting, but also the company made minimal disclosures about its off-the-balance-sheet liabilities that it was carrying.[317] These problems, coupled with the mark-to-market value of the energy contracts, permitted Enron's financial statements to paint a picture that did not adequately reflect the risk investors had.

Enron had created, by the time it collapsed, about 3,000 off-the-books entities, partnerships, limited partnerships, and limited liability companies (called *special purposes entities,* or SPEs, in the accounting profession) that carried Enron debt and obligations that had been spun off but did not have to be disclosed in Enron's financial reports because, under an accounting rule known as FASB 125, the debt and obligations in off-the-books entities did not have to be disclosed so long as Enron's ownership interests in the entities never exceeded 49 percent. Disclosure requirements under GAAP and FASB kicked in at 50 percent ownership at that time. Under the old rules, when a company owned 50 percent or more of a company, it had to disclose transactions with that company in the financials as *related party transactions.*

Enron created a complex network of these entities, and some of the officers of the company even served as principals in these companies and began earning commissions for the sale of Enron assets to them. Andrew Fastow, Enron's CFO, was a principal in many of these off-the-book entities. His wife, Lea, also a senior officer at Enron, was also involved in handling many of the SPEs. In some of the SPEs, the two discussed the possibility of having some of the payments come to their two small children.

In 1999, Enron described one of these relationships in its 10K (an annual report companies must file with the SEC) as follows:

In June 1999, Enron entered into a series of transactions involving a third party and LJM Cayman, L.P. (LJM). LJM is a private investment company, which engages in acquiring or investing in primarily energy-related investments. A senior officer of Enron is the managing member of LJM's general partner.[318]

The effect of all of these partnerships was to allow Enron to transfer an asset from its books, along with the accompanying debt, to the partnership. An outside investor would fund as little as 3 percent of the partnership, with Enron occasionally providing even the front money for the investor. Enron would then guarantee the bank loan to the partnership for the purchase of the asset. Enron would pledge shares as collateral for these loans it guaranteed in cases where the bank felt the asset transferred to the partnership was insufficient collateral for the loan amount.[319] By the time it collapsed, Enron had

---

[316]"Why John Olson Wasn't Bullish on Enron."

[317]Richard A. Oppel Jr. and Andrew Ross Sorkin, "Enron Corp. Files Largest U.S. Claim for Bankruptcy," *New York Times,* December 3, 2001, pp. A1, A16.

[318]Enron Corp. 10K, Filed December 31, 1999, p. 16.

[319]John R. Emshwiller and Rebecca Smith, "Murky Waters: A Primer on Enron Partnerships," *Wall Street Journal,* January 21, 2002, pp. C1, C14.

$38 billion in debt among all the various SPEs, but carried only $13 billion on its balance sheet.[320]

To add to the complexity of these off-the-books loans and the transfer of Enron debt, many of the entities formed to take the asset and debt were corporations in the Cayman Islands. Enron had 881 such corporations, with 700 formed in the Cayman Islands, and, in addition to transferring the debt off its balance sheet, it enjoyed a substantial number of tax benefits because corporations operate tax-free there. The result is that Enron paid little or no federal income taxes between 1997 and 2000.[321] Comedian Robin Williams referred to Enron executives as "the Investment Pirates of the Caribbean."

Relatives and Doing Business with Enron

In addition to these limited liability company and limited partnership asset transfers, there were apparently a series of transactions authorized by Mr. Lay in which Enron did business with companies owned by Mr. Lay's son, Mark, and his sister, Sharon Lay. Jeffrey Skilling had hired Mark Lay in 1989 when Mark graduated with a degree in economics from UCLA. However, Mr. Lay left Enron feeling that he needed to "stand on his own and work outside of Enron."[322] Enron eventually ended up acquiring Mr. Lay's son's company and hired him as an Enron executive with a guaranteed pay package of $1,000,000 over three years as well as 20,000 stock options for Enron shares.[323] There was a criminal investigation into the activities of one of the companies founded by Mark Lay, but he was not charged with wrongdoing. He did pay over $100,000 to settle a civil complaint in the matter, but admitted no wrongdoing. Mark Lay entered a Baptist seminary in Houston and plans to become a minister.[324]

Sharon Lay owned a Houston travel agency and received over $10 million in revenue from Enron during the period from 1998 through 2001 years, one-half of her company's revenue during that period.[325] Both Ms. and the late Mr. Lay say that they made all the necessary disclosures to the board and regulators about their business with Enron.

Enron's Demise

Enron's slow and steady decline began in the November–December 2000 time frame, when its share price was at $85. By the time Jeffrey Skilling announced his departure as CEO on August 14, 2001, with no explanation, the share price was at about $43. Mr. Skilling says that he left the company simply to spend more time with his family, but his departure raised questions among analysts even as Kenneth Lay returned as CEO.[326] The *Wall Street Journal* raised questions about Enron's disclosures on August 28, 2001, as Enron was beginning an aggressive movement for selling off assets.[327] By October, Enron disclosed that it was reporting a third-quarter loss and it took a $1.2 billion reduction in shareholder equity. Within days of those announcements, CFO Andrew Fastow was terminated, and in less than two weeks, Enron restated its earnings dating back to 1997, a $586 million, or 20 percent, reduction.

---

[320]Bethany McLean and Peter Elkind, "Partners in Crime," *Fortune*, October 27, 2003, 79.

[321]David Gonzalez, "Enron Footprints Revive Old Image of Caymans," *New York Times*, January 28, 2002, p. A10.

[322]David Barboza and Kurt Eichenwald, "Son and Sister of Enron Chief Secured Deals," *New York Times*, February 2, 2002, pp. A1, B5.

[323]*Id.*

[324]*Id.*

[325]*Id.*

[326]John E. Emshwiller and Rebecca Smith, "Behind Enron's Fall, a Culture of Operating outside Public View," *Wall Street Journal*, December 5, 2001, pp. A1, A10.

[327]John E. Emshwiller, Rebecca Smith, Robin Sidel, and Jonathan Weil, "Enron Cuts Profit Data of 4 Years by 20%," *Wall Street Journal*, November 9, 2001, p. A3.

Following these disclosures and the announcement of Enron's liability on a previously undisclosed $690 million loan, CEO Kenneth Lay left the company as CEO, but remained as chairman of the board.[328] Mr. Lay waived any rights to his parachute, reportedly worth $60 million, and also agreed to repay a $2 million loan from the company.[329] Mr. Lay's wife, Linda, appeared on NBC with correspondent Lisa Meyer on January 28, 2002, and indicated that she and Mr. Lay were "fighting for liquidity."[330] She indicated that all their property was for sale, but a follow-up check by Ms. Meyer found only one of a dozen homes owned by the Lays was for sale. Mr. Lay consulted privately with the Reverend Jesse Jackson for spiritual advice, according to Mrs. Lay.[331]

The Enron Culture

Enron was a company with a swagger. It had an aggressive culture in which a rating system required that 20 percent of all employees be rated at below performance and encouraged to leave the company. As a result of this policy, no employee wanted to be the bearer of bad news.

Margaret Ceconi, an employee with Enron Energy Services, wrote a five-page memo to Kenneth Lay on August 28, 2001, stating that losses from Enron Energy Services were being moved to another sector in Enron in order to make the Energy Service arm look profitable. One line from her memo read, "Some would say the house of cards are falling."[332] Mr. Lay did not meet with Ms. Ceconi, but she was contacted by Enron Human Resources and counseled on employee morale. When she raised the accounting issues in her meeting with HR managers, she was told they would be investigated and taken very seriously, but she was never contacted by anyone about her memo. Her memo remained dormant until January 2002, when she sent it to the U.S. House of Representatives' Energy and Commerce Committee, the body conducting a series of hearings on the Enron collapse.

Ms. Ceconi's memo followed two weeks after Sherron Watkins, a former executive, wrote of her concerns about "accounting scandals" at Enron. Ms. Watkins was a former Andersen employee who had been hired into the executive ranks by Enron. Ms. Watkins wrote a letter to Kenneth Lay on August 15, 2001, that included the following: "I am incredibly nervous that we will implode in a wave of accounting scandals. I have heard from one manager-level employee from the principal investments group say, 'I know it would be devastating to all of us, but I wish we would get caught. We're such a crooked company.'"[333] She also warned that Mr. Skilling's swift departure would raise questions about accounting improprieties and stated, "It sure looks to the layman on the street that we are hiding losses in a related company."[334] In her memo, she listed J. Clifford Baxter as someone Mr. Lay could talk to in order to verify her facts and affirmed that her concerns about the company were legitimate. Ms. Watkins wrote the memo anonymously on August 15, 2001, but by August 22, and after discussing the memo with former colleagues at Andersen, she told her bosses that she was the one who had written the memo.

[328]*Id.*

[329]Richard A. Oppel Jr. and Floyd Norris, "Enron Chief Will Give Up Severance," *New York Times*, November 14, 2001, pp. C1, C10.

[330]Alessandra Stanley and Jim Yardley, "Lay's Family Is Financially Ruined, His Wife Says," *New York Times*, January 29, 2002, pp. C1, C6.

[331]*Id.*

[332]Julie Mason, "Concerned ex-worker was sent to human resources," *Houston Chronicle*, Jan. 30, 2002, www.chron.com.

[333]Michael Duffy, "What Did They Know and When Did They Know It?" *Time*, January 28, 2002, 16–27.

[334]*Id.*

In the months prior to Enron's collapse, employees became suspicious about what was called "aggressive accounting" and voiced their concerns in online chat rooms.[335] Clayton Verdon was fired in November 2001 for his comments about "overstating profits," made in an employee chat room. A second employee was fired when he revealed in the chat room that the company had paid $55 million in bonuses to executives on the eve of its bankruptcy.[336] Enron indicated that the terminations were necessary because the employees had breached company security.

In his testimony at the trial of his former bosses, Ken Lay and Jeffrey Skilling, former CFO Andrew Fastow offered some insights into the culture at Enron and the tone he set as a senior executive. Andrew Fastow, when confronted by Daniel Petrocelli, lawyer for Jeffrey Skilling, about his clear wrongdoing offered the following: "Within the culture of corruption that Enron had, that valued financial reporting rather than economic value, I believed I was being a hero."[337] He went on to add, "I thought I was being a hero for Enron. At the time, I thought I was helping myself and helping Enron to make its numbers."[338] He explained further, "At Enron, the culture was and the business practice was to do transactions that maximized the financial reporting earnings as opposed to maximizing the true economic value of the transactions."[339] However, Mr. Fastow said he did see the writing on the wall near the end and encouraged others to reveal the true financial picture at Enron: "We have to open up the kimono and show them the skeletons in the closet, what our assets are really worth."[340]

The Enron Board

Some institutional investors have raised questions about conflicts and the lack of independence in Enron's board.[341] Members of Enron's board were well compensated with a total of $380,619 paid to each director in cash and stock for 2001. One member of the board was Dr. Wendy L. Gramm, the former chairwoman of the Commodity Futures Trading Commission and wife of Senator Phil Gramm, the senior U.S. senator from Texas, who has received campaign donations from Enron employees and its PAC. Dr. Gramm opted to own no Enron stock and accepted payment for her board service only in a deferred compensation account.

Dr. John Mendelsohn, the president of the University of Texas M.D. Anderson Cancer Center in Houston, also served on the Enron board, including its audit committee. Dr. Mendelsohn's center received $92,508 from Enron and $240,250 from Linda and Ken Lay after Dr. Mendelsohn joined the Enron board in 1999.[342]

After the Fall

Enron fired 5,100 of its 7,500 employees by December 3, 2001. Although Enron continues to operate as a company today, only 1,900 employees retained their jobs. Each employee received a $4,500 severance package. However, many of the employees were

[335]Alex Berenson, "Enron Fired Workers for Complaining Online," *New York Times*, January 21, 2002, pp. C1, C8.

[336]*Id.*

[337]March 8, 2006, trial testimony of Andrew Fastow, in Greg Farrell, "Fastow 'Juiced' Books," *USA Today*, March 8, 2006, p. 1A.

[338]*Id.*

[339]Farrell, "Fastow 'Juiced' Books," p. 1A.

[340]Alexei Barrionuevo, "Ex-Enron Official Insists Chief Knew He Was Lying," *New York Times*, March 2, 2006, p. C3.

[341]Reed Abelson, "Enron Board Comes under a Storm of Criticism," *New York Times*, December 16, 2001, p. BU4.

[342]Jo Thomas and Reed Abelson, "How a Top Medical Researcher Became Entangled with Enron," *New York Times*, January 28, 2002, pp. C1, C2.

looking forward to a comfortable retirement, basing that assumption on the value of their Enron stock. Many held Enron stock and were compensated with Enron stock options. The stock was trading at $0.40 per share on December 3, 2001, following a high of $90 at its peak. Employee pension funds lost $2 billion. Enron employees' 401(k) plans, funded with Enron stock, lost $1.2 billion in 2001. "Almost everyone is gone. Upper management is not talking. No managing directors are around, and police are on every floor. It's so unreal," said one departing employee.[343] One employee, George Kemper, a maintenance foreman, who is part of a suit filed against Enron related to the employees' 401(k) plans, whose plan was once worth $225,000 and is now worth less than $10,000, said, "How am I going to retire now? Everything I worked for the past 25 years has been wiped out."[344] The auditors have admitted that they simply cannot make sense of the company's books for 2001, but have concluded that the cash flow of $3 billion claimed for 2000 was actually a negative $153 million, and that the profits of $1 billion reported in 2000 did not exist.[345]

Just prior to declaring bankruptcy, Enron paid $55 million in bonuses to executives described as "retention executives," or those the company needs to stay on board in order to continue operations.[346]

Tragically, J. Clifford Baxter, a former Enron vice chairman, and the one officer Ms. Watkins suggested Mr. Lay talk with, took his own life in his 2002 Mercedes Benz about a mile from his $700,000 home in Sugar Land, Texas, a suburb twenty-five miles from Houston. Mr. Baxter, who earned his MBA at Columbia, had left Enron in May 2001, following what some employees say was his voicing of concerns over the accounting practices of Enron and its disclosures.[347] SEC records disclose that Mr. Baxter sold 577,000 shares of Enron stock for $35.2 million between October 1998 and early 2001.[348] He had been asked to appear before Congress to testify, was a defendant in all the pending litigation, and was last seen in public at his yacht club, where he took his yacht out for a sail. Those who saw him indicated that his hair had become substantially grayer since October, when the public disclosures about Enron's condition began. Mr. Baxter was depicted as a philanthropist in the Houston area, having raised money for charities such as Junior Achievement and other organizations to benefit children. He had created the Baxter Foundation with $200,000 from Enron and $20,000 of his own money to assist charities such as Junior Achievement, the American Cancer Society, and the American Diabetes Association.[349]

As noted, Enron had a matching plan for its employees on the 401(k). However, 60 percent of their plan was invested in Enron stock. Between October 17 and November 19, 2001, when the issues surrounding Enron's accounting practices and related transactions began to surface, the company put a lockdown on the plan so that employees could not sell their shares.[350] Prior to the lockdown, most of the executives had sold off large blocks of Enron stock. For example, Jeffrey Skilling, who left the company in August

---

[343]Richard A. Oppel Jr. and Riva D. Atlas, "Hobbled Enron Tries to Stay on Its Feet," *New York Times*, December 4, 2001, pp. C1, C8.

[344]Christine Dugas, "Enron Workers Sue over Retirement Plan," *USA Today*, November 27, 2001, p. 5B.

[345]Cathy Booth Thomas, "The Enron Effect," *Time*, June 5, 2006, 34–36.

[346]Richard A. Oppel Jr. and Kurt Eichenwald, "Enron Paid $55 Million for Bonuses," *New York Times*, December 4, 2001, pp. C1, C4.

[347]Elissa Gootman, "Hometown Remembers Man Who Wore Success Quietly," *New York Times*, January 30, 2002, p. C7.

[348]Mark Babineck, "Deceased Enron Executive Earned Respect in the Ranks," *Houston Chronicle*, January 26, 2002, http://www.chron.com.

[349]*Id.*

[350]*Id.*

2001, sold off 500,000 shares on September 17, 2001.[351] He had sold 240,000 shares in early 2001 and at the time of Enron's bankruptcy owned 600,000 shares and an undisclosed number of options.[352] Mr. Lay also sold a substantial amount of stock in August 2001, but his lawyer had indicated the sale of the stock was necessary in order to repay loans.[353]

Person	Title	Charges	Disposition
Ken Lay	Chairman, CEO	Securities fraud	Convicted; conviction reversed following Mr. Lay's untimely death on July 5, 2006, one month after his conviction.
		Wire fraud	Same as above.
Jeffrey Skilling	CEO	Securities fraud	Convicted on all but two counts; serving a sentence of 24.4 years, but a 2010 U.S. Supreme Court decision on honest services fraud remanded the case after reversing his conviction for honest services fraud because he had not engaged in bribery (required for proof of honest services fraud). With that conviction out of the mix, Mr. Skilling must be resentenced to a lesser period of time.
		Wire fraud	Same as above.
Andrew Fastow	CFO	Securities fraud	Guilty plea; six years (will probably be released in four because of his extensive cooperation in the criminal trials of Skilling and Lay as well as the civil suits)
		Wire fraud	Guilty plea.
		Tax evasion	Guilty plea.
Lea Fastow	Senior Officer	Tax evasion	Guilty plea; one year; served (ended with last month in halfway house in July 2005) her term first so that Andrew Fastow could be at home with their two young children before he began his term in 2006.
David Delainey	CEO Enron North America	Insider trading	Guilty plea; served slightly over one year.

[351]Richard A. Oppel Jr., "Former Head of Enron Denies Wrongdoing," *New York Times*, December 22, 2001, pp. C1, C2.

[352]*Id.*

[353]Richard A. Oppel Jr., "Enron Chief Says His Sale of Stock Was to Pay Loans," *New York Times*, January 21, 2002, pp. A1, A13.

Person	Title	Charges	Disposition
Ben Glisan	Treasurer	Conspiracy	Guilty plea; five years.
Richard Causey	Chief Accounting Officer	Insider trading	Guilty plea to one count of securities fraud in exchange for seven-year sentence recommendation and cooperation with federal prosecutors on Skilling and Lay case.[354] He was sentenced to 5.5 years.
Michael J. Kopper	Officer who worked directly with Fastow	Fraud	Guilty plea to money laundering and conspiracy to commit wire fraud; sentenced to three years and one month.
Kenneth D. Rice	CEO, Enron Broadband		Guilty plea to one count.
Mark Koenig	Vice president of investor relations		Guilty plea to one count of aiding and abetting securities fraud; eighteen months.

Note: Thirty-two Enron executives were indicted in total, with guilty pleas or convictions for all. Mr. Lay was the last Enron official indicted, in July 2004.

In addition to the impact on Enron, its employees, and Houston, there was a worldwide ripple effect. Enron had large stakes in natural gas pipelines in the United States and around the world as well as interests in power plants everywhere from Latin America to Venezuela. It is also a partial owner of utilities, including telecommunications networks. Congressional hearings were held as the House energy and Commerce Committee investigated the company's collapse. Representative Billy Tauzin of Louisiana scheduled the investigations and noted, "How a company can sink so far, so fast, is very troubling. We need to find out if the company's accounting practices masked severe underlying financial problems."[355] Senator Jeff Bingham, then-chairman of the Senate Energy Committee, said, "I believe that our committee is keenly aware of the need for enhanced oversight and market monitoring."[356]

Enron's bankruptcy filing included a list of creditors fifty-four pages long. Although the bankruptcy filing showed $24.76 billion in assets and $13.15 billion in debt, these figures did not include those off-the-balance sheet obligations, estimated to be about $27 billion.[357]

Enron energy customers, which include Pepsico, the California state university system, JCPenney, Owens-Illinois, and Starwood Hotels & Resorts, also felt the effects of the company's collapse. Enron had contracts with 28,500 customers. These customers had to revise their contracts and scramble to place energy contingency plans in place. California's state universities were in negotiations for renewal of their 1998 contract

---

[354]John Emshwiller, "Enron Prosecutors, after Plea Bargain, Can Reduce Technical Jargon at Trial," *Wall Street Journal*, January 4, 2006, pp. C1, C5.

[355]Richard A. Oppel Jr. and Andrew Ross Sorkin, "Ripples Spreading from Enron's Expected Bankruptcy," *New York Times*, November 30, 2001, pp. C1, C6, C7.

[356]"Financial Threat from Enron Failure Continues to Widen," *Financial Times*, December 1, 2001, p. 1.

[357]Rebecca Smith and Mitchell Pacelle, "Enron Files for Chapter 11 Bankruptcy, Sues Dynegy," *Wall Street Journal*, December 3, 2001, p. A2.

with Enron, but those talks went into a stalemate and the university system found another provider.[358]

Trammell Crow halted the groundbreaking ceremony for its planned construction of new Enron headquarters; a building that would have been fifty stories high and included offices, apartments, and stores.[359]

The ripple effect stretched into unrelated investments. Five major Japanese money market funds with heavy Enron investments fell below their face value by December 3, 2001.[360] These losses had additional consumer-level effects because these funds were held by retirees because they were seen as "safe haven" funds for investors.

The Enron board hired Stephen F. Cooper as CEO to replace Mr. Lay. Mr. Cooper is a specialist in leading companies through bankruptcy, including TWA and Federated Department Stores.[361]

Enron's collapse ended the movement toward the deregulation of electricity. Following Enron's collapse, federal and state regulators saw the impact on consumers of allowing energy companies to operate in a regulatory no-man's land, and the state moved back to the model of price regulation of the sale of energy to consumers.[362]

The SEC, a national team of lawyers, and the Justice Department began a six-year investigation of the company, its conduct, and it officers.[363] The civil suits press on, with Andrew Fastow providing the plaintiffs in the cases, many of them former employees, information and details that are aiding them in recovering funds from banks, auditors, and insurers. In the bankruptcy, Enron's creditors received 18.3 cents on the dollar, an amount far below the normal payout in a bankruptcy.[364]

Many noted at the time of Enron's collapse that "evidence of fraud may well be elusive" as the SEC and prosecutors investigate.[365] Professor Douglas Carmichael, a professor of accounting at Baruch College, is one who agrees, "It's conceivable that they complied with the rules. Absent a smoking-gun e-mail or something similar, it is an issue of trying to attack the reasonableness of their assumptions."[366] One auditor said that it never occurred to him that anyone would "use models to try and forecast energy prices for 10 years, and then use those models to report profits, but that the rule had not placed a limit on such trades."[367] When asked about the accounting practices of Enron, Mr. Skilling said, "We are doing God's work. We are on the side of angels."[368]

Mr. Skilling and Mr. Lay were tried in a case that ran from February to June 2006. They were both convicted following six days of deliberations by the jurors. Mr. Fastow was the government's key witness against the two men. Both men took the stand as part of their defense, and both men got angry on the stand when faced with cross-

[358]Rhonda L. Rundle, "Enron Customers Seek Backup Suppliers," *Wall Street Journal*, December 3, 2001, p. A10.

[359]Allen R. Myerson, "With Enron's Fall, Many Dominoes Tremble," *New York Times*, December 2, 2001, pp. 3–1, MB1.

[360]Ken Belson, "Enron Causes 5 Major Japanese Money Market Funds to Plunge," *New York Times*, December 4, 2001, p. C9.

[361]Shaila K. Dewan and Jennifer Lee, "Enron Names an Interim Chief to Oversee Its Bankruptcy," *New York Times*, January 30, 2002, p. C7.

[362]Rebecca Smith, "Enron Continues to Haunt the Energy Industry," *Wall Street Journal*, March 16, 2006, p. C1; and Joseph Kahn and Jeff Gerth, "Collapse May Reshape the Battlefield of Deregulation," *New York Times*, December 4, 2001, pp. C1, C8.

[363]Jo Thomas, "A Specialist in Tough Cases Steps into the Legal Tangle," *New York Times*, January 21, 2002, p. C8.

[364]Mitchell Pacelle, "Enron's Creditors to Get Peanuts," *Wall Street Journal*, July 11, 2003, pp. C1, C7.

[365]Floyd Norris and Kurt Eichenwald, "Fuzzy Rules of Accounting and Enron," *New York Times*, January 30, 2002, pp. C1, C6.

[366]*Id.*

[367]*Id.*

[368]Neil Weinberg and Daniel Fisher, "Power Player," *Forbes*, December 24, 2001, pp. 53–58.

examination. Mr. Lay was convicted on all counts. Mr. Skilling was convicted on 18 of 27 counts, Mr. Lay died of a massive heart attack on July 5, 2006, while at his Colorado vacation home.[369] His conviction was set aside because he had not had the opportunity to appeal the verdict. One comment on his passing was "His death was a cop-out."[370] A former Enron employee told the *Houston Chronicle,* "Glad he's dead. May he burn in hell. I'll dance on his grave."[371]

Mr. Skilling awaits his resentencing following a U.S. Supreme Court reversal of his "honest services" fraud conviction. Mr. Petrocelli was paid $23 million from a trust fund Mr. Skilling had set aside for his defense, and Enron's insurer paid $17 million to Mr. Petrocelli's firm of O'Melveny and Myers, for a total of $40 million. However, the firm and Mr. Petrocelli are still owed $30 million for their defense work, an amount Mr. Skilling is unable to pay.[372]

Discussion Questions

1. Can you see that Enron broke any laws? Andrew Fastow testified at the Lay and Skilling trial as follows: "A significant number of senior management participated in this activity to misrepresent our company. And we all benefited financially from this at the expense of others. And I have come to grips with this. That, in my mind, was stealing."[373] Is Mr. Fastow correct? Was it stealing? How should Fastow's relationships with Enron's partially owned subsidiaries have been handled in terms of disclosure.

2. Do you think that Enron's financial reports gave a false impression? Does it matter that most investors in Enron were relatively sophisticated financial institutions? What about the employees' ownership of stock and their 401(k) plans?

3. What questions could the officers of Enron have used to evaluate the wisdom and ethics of their decisions on the off-the-book entities and mark-to-market accounting? Be sure to apply the various models you have learned.

4. Did Mr. Fastow have a conflict of interest?

5. What elements for your personal credo can you take away from the following testimony from David Delainey and Andrew Fastow? As you think about this question, consider the following from their testimony at the Skilling and Lay trial.

When asked why he did not raise the issue or simply walk away, Mr. Delainey responded, "I wish on my kids' lives I would have stepped up and walked away from the table that day."[374] Mr. Fastow had the following exchange with Daniel Petrocelli, Mr. Skilling's lawyer (Mr. Petrocelli represented the Brown and Goldman families in their civil suit against O. J. Simpson):

Petrocelli: To do those things, you must be consumed with insatiable greed. Is that fair to say?

Fastow: I believe I was very greedy and that I lost my moral compass.[375]

Fastow also testified as follows: "My actions caused my wife to go to prison."[376] Defense attorneys, being the capable souls that they are, extracted even more: "I feel like I've taken a lot of blame for Enron these past few days. It's not relevant to me whether Mr. Skilling's or Mr. Lay's names are on that page. . . . I'm ashamed of the past. What they write about the past I can't affect. I want to focus on the future. Even after being caught, it took me awhile to come to

[369]Bethany McClean and Peter Elkind, "Death of a Disgraced Energy Salesman," *Fortune,* July 30, 2006, 3–32.
[370]*Id.*
[371]*Id.*
[372]Carrie Johnson, "After Enron Trial, Defense Firm Is Stuck with the Tab," *Washington Post,* June 16, 2006, pp. D1, D3.
[373]Alexei Barrionuevo, "Fastow Testifies Lay Knew of Enron's Problems," *New York Times,* March 9, 2006, pp. C1, C4.
[374]*Id.*
[375]John Emshwiller and Gary McWilliams, "Fastow Is Grilled at Enron Trial," *Wall Street Journal,* March 9, 2006, pp. C1, C4.
[376]Emshwiller and McWilliams, "Fastow Is Grilled at Enron Trial," pp. C1, C4.

grips with what I'd done. . . . I've destroyed my life. All I can do is ask for forgiveness and be the best person I can be."[377]

Mr. Fastow also said, "I have asked my family, my friends, and my community for forgiveness. I've agreed to pay a terrible penalty for it. It's an awful thing that I did, and it's shameful. But I wasn't thinking that at the time."[378]

6. Was Ms. Watkins a whistle-blower? Discuss the timing of her disclosures. Compare and contrast her behavior with Paula Reiker's.

Paula H. Reiker, the former manager of investor relations for Enron, was paid $5,000,000 between 2000 and 2001. She testified that she was aware during teleconferences that the numbers being reported were inaccurate. Upon cross-examination she was asked why she didn't speak up as Mr. Petrocelli queried, "Why didn't you just quit?" Her response, "I considered it on a number of occasions. I was very well compensated. I didn't have the nerve to quit."[379] Did she make the right decision?

Compare & Contrast

1. Evaluate Enron's culture. Be sure to compare and contrast with Fannie Mae, Bausch & Lomb, Goldman, and Krispy Kreme. As you evaluate, consider the revelations from the testimony of David W. Delainey at the Skilling and Lay criminal trial. Mr. Delainey, the former head of Enron Energy Services. Energy Services retail unit, testified that he saw the legal and ethical issues unfolding as he worked for Enron. When he was asked to transfer $200 million in losses from his unit to another division in order to then show a profit, he testified, "That was the worst conduct I had ever been a part of and everybody knew exactly what was going on at that meeting."[380]

   Now compare and contrast the decisions and actions of Mr. Olson and Merrill Lynch.

2. Experts have commented that one of the reasons for the success of the Enron task force is that it worked its way up through employees in the company. That is, it got plea agreements and information from lower-level employees and then used the information to go after higher-ranking officers in the company. For example, Mr. Fastow was facing over 180 years in prison if convicted of all of the charges in his indictment. He agreed to turn state's evidence in exchange for a recommendation of a prison sentence of eleven years. He did such a good job in testifying against Mr. Skilling and Mr. Lay that the judge sentenced him to only six years. He is doing such a good job in helping lawyers on the civil cases that he will probably serve only four years before being released. Mr. Skilling, on the other hand, was sentenced to 24.4 years. What is the moral of this story? What can we learn about our role as employees? As officers?

Case 4.16

Arthur Andersen: A Fallen Giant[381]

Arthur Andersen, once known as the "gold standard of auditing," was founded in Chicago in 1913 on a legend of integrity as Andersen, Delaney & Co. In those early years, when the business was struggling, Arthur Andersen was approached by a

[377]Greg Farrell, "Defense Goes after Fastow's 'Greed' with a Vengeance," *USA Today*, March 9, 2006, p; 1; and Alexei Barrionuevo, "Fastow Testifies Lay Knew of Enron's Problems," *New York Times*, March 9, 2006, pp. C1, C4.

[378]Alexei Barrionuevo, "The Courtroom Showdown, Played as Greek Tragedy," *New York Times*, March 12, 2006, pp. 1, 3.

[379]Alexei Barrionuevo, "Enron Defense Chips Away at Witness's Motives," *New York Times*, February 24, 2006, p. C3.

[380]Alexei Barrionuevo, "Ex-Enron Official Insists Chief Knew He Was Lying," *New York Times*, March 2, 2006, p. C3.

[381]Adapted with permission from Marianne M. Jennings, "A Primer on Enron: Lessons from A Perfect Storm of Financial Reporting, Corporate Governance, and Ethical Culture Failures," *California Western Law Review* 39 (2003): 163–262.

well-known railway company about audit work. When the audit was complete, the company CEO was outraged over the results and asked Andersen to change the numbers or lose his only major client. A twenty-eight-year-old Andersen responded, "There's not enough money in the city of Chicago to induce me to change that report!" Months later, the railway filed for bankruptcy.[382]

Over the years Andersen evolved into a multiservice company of management consultants, audit services, information systems, and virtually all aspects of operations and financial reporting. Ultimately, Andersen would serve as auditor for Enron, WorldCom, Waste Management, Sunbeam, and the Baptist Foundation, several of the largest bankruptcies of the century as well as poster companies for the corporate governance and audit reforms of the Sarbanes–Oxley Act, federal legislation enacted in the wake of the Enron and WorldCom collapses. However, it would be Andersen's relationship with Enron that would be its downfall.

Andersen served as Enron's outside auditor, and the following information regarding various conflicts of interest became public both through journalistic investigations and via the Senate hearings held upon Enron's declaration of bankruptcy[383]:

- Andersen earned over one-half ($27 million) of its $52 million in annual fees from consulting services furnished to Enron.[384]
- There was a fluid atmosphere of transfers back and forth between those working for Andersen doing Enron consulting or audit work and those working for Enron who went with Andersen.[385]

David Duncan, the audit partner in the Houston offices of Andersen who was in charge of the Enron account, was a close personal friend of Richard Causey, Enron's chief accounting officer, who had the ultimate responsibility for signing off on all of CFO Andrew Fastow's off-the-books entities.[386] The two men traveled, golfed, and fished together.[387] Employees of both Andersen and Enron have indicated since the time of their companies' collapses that the two firms were so closely connected that they were often not sure who worked for which firm. Many Andersen employees had permanent offices at Enron, including Mr. Duncan. Office decorum thus found Enron employees arranging in-office birthday celebrations for Andersen auditors so as to be certain not to offend anyone. In addition, there was a fluid line between Andersen employment and Enron employment, with auditors joining Enron on a regular basis. For example, in 2000, seven Andersen auditors joined Enron.[388]

Andersen's Imprimatur for Enron Accounting

Enron's executives and internal accountants and the Andersen auditors resorted to two discretionary accounting areas, special purposes entities (SPEs) and mark-to-market accounting, for booking the revenues from its substantial energy contracts,

---

[382]Barbara Ley Toffler, *Final Accounting: Ambition, Greed, and the Fall of Arthur Andersen* (New York: Broadway Books, 2003), p. 12.

[383]"The Role of the Board of Directors in Enron's Collapse," report of the Permanent Subcommittee on Investigations of the Senate Government Affairs Committee, 107th Congress, Report 107-70, July 8, 2002, 39–41 (hereinafter, "PSI Report").

[384]Deborah Solomon, "After Enron, a Push to Limit Accountants to . . . Accounting," *Wall Street Journal*, January 25, 2002, p. C1.

[385]Seven Andersen audit employees became Enron employees in the year 2000 alone. John Schwartz and Reed Abelson, "Auditor Struck Many as Smart and Upright," *New York Times*, January 17, 2002, p. C11.

[386]Anita Raghavan, "How a Bright Star at Andersen Fell along with Enron," *Wall Street Journal*, May 15, 2002, pp. A1, A8. See also Cathy Booth Thomas and Deborah Fowler, "Will Enron's Auditor Sing?" *Time*, February 11, 2002, p. 44.

[387]*Id.*

[388]John Schwartz and Reed Abelson, "Auditor Struck Many as Smart and Upright," *New York Times*, January 17, 2002, p. C11.

approximately 25 percent of all the existing energy contracts in the United States by 2001.[389] Their use of these discretionary areas allowed them to maintain the appearance of sustained financial performance through 2001. One observer who watched the rise and fall of Enron noted, in reference to Enron but clearly applicable to all of the companies examined here, "If they had been going a slower speed, their results would not have been disastrous. It's a lot harder to keep it on the track at 200 miles per hour. You hit a bump and you're off the track."[390] The earnings from 1997 to 2001 were ultimately restated, with a resulting reduction of $568 million, or 20 percent of Enron's earnings for those four years.[391]

Sherron Watkins, who became one of *Time*'s persons of the year for her role in bringing the financial situation of Enron to public light, was the vice president for corporate development at Enron when she first expressed concerns about the company's financial health in August 2001. A former Andersen employee, she was fairly savvy about accounting rules, and with access to the financial records for purposes of her new job, she quickly realized that the large off-the-books structure that had absorbed the company's debt load was problematic.[392] Labeling the SPEs "fuzzy" accounting, she began looking for another job as she prepared her memo detailing the accounting issues, because she understood that raising those issues meant that she would lose her Enron job.[393] Ms. Watkins did write her memo, anonymously, to Kenneth Lay, then chair of Enron's board and former CEO, but she never discussed her concerns or discussed writing the memo with Jeffrey Skilling, then Enron's CEO, or Andrew Fastow, its CFO, because "it would have been a job-terminating move."[394] She did eventually confess to writing the memo when word of its existence permeated the executive suite. Mr. Fastow reacted by noting that Ms. Watkins wrote the memo because she was seeking his job.[395]

Andersen recognized the focus on numbers in an internal memo as it evaluated its exposure in continuing to have Enron as a client. What follows is an excerpt from a 2000 memo that David Duncan and four other Andersen partners prepared as they evaluated what they called the "risk drivers" at Enron. Following a discussion of "Management Pressures" and "Accounting and Financial Management Reporting Risks," the following drivers were listed:

- Enron has aggressive earnings targets and enters into numerous complex transactions to achieve those targets.
- The company's personnel are very sophisticated and enter into numerous complex transactions and are often aggressive in restructuring transactions to achieve derived financial reporting objectives.
- Form-over-substance transactions.[396]

Mr. Duncan presented the board with a one-page summary of Enron's accounting practices.[397] The summary, called "Selected Observations 1998 Financial Reporting,"

[389]Noelle Knox, "Enron to Fire 4,000 from Headquarters," *USA Today*, December 4, 2001, p. 1B.

[390]Bob McNair, a Houston entrepreneur who sold his company to Enron in 1998, quoted in John Schwartz and Richard A. Oppel Jr., "Risk Maker Awaits Fall of Company Built on Risk," *New York Times*, November 29, 2001, p. C1.

[391]John R. Emshwiller, Rebecca Smith, Robin Sidel, and Jonathan Weil, "Enron Cuts Profit Data of 4 Years by 20 percent," *Wall Street Journal*, November 9, 2001, p. A3.

[392]Jodie Morse and Amanda Bower, "The Party Crasher," *Time*, January 6, 2003, pp. 53–55.

[393]*Id.*

[394]Rebecca Smith, "Fastow Memo Defends Enron Partnerships and Sees Criticism as Ploy to Get His Job," *Wall Street Journal*, February 20, 2002, p. A3.

[395]*Id.*

[396]"PSI Report," Hearing Exhibit 2b, Audit Committee Minutes of 2/7/99, p. 18.

[397]"PSI Report," Hearing Exhibit 2b, Audit Committee Minutes of 2/7/99, p. 16.

highlighted Mr. Duncan's areas of concern, and it was presented to the board in 1999, a full two years prior to Enron's collapse. Called "key accounting issues" by Mr. Duncan, the areas of concern included "Highly Structured Transactions," "Commodity and Equity Portfolio," "Purchase Accounting," and "Balance Sheet Issues." Mr. Duncan had assigned three categories of risk for these accounting areas, which included "Accounting Judgments," "Disclosure Judgements [*sic*]," and "Rule Changes," and he then assigned letters to each of these three categories: *H* for high risk, *M* for medium risk, and *L* for low risk.[398] Each accounting issue had at least two *H* grades in the three risk categories.

Andersen's Concerns About Conflicts

Enron's Code of Ethics had both a general and a specific policy on conflicts of interest, both of which had to be waived in order to allow its officers to function as officers of the many off-the-books entities that it was creating. The general ethical principle on conflicts is as follows:

> *Employees of Enron Corp., its subsidiaries, and its affiliated companies (collectively the "Company") are charged with conducting their business affairs in accordance with the highest ethical standards. An employee shall not conduct himself or herself in a manner which directly or indirectly would be detrimental to the best interests of the Company or in a manner which would bring to the employee financial gain separately derived as a direct consequence of his or her employment with the company.*[399]

Enron's code also had a specific provision on conflicts related to ownership of businesses that do business with Enron, which provides,

> *The employer is entitled to expect of such person complete loyalty to the best interests of the Company. . . . Therefore, it follows that no full-time officer or employee should:(c) Own an interest in or participate, directly or indirectly, in the profits of another entity which does business with or is a competitor of the Company, unless such ownership or participation has been previously disclosed in writing to the Chairman of the Board and Chief Executive Officer of Enron Corp., and such officer has determined that such interest or participation does not adversely affect the best interests of the Company.*[400]

The board's minutes show that it waived this policy for Andrew Fastow on at least three different occasions.[401] In post collapse interviews, members of the board have insisted that they were not waiving Enron's code of ethics for Mr. Fastow. In its defense in shareholder lawsuits, the board members and company have argued that in granting a waiver they were simply following the code's policies and procedures.[402] Granting the waiver was a red flag. Even the conflicted Enron board saw the issue and engaged, at least once, in what was called in the minutes "vigorous discussion."[403]

David Duncan was concerned about this conflict of interest, and when Mr. Fastow first proposed his role in the first off-the-books entity, Mr. Duncan, on May 28, 1999, e-mailed a message of inquiry about the Fastow proposal to Benjamin Neuhausen, a member of Andersen's Professional Standards Group in Chicago. Mr. Neuhausen

---

[398]*Id.*

[399]Enron Corporation, "Code of Ethics, Executive and Management," July (Houston: Enron Corporation, 2000), 12.
[400]*Id.*, p. 57.
[401]"PSI Report," p. 26.
[402]"PSI Report," p. 25.
[403]"PSI Report," 28, citing the Hearing Record, 157.

responded, with some of the response in uppercase letters for emphasis, "Setting aside the accounting, idea of a venture entity managed by CFO is terrible from a business point of view. Conflicts galore. Why would any director in his or her right mind ever approve such a scheme?" Mr. Duncan wrote back to Mr. Neuhausen on June 1, 1999, "[O]n your point 1 (i.e., the whole thing is a bad idea), I really couldn't agree more. Rest assured that I have already communicated and it has been agreed to by Andy that CEO, General [Counsel], and Board discussion and approval will be a requirement, on our part, for acceptance of a venture similar to what we have been discussing."[404] Mr. Duncan, the Andersen audit partner responsible for the Enron account, had expressed concern about the aggressive accounting practices Enron sought to use. Attorney Rusty Hardin, who served as Andersen's lead defense lawyer in the obstruction of justice case against the company for document shredding, noted that "no question David Duncan was a client pleaser."[405] Mr. Duncan also experienced pressure from his client and even consulted his pastor about how to resolve the dilemmas he faced in terms of approval of the financial statements: "He basically said it was unrelenting. It was a constant fight. Wherever he drew that line, Enron pushed that line—he was under constant pressure from year to year to push that line."[406]

Enron and Andersen Fall

The special report commissioned by the Enron board following its collapse described Enron's culture as "a flawed idea, self-enrichment by employees, inadequately designed controls, poor implementation, inattentive oversight, simple (and not so simple) accounting mistakes, and overreaching in a culture that appears to have encouraged pushing the limits."[407] In an interview with *CFO Magazine* in 1999, when he was named CFO of the year, Mr. Fastow explained that he was able to keep Enron's share price high because he spun debt off its books into SPEs.[408]

As the problems at Enron began to go from percolating to parboil, there was a cloud of nervousness that hung over Andersen. Based on an increasing number of questions that were coming into the Chicago office as Enron stories continued to appear in the news, Andersen's in-house counsel, Nancy Temple, sent around a memo that included the following advice on the firm's document destruction policy: "It will be helpful to make sure that we have complied with the policy."[409] Andersen's policy allowed for destruction of records when those records "are no longer useful for an audit.[410] There ensued a bit of a fine-line scramble on the Enron papers and documents that Andersen held.

When Enron announced, on October 16, 2001, its third quarter results, the $1.01 billion charge to earnings was not an easy thing for the market to absorb. The release characterized the charge to earnings as "non-recurring." Andersen officials had spoken with Enron executives to express their doubts about this characterization of the charge, but Enron refused to alter the release. Ms. Temple wrote an e-mail to Duncan that "suggested deleting some language that might suggest we have concluded the release is misleading."[411] The following day, the SEC notified Enron by letter that it had opened

---

[404]"PSI Report, p. 26.

[405]Raghavan, "How a Bright Star at Andersen Fell Along with Enron," pp. A1, A8.

[406]*Id.*, p. A8.

[407]Kurt Eichenwald, "Enron Panel Finds Inflated Profits and Few Controls," *New York Times*, February 3, 2002, p. A1.

[408]David Barboza and John Schwartz, "The Finance Wizard behind Enron's Deals," *New York Times*, February 6, 2002, pp. A1, C9.

[409]Tony Mauro, "One Little E-Mail, One Big Legal Issue," *National Law Journal*, April 25, 2005, p. 7.

[410]*Id.*

[411]544 U.S. at 700.

an investigation in August and requested certain information and documents. On October 19, 2001, Enron forwarded a copy of that letter to Andersen.

Also on October 19, 2001, Ms. Temple sent an internal team of accounting experts a memo on document destruction and attached a copy of the document policy. On October 20, 2001, the Enron crisis-response team held a conference call, during which Temple instructed everyone to "[m]ake sure to follow the [document] policy." On October 23, 2001, then–Enron CEO Lay declined to answer questions during a call with analysts because of "potential lawsuits, as well as the SEC inquiry." After the call, Duncan met with other Andersen partners on the Enron engagement team and told them that they should ensure team members were complying with the document policy. Another meeting for all team members followed, during which Duncan distributed the policy and told everyone to comply. These, and other smaller meetings, were followed by substantial destruction of paper and electronic documents.

On October 26, 2001, one of Andersen's senior partners circulated a *New York Times* article discussing the SEC's response to Enron. His e-mail commented that "the problems are just beginning and we will be in the cross hairs. The marketplace is going to keep the pressure on this and is going to force the SEC to be tough."[412] On October 30, the SEC opened a formal investigation and sent Enron a letter that requested accounting documents. Throughout this time period, the document destruction continued, despite reservations by some of Andersen's managers. On November 8, 2001, Enron announced that it would issue a comprehensive restatement of its earnings and assets. Also on November 8, the SEC served Enron and petitioner with subpoenas for records. On November 9, Duncan's secretary sent an e-mail that stated, "Per Dave-No more shredding.. . .We have been officially served for our documents."[413]

Andersen maintained that the shredding was routine, but the federal government indicted the company and Mr. Duncan. Mr. Duncan entered a guilty plea to obstruction of justice and ultimately testified against Andersen in court. Andersen was convicted of obstruction of justice. Its felony conviction meant that it could no longer conduct audits, and those clients that remained were now required to hire other auditors. Within a period of two years, Andersen went from an international firm of 36,000 employees to nonexistence.

However, Andersen did take the case to the U.S. Supreme Court, which ruled in its favor the conviction for obstruction of justice.[414] The court found that although there may have been intent on the part of the individuals involved in the shredding, the jury was not properly instructed on the proof and intent required to convict the accounting firm itself. Following the Supreme Court's reversal of the decision, Mr. Duncan withdrew his guilty plea. The government has the option of prosecuting Mr. Duncan but has, so far, declined to do so.

Discussion Questions

1. With regard to the destruction of the documents, was there a difference between what was legally obstruction of justice and what was ethical in terms of understanding what was happening at Enron? When the U.S. Supreme Court reversed the Andersen decision, the *Wall Street Journal* noted that the Andersen case was a bad legal case and a poor prosecutorial decision on the part of the Bush administration.[415] Why do you think the

[412]544 U.S. at 701.

[413]544 U.S. at 702.

[414]*Arthur Andersen LLP v U.S.*, 544 U.S. 696 (2005).

[415]The editorial is "Arthur Andersen's 'Victory,'" *Wall Street Journal*, June 1, 2005, p. A20. The court decision is *Arthur Andersen LLP v U.S.*, 544 U.S. 696 (2005).

prosecutors took the case forward? What changes under SOX would make the case easier to pursue today?

2. David Duncan was active in his church, a father of three young daughters, and a respected alumnus of Texas A&M. Mr. Duncan's pastor talked with the *New York Times* following Enron's collapse and Duncan's indictment, and discussed with the reporter what a truly decent human being Duncan was.[416] What can we learn about the nature of those who commit these missteps? What can you add to your credo as a result of Duncan's experience? Was the multimillion-dollar compensation he received a factor in his decision-making processes? Can you develop a decision tree on Duncan's thought processes from the time of the first SPE until the shredding? Using the models you learned in Units 1 and 2, what can you see that he missed in his analysis?

3. In 2000, a full two years before WorldCom's collapse, Steven Brabbs, World Com's director of international finance and control, who was based in London, raised objections when he discovered after he had completed his division's books for the year that $33.6 million in line costs had been dropped from his books through a journal entry.[417] He was told that the changes were made pursuant to orders from CFO Scott Sullivan. He next suggested that the treatment be cleared with Arthur Andersen.[418] When there was no response to his suggestion that the external auditor be consulted, Mr. Brabbs again raised his objections in a meeting with internal financial executives a few months later. Following the meeting, Mr. Brabbs was chastised by WorldCom's controller for raising the issue again.[419] The following quarter, Mr. Brabbs received orders from WorldCom headquarters to make another similar change, but to do so at his level rather than having it done from corporate headquarters via journal entry.

Unwilling to have the entries generate from his division, he created another entity and transferred the costs to it.[420] He voiced his concerns again and was told that there was no choice because the accounting was a "Scott Sullivan directive."[421] Mr. Brabbs also had a meeting with Arthur Andersen auditors to discuss his concerns. Following the meeting he received an e-mail from WorldCom's controller, David Myers, which directed that Mr. Brabbs was "not [to] have any more meetings with AA for any reason."[422] When WorldCom's internal audit staff began to raise questions about the reserves and the capitalization of ordinary expenses, they were prohibited from doing further work and, for the most part, worked nights and weekends to untangle the accounting nightmare they had first discovered with a simple question about receipts for some capitalized expenses. CFO Scott Sullivan asked the audit staff to wait at least another quarter before continuing with their investigation. Andersen auditors reported any internal audit inquiries to Sullivan and did not follow through on questions and concerns raised.[423] What controls were missing? Why the reporting lines to Sullivan?

4. One of the tragic ironies to emerge from the collapse of Arthur Andersen, following its audit work for Sunbeam, WorldCom, and Enron, was that it had survived the 1980s savings-and-loan scandals unscathed. In *Final Accounting: Ambition, Greed and the Fall of Arthur Andersen,* the following poignant description appears: "The savings-and-loan crisis, when it came, ensnared almost every one of the Big 8. But Arthur Andersen skated away virtually clean, because it had made the decision, years earlier[,] to resign all of its clients in the industry. S&Ls for years had taken advantage of a loophole that allowed them to boost earnings by recording the value of deferred taxes. Arthur Andersen accountants thought the rule was misleading

[416]Raghavan, "How a Bright Star at Andersen Fell Along with Enron," pp. A1, A8.

[417]Kurt Eichenwald, "Auditing Woes at WorldCom Were Noted Two Years Ago," *New York Times*, July 15, 2002, pp. C1, C9.

[418]*Id.*, p. C9. The information was taken from Mr. Brabbs's statement to the government during its initial investigation of WorldCom.

[419]*Id.*

[420]*Id.*

[421]*Id.*

[422]Jessica Sommar, "E-Mail Blackmail: WorldCom Memo Threatened Conscience-Stricken Exec," *New York Post,* August 27, 2002, p. 27.

[423]Pulliam and Solomon, "How Three Unlikely Sleuths Discovered Fraud at WorldCom," pp. A1, A6.

and tried to convince their clients to change their accounting. When they refused, Andersen did what it felt it had to: It resigned all of its accounts rather than stand behind account-ing that it felt to be wrong."[424] What takes a company from the gold standard to indictment and conviction?

Compare & Contrast

Following its declaration of bankruptcy, Lehman Brothers' trustee released a report that indicated it was able to spin off its risky debt instruments to SPEs under what was known as Repo 105. Lehman controlled 25 percent of the boards of these SPEs although its relationship with the SPEs was depicted as arms-length.[425] As a result of these layers of transfer, Lehman was able to look financially sound right up until the collapse of the market in 2008 when the CDO market collapsed.

The bankruptcy trustee gave this summary of the Lehman practices:

Lehman employed off-balance sheet devices, known within Lehman as "Repo 105" and "Repo 108" transactions, to temporarily remove securities inventory from its balance sheet, usually for a period of seven to ten days, and to create a materially misleading picture of the firm's financial condition in late 2007 and 2008. Repo 105 transactions were nearly identical to standard repurchase and resale ("repo") transactions that Lehman (and other investment banks) used to secure short-term financing, with a critical difference: Lehman accounted for Repo 105 transactions as "sales" as opposed to financing transactions based upon the overcollateralization or higher than normal haircut in a Repo 105 transaction. By recharacterizing the Repo 105 transaction as a "sale," Lehman removed the inventory from its balance sheet.

The bankruptcy trustee does not address whether the transactions complied with accounting rules because he concludes that the failure to disclose their escalating debt and increasingly worthless securities was material. What does the bankruptcy trustee mean that compliance with the accounting rules is not the issue? Analyze why the lessons of other collapsed companies are not internalized by businesses that use the same strategies.

Reading 4.17

The New Shareholder: Taking Over to Change the Culture

Shareholders can submit proposals to be included in proxy solicitation materials. If the company does not oppose what is being proposed, the proposition is included as part of the proxy materials. If management is opposed, the proposing shareholder has the right of a 200-word statement on the proposal in the materials. These proposals are not permitted along with their 200-word statements unless they propose conduct that is legal and related to business operations, as opposed to social, moral, religious, and political views. During the Vietnam era, many shareholders wanted to include proposals in proxy materials for companies that were war suppliers. Their proposals centered on the political opposition to the war and not the business practices of the company.

The proposals have evolved to different sorts of topics, from social responsibility to questions of executive compensation. For example, Iroquois Brands, Ltd., a food company that imports French foie gras, a pâté made from the enlarged livers of force-fed

[424]Toffler, *Final Accounting,* 19.

[425]Louise Story and Eric Dash, "Lehman Channeled Risks Through Alter Ego' Firm," *New York Times,* April 13, 2010, p. A1.

geese, faced shareholder litigation over this French practice in raising the geese. The practice involves funneling corn down the geese's throats and gagging them with rubber bands to keep them from regurgitating. A shareholder asked to have a proposal included in the proxy materials that proposes that the company study the practice as an unethical business practice (cruelty to animals).[426]

Another example involved Steve Hindi, an animal rights activist who owns $5,000 in Pepsi stock. He discovered that Pepsi advertises in bullrings in Spain and Mexico and has attended annual shareholder meetings and put forward shareholder proposals to have the company halt the practice. His proposal has not yet passed, but he has started a website (http://www.pepsibloodbath.com) to increase pressure on the company. Pepsi has withdrawn from bullfighting ads in Mexico, but continues with them in Spain. Mr. Hindi continues his quest.[427]

The SEC and other organizations provide a tally of the types of shareholder proposals included in the proxies for publicly held companies during the 2010 annual meeting season. There has been a shift from social issues to governance issues. The list below shows, in the order of frequency, the types of shareholders' proposals made for the 2010 proxy season.

TOPIC
Advisory vote on compensation
Right to call a special meeting
Repeal board structure with classification of directors
Review of report on company political spending
Independent board chairman
Require a majority to elect directors
Take action on climate change
End super majority vote requirement
Retention period for stock awards
Report on sustainability
Adopt sexual orientation antibias policy

In 1999, the average shareholder support for the measures was 15 percent of all voting shares. By the 2008–2009 season, that number had grown to 46 percent. In 2009, 161 shareholder proposals won majority support. In several companies shareholders dropped proposals after management agreed to comply with the demands in the proposal. Under the Dodd-Frank Wall Street Reform and Consumer Protection Act of 2010, companies are required to give shareholders a say-on-pay and the approval rate for say-on-pay proposals is 86 percent. Also under Dodd-Frank, the SEC will be promulgating rules on shareholder nominations of directors. Some companies negotiate on shareholder proposals. For example, Paychex agreed to seek out more women and minorities for its board and the Calvert Group dropped its diversity proxy proposal. McDonald's agreed to ban workplace discrimination based on sexual orientation.

[426]*Lovenheim v Iroquois Brands, Ltd.,* 618 F.supp. 554 (D.C. 1985).
[427]Constance L. Hays, "A Pepsico Shareholder Meeting and a Very Unhappy Shareholder," *New York Times,* April 22, 2000, pp. B1, B4.

Corporate secretaries who handle proposals and shareholders have their own organization. Their website (www.governanceprofessionals.org) includes information on shareholder proposals and shareholder activism.

Institutional investors can also be very active in shareholder proposals, and the California Public Employee Retirement Service is one of the country's most active institutional shareholders (see http://www.calpers-governance.org).

Shareholders can also flex their muscles in other ways. At Home Depot's annual meeting in 2006, the shareholders showed up in greater numbers than in other years because of concerns about the $245 million compensation package that was awarded to then-CEO Robert L. Nardelli. The shareholders became even more sensitive about the issue when Home Depot's board of directors failed to appear at the annual meeting. When the shareholders were not permitted to ask questions at the meeting, their anger spilled over into negative reports in the financial press. They were limited to one minute at the microphone as their anger boiled. One investor called the board "chicken," and another complained that the company was no longer reporting sales on a per-store basis so that it was difficult to determine how the company was doing.

The company's share price dropped on the day following the meeting. About 30 percent of the shareholders withheld their votes for ten of the eleven directors of the company. Mr. Nardelli was at the time also a director at Home Depot and was also one of the ten from whom support was withheld. The one director who enjoyed shareholder support was the chairman, Angelo R. Mozilo, who was the CEO of Countrywide Financial. Interestingly, Countrywide Financial fell victim to the subprime lending problems. Mr. Mozilo and Countrywide have been charged by the SEC with various violations relating to stock sales as well as financial disclosures in the year prior to the write-downs Countrywide was required to take because of mortgage defaults and foreclosures.

Following the annual meeting, Home Depot announced the following governance changes:

- Shareholders would be permitted to ask questions at the annual meeting.
- Directors will attend all annual meetings.

The company released a statement with its governance announcements:

Consistent with the way we run our company—in which we listen, learn and lead— we will return to our traditional format for next year's annual shareholders meeting, which will include a business overview, the presentation of proposals, an opportunity for shareholder questions and with the board of directors in attendance.[428]

Several months after the quelling of the rebellion, the board announced the termination of Mr. Nardelli. His exit package was valued at $210 million, a figure that outraged the shareholders again.[429] Mr. Nardelli was named as CEO of Chrysler within months after his ouster from Home Depot. Mr. Nardelli resigned as Chrysler's CEO when the federal government took over that company in exchange for a government bailout.

Discussion Questions

1. Are shareholder proposals an effective means for getting corporations to take action?

2. What shift do you see in shareholder activism with their proposals? Why? Are they shifting strategies? Explain your answer.

---

[428]Jeremy W. Peters, "Home Depot Alters Rules for Electing Its Directors," *New York Times*, May 20, 2006, p. C3.

[429]JoAnn S. Lublin, Ann Zimmerman, and Chad Terhune, "Behind Nardelli's Abrupt Exit," *Wall Street Journal*, January 4, 2007, pp. A1, A12.

3. Are these proposals always in the best interests of the shareholders? Why do you think management opposes almost all shareholder proposals?

4. Corporate governance is considered an important part of the ethical culture of a company. What type of tone did the conduct of the Home Depot board set for the company?

Another important aspect of corporate culture is accountability. Was the board dodging accountability?

5. When CEOs fail to provide even an adequate company performance on their watches, should they experience a salary reduction? Is a poor tone-at-the-top established when CEOs are given, and accept, bonuses, even when the company does not perform well?

The Industry Practices and Legal Factors

Reading 4.18

If It's Legal, It's Ethical; and Besides, Everyone Does It[430]

When it comes to buying and selling securities and issuing financial reports on behalf of a company, it is amazing how much you can do and still escape criminal conviction and even more amazing how many folks are doing just what you want to do. The past few years have handed us some landmark cases in finance and trading in which the acquittals seemed to defy facts. The recent round-up via criminal charges of Galleon hedge-fund principals and those who fed them information suggests another round of criminal trials is upon us. However, criminal indictments and trials do not translate into convictions. Criminal fraud sets a high bar when it comes to standards of proof for insider trading as well as for the dissemination of false information by companies to investors.

But, the question is not now nor has it ever been one of mere legality. Nor is the issue how many people are involved in the conduct. The law remains the minimum standard of behavior. And majority vote is not a foolproof method of ethical analysis. Acquittal does not mean those involved acted ethically. Ethics lie as the core of trust and trust is the cornerstone of markets and capitalism. As we glance back at some memorable cases and offer predictions on those that are pending we realize that law and ethics are two very different beasts. If we win hearts and minds on acquittal, what do we accomplish if those who survive live to mislead on another day and another deal?

On Clients and Holding

Theodore Sihpol, a vice president of Bank of America at the time, found himself facing 29 felony charges from then–New York Attorney General, Eliot Spitzer for holding a trade and placing it after the prices for the next day are set. However, the Investment Company Act trading prohibition kicks in at about 5:30. Sihpol had engaged in only "late trading," or placing orders for a client after the 4 PM closing. Mr. Sihpol did not violate the time constraint; he found a window of opportunity and seized it. The jury agreed, and Mr. Sihpol was acquitted of all charges.

Illegal? No. Ethical? Also no. The *Wall Street Journal* argued at the time, and correctly so, that Mr. Sihpol's behavior represented the "criminalization of widespread business practices *ex post facto*."[431] Therein lies the flaw in the *Journal's* analysis. One of the classic rationalizations of unethical behavior is, "Everybody does that!" No one disputes the data that the business practices are widespread. The deeper questions both the *Journal* and those in the business of trading should have explored are:

- Is this a good business practice?
- What would happen if everyone did indeed hold their trades until 4:00 P.M.?
- Can getting a leg up on everyone else in this manner last?
- What happens to markets if everyone follows this practice?

---

[430]Adapted from "Is Acquittal the New Ethical Standard?" *Corporate Finance Review* 14(4):43–47 (2010).

[431]"The Sihpol Verdict," *Wall Street Journal*, June 10, 2005, p. A8.

- What will be the regulatory consequences of using this loophole, of pushing to the edge of the envelope?
- If there is complete innocence of intent and no benefit derived, why hold the trades of one client and not the others?
- Why was the institutional practice not institutionalized across the board and only for one client?
- Mr. Sihpol and his employer, Bank of America, were willing to hold off on trades for their major client, Canary Capital, but did not do so for others. Why are they allowing some clients to take advantage of market outcomes prior to placing trades while others are not permitted to share in that advantage?

When legality is our standard for behavior we do miss in-depth analysis of some strategic issues that can affect our business model as well as how markets will function and be regulated.

On Andersen's and Quattrone's Innocence and Shredding

The Andersen and Quattrone document shredding cases are two examples in which the analyses of the reversals of the convictions of the Andersen firm and Frank Quattrone miss the point.[432] In both cases documents were destroyed while investigations into one of Andersen's clients (Enron) and Quattrone's firm, Credit Suisse First Boston Corporation (CSFB), were pending. The first was an investigation for financial fraud and the latter was related to preferential treatment of clients on access to IPOs. With the SEC breathing down Enron's neck, several employees at Arthur Andersen were working to destroy documents related to the firm's Enron audits. Legal counsel for Andersen, Nancy Temple, reminded those involved of the firm's e-mail policy and then turned away from the events, telling the partners that she no longer wanted to be in on the e-mail loop as they communicated about Enron and the documents.[433]

The acquittal was not one that exonerated Andersen for its complicity in the Byzantine Enron accounting. The acquittal was correctly given because no one was able to establish that the firm itself was aware of destruction of documents that would be relevant for the Enron investigation. The case is one of vicarious criminal liability of firms, not one that decided document shredding was permitted in the circumstances. Neither a company nor its principals can be convicted of a crime unless there is a connection between the *actus reus* and their knowledge of such. The frenzied acts of employees laboring under panic cannot be attributed to those who have a document policy in place that is disregarded. However, the ethical issues are whether the principals did enough to be sure documents were not destroyed, something more than issuing a reminder. In addition, there remained the underlying ethical issue and the reality of what destroyed Andersen. Andersen was not destroyed because of a zealous prosecutor who overreached on obstruction of justice charges. Andersen self-destructed with its willingness to bend too readily to a client's desires when it came to financial structure and reporting.

Mr. Quattrone, upon learning of the SEC investigation, sent the following e-mail:

Subject: Time to clean up those files

With the recent tumble in stock prices, and many deals now trading below issue price, the securities litigation bar is expected to [sic] an all out assault on broken tech IPOs.

---

[432]*U.S. v Arthur Andersen*, 544 U.S. 696 (2005) and *U.S. v Quattrone*, 441 F. 3d 153 (2d Cir. 2006).

[433]David Cay Johnston, "Firm Releases Messages on Destroying Documents," *New York Times*, January 15, 2002, p. BU1.

In the spirit of the end of the year (and the slow down in corporate finance work), we want to remind[ ] you of the CSFB document retention policy. . . . The relevant text is:

> *"For any securities offering, the Designated Member should create a transaction file consisting of (i) all filings made with the SEC in connection with an SEC registered offering or, in an unregistered offering, the final offering memorandum used in a Rule 144A offering or other form of private placement, (ii) the original executed underwriting or placement agent agreements, (iii) the original executed comfort letters from accountants, (iv) the original executed opinions of counsel and (v) a completed document checklist.. . . In order to avoid confusion and ensure greater compliance with these policies, no file categories other than those set forth in Exhibit B may be created in connection with any CSFB managed securities offering without the approval of your time leader and a lawyer in the IBD Legal and Compliance Department or the CDG Manager."*

So what does this mean? Generally speaking, if it is not (i)-(v), it should not be left in the file following completion of the transaction. That means no notes, no drafts, no valuation analysis, no copies of the roadshow, no markups, no selling memos,. . . no internal memos.

Note that if a lawsuit is instituted, our normal document retention policy is suspended and any cleaning of files is prohibited under the CSFB guidelines (since it constitutes the destruction of evidence). We strongly suggest that before you leave for the holidays, you should catch up on file cleanup.[434]

Again, the court correctly noted that a conviction of Mr. Quattrone required that the jury be able to connect the shredding directive with Mr. Quattrone's direct and specific knowledge that the records that would be shredded would be related to the inquiries that CSFB was facing from regulatory authorities. In other words, Mr. Quattrone had to know enough about the specifics of the investigation that the prosecution would be able to tie documents to charges and areas of focus for the investigators. Because his directive was general and based in the firm's shredding policy, Mr. Quattrone's verdict was vacated.

Toes right to the legal line in both cases, there is little doubt that relevant documents were lost in the destruction that followed the announcement of the investigations. However, documents lost does not translate into the crime of obstruction. Obstruction requires direct proof that the document destroyed was evidence necessary to establish a crime and that those who were destroying the documents were aware of the impact of that destruction. Again, such proof is a high bar.

However, the ethical issues do abound:

- Why are we shredding and destroying now?
- What do we hope to accomplish by shredding and destroying?
- If we have nothing to hide, why is the purging necessary at this time?
- What is the likely impact of the disclosure of this activity undertaken at this time?
- If what we are doing complies with the law, why the need for secrecy and turning a blind eye to the activities?

The Bear Stearns Fund Managers, Puffing, and an Acquittal

In April 2007, when some investors holding the now-worthless CDO obligations were trying to pull out as the market was beginning to rumble, Matthew M. Tannin reflected his concerns in an e-mail to fellow fund manager, Ralph R. Cioffi,

---

[434]441 F.3d at 166.

> *"[T]he subprime market looks pretty damn ugly. . . . If we believe [our internal modeling] is ANYWHERE CLOSE to accurate I think we should close the funds now. The reason for this is that if [our internal modeling] is correct then the entire subprime market is toast. . . . If AAA bonds are systematically downgraded then there is simply no way for us to make money—ever."* [435] [Emphasis in original.]

It was fascinating to see that Mr. Tannin did not send the e-mail on the Bear Stearns system, but, rather, through his private e-mail via his wife's e-mail account. In response, Mr. Cioffi had Mr. Tannin, another Bear Stearns colleague, meet at the Cioffi home to discuss the e-mail concerns. Mr. Tannin left the meeting convinced that it was acceptable for him to participate in a positive manner in an upcoming investor call. They did not want Mr. Tannin going rogue during an investor call. And Tannin was known throughout the company as "a worrier," so one more worry from Tannin was another day at the office.[436] The problem is that sometimes worriers are right. Even when the worriers are appeased for the sake of the company, they follow their guts on their worries. Mr. Tannin invested no more of his own money in the funds despite telling investors he would be doing so. The criminal charges related to Mr. Tannin saying one thing to investors that did not turn out to be true.

However, there are plenty of reasons for not investing further despite that pledge being made to investors on a call, none of which rise to the level of *mens rea* needed for a felony conviction of dissemination of false information: a change in strategy in one's personal portfolio, a change in risk tolerance in one's portfolio, a misunderstanding about which funds he planned to invest in, a change in the market following the investor call.

Industry experts say the e-mails were taken out of context because the two men simply mismanaged the risk. "They were not trying to swindle widows out of their future; they were mismanaging a crisis."[437] Of course they saw the risk; they simply doubled down rather than bail out. Therein lies one of the finest of fine lines—was it deception or was it just bad judgment on how the market would go? Deception is the crime; bad judgment is civil liability. But the ethical issues remain:

- If you are uncomfortable enough to keep your own money out of a fund, is it time to tell investors?
- What are the consequences if you are wrong about your choices on others' funds?
- Why are you not disclosing complete information to the investors?
- Why have you withheld from investors the e-mail concerns and the meeting?

So many ethical, not criminal issues, boil down to one simple adage: if you don't want to tell someone something, you probably should. Wouldn't it be lovely if the widows were told that you were indeed managing a crisis?

Galleon: Brace Yourselves for Another Acquittal or Two

In a classic tipper/tippee insider trading case, the SEC and the Justice Department have charged the principals of the Galleon Group hedge fund with receiving information from insiders that they then used to position themselves profitably in the markets. Galleon's returns, earnings, and reputation were legendary. Called the highest profile case of a generation, it involves the founder and owner of Galleon, Raj Rajaratnam, someone who was known throughout the Silicon Valley and was presumed to preside over a mathematical

---

[435]The e-mail is quoted in the indictment against the two men and can be found at www.doj.gov. Accessed May 19, 2010.

[436]Kate Kelly, "Prosecutors in Bear Case Focus In on Emails," *Wall Street Journal*, June 19, 2008, pp. A1, A12.

[437]Emir Eprati, "U.S. Loses Bear Fraud Case," *Wall Street Journal*, November 11, 2009, pp. A1, A6.

model that saw his company outperforming others. Mr. Rajaratnam was also known for his three homes, extravagant parties, and status as a billionaire.

However, the case may not be entirely tipper/tippee. Mr. Rajaratnam carefully cultivated relationships with young executives at companies in the Silicon Valley and then used them as sources of information from things as simple as which customers and suppliers were doing well to, as alleged, eventually gaining inside information from them. For example, one young executive who was formerly at Intel, Roomy Khan, is identified as an informant in the case and had already done six months of house arrest in 2002 for passing along inside proprietary information about Intel (where she worked until her termination following the charges of being a tipper then).

Mr. Rajaratnam often paid for the receptions and dinners of young business school graduates in order to gain access to them and whatever information they had. He was known to sponsor alumni receptions and meetings for the same reason. He was also generous with sponsorships of continuing education programs for young executives.

As with all the acquittal cases that preceded this discussion, there is indeed a fine line. That fine line is one drawn between gathering information (information obtained through the sweat of the brow) and obtaining and using inside information. For example, a young Hambrecht & Quist trader wrote a letter to the SEC when he overheard a Fidelity broker sharing with a Galleon employee the level of volume Fidelity was trading. "Business is booming," is not exactly the stuff of inside information. Indeed, The SEC took no action at that time. But the legality was not the issue at that point; the propriety and evolving contacts were. How propriety slipped and contacts evolved following this simple warning.

There can be little doubt that many of the activities Mr. Rajaratnam engaged in are standard practices for fund managers. They need first-hand, quality information. That level of information is not gleaned from sitting in an office but, rather, comes from discussions and interactions of those who are in business. For example, just knowing how many new hires a company has made is important first-hand information that gives some indication of where the company believes it is headed. Finding out who those hires are and, at one company, funding a reception for alums, recent grads, and soon-to-be-grads gives you that information. More proof than funding a reception is needed for the *actus reus* of insider trading.

In this case there is more, an Octopussy, as the criminal complaint describes it in honor of the center of the large ring of alleged insider trading. Zvi Goffer, a manager with Schottenfeld Group and later Galleon, was command central. Mr. Goffer allegedly obtained information from several sources, including lawyers who were handling acquisitions, Roomy Khan (a former Intel employee), and Deep Shah (an analyst at Moody's). The information that was obtained from these folks found its way to several other financial firms, with all of them profiting by using the information to trade in the shares in advance of the announcements of the information obtained, which included tips on acquisitions and other major events. Allegedly connecting all of them together was Craig Drimal, someone who worked in Galleon office space but was not an employee.

That fine line, ineffective in its ability to halt the trample of desire and the temptation of pure legality, is pushed gradually, not suddenly. The activities are akin to the evolution of teaching in junior high school classes. The first class to take the Algebra I test emerges from the room with this summary, "The test is hard." That evolves to something more following the next exam, "The test is hard and you better know this, this, and this." For the next exam, the first-takers emerge with, "The exam is hard. Here's one of the questions I didn't know." By the time of the final exam, text messages and cell-phone cameras are in full use for the benefit of those who follow. That first report of the test being difficult is not a violation of the honor code. The subsequent discussions deteriorate to the point of cheating.

So it is with this case. Was that fine line between gathering information legally and gaining tippee status crossed? We will not know the answer for some time. However, there are now a total of fourteen under indictment in this case and there is already a great deal of tossing under the bus from five of those who seek to enter pleas early in exchange for testimony and leniency. One lawyer has already stated publicly that his client intends to "cooperate fully" with prosecutors (translate: sing like a canary).[438] Preet Bharara, the U.S. Attorney for the Southern District of New York who is overseeing the prosecution of the case has said, "I urge you to come knocking on our door before we come knocking on yours."[439]

There is a prescience and wisdom in those words. When we are gauging behavior by the strict legal standards, we do come close to the edge of illegality. Rather than waiting for the knock, perhaps some introspection is in order. That's where ethics come in. Toes right at the line, only worrying about *mens rea* and *actus reus,* and proudly proceeding with the phrase, "Prove it" often do win the day in court. But, in the process we chip away at the transparency and forthrightness efficient markets require for long-term progress. Yes, you could do that. Yes, everyone does that and it is standard industry practice. But, "Should it be?" is the question that requires an answer if we would like to avoid having fraud become a routine market correction.

Discussion Questions

1. Walk through each of the examples given and list the advantages gained by their "common" conduct. For those examples for which there is an outcome, describe the costs.

2. Are you at a disadvantage competitively if you do not engage in the same behaviors as those in your industry?

3. Can you give examples of negative consequences for companies that adopted industry practices?

4. What response do you offer to the argument that if everyone is behaving this way it will be difficult for you to be caught?

Reading 4.19

A Primer on Accounting Issues and Ethics and Earnings Management[440]

When Arthur Levitt was the chairman of the Securities Exchange Commission (SEC), the federal agency responsible for regulating accurate disclosures in companies' financial reports, he gave a speech at New York University (NYU) that became known as the "Numbers Game" speech. He spoke about companies and their efforts to use earnings management, a process in which they use accounting rules and financial manipulations to meet goals or make their earnings seem smooth. Mr. Levitt said, "Too many corporate managers, auditors, and analysts are participants in the game of nods and winks. In the zeal to satisfy consensus earnings estimates and project a smooth earnings path, wishful thinking may be winning the day over faithful representation. . . . Managing may be giving way to manipulation; integrity may be losing out to illusion."[441]

Earnings management has been business practice for so long, so often, and by so many that many businesspeople no longer see it as an ethical issue, but an accepted business prac-

---

[438]Susan Pulliam, "Five Cooperating Witnesses Propel Federal Probe," *Wall Street Journal,* November 6, 2009, p. A6.

[439]*New York Times,* November 8, 2009, BU2, in "The Chatter" feature.

[440]Adapted from an article by Marianne M. Jennings in *Corporate Finance Review* 3, no. 5: 39–41 (March/April 1999). Reprinted from *Corporate Finance Review* by RIA, 395 Hudson Street, New York, NY 10014.

[441]Arthur Levitt, Chairman, Securities and Exchange Commission, "The Numbers Game," speech, NYU Center for Law and Business, New York, September 28, 1998.

tice. *Fortune* magazine has even offered a feature piece on the "how to's" and the importance of doing it. It remains an unassailable proposition, based on the financial research, that a firm's stock price attains a quality of stability through earnings management. However, the financial issues in the decision to manage earnings are but one block in the decision tree. In focusing on that one block, firms are losing sight of the impact such activities have on employees, employees' conduct, and eventually on the company and its shareholders.

Issues on financial reporting and earnings management are at the heart of market transparency and trust. Understanding the issue of earnings management is important as you begin to study the cases involving companies that used this process, perhaps to an extreme. What is earnings management? How is it done? How effective is it? How do accountants and managers perceive it from an ethical perspective?

The Tactics in Earnings Management

Earnings management consists of actions by managers used to increase or decrease current reported earnings so as to create a favorable picture for either short-term or long-term economic profitability. Sometimes managers want to make earnings as low as possible so that the next quarter, particularly if they are new managers, the numbers look terrific and it seems as if it is all due to their new management decisions. Earnings management consists of activities by managers to meet or exceed earnings projections in order to increase the company's stock value.

You can pick up just about any company's annual report and see how important consistent and increasing earnings are. Tenneco's 1994 annual report provides this explanation in the management discussion section, "All of our strategic actions are guided by and measured against this goal of delivering consistently high increases in earnings over the long term." Eli Lilly noted it had thirty-three years of earnings without a break. Bank of America's annual report notes, "Increasing earnings per share was our most important objective for the year."

The methods for managing earnings are varied and limited only by manager creativity within the fluid accounting rules. The common physical techniques that have been around since commerce began are as follows:

- Write down inventory.
- Write up inventory product development for profit target.
- Record supplies or next year's expenses ahead of schedule.
- Delay invoices.
- Sell excess assets.
- Defer expenditures.

However, in his NYU speech, Chairman Levitt noted five more transactional and sophisticated methods for earnings management.

1. Large-charge restructuring
2. Creative acquisition accounting
3. Cookie jar reserves
4. Materiality
5. Revenue recognition

Yet another accounting issue, not noted by Mr. Levitt, percolates throughout the financial collapses and misstatements of companies.

6. EBITDA (earnings before interest taxes, depreciation, and amortization) and non-GAAP (GAAP is an acronym for generally accepted accounting principles) financial reporting.

In the following sections, you can find an explanation of each of these accounting issues that present both ethical and legal questions and provide the squishy areas too many companies have used to ultimately mislead investors, creditors, and the markets about their true financial status.

Large-Charge Restructuring

This type of earnings management helps clean up the balance sheet (often referred to as the "big bath"). A company acquiring another company takes large expenses for the acquisition because during the next quarter its new and effective management and control, without those added expenses, makes things look so much better. Often referred to as *spring-loading,* this technique was part of Tyco's acquisition accounting. The strategy here is to toss in as many expenses as possible in the quarter of the acquisition. Even bills not due and charges not accrued are plowed in with the idea of showing a real dog of a performer at the time of the acquisition. Management looks positively brilliant by the next quarter, when the expenses are minimal. Indeed, the next quarter, with its low expenses, may afford the opportunity for some cookie jar reserves (see below) to be set aside for future dry periods of revenues or increased expenses.

Creative Acquisition Accounting

This method, also employed by WorldCom and Tyco and other companies that went on buying binges in the 1990s, is an acceleration of expenses as well. The acquisition price is designated as "in-process" research. The tendency for managers is to overstate the restructuring charges and toss the extra charges, over and above actual charges, into reserves, sometimes referred to as the *cookie jar.*[442] For example, a company makes an acquisition and books $2 billion for restructuring charges. Its earnings picture for that year is painted to look quite awful.[443] However, the actual costs of the restructuring are spread out over the time it takes for the company to restructure, which is actually two to three years, and some of the charges booked may not ever be incurred.[444] The charges taken are often called *soft charges,* or *anticipated costs,* and can include items such as training, new hires, computer consulting, and so forth. It is possible that those services may be necessary, but it is literally a guess as to whether they will be needed and an even bigger guess as to how much they will cost. However, the hit to earnings has already been taken all at once, with the resulting rosier picture of earnings growth in subsequent years. Also, although not entirely properly so, managers have been known to use these in a future year of not-so-great earnings to create a smoother pattern of earnings and earnings growth for investors.[445] Indeed, the reserves have been used to simply meet previously announced earnings targets.[446] So, taking the example further, if the actual charges are $1.5 billion, then the company has $500 million in reserves to feed into earnings in order to demonstrate growth in earnings where there may not be actual growth or to create the appearance of a smooth and upward trend.

For example, in an acquisition, there will be costs associated with merging computer systems. When one airline buys another, the two reservations systems must be merged. Some mergers of computer systems have been done with relative ease and little in the way of either labor costs or consulting fees. However, the acquiring airline has taken a

[442]Geoffrey Colvin, "Scandal Outrage, Part III," *Fortune,* October 28, 2002, p. 56.
[443]"Firms' Stress on 'Operating Earnings' Muddies Efforts to Value Stocks," *Wall Street Journal,* August 21, 2001, pp. A1, A8.
[444]Carol J. Loomis, "Lies, Damned Lies and Managed Earnings: The Crackdown Is Here," *Fortune,* August 2, 1999, pp. 75, 84.
[445]*Id.,* pp. 74, 84.
[446]Louis Uchitelle, "Corporate Profits Are Tasty, but Artificially Flavored," *New York Times,* March 28, 1999, p. BU4.

charge, anticipating a large cost of this merger. Its numbers look low for the quarter and year of the charge. The next quarter and year, however, look dramatically improved. The acquiring airline gains value because of this performance and likely double-digit growth in earnings. The market responds with increased share value. That increased value is not grounded in real performance, changing markets, or superior skill, foresight, and industry on the part of the airline. Rather, the simple manipulation of the timing on reporting expenses yields results. The hit to earnings in one fell swoop means the financial reports do not reflect the airline's expenses and evolving challenges. The hit to earnings may not be real, and certainly we cannot know whether the anticipated costs and expenses actually occur. Again, future earnings look better and the door is open again for cookie jar reserves.

Cookie Jar Reserves

This technique uses unrealistic assumptions to estimate sales returns, loan losses, or warranty costs. These losses are stashed away because, as the argument goes, this is an expense that cannot be tied to one specific quarter or year (and there has been much in the way of interpretation as to what types of expenses fit into this category). Companies then allocate these reserves as they deem appropriate for purposes of smoothing out earnings. They dip into the reserves when earnings are good to take the hit and then also use the reserves when earnings are low to explain away performance issues. The discretionary dip is the key element of the cookie jar. You dip in as needed.

Materiality

Companies avoid recording certain items because, they reason, they are too small to worry about. They are, as the accounting profession calls them, *immaterial.* The problem is that hundreds of immaterial items can and do add up to make material amounts on a single financial statement. Also, these decisions on whether items are material versus immaterial, and to report or not to report certain things, seem to create a psychology in managers that finds them always avoiding reporting bad news or trying to find ways around disclosure. An example comes from Sunbeam, Inc., a maker of home appliances such as electric blankets, the Oster line of blenders, mixers, can openers, and electric skillets. Sunbeam carried a rather large inventory of parts it needed for the repair of these appliances when they came back while under warranty. Sunbeam used a warehouse owned by EPI Printers to store the parts, which were then shipped out as needed. Sunbeam proposed selling the parts to EPI for $11,000,000 and then booking an $8,000,000 profit. However, EPI was not game for the transaction because its appraisal of the parts came in at only $2,000,000. To overcome the EPI objection, Sunbeam let EPI enter into an agreement to agree at the end of 1997. The "agreement to agree" would have EPI buy the parts for $11,000,000, which Sunbeam would then book as a sale with the resulting profit. However, the agreement to agree allowed EPI to back out of the deal in January 1998. The deal was booked, the revenue recognized, Sunbeam's share price went up, and all was well. And all without EPI ever spending a dime.

Arthur Andersen served as the outside auditor for Sunbeam during this time, and its managing partner, Phillip E. Harlow, did raise some questions about the EPI deal and didn't particularly care for the Sunbeam executives' responses. Mr. Harlow asked the executives to restate earnings reflecting changes he deemed necessary. Management refused, but Mr. Harlow and Arthur Andersen certified the Sunbeam financials anyway.

Mr. Harlow reasoned that he did not see the change as "material," something that Sunbeam executives were required to restate prior to his certification. For example, under accounting rules, the "agreement to agree" with EPI, although nothing more than a sham transaction, was not "material" with regard to its amount in relation to

Sunbeam's level of income. However, Mr. Harlow had defined *materiality* only in the sense of percentage of income. Although the amount was immaterial, the transaction itself spoke volumes about management integrity as well as the struggle within Sunbeam to meet earnings projections. Both of those pieces of information are material to investors and creditors. The nondisclosure of the sham transaction meant that the true financial, strategic, and ethical situation in Sunbeam was not revealed through the financial statements intended to give a full and accurate picture of where a company stands.

Further, if one added together the total number of items that were deemed immaterial individually in the Sunbeam situation, the amount of those items (items that the SEC eventually challenged as improper accounting) totaled 16 percent of Sunbeam's profits for 1997.

There is no question that Sunbeam, Mr. Harlow, and Andersen were correct in their handling on the Sunbeam issues, if we measure from a strict application of accounting rules. As the certification reads, Sunbeam's financial statements "present fairly, in all material respects, the financial position of, in conformity with generally accepted accounting principles."

In fact, Mr. Harlow hired PricewaterhouseCoopers to go over Sunbeam's books and his (Harlow's) judgment calls, and those auditors from another firm agreed independently that Mr. Harlow certified "materially accurate financial statements."[447] However, the real issues in materiality are not the technical application of accounting rules. Rather, the issues surround the question of intent in using the materiality trump card.

The amounts involved in many of the noted Sunbeam improprieties were not "material" in a percentage-of-income sense. The problem is that an individual auditor's definition of *materiality* is the cornerstone of a certified audit. All an auditor does is certify that the financial statements "conform with generally accepted accounting principles."

There is no definition of *materiality* for the accounting profession. Research shows that most auditors use a rule of thumb of 5 to 10 percent as a threshold level of disclosure, such as 5 percent of net income or 10 percent of assets or vice versa.[448] They may also use a fixed dollar amount or an index of time and trouble in relation to the amount in question.[449]

However, it is clear just from the amount of regulatory action, shareholder litigation, and judicial definitions that the standard for materiality employed by auditors is not the same as the standard other groups would use in deciding which information should be disclosed. Called the *expectations gap,* this phenomenon means that auditor certification and executive disclosure are at odds from the expectations of investors and creditors. They expect more disclosure even as the technical application of accounting rules allows for less disclosure.

As a company establishes its ethical standards for materiality and disclosure, it should adopt the following questions as a framework for resolution:

- What historically has happened in cases in which these types of items are not disclosed? In our company? In other companies?
- What are the financial implications if this item is not disclosed now?
- What are our motivations for not disclosing this item?[450]

[447]Andersen has settled the suit brought against it by shareholders for $110 million. Floyd Norris, "S.E.C. Accuses Former Sunbeam Official of Fraud," *New York Times*, May 16, 2001, pp. A1, C2.

[448]Marianne M. Jennings, Philip M. Reckers, and Daniel C. Kneer, "A Source of Insecurity: A Discussion and an Empirical Examination of Standards of Disclosure and Levels of Materiality in Financial Statements," 10 *J. Corp. L.* 639 (1985).

[449]Jeffries, "Materiality as Defined by the Courts," 51 *CPA J.* 13 (1981).

[450]In thinking about this question, the words of outgoing SEC Chairman Arthur Levitt are instructive: "In markets where missing an earnings projection by a penny can result in a loss of millions of dollars in market capitalization, I have a hard time accepting that some of these so-called nonevents simply don't matter." *Id.*

- What are our motivations for booking this item in this way?
- What are our motivations for not booking this item?
- How do we expect this issue to be resolved?
- Are our expectations consistent with the actions we are taking vis-à-vis disclosure?
- If I were a shareholder on the outside, would this be the kind of information I would want to know?

Revenue Recognition

These are the operational tools of earnings management, noted earlier in this discussion. Some examples include *channel stuffing,* or shipping inventory before orders are placed. Sales are recognized as final and booked as revenue before delivery or final acceptance, sometimes without the buyer even knowing. The financial reporting issues at Krispy Kreme Donuts resulted from this ploy of reflecting sales of franchise items to franchises without those franchises actually having ordered those items.

The other tools related to revenue recognition can be broken down into categories. Operations earnings management would involve delaying or accelerating research and development expenses (R&D), maintenance costs, or the booking of sales (channel stuffing). Finance earnings management is the early retirement of debt. Investment earnings management consists of sales of securities or fixed assets. Accountings earnings management could include the selection of accounting methods (straight-line vs. accelerated depreciation), inventory valuation (last in first out [LIFO], or first in first out [FIFO]), and the use of reserves (the cookie jar).

EBITDA and Non-GAAP Financial Reporting

Earnings management does hit those roadblocks of the application of accounting rules and their interpretation. So, rather than risk the wrath of the SEC and the litigation of shareholders and creditors, managers began using a different sort of financial statement. Sanjay Kumar, the former CEO of Computer Associates, once said that "standard accounting rules [are] not the best way to measure Computer Associate's results because it had changed to a new business model offering its clients more flexibility."[451]

The "pro forma" financial statement, with all the assumptions and favorable earnings management techniques, was born. Also known as *non-GAAP measures,* this is accounting that does not comply with "Generally Accepted Accounting Principles," the rules established by the American Institute of Certified Public Accountants (AICPA), developed through its work with the SEC, scholars, and practitioners as they debate that elusive question of "Are these financials fair?"

Non-GAAP measures of financial performance can be enormously helpful and insightful in assessing the true financial condition and performance of a company. However, non-GAAP measures can also be used in a way that obfuscates or even conceals the true financial condition and performance of a company.

The Types of Non-GAAP Measurements and Their Use

EBIT (earnings before interest and taxes) and EBITDA (earnings before interest taxes, depreciation, and amortization) are not as much accounting tools as financial analysis tools. They were developed because of concerns on the part of those who evaluated financial performance and worth that the rigidity of GAAP necessarily resulted in the omission of information that was relevant for determining the true value of a company and the richness of its earnings. EBIT and EBITDA were means of factoring out the oranges so that the apples of real earnings growth in a company could be determined.

---

[451]Alex Berenson, "Computer Associates Officials Stand by Their Accounting Methods," *New York Times,* May 1, 2001, p. C1, C7.

Although the dot-coms and other firms of the new economy are often viewed as those that popularized EBITDA as the measure of valuation for companies, its origins actually go back to the time of Michael Milken and the junk bond era of the 1980s. The takeovers of the Milken era, with their characteristics of very little cash, were actually accomplished through the magic of the EBITDA measurement. If an acquirer could reflect an EBITDA of just $100 million per year, that amount was sufficient to attract investors for purposes of acquisition of up to a $1 billion company. Milken, in effect, leveraged EBITDA numbers to structure takeovers.[452] However, the EBITDA figures that Milken used did not include the long-term capital expenditures and principal repayments that were, in effect, assumed to be postponed and postponable, thus allowing a portrayal of a company that could see itself through to a state of profitability. Factoring out expenses such as the cost of equipment replacement meant that earnings growth was reflected at a substantially higher rate. Investors were thus lulled into a sense of exponential earnings growth at the acquired company, not realizing the balloon type of investment that would be required when equipment replacement became inevitable.

EBITDA, for some companies, is perhaps the only forthright way to actually reflect the value of a company. A company dependent on equipment, with its resulting replacement costs, has its earnings growth and value distorted through the use of EBITDA because investors should have the cost of replacement reflected in the numbers. Depreciation is the means whereby that cost is reflected in GAAP measurements. If an equipment-heavy company, such as a manufacturer, has the same EBITDA as a service company, with only minimal equipment investment because of its focus on human resources, then EBITDA is a misleading measure. For example, Sunbeam, the small appliance manufacturer, clearly a company in which replacement of manufacturing equipment is a significant cost, was a proponent and user of EBITDA. Firms in different industries cannot be compared accurately using only EBITDA numbers because the nature of their business attaches significance to those numbers. GAAP measures that include depreciation provide a better means for cross-comparison, with the financial statement user able to note the depreciation component and make independent judgments about the quality of earnings.

The use of these non-GAAP measures in creating pro forma numbers is also particularly useful to investors and analysts when a company changes an accounting practice. For example, when a company switches its inventory evaluation method from LIFO to FIFO, the ability to present to financial statement users the contrast between what the company's performance would have been under the previous accounting practices versus the new methods shows users the real performance versus performance that includes the new methodology.

The original intent in pro forma numbers was a desire on the part of the accounting profession to offer more information and a better view of the financial health of a company. That intent was particularly justified in those cases in which a company has undergone a change in accounting practice that affects income in perhaps a substantial way, but would actually have little impact if prior treatments had continued. The booking of options as an expense is an example. The change in the rule is important, but investors and users of financial statements will want to know what income would have looked like under the old methodology so that they are better able to track trends in real performance. However, these original good intentions in the use of pro forma reports changed. Pro forma became the accepted metric with the pro forma results often manipulated with the idea of meeting earnings expectations, or the practice of earnings management.

Warren Buffett described resorting to non-GAAP methods as a means of "manufacturing desired 'earnings.'"[453] However, among academicians and analysts there

---

[452]Herb Greenberg, "Alphabet Dupe: Why EBITDA Falls Short," *Fortune,* July 10, 2000, p. 240.

[453]Uchitelle, "Corporate Profits Are Tasty, but Artificially Flavored," p. BU4.

was substantial disagreement about whether EBITDA and other non-GAAP measures were meaningful forms of valuation.[454] In 2000, prior to the dot-com bubble bursting, Moody's analyst Pamela Stump created a furor by releasing her twenty-four-page examination of EBITDA in which she concluded that its use was excessive and that it was no substitute for full and complete financial analysis.[455] Former SEC Chief Accountant Lynn Turner was more harsh in his assessment of the pervasive use of EBITDA, calling such usage a means of lulling the "investing public into a trance with imaginary numbers, just as if they had gone to the movies. Little did they know that the theater was burning the entire time."[456] An example of EBITDA in action can be found in the WorldCom case (see Case 4.27).

As early as 1973, the SEC had issued its cautionary advice on the use of pro forma financial statements.[457] Nonetheless, the use of non-GAAP measures continued and expanded, and the accounting profession offered its imprimatur and certification for pro forma releases. By 2001, 57 percent of publicly traded companies used pro forma numbers along with GAAP numbers in their financial reports, whereas 43 percent used only GAAP numbers.[458] For the years 1997 to 1999, Adelphia, the company that collapsed in 2002 and has had two of its officers convicted and sentenced, included on the cover of its annual report charts that reflected its EBITDA growth. Geoffrey Colvin of *Fortune* has said that EBITDA stands for "Earnings Because I Tricked the Dumb Auditor."

Following the passage of Sarbanes–Oxley the SEC defined both EBIT and EBITDA as non-GAAP measures of financial performance.[459] Although both can be offered in financial reports, the SEC requires a joint appearance of the two measures of financial performance.[460] The critical portion of those new rules is that the non-GAAP measures must be accompanied by GAAP measures.[461] These new regulations and appropriate uses of non-GAAP measures are so complex that the SEC has been forced to post responses to the thirty-three most frequently asked questions (FAQs) it has received on non-GAAP financial measures.[462]

---

[454]*Id.* In his 2000 annual report to shareholders, Mr. Buffett wrote, "References to EBITDA make us shudder." Elizabeth McDonald, "The EBITDA Folly," *Forbes,* March 17, 2003, http://www.forbes.com.

[455]Greenberg, "Alphabet Dupe," 240.

[456]MacDonald, "The EBITDA Folly," supra note 393 at p. 3.

[457]Securities and Exchange Commission, Accounting Series Release No. 142, Release No. 33-5337, March 15 (Washington, DC: Securities and Exchange Commission, 1973); and Securities and Exchange Commission, Cautionary Advice regarding the Use of "Pro Forma" Financial Information, Release No. 33-8039 (Washington, DC: Securities and Exchange Commission, n.d.).

[458]Thomas J. Phillips Jr., Michael S. Luehlfing, and Cynthia Waller Vallario, "Hazy Reporting," *Journal of Accountancy* (August 2002), http://www.aicpa.org/pubs/jofa/aug2002/phillips. (original publication URL).

[459]15 C.F.R. § 244.1101(a)(1). The rule provides, "A non-GAAP financial measure is a numerical measure of a registrant's historical or future financial performance, financial position or cash flows that: (i) excludes amounts, or is subject to adjustments that have the effect of excluding amounts, that are included in the most directly comparable measure calculated and presented in accordance with GAAP in the statement of income, balance sheet or statement of cash flows (or equivalent statements) of the issuer or (ii) Includes amounts, or is subject to adjustments that have the effect of including amounts, that are excluded from the most directly comparable measure so calculated and presented." Non-GAAP measures do not include ratios.

[460]SEC Release No. 34-47226, "Conditions for Use of Non-GAAP Financial Measures," 17 C.F.R. §§ 228, 229, 244, and 259 (Washington, DC: Securities and Exchange Commission, n.d.).

[461]Running parallel to the SEC changes is a project by the Financial Accounting Standards Board (FASB) called *Financial Reporting by Business Enterprises.* The purpose of the project is to focus on how key performance measures are presented and the calculation of those measures. The project will also address the general issues of whether current accounting standards and their rigidity prevent the release of full and accurate portrayals of the financial health of a company.

[462]The FAQs on non-GAAP measures can be found at the Securities and Exchange Commission website, http://www.sec.gov/divisions/corpfin/faqs/nongaapfag.

Some of those FAQs have produced the following clear rule interpretations from the SEC:

- Companies should never use a non-GAAP financial measure in an attempt to smooth earnings.
- All public disclosures are covered by Regulation G (the new rule that requires the presentation of GAAP and non-GAAP measures together).
- The fact that analysts find the non-GAAP measures useful is not sufficient justification for their presentation.

Non-GAAP measures make sense in certain circumstances, when their use is actually necessary to provide the financial statement user with a full and fair picture of the company's financial health.

A Follow-Up to Levitt: Ethical Issues in Financial Reporting, Earnings Management, and Accounting

How Effective Is Earnings Management?

Earnings management is effective in increasing shareholder value. A consistent pattern of earnings increases results in higher price-to-earnings ratios. That ratio is larger the longer the series of consistent earnings. Firms that break patterns of consistent earnings experience an average 14 percent decline in stock returns for the year in which the earnings pattern is broken. However, the discovery of earnings manipulation at a company results in a stock price drop of 9 percent. In short, there appears to be a net upside for engaging in earnings management.

In addition to the shareholder value argument, there are other drivers that make earnings management such a treacherous area for managers and employees. Executive and even employee compensation contracts may provide dramatic incentives for managing earnings. Bausch & Lomb, Sears, and Cendant are all examples of companies whose managers manipulated earnings because of incentive systems and goals that brought the managers personal benefits. Incentives for earnings management can also come from sources other than compensation incentives for executives. Covenants in debt contracts, pending proxy contests, pending union negotiations, pending external financing proposals, and pending matters in political or regulatory processes can all be motivational factors for earnings management. Many managers use earnings management as a strategic tool to have an impact on pending matters.

The Ethics of Earnings Management

The question that fails to arise in the context of management decisions on managing earnings is whether the practices are ethical. Managers and accountants comply with the technical rules, but technical compliance may not result in financial statements that are a full and fair picture of how the company is doing financially. In a system dependent upon reliable (known as *transparent*) financial information, the practice of earnings management conceals relevant information. Research shows that firms that engage in earnings management are more likely to have boards with no independence and eventually higher costs of capital.

The new approach to accounting rules and earnings management focuses on the ethical notion of balance: If you were the investor instead of the manager, what information about earnings management would you want disclosed? If you were on the outside looking in, how would you feel about the decision to book extra expenses this year in order to even out earnings in a year not so stellar? In short, when all the complications of LIFO, FIFO, EBITDA, and spring-loading are discussed, we are left with the simple notions of ethical analysis provided in Unit 1, from the categorical imperative to the

Blanchard–Peale and Nash questions of "How would I feel if I were on the other side?" When involved in complex situations, reducing the complexities to their simplest terms gives you the common denominator of those basic tests and analysis methods for all ethical issues.

For example, in evaluating the use of non-GAAP measures, the following questions prove helpful: Why is this measure important for the company? Why do we choose to rely on it? What insight does this measure give that is not afforded by traditional GAAP methods? Does this method of reporting mislead users of financial statements? How reliable is this measure? Is it based on models, or is it simply theory?

In addition to the examination of intent these questions require, those who prepare and audit financial statements should also consider the amount of discussion and analysis that is necessary in order for them to offer a fair explanation on their decisions to use alternative reporting metrics.

An example provides a look at the wide-swath interpretations that these alternative metrics can cut as financial reports are prepared. A company has the following financials:

- Operating revenues: $1,000,000
- Nonrecurring, nonoperating gain: $300,000
- Nonrecurring, nonoperating loss: $800,000
- Operating expenses of $600,000

The questions are as follows: What are the company's earnings? What earnings number should be released to the press? The GAAP answer is that the company has experienced a $100,000 loss. The EBITDA answer is that the company has $400,000 profit because $400,000 does indeed reflect the operating profit. However, some EBITDA proponents would conclude that there was $700,000 in profit because they would eliminate the nonrecurring loss but recognize the nonrecurring gain. WorldCom (see Case 4.27), for example, using its strategy discussed earlier, would have reclassified the operating expenses (inappropriate under GAAP) as nonrecurring and would have boosted its non-GAAP pro forma even beyond the $700,000.[463]

The ultimate ethical question in all financial reporting and accounting practices is "Do these numbers provide fair insight into the true financial health and performance of the company?" Further, the example given illustrates that numbers alone, even if concluded to be fair, may not be sufficient because only MD&A can provide a full and complete picture of what the non-GAAP measures mean, why they were used, and how they should be interpreted. The juxtaposition of GAAP and non-GAAP measures, now mandated by law, has also been a critical component to the effective use of both sets of numbers. The presentation of both provides checks and balances for the excesses in financial reporting during the 1990s as the non-GAAP measures became the standard for financial reports.

Discussion Questions

1. Describe the risks in earnings management.
2. What are the motivations for moving around expenses and revenues in quarters and years?
3. Don't shareholders benefit by earnings management? Who is really harmed by earnings management?
4. Put earnings management into one of the ethical categories you have learned.
5. Make up a headline description of earnings management.
6. How do you respond to a CFO who says, "Everybody does earnings management. If I don't do it, I am at a disadvantage."

---

[463]Modified from an example given in Phillips, Luehlfing, and Vallario, "Hazy Reporting."

Sources

Burgstanler, David, and Ilia Dichev, "Earnings Management to Avoid Earnings Decreases and Losses," *Journal of Accounting and Economics* 24 (1997): 99.

Dechow, Patricia M., Richard G. Sloan, and Amy P. Sweeney, "Causes and Consequences of Earnings Manipulation: An Analysis of Firms Subject to Enforcement Actions by the SEC," *Contemporary Accounting Research,* 13, no. 1 (1996): 1.

Jiabalbo, James, "Discussion of 'Causes and Consequences,'" *Contemporary Accounting Research*, 13, no. 1 (1996): 37.

Levitt, Arthur, "The Numbers Game," September 28, 1998, New York University, http://www.sec.gov/news/speeches/spch220.txt.

Merchant, Kenneth A., and Joanne Rockness, "The Ethics of Managing Earnings: An Empirical Investigation," *Journal of Accounting and Public Policy* 13 (1994): 79–94.

Zweig, Kenneth Rosen, and Marilyn Fischer, "Is Managing Earnings Ethically Acceptable?" *Management Accounting*, March 1994, 31.

Case 4.20

The Ethics of Bankruptcy

In 1980, there were 287,570 personal bankruptcies filed in the United States. In 1996, the number of personal bankruptcies topped 1 million for the first time in history. In 2009, the number of bankruptcies reached 1.5 million.[464] At that time, the number translated to a bankruptcy for 1 of every 100 households in the United States. The rate of bankruptcy filing in the United States for 2009 was five times higher than the bankruptcy rate in 1980 and ten times the rate during the Great Depression.[465]

The following chart shows bankruptcy trends.

Total Bankruptcy Filings		
Year	**Total Business**	**Total Nonbusiness**
2009	60,837	1,412,838
2008	43,546	1,074,225
2007	28,332	822,590
2006	31,206	1,590,575
2005	39,201	2,039,214
2004	34,317	1,563,345
2003	36,183	1,625,813
2002	39,091	1,508,578
2001	29,872	1,117,216
2000	35,472	1,217,972
1999	44,367	1,281,581
1998	44,367	1,398,182
1997	54,027	1,350,118

Source: http://www.uscourts.gov/bankruptcy. Accessed June 30, 2010.

[464]http://www.abiworld.org/research/yearreview. Accessed July 17, 2010.
[465]*Id.*

Nearly 30 percent of all bankruptcy filings were attributed by the petitioner (the party filing for bankruptcy) to simply being "over-extended."[466] Prior to the 2005 bankruptcy reforms through the passage of the Bankruptcy Abuse Prevention and Consumer Protection Act (BAPCPA), over 70 percent of those filing for personal bankruptcy chose Chapter 7, or full bankruptcy, as opposed to Chapter 13 for a consumer debt adjustment plan.[467]

Most consumer debt is owed by those who earn between $50,000 and $100,000 a year. As one lender remarked, "These are people who could afford to save and buy later." (Consumer installment debt is at 85 percent of disposable income—an increase of 23 percent in the past decade.)[468]

Another issue that has been reformed under the bankruptcy code is the homestead exemption. Under this exemption, those who declared bankruptcy are able, under federal and state laws, to keep a portion or all of the equity in their home after emerging from bankruptcy. The examples that emerged during the hearings were that of corporate raider Paul A. Bilzerian being able to emerge from bankruptcy in Florida with his $5 million home because of Florida's rather generous homestead exemption. He had over $300 million in debts. Mr. Bilzerian served twenty months in federal prison following his conviction for securities crimes. Mr. Bilzerian graduated from Harvard Business School and was best known for his hostile takeover of Singer, the sewing machine company.[469] Actor Burt Reynolds also emerged as an example because he was able to keep his $2.5 million home and estate, called Valhalla. After he declared bankruptcy in 1996, Mr. Reynolds had $10 million in debts.[470] As noted in Case 4.27, Scott Sullivan also used Florida's protections.

Some experts have noted that the bankruptcy process has been used for strategic planning and a way to avoid contracts.[471] The following examples illustrate:

TLC was an Atlanta rhythm, blues, and hip-hop band that performed at clubs in 1991. The three-woman group signed a recording contract with LaFace Records. The group's first album that LaFace produced—"Ooooooohhh . . . on the TLC Tip" in 1992—sold almost three million albums. The group's second album, "Crazysexycool," also produced by LaFace, sold five million albums through June 1996. The two albums together had six top-of-the-chart singles.

LaFace had the right to renew TLC's contract in 1996 following renegotiation of the contract terms. Royalty rates in the industry for unknown groups, as TLC was in 1991, are generally 7 percent of the revenues for the first 500,000 albums, and 8 percent for sales on platinum albums (albums that sell over one million copies). The royalty rate increases to 9.5 percent for all sales on an eighth album.

Established artists in the industry who renegotiate often have royalty rates of 13 percent, and artists with two platinum albums can command an even higher royalty.

The three women in TLC, Tionne Watkins (T-Boz), Lisa Lopes (Left-Eye), and Romanda Thomas (Chili), declared bankruptcy in July 1995. All three listed debts that exceeded their assets, which included sums owed to creditors for their cars and

---

[466]Christine Dugas, "Non-Mortgage Debts Top Income for Millions," *USA Today*, October 2, 1997, p. B1.

[467]Fred Waddell, "Easy Credit: A Wall around the Poor," *New York Times*, February 15, 1998, p. BU12.

[468]Timothy L. O'Brien, "Giving Credit Where Debt Is Due," *New York Times*, December 14, 1997, p. 14.

[469]Philip Shenon, "Home Exemptions Snag Bankruptcy Bill," *New York Times*, April 6, 2001, pp. A1, A15.

[470]*Id.*

[471]Jeff Bailey and Scott Kilman, "Here's What's Driving Some Lenders Crazy: Borrowers Who Think," *Wall Street Journal*, February 20, 1998, p. A1.

to Zales and The Limited for credit purchases. Lopes was sued by Lloyd's of London, which claimed Lopes owed it $1.3 million it paid on a policy held by her boyfriend on his home. Lopes pleaded guilty to one count of arson in the destruction of the home but denied that she intended to destroy the house.

Lopes asked that the Lloyd's claim be discharged in her bankruptcy. All three members of TLC asked that their contract with LaFace be discharged in bankruptcy because being bound to their old contract could impede their fresh financial starts. The issue for Ms. Lopes became moot when she was killed in a car accident in 2002.

During 1996, the members of three music groups declared bankruptcy just before their contracts were due for renegotiation. One record company executive has noted that record company owners are frightened by the trend: "You invest all the money and time in making them stars. Then they leave for the bigger companies and a higher take on sales. It has all of us scared."[472]

Pop singer Billy Joel also had a record contract with a small company during the initial stages of his career. When the company refused, during renegotiations, to increase his royalty rate, Joel did not produce another album during the period of the contract renewal option. Instead, he used a clause in the contract that limited him to night club and "piano bar" appearances in the event another album was not produced. For three years, Joel played small clubs and restaurants and did not produce an album. At the end of that period when his contract had expired, he negotiated a contract with Columbia. His first album with Columbia was "Piano Man," a multi-platinum album.[473]

BAPCPA was passed more than ten years after the Bankruptcy Reform Commission was created to study the need for reform, and the changes in bankruptcy law reflect an expressed congressional desire to curb the fifteen-year trend of increases in the number of bankruptcies. Data (see the preceding table) on bankruptcy filings show that the act has been effective. There has been a significant reduction in bankruptcy filings by consumers. The ease with which bankruptcy declaration could be used to avoid contractual obligations is no longer available.

Discussion Questions

1. Do the three women of TLC meet the standards for declaring bankruptcy? Evaluate whether Lopes's Lloyd's claim should have been discharged. What if every recording artist used their strategy?

2. Is declaring bankruptcy by the members of these musical groups legal? Is it ethical? Are the musicians using bankruptcy as a way to avoid contract obligations? Are the musicians using bankruptcy as a way to maximize their income?

3. Is there a presumption of good faith built into the bankruptcy code?

4. What do you learn about a practice that everyone adopts and legislative reforms?

Compare & Contrast

Did Joel take an ethical route? Is his solution more ethical than bankruptcy?

[472]Laura M. Holson, "Music Stars Complain About Stringent Contracts," *New York Times*, September 6, 2001, pp. C1, C12.

[473]Reprinted from *Anderson's Business Law: The Regulatory Environment*, 14th ed. (Cincinnati, Ohio: Anderson, 2001), 658.

Case 4.21

The Ethics of Walking Away[474]

Buyers Have No Moral Duty to Lenders

Brent T. White April 25, 2010

Associate Professor of Law, University of Arizona

As a result of the housing collapse, many Arizonans have seen their homes lose half of their value. Many owe several hundred thousand dollars more than their homes are worth and are unlikely to dig out of their negative equity hole for decades.

For these homeowners, the American dream has become a nightmare—and their financial future is dim.

To compound the stress and anxiety, when they've called their lender to work out a solution, they've discovered that their lender won't even talk to them about a loan modification or a short sale as long as they are current on their mortgage.

With no help in sight, some of these underwater homeowners have decided that they would be better off letting go of their homes and have stopped making their mortgage payments. Many have done so with the hope that defaulting will finally bring their lender to the table, but they are also resigned to the fact that they will likely lose their homes.

It has been suggested that such homeowners are immoral or, at least, irresponsible. I disagree.

Before explaining why, it is important to emphasize that the decision to strategically default on a mortgage involves many complex, localized and individualized factors. No one should decide to strategically default on their mortgage without sitting down first with a knowledgeable professional.

But let's say that you've actually sat down with a professional to do the calculations and have concluded that defaulting on your mortgage is the only way out of your financial nightmare. Would it be immoral or irresponsible for you to do so?

The arguments against homeowners intentionally defaulting on their mortgages generally center on the same three basic points.

First, underwater homeowners "promised" to pay their mortgages when they signed the mortgage contract. Second, foreclosures lead to depreciation of neighborhoods, so underwater homeowners should hang on in order to help preserve their neighbors' property values. And, third, if all underwater homeowners defaulted, the housing market might crash. Homeowners thus have a social obligation to pay their underwater mortgage in order to save the economy.

While all three of these arguments might hold some initial appeal, none holds water.

First, a mortgage contract, like all other contracts, is purely a legal document—not a sacred promise.

Think of it this way: when you got your cell phone, you likely signed a contract with your carrier in which you "promised" to pay a set monthly payment for two years. Would it be immoral for you to break your contractual "promise" to pay for two years if you decided that you no longer needed the cell phone and elect instead to pay the early termination fee? Of course not. The option to breach your "promise" to pay is part of the contract.

---

[474]Brent T. White, "Buyers Have No Moral Duty to Lenders," April 25, 2010. Reprinted with permission of *The Arizona Republic*, p. B11.

Though involving more money and something of great sentimental value to most people, a mortgage contract is simply a contract. Like a cell phone contract, a mortgage contract explicitly sets out the consequences of a breach of contract.

In other words, the lender has contemplated in advance that the mortgagor might be unable or unwilling to continue making payments on his mortgage at some point and has decided in advance what fair compensation to the lender would be. Specifically, the lender included clauses in the contract providing that the lender can foreclose on the property and keep any payments that have been made. By writing this penalty into the contract, the lender has agreed to accept the property and any payments already made in lieu of the remaining payments.

Moreover, lenders charge Arizona borrowers on average an extra $800 per $100,000 borrowed because Arizona is a non-recourse state, meaning the lender cannot come after the borrower for a deficiency judgment on a purchase money loan. In other words, borrowers in Arizona pay for the option to default on a purchase money loan without recourse. The lender can only take the house.

That's the agreement. No one forced the lender to make the loan or sign the contract. Indeed, the lender wrote it. And, to be sure, the lender wouldn't hesitate to exercise his right to take a person's house if it was in his financial interest to do so. Concerns of morality or socially responsibility wouldn't be part of the equation.

In short, as far as the law is concerned, choosing to exercise the default option in a mortgage contract is no more immoral than choosing to cancel a cell phone contract. Indeed, exercising the default option in your mortgage contract is similar to cashing in on an insurance policy. You paid for it—and have you a right to exercise it.

But what about the argument that mortgage default hurts neighborhoods and the economy?

Well, first, in a capitalist society, we don't generally expect individuals to make personal economic decisions for the collective good. Aside from this fact, however, it's unfair, in my opinion, to ask underwater homeowners to prop up neighborhood property values, or the housing market, on their backs—especially if means sacrificing their ability to send their children to college or save adequately for their own retirement.

Why take homeowners, and not lenders, to task for putting their own financial interest ahead of the common good? Indeed, if lenders were less intransigent and more willing to negotiate, underwater homeowners wouldn't have to walk away from their homes in order to save themselves from financial ruin. And we wouldn't have to worry about the fragile housing market crashing again.

Why it is that we speak of morality and social responsibility only when talking about the little guy, who must take his lumps for the common good, while financial institutions are free to protect their bottom line?

It just can't be the case that it's morally acceptable for banks to look out for their financial best interest, but it's not OK for the average American do to exactly the same thing.

Before You Blame the Bums on Wall Street . . .

Marianne M. Jennings
Professor of Legal and Ethical Studies
W.P. Carey School of Business
Arizona State University

Ask folks who's responsible for this economic recession, malaise, recovery . . . (substitute your own ideological bent word here), and you will get a barrage of "B" words: Bush,

Bernanke, Barack, and bums, those of the Wall Street type. However, to continue the "B" alliteration, before you blame the bums, a little introspection on mortgage walk-aways.

Those collateralized debt obligations (CDOs) that felled Lehman, Bear Stearns, and quite nearly AIG, were securities based on pools of mortgages. Wall Streeters sold and analyzed those CDOs based on the usual notions of risk about home mortgages: banks screened for deadbeats, those with home mortgages put in a fairly good chunk of change as a down payment, and monthly mortgage payments were not consuming net income.

Their assumptions about mortgage risks were wrong. During the real estate boom, bubble, etc., mortgages down payments ranged from 0–3%. Pick-a-Pay mortgages allowed borrowers to choose their monthly payments for the first three years of their loan. Of course, there was interest and plenty of hell to pay at that three-year mark. These creative mortgages financed granite countertops, 3500 square feet, and shattered normal lending standards. Once the boom busted, mortgage risks emerged with a vengeance. Wall Street nearly collapsed. We clicked our tongues and blamed greed. Yet, where would we be if creative mortgages hadn't happened? Better yet, where would we be if there had been responsible mortgage borrowers?

Ethical analysis looks at this question: How did you get in this situation in the first place? In the words of the not-so-great Bob Dylan, "When you got nothin', you got nothin' to lose." In the words of the great UT Austin economic, Professor Stan Liebowitz, "skin in the game" is the single most important factor in determining default, think walk-away. If you had a little down payment and no equity to speak of, as creative borrowers do, you walk when your mortgage is more than your property value—under-water. Some walked away with arms full—taking everything that moves (or doesn't) from their homes, including copper plumbing.

USA Today headlines read as if innocents are robbed of their under-water homes by Bush, Bernanke, Barack *et al.* Facts reveal otherwise. One under-water fellow, who was but one year from retirement, confessed that he took a second mortgage of $100,000 on his $642,000 home to put in a theater, fitness room, and bathroom in his basement and expand his living room. He now faces foreclosure because his payments are going up (he signed at a 3.25% rate that goes to 5.85%) and his house value has dropped to $590,000. He cannot get another second mortgage to pay off the first second mortgage for the remodeling lollapalooza. One borrower, grinching about his ineligibility for government foreclosure aid, bought a $1,000,000 home with $4,400 monthly payments, over 50% of the net income of this single-wage earner family.

If the anecdotes don't dispel the myths about hardship, the data are irrefutable. Of the foreclosures in the second half of 2008, only 183,447 resulted from the loss of employment. Other foreclosures? Negative net equity: 283,305; a 3% or less down payment: 130,014; low initial interest rate going higher: 60,942; and poor FICO score: 148,697. So, 624,958 foreclosures for financial folly vs. 183,447 for loss of employment. The 12% of the homes with negative equity are responsible for 47% of the foreclosures. Pick-a-Pay re-default rates are 55%. If you refinance the mortgage challenged, the default rate is 55% on their refinance.

Yet there are economists, largely those who still believe Keynes reigns, who say the walk-away is the smart thing to do because business does it all the time. This trite advice is rationalization. "Everybody does it" is not ethical analysis; it is short-sighted comfort language designed to salve that conscience that pricks, "You have not fulfilled your promise to pay for your not-so-humble abode."

Ethical analysis also looks at the impact our choices and conduct have on others, including neighborhoods, communities, and the economic system. In lieu of, "Hey, I'm just getting what I can just like everyone else," ponder, "What would if everyone behaved as you are?" What would things look like if everyone just walked away? Well, dear readers, you are living through what happens. The market is glutted and prices, even for the above-water mortgage folks, fall further. The drop is about 50% in Phoenix, Atlanta, and even Chula Vista. Detroit has homes for sale for $7,000. Short sales reduce the value of every home in a neighborhood. The presence of so many abandoned properties finds city workers, paid by tax dollars, mowing lawns and doing upkeep on abandoned properties. Vandalized vacant properties attract criminal activity. Baltimore and Detroit are bulldozing areas with high concentrations of walk-away properties.

If you've raised a child you know that consequences for poor choices modify behavior. Keep buying a new bike for your kids each time they leave it outside and it is stolen will find you mortgaging your home to buy replacement bikes. Make them earn the money to pay for their own new bike and that bike will be inside and securely locked, probably to their wrists and beds. Moral hazard does result in economic sensibility and produces long-term prosperity.

So, howl about Wall Street and the failure of executives who walked away unscathed from their companies' collapses. Apply the same standard to those who took out mortgages that put them in over the heads in even the best of economies. They have left messes in neighborhoods, cities, and lenders with their abandoned homes and unpaid mortgages. Accountability and responsibility apply on Main Street too.

Discussion Questions

1. How does the "everybody does it" argument apply here?

2. Apply the analytical models you learned in Units 1 and 2 and determine which piece applies them more completely.

3. Is there a difference between legal and ethical?

4. What is the impact of "everyone doing it"?

The Fear-and-Silence Factors

SECTION 4E

In a true confrontation between personal values and company policy, employees are often faced with the knowledge that their employer is acting unethically in a way that does or could hurt someone else. How should they react? What should they do? Why do employers often ignore employees' concerns? Is it the culture?

Reading 4.22
The Options for Whistle-Blowers

Employees who are faced with a situation at work in which their values are at odds with the actions of their employers are grappling with their sense of loyalty to the company and their coworkers as well as their own value system. For example, an employee who knows that her company's product is defective is torn between her concern for customers who buy the product and her loyalty to the company and her fellow workers, who may also be her friends. She is concerned about her livelihood, her coworkers' livelihood, and the safety of others. Table 4.1 illustrates the options available to those who find their values at odds with the company's conduct.

TABLE 4.1
Employee Concerns and Employee Dissent

Expression of the Concern (Voice)	Illegal, Immoral, or Illegitimate		Not Illegal, Immoral, or Illegitimate	
	Exit Dimension			
	Stay	Go	Stay	Go
External dissent to someone who can take action	External whistle-blowing	Exit with public protest	Secret sharing	Exit with secret sharing
Internal dissent to someone who can take action	Internal whistle-blowing	Protest during exit interview	Employee participation, grievance	Explain reason for resignation in exit
Dissent in some other form	Discussion, confrontation with wrongdoer	Exit with notice to wrongdoer	Sabotage, strikes	Sabotage, strikes with exit
No expressed dissent	Inactive observation	Inactive departure	Silent disgruntlement	Silent departure

Nature of the Perceived Activity Triggering the Concern

Source: Peter B. Jubb, "Whistleblowing: A Restrictive Definition and Interpretation," *Journal of Business Ethics* 21 (1999), 80. Reprinted with kind permission of Springer Science and Business Media.

279

Discussion Questions

1. What choices do whistle-blowers have?

2. As you read the following cases, decide which type of whistle-blower was involved.

Case 4.23

Beech-Nut and the No-Apple-Juice Apple Juice

Beech-Nut was heavily in debt, had only 15 percent of the baby food market, and was operating out of a badly maintained eighty-year-old plant in Canajoharie, New York. Creditors and debt were growing. Beech-Nut needed to keep its costs down, its production up, and increase its market share. In 1977, Beech-Nut made a contract with Inter-juice Trading Corporation (the Universal Juice Corporation) to buy its apple juice concentrate. The contract was a lifesaver for Beech-Nut because Interjuice's prices were 20 percent below market, and apple concentrate was used as a base or sweetener in 30 percent of Beech-Nut's baby food products.

With this much-lower-cost key ingredient (the savings were estimated to be about $250,000 per year), Beech-Nut had reached a turnaround point. Here was a little company that could take on Gerber Baby Foods, the number-one baby food company in the United States. Nestlé Corporation, the international food producer based in Switzerland, saw potential in this little company and bought Beech-Nut in 1979. By the early 1980s, Beech-Nut had become the number-two baby food company in the United States. However, because of its substantially increased marketing costs, Beech-Nut's money pressures remained.

LiCari Raises Questions . . . Often

Dr. Jerome J. LiCari was the director of research and development for Beech-Nut Nutrition Corporation. Beech-Nut still had the low-cost Interjuice contract, but LiCari was worried. There were rumors of adulteration (or the addition or substituted use of inferior substances in a product) flying about in the apple juice industry. Chemists in LiCari's department were suspicious, but they did not yet have tests that could prove the adulteration.

In October 1978, Dr. LiCari learned from other sources that the concentrate might be made of syrups and edible substances that are much cheaper than apples. LiCari reported what he had learned to John Lavery, Beech-Nut's vice president for operations. Lavery's job included management of the purchasing and processing of apple juice concentrates.

Concerned, Lavery sent two employees to inspect Universal's blending operation. What the employees found was only a warehouse without any blending facility. Lavery did nothing more and did not ask about where Interjuice's blending operation was or whether he could have it inspected. Instead, he had Universal officers sign a "hold harmless" agreement, an addendum to the purchase contract that was intended to protect Beech-Nut if any legal claims or suits related to the juice resulted.

Under federal law, a company can sell a product that tastes like apple juice but is not really apple juice so long as the label discloses that it is made from syrups, sweeteners, and flavors. However, Beech-Nut's labels indicated that there was apple product in its apple juice and apple sweetener in the other products in which the concentrate was used, such as the baby fruits, where it provided a sweeter taste. Selling products labeled as apple juice or as containing apple product when they are in fact made with syrups and flavorings is a federal felony. Lavery wanted the hold-harmless agreement for protection against any claims that might be filed under these laws.

During this time, LiCari and his staff were able to develop some tests that did detect the presence of corn starch and other substances in the apple concentrate that were consistent with the composition of adulterated juice. LiCari continued to tell Lavery that he was concerned about the quality of the concentrate supplied by Universal. LiCari told Lavery that if a supplier was willing to adulterate concentrate in the first place, it would likely have little compunction about continuing to supply adulterated product even after signing a hold-harmless document.

Lavery reminded LiCari that Universal's price to Beech-Nut for the concentrate was 50 cents to a dollar per gallon below the price charged by Beech-Nut's previous supplier. He also reminded LiCari of the tremendous economic pressure under which the company was operating. The revenue from Beech-Nut's apple juice was $60 million between 1977 and 1982. Lavery told LiCari that he would not change suppliers unless LiCari brought him tests that would "prove in a court of law that the concentrate was adulterated." He also told Dr. LiCari that any further testing of the product was to be a low item on his list of work assignments and priorities.

In 1979, LiCari sent the concentrate to an outside laboratory for independent analysis. The test results showed that the concentrate consisted primarily of sugar syrup. LiCari told Lavery of the lab results, but Lavery did nothing. In July 1979, Lavery also received a memorandum from the company's plant manager in San Jose, California, that indicated that approximately 95,000 pounds of concentrate inventory was "funny" and "adulterated," in that it was "almost pure corn syrup." The plant manager suggested that Beech-Nut demand its money back from the supplier. Instead, Lavery told the manager to go ahead and use the tainted concentrate in the company's mixed juices. Beech-Nut continued to purchase its apple juice concentrate from Universal.

LiCari and his staff continued their efforts to communicate to Lavery and other company officials that the Interjuice concentrate was adulterated. In August 1981, LiCari sent a memorandum to Charles Jones, the company's purchasing manager, with a copy to Lavery, stating that although the scientists had not proven that the concentrate was adulterated, there was "a tremendous amount of circumstantial evidence" to that effect, "paint[ing] a grave case against the current supplier." LiCari's memorandum concluded that "[i]t is imperative that Beech-Nut establish the authenticity of the Apple Juice Concentrate used to formulate our products. If the authenticity cannot be established, I feel that we have sufficient reason to look for a new supplier."[475]

Lavery took no action to change suppliers. Rather, he instructed Jones to ignore LiCari's memorandum, criticized LiCari for not being a "team player," and called his scientists "Chicken Little." He threatened to fire LiCari.[476] In his evaluation of LiCari's performance for 1981, Lavery wrote that LiCari had great technical ability but that his judgment was "colored by naivete and impractical ideals."[477]

In late 1981, the company received, unsolicited, a report from a Swiss laboratory concluding that Beech-Nut's apple juice product was adulterated, stating, "The apple juice is false, can not see any apple."[478] Lavery reviewed this report, and one of his aides sent it to Universal. Universal made no response, and Beech-Nut took no action.

Nils Hoyvald became the CEO of Beech-Nut in April 1981. Both before and after becoming president of Beech-Nut, Hoyvald was aware, from several sources, about an adulteration problem. In November 1981, Beech-Nut's purchasing manager raised the

---

[475]Chris Welles, "What Led Beech-Nut Down the Road to Disgrace," *Business Week*, February 22, 1988, pp. 124–128.

[476]*U.S. v Beech-Nut, Inc.*, 871 F.2d 1181 (2nd Cir. 1989), at 1185; 925 F.2d 604 (2nd Cir. 1991); cert. denied, 493 U.S. 933 (1989).

[477]Welles, "What Led Beech-Nut Down the Road to Disgrace," p. 128.

[478]*U.S. v Beech-Nut, Inc.*, 871 F.2d 1181 (2nd Cir. 1989), at 1185; 925 F.2d 604 (2nd Cir. 1991); cert. denied, 493 U.S. 933 (1989).

problem. Hoyvald took no action. Rather, he told Lavery that, for budgetary reasons, he would not approve a change in concentrate suppliers until 1983.[479]

In the spring of 1982, Paul Hillabush, the company's director of quality assurance, advised Hoyvald that there would be some adverse publicity about Beech-Nut's purchases of apple juice concentrate. On June 25, 1982, a detective hired by the Processed Apple Institute visited Lavery at Beech-Nut's Canajoharie, New York, plant, and told him that Beech-Nut was about to be involved in a lawsuit as a result of its use of adulterated juice. The investigator showed Canajoharie plant operators documents from the Interjuice dumpster and new tests indicating that the juice was adulterated. The institute invited Beech-Nut to join its lawsuit against Interjuice (a suit that eventually closed Interjuice). Beech-Nut declined. It did cancel its future contracts with Interjuice, but it continued to use its on-hand supplies for production because of the tremendous cost pressures and competition it was facing.

LiCari also took his evidence of adulteration to Hoyvald. Hoyvald told LiCari he would look into the supplier issue. Several months later, after no action had been taken, LiCari resigned. After leaving Beech-Nut, LiCari wrote an anonymous letter to the U.S. Food and Drug Administration (FDA) disclosing the juice adulteration at Beech-Nut. He signed the letter, "Johnny Appleseed." The FDA began an investigation of Beech-Nut and its products and supplier, but Beech-Nut was not cooperative. The explanation managers offered was simple. When the FDA first notified the company of the problem, Beech-Nut had 700,000 cases of the spurious juice. By stalling, Beech-Nut was able to sell off some of those cases and ship others overseas (details follow), leaving it with the destruction of just 200,000 cases of the fake product.

An FDA investigator observed,

> *They played a cat-and-mouse game with us. When FDA would identify a specific apple juice lot as tainted, Beech-Nut would quickly destroy it before the FDA could seize it, an act that would have created negative publicity.*[480]

The Cat-and-Mouse Chase

When New York State government tests first revealed that a batch of Beech-Nut's juice contained little or no apple juice, Beech-Nut had the juice moved during the night, using nine tanker trucks. CEO Hoyvald realized that not being able to sell the inventory of juice the company had on hand would be financially crippling. So, he began delaying tactics designed to give the company time to sell it.

To avoid seizure of the inventory in New York by state officials in August 1982, Hoyvald had this juice moved out of state during the night. It was transported from the New York plant to a warehouse in Secaucus, New Jersey, and the records of this shipment and others were withheld from FDA investigators until the investigators independently located the carrier Beech-Nut had used. While the FDA was searching for the adulterated products but before it had discovered the Secaucus warehouse, Hoyvald ordered virtually the entire stock in that warehouse shipped to Beech-Nut's distributor in Puerto Rico; the Puerto Rico distributor had not placed an order for the product and had twice refused to buy the product even at great discounts offered personally by Hoyvald.

In September 1982, Hoyvald ordered a rush shipment of the inventory of apple juice products held at Beech-Nut's San Jose plant, and took a number of unusual steps to get rid of the entire stock. He authorized price discounts of 50 percent; the largest discount ever offered before had been 10 percent. Hoyvald insisted that the product be shipped

---

[479]*Id.*

[480]Welles, "What Led Beech-Nut Down the Road to Disgrace," p. 128.

"fast, fast, fast," and gave a distributor in the Dominican Republic only two days, instead of the usual thirty, to respond to this product promotion. In order to get the juice out of the warehouse and out of the country as quickly as possible, Beech-Nut shipped it to the Dominican Republic on the first possible sailing date, which was from an unusually distant port, which raised the freight cost to an amount nearly equal to the value of the goods themselves. Finally, this stock was shipped before Beech-Nut had received the necessary financial documentation from the distributor, which, as one Beech-Nut employee testified, was "tantamount to giving the stuff away."[481]

Hoyvald also used Beech-Nut's lawyers to help delay the government investigation, thereby giving the company more time to sell its inventory of adulterated juice before the product could be seized or a recall could be ordered. For example, in September 1982, the FDA informed Beech-Nut that it intended to seize all of Beech-Nut's apple juice products made from Universal concentrate; in October, New York State authorities advised the company that they planned to initiate a local recall of these products. Beech-Nut's lawyers, at Hoyvald's direction, successfully negotiated with the authorities for a limited recall, excluding products held by retailers and stocks of mixed-juice products. Beech-Nut eventually agreed to conduct a nationwide recall of its apple juice, but by the time of the recall Hoyvald had sold more than 97 percent of the earlier stocks of apple juice. In December 1982, in response to Hoyvald's request, Thomas Ward, a member of a law firm retained by Beech-Nut, sent Hoyvald a letter that summarized the events surrounding the apple juice concentrate problem as follows:

From the start, we had two main objectives:

1. to minimize Beech-Nut's potential economic loss, which we understand has been conservatively estimated at $3.5 million, and
2. to minimize any damage to the company's reputation.

We determined that this could be done by delaying, for as long as possible, any market withdrawal of products produced from the Universal Juice concentrate. . . .

In spite of the recognition that FDA might wish to have Beech-Nut recall some of its products, management decided to continue sales of all such products for the time being. . . . The decision to continue sales and some production of the products was based upon the recognition of the significant potential financial loss and loss of goodwill, and the fact that apple juice is a critical lead-in item for Beech-Nut.

Since the mixed fruit juices and other products constituted the bulk of the products produced with Universal concentrate, one of our main goals became to prevent the FDA and state authorities from focusing on these products, and we were in fact successful in limiting the controversy strictly to apple juice.[482]

The Charges and Fates

In November 1986, Beech-Nut, Hoyvald, and Lavery, along with Universal's proprietor Zeev Kaplansky and four others ("suppliers"), were indicted on charges relating to the company's sale of adulterated and misbranded apple juice products. Hoyvald and Lavery were charged with (1) one count of conspiring with the suppliers to violate the FDCA, 21 U.S.C. §§331(a), (k), and 333(b) (1982 & Supp. IV 1986), in violation of 18 U. S. C. §371; (2) twenty counts of mail fraud, in violation of 18 U.S.C. §§1341 and 2; and (3) 429 counts of introducing adulterated and misbranded apple juice into interstate commerce, in

---

[481]*U.S. v Beech-Nut, Inc.*, 871 F.2d, at 1186. This segment of the case was adapted from the judicial opinion.
[482]*Id.*, pp. 1186–1187.

violation of 21 U.S.C. §§331(a) and 333(b) and 18 U.S.C. §2. The suppliers were also charged with introducing adulterated concentrate into interstate commerce.

Hoyvald and Lavery pleaded not guilty to the charges against them. Eventually, Beech-Nut pleaded guilty to 215 felony violations of §§331(a) and 333(b); it received a $2 million fine and was ordered to pay $140,000 to the FDA for the expenses of its investigation. Kaplansky and the other four supplier-defendants also eventually pleaded guilty to some or all of the charges against them. Hoyvald and Lavery thus went to trial alone. LiCari testified at the trials, "I thought apple juice should be made from apples."[483]

The trial began in November 1987 and continued for three months. The government's evidence included that previously discussed. Hoyvald's principal defense was that all of his acts relating to the problem of adulterated concentrate had been performed on the advice of counsel. For example, there was evidence that the Beech-Nut shipment of adulterated juices from its San Jose plant to the Dominican Republic followed the receipt by Hoyvald of a telex sent by Sheldon Klein, an associate of the law firm representing Beech-Nut, which summarized a telephone conference between Beech-Nut officials and its attorneys as follows:

> We understand that approximately 25,000 cases of apple juice manufactured from concentrate purchased from Universal Juice is [sic] currently in San Jose. It is strongly recommended that such product and all other Universal products in Beech-Nut's possession anywhere in the US be destroyed before a meeting with [the FDA] takes place.[484]

Hoyvald and Klein testified that they had a follow-up conversation in which Klein told Hoyvald that, as an alternative, it would be lawful to export the adulterated apple juice products.

The jury returned a verdict of guilty on all of the counts against Lavery. It returned a verdict of guilty against Hoyvald on 359 counts of adulterating and misbranding apple juice, all of which related to shipments after June 25, 1982. It was unable to reach a verdict on the remaining counts against Hoyvald, which related to events prior to that date.

The federal district court sentenced Hoyvald to a term of imprisonment of a year and a day, fined him $100,000, imposed a $9,000 special assessment, and ordered him to pay the costs of prosecution. In March 1989, the federal court of appeals for the second circuit reversed the conviction on the ground that venue was improperly laid in the Eastern District instead of the Northern District of New York. The case was remanded to the district court for a new trial.[485] In August 1989, Hoyvald was retried before Chief Judge Platt on nineteen of the counts on which a mistrial had been declared during his first trial. After four weeks of trial, the jury was unable to agree on a verdict and a mistrial was declared.

Rather than face a third trial, Hoyvald entered into a plea agreement with the government on November 7, 1989. The government recommended that the court impose a suspended sentence; five years of probation, including 1,000 hours of community service; and a $100,000 fine. On November 13, 1989, the district court accepted the plea and imposed sentence. At that plea proceeding Judge Platt agreed, at Hoyvald's request, to defer the beginning of his community service to give him three weeks to travel to Denmark to visit his eighty-four-year-old mother.

---

[483]Welles, "What Led Beech-Nut Down the Road to Disgrace," p. 128.

[484]*U.S. v Beech-Nut, Inc.*, 871 F.2d 1181, at 1194. Again, this material is adapted from the case.

[485]*United States v Beech-Nut Nutrition Corp.*, 871 F.2d 1181 (2nd Cir.), cert. denied, 493 *U.S.* 933, 110 S.Ct. 324, 107 L.Ed.2d 314 (1989).

Six months later, in May 1990, Hoyvald again requested permission from his probation officer to return to Denmark to visit his mother, and then to be permitted to visit "East and West Germany, Switzerland, Hungary, Czechoslovakia, and Greece" on business, a journey that would take slightly more than three weeks. The Probation Department expressed no opposition to the trip so long as he "supplies an appropriate itinerary and documentation as to the business portions of his trip." The United States Attorney did not oppose the request. On May 22, 1990, Hoyvald requested permission to travel to the other European countries to "look for a job and to investigate business opportunities" in those countries. The district court ruled that Hoyvald could visit his mother in Denmark but denied the request to travel to other countries.

Discussion Questions

1. No one was ever made ill or harmed by the fake apple juice. Was LiCari overreacting?

2. Did LiCari follow the lines of authority in his efforts? Is this important for a whistle-blower? Why?

3. What pressures contributed to Beech-Nut's unwillingness to switch suppliers?

4. Using the various models for analysis of ethical dilemmas that you have learned, point out the things that Lavery, Hoyvald, and others in the company failed to consider as they refused to deal with the Interjuice problem.

5. Why did LiCari feel he had to leave Beech-Nut? Why did LiCari write anonymously to the FDA?

6. Is it troublesome that Hoyvald and Lavery escaped sentences on a technicality? Is the sentence too light?

7. Why do you think Hoyvald and the others thought they could get away with the adulterated juice? Why did they play the "cat-and-mouse" game with the FDA? What principles about ethics have you learned that might have helped them analyze their situation more carefully and clearly? Are there some ideas for your credo from both their decisions and LiCari's actions?

8. Beech-Nut's market share went from 19.1 percent of the market to 15.8 percent, where it has hovered ever since. Why? What were the costs of Beech-Nut's fake apple juice and its "cat-and-mouse game"? Do you think consumers still remember this conduct?

Case 4.24

NASA and the Space Shuttle Booster Rockets

Morton Thiokol, Inc., an aerospace company, manufactures the solid-propellant rocket motors for the Peacekeeper missile and the missiles on Trident nuclear submarines. Thiokol also worked closely with the National Aeronautics and Space Administration (NASA) in developing the *Challenger,* one of NASA's reusable space shuttles.

Morton Thiokol served as the manufacturer for the booster rockets used to launch the *Challenger.* NASA had scheduled a special launch of the *Challenger* for January 1986. The launch was highly publicized because NASA had conducted a nationwide search for a teacher to send on the flight. For NASA's twenty-fifth shuttle mission, teacher Christa McAuliffe would be on board.

On the scheduled launch day, January 28, 1986, the weather was cloudy and cold at the John F. Kennedy Space Center in Cape Canaveral, Florida. The launch had already been delayed several times, but NASA officials still contacted Thiokol engineers in Utah to discuss whether the shuttle should be launched in such cold weather. The temperature range for the boosters, as specified in Thiokol's contract with NASA, was between 40°F and 90°F.

The temperature at Cape Canaveral that January morning was below 30°F. The launch of the *Challenger* proceeded nevertheless. A presidential commission later concluded, "Thiokol management reversed its position and recommended the launch of [the *Challenger*] at the urging of [NASA] and contrary to the views of its engineers in order to accommodate a major customer."[486]

Two of the Thiokol engineers involved in the launch, Allan McDonald and Roger Boisjoly, later testified that they had opposed the launch. Boisjoly had done work on the shuttle's booster rockets at the Marshall Space Flight Center in Utah in February 1985, at which time he noted that at low temperatures, an O-ring assembly in the rockets eroded and, consequently, failed to seal properly. Though Boisjoly gave a presentation on the issue, little action was taken over the course of the year. Boisjoly conveyed his frustration in his activity reports. Finally, in July 1985, Boisjoly wrote a confidential memo to R–K. (Bob) Lund, Thiokol's vice president for engineering. An excerpt follows:

> *This letter is written to insure that management is fully aware of the seriousness of the current O-ring erosion problem. . . . The mistakenly accepted position on the joint problem was to fly without fear of failure. . . . [This position] is now drastically changed as a result of the SRM [shuttle recovery mission] 16A nozzle joint erosion which eroded a secondary O-ring with the primary O-ring never sealing. If the same scenario should occur in a field joint (and it could), then it is a jump ball as to the success or failure of the joint. . . . The result would be a catastrophe of the highest order—loss of human life. . . .*
>
> *It is my honest and real fear that if we do not take immediate action to dedicate a team to solve the problem, with the field joint having the number one priority, then we stand in jeopardy of losing a flight along with all the launch pad facilities.*[487]

In October 1985, Boisjoly presented the O-ring issue at a conference of the Society of Automotive Engineers and requested suggestions for resolution.[488]

On January 27, 1986, the day before the launch, Boisjoly attempted to halt the launch. Mr. McDonald also offered his insights to a group of NASA and Thiokol engineers, However, four Thiokol managers, including Lund, voted unanimously to recommend the launch. One manager had urged Lund to "take off his engineering hat and put on his management hat."[489] The managers then developed the following revised recommendations. Engineers were excluded from the final decision and the development of these findings.[490]

- Calculations show that SRM-25 [the designation for the Challenger's January 28 flight] O-rings will be 20°F colder than SRM-15 O-rings.
- Temperature data not conclusive on predicting primary O-ring blow-by.
- Engineering assessment is as follows:
  - Colder O-rings will have increased effective durometer [that is, they will be harder].
  - "Harder" O-rings will take longer to seat.
  - More gas may pass primary [SRM-25] O-ring before the primary seal seats (relative to SRM-15).

---

[486]Judith Dobrzynski, "Morton Thiokol: Reflections on the Shuttle Disaster," *BusinessWeek*, March 14, 1988, p. 82.

[487]Russel Boisjoly et al., "Roger Boisjoly and the Challenger Disaster: The Ethical Dimensions," *Journal of Business Ethics* 8 (1989): 2178–2130.

[488]"No. 2 Official Is Appointed at Thiokol," *New York Times*, June 12, 1992, p. C3; and "Whistle-Blowing: Not Always a Losing Game," *EE Spectrum*, December 1990, 49–52.

[489]Boisjoly et al., "Roger Boisjoly and the *Challenger* Disaster," pp. 217–230.

[490]Paul Hoversten, "Engineers Waver, then Decide to Launch," *USA Today*, January 22, 1996, p. 2A.

- Demonstrated sealing threshold [on SRM-25 O-ring] is three times greater than 0.038" erosion experienced on SRM-15.
- If the primary seal does not seat, the secondary seal will seat.
- Pressure will get to secondary seal before the metal parts rotate.
- O-ring pressure leak check places secondary seal in outboard position which minimizes sealing time.
- MTI recommends STS-51L launch proceed on 28 January 1986.
- SRM-25 will not be significantly different from SRM-15.[491]

After the decision was made, Boisjoly returned to his office and wrote in his journal,

I sincerely hope this launch does not result in a catastrophe. I personally do not agree with some of the statements made in Joe Kilminster's [Kilminster was one of the four Thiokol managers who voted to recommend the launch] written summary stating that SRM-25 is okay to fly.[492]

Seventy-four seconds into the *Challenger* launch, the low temperature caused the seals at the booster rocket joints to fail. The *Challenger* exploded, killing Christa McAuliffe and the six astronauts on board.[493]

The subsequent investigation by the presidential commission placed the blame for the faulty O-rings squarely with Thiokol. Charles S. Locke, Thiokol's CEO, maintained, "I take the position that we never agreed to the launch at the temperature at the time of the launch. The *Challenger* incident resulted more from human error than mechanical error. The decision to launch should have been referred to headquarters. If we'd been consulted here, we'd never have given clearance, because the temperature was not within the contracted specs."[494]

Both Boisjoly and McDonald testified before the presidential panel regarding their opposition to the launch and the decision of their managers (who were also engineers) to override their recommendation. Both Boisjoly and McDonald also testified that following their expressed opposition to the launch and their willingness to come forward, they had been isolated from NASA and subsequently demoted. Since testifying, McDonald has been assigned to "special projects." Boisjoly, who took medical leave for posttraumatic stress disorder, has left Thiokol, but receives disability pay from the company. Currently, Mr. Boisjoly operates a consulting firm in Mesa, Arizona. He speaks frequently on business ethics to professional organizations and companies.[495]

In May 1986, then-CEO Locke stated, in an interview with the *Wall Street Journal*, "This shuttle thing will cost us this year 10¢ a share."[496] Locke later protested that his statement had been taken out of context.[497]

In 1989, Morton Norwich separated from Thiokol Chemical Corporation. The two companies had previously merged to become Morton Thiokol. Following the separation, Thiokol Chemical became Thiokol Corporation. Morton returned to the salt business, and Thiokol, remaining under contract with NASA through 1999, redesigned its space shuttle rocket motor to correct the deficiencies. No one at Thiokol was fired following the *Challenger* accident. Because of this incident and defense contractor indictments,

[491]Boisjoly et al., "Roger Boisjoly and the *Challenger* Disaster," pp. 217–230.

[492]Interview with Roger Boisjoly, June 28, 1993, M. M. Jennings.

[493]Paul Hoversten, Patricia Edmonds, and Haya El Nasser, "Debate Raged Night before Doomed Launch," *USA Today,* January 22, 1996, pp. A1, A2.

[494]Dobrzynski, "Morton Thiokol," p. 82.

[495]Interview with Roger Boisjoly.

[496]Dobrzynski, "Morton Thiokol," p. 82.

[497]"No. 2 Official Is Appointed at Thiokol," p. C3; and "Whistle-Blowing," pp. 49–52.

the Government Accountability Project was established in Washington, D.C. The office provides a staff, legal assistance, and pamphlets to help whistle-blowers working on government projects.

Discussion Questions

1. Who is responsible for the deaths that resulted from the *Challenger* explosion?
2. If you had been in Allan McDonald's or Roger Boisjoly's position on January 28, 1986, what would you have done?
3. Evaluate Locke's comment on the loss of ten cents per share.
4. Should the possibility that the booster rockets might not perform below 30°F have been a factor in the decision to allow the launch to proceed?
5. Roger Boisjoly offers the following advice on whistle-blowing:
   a. You owe your organization an opportunity to respond. Speak to them first verbally. Memos are not appropriate for the first step.
   b. Gather collegial support for your position. If you cannot get the support, then make sure you are correct.
   c. Spell out the problem in a letter.

   Mr. Boisjoly acknowledges he did not gather collegial support. How can such support be obtained? Where would you start? What would you use to persuade others?
6. Scientist William Lourance has written that "a thing is safe if its attendant risks are judged to be acceptable."[498] Had everyone, including the astronauts, accepted the risks attendant to the *Challenger's* launch?
7. *Groupthink* is defined as

   a mode of thinking that people engage in when they are deeply involved in a cohesive in-group, when the members' strivings for unanimity override their motivation to realistically appraise alternative courses of action. . . . Groupthink refers to the deterioration of mental efficiency, reality testing, and moral judgment that results from in-group pressures.[499]

   In another NASA accident, a launch pad fire took the lives of *Apollo I* astronauts Gus Grissom, Ed White, and Roger Chaffee on January 30, 1967. Gene Krantz, the Mission Control Flight Director, addressed his staff by saying, "We were too gung-ho about the schedule and we locked out all of the problems we saw each day in our work. . . . Not one of us stood up and said, "Damn it, STOP!""[500]

   Is this what happened when Thiokol's management group took off its "engineering hats"?

Case 4.25

Westland/Hallmark Meat Packing Company and the Cattle Standers

The U.S. Department of Agriculture issued its biggest meat recall in its history when it ordered a recall of 143 million pounds of meat processed and sold by Westland/Hallmark Meat Packing Company. The Humane Society of the United States had undercover video made at the company's plant that showed how the company handled so-called downer cattle. Under federal law, cattle scheduled for slaughter must be able to stand upright. If the cattle cannot walk or are too ill to stand, the law provides that they must be euthanized, but cannot be put into the meat supply. The rule is based on the reality that cattle that cannot stand or walk are more likely to carry some form of disease such as mad cow or salmonella. The Humane Society video showed workers at the plant using a liberal definition of a "stander," and using shocks and forklifts to get the cattle upright for purposes of inspection so that the cattle could then be slaughtered. Downers

---

[498]Joseph R. Herkert, "Management's Hat Trick: Misuse of 'Engineering Judgment' in the Challenger Incident," *Journal of Business Ethics* 10 (1991): 617.

[499]Irving L. Janis, *Victims of Groupthink* (1972).

[500]http://history.nasa.gov/Apollo204. Accessed May 19, 2010.

are considered unfit for human consumption, but the downers the workers prodded into standing were slaughtered and made their way into the food supply. The workers were compensated on the basis of number of head of cattle slaughtered per day.

Westland/Hallmark was named USDA supplier of the year in 2006; it is a company with a good reputation. However, over 50 million pounds of the meat had made their way into school lunch programs. Some of the meat has already been eaten, with no illnesses reported.

Reforms are already in the works, both in Congress and at the USDA. The video that was taken undercover can be viewed on YouTube. The video was aired at the congressional hearings on Westland/Hallmark and when the general manager saw the video he said, "The video just astounded us. Our jaws dropped. . . . We thought this place was sparkling perfect."[501]

Discussion Questions

1. Was getting the cows to stand up a way of complying with the law? Was it ethical?

2. What effect would Hallmark's compensation system for its employees have on their conduct?

3. Is there something to learn about a manager's role from the general manager's comment that the video surprised him?

For More Information

Julie Schmitt, "Impact of Beef Recall Widens," *USA Today,* February 25, 2008, p. 1A.

Jane Zhang, David Kesmodel, and Elizabeth Williamson, "Meat Recall Sparks Calls for Food-Safety Changes," *Wall Street Journal,* February 20, 2008, p. A3.

Julie Schmitt and Elizabeth Weise, "Feds Still Tracing Some Recalled Meat," *USA Today,* February 22, 2008, p. 1B.

"The Biggest Recall Ever," *New York Times,* February 21, 2008, p. A2.

Reading 4.26

Getting Information from Employees Who Know to Those Who Can and Will Respond[502]

> *In the course of performing my duties for the Firm, I have reason to believe that certain conduct on the part of senior management of the Firm may be in violation of the Code. The following is a summary of the conduct I believe may violate the Code and which I feel compelled, by the terms of the Code, to bring to your attention.*[503]

So wrote Matthew Lee, on May 18, 2008, to the CFO and Chief Risk Officer of Lehman Brothers, a firm that had employed him as an analyst since 1994. Mr. Lee, who headed global balance-sheet and legal-entity accounting, then went on to describe "tens of billions of dollars" on the firm's balance sheet that could not be substantiated. Mr. Lee

---

[501]David Kesmodel and Jane Zhang, "Meatpacker in Cow-Abuse Scandal May Shut as Congress Turns Up Heat," *Wall Street Journal,* February 25, 2008, pp. A1, A10.

[502]Adapted from Marianne M. Jennings., "The Employee We Ignore, the Signs We Miss, and the Reality We Avoid," *Corporate Finance Review* 14(6):42–44 (2010).

[503]Letter of Matthew Lee, dated May 18, 2008, as included and discussed in the Report of the examiner for the bankruptcy trustee in the Lehman bankruptcy.

also highlighted Lehman's use of Repo 105, a means Lehman used to make appear to be solvent. Repo 105 was used to move about $50 billion in debt off the Lehman balance sheet.

The response to Mr. Lee was astonishing but typical: (1) Ernst & Young, the firm's auditor, referred to Mr. Lee's memo as "pretty ugly," but concluded the issues that he raised were immaterial and his allegations unfounded; and (2) Mr. Lee was fired.

Lehman declared bankruptcy on September 15, 2008. Mr. Lee was correct, and the bankruptcy report is a scathing one that demonstrates the top executives at Lehman were aware of both the level of risk exposure as well as the accounting practices used to conceal that exposure.

In the ongoing litigation by Pursuit Partners LLC against UBS AG, there is a similar revelation from an employee about the knowledge floating internally about the quality of its CDOs that were being sold as investment-grade instruments but were anything but. In the fall of 2007, internal documents show that UBS employees were concerned about the debt securities the bank was carrying and were laboring mightily to find a way to unload them on the unwitting. In one e-mail a UBS AG employee, who is discussing the fact that the toxic instruments are on the bank's books, complains, "OK still have this vomit."[504] A judge has ruled that UBS had an "awareness" that the instruments would turn into "toxic waste," but it still persuaded Pursuit to purchase the CDOs based upon the UBS promise that it sold only investment-grade securities. Other e-mails gave employees instructions to "unload" the CDOs, but warned that there was no need to signal this strategy publicly.

These revelations come on the heels of a jailhouse interview with Bernie Madoff in which he commented that he was "astonished" that he escaped detection of his Ponzi scheme through six SEC investigations.[505] There was the controlled and secretive access to the computer trading room, the failure to verify trades with the firms Mr. Madoff said he was using (i.e., no one checked the clearinghouse), and the failure to heed the tips and warnings the agency was receiving from those inside the firm as well as from the industry.

There are two powerful common threads in these three market failures that have once again dissipated market trust: (1) Those involved were aware of their ethical and legal lapses; and (2) The warnings of employees and others were not heeded. These common threads were also present at Enron, WorldCom, HealthSouth and the problem companies that emerged in our turn-of-the-century scandals.

The key to prevention for stopping these schemes and poor ethical choices is getting the information from those in the organization who have it to those who can and will do something about it. Because these issues all involved or affected CFOs it is a good time to review those tools that help employees speak up and get information to the right responders. Those who do take action to resolve an issue are not always the first responders who receive the information. There are some cultural and individual leadership skills changes that CFOs can make to prevent these types of situations in which the issues are obvious and the answers and actions necessary are clear, but fail to surface until post–financial collapse. Firms do fall into the trap of ignoring the employee's warnings. Indeed, too often, the bearer of bad financial reporting news [the messenger] often ends up being killed, which provides the firm with a temporary means of coping.

---

[504]Serena Ng and Carrick Mollenkamp, "In UBS Case, Emails Show CDO Worries," *Wall Street Journal*, September 11, 2009, p. C1.

[505]Diana B. Henriques, "Lapses Kept Scheme Alive, Madoff Told Investigators," *New York Times*, October 31, 2009, p. A1.

Have Your Reporting Systems in Place

Some means of anonymous reporting, either through a hotline or a computer third-party reporting system, is a bare minimum. This company-wide mechanism allows those employees who are uncomfortable in their own environments or, worse, may be working under the folks involved in the unethical or illegal actions, the chance to raise issues. However, these systems do bring out the cranks and, as a result, do give us the reports that have little to do with financial reporting, accounting, or reporting the fact that the folks on the loading dock are using a 32-day month for shipping goods.

However, those reports may come from repeating pockets in the company. Even if the individual report contains no allegations relevant to financial reporting or accounting issues, the employee who submitted may simply not be able to articulate what is happening. However, the pockets of consistent reports indicate something more is afoot than just a manager who irritates employees. Follow sources and patterns to determine whether there may be areas in the company that require more analysis of the complaints to determine the root cause, a cause that may well involve financial reporting issues.

On Dissent and Discussion: The Humble Firm

In a conversation with an executive at a company at the top of its industry and one that is studied by others for its management practices, I asked for a one-line descriptor of the secret to his company's longstanding success. He paused and then gave this pithy response, "We go to work each day and say, 'We suck, now let's get better.'" The Gen X folks are now in management, complete with their jargon. His point is, however, one worth exploring. In these healthy companies, the arrogance of results and top performance is kept at bay. That humility permits a more open environment to take hold. An open environment is one in which a manager with 14 years of experience would not be fired for raising concerns about accounting practices and the code of ethics. Rather, that manager would be given the opportunity to explain his concerns and the issues. Indeed, in a firm of humility a 14-year manager would not need to write a memo of concern—the issues would come up in discussions on the financials, the risk, and certainly with the auditors.

Meetings in the humble firm have lively discussions, not tense ones. As noted many times in this column over the years, another common thread in firms that crash and burn financially is that managers and employees remained sullen and mute in discussions and meetings. However, they certainly did let loose with their concerns only in their e-mails to colleagues, thus providing the documentation that is the stuff of civil litigation and, on occasion, criminal liability. In the humble firm, the e-mail thoughts are the ones stated publicly, discussed, and evaluated.

Develop Your Own Sensing Mechanisms

Even in the humblest of firms, issues still may not emerge. The CFO, as ethical leader, will need to use sensing mechanisms beyond the hotlines and open discussions. The most important sensing mechanism comes from this advice: Get out of your office. That is, what an employee might never utter in a meeting or put in an anonymous report may come out in the cafeteria, the hallways, or at one of the coffee room birthday celebrations. Often spontaneity comes at employee volunteer projects or unannounced visits to plants, divisions, stores, or offices. This egalitarian access has an effect on employees and their willingness to speak up and raise questions. Psychologists could provide more insight into the whys of this situational forthrightness, but once the CFO takes on a new identity as an approachable individual as opposed to an iconic and feared figure, there is new communication. Human translation breaks down the barriers of fear and silence that prevent information from getting it from that place in the company where it is common knowledge to those in the company who can and will take appropriate steps and make changes.

Many CEOs and CFOs do have quarterly or annual meetings with small groups of employees, a means they offer as evidence that they are using sensing mechanisms. Those are scheduled meetings. Those are formal meetings. Spontaneous "blurts" of concern require spontaneous settings. This sensing tool is really an update of the 1970s OB theory, MBWA (Management by Walking Around). This theory is akin to the parents of teens who come home early and unannounced: one never knows what one will find. Some companies are now requiring both executives and boards to have a certain number of "visits" to company sites, plants, offices, and divisions so that they understand what the company does and how it works. Further, those visits cannot be "gaggle" visits, those group visits that are little more than a tour group swoop. Rather, the visits are individual ones with the same goal as the executives' egalitarian interactions.

In the United States a new reality show, "Undercover Boss" finds CEOs, COOs, and CFOs working side-by-side with employees. They have come away with new insights in what worries employees, what their jobs require, and even when the employees are cheating a bit on their time clocks. The greater the isolation an executive has, the less information flows from the frontlines. Ironically, CFO spend their days in non-stop meetings and keep overbooked schedules that find them wondering where this spontaneity can possibly fit. Asking that question provides the answer. The realignment of thinking finds the spontaneity as the priority with the meetings fit nicely in around that interaction.

Don't Look for Absolution; Look for Resolution

In the Lehman, UBS, and Madoff situations, there was another common thread, and one that is typical for companies that experience financial collapse. They all had outsiders who were questioning, looking, and worrying about the companies' true real financial situations. David Einhorn gave public speeches about Lehman's risk and exposure but could not obtain satisfactory answers to his questions. CFO Erin Cowan dismissed his questions, using each conference call as part of a checklist to survive for another day. With Einhorn's persistence, Lehman finally responded by firing Ms. Cowan in June 2008. The termination brought a temporary reprieve, but three months later the bankruptcy revealed that the problem was not Ms. Cowan; the problem was the firm's failed financial strategy based on a risk model that was never fully disclosed.

At UBS, the directive was, "No disclosure; just sell, sell, sell." Mr. Madoff only looked to survive the next government inquiry. Survival that relies on the strategy of dodging bullets is unsustainable. There is a finite period of survival in ignoring issues and hoping for absolution from questions in order to survive another day. In these three firms there was no confrontation of reality—what the real risk levels were, whether there was financial solvency, and how to accurately reflect both in a timely manner in financial statements. Rather the goal was avoiding the painful fixes and hoping the masquerade could continue.

For most companies, it would take some time and a great deal of manipulation to reach the point of the Lehman, UBS, or Madoff meltdowns. However, none began their evasions suddenly. They all began with a few steps in financial strategy and reporting, steps that served to gloss over real and increasing risk. But that glossing must necessarily evolve in Repo 105 programs as the underlying issues remain unaddressed. If the strategy is failing, the solution is not subterfuge; the solution is a new strategy. Taking that hit when you switch strategies seems to be what these firms sought, futilely, to avoid. Resolution, not absolution, is needed when the financial strategy is no longer working.

Discussion Questions

1. What are sensing mechanisms and why are they important?
2. What is the humble firm and how does it encourage ethical behavior?

3. Describe what leads to the types of behaviors at Lehman and others companies that eventually collapse.
4. Why can't managers simply rely on their ethics hotlines?

Case 4.27

WorldCom: The Little Company That Couldn't After All [506]

For a time it seemed as if the little long-distance telephone company headquartered in Hattiesburg, Mississippi, would show the world how to run a telecommunications giant. But dreams turned to dust and credits turned to debits, and WorldCom would be limited to showing the world that you cannot stretch accounting rules and hope to survive.

WorldCom: From Coffee Shop Founding to Merger Giant

It was 1983 when Bernard J. (aka "Bernie") Ebbers founded Long Distance Discount Service (LDDS), a discount long-distance telephone company.[507] Local legend has it that Mr. Ebbers, a former junior high school basketball coach from Edmonton, Alberta, launched the plan for what would become a multi-billion-dollar, international company in a diner at a Days Inn in Hattiesburg, Mississippi.[508] The telephone industry in the United States was about to be deregulated, and a new industry, telecommunications, would be born. Because competitors to the once-formidable Ma Bell, long the nation's dominant phone company, would now be welcome, Mr. Ebbers and a group of small investors saw an opportunity. They followed a basic economic model in developing their company: buy wholesale and sell retail, but cheaper than the other retailers. Their strategy was to buy long-distance phone network access wholesale from AT&T and other long-distance giants and then resell it to consumers at a discount. They were about to undercut long-distance carriers in their own markets, using their own lines. There was enough money even in the planned lower margins to make money for LDDS.[509]

By 1985, Mr. Ebbers was growing weary of the new telephone venture because LDDS was in constant need of cash infusions, and the thirteen-unit budget motel chain Mr. Ebbers owned was the source of the cash. Following another coffee shop meeting, Mr. Ebbers agreed to take over the management of the company.[510] Mr. Ebbers's strategy upon his ascent to management was different from and bolder than just running a Mississippi phone company. Mr. Ebbers envisioned an international phone company and undertook to grow the company through acquisition. One business writer has described the next phase of LDDS as a fifteen-year juggernaut of mergers.[511] LDDS began regionally, and Ebbers acquired phone companies in four neighboring states.

---

[506]Adapted with permission from Marianne M. Jennings, "The Yeehaw Factor," *Wyoming Law Review* 3 (2003): 387–511.

[507]Seth Schiesel and Simon Romero, "WorldCom: Out of Obscurity to under Inquiry," *New York Times*, March 13, 2002, pp. C1, C4; and Susan Pulliam, Jared Sandberg, and Dan Morse, "Prosecutors Gain Key Witness in Criminal Probe of WorldCom," *Wall Street Journal*, July 3, 2002, pp. A1, A6.

[508]Kurt Eichenwald, "For WorldCom, Acquisitions Were behind Its Rise and Fall," *New York Times*, August 8, 2002, p. A1; and Schiesel and Romero, "WorldCom."

[509]Barnaby J. Feder, "An Abrupt Departure Is Seen as a Harbinger," *New York Times*, May 1, 2002, p. C1.

[510]*Id.*

[511]Kurt Eichenwald and Simon Romero, "Inquiry Finds Effort at Delay at WorldCom," *New York Times*, July 4, 2002, p. C1.

Ebbers also expanded the core business of LDDS from cheaper long distance by expanding into local service and data interchange.

By the time LDDS went public in 1989, it was offering telephone services throughout eleven Southern states and had taken on a new name, WorldCom.[512] By 1998, WorldCom had merged sixty-four times, including mergers with MFS Communications, Metromedia, and Resurgens Communications Group.[513] World Com's sixty-fifth merger was its biggest acquisition. WorldCom made a $37 billion offer to purchase MCI in a bidding war with British Telecommunications and GTE.[514] British Telecom had begun the bidding in 1997 with $19 billion, and in a bidding process that enjoyed daily international coverage, the bidding just kept going until Mr. Ebbers offered Bert C. Roberts Jr., the CEO of MCI, the additional perk of making him chair of the newly merged WorldCom–MCI, to be known as WorldCom. WorldCom won the bidding and completed what was at that time the largest merger in history.[515] WorldCom was on a Wall Street roll, a darling of investors and investment banking firms. It was able to acquire CompuServe and ANS Communications before its merger feast ended in 2000. The ending came abruptly when the Justice Department nixed WorldCom's proposed merger with Sprint, citing a resulting lack of competition in long-distance telecommunications if the $129 billion merger were approved.[516]

Despite the Justice Department's rejection of this merger proposal, WorldCom had grown to 61,800 employees, with revenues of $35.18 billion. The bulk of its revenues came from commercial telecommunications services, including data, voice, Internet, and international services, with the second largest source of revenue being the consumer services division.[517]

Mr. Ebbers was a Wall Street favorite. One analyst described Mr. Ebbers's meetings with Wall Street analysts as "prayer meetings" in which no one asked any questions or challenged any numbers.[518] Few analysts ever questioned Mr. Ebbers or WorldCom's nearly impossible financial performance.[519] Mr. Ebbers made it clear to Wall Street as well as WorldCom's employees that his goals rested in the financial end of the business, not in its fundamentals. He reiterated his lack of interest in operations, billing, and customer service and his obsession with not just being the number-one telecommunications company but also being the best on Wall Street. Mr. Ebbers described his business strategy succinctly in 1997: "Our goal is not to capture market share or be global. Our goal is to be the No. 1 stock on Wall Street."[520] In a report commissioned by the bankruptcy court on the company's downfall, former U.S. Attorney General Dick Thornburgh referred to WorldCom as a "culture of greed."[521]

---

[512]Feder, "An Abrupt Departure Is Seen as a Harbinger," p. C1. The company went public on NASDAQ.

[513]Eichenwald, "For WorldCom, Acquisitions Were Behind Its Rise and Fall," p. B1. The MFS merger alone carried a $12 billion price tag; Eichenwald, p. B4.

[514]Feder, "An Abrupt Departure Is Seen as a Harbinger," p. C1.

[515]Schiesel and Romero, "WorldCom," pp. C1, C4.

[516]Rebecca Blumenstein and Jared Sandberg, "WorldCom CEO Quits amid Probe of Firm's Finances," *Wall Street Journal*, April 30, 2002, pp. A1, A9.

[517]Feder, "An Abrupt Departure Is Seen as a Harbinger," pp. C1, C2. The annual reports for 2000 and 2001 could be found at http://www.worldcom.com. Presently, go to http://www.sec.gov and look up "WorldCom" in the Edgar database. The financial statements in those reports have been restated many times, with a resulting impact of about $9 billion less in revenue than originally reported.

[518]Feder, "An Abrupt Departure Is Seen as a Harbinger," pp. C1, C2.

[519]*Id.*

[520]*Id.*

[521]Andrew Backover, "Report Slams Culture at WorldCom," *USA Today*, November 5, 2002, p. 1B.

WorldCom's revenues went from $950 million in 1992 to $4.5 billion by 1996.[522] Mr. Ebbers always promised more and better in each annual report.[523]

The WorldCom era on Wall Street has been likened by those who were competing with the company to being in a race with an athlete who is later discovered to be using steroids. In fact, at AT&T, Michael Keith, the head of the business services division, was replaced after just nine months on the job because he could not match World Com's profit margins. When Mr. Keith told C. Michael Armstrong, CEO of AT&T, that those margins were just not possible, he was removed from his position.[524] William T. Esrey, the CEO of Sprint, said, "Our performance did not quite compare and we were blaming ourselves. We didn't understand what we were doing wrong. We were like, 'What are we missing here?'"[525]

Bernie and His Empire

WorldCom's rollicking Wall Street ride was at least partially enabled by Mr. Ebbers's personality and charisma. He was flamboyant, a 6-foot, 4-inch man who tended toward cowboy boots and blue jeans. Mr. Ebbers's charm worked as well in Jackson, Mississippi, as it did with investment bankers and analysts.[526] He was a "native boy" who was making good. Mr. Ebbers was a 1957 graduate of Mississippi College, located in Clinton, Mississippi, about thirty minutes away from Jackson, Mississippi, where Mr. Ebbers built the headquarters for WorldCom.[527] Even as the company stock was falling, few who lived in Mississippi who had invested in WorldCom would let go of their stock because of an abiding faith in Ebbers.[528] Mr. Ebbers's story was a rags-to-riches one of a Canadian high school basketball player winning a scholarship to a small Mississippi college and then growing an international megabusiness.[529]

Mr. Ebbers's personal life did take some twists and turns. He divorced his wife of twenty-seven years while WorldCom was at its peak and married, in 1998, an executive from WorldCom's Clinton, Mississippi, headquarters who was nearly thirty years his junior. Jack Grubman, the cheerleader analyst for WorldCom who worked at Salomon Brothers, attended the wedding and expensed the trip to Salomon Brothers.[530]

Mr. Ebbers's business acumen with his personal investments presented some problems. He was very good at buying businesses, but not so good at managing them. Most outsiders believed he overpaid for his investments, and he was so distant in day-to-day management that employees referred to him as "the bank," meaning that they could simply turn to him for cash for those things they desired or when they did not operate at a profit or were just plain short of cash.[531] Still, with the value of his WorldCom holdings alone, by 1999 Mr. Ebbers had a net worth of $1.4 billion, earning

[522]These numbers were all computed using the company's annual reports, found under "Investor Relations" at http://www.worldcom.com. Go to http://www.sec.gov and the Edgar database, and plug in "WorldCom" under "Company Name." The numbers were computed using "Selected Financial Data," as called out in each of the annual reports.

[523]In 1998, Mr. Ebbers said that if WorldCom just grew with the market, it would meet its earning targets.

[524]Seth Schiesel, "Trying to Catch WorldCom's Mirage," *New York Times*, June 30, 2002, p. BU1.

[525]*Id.* Sprint has had its own financial difficulties.

[526]Chris Woodyard, "Pressure to Perform Felt as Problems Hit," *USA Today*, July 1, 2002, p. 3A.

[527]*Id.*

[528]*Id.*

[529]Daniel Henninger, "Bye-Bye Bernie Drops the Curtain on the 1990s," *Wall Street Journal*, May 3, 2002, p. A10.

[530]Jayne O'Donnell, "Ebbers Acts as if Nothing Is Amiss," *USA Today*, September 18, 2002, pp. 1B, 2B; and Jessica Sommar, "Here Comes the Bribe: Grubman Expensed Trip to Ebbers' Wedding," *New York Post*, August 30, 2002, p. 39.

[531]Jayne O'Donnell and Andrew Backover, "Ebbers High-Risk Act Came Crashing Down on Him," *USA Today*, December 12, 2002, p. 1B.

him the rank of 174 among the richest Americans. Mr. Ebbers owned a minor-league hockey team (the Mississippi Indoor Bandits), a trucking company, Canada's largest ranch (500,000 acres, 20,000 head of Hereford cattle, a fly-fishing resort, and a general store), an all-terrain cycle ATC dealership, a lumberyard, one plantation, two farms, and forest properties equivalent in acreage to half of Rhode Island.[532]

Mr. Ebbers found himself heavily in debt with his personal investments, and, in need of cash, he used his infallible charm in one more venue, that of his board of directors.[533] Mr. Ebbers was able to persuade the board to allow WorldCom to extend loans in excess of $415 million to him, with the money supposedly to be used to rescue his failing businesses.[534] The problem with the loans, among many others, was that the stock Mr. Ebbers used as security was also the stock he had pledged to WorldCom's creditors in order to obtain financing for the company.[535] The result was that WorldCom's directors were taking a subordinated security interest in stock that had already been pledged, placing it well at the end of the line in terms of creditors, and both the creditors and the board were assuming that the value of the WorldCom stock would remain at an equal or higher level.[536] While the board's loans to Mr. Ebbers put WorldCom at risk of losing $415 million, the control of the company was actually at greater risk because Mr. Ebbers had pledged about $1 billion in WorldCom stock in total to his creditors as security for loans.[537] Further, if the price of the stock declined, and Mr. Ebbers did not meet margin calls, his creditors would be forced to sell the shares. Mr. Ebbers owned 27 million shares of WorldCom stock, and the sale of such large blocks of shares would have had a devastating impact on the price of WorldCom's stock.[538]

Despite all the loans and issues with his personal investments, Mr. Ebbers was a generous philanthropist with his own money as well as with WorldCom's. Clinton Mayor Rosemary Aultman called WorldCom "a wonderful corporate citizen."[539] Ebbers served on the Board of Trustees for Mississippi College and raised $500 million for a fund drive there, more money than had ever been raised by the small college. Interns and graduates from the college worked at WorldCom.

The Burst Bubble and Accounting Myths

Once the Justice Department refused to approve the final proposed merger with Sprint, WorldCom came unraveled. The unraveling had many contributing factors, one of which was the burst in the dot-com bubble and the resulting decline in the need for broadband, Internet access, and all the growth associated with the telecommunications industry.[540] The cuts in the telecom industry began in 2000 and were industry-wide. Between 2000 and 2001, Lucent reduced its employment from 106,000 to 77,000, Verizon went from 263,000 to 247,000, and there was a 52.8 percent decline in employment overall in the

---

[532]Susan Pulliam, Deborah Solomon, and Carrick Mollenkamp, "Former WorldCom CEO Built an Empire on Mountain of Debt," *Wall Street Journal,* December 31, 2002, p. A1.

[533]Jared Sandberg and Susan Pulliam, "Report by WorldCom Examiner Finds New Fraudulent Activities," *Wall Street Journal,* November 5, 2002, pp. A1, A11.

[534]Deborah Solomon and Jared Sandberg, "WorldCom's False Profits Climb," *Wall Street Journal,* November 6, 2002, p. A3.

[535]Jared Sandberg, Deborah Solomon, and Nicole Harris, "WorldCom Investigations Shift Focus to Ousted CEO Ebbers," *Wall Street Journal,* July 1, 2002, pp. A1, A8.

[536]Kurt Eichenwald, "Corporate Loans Used Personally, Report Discloses," *New York Times,* November 5, 2002, p. C1.

[537]Sandberg and Pulliam, "Report by WorldCom Examiner Finds New Fraudulent Activities," p. A1.

[538]*Id.*

[539]As noted earlier, Chris Woodyard, "Pressure to Perform Felt as Problems Hit," *USA Today,* July 1, 2002, p. 3A.

[540]Louis Uchitelle, "Job Cuts Take Heavy Toll on Telecom Industry," *New York Times,* June 29, 2002, p. B1.

telecom industry from 2000 to 2002, cuts that exceeded those in any other industry.[541] When the economy took a general downturn in 2002, WorldCom could no longer sustain what had been phenomenal revenue growth. However, WorldCom's phenomenal revenue growth had not been a function of business acumen. The burst bubble would bring collapses in other industries and regulatory scrutiny of revenues and accounting practices in all industries.

When Enron collapsed, the SEC, under pressure from Congress, state regulators, and investors, announced in March 2002 investigations into the financial statements of many companies. WorldCom and Qwest, two of the country's telecommunications giants, were among the SEC's targets.[542] The SEC listed the areas to be examined at WorldCom: charges against earnings, sales commissions, accounting policies for goodwill, loans to officers or directors, integration of computer systems between WorldCom and MCI, and the company's earnings estimates.[543] The SEC inquiry was referred to as a "cloud of uncertainty" over WorldCom.[544] The announcement of the SEC investigation caused a drop of $8.39 in WorldCom's share price, a 7 percent drop.[545] WorldCom had done so well for so long that many analysts expressed doubt that the SEC would find any improprieties. One noted, "I don't think they are going to find anything that they can prosecute. But you may have people try to rewrite the accounting rules so they are not so loose."[546]

At the time that the SEC announced its investigation, Cynthia Cooper, head of WorldCom's internal audit group, was just beginning her internal investigation of the rampant allegations and rumors of creative and not-so-creative accounting practices within the company.[547] With the pressure of the external regulatory investigation and WorldCom's voluntary disclosure that it had loaned Mr. Ebbers the $415 million, WorldCom came to be called "Worldron" by its own employees.[548]

The Acquisitions, Expenses, and Reserves

WorldCom's acquisition strategy required that there always be a bigger and better merger if the company's numbers were going to continue their double-digit growth.[549] If the mergers stopped, so also did the benefits of the accounting rules WorldCom was using to its advantage in booking the mergers.[550]

The pace of the mergers was so frenetic, and the accounting and financials so different because of interim mergers, that even the most sophisticated analysts had trouble keeping up with the books.[551] WorldCom also benefited from the market bubble of the dot-com era, one in which investors suspended intellectual inquiry about these phenomenal performers.[552]

---

[541]*Id.*

[542]Andrew Backover, "WorldCom, Qwest Face SEC Scrutiny," *USA Today,* March 12, 2002, p. B; and Andrew Backover, "'Cloud of Uncertainty' Rains on WorldCom," *USA Today,* March 13, 2002, p. 3B.

[543]Backover, "'Cloud of Uncertainty' Rains on WorldCom."

[544]*Id.*

[545]*Id.*

[546]*Id.*

[547]Susan Pulliam and Deborah Solomon, "How Three Unlikely Sleuths Discovered Fraud at WorldCom," *Wall Street Journal,* October 30, 2002, p. A1.

[548]Andrew Backover, "Questions on Ebbers Loans May Aid Probes," *USA Today,* November 6, 2002, p. 3B.

[549]Andy Kessler, "Bernie Bites the Dust," *Wall Street Journal,* May 1, 2002, p. A18.

[550]Shawn Tully, "Don't Get Burned," *Fortune,* February 18, 2002, pp. 89, 90.

[551]David Rynecki, "Articles of Faith: How Investors Got Taken in by the False Profits," *Fortune,* April 2, 2001, 76.

[552]*Id.* Securities Exchange Commissioner Cynthia Glassman described the market phenomenon in a speech she gave to the American Society of Corporate Secretaries on September 27, 2002; see http://www.sec.gov/news/speech. Accessed June 30, 2010.

Accounting Professor Mike Willenborg comments on this lax attitude about the confusion and inexplicable numbers during this market era: "You wonder where some of the skepticism was."[553] It almost seemed as if the more confusing the investment, the better the investment. As late as February 2002, analysts were reassuring themselves that all would be well with WorldCom, and one analyst was on the record as telling clients that the rumor swirls surrounding WorldCom would die down.[554] Indeed, the more confusing, the higher the rate of return and even greater the stock price.[555] WorldCom's stock reached $64.50 per share in June 1999, but was at $0.83 on June 26, 2002, following the announcement of the company's accounting reversals.[556]

WorldCom's fancy merger accounting was not unusual, nor is there any allegation that its methods violated accounting rules. The fancy merger accounting goes like this: a company acquires another (as WorldCom did sixty-five times) and is permitted to take a restructuring charge against earnings, the infamous "one-time charge."[557] The restructuring charge is a management determination, and there are professional disagreements among accountants, auditors, and managers as to how much these charges should be.

Scott Sullivan, the CFO of WorldCom, was able to employ reserves to keep World-Com going for two years after the merger with Sprint failed in 2000.[558] Because there were no further mergers, the company's phenomenal earnings record would have ended in 2000 had it not been for WorldCom's rather sizeable reserves.[559] One expert estimates the WorldCom's reserves could have been as high as $10 billion.[560]

The Capitalization of Ordinary Expenses

As WorldCom's executive team grappled with what it believed to be strategic issues that needed attention, Ms. Cooper and her team were working nights and weekends to determine how extensive the accounting issues were. By early June 2002, Ms. Cooper went to WorldCom's CFO, Scott Sullivan, with questions about the booking of operating expenses as capital expenses. When Mr. Sullivan was not as forthcoming as she expected, Ms. Cooper became more concerned. Mr. Sullivan was the most respected person in the company, but Ms. Cooper felt that he seemed hostile, and "when someone is hostile, my instinct is to find out."[561] Mr. Sullivan told Ms. Cooper that he was planning a "write down" in the second quarter if she could just hold off on the investigation.[562]

Ms. Cooper did not feel she could hold off any further on the investigation. She and her internal audit team uncovered layers of accounting issues. With the merger reserves quickly eaten away, Mr. Sullivan had to find a means for maintaining earnings levels, including the expected growth. Although the precise timing for the new accounting

[553]"'Going Concerns': Did Accountants Fail to Flag Problems at Dot-Com Casualties?" *Wall Street Journal*, February 8, 2001, pp. C1, C2.

[554]E. S. Browning, "Burst Bubbles Often Expose Cooked Books and Trigger SEC Probes, Bankruptcy Filings," *Wall Street Journal*, February 11, 2002, pp. C1, C4.

[555]Matt Krantz, "There's Just No Accounting for Teaching Earnings," *USA Today*, June 20, 2001, p. 1B.

[556]Robin Sidel, "Some Untimely Analyst Advice on WorldCom Raises Eyebrows," *Wall Street Journal*, June 27, 2002, p. A12.

[557]Lee Clifford, "Is Your Stock Addicted to Write-Offs?" *Fortune*, April 2, 2001, 166.

[558]Geoffrey Colvin, "Scandal Outrage, Part III," *Fortune*, October 28, 2002, 56.

[559]The reserves and some other creative accounting were often done without the executives in charge knowing that their division's accounting figures were being changed, because the changes were made from headquarters.

[560]Henny Sender, "Call Up the Reserves: WorldCom's Disclosure Is Warning for Investors," *Wall Street Journal*, July 3, 2002, pp. C1, C3.

[561]Amanda Ripley, "The Night Detective," *Time*, December 30, 2002–January 6, 2003, pp. 45, 47.

[562]Kurt Eichenwald and Simon Romero, "Inquiry Finds Effort at Delay at WorldCom," *New York Times*, July 4, 2002, p. C1.

strategy remains unclear,[563] most experts agree that at least by the first quarter of 2001, Mr. Sullivan and staff embarked on an accounting strategy that would keep WorldCom afloat but was not in compliance with GAAP.[564] According to his guilty plea and those filed by others working in WorldCom's financial areas, Mr. Sullivan and colleagues were taking ordinary expenses and booking them as capital expenditures so as to boost earnings.[565]

For example, in 2001, WorldCom had $3.1 billion in long-distance charges.[566] Long-distance wholesale charges are the expenses of a long-distance phone service retailer. The $3.1 billion should have been booked as an operating expense. However, $3.1 billion booked as an expense would have ended the earnings streak of WorldCom with a loss for 2001. So, Mr. Sullivan and his staff charged the $3.1 billion as a capital expense and planned to amortize this amount over ten years, a far lesser hit to earnings. The difference was that WorldCom, by capitalizing the operating expenses, showed net income of $1.38 billion for 2001, its previously announced target.[567]

However, ordinary and capital expenses require receipts and invoices for the property. The accounting lapse began unwinding when Gene Morse, a member of WorldCom's internal audit group, found $500 million in computer expenses, but could not find any documentation or invoices.[568] Mr. Sullivan had demanded that employees keep line costs at 42 percent; anything beyond that was just shifted to capital expenditures.[569] The result was that staff members spun numbers out of whole cloth, but costs were kept down even as profits were pumped artificially high. The initial disclosure of the $3.85 billion sent shock waves through the business world,[570] but before the year was out, that number would rise to $9 billion.[571]

Other Accounting Issues

An investigation and report commissioned by the WorldCom board and completed by former Attorney General Richard Thornburgh indicates that accounting issues extended into the reporting of revenues, not just expenses.[572] Mr. Thornburgh's report, partially excised at the time of its release in deference to the Justice Department investigation, reveals that there were eventually two sets of books prepared for David Myers and Mr. Sullivan by Buford Yates. Mr. Myers was the controller of WorldCom, and Mr. Yates was the head of general accounting. Mr. Myers also held a senior vice president's position at WorldCom and was well liked by the other officers and the staff. Described as a World-Com "cheerleader" by coworkers, Myers was referred to around the company as "Mr. GQ" because he dressed so fashionably.[573] Mr. Yates prepared two charts for Mr. Myers and Mr. Sullivan, with one chart offering the real revenues

---

[563]Disclosures near the end of 2002 put the date at 1999. Stephanie N. Meta, "WorldCom's Latest Headache," *Fortune,* November 25, 2002, 34, 35.

[564]"Big Lapse in Auditing Is Puzzling Some Accountants and Other Experts," *New York Times,* June 28, 2002, p. C4.

[565]Jared Sandberg, Deborah Solomon, and Rebecca Blumenstein, "Inside WorldCom's Unearthing of a Vast Accounting Scandal," *Wall Street Journal,* June 27, 2002, p. A1.

[566]*Id.*

[567]Sandberg, Solomon, and Harris, "WorldCom Investigations Shift Focus to Ousted CEO Ebbers," pp. A1, A8.

[568]Pulliam and Solomon, "How Three Unlikely Sleuths Discovered Fraud at WorldCom," p. A1.

[569]Sandberg, Solomon, and Blumenstein, "Inside WorldCom's Unearthing of a Vast Accounting Scandal," p. A8.

[570]WorldCom's initial $3.8 billion was six times the Enron restatement of earnings. Jared Sandberg, Deborah Solomon, and Rebecca Blumenstein, *Id.,* p. A1.

[571]Kurt Eichenwald and Seth Schiesel, "SEC Files New Charges on WorldCom," *New York Times,* November 6, 2002, pp. C1, C2.

[572]Sandberg and Pulliam, "Report by WorldCom Examiner Finds New Fraudulent Activities," p. A1.

[573]Jim Hopkins, "CFOs Join Their Bosses on the Hot Seat," *USA Today,* July 16, 2002, p. 3B.

and the other chart showing the revenue numbers WorldCom needed to post in order to make the numbers the company had given to Wall Street analysts.[574]

Because of WorldCom's international organization and worldwide offices, those at the corporate level were able to use computer access to these offices' financial records and thereby change the company's final financial statements. For example, Steven Brabbs, a WorldCom executive who was based in London and who was the director of international finance and control, raised the question of the accounting changes, which had affected his division, to David Myers. Mr. Brabbs discovered, after his division's books had been closed, that $33.6 million in line costs had been dropped from his books through a journal entry.[575] Unable to find support or explanation for the entry, Mr. Brabbs raised the question of documentation to Mr. Myers. When he had no response, he suggested that perhaps Arthur Andersen should be consulted to determine the propriety of the changes.[576] Mr. Brabbs also raised his concerns in a meeting with other internal financial executives at WorldCom. Following the meeting, Mr. Myers expressed anger at him for so doing.[577]

When the next quarter financials were due, Mr. Brabbs received instructions to make these transfers at his level rather than having them done by journal entry at the corporate level. Because he was still uncomfortable with the process, but could get no response from headquarters, he established an entity and placed the costs in there. He felt his solution at least kept his books for the international division clean.[578] He continued to raise the question about the accounting propriety, but the only response he ever received was that it was being done as a "Scott Sullivan directive."[579]

Congressional documents verify that many within the company who were concerned about the accounting changes approached Mr. Myers from as far back as July 2000, but he apparently disregarded them and went forward with the accounting changes anyway.[580] Rep. Billy Tauzin described the congressional findings related to the culture of fear and pressure as follows: "The bottom line is people inside this company were trying to tell its leaders you can't do what you want to do, and these leaders were telling them they had to."[581] When Steven Brabbs continued to raise his concerns about the accounting practices at WorldCom, and even with Arthur Andersen, he received an e-mail from David Myers ordering him to "not have any more meetings with AA for any reason."[582] While the accounting issues continued to concern employees, it would be some time before they would percolate to the board level.

It was clear that those involved were aware that they were violating accounting principles.[583] An e-mail sent on July 25, 2000, from Buford Yates, director of general accounting, to David Myers, controller, reflected his doubts about changing the operating expense of purchased wire capacity to a capital expense, "I might be narrow-minded, but

---

[574]Andrew Backover, "Trouble May Have Started in November 2000," *USA Today,* July 1, 2002, p. 3A.

[575]Kurt Eichenwald, "Auditing Woes at WorldCom Were Noted Two Years Ago," *New York Times,* July 15, 2002, pp. C1, C9.

[576]*Id.,* p. C9.

[577]*Id.*

[578]*Id.*

[579]*Id.*

[580]*Id.*

[581]Jayne O'Donnell and Andrew Backover, "WorldCom's Bad Math May Date Back to 1999," *USA Today,* July 16, 2002, p. 1B.

[582]Jessica Sommar, "E-Mail Blackmail: WorldCom Memo Threatened Conscience-Stricken Exec," *New York Post,* August 27, 2002, p. 27.

[583]A 2001 survey of CFOs indicated that 17 percent of CFOs at public corporations feel pressure from their CEOs to misrepresent financial results. Hopkins, "CFOs Join Their Bosses on the Hot Seat," p. 3B.

I can't see a logical path for capitalizing excess capacity."[584] Mr. Yates sent an e-mail to Scott Sullivan that read, "David and I have reviewed and discussed your logic of capitalizing excess capacity and can find no support within the current accounting guidelines that would allow for this accounting treatment."[585] Mr. Myers admitted to investigators that "this approach had no basis in accounting principles."[586] Nonetheless, the change from operating expenses to capitalization went forward, with Betty Vinson and Troy Normand, employees in accounting, making the adjustments in the books per orders from Mr. Myers.[587] Ms. Vinson and Mr. Normand were both fired, and Mr. Yates resigned shortly after he was indicted.

Before making the decision on the accounting changes, neither Mr. Myers nor Mr. Sullivan consulted with WorldCom's outside auditor, Arthur Andersen.[588] The criminal complaint in Mr. Myers's case, and the one to which he entered a guilty plea, included the following description of the role of financial pressures in their decisions and accounting practices: "Sullivan and Myers decided to work backward, picking the earnings numbers that they knew the analysts expected to see, and then forcing WorldCom's financials to match those numbers."[589]

Mr. Sullivan had assumed the helm of WorldCom's finances as CFO in 1994, at age thirty-two.[590] The joke around the WorldCom offices when Mr. Sullivan assumed the CFO slot was that he was "barely shaving."[591] Arriving at WorldCom in 1992 through its merger with Advanced Telecommunications, where he had been since 1987, Mr. Sullivan and Mr. Ebbers became inseparable in the mergers and deals they put together over the next eight years.[592] He earned the nickname *whiz kid,* and whereas Mr. Ebbers was the showman for WorldCom, Mr. Sullivan was the detail person. Mr. Ebbers frequently answered questions from analysts and others with "We'll have to ask Scott."[593]

Mr. Ebbers praised Mr. Sullivan publicly and saw to it that he was well compensated for his efforts.[594] Mr. Ebbers rewarded Mr. Sullivan with both compensation and titles. In addition to his role as CFO, he served as the secretary for the board.[595] When Mr. Sullivan was appointed to the WorldCom board at age thirty-four, in 1996, the company press release included this quote from Mr. Ebbers: "Over the years WorldCom, Inc. has benefited immensely from the outstanding array of talent and business acumen of our Board of Directors, and Scott Sullivan will be an excellent addition to that group.

[584]Kevin Maney, Andrew Backover, and Paul Davidson, "Prosecutors Target World Com's Ex-CFO," *USA Today,* August 29, 2002, pp. 1B, 2B.

[585]*Id.,* p. 2B.

[586]Kurt Eichenwald, "2 Ex-Officials at WorldCom Are Charged in Huge Fraud," *New York Times,* August 2, 2002, pp. A1, C5.

[587]Kevin Maney, Andrew Backover, and Paul Davidson, "Prosecutors Target WorldCom's Ex-CFO," *USA Today,* August 29, 2002, pp. 1B, 2B. See also Simon Romero and Jonathan D. Glater, "Wider WorldCom Case Is Called Likely," *New York Times,* September 5, 2002, p. C9, for background given on titles of employees noted.

[588]Eichenwald, "2 Ex-Officials at WorldCom Are Charged in Huge Fraud," p. C5.

[589]*Id.* Yochi J. Dreazen, Shawn Young, and Carrick Mollenkamp, "WorldCom Probers Say Sullivan Implicates Ebbers," *Wall Street Journal,* July 12, 2002, p. A3; and Andrew Backover and Paul Davidson, "WorldCom Grilling Turns Up No Definitive Answers," *USA Today,* July 9, 2002, pp. 1B, 2B.

[590]Shawn Young and Evan Perez, "Wall Street Thought Highly of WorldCom's Finance Chief," *Wall Street Journal,* June 27, 2002, pp. B1, B3.

[591]*Id.*

[592]Barnaby J. Feder and David Leonhardt, "From Low Profile to No Profile," *New York Times,* June 27, 2002, p. C1.

[593]*Id.*

[594]*Id.,* p. C6. Sullivan still lives with his wife, who has chronic health problems, in a home in Florida that is valued at $178,000, but they were in the process of constructing a home in the Boca Raton, Florida, area at a cost estimated to be $10 million, with the lot costing $2.45 million. Because of the unlimited homestead exemption in Florida, many financially troubled executives have retained significant assets while still discharging debts in bankruptcy.

[595]WorldCom, WorldCom Proxy Statement, April 22, 2002, http://www.sec.gov. Accessed June 30, 2010.

He brings to the table a proven background of expertise and dedication to the Company."[596]

According to WorldCom proxy statements, Mr. Sullivan's compensation was as follows: 1997, $500,000 salary and $3.5 million bonus; 1998, $500,000 salary and $2 million bonus; 1999, $600,000 salary and $2.76 million bonus; 2000, $700,000 salary and $10 million bonus; and for 2001, Mr. Sullivan earned a salary of $700,000 and a bonus of $10 million. These figures do not include the stock options, which for the years from 1997 to 2001 totaled $1.5 million, $900,000, $900,000, $619,140, and $928,710, respectively.[597]

Congressional documents indicate that both Mr. Myers and Mr. Sullivan met with other executives indicating the need to "do whatever necessary to get Telco/Margins back in line."[598] Mr. Myers has subsequently indicated that once they started down the road, it was tough to stop.[599]

Later discussions between Mr. Myers and the head of WorldCom's internal audit group, Cynthia Cooper, reflect that he understood "there were no specific accounting pronouncements" that would justify the changes.[600] When Ms. Cooper raised the question to Mr. Myers about how the changes could be explained to the SEC, Mr. Myers, reflecting the view that it was a temporary change to see the company through until the financial picture changed, said that "he had hoped it would not have to be explained."[601]

Corporate Governance at WorldCom

The board at WorldCom was often referred to as "Bernie's Board."[602] Carl Aycock had been a member of the board since 1983 when the original company was founded.[603] Max Bobbitt and Francesco Galesi, who were friends of Mr. Ebbers, joined the board in 1992.[604] And one board member, Stiles A. Kellett Jr., an original board member and friend of Mr. Ebbers from the early motel-meeting days, resigned in October 2002 after revelations about his extensive use of the company jet.[605] All of the directors became millionaires after the days of their humble beginnings, when the board meetings were held at the Western Sizzlin' Steakhouse in Hattiesburg, Mississippi.[606] A former board member, Mike Lewis, said few board members would disagree with Mr. Ebbers: "Rule No. 1: Don't bet against Bernie. Rule No. 2: See Rule No. 1."[607]

Although board members were entitled to WorldCom or MCI stock in lieu of fees and were awarded options each year, their annual retainer was $35,000 per year, with $750 for committee meetings attended on the same day as the board meetings and

[596]"WorldCom, Inc. Appoints New Board Member," press release, March 12, 1996. http://www.worldcom.com. Accessed January 22, 2003.

[597]See proxy statements, 14-A, at http://www.sec.gov under WorldCom for 1997–2001.

[598]O'Donnell and Backover, "WorldCom's Bad Math May Date Back to 1999," p. 1B.

[599]Id.

[600]Yochi J. Dreazen and Deborah Solomon, "WorldCom Aide Conceded Flaws," *Wall Street Journal*, July 16, 2002, p. A3.

[601]Id.

[602]Jared Sandberg and Joann S. Lublin, "An Already Tarnished Board also Faces Tough Questions over Accounting Fiasco," *Wall Street Journal*, June 28, 2002, p. A3.

[603]Seth Schiebel, "Most of Board at WorldCom Resign Post," *New York Times*, December 18, 2002, p. C7.

[604]Id.

[605]Susan Pulliam, Jared Sandberg and Deborah Solomon, "WorldCom Board Will Consider Rescinding Ebbers's Severance," *Wall Street Journal*, September 10, 2002, p. A1.

[606]Jared Sandberg, "Six Directors Quit as WorldCom Breaks with Past," *Wall Street Journal*, December 18, 2002, p. A3.

[607]Sandberg and Lublin, "An Already Tarnished Board also Faces Tough Questions over Accounting Fiasco," p. A3

$1,000 for other committee meetings.[608] But this was a generous board when it came to Mr. Ebbers. Even upon Mr. Ebbers's departure, with significant loans due and owing, the board gave Mr. Ebbers a severance package that included $1.5 million per year for the rest of his life, thirty hours of use of the company jet, full medical and life insurance coverage, and the possibility of consulting fees beyond a minimum amount required under the terms of the package.[609]

The WorldCom board was not an active or curious one. Despite experiencing a lawsuit in which employees with specific knowledge about the company's accounting practices filed affidavits, the board made no further inquiries. In fact, the company dismissed the employees and ignored their affidavits when a judge dismissed the class-action suit.[610] The board was not aware of $75 million in loans to Mr. Ebbers or a $100 million loan guarantee for Mr. Ebbers's personal loans until two months after the loans and guarantees had been signed for him. Two board meetings went by after the loan approvals before the board was informed and approval given. Further, the board's approval came without any request for advice from WorldCom's general counsel.[611]

What Went Wrong: Management and Operations

The creative and not-so-creative accounting at WorldCom may have been a symptom, and not the problem. Mr. Ebbers made no secret of the fact that he was often bored by business details, operations, and fundamentals. He far preferred the art of the deal.[612] When Mr. Ebbers did get involved in operations, his involvement was more like that of an entrepreneur or small businessperson trying to micromanage details. For example, when Mr. Ebbers visited his dealerships in Mississippi, he usually went in with the idea of cutting costs and would do so by focusing on things such as allotting cell phones to sales personnel, eliminating the water cooler, and even requiring that the heating bills be reduced.[613] As a result, WorldCom could hardly be said to have a crackerjack management team.[614] It had an abysmal record on receivables, being lax in bringing in cash from regular billings.[615] One analyst described the operations side of WorldCom as follows: "WorldCom wasn't operated at all, it was just on auto pilot, using bubble gum and Band-Aids as solutions to its problems."[616]

The constant mergers threw the billing system for WorldCom customers into turmoil.[617] WorldCom had fifty-five different billing systems and the litigation from customers to show that the billing systems were not studies in accuracy.[618] MCI customers would find their service disconnected for nonpayment because the WorldCom side,

---

[608]http://www.sec.gov; and WorldCom proxy for 2001, p. 6. Accessed June 30, 2010.

[609]*Id.*

[610]Neil Weinberg, "WorldCom's Board Alerted to Fraud in 2001," *Forbes*, August 12, 2002, p. 56. See also Kurt Eichenwald, "Auditing Woes at WorldCom Were Noted Two Years Ago," *New York Times*, July 15, 2002, p. C1.

[611]Andrew Backover, "Questions on Ebbers Loans May Aid Probes," *USA Today*, November 6, 2002, p. 3B.

[612]Feder, "An Abrupt Departure Is Seen as a Harbinger," pp. C1, C2; and Eichenwald, "For WorldCom, Acquisitions Were behind Its Rise and Fall," p. A1.

[613]Jayne O'Donnell and Andrew Backover, "Ebbers' High-Risk Act Came Crashing Down on Him," *USA Today*, December 12, 2002, pp. 1B, 2B.

[614]Feder, "An Abrupt Departure Is Seen as a Harbinger," pp. C1, C2.

[615]Marcy Gordon, "WorldCom CEO Blames Former Execs for Woes," *The Tribune*, from the Associated Press, July 2, 2002, p. B1.

[616]Eichenwald, "For WorldCom, Acquisitions Were behind Its Rise and Fall," p. A1.

[617]One analyst noted that Mr. Ebbers may not have even seen the importance of operations: "Bernie viewed this as a series of financial-engineering maneuvers and never truly understood the business that he was in"; *Id.*, p. C2.

[618]The CEO of one WorldCom customer said, "They can't even tell you what they're owed." Scott Woolley, "Bernie at Bay," *Fortune*, April 15, 2002, p. 63.

which did the billing, never got the payments, which went to the MCI side.[619] Even when the customer's account was located, there was a great deal of foot-dragging by WorldCom in terms of both bill payment and acknowledgment of customer corrections.[620] Cherry Communications, a large customer of WorldCom, filed suit against WorldCom for $100 million in "false and questionable" bills from 1992 to 1996.[621] Cherry went into Chapter 11 bankruptcy owing WorldCom $200 million in uncollectable revenues, less the $100 million in disputes spread across the fifty-five billing systems. WorldCom did get stock in a reorganized Cherry Communications—a typical result, because WorldCom extended credit to small companies that were high credit risks. On average, two to three of World-Com's commercial customers filed for bankruptcy during any given quarter.[622]

One part of the SEC investigation of WorldCom focused on whether WorldCom capitalized on the chaotic billing system to boost revenues. One technique investigated was whether services sold to one customer were then booked twice as revenues in different divisions, all at different rates and under multiple billing systems.[623] In fact, three stellar performers at WorldCom were fired because they had used the fact that revenues could often be booked twice in the confusing systems to pump up the commission figures for their sales teams. The three simply listed sales from other divisions for their employees and were able to boost commissions substantially.[624] In September 2000, WorldCom did take a write-down of $685 million for uncollectable revenues.[625]

The rapidity of the mergers left employees and managers with the day-to-day work of trying to integrate the acquired company's technology with WorldCom's in order to create a seamless communications network. That seamless network never happened because technical problems and employees consumed with constant troubleshooting meant that customer service suffered and the overall systemic issues could not be addressed.[626]

The problems were never solved because of one additional management issue, and that was the constant merger of executives from other companies with WorldCom managers.[627] One former WorldCom employee summarized the company atmosphere: "Nobody had time to adjust. There was a [reorganization] every couple of months, so people didn't know who they were supposed to be reporting to or what they were supposed to be working on."[628] MCI had the experience, but WorldCom had control. No one took the lead in an integration effort, and the result was that WorldCom was saddled with excess and expensive capacity from improperly integrated dual systems. Power struggles apparently contributed to a type of nepotism in which Mississippi-based executives were awarded the vice president positions in charge of operations and billing, and they lacked the experience and expertise that was necessary to fix the problems created by the mergers and create an effective billing system and integrated technology.

[619]Eichenwald, "For WorldCom, Acquisitions Were behind Its Rise and Fall," p. A1.

[620]Kevin Maney, "WorldCom Unraveled as Top Execs' Unity Crumbled," *USA Today*, June 28, 2002, pp. 1B, 2B.

[621]*Id.*

[622]Scott Woolley, "Bernie at Bay," *Fortune*, April 15, 2002, p. 64.

[623]*Id.*

[624]Yochi J. Dreazen, "WorldCom Suspends Executives in Scandal over Order Booking," *Wall Street Journal*, February 15, 2002, p. A3.

[625]Eichenwald, "For WorldCom, Acquisitions Were behind Its Rise and Fall," p. A1.

[626]*Id.*

[627]Maney, "WorldCom Unraveled as Top Execs' Unity Unraveled," pp. 1B, 2B.

[628]Eichenwald, "For WorldCom, Acquisitions Were behind Its Rise and Fall," p. A1.

WorldCom Bubble Bursts

While the operations in the company became more and more fractured, the internal auditors' work continued. However, they were forced to work secretly.[629] The internal auditors worked at night to avoid detection and, at one point, concerned that their work might be sabotaged, purchased a CD-ROM burner privately and began recording the data they were gathering and storing the CDs elsewhere.[630] Indeed, so chilly was their reception when they met with Mr. Sullivan that Ms. Cooper arranged to meet with Max Bobbitt, the head of the board's audit committee, in secret fashion at a local Hampton Inn so that there would be no repercussions for her or her staff as they completed their work.[631] Ms. Cooper was forced to go to the board and the audit committee because she was unable to secure an adequate explanation from Mr. Sullivan, who, as noted earlier, had even asked her to delay her audit.

At one point, while Ms. Cooper's internal audit team was conducting its investigation, Mr. Sullivan confronted one of her auditors, Gene Morse, in the cafeteria. During his five years at WorldCom, he had only spoken to Mr. Sullivan twice. Mr. Sullivan asked what he was working on, and Mr. Morse responded with information about another project, "International capital expenditures," which seemed to satisfy Mr. Sullivan.[632]

Mr. Sullivan was given an opportunity to respond at that board meeting, but could offer no explanation other than his belief that the expenses were correctly booked. He refused to resign and defended his accounting practices until that final meeting, when he was fired that day by the board.[633] David Myers, the controller for the company, resigned the following day.[634] Following sufficient review by Ms. Cooper and the company's new auditor, KPMG, WorldCom announced on June 25, 2002, that it had overstated cash flow by $3.9 billion for 2001 and the first quarter of 2002 by booking ordinary expenses as capital expenditures.[635] WorldCom's shares dropped 76 percent, to 20 cents per share.[636] Trading was halted for three sessions, and when it was reopened, more than 1.5 billion shares of WorldCom were dumped on the market, sending the share price down from 20 cents to 6 cents in what was then the highest-volume selling frenzy in the history of the market. It was the first time in the history of the market that more than 1 billion shares had ever been traded in one day. The pace exceeded the previous record of 671 million shares sold in one day, a record WorldCom held only for a few days until this trading reopened. WorldCom was delisted from the NASDAQ on July 5, 2002.[637]

WorldCom's bonds dropped from 79 cents just before the announcement of the accounting irregularities to 13 cents just following the announcement.[638] There was a

---

[629]Pulliam and Solomon, "How Three Unlikely Sleuths Discovered Fraud at WorldCom," pp. A1, A6.

[630]Ripley, "The Night Detective," pp. 45, 47.

[631]There is a certain irony here. WorldCom was hatched in a low-priced motel, and its unraveling began at a similar location.

[632]Pulliam and Solomon, "How Three Unlikely Sleuths Discovered Fraud at WorldCom," pp. A1, A6.

[633]Ripley, "The Night Detective," p. 49.

[634]*Id.*

[635]Andrew Backover, Thor Valdmanis, and Matt Krantz, "WorldCom Finds Accounting Fraud," *USA Today*, June 26, 2002, p. 1B.

[636]*Id.* This restatement remained the largest in history, more than doubling the previous record set by Rite-Aid of $1.6 billion, until Parmalat collapsed. See http://www.bankruptcydata.com.

[637]Matt Krantz, "Investors Dump WorldCom Stock at Record Pace," *USA Today*, July 3, 2002, p. 3B; and WorldCom, "Press Releases, 2001," July 29, 2002, http://www.worldcom.com. These press releases may or may not be available at http://www.mci.com. However, they were researched when the WorldCom site was functioning.

[638]Henny Sender and Carrick Mollenkamp, "WorldCom Bondholders Study Plan," *Wall Street Journal*, July 5, 2002, p. A6.

flurry of subpoenas from Congress for the officers of the company.[639] The officers all took the Fifth Amendment, and $2 billion in federal contracts held by WorldCom were under review by the General Services Administration because federal regulations prohibit federal agencies from doing business with companies under investigation for financial improprieties.[640]

The SEC filed fraud charges within three days and asked for an explanation from WorldCom about exactly what had been done in its accounting.[641] On August 8, 2002, WorldCom announced that it had found an additional $3.3 billion in earnings misstatements, from 2000, with portions from 1999.[642] WorldCom declared bankruptcy on July 22, 2002, the largest bankruptcy in the history of the United States.[643]

Shortly after WorldCom filed for bankruptcy, the federal government indicted Scott Sullivan, David Myers, Betty Vinson, Buford Yates, Troy Normand, and a host of other characters involved in developing the company's financial reports.[644] Mr. Ebbers was not indicted until after Mr. Sullivan entered a guilty plea.[645]

Mr. Sullivan was indicted on federal charges of fraud and conspiracy on August 1, 2002.[646] Mr. Myers entered a guilty plea to three felony counts of fraud on September 26, 2002.[647] Mr. Yates initially entered a not guilty plea.[648] However, just one month later, Mr. Yates entered a guilty plea to securities fraud and conspiracy and agreed to cooperate with the Justice Department.[649] Ms. Vinson and Mr. Normand also entered guilty pleas to fraud and conspiracy just three days after Mr. Yates' plea.[650] When Ms. Vinson testified she was asked why she made the accounting entries that she knew were wrong, she said she considered quitting, but, as the primary breadwinner in her household, she succumbed: "I felt like if I didn't make the entries, I wouldn't be working there."[651] Ms. Vinson and Troy Normand raised their concerns to Mr. Sullivan, but he was able to convince them to go along.[652] His colorful analogy was that WorldCom was akin to an aircraft carrier. He had some planes out there that he needed to land on deck before they came clean on the creative interpretations.[653] When Betty Vinson was asked how she

---

[639]Andrew Backover and Thor Valdmanis, "WorldCom Scandal Brings Subpoenas, Condemnation," *USA Today*, June 28, 2002, p. 1A; and Michael Schroder, Jerry Markon, Tom Hamburger, and Greg Hitt, "Congress Begins WorldCom Investigation," *Wall Street Journal*, June 28, 2002, p. A3.

[640]Yochi J. Dreazen, "WorldCom's Federal Contracts May Be Vital," *Wall Street Journal*, July 10, 2002, p. C4. For information on the Fifth Amendment, see Andrew Backover and Paul Davidson, "WorldCom Grilling Turns Up No Definitive Answers," *USA Today*, July 9, 2002, p. 1B.

[641]Andrew Backover and Thor Valdmanis, "WorldCom Report Will Face Scrutiny," *USA Today*, July 1, 2002, p. 1B.

[642]Kevin Maney and Thor Valdmanis, "WorldCom Reveals $3.3B More in Discrepancies," *USA Today*, August 9, 2002, p. 1B.

[643]Simon Romero and Riva D. Atlas, "WorldCom Files for Bankruptcy; Largest U.S. Case," *New York Times*, July 22, 2002, p. A1; and Kevin Maney and Andrew Backover, "WorldCom's Bomb," *USA Today*, July 22, 2002, pp. 1B, 2B.

[644]Kurt Eichenwald, "2 Ex-Officials at WorldCom Are Charged in Huge Fraud," *New York Times*, August 2, 2002, p. A1. See also Deborah Solomon and Susan Pulliam, "U.S., Pushing WorldCom Case, Indicts Ex-CFO and His Aide," *Wall Street Journal*, August 29, 2002, p. A1.

[645]Simon Romero and Jonathan D. Glater, "Wider WorldCom Case Is Called Likely," *New York Times*, September 5, 2002, p. C9.

[646]Eichenwald, "2 Ex-Officials at WorldCom Are Charged in Huge Fraud," p. A1.

[647]Deborah Solomon, "WorldCom's Ex-Controller Pleads Guilty to Fraud," *Wall Street Journal*, September 27, 2002, p. A3.

[648]Jerry Markon, "WorldCom's Yates Pleads Guilty," *Wall Street Journal*, October 8, 2002, p. A3.

[649]*Id.*

[650]"2 Ex-Officials of WorldCom Plead Guilty," *New York Times*, October 11, 2002, p. C10.

[651]Susan Pulliam, "A Staffer Ordered to Commit Fraud Balked, Then Caved," *Wall Street Journal*, June 23, 2003, pp. A1, at A6; and "Ex-WorldCom Accountant Gets Prison Term," *New York Times*, August 6, 2005, p. B13.

[652]See Simon Romero and Jonathan D. Glater, "Wider WorldCom Case Is Called Likely," *New York Times*, September 5, 2002, p. C9, for background and titles of employees.

[653]Pulliam, "A Staffer Ordered to Commit Fraud Balked," pp. A1, at A6.

decided which accounts she would change, her response in court was dramatic and sadly illegal: "I just really pulled some out of the air. I used the spreadsheets."[654] Troy Normand got three years of probation. Betty Vinson was sentenced to five months in jail, and Yates and Myers received one-year-and-a-day sentences.[655] Mr. Sullivan was sentenced to five years.

Before the year ended, most of the WorldCom board had resigned, Michael D. Capellas, the former CEO of Compaq Computers, replaced John Sidgmore, and there was another revision of WorldCom revenues, bringing the total revisions to $9 billion.[656] However, WorldCom did reach a settlement with the SEC on the $9 billion accounting problems. The civil fraud suit settlement did not admit any wrongdoing, and required the payment of fines totaling $500 million.[657] The consent decree required WorldCom, now MCI, to submit to oversight by a type of probation officer over the company's activities and gave the SEC discretion in terms of the amount of fines that could be assessed in the future.[658] On December 9, 2002, WorldCom ran full-page ads in the country's major newspapers with the following message: "We're changing management. We're changing business practices. We're changing WorldCom."[659]

In what was an unprecedented move, ten of WorldCom's former directors agreed to personally pay restitution to shareholders as part of the settlement of the lawsuit. The ten directors paid a total of $18 million to the shareholders in order to be released from liability in the suit.[660] The funds had to be paid from their own assets; they were not permitted to use insurance funds to pay the settlement. Mr. Ebbers was tried and convicted on multiple counts of conspiracy and fraud in March 2005. In exchange for a sentence of five years, Scott Sullivan testified against his former boss. He testified on his own behalf as part of the defense. There was uniform agreement among trial lawyers, experts, and, apparently, the jury that he did not help his case. Mr. Ebbers appealed his case to the federal court of appeals, but the verdict was affirmed.[661]

In July 2005, Mr. Ebbers was sentenced to twenty-five years in prison. In addition, Ebbers had to turn over all of his assets as part of his fine. A federal marshal who was responsible for collecting the property indicated that the government took between $35 and $40 million in assets and left Mr. and Mrs. Ebbers with the furniture in their home and their silverware. They will sell their home and all of Mr. Ebbers's personal investments. Mrs. Ebbers was allowed to retain $50,000 as a means for transitioning to self-support.

Mr. Ebbers was sentenced following a ninety-minute hearing. The judge, in sentencing Ebbers, said,

> *Mr. Ebbers was the instigator in this fraud. Mr. Ebbers's statements deprived investors of their money. They might have made different decisions had they known the truth.*[662]

---

[654]"Ex-WorldCom Accountant Gets Prison Term," p. B13.

[655]Greg Farrell, "Final WorldCom Sentence Due Today," *USA Today*, August 11, 2005, p. 1B.

[656]Seth Schiesel, "WorldCom Sees More Revisions of Its Figures," *New York Times*, November 11, 2002, p. C1; Jared Sandberg, "Six Directors Quit as WorldCom Breaks with Past," *New York Times*, December 18, 2002, p. A3; Andrew Backover and Kevin Maney, "WorldCom to Replace Sidgmore," *USA Today*, September 11, 2002, p. 1B; and Stephanie N. Mehta, "Can Mike Save WorldCom?" *Fortune*, December 9, 2002, p. 163.

[657]Seth Schiesel and Simon Romero, "WorldCom Strikes a Deal with S.E.C.," *New York Times*, November 27, 2002, p. C1.

[658]Jon Swartz, "WorldCom Settles Big Issues with SEC," *USA Today*, November 27, 2002, p. 1B; and *SEC v WorldCom, Inc.*, 2002 WL 31760246 (S.D.N.Y. 2002).

[659]*New York Times*, December 9, 2002, p. C3; and *USA Today*, December 11, 2002, p. 4A.

[660]Gretchen Morgenson, "10 Ex-Directors from WorldCom to Pay Millions," *New York Times*, January 6, 2005, p. A1.

[661]*Ebbers v* U.S., 453 F.3d 110 (2nd Cir. 2006). cert. den.127 S.Ct. 1483 (2007).

[662]Ken Belson, "WorldCom Head Is Given 25 years for Huge Fraud," *New York Times*, July 14, 2005, p. A1.

I recognize that this sentence is likely to be a life sentence. But I find a sentence of anything less would not reflect the seriousness of this crime.[663]

Mr. Ebbers did not speak on his own behalf at the hearing, but he had submitted evidence of a heart condition as well as 169 letters from friends and colleagues. Interestingly, Mr. Ebbers is the one executive among all those indicted who was not selling his stock as the market and company collapsed. He retained all of his stock and saw his $1 billion in WorldCom holdings all but disappear as the stock dropped from a high of $64 to about $0.10. However, the judge found that neither the letters nor his stock retention was compelling and that Ebbers's heart condition was not serious. She did agree to let Ebbers serve his time in a prison near his home in Mississippi.

The maximum sentence was thirty years. Mr. Ebbers can shave off 10 percent for good behavior. The earliest he could be released is 2027, when he turns eighty-five (Mr. Ebbers was sixty-three at the time of his sentencing).

Mr. Ebbers's sentence is the longest of any for the so-called bubble crimes. Jeffrey Skilling received 24.4 years. Timothy Rigas of Adelphia was sentenced to twenty years, and his father, John, to fifteen.

Discussion Questions

1. Consider the following statement by a government official. Securities Exchange Commissioner Cynthia Glassman included the following in a speech she gave to the American Society of Corporate Secretaries on September 27, 2002:

   [T]he distribution of securities by companies that had not made a previous public offering reached the highest level in history. This activity in new issues took place in a climate of general optimism and speculative interest. The public eagerly sought stocks of companies in certain "glamour" industries, especially the electronics industry, in the expectation that they would rise to a substantial premium—an expectation that was often fulfilled. Within a few days or even hours after the initial distribution, these so-called hot issues would be traded at premiums of as much as 300 percent above the original offering price. In many cases the price of a "hot" issue later fell to a fraction of its original offering price.

   What impact do you think the psychology of the market had on allowing WorldCom, Mr. Ebbers, and others to engage in creative accounting? Is this "everyone does it"?

2. Consider the following:

   This phenomenon of confusion ruling in a bullish market is not unique to the 1990s stock market. Following the 1929 stock market crash, one of the biggest collapses, and a shocker to the investment world, was the bankruptcy of Middle West Utilities. The company was run by Samuel Insull according to the prevailing, and confusing, structure of the time, "elaborate webs of holding companies, each helping hide the others' financial weaknesses, an artifice strangely similar to what Enron did with its partnerships."[664] Following the bubble burst in the early 1970s, accounting firm Peat Marwick, Mitchell was censured for its failure to conduct proper audits of five companies that crashed after PMM had given the firms clean and ongoing entity opinions. After the October 1987 crash, Drexel, Burnham & Lambert, Michael Milken's junk bond firm, collapsed along with a host of other companies and the savings and loan industry.[665]

   What does this market history tell you about WorldCom? How could the employees in WorldCom who went along benefit from this

---

[663]Dionne Searcey, Shawn Young, and Kara Scannell, "Ebbers Is Sentenced to 25 Years for $11 Billion WorldCom Fraud," *Wall Street Journal*, July 14, 2005, pp. A1, A8.

[664]E. S. Browning, "Burst Bubbles Often Expose Cooked Books and Trigger SEC Probes, Bankruptcy Filings," *Wall Street Journal*, February 11, 2002, pp. C1, C4.

[665]*Id.*

information? What fears did these employees have?

3. Bill Parish, investment manager for Parish & Co., explained the collapse of Enron, WorldCom, and others with this insight: "There's massive corruption of the system. Earnings are grossly overstated."[666] Accounting Professor Brent Trueman at the University of California, Berkeley, added, "Reported numbers may not reflect the true income from operations." The phenomenon accompanies bubbles. "It is absolutely what almost invariably happens after every bubble. You should expect them [bankruptcies, scandals, and accounting disclosures], but that doesn't mean that people who haven't been through it before aren't going to be surprised. The bigger the binge, the longer and more severe the hangover."[667]

Is he right? Is fraud inevitable in a fast-paced market? Are these just natural market corrections? Is this "everyone does it"?

4. WorldCom was eerily meeting its earnings targets precisely. One analyst did, however, notice that WorldCom was making its targets for several quarters in a row within fractions of cents. "When you see that they're making it by one one-hundredth of a penny you know the odds of that happening twice in a row are very slim. It indicates they're willing to stretch to make the quarter."[668] Are investors to blame for relying on the precise numbers and predictions? Shouldn't they have acted with greater skepticism?

5. Mr. Ebbers's conduct shows that he still believes he has done nothing wrong. At church services in Mississippi immediately following the revelation of the WorldCom accounting impropriety, Mr. Ebbers arrived as usual to teach his Sunday school class and attend services. He addressed the congregation, "I just want you to know you aren't going to church with a crook. This has been a strange week at best. . . . On Tuesday I received a call telling me what was happening at WorldCom. I don't know what the situation is with all that has been reported. I don't know what all is going to happen or what mistakes have been made. . . . No one will find me to have knowingly committed fraud. More than anything else, I hope that my witness for Jesus Christ [will not be jeopardized]." The congregation gave Mr. Ebbers a standing ovation.[669] Mr. Ebbers continues to teach Sunday school each Sunday at 9:15 A.M., and then stays for the ninety-minute service held afterward.[670] What relationship do religious views and affiliations play in business ethics?

6. What did Scott Sullivan miss in making his analysis to capitalize ordinary expenses? What skills you learned in Units 1 and 2 might have helped him see the decision and the impact of his decision differently? Why did he not listen to employees and block questions?

7. Even when the first multi-billion-dollar restatement came, many near Clinton, Mississippi, appeared to be more in mourning than angry. One employee, sharing the shock with bar patrons at Bravo Italian Restaurant & Bar, said, "People are taking it with exceptional grace. In my experience with MCI, I have never worked for a better company."[671] Others, such as Bernie's minister, give him the benefit of the doubt, concluding that he might not have known about the distortion of the numbers: "We've kind of held judgment until we know the entire story and whether he had knowledge."[672]

Evaluate the effect of these companies on the home towns in which they operate. What role do hubris and the fear of letting the locals down play in situations such as WorldCom's?

[666]Matt Krantz, "There's Just No Accounting for Teaching Earnings," *USA Today*, June 20, 2001, p. 1B.

[667]E. S. Browning, "Burst Bubbles Often Expose Cooked Books and Trigger SEC Probes, Bankruptcy Filings," *Wall Street Journal*, February 11, 2002, pp. C1, C4.

[668]Jared Sandberg, Deborah Solomon, and Nicole Harris, "WorldCom Investigations Shift Focus to Ousted CEO Ebbers," *Wall Street Journal*, July 1, 2002, pp. A1, A8.

[669]*Id.*, p. A1.

[670]Jayne O'Donnell, "Ebbers Acts as if Nothing Is Amiss," *USA Today*, September 19, 2002, pp. 1B, 2B.

[671]Kelly Greene and Rick Brooks, "WorldCom Staff Now Are Saying 'Just Like Enron,'" *Wall Street Journal*, June 27, 2002, p. A9.

[672]O'Donnell, "Ebbers Acts as if Nothing Is Amiss," pp. 1B, 2B.

Compare & Contrast

1. At his sentencing, Scott Sullivan told the federal judge of his diabetic wife's need for care and of their four-year-old daughter and said, "Every day I regret what happened at WorldCom. I am sorry for the hurt caused by my cowardly decisions."[673] Scott Sullivan stated at his sentencing hearing, "I chose the wrong road, and in the face of intense pressure I turned away from the truth."[674] He added, "It was a misguided attempt to save the company."[675]

   What is the difference between Sullivan at the sentencing hearing and Sullivan at WorldCom making the accounting decisions? What elements for your credo can you find in this tale?

2. One analyst noted, "You always had this question about whether WorldCom was a house of cards. Everything was pro-forma. It drove us nuts."[676] Yet another analyst described the WorldCom phenomenon as "a game of chicken, where you get as close as possible to the end before getting out. We all knew WorldCom couldn't go on forever."[677] Competitors were flummoxed by the company's performance. Recall the observations of William T. Esrey, the CEO of Sprint, and the replacement of Michael G. Keith, the head of AT&T's business service division, for his failure to reach WorldCom heights. During this time, Sprint and AT&T were considered "dogs," whereas WorldCom was the darling of Wall Street. Howard Anderson of the Yankee Group, a research firm in Boston, said, "Wall Street was more than captivated by these new guys; they were eating the lotus leaves and it made companies like AT&T and Sprint look stodgy in comparison, "There was never any question that in terms of the strength and reliability of the network, none of these new guys compared to AT&T. AT&T made a lot of legitimate moves and the stock market did not reward them."[678]

   Another analyst observed about WorldCom upon its collapse, "The real issue isn't accounting. It is the incentive people had to use questionable accounting. The truth is that this never was an industry [that] made phenomenal returns. People forget this was foremost a utility business."[679] WorldCom's numbers, like Enron's, defied market possibilities:
   - WorldCom's revenues went from $950 million in 1992 to $4.5 billion by 1996.[680]
   - Operating income rose 132 percent from 1997 to 1998.
   - Sales increased to $800 billion, and the price of WorldCom's stock rose 137 percent.[681]
   - In 1999, WorldCom's increase in net income was 217 percent.[682]

   How are Sprint and AT&T doing today? In comparison to WorldCom? What lessons can competitors and analysts learn from these insights they had at the time of WorldCom's pinnacle? Do you think Michael Keith has new credibility?

3. Compare and contrast the WorldCom case with the others you have studied, and develop a list of common threads and "take-aways" you would have to incorporate into a company as prevention tools. Be sure to consider elements for your credo in the process.

---

[673]Greg Farrell, "Sullivan Gets a 5-Year Prison Sentence," *USA Today*, August 12, 2005, p. 1B.

[674]Jennifer Bayot and Roben Farzad, "WorldCom Executive Sentenced," *New York Times*, August 12, 2005, pp. C1, C14.

[675]*Id.*

[676]Rebecca Blumenstein and Jared Sandberg, "WorldCom CEO Quits amid Probe of Firm's Finances," *Wall Street Journal*, April 30, 2002, pp. A1, at A9.

[677]Kurt Eichenwald, "Corporate Loans Used Personally, Report Discloses," *New York Times*, November 5, 2002, p. C1.

[678]*Id.*

[679]Henny Sender, "WorldCom Discovers It Has Few Friends," *Wall Street Journal*, June 28, 2002, pp. C1, C3.

[680]These numbers were all computed using the company's annual reports found under WorldCom, "Investor Relations," http://www.worldcom.com. The numbers were computed using "Selected Financial Data" as called out in each of the annual reports.

[681]WorldCom, *Annual Report*, 1998, http://www.worldcom.com. No longer available on the web. Go to www.sec.gov and use the eDGAR database to access annual reports.

[682]Bernard Ebbers's letter to shareholders, in WorldCom's: *Annual Report*, 1999, http://www.worldcom.com. No longer available on the web. Go to www.sec.gov and use the EDGAR database to access annual reports.

Case 4.28

Bernie Madoff: Just Stay Away from the 17th Floor

Bernard Madoff and his securities firm were an operation that, for over 18 years, managed to lose $50 billion in investors' funds. Madoff, the former chairman of NASDAQ, was able to dupe employees, regulators, and, of course, investors, with nothing more sophisticated than a Ponzi scheme for 18 years. When Mr. Madoff was indicted for federal securities fraud, Mr. Madoff's lawyer offered, "We will fight to get through this unfortunate series of events." "Unfortunate series of events" is the name of a children's book series, but may not be appropriately descriptive of a gigantic fraud.

Madoff was an iconic CEO. He was instrumental in creating NASDAQ and had served as a board member at NASD, the precursor organization to FINRA. Even Arthur Levitt Jr., the former head of the SEC for eight years, was known to consult with Madoff on market issues. Mr. Madoff was an icon, and in classic Ponzi fashion, when anyone questioned his operation, he gave their money back. Folks clamored to get their money in with Bernie.

Still, Mr. Madoff kept his operation close to the vest. Bernie Madoff's direct reports were his sons and brother. Mr. Madoff limited access to the 17th floor of his headquarters, the Lipstick Building, where the supposed trading computer was housed. However, the computer was terribly outdated. No one ever wondered why it was never replaced. The reason was simple: a new computer would require someone looking at the old computer and transferring files. Files for nonexistent trades. No one ever wondered why such a large investment firm employed a strip-mall accountant.[683] No one never wondered how Madoff was able to use only 20 people to do the work that would have required 200 in another firm. They just knew only those 20 people ever got access to the 17th floor. The SEC was in to investigate at least three times, but the red flags were not obvious. Mr. Madoff even commented on how his niece had married an investigator from the SEC.

The 17th floor was where the money of investors such as Mort Zuckerman, Kevin Bacon, and many of Palm Beach's movers and shakers, was never really invested but was funneled to Mr. Madoff and the charities he favored. Mr. Madoff contributed to his church, universities, and so many philanthropies that he was known in both New York and Florida for his generosity. Mr. Madoff followed the pattern of all Ponzi schemers. They never begin with the idea of a fraud. Indeed, Mr. Madoff was even more true to form. He offered good, but not excessive returns. He was a consistent performer with a steady 12 percent; enough to be better than the rest, but not enough to turn regulatory heads too far in the direction of the 17th floor. Also Ponzi schemers continue to believe that they are just one dramatic trade or market move from pulling a rabbit out of a hat and making it all work for everyone. Generally, Ponzi schemes last no longer than one year. Mr. Ponzi himself made it only 9 months. Mr. Madoff lasted 18 years.[684]

There were those outside the regulatory agencies and New York's and Palm Beach's movers and shakers who were wondering. For example, Harry Markopolos wrote in a November 7, 2005, e-mail to the SEC of his concerns about the Madoff operations and concluded, "Madoff Investment Securities LLC is likely a Ponzi scheme."[685] The SEC investigated and closed its investigation 11 months later, writing, "The staff found no evidence of fraud." [686]

---

[683]Gregory Zuckerman, "Chasing Bernard Madoff," *Wall Street Journal*, December 18, 2008, p. A1.

[684]Catherine Rampell, "A Scheme with No Off Button," *New York Times*, December 21, 2008, WK, p. 8.

[685]Zuckerman, "Chasing Bernard Madoff," p. A1.

[686]*Id.*

After entering a guilty plea, Mr. Madoff was sentenced to 150 years in prison. The federal judge who sentenced him said that Madoff's conduct was "extraordinarily evil." The Ponzi scheme is the largest in history. The sentence is three times longer than what was recommended by the prosecution and ten times longer than what Mr. Madoff's lawyers proposed.

Mrs. Madoff was required to vacate the couple's penthouse apartment, and U.S. Marshalls took possession of it. The Madoffs' assets, including properties in the Hamptons, Palm Beach, and Switzerland, are being sold, with the funds being used to compensate victims of the fraud as well as pay the fines imposed by the judge.

Mr. Madoff turned to the courtroom full of his victims and said that he was sorry and, "I know that doesn't help you."[687] Mr. Madoff blamed his pride for his actions stating that he could not bring himself to admit his failure as a money manager and created the Ponzi scheme to cover up his shortcoming in terms of the returns on investments of his clients.

Discussion Questions

1. Should investors have suspected the continuing higher levels of returns that never faltered?

2. Mr. Markopolos was dismissed by his bosses and friends even as he provided a list of 28 red flags. What do we learn from his experience about raising questions on the accounting and returns of companies? What can we learn about the reception whistle-blowers receive? Did the market, regulators, and investors not want to raise questions because of the steady returns Madoff provided? What role does a questioning attitude play in preventing company collapses?

3. The Madoff empire could not have lasted as long as it did without complicity from employees.[688] Mr. Madoff's second-in-command, Frank DiPascali, who entered a guilty plea, told the federal judge,

   > I'm standing here to say that from the early 1990s until December 2008, I helped Bernie Madoff and other people carry out a fraud. I knew no trades were happening. I knew what I was doing was criminal. But I did it anyway.[689]

   Mr. DiPascali's compensation was $2,000,000 per year. He had not completed college at the time Mr. Madoff hired him in the early years of the firm. What might have helped Mr. DiPascali resist the temptation to participate in the fraud?

---

[687]Diana B. Henriques, "Madoff, Apologizing, Is Given 150 Years," *New York Times*, June 30, 2009, p. A1.

[688]Kevin McCoy, "Madoff Insider Pleads Guilty to 9 Charges," *USA Today*, November 4, 2009, p. 4B.

[689]Kevin McCoy and Kathy Chu, "Madoff's CFO Pleads Guilty," *USA Today*, August 12, 2009, p 1B.

Ethics in International Business

"The world is your oyster."

—William Shakespeare

"If a foreign country can supply us with a commodity cheaper than we ourselves can make it, better buy it of them with some part of our own industry, employed in a way in which we have some advantage."

—Adam Smith
The Wealth of Nations

"We didn't think of the payments as bribes. We thought of them as useful expenditures."

—Reinhard Siekaczek, former Siemens employee, after Siemens paid the largest fine in U.S. history for violations of the Foreign Corrupt Practices Act

Although we have a global market, we do not have global safety laws, ethical standards, or cultural customs. Businesses face many dilemmas as they decide whether to conform to the varying standards of their host nations or to attempt to operate with universal (global) standards. What we would call a bribe and illegal activity in the United States may be culturally acceptable and necessary in another country. Could you participate in such a practice?

Conflicts Between the Corporation's Ethics and Business Practices in Foreign Countries

Reading 5.1

Why an International Code of Ethics Would Be Good for Business[1]

The global market presents firms with more complex ethical issues than they would experience if operations were limited to one country and one culture. Moral standards vary across cultures. In some cases, cultures change and evolve to accept conduct that was not previously acceptable. For example, in some countries, it is permissible for donors to sell body organs for transplantation. Residents of other countries have sold their kidneys to buy televisions or just to improve their standard of living. In the United States, the buying and selling of organs by individuals is not permitted, but recently experts have called for such a system as a means of resolving the supply-and-demand dilemma that exists because of limited availability of donors and a relative excess of needy recipients.

In many executive training seminars for international business, executives are taught to honor customs in other countries and to "Do as the Romans do." Employees are often confused by this direction. A manager for a U.S. title insurer provides a typical example. He complained that if he tipped employees in the U.S. public-recording agencies for expediting property filings, the manager would not only be violating the company's code of ethics but could also be charged with violations of the Real Estate Settlement Procedures Act and state and federal antibribery provisions. Yet, that same type of practice is permitted, recognized, and encouraged in other countries as a cost of doing business. Paying a regulatory agency in the United States to expedite a licensing process would be considered bribery of a public official. Yet, many businesses maintain that they cannot obtain such authorizations to do business in other countries unless such payments are made. So-called grease or facilitation payments are permitted under the Foreign Corrupt Practices Act, but legality does not necessarily make such payments ethical.

An inevitable question arises when custom and culture clash with ethical standards and moral values adopted by a firm. Should the national culture or the company code of ethics be the controlling factor?

Typical business responses to the question of whether cultural norms or company codes of ethics should take precedence in international business operations are the following: Who am I to question the culture of another country? Who am I to impose U.S. standards on all the other nations of the world? Isn't legality the equivalent of ethical behavior? The attitude of businesses is one that permits ethical deviations in the name of cultural sensitivity. Many businesses fear that the risk of offending is far too high to impose U.S. ethical standards on the conduct of business in other countries.

Tip: One of the misunderstandings of U.S.-based businesses is that ethical standards in the United States vary significantly from the ethical standards in other countries. Operating under this misconception can create a great deal of ethical confusion among

---

[1]From Larry Smeltzer and Marianne M. Jennings, "Why an International Code of Business Ethics Would Be Good for Business," *Journal of Business Ethics* 17 (1998), 57–66.

employees. What is known as the "Golden Rule" in the United States actually has existed for some time in other religions and cultures and among philosophers. Following is a list of how this simple rule is phrased in different writings. The principle is the same even if the words vary slightly. Strategically, businesses and their employees are more comfortable when they operate under uniform standards. This simple rule may provide them with that standard.

Categorical Imperative: How Would You Want to Be Treated?

Would you be comfortable with a world in which your standards were followed?

"Christian Principle: The Golden Rule"

And as ye would that men should do to you, do ye also to them likewise.
— LUKE 6:31

Thou shalt love . . . thy neighbor as thyself.
— LUKE 10:27

"Confucius:"

What you do not want done to yourself, do not do to others.

"Aristotle:"

We should behave to our friends as we wish our friends to behave to us.

"Judaism:"

What you hate, do not do to anyone.

"Buddhism:"

Hurt not others with that which pains thyself.

"Islam:"

No one of you is a believer until he loves for his brother what he loves for himself.

"Hinduism:"

Do nothing to thy neighbor which thou wouldst not have him do to thee.

"Sikhism:"

Treat others as you would be treated yourself.

"Plato:"

May I do to others as I would that they should do unto me.

The successful operation of commerce is dependent on an ethical business foundation. A look at the three major parties in business explains this point. These parties are the risk takers, the employees, and the customers. Risk takers—those furnishing the capital necessary for production—are willing to take risks on the assumption that their products will be judged by customers' assessment of their value. Employees are willing to offer production input, skills, and ideas in exchange for wages, rewards, and other incentives. Consumers and customers are willing to purchase products and services so long as they receive value in exchange for their furnishing, through payment, income and profits to the risk takers and employers. To the extent that the interdependency of the parties in the system is affected by factors outside of their perceived roles and control, the intended business system does not function on its underlying assumptions.

The business system is, in short, an economic system endorsed by society that allows risk takers, employees, and customers to allocate scarce resources to competing ends. Although the roots of business have been described as primarily economic, this economic system cannot survive without recognition of some fundamental values. Some of the inherent—indeed, universal—values built into our capitalistic economic system, as described here, are as follows: (1) the consumer is given value in exchange for the funds expended, (2) employees are rewarded according to their contribution to production, and (3) the risk takers are rewarded for their investment in the form of a return on that investment. This relationship is depicted in Figure 5.1.

Everyone in the system must be ethical. An economic system can be thought of as a four-legged stool. If corruption seeps into one leg, the economic system becomes unbalanced. In international business, very often the government slips into corruption with bribes controlling which businesses are permitted to enter the country and who is awarded contracts in that country. In the United States, the current wave of reforms at the federal level is the result of perceived corruption by business in their operations in the economic system.

To a large extent, all business is based on trust. The tenets for doing business are dissolved as an economy moves toward a system in which one individual can control the market in order to maximize personal income.

Suppose, for example, that the sale of a firm's product is determined not by perceived consumer value but rather by access to consumers, which is controlled by government officials. That is, your company's product cannot be sold to consumers in a particular country unless and until you are licensed within that country. Suppose further that the licensing procedures are controlled by government officials and that those officials demand personal payment in exchange for your company's right to even apply for a business license. Payment size may be arbitrarily determined by officials who withhold

FIGURE 5.1

Interdependence of Trust, Business, and Government

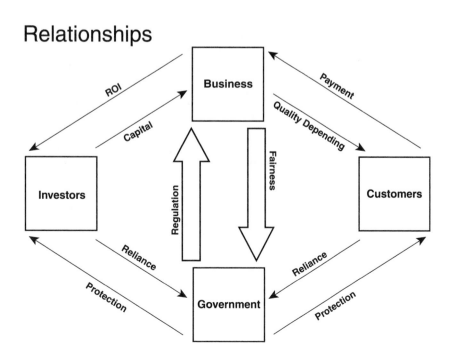

Relationships

portions for themselves. The basic values of the system have been changed. Consumers no longer directly determine the demand.

Beyond just the impact on the basic economic system, ethical breaches involving grease payments introduce an element beyond a now recognized component in economic performance: consumer confidence in long-term economic performance. Economist Douglas Brown has described the differences between the United States and other countries in explaining why capitalism works here and not in all nations. His theory is that capitalism is dependent on an interdependent system of production. For economic growth to be possible, consumers, risk takers, and employees must all feel confident about the future, about the concept of a level playing field, and about the absence of corruption. To the extent that consumers, risk takers, and employees feel comfortable about a market driven by the basic assumptions, the investment and commitments necessary for economic growth via capitalism will be made. Significant monetary costs are incurred by business systems based on factors other than customer value, as discussed earlier.

In developing countries where there are "speed" or grease payments and resulting corruption by government officials, the actual money involved may not be significant in terms of the nation's culture. Such activities and payments introduce an element of demoralization and cynicism that thwart entrepreneurial activity when these nations most need risk takers to step forward.

Bribes and *guanxi* (gifts) in China given to establish connections with the Chinese government are estimated at 3 to 5 percent of operating costs for companies, totaling $3 billion to $5 billion of foreign investment in 1993. But China incurs costs from the choices government officials make in return for payments. For example, *guanxi* are often used to persuade government officials to transfer government assets to foreign investors for substantially less than their value. Chinese government assets have fallen over $50 billion in value over the same period of economic growth, primarily because of the large undervaluation by government officials in these transactions with foreign companies.

Perhaps Italy and Brazil provide the best examples of the long-term impact of foreign business corruption. Although the United States, Japan, and Great Britain have scandals such as the savings and loan failures, political corruption, and insurance regulation, these forms of misconduct are not indicative of corruption that pervades entire economic systems. The same cannot be said about Italy. Elaborate connections between government officials, the Mafia, and business executives have been unearthed. As a result, half of Italy's cabinet has resigned, and hundreds of business executives have been indicted. It has been estimated that the interconnections of these three groups have cost the Italian government $200 billion, as well as compromising the completion of government projects.

In Brazil, the level of corruption has led to a climate of murder and espionage. Many foreign firms have elected not to do business in Brazil because of so much uncertainty and risk—beyond the normal financial risks of international investment. Why send an executive to a country where officials may use force when soliciting huge bribes?

The *Wall Street Journal* offered an example of how Brazil's corruption has damaged the country's economy despite growth and opportunity in surrounding nations. The governor of the northeastern state of Paraiba in Brazil, Ronaldo Cunha Lima, was angry because his predecessor, Tarcisio Burity, had accused Lima's son of corruption. Lima shot Burity twice in the chest while Burity was having lunch at a restaurant. The speaker of Brazil's Senate praised Lima for his courage in doing the shooting himself as opposed to sending someone else. Lima was given a medal by the local city council and granted immunity from prosecution by Paraiba's state legislature. No one spoke for the victim, and the lack of support was reflective of a culture controlled by self-interest that benefits those in control. Unfortunately, these self-interests preclude economic development.

Economists in Brazil document hyperinflation and systemic corruption. A São Paulo businessman observed, "The fundamental reason we can't get our act together is we're an amoral society." This businessperson probably understands capitalism. Privatization that has helped the economies of Chile, Argentina, and Mexico cannot take hold in Brazil because government officials enjoy the benefits of generous wages and returns from the businesses they control. The result is that workers are unable to earn enough even to clothe their families, 20 percent of the Brazilian population lives below the poverty line, and crime has reached levels of nightly firefights. Brazil's predicament has occurred over time, as graft, collusion, and fraud have become entrenched in the government-controlled economy.[2]

Discussion Questions

1. What did you learn about universal values and ethics from the categorical imperative list?
2. What happens when a society does not have ethical standards? Be sure to discuss the example of the situation in Brazil.
3. Who are the victims of corruption and graft?
4. Do you think following U.S. ethical standards in other countries is wise? Would it be unethical not to follow those standards? Explain your answer.

Case 5.2

Chiquita Banana and Mercenary Protection

Chiquita Banana has been known for its poor labor and farming practices in other countries. However, in 1992, the Rainforest Alliance, a group that worked closely with logging companies to minimize harm to rainforests, sent its environmental and worker rights standards to banana companies around the world. Chiquita took the standards to heart and is now ranked as number one among producers in terms of its corporate responsibility. Among the changes Chiquita made are as follows:

- It recycles 100 percent of the plastic bags and twines used on its farms.
- It provided protective gear for its workers using pesticides.
- It cut pesticide use by 26 percent.
- It improved working conditions for plantation workers.
- It provided housing for workers.
- It provided schools for employees' families.
- It purchased buffer zones around plantations in order to prevent chemical runoff.
- All 110 Chiquita farms are certified by the alliance.

Chiquita notes that its pesticide costs are down and productivity among workers is up 27 percent. Chiquita's CEO says of the changes he implemented, "This is the first time I've made an investment decision without having a spreadsheet in front of me, and it's one of the best."[3]

As Chiquita was able to put these sustainability issues behind it and earn the respect of human rights and environmental groups, another issue emerged. Between 1997 and 2004, executives in Chiquita operations in Colombia paid $1.7 million to the United Self-Defense Forces of Colombia (AUC, named for its initials in Spanish). The AUC, according to the U.S. Justice Department, "has been responsible for some of the worst massacres in Colombia's civil conflict and for a sizable percentage of the country's cocaine exports. The U.S. government designated the right-wing militia a terrorist

[2]Thomas Kamm, "Why Does Brazil Face Such Woes? Some See a Basic Ethical Lapse," *Wall Street Journal*, February 4, 1994, p. A1.

[3]Jennifer Alsever, "Chiquita Cleans Up Its Act," *Fortune*, November 27, 2006, p. 73.

organization in September 2001."[4] The payments were made through a Chiquita wholly owned subsidiary known as Banadex, the company's most profitable unit by 2003.

The payments began in 1997 following a meeting between the then-leader of the AUC, Carlos Castaño, and a senior executive of Banadex. No one disputes that during that meeting, Castaño implied that Chiquita's failure to make the payments could result in physical harm to Banadex employees and property. Likewise, no one disputes either that the AUC was known for such violence and had been successful in obtaining payments from other companies, either following Castaño's meetings with company officials or, when the companies declined, by carrying out the threat of harm as a form of warning. By September 2000, Chiquita's senior executives, its board, and many employees were aware that the payments were being made and were also aware that the AUC was a violent paramilitary organization. Chiquita officers, directors, and employees were also aware of the Banadex payments to the AUC. Chiquita recorded these payments in its financial reports and other records as "security payments" or payments for "security" or "security services." Chiquita never received any actual security services in exchange for the payments.

Beginning in June 2002, Chiquita began paying the AUC in cash according to new procedures established by senior executives of Chiquita. These new procedures concealed direct cash payments to the AUC. However, a senior Chiquita officer had described these new procedures to Chiquita's Audit Committee on April 23, 2002. These procedures were implemented well after the U.S. government designated the AUC as a terrorist organization on September 10, 2001. Under federal law, once an organization is designated by the U.S. government as a terrorist organization, companies cannot continue to do business with them because such restrictions were a means of curbing funding to and money laundering by terrorist groups. The designation of terrorist groups is available from a website the government provides to businesses via subscription. Nonetheless, from September 10, 2001, through February 4, 2004, Chiquita made fifty payments to the AUC totaling over $825,000 of the total $1.7 million paid from 1997 through 2004.

On February 20, 2003, a Chiquita employee, aware of the payments to the AUC, told a senior Chiquita officer that he had discovered that the AUC had been designated by the U.S. government as a foreign terrorist organization (FTO). The Justice Department discovered the following sequence of events in response to the employee having raised the issue:

Shortly thereafter, these Chiquita officials spoke with attorneys in the District of Columbia office of a national law firm ("outside counsel") about Chiquita's ongoing payments to the AUC. Beginning on Feb. 21, 2003, outside counsel emphatically advised Chiquita that the payments were illegal under United States law and that Chiquita should immediately stop paying the AUC directly or indirectly. Outside counsel advised Chiquita:

"Must stop payments."

"Bottom Line: Cannot Make the Payment[.]"

"Advised Not to Make Alternative Payment through Convivir[.]"

"General Rule: Cannot do indirectly what you cannot do directly[.]"

Concluded with: "Cannot Make the Payment[.]"

"You voluntarily put yourself in this position. Duress defense can wear out through repetition. Buz [business] decision to stay in harm's way. Chiquita should leave Colombia."

"[T]he company should not continue to make the Santa Marta payments, given the AUC's designation as a foreign terrorist organization[.]"

"[T]he company should not make the payment."

---

[4]U.S. Department of Justice, press release, March 19, 2007. www.doj.gov.

On April 3, 2003, a senior Chiquita officer and a member of Chiquita's Board of Directors first reported to the full Board that Chiquita was making payments to a designated FTO. A Board member objected to the payments and recommended that Chiquita consider taking immediate corrective action, including withdrawing from Colombia. The Board did not follow that recommendation, but instead agreed to disclose promptly to the Department of Justice the fact that Chiquita had been making payments to the AUC. Meanwhile, Banadex personnel were instructed to continue making the payments.[5]

On April 24, 2003, Roderick M. Hills, a member of Chiquita's board and head of its audit committee, Chiquita general counsel Robert Olson, and, some reports indicate, the company's outside counsel met with members of the Justice Department to disclose the payments and explain that they had been made under duress. Mr. Hills, a former chairman of the Securities Exchange Commission, and the Chiquita officer (and perhaps its lawyer) were told that the payments were illegal and had to stop. The payments did not stop, and the company's outside counsel wrote to the board on September 8, 2003, advising that "[Department of Justice] officials have been unwilling to give assurances or guarantees of non-prosecution; in fact, officials have repeatedly stated that they view the circumstances presented as a technical violation and cannot endorse current or future payments."[6]

Nonetheless, the payments continued. From April 24, 2003, through February 4, 2004, Chiquita made twenty payments to the AUC totaling $300,000. On February 4, 2004, Chiquita sold the Banadex operations to a Colombian-owned company.

Chiquita then cooperated with the government by making its records available. In March 2007, Chiquita entered a guilty plea and agreed to pay a $25 million fine. Chiquita will be on probation for five years and has agreed to create and maintain an effective ethics program. As of August 2007, Mr. Hills and four former Chiquita officers, including Mr. Olson, were under investigation by the Justice Department for their failure to stop the payments. A Justice Department official said of the investigation, "If the only way that a company can conduct business in a particular location is to do so illegally, then the company shouldn't be doing business there."[7]

Discussion Questions

1. Refer back to the Laura Nash question (see Reading 1.8). "How did Chiquita get into this position in the first place?" What of the sale of its most profitable unit in 2004?

2. Why does the term *technical violation* creep into our discussions of ethical and legal issues? Reid Weingarten, Mr. Hills's attorney has said, "That Rod Hills would find himself under investigation for a crime he himself reported is absurd."[8] Evaluate Mr. Weingarten's analysis of the situation.

3. Are there any lines you could draw (some elements for your credo) based on what happened at Chiquita?

4. Discuss the relationship between social responsibility and the sustainability initiative and compliance with the law. What benefits do companies gain from social responsibility actions?

Compare & Contrast

Chiquita's chief executive, Fernando Aguirre, said in a statement, "The payments made by the company were always motivated by our good faith concern for the safety of our

---

[5]U.S. Department of Justice, press release #07-161:03, http://www.doj.gov.

[6]*Id.*

[7]Neil A. Lewis, "Inquiry Threatens Ex-Leader of Security Agency," *New York Times*, August 16, 2007, p. A18.

[8]Laurie P. Cohen, "Chiquita Under the Gun," *Wall Street Journal*, August 2, 2007, pp. A1, A9.

employees."[9] However, Assistant Attorney General Kenneth L. Wainstein of the National Security Division of the U.S. Department of Justice offered the following thoughts in announcing the guilty plea:

> *Like any criminal enterprise, a terrorist organization needs a funding stream to support its operations. For several years, the AUC terrorist group found one in the payments they demanded from Chiquita Brands International. Thanks to Chiquita's cooperation and this prosecution, that funding stream is now dry and corporations are on notice that they cannot make protection payments to terrorists. Funding a terrorist organization can never be treated as a cost of doing business. American businesses must take note that payments to terrorists are of a whole different category. They are crimes. But like adjustments that American businesses made to the passage of the Foreign Corrupt Practices Act decades ago, American businesses, as good corporate citizens, will find ways to conform their conduct to the requirements of the law and still remain competitive.*[10]

Reconcile the two positions for the company. What alternatives were there? Is this the either/or conundrum you learned about in Units 1 and 2?

Case 5.3

Transnational Shipping and the Pirates

Transnational is an international company that arranges transportation for large cargo items and shipments of large orders. Transnational has a fleet of cargo ships. Each cargo ship has a crew of 25 employees.

Transnational's head of security, Jack Davis, is a retired U.S. Navy officer who, until January 2009, worked for the U.S. Department of Homeland Security. Davis has, since the time of his being hired at Transnational, alerted senior management to the evolving issue of pirates. Despite an international incident involving a U.S. ship in the spring of 2009, the response of management to Davis's concerns has been one of postponement.

On September 11, 2009, a group of pirates boarded a Transnational ship that was, at the time of the takeover, sailing off the coast of Africa. The pirates have demanded payment of $25 million, or $1,000,000 for each crew member. The pirates have imposed a deadline of 5 hours for Transnational's decision and promise of payment. The pirates have also indicated that they will begin killing crew members one at a time if their deadline for Transnational's agreement to the payment is not met. Davis has advised Transnational to go ahead and simply pay the pirates because, "Lives of employees are at stake and my job is protecting employees." However, a Transnational senior officer has cautioned in a meeting, "That's a bribe, and Transnational has a longstanding practice of not paying bribes."

Discussion Questions

1. The officers, the board, and Davis seek your advice. Be sure to apply all applicable principles, forms of analyses, readings, etc. you have studied to date. What advice would you give?

2. Is the description of "bribe" accurate?
3. Is this situation different because human life is involved?
4. What values of Transnational are in conflict?

---

[9]Matt Apuzzo, "Chiquita to Pay $25 Million in Terrorist Case," AP, http://www.yahoo.com, March 14, 2007.
[10]U.S. Department of Justice, press release #07-161:03.

Case 5.4

The Former Soviet Union: A Study of Three Companies: PwC, Ikea, and AES

PwC and the Russian Tax Authorities[11]

PriceWaterhouseCoopers (or PwC, as it is known), one of the United States' "Big 4" accounting firms, has had a tax practice in Russia since the time that country changed from Communist rule. One of PwC's clients in Russia was Yukos, a major Russian oil company that is now bankrupt.

Russia's Federal Tax Service, an agency similar to the United States' IRS, has filed suit against PwC, alleging that it concealed tax evasion by Yukos for the years 2002 to 2004. The Tax Service also announced a criminal probe of PwC's conduct with regard to its tax services for Yukos. Twenty Tax Service agents searched PwC's offices in Moscow and questioned PwC employees about the Yukos account. Yukos lost its tax case and has paid $9.2 million in charges for the nonpayment of taxes. However, Yukos and PwC do have the case on appeal.

Many see the battle between PwC and the Tax Service as part of the Russian government's ongoing battle to sell off the assets of Yukos and avoid the surrender of the company's assets to investors and creditors who have filed claims. Those suits are pending in courts in The Hague. Some analysts believe that the Russian government is hoping to press PwC into revealing information that would help it take back the Yukos assets.

If PwC is found to have engaged in evasion, it loses its license to do business in Russia, but if it turns over information, it is likely to lose its clients in Russia.

Discussion Questions

1. Referring back to the Laura Nash model (Reading 1.8), how did PwC get into this situation in the first place? What issues should a company consider before doing business in an economically developing country? What are the risks? Did this ethical dilemma begin long before the Russian government's demands of PwC?

2. When countries open up to capitalism and economic freedom, there is much cream— that is, businesses can move in easily and capture markets with little effort. However, what are the issues that accompany this ease of initial introduction?

3. What two PwC values would be in conflict if the Russian government demands disclosure by PwC?

Ikea and the Generators

When Ikea was poised to open a flagship store outside Moscow in 2001, its executives were approached by employees of a local utility. If Ikea wanted electricity for its planned grand opening, some bribes were needed. Ikea is known for its stringent policy of, "No bribes." However, Ikea was on the eve of a grand opening, complete with creditors and employees. Ikea's solution was to rent diesel generators. But, corruption does have ways. Ikea discovered that one of its managers was accepting kickbacks from the rental company that furnishes Ikea with the generators for operating its stores. Ikea ended the manager's Ikea career as well as the contract with the rental company and went to court in Russia to seek damages.

Ah, but who runs the courts? Judges who are, apparently, quite fond of utility workers who demand bribes. Ikea ended up owing damages to the rental company for its breach of contract. As one Ikea board member noted, "this is unlike anything" the international

[11]From Neil Buckley and Catherine Belton, "Moscow Raids PwC ahead of Yukos Case," *Financial Times*, March 11, 2007, p. 1.

company has encountered in any of its operations. Ikea is still running stores in Russia, but not expanding. Its disclosure of the details of its electricity/generator experience was done by design: The company hopes that the public can sway corrupt officials into a more transparent atmosphere for doing business.

Discussion Questions

1. By not succumbing to, "Well, you either bribe or you don't do business there," Ikea found an end-run, a creative solution to international business's ubiquitous either/or conundrum: To bribe or not to bribe. However, what issues did Ikea miss in its analysis of the situation?

2. Ikea discovered in 2010 that one of its executives responsible for leasing the generators was accepting kickbacks for awarding those contracts. Ikea fired the executive, but what issues arise from this conduct?

AES and the Power Plant

AES, the U.S.-based energy company, provides power in developing countries. Because it does business in Colombia and Brazil, the problems of regimes, corruption, and expropriation are not unusual ones for the company. However, its operation of the Maikuben coal mine in northern Kazakhstan was new and different even for the seasoned international player AES had come to be.

When AES opened the mine in the former Soviet republic in 1996, it had a management experience about which most companies will only dream. The local residents who were miners there dug coal in freezing temperatures and took only tea breaks every other hour to warm up before going right back to digging. As AES expanded its operations to include power plants and transmission lines it found a work force with high technical abilities. Further, the work ethic of the Kazakhs was remarkable. It took only five to seven AES managers to supervise 6,500 Kazakhs.

If the employees were great, the customers were terrific. Electric utility customers, grateful for the consistency of electric service, paid on time, even with 20 percent rate increases in some years.

However, the company's relations with the Kazakhstan government were also a unique experience. At one point, in 2005, 24 foot soldiers, armed with AK-47s entered the office of the Maikuben mine and demanded documents for a tax case the government had brought against AES. AES officials were able to negotiate a pull-back of the forces after 2 days of phone conversations with regional government officials. The soldiers left, AES paid a fine, and the tax case continued. By 2008, with continuing tense relationships and demands, AES, despite a $200 million investment in a power plant in the country, walked away. AES sold its assets there at fire-sale prices.

The tax rate for companies in Kazakhstan is 30 percent, plus the country's value-added tax. In addition, the regional tax officials do come calling on the companies for collection of additional revenues. Kazakhstan is a country that is rich in resources, but also abundant in corruption. Parker Drilling, a company with $655 million in revenue and $104 in net profits in 2008, paid $51 million that same year in taxes for its drilling rights to Kazakhstan. ExxonMobil paid a $5 billion fine for project delays.

AES managers were grilled about their political affiliations and placed under investigation because, as local officials explained, they worked for "Americans who steal from us."[12] Many managers left the country once AES was charged with antitrust violations because of a fear that they would be arrested. One manager explained that what was once at least considered taboo, that is, the jailing of business managers, has become the norm in the country.

[12]Nathan Vardi, "Power Putsch," *Forbes,* June 2, 2008, pp. 84, 90.

AES and others continue to pursue the assets taken by the government through arbitration in London.

Discussion Questions

1. What is the underlying cause of AES's difficulty in doing business in Kazakhstan?
2. Take the three cases in this segment and develop a list of questions and concerns for companies considering expansion into countries with rich resources but rugged due process and governance.
3. What factor must be evaluated in doing the numbers related to operations or drilling?

Case 5.5

Product Dumping

Once the Consumer Product Safety Commission prohibits the sale of a particular product in the United States, a manufacturer can no longer sell the product to U.S. wholesalers or retailers. However, the product can be sold in other countries that have not prohibited its sale. The same is true of other countries' sales to the United States. For example, Great Britain outlawed the sale of the prescription sleeping pill Halcion, but sales of the drug continue in the United States.[13] The British medical community reached conclusions regarding the pill's safety that differed from the conclusions reached by the medical community and the Food and Drug Administration here. Some researchers who conducted studies on the drug in the United States simply concluded that stronger warning labels were needed.

The Consumer Product Safety Commission outlawed the sale of three-wheel all-terrain cycles in the United States in 1988.[14] Although some manufacturers had already turned to four-wheel models, other manufacturers still had inventories of three-wheel cycles. Testimony on the cycles ranged from contentions that although the vehicles themselves were safe, the drivers were too young, too inexperienced, and more inclined to take risks (i.e., to "hot dog"). However, even after the three-wheel product was banned here, outlawed vehicles could still be sold outside the United States.

For many companies, chaos follows a product recall because inventory of the recalled product may be high. Often, firms must decide whether to "dump" the product in other countries or to take a write-off that could damage earnings, stock prices, and employment stability.

Discussion Questions

1. If you were a manufacturer holding a substantial inventory of a product that has been outlawed in the United States, would you have any ethical concerns about selling the product in countries that do not prohibit its sale?
2. Suppose the inventory write-down that you will be forced to take because of the regulatory obsolescence is material—nearly a 20 percent reduction in income will result. If you can sell the inventory in a foreign market, legally, there will be no write-down and no income reduction. A reduction of that magnitude would substantially lower share market price, which in turn would lead your large, institutional shareholders to demand explanations and possibly seek changes in your company's board of directors. In short, the write-down would set off a wave of events that would change the structure and stability of your firm. Do you now feel justified in selling the product legally in another country?

---

[13]"The Price of a Good Night's Sleep," *New York Times*, January 26, 1992, p. E9.
[14]"Outlawing a Three-Wheeler," *Time, January* 11, 1988, 59.

3. Is selling the product in another country simply a matter of believing one aspect of the evidence—that the product is safe? Is this decision a matter of the credo as well?

4. Would you include any warnings with the product?

Case 5.6

On Sweatshops, Nike, and Kathie Lee

With the passage of the General Agreement on Tariffs and Trade (GATT) and the North American Free Trade Agreement (NAFTA), a worldwide market emerged. In addition to the international market for goods, there is also an international market for labor. Many U.S. firms have subcontracted the production of their products to factories in China, Southeast Asia, and Central and South America.

The National Labor Committee (NLC), an activist group, periodically releases information on conditions in foreign factories and the companies utilizing those factories. In 1998, the NLC issued a report that Liz Claiborne, Walmart, Ann Taylor, Esprit, Ralph Lauren, JCPenney, and Kmart were using subcontractors in China that use Chinese women (between the ages of seventeen and twenty-five) to work 60 to 90 hours per week for as little as 13 to 23 cents per hour. The Chinese subcontractors do not pay overtime, and they house the workers in crowded dormitories, feed them a poor diet, and operate unsafe factories.[15]

Levi Strauss pulled its manufacturing and sales operations out of China in 1993 because of human rights violations, but announced in 1998 that it would expand its manufacturing there and begin selling clothing there. Peter Jacobi, the then-president of Levi Strauss, indicated that the company had the assurance of local contractors that they would adhere to Levi's guides on labor conditions. Jacobi stated, "Levi Strauss is not in the human rights business. But to the degree that human rights affect our business, we care about it."[16]

The Mariana Islands was the site of an investigation by the U.S. Department of the Interior (because these islands are a U.S. territory) for alleged indentured servitude of children as young as fourteen in factories there.[17] Wendy Doromal, a human rights activist, issued a report that workers there have tuberculosis and oozing sores. Approximately $820 million worth of clothing items are manufactured each year on the islands. Labels manufactured there include The Gap, Liz Claiborne, Banana Republic, JCPenney, Ralph Lauren, and Brooks Brothers.[18]

U.S. companies' investments in foreign manufacturing in major developing nations like China, Indonesia, and Mexico have tripled in fifteen years to $56 billion, a figure that does not include the subcontracting work. In Hong Kong, Singapore, South Korea, and Taiwan, where plants make apparel, toys, shoes, and wigs, national incomes have risen from 10 percent to 40 percent of American incomes over the past ten years. In Indonesia, since the introduction of U.S. plants and subcontractors, the proportion of malnourished children in the country has gone from one-half to one-third.[19]

In a practice that is widely accepted in other countries, children, ages ten to fourteen, labor in factories for fifty or more hours per week. Their wages enable their families to

[15]Jon Frandsen, "Chinese Labor Practices Assailed," *Mesa (Arizona) Tribune,* March 19, 1998, p. B2.

[16]Mark Landler, "Reversing Course, Levi Strauss Will Expand Its Output in China," *New York Times,* April 9, 1998, p. C1.; and G. Pascal Zachary, "Levi Tries to Make Sure Contract Plants in Asia Treat Workers Well," *Wall Street Journal,* July 28, 1994, pp. A1, A5.

[17]Zachary, "Levi Tries to Make Sure Contract Plants in Asia Treat Workers Well," pp. A1, A5.

[18]John McCormick and Marc Levinson, "The Supply Police," *Newsweek,* February 15, 1993, pp. 48–49.

[19]Allen R. Myerson, "In Principle, a Case for More 'Sweatshops,'" *New York Times,* June 22, 1997, p. E5.

survive. School is a luxury, and a child attends only until he or she is able to work in a factory. The Gap, Levi Strauss, Esprit, and Leslie Fay have all been listed in social responsibility literature as exploiting their workers.[20] In 1994, the following appeared in a quarter-page ad in the *New York Times*:

The Price of Corporate Greed at Leslie Fay

Marie Whitt is fighting to keep the job she has held for 17 years at a Leslie Fay plant in Wilkes-Barre. Marie earns $7.80 an hour—hardly a fortune. On June 1st, she and 1,800 coworkers were forced to strike because Leslie Fay plans to dump them. Ninety percent are women whose average age is 50. They have given their whole working lives to the company and losing their jobs would be a disaster. Marie knows she will never find a comparable job in today's economy. Without her union benefits, she and her husband won't be able to pay for his anti-cancer medication. "What Leslie Fay wants to do is so rotten," she says. "You've got to draw the line somewhere and fight."

Dorka Diaz worked for Leslie Fay in Honduras, alongside 12- and 13-year-old girls locked inside a factory where the temperature often hits 100° and where there is no clean drinking water. For a 54-hour week, including forced overtime, Dorka was paid a little over $20. With food prices high—a quart of milk costs 44 cents— Dorka and her three-year-old son live at the edge of starvation. In April, Dorka was fired for trying to organize a union. "We need jobs desperate," she says, "but not under such terrible conditions."[21]

Leslie Fay executives claim they can only "compete" by producing in factories like Dorka's. But identical skirts—one made by Dorka, the other by Marie—were recently purchased at a big retail chain here. Both cost $40. Searching the world for ever-cheaper sources of labor is not the kind of competition America needs. Leslie Fay already does 75% of its production overseas. If it really wants to compete successfully in the global economy, it would modernize its facilities here in the U.S. as many of its competitors have done. But Leslie Fay wants to make a fast buck by squeezing every last drop of sweat and blood out of its workers. Marie Whitt and Dorka Diaz don't think that's right. And they know it's a formula for disaster—for all of us.

You can help by not buying Leslie Fay products—until Leslie Fay lives up to its corporate responsibilities at home and overseas.

Don't buy Leslie Fay! Boycott all clothing made by Leslie Fay and sold under these labels: Leslie Fay, Joan Leslie, Albert Nipon, Theo Miles, Kasper, Le Suit, Nolan Miller, Castleberry, Castlebrook.[22]

In the United States, the issue of sweatshops came to the public's attention when several media sources disclosed that talk-show host Kathie Lee Gifford's line of clothing at Walmart had been manufactured in sweatshops in Guatemala, and CBS ran a report on conditions in Nike subcontractor factories in Vietnam and Indonesia.[23] The reports on Nike's factories issued by Vietnam Labor Watch included the following: women required to run laps around the factory for wearing nonregulation shoes to work; payment of

[20]Dana Canedy, "Peering into the Shadows of Corporate Dealings," *New York Times,* March 25, 1997, pp. C1, C6.

[21]From Ms. Diaz's testimony before a hearing of the Subcommittee on Labor-Management Relations, Committee on Education and Labor, U.S. House of Representatives, Wilkes-Barre, Pennsylvania, June 7, 1994.

[22]From a statement published by the International Ladies Garment Workers Union in *New York Times,* June 9, 1994, p. A16.

[23]Jeff Ballinger and Claes Olsson, *Beyond the Swoosh: The Struggle of Indonesians Making Nike Shoes* (Uppsala, Sweden: ICDA/Global Publications Foundations, 1997).

subminimum wages; physical beatings, including with shoes, by factory supervisors; and most employees are women between the ages of fifteen and twenty-eight. Philip Knight, CEO of Nike, included the following in a letter to shareholders:

Q: Why on earth did NIKE pick such a terrible place as Indonesia to have shoes made?

A: Effectively the US State Department asked us to. In 1976, when zero percent of Nike's production was in Taiwan and Korea, Secretary of State Cyrus Vance asked Charles Robinson…to start the US-ASEAN Business Council to fill the vacuum left by the withdrawal of the American military from that part of the world. . . . Chuck Robinson accepted the challenge, put together the council and served as Chairman of the US side for three years. Mr. Robinson was a Nike Board member at that time as he is today. . . . "Nike's presence in that part of the world," according to a senior state department official at that time, "is American foreign policy in action."[24]

Nike sent former UN Ambassador Andrew Young to its overseas factories in order to issue a report to Knight, the board, and the shareholders.[25] Young did tour factories, but only with Nike staff and only for a few hours. Young issued the following findings:

- Factories that produce Nike goods are "clean, organized, adequately ventilated, and well-lit."
- No evidence of a "pattern of widespread or systematic abuse or mistreatment of workers."
- Workers don't know enough about their rights or about Nike's own code of conduct.
- Few factory managers speak the local language, which inhibits workers from lodging complaints or grievances.
- Independent monitoring is needed because factories are controlled by absentee owners and Nike has too few supervisors on-site.[26]

On October 18, 1997, there were international protests against Nike in thirteen countries and seventy cities. On October 13, 1997, 6,000 Nike workers went on strike in Indonesia followed by a strike of 1,300 in Vietnam.[27]

On November 8, 1997, an Ernst & Young audit about unsafe conditions in a Nike factory in Vietnam was leaked to the *New York Times* and made front-page news.[28]

Michael Jordan, then-NBA superstar and Nike's endorser, agreed to tour Nike's factories in July 1998, stating that "the best thing I can do is go to Asia and see for myself. The last thing I want to do is pursue a business with a negative over my head that I don't have an understanding of. If there are issues . . . . if it's an issue of slavery or sweatshops, [Nike executives] have to revise the situation."[29]

From June 1997 to January 1998, Nike distributed 100,000 plastic "code of conduct" cards to plant workers. The cards list workers' rights. Nike's market performance dropped during this period. Its stock price went from a 1996 high of $75.75 per share to a March 1998 low of $43 per share.[30] (Its share price rebounded to $62 by March 2002 and increased to $91.70 by December 2004. As of mid-2010, Nike stock was trading at $72.25.)

Retail order cancellations caused sales to decrease by 3 percent in 1997. As a result, Nike planned to reduce its labor force by 10 to 15 percent, or 2,100 to 3,100 positions.[31]

[24]Sharon R. King, "Flying the Swoosh and Stripes," *New York Times,* March 19, 1998, pp. C1, C6.

[25]Ellen Neuborne, "Nike to Take a Hit in Labor Report," *USA Today,* March 27, 1997, p. 1A.

[26]"Nike Tries to Quell Exploitation Charges," *Wall Street Journal,* June 25, 1997, p. A16.

[27]Patricia Seller, "Four Reasons Nike's Not Cool," *Fortune,* March 30, 1998, pp. 26–28.

[28]Bob Herbert, "Brutality in Vietnam," *New York Times,* March 28, 1997, p. A19.

[29]Bill Richards, "Tripped Up by Too Many Shoes, Nike Regroups," *Wall Street Journal,* March 3, 1998, pp. B1, B15.

[30]Tom Lowry and Bill Beyers, "Earnings Woes Trip Nike; Layoffs Loom," *USA Today,* February 25, 1998, p. 1B.

[31]*Id.;* and "Nike Refuses to 'Just Do It,'" *Business Ethics,* January/February 1998, p. 8.

Press for Change and Global Exchange, an activist group, made the following demands of Nike in 1998:

1. **Accept independent monitoring by local human rights groups to ensure that Nike's Code of Conduct is respected by its subcontractors.** The Gap has already accepted independent monitoring for its factories in El Salvador, setting an important precedent in the garment industry. If Nike were to accept such monitoring in Indonesia, it would set a similar positive precedent in the shoe industry, making Nike a true leader in its field.
2. **Settle disputes with workers who have been unfairly dismissed for seeking decent wages and work conditions.** There are dozens of Indonesian workers who have been fired for their organizing efforts, and thousands who have been cheated out of legally promised wages. Nike must take responsibility for the practices of its subcontractors, and should offer to reinstate fired workers and repay unpaid wages.
3. **Improve the wages paid to Indonesian workers.** The minimum wage in Indonesia is $2.26 a day. Subsistence needs are estimated to cost at least $4 a day. While Nike claims to pay double the minimum wage, this claim includes endless hours of overtime. We call on Nike to pay a minimum of $4 a day for an eight-hour day, and to end all forced overtime.[32]

The American Apparel Manufacturers Association (AAMA), which counts 70 percent of all U.S. garment makers in its membership, has a database for its members to check labor compliance by contractors.[33] The National Retail Federation has established the following statement of Principles on Supplier Legal Compliance (now signed by 250 retailers):

1. We are committed to legal compliance and ethical business practices in all of our operations.
2. We choose suppliers that we believe share that commitment.
3. In our purchase contracts, we require our suppliers to comply with all applicable laws and regulations.
4. If it is found that a factory used by a supplier for the production of our merchandise has committed legal violations, we will take appropriate action, which may include canceling the affected purchase contracts, terminating our relationship with the supplier, commencing legal actions against the supplier, or other actions as warranted.
5. We support law enforcement and cooperate with law enforcement authorities in the proper execution of their responsibilities.
6. We support educational efforts designed to enhance legal compliance on the part of the U.S. apparel manufacturing industry.[34]

The U.S. Department of Labor made the following recommendations to companies in order to improve the international labor situation:

1. All sectors of the apparel industry, including manufacturers, retailers, buying agents and merchandisers, should consider the adoption of a code of conduct.
2. All parties should consider whether there would be any additional benefits to adopting more standardized codes of conduct [to eliminate confusion resulting from a proliferation of different codes with varying definitions of child labor].
3. U.S. apparel importers should do more to monitor subcontractors and homeworkers [the areas where child labor violations occur].
4. U.S. garment importers—particularly retailers—should consider taking a more active and direct role in the monitoring and implementation of their codes of conduct.
5. All parties, particularly workers, should be adequately informed about codes of conduct so that the codes can fully serve their purpose.[35]

---

[32]Lowry and Beyers, "Earnings Woes Trip Nike," p. 1B; and "Nike Refuses to 'Just Do It,'" p. 8.

[33]"Slave Labor," *Fortune*, December 9, 1996, p. 12.

[34]Martha Nichols, "Third-World Families at Work: Child Labor or Child Care?" *Harvard Business Review* (January–February 1993): 12–23.

[35]Daniela Deane, "Senators to Hear of Slave Labor on U.S. Soil," *USA Today*, March 31, 1998, p. 9A.

By 2000, Nike, still the target of campus protests for its overseas plant conditions, began to experience economic impact as the students protested their colleges and universities signing licensing agreements with Nike. For example, Nike ended negotiations with the University of Michigan for a six-year, multimillion dollar licensing agreement because Michigan joined the consortium. And Phil Knight withdrew a pledge to make a $30 million donation to the University of Oregon because the university joined the consortium. Nonetheless, Knight acknowledged a brand image problem, "Nike product has become synonymous with slave wages, forced overtime, and arbitrary abuse."[36]

Nike continues to support the Fair Labor Association, an organization backed by the White House with about 135 colleges and universities as members, but its membership there has not halted the consortium's activities.[37]

Despite its efforts, Nike remained a target in op-ed pieces and various magazine articles regarding its labor practices around the world. Nike CEO Phil Knight often responds to these opinion pieces and articles by writing letters to the editor, citing Nike's standards and independent and outside reviews of its factories' conditions. One such letter went to the editor of the *New York Times* in response to a negative op-ed piece there on Nike's labor practices.

Marc Kasky filed suit against Nike in California alleging that the op-ed pieces and letters in response to negative op-ed pieces about Nike violated the False Advertising Act of California. The act permits state agencies to take action to fine corporate violators of the act as well as obtain remedies such as injunctions to halt the ads.

Nike challenged the suit on the grounds that such an interpretation and application of the advertising regulation violated its rights of free speech. The lower court agreed with Kasky and held that the advertising statute applied to Nike's defense of its labor practices, even when that defense appeared on the op-ed pages of newspapers. Nike appealed to the U.S. Supreme Court. The U.S. Supreme Court held that the case could not be reviewed until Nike had actually gone through the state process for finding it in violation of the False Advertising Act.[38] The case was remanded for trial, but Nike settled the matter with the California authorities before a trial was held. The terms of that settlement were not disclosed.

In 2004, *Business Ethics* magazine presented its Social Reporting Award to Gap, Inc., for being the first company to issue a report on vendor compliance with its factory standards. The report disclosed both positive aspects and contractor failures. For example, Gap disclosed that 25 percent of its factories in Mexico paid subminimum wages and that factories in China had obstructions in the aisles. The company has been recognized for its candor and pledge to improve.[39] However, disclosure about the problems, to some labor activists note, is not enough. Efforts that prevent the problems is the new focus of these groups, and they are asking companies to implement prevention mechanisms in international operations.

In 2008, public reports emerged about conditions in Nike's factories in Malaysia. When the stories broke, Nike called representatives from its 30 factories in the country to its headquarters and held several days of discussion and training on the importance of enforcing the company's labor standards. A labor activist from Australia praised the company for its prompt action, noting that ten years earlier a response from Nike would have been slow in coming. However, the activist also noted, "But, we're looking for systematic change that improves conditions across the supply chain, not solutions once problems are exposed."[40]

[36]Eugenia Levenson, "Citizen Nike," *Fortune*, November 24, 2008, p. 165.

[37]Steven Greenhouse, "Anti-Sweatshop Group Invites Input by Apparel Makers," *New York Times*, April 29, 2000, p. A9.

[38]*Nike v Kasky*, 539 U.S. 654 (2003). Lower court decisions at *Kasky v Nike*, 2 P.3d 1065 (2000); and *Kasky v Nike*, 45, P.3d 243 (2002).

[39]"Gap, Inc. Social Reporting Award," *Business Ethics* (Fall 2004): 9.

[40]Levenson, "Citizen Nike," p. 165.

As a result, Nike has introduced "lean manufacturing" into the supply chain. This form of production shifts from low-skill assembly lines to organizing workers into multi-task teams. The team members require more training, something that requires factory owners to invest in their workers. With that investment, the worker abuse is reduced or stops because the factory owners want to hang on to the trained employees in order to enjoy returns on the skills training they have given.

Another change Nike has made focuses on its decision processes for shoe design and production. The teams in Beaverton, Oregon, learned that their last-minute changes placed unnecessary stress on the factories and, as a result, the workers. Reducing the production crunch has also reduced the hours, stress, and likelihood of abuse. Beaverton has now developed a sensitivity that its design changes, schedule, and final decisions do impact the supply chain, including the labor conditions.

Another new focus is working with suppliers to solve the strains rather than pushing all of the responsibility onto them for compliance with company standards. The adoption of this quasi-partnership means of solving labor issues is also a result of Nike's realization that just terminating contracts is problematic. When Nike simply ended a contract with a company that produced its soccer balls in Pakistan because of labor issues there, Nike experienced backlash from that country for the loss of jobs. Nike and other retailers have learned that international production does provide cost savings but also requires a tough balancing act that is sensitive to workers, the nature of the country and its economy, and the needs and practices of their suppliers.

Discussion Questions

1. One executive noted, "We're damned if we do because we exploit. We're damned if we don't because these foreign economies don't develop. Who's to know what's right?" How does this observation compare with the Nike changes and experiences?

2. Would you employ a twelve-year-old in one of your factories if it were legal to do so?

3. Would you limit hours and require a minimum wage even if it were not legally mandated?

4. Would you work to provide educational opportunities for these child laborers?

5. Why do you think the public seized on the Kathie Lee Gifford and Nike issues?

Compare & Contrast

Levi Strauss & Company, discovering that youngsters under the age of fourteen were routinely employed in its Bangladesh factories, could either fire forty underage youngsters and impoverish their families or allow them to continue working. Levi compromised and provided the children both access to education and full adult wages.

Nike has shoe factories in Indonesia, and the women who work in those factories net $37.46 per month. However, as Nike points out, their wages far exceed those of other factory workers. Nike's Dusty Kidd notes, "Americans focus on wages paid, not what standard of living those wages relate to."

Economist Jeffrey D. Sachs of Harvard has served as a consultant to developing nations such as Bolivia, Russia, Poland, and Malawi. He observes that the conditions in sweatshops are horrible, but they are an essential first step toward modern prosperity. "My concern is not that there are too many sweatshops, but that there are too few. These are precisely the jobs that were the stepping stone for Singapore and Hong Kong, and those are the jobs that have to come to Africa to get them out of their backbreaking rural poverty."[41]

[41]"Slave Labor," p. 12.

Business executives respond as follows,

If someone is willing to work for 31 cents an hour, so be it—that's capitalism. But throw in long hours, abusive working conditions, poor safety conditions, and no benefits, and that's slavery. It was exactly those same conditions that spawned the union movement here in the U.S.

— JOHN WALDRON

If the wages of 31 cents per hour were actually fair wages, adults would gladly do the work instead of children.

— WESLEY M. JOHN

Just when you think the vile remnants of those who would build empires on the blood and bones of those less fortunate than ourselves have slithered off into the history books, you come across this kind of tripe. For shame for rationalizing throwing crumbs to your fellow human beings so that you and your ilk can benefit at their expense.

— JOSE GUARDIOLA

Economists have made some critical points about wages in developing countries. One point is that the employees hired at the wages in these countries lack the skills necessary for the pace of production that would exist in a country with a trained work force. The lower wages are a means of pricing the lower productivity. Another point economists make is that joblessness in developing countries presents a greater social cost and precludes the country from evolving economically. For example, there was child labor in the United States until the federal labor legislation addressed it fully during the 1930s. Economists maintain that wages increase as skills do and the initial wages are a just a first step in economic development for the country.[42]

Discuss the economic, social, and ethical issues of plants and wages in developing countries.

Discuss the merits in the various positions on child labor and sweat shops in a company's supply chain.

Sources

Gibbs, Nancy, "Suffer the Little Children," *Time,* March 26, 1990, p. 18.
Mitchell, Russell, and Michael O'Neal, "Managing by Values," *Business Week,* August 1, 1994, pp. 40–52.
"Nike's Workers in Third World Abused, Report Says," *(Phoenix) Arizona Republic,* March 28, 1997, p. A10.
"Susie Tompkins," *Business Ethics,* January/February 1995, pp. 21–23.

[42]For additional perspective on these issues, see "Invasion of the Job Snatchers," *The Economist,* November 2, 1996, p. 18. © 1996 The Economist Newspaper Group Inc.

Case 5.7

Bhopal: When Safety Standards Differ[43]

Bhopal is a city in central India with a population, in 1984, of 800,000. Because it was, at that time, home to the largest mosque in India, Bhopal was a major railway junction. Its main industries consisted of manufacturing heavy electrical equipment, weaving and printing cotton cloth, and milling flour.

In 1969, American Union Carbide Corporation, a company headquartered in Danbury, Connecticut, reached an agreement with the Indian government for the construction of a Union Carbide plant in Bhopal. Union Carbide would hold a 51 percent interest in the plant through its share of ownership of an Indian subsidiary of American Union Carbide. The agreement was seen as a win–win situation. India would have the plant and its jobs as well as the production of produce pesticides, a product needed badly by Indian farmers in order to increase agricultural productivity. In addition, Union Carbide also agreed that it would use local managers, who would be provided with the necessary skills and management training so that the plant would be truly locally operated.

The plant used methyl isocyanate (MIC) gas as part of the production process for the pesticides. MIC is highly toxic and reacts strongly with other agents, including water. Operation of a plant with MIC processes requires detailed monitoring as well as security processes to prevent sabotage.

While the plant began operations with high hopes, by 1980 the relationships were strained because the plant was not profitable. Union Carbide had asked the Indian government for permission to close the plant but the government felt the products from the plant as well as the jobs were needed for the Indian economy.

Sometime in the early morning hours of December 3, 1984, MIC stored in a tank at the Bhopal plant came in contact with water, and the result was a boiling effect in the tank. The back-up safety systems at the plant, including cooling components for the tanks, did not work. The result was the toxic mixture began to leak and workers at the plant felt a burning sensation in their eyes. The boiling of the water and MIC caused the safety valves on the tank to explode. Following the explosion, the white smoke from the lethal mixture escaped through a smoke stack and began to spread across the area to the city of Bhopal.

As the gas spread, it wove its way through the shanty towns that were located near the plant. The occupants of these shanty towns were Bhopal's poorest. As the gas floated through these makeshift neighborhoods, 3,500 lives were lost and 200,000 were injured. The injuries included blindness, burns, and lesions in the respiratory system.

The initial deaths and injuries were followed by long-term health effects. Of the women who were pregnant and exposed to the MIC, one-fourth either miscarried or had babies with birth defects. Children developed chronic respiratory problems. Smaller children who survived the toxic gas were sick for months and, weak from a lack of nutrition and ongoing illnesses, also died. MIC also produced strange boils on the bodies of many residents, boils that could not be healed. The problem of tuberculosis in the area was exacerbated by the lung injuries caused by the leaking MIC.

In the year following the accident, the Indian government spent $40 million on food and health care for the Bhopal victims. Warren M. Anderson, Union Carbide's chairman of the board at the time of the accident, pledged that he would devote the remainder of his career to solving the problems that resulted from the accident. However, by the end

---

[43]Adapted from Marianne M. Jennings, *Case Studies in Business Ethics,* 2nd ed.

of the first year, Mr. Anderson told *Business Week,* "I overreacted. Maybe they, early on, thought we'd give the store away. [Now] we're in litigation mode. I'm not going to roll over and play dead."[44]

Following the accident, Union Carbide's stock fell 16 points and it became, in the go-go 80s, a takeover target. When GAF Corporation made an offer, Union Carbide incurred $3.3 billion in debt in order to buy 56 percent of its own stock to avert a takeover. Through 1992, Union Carbide remained in a defensive mode as it coped with litigation, takeover attempts, and the actions of the Indian government in seeking to charge officers, including Anderson, with crimes.[45]

U.S. lawyers brought suit in the United States against Union Carbide on behalf of hundreds of Bhopal victims, but the case was dismissed because the court lacked jurisdiction over the victims as well as the plant. Union Carbide did settle the case with the Indian government for a payment of $470 million. There were 592,635 claims filed by Bhopal victims. The victims received, on average, about $1,000 each. The ordinary payment from the Indian government, as when a government bus harms an individual, is $130 to $700, depending upon the level of the injury. Individual awards were based on earning capacity, so, for example, widows of the Bhopal accident received $7,000.

The Indian government also pursued criminal charges, including against Mr. Anderson. Lawyers for the company and Mr. Anderson continued to fight the charges, largely on the basis that the court had no jurisdiction over Mr. Anderson. However, to be on the safe side, Mr. Anderson did not return to India because of his fear of an arrest.

In May 1992, the Indian government seized the plant and its assets and announced the sale of its 50 percent interest in the plant. When the sale occurred and Union Carbide received its share of the proceeds, it contributed $17 million to the Indian government for purposes of constructing a hospital near Bhopal. The plant now makes dry-cell batteries.

Following the accident, Union Carbide reduced its workforce by 90 percent. Because of the share purchase, Union Carbide had a debt-to-equity ratio of 80 percent. In addition, the Union Carbide brand was affected by the accident and the company could not seem to gain traction. Dow Chemical would acquire the company in 1999 for $11.6 billion.

In 2008, a study revealed that pesticide residues in the water supply for the area surrounding the plant were at levels above permissible ones. There are about 425 tons of waste buried near the former plant. Advocates continue to appear at Dow shareholder meetings in order to demand clean-up. Dow's response is, "As there was never any ownership, there is no responsibility and no liability—for the Bhopal tragedy or its aftermath."[46]

Discussion Questions

1. Should the Bhopal plant have been operated using U.S. safety and environmental standards? What would the U.S. policy be on the shanty towns?
2. Should the case have been moved to the United States for recover?
3. List all of the costs of the accident to Union Carbide.
4. Evaluate Dow's position on the clean-up.
5. Later studies seem to indicate that the cause of the accident was sabotage. How does this affect your analysis?

[44]Leslie Helm, *et al.,* "Bhopal, A Year Later: Union Carbide Takes a Tougher Line," *Business Week,* November 25, 1985, p. 96.

[45]Scott McMurray, "Union Carbide Offers Some Sober Lessons in Crisis Management," *Wall Street Journal,* January 28, 1992, p. A1.

[46]Somini Sengupta, "Decades Later, Toxic Sludge Torments Bhopal," *New York Times,* July 7, 2008, p. A1.

Case 5.8

Nestlé: When Products Translate Differently

Nestlé Infant Formula

Although the merits and problems of breast-feeding versus using infant formula are debated in the United States and other developed countries, the issue is not so balanced in third-world nations. Studies have demonstrated the difficulties and risks of bottle-feeding babies in such places.

First, refrigeration is not generally available, so the formula, once it is mixed or opened (in the case of premixed types), cannot be stored properly. Second, the lack of purified water for mixing with the formula powder results in diarrhea or other diseases in formula-fed infants. Third, inadequate education and income, along with cultural differences, often lead to the dilution of formula and thus greatly reduced nutrition.

Medical studies also suggest that regardless of the mother's nourishment, sanitation, and income level, an infant can be adequately nourished through breast-feeding.

In spite of medical concerns about using their products in these countries, some infant formula manufacturers heavily promoted bottle-feeding.

These promotions, which went largely unchecked through 1970, included billboards, radio jingles, and posters of healthy, happy infants, as well as baby books and formula samples distributed through the health care systems of various countries.

Also, some firms used "milk nurses" as part of their promotions. Dressed in nurse uniforms, "milk nurses" were assigned to maternity wards by their companies and paid commissions to get new mothers to feed their babies formula. Mothers who did so soon discovered that lactation could not be achieved and the commitment to bottle-feeding was irreversible.

In the early 1970s, physicians working in nations where milk nurses were used began vocalizing their concerns. For example, Dr. Derrick Jelliffe, then the director of the Caribbean Food and Nutrition Institute, had the Protein-Calorie Advisory Group of the United Nations place infant formula promotion methods on its agenda for several of its meetings.

Journalist Mike Muller first brought the issue to public awareness with a series of articles in the *New Internationalist* in the 1970s. He also wrote a pamphlet on the promotion of infant formulas called "The Baby Killer," which was published by a British charity, War on Want. The same pamphlet was published in Switzerland, the headquarters of Nestlé, a major formula maker, under the title "Nestlé Kills Babies." Nestlé sued in 1975, which resulted in extensive media coverage.

In response to the bad publicity, manufacturers of infant formula representing about 75 percent of the market formed the International Council of Infant Food Industries to establish standards for infant formula marketing. The new code banned the milk nurse commissions and required the milk nurses to have identification that would eliminate confusion about their "nurse" status.

The code failed to curb advertising of formulas. In fact, distribution of samples increased. By 1977, groups in the United States began a boycott against formula makers over what Jelliffe called "comerciogenic malnutrition."

One U.S. group, Infant Formula Action Coalition (INFACT), worked with the staff of U.S. Senator Edward Kennedy of Massachusetts to have hearings on the issue by the Senate Subcommittee on Health and Human Resources, which Kennedy chaired. The hearings produced evidence that 40 percent of the worldwide market for infant formula, which totaled $1.5 billion at the time, was in third-world countries. No regulations resulted, but Congress did tie certain forms of foreign aid to the development by recipient countries of programs to encourage breast-feeding.

Boycotts against Nestlé products began in Switzerland in 1975 and in the United States in 1977. The boycotts and Senator Kennedy's involvement heightened media interest in the issue and led to the World Health Organization (WHO) debating the issue of infant formula marketing in 1979 and agreeing to draft a code to govern it.

After four drafts and two U.S. presidential administrations (Jimmy Carter and Ronald Reagan), the 118 member nations of WHO finally voted on a code for infant formula marketing. The United States was the only nation to vote against it; the Reagan administration opposed the code being mandatory. In the end, WHO made the code a recommendation only, but the United States still refused to support it.

The publicity on the vote fueled the boycott of Nestlé, which continued until the formula maker announced it would meet the WHO standards for infant formula marketing. Nestlé created the Nestlé Infant Formula Audit Commission (NIFAC) to demonstrate its commitment to and ensure its implementation of the WHO code.

In 1988, Nestlé introduced a new infant formula, Good Start, through its subsidiary, Carnation. The industry leader, Abbott Laboratories, which held 54 percent of the market with its Similac brand, revealed Carnation's affiliation: "They are Nestlé," said Robert A. Schoellhorn, Abbott's chairman and CEO.[47] Schoellhorn also disclosed that Nestlé was the owner of Beech-Nut Nutrition Corporation, officers of which had been indicted and convicted (later reversed) for selling adulterated apple juice for babies.[48]

Carnation advertised Good Start in magazines and on television. The American Academy of Pediatrics (AAP) objected to this direct advertising, and grocers feared boycotts.

The letters "H.A." came after the name "Good Start," indicating the formula was hypoallergenic. Touted as a medical breakthrough by Carnation, the formula was made from whey and advertised as ideal for babies who were colicky or could not tolerate milk-based formulas.

Within four months of Good Start's introduction in November 1988, the FDA was investigating the formula because of six reported cases of vomiting due to the formula. Carnation then agreed not to label the formula hypoallergenic and to include a warning that milk-allergic babies should be given Good Start only with a doctor's approval and supervision.

In 1990, with its infant formula market share at 2.8 percent, Carnation's president, Timm F. Crull, called on the AAP to "examine all marketing practices that might hinder breast-feeding."[49] Crull specifically cited manufacturers' practices of giving hospitals education and research grants, as well as free bottles, in exchange for having exclusive rights to supply the hospital with formula and to give free samples to mothers. He also called for scrutiny of the practice of paying pediatricians' expenses to attend conferences on infant formulas.

The AAP looked into prohibiting direct marketing of formula to mothers and physicians' accepting cash awards for research from formula manufacturers.

The distribution of samples in third-world countries continued during this time. Studies by the United Nations Children's Fund found that a million infants were dying every year because they were not breast-fed adequately. In many cases, the infant starved because the mother used free formula samples and could not buy more, while her own milk had dried up. In 1991, the International Association of Infant Food Manufacturers agreed to stop distributing infant formula samples by the end of 1992.

In the United States in 1980, the surgeon general established a goal that the nation's breast-feeding rate be 75 percent by 1990. The rate remains below 60 percent, however,

[47]Rick Reiff, "Baby Bottle Battle," Forbes, November 28, 1988, pp. 222–224.

[48]For details of the Beech-Nut apple juice case, see Case 4.23.

[49]Julia F. Siler and D. Woodruff, "The Furor over Formula Is Coming to a Boil," Business Week, April 9, 1990, pp. 52–53.

despite overwhelming evidence that breast milk reduces susceptibility to illness, especially ear infections and gastrointestinal illnesses. The AAP took a strong position that infant formula makers should not advertise to the public, but, as a result, new entrants into the market (such as Nestlé with its Carnation Good Start) were disadvantaged because long-time formula makers Abbott and Mead Johnson were well-established through physicians. In 1993, Nestlé filed an antitrust suit alleging a conspiracy among the AAP, Abbott, and Mead Johnson.

Some 200 U.S. hospitals have voluntarily stopped distributing discharge packs from formula makers to their maternity patients because they felt it "important not to appear to be endorsing any products or acting as commercial agents."[50] A study at Boston City Hospital showed that mothers who receive discharge packs are less likely to continue nursing, if they nurse at all. UNICEF and WHO offer "Baby Friendly" certification to maternity wards that take steps to eliminate discharge packs and formula samples.

Discussion Questions

1. If you had been an executive with Nestlé, would you have changed your marketing approach after the boycotts began?
2. Did Nestlé suffer long-term damage because of its third world marketing techniques?
3. How could a marketing plan address the concerns of the AAP and WHO?
4. Is anyone who worked in the infant formula companies responsible for the deaths of infants described in the United Nations study? Is there a line that companies could draw that emerges in this case?
5. Is the moratorium on distributing free formula samples voluntary? Would your company comply?
6. If you were a hospital administrator, what policy would you adopt on discharge packs?
7. Should formula makers advertise directly to the public? What if their ads read, "Remember, breast is best"?

Sources

"Breast Milk for the World's Babies," *New York Times,* March 12, 1992, p. A18.

Burton, Thomas B., "Methods of Marketing Infant Formula Land Abbott in Hot Water," *Wall Street Journal,* May 25, 1993, pp. A1, A6.

Freedman, Alix M., "Nestlé's Bid to Crash Baby-Formula Market in the U.S. Stirs a Row," *Wall Street Journal,* February 6, 1989, pp. A1, A10.

Garland, Susan B., "Are Formula Makers Putting the Squeeze on the States?" *BusinessWeek,* June 18, 1990, p. 31.

Meier, Barry, "Battle over the Market for Baby Formula," *New York Times,* June 15, 1993, pp. C1, C15.

"Nestlé Unit Sues Baby Formula Firms, Alleging Conspiracy with Pediatricians," *Wall Street Journal,* June 1, 1993, p. B4.

Post, James E., "Assessing the Nestlé Boycott: Corporate Accountability and Human Rights," *California Management Review* 27 (1985): 113–131.

Star, Marlene G., "Breast Is Best," *Vegetarian Times,* June (1991): 25–26.

"What's in a Name?" *Time,* March 29, 1989, p. 58.

Case 5.9

Google, Yahoo, and Human Rights in China

In 2006, at the request of the Chinese government, Yahoo's Chinese subsidiary turned over the name of journalist Shi Tao. Tao was a dissident who was posting information about the government's activities on the Internet. Tao was arrested and is now serving a ten-year term. His crime was disclosing "state secrets." Yahoo's subsidiary there is now

---

[50]Andrea Gerlin, "Hospitals Wean from Formula Makers' Freebies," *Wall Street Journal,* December 29, 1994, p. A1.

defunct, and it has created a committee within the company to address issues of privacy and freedom of expression.

However, Rep. Chris Smith has proposed a bill in the House that would ban companies from disclosing information to governments such as China's information that would identify individual Internet users. Yahoo's CEO Jerry Yang and its general counsel, Michael Callahan, appeared before the House Foreign Affairs Committee to testify regarding the bill. Both apologized for Yahoo's role in the journalist's imprisonment, but both also refused to endorse the bill. They did agree to work closely with Congress in developing a solution to the complex issue of disclosure of information about customers to foreign governments. The Electronic Frontier Foundation has been working with Internet companies to develop a code of Internet privacy policies that would address issues such as the Tao disclosure, but the effort has been very slow-moving.

Yahoo's shares dropped 7.7 percent following the testimony of the two executives. There was a 2.7 percent NASDAQ drop the same day because of a weakening market. Yahoo does own a 39 percent interest in Alibaba.com Ltd., a Chinese Internet firm that completed a successful IPO in Hong Kong the same week as the hearings on the Chinese dissidents. Because of the transfer of assets and goodwill to Alibaba, Yahoo maintains that it does not do business in China. Mr. Yang does serve on Alibaba's board.

Rep. Smith said he was "absolutely bewildered and angered" by Yahoo's position.[51] Goa Qin Sheng, mother of Tao, wept in the hearing room as Yang testified. Rep. Tom Lantos told Mr. Yang, "While technologically and financially you are giants, morally, you are pygmies." Yang added, in addressing the family member present, "I want to say we are committed to doing what we can to secure their freedom. And I want to personally apologize for what they are going through."[52]

Another issue that emerged was that Mr. Callahan's testimony, given to Congress in 2006 when the imprisonment in China first occurred, was incorrect. Mr. Callahan testified that Yahoo did not know the nature of the reason for the Chinese government's request when it turned over the information. However, congressional staff members established that Yahoo employees did know the nature of the request even if Mr. Callahan did not. When Mr. Callahan learned the full story on what had happened, he failed to take steps to inform Congress about the incorrect testimony. However, members of the committee felt that Yahoo was either "negligent" or "deliberately deceptive." "How could a dozen lawyers prepare another lawyer to testify before Congress without anyone thinking to look at the document that had caused the hearing to be called? This is astonishing," was the response of Rep. Smith.

The committee urged Yahoo to get involved in humanitarian efforts to assist the families of the jailed dissidents. Professor John Palfrey of the Berkman Center for the Internet & Society at Harvard Law School said, "There's no avoiding the ethical consequences of doing business as a technology company in regimes like China, where human rights are not held so dear as they are in the United States."

The World Organization for Human Rights USA has launched a campaign against Yahoo. Yahoo defended its actions by indicating that its employees in China faced both civil and criminal sanctions if they refused to comply with the government's requests for the information.

When Google began doing business in China, it agreed to place restrictions on the types of materials that residents of China could pull up using the Google search tool. The government dictated the type of information that had to be filtered out by Google

---

[51]Jim Hopkins and Jefferson Graham, "Yahoo Shares Savaged over China Journalist," *USA Today*, November 8, 2007, p. 3B.

[52]Corey Boles, Don Clark, Pui-Wing Tam, "Yahoo's Lashing Highlights Risks of China Market," *Wall Street Journal*, November 7, 2007, pp. A1, A14.

before it could begin doing business there. In early 2010, Google reversed its position on doing business with China and threatened to withdraw from China unless the government negotiated on issues of privacy and restrictions. Google co-founder Sergey Brin said that previously the company was doing business there in order to "advance the bar." However, he added, "Ultimately, I guess it is where your threshold of discomfort is."[53] By mid-2010, Google was again doing business in China with some change in government policies on censorship but not an end result of open Internet access.

Discussion Questions

1. Did Yahoo and Google act ethically in making their decisions to do business in China?
2. What questions did Google and Yahoo fail to answer in making their business decision to enter this large untapped market?

3. Evaluate Brin's discomfort test for doing business in China.

Compare & Contrast

A Google spokesperson indicated that it was better to be in China in some way, even with restrictions, than to deprive the citizens there of access to the Internet's information. Google argued for progress in China in small steps.[54] There is some historical perspective for Google in making its decision. Has this approach been used in other countries at points in their development? Consider the issues in South Africa during apartheid. Some companies stayed, and some refused to do business there. Those companies that stayed helped the country develop, and eventually the rights issues were addressed. Was it ethical to stay or boycott? What is the same about the issues in South Africa in comparison to those in China? What is different?

---

[53]Mark Landler, "Google Searches for a Foreign Policy," *New York Times,* March 28, 2010, WK, p. 4.

[54]"Rights Group Says Yahoo Helped China," *USA Today,* April 19, 2007, p. 1B.

Bribes, Grease Payments, and When in Rome...

Reading 5.10

A Primer on the FCPA[55]

Perhaps the most widely known criminal statute affecting firms that operate internationally is the **Foreign Corrupt Practices Act** (FCPA).[56] The FCPA applies to business concerns that have their principal offices in the United States. It contains antibribery provisions as well as accounting controls for these firms, and was passed to curb the use of bribery in foreign operations of these companies.

The act prohibits making, authorizing, or promising payments or gifts of money or anything of value to government officials with the intent to corrupt for the purpose of *obtaining* or *retaining business* for or with, or *directing business*. Under the FCPA, payments designed to influence the official acts of foreign officials, political parties, party officials, candidates for office, any nongovernmental organization (NGO), or any person who will transmit the gift or money to one of the other types of persons are prohibited. Changes in 1998 added the NGO coverage so that foreign officials are now defined to include public international figures, such as officials with the United Nations, the Olympics, or the International Monetary Fund (IMF).

First passed in 1977, the FCPA is the result of an SEC investigation that uncovered questionable foreign payments by large stock issuers who were based in the United States. Approximately 435 U.S. corporations had made improper or questionable payments totaling $300 million in Japan, the Netherlands, and Korea. Under the 1998 amendments to the FCPA, any payment made to those designated in the statute, including government and NGO officials, to "secure any improper advantage" in doing business in that country would be a violation. For example, if an American company trying to win a bid on a contract for the construction of highways in a foreign country paid a government official there who was responsible for awarding such construction contracts a "consulting fee" of $25,000, the American company would be in violation of the FCPA. The payment was of money, it was made to a foreign official, and it was made for the purpose of obtaining business within that country. Titan Corporation violated the FCPA when money it paid to an agent in Benin was passed along to the reelection campaign of the president of Benin. The result was an increased management fee for Titan's operation of the telecommunications system in Benin. The payments were uncovered as Lockheed Martin was conducting due diligence for purposes of a merger with Titan. Titan voluntarily disclosed the payment and paid a total fine of $28.5 million as follows: $13 million criminal penalty, $12.6 million disgorgement (benefit), and $2.9 million in interest.

Use of Agents and the FCPA

When the FCPA was passed initially, many companies tried to find ways around the bribery prohibitions. Companies would hire foreign agents or consultants to help them gain business in countries and allowed these "third parties" to act independently. However,

---

[55]Adapted from Marianne M. Jennings, *Business: Its Legal, Ethical, and Global Environment*, 9th ed.
[56]15 U.S.C. §§ 78dd-1

many of these consultants then paid others who then actually paid bribes to officials. Under the FCPA, even these types of arrangements can constitute a violation if the consulting fees are high, odd payment arrangements occur, or the company has reason to know of a potential or actual violation. Companies must be able to establish that they have performed due diligence in investigating those hired as their agents and consultants in foreign countries. For example, if a U.S. company hired a consultant who charged the company $25,000 in fees and $250,000 in expenses, the U.S. company is, under Justice Department guidelines, on notice for excessive expenses that could signal potential bribes being paid. These types of expenses are known as "red flags" for U.S. companies. The Justice Department uses this information as a means of establishing intent even when the company may not know precisely what was done with the funds and what was paid to whom.

FCPA and "Grease," or Facilitation Payments

Payments to any foreign official for "facilitation," often referred to as "grease payments," are not prohibited under FCPA so long as these payments are made only to get these officials to do their normal jobs that they might not do or would do slowly without some payment. These grease payments can be made for obtaining permits, licenses, or other official documents; processing governmental papers, such as visas and work orders; providing police protection and mail pickup and delivery; providing phone service, power, and water supply; loading and unloading cargo, or protecting perishable products; and scheduling inspections associated with contract performance or transit of goods across the country.

Penalties for Violation of FCPA

Penalties for violations of the FCPA can run up to $250,000 per violation and five years' imprisonment for individuals. Corporate fines are up to $2 million per violation. Also, under the Alternative Fines Act, the Justice Department can seek to obtain two times the benefit that the bribe attempted to gain, known as disgorgement. The government's methods for computation of the profits on the contracts that involved FCPA violations are often difficult to discern, but the Justice Department has been using disgorgement consistently as a penalty for companies during the past five years and the amounts recouped through disgorgement have been increasing steadily. The Dodd-Frank Wall Street Reform Act allows whistle-blowers who report FCPA violations to receive between 10 to 30 percent of the amount of the fine collected from the company.

Investigations and prosecutions under the FCPA are on the rise. The following chart shows the number of U.S. companies that have self-reported FCPA violations.

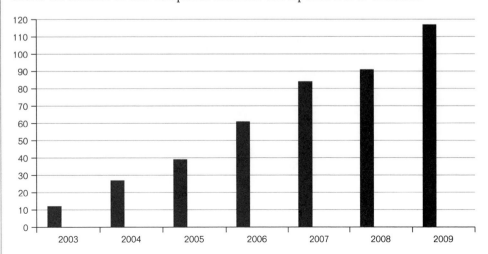

The U.S. Justice Department has been stepping up enforcement because, "U.S. companies that are paying bribes to foreign officials are undermining government institutions around the world. It is a hugely destabilizing force."[57] This year, the guilty plea of former Halliburton executive Albert J. Stanley (a.k.a. Jack Stanley) led to his seven-year sentence—the longest one ever imposed since the FCPA was passed in 1977.[58] In 2008, Siemens agreed to pay a $800 million fine, the largest since the FCPA passage.

The Justice Department also notes that cooperation from foreign officials and governments in these prosecutions is also at an all-time high. In the past, requests from the Justice Department for information from foreign governments went unanswered or were ignored. Now, with increased enforcement in those countries as well as negotiated treaties and agreements, the countries are cooperating more. For example, prosecutors from the OECD nations[59] met in Paris in summer 2008 to discuss ongoing cases and investigations so that they could share information.

Discussion Questions

1. What are the risks associated with making facilitation payments?
2. If you had to draft a policy for a company on FCPA compliance, what would that policy contain?
3. There were complaints from companies in 2010 that Justice Department lawyers were pursuing FCPA cases and building the department's FCPA focus during their government service and then crossing over into the private sector and commanding large salaries for their FCPA expertise.[60] Discuss any ethical issues you see with regard to the conduct of the lawyers.

Case 5.11

Siemens and Bribery, Everywhere

Siemens is a German conglomerate that has been in business since 1847 with its three divisions of Energy, Health Care, and Industry. Siemens has 428,200 employees and operates in 190 countries. Siemens produces wind turbines and high-speed trains and provides engineering services on all types of construction projects. Siemens's net income for 2008 was $8.9 billion on net revenue of $116.5 billion. However, a large portion of Siemens's revenues came from projects with governments and their agencies. As a result of a multicountry investigation, authorities uncovered a four-year pattern of bribery by Siemens that is shown in the chart below.

Country	Product	Bribes Paid	Period
Russia	Medical devices	$55 million	2000–2007
Argentina	Identity cards project	$40 million	1998–2004
China	High-voltage transmission lines	$25 million	2002–2003
China	Metro trains	$22 million	2002–2007

[57]Russell Gold and David Crawford, "U.S., Other Nations Step Up Bribery Battle," *Wall Street Journal,* September 12, 2008, pp. B1, B6.

[58]Because of Mr. Stanley's plea deal, more indictments are expected as he shares information.

[59]OECD is the Organization for Economic Cooperation and Development. Its 1997 agreement resulted in uniform FCPA acts around the world, a beginning point for the cooperation among the countries that are signatories to the OECD agreement.

[60]Nathan Vardi, "How Federal Crackdown on Bribery Hurts Business and Enriches Insiders," *Forbes,* May 24, 2010, p. 54. Blog, "DOJ, Defense Lawyers Spar Over Pace of FCPA Cases," *Legal Times*, May 7, 2010. http://legaltimes. typepad.com/blt/2010/05/doj-defense-lawyers-spar-over-pace-of-fcpa-prosecution.html. Accessed August 6, 2010.

Country	Product	Bribes Paid	Period
Israel	Power plants	$20 million	2002–2005
Bangladesh	Mobile telephone works	$5.3 million	2004–2006
Venezuela	High-speed trains	$16.7 million	2001–2007
Russia	Traffic-control systems	$0.75 million	2004–2006
Vietnam	Medical devices	$0.5 million	2005
China	Medical devices	$14.4 million	2003–2007
Nigeria	Telecommunications projects	€4.2 million	2003
Iraq	Power station	$1.7 million	2000
Italy	Power station	€6.0 million	2003
Greece	Telecommunications	€37 million	2006

Both the SEC and the Justice Department were investigating Siemens. The two agencies concluded that Siemens had paid more than 4,283 bribes totaling $1.4 billion to government officials to secure contracts. The SEC concluded that the bribes resulted in the company obtaining $1.1 billion in profits. Siemens did follow what is known as "the four-eyes principle" of internal control for the FCPA, which is that all payments required two signatures. However, the company had made so many exceptions to the four-eyes principle that, operationally, it was not in effect. The SEC complaint notes how many "red flags" the board ignored in the years during which the bribery was occurring. Since 1999, when Germany signed on to the anti-bribery provisions of the OECD, Siemens's executives were concerned about all the companies involved in bribery around the world. Siemen's CEO at the time of the OECD adoption also voiced concern to the board about the number of Siemens executives who were under investigation by the German government for bribery activities. He asked the board to take protective measures because its members could be held responsible for inaction. Despite his plea, the bribes continued with support from some board members.

In 2001, general counsel for the board notified the members that in order for the company to meet U.S. standards for its new New York Stock Exchange (NYSE) listing, it needed to end its practices of having off-the-books accounts for the payment of the bribes. The company took no steps to investigate or end its practices. The SEC noted there was a stunning lack of internal controls as well as a tone at the top that did not take the FCPA seriously.

The U.S. Justice Department and Siemens AG reached an agreement to settle the company's ongoing violations of the FCPA. Siemens agreed to pay $800 million to the United States, a fine 20 times higher than the largest fine ever collected under the FCPA. Siemens is also settling charges with 10 other countries and will be paying fines that total $5.8 billion. The SEC complaint states that the bribes involved employees at all levels of the company and revealed a culture that had long been at odds with the FCPA.[61]

The company's cooperation with the U.S. government since 2006 as well as its efforts to correct the violations caused government officials to reduce the fine from $2.7 billion to the $800 million. Siemens's efforts to correct its culture included cooperating with the government, turning over all documents it found, and replacing all but one officer and

---

[61]www.sec.gov/litigation. Accessed May 19, 2010.

the board. Three of the company's former officers are under investigation by German authorities for their role in the ongoing bribery web. Siemens has paid a total of $1.3 billion in fines in other countries for the violations.

Discussion Questions

1. Add together all the fines and compare with the profits made from the bribes and determine whether Siemens made a good business decision with its approach to winning contracts.
2. Peter Löscher, the new CEO hired to take over following the settlement of the FCPA charges, indicates that the company was a great innovator but no longer had marketing skills because it had relied on the facile approach of bribery for so long.[62] Thinking about his statement, offer a risk associated with using bribes as a business model.
3. Reinhard Siekaczek, the former Siemens employee, largely responsible for Siemens accounting system that hid bribes for 5 years, and who has been charged with breach of trust under German law, has made the following statements about his activities, the bribes, and the consequences:

"People will only say about Siemens that they were unlucky and that they broke the 11th Commandment. The 11th Commandment is: 'Don't get caught.'"[63]

"It was about keeping the business unit alive and not jeopardizing thousands of jobs overnight."

"I was not the man responsible for the bribery. I organized the cash."

"I would have never thought I'd go to jail for my company. Sure, we joked about it, but we thought if our actions ever came to light, we'd get together and there would be enough people to play a game of cards."

Can you describe what type of moral development is involved here? What did he miss in his evaluation of his conduct and the risks? What lines did Siemens cross in getting to this level of bribery payments?

Case 5.12

Salt Lake City, the Olympics, and Bribery

Officials in Salt Lake City had been trying to win the International Olympic Committee (IOC) nod for the Winter Olympics since 1966. For the IOC meeting in Rome at which the 1966 decision would be made, the Salt Lake City Olympic Committee raised $24,000 by selling Olympic pins for $1 each. Following a trip to Rome, there was $10,305 left and a two-page audit documented all the expenses for the failed try.

Business and government leaders kept trying to win over the IOC, but continued to do so on a spartan budget. For example, in 1989 the Salt Lake leaders journeyed to Greece to meet with the IOC and noted that other cities were giving the IOC members jewelry and crystal vases. Atlanta had created "The Atlanta House" and had furniture shipped from Atlanta to create an authentic Southern home. Other cities had created rooms for breakfast and lunch buffets for the IOC members. That year, Salt Lake City leaders, concerned about their lack of gifts, had some letter openers flown in to give to the IOC members.

When Salt Lake City officials were trying for the 1998 Winter Games, they were told in a letter from the head of Ireland's Olympic Committee that some of the IOC members were selling their votes for $100,000 in exchange for a vote for Nagano, Japan (the site eventually chosen). One of the children of a member of the IOC approached Thomas Welch, the head of the Salt Lake City Olympic Committee, and said that he could help get Salt Lake City the votes in exchange for $35,000. Mr. Welch and the members of the Salt Lake City Olympic Committee (SLCOC) refused to pay the money, although many

[62]Anita Raghavan, "No More Excuses," *Forbes,* April 27, 2009, p. 121.
[63]*U.S. v Siemens*, SEC Complaint, 1 :08-cv-02167 (December 12, 2008).

have said it was only because they could not raise the $35,000 at the last minute. The SLCOC had simply paid for travel expenses for IOC members. For example, an audit of the 1991 expenses for the unsuccessful bid for the 1998 Winter Olympics revealed that Mr. David R. Johnson was reimbursed $2.73 for a receipt from a 7-Eleven convenience store near Utah's ski areas and an accompanying note that read, "juice for Prince Albert." Prince Albert of Monaco was an IOC member at the time and had traveled to Utah to view the sites for events. Prince Albert refused any special treatment, including limousines and any types of events or dinners in his honor. Such simplicity from a member of a royal family and also an IOC member perhaps also convinced the SLCOC members that the exchange of cash was unnecessary.

However, when the SLCOC lost its bid to Nagano, despite its hopes that the issues of cash payments were not effective, its members began to talk openly about "what it took to win the Olympics" for their city. When the SLCOC began its planning in 1991 for its bid for the 2002 Winter Olympics, even the minutes from the meetings make it clear that committee members were single-minded in doing all it took to get the Olympics. Mr. Johnson, a continuing and prominent member of the 2002 SLCOC, said, "Everything we had was about getting the bid. All our money was to get votes." Others have described the attitude of "doing whatever it takes" to get the Winter Olympics because the cause was a good one and it seemed that Salt Lake City was losing "for not playing the game" and "doing what everyone else was doing." There was an attitude of "If we don't do it, someone else will" and "This is the way it's always been done—we just didn't understand that."

Beginning in 1991, on the heels of their loss to Nagano, the SLCOC began its new style of garnering votes, particularly, as they thought through their strategy, the African votes. From 1991 through 1995, the SLCOC gave an estimated $1.2 million to members of the IOC or their families. Nearly $100,000 in scholarships went to children of members of the IOC. Other children of IOC members stopped by the SLCOC offices on a regular basis and picked up checks for themselves. Sibo Sibandze, son of an IOC member from Swaziland, picked up weekly checks from the SLCOC offices that ranged from $250 to $590.

A volunteer staff member described the situation on the payments and checks as follows:

> You knew these guys, they came in weekly. You saw them pick up their checks. You took them places. You didn't have to be a brain surgeon to know what was going on. It was always whispered, "Whose son is he? How much of a scholarship is he getting? How does that work?" People freaked out the first time they heard about it. Then it became second nature.[64]

Audits of the SLCOC's books from this time period reveal a dramatic drop-off in documentation for payments, with many never explained. There were a series of payments to Raouf Scally totaling $14,500 in $500 installments with a notation that Mr. Scally was a son of a member of the IOC. No one has ever been able to tie him to any IOC member, and subsequent investigations have not determined who he is and what role he played in the SLCOC's successful bid.

An examination of the records also revealed that the members of the SLCOC had done their homework in terms of vulnerability. Some of the dossiers on IOC members made reference to those who had complained about financial difficulties, including issues of making their mortgage payments. Although IOC members are prohibited from

[64]Jo Thomas, Kirk Johnson, and Jere Longman, "From an Innocent Bid to Olympic Scandal," *New York Times*, March 11, 1999, pp. A1, A14, A15.

accepting gifts valued over $150, the following are documented benefits to IOC members from the SLCOC:

- Lawn equipment, $268.
- Violin, $524.
- Doorknobs, $673 (one of the IOC members, Jean-Claude Ganga, an IOC member from Congo Republic, was remodeling his home).
- Jean-Claude Ganga received more than $200,000 in cash and medical treatment.
- Ganga's wife used an SLCOC member's credit card at Walmart for various items and reached the maximum credit limit on the member's card.
- Bathroom fixtures, $1,488.
- Draperies, $3,117.
- Dogs, $1,010.
- Letterhead stationery for one of the IOC member countries, $6,934.
- Super Bowl trip for Mr. Welch and IOC members Philip Coles of Australia and Willi Kaltschmitt of Guatemala, $19,991. These two IOC members never visited Salt Lake City.
- Two-week Park City condominium rental for a vacation for Agustin Arroyo, the ICO member from Ecuador, $10,000.
- The daughter of Kim Un Yung, an IOC member from South Korea, was given a contract playing with the Utah Symphony.
- English-language training, $1,390.
- Disneyland trip, $1,202.
- Yellowstone trip, $926.
- Ski lessons for a child, $414.
- Furniture rental for a child, $250.

Ernst & Young, the auditors for the SLCOC, uncovered most of the questionable items during a 1995 audit. The auditors' work papers indicate that they talked to SLCOC members about the scholarship programs, the amounts, and the purposes. These committee members deny that they were informed of these issues by the auditors. However, the auditors did not uncover any evidence that any of the checks that were issued were unauthorized.

What happened following the audit and the eventual public disclosure of these payments was a complex tale of several individuals trying to have someone review what the SLCOC was doing. Mr. Ken Bullock, a member of the SLCOC Board of Trustees, talked with both Governor Michael O. Leavitt's staff and members of Salt Lake City's city council. In many cases, he was dismissed as being "a little out there." Friends said that Mr. Bullock was frustrated, bloodied, and bruised as he tried to bring the matters to someone's attention. One city council member did have a meeting with Rod Decker, a television reporter, about the scholarship issues on June 3, 1997. However, Mr. Decker accepted Mr. Johnson's explanation that children of members of the IOC had simply toured the University of Utah and that there were no scholarships. It was during this time that the law firm housing the records of the SLCOC meetings ordered the destruction of firm documents with no indication of who had given the order for their destruction. The destruction was accomplished at a time when the time frame for retention of the client's documents would not have provided for their destruction.

The story finally came to public light when a staff member from the SLCOC offices sent an anonymous letter reflecting the payment of scholarship monies to one of the children of an IOC member to a different television station from Mr. Decker's that did not run the story. On November 4, 1998, the first television story ran about possible scholarship and other payments to IOC members and their children. Both local and national news outlets descended on Salt Lake City to investigate the full extent of the payments. When a high-ranking member of the IOC used the word *bribes* in connection with the SLCOC bid, government agencies began investigations. Mr. Welch resigned from his $10,000-per-month job as head of the SLCOC, and Mitt Romney, former candidate for the U.S. Senate in Massachusetts and the presidency, the owner of Staples, Inc., and former Massachusetts governor, took over as head of the SLCOC.

Once the news stories began, the following investigations and their outcomes resulted:

- Ethics investigation by Gordon R. Hall, former chief justice of the Utah Supreme Court: issued a 300-page report in February 1999 that concluded no criminal activity but a host of ethical issues and violations of trust in the SLCOC's bid for the 2002 games; twenty-four members of the IOC are mentioned by name in the report as having received gifts and other items from the SLCOC.

- United States Olympic Committee (USOC) investigation by George Mitchell (former U.S. senator, ambassador to Ireland, and head of the USOC Ethics Committee): recommends processes, procedures, checks, and balances for future bids for games from the United States.

- U.S. Justice Department: investigation of SLCOC activities that resulted in indictments. David Simmons entered a guilty plea to charges of tax evasion after admitting that he set up a sham job for John Kim, the son of Yong Kim, an IOC member from Korea (in response to a request from Mr. Welch); John Kim is charged with lying to the FBI about his job and lying to obtain a green card. David Simmons was the head of Keystone Communications. He set up a job for John Kim that paid between $75,000 and $100,000; Keystone was then reimbursed by the SLCOC for the salary. The investigation was referred to the Reno Justice Department after the U.S. attorney for Utah, Paul Warner, recused himself and his office from any SLCOC investigations and related matters. Justice Department investigators zeroed in on violations of the Foreign Corrupt Practices Act and tax fraud. Mr. Johnson and Mr. Welch were charged with RICO (racketeering) violations, bribery, and conspiracy in a grand jury indictment handed down in July 2000. Both rejected plea bargain agreements from the Justice Department.[65] Their trial was scheduled to begin on July 16, 2001; however, the federal district judge dismissed the charges, noting that the state of Utah had declined to prosecute. The U.S. attorney filed an appeal of the dismissal.[66] The Tenth Circuit Court of Appeals held that the Utah antibribery statute was constitutional and that the two men could be tried for RICO violations under federal law.[67]

- IOC internal investigation: resulted in the expulsion of six IOC members; a reprimand to Phillip Coles of Australia, who also resigned his position as a member of the Sydney Olympics Board; and revisions in rules on choosing an Olympic site. A new code of ethics was also adopted. The final years of IOC President Juan Antonio Samaranch's tenure were rocky because of the SLCOC scandal. Many had called for his resignation, but he stayed until July 2001 when his tenure expired, promising ethics reform during those final years.

- U.S. Congress: conducted hearings on IOC reforms with a stern admonition to IOC members that there would be continuing oversight on the gifts aspects of the IOC's code of ethics and that reforms were not yet complete. Congressional budget committees also examined the award of federal funds to Utah and Salt Lake City for Olympics-related transit and highway improvements.

Salt Lake City was permitted to keep the 2002 Winter Olympics after the news of the "gifts" broke, but it had trouble with corporate sponsorships and raising funds during 1999–2000 because confidence in the games was so shaken.[68] Mitt Romney headed the Olympic efforts in Salt Lake City after the bribery scandal erupted. Mr. Romney was able to bring back corporate sponsors. In November 1999, when Mr. Romney announced that Gateway Computer would be a $20 million sponsor, the tide on fund-raising turned.[69] Visa followed later in November.[70] Further, the Sydney Summer Olympics in 2000

---

[65]*U.S. v Welch*, 327 F.3d 1081, at 1085 (10th Cir. 2003).

[66]*Id.*

[67]*Id.*

[68]For example, Johnson & Johnson withdrew its sponsorship. "Johnson & Johnson Decides against Olympic Scholarship," *(Phoenix) Arizona Republic*, April 19, 1999, p. A5.

[69]Bruce Horovitz, "Gateway Logs On as Salt Lake Olympics Sponsor," *USA Today*, November 3, 1999, p. 1B.

[70]Bruce Horovitz, "Visa Reviews Support for Olympic Games," *USA Today*, November 12, 1999, p. 1B.

experienced many sponsorship withdrawals because of the Salt Lake City bid scandal.[71] Although John Hancock Mutual Life Insurance Company criticized the IOC for the scandal[72] and initially indicated it would withdraw its support, it re-upped as a sponsor for $55 million.[73] Mr. Romney, through the use of large numbers of volunteers, finished the 2002 Winter Olympics with a surplus in funds, a first in the history of the games.

The bribery case against Mr. Welch and Mr. Johnson went to trial in October 2003 after the case was remanded by the court of appeals.[74] Federal U.S. District Judge David Sam acquitted Mr. Welch and Mr. Johnson of the fifteen felony counts because of a lack of evidence. Judge Sam said, "I have never seen a criminal case brought to trial that was so devoid of . . . criminal intent or evil purpose," and called the prosecution "misplaced." Judge Sam also said that the case "offends my sense of justice."[75] The evidence was weak in the case because the federal government's key witness refused to return to the country to testify. John Kim, of South Korea, refused to return because he did not want to take the stand to testify against Mr. Welch and Mr. Johnson. Kim, in a telephone interview with the *Los Angeles Times,* said he is "happy I am not considered a rat. I can walk away with my dignity and my manhood in place."[76] The U.S. attorney also dropped the charges against Kim following his refusal to testify against the other two defendants in the case. Mr. Kim is the son of a vice president of the International Olympic Committee who was, at the time of the case dismissal, hiding in Bulgaria. He was charged, as mentioned above, with lying to the FBI and obtaining a green card fraudulently.

Discussion Questions

1. Tom Schaffer, the attorney for Mr. Welch, said that his client and Mr. Johnson did "what they had to do" to win a bid in a system that "stinks."[77] Are the flaws in a system a justification for the payments? Ken Bullock has noted, "The Games are an aphrodisiac. If you want something bad enough, you stretch the boundaries. The IOC allowed this sucking up."[78]

2. In one discussion of exchanges with IOC committee members, SLCOC members brought athletes from the Sudan to the United States for training as part of an exchange for Sudan members' votes. One person associated with the exchange has said, "In our minds, we distinguished the transactions in which Sudanese athletes were brought to the United States, apparently with some understanding that we would receive Sudanese votes, from an example in which an IOC member sells their vote. It's a different thing. A distinction needs to be made."[79] Do you agree? However, another e-mail exchange raises some concerns about the funding being taken from U.S. athletes. One USOC member wrote, "Should I take financial support away from American athletes? Or does your budget cover these international political initiatives?" A response from another USOC member was as follows: "You can take it away from the additional revenue we will ALL benefit from after having won the 2002 Games for SLC."[80] Was there harm in this benefit to the athletes? Dick Schultz, the executive director of the USOC, said of the e-mail exchanges that they were "unfortunate," and,

[71]A. Craig Copetas, "After Scandal, Local Sponsors Shun Olympics," *Wall Street Journal*, April 4, 2000, pp. B1, B4.

[72]Joseph B. Treaster, "Monitor of the Olympic Mettle," *New York Times*, March 28, 1999, p. BU2.

[73]Bruce Horovitz, "Reaching for Rings," *USA Today*, March 16, 2000, p. 1B.

[74]*U.S. v Welch*, 327 F.3d 1081 (10th Cir. 2003).

[75]Dennis Romboy and Lisa Riley Roche, "Judge Tosses Olympic Bribery Case," (*Salt Lake City, Utah*) *Deseret News*, online ed., December 5, 2003.

[76]Lisa Riley Roche, "Charges Dropped in IOC Case," (*Salt Lake City, Utah*) *Deseret News*, December 17, 2003, p. B1.

[77]Kirk Johnson, "E-Mail Trail Adds Details to U.S.O.C.'s Role," *New York Times*, February 10, 1999, pp. C1, C25.

[78]Nadya Labi, "The Olympics Turn into a Five-Ring Circus," *Time*, January 11, 1999, P. 33.

[79]*Id.*

[80]*Id.*

"People make flippant remarks on E-mails that aren't always accurate. It seems like it was handled appropriately. 'If you do this they'll vote for us'—I don't see that in any records we've turned up."[81] Do you think that the statement must be made expressly for exchanges for votes to take place?

3. Richard Pound, an IOC member and a lawyer from Montreal, was the lead investigator for the IOC report. His twenty-four-page summary indicated that "inappropriate activities of certain members of the IOC did not commence with the candidacy of Salt Lake City." The report also notes, "It is clear the matter of gifts is going to be troublesome. In some cases, the value of the gifts was . . . not reasonably perceived as ordinary or routine."[82] How does one define appropriate gifts? What are ordinary and routine gifts? Does it make a difference that Salt Lake City was not the first site bidder to give these types of gifts?

4. When Pound issued his report and recommended a reprimand for Phil Coles, *USA Today* columnist Christine Brennan wrote the following:

   This reminds me of the fabulous way the IOC handled a messy gift-taking situation involving member Phil Coles earlier this year. The IOC refused to use an independent investigator and instead let vice president Dick Pound handle the case. First Pound interrogated Coles, then he went to dinner with him. The two men, it turns out, are good friends. When the investigation was completed do you think the IOC expelled Coles? Heavens no.[83]

   Why does Brennan make this point?

5. Why do you think the expelled members were from third-world nations (Togo, India, Mauritius, Nigeria, Mongolia, and Algeria)?

6. One member of the SLCOC noted that a shopping trip to Walmart was a "good value" and could not be corruption. Do you agree?

7. A lawyer representing the SLCOC in the Justice Department probe has stated, "There were a lot of things that were unethical, but that's a long way from being criminal."[84] Given the outcome of the criminal trial, was she correct?

8. Tom Welch sent a fax to his friends and copied reporters. The note contained the following language:

   I am saddened and dismayed that so many feel the need to isolate responsibility for what—at the time—were cooperative decisions. Had our agreed course of action been questioned at the time by those to whom we reported, no doubt we would have been pleased to pursue other avenues. It is ironic that those who were so supportive of our efforts to secure the Games now feel the need to distance themselves.[85]

   Do you think others knew and abandoned him once the information was public?

9. A letter to the editor of the Salt Lake City paper, the *Deseret News,* read as follows:

   Instead of pursuing legal proceedings, we should be erecting a statue of Tom Welch in Washington Square and put a canopy to keep the pigeons, vultures, the Chris Vancours, and the Steve Paces off of him. It is people like Tom, with deep passions, who accomplish much and who almost single-handedly brought the Olympics to Salt Lake and Utah. There is a lot of truth in the adage, no good deed goes unpunished. I know to be politically correct we had to dump him but only because he played the age-old game of favor for favor, something everyone of us plays daily. Good luck, Tom and Dave. I wish I could be on the jury.[86]

   Is the writer correct? Was it a favor-for-favor game that all of us play every day?

10. Evaluate Mr. Kim's remark about being a "rat."

[81]*Id.*

[82]A. Craig Copetas and Roger Thurow, "A Preliminary Report on Salt Lake Scandal Certain to Rile the IOC," *Wall Street Journal,* January 20, 1999, pp. A1, A8.

[83]Christine Brennan, "Some IOC Fixes Sound Like Trouble," *USA Today,* December 16, 1999, p. 3C.

[84]Laurie P. Cohen and David S. Cloud, "U.S. Probe into Salt Lake Bid Scandal to Explore Possible Federal Violations," *Wall Street Journal,* February 18, 1999, p. A6.

[85]Kristen Moulton, "Welch Defends Actions in Olympics," *LATimes.com,* http://www.latimes.com, Thursday, February 4, 1999.

[86](*Salt Lake City, Utah*) *Deseret News,* June 24, 2001, http://www.desnews.com.

Sources

Caldwell, Christopher, "Pillars of Salt Lake," *National Review,* March 8, 1999, 35–36.

Copetas, Craig, and Roger Thurow, "Closing Ceremony: The Olympics Say Farewell to Samaranch," *Wall Street Journal,* August 12, 2001, pp. A1, A10.

Dodd, Mike, "10 More Are Cited for Misconduct," *USA Today,* February 10, 1999, p. 4C

Fatis, Stefan, "Olympic Broadcaster's IOC Ties Raise Questions," *Wall Street Journal,* January 19, 1999, pp. B1, B6.

Longman, Jere, and Jo Thomas, "Report Details Lavish Spending in Salt Lake's Bid to Win Games," *New York Times,* February 10, 1999, pp. A1, C25.

"Probe Won't Have Salt Lake Federal Prosecutor," *USA Today,* December 22, 1998, p. 3C.

Raboin, Sharon, and Kevin Johnson, "Salt Lake Fund-Raising Slowed," *USA Today,* January 14, 1999, p. 2C.

"A Time of Turmoil," *USA Today,* December 8, 1999, p. 10C.

Titze, Maria, "Bid-Scandal Lawyers File Objection," *(Salt Lake City, Utah) Deseret News,* June 26, 2001, http://www.desnews.com.

Ethics, Business Operations, and Rights

This unit deals with the interrelationships of companies, managers, and employees and the rights of all of those employees. From safety risks to questions of employee privacy and on through to the obligations of employees to throw down the flag when they are concerned about issues and practices in the workplace, this section grapples with the delicate balances required for preserving a safe work environment with open communication.

Workplace Safety

Reading 6.1

Two Sets of Books on Safety

A study in the June 2010 issue of *Annals of Epidemiology* finds that employers have two sets of books when it comes to injuries in the workplace. OSHA reportable figures (as found in the Bureau of Labor Statistics), or those injury stats reported by employers, are 24 percent to 49 percent lower than the number of injuries the study found in worker compensation claims. Injuries have declined since 2000, but fatalities have not.

Workers' comp numbers are the real thing. Employees don't care what employers report to OSHA—they want coverage for work-related injuries. Why the disparity? Some believe that because incentive plans include safety goals related to the injury rate, managers are motivated to put pressure on workers to not report injuries. Some managers even pressure doctors into characterizing an injury as non-work-related. Other managers ask doctors to write a different diagnosis so as to avoid a reportable injury. Employees often share stories about their managers going with them to the hospital or doctor to get the injury characterized in the "right" way.

There is always the wiggle room of technical compliance with the lost workday reporting requirements. There is no question that federal regulations on reportable injuries are confusing and that reasonable minds could differ on some close calls. However, this study seems to indicate that something more than just differing interpretations is driving the disparity. Interpretations seem to cut a wide swath. For example, if an employee can return to work, the injury is not classified as a lost workday. Dr. Robert McClellan, formerly the president of the American College of Occupational and Environmental Medicine, often cites an example of a worker being wheeled onto a construction site with his broken leg so as to avoid a lost workday report. So an employee reported for beam work with a cast and in a wheelchair and there was no OSHA reportable injury.

Discussion Questions

1. What are the parallels between this part of business reporting and financial reports?
2. What risks do you see with the two sets of books?
3. What might happen to safety as a result of these approaches to reporting injuries?

Case 6.2

Sleeping on the Job and on the Way Home

Matt Theurer was an 18-year-old high school senior with many extracurricular activities, including being a member of the National Guard. Mr. Theurer was employed by a McDonald's restaurant (defendant) in Portland, Oregon, on a part-time basis. While his employer called Mr. Theurer an enthusiastic worker, his friends and family felt that he was doing too much and getting too little sleep.

McDonald's employed many high school students on a part-time basis, and their restaurants closed at 11:00 P.M., with clean-up and other procedures taking up another hour until midnight. McDonald's informal policy did not permit high school students to work more than one midnight shift per week or allow split shifts. Split shifts forced the students to work in the morning and then evening. McDonald's felt the commuting time between the shifts prevented "people from getting their rest." Despite these policies, high school employees frequently complained about being tired, and at least two of McDonald's employees had accidents while driving home after working the closing shift until midnight.

A few times each year, McDonald's scheduled special cleanup projects at the restaurant that required employees to work after the midnight closing until 5 A.M. Student workers were to be used for cleanup shifts only on weekends or during spring break. However, for one scheduled cleanup project, there were not enough regular employees, and the manager asked for volunteers for a midnight to 5 A.M. cleanup shift. Mr. Theurer volunteered; the manager knew that Mr. Theurer had to drive about twenty minutes to and from work.

During the week of the scheduled special cleanup, Mr. Theurer had worked five nights. One night he worked until midnight, another until 11:30 P.M., two until 9 P.M., and another until 11 P.M. On Monday, April 4, 1988, Mr. Theurer worked his regular shift from 3:30 until 7:30 P.M., followed by a cleanup shift from midnight until 5 A.M. on April 5, and then worked another shift from 5 A.M. until 8:21 A.M. During that shift Mr. Theurer told his manager that he was tired and asked to be excused from his next regular shift. The manager excused him, and Mr. Theurer began his drive home.

Mr. Theurer was driving 45 miles per hour on a two-lane road when he became drowsy or fell asleep, crossed the dividing line into oncoming traffic, crashed into the van of Frederic Faverty (plaintiff), and was killed. Mr. Faverty was seriously injured. Mr. Faverty settled his claims with Mr. Theurer's estate and then filed suit against McDonald's.[1]

Discussion Questions

1. Does McDonald's have responsibility for employee fatigue?
2. Who is affected by McDonald's work-hour policies?
3. What other industries would be affected by sleep-deprivation liability issues?

Case 6.3

Cintas and OSHA

In 2007, Eleazar Torres-Gomez fell into an industrial dryer at the Cintas plant where he worked. He was killed before anyone even noticed that he had fallen into the dryer from the moving conveyor belt where he was picking up loose clothes. The manufacturer of the equipment provides warnings about not having people on the conveyor belt while it is moving. There are warnings on the belt for Cintas employees not to get on the belt while it is moving. All Cintas employees receive training that warns them against getting onto the moving belts at any time. However, surveillance tapes shows that at the Tulsa plant where Mr. Torres-Gomez worked and other Cintas plants the practice was routine. The tapes show employees jumping on the moving belts to clears jams of clothing as

[1]*Faverty v McDonald's Restaurants of Oregon, Inc.* 892 P.2D 703 (Ct. App. Or. 1995).

they headed into the dryer chutes. Some tapes even showed employees sticking their knees into the chutes as a means of unclogging the clumps of wet laundry making their way into the dryer from the moving belts.

Cintas has an internal memo from its director of safety in 2004 that cautioned the plants about the problem and required plant managers to implement several safety procedures before trying to dislodge laundry. The procedures were not followed at the Tulsa plant.

In interviews with OSHA officials, employees said that they were under a great deal of pressure to keep the laundry moving and not shut down the belt. Cintas has per-piece goals for employees to meet, but Cintas officials say that the goals established for employees are reasonable.

Cintas has had 70 OSHA investigations since 2002, more than any other laundry company, and OSHA has found violations in forty of the investigations. Forty-two of the violations found were "willful." Cintas feels that it has had more inspections because there is a union organizing effort that is ongoing and that employees are reporting violations even when there are no violations.

Discussion Questions

1. Would an employee's compensation package have any effect on his or her decisions at work about risk?

2. What are the values in conflict at Cintas that resulted in the accident and death?

3. What are the ethical issues in employee safety?

Source

James Bandler and Kris Maher, "House Panel to Examine Cintas Plants' Safety Record," *Wall Street Journal,* April 23, 2008, pp. B1, B2.

Workplace Loyalty

SECTION 6B

Case 6.4

Aaron Feuerstein and Malden Mills[2]

Aaron Feuerstein is the chief executive officer and chairman of the board of Malden Mills, a ninety-three-year-old privately held company that manufactures Polartec and is located in Methuen, Massachusetts. Polartec is a fabric made from recycled plastic that stays dry and provides warmth. It is used in everything from ski parkas to blankets by companies such as L.L. Bean, Patagonia, Lands' End, and Eddie Bauer. Malden employs 2,400 locals, and Mr. Feuerstein and his family have steadfastly refused to move production overseas. Their labor costs are the highest in the industry—an average of $12.50 per hour. Malden Mills is the largest employer in what is one of Massachusetts' poorest towns.

On December 11, 1995, a boiler explosion at Malden Mills resulted in a fire that injured twenty-seven people and destroyed three of the buildings at Malden Mills' factory site. With only one building left in functioning order, many employees assumed they would be laid off temporarily. Other employees worried that Mr. Feuerstein, then seventy years old, would simply take the insurance money and retire. Mr. Feuerstein could have retired with about $300 million in insurance proceeds from the fire.

Instead, Mr. Feuerstein announced on December 14, 1995, that he would pay the employees their salaries for at least thirty days. He continued that promise for six months, when 90 percent of the employees were back to work. The cost to the company of covering the wages was approximately $25 million. During that time, Malden ran its Polartec through its one working facility as it began and completed the reconstruction of the plant, at a cost of $430 million. Only $300 million of that amount was covered by the insurance on the plant; the remainder was borrowed so that Malden Mills would be a state-of-the-art, environmentally friendly plant. Interestingly, production output during this time was nine times what it had been before the fire. One worker noted, "I owe him everything. I'm paying him back."[3] After the fire and Feuerstein's announcement, customers pledged their support, with one customer, Dakotah, sending in $30,000 to help. Within the first month following the fire, $1 million in donations was received.[4]

Malden Mills was rededicated in September 1997 with new buildings and technology. About 10 percent of the 2,400 employees were displaced by the upgraded facilities and equipment, but Feuerstein created a job training and placement center on site in order to ease these employees' transition.

By the end of 2001, six years after the fire, Malden Mills had debts of $140 million and was teetering near bankruptcy. However, Malden Mills has been through bankruptcy before, in the 1980s, and emerged very strongly with its then new product, Polartec, developed through the company's R&D program.

---

[2]Adapted from Marianne M. Jennings, "Aaron Feuerstein—an Odd CEO," in *Business: Its Legal, Ethical and Global Environment*, 9th ed. (2011), 634–635.

[3]"Malden Mills," *Dateline NBC*, August 9, 1996.

[4]Steve Wulf, "The Glow from a Fire," *Time*, January 8, 1996, 49.

Some have suggested that Mr. Feuerstein's generosity during that time is responsible for the present financial crisis. However, the fire destroyed the company's furniture upholstery division and customers were impatient at that time. They were not inclined to wait for production to ramp up, and Malden Mills lost most of those customers. It closed the upholstery division in 1996.

Also, there was the threat of inexpensive fleece from the Asian markets that was ignored largely because of the plant rebuilding and the efforts focused there. Finally, in 2000, the company had a shakeup in its marketing team just as it was launching its electric fabrics—fabrics with heatable wires that are powered by batteries embedded in the fleece.

Once again, however, the goodwill from 1995 remains. Residents of the town have been sending in checks to help the company, some as small as $10. An Internet campaign was begun by town residents to "Buy Fleece." The campaign is enjoying some success as Patagonia, Lands' End, and L.L. Bean report increased demand. In addition, the U.S. military placed large orders for fleece jackets for soldiers fighting in Operation Enduring Freedom in Afghanistan.

Senators Ted Kennedy and John Kerry lobbied GE not to involuntarily petition Malden Mills into bankruptcy. GE Capital held one fourth of Malden Mills' debts. Its other creditors included Finova Capital, SAI Investment, Pilgrim Investment, LaSalle Bank, and PNC Bank. The lobbying was to no avail. By 2002, Malden Mills was in bankruptcy. Feuerstein labored to raise the money to pay off creditors and buy his company back, but he was unable to meet the bankruptcy deadline. Malden Mills emerged from bankruptcy on September 30, 2003, but under management other than Mr. Feuerstein. He still hopes to buy the company back, but the price, originally $93 million, has increased to $120 million. Feuerstein is the president of Malden Mills, serves on its board, and earns a salary of $425,000 per year, but he is no longer in charge and cannot be until the creditors are repaid.

In January 2004, members of the U.S. House and Senate lobbied to convince the Export-Import Bank to loan Mr. Feuerstein the money he needed to buy back his company. The Ex-Im Bank, swayed by Mr. Feuerstein's commitment to keep Malden's production in the United States, increased the loan amount from the $20 million it had originally pledged to the $35 million Mr. Feuerstein needed.

By the end of January 2004, Malden Mills had three new strategies: Mr. Feuerstein was selling Polarfleece blankets on QVC, the company would be in partnership in China with Shanghai Mills, and the company announced it would expand its military contracts. Mr. Feuerstein remains as president and chairman of the board.

The company's patient union had its patience wearing thin. During the 2002–2003 time frame of the bankruptcy, the union leader said, "We're ready to make sacrifices for a little while. Whatever he asks us to do to keep the place going."[5] However, a threatened strike in December 2004 resulted in negotiations and a new union three-year contract, a more expensive one for the company.

As for Mr. Feuerstein, his view is simple: "There are times in business when you don't think of the financial consequences, but of the human consequences. There is no doubt this company will survive."[6] Mr. Feuerstein appears to have been correct. In 2006, Malden Mills landed a multimillion-dollar contract with the U.S. Department of Defense to be a supplier of the lightweight Polartec blankets for the U.S. military branches.

[5]Lynnley Browning, "Fire Could Not Stop a Mill, but Debts May," *New York Times*, November 28, 2001, pp. C1, C5.
[6]*Id.*, p. C1.

Discussion Questions

1. Mr. Feuerstein has stated, "I don't deserve credit. Corporate America has made it so that when you behave the way I did, it's abnormal." Is he right? Was he right in continuing the salaries?

2. Mr. Feuerstein is a Talmudic scholar who often quotes the following proverbs:

   "In a situation where there is no righteous person, try to be a righteous person."

   "Not all who increase their wealth are wise."[7]

   What wisdom for your credo comes from these two insights?

3. What impact would a closure of Malden Mills have had on Methuen?

4. Did the fact that Malden Mills is privately held make a difference in Mr. Feuerstein's flexibility?

5. Did Mr. Feuerstein focus too much on benevolence and not enough on business? Did he rely only on goodwill to survive, and did he neglect the basics of strategy, marketing, and addressing the competition?

Case 6.5

Plant Closings, Downsizings, Company Closings, Government Takeovers, Bankruptcies, and Pensions

United, GM, and the Pension Obligations

As part of its Chapter 11 bankruptcy, United Airlines was relieved of its pension liabilities. Questions have arisen as to how a company can be permitted to renege on those benefits when so many protections were built into the law under the Employee Retirement Income Security Act (ERISA). Congressional hearings now reveal that there were loopholes in the accounting processes for pension fund reporting that permitted United, and many others, to report pension numbers that made the health of the fund look better than it actually was. The loopholes were Enron-esque in nature, allowing obligations to be spun off the books so that the existing levels of obligations of the plan looked small and the assets very rich.

These financial-reporting accounting loopholes for general financial reports have been changed. Because of United's bailout, Congress has changed the accounting for pension plans to avoid the problem of the rosy picture when the funds need further funding. The Pension Protection Act of 2006 also made other changes to close loopholes and provide greater assurance for employees that their promised pensions and the funding for them would be available upon their retirement. The effect of the changes is to require companies to fund their pension plans according to the numbers they have reported to the SEC in their financials. Apparently the numbers reported to the SEC vis-à-vis pensions are accurate, whereas the numbers reported for ERISA purposes are inflated. If United had funded its plans when its SEC numbers indicated it needed to (e.g., 1998 would have been the year when funding was first needed), the plan would have been sufficiently funded at the time of the United bankruptcy. However, under ERISA guidelines, it was not required to kick in funds until 2002, when it was grossly underfunded.

The entire reduction in force (RIF) process that became a political hot-button issue in the 1980s has changed over the past two decades. The RIF process now incorporates the pension and retirement components. Since 2001, companies that have had to downsize have taken an approach of offering employees buyouts. Since the market crash of 2008, downsizings have been ongoing. Indeed, 100 national and regional retailers went out of business between 2008 and 2010, with other national retailers closing large numbers of

---

[7]Rabbi Avri Shafran, "Bankruptcy and Wealthy," *Society Today,* July 29, 2007, http://www.aish.com/societyWork/work/Aaron_Feuerstein_ Bankrupt_and_Wealthy.asp.

their locations. For example, Arby's closed 80 of its outlets in 2010. Closures are the ultimate form of downsizing. The following list provides some data on some of the larger companies and the steps they took as well as some general figures for the recession that followed the 2008 market crash:

2001	Lucent Technologies offered 13,000 employees early retirement incentives.
2001	Merrill Lynch offered voluntary severance packages to a majority of its 65,900 employees.
2003	Almost 10 percent of the 221,000 employees of Verizon accepted an early retirement–buyout offer.
2004	Southwest Airlines offered 33,000 of its employees cash, travel privileges, and other benefits as part of a voluntary termination package.
2005	Safeway offered 5,800 clerks voluntary buyouts.
2006	GM offered 131,000 GM and Delphi employees (including 105,000 union workers in that group) buyouts with figures ranging from $35,000 to $140,000 per employee, depending upon their years of employment with GM or Delphi.
2008	30% of U.S. employers laid off employees.
2009	Boeing cut 10,000 jobs. Caterpillar cut 22,000 jobs. Delta forced 2,000 early retirements.
2010	50% of U.S. companies did some form of downsizing.

Because of the extensive benefits employees at these companies have, the average cost of keeping an employee is about $67 per hour, with $27 being wages and the remainder made up of pensions and health care benefits. One employee who works in the paint-repair shop at GM's Pontiac plant said that he would give up his $100,000 per year salary to retire, spend more time with grandchildren, and get away from the paint fumes. However, one worker noted, "Where is anybody going to find a job paying $28 per hour with [only] a high-school diploma?"[8]

One worker, who will receive a $140,000 payment, has a small dealership in Doraville, Georgia, where the GM plant is located, at which he sells used pickup trucks. He is not married and has no children, rents out six homes that he owns, and co-owns a beauty parlor. He will retire comfortably.

In 2008, the U.S. government provided General Motors with $5.8 billion in funds in order to allow the company to emerge from bankruptcy. As security for the loan and for the advancement of $43 billion in bailout funds to the company, the U.S. government held a 10 percent ownership stake in the auto company. As part of the deal with the government, GM had to agree to certain management changes and promise to repay the funds. GM also had to agree to provide 39 percent share ownership of the company to employees of the company. GM promised to cut 40 percent of its car dealers and eliminate 7,000 jobs. Following its emergence from bankruptcy, GM did cut its car dealers by 40 percent, but following public outcry on the termination of longstanding dealers, it reinstated many of those who had been terminated. GM consolidated plants and closed its Saturn division to push toward the 7,000-job cutback. A government official said that the loss of jobs if the auto maker failed was too great to risk and thus required government intervention.

---

[8]Jeffrey McCracken and Lee Hawkins Jr., "Massive Job Cuts Will Reshape GM," *Wall Street Journal*, March 23, 2006, pp. A1, A15.

Discussion Questions

1. Describe the regulatory cycle on pension fund accounting. Discuss, again, the issue of the legal versus ethical accounting and interpretation of ERISA.

2. Give a list of the economic and ethical issues in pension funding, employee wages, and RIFs.

3. Did noble goals on all sides result in unintended consequences at United and GM?

4. What ethical issues do you see in the government intervention to save GM?

Compare & Contrast

Drawing on the Malden Mills case (Case 6.4), what have we learned about balancing social goals and operating a business? What were the drivers for the Feuerstein decision versus the United decision?

Sources

Micheline Maynard, "G.M. Will Offer Buyouts to All Its Union Workers," *New York Times*, March 23, 2006, pp. A1, C4.

Marry Williams Walsh, "Pension Law Loopholes Helped United Hide Its Troubles," *New York Times*, June 7, 2005, p. C1.

Workplace Conflicts

SECTION 6C

Purchasing agents hold powerful positions. They make the choices to award business to other companies. Often, contractors use tools of influence to gain favor. When are such tools unethical? Can an agent accept gifts for the award of business?

Case 6.6

JCPenney and Its Wealthy Buyer

Purchasing agent Jim G. Locklear began his career as a retail buyer with Federated Department Stores in Dallas, where he became known for his eye for fashion and ability to negotiate low prices. After ten years with Federated, he went to work for Jordan Marsh in Boston in 1987 with an annual salary of $96,000. But three months later, Locklear quit that job to take a position as a housewares buyer with JCPenney so he could return to Dallas. His salary was $56,000 per year, he was thirty-eight years old, he owed support payments totaling $900 per month for four children from four marriages, and the bank was threatening to foreclose on his $500,000 mortgage.[9]

Locklear was a good performer for Penney. His products sold well, and he was responsible for the very successful JCPenney Home Collection, a color-coordinated line of dinnerware, flatware, and glasses that was eventually copied by most other tabletop retailers. Locklear took sales of Penney's tabletop line from $25 million to $45 million per year and was named the company's "Buyer of the Year" several times.

However, Locklear was taking payments from Penney's vendors directly and through front companies. Some paid him to get information about bids or to obtain contracts, whereas others paid what they believed to be advertising fees to various companies that were fronts owned by Locklear. Between 1987 and 1992, Locklear took in $1.5 million in "fees" from Penney's vendors.

Penney hired an investigator in 1989 to look into Locklear's activities, but the investigator uncovered only Mr. Locklear's personal financial difficulties.

During his time as a buyer, Locklear was able to afford a country club membership, resort vacations, luxury vehicles, and large securities accounts. Although his lifestyle was known to those who worked with him, no questions were asked again until 1992, when Penney received an anonymous letter about Locklear and his relationship with a Dallas manufacturer's representative. Penney investigated and uncovered sufficient evidence of payments to file a civil suit to recover those payments and referred the case to the U.S. attorney in Dallas for criminal prosecution.

Mr. Locklear was charged by the U.S. attorney with mail and wire fraud. Mr. Locklear entered a guilty plea and provided information to the U.S. attorney on suppliers, agents, and manufacturers' reps who had paid him "fees." Mr. Locklear was sentenced to eighteen months in prison and fined $50,000. Penney won a $789,000 judgment against him, and Mr. Locklear's assets have been attached for collection purposes.[10]

[9]Andrea Gerlin, "How a Penney Buyer Made Up to $1.5 Million on Vendors' Kickbacks," *Wall Street Journal*, February 7, 1995, pp. A1, A18.

[10]Andrea Gerlin, "J. C. Penney Ex-Employee Sentenced to Jail," *Wall Street Journal*, August 28, 1995, p. A9.

Discussion Questions

1. Given Locklear's lifestyle, why did it take so long for Penney to take action? Do you see any red flags in the facts given?

2. A vendor who paid Locklear $25,000 in exchange for a Penney order stated, "It was either pay it or go out of business." Evaluate the ethics of this seller.

3. Do you agree that both the buyer and the seller are guilty in commercial bribery cases? Is the purchasing agent "more" wrong?

4. Many companies provide guidelines for their purchasing agents on accepting gifts, samples, and favors. For example, under Walmart's "no coffee" policy, its buyers cannot accept even a cup of coffee from a vendor. Any samples or models must be returned to vendors once a sales demonstration is complete. Other companies allow buyers to accept items of minimal value. Still others place a specific dollar limit on the value, such as $25. What problems do you see with any of these policies? What advantages do you see?

5. Describe the problems that can result when buyers accept gifts from vendors and manufacturer's representatives.

6. Mr. Locklear said at his sentencing, "I became captive to greed. Once it was discovered, I felt tremendous relief." Mr. Locklear's pastor said Locklear coached Little League and added, "Our country needs more role models like Jim Locklear."[11] Evaluate these two quotes from an ethical perspective. Are there any lessons for your credo in Mr. Locklear's experience?

Case 6.7

The Trading Desk, Perks, and "Dwarf Tossing"

Wall Street firms dream of acquiring the trading business of a mutual fund like Fidelity Investments. Wooing those Fidelity traders during 2006 resulted in at least one Wall Street firm, Jeffries & Co., going well over the $100 limit that the National Association of Securities Dealers (NASD) places as the upper edge for "stuff" that can be given by investment firms to traders. The traders were wooed with, among other things:

- A bachelor party in Miami for Fidelity Boston traders, complete with bikini-clad women, free charter flights from Boston to Miami that cost $31,000, and hotel suites with a party that included "dwarf tossing"
- Trips to the Super Bowl, all free
- $19,000 for Wimbledon tickets
- $7,000 for U.S. Open tickets
- $2,600 for six bottles of 1998 Opus One wine
- $47,000 in chartered flights from Boston to the Caicos Islands
- $1,200 for Justin Timberlake and Christina Aguilera tickets
- $1,000 for a portable DVD player
- $500 for golf clubs

Jeffries spent a total of $1.6 million on fourteen Fidelity traders.[12]

The SEC and the National Association of Securities Dealers (NASD) (now FINRA—Financial Industry Regulatory Authority) brought civil charges against Jeffries and required the firm to pay $5.5 million in fines and $4.2 million to disgorge profits made as a result of the gifts to the Fidelity traders. The SEC was able to tie the bestowing of the gifts to the timing of trades made by the Fidelity traders.[13]

Fidelity disciplined the brokers when news of the bachelor party trickled back to Boston and the company began looking beneath the tip-of-the-iceberg party.[14]

---

[11]*Id.*

[12]Greg Farrell, "Jeffries to Pay $9.7 Million to Settle Fidelity Gift Case," *USA Today*, December 5, 2006, p. 9B.

[13]See http://www.sec.gov/enforcement for press releases. Accessed May 19, 2010.

[14]http://www.nasd.com. Accessed May 19, 2010.

Following the Fidelity settlement for the employees, Peter Lynch, one of the firm's principals, was investigated and the SEC discovered that Mr. Lynch was getting tickets to events such as the Ryder Golf Classic and U2 and Santana concerts. Lynch's eclectic tastes aside, he was earning between $3 million and $10 million per year when he solicited through Fidelity employees the $15,948 for tickets. Mr. Lynch agreed to repay the value of the tickets plus interest of $4,183, and also expressed regret, "In asking the Fidelity equity trading desk for occasional help locating tickets, I never intended to do anything inappropriate and I regret having made those requests."

Through his use of the Fidelity traders for tickets, Lynch placed his imprimatur on a system of getting and giving "stuff" for Fidelity's trades. In addition to Mr. Lynch, other Fidelity traders and officers racked up $1.6 million in goodies from brokers who were wooing Fidelity trades. One Fidelity trader commented, "Word is out that the order flow is for sale."

The various reports Fidelity had prepared on the trader goodies and stuff from brokers concluded that the conduct resulted in "adverse publicity, loss of credibility with principal regulators, and a loss of Fund shareholders." The SEC noted, "The tone is set at the top. If higher-ups request tickets from a trading desk, it may send a message that such misconduct is tolerated and could contribute to the breakdown of compliance on the desk."[15] It seems there is a relatively short leap from U2 concert tickets to bachelor parties with dwarf tossing as entertainment than most of those at the top realize.

Discussion Questions

1. Why should we worry about gifts here and there to traders? Aren't all investment firms about the same and offer the same levels of service?
2. Why do NASD, now FINRA, and the SEC worry about traders receiving stuff?
3. Is there a definitive line that you could draw for your credo from what this case involves?
4. What level of discipline would be appropriate for the Fidelity brokers? Was the discipline for Mr. Lynch sufficient?
5. What signals did Mr. Lynch's conduct send to the traders?

Case 6.8

Docs, Pharmas, Medical Journals, Funded Research, and Pizza

Pharmaceutical companies (or *pharmas*), faced with the uphill battle of getting information about their new drugs to doctors and the public, have developed complex layers of marketing and access programs. Those marketing programs and the tools used to capture doctors' attention in order to give them information on the drugs have raised some questions about the need for more than self-regulation of both the pharmaceuticals and the physicians.

Perks for the Docs from the Pharmas

Below is a list of the various types of benefits and gifts drug companies have given doctors over the past few years to try and get them to consider prescribing their new offerings:

- An event called "Why Cook?" in which doctors are given the chance to review drug studies and product information at a restaurant as their meals are being prepared—they can leave as soon as their meals are ready and they are treated to appetizers and drinks as they wait.

[15]Kara Scannell, Susanne Craig, and Jennifer Levitz, "'Gifts' Case Nabs a Star," *Wall Street Journal*, March 6, 2008, p. C1.

- An event at Christmas tree lots at which doctors can come and review materials and pick up free Christmas trees.
- Flowers sent to the doctors' offices on Valentine's Day with materials attached.
- Manicures as they study materials on new drugs.
- Pedicures as they study materials on new drugs.
- Free car washes during which they can study materials.
- Free books with materials enclosed.
- Free CDs with materials attached.
- Bottles of wine sent with materials attached.
- Events at Barnes & Noble where doctors can browse and pick out a book for themselves for free so long as they take along some materials on a new drug.

Some doctors say that they can often enjoy dinner on a drug company as often as five times per week.

The American Medical Association (AMA) frowns on the "dine and dash" format because its rules provide that dinners are acceptable so long as the doctors sit and learn something from a featured speaker. The AMA also limits gifts to those of a "minimal value" that should be related to their patients, such as note pads and pens with the new drug's name imprinted on them. The chairman of the AMA Committee says the following about the gifts: "There are doctors who say, 'I always do what's best for my patients, and these gifts and dinners and trips do not influence me.' They are wrong."[16] One Georgetown medical student, offended by the requirement of ethics training noted, "I'm too smart to be bought by a slice of pizza. " However, a study of doc–pharma rep interaction concluded:

- One minute with a pharma sales rep translates to prescribing 16 percent more of the rep's products than the doc was prescribing
- Four minutes with a pharma sales rep translates to prescribing 52 percent more of the rep's products than the doc was prescribing[17]

Experts estimate that drug companies spend about $1,500 per physician per year in trying to attract the physicians' attention to particular drugs in order to have the doctors prescribe them. Those figures come from the $15.7 billion drug companies spent on marketing in 2000. That figure for marketing was $9 billion in 1996.

The AMA has created a $1 million educational campaign to discourage doctors from accepting even the smallest of gifts from pharmaceuticals because of the reality and perception that these gifts influence doctors' decisions on which drugs to prescribe. Interestingly, the pharmaceutical companies themselves donated $675,000 of the $1 million.

At the same time of the announcement of the AMA campaign, Dr. Joseph Bailey proposed that the physicians in his specialty practice group simply charge pharmaceutical company representatives $65 in order to make a ten-minute pitch to a doctor about their drug(s). One doctor describes the proposal as follows: "There are some doctors who would like to have access to that information who don't want to give up two hours of their time to go to dinner. Rather than getting a free ham or a free turkey from a pharmaceutical rep, I would rather see that money put to use to directly benefit the patient."[18] The reps sign up through a separate for-profit corporation, and the corporation then distributes its funds to the physicians so that there is no taint or influence from a particular company.

---

[16]Chris Adams, "Doctors on the Run Can 'Dine 'n' Dash' in Style in New Orleans," *Wall Street Journal*, May 14, 2001, pp. A1, A6.

[17]Arlene Weintraub, "Just Say No to Drug Reps," *BusinessWeek*, February 4, 2008, p. 69.

[18]Cheryl Jackson, "Ohio Group Tells Drug Reps: We'll Listen—If You Pay," *American Medical News*, August 20, 2001, pp. 1, 4.

There is a new organization among doctors known as "No Free Lunch." The goal of the organization is to have physicians refuse all gift offers from pharmaceutical companies, including both prescription and consumer drugs.[19] The American Medical Students Association (AMSA) has begun a campaign to limit these activities and encourage doctors to stop accepting the gifts because they influence doctors in inappropriate ways and create a sense of indebtedness. Students from 150 medical schools in the United States will be making calls on 40,000 doctors, encouraging them to join the students in turning a new leaf on accepting these perks.

The pharmas have responded to all the movements for change by noting that all they want is "face time" with the doctors to discuss the drugs. Some pharmas have noted that the doctors do not have to accept the perks; they can simply listen to the information about the new drugs.

The Academic and Research Route to "Face Time"

With so many avenues of direct access to the docs closed, pharmas have been using different ways to obtain access to physicians for purposes of getting information about new drugs to them. Having studies about the drugs appear in the medical journals was a logical approach because docs do read medical journals. To get that kind of information to the journals, pharmas began funding research projects and providing consulting fees to physician scientists and physician editors who then touted the new drugs of the companies that paid the fees.

Since 2002, medical publications have touted articles and research on "aspirin resistance." The articles and research suggest that those who are taking aspirin to prevent heart attacks are wasting their money and effort because they are resistant to the effects aspirin is said to have in preventing clotting. The articles also suggest that the solution is for those taking aspirin to take aspirin substitutes that will have similar effects. These substitutes are manufactured by pharmaceutical firms and cost about $4.00 per day.

However, the journals in which the "aspirin-resistant" articles have appeared have failed to disclose ties between the researchers and authors and the drug companies manufacturing the aspirin substitutes that they tout. For example, in July 2005, Dr. Daniel Simon, an associate professor of medicine at the Harvard Medical School, wrote in *Physicians Weekly*, a trade magazine for the profession, that aspirin resistance could affect 30 percent of those who are taking aspirin to prevent heart attacks. He went on to suggest that these aspirin-resistant souls needed other anticlotting drugs. *Physicians Weekly* did not disclose that Dr. Simon is the recipient of research funding from Accumetrics, Inc., a company that produces a test for aspirin resistance. Neither did the publication mention that Dr. Simon also receives research funding from Schering-Plough Corp., a company now testing a drug to be used to help the aspirin-resistant heart patient. Stunningly, editor Keith D'Oria indicated that he was aware of Dr. Simon's ties but that *Physicians Weekly*'s policy is not to disclose the ties but rather to use the information for different purposes such as contacting Accumetrics or Schering-Plough to determine whether they would like to place ads near the good doctor's discussion of aspirin resistance and resolutions therefore. Dr. Simon's response to questions about conflicts of interest is that one cannot rely on independent researchers because they "are not truly expert."[20]

Sales of anticlotting drugs for the aspirin resistant are up 59 percent. A study appearing in the *New England Journal of Medicine* concluded that combinations of the

[19]G. Jeffrey MacDonald, "Fighting the Freebies," *Time*, December 2005, Inside Business, A20.

[20]David Armstrong, "Doctors with Ties to Companies Push Aspirin Objections," *Wall Street Journal*, April 24, 2006, pp. A1, A12.

prescription drugs with aspirin were no more effective than just taking aspirin, but cardiologists have cautioned their patients about eliminating the drugs.

Discussion Questions

1. What category of ethical issue are the gifts to physicians? The consulting arrangements? The research arrangements?

2. Do you think the doctors act ethically in accepting the gifts, meals, and favors?

3. Do you think the conflict of interest with regard to physicians and their relationships with pharmas is resolved? Discuss the pizza studies and their conclusion.

4. If you were a doctor, how would you handle funded research from a company whose drug you are testing? Are there credo issues here?

5. A lawsuit filed by Ami P. Kelley, a former senior legal counsel for Medtronic, against the company and ten physicians alleges that Medtronic provided considerable "goodies" to doctors in exchange for the doctors' use of Medtronic products. The suit alleges that Medtronic staff members "routinely" took physicians to the Platinum Plus, a strip club in Memphis and also paid for the physicians to have VIP visits there.[21] The suit also alleges that Medtronic had hundreds of consulting contracts with doctors for which the doctors did little or no work and that were entered into in order to have the doctors use Medtronic devices. According to the suit, Medtronic also paid almost $25,000 to allow physicians to ride on a Mardi Gras float during a New Orleans "seminar" and also provided the doctors with $15,000 worth of Mardi Gras beads for use during the ride.[22]

   Medtronic has actually settled charges of kickbacks with the federal government and paid a $40 million fine. Ms. Kelley seeks private remedies because she was fired after she threw down the flag on the various forms of payment and entertainment that flowed from Medtronic to the docs. Medtronic has since changed its policies on trips and consulting for physicians. Under federal law, a whistle-blower is entitled to a percentage of the amount the government recovers because of the information the whistleblower has provided. Ms. Kelley seeks recovery for her termination.

   Describe the role and rights of whistle-blowers in situations such as these. Why do you think Ms. Kelley was fired for raising such a simple concern?

6. Several doctors received compensation from GlaxoSmithKline for their work in discussing Glaxo products at professional meetings. The amounts that the good doctors received are minimal. For example, Dr. David Capuzzi received $3,750 over a one-year period from Glaxo. However, during the same period, Avandia, a Glaxo product, was facing increasing scrutiny for its side effects. The FDA was considering whether to halt sales of Avandia. The FDA faced a critical decision because of the importance of Avandia for treatment of diabetes. Yet the FDA was also facing serious questions about the drug's risks. Dr. Capuzzi served on the FDA Advisory Committee that voted to allow Avandia to remain on the market. Dr. Capuzzi's disclosure of his Glaxo consulting fees never made its way to the FDA Advisory Committee prior to the vote. Dr. Capuzzi does not see the payments as a conflict because, "I have not given any talks to doctors' groups promoting Avandia."[23] Evaluate Dr. Capuzzi's analysis.

Sources

For a look at more information on this issue and various policies relating to it, visit the following websites:

http://www.ama.org

http://www.kaisernetwork.org

---

[21]As an aside, the owner of Platinum Plus entered a guilty plea to charges of prostitution against the club, and the club has since closed.

[22]David Armstrong, "Lawsuit Says Medtronic Gave Doctors Array of Perks," *Wall Street Journal*, September 25, 2008, pp. B1, B6.

[23]Alicia Mundy, "Panelist Paid Fees By Glaxo," *Wall Street Journal*, July 20, 2010, p. B2.

Case 6.9

The Analyst Who Needed a Preschool

The stock market of the late 1990s and early 2000s represented a period of irrational exuberance. Investors invested as they never had, but they were egged on by analysts who could say no evil of the companies they were to evaluate. For example, Citigroup is the parent company of Salomon Smith Barney, an investment banker and broker whose star telecommunications analyst, Jack Grubman, was perhaps WorldCom's biggest cheerleader.[24] Jack Grubman's calls on WorldCom were so positive that the company came to be known as "his beloved WorldCom." For example, WorldCom had the following quote from Mr. Grubman that was included in WorldCom's 1997 annual report that was still posted on its Web site through July 2002, "If one were to find comparables to WorldCom . . . the list would be very short and would include the likes of Merck, Home Depot, Walmart, Coke, Microsoft, Gillette and Disney."[25] The sycophantism of Mr. Grubman is difficult to describe because it seems almost parody, as the WorldCom ending is now known. Mr. Grubman introduced Mr. Ebbers at analyst meetings as "the smartest guy in the industry."[26] It was not until the stock had lost 90 percent of its value, and just six weeks before its collapse, that Mr. Grubman issued a negative recommendation on WorldCom.[27] Mr. Grubman was free with his negative recommendations on other telecom companies. And Salomon would earn $21 million in fees if the WorldCom–Sprint merger was approved in 1999. He wrote, "We do not think any other telco will be as fully integrated and growth-oriented as this combination,"[28] Mr. Grubman attended WorldCom board meetings and offered advice.[29]

The Loans From Citi

Citicorp was WorldCom's biggest lender as well as a personal lender for Bernie Ebbers, WorldCom's CEO (see Case 4.27). Mr. Ebbers's personal loans are reflected in the following chart.

Lender	Amount ($ million)	Status
Citigroup	$552	$88 million repaid
WorldCom	$415	Collateral seized
Bank of America	$253	Repaid
UBS Paine Webber	$51	Repaid
Toronto-Dominion	$40	Repaid
Morgan Keegan	$11.6	Repaid
J.P. Morgan Chase	$10.8	Repaid
Bank of North Georgia	$10.8	Repaid

Source: Susan Pulliam, Deborah Solomon, and Carrick Mollenkamp, "Former WorldCom CEO Built an Empire on Mountain of Debt," *Wall Street Journal*, December 31, 2002, p. A1.

---

[24]Neil Weinberg, "Walmart Could Sue for Libel," *Forbes*, August 12, 2002, p. 56.

[25]*Id.*

[26]Randall Smith and Deborah Solomon, "Ebbers's Exit Hurts WorldCom's Biggest Fan," *Wall Street Journal*, May 3, 2002, p. C1.

[27]*Id.*

[28]*Id.*, p. C3.

[29]*Id.*

The personal loans to Ebbers brought results for the banks in terms of WorldCom business.[30] Mr. Grubman's continuing positive reports on WorldCom, despite the slide of the company's stock and the clear signals from the market, earned him a subpoena to the congressional hearings, alongside Mr. Ebbers and CFO Scott Sullivan.[31] Former WorldCom employees who were directed to a special number when they wished to exercise their options and were discouraged from doing so by Salomon brokers who handled the WorldCom employee options program have filed a lawsuit.[32]

The IPO Allocations

Mr. Grubman's relationship with WorldCom's senior management was a target of investigation at the congressional level and elsewhere for reasons other than the personal loan relationships and the glowing reports from Mr. Grubman.[33] WorldCom gave the bulk of its investment banking business to Salomon Smith Barney and it gave Mr. Ebbers and others the first shot at hot initial public offering (IPO) stocks.[34] The figures in congressional records indicate that Mr. Ebbers made $11 million in profits from investments in twenty-one IPOs recommended to him by Salomon Smith Barney, and, more particularly, Mr. Grubman.[35] Apparently, there were complex games going on in terms of how those shares were allocated initially, and Ebbers was one of the players let in on the best IPOs by Salomon Smith Barney. One expert described the allocation system as follows:

> *Looking back, it looks more and more like a pyramid scheme. The deals explain why people weren't more diligent in making decisions about funding these small companies. If the money was spread all over the place and everyone who participated early was almost guaranteed a return because of the hype, they had no incentive to try and differentiate the technology. And in the end, all the technology turned out to be identical and commodity-like.[36]*

The Glowing Reports

Mr. Grubman continued to issue nothing but positive reports on WorldCom as he became completely intertwined with the company, Mr. Ebbers, and the company's success.[37] In e-mails uncovered by an investigation of analysts conducted by then–New York Attorney General Eliot Spitzer, Mr. Grubman had complained privately that he was forced to continue his "buy" ratings on stocks that he considered "dogs." Mr. Spitzer filed suit against the analysts for "profiteering" in IPOs.[38]

---

[30]At least one lawsuit by a shareholder alleges that the loans were made in exchange for business with WorldCom. Andrew Backover, "Suit Links Loans, WorldCom Stock," *USA Today*, October 15, 2002, p. 3B.

[31]Susan Pulliam, Deborah Solomon, and Randall Smith, "WorldCom Is Denounced at Hearing," *Wall Street Journal*, July 9, 2002, p. A3; and Gretchen Morgenson, "Salomon under Inquiry on WorldCom Options," *New York Times*, March 13, 2002, p. C9.

[32]Gretchen Morgenson, "Outrage Is Rising as Options Turn to Dust," *New York Times*, March 11, 2002, p. BU1.

[33]Charles Gasparino, Tom Hamburger, and Deborah Solomon, "Salomon Made IPO Allocations Available to Ebbers, Others," *Wall Street Journal*, August 28, 2002, p. A1.

[34]Gretchen Morgenson, "Ebbers Made $11 Million on 21 Stock Offerings," *New York Times*, August 31, 2002, p. B1; Gretchen Morgenson, "Ebbers Got Million Shares in Hot Deals," *New York Times*, August 28, 2002, p. C1; and Gretchen Morgenson, "Deals within Telecom Deals," *New York Times*, August 28, 2002, pp. BU1, BU10.

[35]See Morgenson, "Ebbers Got Million Shares in Hot Deals," for Ebbers information; and Andrew Backover, "WorldCom, Qwest Face SEC Scrutiny," *USA Today*, March 12, 2002, p. 1B, for information on Qwest inquiry; see also Thor Valdmanis and Andrew Backover, "Lawsuit Targets Telecom Execs' Stock Windfalls," *USA Today*, October 1, 2002, p. 1B.

[36]Backover, "WorldCom, Qwest Face SEC Scrutiny," p. 1B; and Valdmanis and Backover, "Lawsuit Targets Telecom Execs' Stock Windfalls," p. 1B.

[37]Smith and Solomon, "Ebbers's Exit Hurts WorldCom's Biggest Fan," p. C1; and Andrew Backover and Jayne O'Donnell, "WorldCom Scrutiny Touches on E-mail," *USA Today*, July 8, 2002, p. 1B.

[38]Valdmanis and Backover, "Lawsuit Targets Telecom Execs' Stock Windfalls," p. 1B.

Further, Mr. Ebbers was not the sole beneficiary of the Salomon Smith Barney IPO allocations, although he was the largest beneficiary.[39] Others who benefited from the IPO allocations and who were affiliated with WorldCom included: Stiles A. Kellett Jr. (director, 31,500 shares), Scott Sullivan (CFO, 32,300 shares), Francesco Galesi (director), John Sidgmore (officer, director, and CEO after Ebbers's ouster), and James Crowe (former director of WorldCom).[40] Apparently, those who enjoyed the benefits of Salomon's allocations also stuck with Mr. Grubman in terms of his advice once the shares were allocated, often keeping the shares for too long because of Mr. Grubman's overly optimistic views on telecommunications-related companies' stock. However, Citigroup and Salomon both denied that there was any quid pro quo between Ebbers, WorldCom, and the companies for WorldCom's investment banking business.[41]

The Pre-School Deal

No charges were ever brought against Mr. Grubman. He operates his own firm today. However, there is one additional story related to Mr. Grubman's role as an analyst that illustrates that financial analysis may not be as math-oriented as we believed. Through a series of e-mails, we learned that Mr. Grubman used his position for some help on the home front. Mr. Grubman was the father of twins whom he wanted to see admitted to one of Manhattan's most prestigious preschools—the 92nd Street Y.

Mr. Grubman wrote a memo to Sanford Weill, the then-chairman of Citigroup, with the following language:

> On another matter, as I alluded to you the other day, we are going through the ridiculous but necessary process of pre-school applications in Manhattan. For someone who grew up in a household with a father making $8,000 a year and for someone who attended public schools, I do find this process a bit strange, but there are no bounds for what you do for your children.
>
> Anything, anything you could do Sandy would be greatly appreciated. I will keep you posted on the progress with AT&T which I think is going well.
>
> Thank you.

The backdrop for the memo is important. Citigroup pledged $1 million to the school at about the same time Grubman's children were admitted.

Mr. Weill, Mr. Grubman's CEO, asked Mr. Grubman to "take a fresh look" at AT&T, a major corporate client of Citigroup.

Mr. Weill served on the board of AT&T; AT&T's CEO, C. Michael Armstrong, served as a Citigroup director; and Mr. Weill was courting Armstrong's vote for the ouster of his co-chairman at Citigroup, John Reed.

A follow-up e-mail from Mr. Grubman to Carol Cutler, another New York analyst, connected the dots:

> I used Sandy to get my kids in the 92nd Street Y pre-school (which is harder than Harvard) and Sandy needed Armstrong's vote on our board to nuke Reed in showdown. Once the coast was clear for both of us (ie Sandy clear victor and my kids confirmed) I went back to my normal self on AT&T.

---

[39]Charles Gasparino, Tom Hamburger, and Deborah Solomon, "Salomon Made IPO Allocations Available to Ebbers, Others," *Wall Street Journal,* August 28, 2002, p. A1.

[40]Morgenson, "Deals within Telecom Deals," pp. BU1, BU10.

[41]Gretchen Morgenson, "Ebbers Got Million Shares in Hot Deal," *New York Times,* August 28, 2002, p. C15.

At the same time as all the other movements, Mr. Grubman upgraded AT&T from a "hold" to a "strong buy." After Mr. Reed was ousted, Mr. Grubman downgraded AT&T again.

Mr. Grubman said that he sent the e-mail "in an effort to inflate my professional importance."

In another e-mail, Mr. Grubman wrote, "I have always viewed [AT&T] as a business deal between me and Sandy."

Discussion Questions

1. Were there conflicts of interest?
2. What personal insights do you gain from Mr. Grubman's e-mails and conduct? What elements can be added to your credo from this case?
3. All analysts were participating in the same types of favors and quid pro quo as Grubman. Does industry practice control ethics?
4. Then–Attorney General Eliot Spitzer (now ex-governor of New York) pursued the analysts and the investment houses for their lack of independence. Although they all settled the cases brought against them, what types of criminal conduct could they be charged with?
5. Mr. Spitzer found the bulk of his evidence for his cases in candid e-mails the analysts sent describing the eventual collapse of these companies even as their face-to-face evaluations of companies were most positive. Does he have the right to view their e-mails?

Compare & Contrast

What is different about someone such as Matthew Whitley (the Coke employee who raised questions about the payments to the consultant in Case 7.17) and Jack Grubman? Why is one willing to label actions for what they are whereas the other hangs on despite the evolving problems? Consider their personal interests and then think about whether their personal credos had an impact on their careers and decisions.

Case 6.10

Julie Roehm: The Walmart Ad Exec with Expensive Tastes

In 2007, Walmart was in litigation with a former advertising executive, Ms. Julie Roehm, who filed a wrongful termination suit against the company, seeking money under her contract with Walmart because the company had not given her a valid reason for termination. Walmart counterclaimed for its legal fees as well as for the damages (costs) it experienced when it had to rebid the advertising agency contract Ms. Roehm had awarded. Walmart alleged that there was a conflict of interest in the award of that advertising contract because Ms. Roehm had accepted expensive meals and other gifts from the agency, a violation of Walmart's code of ethics.

In its counterclaim, Walmart alleged that Ms. Roehm had an affair with Sean Womack (both are married with children), her second-in-command at the company. E-mails allegedly were sent to Mr. Womack from Ms. Roehm. Mrs. Womack had provided Walmart with copies of the e-mails from the Womacks' personal computer such as:

> I hate not being able to call you or write you. I think about us together all the time. Little moments like watching your face when you kiss me.[42]

The filing also accuses the two of seeking employment with Draft FCB. Draft FCB was the company that was awarded the Walmart ad account by Ms. Roehm. As noted earlier, Walmart fired Draft FCB after the revelations about the conflicts and has since

---

[42]Louise Story and Michael Barbaro, "Walmart Criticizes 2 in a Filing," *New York Times*, March 20, 2007, pp. C1, C5. Ms. Roehm says the e-mail is out of context and not from her.

hired Interpublic Group. Walmart's decision to terminate Draft FCB's contract came after Walmart learned the following information, perks that Roehm and Womack enjoyed via Draft FCB (and which were included in Walmart's counterclaim filings):

- $1,100 dinner
- $700 LuxBar in Chicago
- $440 at the bar in the Peninsula Hotel

Draft FCB cooperated with Walmart by providing copies of the e-mail communications between its employees and Roehm and Womack. However, Draft FCB also released a statement indicating that the employee who was communicating with Womack about employment for the two had no authority to negotiate such employment contracts and even lacked any authority to engage in business development.

Once Walmart counterclaimed, Ms. Roehm fired back with her own allegations, ones that basically argued that "what's sauce for the goose is sauce for the gander," a timeless legal principle in these battles of will. She alleged that Lee Scott, Walmart's CEO, enjoyed favorable prices from Irwin Jacobs, a supplier of Walmart's, on everything from jewelry to boats and that Mr. Scott's son, Eric, has worked for Mr. Jacobs for years.[43] Her allegation was that Mr. Scott was not fired for these conflicts and, ergo, she was dismissed wrongfully or inconsistently for her alleged breach of Walmart's conflicts policies. Walmart's code of ethics states that employees are not to have social relationships with suppliers if those relationships create even the appearance of impropriety.[44]

Although Walmart and Mr. Jacobs dismissed the allegations as false and outrageous, Mr. Jacobs and Mr. Scott acknowledged that their families have vacationed together and that Mr. Jacobs attended Mr. Scott's daughter's wedding. Mr. Jacobs has also stated that when the two are out together, Mr. Scott always pays and will not allow Mr. Jacobs to pay for even a lunch or other meal. Mr. Jacobs also says, "I swear to God Lee never called me about [putting Eric to work]."[45]

Less than a year following its filing, Julie Roehm ended her wrongful termination suit against Walmart, and Walmart has agreed not to pursue its claims against Ms. Roehm. Ms. Roehm also noted that some of the allegations she made about Irwin Jacobs, one of Walmart's suppliers, were inaccurate. Ms. Roehm said she was dropping her suit because it was financially draining and because she had been given information that indicated her allegations about Mr. Jacobs were not true. Walmart indicated it was satisfied with the withdrawal of the suit, would not pursue the matter further, and was pleased to be able to move forward. Ms. Roehm did not receive any money in the dismissal settlement.[46]

Discussion Questions

1. How does this case relate to the phrase "tone at the top," and what does "tone at the top" mean as it relates to ethics and ethical culture in a company?

2. What problems do inconsistencies in enforcing rules present to a company? How does inconsistency relate to due process?

---

[43]Gary McWilliams and James Covert, "Roehm Claims Walmart Brass Defy Ethics Rules," *Wall Street Journal*, May 27, 2007, pp. A1, A5.

[44]*Id.*

[45]*Id.*

[46]Ann Zimmerman, "Walmart, Roehm Drop Lawsuits," *Wall Street Journal*, November 5, 2007, p. A4.

Compare & Contrast

1. Ms. Roehm has also alleged that she was terminated because she did not fit into Walmart's simple and conservative culture. Ms. Roehm is a nationally known advertising executive whose ads for Chrysler caused a stir when the ads showed car buyers telling their child that he was conceived in the back seat of a car. How does this "culture fit" issue relate to the Hopkins case? Is it possible for employers to articulate "fit" as a criterion for continuation of employment, or is subjectivity automatically a part of that standard?

2. Why did Ms. Roehm and Mr. Womack feel that the strict and clear Walmart policies on relationships with suppliers and vendors of the company did not apply to them? Why did they accept the expensive restaurant and bar perks while Mr. Scott insisted on paying when he was out with Mr. Jacobs?

Workplace Diversity and Atmosphere

Case 6.11

English-Only Employer Policies

English-only policies in the workplace have become the fastest-growing area of Equal Employment Opportunity Commission (EEOC) complaints as well as litigation under Title VII. In 1996, the EEOC had 30 discrimination complaints related to English-only policies of employers. Since 1996, the EEOC has had a 500 percent increase in those complaints.[47] Employers that have implemented English-only policies include the Salvation Army, All-Island Transportation (a Long Island taxi company), a geriatric center in New York, and Oglethorpe University in Atlanta.

One lawyer noted that employers seem more willing to make the policies and risk the legal battles because they think such policies are appropriate and necessary in order to provide adequate customer service, or in the case of health operations such as the geriatric center, correct medical care. Employers are, however, warned by their lawyers, that they will have "a target on their backs" if they implement the policies.

A case that an employer lost was *Maldonado v City of Altus,* 433 F.3d 1294 (10th Cir. 2006). In that case, the city of Altus promulgated an English-only policy that affected twenty-nine of the city's employees who are Hispanic. All twenty-nine of the employees are fluently bilingual. In the spring of 2002, the city's street commissioner issued a rule that employees in his division could speak only English while on the job. The city's HR director told the commissioner that the policy would be upheld only if limited to when the employees were using the radio to communicate for purposes of city business. However, the rule was enforced throughout the workday, even during lunch and breaks. The employees filed suit alleging that the rule created a hostile environment for them. The tenth circuit agreed with the employees and reversed the summary judgment for the city. A portion of the court's decision appears below:

> *Defendants' evidence of business necessity in this case is scant. As observed by the district court, "[T]here was no written record of any communication problems, morale problems or safety problems resulting from the use of languages other than English prior to implementation of the policy." And there was little undocumented evidence. Defendants cited only one example of an employee's complaining about the use of Spanish prior to implementation of the policy. Mr. Willis admitted that he had no knowledge of City business being disrupted or delayed because Spanish was used on the radio. In addition, "city officials who were deposed could give no specific examples of safety problems resulting from the use of languages other than English. . . ." Moreover, Plaintiffs produced evidence that the policy encompassed lunch hours, breaks, and private phone conversations; and Defendants conceded that there would be no business reason for such a restriction.*

---

[47]www.eeoc.gov. Click on litigation statistics. Accessed May 19, 2010.

Lawyers offer the following guidelines for enforceable English-only policies:

1. Such policies are permitted if they are needed to promote safe or efficient operations;
2. Such policies are permitted where communication with customers, co-workers, supervisors (who speak only English) is also important;
3. Such policies are permitted where there are frequent emergency encounters in which a common language is necessary for purposes of being able to manage the situation; and
4. Such policies are necessary in situations in which cooperation and close working relationships demand a common language and some workers speak only English.

Discussion Questions

1. Do you think the policies are discriminatory?
2. Do you think they create a hostile environment?
3. Give a list of the types of employers you believe could qualify for an English-only policy under the EEOC guidelines.

Source

Tresa Baldas, "Language Policies Trigger Lawsuits," *National Law Journal,* June 11, 2007, pp. 1 and 17.

Case 6.12

On-the-Job Fetal Injuries

Johnson Controls, Inc., is a battery manufacturer. In the battery-manufacturing process, the primary ingredient is lead. Exposure to lead endangers health and can harm a fetus carried by a female who is exposed to lead.

Before Congress passed the Civil Rights Act of 1964, Johnson Controls did not employ any women in the battery manufacturing process. In June 1977, Johnson Controls announced its first official policy with regard to women who desired to work in battery manufacturing, which would expose them to lead:

> *Protection of the health of the unborn child is the immediate and direct responsibility of the prospective parents. While the medical professional and the company can support them in the exercise of this responsibility, it cannot assume it for them without simultaneously infringing their rights as persons.*

> *Since not all women who can become mothers wish to become mothers (or will become mothers), it would appear to be illegal discrimination to treat all who are capable of pregnancy as though they will become pregnant.*[48]

The policy stopped short of excluding women capable of bearing children from jobs involving lead exposure but emphasized that a woman who expected to have a child should not choose a job that involved such exposure.

Johnson Controls required women who wished to be considered for employment in the lead exposure jobs to sign statements indicating that they had been told of the risks lead exposure posed to an unborn child: "that women exposed to lead have a higher rate of abortion . . . not as clear as the relationship between cigarette smoking and cancer . . . but medically speaking, just good sense not to run that risk if you want children and do not want to expose the unborn child to risk, however small."

By 1982, however, the policy of warning had been changed to a policy of exclusion. Johnson Controls was responding to the fact that between 1979 and 1982, eight employees became pregnant while maintaining blood lead levels in excess of thirty micrograms

---

[48]*International Union v Johnson Controls, Inc.*, 499 U.S. 187, 191 (1991).

per deciliter, an exposure level that OSHA categorizes as critical. The company's new policy was as follows:

> *It is Johnson Controls' policy that women who are pregnant or who are capable of bearing children will not be placed into jobs involving lead exposure or which would expose them to lead through the exercise of job bidding, bumping, transfer or promotion rights.*[49]

The policy defined women capable of bearing children as "all women except those whose inability to bear children is medically documented."[50] The policy defined unacceptable lead exposure as the OSHA standard of thirty micrograms per deciliter in the blood or thirty micrograms per cubic centimeter in the air.

In 1984, three Johnson Controls employees filed suit against the company on the grounds that the fetal-protection policy was a form of sex discrimination that violated Title VII of the Civil Rights Act. The three employees included Mary Craig, who had chosen to be sterilized to avoid losing a job that involved lead exposure; Elsie Nason, a fifty-year-old divorcee who experienced a wage decrease when she transferred out of a job in which she was exposed to lead; and Donald Penney, a man who was denied a leave of absence so that he could lower his lead level because he intended to become a father. The trial court certified a class action that included all past, present, and future Johnson Controls' employees who had been or would continue to be affected by the fetal protection policy Johnson Controls implemented in 1982.

At the trial, uncontroverted evidence showed that lead exposure affects the reproductive abilities of men and women and that the effects of exposure on adults are as great as those on a fetus, although the fetus appears to be more vulnerable to exposure. Johnson Controls maintained that its policy was a product of business necessity.

The employees argued in turn that the company allowed fertile men, but not fertile women, to choose whether they wished to risk their reproductive health for a particular job. Johnson Controls responded that it had based its policy not on any intent to discriminate, but rather on its concern for the health of unborn children. Johnson Controls also pointed out that inasmuch as more than forty states recognize a parent's right to recover for a prenatal injury based on negligence or wrongful death, its policy was designed to prevent its liability for such fetal injury or death. The company maintained that simple compliance with Title VII would not shelter it from state tort liability for injury to a parent or child.

Johnson Controls also maintained that its policy represented a bona fide occupational qualification and that it was requiring medical certification of nonchildbearing status to avoid substantial liability for injuries.

Discussion Questions

1. To what extent should a woman have the right to make decisions that will affect not only her health but also the health of her unborn child? To what extent should a woman's consent to or acknowledgment of danger mitigate an employer's liability? What if a child born with lead-induced birth defects sues? Should the mother's consent apply as a defense?

2. The U.S. Supreme Court eventually decided Johnson Controls' policy was discriminatory and a violation of Title VII.[51] What steps would you take as director of human resources to create a "policy-free" work setting?

3. The fallout from the *Johnson Controls* decision has been that many women have been

---

[49]*Id.*, p. 191.

[50]*Id.*, p. 192.

[51]*International Union v Johnson Controls, Inc.*, 499 U.S. 187 (1991).

working in jobs that expose them to toxins. The U.S. Supreme Court did acknowledge in its holding that there might be tort liability resulting from its decision but that such liability was often used as a guise or cover for gender discrimination. However, fourteen years after the decision, women who were held to be entitled to the high-risk jobs are now suing their employers for the birth defects in their children. For example, IBM has several suits from employees and their children against it for defects allegedly tied to production line toxins.[52] The position of many of the employers is that even if there were evidence linking the toxins to birth defects, the women took the jobs with knowledge about the risk and agreed to that risk. How can employers, legislators, and public policy specialists reconcile antidiscrimination laws and these risks of exposure?

4. At what times, if any, should discrimination issues be subordinate to other issues, such as the risk of danger to unborn children?

Reading 6.13

The Benefits of Diversity: Remarks of Doug Daft, Former CEO of Coca-Cola

Coca-Cola, Inc. entered into a settlement with the EEOC in order to dismiss complaints of 2,000 employees for racial discrimination. The total settlement amount is $191.5 million (plus costs), the largest settlement ever in a discrimination case, topping the Texaco settlement in 1996 of $176 million.[53]

The payments will be made to current and former African American employees of Coke as follows:

- $92.4 million in compensatory damages to employees
- $20.6 million in attorneys' fee
- $43.5 million to promote pay equity within the company
- $35 million invested in diversity reform programs[54]

Coke also agreed to link management pay to diversity efforts by managers and form a seven-member independent panel to oversee diversity efforts at Coke and measure progress.

The settlement with the EEOC does not dispose of individual employee claims in a $1.5 billion racial bias class action suit still pending, which employees who benefit from this settlement may still join.

The following speech by the former CEO indicates a new commitment to diversity by Coca-Cola.[55] Mr. Daft is now retired.

Good evening everyone and welcome.

Thank you, Ralph, for your kind words and thanks to everyone here at King and Spalding for inviting me to speak tonight. The link between The Coca-Cola Company and King & Spalding certainly predates my thirty-year career with Coca-Cola. A number of our Directors and General Counsels have hailed from King & Spalding, including Sam Nunn, Joe Gladden, Jimmy Sibley and his father John Sibley . . . just to name a few. I am honored to be here.

Tonight, I have been asked to share a few thoughts with you about diversity . . . diversity is a simple word, but a complex subject. Complex, in part, because it is

---

[52]Stephanie Armour, "Workers Take Employers to Court over Birth Defects," *USA Today*, February 26, 2002, pp. 1A, 2A. For more information, go to http://www.cdc.gov/niosh.

[53]Theresa Howard, "Coke Settles Bias Lawsuit for $192.5 Million," *USA Today*, November 17, 2000, p. 1B.

[54]Betsy McKay, "Coke Settles Bias Suit for $192.5 Million," *Wall Street Journal*, November 17, 2000, p. A3.

[55]Viewpoints, October, 9, 2001, Atlanta, GA Remarks by Doug Daft, Importance of Diversity, King & Spalding Fall Executive Dinner. http://www2.coca-cola.com/presscenter/viewpointskingspalding.html. Accessed May 19, 2010.

rooted in deeply personal and emotional attitudes connected to race and gender. Complex, too, because there are so many things that come together to make every individual unique, and at the same time a part of an interdependent community.

What sort of characteristics am I talking about? Ones that go well beyond race and gender . . . characteristics like professional experiences, educational backgrounds, working styles and career aspirations. Also family values, our childhood communities and the books we have read and the people we have met.

There is a near endless list of factors that help shape our perspectives. And each individual's perspective—like every individual—is indeed unique.

But that's both the beauty and the power of diversity. . . . Bringing those unique perspectives together to solve a problem or capture an opportunity is what managing diversity is all about.

And as we look at the changed world after the tragedies of September 11, we can only be reminded that diversity of different peoples, with different experiences and opinions not only made this country great, but also made it a prime target of the terrorists who seek to destroy our way of life.

These terrible events remind us of the importance of understanding and embracing diversity in our country, our communities and our companies.

The reality is that managing diversity . . . simply understanding diversity . . . requires an investment on our part. An investment of time . . . an investment of focus . . . and more than anything, an investment in people. If you take anything away from my remarks this evening, I hope it will be that such investment is well worth making.

Diversity is a subject I am continually learning more about. I have spent much of my working career in places and situations where I was one of the persons who brought diversity to the team . . . including my current role as an Australian CEO of a worldwide corporation, headquartered here in Atlanta.

During my years with Coca-Cola, I have lived and worked in communities throughout Asia, Europe and the United States. Most of the time, I was a minority learning to operate with respect and consideration in a societal culture very different from my own.

These experiences have helped me to appreciate the complexity of diversity and have given me an opportunity to experience its enormous power.

My commitment to diversity is rooted in seeing how a rich mosaic of perspectives builds a brand that transcends demographics. . . . A brand that makes more than a billion people feel just a little bit better, a little more refreshed, and a little more connected to one another every day. . . . A brand that is as at home in Brussels, as it is in Buckhead.

I am fortunate to work for The Coca-Cola Company . . . because we have a brand that lives and breathes the paradox of diversity. It is the same simple formula all over the world. And yet each individual . . . each community . . . each culture, experiences this wonderful beverage in a unique way.

People like to talk about Coca-Cola as a global brand. . . . But the reality is that no one drinks a Coke globally. . . . Local people in every market get thirsty, go to their local retailer, and buy locally-produced Cokes.

So our communication to consumers . . . their interaction with the brand . . . has to address their local needs and wants. Only if we understand them can we address them. And that understanding comes from devoting ourselves to recognizing, respecting, and celebrating the diversity of those local needs and wants.

At one point, we struggled with our advertising in China. We just could not seem to get traction. Well, when we talked to the Chinese about our advertising, we learned that we were not connecting with them culturally. Needless to say, we changed our processes, and now we have successful advertising in China. Here's another example. . . . In Japan, we have a ready-to-drink coffee brand called Georgia. I am proud to say that it is the number one coffee brand in Japan. When we talked to Japanese consumers about growing the brand, we learned that they wanted variety.

So, we responded to their needs and wants by introducing multiple flavors of Georgia Coffee. We now have Georgia original, Espresso, Cappuccino and Café au-lait . . . and we now have dramatic growth of the brand.

We would not be able to grow our business the way we have around the world if we didn't open ourselves up to the perspectives of others. Genuinely expressed interest in another's point of view in a way to build bridges and mutual respect . . . it is about the power of relationships.

One more example illustrates how one product can be viewed differently by different people in different parts of the world.

Here in the U.S., you may have noticed the relaunch of POWERade, which is producing truly spectacular results . . . our overall volume for POWERade is up 17% this year! In our home country, the brand is aimed at athletes—from the professional to the weekend warrior. We tap into the desire for a beverage that replenishes you while you are working out.

However, in Japan, sports drinks are viewed very differently. They are a component of relaxation. Japanese consumers might enjoy a sports beverage, not during their workout, but after it, while they bathe. Understanding that difference has helped us make our Aquarius brand the biggest selling sports drink in Japan.

Understanding diversity has led to innovation for our carbonated brands too. For example, I hope that all of you will try our newest brand extension, diet Coke with Lemon.

Sometime ago, some of our people came up with an idea. . . . In the U.S., they said, "People sit at cafes and restaurants and enjoy diet Coke with a lemon in their drink." They asked, "Why don't we put that flavor into the beverage itself, so that consumers can enjoy the same taste while they are on the go?"

As a result, diet Coke with Lemon is currently being introduced in the Midwest to rave reviews and will be rolled out nationwide later this month.

These are all a result of listening to new and different perspectives—from inside and outside our Company—and incorporating them into our decision-making to grow our business. In short . . . diversity marketing.

And even if you don't operate in two hundred countries around the world, any organization will be more successful if it can access a broader array of perspectives and then channel them towards the organization's mission. Those perspectives can be driven not only by race or gender, but also by functional background or professional expertise.

Put simply . . . you are not taking advantage of your diversity if, in developing a new strategy, you gather a group of people with the same perspective or business expertise, say a group of marketers, or a group of accountants, or even lawyers . . . sorry. . . . You'll get limited, narrow points of view.

At Coca-Cola, we value a workforce that mirrors the consumers we serve, and we continue to build towards that objective. And let's be clear about what that means. Yes, it is including African-Americans, Latinos, and Asian-Americans. And it is also bringing together young people with those closer to my age. . . . It's single parents. . . . It's liberals and conservatives. It is working diligently to maintain a workforce that possesses the experiences, backgrounds and influences that can enrich our lives and enhance our business.

It starts with education. All of us, from myself on, have participated in strategic diversity management sessions—to educate ourselves, to understand how we can best leverage our diversity to support our business, and to apply what we learn to our operations.

This commitment to bring diversity to the way we do business extends beyond the Company and into society at large, through the communities of which we are a part. Through our local people and those of our bottling partners, we are part of the community connecting with local residents through local marketing and local civic programs. We create opportunities for our consumers to[o]. For example, our Urban Economic Partnership in Harlem developed with our largest U.S. bottler, Coca-Cola Enterprises, has expanded to several other communities in the Northeast. Many of the people hired in those new jobs have been promoted from account managers to district managers and sales managers.

Last fall we donated $1.5 million to the American Institute of Managing Diversity for the establishment of the Diversity Leadership Academy, right here in Atlanta.

The Diversity Leadership Academy is designed to build diversity management skills and capabilities in leaders from various sectors within the community—including government, nonprofits, education and business—so they all can benefit from better diversity management.

Diversity has a direct impact on The Coca-Cola Company:

- It improves our understanding of local markets;
- It makes us a better employer and business partner;
- It helps us compete more effectively;
- It makes us better neighbors in our communities; and ultimately,
- It builds value for our shareowners.

Respecting and benefiting from diversity in our businesses and in our communities is not only a guiding principle but also a core value of The Coca-Cola Company.

That's why our success demands that we continue to develop a worldwide team rich in its diversity of thinking, perspectives, backgrounds and culture.

Only when we do that can we keep developing a unique intellectual and physical system throughout the world, a system with the people and assets to refresh consumers in local communities in over 200 countries.

Thank you.

Discussion Questions

1. Why does Mr. Daft believe diversity is important? What personal experiences does he have with the issue of diversity?

2. What are the five components of Coke's diversity program?

3. Was the program put into place because of the EEOC issues? Will the program prevent future EEOC issues?

4. You can study Coca-Cola's actions in ginning up data in order to sell Frozen Coke to Burger King in Case 7.17. Do you think a company that adopts a good posture on diversity is immune from honesty issues and vice versa?

5. Diet Coke with Lemon failed as a product and is no longer sold. What do you learn from this result and diversity?

Case 6.14

Seinfeld *in the Workplace*

Jerold J. Mackenzie was hired by Miller Brewing Company in 1974 as an area manager of Miller distributors with a salary grade level of 7. In 1982 he had progressed to grade level 14, and he attained the position of sales services and development manager, reporting to Robert L. Smith in 1987. In late 1987 Miller undertook a corporate reorganization, which led to a transfer of many of Mackenzie's responsibilities.[56]

Concerned, Mackenzie asked Smith whether the reorganization affected his grade level. Smith responded that it did not. In 1989 Miller reevaluated the grade levels of 716 positions, including Mackenzie's. As a result, Mackenzie's position was downgraded to grade level 13. The reevaluation, however, was prospective and applied to the position, not the employee. Therefore, Mackenzie was grandfathered as a grade level 14, even though his position was a grade level 13. That same year, Mackenzie's secretary, Linda Braun, made a sexual harassment complaint against him. She made another sexual harassment complaint against him in 1990.

In August 1992 Miller sent a memo to employees whose positions had been downgraded but who had been grandfathered to their current grade level informing them that they would be downgraded to their position grade level. Therefore, as of January 1, 1993, Mackenzie would be at grade level 13. He would receive the same salary and benefits of a grade level 14, but he would not be entitled to any future grants of stock options.

On March 23, 1993, Patricia Best, a Miller distributor services manager who had previously reported to Mackenzie, told her supervisor, Dave Goulet, that Mackenzie had told her about a sexually suggestive episode of the *Seinfeld* television show, which made her uncomfortable. The *Seinfeld* episode is one in which Jerry forgets the first name of a woman he is dating but does recall that her name rhymes with a part of the female anatomy (Dolores was the woman's name). Ms. Best said she didn't "get it," and Mackenzie made a photocopy of the word *clitoris* from the dictionary. Best reported the incident to her supervisor. Miller immediately investigated the matter, and Mackenzie denied sexually harassing Ms. Best. After concluding its investigation, Miller fired Mackenzie for "unacceptable managerial performance" and "exercising poor judgment."

Mackenzie filed suit against Miller on September 29, 1994. He alleged four causes of action in tort against Miller, Smith, and Best: (1) intentional misrepresentation against Smith and Miller, (2) tortious interference with prospective contract against Smith, (3) tortious interference with contract against Best, and (4) wrongful termination against Miller. His theory supporting the intentional misrepresentation torts against Smith and Miller was that Miller had a duty to disclose after the 1987 reorganization that his position had been grandfathered and that Smith misrepresented to Mackenzie that he would not be affected by the reorganization. In support of the tortious interference claim

---

[56]James L. Graff and Andrea Sachs, "It Was a Joke!" *Time*, July 28, 1997, 62.

against Best, he contended that she improperly induced Miller to terminate Mackenzie by fraudulently misrepresenting to Miller that she felt harassed by his discussion of the *Seinfeld* program. The circuit court denied the defendants' motion to dismiss.

On June 23, 1997, a jury trial began and resulted in a verdict three weeks later. The jury awarded $6,501,500 in compensatory damages and $18,000,000 in punitive damages against Miller on the intentional misrepresentation claim. The jury also awarded $1,500 in compensatory damages and $500,000 in punitive damages against Smith on the same tort. The jury found Smith liable for tortious interference with Mackenzie's promotion and awarded him compensatory damages of $100,000. Finally, the jury failed to award Mackenzie any compensatory damages for tortious interference with contract against Best, but did award him $1.5 million in punitive damages. The jurors in the case (ten women and two men) said the *Seinfeld* story did not offend them and they wanted to send a message with the size of the award that "sexual harassment has to be more important" than a story from a TV show.

The circuit court reduced the punitive damages against Smith to $100,000—giving Mackenzie the option to take the reduction or risk a new trial on the issue of damages—and dismissed Mackenzie's claim against Best because the jury failed to award compensatory damages. Miller and Smith appealed.

In an exhaustive opinion, the court of appeals reversed the judgment of the circuit court.[57] Mackenzie appealed, and the Wisconsin Supreme Court affirmed the appellate court's decision.[58]

Discussion Questions

1. Do you think Mackenzie's conduct was sexual harassment?
2. Do you think Mackenzie's conduct was professional? Do you think Mackenzie showed poor judgment?
3. Was the award excessive? Was the court of appeals correct in reversing the decision?
4. Do you think Mackenzie was wrongfully terminated? Was he already having difficulty at work? What about the previous allegations of harassment? Should Miller have taken action then to prevent the so-called "*Seinfeld* episode" from entering into workplace conversations?

Case 6.15

Toyota, the CEO, the Assistant, and Inaction

Sayaka Kobayashi sent a letter to the senior vice president of Toyota North America to notify him that her boss, Hideaki Otaka, CEO of Toyota North America, had been making romantic and sexual advances to her for three months. She told the vice president, Dennis Cuneo, that she felt helpless. The vice president told her that she should meet privately with Mr. Otaka to discuss her concerns. When she did meet with Mr. Otaka, he indicated that she "lacked quality" and had not been sufficiently grateful for his efforts to advance her career.[59]

Kobayashi then informed Toyota's general counsel of the issues, and he suggested that she should consider her options, including leaving the company.

As a result of that meeting, Kobayashi filed a lawsuit in New York with full details that had the tabloids clucking over the lurid details. The lawsuit asked for $40 million in compensatory damages for Ms. Kobayashi's career and $190 million in punitive damages. The detailed account lists several occasions in which Kobayashi was required

[57]*Mackenzie v Miller Brewing Co.*, 2000 Wis. App 48, 234 Wis.2d 1, 608 N.W.2d 331 (2000).

[58]*Mackenzie v Miller Brewing Co.*, 241 Wis.2d 700, 623 N.W.2d 739 (Wis. 2001).

[59]"Woman Sues Toyota, Says U.S. Chief Harassed Her," *USA Today*, May 2, 2006, p. 1B.

to accompany her boss alone on trips, dinners, and outings, and states that he attempted sexual contact several times, once in Central Park in New York City. When she wrote to the senior vice president to seek his help with the harassment, her letter included the following:

> Nowadays, I come to work with anxiety and pray that Mr. Otaka will not ask me to accompany with him to another lunch, another dinner, another business trip. I would like to seek advice from you on the issue that I feel helpless.[60]

Otaka, sixty-five, is married. Kobayashi married recently and received a note from Otaka, "If I had known you were getting married, I wouldn't have bothered you." Experts have noted that training on U.S. harassment laws for international executives is necessary.

Discussion Questions

1. Corporate governance experts advise that when a CEO is involved in any allegation of misconduct (whether harassment or financial reporting or any misstep) the board should be involved. To not involve the board leaves the officers dangling, as they were in this case.[61] Why do you think the other officers took no action to report the issue to the board?

2. What are the requirements when sexual harassment is reported?

3. Toyota took the following steps:
   a. Mr. Otaka was put on leave, eventually reassigned to Toyota Japan, and then retired there.
   b. Dennis Cuneo was no longer head of HR at Toyota North America.
   c. Alexis Herman, a former secretary of labor, was retained to review and revamp, as it were, Toyota's sexual harassment policies. Toyota settled the suit with Ms. Kobayashi for an undisclosed amount.

   What signals did Toyota send to its employees about its corporate culture through the steps it took, as outlined above?

Compare & Contrast

Compare the path of the sexual harassment issues raised in the Miller Brewing case and in this, the Toyota case. What reporting issues did both cases have? What is different about the way Miller handled its situation versus Toyota's response? Be sure to consider the final outcomes in the two cases and how the victims were treated. Using the two cases, develop some guidelines, policies, and reporting systems that would result in faster resolution of these situations.

Case 6.16

Arizona Senate Bill 1070: Immigration Laws, Employers, Enforcement, and Emotion

On April 21, 2010, Arizona Governor Jan Brewer signed Arizona Senate Bill 1070, a state legislative enactment that has been described as the "broadest and strictest immigration measure in generations."[62] From the moment of its passage, the law created a firestorm of controversy, including boycotts from the cities of Los Angeles, Seattle, and Columbus,

---

[60]Michael Orey, "Trouble at Toyota," *BusinessWeek*, May 22, 2006, pp. 46–48.
[61]Joann S. Lublin, "Harassment Law in U.S. Is Strict, Foreigners Find," *Wall Street Journal*, May 15, 2006, pp. B1, B3.
[62]Randal C. Archibald, "Arizona Enacts Stringent Law on Immigration," *New York Times*, April 23, 2010, p. A1.

Ohio, from doing business with Arizona. Arizona fired back with a letter from its public utility commission reminding the mayor of Los Angeles that Arizona power plants generated 25 percent of the electricity for his city and asking him to include the power contracts as part of his boycott, a move that would result in brown-outs in Los Angeles. The Phoenix Suns players wore jerseys for one of their May playoff games that read, "Los Suns." Los Angeles Lakers' coach, Phil Jackson, coach of the Suns' opposition team, spoke out and reflected that sports franchises should stay away from political issues and let fans enjoy the sport. The Lakers then had protestors outside their arena the following night who demanded a retraction from Mr. Jackson.

The emotionally charged discussion of the bill did not focus on the language and provisions of the bill. Consider the following portions of the law:

Unlawful stopping to hire and pick up passengers for work; unlawful application, solicitation or employment; classification; definitions[63]:

A. It is unlawful for an occupant of a motor vehicle that is stopped on a street, roadway or highway to attempt to hire or hire and pick up passengers for work at a different location if the motor vehicle blocks or impedes the normal movement of traffic.

B. It is unlawful for a person to enter a motor vehicle that is stopped on a street, roadway or highway in order to be hired by an occupant of the motor vehicle and to be transported to work at a different location if the motor vehicle blocks or impedes the normal movement of traffic.

Knowingly employing unauthorized aliens; prohibition; false and frivolous complaints; violation; classification; license suspension and revocation; affirmative defense[64]:

A. An employer shall not knowingly employ an unauthorized alien. If, in the case when an employer uses a contract, subcontract or other independent contractor agreement to obtain the labor of an alien in this state, the employer knowingly contracts with an unauthorized alien or with a person who employs or contracts with an unauthorized alien to perform the labor, the employer violates this subsection.

Discussion Questions

1. What restrictions do these provisions of the law impose on employers?
2. Will the employers have to profile by race to be in compliance with either of these sections?
3. Is this bill an ethical issue?
4. Consider the following illustration of one employer's conduct with respect to its workforce and the lack of documentation.

> The Agriprocessor Inc. plant in Postville, Iowa, has been called the largest kosher slaughterhouse in the country. Federal authorities conducted a raid at the plant in April 2008 and arrested 400 undocumented workers at the plant.
>
> The company had received more than 12 letters in 2005 and 2006 that indicated the Social Security numbers that the company was using for its workers did not match the information that the federal agency had in its files. The 3,000 discrepancies the agency found affected 78% of the plant's workers. The letters did not result in any response from the company and the Social Security Administration stopped sending letters after 2007.
>
> The following chart, from the Social Security website, shows the discrepancies pointed out to the company by the agency:

---

[63]A.R.S. §13-2928(2010).

[64]A.R.S. §23-212 (2010).

Social Security Administration Correspondence with Agriprocessors		
Date	SS# Discrepencies	Tax Year
May 9, 2002	22	2001
May 19, 2005	500	2004
May 19, 2005	500	2003
May 19, 2005	500	2002
May 19, 2005	500	2001
May 19, 2005	461	2000
March 24, 2006	52	2004
March 24, 2006	42	2003
March 24, 2006	37	2002
March 24, 2006	24	2000
April 21, 2006	68	2005
May 5, 2006	500	2005

In 2008, federal authorities served a search warrant on the Postville, Iowa, company and arrested over 900 employees for violations of immigration laws as well as fraud in the use of Social Security numbers. Also charged with violations were the following officers of the company:

- Abraham Aaron Rubashkin—principal owner and president of Agriprocessors, Inc.
- Sholom M. Rubashkin—son of Mr. Rubaskin, manager of the slaughtering and meat packing plant at Postville and a company officer
- Elizabeth Billmeyer—human resources manager of Agriprocessors, Inc.
- Laura Althouse—management employee in the human resources department at Agriprocessors in Postville
- Karina Freund—management employee in the human resources department at Agriprocessors in Postville

In September, 2008, the Iowa Attorney general charged the food processor with over 9,000 violations of child labor laws. The charges focused on 32 minors who were working at the company and had been assigned work tasks or worked in areas not permitted for minors under Iowa law. The charges filed included the following:

During the period of Sept. 9, 2007, through May 12, 2008, the persons as listed as employee-victims in the attached Complaint were employed and permitted to work at Agriprocessors' slaughtering and meat packing establishment. All were under eighteen years of age on each of the dates listed. Throughout their employment these children were exposed to dangerous and/or poisonous chemicals, including, but not limited to, dry ice and chlorine solutions. Several of these employee-victims were also under sixteen years of age during the dates for which they are identified as such in the Complaint. Throughout their employment, these children, while under sixteen years of age, were employed in the operation of or tending of power-driven machinery, including, but not limited to, conveyor belts, meat grinders, circular saws, power washers, and power shears.

Agriprocessor filed for bankruptcy in 2008, was purchased by a Canadian company, and is now known as Agristar. Agriprocessor and the Rubashkin family were known for their generosity in the community and the convictions and change in ownership have resulted in a different complexion for the community. Discuss who is harmed when federal immigration laws are not followed. Does the Agriprocessor situation present additional issues not envisioned in the objections to the 1070 law?

Workplace Privacy and Personal Lives

SECTION 6E

Case 6.17

Facebook, MySpace, and YouTube Screening of Employees

Employers are using new methods for doing background searches on their potential employees:

- 61 percent of professional service firms, including accounting, consulting, engineering, and law firms, do Google searches on their job candidates and use what they find, including YouTube and MySpace references, in the search to gather background on applicants.
- 50 percent of professional services employers hired to do background checks use Google. They also use YouTube and MySpace.

One employer commented that a Google search is so simple that it would be irresponsible not to conduct such a search.

Colleges and universities are continuing to work to help students understand that what they post on the web is not private information and can often have unintended consequences. The following examples resulted in student disciplinary proceedings:

- Several students at Ohio State boasted on Facebook (a networking/socializing site) that they had stormed the field after Ohio State beat Penn State and taken part in what erupted into a riot. Law enforcement officials were able to trace the students through the university system and fifty Ohio State students were referred to the office of judicial affairs for disciplinary proceedings.
- Students at the University of Mississippi were disciplined for stating on an open site that they wanted to have sex with a professor.
- A student at Fisher College was expelled for threatening to take steps to silence a campus police officer.

Another problem with the open sites is that the students are posting personal information with the result that they are accessible by a nefarious element. Students' cell phone numbers, addresses, whereabouts, and other information is easily obtained from these sites and can enable stalkers and identity thieves.

The most popular college site, Facebook, indicates that students spend an average of 17 minutes per day on the site.[65] A great deal of information can be conveyed during that time period. Students do so without thinking through the possibility that outsiders with bad intentions may be seeking and using information about them that is posted there.

As a result of the increased activity levels on websites and the problems, many colleges and universities are offering their entering students sessions on Internet security and safety. Helping the students understand issues of privacy and risk is a critical part of orientation.

The advice experts offer to job-seekers is to remember that what may seem to be something noncontroversial in your youth can later come back to haunt you when you

---

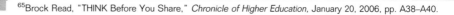

[65]Brock Read, "THINK Before You Share," *Chronicle of Higher Education*, January 20, 2006, pp. A38–A40.

385

begin your professional careers. They also advise that job-seekers watch what they put online in MySpace, Facebook, and all other Internet sites.

Discussion Questions

1. Discuss privacy rights and whether there is an issue of privacy when Information is posted voluntarily on the Internet.

2. Would using these sources for background checks involve any sort of discrimination?

3. Professor Harold Abelson has explained rights, privacy, and the Internet as follows, "In today's online world, what your mother told you is true, only more so: people can really judge you by your friends."[66] In which school of ethical thought would you place Professor Abelson in relation to his views on this question of the Internet and privacy?

Source

Sandhya Bathija, "Have a Profile on MySpace? Better Keep It Clean," *National Law Journal*, June 4, 2007, p. 10.

Case 6.18

Bloggers, Chat Rooms, and E-Mail: Your Employer Is Watching

"Troll Tracker" was a popular blogger in the world of patent litigation. In fact, the blogger confessed to being a patent lawyer. The focus of the blog was "patent trolls," the name patent lawyers give to businesses that purchase patents and then sue large companies to recover for infringement. Whilst Troll Tracker was blogging away, Cisco and other companies that were ending up as defendants in patent troll suits were lobbying Congress for changes in the law that could afford them some protection from what they felt were the willy-nilly attacks of the trolls. However, Cisco was not aware that "Troll Tracker," whose site the company had commended to members of Congress, was its own in-house patent counsel, Rick Frenkel.

Frenkel had blogged that two plaintiffs' patent lawyers had altered dates on documents, a charge that amounted to an accusation of felony misconduct by the lawyers (and the lawyers were named). In addition, Frenkel had allowed posts on his Troll Tracker blog such as, "If you shoot and kill Ray Niro tonight, I would consider it a justifiable killing." (Niro was a plaintiff's patent lawyer).

Eventually, through a subpoena to Google, the lawyers affected were able to track down Frenkel's identity even though he had his blog hosted by a server in Korea and put down his address as one in Afghanistan.

The lawyers have sued both Frenkel and Cisco for defamation. Cisco has taken full responsibility for the problems, but notes that Troll Tracker played an important role in highlighting issues and that it does not want to cut off blogs all together.

The blogosphere represents a risk for companies, despite the fact that many are embracing it. Sun Microsystems indicates that it has 4,000 employees with blogs (its CEO and general counsel are part of the group of blogging employees). Cisco has twelve in-house blogs and seventy-five employees who blog, including its CEO. However, since the Troll Tracker "outing," Cisco has developed new policies that require the bloggers to state that they are employees of Cisco when they are discussing opinions related to matters that affect Cisco.

Experts worry that there is a tendency to be more reckless with facts and assertions when there is anonymity and that it is tough for those who are affected by the bloggers to track down sources and halt the spread of false information.

---

[66]"Quotation of the Week," *New York Times*, March 21, 2010, p. SB2.

Blogging issues arise even when we are blogging away on our own time and our own computers. Shellee Hale put a post on several blogs indicating that a company that manufactured software for tracking sales of adult entertainment had its files tapped into and, as a result, customer information had been compromised.

Three months later, Ms. Hale was served with a suit by the software company for defamation. The company maintains that its files were not compromised. Ms. Hale is defending against the suit on the grounds that she is a reporter and protected by a reporter's privilege of retraction and, absent malice, no liability for defamation.

The most recent data available indicate that there are 207 such suits against bloggers for the content of their postings. Courtney Love has been sued by a fashion designer for her negative remarks about the designer's line and abilities. Referred to as "impetuous remarks," these tweets, blogs, postings, and comments can reach thousands in a matter of minutes, inflicting damage on everything from reputation to stock price. One lawyer has said that what used to be posted on a bathroom wall can now be blasted across the Internet with exponential effects in terms of how many people are reached and how much damage is done.

As the *Wall Street Journal* notes, your homeowner's insurance policy will not cover these defamation suits, but an umbrella policy can. The umbrella policy is one that protects you from liabilities not covered by your other insurance. Former President Clinton used his umbrella policy to pay the damages in the Paula Jones litigation. Ms. Hale has her lawyer's fees covered by her umbrella policy. In fact, Ms. Hale has some advice: 1. Be careful when blogging. 2. Get an umbrella policy.

Discussion Questions

1. What are the rights of employees on blogs?
2. What are the companies' obligations to them?

Sources

Michael Orey, "Busting a Rogue Blogger," *BusinessWeek,* April 7, 2008, p. 75.
M.P. McQueen, "Bloggers, Beware: What You Write Can Get You Sued," *Wall Street Journal,* May 21, 2009, p. D1.

Case 6.19

Jack Welch and the Harvard Interview

Ms. Suzy Wetlaufer, then-editor of the *Harvard Business Review,* interviewed former GE CEO and business legend, Jack Welch, for a piece in the business magazine. She asked in December 2001 that the piece be withdrawn because her objectivity might have been compromised. Those at the magazine did another interview and published that interview in the February issue of the magazine.

Soon afterward, the editorial director of the magazine, Walter Kiechel, who supervised Ms. Wetlaufer, acknowledged that a report in the *Wall Street Journal* about an alleged affair between Ms. Wetlaufer and Mr. Welch was correct and that Mr. Welch's wife, Jane, had called to protest the article's objectivity. At that time, Mr. Welch refused to confirm or deny that there had been an affair. Ms. Wetlaufer was, at the time of the interview, divorced.

Some staff members asked that Ms. Wetlaufer resign from her $277,000 per year job, but she initially survived termination. Their objections were that she compromised her journalistic integrity. Mr. Kiechel, on the other hand, noted that she did "the right thing in raising her concerns."[67]

[67]Del Jones, "Editor Linked with Welch Finds Job at Risk," *USA Today,* March 5, 2002, p. 3B.

After the article appeared in print and following thirteen years of marriage, Jane filed for divorce. The Welches did have a prenuptial agreement, but that agreement expired after ten years, leaving Mrs. Welch entitled to one-half of what was estimated at that time to be Welch's nearly $1 billion net worth.[68] The result was a battle over assets that spilled over into the business and popular press. The documents filed in the divorce proceedings proved to be quite revealing about Mr. Welch, his finances, and GE.

Mr. Welch asked the judge to deduct $200 million from his assets as the amount he has pledged to his four children from his first marriage, an arrangement that was part of his divorce settlement with Carolyn B. Welch.[69] That request was refused because the pledge only takes effect at Mr. Welch's death and does not eliminate lifetime obligations to any current spouses. Mr. Welch told the judge, "This is taking up too much time. I'd like to get on with my life and have her get on with her life. These issues are all resolvable."[70]

Jane earned the upper hand in the divorce proceedings by revealing Mr. Welch's retirement perks from General Electric, including:

- An apartment in New York owned by GE
- Courtside seats at the U.S. Open
- Security personnel for international travel
- Satellite TV at four of their homes
- $17,307 per day in consulting fees
- Wine
- Car and driver[71]

The revelations brought instant reactions from shareholders, who felt that the extensive perks indicated a board that was either asleep at the wheel or not concerned about lavish expenses.[72] The SEC opened an investigation examining the following issues with GE:

- Whether there had been adequate disclosure about the nature of Mr. Welch's retirement contract
- Whether there had been adequate disclosure of Mr. Welch's perks while he was CEO
- Whether all retirement benefits bestowed have been disclosed by GE[73]

Mr. Welch reached a new agreement with GE, published an op-ed piece in the *Wall Street Journal*, and agreed to pay for his retirement perks.[74]

In part, the *Wall Street Journal* op-ed stated,

I want to share a helluva problem that I've been dealing with recently.

Papers filed by my wife in our divorce proceeding became public and grossly misrepresented many aspects of my employment contract with General Electric. I'm not going to get into a public fight refuting every allegation in that filing. But some

[68]Christine Dugas, "Some Prenups Are Set Up to Expire," *USA Today*, March 15, 2002, p. 3B.

[69]Geraldine Fabrikant, "Judge Permits a Litigator to Join the Welch Divorce Team," *New York Times*, October 31, 2002, p. C3.

[70]*Id.*

[71]Rachel Emma Silverman, "Here's the Retirement Jack Welch Built: $1.4 Million a Month," *Wall Street Journal*, October 31, 2002, pp. A1, A15.

[72]Del Jones and Garry Strauss, "Jane Welch Reveals Jack's GE Perks in Divorce Case," *USA Today*, September 9, 2002, p. 4B.

[73]Matt Murray, "SEC Investigates GE's Retirement Deal with Jack Welch," *Wall Street Journal*, September 17, 2002, pp. B1, B3.

[74]David Cay Johnston and Reed Abelson, "G.E.'s Ex-Chief to Pay for Perks, but the Question Is: How Much?" *New York Times*, September 17, 2002, pp. C1, C2.

charges have gotten a lot of media attention. So, for the record, I've always paid for my personal meals, don't have a cook, have no personal tickets to cultural and sporting events. In fact, my favorite team, the Red Sox, has played 162 home games over the past two years, and I've attended just one.

I spent 41 years at GE, the past 21 as chairman. My respect for the company and my fondness for its employees make me hate the fact that my private life has brought unwelcome and inaccurate attention to the company.

I've debated what to do about this. In my mind, it comes down to two choices. I could keep the contract as it is, and tough-out the public attention. Or I could modify the contract and open myself to charges that the contract was unfair in the first place.

My employment contract was drawn up in 1996. GE was enjoying great results and was in the second year of a succession plan for a new CEO. The GE board knew I loved my job, and, frankly, I had no plans to leave, despite persistent rumors in the media that other companies were recruiting me.

But GE's two previous CEOs had retired at ages 62 and 63, and the board wanted to make sure I wouldn't do the same, especially in light of the quintuple bypass surgery I had undergone the year before. With these facts in mind, the board came to me and suggested an employment contract, which offered me a special one-time payment of tens of millions of dollars to remain as CEO until December 2000, when I would be 65.

I instead suggested an employment contract that spelled out my obligations to GE, including my post-retirement obligations, and the benefits I would receive in return. For six years, the contract was disclosed to shareholders through the proxy statement, posted on the Securities and Exchange Commission website, and discussed in the media. I agreed to take the post-retirement benefits that are now being questioned instead of cash compensation—cash compensation that would have been much more expensive for the company.

Over the next five years, GE prospered and I lived up to my end of the bargain.

That said, in spite of the contract's validity and benefits to GE, a good argument can be made for modifying it today.[75]

The Welch divorce was finalized, and Mr. Welch married Ms. Wetlaufer on April 24, 2004, in Boston's Park Street Church. The two now live in a 26,000-square-foot home on Beacon Street in Boston with Ms. Wetlaufer's four children, who were ages 9 to 15 when the couple married.[76] They co-wrote Mr. Welch's second book, which the two sold to Random House for $4 million based on a two-page proposal.[77] The book, *Winning,* has not reached sales levels anywhere near those of Mr. Welch's first book, *Jack: Straight From the Gut.* However, the book was a bestseller and there have been two follow-up books, *Winning: The Answers* and *The Welch Way.* Mr. Welch said that his wife/coauthor and he make a good team: "We have a lot going on. We've got my greasy fingernails and her brains."[78] The two wrote a weekly column in *BusinessWeek* that began in 2005 and ended in 2009. The column appeared on the last page of the magazine and

[75]Jack Welch, "My Dilemma—and How I Resolved It," *Wall Street Journal,* September 16, 2002, p. A14.
[76]"Jack and Suzy Wetlaufer," *People,* May 10, 2004, 215.
[77]Hugo Lindgren, "Welch Makes another Major Book Deal," *New York Times,* February 4, 2004, pp. C1, C4.
[78]*Id.*

addressed questions from readers on management, strategy, and a wide range of business issues. In 2010, the two launched an online MBA Program through Chancellor University. Mrs. Welch published her own book, *10-10-10: A Life-Transforming Idea,* in 2009, a book that became a *New York Times* bestseller.

Following its investigation, the SEC brought charges against GE for its failure to fully disclose Mr. Welch's compensation package. Those charges were settled in September 2004 in a consent decree in which GE neither admitted nor denied the SEC's accusations but agreed to make full disclosure of Mr. Welch's compensation package. The SEC was troubled by a proxy disclosure that put the compensation at $399,925 when the real figure was $2.5 million.[79] As a result of the Welch disclosure issues, the SEC promulgated new rules that now mandate the disclosure of perks granted to the top five officers of a publicly traded company. The first perk disclosure season was in Spring 2007, and shareholders discovered that the perks of many executives were similar to the Welch perks but included some additional benefits such as payments for financial advisers for officers, discount shopping for spouses of officers, and significant private jet travel for family and friends.

Discussion Questions

1. Was there a conflict of interest for Ms. Wetlaufer if there was an affair between her and Mr. Welch?
2. Were the staff members correct to protest?
3. What were the consequences of Mr. Welch's affair and divorce? Is it troublesome that he and Ms. Wetlaufer are so successful?
4. Does Mr. Welch rationalize his postemployment perks?
5. Did the headline of the newspaper test apply to Mr. Welch's original contract terms?
6. Are there any credo elements you find from either Mr. Welch or Ms. Wetlaufer?

Reading 6.20

Is It None of Our Business?[80]

Introduction

Reaction to the Boeing board's ouster of CEO Harry Stonecipher for an improper relationship with a Boeing employee ranged from "Good for Boeing," to television analyst Bill Maher's nonchalant irritation reflected in his show's monologue, "Who cares what a 68-year-old guy does?" There has also been great murmuring from my colleagues in business ethics about "private lives," "police state," and "moralizing." The Boeing Stonecipher issue brought the reemergence of the question of compartmentalization. The compartmentalization theory ran rampant during the Clinton presidency. During l'affair Bill Clinton/Monica Lewinsky many were outraged at the investigation and intrusion into his private life. Others argued that it was not his private life that was at issue but, rather, perjury related to his conduct in his private life. Still others formed a third school of thought with their "Never mind the perjury, what about the adultery?"

Can we isolate the private unethical conduct of executives, political leaders, officers and directors from our evaluations and determinations of whether they are or will behave ethically as fiduciaries, the managers of others' funds? The question has no facile answer and an exploration of the private lives of those who yielded our greatest corporate scandals nets some inconsistencies in concluding whether private standards and

[79]Geraldine Fabrikant, "G.E. Settles S.E.C. Case on Welch Retirement Perks," *New York Times,* September 24, 2004, p. C2.

[80]Reprinted with permission from "Does Officer Personal Conduct Matter When It Comes to Company Ethics?" *Corporate Finance Review* 10, no. 1 (2005):43–46.

behaviors are important predictors or determinants of ethical conduct in business. The answer to the question of whether private conduct is relevant yields a definite answer only in its indefiniteness. The answer on compartmentalization and relevance of private conduct as a determinant of behavior in business is, "Maybe." The nature and extent of the private conduct and whether it is part of a pattern may provide a better framework and a more definitive answer than, "Maybe."

A Look at The Scandals of Officers in the Scandalous Companies

They All Turned On Each Other

Perhaps there is one definitive observation from all of the misconduct and resulting criminal trials of corporate executives since the crash of Enron in 2001. That observation is one that is a familiar refrain to my students, "Never trust the people you cheat with, whether in adultery or cooking the books." Former WorldCom CEO Bernie Ebbers was convicted on all counts with the critical evidence against him coming from his CFO, Scott Sullivan, who turned state's evidence as part of a guilty plea with promised lesser sentencing recommendations. Beneath Scott Sullivan there was a host of financial and accounting employees who also testified on behalf of the prosecution and against Mr. Ebbers. His CFO, his head of accounting, his controller, and even run-of-the-mill CPAs who did the entries all testified for the federal government. Scott Sullivan, David Myers, Betty Vinson, Buford Yates, Troy Normand, and a host of other characters involved in developing the company's financial reports.[81]

There were very few officers, including the final five CFOs of HealthSouth, who did not testify against their former boss and HealthSouth CEO, Richard Scrushy.[82] They are lined up to testify against Jeffrey Skilling and Ken Lay, the former CEO and chairman of the board, respectively, at Enron.[83] Enron's former CFO, Andrew Fastow, its treasurer, Ben Gilsan, Lea Fastow, Andrew's wife,[84] and even the Andersen audit partner, all entered guilty pleas to some form of federal charges from obstruction to fraud to tax evasion and those pleas were the key to the government's indictment of former chairman, Ken Lay, and former CEO Jeffrey Skilling.[85] The guilty pleas, the guilty verdicts, and even some of the sentencing are over and all will testify against their former bosses.[86]

Perhaps the message is that everyone turns on everyone else in a corporate scandal in order to save themselves. However, there is a chicken and egg issue here. Did they turn

---

[81]Kurt Eichenwald, "2 Ex-Officials at WorldCom Are Charged in Huge Fraud," *New York Times,* August 2, 2002, p. A1. See also Deborah Solomon and Susan Pulliam, "U.S., Pushing WorldCom Case, Indicts Ex-CFO and His Aide," *Wall Street Journal,* August 29, 2002, p. A1. Yates was the former director of general accounting, Myers was the former controller, Vinson was the former director of management reporting, and Normand was the former director of legal entity accounting. Jayne O'Donnell, "Workaholic Sullivan Turns on Former Boss," *USA Today,* March 3, 2004, p. 3B.

[82]Carrick Mollenkamp and Ann Carrns, "HealthSouth Ex-CFO Helps Suits," *Wall Street Journal,* July 26, 2004, pp. C1, C3; Dan Morse and Evelina Shmulker, "HealthSouth Ex-Treasurer Says He Found Fraud, Told Scrushy," *Wall Street Journal,* February 17, 2005, p. C4; and Carrick Mollenkamp and Ann Carrns, "Scrushy 'Coup' Defense Presses On," *Wall Street Journal,* April 18, 2003, p. B3.

[83]Greg Farrell, "Prosecutors Zero In on Enron's Lay," *USA Today,* June 21, 2004, 1B; and Julie Rawe, "The Case against Ken Lay," *Time,* July 19, 2004, p. 62.

[84]Kurt Eichenwald, "Ex-Chief Financial Officer of Enron and Wife Plead Guilty," *New York Times,* January 15, 2004, pp. C1, C9.

[85]Kurt Eichenwald, "Enron's Skilling Is Indicted by U.S. in Fraud Inquiry," *New York Times,* February 20, 2004, pp. A1, C3.

[86]Reed Abelson, "4 of 5 HealthSouth Executives Spared Prison Terms," *New York Times,* December 11, 2004, pp. C1, C2. Sixteen officers and managers beneath Richard Scrushy were charged, with the remaining nine to be sentenced following the completion of Scrushy's trial. John Emshwiller, "Enron Ex-Official Pleads Guilty to Fraud, Agrees to Aid Probe," *Wall Street Journal,* August 2, 2004, p. C3. Ken Rice, head of the broadband unit, agreed to cooperate, as did Richard Causey, the head of accounting; as did Andrew Fastow, the former CFO; and as did a host of others in the company who reported to Mr. Fastow, who, in turn, reported to Mr. Skilling and Mr. Lay.

on others because of the business scandal or was the business scandal the result of their character flaws in the first place?

They Had "Extreme" Personal Lives

The companies in which these frauds occurred all had both peculiar habits and executives with peculiar spending habits. Dennis Kozlowski, the former CEO of Tyco, now slogs through what might be called his "technically not embezzlement" trial. [Mr. Kozlowski was convicted following a retrial after an initial acquittal.] If Tyco had acted on the egregiously unethical personal conduct of its then-CEO, it might not be struggling to recover now. On March 23, 2000, fully two years before Tyco's real numbers and Kozlowski's sales tax evasion and spending problems came to light, partner Lewis Liman at Wilmer Cutler sent an e-mail to then–Tyco general counsel Mark Belnick that read, "There are payments to a woman whom the folks in finance describe as Dennis's girlfriend. I do not know Dennis's situation, but this is an embarrassing fact."[87] If only someone had confronted the issue of the affair, they might have cleaned up the lax personal loans and spending procedures as well as the weak board before Tyco shareholders suffered.

Scott Sullivan's adultery via the workplace as well as marijuana and cocaine use came out during defense lawyers' cross-examination in Bernie Ebbers' trial. These moral missteps occurred even as Sullivan was busily capitalizing $11 billion in ordinary expenses.[88] Bernie divorced his wife of decades and married a WorldCom employee during the years of inflated earnings.

Enron's officer retreats had a Tailhook flavor. They allowed themselves to be photographed with scantily-clad dancing girls for, one presumes, the retreat scrapbook?[89]

HealthSouth's former CEO Richard Scrushy, now in the midst of his trial for various frauds, is on wife number three, and he carries a string of eight children among the three wives.[90] Scrushy's radio show, singing, and female rock group promotion activities also cut into his day and, apparently, his concentration on earnings and financial reports.[91]

The scandals could go on, and they do, even when executives retire. Does it matter? . . .

Why Personal Conduct Matters

There are the obvious lessons from the financial collapses of these companies and the seeming moral collapse of the individual executives. Those lessons relate to Sarbanes–Oxley types of reforms in everything from the officer imprimatur on the financials to the independence of the boards. However, those steps are largely irrelevant and certainly not preventive in the sense of fraud.

A Precursor to Fraud?

How does one detect and prevent fraud? Consulting industries and audit specialists have been working at developing measures, tools, and signs for decades, if not a full century or so. Those means clearly have their flaws. Perhaps what we need is a scale for measuring the moral development or character of those officers to whom the financial status and

---

[87]Laurie P. Cohen and Mark Maremont, "E-Mails Show Tyco's Lawyers Had Concerns," *Wall Street Journal*, December 27, 2002, p. C1. The payments were made to Karen Mayo (then-girlfriend, now wife, who can't be happy about the ex-wife posting the bond) from the Key Employee Loan Account in 1997.

[88]Ken Belson, "Key Witness on WorldCom Says He Frequently Lied," *New York Times*, February 11, 2005, p. C14; and Ken Belson, "Can a Cool-Headed Star Witness Take the Heat from the Ebbers Defense Team?" *New York Times*, February 14, 2005, p. C2.

[89]Bethany McLean and Peter Elkind, *The Smartest Guys in the Room: The Amazing Rise and Scandalous Fall of Enron* (2003). This book gives the full detail and flavor of the lying, cheating, partying nature of the Enron culture.

[90]Greg Farrell, "From Emperor to Outcast," *USA Today*, May 29, 2003, p. 2B.

[91]*Id*; and John Helyar, "King Richard," *Fortune*, July 7, 2003, p. 77.

reports of the company are entrusted. One measure of moral development is the private conduct of executives. How we treat those who are the closest to us and, at least in theory, the most important is telling. If they can be treated with disregard and breaches of trust, it is not a leap in logic to conclude that the same character can see its way clear to be dishonest with those who are not even acquaintances. Such a theory of "morality matters" will hardly be embraced for the sake of morality. However, there are other reasons for invoking a standard of personal moral fiber as a requirement for employment at the executive level. The following subsections make the case for immorality dismissals.

The Impact on the Culture

Sacking people for affairs is not all that bad of an HR or ethics principle because there is much more accomplished by doing so than mere moralizing. What darts through my mind and, through many conversations I have discovered, through the minds of many employees, is, "How on earth do these people have time for this stuff?" A factory line worker can't take time for an officer retreat or have a break long enough to spark a romance. Employees juggle demands of home, job, family, and, for some, education at night. Yet, those to whom they report and who demand private jets to maximize their efficiency somehow find the time to take on all the complexities of a new relationship while maintaining a marriage? Just the thought of the lies needed for the cover-up is exhausting to the frontline employee. One employee asked me, "How can anyone think clearly by dating while married?"

Adultery matters for the moral reasons, but it matters for the fundamental governance reason that an officer consumed with romance, secret meetings, and a cheating partner is not at optimum performance level, as it were. Employees understand this element of distraction and its attendant risk, irrespective of moral issues. They know they could not do their jobs as well, and also know their codes of ethics on affairs between those who share reporting lines, and the failure to take action sends confusing signals about codes, expectations, propriety, culture, and even what is and is not appropriate conduct in their workplaces. Cleaning up a culture and maintaining it requires definitive, egalitarian, and unequivocal signals when violations of codes and standard occur, regardless of who is involved in those violations.

Having worked with Boeing following its first ethical issues surrounding the use of Lockheed-Martin proprietary information in a defense contractor bid and its second involving CFO Michael Sears's premature post-retirement employment discussion with Defense Department contract official, Darlene Druyun (see Case 9.16), I fall in the school that concludes there was no choice but to end the Stonecipher relationship with Boeing, either through termination or resignation. Cleaning up a culture requires definitive signals. As signals go, this was a dandy.

The Issue of Judgment

Adultery also matters as a workplace issue because those who seek respect from employees must earn it. The rush of forbidden lust is short-term pleasure. We like to think that those who establish and enforce the rules have progressed beyond addictions and indiscretions. We particularly like to think so when they are preaching ethics to us as employees. Those who would lead should assume the role of role model. The corporate disasters outlined earlier tell us that the captains of industry were busily involved in activities that not only distract from the intense focus demanded at these higher levels of business, but serve as a risk to the company itself when exposure inevitably comes. If the review of the collapsed companies is a representative set, checking the personal lives, and in particular, the adultery of the CEO and/or CFO may be a formula for saving the company.

The Issue of Integrity

There's a fine line between an office romance and sexual harassment, and there seems to be somewhat of a direct line between executive adultery and executive-induced accounting fraud. The Nashville folks don't refer to adultery as "your *cheatin'* heart" without good reason.

Most are loathe to admit it, but sexual tomfoolery reveals a character flaw that serves those well who would perpetuate corporate shenanigans. A quick review of the scandals over the past four years shows that the two go hand-in-hand. While we may never know which came first, wandering corporate officers' eyes, whether on-the-job or in retirement, do not bode well for the company. The effect on the company culture may not be measurable, even if the same officers never graduate to Ponzi schemes and other forms of fraud. Not every monogamous CEO is a winner and not every adulterer fails in business. However, when officers are dishonest with the single most important person in their lives, i.e., their spouses, it is not a great leap in logic to conclude that they are capable of being dishonest with those with whom they do not share a day-to-day relationship: investors, suppliers, customers.

The examination of this issue and its necessary infringement upon personal lives is a difficult one that finds many officers and employees rankled because of the intrusion. However, the study of collapsed companies shows that indiscretions in private lives go hand-in-hand with individual moral lapses. Knowing which came first may not be critical because they key observation is that those to whom officers are accountable, the boards and eventually the shareholders, send clear signals to those officers about behavior expectations. In so doing they send clear signals to employees and create or preserve a culture of honor and forthrightness, whether in private lives or financial reports.

Discussion Questions

1. Is there a correlation between personal conduct and business ethics missteps? On August 6, 2010, Hewlett-Packard CEO Mark Hurd tendered his resignation. He was following the board's request after they conducted an investigation into charges of sexual harassment made by Jodie Fisher, a contractor hired to conduct marketing research. The investigation report given to the board found no evidence of a sexual relationship but also concluded that Mr. Hurd had a personal relationship with the contractor, that he submitted false expense reports for dinners with Ms. Fisher, and that there were several unauthorized payments made to Ms. Fisher without documentation of work performed. Mr. Hurd submitted expenses that ranged from $1,000 to $20,000 for payments, meals, and gifts for the contractor. Mr. Hurd offered to pay back the money and wanted to stay on as CEO, but the company's CFO, Cathie Lesjak, who assumed the CEO role, released a statement that included the following, "Mark Hurd demonstrated a profound lack of judgment that seriously undermined his credibility and damaged his effectiveness in leading HP."[92] Following the late-Friday-afternoon announcement, HP shares dropped 9.3%. What does the CFO mean by this statement? What role does judgment play in ethical leadership?

2. List the reasons shareholders should worry about officers' personal lives.

3. List the problems you see in corporations taking officers' personal lives into account as part of their contracts and conditions of employment.

4. Are there any personal credo issues in controlling personal conduct and decisions? Are the lines in their personal lives crossed because of the power and success they attain in their professional lives? Can your personal credo be different from your business and professional credo?

---

[92] "HP CEO Resigns," *Wall Street Journal*, August 7–8, 2010, p. A1.

Workplace Confrontation

Reading 6.21

The Glowing Recommendation[93]

Randi W. was a thirteen-year-old minor who attended the Livingston Middle School where Robert Gadams served as vice principal. On February 1, 1992, while Randi was in Gadams's office, Gadams sexually molested Randi.

Gadams had previously been employed at the Mendota Unified School District (from 1985 to 1988). During his time of employment there, Gadams had been investigated and reprimanded for improper conduct with female junior high students, including giving them back massages, making sexual remarks to them, and being involved in "sexual situations" with them.

Gilbert Rossette, an official with Mendota, provided a letter of recommendation for Gadams in May 1990. The letter was part of Gadams's placement file at Fresno Pacific College, where he had received his teaching credentials. The recommendation was extensive and referred to Gadams's "genuine concern" for students and his "outstanding rapport" with everyone, and concluded, "I wouldn't hesitate to recommend Mr. Gadams for any position."

Gadams had also previously been employed at the Tranquility High School District and Golden Plains Unified District (1987–1990). Richard Cole, an administrator at Golden Plains, also provided a letter of recommendation for the Fresno placement file that listed Gadams's "favorable" qualities and concluded that Cole "would recommend him for almost any administrative position he wishes to pursue." Cole knew at the time he provided the recommendation that Gadams had been the subject of various parents' complaints, including that he "led a panty raid, made sexual overtures to students, [and made] sexual remarks to students." Cole also knew that Gadams had resigned under pressure because of these sexual misconduct charges.

Gadams's last place of employment (1990–1991) before Livingston was Muroc Unified School District, where disciplinary actions were taken against him for sexual harassment. When allegations of "sexual touching" of female students were made, Gadams was forced to resign from Muroc. Nonetheless, Gary Rice and David Malcolm, officials at Muroc, provided a letter of recommendation for Gadams that described him as "an upbeat, enthusiastic administrator who relates well to the students" and who was responsible "in large part" for making Boron Junior High School (located in Muroc) "a safe, orderly and clean environment for students and staff." The letter concluded that they recommended Gadams "for an assistant principalship or equivalent position without reservation."

All of the letters provided by previous administrators of Gadams were sent in on forms that included a disclosure that the information provided "will be sent to prospective employers."

---

[93]Adapted from *Randi W. v Muroc Joint Unified School District*, 929 P.2d 582 (Cal. 1997).

Through her guardian, Randi W. filed suit against the districts, alleging that her injuries from Gadams's sexual touching were proximately caused by their failure to provide full and accurate information about Gadams to the placement service.

Discussion Questions

1. If you were a former administrator to whom Gadams reported, what kind of recommendation would you give?
2. Should the previous administrators have done something about Gadams prior to being placed in this dilemma?
3. Do administrators owe their loyalty to employees? to students? to the school district? to the parents?
4. Is this type of recommendation commonly given to get rid of employees?
5. Should friendship have a higher value than honesty?
6. Why do you think the administrators said nothing?

Reading 6.22

The Ethics of Confrontation[94]

Why We Avoid Confrontation

The "Don't rock the boat" attitude is frequently seen as the virtuous road. Confrontation is messy—there are often hurt feelings. There are embarrassing revelations. There are destroyed careers. There are costs. Whether confrontation involves sexual misconduct by an assistant school principal or cooking the books by a manager or bond trader, the impact is the same.

Human nature flees from such situations. Further, there is within human nature that rationalization that avoiding confrontation is being "nice," and nice is associated with ethics.

There are also the harsh realities of confrontation. To confront the assistant school principal with allegations and carry through with a disciplinary process for the loss of a license to teach are time consuming and reflect on the school and administrators who hired him in the first place. There is exposure to liability.

A good employee evaluation means that the employee is happy, there are no reviews, no messy discussions, and no allegations of discrimination. Not confronting a rogue trader means enjoying the ride of his performance and earnings and worrying about consequences at another time when perhaps something else will come along to counterbalance any of the harmful activities. Not insisting that a loan be written down carries with it the comfort of steady growth and earnings and a hope that future financial performance can make up for the loss when it eventually must be disclosed.

There is a great deal of rationalization that goes into the avoidance of confrontation. There is a comfort in maintaining status quo. There is at least a postponement of legal issues and liabilities. Often, avoiding confrontation is a painless road that carries with it the hope that whatever lies beneath does not break through and reveal its ugliness. Often, confrontation carries with it the hope that a problem will solve itself or become a moot issue.

[94]From Marianne M. Jennings, "The Ethics of Confrontation: The Virtues and Vice in Remaining Silent," *Corporate Finance Review* 6(4) (2002), 42–46. Reprinted from *Corporate Finance Review* by RIA, 395 Hudson Street, New York, NY 10014.

The Harms of Avoiding Confrontation

Postponing confrontation does not produce a better result when the issue at the heart of the needed confrontation inevitably emerges. Those harms include liability, individual harms, reputational damage, and the loss of income as the issue chugs along without resolution.

Physical Harm

In the *Muroc* case (Reading 6.21), all of the districts were liable for failing to take action and then issuing glowing letters of recommendation. Had the issue of sexual misconduct and the assistant principal been confronted the first time there was misconduct, there would not have been the remaining three schools and victims.

Liability Increased

Another example is the eventual confrontation between Ford and Firestone over who and what was responsible for the Ford Explorer debacle and the accidents and deaths. The two companies' long-standing business relationship and an unwillingness to deal with data and questions accomplished little. With more information percolating on a regular basis, both companies acknowledged, even as they battled with each other in a media confrontation, that neither has emerged with its reputation intact in the public eye. Civil litigation and an investigation by the federal government as well as depositions of top executives in the companies trickled out to the public. Those depositions have had some inconsistencies with some of the public statements by Bridgestone/Firestone.

For example, Bridgestone/Firestone has issued public statements that it was not aware of peeling issues with its tires used on the Ford Explorer. However, a deposition of Firestone's chief of quality reveals that he believes he discussed the issue of the tires with the company's CEO in 1999, a full year before the issue became public with the resulting recall. David Laubie, who retired from the company in May 2000, said that he handled consumer claims and quality control issues for the company and had received complaints that he passed along to the CEO in memo form as well as in their regular meetings.

In testimony before Congress in September 2000, Firestone's executive vice president, Gary Crigger, testified that the company only became aware of the problem in July or August 2000.

Another issue in the case has been Firestone's allegation that Ford did not put the proper tire pressure instructions with the Ford Explorer. Firestone said that Ford's recommendation of an unusually low tire pressure, 26 pounds per square inch, caused the sidewalls to flex and get hot, which then weakened the tires. However, the depositions of both Mr. Laubie and the current quality control chief of Firestone indicate that no one from Firestone ever discussed the low tire pressure issue with anyone at Ford.[95] The lack of confrontation before, during, and after the public revelations about some issue, whatever that may prove to be, surrounding the Ford Explorer and its tires cost both companies in terms of reputation and perhaps liability.

The Deceptive Lull of "Being Nice"

One of the faulty assumptions in avoiding confrontation is that the "niceness" benefits the individuals affected. A good performance evaluation is beneficial to the employee. Not taking disciplinary action permits a teacher or administrator to continue his career and earn a living. Not raising a financial reporting issue means that shareholders can

---

[95] James R. Healey and Sara Nathan, "Depositions in Tire Lawsuits Don't Match Company's Lines," *USA Today*, December 11, 2000, p. 3B.

continue to enjoy returns and market value. Not questioning an employee's unusual success means that the earnings figures stand unscathed. Many are protected when confrontation is avoided.

The difficulty with the protection argument is that it presumes that the truth will not emerge. When it does, the preservation of a career in light of information introduces greater liability. Termination of an employee for cause may carry with it the difficulties of challenge and even litigation. Not terminating an employee for cause who goes on later to do more harm exposes the company to liability. The difficulty with not disclosing matters that affect earnings is that when those matters do emerge, there is not just the resulting restatement of earnings but also the accompanying lack of investor trust and resulting reduction in market value. The greatest harm in avoiding confrontation is that what the confrontation could have minimized is exacerbated by the postponement.

The Ethics of Confrontation

Although not widely accepted as a principle of virtue, there is an ethical duty of confrontation. Edmund Burke was a proponent of such a duty with his admonition of two centuries ago, "All that is necessary for evil to triumph is for good men to do nothing." There is the more modern phraseology that holds that if there is a legal or ethical problem in a company and an employee or manager or executive says nothing, they become part of the problem.

However, one of the reasons for the hesitancy in confrontation not discussed earlier is a certain degree of ineptness on the part of those who must do the confronting. If confrontation is indeed a virtue, are there guides for its exercise? The following offers a model for confrontation.

Determine the Facts

An underlying disdain for confrontation arises because too often those who do the confronting are wrong. Prior to confrontation, prepare as if you were working on a budget, a product launch, or a financing. Know what is happening or what has happened, and obtain as much background information as possible. Preparation also serves as protection for any fears of liability from taking action. Employers need to understand that well-documented personnel actions are not a basis for discrimination suits. And termination of employees who are harming others is not actionable if the harm is established.

If You Don't Know the Facts, or Can't Know the Facts, Present the Issue to Those Involved and Affected

Ford and Firestone will perhaps not know the issues of liability and accountability for years to come with regard to the Explorer and the tires. However, their lack of information should not have prevented them from confronting each other or confronting the customers and public with the information they did have.

In the case of allegations or when an employee has raised a question about how a particular matter is being carried on the books, you may only be presented with one side. That lack of information need not preclude you from raising the question. In the case of the school administrator, the students made an allegation against the assistant principal. The principal has no way of knowing whether the allegation is true or false, but he can go to the assistant principal and raise the issue and then can proceed with the types of hearings or inquiries that can provide the information or at least constitute the confrontation.

A financial officer can hear from employees a number of views on carrying certain items on the books. The very definition of materiality opens the door to that type of disagreement. But a good financial officer knows that an open discussion of the issue, and confrontation of the issue with those who tout various views, is the solution that serves the company best in the long run. Without such confrontation, the failure to listen to an employee's view exacerbates the eventual fallout from a bad decision. The public confrontation of the issue is, in and of itself, insurance against the fallout should that decision prove to be wrong.

Always Give the Opportunity for Self-Remedy

One of the reasons confrontation enjoys such universal disdain is that very often the confrontation is done circuitously. If your attorney has done something questionable, confront him or her first, and then report them to the state bar for discipline. If an employee has engaged in misconduct, tell them, and don't let him or her hear it from someone else. If earnings are overstated, employees should work within the company for self-remedy before heading to the SEC.

One of the virtue constraints in the ethics of confrontation is having the courage to discuss the issues and concerns with those who are involved in creating them. An end run is not a confrontation. It is an act of cowardice that can result in the liability discussed earlier.

Don't Fear the Fallout and Hassle

The reasons for the lack of confrontation discussed earlier included the realistic observation that many avoid confrontation because it is too much trouble. However, as also noted earlier, if there is a problem that remains unconfronted, it does not improve with age. Indeed, the failure to make a timely confrontation often proves to result in more costs in the long run. Hassles don't dissipate as confrontation is postponed or avoided.

Conclusion

The ethics of confrontation are quite simply that confrontation is a necessary part of managing an honest business. Confrontation openly airs disagreement. Confrontation prevents the damage that comes from concealed truth. Confrontation preserves reputations when it produces the self-remedies that are nearly always cheaper than those imposed from the lack of confrontation. Niceness is rarely the ethical route when issues and facts need to be aired. Confrontation, although not always pleasant, is often the only resolution of a problem.

Discussion Questions

1. What are the consequences of the failure to raise an issue, whether legal or ethical, when it first arises?

2. What factors contribute to the failure to confront an issue?

3. What steps could a business take to encourage confrontation?

Case 6.23

Ann Hopkins and Price Waterhouse

Ann Hopkins was a senior manager in the Management Advisory Services division of the Price Waterhouse Office of Government Services (OGS) in Washington, D.C. After earning undergraduate and graduate degrees in mathematics, she taught mathematics at her alma mater, Hollins College, and worked for IBM, NASA, Touche Ross, and American Management Systems before beginning her career with Price Waterhouse in 1977.[96] She became the

---

[96]Reports conflict in regard to her starting date at Price Waterhouse. Some reports indicate 1977, and some indicate 1978.

firm's specialist in large-scale computer system design and operations for the federal government. Although salaries in the accounting profession are not published, estimates put her salary as a senior manager at about $65,000.

At that time, Price Waterhouse was known as one of the "Big 8," or one of the top public accounting firms in the United States.[97] A senior manager became a candidate for partnership when the partners in her office submitted her name for partnership status. In August 1982, at the end of a nomination process that began in June, the partners in Hopkins's office proposed her as a candidate for partner for the 1983 class of partners. Of the eighty-eight candidates who were submitted for consideration, Hopkins was the only woman. At that time, Price Waterhouse had 662 partners, 7 of whom were women.[98] Hopkins was, however, a stellar performer and was often called a "rainmaker." She was responsible for bringing to Price Waterhouse a two-year, $25 million contract with the U.S. Department of State, the largest contract ever obtained by the firm.[99] Being a partner would not only bring Hopkins status. Her earnings would increase substantially. Estimates of the increase in salary were that she would earn almost double, or $125,000 annually, on average (1980 figures).

The partner process was a collaborative one. All of the firm's partners were invited to submit written comments regarding each candidate on either "long" or "short" evaluation forms. Partners chose a form according to their exposure to the candidate. All partners were invited to submit comments, but not every partner did so. Of the thirty-two partners who submitted comments on Hopkins, one stated that "none of the other partnership candidates at Price Waterhouse that year [has] a comparable record in terms of successfully procuring major contracts for the partnership."[100] In addition, Hopkins' billable hours were impressive, with 2,442 in 1982 and 2,507 in 1981, amounts that none of the other partnership candidates' billable hours even approached.

After reviewing the comments, the firm's Admissions Committee made recommendations about the partnership candidates to the Price Waterhouse Policy Board. The recommendations consisted of accepting the candidate, denying the promotion, or putting the application on hold. The Policy Board then decided whether to submit the candidate to a vote, reject the candidate, or hold the candidacy. There were no limits on the number of persons to whom partnership could be awarded and no guidelines for evaluating positive and negative comments about candidates. Price Waterhouse offered forty-seven partnerships to the eighty-eight candidates in the 1983 round, another twenty-seven were denied partnerships, and twenty, including Ms. Hopkins, were put on hold. Ms. Hopkins had received more "no" votes than any other candidate for partnership, with most of those votes coming from members of the partnership committee outside the firm's government services unit.

The comments on Hopkins were extensive and telling. Thirteen of the thirty-two partners who submitted comments on Hopkins supported her, three recommended putting her on hold, eight said they did not have enough information, and eight recommended denial. The partners in Hopkins's office praised her character as well as her accomplishments, describing her in their joint statement as "an outstanding professional" who had a "deft touch," a "strong character, independence, and integrity." Clients appear to have agreed with these assessments. One official from the State Department described

[97]Price Waterhouse no longer exists, having merged into PriceWaterhouseCoopers, and the "Big 8," is now the "Big 4," due to the collapse of Arthur Andersen and the mergers of most of the other firms.

[98]There are factual disputes over the number. Hopkins maintains that there were only six female partners at the time.

[99]Ann Hopkins, "Price Waterhouse v Hopkins: A Personal Account of a Sexual Discrimination Plaintiff," 22 *Hofstra Lab. & Emp. L.J.* 357 (2005).

[100]*Price Waterhouse v Hopkins*, 490 U.S. 228 (1989).

her as "extremely competent, intelligent," "strong and forthright, very productive, energetic, and creative." Another high-ranking official praised Hopkins's decisiveness, broadmindedness, and "intellectual clarity"; she was, in his words, "a stimulating conversationalist."[101] Hopkins "had no difficulty dealing with clients and her clients appear to have been very pleased with her work."[102] She "was generally viewed as a highly competent project leader who worked long hours, pushed vigorously to meet deadlines, and demanded much from the multidisciplinary staffs with which she worked."[103]

On too many occasions, however, Hopkins's aggressiveness apparently spilled over into abrasiveness. Staff members seem to have borne the brunt of Hopkins's brusqueness. Long before her bid for partnership, partners evaluating her work had counseled her to improve her relations with staff members. Although later evaluations indicate an improvement, Hopkins's perceived shortcomings in this important area eventually doomed her bid for partnership. Virtually all of the partners' negative remarks about Hopkins—even those of partners who supported her—concerned her "interpersonal skills." Both "[s]upporters and opponents of her candidacy indicated that she was sometimes overly aggressive, unduly harsh, difficult to work with, and impatient with staff."[104]

Another partner testified at trial that he had questioned her billing records and was left with concern because he found her answers unsatisfying:

I was informed by Ann that the project had been completed on sked within budget. My subsequent review indicated a significant discrepancy of approximately $35,000 between the proposed fees, billed fees [and] actuals in the WIPS. I discussed this matter with Ann who attempted to try and explain away or play down the discrepancy. She insisted there had not been a discrepancy in the amount of the underrealization. Unsatisfied with her responses, I continued to question the matter until she admitted there was a problem but I should discuss it with Krulwich [a partner at OGS]. My subsequent discussion with Lew indicated that the discrepancy was a result of 500 additional hours being charged to the job (at the request of Bill Devaney. . . agreed to by Krulwich) after it was determined that Linda Pegues, a senior consultant from the Houston office working on the project had been instructed by Ann to work 12–14 hrs per day during the project but only to charge 8 hours per day. The entire incident left me questioning Ann's staff management methods and the honesty of her responses to my questions.[105]

Clear signs indicated, though, that some of the partners reacted negatively to Hopkins's personality because she was a woman. One partner described her as "macho," whereas another suggested that she "overcompensated for being a woman," a third advised her to take "a course at charm school."[106] One partner wrote that Hopkins was "universally disliked."[107] Several partners criticized her use of profanity. In response, one partner suggested that those partners objected to her swearing only "because it[']s a lady using foul language."[108] Another supporter explained that Hopkins "ha[d] matured from a tough-talking somewhat masculine hardnosed manager to an authoritative, formidable,

---

[101] *Id.*, p. 234.

[102] *Id.*

[103] *Id.*

[104] *Price Waterhouse v Hopkins*, 490 U.S. 228 (1989), at p. 235.

[105] Appellant's brief, *Price Waterhouse v Hopkins*, 490 U.S. 228 (1989).

[106] *Price Waterhouse v Hopkins*, 490 U.S. 228 (1989), p. 235.

[107] Hopkins, "Price Waterhouse v Hopkins."

[108] *Id.*

but much more appealing lady partner candidate."[109] In order for Hopkins to improve her chances for partnership, Thomas Beyer, a partner who supervised Hopkins at OGS, suggested that she "walk more femininely, talk more femininely, dress more femininely, wear make-up, have her hair styled, and wear jewelry."[110] Ms. Hopkins said she could not apply makeup because that would require removing her trifocals and she would not be able to see. Also, her allergy to cosmetics made it difficult for her to find appropriate makeup. Mr. Beyer also suggested that she should not carry a briefcase, should stop smoking, and should not drink beer at luncheon meetings. Dr. Susan Fiske, a social psychologist and associate professor of psychology at Carnegie-Mellon University who would testify for Hopkins in her suit against Price Waterhouse, reviewed the Price Waterhouse selection process and concluded that it was likely influenced by sex stereotyping. Dr. Fiske indicated that some of the partners' comments were gender-biased, and even those comments that were gender-neutral were intensely critical and made by partners who barely knew Hopkins. Dr. Fiske concluded that the subjectivity of the evaluations and their sharply critical nature were probably the result of sex stereotyping.[111]

However, there were numerous comments such as the following that voiced concerns about nongender issues:

In July/Aug 82 Ann assisted the St. Louis MAS practice in preparing an extensive proposal to the Farmers Home Admin (the proposal inc 2800 pgs for $3.1 mil in fees/expenses & 65,000 hrs of work). The proposal was completed over a 4 wk period with approx 2000 plus staff/ptr hrs required based on my participation in the proposal effort & sub discussions with St. L MAS staff involved. Ann's mgmt style of using "trial & error techniques" (ie, sending staff assigned off to prepare portions of the proposal with little or no guidance from her & then her subsequent rejection of the products developed) caused a complete alienation of the staff towards Ann & a fear that they would have to work with Ann if we won the project. In addition, Ann's manner of dealing with our staff & with the Houston sr consultant on the BIA project, raises questions in my mind about her ability to develop & motivate our staff as a ptr. (No) [indicates partner's vote][112]

I worked with Ann in the early stages of the 1st State Whelan Dept proposal. I found her to be a) singularly dedicated. b) rather unpleasant. I wonder whether her 4 yrs with us have really demonstrated ptr qualities or whether we have simply taken advantage of "workaholic" tendencies. Note that she has held 6 jobs in the last 15 yrs, all with outstanding companies. I'm also troubled about her being (having been) married to a ptr of a serious competitor.[113] (Insuff—but favor hold. at a minimum)

Ann's exposure to me was on the Farmers Home Admin Blythe proposal. Despite many negative comments from other people involved I think she did a great job and turned out a first class proposal. Great intellectual capacity but very abrasive in her dealings with staff. I suggest we hold, counsel her and if she makes progress with her interpersonal skills, then admit next year. (Hold)[114]

---

[109]*Id.*

[110]*Id.*

[111]Cynthia Cohen, "Perils of Partnership Reviews: Lessons from Price Waterhouse v Hopkins, "*Labor Law Journal* (October 1991): 677–82.

[112]*Price Waterhouse v Hopkins,* 490 U.S. 228 (1989).

[113]Ms. Hopkins left Deloitte Touche when her husband was made a partner there and firm policy prohibited partners' spouses from working for the company.

[114]*Price Waterhouse v Hopkins,* 490 U.S. 228 (1989).

Although Hopkins and nineteen others were put on hold for the following year, her future looked dim. Later, two partners withdrew their support for Hopkins, and she was informed that she would not be reconsidered the following year. Hopkins, who maintains that she was told after the second nomination cycle that she would never be a partner, then resigned and filed a discrimination complaint with the Equal Employment Opportunity Commission (EEOC).[115]

The EEOC did not find a violation of Title VII of the Civil Rights Act of 1964 (which prohibits discrimination in employment practices) because of the following: (1) Hopkins had resigned and not been terminated; and (2) at that time, the law was not clear and the assumption was that Title VII did not apply to partnership decisions in companies. With the EEOC refusing to take action, Hopkins filed suit against Price Waterhouse. She has stated she filed the suit to find out why Price Waterhouse made "such a bad business decision."[116] After a lengthy trial and numerous complex appeals through the federal system, the Supreme Court found that Ms. Hopkins did indeed have a cause of action for discrimination in the partnership decision.

Hopkins was an important employment discrimination case because the Supreme Court recognized stereotyping as a way of establishing discrimination. However, the case is also known for its clarification of the law on situations in which employers take action against employees for both lawful and unlawful reasons. Known as *mixed-motive cases,* these cases involved forms of discrimination that shift the burden of proof to the employer to establish that it would have made the same decision if using only the lawful considerations and in spite of unlawful considerations that entered into the process. The "same-decision" defense requires employers to establish sufficient grounds for termination or other actions taken against employees that are independent of the unlawful considerations.

In 1990, on remand, Ms. Hopkins was awarded her partnership[117] and damages. She was awarded back pay plus interest, and although the exact amount of the award is unclear, Hopkins later verified that she paid $300,000 in taxes on her award that year and also paid her attorneys the $500,000 due to them. Ms. Hopkins was also awarded her partnership and rejoined Price Waterhouse as a partner in 1991.

In accounting firms generally, the number of female principals has grown from 1 percent in 1983 to 18 percent today. Ms. Hopkins retired from PriceWaterhouseCoopers in 2002; she has written a book about her experience as a litigant, gardens, does carpentry work, and enjoys spending time with her grandchildren. She is still in litigation over the death of her youngest son, who was struck by a drunk driver.

Discussion Questions

1. What ethical problems do you see with the Price Waterhouse partnership evaluation system?

2. Suppose that you were a partner and a member of either the admissions committee or the policy board. What objections, if any, would you have made to any of the comments by the partners? What would have made it difficult for you to object? How might your being a female partner in that position have made objection more difficult?

3. In what ways, if any, do you find the subjectivity of the evaluation troublesome? What aspects of the evaluation would you change?

4. To what extent did the partners' comments reflect mixed motives (i.e., to what extent did their points express legal factors while at the same time expressing illegal ones)?

---

[115]*Id.,* p. 233.

[116]M. Jennings, Interview with Ann Hopkins, June 18, 1993.

[117]Technically, Ms. Hopkins was made a principal, a title reserved for those reaching partner status who do not hold CPA licenses. *Id.,* p. 366.

5. Ms. Hopkins listed three factors to help companies avoid what happened to her: clear direction from the top of the enterprise, (b) diversity in management, and specificity in evaluation criteria. Give examples of how a company could implement these factors.

Compare & Contrast

Ms. Hopkins described her interactions with and reactions to Kay Oberly, the lawyer who argued Price Waterhouse's case before the U.S. Supreme Court:

In the years since she argued the firm's case before the Supreme Court, I have had the pleasure of meeting Kay Oberly on several occasions.

"Nothing personal. Litigation polarizes," she said when we were first introduced. The warmth of her smile and the sincerity that radiated from troubled eyes banished any recollection I had of her at the arguments. I gave her a ride to the airport once. I was driving to work and noticed her unsuccessfully trying to hail a cab. We chatted about being single parents and the trauma of divorce proceedings, matters that we had in common. I like Kay. "Nothing personal. Litigation polarizes." I'm sure it wasn't personal to her, but it was to me. Discrimination cases tend to get very personal, very fast. My life became a matter of public record. Attorneys pored over my tax returns. People testified about expletives I used, people I chewed out, work I reviewed and criticized, and they did so with the most negative spin they could come up with. I'm no angel, but I'm not as totally lacking in interpersonal skills as the firm's attorneys made me out to be.[118]

Offer your thoughts on personal feelings, personal ethics, and litigation. Why did some partners evaluate Ms. Hopkins on the basis of work issues such as billing discrepancies and staff relationships whereas other partners focused on Ms. Hopkins' appearance? What role does fairness play in the differences in approaches by the partners?

---

[118]*Id.*, p. 366.

Workplace and the Environment

Case 6.24

Exxon and Alaska

On March 24, 1989, the Exxon *Valdez* ran aground on Bligh Reef, south of Valdez, Alaska, and spilled nearly 11 million gallons of oil into Prince William Sound. The captain of the tanker was Joseph Hazelwood.

The Spill

The Ninth Circuit Court of Appeals offered the following description of the accident in its review of the federal district court's award of damages against Exxon:

> *The vessel left the port of Valdez at night. In March, it is still dark at night in Valdez, the white nights of the summer solstice being three months away. There is an established sea lane that takes vessels well to the west of Bligh Reef, but Captain Hazelwood prudently took the vessel east of the shipping lanes to avoid a heavy concentration of ice in the shipping lane, which is a serious hazard. Plaintiffs have not claimed that Captain Hazelwood violated any law or regulation by traveling outside the sea lane. The problem with being outside the sea lane was that the ship's course was directly toward Bligh Reef.*
>
> *Bligh Reef was not hard to avoid. All that needed to be done was to bear west about the time the ship got abeam of the navigation light at Busby Island, which is visible even at night, some distance north of the reef. The real puzzle of this case was how the ship managed to run aground on this known and foreseen hazard.*
>
> *There was less than a mile between the ice in the water, visible at night only on radar, and the reef. Captain Michael Clark, an expert witness for the plaintiffs, testified that an oil tanker is hard to turn, more like a car on glare ice than a car on asphalt:*

Q: Let's talk a minute about how you turn one of these vessels. Now, this we're talking about a vessel here that's in excess of 900 feet long, all right? Over three football fields. What's it like to turn one of these?

A: Well, it's not like turning a car or a fishing boat or something. There is a—as you are traveling in one direction and you put the rudder over, even though the head of the vessel will turn, your actual direction of travel keeps going in the old direction. Sort of like you're steering a car on ice; you turn the wheel and you just keep going in the same direction. Eventually you'll start to turn and move in the direction you're headed for.

Q: Okay. Is it just as easy as turning a car?

A: No.

Q: And does it make any sense to try to compare changing course in one of these vessels fully laden to that of turning a corner with a car?

A: No.

Q: To make it turn on a vessel, there has to be a rudder command given?

A: Yes.

Q: And once you give that rudder command, is that the end of the turn?

A: No. No, you have to watch and make sure that the rudder command is made as you ordered it and to make sure that it's having the desired effect.

Q: Is there anything else that has to be done in order to put it on the course that you want it on?

A: Yes, you usually have to give counter rudder to slow the turn down.

Considering the ice in the water, the darkness, the importance of turning the vessel away from Bligh Reef before hitting it, and the tricky nature of turning this behemoth, one would expect an experienced captain of the ship to manage this critical turn.

But Captain Hazelwood left the bridge. He went downstairs to his cabin, he said, to do some paperwork. A special license is needed to navigate the oil tanker in this part of Prince William Sound, and Captain Hazelwood was the only person on board with the license. There was testimony that captains simply do not leave the bridge during maneuvers such as this one and that there is no good reason for the captain to go to his cabin to do paperwork at such a time. Captain Hazelwood left the bridge just two minutes before the turn needed to be commenced, which makes it all the more strange that he left at all.

Before leaving, Captain Hazelwood added to the complexity of the maneuver that needed to be made: he put the vessel on autopilot, which is not usually done when a vessel is out of the shipping lanes, and the autopilot program sped the vessel up, making it approach the reef faster and reducing the time during which error could be corrected. As Captain Hazelwood left, he told [Gregory] Cousins, the third mate, to turn back into the shipping lane once the ship was abeam of Busby Light. Though this sounds plain enough, expert witnesses testified that it was a great deal less clear and precise than it sounds.

There are supposed to be two officers on the bridge, but after Hazelwood left, there was only one. The bridge was left to the fatigued third mate, Gregory Cousins, a man in the habit of drinking sixteen cups of coffee per day to keep awake. Cousins was not supposed to be on watch—his watch was ending and he was supposed to be able to go to sleep—but his relief had not shown up, and Cousins felt that it was his responsibility not to abandon the bridge. He was assisted only by the helmsman, Robert Kagan. Kagan, meanwhile, had forgotten his jacket, ran back to his cabin for it, and returned to the bridge a couple of minutes before the time the turn had to be initiated. Cousins and Kagan thought they had conducted the maneuver, but evidently they had not. When Cousins realized that the vessel was not turning, he directed an emergency maneuver that did not work.[119]

Hazelwood had a history of drinking problems and had lost his New York driver's license after two drunken-driving convictions. The court described the problem as follows:

Captain Hazelwood's departure from the bridge, though unusual, was not inexplicable. The explanation put before the jury was that his judgment was impaired by alcohol. He was an alcoholic. He had been treated medically, in a 28 day residential program, but had dropped out of the rehabilitation program and fallen off the

---

[119]From *In re Exxon Valdez*, 270 F.3d 1215 (9th Cir. 2002).

wagon. He had joined Alcoholics Anonymous, but had quit going to meetings and resumed drinking. Testimony established that prior to boarding his ship, he drank at least five doubles (about fifteen ounces of 80 proof alcohol) in waterfront bars in Valdez. The jury could have concluded from the evidence before them that leaving the bridge was an extraordinary lapse of judgment caused by Captain Hazelwood's intoxication. There was also testimony that the highest executives in Exxon Shipping knew Hazelwood had an alcohol problem, knew he had been treated for it, and knew that he had fallen off the wagon and was drinking on board their ships and in waterfront bars.[120]

Hazelwood had joined a twenty-eight-day alcohol rehabilitation program mentioned in 1985. Almost a week after the Prince William Sound accident, Exxon revealed that Hazelwood's blood-alcohol reading was 0.061 in a test taken ten and one-half hours after the spill occurred—a level that would indicate intoxication. Exxon also announced it had fired Hazelwood.

Actions Taken . . . On All Sides

The magnitude of the spill seemed almost incomprehensible. Then-U.S. Interior Secretary Manual Lujan called the spill the oil industry's "Three Mile Island." After ten days, the spill covered 1,000 square miles and leaked out of Prince William Sound onto beaches along the Gulf of Alaska and Cook Inlet. A cleanup army of 12,000 was sent in with hot water and oil-eating microbes. The workers found more than 1,000 dead otters, 34,400 dead seabirds, and 151 bald eagles that had died from eating the oil-contaminated remains of seabirds.

By September 15, Exxon pulled out of the cleanup efforts after having spent $2 billion but recovering only 5 to 9 percent of the oil spilled. Alaskan officials said about 20 to 40 percent of the oil had evaporated. This meant that 50 to 75 percent of the oil was either on the ocean floor or on the beaches.

Hazelwood was indicted by the State of Alaska on several charges, including criminal mischief, operating a watercraft while intoxicated, reckless endangerment, and negligent discharge of oil. He was found innocent of all charges except the negligent discharge of oil, fined $50,000, and required to spend 1,000 hours helping with the cleanup of the beaches. Exxon paid Hazelwood's legal fees. Hazelwood now works as a maritime consultant for a New York City law firm and still holds a valid sea license.

When the *Valdez* was being repaired, ship workers observed that Hazelwood and his crew had kept the tanker from sinking by quickly sealing off the hatches to the ship's tank, thus making a bubble that helped stabilize the ship. Citing incredible seamanship, the workers noted that an 11-million-gallon spill was preferable to a 60-million one—the tanker's load.

Continuing Contention with Exxon

Following the spill, critics of Exxon maintained that the company's huge personnel cutbacks during the 1980s affected the safety and maintenance levels aboard its tankers. Later hearings revealed that the crew of the *Valdez* was overburdened with demands for speed and efficiency. The crew worked ten- to twelve-hour days and often had their sleep interrupted. Lookouts frequently were not properly posted, and junior officers were permitted to control the bridge without the required supervision. Robert LeResche, oil-spill coordinator for Alaska, said, "It wasn't Captain Ahab on the bridge. It was Larry and Curly in the Exxon boardroom."[121] In response to critics, Exxon's CEO Lawrence Rawl stated,

---

[120]270 F.3d 1222.

[121]*In re Exxon Valdez*, 296 F.Supp.2d 1071 (D. Alask. 2004).

And we say, "We're sorry, and we're doing all we can." There were 30 million birds that went through the sound last summer, and only 30,000 carcasses have been recovered. Just look at how many ducks were killed in the Mississippi Delta in one hunting day in December! People have come up to me and said, "This is worse than Bhopal." I say, "Hell, Bhopal killed more than 3,000 people and injured 200,000 others!" Then they say, "Well, if you leave the people out, it was worse than Bhopal."[122]

On January 1, 1990, a second Exxon oil spill occurred when a pipeline under the Arthur Kill waterway between Staten Island and New Jersey burst and spilled 567,000 gallons of heating oil. New York and New Jersey officials criticized Exxon, citing shoddy equipment and poor maintenance. It was six hours after an alarm from the pipeline safety system went off before Exxon workers shut down the pipeline. Albert Appleton, New York City commissioner on the environment, said, "Exxon has a corporate philosophy that the environment is some kind of nuisance problem and a distraction from the real business of moving oil around."[123]

Late in February 1990, Exxon was indicted on federal felony charges of violating maritime safety and antipollution laws in the *Valdez* spill. The charges were brought after Exxon and the Justice Department failed to reach a settlement. The oil company also faced state criminal charges. Alaska and the Justice Department also brought civil suits against Exxon for the costs of cleaning up the spill. Approximately 150 other civil suits were filed by fishing and tour boat operators whose incomes were eliminated by the spill. At the time of the federal indictment, Exxon had paid out $180 million to 13,000 fishermen and other claimants.

The Clean-Ups and the Pay-Outs

By May 1990, Exxon had renewed its cleanup efforts at targeted sites with 110 employees. Twice during 1991, Exxon reached a plea agreement with the federal government and the state on the criminal charges. After Alaska disagreed with the terms of the first, a second agreement was reached in which Exxon consented to plead guilty to three misdemeanors and pay a $1.15 billion fine. The civil litigation was settled when Exxon agreed to pay $900 million to both Alaska and the federal government over ten years.

The plea agreement with the governments did not address the civil suits pending against Exxon. At the end of 1991, an Alaska jury awarded sixteen fishers more than $2.5 million in damages and established a payout formula for similar plaintiffs in future litigation against Exxon. As of September 1994, Exxon had spent $2 billion to clean up shores in Alaska.

Exxon has had a stream of payouts since 1991—a total of $3.4 billion of its $5.7 billion in profits for that period. Payouts included the following:

- $20 million to 3,500 native Alaskans for damages to their villages
- $287 million to 10,000 fishers
- $1.5 billion for damages to wildlife
- $9.7 million for damages to Native American land

In September 1994, a federal jury awarded an additional $5 billion in punitive damages against Exxon for the suits filed since 1991. The original verdict of Exxon's recklessness and the resulting damage awards were made by a jury following a trial that ended in 1994. The damage award was the largest in history at that time. Exxon's stock fell two and five-eighths points following the verdict. Exxon appealed the verdict to the 9th Circuit.

---

[122]Jay Mathews, "Problems Preceded Oil Spill," *Washington Post*, May 18, 1989, pp. A1, A18.

[123]Chris Welles, "Exxon's Future: What Has Larry Rawl Wrought?" *Business Week*, April 2, 1990, 72–76.

In 1996, during a court review of the distribution of an award in an Alaskan case, a *Wall Street Journal* article revealed that Exxon had reached secret agreements with fish processors that would require them to refund the punitive damages awarded by juries. Apparently, some type of high-low settlement was reached with the plaintiffs prior to trial, but the jury trial proceeded without disclosure of the settlement and potential refund by the plaintiffs. Under a high–low settlement, the parties agree to a ceiling and a floor on the amount of damages that can be awarded. If the parties reach a $1 million–$5 million high-low agreement, they mean that $5 million will be the maximum damage award (including punitive damages and lawyers' fees) and $1 million will be the minimum award, regardless of the jury's actual verdict. The parties are guaranteed an outcome they can live with regardless of what the jury comes back with as a verdict. Often companies reach high–low verdicts because they need a court decision in order to take issues up on appeal, but they are concerned about their exposure in allowing a jury carte blanche on their liability. Further, even without an appeal, a verdict can bring a certain finality as well as precedent to what could be a number of cases or cases that will be brought in the future. Some believe that in the Exxon high–low agreement, there was a refund provision that required the plaintiffs to return or refund part of the settlement if the verdict came in at a lower range.

U.S. District Judge H. Russel Holland learned of the high–low agreements and called them an "astonishing ruse" to "mislead" the jury. Judge Holland set aside the agreements and allowed punitive damages to stand.

By November 1, 1996, Exxon had settled all of the *Valdez* cases and settled with its insurers for its claims. Exxon recovered $780 million of its $2.5 billion in costs, including attorney fees, from its insurers. Exxon had been in litigation with its insurers over coverage. Eugene Anderson, a lawyer who represents corporations in insurance actions, noted that insurance companies virtually always deny all large claims because "they pay lawyers much less each year in these cases than they earn in interest."[124]

In November 2001, the U.S. Court of Appeals for the 9th Circuit ruled that the $5 billion verdict in the Exxon *Valdez* case for punitive damages was excessive. The case was remanded to the federal district court for a redetermination of that damage figure.[125] On remand, the verdict was reduced to $4 billion and appealed again. It was remanded again for damage redetermination because of new U.S. Supreme case law on damages, and the last amount entered on record in 2004 was $4.5 billion.[126]

Exxon has since publicly admitted responsibility for the spill and has paid in excess of $3 billion to clean up the area along the Alaska coastline that has been a prime fishing area and an economic base for people of the area.[127]

The $287 million verdict for the fishermen, awarded as compensatory damages for the loss of their fishing rights during the cleanup, was upheld by the 9th Circuit.

The Impact of Exxon's Valdez

Congress passed the Oil Spill Act in response to the *Valdez* disaster as well as other provisions that effectively preclude the *Valdez* from ever entering Prince William Sound again.[128]

After the ten-year marking point of the spill, many scientists undertook studies of Prince William Sound and reached conclusions along the lines of the following, from a

[124]Barbara Rudolph, "Exxon's Attitude Problem," *Time*, January 22, 1990, 51.

[125]Joseph B. Treaster, "With Insurers' Payment, Exxon Says Valdez Case Is Ended," *New York Times*, November 1, 1996, p. C3.

[126]*In re Exxon*, 270 F.3d 1215 (9th Cir. 2001).

[127]"$5 B Exxon Verdict Is Tossed Out," *National Law Journal*, November 19, 2001–November 26, 2001, A6. See also http://www.exxon.com.

[128]33 U.S.C. §2732 (2001).

website that archives summaries of all the papers presented at the conference on the ten-year anniversary of the *Valdez* spill:

> *Natural interannual variability in the structure of the biological infaunal communities is the largest and most consistent signal observed in this study, not any residual effects of the oil spill. The results of statistical analyses of the data (ANCOVA) showed no indication of continuing oiling effects in 1998.*[129]

The scientists also noted a natural weathering process that appears to dissipate the oil and diminish its toxicity through the effects of weather and water, even before the oil disappears.

The 1991 settlement had a loophole that allowed the government (either federal or state) to claim up to $100 million in additional damages for a fifteen-year period. On Thursday, June 2, 2006, the State of Alaska and the Justice Department, relying on the loophole, demanded an additional $92 million in damages. The amount is needed, according to the exercise of the clause in the agreement, because of oil still present along the beaches.

Exxon argued that there is $145 million still left in the trust fund and that if there were any ongoing damage or concerns, the trustees had the responsibility to fix it with those funds. After three remands of the case, a federal district judge entered an award of $4.5 billion in punitive damages against Exxon. Exxon appealed the punitive damage awards as excessive and the U.S. Supreme Court agreed in *Exxon Shipping Co. v Baker*, 128 S.Ct. 2605 (2008), holding that maritime cases limited the amount of punitive damages. The court reduced the punitive damages to the amount of the compensatory damages, or $507.5 million.

Discussion Questions

1. Evaluate Exxon's "attitude" with regard to the spill. Following the explosion and resulting ninety-day oil spill at BP's Deepwater Horizon well in the Gulf, Exxon took on the mantle of a responsible corporate citizen (see Case 6.25). Why the change? Is the concept of a socially responsible company a fluid one?

2. Why did the company cut back on staff and maintenance expenditures?

3. What are the risks of a company becoming too cost-conscious? Complacent on safety? Complacent because of accolades for its actions? How do these types of budget deci-

sions differ from decisions by employees to supervisors to violate safety rules?

4. Would Exxon make the same decisions about Hazelwood and cost cutting given the costs of the spill?

5. Evaluate the ethics in Exxon's secret deal on punitive damages.

6. Evaluate the ethics of the insurers in denying large claims in order to earn the interest while litigation over the claim is pending.

7. Why do you think the court held that the punitive damage verdict was excessive? Is there another social issue regarding litigation here?

Compare & Contrast

What are the differences between environmental policy and approaches at Herman Miller (Case 3.17) versus Exxon vs. BP's handling of the Deepwater Horizon spill (Case 6.25)? Does the Exxon spill seem irrelevant now?

Sources

Barringer, Felicity, "$92 Million More Is Sought for Exxon Valdez Cleanup," *New York Times*, June 2, 2006, p. A13.

Dietrich, Bill, "Is Oil-Spill Skipper a Fall Guy?" *(Phoenix) Arizona Republic*, January 28, 1990, p. A2.

"Exxon Labeled No. 1 in Bungling a Crisis," *(Phoenix) Arizona Republic*, March 24, 1990, p. A8.

---

[129]http://www.valdezscience.com/page/index.html. (as accessed in original research).

"Exxon, Lloyd's Agree to Valdez Settlement," *Wall Street Journal,* November 1, 1996, p. B2.

"Exxon Stops the Flow," *Time,* March 25, 1992, p. 51.

"Exxon to Pay $1.1 Billion in Spill," *(Phoenix) Arizona Republic,* March 13, 1991, p. A3.

Foster, David, "Oily Legacy," Mesa *(Arizona) Tribune,* March 18, 1990, p. D1.

Galen, Michele, and Vicky Cahan, "Getting Ready for Exxon vs. Practically Everybody," *Business-Week,* September 25, 1989, pp. 190–192.

Galen, Michele, and Vicky Cahan, "The Legal Reef Ahead for Exxon," *BusinessWeek,* March 12, 1990, p. 39.

Hayes, Arthur S., and Milo Geyelin, "Oil Spill Trial Yields $2.5 Million," *Wall Street Journal,* September 11, 1991, p. B2.

Kangmine, Linda, and Carol Castaneda, "For Alaska, Tide Has Changed," *USA Today,* June 14, 1994, p. 3A.

"Like Punch in Gut: Exxon Skipper Talks," *(Phoenix) Arizona Republic,* March 25, 1990, pp. A1, A12.

Marshall, Steve, "Jury Rules Exxon Must Pay $287 Million to Alaska Fishermen," *USA Today,* August 12, 1994, p. 3A.

McCoy, Charles, "Exxon Reaches $1.15 Billion Spill Pact That Resembles Earlier Failed Accord," *Wall Street Journal,* October 1, 1991, p. A3.

McCoy, Charles, and Peter Fritsch, "Legal Experts Surprised by Exxon Deals with Fish Processors in Valdez Case," *Wall Street Journal,* June 14, 1996, p. B5.

"Native Americans Awarded $9.7 Million from Exxon," *National Law Journal,* October 10, 1994, A19.

"Nice Work, Joe," *Time,* December 4, 1989, 48.

"Paying up for the Exxon Valdez," *Time,* August 8, 1994, 18.

Rempel, William C., "Exxon Captain Acquitted," *(Phoenix) Arizona Republic,* March 23, 1990, p. A1.

Rubin, Julia, "Exxon Submits Final Oil-Spill Cleanup Plan," *Burlington Vermont Free Press,* April 28, 1990, p. 2A.

Satchell, Michael, and Betsy Carpenter, "A Disaster That Wasn't," *U.S. News & World Report,* September 18, 1989, pp. 60–69.

Schneider, Keith, "Jury Finds Exxon Acted Recklessly in Valdez Oil Spill," *New York Times,* June 14,1994, pp. A1, A8.

Schneider, Keith, "$20 Million Settlement in Exxon Case," *New York Times,* July 26, 1994, p. A8.

Solomon, Caleb, "Exxon Attacks Scientific Views of Valdez Spill," *Wall Street Journal,* April 15, 1993, pp. B1, B10.

Solomon, Caleb, "Exxon's Real Problem: Many of Its Oil Fields Are Old and Declining," *Wall Street Journal,* September 19, 1994, pp. A1, A6.

Solomon, Caleb, "Jury to Weigh Exxon's Actions in Spill," *Wall Street Journal,* June 7, 1994, p. B5.

Sullivan, Allanna, "Exxon Begins Final Defense in Valdez Spill," *Wall Street Journal,* May 2, 1994, pp. B1, B3.

Sullivan, Allanna, and Arthur S. Hayes, "Exxon's Plea Bargaining," *Wall Street Journal,* February 21, 1990, p. B8.

Tyson, Rae, "Valdez Cleanup Is Skin Deep," *USA Today,* March 22, 1994, p. 3A.

Case 6.25

BP: Pipeline, Refinery, and Offshore-Drilling Safety

Background and Nature of Market

BP PLC is a holding company with three operating segments: Exploration and Production; Refining and Marketing; and Gas, Power, and Renewables. Exploration and Production's activities include oil and natural gas exploration and field development and production, together with pipeline transportation and natural gas processing. Refining and Marketing includes oil supply and trading, as well as refining and petrochemicals manufacturing and marketing, including the marketing and trading of natural gas. BP is also involved in low-carbon power development, including solar and wholesale marketing and trading (BP Alternative Energy). BP has a presence in 100 countries and employs 96,000 people in these countries. It has nearly 24,000 retail service stations around the world, and its stations sell coffee made from fair-trade beans. It is the second largest oil company in the world and one of the world's ten largest corporations.

Until 2007, BP had been a perennial favorite of nongovernmental organizations (NGOs) and environmental groups. For example, *Business Ethics* named BP the world's most admired company and one of its top corporate citizens. Green Investors named BP its top company because of BP's continuing commitment to investment in alternative energy sources. BP lists its social and community policy as follows:

Objectives:

- To earn and build our reputation as a responsible corporate citizen
- To promote and help the company achieve its business objectives
- To encourage and promote employee involvement in community upliftment
- To contribute to social and economic development

BP has been recognized for its work in helping AIDS victims in Africa. BP Alternative Energy was launched in 2005 and anticipates investing some $8 billion in BP Alternative Energy over the next decade, reinforcing its determination to grow its businesses "beyond petroleum."

In July 2006 BP and GE announced their intention to jointly develop and deploy hydrogen power projects that dramatically reduce emissions of the greenhouse gas carbon dioxide from electricity generation. Vivienne Cox, BP's chief executive of Gas, Power, and Renewables, said, on announcing the joint venture, "The combination of our two companies' skills and resources in this area is formidable, and is the latest example of our intent to make a real difference in the face of the challenge of climate change."

In 2001, BP admitted that it had hired private investigators to collect information on Greenpeace and The Body Shop. Also in 2001, its annual meeting created a stir when a shareholder proposal to stop the erection of a pipeline in mainline China was defeated when the board of directors opposed the proposal.

BP's political donations were also a controversial and newsworthy subject until it abandoned the practice with the following statement:

> *In early 2002 the company Chairman, Lord Browne, announced that it will no longer make donations to political parties anywhere in the world. In a speech to the Royal Institute of International Affairs, Browne, said "we have to remember that however large our turnover might be, we still have no democratic legitimacy anywhere in the world. . . . We've decided, as a global policy, that from now on we will make no political contributions from corporate funds anywhere in the world." However, BP will continue to participate in industry lobbying campaigns and the funding of think-tanks. "We will engage in the policy debate, stating our views and encouraging the development of ideas—but we won't fund any political activity or any political party," he said. In response to a question, Browne said that over the long term donations to political parties were not effective.*[130]

The energy market was volatile during 2006. Crude oil futures slid below $60 in mid-September 2006 when the government report on winter heating fuel was released. The

---

[130]Adapted from BP political donation press release, original link http://www.bp.com/centres/press_detail.asp?id=147. (as accessed in original research).

El Niño weather patterns resulted in a warm winter and very little demand for home heating oil, and a resulting glut in supply with the accompanying dip in price.

Natural gas prices declined during the same period because of mild temperatures. With no hurricane activity and resulting disruption in production or damage to pipelines, the natural gas inventory remained high. Also, the warmer temperatures meant that the utilities' peaker plants, or plants used in periods of high demand, were not fired up, as it were. With peaker plants run by natural gas, the lower demand crossed into commercial contracts. Amaranth Advisors, the internationally known hedge fund that is based in Connecticut, lost $3 billion in September 2006 because of its position in natural gas.

An Unfortunate Series of Events

From January 2005 through May 2010, BP experienced some production, legal, and operations setbacks. These events have changed BP's public image even further.[64]

The Texas City Refinery Explosion

In 2005 BP had a deadly explosion at one of its refineries, located in Texas City, Texas. Fifteen employees were killed and 500 other employees were injured. OSHA levied the largest fine in its history against BP for its failure to correct safety violations at the refinery, a violation that resulted in a fine of $87 million—four times larger than any fine OSHA had ever before issued against a company.

BP had entered into a 2005 agreement with OSHA to fix the safety violations, but it had failed to do so. At that time, OSHA had found 271 violations at the refinery. After completing its investigation following the explosion, OSHA found 439 "willful and egregious" violations, a finding that resulted in the large fine.

OSHA attributed many of the violations at the plant to overzealous cost-cutting on maintenance and safety, undue production pressures, antiquated equipment, and fatigued employees. The OSHA report concluded, "BP often ignored or severely delayed fixing known hazards in its refineries."[131] Jordan Barab, a deputy assistant secretary of labor stated following the OSHA findings, "The only thing you can conclude is that BP has a serious, systemic safety problem in their company."[132] The Chemical Safety Board (CSB) Report concluded that cost-cutting played a role in BP's failure to address the ongoing OSHA violations,

> *Beginning in 2002, BP commissioned a series of audits and studies that revealed serious safety problems at the Texas City refinery, including a lack of necessary preventative maintenance and training. These audits and studies were shared with BP executives in London, and were provided to at least one member of the executive board. BP's response was too little and too late. Some additional investments were made, but they did not address the core problems in Texas City. Rather, BP executives in 2004 challenged their refineries to cut yet another 25 percent from their budgets for the following year.[133]*

Carolyn Merritt, the chair of the CSB, said, "As the investigation unfolded, we were absolutely terrified that such a culture could exist at BP."[134] CSB ordered that the company launch its own investigation by an independent panel. The panel, headed by former Secretary of State James A. Baker, found "instances of a lack of operating discipline,

---

[131]Guy Chazan, "BP Faces Fine Over Safety at Ohio Refinery," *Wall Street Journal*, March 9, 2010, p. A4.

[132]http://www.publicintegrity.org/articles/entry/2085. Accessed May 19, 2010.

[133]The report recommended that BP comply with 29 CFR 1910.119, Process Safety Management of Highly Hazardous Chemicals and implement an effective means of process safety management.

[134]Sheila McNulty, "BP Safety Culture under Attack," *Financial Times*, March 20, 2007, p. 15.

toleration of serious deviations from safe operating practices and apparent complacency toward serious process safety risks at each refinery."[135]

The CSB report noted that cost cutting at the refinery had "drastic effects," with "[m]aintenance and infrastructure deteriorating over time, setting the stage for the disaster."[136]

The following chart shows workplace deaths in the oil and gas industry.

Company	2003	2004	2005	2006
Exxon-Mobil	23	6	8	10
Royal Dutch Shell	45	37	36	37
BP	20	11	27	7
Total (oil co.)	23	16	22	NA
Chevron	12	17	6	NA[137]

The International Association of Oil and Gas Producers points to progress, with fatalities now at a rate of 3.5 per 100 man hours worked in 2005 versus 5.2 in 2004. The companies also note the extraordinary danger of the industry. For example, all thirty-seven of Royal Dutch's fatalities in 2006 were from kidnappings of workers.

BP had already entered into an agreement with the EPA for a guilty plea to Clean Air Act violations and paid a $50 million fine. BP has also settled civil suits (4,000 in total) and paid them from a fund of $2.1 billion that the company set aside for the litigation.

Prudhoe Bay

Prudhoe Bay is one of BP's refineries located on the 478,000 acres of land BP owns in Alaska.[138] In March 2006, a pipeline at BP's Prudhoe Bay, Alaska, facility burst and spilled 267,000 gallons of oil. The twenty-two-mile pipeline carries oil from BP's facility to the Trans-Alaska Pipeline. State and federal investigators on-site following the spill indicated that the pipeline was severely corroded. As a result of the spill, both internal and government investigations of Prudhoe Bay and BP began. Currently, the Justice Department is presenting evidence to a grand jury regarding the company's conduct. A grand jury has also been impaneled in Anchorage, Alaska. As of June 2010, there had been no indictment.

The Inspecting and Cleaning of Pipes

BP used a coupon method of pipe inspection, one that sends pieces of metal into the pipeline to run with the flow. The "coupons" are then inspected to detect for corrosion. Of the 1,495 locations that BP monitored using the coupon method, only five were located in the area of the spill. BP did not use "smart pig" technology, the industry standard, as other companies do. The *smart pig* is a detection device that runs along the inside of a pipeline to detect corrosion. Larry Tatum, an engineer with corrosion expertise and an officer of the National Association of Corrosion Engineers, said of smart pigging, "If you want to find this type of random, spotty corrosion, you've got to do 100 percent ultrasonic scanning, or the smart pig approach."[139] Industry standards

---

[135]*Id.*

[136]*Id.*

[137]Ed Crooks, "BP's Record on Safety Pinned Down," *Financial Times,* March 20, 2007, p. 17.

[138]For complete information about BP's presence in Alaska and its contribution to the economic base there, go to http://www.alaska.bp.com. (as used in original research).

[139]Matthew Dalton and John M. Biers, "Consultant Warned BP of Pipe-Network Corrosion," *Wall Street Journal,* August 24, 2006, p. A3.

require smart pigging every five years. BP had not done smart pigging on the Prudhoe Bay line since 1998. The pipes had not been cleaned since 1992. BP had increased its pipeline maintenance budget to $71 million for 2006, an increase of 80 percent since 2001. The speed of the oil through the pipes had declined over the years, and the flow in 2006 was at a speed one-fourth of the flow rate that existed when the pipes first opened. The BP field manager at Prudhoe Bay said, following the spill, "If we had it to do over again, we would have been pigging those lines."[140]

During the 1990s, when oil was at $20 per barrel, all companies cut down on pipeline maintenance. There were more pipeline accidents and spills during the 1990s, but they did not receive the attention that Prudhoe Bay did because gas prices were low. A family of twelve was killed in 2000 when a BP pipeline near its New Mexico campground exploded. The only coverage of the explosion was a small paragraph in the *New York Times*. BP's circa 2000 spill and pipeline issues occurred at a time when gasoline prices were at an all-time high and the talk of oil company profits was pervasive and across all forms of the media. The number of accidents in 1995 was 250; by 2005, that number had dropped to 50, after a steady decline. However, as the price of oil increased, the incentives for not shutting the pipes down increased. BP employees described Lord John Browne, the former head of BP (see earlier discussion on the company background), as the industry's best cost cutter, who created "a ruthless culture."[141]

The economic life of the pipes was estimated at twenty-five years when the pipes were first installed in 1977. At the time, no one believed that the oil production in the area would last longer than twenty-five years. One expert likened anticorrosion sensing and repairs to maintenance on a car: they have to be done regularly in order to keep the car running.

The External Pressure on the Pipes

In 2004, Walter Massey, the chair of BP's board's environmental committee, wrote a memo to fellow board members expressing concerns about the corrosion problems. Mr. Massey's memo described "[c]ost cutting, causing serious corrosion damage" to the pipes and creating the possibility of a catastrophic event that would put the Prudhoe Bay employees at risk. Internal documents uncovered in the government investigation show that a corrosion consultant who BP hired in 2004 issued a report that described the twenty-two-mile pipeline as experiencing "accelerated corrosion."

Environmental groups called for additional government investigations into BP's environmental record and oil pipeline, refinery, and drilling activities: "The North Slope corrosion problem is simply the latest example of a pattern of neglect and less-than-adequate maintenance over the years."[142] The groups released information about BP's environmental record. The groups' releases were printed in newspapers around the world, including lengthy stories in the newspapers of London, where BP headquarters are located. A 2003 leak from the BP pipeline had harmed caribou in the area. BP officials promised government officials that it would conduct inspections of the pipeline to determine whether corrosion was causing the leaks. In 1999, BP paid a $6.5 million penalty for dumping hazardous waste at the Prudhoe Bay site. BP did report the hazardous waste spill voluntarily.

BP had been operating on borrowed goodwill when it came to regulatory relations. In 1999, the State of Alaska agreed to approve the proposed Arco–BP merger provided BP would agree to semiannual meetings with state officials to discuss progress on the

[140]Chris Woodward, Paul Davidson, and Brad Heath, "BP Spill Highlights Aging Oil Field's Increasing Problems," *USA Today,* August 14, 2006, p. 1B, at 2B.

[141]Jon Birger, "What Pipeline Problem?" *Fortune,* September 4, 2006, pp. 23–24.

[142]Woodward, Davidson, and Heath, "BP Spill Highlights Aging Oil Field's Increasing Problems," p. 1B.

"serious" corrosion problems for the Prudhoe Bay pipelines. The meetings did not take place as promised.

In the same year as the merger and the promises to Alaska, Chuck Hamel, a union advocate, corporate gadfly, and close friend of actress Sissy Spacek, filed a report with BP management about worker safety concerns based on the corrosion problems with Prudhoe Bay pipes. The memo indicated that workers were asked to skimp on the use of anticorrosion chemicals in the pipe because of expense. Prudhoe Bay BP employees were paid very well and were loyal. They earned $100,000 to $150,000 per year. They worked for two weeks and then had two weeks off because of the remote location of the facility, and the near-total darkness twenty-four hours per day during the winter months.

Hamel took his complaints and information to the U.S. Environmental Protection Agency (EPA) that year based on the lack of response from BP management.[143] Mr. Hamel at one point owned an oil field in Prudhoe Bay, but subsequently sold it to Exxon. Exxon would later hit a gusher on the field, and Hamel sued for Exxon's failure to disclose to him the potential for oil discovery on his field. Ms. Spacek says Hamel is like an uncle to her: someone who is kind, generous, and trustworthy, and someone who speaks for those who cannot speak for themselves.

One executive at BP describes the Prudhoe Bay spill and pipeline problems as follows: "Sometimes bad things happen to good companies."[144] A Kinder Morgan (a pipeline company) executive said that Prudhoe Bay has been blown out of proportion: "That pipeline is still the safest part of the journey, including safer than when you put gas in your tank."[145]

One environmentalist wondered how BP can call itself a "green company" when its environmental record is so poor. The BP response was that "[w]e are investing in alternative energy sources. We are putting our money where our mouth is."[146] Environmental groups have taken the position that the conduct of BP should be the "nail in the coffin" for any plans to allow drilling in the north refuge area of Alaska (the Arctic National Wildlife Refuge, or ANWR, one of the world's greatest, yet untapped, sources of oil). "These companies simply cannot behave responsibly," stated one environmentalist leader in reaction to BP's conduct over the past four years at Prudhoe Bay.

In September 2006, the executives of BP were summoned to appear at congressional hearings on oil pipelines. The executives found few friends during their hearings. The chair of the House Energy and Commerce Committee told BP's CEO, "Years of neglecting to inspect the most vital oil-gathering pipeline in this country is not acceptable."[147]

The committee heard testimony from an employee who raised concerns about Prudhoe Bay corrosion in 2004 and was then transferred from the facility. Richard Woolham, BP's chief inspector for the Alaska pipelines, was subpoenaed to testify but took the Fifth Amendment.[148] Another BP executive testified that BP had fallen short of the high standards the public had come to expect of it.

The Trading Markets

In June 2006, the Commodities Futures Trading Commission filed a civil complaint against BP alleging that its brokers tried to manipulate the price of propane by

---

[143]Jim Carlton, "BP's Alaska Woes Are No Surprise for One Gadfly," *Wall Street Journal,* August 12–13, 2006, pp. B1, B5.

[144]*Id.*

[145]Birger, "What Pipeline Problem?" *pp.* 23–24.

[146]*Id.*

[147]Paul Davidson, "Congressmen Slam BP Executive at Oil Leak Hearings," *USA Today,* September 8, 2006, p. 2B.

[148]John J. Fialka, "BP's Top U.S. Pipeline Inspector Refuses to Testify," *Wall Street Journal,* September 8, 2006, p. A3.

manipulating the supply, or at least access to information about the real supply levels. One broker wrote in an e-mail that if they "squeezed" the pipeline, they could drive up the price of propane, "and then we could control the market at will," and ". . . we would own them."[149] The brokers commented to each other about how easily they could control the supply and, therefore, the market price for propane.

Following the Prudhoe Bay pipeline incident, government investigators also began looking into BP's trading practices. On August 29, 2006, the Justice Department announced investigations into BP's energy trading and stock sales by executives and others. BP officials said it gets such requests regularly.

One of the investigations focused on alleged insider trading by BP brokers. BP runs one of the world's largest energy-trading firms, dealing not only in the sale of oil and gas but also in energy futures. BP also provides risk-management services for other companies. One regulator has referred to the BP operation as one large commodities trading desk. Based on information about BP's storage, refinery, and pipeline facilities as well as a wide expanse of information about other companies and their risk and exposure, the brokers were indicted for trading in commodities prior to announcements about BP's production quantity and transport systems, information that affects market prices and hence stock prices of companies affected by energy prices.[150] BP had warned its brokers about the inability to use information gained from their positions to profit personally in the markets, commodities or stock, but there are no guarantees that such an artificial wall between information gained but not used in a personal context was effective. For example, when the Texas City refinery explosion occurred, BP traders were warned not to trade on that information prior to its dissemination to the public. The shutdown of a major refinery can impact market prices for oil.

Following the indictments, one BP trader entered a guilty plea. BP also entered into a deferred prosecution agreement and paid a $303-million fine, $53 million of which was used to repay investors for the losses they experienced as a result of BP's advance trading. However, in September 2009, a federal judge tossed the indictments of the BP traders because he concluded that the law used for the basis of the indictments was not violated.[151]

The series of events resulted in negative press coverage. One London newspaper has carried the headline "BP = Big Problems for Oil Giant."[152] From this headline, the public began developing its own translations for the BP acronym such as, "Beyond Pitiful" and "Big Putzes." The BP brand was damaged significantly by the unfortunate series of events.

BP Responses

In August 2006, when BP shut down the Prudhoe Bay pipeline for repair and replacement, it announced that it will replace sixteen of the twenty-two miles of pipe from Prudhoe Bay.

On Tuesday, September 19, 2006, BP was downgraded by several agencies when it announced further delay in bringing Project Thunder Horse up and on line. Thunder Horse is a subsea drill in the Gulf of Mexico that suffered a severe setback last year when Hurricane Dennis hit the area and caused substantial damage to the work to date on the project. BP had anticipated having the site on line by early 2007.

---

[149]Tom Fowler, "How the Case Against BP Traders Went Wrong," *Houston Chronicle,* September 18, 2009, http://www.chron.com/disp/story.mpl/business/energy/6626251.html.

[150]Ann Davis, "Probes of BP Point to Hurdles U.S. Case Faces," *Wall Street Journal,* August 30, 2006, p. C1.

[151]Fowler, "How the Case Against BP Traders Went Wrong," http://www.chron.com/disp/story.mpl/business/energy/6626251.html

[152]*Red Independent,* August 30, 2006, http://news.independent.co.uk/business/analysis_and_features/article1222607.ece. (as used in original research).

The following is an excerpt from a lengthy announcement that BP issued in August 2006:

BP today announced an acceleration of actions to improve the operational integrity and monitoring of its US businesses. BP announced the addition of smart-pigging technology to the monitoring of all of its pipelines, worldwide.

The company said it would add a further $1 billion to the $6 billion already earmarked over the next four years to upgrade all aspects of safety at its US refineries and to repair and replace infield pipelines in Alaska.

Speaking in London, BP chief executive Lord Browne said: "These events in our US businesses have all caused great shock within the BP Group. They have prompted us to look very critically at what we can learn from ourselves and others and at what more we can do in certain key areas to assure ourselves and the outside world that our US businesses are consistently operating safely, and with honesty and integrity.

"We are, of course, continuing to co-operate to the fullest possible extent with the US regulatory bodies investigating these events. But we do not believe we can simply await the outcome of those investigations. In addition to the significant steps we have already taken we have decided we must do more now." Browne said it is intended to appoint an advisory board to assist and advise the Group's wholly-owned US subsidiary, BP America Inc. and its newly-appointed chairman, Robert A. Malone, in monitoring the operations of BP's US businesses with particular focus on compliance, safety and regulatory affairs.

The measures Browne announced today include a step-up in the scale and pace of spending at BP's five US refineries on maintenance, turnarounds, inspections and staff training. Spending will now rise to $1.5 billion this year from $1.2 billion in 2005 and will jump further to an average [of] $1.7 billion each year from 2007 to 2010.

Systems to manage process safety at the refineries will undergo a major upgrade, with some $200 million earmarked to pay for 300 external experts who will conduct comprehensive audits, and re-designs where necessary, of all safety process systems. The new systems are targeted to be installed and working by the end of 2007, a year ahead of the original schedule.

BP today also pledged more rapid action to restore the integrity of its infield pipelines in Alaska. With corrosion monitoring already upgraded, it now plans to remove pipeline residues—through a process known as "pigging"—by November, six months ahead of the original schedule.

The pipeline which leaked in the recent oil spill has been taken out of service and will be replaced by a new line which has already been ordered. If other transit lines are found to be faulty, they will also be replaced.

Browne said a major review by independent external auditors had also been set in train of the BP's compliance systems in its US trading business. In the wake of allegations of market manipulation in US propane trading, the auditors will examine the design of the trading organisation, delegations of authority, standards and guidelines, resources and the effectiveness of control and compliance. The results of the review will be shared with relevant US regulatory authorities and the auditors' recommendations will be urgently acted upon by BP.[153]

---

[153]From Securities and Exchange Commission, BP 6-k, http://www.sec.gov, August 6, 2006.

BP also announced that it had hired former federal judge Stanley Sporkin to investigate what happened at Prudhoe Bay and why. Judge Sporkin was famous for one line in his work in handling the criminal and civil cases resulting from the savings and loans frauds of the 1990s: "Where were the lawyers? Where were the auditors and the other professionals when this fraud was occurring?" Upon his appointment to the BP position, Judge Sporkin said, "I'll call them as I see them."[154]

On September 20, 2006, BP announced that it would spend $3 billion to upgrade its oil refinery in northwest Indiana so it can process significantly more heavy crude from Canada while also boosting its production of motor fuels at the site by up to 15 percent. The heavy crude from Canada is taken from Canada's vast oil sands resources, a source that has been left untapped and is seen as an alternative to the switch to ethanol. BP PLC's U.S. division said the upgrade would create up to eighty new permanent full-time jobs and 2,500 jobs during the three-year construction phase. The Whiting refinery, about ten miles from Gary, Indiana, currently produces about 290,000 barrels a day of transportation fuels such as gasoline and diesel. Mike Hoffman, BP's group vice president for refining, said the project will modernize the equipment at the refinery, include environmental precautions beyond regulatory requirements, "and competitively reposition it as a top tier refinery well into the future." BP indicated that it would deliver the oil to the refinery by an existing pipeline but that the pipeline would be upgraded. The Indiana Economic Development Corporation provided $450,000 in training grants and $1.2 million in tax credits in order to attract the BP refinery.

Offshore Oil Rigs and Safety

As BP was working to recover from its unfortunate series of events, there was another evolving area it would need to address: its offshore oil production. Almost two years after Texas City and Prudhoe and nearly two years before the April 2010 Deepwater Horizon rig explosion and spill in the Gulf of Mexico, BP had a 193-barrel oil spill on June 5, 2008, at its Atlantis rig (also in the Gulf of Mexico). The internal report included the following information:

> "[Managers] put off repairing the pump in the context of a tight cost budget."

> "Leadership did not clearly question the safety impact of the delay in repair."

> A BP safety officer told company investigators, "You only ever got questioned on why you couldn't spend less."[155]

The same problems that dogged refinery and pipeline operations had carried over into offshore production. Nonetheless, during this period of ongoing safety lapses and resulting casualties, BP continued its stellar financial performance. In 2007, BP's shares were at $77. Its debt/equity ratio was .31, its dividend rate was 15%, and it had a 20% ROE, with gross margins of 27% and net margins of 7.47%. EPS growth in 2008 was at 64%. Managers were rewarded for their performance at the well for trimming 4 percent off costs.

However, that financial performance suffered a blow when one of BP's oil-drilling platforms, located about 50 miles off the coast of Louisiana in the Gulf of Mexico, experienced an explosion followed by an oil spill. The Deepwater Horizon rig, one that drilled at levels down to 18,000 feet, also experienced a fire on that fateful date of April 20, 2010. Eleven workers were killed. Oil began leaking from the rig in three places and had drifted

---

[154]Jim Carlton, "BP Hires Former Judge to Be U.S. Ombudsman," *Wall Street Journal*, September 5, 2006, p. A3.

[155]Guy Chazan, Benoit Faucon, and Ben Casselman, "Safety and Cost Drives Clashed as CEO Hayward Remade BP," *Wall Street Journal*, June 30, 2010, p. A1.

ashore in Alabama by May 14 and in Louisiana by May 19. By July 7, 2010, the oil had reached Houston and Lake Ponchartrain in New Orleans.

Following the spill, BP lost $30 billion, or 16 percent, of its market value.[156] Since the time of the explosion, BP has spent $7 million per day trying to contain the spill, not much of which has worked. Tony Hayward, then-CEO who took over following Browne's tenure, was on-site in Louisiana, overseeing the work to stop the leak, and pledged to pay for all damages and summarized his experience with the tragedy by quoting Winston Churchill, "When you are going through hell, keep going."[157] BP struggled, trying to contain the spill. Several engineering fixes did not work, and the relief wells took months to complete. As BP worked to stop the spill, oil drifted ashore. In total, there would be 200 million gallons of oil spilled. On August 2, 2010, engineers were able to contain the spill.

A whistle-blower allegation that had emerged early in 2010 resurfaced, as it were, following the explosion with the release of e-mails related to government investigations of BP, the rig, the well, the explosion, and the deaths and injuries. The e-mails express concern about whether other companies had completed crucial engineering drawings and paperwork necessary prior to operation of offshore rigs. There is other information that is emerging related to BP's focus on costs versus best practices. E-mails indicate that engineers who asked for an additional 10 hours in the critical path to address their concerns about the well by installing twenty-one centralizers instead of just six were dismissed by the lead engineer with a, "I do not like this."[158] At hearings before the House of Representatives, other oil company CEOs testified that BP did not follow appropriate design standards in drilling the well.[159] A *Wall Street Journal* study found that BP used a risky design for one out of three of its deep-water wells that was cheaper than the preferred type of design. The so-called long string design is one that uses a single pipe for bringing the oil to the surface. Experts indicate that the result of using one long pipe is that natural gas accumulates around the pipe and can rise unchecked. Most experts recommend its use only in low-pressure wells, not wells such as Deepwater Horizon. They also note that long-string drilling would not be appropriate when a company does not know the area, something that was true about this well for BP.

Deepwater Horizon is the largest oil spill in history and has been called the largest environmental disaster in history. BP agreed to a $20-billion fund that would be used to compensate businesses, workers, and others who have been damaged as a result of the spill. The costs, in terms of cash outlays, continue for BP. From April through July, BP spent $7 million per day trying to contain the spill. BP was given an ultimatum by the Obama administration and, shortly after a White House meeting, placed $20 billion in an escrow account for the U.S. government to distribute to those in the Gulf-area states who have been harmed by the spill. BP sold off $7 billion in assets to cover the expenses and the $20 billion. BP took a $32 billion charge in July 2010 for the Gulf Oil spill costs and added the following about it losses in its July 27, 2010, SEC filing:

> *The costs and charges involved in meeting our commitments in responding to the Gulf of Mexico oil spill are very significant and this $17 billion reported loss reflects that. However, outside the Gulf it is very encouraging that BP's global business has delivered another strong underlying performance, which means that the company*

[156]Peter Coy and Stanley Reed, "Lessons of the Spill," *Bloomberg BusinessWeek,* May 10–16, 2010, p. 48.

[157]*Id,* p. 61.

[158]Neil King Jr. and Russell Gold, "BP Crew Focused on Costs: Congress," *Wall Street Journal,* June 15, 2010, p. A1, A5.

[159]Julie Schmit, "Oil Execs: BP Didn't Meet Standards," *USA Today,* June 16, 2010, p. 1B.

is in robust shape to meet its responsibilities in dealing with the human tragedy and oil spill in the Gulf of Mexico.

The Oil Industry Post–Deepwater Horizon

The federal government placed a moratorium on all new offshore drilling following the Deepwater Horizon explosion and spill. However, a federal court issued an injunction against the moratorium taking effect on the grounds that the federal government had acted arbitrarily and capriciously.[160] The Secretary of the Interior redrafted the moratorium, which stayed in effect until the Obama administration lifted it in October 2010. In the initial decision, Federal District Judge Martin Feldman concluded that the failure of one well, even with safety issues, was not grounds for prohibiting all offshore drilling.

> *After reviewing the Secretary's Report, the Moratorium Memorandum, and the Notice to Lessees, the Court is unable to divine or fathom a relationship between the findings and the immense scope of the moratorium. The Report, invoked by the Secretary, describes the offshore oil industry in the Gulf and offers many compelling recommendations to improve safety. But it offers no time line for implementation, though many of the proposed changes are represented to be implemented immediately. The Report patently lacks any analysis of the asserted fear of threat of irreparable injury or safety hazards posed by the thirty-three permitted rigs also reached by the moratorium. It is incident-specific and driven: Deepwater Horizon and BP only. None others. While the Report notes the increase in deepwater drilling over the past ten years and the increased safety risk associated with deepwater drilling, the parameters of "deepwater" remain confused. And drilling elsewhere simply seems driven by political or social agendas on all sides. The Report seems to define "deepwater" as drilling beyond a depth of 1000 feet by referencing the increased difficulty of drilling beyond this depth; similarly, the shallowest depth referenced in the maps and facts included in the Report is "less than 1000 feet." But while there is no mention of the 500 feet depth anywhere in the Report itself, the Notice to Lessees suddenly defines "deepwater" as more than 500 feet.*

> *The Deepwater Horizon oil spill is an unprecedented, sad, ugly and inhuman disaster. What seems clear is that the federal government has been pressed by what happened on the Deepwater Horizon into an otherwise sweeping confirmation that all Gulf deepwater drilling activities put us all in a universal threat of irreparable harm. While the implementation of regulations and a new culture of safety are supportable by the Report and the documents presented, the blanket moratorium, with no parameters, seems to assume that because one rig failed and although no one yet fully knows why, all companies and rigs drilling new wells over 500 feet also universally present an imminent danger.[161]*

Tony Hayward was replaced as CEO of BP on July 27, 2010. Robert Dudley, a U.S. citizen and native of Mississippi, was chosen to replace Mr. Hayward. Mr. Hayward issued a statement upon his forced retirement, "The Gulf of Mexico explosion was a terrible tragedy for which—as the man in charge of BP when it happened—I will always feel a deep responsibility, regardless of where blame is ultimately found to lie."[162] The Deepwater Horizon well was plugged permanently in September 2010.

---

[160]*Hornbeck Offshore Services, LLC v Salazar,* 696 F.Supp.2d 627 (E.D. La. 2010).

[161]*Hornbeck Offshore Services, LLC v Salazar,* 696 F.Supp.2d 627 (E.D. La. 2010).

[162]www.bp.com. Click on Press Releases, July 27, 2010. Last visited August 6, 2010.

Discussion Questions

1. Discuss the ethical, negligence, and environmental issues you see in this case.

2. BP had rented the rig from Transocean for $500,000 per day. Transocean had been recognized by the U.S. government for its safety record.[163] Can companies distance themselves from liability and responsibility through the use of contractors? What are the risks of using third-party contractors?

3. Discuss how BP got into the position in which it found itself in late 2006 and what might have prevented the spill, the financial fallout, and the loss of reputation. Be sure to factor in the financial implications of any decision made during the period from 2001 to 2006.

4. What was the impact of the emphasis on cost cutting on BP's culture? What was the impact on the company's performance?

5. Evaluate the social responsibility positions of BP in light of the refinery explosion and the pipeline issue. What can companies learn from the BP experience?

6. Applying the regulatory cycle, what do you see happening with regulation in offshore drilling and the refinery and drilling portions of the oil and gas business?

7. When does OSHA assess criminal penalties? When does the Clean Air Act require criminal penalties? Wouldn't workers' comp cover the employees for the deaths and injuries? Why is there civil litigation?

8. The judge's opinion on the moratorium contained this discussion of the government's use of a report by experts on offshore drilling:

   Much to the government's discomfort and this Court's uneasiness, the Summary also states that "the recommendations contained in this report have been peer-reviewed by seven experts identified by the National Academy of Engineering." As the plaintiffs, and the experts themselves, pointedly observe, this statement was misleading. The experts charge it was a "misrepresentation." It was factually incorrect. Although the experts agreed with the safety recommendations contained in the body of the main Report, five of the National Academy experts and three of the other experts have publicly stated that they "do not agree with the six month blanket moratorium" on floating drilling. They envisioned a more limited kind of moratorium, but a blanket moratorium was added after their final review, they complain, and was never agreed to by them. A factor that might cause some apprehension about the probity of the process that led to the Report.

   The draft reviewed by the experts, for example, recommended a six-month moratorium on exploratory wells deeper than 1000 feet (not 500 feet) to allow for implementation of suggested safety measures.

   The Report makes no effort to explicitly justify the moratorium: it does not discuss any irreparable harm that would warrant a suspension of operations, it does not explain how long it would take to implement the recommended safety measures. The Report does generalize that "[w]hile technological progress has enabled the pursuit of deeper oil and gas deposits in deeper water, the risks associated with operating in water depths in excess of 1,000 feet are significantly more complex than in shallow water."[164]

   Evaluate the ethics of the Secretary of Interior regarding the representations of what the experts concluded.

9. Evaluate Mr. Hayward's parting statement and his views on accountability.

---

[163]Ben Casselman, Russell Gold, and Angel Gonzalez, "Workers Missing After Gulf Rig Explodes," *Wall Street Journal*, April 22, 2010, pp. A1, A4.

[164]*Id.*

Ethics and Products

Products are points of pressure. There is pressure to get those products out there on the market. There is the pressure to sell, sell, sell those products. Even buyers, on occasion, feel the pressure to buy, buy, buy. And there is even the pressure that comes when problems with a product arise—to recall or not to recall, that is the question, or is it?

Advertising Content

Ads sell products. But how much can the truth be stretched? Are ads ever irresponsible by encouraging harmful behavior?

Case 7.1

Joe Camel: The Cartoon Character Who Sold Cigarettes and Nearly Felled an Industry

Old Joe Camel, originally a member of a circus that passed through Winston-Salem, North Carolina, each year, was adopted by R.J. Reynolds (RJR) marketers in 1913 as the symbol for a brand being changed from "Red Kamel" to "Camel." In the late 1980s, RJR revived Old Joe with a new look in the form of a cartoon. He became the camel with a "Top Gun" flier jacket, sunglasses, a smirk, and a lot of appeal to young people.

In December 1991, the *Journal of the American Medical Association* (JAMA) published three surveys that found that the cartoon character Joe Camel reached children very effectively. Of children between the ages of three and six who were surveyed, 51.1 percent recognized Joe Camel as being associated with Camel cigarettes.[1] The six-year-olds were as familiar with Joe Camel as they were with the Mickey Mouse logo for the Disney Channel. The surveys also established that 97.7 percent of students between the ages of twelve and nineteen had seen Old Joe and 58 percent thought the ads he was used in were cool. Camel was identified by 33 percent of the students who smoke as their favorite brand.[2]

Before the survey results appeared in JAMA, the American Cancer Society, the American Heart Association, and the American Lung Association had petitioned the Federal Trade Commission (FTC) to ban the ads as "one of the most egregious examples in recent history of tobacco advertising that targets children."[3]

In 1990, Camel shipments rose 11.3 percent. Joe Camel helped RJR take its Camel cigarettes from 2.7 to 3.1 percent of the market.[4]

Michael Pertschuk, former FTC head and co-director of the Advocacy Institute, an antismoking group, said, "These are the first studies to give us hard evidence, proving what everybody already knows is true: These ads target kids. I think this will add impetus to the movement to further limit tobacco advertising.[5] Joe Tye, founder of Stop Teenage Addictions to Tobacco, stated, "There is a growing body of evidence that teen smoking is increasing. And it's 100 percent related to Camel."[6]

A researcher who worked on the December 1991 JAMA study, Dr. Joseph R. DiFranza, stated, "We're hoping this information leads to a complete ban of cigarette

---

[1]Kathleen Deveny, "Joe Camel Ads Reach Children, Research Finds," *Wall Street Journal,* December 11, 1991, p. B1.

[2]Walecia Konrad, "I'd Toddle a Mile for a Camel," *BusinessWeek,* December 23, 1991, 34. Although the studies and their methodology have been questioned, their impact was made before the challenges and questions were raised.

[3]Deveny, "Joe Camel Ads Reach Children," p. B1.

[4]Konrad, "I'd Toddle a Mile for a Camel," p. 34.I

[5]Deveny, "Joe Camel Ads Reach Children," p. B6.

[6]Laura Bird, "Joe Smooth for President," *Adweek's Marketing Week,* May 20, 1991, p. 21.

advertising."[7] Dr. John Richards summarized the study as follows: "The fact is that the ad is reaching kids, and it is changing their behavior."[8]

RJR spokesman David Fishel responded to the allegations with sales evidence: "We can track 98 percent of Camel sales; and they're not going to youngsters. It's simply not in our best interest for young people to smoke, because that opens the door for the government to interfere with our product."[9] At the time the survey results were published, RJR, along with other manufacturers and the Tobacco Institute, began a multimillion-dollar campaign with billboards and bumper stickers to discourage children from smoking but announced it had no intention of abandoning Joe Camel. The Tobacco Institute publishes a free popular pamphlet called "Tobacco: Helping Youth Say No."

Former U.S. Surgeon General Antonia Novello was very vocal in her desire to change alcohol and cigarette advertising. In March 1992, she called for the withdrawal of the Joe Camel ad campaign: "In years past, R.J. Reynolds would have us walk a mile for a Camel. Today it's time that we invite old Joe Camel himself to take a hike."[10] The AMA's executive vice president, Dr. James S. Todd, concurred:

This is an industry that kills 400,000 per year, and they have got to pick up new customers. We believe the company is directing its ads to the children who are 3, 6 and 9 years old.[11]

Cigarette sales are, in fact, declining 3 percent per year in the United States.

The average Camel smoker is thirty-five years old, responded an RJR spokeswoman: "Just because children can identify our logo doesn't mean they will use our product."[12] Since the introduction of Joe Camel, however, Camel's share of the under-eighteen market has climbed to 33 percent from 5 percent. Among eighteen- to twenty-five-year-olds, Camel's market share has climbed to 7.9 percent from 4.4 percent.

The Centers for Disease Control reported in March 1992 that smokers between the ages of twelve and eighteen prefer Marlboro, Newport, or Camel cigarettes, the three brands with the most extensive advertising.[13]

Teenagers throughout the country were wearing Joe Camel T-shirts. Brown & Williamson, the producer of Kool cigarettes, began testing a cartoon character for its ads, a penguin wearing sunglasses and Day-Glo sneakers. Company spokesman Joseph Helewicz stated that the ads are geared to smokers between twenty-one and thirty-five years old. Helewicz added that cartoon advertisements for adults are not new and cited the Pillsbury Doughboy and the Pink Panther as effective advertising images.

In mid-1992, then–Surgeon General Novello, along with the American Medical Association, began a campaign called "Dump the Hump" to pressure the tobacco industry to stop ad campaigns that teach kids to smoke. In 1993, the FTC staff recommended a ban on the Joe Camel ads. In 1994, then–Surgeon General Joycelyn Elders blamed the tobacco industry's $4 billion in ads for increased smoking rates among teens. RJR's tobacco division chief, James W. Johnston, responded, "I'll be damned if I'll pull the ads."[14] RJR put together a team of lawyers and others it referred to as in-house censors

[7]Konrad, "I'd Toddle a Mile for a Camel," p. 34.

[8]"Camels for Kids," *Time,* December 23, 1991, p. 52.

[9]*Id.*

[10]William Chesire, "Don't Shoot: It's Only Joe Camel," *(Phoenix) Arizona Republic,* March 15, 1992, p. C1.

[11]*Id.*

[12]Konrad, "I'd Toddle a Mile for a Camel," p. 34.

[13]"Selling Death," *Mesa (Arizona) Tribune,* March 16, 1992, p. A8.

[14]Anna White, "Joe Camel's World Tour," *New York Times,* April 23, 1997, p. A21.

to control Joe's influence. A campaign to have Joe wear a bandana was nixed, as was one for a punker Joe with pink hair.[15]

In 1994, RJR CEO James Johnston testified before a congressional panel on the Joe Camel controversy and stated, "We do not market to children and will not," and added, "We do not survey anyone under the age of 18."[16]

As health issues related to smokers continued to expand, along with product liability litigation and state attorneys general's pursuit of compensation for their states' health system costs of smokers, more information about the Joe Camel campaign was discovered. Lawyers in a California suit against RJR discovered charts from a presentation at a September 30, 1974, Hilton Head, South Carolina, retreat of RJR top executives and board.[17] The charts offered the following information:

Company	Brand	Share of 14- to 24-Year-Old Market (%)
Philip Morris	Marlboro	33
Brown & Williamson	Kool	17
Reynolds	Winston	14
Reynolds	Salem	9[18]

RJR's then–vice president of marketing, C.A. Tucker, said, "As this 14–24 age group matures, they will account for a key share of total cigarette volume for at least the next 25 years."[19] The meeting then produced a plan for increasing RJR's presence among the under-thirty-five age group, which included sponsoring NASCAR auto racing. Another memo described plans to study "the demographics and smoking behavior of 14- to 17-year-olds."[20]

Internal documents that discussed targeting young people were damaging. A 1981 RJR internal memo on marketing surveys cautioned research personnel to tally underage smokers as "age 18."[21] A 1981 Philip Morris internal document indicated information about smoking habits in children as young as fifteen was important because "today's teenager is tomorrow's potential regular customer."[22] Other Philip Morris documents from the 1980s expressed concerns that Marlboro sales would soon decline because teenage smoking rates were falling.[23]

A 1987 marketing survey in France and Canada by RJR before it launched the Joe Camel campaign showed that the cartoon image with its fun and humor attracted attention. One 1987 internal document uses the phrase "young adult smokers"[24] and notes a target campaign to the competition's "male Marlboro smokers ages 13–24."[25]

---

[15]Melanie Wells and Chris Woodyard, "FTC Says Joe Camel Tobacco Icon Targeted Young," *USA Today,* May 29, 1991, p. 1A.

[16]Milo Geyelin, "Reynolds Aimed Specially to Lure Young Smokers Years Ago Data Suggest," *Wall Street Journal,* January 15, 1998, p. A4.

[17]Doug Levy and Melanie Wells, "Papers: RJR Did Court Teens," *USA Today,* January 15, 1998, pp. 1A, 1B.

[18]Eben Shapiro, "FTC Staff Recommends Ban of Joe Camel Campaign," *Wall Street Journal,* August 11, 1994, pp. B1, B8.

[19]Bruce Horovitz and Doug Levy, "Tobacco Firms Try to Sow Seeds of Self-Regulation," *USA Today,* May 16, 1996, pp. 1B, 2B.

[20]Bruce Ingersoll, "Joe Camel Ads Illegally Target Kids, FTC Says," *Wall Street Journal,* May 29, 1997, pp. B1, B8.

[21]Geyelin, "Reynolds Aimed Specifically to Lure Young Smokers Years Ago," p. A4.

[22]Suein L. Hwang, Timothy Noah, and Laurie McGinley, "Philip Morris Has Its Own Youth-Smoking Plan," *Wall Street Journal,* May 16, 1996, pp. B1, B4.

[23]Barry Meier, "Tobacco Executives Wax Penitent before House Panel in Hopes of Preserving Accord," *New York Times,* January 30, 1998, p. A15.

[24]Wells and Woodyard, "FTC Says Joe Camel Tobacco Icon Targeted Young," p. 1A.

[25]*Id.*

A 1997 survey of 534 teens by *USA Today* revealed the following:

Ad	Have Seen Ad (%)	Liked Ad (%)
Joe Camel	95	65[26]
Marlboro Man	94	44[27]
Budweiser Frogs	99	92

In 1987, Camels were the cigarette of choice for 3 percent of teenagers when Joe Camel debuted. By 1993, the share had climbed to 16 percent.[28]

In early 1990, the FTC began an investigation of RJR and its Joe Camel ads to determine whether underage smokers were illegally targeted by the ten-year Joe Camel Campaign.[29] The FTC had dismissed a complaint in 1994, but did not have the benefits of the newly discovered internal memos.[30]

By late 1997, RJR began phasing out Joe Camel.[31] New Camel ads feature men and women in their twenties, with a healthy look, in clubs and swimming pools with just a dromedary logo somewhere in the ad. Joe continued as a youth icon. A "Save Joe Camel" website developed, and Joe Camel paraphernalia brought top dollar. A Joe Camel shower curtain sold for $200. RJR also vowed not to feature the Joe Camel character on nontobacco items such as T-shirts. The cost of the abandonment was estimated at $250 million.[32]

Philip Morris proposed its own plan to halt youth smoking in 1996, which includes no vending machine ads, no billboard ads, no tobacco ads in magazines with 15 percent or more of youth subscribers, and limits on sponsorships of events (rodeos, motor sports) to those in which at least 75 percent of attendees are adults.[33]

It was also in 1997 that the combined pressure from Congress, the state attorneys general, and ongoing class action suits produced what came to be known as "the tobacco settlement." The tobacco settlement in all of its various forms bars outdoor advertising, the use of human images (Marlboro man) and cartoon characters, and vending-machine sales. This portion of the settlement was advocated by those who were concerned that teenagers would be attracted to cigarette smoking via these ads and that cigarettes were readily available in machines.[34]

Although the governmental suits were settled, those suits focused simply on reimbursement for government program costs in treating smokers for their health issues related to smoking. The private litigation has not ended. The bulk of the awards consisted of punitive damages. The total losses to date are as follows:

$144 billion—verdict in Florida class action suit

$40 billion—settlement of Florida, Texas, and Minnesota suits

$206 billion—settlement of suits by forty-six states and five territories

$3.4 billion—settlement of Mississippi Medicaid suit

[26]"Joe Camel Shills to Kids," *USA Today,* June 2, 1997, p. 12A.
[27]*Id.*
[28]Alan Kline, "Joe Camel Is One Species the Government Wants Extinct," *Washington Times,* June 8, 1997, p. 10.
[29]Doug Levy, "Blowing Smoke?" *USA Today,* January 15, 1998, pp. 1B, 2B.
[30]Shapiro, "FTC Staff Recommends Ban of Joe Camel Campaign," pp. B1, B8.
[31]"Smokin' Joe Camel Near His Last Gasp," *Time,* June 9, 1997, p. 47.
[32]Maria Mallory, "That's One Angry Camel," *BusinessWeek,* March 7, 1994, pp. 94, 95.
[33]Horovitz and Levy, "Tobacco Firms Try to Sow Seeds of Self-Regulation," pp. 1B, 2B; and Gary Rausch, "Tobacco Firms Unite to Curb Teen Smoking," *Mesa Tribune,* June 24, 1991, pp. B1, B6.
[34]Meier, "Tobacco Executives Wax Penitent before House Panel," *New York Times,* January 30, 1998, p. A15.

A Florida jury verdict of $144 billion would be allocated among the tobacco companies as follows:

Phillip Morris—50 percent, or $73.96 billion

Lorillard—10 percent, or $16.25 billion

Brown & Williamson—13 percent, or $17.59 billion

R.J. Reynolds—24 percent, or $36.28 billion[35]

Since the time of the tobacco settlement and the Joe Camel ad campaign, the industry has changed in some ways, but in other ways remains unbowed by the events described here. For example, in 2002, Philip Morris was poised to introduce a new cigarette that was designed to save lives. If left unattended, the cigarette would extinguish itself, thus eliminating the tremendous fire risk that results from smokers falling asleep while their cigarettes are still burning. Nonextinguished cigarettes are the leading cause of fire fatalities in the United States. The cigarette was to be released under the company's Merit brand.

However, a company scientist, Michael Lee Watkins, told his superiors that the cigarettes were, in fact, a greater fire risk than conventional cigarettes because chunks of them fell off onto smokers and nearby objects. He was fired, and Philip Morris released the Merit cigarette with special advertising emphasizing its safety. The U.S. Justice Department got wind, as it were, of the problem from Dr. Watkins, and has led suit against Morris and other tobacco companies for deception as well as for the safety issues related to the cigarettes. Dr. Watkins has agreed to serve as a witness for the government.

Philip Morris indicates that Dr. Watkins was fired for failing to attend meetings, for speaking negatively of his colleagues, and for failing to document his research.

Philip Morris says that Dr. Watkins was correct in that chunks of the Merit safety cigarette did tend to fall off, thereby creating a different fire hazard, but the company fixed that problem by substituting a different paper before Merit was released to the market.

The suit is but one part of the legal and regulatory quagmire the tobacco companies face. New York passed a statute, which took effect in 2004 and which requires that cigarettes sold in the state be "self-extinguishing" according to rules and guidelines contained in the statute. Twenty-one other states, including California, Illinois, North Carolina, Massachusetts, and Vermont have similar legislation, with the issue reemerging when there are accidental deaths from fires caused by a smoker falling asleep with a lighted cigarette.[36] Canadian and EU health authorities are also working on fire-safe cigarette requirements.

Customers have complained about being burned when chunks of the new cigarettes fall off onto them and their clothing. The test cigarettes appeared in New York in June 2004, and the problems with them continue. The Justice Department litigation also continues, with depositions and document production.

However, there are positive signs from the industry. In the summer of 2004, Philip Morris launched a massive ad campaign directed at children and teens, warning them not to begin smoking. The company ran radio and television ads directing kids and parents to a website for help on peer pressure, smoking, and talking about the dangers of smoking. The company also inserted multipage glossy pamphlet inserts, titled "Raising Kids Who Don't Smoke: Peer Pressure & Smoking," in major magazines. The pamphlets tell parents, "Talk to your kids about not smoking. They'll listen."

---

[35]Rick Bragg and Sarah Kershaw, "Juror Says a 'Sense of Mission' Led to Huge Tobacco Damages," *New York Times*, July 16, 2000, pp. A1, A16.

[36]These states' self-extinguishing requirements were all in effect by the end of 2009.

Discussion Questions

1. Suppose you were the executive in charge of marketing for R.J. Reynolds. Would you have recommended an alternative to the Joe Camel character? What if RJR insisted on the Joe Camel ad despite your reservations?

2. Suppose you work with a pension fund that has a large investment in RJR. Would you consider selling your RJR holdings?

3. Do you agree with the statement that identification of the logo does not equate with smoking or with smoking Camels? Do regulators agree? Did the Joe Camel ads generate market growth?

4. Antitobacco activist Alan Blum said, "This business of saying 'Oh, my God, they went after kids' is ex post facto rationalization for not having done anything. It's not as if we on the do-good side didn't know that." Is he right?

5. What do you make of its new antismoking ad campaign targeted at children and teens? Is it significant that the company with the highest percentage of the youth market undertook the campaign to prevent kids from smoking?

6. Internationally, the tobacco companies are doing well in developing economies. What lessons learned here should be applied as the tobacco companies expand into other countries?

Compare & Contrast

Philip Morris is a company known for a phenomenal atmosphere of diversity. Government regulators in the EEOC often point to Philip Morris and its programs as an example of how companies should structure their diversity programs to make them effective. The company culture is known for being warm, accepting, and supportive. What can we learn from this aspect of the company versus it strategic policies on marketing?

Sources

Beatty, Sally Goll, "Marlboro's Billboard Man May Soon Ride into the Sunset," *Wall Street Journal*, July 1, 1997, pp. B1, B6.

Boot, Max, "Turning a Camel into a Scapegoat," *Wall Street Journal*, June 4, 1997, p. A19.

Burger, Katrina, "Joe Cashes In," *Forbes*, August 11, 1997, p. 39.

Dagnoli, Judann, "RJR Aims New Ads at Young Smokers," *Advertising Age*, July 11, 1988, pp. 2–3.

Horovitz, Bruce, and Melanie Wells, "How Ad Images Shape Habits," *USA Today*, January 31–February 2, 1997, pp. 1A, 2A.

Lippert, Barbara, "Camel's Old Joe Poses the Question: What Is Sexy?" *Adweek's Marketing Week*, October 3, 1988, p. 55.

"March against Smoking Joe," *Arizona Republic*, June 22, 1992, p. A3.

Martinez, Barbara, "Antismoking Ads Aim to Gross Out Teens," *Wall Street Journal*, March 31, 1997, pp. B1, B5.

O'Connell, Vanessa, "U.S. Suit Alleges Philip Morris Hid Cigarette-Fire Risk," *Wall Street Journal*, April 23, 2004, pp. A1, A8.

Case 7.2

Spring Break, Beer, and Alcohol on Campus

The mix is unquestionably there. Alcohol ads mix youth, fun, and enticing activities like scuba diving, beach parties, and skiing. As early as 1991, then–U.S. Surgeon General Antonia Novello asked the industry to voluntarily cut ads that attract minors. Novello stated, "I must call for industry's voluntary elimination of the types of alcohol advertising that appeal to youth on the bases of certain life-style appeals, sexual appeals, sports appeal, or risky activities, as well as advertising with the more blatant youth appeals of cartoon characters and youth slang."[37]

---

[37]Hilary Sout, "Surgeon General Wants to Age Alcohol Ads," *Wall Street Journal*, November 5, 1991, p. B1.

However, by 2003, Bud Light, Miller Lite, Coors Light, and Skyy Blue Malt Liquor were still heavy, as it were, advertisers on college sports broadcasts. All of the major companies, with the exception of Anheuser-Busch, advertise on MTV.[38] The issue of the ads targeted at college students has become an increasingly sensitive one because fatal injuries related to alcohol use climbed from about 1,500 in 1998 to 1,825 in 2009 among U.S. college students 18 to 24 years of age. There were 599,000 injuries, 696,000 assaults, and 150,000 health problems attributed to alcohol use on college campuses during 2009. There were 35 binge-drinking deaths (i.e., alcohol-poisoning deaths) on college campuses in 2008. The studies show that freshmen are at greatest risk for alcohol deaths, with 11 of the 18 binge deaths in 2002 being freshmen. Twenty-five percent of academic probations and disqualifications are attributed to alcohol use and abuse. The 21-shots-on-your-21st birthday drinking game resulted in 21 of the binge deaths in 2008. Over the same period, the number of college students who drove under the influence of alcohol increased by 500,000, from 2.3 million to 2.8 million.[39] Anheuser-Busch spends $20 million of its $260 million ad budget on a campaign that features the slogan "Know when to say when." Miller Brewing Company runs a thirty-second television ad with the slogan "Think when you drink" as part of the $8 million per year that it spends to promote responsible drinking.

Shortly after the Novello request, Miller and Anheuser-Busch stopped using their multistory inflatable beer cans on popular beaches in Florida, Texas, and Mexico. Several of the beer companies began ad campaigns related to alcohol use and abuse, especially at spring break locations. For example, in Daytona Beach, Florida, Miller put billboards along the highways with the slogan "Good beer is properly aged. You should be too." Miller's manager for alcohol and consumer issues, John Shafer, explained, "It's just good business sense to make sure we're on the right side of these issues."[40] By 2000, many of the inflatable bottles for the companies had returned to the beaches of spring break.

Patricia Taylor, a director at the Center for Science in the Public Interest, responded to the efforts by saying, "The beer companies are spending hundreds of millions every year to present a very positive image of drinking. That overwhelms all attempts to talk about the other side of the issue."[41]

Because of concerns about liability as well as concerns about image, the notion of college-student spring break marketing has been downplayed during the past few years by U.S. businesses. In 2010, one college student and a high school student who had just earned an athletic scholarship jumped to their deaths from hotel rooms in Florida after binge drinking. Many U.S. businesses, for reasons of costs springing from damages to property and others from liability for alcohol-induced accidents, have declined to market their products or facilities to the spring-break crowd.

San Diego passed a ban on drinking on its beaches in order to avoid the college spring-break problems. However, the students created a flotilla of rafts and conducted their drinking offshore, a problem the city council is grappling to address because the flotilla is not part of the city's beaches or under its jurisdiction.[42]

To fill the void, U.S. companies have begun to use Mexico, Amsterdam, and the Caribbean as liability-free spring-break areas and are intensely marketing these sites to

---

[38]Anheuser-Busch pulled its MTV ads in 1996.

[39]The National Institutes of Health keeps records of campus alcohol-related deaths. Data can be found at http://www.niaaa.nih.gov/NewsEvents/NewsReleases/College.htm.

[40]*Id.*

[41]*Id.*

[42]Connor Dougherty, "Boozy Flotilla About to Run Aground in San Diego," *wsj.com.*, July 24, 2010, http://online.wsj.com/article/SB10001424052748704895004575395491314812452.html?mod=WSJ_newsreel_us. (Last visited August 9, 2010).

college students. StudentSpringBreak.com encourages students to take a trip to Amsterdam, a "pot-smoker's paradise." It also notes, "Your yearly intake of alcohol could happen in one small week in Cancun, Mexico, on spring break." Hotels and travel agencies sell $179 passes for seven bars with one all-you-can-drink-night in each one.[43]

Cancun, Jamaica, Mazatlán, Acapulco, the Bahamas, Cabo San Lucas, and Amsterdam now top Miami, Fort Lauderdale, Daytona Beach, and South Padre Island for spring-break destinations. The drinking age in the U.S. locations is twenty-one, but it is only eighteen in the travel destinations abroad.

Because of the increasing numbers of college-age drinkers, accidents, and fatalities, colleges and universities have begun a number of programs to curb student drinking. Those programs include:

1. Greater enforcement of the drinking age through college and university disciplinary actions taken against students who engage in underage drinking, on or off campus.
2. Faculty mentor programs, in which faculty volunteer to counsel students and provide assistance if they find themselves in situations in which they cannot stop their friends from excessive drinking.
3. Prohibiting bars and hotels from providing shuttle buses from campus to and from their facilities to permit drinking without transportation and DUI worries.

Discussion Questions

1. Suppose you were an officer of a brewery whose advertising campaign targets young adults (18 to 21). Would you change the campaign?
2. Are campaigns on responsible drinking sufficient?
3. What do you see evolving in a regulatory cycle sense? Why should beer companies impose more self-restraint?
4. Is the shift to an international strategy a means of circumventing the law? Is it a means of avoiding social responsibility as well as liability?

Sources

Balu, Rekha, "Anheuser-Busch Amphibian Ads Called Cold-Blooded by Doctors," *Wall Street Journal*, April 10, 1998, p. B6.
Buck, Rinker, "Ode to Miller Beer," *Adweek's Marketing Week*, May 27, 1991, p. 16.
Colford, Steven W., "FTC May Crash Beer Promos' Campus Party," *Advertising Age*, March 25, 1991, pp. 3–4.
Horovitz, Bruce, "Brewer to Stop Ads on MTV," *USA Today*, December 23, 1996, p. 1A.
Wells, Melanie, "Budweiser Frogs Will Be Put Out to Pasture," *USA Today*, January 14, 1997, pp. 1B, 8B.
Yang, Catherine, and Stan Crock, "The Spirited Brawl Ahead Over Liquor Ads on TV," *BusinessWeek*, December 16, 1996, p. 47.

Case 7.3

Cheerios and Cholesterol and Rice Krispies and Immunity

The Food and Drug Administration (FDA) warned General Mills about the content of its ads for Cheerios. The warning letter that the agency sent to General Mills focused on the company's claims that its cereal, Cheerios, was "clinically proven to help lower cholesterol." The ads also claimed that the cereal could reduce bad cholesterol by 4 percent in six weeks. General Mills indicated that it has used the claim in its ads for more than two years and that the clinical study supporting the claim is very strong.

[43]Donna Leinwand, "Alcohol-Soaked Spring Break Lures Students Abroad," *USA Today*, January 6, 2003, pp. 1A, 2A.

However, the FDA says that government regulations prohibit such claims for anything other than drugs and that Cheerios would have to be approved as a drug in order to make the claims. The FDA indicated that it wants to keep a bright line between what companies can say about a product versus what it can say about a drug. The FDA and Federal Trade Commission (FTC) also pointed to the following analysis of the studies that were used as the basis for the General Mills claims:

But the average LDL ("bad") cholesterol of the Cheerios eaters fell by only 7 points (from 160 to 153). In fact, a 7-point fall would be a decent drop from just one food, but it was actually three servings of one food. On average, participants ate 450 calories' worth of cereal a day (3 cups of Cheerios plus 1½ cups of fat-free milk). That's a big chunk of the average American's 2,200-calorie diet, especially for such a modest payoff.

And it would take even more than 450 calories to get the same LDL drop from Honey Nut or Berry Burst Cheerios (both of which contain less soluble fiber and more sugar than regular Cheerios).[44]

The General Mills ads features Cheerios eaters who appear to be celebrating more than just a 7-point drop in cholesterol. One commentator commented wryly that those in the ads appear to have conquered heart disease.

Other companies have been facing the same increasing scrutiny on their health benefit ads claims. For example, the FTC reached one settlement with Kellogg's Cereals for its claim that Frosted Mini-Wheats improve children's attentiveness by 20 percent and another for claiming that Rice Krispies bolstered immunity. The Rice Krispies boxes claimed, "Now helps support your child's immunity with 25 percent daily value of antioxidants and nutrients—vitamins A, B, C, and E." Kellogg's said it stood behind its research but agreed to remove the claims related to health from its boxes.[45] Kellogg's also agreed to change its boxes for Frosted Mini-Wheats to remove the claim that this cereal would "increase your child's attentiveness by 20%."

Discussion Questions

1. Are the ads misleading?
2. What are the companies trying to accomplish with their health claims?
3. Perhaps the cereals could help consumers if the companies could get the word out about the benefits. The website for Cheerios still includes the following:

Good news for your heart!

As part of a heart healthy diet, the soluble fiber in Cheerios and Honey Nut Cheerios can help lower cholesterol and reduce the risk of heart disease.[46]

In addition, Cheerios has the seal of approval of the American Heart Association, and the following language appears on the Cheerios boxes, along with the seal of the AHA:

Products displaying the heart-check mark meet American Heart Association food criteria for saturated fat and cholesterol for healthy people over the age of 2.[47]

Are the actions of General Mills in using this language and displaying the seal acts of civil disobedience? Or is the company just not using the claim in its ads? Is a website an ad? Is this a gray area? Is this puffing or are the medical claims the ad content that move the claims from salesmanship to factual claims?

---

[44]David Schardt, "Hook, Line, and Cheerios," *Nutrition Action Newsletter*, October 5, 2005. http://findarticles.com/p/articles/mi_m0813/is_8_32/ai_n15691320. Accessed June 10, 2010.

[45]Susan Carey, "Snap, Crackle, Slap: FTC Forbids Rice Krispies' Claim," *Wall Street Journal*, June 4, 2010, p. B1.

[46]www.cheerios.com. Accessed June 10, 2010.

[47]www.heartcheckmark.org. Accessed June 10, 2010.

Compare & Contrast

The claims about cholesterol reduction and immunity bolstering appear to be at least marginally true but regulation prohibits the companies from using those claims in advertising. There are some actions that are *malum in se,* that is, they are ethically and morally wrong (murder). There are other actions that are *malum prohibitum,* or wrong because they have been prohibited. Which are the ad claims? Is this distinction important in ethical analysis?

Sources

Jennifer Corbett Dooren, "Health Claims For Cheerios Break Rules, FDA Warns," *Wall Street Journal*, May 13, 2009, p. B1.
www.ftc.gov
www.fda.gov

Case 7.4

Subprime Loans—The Under-the-Radar Loans That Felled a Market

What Is a Subprime Loan?

Troubled credit history is a problem for debtors when they want to buy a home. Nonetheless, there is bad credit repentance and lender-induced redemption, and the latter can be profitable. Between 2004 and 2008, there was significant growth in the subprime mortgage market. The *subprime mortgage market* is defined to include those borrowers with a FICO (Fair Isaac Co.) score below 570. The median FICO score is 720, with a perfect score being 850. The subprime home mortgage market, from 1994 to 2004, grew from $35 billion to $401 billion. The foreclosure rates range from 20 to 50 percent on subprime loans, with the likelihood of default higher on many of the loans because of loan structures that include high interest rates as well as balloon payments.

The Subprime Lending Market and Risk

During its period of expansion, the subprime market was a source of great wealth for many lenders. "We made so much money, you couldn't believe it. And you didn't have to do anything. You just had to show up,"[48] commented Kal Elsayed, a former executive at New Century Financial, a mortgage brokerage firm based in Irvine, California. With his red Ferrari, Mr. Elsayed enjoyed the benefits of the growth in the subprime mortgage market, which grew from $100 billion in 2000 to over $600 billion in 2007. It was during 2007 that the defaults began to surface and the rate of subprime lending declined.

Despite its success, the subprime market is risky for both borrowers and lenders. These types of loans are risky for lenders because they are given to those who do not qualify under traditional lending standards that require larger down payments and higher income levels. For example, Countrywide Mortgages had a "Fast and Easy" loan program, which lowered the required debtor credit score from 700 to 650. There was little verification of income or other information that was often provided via online applications.

The relaxed standards attracted mortgage brokers who worked to process as many loans as possible, sometimes using the same applicant. In 2004, Countrywide hired mortgage broker Kourosh Partow at its Anchorage, Alaska, office. Countrywide made the

---

[48]Julie Creswell and Vikas Bajas, "A Mortgage Crisis Begins to Spiral, and the Casualties Mount," *New York Times*, March 5, 2007, pp. C1, C4.

offer to Mr. Partow despite the fact that Partow was under investigation in Wisconsin for lending abuses. Several months later, the state of Wisconsin revoked his broker's license. Countrywide, however, continued him in their employ. Partow submitted an application for a $295,000 loan for Agim Delolli that listed Mr. Delolli as being in the construction business with $24,000 per month in income. Ten months later, in 2005, Partow submitted another Fast-and-Easy application for Mr. Delolli for a $202,500 loan. This application stated that Mr. Delolli was in car sales and that his income was $15,000 per month. However, both applications had the same phone number for Mr. Delolli.[49]

When both men were indicted for their roles in a mortgage fraud ring, Mr. Delolli agreed to testify against Mr. Partow and others involved in the fraud in exchange for immunity. Mr. Partow and others were convicted of mortgage fraud.

The Partow loans were sold to Fannie Mae, and the FBI opened an investigation as the conflicting Partow loans came through. By the time the federal investigation began in 2006, the "Fast and Easy" program had taken hold and Countrywide had a full portfolio of loans with buyers who were either not qualified or who had not actually made the 10 percent down payment required.

For borrowers, the subprime loans are fraught with complexities that the average consumer may not fully understand as he or she realizes the dream of home ownership or a means for paying off credit card debt through a home equity loan. Some subprime borrowers are able to make payments initially because they have interest-only loans for a three- to five-year period, such as with pick-a-pay loans where borrowers chose their initial monthly payments, not realizing how much their payments would increase because they were not paying interest during this time. The result was a payment that was beyond their means. In many subprime loans, the lender builds in very high costs for closing, appraisal, and other fees, with a result known as *equity stripping*. The loan amount is so high that the borrower owes more than 100 percent of the value of the home. The lenders often return to customers and use a practice known as *flipping*. The borrowers refinance their homes on the promise of lower payments, a lower rate, or some benefit that may actually be real. However, the costs of refinancing, known as *packing* the loan increases the lender's interest in the home as well as the interest rate. The end result was a higher loan amount with a longer payment period and greater likelihood of default and foreclosure.

These risky debtors, whose credit histories spelled trouble even without the terms of subprime loans, defaulted. Their defaults meant that the loan portfolios of subprime lenders had to be written down, write-downs that were so significant that lenders collapsed. New Century Financial was among the first of the subprime lenders to declare bankruptcy, and a federal investigation found accounting irregularities as well as a portfolio of $39.4 billion in subprime loans. Following New Century into collapse was Countrywide, a firm that was acquired by Bank of America. This acquisition resulted in significant litigation for Bank of America for its failure to disclose the full scope of lending losses at Countrywide.

Regulating the Subprime Market

These defaults and institutional failures, coupled with marketing techniques for subprime lenders that often targeted the poor and elderly, have resulted in significant state and local legislation designed to curb subprime lender activities. Known as "Homeowner Security Protection Acts" or "High Cost Home Loan Acts" or "Home Loan Protection Acts," these state laws take various approaches to protecting consumers from predatory

---

[49]Glenn R. Simpson and James R. Hagerty, "Countrywide Loss Focuses Attention on Underwriting," *Wall Street Journal*, April 30, 2008, pp. B1, B4.

lending practices.[50] Some states limit charges or interest rates. Other states limit foreclosures or refinancings within certain time frames. Some, such as Cleveland's ordinance, simply prohibit predatory practices, making such activity a criminal misdemeanor. Cleveland's ordinance was described by a court in a successful challenge by a lender as follows:

> *"Predatory loan" in Cleveland is defined as any residential loan bearing interest at an annual rate that exceeds the yield on comparable Treasury securities by either four and one-half to eight percentage points for first mortgage loans or six and one-half to ten percentage points for junior mortgages. In addition, loans are considered predatory if they were made under circumstances involving the following practices or include the following terms: loan flipping, balloon payments, negative amortization, points and fees in excess of four percent of the loan amount or in excess of $800 on loans below $16,000, an increased interest rate on default, advance payments, mandatory arbitration, prepayment penalties, financing of credit insurance, lending without home counseling, lending without due regard to repayment, or certain payments to home-improvement contractors under certain circumstances.[51]*

Cleveland's ordinance, like so many of the antipredatory statutes, was declared unconstitutional by a federal court because the court ruled that the regulation of home loans is preempted by the extensive federal regulation of both home mortgages and consumer credit.[52] Other challenges are pending.

The Secondary Impact of Subprime Loans

The high default and foreclosure rates of subprime loans carried a secondary market impact at the beginning of 2007 as subprime lenders collapsed under the weight of their foreclosure portfolios in a soft real estate market. The financial instruments based on these mortgage portfolios dropped in value, something that not only resulted in investor losses but also in the collapse of firms such as Bear Stearns and Lehman Brothers as well as the need for government support for AIG, Fannie Mae, and others. The stock market declined 18 percent in one week as these institutions teetered.

There was a failure or unwillingness on the part of investment banks and analysts to process accurately the risk and exposure their companies had in their ties to subprime lending. A *Fortune* cover story featured the words, "What were they smoking?" in a 3.5-inch headline as well as photos of Chuck Prince, Citigroup ($9.8 billion loss), Jimmy Cayne, Bear Stearns ($450 million loss), John Mack, Morgan Stanley ($3.7 billion loss), and Stan O'Neal, Merrill Lynch ($7.9 billion), with their firms' losses as of November 2007 appearing in parentheses following their names.[53] As a result of these firms' losses, and the eventual bankruptcies of Bear Stearns and Lehman Brothers, the stock market lost one-third of its value and the U.S. government had to shore up the remaining firms as well as AIG, the company that had provided insurance for the subprime investments.

[50]For a summary of the state legislation on predatory lending practices, see Therese G. Fanzén and Leslie M. Howell, "Predatory Lending Legislation in 2004," 60 *Business Lawyer* 677 (2005).

[51]*Am. Financial Serv. Assn. v Cleveland*, 824 N.E.2d 553 at 557 (Oh. App. 2004).

[52]*Am. Fin. Servs. Ass'n v City of Cleveland*, No. 83676, 2004 WL 2755808, (Ohio Ct. App. 2004); *City of Dayton v State*, No.02-CV-3441 (Ohio Ct. Common Pleas Aug. 26, 2003); 813 N.E.2d 707 (Ohio Ct. App. 2004); *Am. Fin. Servs. Ass'n v City of Oakland*, 23 Cal. Rptr. 3d 453, 461–62 (Cal. 2005); and *Mayor of New York v Council of New York*, 780 N.Y.S.2d 266 (N.Y. Sup. Ct. 2004). Cleveland's ordinance was held to be preempted by Ohio's laws on predatory lending.

[53]*Fortune*, November 26, 2007, cover story.

Discussion Questions

1. Evaluate the ethics of the subprime mortgage brokers. Subprime default rates caused ripple effects in the stock market. What can we learn about the isolation of individual ethical choices?

2. A study by Freddie Mac shows that 38 percent of those who borrowed in the subprime market (a lending market for those who are high credit risks that carries higher interest rates) were actually qualified to obtain loans in the prime rate market. How do incentives affect lenders in terms of the types of loan products offered to potential borrowers?

3. Martin Eakes, one of the businesspeople (and a trained lawyer), who worked to get North Carolina's antipredatory lending law in place said, "Subprime mortgages can be productive and fruitful. We just have to put boundaries in place."[54] What is the place and role of subprime mortgages?

4. Give an analysis of the systemic effects of the subprime market. How many stakeholders were there in the relationship between subprime lender and borrower?

Compare & Contrast

Reverse mortgages are often lumped in with subprime mortgages, but there are some difference. Reverse mortgages are a tool generally used by retirees to tap into the equity in their homes for purposes of obtaining additional cash flow on which to live during their retirement years. For example, a seventy-eight–year-old retiree may be living in a home that he owns free and clear of any mortgage and that is worth $270,000. His retirement income may be limited to his pension and Social Security payments, two sources that may give him $2,000 per month. However, he would like to travel and have a little extra discretionary spending money. Under a reverse mortgage, the retiree can turn over a portion of the equity in his home to a lender. That lender, relying on recoupment from the eventual sale of the property, then provides the desired cash through the payments for the equity. The lender is, in effect, paying the retiree mortgage payments for the equity rights.

However, if the retiree no longer uses the home as his chief residence or moves, the lender has the right to demand the sale of the home. That sale option has not been readily available over the past few years and the result is that the retiree turns the home back over to the lender, with the resulting loss of any equity not used for the reverse mortgage. Also, a substantial portion of the value of the retiree's estate is tied up in the home. Upon the retiree's death, the home is also sold with the lender recouping its investment first and the remainder, if any, turned over to the retiree's heirs. Again, when a sale is not possible in the time limits provided for in the reverse mortgage, the heirs lose most of the value of the estate.

What are the ethical issues for lenders who make reverse mortgages? Isn't this a way for retirees to improve their standard of living? Would it be easy to take advantage of retirees if you were a loan representative for a lender who offers reverse mortgages? If you were an employee with such a lender, what policies would you put in place to be sure that loan representatives do not take advantage of retirees? Would a profile of who reverse mortgages can help provide some standards for your representatives and their representations to potential customers for reverse mortgages?[55]

Source

White, Ben, Saski Scholtes, and Peter Thai Larsen, "Subprime Mortgage Meltdown Intensifies," *Financial Times,* March 6, 2007, p. 10.

---

[54]Nanette Byrnes, "These Tough Lending Laws Could Travel," *BusinessWeek,* November 5, 2007, pp. 70–71.

[55]Professor Eric Yordy of Northern Arizona University has done significant and important work on the ethical issues in reverse mortgages. Eric D. Yordy, "Grandma's Living Large: Her Reverse Mortgage: Saving Grace or Terrific Waste?" *Proceedings of the Academy of Legal Studies in Business,* August 2010.

Case 7.5

Hollywood Ads

Actress Demi Moore starred in the 1995 movie entitled *The Scarlet Letter,* which was based on Nathaniel Hawthorne's book of the same name. Hollywood Pictures ran the following quote from a *Time* magazine review: "'Scarlet Letter' Gets What It Always Needed: Demi Moore." The actual review by *Time* magazine read, "Stuffy old Scarlet Letter gets what it always needed: Demi Moore and a happier ending." A *Time* spokesman noted that the statement was clearly ironic. In the same review, the *Time* critic, Richard Corliss, referred to the movie as "revisionist slog" and gave it an "F."

An ad for the 1995 movie *Seven* quoted *Entertainment Weekly* as calling it a "masterpiece." The actual review read, "The credits sequence... is a small masterpiece of dementia."

A movie industry observer stated in response to these examples, "The practice of fudging critics' quotes [in ads] is common." However, there are other types of nuances in the movie ads. For example, ads for the movie *Thirteen Days* included the descriptive phrases "by-the-numbers recreation" and "close to perfect" in order to reflect what producers touted as the strength of the film—its historical accuracy. But the ads also included pictures of the Spruance-class destroyer and F-15 jet fighters. Neither of these defense systems was available in 1962, the time of the movie, which is a depiction of the thirteen-day Cuban missile crisis during the Kennedy administration. These systems were not developed until the 1970s.

The movie studios pulled the ads after they had run for one weekend. They also pulled those ads that showed the movie's star, Kevin Costner, walking with the actors who played John and Robert Kennedy because that scene was not part of the movie.

In 2001, ads by Sony Studios had theater critic David Manning proclaiming that *The Animal,* starring Rob Schneider and ex-"Survivor" Colleen Haskell, was "another winner." Mr. Manning also gave a favorable review of Sony's *A Knight's Tale.* However, David Manning is fictitious. He is a critic created out of whole cloth by young marketing staff members at Sony.[56]

Discussion Questions

1. Is the practice of fudging quotes ethical? Should Hollywood Pictures have pulled the *Scarlet Letter* ads?
2. How do you respond to the statement that these types of issues in movie ads are "common"?
3. Some companies hire individuals to write reviews of apps, products, and services, and post them online. The individuals have often not used the app, product, or service. Is this similar to the fake movie reviews? Any ethical issues?

Case 7.6

Kraft, Barney Rubble, and Shrek

Kraft Foods has decided to ban certain food ads from children's websites for Kraft Foods. Kraft has created a group of outside independent advisers who analyzed the company websites and were disturbed by the sites' games for children involving Barney Rubble and Shrek that led the kids to chases for Kraft products such as ChipsAhoy, Lunchables, and Kool-Aid. Professor Ellen Wartella, dean of the College of Communications at University of Texas at Austin, called the web ads "indefensible." Kraft agreed to pull the ads from the web. The ads were placed there as a sort of loophole to its long-standing policy (since the 1980s) of not advertising its products in children's TV and

[56]"Ads for Missile Crisis Movie Are Pulled Because of Errors," *New York Times,* January 13, 2001, p. A8.

radio programs. Kraft does market "healthier" products to children between the ages of six and twelve. Kraft also uses cartoon characters on its products such as Sponge Bob on its crackers and Dora the Explorer on Teddy Grahams cookies.

About eighteen months after Kraft heeded the advice of this advisory board and made changes, eleven U.S. companies, including Kraft, announced that they would put stricter controls on their advertisements for products for children. The companies that participated in the voluntary initiative are as follows:

- Kraft
- McDonald's
- Pepsico
- Coca-Cola
- General Mills
- Campbell's
- Cadbury Adam's
- Kellogg's
- Hershey's
- Mars, Inc.
- Unilever

The companies all took a pledge to impose stricter controls on their ads directed at children. The controls take different forms. For example, Pepsico and Coke will eliminate ads at elementary schools. Pepsico is also eliminating ads at middle schools. Cadbury Adam's will stop advertising its Bubblicious to children under twelve.

Margo Wootan, the head of the Center for Science in the Public Interest, praised the group. However, members of Congress indicated that the media outlets, including the Cartoon Network and Nickelodeon, also needed to step forward with voluntary steps on running ads from companies that were not part of the group.[57]

Discussion Questions

1. Is it possible to have a nondeceptive ad for children?

2. What relationship does the regulatory cycle have with the Kraft decision and the follow-up actions by the other ten companies?

Compare & Contrast

Refer back to the Joe Camel case (Case 7.1), and consider why Kraft and the other ten companies made their decisions on self-regulation when they did versus the actions of RJR and the timing.

Source

Sarah Ellison, "Kraft Is Banning Some Food Ads to Kids," *Wall Street Journal*, October 30, 2005, pp. A1, A13.

Case 7.7

Craigslist and Ad Screening

Garage sale listings on Craigslist increased 60 percent from 2008 to 2009.[58] Craigslist has been called the world's largest classified advertising listing. However, the expansion has brought with it some attention for the company as well as some questions. The

---

[57]"McDonald's, Kraft Tighten Advertising Policies," ChicagoBusiness.com, July 19, 2007, http://www.chicagobusiness.com. Accessed June 10, 2010.

[58]Anjali Athavaley, "Seller, Beware: the New Yard-Sale Rules," *Wall Street Journal*, July 8, 2009, p. D1.

Consumer Product Safety Improvement Act of 2008 (CPSIA) includes several sections on the resale of goods, including resales through garage sales and Internet listings. The CPSC has published a *Handbook for Resale Stores and Product Resellers.* The handbook was published after CPSC discovered that recalled products do find their way into garage sales and that buyers may not be aware that the goods are no longer legal. The CPSC does not have the resources to police garage sales but is encouraging sellers to be safe and do their research on the goods they are selling. Craigslist has assumed a policy of accepting ads but not screening those ads for product safety.

Craigslist had a bright light shone on it in 2009 when murder charges were brought against Philip H. Markoff, a medical student charged with the murder of a young woman he contacted and met through classifieds placed on Craigslist. Mr. Markoff committed suicide in jail in 2010.

Craigslist did not screen out erotic ads and when the murder occurred there was at least one investigation pending into a possible prostitution ring. Because of the negative publicity and investigation, Craigslist announced that it would remove the erotic ads. The ads would be shifted to a new category called "Adult Services." By September 2010, Craigslist announced that it would no longer accept sex ads for ads in the United States.

The experience of Craigslist repeats one that involved *Soldier of Fortune* magazine. In *Norwood v Soldier of Fortune Magazine, Inc.* 651 F.Supp. 1397 (W.D. Wash. 1987), the fact pattern involved a connection for a murder that was made via the classified ads in that magazine. In that case, Norman Douglas Norwood filed suit against Soldier of Fortune Magazine, Inc. because of several attempts that were made on his life by individuals who were hired via the following ads that ran in the magazine that has national circulation:

> GUN FOR HIRE: 37-year-old professional mercenary desires jobs. Vietnam Veteran. Discreet and very private. Bodyguard, courier, and other special skills. All jobs considered. Phone (615) 891-3306 (I-03).

> GUN FOR HIRE. NAM sniper instructor. SWAT. Pistol, rifle, security specialist, body guard, courier plus. All jobs considered. Privacy guaranteed. Mike (214) 756-5941 (101).

The two individuals who placed the ad were hired by Larry Gray to kill Mr. Norwood. They made several attempts and eventually shot and wounded Mr. Norwood. Norwood wanted to recover for his injuries from Soldier of Fortune. The court found for the magazine but Solider of Fortune also began a screening process.

Discussion Questions

1. Why would these two publishers take voluntary screening steps if they have no liability?
2. Does the use of the Internet for ads exacerbate the problems of magazine and newspaper ads?
3. What type of screening process could a company use for ads?

Product Safety

A bad reputation is like a hangover. It takes a while to get rid of and it makes everything else hurt.

JAMES PRESTON, FORMER CEO, AVON

Quality, safety, service, and social responsibility—customers want these elements in a product and a company. Does the profit motive interfere with these traits?

When is a product safe enough for sale? What happens if the product develops problems after it has been sold? What if a product cannot be made safe?

Reading 7.8

A Primer on Product Liability

From Shunning to Anonymity

When someone purchased the butter churner or the wagon wheel from a neighbor in the era of wagons and churning, there was no need for the Restatement of the Law of Torts. If the churner or the wheel was defective, the neighbor simply made good on the product or risked the mighty shunning that the community would dish out for those who dared to be less than virtuous, forthright, and of good rapport with one's fellow village dwellers. When neighbor manufactured for neighbor, the rule of law was *caveat vendor*, which, loosely translated, meant "If you want to continue living here, you had better take care of the problem with the crooked wagon wheel."

The birth of the industrialized society changed the community dynamic so that some communities made wheels, some made churners, and those in other communities purchased those goods even as they sold their specialties that they produced. The result was that buyers knew the merchant who sold them the wheel or the churn, but had no idea who really put together either, and, in many cases, were not even sure which community produced either. The one-to-one process of implementing product quality and guarantees disappeared. Even the ads for the wheels and churns were written by some copy writer far, far away who was a subcontractor of an advertising agency working for the manufacturing companies of these products. The physical and production distance between seller and buyer meant that the one-on-one confrontation and shunning methods were no longer effective. The law shifted from *caveat vendor* to *caveat emptor*, which, actually translated, means "Buyer beware." Now the buyer had to be on guard, ever vigilant in inspecting goods before buying and investigating the company doing the selling so that the buyer could at least be sure of reputation to date. The greater these physical and supply chain distances, the less likely the buyer was to have any information about the company, the product, or the history of either. And there was even less likelihood that the buyer could count on a seller repairing or replacing defective goods. Anonymity created a marketplace in which there were few or no buyer remedies.

Ralph Nader and Unsafe at Any Speed

During the 1960s, the law began to whittle away at the anonymity protections and immunity that manufacturers and sellers enjoyed when they sold their wares. In 1965, Ralph Nader published *Unsafe at Any Speed: The Designed-In Dangers of the American Automobile*, a book that was directed in its specific analysis at General Motors' Corvair, but that urged liability for auto manufacturers for their failure to research and implement product safety standards in their automobiles. Because of the stir the book created, a U.S. Senate subcommittee asked the CEOs of the automakers to testify about their commitment to auto safety research. Then–U.S. Senator Robert Kennedy had the following exchanges with James Roche, then–CEO, and Frederic Donner, then–chairman of the board, of General Motors:

Kennedy:	What was the profit of General Motors last year?
Roche:	I don't think that has anything to do—
Kennedy:	I would like to have that answer if I may. I think I am entitled to know that figure. I think it has been published. You spend a million and a quarter dollars, as I understand it, on this aspect of safety. I would like to know what the profit is.
Donner:	The aspect we are talking about is safety.
Kennedy:	What was the profit of General Motors last year?
Donner:	I would have to ask one of my associates.
Kennedy:	Could you, please?
Roche:	$1,700,000,000.
Kennedy:	What?
Donner:	About a billion and a half, I think.
Kennedy:	About a billion and a half?
Donner:	Yes.
Kennedy:	Or $1.7 billion. you made $1.7 billion last year?
Donner:	That is correct.
Kennedy:	And you spent $1 million on this?
Donner:	In this particular facet we are talking about. . . .
Kennedy:	If you gave just 1 percent of your profits, that is $17 million.

The drama of the moment was historically significant. From that point forward, the nature of seller and manufacturer liability, in the auto industry and consumer products generally, changed. The message was clear: part of the cost of manufacturing consumer products is ensuring their safety. Within the decade we would see the first appellate court decision that held Johns-Manville responsible for the damage to workers' lungs from asbestos exposure. Strict liability, or full accountability for one's products akin to the days of one-on-one sales, had returned.

The Legal Basis for Product Liability

Product liability has two foundations in law. The first is in contract, found in the Uniform Commercial Code. An **express warranty** as provided in the Uniform Commercial Code (UCC) is an express promise (oral or written) by the seller as to the quality, abilities, or performance of a product (UCC § 2–313). The seller need not use the words *promise* or *guarantee* to make an express warranty. A sample, a model, or just a description of the goods is a warranty. Promises of what the goods will do are also express warranties. "22 mpg" is an express warranty, which is why the claim is always followed by "Your mileage may vary." Other examples of express warranties are "These goods are 100 percent wool," "This tire cannot be punctured," and "These jeans will not shrink."

Any statements made by the seller to the buyer before the sale is actually made that are part of the basis of the sale or bargain are express warranties. Also, the information included on the product packaging constitutes an express warranty if those are statements of fact or promises of performance. So, ads count as warranties. Statements by salespeople count as warranties.

The **implied warranty of merchantability** (UCC § 2–314) is given in every sale of goods by a merchant seller. Merchants are those sellers who are engaged in the business of selling the good(s) that are the subject of the contract. This warranty requires that goods sold by a merchant "(c) are fit for the ordinary purposes for which goods of that description are used." This warranty means that food items are not contaminated and that cars' steering wheels do not break apart. Basketballs bounce, mobile homes do not leak when it rains, and brakes on cars do not fail.

The **implied warranty of fitness for a particular purpose** (UCC § 2–315) is the salesperson's warranty. If a buyer asks the owner of a nursery what weed killer would work in his garden and the nursery owner makes a recommendation that proves to kill the roses, the nursery owner has breached this warranty and has liability to the rose gardener. An exercise enthusiast who relies on an athletic shoe store owner for advice on which particular shoe is appropriate for aerobics also gets the protection of this warranty.

The second basis for product liability lies in tort law. Under the **Restatement of Torts (Section 402A),** anyone who manufactures or sells a product is liable to the buyer if the product is in a defective condition that makes it unreasonably dangerous. A product can be defective by design, the allegation that Mr. Nader made against GM for its Corvair when he stated that the position of the engine in the rear of the car made it dangerous for the occupants of the car. A product can also be dangerous because of shoddy manufacturing, as when there is a forgotten bolt or a failure to attach a part correctly. Finally, a product can be defective because the instructions or warnings are inadequate. "Do not stand on the top of the ladder," "Do not use this hair dryer near water," and "Not suitable for children under the age of 3" are all examples of warnings that are given to prevent injuries through use of the product.

Tort liability exists even when the manufacturer or seller is not aware of the problem. For example, a prescription drug may cause a reaction in adults who take aspirin. The manufacturer may not have been aware of this side effect, but the manufacturer is still responsible for the harm caused to those who have the reaction. The idea behind strict liability rests in the Senate hearings exchange: manufacturers need to devote enough resources to product development and research to determine that their products are made safely and that risks are discovered and disclosed before consumers are harmed.

The expansion of product liability from just UCC/contract law to tort law also meant that the traditional notion of "privity of contract" was no longer required. *Privity of contract* is a direct contract relationship between parties. Prior to the restatement standard, a buyer would not have a remedy against a manufacturer for its defective product and certainly could not go back to the bolt supplier or to the manufacturer if the bolt in a product turned out to be defective. The effect of strict tort liability is to hold sellers and manufacturers fully accountable for products up and down the supply chain. The defect may begin with a supplier, but the manufacturer and seller are not excused from liability because "someone else did it." Under strict tort liability standards, all companies associated with the design, production, and sale of defective products have responsibility for damages and injuries caused by that product.

Discussion Questions

1. Who are the stakeholders in dealing with the question of who should bear the costs of defective products?

2. Relate the discussion of the development of product liability theories for recovery to the regulatory cycle (Reading 3.9).

Case 7.9

Tylenol: Decades of Dilemmas

The Chicago Capsule Poisonings

In 1982, twenty-three-year-old Diane Elsroth died after taking a Tylenol capsule laced with cyanide. Within five days of her death, seven more people died from taking tainted Tylenol purchased from stores in the Chicago area.

At that time, Tylenol generated $525 million per year for McNeil Consumer Products, Inc., a subsidiary of Johnson & Johnson. The capsule form of the pain reliever represented 30 percent of Tylenol sales. McNeil's marketing studies indicated that consumers found the capsules easy to swallow and believed, without substantiation, that Tylenol in capsule form worked faster than Tylenol tablets.

The capsule's design, however, meant they could be taken apart, tainted, and then restored to the packaging without evidence of tampering. After the Chicago poisonings, which were never solved, McNeil and Johnson & Johnson executives were told at a meeting that processes for sealing the capsules had been greatly improved, but no one could give the assurance that they were tamperproof.

The executives realized that abandoning the capsule would give their competitors, Bristol-Myers (Excedrin) and American Home Products (Anacin), a market advantage, plus the cost would be $150 million just for 1982. Jim Burke, CEO of Johnson & Johnson, told the others that without a tamperproof package for the capsules, they would risk the survival of not only Tylenol but also Johnson & Johnson. The executives decided to abandon the capsule.

Frank Young, a Food and Drug Administration (FDA) commissioner, stated at the time, "This is a matter of Johnson & Johnson's own business judgment, and represents a responsible action under tough circumstances."[59]

Johnson & Johnson quickly developed "caplets"—tablets in the shape of a capsule—then offered consumers a coupon for a bottle of the new caplets if they turned in their capsules. Within five days of the announcement of the capsule recall and caplets offer, 200,000 consumers had responded. Johnson & Johnson had eliminated a key product in its line—one that customers clearly preferred—in the interest of safety. Otto Lerbinger of Boston University's College of Communication cited Johnson & Johnson as a "model of corporate social responsibility for its actions."[60]

President Ronald Reagan, addressing a group of business executives, said, "Jim Burke, of Johnson & Johnson, you have our deepest admiration. In recent days you have lived up to the very highest ideals of corporate responsibility and grace under pressure."[61]

Within one year of the Tylenol poisonings, Johnson & Johnson regained its 40 percent market share for Tylenol. While many attribute the regain of market share to tamperproof packaging, the other companies had moved to that form as well. However, it is interesting to note that McNeil was able to have its new product and packaging on the shelves within weeks of the fatal incidents. There had been some preparation for the change prior to the fatalities, but the tragedy was the motivation for the change to safer packaging and product forms.

McNeil has continued to enjoy the goodwill from its rapid response to the poisonings as well as its willingness to take the financial hit for what experts believed was a very small risk that there was more cyanide-laced Tylenol out on the shelves. In fact, the

---

[59] "Drug Firm Pulls All Its Capsules off the Market," *(Phoenix) Arizona Republic*, February 18, 1986, p. A2.

[60] Pat Guy and Clifford Glickman, "J & J Uses Candor in Crisis," *USA Today*, February 12, 1986, p. 2B.

[61] "The Tylenol Rescue," *Newsweek*, March 3, 1986, p. 52.

recall was so indelibly etched in the public's mind and in the minds of those in the field of business ethics that McNeil, Johnson & Johnson, and Tylenol itself were often given free passes on conduct that did pose safety risks to customers. As new issues with Tylenol have developed, McNeil seems to be given the benefit of the doubt because of the goodwill and reputational capital it purchased with the capsule recalls.[62]

Tylenol and Liver Damage

On December 21, 1994, the *Journal of the American Medical Association* published the results of a five-and-one-half-year study showing that moderate overdoses of acetaminophen (known most widely by the brand name Tylenol) led to liver damage in ten patients.[63] The damage occurred even in patients who did not drink and was most pronounced in those who did drink or had not been eating. Further, the study by Dr. David Whitcomb at the University of Pittsburgh Medical School found that taking one pill of acetaminophen per day for a year may double the risk of kidney failure.[64] By 2001, there were 450 deaths due to liver failure from Tylenol overdoses.

At that time, the American Association of Poison Control Centers called acetaminophen poisonings the most common of all reported poisonings.[65] The number of pediatric poisonings from overdoses of acetaminophen has more than tripled since 1996. As a result, the FDA adjusted the adult and pediatric doses that were acceptable in 2009. However, adult deaths from overexposure are more likely to be the result of suicidal ingestion.

Tylenol is a stunning source of revenue for McNeil and Johnson & Johnson, with revenue totals growing at double-digit rates as Tylenol expands market presence into 5,000 convenience stores with new and smaller packaging of its product and its new formulas such as Tylenol PM.[66]

Tylenol users who claimed they were victims of overdose and liver damage and the lack of effective warnings have not been successful against Johnson & Johnson.[67] McNeil has modified the recommended dosages, the ad claims, and language on its labels. The product labels before current modification read, "Gentle on an infant's stomach," and Tylenol's ad slogan was "Nothing's safer." That language has been removed and McNeil added to its infant Tylenol label: "Taking more than the recommended dose . . . could cause serious health risks" because of liver damage in children.[68]

McNeil also responded to data that showed patients who combine Tylenol with alcohol have produced 200 cases of liver damage in the past twenty years, with fatality in 20 percent of those cases. The level of alcohol use by patients among these cases was multiple drinks every day. McNeil modified its labels to include bold warnings about alcohol use and the dangers of combining Tylenol with any drinking.

Despite the extensive coverage of the issues surrounding Infant Tylenol, Tylenol overdoses, and issues with liver damage from combining alcohol and Tylenol, the company did not experience any loss of market share or even extensive negative media coverage. The goodwill from Tylenol's earlier recall appeared to see it through these crises. However, others issues were emerging.

[62]"Legacy of Tampering," *(Phoenix) Arizona Republic,* September 29, 1992, p. A1.

[63]"Acetaminophen Overdoses Linked to Liver Damage," *Mesa (Arizona) Tribune,* December 21, 1994, p. A12; and Doug Levy, "Acetaminophen Overuse Can Lead to Liver Damage," *USA Today,* December 22, 1994, p. 1D.

[64]"Second Tylenol Study Links Heavy Use to Kidney Risk," *(Phoenix) Arizona Republic,* December 22, 1994, p. A6.

[65]www.aapcc.com. Accessed June 10, 2010.

[66]Thomas Easton and Stephan Herrera, "J&J's Dirty Little Secret," *Forbes,* January 12, 1998, 42–44.

[67]Deborah Sharp, "Alcohol-Tylenol Death Goes to Trial in Florida," *USA Today,* March 24, 1997, p. 3A.

[68]Richard Cole, "Tylenol Agrees to Warning on Labels of Risk to Children," *(Phoenix) Arizona Republic,* October 19, 1997, p. A5.

The Tylenol Quality Control Program

In May 2010, the FDA was considering bringing criminal charges against McNeil for a pattern of violations in its quality control in the production of children's Tylenol. The charges would spring from the April 30, 2010, recall by McNeil of 136 million bottles of liquid pediatric Tylenol, Motrin, Benadryl, and Zyrtec because the medicines contained too much metal debris or too much of the necessary active ingredient in these over-the-counter drugs. Because of the presence of metal debris, the medicine batches failed FDA testing. However, prior to the FDA testing and the recall, there was evidence that McNeil was aware of the developing problem but took no public action. A purchase order that the company turned over to congressional investigators indicated that McNeil had hired a contractor in 2009 to visit 5,000 stores and buy Motrin from the shelves. The contractor's PowerPoint materials instructed employees to act like any other customer and make "no mention of this being a recall when making a purchase."[69] McNeil indicated to congressional investigators that "The Motrin Purchase Project" was created by a McNeil subcontractor without its knowledge and approval. McNeil said it notified the FDA about two Motrin lots that did not dissolve properly and that it was removing the Motrin from the shelves.

The evidence submitted for the hearings showed that McNeil had received forty-six complaints from consumers about black particles in Tylenol and other McNeil products. However, McNeil did not notify the FDA nor did it recall the medicines. The inaction in the face of customer harm represented the straw that broke the FDA's back of tolerance because the company, at that point, was finishing two years of an ongoing tussle with regulators over quality control. At one plant that manufactured Children's Tylenol, seven batches of product were released after testing revealed problems in three batches. The agency's frustration in dealing with the plants and managers for inaction and ongoing violations led to the review of the company for possible criminal charges.

The surreptitious removal of Motrin from retail stores because McNeil had discovered quality control problems with that product was referred to by the FDA as, in effect, an unannounced or "phantom" recall.[70] Also in 2008, McNeil failed to notify the FDA that it had received complaints from customers about a moldy smell in some of the products made in its Puerto Rico production facilities and, at the same time, failed to disclose complaints from customers about stomach problems experienced after they had used the "moldy" products. McNeil tested the products and found no problems, but the complaints continued through 2009. Further testing showed that the medicine had been contaminated by a chemical used in the plant for the treatment of wooden shipping pallets. One member of Congress noted that the recall on the "smell" issue took one year and that it should have taken 3 days. At another plant, the FDA found that the company "knowingly" used an ingredient that was tainted with *Burkholderia cepacia,* a bacteria that most healthy people can handle but that can cause serious infections in those with chronic illnesses such as cystic fibrosis.[71] Another member of Congress said of the congressional inquiry, "We are not getting the kind of information and cooperation from Johnson that I would like."[72]

As consumers purchased generic brands to substitute for the recalled Tylenol products, quality problems emerged in those medicines as well. In addition to the criminal

[69]Natasha Singer, "Johnson & Johnson Seen as Uncooperative on Recall Inquiry," *New York Times,* June 11, 2010, pp. B1, B4.

[70]Natasha Singer, "F.D.A. Weighs More Penalties In Drug Recall," *New York Times,* May 28, 2010, p. A1.

[71]Alison Young, "Plant in Recall Had Other Violations," *USA Today,* May 27, 2010, p. 3A.

[72]Natasha Singer, "Johnson & Johnson Seen as Uncooperative on Recall Inquiry," *New York Times,* June 11, 2010, p. B1.

charges, the FDA is studying the production quality issue from an industry perspective and is considering revamping the production and testing requirements for all over-the-counter drug manufacturers. The agency released the letters that it sent to forty-three drug factories for their failure to correct "shoddy manufacturing practices that may have exposed patients to health risks."[73] The letters indicated that FDA inspectors had found insects in equipment and ingredients, improper testing, failure to conduct required tests, and disregard for customer complaints. More than half of the plants inspected had violations, even if those violations did not rise to the level of receiving the agency's letter warning.

Discussion Questions

1. Were the shareholders' interests ignored in the decision to take a $150 million write-off and a possible loss of $525 million in annual sales by abandoning the capsules?
2. Suppose that you were a Tylenol competitor. Would you have continued selling your capsules?
3. Was Mr. Burke's action a long-term decision? Did it take into account the interests of all stakeholders? How did Mr. Burke's action help the company with the liver-damage issues?
4. What can you conclude from the quick development and appearance of the new product line?
5. Following the 2010 misstep, Tylenol's competitors have been sending out free samples and coupons to Tylenol customers who participated in the Tylenol recall as a way of getting them to try their products. Why would such a campaign at this time result in more sales of their products? What is different about this issue versus the cyanide poisonings? Make a list of the distinctions between the two series of events, including descriptions of company and customer responses.
6. General Robert Wood Johnson, the CEO of Johnson & Johnson from 1932 to 1963, wrote a credo for his company that states the company's first responsibility is to the people

who use its products and services, the second responsibility is to its employees, the third to the community and its environment, and the fourth to the stockholders.[74] Johnson and his successors have believed that if the credo's first three responsibilities are met, the stockholders will be well served. Does Johnson & Johnson follow its credo?
7. Why did the company drag its heels on the later recalls? What was the purpose of the phantom contractor and the resulting unannounced recall?
8. Did the company ride the coattails of its recall recognition from the 1987 poisonings for too long? Was there hubris involved?
9. A lawyer who represents clients suing McNeil offered the following observations: "It [McNeil] markets itself as a company that takes children's safety very seriously and that's why they can charge a premium price for the Tylenol. People are willing to pay a premium price because of a reputation for safety. Now they're being deceived."[75] Another lawyer who represents companies before the FDA added, "The value of the brand is such that that's got to be the first thought."[76] What thoughts are the lawyers offering on cost analysis in ethical issues through their experiences and observations?

Case 7.10
Merck and Vioxx

A Company with a Rich History and Excellent Reputation

Merck was founded as a chemical manufacturer in Germany in 1668. Run by the Merck family for generations, the company moved to the United States in 1891 under the direction of George Merck. George Merck Jr. once said, "We try never to forget that medicine

[73]Alison Young, "FDA Warns 43 Drug Manufacturers," *USA Today,* May 27, 2010, p. 3A.
[74]"Brief History of Johnson & Johnson," company pamphlet, 1992.
[75]Carrie Levine, "Tylenol's Growing Headache," *National Law Journal,* June 7, 2010, p.A1.
[76]*Id.*

is for the people. It is not for the profits. The profits follow, and if we have remembered that, they have never failed to appear."

Merck continued as a chemical manufacturer until the 1930s, when it began to do research and development (R&D) in pharmaceuticals. Two mergers, one in 1953 with Sharp & Dohme, a pharmaceutical firm, and another with Medco, a prescription benefits management company, found Merck leaving its chemical production roots and moving exclusively to producing and selling pharmaceuticals.

With this focus, Merck—still headquartered in New York, where George Merck originally located the German chemical company after coming to the United States—has 100,000 employees in 96 plants in 120 countries. A merger with Schering-Plough increased the number of employees from 73,000 in 2008 to the 100,000 figure at the end of 2009. There are thirty-one Merck pharmaceutical factories around the world, and Merck sells its drugs in over 200 countries.

Merck has long been known as a responsible and generous corporation. Merck was named one of *Fortune*'s "Most Admired Companies in America" for seven years during the 1980s. In 2004, *Business Ethics* named Merck one of its Top 100 Most Ethical Companies in America. Merck has donated billions in AIDS and river blindness drugs, particularly in Africa. Its scientists have focused on R&D related to disease and prevention in undeveloped countries. Its name carries tremendous goodwill around the world. Its drugs for treating high cholesterol levels, osteoporosis, and hypertension have proven to be lifesavers for billions around the world.

The Lackluster Performance and New Drug with Promise and Perils

Despite, however, Merck's excellent philanthropic reputation, analysts were disgruntled during the 1990s over Merck, its performance, and its promise. One analyst concluded, "Merck is living in the past."[77] Merck had launched six new drugs, but its patent exclusivity had expired on five of its drugs. Another analyst expressed dismay that such a grand company had slipped so far from its once impeccable gold standard of achievement in sales and R&D.

In 1994, Merck's R&D program discovered Vioxx (its generic name is rofecoxib), one of a group of COX-2 inhibitors. COX-2 inhibitors include over-the-counter (OTC) medications such as Advil (ibuprofen) and Aleve (naproxen) that serve to reduce both pain and inflammation. COX-2 inhibitors are particularly effective for arthritis pain relief without the side effects that come with the use of steroids for treatment of the aches, pains, stiffness, and swelling of arthritis. Other nonsteroidal medications for these symptoms produce the undesirable side effects of gastrointestinal bleeding and stomach ulcers. Vioxx actually helped with stomach ulcers and curbed intestinal bleeding.

From 1994 through 1999, Merck navigated the Food and Drug Administration approval process, one that has incremental steps for approval. The Phase 1 test for an experimental drug requires that the medication be given to 20 to 100 patients and be administered over a period of months. This basic and limited testing is for safety issues, and about 70 percent of all drugs make it through the Phase 1 test. Once the initial test is complete, Phase 2 begins. Phase 2 is testing for the effectiveness of the drug as well as its safety. The number of patients in Phase 2 is 200 to 300, and a Phase 2 screening can take months or up to two years. About 33 percent of the drugs that make it to Phase 2 pass. The final phase, Phase 3, requires 300 to 5,000 patients in a process that will run from one to four years, depending upon the nature of the drug and the type of medical issue it addresses.[78] Phase 3 tests for dosage as well as safety and effectiveness. Only

---

[77] "Merck: Will They Survive Vioxx?" *Fortune*, November 1, 2004, pp. 91, 92, 94.

[78] With chronic illness drugs, such as anticancer drugs, the tests run longer because of issues of relapse.

25 to 30 percent of the drugs that go through Phase 3 make it through for approval for sale to the public. During the Phase 3 trial, in 1997, Dr. Alise Reicin, a Merck physician and scientist, wrote in an e-mail to a fellow Merck scientist on her discovery of "C.V. events" (cardiovascular effects of Vioxx) and her concern about a setback, "I just can't wait to be the one to present those results to senior management." Those study results were not disclosed to the FDA. The FDA would not become aware of them until 2001.

Vioxx made it through all of the phases, and in May 1999 sales of Vioxx began in the United States, complete with ads featuring former Olympic ice skater Peggy Fleming, who endorsed the product as effective for her arthritis pain. Vioxx had competition from Pfizer's Celebrex and Bextra, as well as OTC products such as Advil and Tylenol, Arthritic Formula.

Questions Arise

In 2001, then–Merck CEO Ray Gilmartin received an eight-page letter from the FDA about a Vioxx study and the FDA's concerns about Merck's lack of disclosure of the information from the studies to the public (through its media campaigns for the drug) and to doctors prescribing the drug.[79] A study that would come to be referred to as "the Cleveland study" concluded that Vioxx users were at five times greater risk for a heart attack than those who used just naproxen (Aleve being the OTC example). An excerpt from the letter appears below:

> Additionally, your claim in the press release that "Vioxx has a favorable cardiovascular safety profile," is simply incomprehensible, given the rate of MI [myocardial infarction, or heart attack] [clarification added] and serious cardiovascular events compared to naproxen.[80]

The press release referenced in the FDA letter was one made by Merck after the Cleveland studies went public and was titled "Merck Confirms Favorable Cardiovascular Safety Profile of Vioxx." Merck described Vioxx as "heart protective."

After the Cleveland study became public in 2001, several class action lawsuits were filed on behalf of Vioxx users around the country. The plaintiffs in the cases were surviving relatives of Vioxx patients who had experienced fatal heart attacks or patients who were suffering from heart disease or recovering from heart attacks.

Following the release of the 2001 study, Merck's sales force began to experience questions about Vioxx and cardiovascular events (CVEs). The following are excerpts from Merck's training materials for its sales force:

- "Obstacles": reference for negative CVE data on Vioxx; used in videotaped sales training for Merck sales reps
- "Dodgeball": term used to describe what sales reps should do when asked questions about CVEs and Vioxx and medical data

In April 2002, Merck added to its Vioxx bottle labels that there was a risk of cardiovascular and stroke events. All scientists agreed that there was no elevated risk until patients took Vioxx for at least eighteen months.[81]

By 2000, with Vioxx taking off with its approval and fast first sales, Merck's stock would peak at $95 per share. By 2003, Vioxx had proved to be a winner. Vioxx sales totaled $2.5 billion, or 11 percent of the company's total revenue. Vioxx's contribution to net income was $1.2 billion, or 18 percent.

[79]Barbara Martinez, "Vioxx Lawsuits May Focus on FDA Warning in 2001," *Wall Street Journal,* October 5, 2004, pp. B1 and B4.
[80]*Id.*
[81]Andrea Peterson, "Putting Side Effects in Perspective," *Wall Street Journal,* October 5, 2004, p. D1.

However, after the Vioxx approval in 1999, Merck realized, in early 2000, that Vioxx may have other potential uses. Merck commissioned a study to determine whether Vioxx had additional efficacy in treating colon polyps. The study was monitored by a safety committee of Merck employees as well as outside scientists, which one Merck scientist described as "50% scientific need and 50% appearance."[82] Two of the outside scientists on the committee had continuing consulting arrangements with Merck. The outside committee continued to meet to monitor the polyps study. At the committee meeting in September 2003, the minutes reflect a discussion of the findings of the ongoing studies that concluded that there was a 20 percent higher chance of a heart attack or stroke in Vioxx users. The study continued, with the numbers climbing to 40 percent, then 80 percent, and finally 120 percent by the data shown to the committee in September 2004.[83]

In May 2004, the medical journal *Circulation* was in the process of preparing an article for publication that highlighted the serious CV effects of Vioxx. One of the authors of the study, Dr. Carolyn C. Cannuscio, was a Merck scientist. While the editor was unaware of the change, the Merck employee's name was removed from the study prior to publication of the article. No one at the journal was certain how the name, which was on the paper at the time of its submission for review, was removed from the article during the course of its production, after its acceptance for publication.[84] Merck indicated, through a spokesperson, "Merck disagreed with the conclusions and didn't think it was appropriate to have a Merck author."[85] The study concluded that Vioxx users had an elevated risk of myocardial infarction. Dr. Cannuscio said that she requested that her name be removed because people would conclude, with her name on it, that Merck agreed with the study. One scientist commented that Merck missed the boat on the name removal: "They missed a wonderful opportunity to get some good publicity for the pharmaceutical industry."[86]

When asked about these minutes and numbers, Merck spokeswoman Joan Wainwright would explain in 2004, "Those percentages are based on very small numbers of events."[87] She also indicated that the outside committee had concluded that those numbers were not statistically significant when compared with events in the placebo group. Ms. Wainwright's description is correct according to the minutes of the meetings. While the committee discussed the numbers, issues, and concerns, there was no dissent in their decision to continue with the testing and do so without disclosure.

When the conduct of the safety committee was reviewed, outside scientists felt that the committee was just doing what scientists do in these clinical trials. "Sometimes you see something significant, and then it goes away," and so there is a delay on disclosure.[88]

Dr. David Bjorkman, one of the outside scientists on the committee, indicated that he had received, at most, $20,000 as a Merck consultant. Cardiologist Dr. Martin Konstam, another scientist on the panel, had conducted research with Merck employees on CVEs and Vioxx and was the lead author on an article that appeared in the medical journal *Circulation*. The article, which had been published in 2001, concluded that there was "no evidence for an excess of cardiovascular effects of Vioxx."[89] The article was critical of a study that had appeared two months earlier in the *Journal of the American Medical Association* (JAMA) that warned of the CVEs of Vioxx.

---

[82]*Id.*

[83]*Id.*

[84]Thomas M. Burton, "Merck Takes Author's Name off Study," *Wall Street Journal,* May 18, 2004, p. B1.

[85]*Id.*

[86]*Id.*

[87]*Id.*

[88]*Id.*

[89]*Id.*

When the number of 120 percent appeared at the September 2004 safety committee meeting, the committee warned the company, and the company stopped selling Vioxx and issued a recall of the drug.[90] R&D head Dr. Peter Kim said, "I am proud that we did the right thing."[91]

The Impact of Vioxx CV Effects

Upon the announcement of the Vioxx recall, Merck's shares dropped from $45.07 to $33 in one day.[92] Even after the recall, Moody's and Standard & Poor's kept Merck's Triple-A bond rating. Analysts estimate that Merck has, easily, $10 billion in highly liquid assets, more than enough to manage the crisis.[93] Most analysts place the final tally for the litigation at $10 billion.

The estimate of fatal and nonfatal heart attacks in Vioxx users since 1999 is 140,000. By the time of the recall, 20 million Americans had used Vioxx. In early 2005, Merck announced the creation of a $675 million reserve for handling both the recall–refund program and the pending litigation.[94] There were 625 lawsuits, including class action suits, filed against the company by February 2005. Also in February 2005, the SEC announced that it was opening an investigation into Merck's disclosures about Vioxx and its safety in the company's 10-K's and periodic filings. The Justice Department subpoenaed company records on the handling of the warnings and disclosures related to Vioxx. Congress opened hearings in February 2005 into the role of the FDA in the Vioxx issues. In May 2005, the Merck board replaced CEO Gilmartin with Richard Clark.[95] At the time, its stock price had dipped below $25.

The jury verdicts in the cases have been split—50 percent finding for Merck, and 50 percent for the plaintiffs. Verdicts in four of the eight cases decided through November 2007 totaled $39.75 million. Merck's strategy for the suits was to ensure that the suits were not grouped together as one class action. Merck's lawyers reasoned that, because the Vioxx users were so different in age, health, and heart conditions, there would be different verdicts, since not all of the health issues or deaths could be attributed to Vioxx. Merck achieved a major victory in September 2007 when the New Jersey Supreme Court ruled that a group of Vioxx plaintiffs could not be certified for purposes of a consumer fraud class action.[96] The judge found, as Merck had reasoned, that the plaintiffs were very different, in age, in health, and in terms of preexisting health conditions. However, the case-by-case strategy proved expensive and the legal bills remained steep.

In November 2007, Merck was able to settle the lawsuits brought against it by patients who used Vioxx. Merck pulled the antiarthritis drug completely from the market in September 2004 after there was evidence that use of the drug was tied to a higher risk of heart attack and stroke. At the time there were 26,600 cases pending against Merck. The cases had not been consolidated into one class action.

Merck's legal strategy had been one of fighting each of the cases independently. Merck announced a $1.9 billion set aside for defending the legal cases, and, as of November 2007, had spent $1.2 billion of that amount. With litigation costs mounting, Merck

[90]Barnaby J. Feder, "Merck's Actions on Vioxx Face Scrutiny," *New York Times,* February 15, 2005, p. C1.

[91]"Merck: Will They Survive Vioxx?" pp. 91, 92.

[92]David Henry, "Market Lessons from Merck's Decline," *BusinessWeek,* October 18, 2004.

[93]"Merck: Will They Survive Vioxx?" pp. 91, 92.

[94]Feder, "Merck's Actions on Vioxx Face Scrutiny," pp. C1, C4.

[95]Barbara Martinez and Joann A. Lublin, "Merck Replaces Embattled CEO with Insider Richard Clark," *Wall Street Journal,* May 6, 2005, p. A1.

[96]International Union of Operating Engineers Local No. 68 *Welfare Fund v Merck & Co.,* Inc., 2007 WL 2493917 (NJ 2007).

made the decision to settle the cases. The biggest problem with such massive settlements is the ability of plaintiffs to opt out of the settlement and pursue litigation. Merck was trying to avoid what happened to Wyeth when it settled its suits on the diet drug fen-phen. The suits were settled for $3.75 billion, but so many fen-phen users opted out that Wyeth ended up with a total pay-out of $21 billion. Merck negotiated limits on who could opt out, especially with regard to statutes of limitation for suits by those who opt out.

Merck's share price climbed 2.1 percent, or $1.13, when, in 2007, the settlement of $4.85 billion was announced.[97]

Discussion Questions

1. Applying the background on the law for product liability, why do you think some jurors found Merck liable? Applying the law again, why do you think some found the company not liable?

2. List the facts that work in Merck's favor in terms of being forthright. List the facts that work against Merck. Compare the list and offer suggestions on what Merck might have done differently in handling Vioxx issues.

3. Describe other ethical issues you see arising peripherally in this case.

Compare & Contrast

Since the Merck Vioxx experience, a number of pharmaceutical firms have voluntarily withdrawn many of their drugs when the smallest question arises, even just a negative reaction in one patient. Why the quick reaction by these companies? What analyses are they performing that is perhaps different from the one Merck performed with Vioxx? What general lessons could pharmaceutical firms take from the Vioxx experience?

Case 7.11

Ford and Its Pinto and GM and Its Malibu: The Repeating Exploding Gas Tank Problem

The Ford Pinto

In 1968, Ford began designing a subcompact automobile that ultimately became the Pinto. Lee Iacocca, then a Ford vice president, conceived the idea of a subcompact car and was its moving force. Ford's objective was to build a car weighing 2,000 pounds or less to sell for no more than $2,000. At that time, prices for gasoline were increasing, and the American auto industry was losing competitive ground to the small vehicles of Japanese and German manufacturers.

The Rushed Project

The Pinto was a rush project. Ordinarily, auto manufacturers work to blend the engineering concerns with the style preferences of consumers that they determine from marketing surveys. As a result, the placement of the Pinto fuel tank was dictated by style, not engineering. The preferred practice in Europe and Japan was to locate the gas tank over the rear axle in subcompacts because a small vehicle has less "crush space" between the

[97]Heather Won Tesoriero, Sarah Rubenstein, and Jamie Heller, "Vioxx Settlement for $4.85 Billion Large Vindicates Merck's Tactics," *Wall Street Journal,* November 10–11, 2007, pp. Al, A5; Alex Berenson, "Analysts See Merck Victory in Vioxx Deal," *New York Times,* November 10, 2007, pp. A1, Al2; and "Merck Agrees to $4.85B Settlement over Vioxx," *National Law Journal,* September 12, 2007, p. 3.

rear axle and the bumper than larger cars.[98] The Pinto's styling, however, required the tank to be placed behind the rear axle, leaving only nine to ten inches of "crush space"—far less than in any other American automobile or Ford overseas subcompact. In addition, the Pinto's bumper was little more than a chrome strip, less substantial than the bumper of any other American car produced then or later. The Pinto's rear structure also lacked reinforcing longitudinal side members, known as "hat sections," and horizontal cross members running between them, such as those in larger cars produced by Ford. The result of these style-driven changes was that the Pinto was less crush-resistant than other vehicles. But, there was one more problem, which was that the Pinto's differential housing had an exposed flange and bolt heads. These resulting protrusions meant that a gas tank driven forward against the differential by a rear impact would be punctured.[99]

Pinto prototypes were built and tested. Ford tested these prototypes, as well as two production Pintos, to determine the integrity of the fuel system in rear-end accidents. It also tested to see if the Pinto would meet a proposed federal regulation requiring all automobiles manufactured in 1972 to be able to withstand a twenty-mile-per-hour fixed-barrier impact and those made after January 1, 1973, to withstand a thirty-mile-per-hour fixed-barrier impact without significant fuel spillage.[100]

The crash tests revealed that the Pinto's fuel system as designed could not meet the proposed twenty-mile-per-hour standard. When mechanical prototypes were struck from the rear with a moving barrier at twenty-one miles per hour, the fuel tanks were driven forward and punctured, causing fuel leakage in excess of the proposed regulation standard. A production Pinto crashing at twenty-one miles per hour into a fixed barrier resulted in the fuel neck being torn from the gas tank and the tank being punctured by a bolt head on the differential housing. In at least one test, spilled fuel entered the driver's compartment through gaps resulting from the separation of the seams joining the rear wheel wells to the floor pan.

Ford tested other vehicles, including modified or reinforced mechanical Pinto prototypes, that proved safe at speeds at which the Pinto failed. Vehicles in which rubber bladders had been installed in the tank and were then crashed into fixed barriers at twenty-one miles per hour had no leakage from punctures in the gas tank. Vehicles with fuel tanks installed above rather than behind the rear axle passed the fuel system integrity test at thirty-one miles per hour against a fixed barrier. A Pinto with two longitudinal hat sections added to firm up the rear structure passed a twenty-mile-per-hour fixed-barrier test with no fuel leakage.[101]

The vulnerability of the Pinto's fuel tank at speeds of twenty and thirty miles per hour in fixed-barrier tests could have been remedied inexpensively, but Ford produced and sold the Pinto without doing anything to fix the defects. Among the design changes that could have been made were side and cross members at $2.40 and $1.80 per car, respectively; a shock-absorbent "flak suit" to protect the tank at $4; a tank within a tank and placement of the tank over the axle at $5.08 to $5.79; a nylon bladder within the tank at $5.25 to $8; placement of the tank over the axle surrounded with a protective barrier at $9.59 per car; imposition of a protective shield between the differential housing and the tank at $2.35; improvement and reinforcement of the bumper at $2.60; and addition of eight inches of crush space at a cost of $6.40. Equipping the car with a reinforced

---

[98]Rachel Dardis and Claudia Zent, "The Economics of the Pinto Recall," *Journal of Consumer Affairs* (Winter 1982): 261–277.

[99]*Id.*

[100]*Id.*

[101]*Grimshaw v Ford Motor Co.,* 174 Cal. Rptr. 378 (1981).

rear structure, smooth axle, improved bumper, and additional crush space at a total of $15.30 would have made the fuel tank safe when hit from the rear by a vehicle the size of a Ford Galaxy. If, in addition, a bladder or tank within a tank had been used or if the tank had been protected with a shield, the tank would have been safe in a rear-end collision of forty to forty-five miles per hour. If the tank had been located over the rear axle, it would have been safe in a rear impact at fifty miles per hour or more.[102]

Engineering Doubts

As the Pinto approached actual production, the engineers responsible for the components of the project "signed off" to their immediate supervisors, who in turn "signed off" to their superiors, and so on up the chain of command until the entire project was approved for release by the lead engineers, and ultimately, Iacocca. The Pinto crash test results were known to these decision makers when they decided to go forward with production.

At an April 1971 product review meeting, a report by Ford engineers on the financial impact of a proposed federal standard on fuel-system integrity and the cost savings that would accrue from deferring even minimal "fixes" of the Pinto was discussed.

In 1969, the chief assistant research engineer in charge of cost-weight evaluation of the Pinto and the chief chassis engineer in charge of crash testing the early prototype both expressed concern about the integrity of the Pinto's fuel system and complained about management's unwillingness to deviate from the design if the change would cost money.

J. C. Echold, Ford's director of automotive safety, studied the issue of gas-tank design in anticipation of government regulations requiring modification. His study, "Fatalities Associated with Crash Induced Fuel Leakage and Fires," included the following cost–benefit analysis:

The total benefit is shown to be just under $50 million, while the associated cost is $137 million. Thus, the cost is almost three times the benefits, even using a number of highly favorable benefit assumptions.[103]

Benefits

Savings—180 burn deaths, 180 serious burn injuries, 2,100 burned vehicles

Unit cost—$200,000 per death, $67,000 per injury, $700 per vehicle

Total benefits—(180 × $200,000) + (180 × $67,000) + (2,100 × $700) = $49.15 million

Costs

Sales—11 million cars, 1.5 million light trucks

Unit cost—$11 per car, $11 per truck

Total costs—(11,000,000 × $11) + (1,500,000 × $11) = $137 million

Ford's unit cost of $200,000 for one life was based on a National Highway Traffic Safety Administration calculation developed as shown in Table 7.1.

Despite the concerns of the engineers and the above report, Ford went forward with production of the Pinto without any design change or any of the proposed modifications. Shortly after the release of the car, significant mechanical issues were recurring, with complaints by vehicle owners as well as a number of fiery rear-end collisions. One of the most public cases happened in 1971, when the Gray family purchased a 1972 Pinto hatchback

---

[102]*Id.*

[103]Ralph Drayton, "One Manufacturer's Approach to Automobile Safety Standards," *CTLA News*, February 8, 1968, p. 11.

TABLE **7.1**		
Ford's Unit Cost of $200,000 for One Life		

Component	1971 Costs ($)
Future productivity losses	
Direct	132,000
Indirect	41,300
Medical costs	
Hospital	700
Other	425
Property damage	1,500
Insurance administration	4,700
Legal and court	3,000
Employer losses	1,000
Victim's pain and suffering	10,000
Funeral	900
Assets (lost consumption)	5,000
Miscellaneous accident cost	200
Total per family	$200,725

Source: Mark Dowie, "Pinto Madness," *Mother Jones*, September/October 1977, p. 28.

(the 1972 models were made available in the fall of 1971) manufactured by Ford in October 1971. The Grays had trouble with the car from the outset. During the first few months of ownership, they had to return the car to the dealer for repairs a number of times. The problems included excessive gas and oil consumption, down-shifting of the automatic transmission, lack of power, and occasional stalling. It was later learned that the stalling and excessive fuel consumption were caused by a heavy carburetor float.

The Accidents and Injuries

On May 28, 1972, Mrs. Gray, accompanied by thirteen-year-old Richard Grimshaw, set out in the Pinto from Anaheim, California, for Barstow to meet Mr. Gray. The Pinto was then six months old and had been driven approximately 3,000 miles. Mrs. Gray stopped in San Bernardino for gasoline, then got back onto Interstate 15 and proceeded toward Barstow at sixty to sixty-five miles per hour. As she approached the Route 30 off-ramp where traffic was congested, she moved from the outside fast lane into the middle lane. The Pinto then suddenly stalled and coasted to a halt. It was later established that the carburetor float had become so saturated with gasoline that it sank, opening the float chamber and causing the engine to flood. The driver of the vehicle immediately behind Mrs. Gray's car was able to swerve and pass it, but the driver of a 1962 Ford Galaxy was unable to avoid hitting the Pinto. The Galaxy had been traveling from fifty to fifty-five miles per hour but had slowed to between twenty-eight and thirty-seven miles per hour at the time of impact.[104]

---

[104]"Who Pays for the Damage?" *Time*, January 21, 1980, p. 61.

The Pinto burst into flames that engulfed its interior. According to one expert, the impact of the Galaxy had driven the Pinto's gas tank forward and caused it to be punctured by the flange or one of the bolts on the differential housing so that fuel sprayed from the punctured tank and entered the passenger compartment through gaps opening between the rear wheel well sections and the floor pan. By the time the Pinto came to rest after the collision, both occupants had been seriously burned. When they emerged from the vehicle, their clothing was almost completely burned off. Mrs. Gray died a few days later of congestive heart failure as a result of the burns. Grimshaw survived only through heroic medical measures. He underwent numerous and extensive surgeries and skin grafts, some occurring over the ten years following the collision. He lost parts of several fingers on his left hand and his left ear, and his face required many skin grafts.[105]

As Ford continued to litigate Mrs. Gray's lawsuit and thousands of other rear-impact Pinto suits, damages reaching $6 million had been awarded to plaintiffs by 1980. In 1979, Indiana filed criminal charges against Ford for reckless homicide.

Discussion Questions

1. Calculate the total cost if all the "fixes" for the Pinto gas tank problem had been performed.
2. What was management's position on the fixes?
3. Using the decision models you have learned, list some of the analysis questions and issues management missed in making its decision to go forward with production without any design changes.

4. Don't all automobiles present the potential for injuries? Do we assume risks in driving and buying an automobile?
5. If you had been one of the engineers who was concerned, what would you have done differently? Do you think there was anything you could do? What if you resigned, as Dr. LiCari at Beech-Nut did (Case 4.23)? Could you then notify a government agency?

Compare & Contrast

In 1996, Ford issued a recall on 8.7 million vehicles because a joint investigation with the National Highway Traffic Safety Administration (NHTSA) revealed that the ignition in certain cars could short-circuit and cause a fire. Ford ran full-page ads in major newspapers. The ad from the *Wall Street Journal* (May 8, 1996, p. B7) is reproduced below:

T.J. Wagner

Vice President

Ford Motor Company

Dearborn, MI 48121

Customer Communication & Satisfaction

To Our Ford, Lincoln and Mercury Owners:

As I am sure you have read, Ford Motor Company recently announced a program to voluntarily recall 8.7 million vehicles to replace ignition switches. You should know that at the time we announced the recall, the actual number of complaints which may be related to the ignition switch in question was less than two hundredths of one percent of that total. We regret the inconvenience this has caused the customers who have placed their trust in our products.

Q: What happened?

A: Following an intensive investigation in cooperation with the U.S. National Highway Traffic Safety Administration and Transport Canada, we determined that the ignition switch in a

---

[105]Adapted from *Grimshaw v Ford Motor Co.*, 174 Cal. Rptr. 348 (1981).

very small percentage of certain models could develop a short circuit—creating the potential for overheating, smoke, and possibly fire in the steering column of the vehicle. The factors that contribute to this are a manufacturing process change to the ignition switch in combination with the electrical load through the switch.

Q: What should I do?

A: If you own one of these vehicles, you will receive a letter from us instructing you to take your vehicle to the Ford or Lincoln/Mercury dealer of your choice and have the switch replaced free of charge. However, you do not have to wait for our letter. You may contact your dealer and arrange to have the switch replaced immediately if you choose, free of charge.

Q: How long will it take?

A: The repair procedure should take about one hour. But please contact your dealer in advance to schedule a time that is convenient for you.

Q: What if I need additional help?

A: You may contact your dealer anytime, or call our Ford Ignition Switch Recall Customer Information Line at 1-800-323-8400.

We're in business because people believe in our products. We make improvements because we believe we can make our products better. And at times we'll take a major step like this to make sure that people who buy a Ford, Lincoln or Mercury vehicle know that they bought more than a vehicle, they bought a company and a dealer organization that stands behind the cars and trucks they build and sell. This is our Quality is Job 1 *promise to you. Thank you for your patience and support.*

What was different about Ford's conduct in this case? Has Ford had an ethical cultural change on product safety? Why did Ford voluntarily agree to fix almost 9 million vehicles?

The Chevrolet (GM) Malibu

On July 9, 1999, a Los Angeles jury awarded Patricia Anderson, her four children, and her friend, Jo Tigner, $107 million in actual damages and $4.8 billion in punitive damages from General Motors in a lawsuit the six brought against GM because they were trapped and burned in their Chevrolet Malibu when it exploded on impact following a rear-end collision.[106]

Jury foreman Coleman Thorton, in explaining the large verdict, said, "GM has no regard for the people in their cars, and they should be held responsible for it." Richard Shapiro, an attorney for GM, said, "We're very disappointed. This was a very sympathetic case. The people who were injured were innocent in this matter. They were the victims of a drunk driver."[107]

The accident occurred on Christmas Eve 1993 and was the result of a drunk driver striking the Andersons' Malibu at 70 mph. The driver's blood alcohol level was .20, but the defense lawyers noted they were not permitted to disclose to the jury that the driver of the auto that struck the Malibu was drunk.

The discovery process in the case uncovered a 1973 internal "value analysis" memo on "post-collision fuel-tank fires" written by a low-level GM engineer, Edward C. Ivey, in which he calculated the value of preventing fuel-fed fires. Mr. Ivey used a figure of $200,000 for the cost of a fatality and noted that there are 500 fatalities per year in GM auto fuel fire accidents. The memo also stated that his analysis must be read in the

[106]Ann W. O'Neill, Henry Weinstein, and Eric Malnic, "Jury Orders GM to Pay Record Sum," *Arizona Republic*, July 10, 1999, pp. A1, A2.
[107]*Id.*

context of "it is really impossible to put a value on human life." Mr. Ivey wrote, using an estimate of $200,000 as the value of human life, that the cost of these explosions to GM would be $2.40 per car. After an in-house lawyer discovered the memo in 1981, he wrote,

> Obviously Ivey is not an individual whom we would ever, in any conceivable situation, want identified to the plaintiffs in a post-collision fuel-fed fire case, and the documents he generated are undoubtedly some of the potentially most harmful and most damaging were they ever to be produced.[108]

In the initial cases brought against GM, the company's defense was that the engineer's thinking was his own and did not reflect company policy. However, when the 1981 lawyer commentary was found as part of discovery in a Florida case in 1998, GM lost that line of defense. In the Florida case in which a thirteen-year-old boy was burned to death in a 1983 Oldsmobile Cutlass station wagon, the jury awarded his family $33 million.

The two documents have become the center of each case. Judge Ernest G. Williams of Los Angeles Superior Court, who upheld the verdict in the $4.9 billion Los Angeles case but reduced the damages, wrote in his opinion,

> The court finds that clear and convincing evidence demonstrated that defendants' fuel tank was placed behind the axle of the automobiles of the make and model here in order to maximize profits—to the disregard of public safety.[109]

As of 2006, there were still class-action lawsuits pending around the country. The suits center on GM's midsize "A-cars," which include the Malibu, Buick Century, Oldsmobile Cutlass, and Pontiac Grand Prix. Approximately 7.5 million cars are equipped with this gas-tank design. On appeal, the Los Angeles verdict was, as mentioned above, reduced from $4.9 billion (total) to $1.2 billion.[110]

Discussion Questions

1. Why do you think the drunk driver was not held responsible for the Los Angeles accident?
2. If you had found the 1973 memo, what would you have done with it?
3. What happens over time when memos such as this engineer's discussion are concealed?
4. What did the GM managers miss in ignoring the engineer's concerns? Why do you think they said he was acting on his own? If an employee writes a memo about the company's product, is the employee ever acting on his or her own?
5. Offer some general lessons from these two cases for business managers and for yourself when you enter the business world.

Case 7.12

Toyota: Sudden Acceleration or Bad Drivers or Pesky Floor Mats?

Introduction and History of SUA

Audi barely survived its sudden-acceleration problem in the 1980s, when about 1,000 Audi 5000 owners said that their cars were suddenly accelerating. Audi would issue five recalls on the cars before it and the National Highway Safety Traffic Administration (NHSTA) were able to conclude that it was driver error, the accidental placement of

---

[108]Milo Geyelin, "How an Internal Memo Written 26 Years Ago Is Costing GM Dearly," *Wall Street Journal*, September 29, 1999, pp. A1, A6.

[109]*Id.*

[110]Margaret A. Jacobs, "BMW Decision Used to Whittle Punitive Awards," *Wall Street Journal*, September 13, 1999, p. B2.

the foot on the accelerator instead of the brake. However, there were dissenters among the causation teams. The dissenters felt that there was indeed a problem with sudden unintended acceleration (SUA) that could be solved only with the installation of a shift-interlock system, something the NHTSA was not willing to mandate on the basis of the Audi or isolated SUA cases that followed. However, SUA would reemerge in 2007 as another auto maker, Toyota, experienced the mysterious phenomenon.

Toyota's Issues Begin

The Audi SUA problem unfolded quickly and furiously and quite nearly destroyed a brand. The problems with Toyota's cars and sudden acceleration progressed like a slow simmer of soup on a stove. One bubble would pop up, but then there was quiet. For example, in 2007, Bulent and Anne Ezal drove their 2005 Toyota Camry to the Pelican Beach Restaurant in Pismo Beach, California. The restaurant is on a cliff that overlooks the Pacific Ocean. Mr. Ezal was applying the brakes as he drove the car down the steep grade to its parking lot below. When he stopped after finding a parking place, he said the Camry accelerated suddenly and took its two occupants over the seaside cliff, plunging 70 feet onto rocks below and overturning. Anne was killed, but Ezal recovered.[111]

Later in 2007, Jean Bookout tried to stop her 2005 Toyota Camry on a freeway ramp as she exited. The brakes would not respond. Her use of the parking brake left 100 feet of skid marks, but still the car did not stop. The car came to a halt when it hit a bank of dirt. Jean's passenger was killed and Jean's injuries were severe.[112]

There were other accidents in between these two and reports to the NHTSA requesting an investigation of the root cause of SUA in Toyotas and Lexus cars. The agency did not pursue the issue at that time because investigations into cause did not reveal any issues with the accelerator or component parts.

Trying to Establish a Causal Connection

However, the SUA cases continued, percolating up here and there around the country, in various Toyota and Lexus models. No two accidents were identical, and patterns eluded the NHTSA and others as they attributed the causes of the accident to these factors:

- For elderly drivers, it was driver error or a foot misplaced on the gas instead of the brake
- Floor-mat interference with the accelerator
- Poor pedal placement in certain models
- Mechanical defects
- Electronic defects
- Poor quality suppliers for parts
- A combination of the above
- Intermittent misfires in electronic systems

But following each explanation was another accident in which the previous explanation could not be applied. For example, a Toyota September 2007 internal newsletter praised its engineering safety group with the following kudos, "Wins for Toyota—Safety Group: The company saved $100 million by convincing NHTSA that replacing the floor mats in 55,000 vehicles solved the sudden acceleration issue."[113] However, four days later four people were killed in their Toyota following an SUA and the floor mats were in the trunk at the time of the accident.

---

[111] "Sudden Unintended Acceleration Redux: The Unresolved Issue," 6 *The Safety Record* 13 (June 2009).

[112] *Id.*

[113] James R. Healey and Sharon Silke Carty, "Toyota Memo: Savings on Safety," *USA Today*, February 21 , 2010, p. 2B.

On August 28, 2009, the SUA accident that would find Toyota in the news daily and result in the largest fine and recall in automotive history occurred near San Diego. Mark Saylor, a California highway patrol officer, his wife, their daughter, and his brother-in-law were all killed in a fiery crash in their Lexus that some believed had suddenly accelerated to a speed estimated at 120 mph. Saylor's brother-in-law called 9-1-1 to get help but there was nothing to be done. Officer Saylor can be heard in the background saying, "Hold on guys, pray. Pray." Screams can be heard as the Lexus struck another car, flew off the side of the road, went airborne, and then landed in the San Diego River basin.[114] The emotional reaction to the accident was nationwide and it served to bring Toyota and Lexus owners forward with their complaints about SUA issues.

The Largest Recalls in History

Following the Saylor accidents, more SUA reports and accidents became public. Toyota was left with few choices. For a time it had to suspend sales of new cars. By January 2010, Toyota would issue recalls on 7.7 million vehicles: 5.4 million for floor-mat replacement and 2.3 million to replace gas-pedal assemblies. By May 2010, the NHSTA had received 6,200 complaints from Toyota owners about SUA and released a report indicating that there had been 89 deaths attributable to SUA.[115] However, the NHTSA assessed a $16.4 million fine against Toyota, the highest the agency could assess, for its failure to timely report the complaints that were coming in about SUA.[116] Transportation Secretary Ray LaHood, in assessing the fine said, "We now have proof that Toyota failed to live up to its legal obligations. Worse yet, they knowingly hid a dangerous defect from U.S. officials and did not take action to protect millions of drivers and their families."[117] According to NHTSA, Toyota issued recalls in Europe and Canada in September 2009 on its vehicles there but did not disclose its recall campaign to U.S. regulators. In fact, Toyota had already begun producing redesigned vehicles that included the fixes taken care of in the European and Canadian recalls, but had still not alerted regulators. Further, Toyota did not issue recalls on the same vehicles in the United States until late January 2010.

The Legal Proceedings

As plaintiff's lawyers began class-action suits against Toyota, they released figures on consumers reporting problems to various agencies that indicated there had been 38,000 such complaints filed over SUA events. There are 140 class-action lawsuits pending against Toyota in federal court and dozens more in state courts.

A grand jury in the Southern District of New York has subpoenaed documents from Toyota for its investigation into whether there was any criminal conduct in Toyota's failure to disclose the SUA issues. The Transportation Recall Enhancement and Documentation Act (TREAD) imposes criminal charges against companies that intentionally mislead federal regulators. TREAD was passed following the Ford/Firestone/Explorer vehicle rollovers, a situation that indicated the companies were aware of the issues in other countries but did not disclose the problems to U.S. regulators.[118]

The Doubts

Several studies reached the conclusion that driver error, not Toyota design or production, was responsible in some of the cases of claimed SUA. At least one of the cases

[114]Sharon Silke Carty, "They Died in Toyotas, Leaving Many Questions," *USA Today*, March 1, 2010, p. 1A.

[115]James R. Healey, "89 Deaths May be Linked to Toyota," *USA Today*, May 26, 2010, p. 1B.

[116]Micheline Maynard, "U.S. Is Seeking Maximum Fine Against Toyota," *New York Times*, April 6, 2010, p. A1.

[117]*Id.*

[118]Jayne O'Donnell, "Toyota Could Face Criminal Charges Related to Recall," *USA Today*, March 11, 2010, p. 3B.

that made the news, in which a Prius driver sped along at 90 mph on a San Diego freeway as he talked with a 9-1-1 operator about his SUA problems, has resulted in police concluding that the driver had committed a hoax.

Despite the doubts, Toyota apologized through newspaper and television ads and continued to respond to customers who complained about SUA as it continued the repairs on the recalled vehicles. Some experts wondered whether the company handled the initial stages of the emerging problem appropriately because the public perception of the cars and SUA became irreversible.

Discussion Questions

1. Why do you think the managers at Toyota did not disclose the complaints it was receiving from U.S. Toyota owners or the fact that it was having trouble with SUA in other countries? What is the risk in assuming you have an issue under control?

2. The driver who called 9-1-1 and claimed an SUA event was behind on his payments for his Prius. Evaluate the ethics of this driver.

3. What can you glean about the culture of Toyota from the content of the internal memo on the "win" for the safety team on the mats?

4. Give a list of lessons learned from both the Audi and Toyota SUA experiences.

5. Place the issues with SUA within the legal framework for product liability. What would be the basis of finding Toyota liable?

Case 7.13

E. coli, *Jack-in-the-Box, and Cooking Temperatures*

On January 11, 1993, young Michael Nole and his family ate dinner at a Jack-in-the-Box restaurant in Tacoma, Washington, where Michael enjoyed his $2.69 "Kid's Meal." The next day, Michael was admitted to Children's Hospital and Medical Center in Seattle with severe stomach cramps and bloody diarrhea. Several days later, Michael died of kidney and heart failure.[119]

At the same time, 300 other people in Idaho, Nevada, and Washington who had eaten at Jack-in-the-Box restaurants were poisoned with *E. coli* bacteria, the cause of Michael's death. By the end of the outbreak, more than 600 people nationwide were affected.[120]

Jack-in-the-Box, based in San Diego, California, was not in the best financial health, having just restructured $501 million in debt. The outbreak of poisonings came at a difficult time for the company. However, the company was also at the beginning of what was proving to be an effective ad campaign with the introduction of "Jack," the executive with a white-spherelike head and clown features. The company was making inroads in the market shares of Burger King and Wendy's.

Federal guidelines require that meat be cooked to an internal temperature of 140 degrees Fahrenheit. Jack-in-the-Box followed those guidelines. In May 1992 and September 1992, the state of Washington notified all restaurants, including Jack-in-the-Box, of new regulations requiring hamburgers to be cooked to 155 degrees Fahrenheit. The change would increase restaurants' costs because cooking to 155 degrees slows delivery of food to customers and increases energy costs.

At a news conference one week after the poisonings, Jack-in-the-Box president Robert J. Nugent criticized state authorities for not notifying the company of the 155-degree rule. A week later, the company found the notifications, which it had misplaced, and issued a statement.

---

[119]Catherine Yang and Amy Barrett, "In a Stew over Tainted Meat," *BusinessWeek*, April 12, 1993, p. 36.

[120]Fred Bayles, "Meat Safety," *USA Today,* October 8, 1997, p. 1A.

After the Jack-in-the-Box poisonings, the federal government recommended that all states increase their cooking temperature requirements to 155 degrees. Burger King cooks to 160 degrees; Hardee's, Wendy's, and Taco Bell cook to 165 degrees. The U.S. Agriculture Department also changed its meat-inspection standards.[121]

The poisonings cut sales at Jack-in-the-Box by 20 percent.[122] Three store managers were laid off, and the company's plan to build five new restaurants was put on hold until sales picked up. Jack-in-the-Box scrapped 20,000 pounds of hamburger patties produced at meat plants where the bacteria was suspected to have originated. It also changed meat suppliers and added extra meat inspections of its own at an expected cost of $2 million a year.[123]

Consumer groups advocated a 160-degree internal temperature for cooking and a requirement that the meat no longer be pink or red inside.

A class action lawsuit brought by plaintiffs with minor *E. coli* effects was settled for $12 million. Two other suits, brought on behalf of children who went into comas, were settled for $3 million and $15.6 million, respectively.[124] All of the suits were settled by the end of 1997, with most of the settlements coming from a pool of $100 million established by the company's ten insurers.[125]

Discussion Questions

1. In 1993, Jack-in-the-Box adopted tougher standards for its meat suppliers than those required by the federal government so that suppliers test more frequently for *E. coli*. Could Jack-in-the-Box have done more before the outbreak occurred?

2. The link between cooking to a 155-degree internal temperature and the destruction of *E. coli* bacteria had been publicly known for five years at the time of the outbreak. The Centers for Disease Control and Prevention tests showed Jack-in-the-Box hamburgers were cooked to 120 degrees. Should Jack-in-the-Box have increased cooking temperatures voluntarily and sooner?

3. What does the misplacement of the state health department notices on cooking temperature say about the culture at Jack-in-the Box?

4. A plaintiff's lawyer praised Jack-in-the-Box, saying, "They paid out in a way that made everybody walking away from the settlement table think they had been treated fairly." What do we learn about the company from this statement?

Case 7.14

Peanut Corporation of America and Salmonella

The Peanut Corporation of America was a supplier of processed peanuts to some of the largest food-production companies in the United States, including ConAgra, a major producer of peanut butter. The company was founded by Hugh Parnell Sr. when he was selling ice cream vending machines in the 1960s. When he was restocking a machine he noticed that the peanuts on the Nutty Buddy ice cream cones came from a plant in the North. He decided to begin a company that processed peanuts in the South, where they were grown. The company grew and had plants in Virginia, Georgia, and Texas. Stewart Parnell entered the business in the 1970s, when he complained to his father that those in

---

[121]Richard Gibson and Scott Kilman, "Tainted Hamburger Incident Heats Up Debate over U.S. Meat-Inspection System," *Wall Street Journal*, February 12, 1993, pp. B1, B7; and Martin Tolchin, "Clinton Orders Hiring of 160 Meat Inspectors," *New York Times*, February 12, 1993, p. A11.

[122]Ronald Grover, Dori Jones Yang, and Laura Holson, "Boxed in at Jack-in-the-Box," *BusinessWeek*, February 15, 1993, p. 40.

[123]Adam Bryant, "Foodmaker Cancels Expansion," *New York Times*, February 15, 1993, p. C3.

[124]Bob Van Voris, "Jack-in-the-Box Ends E-Coli Suits," *National Law Journal*, November 17, 1997, A8.

[125]*Id.*

his major, oceanography, often ended up working on oil rigs. His father offered him a job, and Stewart left college to begin work in the Virginia facilities. The company's sales grew and in 1995, the Parnells sold the company to Morvan Partners LLP. Stewart worked as a consultant for the new buyer, but bought back the company in 2000.

Peanut Corporation's base was sold to its customers for use in peanut butter, ice cream, cookies, and crackers. Peanut Corporation was known for its cost-cutting. When a customer came back with a bid from another peanut product base that was lower, Stewart Parnell, the CEO of Peanut Corporation would always cut the price by a few cents in order to win over the potential customer.

The price cuts were possible because of cost-cutting at the plant. Peanut Corporation paid low wages to temporary workers and offered few benefits programs. E-mails reflect Parnell's concerns about costs. When a salmonella test was positive, Peanut Corporation was required to hold off shipment for a retest. However, in response, Parnell wrote in an e-mail, "We need to discuss this. Beside the cost, this time lapse is costing us $$$$ and causing us obviously a huge lapse from the time when we pick up the peanuts until the time we can invoice."[126] He also wrote, about the product he was informed had tested positive for salmonella, "Turn them loose."[127] When the FDA made the connection between Peanut Corporation and the salmonella poisonings, Mr. Parnell wrote that, "Obviously we are not shipping any peanut butter products affected by the recall but desperately at least need to turn the raw peanuts on the floor into money."[128]

Following the discovery of Peanut Corporation as the source of salmonella in peanut products that were sickening customers in forty-four states, Congress held hearings into Peanut Corporation's operations. Stewart Parnell took the Fifth Amendment when members of the Commerce Committee in the House of Representatives asked him questions about his company.

The peanut product caused 644 illnesses in forty-four states and probably resulted in eight deaths because of the salmonella that then made its way into peanut butter, peanut butter crackers, and other products that use a peanut base. The company declared Chapter 7 bankruptcy on February 13, 2009.

Discussion Questions

1. Discuss the theories for imposing liability on Peanut Corp.
2. Discuss whether Mr. Parnell could be held criminally liable.
3. Are the e-mails admissible as evidence?
4. Mr. Parnell's father, Hugh Parnell Sr., said, "He's being railroaded. Why would anybody send something out that would ruin his own company? It's like an auto dealer sending a car out with no brakes."[129] What defense is he raising for his son?

Sources

Jane Zhang, "Peanut Corp. for Bankruptcy," *Wall Street Journal*, February 14–15, 2009, p. A3.
Julie Schmidt, "Peanut President Refuses to Testify," *USA Today*, February 12, 2009, p. 2B.

[126]Jane Zhang and Julie Jargon, "Peanut Corp. Emails Cast Harsh Light on Executive," *Wall Street Journal*, February 12, 2009, p. A3.
[127]*Id.*
[128]*Id.*
[129]Ilan Bray and Julie Jargon, "Career in Peanuts Began as a Detour From Oceanography," *Wall Street Journal*, Feb. 19, 2009, p. A6.

Product Sales

The way a company sells is as important as what it sells. Good hustle wins sales, but too much hustle can cross ethical and then legal lines.

Case 7.15

Pfizer and the $2.3 Billion Fine for Sales Tactics

Pfizer has agreed to pay the largest health care fraud settlement in the history of the United States—$2.3 billion. The criminal portion of the fine, $1.195 billion, is the largest criminal fine ever imposed in any crime or matter in the United States. The remaining $1 billion is being paid to settle civil damages. Pfizer has agreed to pay the civil and criminal penalties because of its practices related to off-label marketing. Off-label marketing is prohibited by federal law and occurs when a company makes representations about one of its products that are not approved by the Food and Drug Administration (FDA). Prescription drugs are approved for sales only for the FDA-designated uses. Physicians are able to use their discretion in treatment to prescribe drugs for what research may show are beneficial uses, but sales representatives of pharmaceutical (pharma) companies cannot then tout those off-label uses.

There are many prescription drugs on the market that are approved for one use but are then prescribed by physicians to treat other illnesses for which they have not been approved. The difficulties for pharma companies arise when the sales force is asked about the nonapproved use. The reps are not permitted to make any representations about the nonapproved use, but the line is a fine one between disclosure of nonapproved uses and marketing for that nonapproved use.

The Justice Department referred to Pfizer as a four-time offender. One of those previous violations began when former sales representative, John Kopchinski, questioned Pfizer's marketing of Bextra. Bextra, which has since been removed from the market because of a side effect of a rare, but sometimes fatal skin reaction, was approved by the FDA for treating rheumatoid arthritis, osteoarthritis, and menstrual pain. However, doctors were prescribing Bextra for relieving pain following joint replacement, such as knee replacements. When Kopchinski questioned Pfizer's marketing tools and materials, he was fired. He filed a wrongful termination suit. Five other Pfizer employees would also file similar suits and the six will be splitting $102 million, their take of the fine Pfizer will pay. Mr. Kopchinski will receive $51.5 million of that amount. He has said, "At Pfizer, I was expected to increase profits at all costs, even when sales meant endangering lives."

Mr. Kopchinski also told the BBC, "It's hard to do what's right when everyone around you is following management sales directives." He also referred to his experience as one of "swimming upstream."

At the time Mr. Kopchinski raised his concerns to his managers, he was earning $125,000 per year and his wife was pregnant with twins. After he was fired, he resorted to living on his retirement pay from the military of $40,000 per year. He is a Gulf War veteran. He also depleted his savings from the point at which he was fired in 2003 until the settlement on September 2, 2009. Mr. Kopchinski was a valued Pfizer employee, having been hired by then-CEO Edward Pratt in 1992 after their correspondence during the Gulf War sparked a friendship.

However, Pfizer's record was not clean when the Mr. Kopchinski suit emerged. Mr. Kopchinski had been with Pfizer, selling Pfizer's drug Neurontin, when the company was hit with fines and another whistle-blower suit in the late 1990s over off-label marketing for Neurontin. Mr. Kopchinski said at the time that he was told by company managers that when physicians asked about the news stories on Neurontin that they were to explain that the litigation was the result of disgruntled former employees seeking revenge. Neurontin was approved as an anticonvulsant for use in treating patients with epilepsy. However, doctors had been prescribing it for psychiatric patients with anxiety as well as for treating the pain associated with shingles. The markets for the nonapproved uses are much larger than the market for anticonvulsants.

In the pharma industry, employees who are terminated and win wrongful termination suits often receive large settlements or verdicts because they are, in effect, blackballed in the industry and are unable to return to their former line of work, no matter which company.

Discussion Questions

1. Discuss the restrictions the FDA puts on marketing. Do they make it difficult for sale reps? Do they deprive patients of useful drugs?
2. Discuss what happens with a corporation convicted of a crime.
3. What are the cultural issues when employees raise questions in a company? Why do some situations require employees to go outside the company to obtain a response to their concerns?
4. Discuss the fine line pharma reps may have to walk when discussing their companies' drugs with physicians who are curious about off-label uses. For example, what if a physician who is accepting payments from Pfizer speaks at a conference and discusses the research on off-label use of Pfizer's drugs? Could the reps cite the doctor? Could the reps cite the research? Would doctors who accept the payments from Pfizer also need to abide by the off-label rules? One doctor has noted that he knew exactly what to say to get in the off-label use information without violating FDA regulations. Describe this doctor's ethical posture and discuss its impact on Pfizer.

Sources

Rita Rubin, "Pfizer Fined $2.3B for Illegal Marketing," *USA Today*, September 3, 2009, p. 1B.
www.doj.gov. Accessed June 10, 2010.
www.pharmablog.com. Accessed June 10, 2010.

Case 7.16

The Mess at Marsh McLennan

Background and Structure

Marsh McLennan (MMC) is a multinational insurance broker that, at its peak in 2004, had 43,000 employees at offices around the world.[130] MMC's revenues were $2 billion more than its closest competitor, Aon Corporation.[131] MMC is actually a conglomerate

---

[130]Monica Langley and Ianthe Jeanne Dugan, "How a Top Marsh Employee Turned the Tables on Insurers," *Wall Street Journal*, October 23, 2004, pp. A1, A9. Some put the number of employees at 60,000. Gretchen Morgenson, "Who Loses the Most at Marsh? Its Workers," *New York Times*, October 24, 2004, pp. 3–1 (Sunday Business 1), 9.

[131]Monica Langley and Theo Francis, "Insurers Reel from Bust of a 'Cartel,'" *Wall Street Journal*, October 18, 2004, pp. A1, A14.

that consists of Marsh, its risk and insurance division; Putnam Investments, a mutual fund and investment management company; and Mercer, Inc., a human resources consulting company.

Regulatory and Legal Problems Emerge

Following a series of earnings restatements in the 2001 through 2003 period, MMC was hit with additional Securities and Exchange Commission (SEC) investigations on its Putnam Investments. The result was suits by Putnam's mutual fund customers, and fines paid to the SEC to settle allegations with that agency. The suits by the mutual fund holders were settled with payouts. In 2003, Putnam was the first of the mutual fund companies charged with showing favoritism to certain customers by allowing them to buy and sell shares at the expense of lesser customers in order to retain the greater (larger-investor) customers.[132]

Running parallel to the restatements and the mutual fund issues were problems at Mercer. Mercer settled charges related to conflicts of interest that had arisen in trying to retain clients by not making disclosures about its relationships. Also, Mercer was involved with former New York Stock Exchange (NYSE) Chairman Richard Grasso's compensation package, an issue that would later cause Mr. Grasso to lose his position for the failure to disclose the full extent of his compensation, something Mercer was fully aware of but did not discuss with NYSE board members.[133]

The Pay-to-Play Ploy

MMC employees, who were generously rewarded for more clients, had developed a "pay-to-play" format for obtaining bids for insurance coverage that was almost a sure thing. The pay-to-play scheme came into play, as it were, when MMC corporate customers came up for renewal on their policies. MMC, as the world's largest insurance broker, had all of its insurers for its corporate customers agree to just roll over their coverage on renewals. MMC's plan was to eliminate all the nastiness of rebidding and competition among insurers for the renewal. Rolling over is, in many ways, both literally and figuratively easier. For example, if Insurer A was up for renewal with Customer Y, Insurers B and C would submit fake and higher bids for Customer Y that MMC would then take to Customer Y. And the no-brainer for executives at Customer Y was to go with the lowest bidder. Then–New York State Attorney General Eliot Spitzer was able to show that MMC did not even have official bids from the competing insurers in some of these rollover situations. MMC sometimes sent bids forward that had not even been signed by the insurers who were playing along at the higher bid. Of course, those who played along and didn't get the renewal had the others play along when their turn came for renewal with an existing customer. There was no competitive bidding, only a façade.

Mr. Spitzer, in filing suit against MMC, referred to it as part of a cartel.[134] In the complaint, Mr. Spitzer quoted this e-mail from an ACE assistant vice president to ACE's vice president of underwriting (ACE is a "competitor" of MMC and American International): "Original quote $990,000. . . . We were more competitive than AIG in

---

[132]Marcia Vickers, "The Secret World of Marsh Mac," *Fortune*, November 1, 2004, pp. 78, 80; and Monica Langley and Ian McDonald, "Marsh Directors Consider Having CEO Step Aside," *Wall Street Journal*, October 23, 2004, pp. A1, A11.

[133]Monica Langley and Ian McDonald, "Marsh's Chief Is Expected to Step Down," *Wall Street Journal*, October 25, 2004, pp. C1, C4.

[134]Alex Berenson, "To Survive the Dance, Marsh Must Follow Spitzer's Lead," *New York Times*, October 25, 2004, pp. C1, C8.

price and terms. MMGB (Marsh McLennan Global Broking) requested we increase the premium to $1.1M to be less competitive, so AIG does not lose the business."[135]

Once MMC got the pay-to-play system in place, its insurance revenue was 67.1 percent of its total revenue.[136] Commissions from these rollovers represented one-half of MMC's 2003 income of $1.5 billion.[137] When MMC agreed to drop the system as part of a settlement with Spitzer's office, it reported a 94 percent drop in its third-quarter profit for 2004 from 2003. MMC's income for 2003 was $357 million, but for 2004, it was just $21 million.[138]

E-mails show that employees understood that they were violating antitrust laws. In one e-mail quoted in the Spitzer suit, an MMC executive (whose name is redacted) even jokes about the practice of sending a fake emissary to a meeting with a customer who was taking bids for insurance renewal. The e-mail read, "This month's recipient of our Coordinator of the Month Award requests a body at the rescheduled April 23 meeting. He just needs a live body. Anyone from New York office would do. Given recent activities, perhaps you can send someone from your janitorial staff—preferably a recent hire from the U.S. Postal Service."[139] The response to this e-mail, in ALL CAPITAL LETTERS, showed some disgust with the process: "We don't have the staff to attend meeting just for the sake of being a 'body.' While you may need 'a live body,' we need a 'live opportunity.' We'll take a pass."[140]

An executive at Munich RE, an insurer that worked with MMC, indicated some concerns in another e-mail:

> I am not some Goody Two Shoes who believes that truth is absolute, but I do feel I have a pretty strict ethical code about being truthful and honest. This idea of "throwing the quote" by quoting artificially high numbers in some predetermined arrangement for us to lose is repugnant to me, not so much because I hate to lose, but because it is basically dishonest. And I basically agree with the comments of others that it comes awfully close to collusion and price-fixing.[141]

As MMC's profitability increased under the pay-to-play scheme, it became more and more difficult to meet the past numbers and even increase them as management was demanding. One branch manager explained, "We had to do our very best to hit our numbers. Each year our goals were more aggressive."[142] Jeff Greenberg, the MMC CEO, frightened even his direct report, Roger Egan, the president and chief operating officer of MMC, who stated to his direct reports in a meeting on the goals and achieving them, "Each time I see Jeff [Greenberg] I feel like I have a bull's eye on my forehead."[143] An accounting employee who was at that meeting provided the information to Mr. Spitzer and agreed to testify if it became necessary. It was never necessary for him to testify because MMC settled the suit, agreeing to pay an $850 million fine.[144] Within two

---

[135]Thor Valdmanis, Adam Shell, and Elliot Blair Smith, "Marsh & McLennan Accused of Price Fixing, Collusion," *USA Today,* October 15, 2004, pp. 1B, 2B.

[136]Langley and Dugan, "How a Top Marsh Employee Turned the Tables on Insurers," pp. A1, A9.

[137]*Id.*

[138]Thor Valdmanis, "Marsh & McLennan Lops off 3,000 Jobs," *USA Today,* November 10, 2004, p. 1B.

[139]Alex Berenson, "Once Again, Spitzer Follows E-Mail Trail," *New York Times,* October 18, 2004, pp. C1, C2.

[140]*Id.,* p. C1.

[141]*Id.,* p. C2.

[142]*Id.,* p. C2.

[143]Langley and Dugan, "How a Top Marsh Employee Turned the Tables on Insurers," pp. A1, A9.

[144]Ian McDonald, "Marsh & McLennan Posts Loss, Unveils Dividend and Job Cuts," *Wall Street Journal,* March 2, 2005, p. C3.

months of the settlement, MMC had cut 5,500 jobs. MMC's share price dropped 28 percent over the same time period. Its revenues dropped 70 percent.[145]

Discussion Questions

1. What cultural issues do you see that affected decisions at MMC?

2. Whose interests were served by the pay-to-play cartel?

3. What thoughts does this case offer for your credo?

Compare & Contrast

Evaluate the thoughts of the insurer who indicates there is no absolute truth. Why did he react differently from the others who were involved in the pay-to-play scheme?

Case 7.17

Frozen Coke and Burger King and the Richmond Rigging[146]

Tom Moore, president of Coca-Cola's Foodservice and Hospitality Division, was looking at sales in the fountain division, a division responsible for one-third of all of Coke's revenues. The fountain division sells fountain-dispensed soda to restaurants, convenience marts, and theaters. Sales were stagnant and he knew from feedback from the salespeople that Pepsi was moving aggressively in the area. In 1999, Pepsi had waged a bidding war to try and seize Coke's customers. Coke held about 66 percent of the fountain drink business and 44.3 percent of the soda market overall. Pepsi held 22 percent of the fountain market and 31.4 percent of the overall soda market. The war between the two giants had been reduced to a price war. One might say that Coke's fountain sales were flat.

However, Moore noted that there was a potential new product line as he looked at the Frozen Coke products. At that time, Frozen Coke was a convenience store item only. Frozen Coke was still a little-known product, and Moore's team at Coke pitched the idea of having Frozen Coke at Burger King along with a national advertising push that would push Coke's fountain sales but also increase food sales at Burger King as customers came in to try the newly available product. Their pitch to Burger King was that Frozen Coke would draw customers and that the sales of all menu items would increase as a result. Burger King was not ready for a marketing push because it had just lived through two marketing disasters. The first was the failure of the introduction of its new fries and another was a costly ad campaign to boost sales of the Whopper, with no impact but a great many angry franchise owners who had been required to help pay for the ads. Before Burger King would invest in another ad campaign, it wanted to see some test marketing results. Burger King asked Coke to do a promotion of Frozen Coke in a test market. Burger King chose the Richmond, Virginia, area as a good test market.

If the Richmond market did not show sales during the marketing test, Moore knew that Coke risked not only no more growth in fountain sales, but also loss of Burger King's confidence and perhaps an open door for Pepsi to win Burger King over.

Promotions and the marketing test in Richmond began in February 2000. Initial sales were not good. Burger King executives made what Coke employees called "excoriating" calls to Coke team members about the poor performance. Coke pulled out all the stops

[145]Ian McDonald, "Marsh Post 70% Drop in Earnings," *Wall Street Journal*, May 4, 2005, p. C3.

[146]The author has done consulting work with the Burger King team of Coca-Cola. All information in this case is from public records and/or third-party publications.

and hired mystery shoppers to make sure that Burger King employees were offering the Frozen Coke to customers as had been directed during the promotion. Coke gave T-shirts and other promotional items to Burger King managers to encourage them to promote Coke sales. John Fisher, the Coke executive who had just been given the Burger King account to manage, was getting more nervous the closer Coke got to the end of the Richmond promotion time frame.

The Coke team told its own employees to buy more value meals at Burger King, the menu item that was being promoted with the Frozen Coke. Finally, Robert Bader, the Coke marketing manager who was in charge of the Richmond test, decided to hire a marketing consultant, Ronald Berryman, to get more purchases at Burger King. Mr. Berryman, who had worked with Coke in the past, developed a plan that included working with the Boys & Girls Clubs in the area. Using $9,000 wired to him by Mr. Bader from Mr. Bader's personal Visa card, Berryman gave cash to directors of these clubs and developed a homework reward program: if the kids came to the clubs and did their homework, they could go and buy a value meal at Burger King. The directors at the clubs assumed that the money for the value meals was a donation from either Burger King or Coke.

The result of the Berryman plan was that the Richmond area Burger Kings had a 6 percent increase in sales during the Frozen Coke promotion. Other Burger King stores had only 0 to 2 percent growth during the same period. As a result, Burger King agreed to invest $10 million in an ad program to promote Frozen Coke. Burger King also invested $37 million in equipment, training, and distribution in order to carry the Frozen Coke in its franchises, but sales did not follow the Richmond pattern. Estimates are that Burger King's total investment in the Frozen Coke promotion was $65 million.

Matthew Whitley, who had been with Coke since 1992, was its finance director in 2000. During some routine audit work at Coke, he ran across an expenses claim from Mr. Berryman in the amount of $4,432.01, a claim that was labeled as expenses for the "mystery shop." Mr. Whitley questioned Mr. Bader about this amount and others, what the funds were for, who Mr. Berryman was, and what the "mystery shop" submission label represented. Mr. Bader responded that the methods might be "unconventional," but they were "entrepreneurial." Mr. Fisher wrote in a memo in response:

> *I would never have agreed to move forward if I believed I was being asked to commit an ethics code or legal transgression. . . . We had to deseasonalize the data in order to have an accurate measure. I am not completely aware of the details of how the shops were executed but take full responsibility for the decision to execute the program.*[147]

Mr. Whitley recommended that Mr. Fisher be fired because of the excessive expense and his authorization for it. Coke did not fire Mr. Fisher, but Mr. Moore took away one half of his bonus for the year, saying in his memo of explanation to Mr. Fisher, "These actions exposed the Coca-Cola Co. to a risk of damage to its reputation as well as to the relationship with a major customer."[148]

However, Coke did fire Mr. Whitley, who then filed suit for wrongful termination. Coke first told Burger King of the issues the day before Mr. Whitley filed his suit. Mr. Whitley's lawyer had contacted Coke and offered to not file the suit if Coke would pay Mr. Whitley $44.4 million within one week. Coke declined the offer and disclosed the Whitley and Frozen Coke issues to Burger King. The Coca-Cola board hired the

---

[147]Chad Terhune, "How Coke Officials Beefed Up Results of Marketing Test," *Wall Street Journal*, August 20, 2003, pp. A1, A6.

[148]*Id.*

law firm of Gibson, Dunn & Crutcher and auditors Deloitte & Touche to investigate Whitley's claim.

Mr. Whitley then filed his suit. The *Wall Street Journal* uncovered the lawsuit in court documents when a reporter was doing some routine checking on Coke and ran a story on August 20, 2003, describing Mr. Whitley's experience and suit.

The reports of the law and audit firms concluded that the employees had acted improperly on the Richmond marketing test. Also, as a result, Coca-Cola issued an earnings restatement of $9 million in its fountain sales.

Burger King's CEO, Brad Blum, was informed of the report following the investigation and calling the actions of the Coke employees "unacceptable," and he issued the following statement:

> We are very disappointed in the actions . . . confirmed today by the Coca-Cola audit committee. We expect and demand the highest standards of conduct and integrity in all our vendor relationships, and will not tolerate any deviation from these standards.

Coke's president and chief operating officer, Steve Heyer, sent an apology to Mr. Blum:

> These actions were wrong and inconsistent with values of the Coca-Cola Co. Our relationships with Burger King and all our customers are of the utmost importance to us and should be firmly grounded in only the highest-integrity actions.[149]

Coke had to scramble to retain Burger King's business because Burger King threatened to withdraw Coca-Cola products from its restaurants. Burger King is Coke's second largest fountain customer (McDonald's is its largest). The settlement requires Coke to pay $10 million to Burger King and up to $21.2 million to franchisees who will still have the right to determine whether they will continue to carry the Frozen Coke products.

Coke continued with its litigation against Whitley, maintaining that he was "separated" from the company because of a restructuring and that his "separation" had nothing to do with his raising the allegations. However, in October 2003, Coke settled the lawsuit for $540,000: $100,000 in cash, $140,000 in benefits including health insurance, and $300,000 in lawyer's fees. Mr. Whitley said when the settlement was reached, "Over the past several weeks I have reflected on my relationship with Coca-Cola, a company I still respect and love. It's become increasingly clear to me that the company has taken seriously the issues I raised. That's all I ever wanted."[150]

Deval Patrick, then–executive vice president and Coke's general counsel, also issued the following statement when the settlement was reached:

> Mr. Whitley was a diligent employee with a solid record. It is disappointing that he felt he needed to file a lawsuit in order to be heard. We want everyone in this company to bring their issues to the attention of management through appropriate channels, and every manager to take them seriously, investigate them, and make necessary changes.[151]

Mr. Fisher was promoted to a top marketing position in the fountain division at Coke in 2003. However, In April 2003, Coke's internal auditors raised questions with

---

[149]Chad Terhune, "Coke Employees Acted Improperly in Marketing Test," *Wall Street Journal*, June 18, 2003, pp. A3, A6.

[150]Sherri Day, "Coca-Cola Settles Whistle-Blower Suit for $540,000," *New York Times*, August 26, 2003, pp. C1, C2.

[151]*Id.*

Mr. Fisher about why he exchanged two Disney theme park tickets that had been purchased by the company for Notre Dame football tickets. Mr. Fisher resigned shortly after, but no one at Coke has offered an explanation.

Mr. Bader is still a marketing manager in the fountain division, but he does not work on the Burger King account.

Tom Moore resigned following both the settlements. A spokesperson for Coca-Cola said, "As he reflected on the events, he felt that change was necessary to avoid distractions and move the business forward."[152] Sales of Frozen Coke at Burger King have fallen to half of Coke's original estimates. Burger King has proposed changing the name to Icee.[153] Coke did sign the Subway chain for its fountain beverages, a contract that gave Coke the three largest fountain drink contracts in the country: McDonald's, Burger King, and Subway.[154] Pepsi had previously held the Subway contract.

As a result of the Whitley lawsuit, the SEC and the FBI began investigating Coke. Coke cooperated fully with the government investigations. In 2005, those investigations were closed with no action taken against the company or any individuals with regard to the marketing scenario or the response to Mr. Whitley's report on the consultant's conduct in the Richmond test market.[155] Coke also settled the channel-stuffing charges in 2005. Although channel-stuffing issues at Coke had emerged in the 1997–1999 time frame, regulatory interest was rekindled when the Burger King issue became public.[156] As part of the settlement, in which Coke neither admitted nor denied the allegations, Coke agreed to put compliance and internal control processes in place and work to ensure an ethical culture. Coke was also able to settle private suits on the channel-stuffing issues.[157] Federal prosecutors investigated the Frozen Coke marketing tests for possible fraud.[158]

Discussion Questions

1. Why did the executives at Coke decide to go forward with the marketing studies? What questions from the models you have studied could they have asked themselves in order to avoid the problems that resulted?

2. Make a list of everyone who was affected by the decision to fix the numbers in the Richmond test market.

3. Make a list of all of the consequences Coke experienced as a result of the Richmond rigging. "The initial decision was flawed, and the rest of the problems resulted from that flawed decision," was an observation of an industry expert on the Richmond marketing test. What did the expert mean with this observation?

4. List the total costs to Coke of the Richmond rigging. Be sure to list any costs that you don't have figures for but that Coke would have to pay. Do you think those costs are done and over?

5. What lessons should companies learn from the Whitley firing and lawsuit? What changes do you think Coke has made in its culture to comply with the SEC settlement requirements? Are there some lessons and elements for a credo in the conduct of individuals in this case?

[152]Sherri Day, "Coke Executive to Leave His Job after Rigged Test at Burger King," *New York Times*, August 26, 2003, pp. C1, C2.

[153]Terhune, "How Coke Officials Beefed Up Results of Marketing Test," pp. A1, A6.

[154]Sherri Day, "Subway Chain Chooses Coke Displacing Pepsi," *New York Times*, November 27, 2003, pp. C1, C2.

[155]"Coke Settles with SEC," http://www.BevNet.Com, April 19, 2005. Accessed June 10, 2010.

[156]Betsy McKay and Chad Terhune, "Coca-Cola Settles Regulatory Probe," *Wall Street Journal*, April 19, 2005, p. A3.

[157]Sherri Day, "Coke Employees Are Questioned in Fraud Inquiry," *New York Times*, January 31, 2004, pp. B1, B14.

[158]Kenneth N. Gilpin, "Prosecutors Investigating Suit's Claims against Coke, *New York Times*, July 13, 2003, pp. B1, B4; and Chad Terhune, "Coca-Cola Says U.S. Is Probing Fraud Allegations," *Wall Street Journal*, July 14, 2003, p. B3.

Case 7.18

Slotting: Facilitation, Costs, or Bribery?[159]

Finding "Bearwiches" on the cookie shelf in your grocery store will be a daunting task. Locating some "Frookies," a line of fat-free, sugarless cookies, will take you on a journey through various aisles in the store, and you may find them at knee level in the health foods section. You can find packaged Lee's Ice Cream from Baltimore in Saudi Arabia and South Korea, but it will not be found on the grocery store shelves in Baltimore. The difficulty with finding these items is not that they are not good products. The manufacturers of these products cannot afford to buy shelf space. The shelf space in grocery stores is not awarded on the basis of consumer demand for Bearwiches or Frookies. Shelf space in grocery stores is awarded on the basis of the manufacturer's willingness to pay "slotting" fees. If manufacturers pay, they are given a space on the grocer's shelf. If the slotting fees are not paid, the product is not sold by the grocer.

Slotting fees are fees manufacturers pay to retailers in order to obtain retail shelf space.[160] The practice has been common in the retail grocery industry since 1987. The origins of slotting fees are unclear, with different parties in the food chain offering various explanations. Retailers claim slotting was started by manufacturers with the fees paid to retailers as an inducement to secure shelf space. Another theory of origin offered by retailers is that manufacturers use slotting fees to curtail market entrants. If a manufacturer buys more space with additional fees, the market can be controlled by existing manufacturers. Manufacturers claim slotting was started by retail grocers as a means of covering the bookkeeping and warehousing costs of the introduction of a new product. However, two things are clear. First, the practice of affiliated fees for sale has expanded to other industries. The retail book industry, particularly the large chains, now demands fees from publishers for shelf slots and displays for their books. In malls, developers and landlords now demand sums as large as $50,000 from tenants or prospective tenants before a lease can be negotiated or renegotiated. These fees for a position in the mall are referred to as *key money* or *negative allowances*. In certain areas, home builders are demanding "access fees" or "marketing premiums" from appliance makers and other residential construction suppliers for use of their products in the builders' developments. In the computer software industry, the packaging of software programs with computers ensures sales and requires a fee. Even the display of programs in electronic stores is subject to a fee. The second clearly evolving trend in affiliated fees is that the practice is inconsistent and the purposes of the fees are unknown. Fees differ from manufacturer to manufacturer, from product to product, and from retailer to retailer.

How Slotting Works

Food manufacturers produce more than 10,000 new products each year. However, store shelf space remains fixed. Because profit margins at grocery stores hover at very narrow levels of only 1 to 2 percent of sales,[161] additional shelf space would not increase profits or produce guaranteed returns from the new products displayed there. In addition, grocers must assume the risk of allocating shelf space to a new product that would not sell

---

[159]Portions adapted from Robert J. Aalberts and Marianne M. Jennings, "The Ethics of Slotting: Is This Bribery, Facilitation, Marketing or Just Plain Compensation?" *Journal of Business Ethics* 20 (1999): 207–15. Reprinted with kind permission of Kluwer Academic Publishers.

[160]*Slotting fees* actually pertain to obtaining space in the grocer's warehouse. *Shelf fees*, which are fees for placement on the shelf, are also charged by some grocery retailers.

[161]Costs in the retail grocery industry are relatively fixed and cannot be readily reduced. Union wages and other unmanageable cost elements preclude effective efforts at increasing profit margins. Further, competition from the "club" stores (e.g., Costco, Sam's Club, and Price Club) is intense.

at a level sufficient to provide even the narrow margins. Retail grocers must absorb the cost of warehousing the product, accounting for it in inventory, bar coding it, and eventually stocking the shelves with it.[162] In many cases, particularly where the manufacturer is a small company, there has been little or no advertising of the product, and the retail grocer must also incur the cost of advertising the product in some way or offer in-store coupons to entice customer purchases. To the retail grocer, the introduction of a new product and the allocation of precious shelf space is a high-cost risk. There are no guarantees that a new product will garner sales, and there is the downside of the loss of revenue from whatever product is displaced by the new product. To retail grocers, a slotting fee is a means of insulation from the risk of new product introduction and a means of advance recoupment of costs.

Within some retail grocery chains, slotting fees represent the net profits for the organization. Similar to the rental car industry in which earnings come from renters' fees for insurance, car seats, and additional driver coverage, some retail grocers' profits come not from the sales of food but from the fees manufacturers pay for access.

The level and nature of slotting fees vary significantly. Some retailers have a flat fee of $5,000 per product for introduction. Other retailers have a graduated fee schedule tied to the shelf space location. Eye-level slots cost more than the knee- or ground-level slots. The prime spaces at the ends of grocery aisles bring premium slotting fees because those spaces virtually ensure customer attention.[163] Other stores require that a "kill fee" be paid when a product does not sell. One supermarket chain requires $500 just for a manufacturer to make an appointment to present a new product. Some retailers will not accept a new product even with a slotting fee. Small businesses often incur the cost of product development only to be unable to place the product with grocery stores.

Some stores charge a slotting fee, an additional fee if the product is new, and a "failure fee" on new products to cover the losses if the product fails to sell. A new fee, called the *staying fee,* has also developed. A staying fee is an annual rent fee that prevents the retailer from giving a manufacturer's product slot to someone else. Some manufacturers offer to buy out the product in existing space in order to make room for their product. A 1988 survey found that 70 percent of all grocery retailers charge slotting fees, with one retail store disclosing that its $15-per-store per-product slotting fees bring in an additional $50 million in revenue each year.[164] Examples of various slotting fees paid and documented are found in Table 7.2. The most typical slotting fee for a new product to be placed with a grocery retailer was $10,000. Slotting fees do not typically come down over time, even if the product sells well. At the retail level for CD-ROM sales, the producers pay a 20 percent fee per shipment, regardless of whether their product is in demand.

The Legal Issues Surrounding Slotting

The chairman of the board of a small food manufacturer in Ohio wrote to his congressman and described slotting fees in this way: "This is nothing but a device to extort money from packers and squeeze all the independent and smaller processors off the shelves and out of business. We believe this is the most flagrant restraint of trade device

---

[162]The cost of shelving is that of the labor and materials involved in simply changing the shelf sign. Shelf fees are typically a minimal amount, such as $50.

[163]Referred to as *prime real estate* in the industry, slotting fees follow a graduated schedule for the locations. Amounts vary according to aisle space. Bread-slotting fees are $500 to $1,000 per bread type. Ice cream, with one small segment in frozen foods, brings $25,000 per flavor.

[164]No convenience store chains charge slotting fees. However, convenience stores do not warehouse inventory. Manufacturers deliver directly to the convenience stores (from interviews conducted by the author).

Payer	Amount	Terms	Payee
Truzzolino Pizza Roll	$25,000	Chain-wide	
Old Capital Micro-wave Popcorn	$86,000	Chain-wide for $172,000	ShopRite stores
United Brands	$375,000	Frozen fruit juice bar	New York City–area stores
Apple & Eve	$150,000	Fruit punch product	Limited stores in Northeast
Frookies	50 cents per box Increased price (from $1.79 to $2.29)	Sugar-free cookies	100 stores Various
Frito-Lay	$100,000	New product	Each grocery store chain
Lee's Ice Cream	$25,000 per flavor	Ice cream	Each grocery
Bread	$1,500 per store per bread	Chain-wide cost is $100,000	Chains
General, manufacturers, and producers	$15,000–$30,000 per SKU (item)	New products—chain-wide	Chains[165]

yet conceived."[166] The Senate Small Business Committee's investigation included a report on an interview with one small manufacturer who said, "I know for a fact that my competition is paying the lease on the buyer's BMW."[167] When the Senate hearings were held, many of the manufacturers appeared behind a screen at the hearing and used voice-altering technology because of their expressed fear of retaliation from distributors and stores for speaking out on the extent of the fees and the problems of under-the-table payments that have sprung from the practice. One manufacturer testified with a grocery bag on his head.

The Federal Trade Commission has investigated both slotting and rebate fees for possible antitrust implications. The American Antitrust Institute notes that there is an "absence of reliable industry-wide information" on slotting fees and a "pervasive secrecy surrounding what actually occurs among the major players."[168] It is possible that a slotting fee might fall under the legally prohibited conduct of commercial bribery. However, for a successful prosecution for payment of a bribe, the conduct required must be that in which funds are paid by a seller to a buyer solely for the purpose of acquiring a contract or business opportunity (in the case of slotting, a space on the shelf). As noted earlier, however, the reality is that there are costs associated with awarding an item shelf space.

---

[165]Updated from Robert J. Aalberts and Marianne M. Jennings, "The Ethics of Slotting: Is This Bribery, Facilitation, Marketing or Just Plain Compensation?" *20 Journal of Business Ethics* 207 (1999). A 1997 survey indicates the following: Usual slotting fees: Retailers vary from free to $20,000 per SKU (product). Wholesalers: $500 to 10,000 per SKU. Manufacturers: $500 to 10,000 per SKU. The figures in the chart were updated through May 2001.

[166]Slotting: Fair for Small Business and Consumers? Hearing before the Committee on Small Business, U.S. Senate, 106th Congress, 1999.

[167]Roger K. Lowe, "Stores Demanding Pay to Display Products on Shelves, Panel Told," *Columbus Dispatch*, September 15, 1999, p. 1H.

[168]Aalberts and Jennings, "The Ethics of Slotting," p. 207.

If the funds are simply received by the retailer and used for general operating expenses that include advertising, bookkeeping, and warehousing, then the notion that a slotting fee is commercial bribery does not fit within the *actus reus,* or the required conduct, for criminal prosecution.[169]

Regardless of legalities, the use of slotting fees creates an atmosphere of confusion. It is unclear how slotting payments are made and where the payments are reported. Many small business owners report that the payments they make to grocery retailers must be made in cash. Some owners report that payments are made in cash both to the chain and to individual store managers. The atmospheric result is that there are large amounts of cash changing hands among sellers, managers, and purchasers. The former CEO of Harvest Foods, a food retailer in the South, has been indicted on charges of bribery and other related offenses for the alleged receipt of hundreds of thousands of dollars in cash for slotting fees.

Because slotting fees are nonuniform and even nonuniversal, it is impossible to understand how the fee structure works, how much the fees should be, and whether the fees are actually related to the costs incurred by retailers in getting a new product to the shelf. The secretive and inconsistent nature of slotting fees and their payment in cash create an atmosphere similar to that in the drug trade.[170] Market entry rights are unclear, fees change, not everyone is permitted to buy into the system, and the use and declaration of revenues are unknown. In at least four reports on the practice of slotting fees, parties on both sides referred to slotting as the grocery industry's "dirty little secret." Cost recoupment, the public airing of the fees, and public accounting disclosures are nonexistent for slotting fees. The secrecy of the fees and the industry's unwillingness to discuss or disclose them are problematic for manufacturers.

From the cost figures offered in Table 7.2, it is safe to conclude that slotting fees could make market entry prohibitive for many small companies. In some instances, fees have gone beyond the initial slotting costs, with some grocery chains now demanding up to $40,000 per year for a company to maintain just a square foot of retail space for its product. Even some of the larger companies have difficulty competing because of the large fees. Frito-Lay recently purchased Anheuser-Busch's Eagle Snacks after Anheuser had spent over $500 million trying to increase its 17 percent market share. Frito-Lay now holds 55 percent of the snack market and pays the largest slotting fees in the grocery industry. Borden ended its foray into the snack market in 1995, and barely survived before it did so. Nearly thirty regional snack companies went out of business between 1995 and 1998. A vice president of Clover Club Foods, a Utah-based snack company, believes Frito-Lay's goal is to be the only salted-snack food company in the country. The Independent Baker's Association has described slotting fees as being "out of control."

The following data were obtained from surveys of members of the retail food industry:

Slotting allowances are a way of penalizing manufacturers for inadequate market tests.

52 percent of retailers, 72 percent of wholesalers, and 77 percent of manufacturers said they disagreed or disagreed strongly.

[169]Again, it is important to note that a retailer may also charge an "advertising fee."

[170]The authors could find only three manufacturers willing to discuss their personal experiences with slotting fees or industry practices. Retribution (i.e., denial of retail access) was cited as the reason for their reluctance. These three manufacturers spoke on condition of anonymity. Two other manufacturers, Richard Worth (Frookies) and Scott Garfield (Lee's Ice Cream), have been public in their discussion of slotting fees. Grocery retailers referred all questions to legal counsel or corporate officers, who declined to be interviewed.

If a supplier can demonstrate adequate market testing of a new product, slotting fees should not be charged.

54 percent of retailers, 50 percent of wholesalers, and 0 percent of manufacturers said they disagreed or disagreed strongly.

Slotting fees hamper a retailer's ability to maximize the effectiveness of his product assortment.

58 percent of retailers, 54 percent of wholesalers, and 94 percent of manufacturers agreed strongly or agreed somewhat.[171]

A 1997 survey by Supermarket Business found the following:

At present, some slotting fees are an "under the table" form of payment.

83 percent of retailers, 85 percent of wholesalers, and 79 percent of manufacturers strongly agreed or agreed somewhat with the statement.

Slotting and Accounting Issues

Slotting has received additional attention since 2003 because of questions and confusion surrounding the accounting for such fees. For example, if promotional fees are to be paid as part of an arrangement between a manufacturer and a retailer, how are those fees to be carried on the retailer's financial statements? Promotional fees may be paid over time, may be tied to the amount sold, or may be conditioned on certain forms of advertising and results. The flexibility in booking those promotional fee revenues has brought attention to several major retailers, including Royal Ahold N.V. and its U.S. subsidiary, U.S. Foodservice. The *New York Times* ran the following description of the activities and issues that resulted in the U.S. Food Services investigation and accounting restatement:

> *Representatives of U.S. Foodservice are rewarded regularly with goodies like Palm hand-held computers, fax machines, vacation travel and even help with college tuition. All they have to do is earn points by persuading their customers to buy more crackers, coffeecake, plastic forks or other products that have made the company's list for intense promotion.*
>
> *Under the program, known as Points of Focus, U.S. Foodservice sales representatives amass points if they increase their sales of certain brands, which include the company's own labels as well as brands from nationally known "preferred vendors."*
>
> *Preferred-vendor status may have more to do with cash than cachet. The companies that get it have been willing to pay U.S. Foodservice for special treatment, former executives of the company say. Such payments are not illegal, and many other food companies have similar programs. But the former executives and others say that the passion with which U.S. Foodservice managers chased those payments shaped the culture of the company, the second-largest food service supplier in the country.*
>
> *The parent company of U.S. Foodservice, Royal Ahold N.V., one of the biggest supermarket operators in the world, is under investigation in the United States after acknowledging that it overstated earnings by at least $500 million over the last two years. The problem, which Ahold disclosed last month, involved U.S. Foodservice inflating promotional payments from its suppliers, falsely increasing its profit. Two top Ahold executives have quit, and others from U.S. Foodservice have been*

---

[171]Adapted from Robert Aalberts, Marianne Jennings, and Stephen Happel, "The Economics, Legalities and Ethics of Slotting Fees," 21 *Journal of Law and Commerce* 1 (2001).

suspended. The Justice Department and the Securities and Exchange Commission are now investigating the company's accounting.[172]

Every major food distributor, with the exception of Sysco, has been the subject of accounting restatements or SEC investigation for issues related to the booking of revenues.[173] Two former vice presidents of Kmart were indicted on federal charges that they lied to accountants about a payment from a supplier and that they used that payment to supplement earnings for the company. Joseph Hofmeister was a divisional vice president of merchandising in Kmart's drugstore division. Enio Montini was a senior vice president and general manager of the same division. Former CEO Charles Conaway and Chief Financial Officer John McDonald were also charged by the SEC with making materially false financial disclosures about Kmart.[174] They are charged with attributing larger amounts of inventory to seasonable demand (i.e., it was being carried for the Christmas season as opposed to disclosing that sales were down) and with failing to disclose agreements to postpone payments to creditors. Interestingly, a panel used by Kmart's board to arbitrate Conaway's termination found that Mr. Conaway acted in good faith and had not committed any fraud. The panel ruled that Mr. Conaway was entitled to his compensation package. The SEC charges, accusing Mr. Conaway of fraudulent reporting, followed several days later.[175]

The charges center on a payment of $42.4 million from American Greetings in 2001. The payment was called an *allowance* or *rebate,* and covered joint advertising as well as rebates and markdowns.[176] The payment was fully booked for that quarter despite accounting rules that require an examination of possible refunds for those fees. Many argue that the accounting there is a gray area on which experts disagree and that there was no criminal intent. In fact, the area of allowances between manufacturers and retailers is one in which many stores are under SEC investigation. Kmart purchased Sears in November 2004 under new ownership.[177]

Discussion Questions

1. Are slotting fees a means of allocating risk?
2. What possible employee temptations exist?
3. Would a schedule of fees change the ethical and economics issues in slotting fees?
4. Are the perceptions of the industry participants a reflection of their questions about the ethics of slotting?
5. Are the accounting issues the result of the secretive nature of the payments?

Compare & Contrast

Note that Sysco, one of the largest food distributors in the United States, was the only food distributor in the industry that did not have to restate its financials based on the accounting for these types of fees. What made Sysco behave so differently from the rest of the industry? Sysco remains financially sound today and is not involved with SEC charges. Were these long-term factors part of the decision process on its accounting practices?

[172]Constance Hays, "At a Food Distributor, Vendors Often Pay to Play," *New York Times,* March 30, 2003, p. C1.

[173]Constance Hays, "Rules Are Loosely Defined in the Food Service Industry," *New York Times,* March 5, 2003, p. C1.

[174]Lorrie Grant, "K-Mart's Former CEO, CFO Face Charges," *USA Today,* August 24, 2005, p. 1B.

[175]Susan Carey, "K-Mart Ex-CEO Cleared of Wrongdoing," *Wall Street Journal,* August 16, 2005, p. A3.

[176]Lorrie Grant, "Former Kmart Executives Face 3-Count Federal Indictment," *USA Today,* February 27, 2003, p. 1B; Amy Merrick, "U.S. Indicts 2 Ex-Executives of Kmart Corp.," *Wall Street Journal,* February 27, 2003, pp. A3, A14; and Constance L. Hays, "2 Officials at Kmart Face Fraud Charges," *New York Times,* February 27, 2003, pp. C1, C7.

[177]Robert Berner, "The Next Warren Buffett?" *BusinessWeek,* November 22, 2004.

Contracts

My word is my bond, unless, perhaps you misunderstood the words that I used? Honoring contract commitments is often costly, and being forthright in negotiations is a challenge many have failed to undertake.

Case 7.19

Intel and the Chips: When You Have Made a Mistake

Intel, which makes components used in 80 percent of all personal computers, introduced the powerful Pentium chip in 1993. Intel had spent $1 billion developing the chip, and the cost of producing it was estimated to be between $50 and $150 each. When the Pentium chip was finally rolled out, Intel shipped 4 million of the chips to computer manufacturers, including IBM.

In July 1994, Intel discovered a flaw in the "floating-point unit" of the chip, which is the section that completes complex calculations quickly.[178]

The flaw caused errors in division calculations involving numbers with more than eight digits to the right of the decimal, such as in this type of equation[179]:

$$\frac{4,195,835}{3,145,727} \times 3,145,727 = 4,195,835$$

Pentium-equipped computers computed the answer, in error, as 4,195,579. Before introducing the Pentium chip, Intel had run 1 trillion tests on it. Those tests showed that the Pentium chip would produce an error once every 27,000 years, making the chance of an average user getting an error one in 9 billion.

In November, Thomas Nicely, a mathematician at Lynchburg College in Virginia, discovered the Pentium calculations flaw described above. On Thanksgiving Day 1994, Intel publicly acknowledged the flaw in the Pentium chip, and the next day its stock fell from 651/8 to 637/8. Intel stated that the problem had been corrected, but flawed chips were still being shipped because a three-month production schedule was just ending. Intel initially offered to replace the chips but only for users who ran complicated calculations as part of their jobs. The replacement offer carried numerous conditions.[180]

On December 12, 1994, IBM announced that it would stop all shipments of its personal computers because its own tests indicated that the Pentium flaw was far more frequent than Intel had indicated.[181] IBM's tests concluded that computer users working on spreadsheets for as little as fifteen minutes per day could produce a mistake every twenty-four days. Intel's then-CEO Andrew Grove called IBM's reaction "unwarranted." No other computer manufacturer adopted IBM's position. IBM's chief of its personal computing division, G. Richard Thoman, emphasized that IBM had little choice: "It is absolutely critical for this industry to grow, that people trust that our products work

---

[178]Evan Ramstad, "Pentium: A Cautionary Tale," *(Phoenix) Arizona Republic*, December 21, 1994, p. C1.

[179]Janice Castro, "When the Chips Are Down," *Time*, December 26, 1994, p. 126.

[180]James Overstreet, "Pentium Jokes Fly, but Sales Stay Strong," *USA Today*, December 7, 1994, p. 1B.

[181]Ira Sager and Robert D. Hof, "Bare Knuckles at Big Blue," *BusinessWeek*, December 26, 1994, PP. 60–62.

right."[182] Following the IBM announcement, Intel's stock price dropped 6.5 percent, and trading had to be halted temporarily.

On December 20, 1994, CEO Grove announced that Intel would replace all Pentium chips:

> *We were dealing with a consumer community that was upset with us. That they were upset with us—it has finally dawned on us—is because we were telling them what's good for them. . . . I think we insulted them.*[183]

Replacing the chips could have cost up to $360 million. Intel offered to send owners a new chip that they could install or to have service firms replace chips for customers who were uncomfortable doing it themselves.

Robert Sombric, the data-processing manager for the city of Portsmouth, New Hampshire, found Intel's decision to continue selling flawed chips for months inexcusable: "I treat the city's money just as if it were my own. And I'm telling you: I wouldn't buy one of these things right now until we really know the truth about it."[184]

Following the replacement announcement, Intel's stock rose $3.44 to $61.25. One market strategist praised the replacement program: "It's about time. It's very clear they were fighting a losing battle, both in public relations as well as user confidence."[185]

Grove responded that Intel's delay in offering replacements was based on concerns about precedent. "If we live by an uncompromising standard that demands perfection, it will be bad for everybody," he said.[186] He also acknowledged that Intel had agreed to sell the flawed Pentium chips to a jewelry manufacturer.[187]

By December 16, 1994, ten lawsuits in three states involving eighteen law firms had been filed against Intel for the faulty chips. Chip replacement demands by customers, however, were minimal.

Intel's internal employee newsletter had an April 1, 1995, edition that spoofed the infamous chip.[188] A spoof form provided in the newsletter required customers with Pentium chips to submit a 5,000-word essay on "Why My Pentium Should Be Replaced."

In 1997, Intel launched two new products: Pentium Pro and Pentium II. A new potential bug, again affecting only intensive engineering and scientific mathematical operations, was uncovered. Intel, however, published the list of bugs with technical information and remedies for both of the new processors. One analyst commented on the new approach, "They have learned a lot since then. You can't approach the consumer market with an engineering mindset."[189]

---

[182]Bart Ziegler and Don Clark, "Computer Giants' War over Flaw in Pentium Jolts the PC Industry," *Wall Street Journal,* December 13, 1994, pp. A1–A11.

[183]Jim Carlton and Stephen Kreider Yoder, "Humble Pie: Intel to Replace Its Pentium Chips," *Wall Street Journal,* December 21, 1994, pp. B1–B9.

[184]Jim Carlton and Scott McCartney, "Corporations Await More Information: Will Consumers Balk?" *Wall Street Journal,* December 14, 1994, pp. B1–B5; and Stephen Kreider Yoder, "The Pentium Proposition: To Buy or Not to Buy," *Wall Street Journal,* December 14, 1994, p. B1.

[185]Carlton and Kreider Yoder, "Humble Pie," pp. B1–B9; "Intel Eats Crow, Replaces Pentiums," *Mesa (Arizona) Tribune,* December 21, 1994, p. F1; and Catalina Ortiz, "Intel to Replace Flawed Pentium Chips," *(Phoenix) Arizona Republic,* December 21, 1994, pp. A1–A8.

[186]Ziegler and Clark, "Computer Giants' War over Flaw in Pentium Jolts the PC Industry," pp. A1–A11.

[187]Otis Port, "A Chip on Your Shoulder—or Your Cuffs," *BusinessWeek,* January 23, 1995, p. 8.

[188]Richard B. Schmitt, "Flurry of Lawsuits Filed against Intel over Pentium Flaw," *Wall Street Journal,* December 16, 1994, p. B3.

[189]James Kim, "Intel Proactive with Potential Buy," *USA Today,* May 6, 1997, p. 1B.

Discussion Questions

1. Should Intel have disclosed the flaw in the Pentium chip when it first discovered it in July 1994?

2. Should Intel have issued an immediate recall? Why do you think the company didn't do that? Discuss what issues their executives missed by applying the models you learned in Unit 1.

3. Was it ethical to offer limited replacement of the chip?

4. A joke about Intel's Pentium chip (source unknown) circulated on the Internet: Top Ten Reasons to Buy a Pentium-Equipped Computer:

   10. Your current computer is too accurate.
   9. You want to get into the Guinness Book of World Records as "owner of most expensive paperweight."
   8. Math errors add zest to life.
   7. You need an alibi for the IRS.
   6. You want to see what all the fuss is about.
   5. You've always wondered what it would be like to be a plaintiff.
   4. The "Intel Inside" logo matches your decor perfectly.
   3. You no longer have to worry about CPU overheating.
   2. You got a great deal from the Jet Propulsion Laboratory.

   And, the number one reason to buy a Pentium-equipped computer: It'll probably work.[190]

   Based on this circulating joke, discuss the long-term impact on Intel of this chip and Intel's decisions on how to handle it.

5. Assume that you are an Intel manager invited to the 1994 post-Thanksgiving meeting on how to respond to the public revelation of the flawed chips. You believe the failure to offer replacements will damage the company over the long term. Further, you feel strongly that providing a replacement is a balanced and ethical thing to do. However, CEO Grove disagrees. How would you persuade him to offer replacements to all purchasers?

6. If you could not persuade Grove to replace the chips, would you stay at the company?

Compare & Contrast

Consider the following analysis (from "Intel Eats Crow, Replaces Pentium," *Mesa Tribune*, December 21, 1994, p. F1):

Regarding your article "Bare Knuckles at Big Blue" (News: Analysis & Commentary, Dec. 26), future generations of business school students will study Intel Corp.'s response to the problems with the Pentium chip as a classic case study in how to transform a technical problem into a public-relations nightmare. Intel's five-point plan consisted of:

1. *Initially deny that the problem exists;*
2. *When irrefutable evidence is presented that the problem exists, downplay its significance;*
3. *Agree to only replace items for people who can demonstrate extreme hardship;*
4. *Continue running your current ad campaign extolling the virtues of the product as if nothing has happened;*
5. *Count the short-term profits.*[191]

List other companies discussed in this book or in other readings that followed this same five-point pattern.

Compare & Contrast

In 2003, the math department at the University of Texas at Austin complained to Dell Computers that its computers were failing. Dell examined the computers for the

---

[190]From memo furnished to author by Intel employee at the time of the Intel chip problems.

[191]"Intel Eats Crow, Replaces Pentiums," p. F1.

university, one of its major customers, and a major tie-in to the student body there, and concluded that the computers were failing because those using them in the math department were performing too many complex math calculations that overtaxed the computers.

However, internal e-mails that surfaced in the discovery process of a class-action lawsuit indicate that the computers sent to UT–Austin had faulty electrical components that were leaking chemicals into the computer, thus resulting in the failures. Ironically, the cause was so clear and so common that all of the computers shipped with these faulty parts failed at the same time.

Despite this knowledge, Dell employees were instructed to tell customers that the problems were not a big issue. Many companies using the computers were relying on the faulty calculations that resulted prior to the failure.

There were also e-mails and instructions to employees about downplaying the problem and "Don't bring this to the attention of the customer proactively. Emphasize uncertainty."[192] In fact, there were safety issues because of the risk of fire from the failed computers with leaking components.

Was Dell's response similar to or different from Intel's?

Dell has settled the litigation that resulted from the failed computers. Is this a difference from Intel's response?

Dell has been a Harvard Business School case since its initial success for its unique strategy, supply chain, production, and distribution. What conclusions can you draw about business acumen and praise and ethical lapses? Why do you think the employees participated in the cover-up of the underlying problems with the computers?

Case 7.20

Sears and High-Cost Auto Repairs

In 1991, the California Department of Consumer Affairs began investigating Sears Auto Repair Centers. Sears' automotive unit, with 850 repair shops nationwide, generated 9 percent of the merchandise group's $19.4 billion in revenues. It was one of the fastest growing and most profitable divisions of Sears over the previous two years.

In the California investigation, agents posed as customers at thirty-three of the seventy-two Sears automotive repair shops located from Los Angeles to Sacramento. They found that they were overcharged 90 percent of the time by an average of $223. In the first phase of the investigation, the agents took thirty-eight cars with worn-out brakes but no other mechanical problems to twenty-seven Sears shops between December 1990 and December 1991. In thirty-four of the cases, the agents were told that their cars needed additional work. At the Sears shop in Concord, a San Francisco suburb, the agent was overcharged $585 to replace the front brake pads, front and rear springs, and control-arm bushings. Sears advertised brake jobs at prices of $48 and $58.[193]

In the second phase of the investigation, Sears was notified of the investigation and ten shops were targeted. In seven of those cases, the agents were overcharged. No springs and shocks were sold in these cases, but the average overcharge was $100 per agent.

Up until 1990, Sears had paid its repair center service advisors by the hour rather than by the amount of work.[194] But in February 1990, Sears instituted an incentive compensation policy under which employees were paid based on the amount of repairs

---

[192]Ashlee Vance, "Suit Over Faulty Computers Highlights Dell's Decline," *New York Times*, June 29, 2010, pp. B1, B2.

[193]James R. Healey, "Shops under Pressure to Boost Profits," *USA Today*, July 14, 1992, p. 1A.

[194]Gregory A. Patterson, "Distressed Shoppers, Disaffected Workers Prompt Stores to Alter Sales Commissions," *Wall Street Journal*, July 1, 1992, pp. B1, B4.

customers authorized.[195] Service advisors also had to meet sales quotas on specific auto parts; those who did not meet the quotas often had their hours reduced or were assigned to work in other departments in the Sears stores. California regulators said the number of consumer complaints they received about Sears shops increased dramatically after the commission structure was implemented.

The California Department of Consumer Affairs charged all seventy-two Sears automotive shops in the state with fraud, false advertising, and failure to clearly state parts and labor on invoices.

Jim Conran, the director of the consumer affairs department, stated:

This is a flagrant breach of the trust and confidence the people of California have placed in Sears for generations. Sears has used trust as a marketing tool, and we don't believe they've lived up to that trust. The violation of the faith that was placed in Sears cannot be allowed to continue, and for past violations of law, a penalty must be paid.[196]

Dick Schenkkan, a San Francisco lawyer representing Sears, charged that Conran issued the complaint in response to bipartisan legislative efforts to cut his agency's funding because of a state budget crunch and claimed, "He is garnering as much publicity as he can as quickly as he can. If you wanted to embark on a massive publicity campaign to demonstrate how aggressive you are and how much need there is for your services in the state, what better target than a big, respected business that would guarantee massive press coverage?"[197]

Richard Kessel, the executive director of the New York State Consumer Protection Board, stated that he also had "some real problems" with Sears' policy of paying people by commission. "If that's the policy," Kessel said, "that in my mind could certainly lead to abuses in car repairs."[198]

Immediately following the issuing of the California complaint, Sears said that the state's investigation was "very seriously flawed and simply does not support the allegations. The service we recommend and the work we perform are in accordance with the highest industry standards."[199]

It then ran the following ad:

With over two million automotive customers serviced last year in California alone, mistakes may have occurred. However, Sears wants you to know that we would never intentionally violate the trust customers have shown in our company for 105 years.

Ten days after the complaint was announced, the chairman of Sears, Edward A. Brennan, announced that Sears was eliminating the commission-based pay structure for employees who propose auto repairs.[200] He conceded that the pay structure may have created an environment in which mistakes were made because of rigid attention to goals. Brennan announced the compensation system would be replaced with one in which customer satisfaction would now be the primary factor in determining service personnel rewards, shifting the emphasis away from quantity to quality. An outside firm would be hired to conduct unannounced shopping audits of Sears auto centers to be certain the hard sells

[195]James R. Healey, "Sears Auto Cuts Commissions," *USA Today*, June 23, 1992, p. 2B.

[196]Lawrence M. Fisher, "Accusation of Fraud at Sears," *New York Times*, June 12, 1992, pp. C2, C12.

[197]*Id.*

[198]*Id.*

[199]Tung Yin, "Sears Is Accused of Billing Fraud at Auto Centers," *Wall Street Journal*, June 12, 1992, p. B1.

[200]Lawrence M. Fisher, "Sears' Auto Centers to Halt Commissions," *New York Times*, June 23, 1992, p. C1.

were eliminated. Further, Brennan said, the sales quotas on parts would be discontinued. While he did not admit to any scheme to recommend unnecessary repairs, he emphasized that the system encouraged mistakes and he accepted full responsibility for the policies. "The buck stops with me," he said.[201]

Sears auto repair customers filed class action lawsuits in California, and a New Jersey undercover investigation produced similar findings of overcharging. New Jersey officials found that 100 percent of the Sears stores in its investigation recommended unneeded work compared to 16 percent of stores not owned by Sears.[202] On June 25, 1992, Sears ran a full-page ad in all major newspapers throughout the country. The ad, a letter signed by Brennan, had the following text:

An Open Letter to Sears Customers:

You may have heard recent allegations that some Sears Auto Centers in California and New Jersey have sold customers parts and services they didn't need. We take such charges very seriously, because they strike at the core of our company—our reputation for trust and integrity.

We are confident that our Auto Center customers' satisfaction rate is among the highest in the industry. But after an extensive review, we have concluded that our incentive compensation and goal-setting program inadvertently created an environment in which mistakes have occurred. We are moving quickly and aggressively to eliminate that environment.

To guard against such things happening in the future, we're taking significant action:

We have eliminated incentive compensation and goal-setting systems for automotive service advisors—the folks who diagnose problems and recommend repairs to you. We have replaced these practices with a new non-commission program designed to achieve even higher levels of customer satisfaction. Rewards will now be based on customer satisfaction.

We're augmenting our own quality control efforts by retaining an independent organization to conduct ongoing, unannounced "shopping audits" of our automotive services to ensure that company policies are being met.

We have written to all state attorneys general, inviting them to compare our auto repair standards and practices with those of their states in order to determine whether differences exist.

And we are helping to organize and fund a joint industry-consumer-government effort to review current auto repair practices and recommend uniform industry standards.

We're taking these actions so you'll continue to come to Sears with complete confidence. However, one thing we will never change is our commitment to customer safety. Our policy of preventive maintenance—recommending replacement of worn parts before they fail—has been criticized by the California Bureau of Automotive Repair as constituting unneeded repairs. We don't see it that way. We recommend preventive maintenance because that's what our customers want, and because it makes for safer cars on the road. In fact, 75 percent of the consumers we talked to

---

[201]Gregory A. Patterson, "Sears' Brennan Accepts Blame for Auto Flap," *Wall Street Journal*, June 23, 1992, p. B1.

[202]Jennifer Steinhauer, "Time to Call a Sears Repairman," *New York Times*, January 15, 1998, pp. B1, B2.

in a nationwide survey last weekend told us that auto repair centers should recommend replacement parts for preventive maintenance. As always, no work will ever be performed without your approval.

We understand that when your car needs service, you look for, above all, someone you can trust. And when trust is at stake, you can't merely react, we must overreact.

We at Sears are totally committed to maintaining your confidence. You have my word on it.

Ed Brennan

Chairman and Chief Executive Officer

Sears, Roebuck and Co.[203]

On September 2, 1992, Sears agreed to pay $8 million to resolve the consumer affairs agency claims on overcharging in California. The $8 million included reimbursement costs, new employee training, and coupons for discounts at the service center. Another $15 million in fines was paid in forty-one other states to settle class action suits.[204]

In December 1992, Sears fired John T. Lundegard, the director of its automotive operations. Sears indicated that Lundegard's termination was not related to the controversy surrounding the auto centers.

Sears recorded a net loss of $3.9 billion despite $52.3 billion in sales in 1992—the worst performance ever by the retailer in its 108-year history and its first loss since 1933. Its Allstate Insurance division was reeling from damage claims for Hurricane Andrew in the Gulf Coast and Hurricane Iniki in Hawaii ($1.25 billion). Auto center revenue dropped $80 million in the last quarter of 1992, and Sears paid out a total of $27 million to settle state overcharging claims. Moody's downgraded Sears debt following the loss announcement.

In 1994, Sears partially reinstated its sales incentive practices in its auto centers. Service advisors must earn at least 40 percent of their total pay in commissions on the sale and installation of tires, batteries, shock absorbers, and struts. Not included on commission scales are brakes and front-end alignments (the core of the 1992 problems). Earnings in auto centers have not yet returned to pre-1992 levels. Many of the auto centers have been closed.

There are some who have expressed concerns about the ethical culture at Sears. While incentive systems may have created the auto center fraud problems, consider the following dilemmas involving Sears since the time of its auto center fraud cases:

- Montgomery Ward obtained an order from a federal court prohibiting Sears from hiring employees away from Ward as it works its way through Chapter 11 bankruptcy. The order was based on an e-mail sent from Sears' regional vice president, Mary Conway, in which Sears managers are instructed to "be predatory" about hiring away Montgomery Ward managers.
- A class action civil suit was filed in Atlanta against Sears by consumers who allege that Sears sold them used batteries as new. One of the plaintiffs in the suit alleges that an investigator purchased one hundred "new" batteries from Sears in 1995 (in thirty-two states) and that seventy-eight of them showed signs of previous usage. A Sears internal auto center document explains that the high allowances the centers must give customers on returns of batteries cut into profits and induce the sale of used batteries to compensate. (Sears denies the allegation and attributes it to

[203]"Open Letter," *(Phoenix) Arizona Republic*, June 25, 1992, p. A9.

[204]Barnaby J. Feder, "Sears Post First Loss since 1933," *New York Times*, October 23, 1992, p. C1; and "Sears Gets Handed a Huge Repair Bill," *BusinessWeek*, September 14, 1992, p. 38.

disgruntled former employees and not understanding that a nick does not necessarily mean a battery is used.)[205]

- Sears admitted to "flawed legal judgment" when it made repayment agreements with its credit card customers who were already in bankruptcy, a practice in violation of creditors' rights and priorities. Sears agreed to refund the amounts collected from the 2,700 customers who were put into the program. Sears warned the refunds could have a "material effect" on earnings. The announcement caused a drop in Sears' stock price of 37/8. Sears included the following notice to its credit card customers:

> NOTICE: If you previously filed for personal bankruptcy under Chapter 7 and entered into a reaffirmation agreement with Sears, you may be a member of a Settlement Class in a proposed class action settlement. For information, please call 1-800-529-4500. There are deadlines as early as October 8, 1997 applicable to the settlement.

Sears entered a guilty plea to criminal fraud charges in connection with the bankruptcy issues and agreed to pay a $60 million fine, the largest in the history of bankruptcy fraud cases.[206] The company also settled with the fifty state attorneys general, which included $40 million in state fines, $12 million for state shareholder suits, and a write-off of the $126 million owed by the cardholders involved, which was forgiven as part of the settlement.[207]

Sears also settled the class action suit on the bankruptcy issue by agreeing to pay $36 million in cash and issuing $118 million in coupons to those cardholders affected by its conduct with regard to bankruptcy customers. Sears did not admit any wrongdoing as part of the settlement but indicated the action was taken "to avoid the litigation."[208] Sears spent $56 million in legal and administrative costs in handling the bankruptcy cases.

Sears has been struggling to find its market niche for some time. In 2001, it was forced to close eighty-nine stores as it watched its competitor, Montgomery Ward, close its doors for good.[209] In 2004, Kmart purchased Sears.

Discussion Questions

1. What temptations did the employee compensation system present?
2. If you had been a service advisor, would you have felt comfortable recommending repairs that were not immediately necessary but would be eventually?
3. A public relations expert has said of the Sears debacle: "Don't make the Sears mistake. When responding to a crisis, tell the public what happened and why. Apologize with no crossed fingers. Then say what you're going to do to make sure it doesn't happen again."[210] What

are the ethical standards in this public relations formula?
4. What do you believe creates Sears' culture?
5. Sears' stock price and earnings fell. What lesson is there in these consequences?
6. Compute the total costs of the bankruptcy cases to Sears.
7. Are there principles for a credo for, as an example, the mechanics at the auto centers? What about the lawyers who worked for Sears on the bankruptcy issues?

---

[205]There were questions and investigations surrounding Exide Corporation, Sears' battery supplier. The questions related to the quality of the batteries, and Exide at one point announced that it expected to face criminal indictment for certain of its business practices. Keith Bradsher, "Exide Says Indictment Is Likely over Its Car Battery Sales to Sears," *New York Times*, January 11, 2001, pp. B1, B7.

[206]Joseph B. Cahill, "Sears Agrees to Plead Guilty to Charges of Criminal Fraud in Credit-Card Case," *Wall Street Journal*, February 10, 1999, p. B2.

[207]Id.

[208]Leslie Kaufman, "Sears Settles Suit on Raising of Its Credit Card Rates," *New York Times*, March 11, 1999, p. C2.

[209]Amy Merrick, "Sears to Shut 89 Stores and Report Big Changes," *Wall Street Journal*, January 5, 2001, p. A4.

[210]Nat B. Read, "Sears PR Debacle Shows How Not to Handle a Crisis," *Wall Street Journal*, January 11, 1993, p. A14.

Sources

Berner, Robert, "Sears Faces Controversy over Car Batteries," *Wall Street Journal*, August 26, 1997, p. B2.

Berner, Robert, and JoAnn S. Lublin, "Sears Is Told It Can't Shop for Ward Brass," *Wall Street Journal*, August 13, 1997, pp. B1, B6.

Conlin, Michelle, "Sears: The Turnaround Is for Real," *Forbes*, December 15, 1997.

Flynn, Julia, Christina Del Valle, and Russell Mitchell, "Did Sears Take Other Customers for a Ride?" *BusinessWeek*, August 3, 1992, pp. 24–25.

Fuchsberg, Gilbert, "Sears Reinstates Sales Incentives in Some Centers," *Wall Street Journal*, March 7, 1994, p. B1.

Miller, James, "Sears Roebuck Expects Loss in Third Period," *Wall Street Journal*, September 8, 1992, p. A3.

Patterson, Gregory A., "Sears Debt of $11 Billion Is Downgraded," *Wall Street Journal*, December 11, 1992, p. A3.

"Sears Roebuck Fires Head of Its Auto Unit," *Wall Street Journal*, December 21, 1992, p. B6.

Stevenson, Richard W., "Sears' Crisis: How Did It Do?" *New York Times*, June 17, 1992, p. C1.

Woodyard, Chris, "Sears to Refund Millions to Bankrupt Customers," *USA Today*, April 11–13, 1997, p. 1A.

Products and Social Issues

Sometimes the product is legal, the quality is good, and yet the product does have its issues. In this section, the issues are ones of social responsibility.

Case 7.21

The Mommy Doll

Villy Nielsen, APS, a Danish toy company, introduced the Mommy-To-Be doll in the United States. The doll, named Judith, looks like it is pregnant. When its belly is removed, a baby is revealed inside that can be popped out. Once the baby is removed, the doll's original stomach pops into place. The new stomach is flat and instantly restores Judith's youthful figure.

Teenage girls are intrigued by the doll and call it "neat." However, Diane Welsh, the president of the New York chapter of the National Organization for Women, stated, "A doll that magically becomes pregnant and unpregnant is an irresponsible toy. We need to understand having a child is a very serious business. We have enough unwanted children in this world."[211]

Mommy-To-Be comes with Charles, her husband, and baby accessories. An eleven-year-old shopper said of the doll, "I don't think she looks like a mommy. . . . She looks like a teenager."[212] Mattel also had an expectant mother doll, but, in the background on the box the doll and baby came in, there was a picture of a father standing at-the-ready to help.

Discussion Questions

1. Is the doll a socially responsible toy?
2. Would you carry the doll if you owned a toy store?
3. Would you want your children to have the doll?
4. Why did Mattel take a different approach in its packaging?

Case 7.22

Stem-Cell Research

During the summer of 2001, there was extensive debate over stem-cell research because President George W. Bush was faced with the decision of whether to allow federal funding for the extraction of stem cells from human embryos.

Stem-cell research has strong advocates in the medical and scientific community because of their belief that the research holds great potential for cures for Alzheimer's disease, cancer, spinal cord injuries, Parkinson's disease, diabetes, and a range of other related illnesses.[213] The advocates had strong support from Mrs. Nancy Reagan, wife of President Ronald Reagan, who had suffered from Alzheimer's for nearly a decade, and the late Christopher Reeve, a Hollywood actor with a spinal cord injury. Ron Reagan,

---

[211] "Mommy Doll Makes Birth a Snap," *Mesa (Arizona) Tribune*, May 9, 1992, p. A7.
[212] *Id.*
[213] Robert P. George, "Don't Destroy Human Life," *Wall Street Journal*, July 30, 2001, p. A16.

Mr. Reagan's son, spoke at the Democratic National Convention in 2004 urging the delegates to support embryonic stem-cell research and to vote for Democratic candidate John Kerry for president to ensure that the research developed with federal funding.

However, stem-cell research has its strong opponents among those who believe that life begins at conception, that the "harvesting" of stem cells from embryos is the taking of life, and that encouraging such research is likely to result in the creation of human embryos for purposes of harvesting the cells. These opponents tout adult stem-cell research as an alternative that has been pursued with some success and a solution that avoids what they see as a moral dilemma. They also fear the likelihood of the slippery slope to cloning.[214] Indeed, the U.S. House of Representatives voted to ban human cloning during this time period because of concerns that any federal funding that would be approved might lead to further experimentation.[215] Richard M. Doerflinger, of the U.S. Conference of Catholic Bishops, has called the research "grotesque" and said, "Those who have become accustomed to destroying 'spare' embryos for research now think nothing of taking the next horrible step, creating human life for the purpose of destroying it."[216]

During the time of the debate, the media revealed that the Jones Institute, a private fertility clinic in Norfolk, Virginia, was mixing eggs and sperm to create human embryos.[217]

Mr. Bush, as a compromise position on a hotly debated issue, approved limited federal funding for lines of research on stem cells that were already "harvested." His reasoning was that the cells should not be thrown away.

While the public continued its debate, biotech businesses were gearing up for what they felt would be the new direction for medical research and treatment. For example, Advanced Cell Technology, Inc., began acquiring eggs from female donors for purposes of future research.[218] Later in 2001, Advanced Cell Technology announced that it has successfully cloned a human embryo.[219]

Universities such as Georgetown and Michigan, with extensive cancer research programs, stand to benefit substantially from federal research dollars. Upon President Bush's announcement of his partial approval, biotech stocks soared.

Late in 2007, scientists announced that they had been able to glean all that they needed for stem-cell research without killing the embryos. The *New York Times* included the following observation on the new science:

It has been more than six years since President Bush, in the first major televised address of his presidency, drew a stark moral line against the destruction of human embryos in medical research.

Since then, he has steadfastly maintained that scientists would come up with an alternative method of developing embryonic stem cells, one that did not involve killing embryos.

Critics were skeptical. But now that scientists in Japan and Wisconsin have apparently achieved what Mr. Bush envisioned, the White House is saying, "I told you so."[220]

[214]David Baltimore, "Don't Impede Medical Progress," *Wall Street Journal*, July 30, 2001, p. A16.

[215]Sheryl Gay Stolberg, "House Backs Ban on Human Cloning for Any Objective," *New York Times*, August 1, 2001, pp. A1, A11.

[216]Laurie McGinley, "Nancy Reagan Urges GOP to Back Stem-Cell Research," *Wall Street Journal*, July 12, 2001, p. B2.

[217]Sheryl Gay Stolberg, "Bioethicists Find Themselves the Ones Being Scrutinized," *New York Times*, August 2, 2001, pp. A1, A14.

[218]"Cloning of Embryos for Research Raises Ethics Questions," *Wall Street Journal*, July 12, 2001, p. B2.

[219]Sheryl Gay Stolberg, "Cloning Executive Presses Senate," *New York Times*, December 5, 2001, p. A22.

[220]Sheryl Gay Stolberg, "Method Equalizes Stem Cell Debate," *New York Times*, November 21, 2007, p. A1.

Upon taking office in 2009, President Barack Obama lifted the eight-year ban on federal funding for stem-cell research. In making the announcement of his executive order on March 9, 2009, Mr. Obama said, "These tiny cells may have the potential to help us understand, and possibly cure, some of our most devastating diseases."[221]

Discussion Questions

1. Is it ethical for the Jones Institute to create embryos? What of Advanced Cell Technology's cloning?
2. One bioethicist has questioned the role of bioethicists in the debate, raising the question "Are we being ethical even as we say what is ethical?" What if they are funded by hospitals, biotech companies, and pharmaceutical firms in their research or at their colleges and universities?
3. Is stem-cell research a moral issue that breaks down along religious lines, or are there implications for each side's position?
4. Pope John Paul II, believed to have suffered from Parkinson's disease before his death in 2005, had taken a strong position against stem-cell research and indicated, "The end never justifies the means."[222] What did he mean? Are businesses using this rationalization?
5. Why is the new research so significant as part of this discussion of the use of an embryo?

Case 7.23

Toro and Its Product Liability Program

Toro Company is a manufacturer of lawnmowers, snowblowers, and other forms of household equipment that we think of as just generally smelling of product liability. However, in 1991, Toro began a program of early case resolution that has not only cut its litigation and liability costs but also reduced the time for resolution as well as the number of claims. The program works as follows:

- Within days of hearing from a customer or about an accident, Toro sends one of two paralegals to the customer's home to discuss the accident.
- The paralegals are not accompanied by lawyers, but by engineers.
- The paralegals are dressed casually, in khakis and a Toro polo shirt.
- The paralegals listen to the customer's story about the accident. Sometimes they offer hugs, sometimes they cry, and sometimes they just listen.
- They are authorized to settle cases on the spot, up to five figures.
- They obtain a waiver from the customer in exchange for the payment.
- They are authorized to settle cases that are not Toro's fault. For example, in one case a man was cleaning his Toro lawnmower with the motor running as he sprayed a hose on the blades. The instructions for the mower state specifically that cleaning the mower in this way is very dangerous and that parts could be dislodged and fly in the air or at the customer. The latter is what happened to the customer, but Toro still settled the case and received a "Thank You" note from the customer.
- If the customer does not settle, the complaint then goes to a mediation handled by a Toro lawyer who will offer a settlement that, if not taken, will be Toro's last offer. Those who do not take the settlement go to trial, a very rare event these days at Toro.

Toro's costs for resolving claims have been reduced from an average of $115,000 to $35,000, and its claims have gone down from 640 between 1986 to 1991 to 536 between 1991 and 1996 to 404 from 1996 to 2001. The average time for the settlement of cases has gone from twenty-four months to six months.

[221]www.Whitehouse.gov. Go to March 9, 2009 press releases. Accessed June 10, 2010.
[222]Robert A. Sirico, "No Compromise on Stem Cells," *Wall Street Journal*, July 11, 2001, p. A16.

Discussion Questions

1. What benefit to the shareholders come from the program, if any?
2. List the reasons why Toro would create and use such a program.
3. One law professor has stated that she believes Toro takes advantage of customers before they have the chance to speak with a lawyer. The Toro representatives share with the customers that they have no obligation to meet with them and that they are welcome to halt the meeting and discussion at any time. Also, customers can meet with a lawyer before the meeting if they choose to do so. Do you think Toro takes advantage of injured customers who have not consulted with a lawyer?

Compare & Contrast

Other companies that have followed the pioneering Toro include DuPont and General Electric. Companies that do not follow the Toro model insist that they litigate because they stand behind their products. Others indicate that they don't want to be seen as pushovers and easy marks. Which model do you think serves customers best? Which serves shareholders best?

Sources

Ashby Jones, "House Calls," *Corporate Counsel*, October 2004, 88.
Letter from Ken Melrose, CEO of Toro Company.

Case 7.24

Fast Food Liability

Ashley Pelman, Roberta Pelman, Jazlen Bradley, and Israel Bradley (all youths under the age of eighteen) brought suit against McDonald's Corporation and several of its franchisees, alleging that in making and selling their products they have engaged in deception and that this deception has caused them to consume McDonald's products to such an extent that they have injured their health. Their health problems include being overweight and diabetic. Three of them also have coronary heart disease, high blood pressure, and elevated cholesterol intake.

The following is an excerpt from the district court decision that dismissed the suit brought by the parents of the young people on their behalf.

Sweet, District Judge

Questions of personal responsibility, common knowledge and public health are presented, and the role of society and the courts in addressing such issues. Laws are created in those situations where individuals are somehow unable to protect themselves and where society needs to provide a buffer between the individual and some other entity—whether herself, another individual or a behemoth corporation that spans the globe. Thus Congress provided that essentially all packaged foods sold at retail shall be appropriately labeled and their contents described. The Nutrition Labeling and Education Act of 1990, Pub.L. 101-535, 104 Stat. 2353 (Nov. 8, 1990) (the "NLEA"), 21 U.S.C. § 343(q). Also as a matter of federal regulation, all alcoholic beverages must warn pregnant women against their use. 27 U.S.C. § 215 (forbidding sale of alcohol unless it bears the following statement: "GOVERNMENT WARNING: (1) According to the Surgeon General, women should not drink alcoholic beverages during pregnancy because of the risk of birth defects. . . ."); 27 C.F.R. § 16.21.

Congress has gone further and made the possession and consumption of certain products criminal because of their presumed effect on the health of consumers.

This opinion is guided by the principle that legal consequences should not attach to the consumption of hamburgers and other fast food fare unless consumers are unaware of the dangers of eating such food. . . . [T]his guiding principle comports with the law of products liability under New York law. As Sir Francis Bacon noted, "Nam et ipsa scientia potestas est," or knowledge is power. Following from this aphorism, one important principle in assigning legal responsibility is the common knowledge of consumers. If consumers know (or reasonably should know) the potential ill health effects of eating at McDonald's, they cannot blame McDonald's if they, nonetheless, choose to satiate their appetite with a surfeit of supersized McDonald's products. On the other hand, consumers cannot be expected to protect against a danger that was solely within McDonald's knowledge. Thus, one necessary element of any potentially viable claim must be that McDonald's products involve a danger that is not within the common knowledge of consumers.

McDonald's has also, rightfully, pointed out that this case, the first of its kind to progress far enough along to reach the stage of a dispositive motion, could spawn thousands of similar "McLawsuits" against restaurants. Even if limited to that ilk of fare dubbed "fast food," the potential for lawsuits is great: Americans now spend more than $110 billion on fast food each year, and on any given day in the United States, almost one in four adults visits a fast food restaurant.[223] The potential for lawsuits is even greater given the numbers of persons who eat food prepared at other restaurants in addition to those serving fast food.

The interplay of these issues and forces has created public interest in this action, ranging from reports and letters to the Court to television satire. Obesity, personal liberty and public accountability affect virtually every American consumer.

. . . [T]here is no allegation that McDonald's of New York had in its possession any particular knowledge that consumers did not have that would require it to promulgate information about the nutritional contents of the products.

. . . [T]he plaintiffs only cite two advertising campaigns ("McChicken Everyday!" and "Big N' Tasty Everyday") and to a statement on the McDonald's website that "McDonald's can be part of any balanced diet and lifestyle." These are specific examples of practices, act[s] or advertisements and would survive a motion to dismiss based on lack of specificity. Whether they would survive a motion to dismiss on the substantive issue of whether such practices, act[s] and advertisements are deceptive is less clear. The two campaigns encouraging daily forays to McDonald's and the statement regarding making McDonald's a part of a balanced diet, if read together, may be seen as contradictory—a balanced diet likely does not permit eating at McDonald's everyday. However, the advertisements encouraging persons to eat at McDonald's "everyday!" do not include any indication that doing so is part of a well-balanced diet, and the plaintiffs fail to cite any advertisement where McDonald's asserts that its products may be eaten for every meal of every day without any ill consequences. Merely encouraging consumers to eat its products "everyday" is mere puffery, at most, in the absence of a claim that to do so will result in a specific effect on health. As a result, the claims likely would not be actionable.

---

[223]Eric Schlosser, *Fast Food Nation* 3 (2002).

As noted, the trial court dismissed the suit. However, the appellate court reversed the decision, and the case is now in the discovery and trial stage.[224]

Discussion Questions

1. Are the following questions, raised by lawyers for McDonald's, relevant in resolving this situation: What else did the young people eat? How much did they exercise? Is there a family history of the diseases that are alleged to have been caused by McDonald's products?

2. Why does the court bring up the issue of personal accountability?

3. What would happen if there were a flurry (as it were) of McLawsuits?

4. McDonald's has added a choice of fruit pieces, yogurt, and salads to its menus, with a resulting boost in revenues. What business lessons are there in this decision?

Sources

Pelman ex rel. Pelman v McDonald's Corp., 396 F.3d 508 (C.A. 2 2005).
Pelman v McDonald's Corp., 237 F.Supp.2d 512 (S.D. N.Y. 2003).

---

[224]The full history of the case is as follows: *Pelman v McDonald's Corp.* (Pelman III), 396 F.3d 508, 510 (2nd Cir. 2005). *Pelman* was initially dismissed. *Pelman I*, 237 F. Supp. 2d at 543. An amended complaint was refiled and dismissed. *Pelman v McDonald's Corp.* (*Pelman II*), No. 02 Civ. 7821(RWS), 2003 WL 22052778, at 15 (S.D.N.Y. Sep. 3, 2003). The U.S. Court of Appeals vacated the court's dismissal and remanded the case, see *Pelman III*, 396 F.3d 508, which is pending. See also *Pelman v McDonald's Corp.* (*Pelman IV*), 396 F. Supp. 2d 439, 446 (S.D.N.Y. 2005); *Pelman v McDonald's Corp.* (*Pelman V*), 452 F. Supp. 2d 320, 328 (S.D.N.Y. 2006).

Ethics and Competition

"Capitalism without failure is like religion without sin."

Irwin M. Stelzer, "Our Hapless Automakers," *The Weekly Standard*, June 16, 2010

"I would say everybody out here on the PGA Tour would do the same thing. It's not the end of the world. It will be fine. It is fine."

Golfer J.P. Hayes on his decision to self-report his mistaken use of a non–PGA-approved golf ball, November 21, 2008

A business's relations with its competitors can be a sticky wicket. Producing similar products, poaching employees, and pricing all present areas of ethical challenges that are often about as close to the legal line as ethical issues come. The heat of competition often creates dilemmas on what you can take with you to your new job or just how similar you can make a product to that of your competition.

Covenants Not to Compete

Reading 8.1

A Primer on Covenants Not to Compete: Are They Valid?[1]

Covenants not to compete take two forms. The first type is found in the sale of a business. To keep the seller of the business from trotting down the street and opening up another business to compete, courts enforce covenants not to compete in these business purchase agreements as long as they are reasonable in length and geographic scope. The questions of time and scope are based in economics; that is, how many dry cleaners can be located within this radius and still find a sufficient customer base?

The second type of covenant not to compete is a bit more testy than those found in the sale of a business. This type of covenant applies to employees. Employers require their new hires, as part of their contractual arrangement, to agree not to compete with their employer should they decide to leave their employ. When an owner sells a business, he or she has the income from the sale as a means of a support. When an employee leaves his or her employ, a banishment from that area of doing business, i.e., from using their skills, can be tantamount to a ban on employment.

In dealing with these covenants, courts strike a balance between employees' right to work and employers' right to protect the trade secrets, training, etc. that former employees have and then take with them to another company or use to start a business.

Requirements for Noncompete Agreements

1. The Need for Protection

The laws on noncompete agreements vary from state to state, with California's being the most protective of employees. California's statute in essence prohibits employers from enforcing agreements that prohibit employees from working in their chosen fields.[2] However, across all states, courts are clear in their positions that there must first be an underlying need or reason for the noncompete agreement. The employee must have had access to trade secrets and then start a business in competition with the principal/employer.

2. Reasonableness in Scope

The covenant must also be reasonable in geographic scope and time. These factors depend upon the economic base and the nature of the business. For example, a noncompete in a high-tech employee's contract could be global but must be shorter in duration because technology changes so rapidly. A noncompete for a collection agency could not be global but might be longer in duration because business is one of relationships.

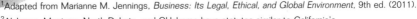

---

[1]Adapted from Marianne M. Jennings, *Business: Its Legal, Ethical, and Global Environment*, 9th ed. (2011).

[2]Alabama, Montana, North Dakota, and Oklahoma have statutes similar to California's.

3. Valid Formation

Noncompete agreements are also subject to the basics of contract law. There must be consideration and there cannot be duress. For example, one dot-com agreed to give its employees stock options if they would sign a noncompete agreement. Amazon.com offered downsized employees an additional ten weeks' pay plus $500 if they would sign a three-page "separation agreement and general release" in which they promised not to sue Amazon over the layoff or disparage it in any way. Amazon has had employees sign a confidentiality agreement at the beginning of their employment that restricts their use of information and knowledge gained whilst working at Amazon.

California has provided protection for employees who refuse to sign noncompete agreements by imposing punitive damages on employers that terminate employees who refuse to sign.

4. Other Theories for Noncompete Enforcement

Some employers have begun to use the tort of tortious interference with contracts as a means of preventing former employees from working for competitors or beginning their own competing business. In those states in which noncompete clauses are unenforceable, interference is used as a means of enjoining the former employee's business activities. For example, in *TruGreen Companies, L.L.C. v Mower Brothers, Inc.* (199 P.3d 929 Utah 2008), the Utah Supreme Court held that a company whose former employer had gone to work for a competing company and recruited other employees to join him was liable for tortious interference.

Another possible avenue of protection is a confidentiality agreement, one signed with employees that prohibits them from disclosing confidential and proprietary information they learned of during their employment. For example, the information in a sealed bid is proprietary. An employee who takes that information along when hired by a competitor breaches a confidentiality agreement. This type of agreement does not prohibit employment, but it does control the type of work the employee can do at the new company.

Discussion Questions

1. What is the balance in covenants?

2. What types of covenants are enforced?

Case 8.2

Boeing, Lockheed, and the Documents[3]

In 1996, Boeing and Lockheed Martin were in a head-to-head competition for a multibillion-dollar government contract for furnishing the rockets that are used for launching satellites into space (a project referred to in the industry as the Evolved Expendable Launch Vehicle, or EELV). The satellites perform various functions and could be communication or spy satellites.

It was during this competitive time frame (1996) for the rocket launcher project that Kenneth Branch, a space engineer and manager at Lockheed facilities in Florida, traveled to McDonnell Douglas facilities at Huntington Beach, California, for a job interview. McDonnell Douglas was working on the rocket bid at the same time that it was being acquired by Boeing. Boeing's acquisition of McDonnell Douglas had been finalized at the time of the Branch interview, but the logistics of acquisition had not yet been completed (it would be completed in August 1997). Boeing's acquisition of

---

[3]The author consulted with Boeing following the ethical scandals to help with employee ethics training. The information here was taken from public documents.

McDonnell Douglas and the combination of Lockheed with Martin Marietta meant that in the future, the federal government would basically be dealing with two large contractors on all of its projects.

Near the end of his interview at McDonnell Douglas, Branch showed the participants in the interview process a copy of Lockheed's proposed presentation for the government project. Six months after his interview, in January 1997, Branch began work at Boeing on Boeing's rocket project, a $5 billion project. The pressure for Boeing to win the contract became intense at that time. Boeing executive Frank Slazer, the director of business development for the project, encouraged Boeing employees working on EELV to develop "an improved Lockheed Martin EELV competitive assessment." He also encouraged the employees to find former Lockheed employees to get their thoughts and impressions about the project.

Sometime during the first quarter of 1997, Lockheed sent Mr. Branch a letter reminding him of his confidentiality agreement with Lockheed and his duty not to disclose any proprietary information in his new position at Boeing. During this same period, a Boeing employee filed a report that she had seen Mr. Branch in the hallway with a notebook that had the Lockheed logo on the outside. She was reprimanded by Tom Alexiou, Mr. Branch's supervisor, for doing so, and no one took any action with regard to Mr. Branch or the notebook.

Shortly after, the project was awarded in what is called a "leader–follower" contract, in which the two companies compete for the term of the satellite launcher program. Boeing did emerge as the leader in that project and was awarded nineteen of the planned twenty-eight rocket launches, a total contract value of $1.88 billion. Shortly after, there were rumblings around the industry and government agencies about Boeing's conduct and possible possession of proprietary documents during the time of the bids. The government began an investigation into whether proprietary documents had passed from Lockheed to Boeing. Boeing also launched, as it were, an internal investigation and fired Mr. Branch as well as one of his supervisors, William Erskine, because it found that the two were in possession of thousands of pages of proprietary documents that included Lockheed Martin information on specifications and cost. The terminations were reported to the federal government along with Boeing's assurances that it had dealt with the situation and completed cleansing its own house.

Mr. Branch and Mr. Erskine filed suit against Boeing for wrongful termination, and document production began as part of the discovery process in the suit. Although the suit was dismissed in 2002, the details of Boeing's internal investigation still made their way into the court case, including documents and a memo describing the conduct of Mr. Branch, Mr. Erskine, and Boeing executives. The interest of the Justice Department was piqued, and its investigation into Boeing's conduct also began in 2002. In one telling exchange, a project specialist, Steve Griffin, confronted Mr. Erskine with his conduct related to the EELV project: Mr. Erskine admitted that he had an "under-the-table" arrangement to get Lockheed bid documents from Mr. Branch and that he did ultimately incorporate what he learned into Boeing's bid. The internal investigation revealed this conversation between the two following that disclosure:

Griffin: We just took a Procurement Integrity Law class. I can't believe you did that.

Erskine: I was hired to win . . . and I was going to do whatever it took to do it.

Mr. Griffin ultimately reported the information to his boss, and the internal investigation resulted.

Boeing and Lockheed had been in a virtual dead heat for military contracts for some time, with Lockheed Martin slightly ahead in 2000 and 2001 and the two nearly tied at

$15 billion each in 2002. There was, as a result, significant bad blood between the two, and each new disclosure led to further investigations by more agencies.

The judge in the Branch and Erskine wrongful termination suit ordered the men to pay Boeing's legal fees, but the two men signed agreements promising not to disclose details about the case or discuss it with the media in exchange for Boeing waiving its rights to collect its legal fees.

At the end of April 2003, Boeing shipped eleven boxes of documents to Lockheed Martin. The documents in the boxes had the Lockheed Martin logo and were stamped "Proprietary." When those documents arrived, the entire sordid history emerged in the press.[4] Boeing did not disclose the issues and investigations surrounding EELV in its SEC documents until May 2003, after a *Wall Street Journal* report on the investigations and litigation appeared. Jim Albaugh, CEO of the Defense Systems Division, indicated that management had not really focused on the inquiries and investigations until that public disclosure.[5]

The scandal then reached Congress, where concerns about government contracts with Boeing arose.[6] Pending at the time of the erupting investigation into the EELV contracts was an $18 billion contract with the U.S. Air Force for the delivery of Boeing 767 tankers, aircraft used to refuel fighter jets in midair. Congress held hearings on the Defense Department's decision to award a tanker contract to Boeing because CEO Albaugh had called Air Force Assistant Secretary Marvin Sambur for help in closing the deal. Mr. Sambur did step in to help, and congressional wrath resulted. U.S. Senator John McCain (R-Ariz.) noted, "It's astonishing. Even in light of serious allegations, they [Boeing] continued to push to railroad the [tanker] deal through, and they still are."[7]

The public relations fallout from the tankers issue not only created a negative reaction in Congress but also created public perception problems. In order to win back public favor and attempt to refute the charges, Boeing ran a series of one-page ads in newspapers around the country, including the *Wall Street Journal*.[8]

Continuing ethical lapses (see Case 9.16 on Boeing's recruitment while bids were pending of a government official who had not recused herself) forced a shake-up in Boeing, with the termination of its chief financial officer (CFO), Michael Sears.[9] On July 24, 2003, the USAF suspended the space launch services business and the three former employees from receiving government contracts for an indefinite period because of Boeing's possession of the Lockheed Martin information during the EELV source selection in 1998. The USAF also terminated seven out of twenty-one contracts from Boeing as a penalty for its conduct with the Lockheed documents.[10] The USAF also disqualified the launch services business from competing for three additional launches under a

[4]Anne Marie Squeo and Andy Pasztor, "U.S. Probes Whether Boeing Misused a Rival's Documents," *Wall Street Journal*, May 5, 2003, pp. A1, A7.

[5]Anne Marie Squeo, J. Lynn Lunsford, and Andy Pasztor, "Boeing's Plan to Smooth Bumps of Jet Market Hits Turbulence," *Wall Street Journal*, August 25, 2003, pp. A1, A6.

[6]Stanley Holmes, "Boeing: Caught in Its Own Turbulence," *BusinessWeek*, December 8, 2003, p. 37.

[7]Byron Acohido, "Boeing's Call for Help from Air Force Raise More Questions," *USA Today*, December 8, 2003, p. 3B.

[8]See *Wall Street Journal*, May 4, 2004, p. A7.

[9]Ironically, Mr. Sears's book *Soaring through Turbulence* was scheduled for release from the publisher at the same time; Julie Creswell, "Boeing Plays Defense," *Fortune*, April 19, 2004, p. 91. Its publication was delayed indefinitely; Del Jones, "Fired Boeing Executive Encounters Book Turbulence," *USA Today*, November 28, 2003, p. 2B. Some quotes from the book: "Corporate leaders need a model that will keep them clear of impropriety and the appearance of impropriety," and "Either you are ethical or you are not. You have to make that decision; all of us do. And there is no in between."

[10]J. Lynn Lunsford and Anne Marie Squeo, "Boeing CEO Condit Resigns in Shake-Up at Aerospace Titan," *Wall Street Journal*, December 2, 2003, pp. A1, A12.

follow-on procurement. Air Force Undersecretary Peter Teets released the following statement in making the announcement:

> *We do not tolerate breaches of procurement integrity, and we hold industry account-able for the actions of their employees.*[11]

Just prior to the Air Force announcement, Boeing had issued its own announcement that the expected revenues from commercial satellites and rocket launchers had been greatly overestimated by that division. Boeing took a $1.1 billion charge to reflect the fact that those revenues had already been overestimated.[12] Two of Boeing's former executives were indicted for their role in the documents scandal. The fallout from the problems at Boeing has caused the contract for the tankers to go back and forth several times, with the Air Force ultimately, in 2009, suspending the bidding and ordering a new process of bidding for those planes. The bidding will not close until November 2010.

Lockheed filed suit against Boeing for the appropriation of the documents. CEO Philip Condit had fired CFO Sears, saying, "Boeing must and will live by the highest standards of ethical conduct."[13] However, Condit departed abruptly on December 1, 2003.[14] When Condit resigned, analysts, observers, employees, and others took stock of Boeing and what had gone wrong. One wrote, "Under Condit, engineering skills and ethics seemed to lose sway over senior management." Condit's four marriages, two to Boeing employees, one of whom was pink-slipped during her relationship with Condit, created a culture that ran contra to the conservative traditions of Boeing. When Condit moved into the Four Seasons Olympic Hotel in Seattle and had the suite remodeled at company expense, even the board members became nervous, quietly saying among themselves that they had "another Clinton" on their hands.[15]

As the culture of the company deteriorated, Boeing missed strategic opportunities. Doubting the ability of Airbus to bring the A380 555-passenger jet to market, Boeing opted out of that jumbo-jet market. Airbus won 120 orders for the super jumbo jet and seized Boeing's market for large jetliners. Shareholders were in revolt. Boeing did develop the Dreamliner 7E7 jetliner following its withdrawal from the jumbo-jet competition with Airbus, but its commercial production has been delayed numerous times for both design flaws and supplier issues. Boeing was scheduled to deliver fifty of the new aircraft to All Nippon Airways, for a total contract price of $6 billion in 2008, but the jet was not unveiled in Everett, Washington, until July 8, 2007. And its maiden public flight did not occur until 2009.

After the management shake-up and all the fallout from the documents and the defense employee recruitment, Boeing worked toward a culture change. However, the issues continued to arise. In April 2004, the U.S. Attorney's Office in Los Angeles expanded its investigation of the Lockheed Martin document case into Boeing work for NASA and the possibility that other Lockheed documents were used on NASA projects. The documents are different and involve different managers, but the pattern of abuse is the same.[16]

---

[11]Edward Iwata, "Air Force Punishes Boeing by Taking 7 Contracts," *USA Today,* July 25, 2003, p. 1B.

[12]Squeo, Lunsford, and Pasztor, "Boeing's Plan to Smooth Bumps of Jet Market Hits Turbulence," pp. A1, A6.

[13]Gary Strauss, Byron Acohido, Elliot Blaire Smith, and Marilyn Adams, "Boeing CEO Abruptly Quits after Controversy," *USA Today,* December 2, 2003, p. 1B.

[14]Stanley Holmes, "Boeing: What Really Happened," *BusinessWeek,* December 15, 2003. p. 33.

[15]*Id.*

[16]Andy Pasztor and Jonathan Karp, "Federal Officials Widen Probe into Boeing's Use of Rival's Data," *Wall Street Journal,* April 27, 2004, pp. A7, A10.

In 2003, the U.S. Navy selected Boeing to deliver up to 210 F/A 18 fighter jets for a total contract price of $9.6 billion.[17] In June 2004, the Navy awarded a $23 billion contract to Boeing to convert 737 jets into antisubmarine aircraft, a contract that replaces plans that had been supplied by Lockheed Martin originally.[18] The contract was awarded even as the government investigation on the EELV was still ongoing. When former CEO Harry Stonecipher returned from retirement to reassume his role following Mr. Condit's resignation, he told the business press, "We're cleaning up our own house."[19] When asked if he could provide assurance to investors and customers that the scandals were behind Boeing, Mr. Stonecipher said, "Well, as in definitely behind us, they'll never be definitely behind us until all the lawsuits are finished. Rather than trying to convince people that it's all behind us, I have convinced them that we have a process and a will to deal with it, vigorously and summarily."[20] In 2005, the federal government lifted the sanctions against Boeing that had banished it from the line of defense contracts that were related to the Lockheed documents.[21]

In 2005, Mr. Stonecipher was removed as CEO after an internal investigation revealed that he had had an affair with one of the company executives. The affair was uncovered by an employee responsible for monitoring e-mails, and Mr. Stonecipher's e-mails to the executive demonstrated not only an affair but also poor judgment in the use of company e-mail. The employee reported anonymously the content of the e-mails, including information about the affair and other "graphic content," to an ethics officer.[22] The ethics officer investigated the concern and then turned over the findings to general counsel, who then took the information to the Boeing board. When confronted with the issue, even Mr. Stonecipher agreed that he was no longer the right person to lead the company in its recommitment to ethics, "We set—hell, I set—a higher standard here. I violated my own standards. I used poor judgment."[23] Mr. Stonecipher's departure was announced within ten days following the employee's anonymous tip. The board found that he had violated the following provisions of Boeing's code of ethics:

> In conducting its business, integrity must underlie all company relationships, including those with customers, suppliers, communities, and other employees.

> Employees will not engage in conduct or activity that may raise questions about the company's honesty, impartiality, [or] reputation or otherwise cause embarrassment to the company.

Lou Platt, chairman of the board, said that Mr. Stonecipher's "poor judgment . . . impaired his ability to lead."[24]

On May 15, 2006, Boeing announced that it had settled the charges with the federal government related to the federal contracts and the Darlene Druyun matter (Case 9.16). Boeing agreed to pay a $615 million fine, but the government did not require the

---

[17]"Closing Bell," *BusinessWeek*, January 12, 2004, p. 42.

[18]Leslie Wayen, "Boeing Wins Navy Contract to Replace Sub Chasers," *New York Times*, June 15, 2004, pp. C1, C9.

[19]Ron Insana, "We're Cleaning Up Our Own House," *USA Today*, January 5, 2004, p. 4B.

[20]Laura Rich, "A Boeing Stalwart, War or Peace," *New York Times*, July 18, 2004, p. BU4.

[21]Floyd Norris, "Moving from Scandal to Scandal, Boeing Finds Its Road to Redemption Paved with Affairs, Great and Small," *New York Times*, March 8, 2005, p. C5.

[22]J. Lynn Lunsford, Andy Pasztor, and JoAnn S. Lublin, "Boeing CEO Forced to Resign over His Affair with an Employee," *Wall Street Journal*, March 8, 2005, pp. A1, A8.

[23]*Id.*

[24]Bryan Acohido and Jayne O'Donnell, "Extramarital Affair Topples Boeing CEO," *USA Today*, March 8, 2005, p. B1.

company to admit any wrongdoing and acknowledged that employees had acted without "authority and against company policy."[25]

Discussion Questions

1. What made the engineers and executives want the Lockheed documents and then use them? Do you have some ideas for lines for your credo that come from seeing what happened with the engineers and the executives who were complicit?

2. List the long-term costs and consequences of Boeing's use of the documents. Consider others you may see that are not called out in the case.

3. Do you think the fact that Boeing continued to receive contracts is evidence that ethics don't matter?

4. One analyst has said that the problem with Boeing is that it cannot admit that the problems were internal but always seeks to blame the problems on a "few bad apples." Is this statement valid?

5. List the categories of ethical breaches that you see in this scenario.

Compare & Contrast

When Mr. Stonecipher left the company, analysts disagreed on whether his ouster was appropriate. One analyst said that "the board has done the right thing inasmuch as the firm still needs a moral rudder to return to its storied reputation."[26] Another analyst added, "It's a board that's become overly sensitized by all the negative publicity about Boeing employees and their ethics, and they reacted more strongly than I think was appropriate."[27] Discuss the two views, and using what you have learned, determine what was best for the company. Why did they reach different conclusions? Can you draw any additional lines for conduct in business based on this case?

Case 8.3

Starwood, Hilton, and the Suspiciously Similar New Hotel Designs

The Hotel Set-Up and Background

Starwood and Hilton are direct, head-to-head competitors. In 2007, the Blackstone Group, a private equity firm, acquired Hilton for over $20 billion in a top-of-the-market, highly leveraged buyout. Financial analysts suggested that because Blackstone had paid a super-premium price for Hilton, the hotel chain would be under intense pressure to deliver immediate results. Ross Klein and Amar Lalvani were President and Senior Vice President, respectively, of Starwood's Luxury Brands Group. Both were intimately involved in and aware of the strategy and planned future development of Starwood's lifestyle and luxury hotel brands: the St. Regis, W Hotels, and The Luxury Collection. Both Messrs. Klein and Lalvani had access to strategic development plans and both had signed written confidentiality agreements with Starwood.

Hilton Recruits from Starwood

In February 2008 Christopher Nassetta, Hilton's President & Chief Executive Officer, began recruiting Mr. Klein to join Hilton. Mr. Klein then began requesting large volumes of confidential information from Starwood employees, which he took home and loaded

[25]"Boeing Pays a Biggie," *BusinessWeek*, May 29, 2006, p. 30.
[26]Dave Carpenter, "Boeing Chief Ousted over Affair with Employee," *The Tribune*, March 8, 2005, pp. B1, B2.
[27]*Id.*

onto a personal laptop computer and/or forwarded to a personal e-mail account before joining Hilton. After Mr. Klein obtained a severance payment of more than $600,000 from Starwood, he joined Hilton and used the information there in the development of a new Hilton high-scale hotel known as Denizen.

In March 2008 Steven Goldman, Hilton's President of Global Development & Real Estate, began recruiting Mr. Lalvani to join Hilton. Goldman told Lalvani that Hilton was a "clean slate" and "you're the first guy on my list." Mr. Lalvani provided Mr. Goldman with his ideas for Hilton, including the following from an e-mail: "Other idea is bring over the core W team which has created an enormous amount of value and is very loyal to me to build a new brand for you guys. Not sure your appetite but I know I could make that happen as well."[28] Before joining Mr. Goldman at Hilton, Mr. Lalvani, too, secretly downloaded large quantities of confidential Starwood documents, which he brought with him to and used at Hilton.

By June 2008, Messrs. Klein and Lalvani were both at Hilton as Hilton's Global Head of Luxury & Lifestyle Brands and Global Head of Luxury & Lifestyle Brand Development, respectively.

Hilton's press release included the following statement upon the arrival of the two:

These new hires will help advance Hilton's strategic goal of further developing its presence in the luxury and lifestyle sectors. At Hilton, Mr. Klein will oversee the company's global luxury and lifestyle brand portfolio, including Waldorf-Astoria, the Waldorf-Astoria Collection and Conrad, and will spearhead the company's entry into the lifestyle segment. Mr. Lalvani will lead the global development of Hilton's luxury and lifestyle segments.[29]

The Paper Hiring Bonus

Between the two men, they brought along to Hilton over 100,000 electronic Starwood documents that contained proprietary information that Hilton then used in creating its new Denizen hotel chain. The documents included the following:

Starwood's Forward-Looking Strategic Development Plans

- Starwood's Principal Term Prioritization Worksheets, containing Starwood's highly confidential and proprietary current and prospective negotiation strategies with owners ranked by importance to Starwood for numerous deal terms.
- Starwood's Property Improvement Plan templates for how to create "the Ultimate W Experience" in conversion properties, providing step-by-step details for how to convert a hotel property to a W branded hotel.
- Starwood's confidential computer files containing the names, addresses, and other nonpublic information for its Luxury Brands Group owners, developers, and designers compiled by Starwood.
- Recent presentations to Starwood's executive leadership team containing current and prospective financial, branding, and marketing information for Starwood's lifestyle and luxury brands.
- Starwood's site-specific Project Approval Requests, which set out in detail highly sensitive and competitively useful information for Starwood properties and targeted properties around the world.
- Confidential and proprietary marketing and demographic studies for which Starwood paid third parties over $1 million.
- Starwood's W Residential Guidelines 2008, containing Starwood's strategies and proprietary toolkits for residential development in or at W hotels.

---

[28]*Starwood Hotels & Resorts Worldwide, Inc. v Hilton Hotels Corporation,* Klein, & Levine, trial pleading, 2009 WL 1025597 (S.D.N.Y.)

[29]*Id.*

- Starwood's W Hotels "Brand in a Box" modules and training materials, containing Starwood's proprietary training, operational materials, and procedures for opening a new lifestyle hotel.
- A board presentation on future strategies for the chain.
- Starwood's Luxury Brands Group "Brand Bibles," brand handbooks, brand immersion materials, and brand marketing plans.

The Recruiting Raids

Upon their arrival at Hilton, Messrs. Klein and Lalvani also recruited additional Starwood employees to join them at Hilton and to bring with them to Hilton additional confidential, competitively sensitive Starwood information. A list appears below:

Individual	Former Starwood Position	Current Hilton Position
Christopher Kochuba	Vice President, Development Planning & Design Management, Luxury Brands Group	Vice President, Planning and Programming, Global Luxury and Lifestyle Brands
Erin Shaffer	Senior Manager, Brand Marketing, Luxury Brands Group	Senior Director, Communications and Partnerships
Jeff Darnell	General Manager, W Hotel Los Angeles	Vice President, Brand Operations
Stephanie Heer	Marketing Manager, W Hotel Los Angeles	Brand Marketing Manager, Conrad Hotels
Erin Green	Director, W Development, Europe, Africa, and Middle East	Senior Development Director, Luxury and Lifestyle (Europe and Africa)
Elie Younes	Senior Director, Acquisitions & Development, Europe, Africa, and Middle East	Vice President, Development (Middle East)
Leah Corradino	Marketing Manager, W Hotel San Diego	Brand Marketing Manager, Waldorf Astoria and Waldorf Astoria Collection
Susan Manrao	Senior Manager, Interior Style & Design Standards	Senior Director of Design and Brand Experience[30]

The Arbitration and Truth Percolates

Because of the ongoing poaching, Starwood brought and commenced an arbitration action against Mr. Klein in November 2008 to enforce the nonsolicitation provisions in his employment contract and his separation agreement with Starwood.

In February 2009, pursuant to a Starwood discovery request of Hilton, Hilton delivered eight large boxes of computer hard drives, zip drives, thumb drives, and paper records containing the information listed above. Hilton also acknowledged that the former employees had additional Starwood materials "at home." However, Hilton took no action against Mr. Klein or any of the other former Starwood employees.

[30]*Id.*

Hilton's general counsel said in a cover letter included with the eight boxes of documents that he did not think the information was proprietary or confidential but that he was sending them back as a precaution.

However, Starwood noted that files that had been taken included its development plans for its "zen den" that it was going to put in its upscale "W" hotels. Hilton's development plans for Denizen referred to it as their "den of zen."

The suit is ongoing.

Discussion Questions

1. In developing a concept for a new chain (Denizen is geared at the high-end market), companies spend years and millions of dollars on studying consumer needs and preferences, social trends, lighting, costs, food choices, and even fabrics and designs. What ethical category does the conduct of the former Starwood executives fall into beyond just the breach of their employment contract covenants?

2. The following clause appears in the former Starwood employees' contracts:

   > acknowledges that during the course of his/her employment with [Starwood], Employee will receive, and will have access to, 'Confidential Information' . . . of [Starwood] and that such information is a special, valuable and unique asset belonging to [Starwood] . . . All [Documents (broadly defined)] which from time to time may be in Employee's possession . . . relating, directly or indirectly, to the business of [Starwood] shall be and remain the property of [Starwood] and shall be delivered by Employee to [Starwood] immediately upon request, and in any event promptly upon termination of Employee's employment, and Employee shall not make or keep any copies or extracts of the Documents. . . . Employee shall not disclose to any third person any information concerning the business of [Starwood], including, without limitation, any trade secrets, customer lists and details of contracts with or requirements of customers, the identity of any owner of a managed hotel, information relating to any current, past or prospective management agreement or joint venture, information pertaining to business methods, sales plans, design plans and strategies, management organization, computer systems and software, operating policies or manuals . . . financial records or other financial, commercial, business or technical information relating to the company. . . ."(Emphasis added.)

   Is this an enforceable provision? Do you believe the employees violated this provision by their conduct?

3. What components of a personal credo would have helped in this situation?

4. Where does "fair play" fit into ethics? Competition? Law?

All's Fair, or Is It?

We all look for that angle, that piece of information, that extra effort that gives us a winning moment financially. But ethical issues arise in how we obtain that one piece of information and how we use it.

Reading 8.4

Adam Smith: An Excerpt from The Theory of Moral Sentiments

How selfish soever man may be supposed, there are evidently some principles in his nature, which interest him in the fortune of others, and render their happiness necessary to him, though he derives nothing from it, except the pleasure of seeing it.

I.I.27

Philosophers have, of late years, considered chiefly the tendency of affections, and have given little attention to the relation which they stand in to the cause which excites them. In common life, however, when we judge of any person's conduct, and of the sentiments which directed it, we constantly consider them under both these aspects. When we blame in another man the excesses of love, of grief, of resentment, we not only consider the ruinous effects which they tend to produce, but the little occasion which was given for them. The merit of his favourite, we say, is not so great, his misfortune is not so dreadful, his provocation is not so extraordinary, as to justify so violent a passion. We should have indulged, we say; perhaps, have approved of the violence of his emotion, had the cause been in any respect proportioned to it.

I.I.28

When we judge in this manner of any affection, as proportioned or disproportioned to the cause which excites it, it is scarce possible that we should make use of any other rule or canon but the correspondent affection in ourselves. If, upon bringing the case home to our own breast, we find that the sentiments which it gives occasion to, coincide and tally with our own, we necessarily approve of them as proportioned and suitable to their objects; if otherwise, we necessarily disapprove of them, as extravagant and out of proportion.

Every faculty in one man is the measure by which he judges of the like faculty in another. I judge of your sight by my sight, of your ear by my ear, of your reason by my reason, of your resentment by my resentment, of your love by my love. I neither have, nor can have, any other way of judging about them.

The man who, by some sudden revolution of fortune, is lifted up all at once into a condition of life, greatly above what he had formerly lived in, may be assured that the congratulations of his best friends are not all of them perfectly sincere. An upstart, though of the greatest merit, is generally disagreeable, and a sentiment of envy commonly prevents us from heartily sympathizing with his joy. If he has any judgment, he

505

is sensible of this, and instead of appearing to be elated with his good fortune, he endeavours, as much as he can, to smother his joy, and keep down that elevation of mind with which his new circumstances naturally inspire him. He affects the same plainness of dress, and the same modesty of behaviour, which became him in his former station. He redoubles his attention to his old friends, and endeavours more than ever to be humble, assiduous, and complaisant. And this is the behaviour which in his situation we most approve of; because we expect, it seems, that he should have more sympathy with our envy and aversion to his happiness, than we have with his happiness. It is seldom that with all this he succeeds. We suspect the sincerity of his humility, and he grows weary of this constraint. In a little time, therefore, he generally leaves all his old friends behind him, some of the meanest of them excepted, who may, perhaps, condescend to become his dependents: nor does he always acquire any new ones; the pride of his new connections is as much affronted at finding him their equal, as that of his old ones had been by his becoming their superior: and it requires the most obstinate and persevering modesty to atone for this mortification to either. He generally grows weary too soon, and is provoked, by the sullen and suspicious pride of the one, and by the saucy contempt of the other, to treat the first with neglect, and the second with petulance, till at last he grows habitually insolent, and forfeits the esteem of all. If the chief part of human happiness arises from the consciousness of being beloved, as I believe it does, those sudden changes of fortune seldom contribute much to happiness. He is happiest who advances more gradually to greatness, whom the public destines to every step of his preferment long before he arrives at it, in whom, upon that account, when it comes, it can excite no extravagant joy, and with regard to whom it cannot reasonably create either any jealousy in those he overtakes, or any envy in those he leaves behind.

Discussion Questions

1. How do we relate to and judge others? Why?
2. How do we determine when someone is wrong in their behavior?
3. What happens to our relationships with those who enjoy success very quickly?

Case 8.5

The Coke Employee Who Offered Inside Information to Pepsi

A former executive administrative assistant to Coca-Cola's global brand director, Joya Williams was sentenced to eight years in prison for her role in an attempt to sell confidential materials to Pepsi. Working with Ibrahim Dimson and Edmund Duhaney, the three hatched a plan to make money by selling the confidential materials. A man named "Dirk" sent a letter to Pepsi headquarters in May 2006 offering secrets for sale. The "secrets for sale" included recipes for some Coca-Cola products and details of future promotions (these two bits of information were selling for $15,000) as well as the formula for a new beverage ($75,000).

When Pepsi got the letter, it called Coke, Coke called the FBI, and the FBI set up a sting operation that included videotaping Ms. Williams. Ms. Williams was observed on the videotape putting the confidential materials, including bottles of prototype beverages identified by their eight-ounce size and plain white labels, into her personal handbag.

Also as part of the sting operation, an undercover FBI agent met the infamous "Dirk," who turned out to be Mr. Dimson, on June 16, 2006, at Atlanta's Hartsfield-Jackson Airport. Mr. Dimson handed over some of the documents and a beverage sample. The documents included fourteen pages of Coca-Cola documents with the company logo, marked "Classified—Confidential" and "CLASSIFIED—Highly Restricted." Coke later confirmed that these documents were real and highly confidential and contained classified proprietary information—in other words, trade secrets. The undercover agent gave Mr. Dimson $30,000 in cash (in $50 and $100 bills) that was in a Girl Scout cookie box. The undercover agent told Mr. Dimson that the cash was a down payment with the remainder to come after the items were authenticated. The two then agreed that there would be more secrets coming for a total price of $1.5 million.

According to FBI press releases, Mr. Dimson later e-mailed the undercover agent the following:

> I must see some type of seriousness on there [sic] part, if I'm to maintain the faith to continue with you guys, or if I need to look towards another entity that will be interested in a relationship with me. I have the capability of obtaining information per request. I have information that's all Classified and extremely confidential, that only a handful of the top execs at my company have seen. I can even provide actual products and packaging of certain products, that no eye has seen, outside of maybe 5 top execs. I need to know today, if I have a serious partner or not. If the good faith moneys [sic] is in my account by Monday, that will be an indication of your seriousness.

After leaving the airport meeting with the undercover agent, Mr. Dimson met in a rental car with Edmund Duhaney, and they drove to Mr. Duhaney's home in Decatur, Georgia. Call records showed that Mr. Duhaney was in contact with Mr. Dimson and Ms. Williams on that day. Following these events, the undercover agent arranged for a July 5, 2007, meeting to transfer documents and $1.5 million. Following that meeting, the three were arrested.

When news of the arrests was made public, Pepsi released a statement that included the following: "Competition can be fierce, but must also be fair and legal."[31]

The prosecutor indicated that Ms. Williams chose to go to trial, a trial that lasted seven days, and that she lied on the stand. "Choices have consequences, and she made those choices."[32] Ms. Williams testified that Messrs. Dimson and Duhaney took the information from her home without her knowledge. However, the videotape of her at the company contradicted her testimony. Ms. Williams testified that she had a habit of just "hoarding" company documents and e-mails. There was also, however, a recorded tape of her accomplices deciding how to divvy up the money among the three of them. The day after the Girl Scout cookie box handover (also on videotape), Ms. Williams deposited $4,000 into her checking account. She testified that the $4,000 was a loan from a friend. However, the friend did not testify. Mr. Duhaney created an account the next day in the name of Noblehouse Group, LLC, with the address used on the account being Mr. Duhaney's Decatur residence. Bizarrely, Ms. Williams's residence was destroyed by fire in February 2007 within one hour of her conviction that same day.

Both Messrs. Dimson and Duhaney entered guilty pleas, and Mr. Duhaney testified against Ms. Williams at her trial. Mr. Dimson was sentenced to five years in prison, and both Mr. Dimson and Ms. Williams were ordered to pay $40,000 in restitution. Mr. Duhaney's sentence was postponed because of his lawyer's schedule and also because of his fifteen-year-old daughter's surgery. Mr. Duhaney and Ms. Williams had been friends for many years. Mr. Duhaney was released for a few days to be with his daughter but was sentenced to eight years in May 2007.

At her sentencing hearing, Ms. Williams offered the following: "Your honor, I have expanded my consciousness through this devastating experience. This has been a very

---

[31]Kathleen Kingsbury, "You Can't Beat the Real Thing," *Time*, July 9, 2006, http://www.time.com.

[32]"Ex-Secretary Gets 8-Year Term in Coca-Cola Secrets Case," *New York Times*, May 24, 2007, p. C3.

defining moment in my life. I have become infamous when I never wanted to become famous. . . . I am sorry to Coke and I'm sorry to my boss and to you and to my family as well."[33] She also added, "Punishment is the memories and the moments that I'm going to miss. Punishment is never having a family of my own."[34]

Ms. Williams's sentence is two years longer than prosecutors recommended (although two years shorter than the possible ten years) because the federal judge, J. Owen Forrester, said, "I can't think of another case in 25 years that there's been so much obstruction of justice."[35] Judge Forrester also added, "The [sentencing] guidelines as they are written don't begin to approach the seriousness of this case."

Following the Dimson and Williams sentencings, the U.S. attorney issued the following statement:

> As the market becomes more global, the need to protect intellectual property becomes even more vital to protecting American companies and our economic growth. This case is an example of good corporate citizenship leading to a successful prosecution, and that unlawfully gaining a competitive advantage by stealing another's trade secrets can lead straight to federal prison.[36]

Discussion Questions

1. What thoughts did Pepsi offer that showed its value system and helped to explain why it turned over the materials to Coke and, eventually, the FBI?[37]

2. Why are ethical standards and values critical at all levels of an organization?

3. Discuss the importance of long-term thinking in resolving ethical dilemmas.

4. How does the phrase "Truth percolates" apply to analysis by employees at both companies?

Compare & Contrast

What was different about the Coke employees from the Pepsi employees who were on the receiving end of the potentially valuable information?

Case 8.6

The Compliance Officer Who Strayed

Marisa Baridis, then twenty-nine, was the legal compliance officer at Morgan Stanley, Dean Witter, Discover and Company. Ms. Baridis was in charge of what is commonly referred to as the "Chinese wall" in brokerage houses. Her job was to be certain that sensitive information did not cross from the side of the house putting together deals to the side of the house that buys stock. Her responsibilities included making certain that confidential information about Morgan Stanley clients did not leak to the brokerage side of the business so that Morgan Stanley brokers would not use inside information for trading.

Ms. Baridis met Jeffrey Streich, then thirty-one, in the summer of 1997. Mr. Streich was a broker who specialized in speculative stocks. Over a six-month period, Ms. Baridis allegedly provided Mr. Streich with information in exchange for $2,500 for each tip.

---

[33]*Id.*

[34]FBI, press release. http://www.fbi.gov. Accessed June 10, 2010.

[35]"Ex-Secretary Gets 8-Year Term in Coca-Cola Secrets Case," p. C3.

[36]From FBI, press release. http://www.fbi.gov. Accessed June 10, 2010.

[37]*Note*: The author has conducted a seminar for Pepsi employees on ethics.

However, late in October 1997, Mr. Streich and Ms. Baridis would have their last meeting when Mr. Streich went to their meeting wearing a hidden recorder, and there was a camera across the street that videotaped them both sitting in the window of a restaurant. The tape shows Mr. Streich handing Ms. Baridis $2,500 in one-hundred-dollar bills.

Ms. Baridis, who was indicted on charges of trading on inside information to make a profit, was fired from her $70,000-a-year job. Her father posted her $250,000 bail. Her indictment included statements by her obtained via a surveillance tape. When asked by Mr. Streich if she understood the implications of the tips and their scheme to profit, she said, "It's the most illegalest thing you can do."[38] Ms. Baridis received kickbacks totaling $40,000. In another segment of the tape, she is asked if she understands what would happen if they were caught: "We'd be interviewed in every magazine. We'd be in like . . . we'd be, who were the people of the '80s? Boesky? Michael Milken. We'd be bigger than that."[39] She added, "It's fun. If you don't get greedy."[40]

Prior to her indictment, Ms. Baridis had an upscale Manhattan apartment with rent of $2,400 per month. The extra money from the sale of information had afforded her a comfortable New York lifestyle. Her assets were frozen, and prosecutors obtained $100,000 in a seizure of those assets. Overall, the insider tips involved thirteen companies and netted those involved in the trading over $1 million.[41]

Ms. Baridis entered a guilty plea in exchange for a lighter sentence contingent upon her cooperation. A college friend of Ms. Baridis also entered a guilty plea in federal court to charges of insider trading. Mr. Mitchell Sher, then thirty-two, admitted that he made cash payments to Ms. Baridis in exchange for her furnishing confidential information about pending events such as mergers for Morgan Stanley clients.[42]

Mr. Sher admitted that he used information provided to him by Ms. Baridis to trade in shares of Georgia-Pacific Corp., Burlington Resources, and two other companies. Unlike the ten other individuals charged in the case, Mr. Sher was not a broker but rather a vice president for a book distributor. He also admitted in his plea that Ms. Baridis had fed him confidential information in exchange for cash when she worked for Smith Barney earlier in her career.

When asked to comment on the Baridis case, an executive with Smith Barney said, "We had trusted the individual with great responsibility and that trust was misplaced."[43]

Discussion Questions

1. What is troublesome about insiders using information in advance of public disclosure to make money?

2. Are there any elements for a credo that you can gain from her experience?

Compare & Contrast

Ms. Baridis makes reference to Ivan Boesky and Michael Milken, the "greed is good" Wall Street icons of the 1980s. It has been thirty years since Drexel Burnham, the Wall

[38]Dean Starkman, "Three Indicted for Insider Trading Tied to Ex-Morgan Stanley Aide," *Wall Street Journal,* November 26, 1997, p. B2.

[39]Elise Ackerman, "Remember Boesky? Many Gen Xers Don't," *U.S. News & World Report,* November 22, 1999, p. 52.

[40]Peter Truell, "Lessons of Boesky and Milken Go Unheeded in Fraud Case," *New York Times,* November 26, 1997, pp. C1, C10.

[41]Peter Truell, "Sparring for Pieces of the Wall Street Action," *New York Times,* December 26, 1997, pp. C1, C2.

[42]Dean Starkman, "Five Brokers Indicted for Insider Trades Linked to Ex-Morgan Stanley Officer," *Wall Street Journal,* December 23, 1997, p. B9.

[43]Peter Truell, "An Employee on Wall Street Is Arrested," *New York Times,* November 7, 1997, p. C8.

Street investment banking firm, collapsed into bankruptcy under the weight of its investments in risky businesses via what became a household word for the 1980s: *junk bonds.* Michael Milken, the Wharton MBA who was the mastermind behind the risky financial instruments used to fund takeovers for the sake of takeovers, would enter a guilty plea to six of the ninety-eight felony charges brought against him by the federal government and, after paying a $600 million fine, serve two years in prison. The *New York Times* reports that the young investment bankers who worked at Drexel at the time of its collapse have done very well, most of them on Wall Street, either with other companies or in firms they started on their own. They all speak favorably of their former, collapsed company, and many still see Mr. Milken as responsible for their success. One noted, "He's so brilliant, it's like getting near the sun." Another said, "He was the best visionary Wall Street ever had."[44] Another, Leon Wagner, who served on Drexel's trading desk and now is chairman of GoldTree Asset Management, said, "Just to be able to sit on the desk and see the calls start at 4:15 in the morning, Boesky and Perelman and Diller and Murdoch."[45] But Mr. Wagner said that he took not just the memories of the power of Drexel with him but a powerful lesson as well: "There's a difference between being very competitive and can-do, and winning at all costs. All costs is costly."[46]

What insight do you gain from these Wall Street executives who were there during the Boesky and Milken period? What do they see that Ms. Baridis did not?

Case 8.7

Jonathan Lebed: The Middle School Tycoon

Jonathan Lebed, a fifteen-year-old New Jersey middle school student at the time, shocked the investment world when the SEC came knocking at his parents' door with a charge of securities fraud. It seems that Jonathan had turned his $8,000 in savings and gifts from family members into nearly $900,000 in gains on stocks traded using a pump-and-dump strategy. Jonathan did so without ever missing a day of school.

Master Jonathan, using over twenty screen names on a computer his parents had given him as a gift, would buy shares of stock and then post positive information about the stock around the Internet in various chat rooms. When the price of his chosen stock would rise, he would then sell it and move on to another stock. He did the bulk of his "pump-and-dump" trading between September 1999 and February 2000. During that time he traded, on average, 60,000 shares per day; his smallest gain in a day was $12,000, and his largest was $74,000.

Mrs. Lebed said that Jonathan had always been fascinated with the market and would often sit by the TV and watch the stock prices go across the screen on MSNBC and CNN. His mother also indicated he was not a bad stock picker, having given some of her friends and family members some good investment advice on stocks.

When the SEC stepped in to halt his trading and take his computer, Jonathan became the first minor ever prosecuted by the SEC for securities fraud. His father noted that his son did nothing more than what others in the market do and yet the SEC chose to come after "a kid." Mr. Lebed stated during a "60 Minutes" interview, "I'm proud of my son. It's not like he was out stealing the hubcaps off cars or peddling drugs to the neighbors."[47]

---

[44]Jenny Anderson, "The Drexel Diaspora," *New York Times,* Money & Business sec., February 6, 2005, p. 3–1.

[45]*Id.* Mr. Wagner is referring to Ivan Boesky, who also served a prison sentence; Ron Perelman, the chairman of Revlon, Inc.; Barry Diller; and Rupert Murdoch, the media mogul.

[46]*Id.*

[47]Michael Lewis, "Jonathan Lebed: Stock Manipulator, S.E.C. Nemesis—and 15," *New York Times,* February 25, 2001, pp. 1–18.

Mr. Lebed also noted that analysts behaved in the same fashion and that his son had been singled out for prosecution.

Michael Lewis, who conducted an investigation into the case, interviewed Richard Walker, the head of enforcement for the SEC, and asked what was different about Master Lebed's conduct from that of analysts. The following is their exchange:

"Jonathan Lebed was seeking to manipulate the market," said Walker.

"But that only begs the question. If Wall Street analysts and fund managers and corporate CEOs who appear on CNBC and CNNfn to plug stocks are not guilty of seeking to manipulate the market, what on earth does it mean to manipulate the market?"

"It's when you promote a stock for the purpose of artificially raising its price."

"But when a Wall Street analyst can send the price of a stock of a company that is losing billions of dollars up 50 points in a day, what does it mean to 'artificially raise' the price of a stock? The law sounded perfectly circular."[48]

The Lebeds entered into a consent decree.[49] They repaid all of the money Jonathan had made except for $273,000, a sum equal to about what is no doubt owed by his parents as taxes on the gains Jonathan made in his trading activity.[50]

Following his high school graduation, Master Lebed launched a website where he again touts stocks (http://lebed.biz), but now he does not take positions in the stocks he is advancing. And he adds, "I never thought there was anything wrong with what I did."[51]

He also has an investor relations firm, Lebed & Lara, that now has about 100 clients who pay $200 per year for access to stock information. He also offers a newsletter.

At one point Lebed ran for city council in Cedar Grove, New Jersey, and was in negotiations for a movie deal for his story.

Discussion Questions

1. Do you think Master Lebed violated the law? Why or why not?
2. Can you distinguish his conduct from a CEO or analyst plugging a particular stock?
3. Did Master Lebed take unfair advantage, or should investors be more wary of information they get over the Internet?
4. Do you think Master Lebed's conduct was ethical? Why or why not? Was it honest? Was it fair?
5. Does his apparent success following the pump-and-dump scheme show that being honest and fair doesn't really matter? Why or why not?

Case 8.8

Simmons, Mervyn's, and the Private Equity Firms That Bankrupt Them

The Story of a Cash-Strapped Mervyn's

Mervyn's LLC filed an interesting lawsuit against its former private equity holders because of the structure of the acquisition deal that hobbled the retailer but allowed the private equity firms to double their investment.

---

[48]*Id.*

[49]Noelle Knox, "Teen Settles Stock-Manipulation Case for $285,000," *USA Today,* September 21, 2000, p. 1B.

[50]Gretchen Morgenson, "S.E.C. Says Teenager Had After-School Hobby: Online Stock Fraud," *New York Times,* September 21, 2000, pp. A1, C10.

[51]Gary Weiss, "The Kid Stays in the Picture," *BusinessWeek,* April 7, 2003, pp. 70–72.

In 2004, Cerberus Capital Management and Sun Capital Partners bought Mervyn's from Target (parent company) for $1.26 billion. The deal consisted of two parts: one part is the sale of the company and the other part is the sale of the company's real estate, i.e., its store properties. The result of the two-part deal was that Mervyn's had to pay rent to its acquirers because of the real estate transfers. Because the transaction occurred just at the beginning of the real estate bubble, the value of real estate increased, and the acquisition firm kept increasing Mervyn's lease payments. With the cash flow from the $172 million in annual rent, the acquirers doubled their investment in the purchase. In addition, Mervyn's had to pay its acquirers an annual dividend payment.

Mervyn's tried to cope with the cash drain by closing some stores, but closing required permission of the private equity acquirers, permission that was withheld. Without an ability to downsize and the decline in retail sales as the real estate bubble burst, Mervyn's had to declare bankruptcy.

Mervyn's suit alleges that Capital Management and Sun Capital stripped the company, without regard for its employees and operations.

Serial Acquisitions of Simmons

The Simmons Mattress Company will be filing for bankruptcy. The 133-year-old company has been a part of U.S. history, furnishing mattresses for the Lincoln Bedroom as well as Air Force One. The spokespersons for the company and its magnificent mattresses have included Henry Ford, H.G. Wells, and Eleanor Roosevelt. Cole Porter used the mattress name in his Broadway musical, *Anything Goes*.

The hope of the bankruptcy is that the company can be sold. This sale would be the seventh time the company has been transferred in 20 years. Simmons has been a favorite target for private equity groups. However, their acquisition of the company has not proved helpful to the business. As a result of the acquisitions, Simmons has been saddled with management fees, rental costs, and other charges levied on it by these firms. With little cash, Simmons is insolvent.

However, the equity firms have always managed to make a profit. Thomas H. Lee Partners, the current owner, received increases in its management fees and showed a profit in its management of the company. Simmons continues to grapple with the debt Lee incurred in acquiring and running the company.

Before Simmons was acquired for the first time, in 1991, it had $164 million in debt. It enters bankruptcy with $1.3 billion in debt. During the mortgage market run-up, it was easy to borrow money, and Lee continued to use Simmons's assets to borrow money that it was then investing. However, with the market downturn there followed the realization of the true value of many of their mortgage-backed investments. The assets were a small percentage of the debt at Simmons, and the cash is gone. Simmons is left holding the debt that the investors incurred and from which they profited.

Discussion Questions

1. Discuss the ethical and legal issues in the acquisition and bankruptcy as well as the role of Lee partners in running the company.

2. Who are the stakeholders in this situation? For example, Simmons has closed a number of factories, including recently one just outside of Atlanta that employed 1,000 long-term Simmons's employees. Be sure to think about the social responsibility issues.

3. Discuss the ethical issues in the transaction, its terms, and the conduct of the private equity firms.

4. Isn't this just business? Didn't Target benefit from the deal?

5. Is this creative destruction, per Joseph Schumpeter?

Sources

Jeffrey McCracken and Peter Lattman, "Mervyn's Sues Ex-Owners, Charges They 'Stripped' It,'"
Wall Street Journal, September 4, 2008, pp. B1, B6.

Julie Creswell, "Buyout Firms Profited as Company Debt Soared," *New York Times,* October 5,
2009, p. A1

Intellectual Property and Ethics

When does an idea belong to someone else? Laws on patents and copyrights afford protection in some cases, but other situations are too close to call—or are they?

Case 8.9

Tiffany, Louis Vuitton, eBay, Landlords, and Knock-Offs

The luxury goods industry has gone global. Cartier watches, Louis Vuitton bags, and anything Gucci are among the most popular items. However, where there is high demand for brand-name goods, there are also the "knock-off merchants." Knock-off merchants are those who sell fake designer goods. You can find knock-off merchants on the Internet, on the streets of New York City, in strip malls, and in beauty parlors. These are the businesspeople who produce goods that look like the luxury brand items, but sell for between $12 and $25 to beauty parlors, street vendors, and Internet sellers. Consumers pay up to $250 for the Cartier watches, for example, especially those who buy the watches over the Internet. A real Cartier watch starts at $1,800.

The global market gives those in China, the main area for production of counterfeit goods, increased access to view the designer goods and make the replications more authentic. The Internet allows the posting of photos of the real thing and the selling of knock-offs.

The profit margins in counterfeit goods are phenomenal—better than other forms of illegal activity. Profit in cocaine sales is 100%. Profit in the sale of Microsoft counterfeit products is 900%.[52] Further, those profits have become a source of revenue for terrorist groups. Interpol (the international police organization based in Lyon, France) has connected Hezbollah to a ring of auto parts counterfeiters in Germany that resulted in a seizure of $1.2 million in brake pads.[53]

The annual revenue from counterfeit goods is about $540 billion and, according to Interpol is the main source of income for terrorist groups such as Hezbollah as well as the Chinese triad.

One private investigator who works for brand-name companies says that handbag counterfeiters can make as much money as someone who sells cocaine. Profits are estimated at $10 for every $1 invested. Those margins are significantly higher than those for the drug trade. One businessman had watch components imported from China, assembled them in the United States, and slapped on fake Cartier labels—all for a cost of 27 cents. He then sold them for between $12 and $20.

To cut back on the increasing problem, countries are taking different steps. France has passed a new law making it a crime for someone to buy or carry a knock-off bag. A violation carries up to a three-year sentence in France. In the United States, a first-time violation of counterfeit laws carries up to a ten-year sentence and a $2 million

---

[52]Zachary Pollinger, "Counterfeit Goods and Their Potential Financing of International Terrorism," 1 *Michigan Journal of Business* 85 (2008).

[53]*Id.*, p. 89.

fine. Enforcement has increased, and U.S. Customs seized the following amounts of counterfeit goods in the years noted below:

Year	Amount Seized
2000	$40 million
2001	$53 million
2002	$95 million
2003	$80 million
2004	$130 million
2009	$260 million[54]
2009 (worldwide)	$606 billion

The counterfeiters are a tough group to rein in, but the trademark owners have become diligent in their pursuit up and down the economic chain—they are going after those who own the shops and the Internet sites that sell counterfeit merchandise.

Tiffany and eBay

Tiffany & Co. and eBay have been in litigation in San Francisco for several years. The litigation culminated in a week-long bench trial in December 2007. Tiffany accused eBay of being, in effect, a distributor of goods that infringe Tiffany's trademarks and copyrights. Tiffany has established that eBay sellers are selling counterfeit and knock-off Tiffany items and that eBay is facilitating the exchanges. eBay counters that it simply provides a marketplace and cannot police every item that is sold via its network of buyers and sellers. eBay's lawyers maintain that as a marketplace they never take possession of any of the goods so that it would be impossible for the company to check for the authenticity of the goods being bought and sold.

However, Tiffany lawyers have argued that eBay benefits from the transactions because it advertises the availability of Tiffany jewelry through its marketplace and thereby profits from these counterfeit sales.

Flea markets and retail stores have been held responsible for determining the authenticity of their goods. The question is whether such a vicarious duty applies to eBay.

Tiffany did notify eBay of the counterfeit problems on the site in 2003, but eBay elected not to look into the problem. Tiffany maintains that eBay could police the situation simply by requiring sellers to provide proof of authenticity such as a receipt from a Tiffany's store. Tiffany has tried to chase down the counterfeit sellers but finds phantom sites and disappearing and changing identities. Tiffany would shut down one site only to have another site appear under a different name within a matter of days. "We were chasing ourselves," was the comment of Michael J. Kowalski, Tiffany's chairman.[55]

A French court has ordered eBay Inc. to pay several luxury brand manufacturers €40 million, or about $63.2 million for its failure to take steps to ensure that the goods being sold through the Internet auction site were not counterfeit. Louis Vuitton and Christian Dior had brought suit against the online retailer because of the large numbers of fake and unauthorized products of the two companies that were being sold at the site. In addition, the judge found that eBay had permitted the unauthorized sales of certain perfumes manufactured by the two companies. The perfumes that were sold were indeed

---

[54]www.cbp.gov, from press release. Accessed June 10, 2010.

[55]Katie Hafner, "Tiffany and eBay in Fight Over Fakes," *New York Times*, November 27, 2007, pp. C1, C9.

authentic. However, the two companies have exclusive deal arrangements with retailers, and the perfumes can only be sold at department stores and other specialized retail outlets.

The French court decision means that online retailers cannot assume a passive role in allowing the sale of goods. They must undertake some form of screening to eliminate the obvious forms of infringement and the selling of counterfeit items.

eBay is appealing the court's decision. The company says that it has 2,000 employees and a $20 million per annum budget devoted to ferreting out counterfeit goods but that the task is so large that there are some items that slip through the oversight system.

This decision is not the first from the EU:

- eBay was ordered by a French court last year to pay Hermes €20,000 for the sale of fake products
- A German court ordered eBay to do more to stop the sale of counterfeit Rolex watches

In *Tiffany, Inc. v eBay, Inc.*, 576 F.Supp.2d 463 (S.D.N.Y. 2008), the federal court ruled that eBay cannot be held vicariously responsible for the infringing goods being sold on eBay. The court held that although eBay had generalized knowledge that there were counterfeit Tiffany goods being sold, it also used search engines to try and flag obvious infringements. Further, the court noted that there are, in fact, authentic items sold on eBay, and courts cannot impose vicarious liability on eBay because of suspicions. The federal court of appeals reversed that decision and found for eBay (600 F.3d 93 (2010)), and Tiffany has appealed to the U.S. Supreme Court.

Louis Vuitton and the Web

Two web-hosting companies had a verdict of $32 million entered against them by a California jury for contributory trademark infringement. The case is *Louis Vuitton v Akanoc Solutions, Inc.,* and the jury returned the verdict against the web-hosting companies for "contributory trademark infringement."

The lawyers for Louis Vuitton, and the company employs forty of them each year, were able to put their case together from internal e-mails obtained through discovery from Akanac Solutions and Managed Solutions Group, two web-hosting companies owned by Steven Chen. The e-mails indicated that employees at both companies were aware that there were counterfeit Vuitton bags and merchandise being sold by others using their service, but they took no steps to warn or stop the sales. Louis Vuitton also employs 250 investigators at a cost of $20 million per year to track down the fake goods, which, in this case, are almost identical to the company's actual products.[56]

While the courts have held that it is primarily the responsibility of the trademark holder to enforce against counterfeiters and the eBay case was decided prior to this one, there are an increasing number of decisions holding websites liable on the grounds that they cannot turn a blind eye when they are aware that there is infringement occurring using their websites, such as when the sellers advertise "fake designer handbags" or "No one will know they are not the original Louis Vuitton purse."

The case between eBay and Tiffany is on appeal to the U.S. Supreme Court, and the $32 million verdict in the *Akanoc* case is also expected to go up on appeal.

Landlords, Louis Vuitton, and Liability for Counterfeit Tenants

Buyers of counterfeit goods are not prosecuted in the United States, but the goal is to frighten them away. Also, companies such as Louis Vuitton are turning to landlords, property owners, shippers, credit card companies, and any others in the supply chain to

---

[56]Pollinger, "Counterfeit Goods and Their Potential Financing of International Terrorism."

stop the flow of goods with suits for vicarious or contributory liability. A settlement in one case found landlords promising to evict tenants who sell fake goods as well as hang warning signs permanently. Companies that have joined with Louis Vuitton include Burberry, Gucci, and Prada. They refer to their work with the supply chain as "the Landlord Program." Although a judge has awarded the companies $464 million in one case for infringement by tenants, the companies are unable to collect such a large judgment from these small businesses. The result is the pursuit of the landlords, and landlords are generally larger companies with more funds and less likelihood of having judgment-proof status.

In *Polo Ralph Lauren Corp. v Chinatown Gift Shop*, 855 F. Supp. 648 (S.D. N.Y. 1994), Polo Ralph Lauren, Rolex Watch USA, and Louis Vuitton brought suit against a landlord who was leasing property to three retailers who were selling goods that infringed on their trademarks for their clothing, watches, and leather goods, respectively. The court held that the landlord could have vicarious liability under federal law for facilitating the infringement by the tenants. In *Habeeba's Dance of the Arts, Ltd. v Knoblauch*, 430 F.Supp.2d 709 (Ohio 2006), the court held that the landlord (YWCA) could be held liable for contributory infringement for leasing a portion of its facilities to Habeeba's when it knew that Habeeba's was teaching the Habiba form of dancing, a trademarked method that belonged to Habiba, and that such use was likely to cause confusion about ownership of the dance method.[57]

The bags are still there on Canal Street in New York City, but, as the buyers note, you are taken back into secret rooms through two locked doors. The bags no longer hang out in the open, something that makes everyone vulnerable. The extra steps have not, however, made a dent in the counterfeit trade. The companies estimate that their intense program has cut back on counterfeit sales about 5 percent. Still, the companies continue because they feel that the precedent for third-party liability is their only hope of curbing the huge counterfeit market.

Because of their potential liability, even property owners have joined in to help with enforcement. On New York's Canal Street, owners post signs (furnished by Louis Vuitton) with the following information:

This retailer is not authorized or licensed to sell Louis Vuitton merchandise. Counterfeiting is criminally and civilly punishable under federal and state law by up to 10 years of imprisonment and $2,000,000 in fines.

Discussion Questions

1. Why should we worry about knock-offs of luxury goods? What ethical issues exist?
2. If you were a landlord, would you turn a blind eye to counterfeit sales? Should landlords be held responsible if they don't know about the sales?
3. Would you, or do you, buy knock-offs? Who is harmed? Make a list of stakeholders.
4. What are the ethical issues in taking no action when someone else is harmed—that is, you know it is happening, but you aren't doing it and you do nothing to stop it?

Sources

Galloni, Alessandra, "As Luxury Industry Goes Global, Knock-Off Merchants Follow," *Wall Street Journal*, January 31, 2006, pp. A1, A13.

Galloni, Alessandra, "Bagging Fakers and Sellers," *Wall Street Journal*, January 31, 2006, pp. B1, B2.

[57]This discussion was adapted from Marianne M. Jennings, *Real Estate Law*, 9th ed. (2010), p. 235.

Christina Passariello and Mylebe Mangalindan, "EBay Fined Over Selling Counterfeits," *Wall Street Journal*, July 1, 2008, p. B1.

Dorene Carvajal, "EBay Told to Pay $61 Million In Sale of Counterfeit Goods," *New York Times*, July 1, 2008, p. C1

Tresa Baldas, "Add Knockoff Handbags to Web Hosts' Woes," *National Law Journal*, September 28, 2009, p. 4.

Case 8.10

Copyright, Songs, and Charities

Children at camps around the country in the summer of 1996 were not able to dance the "Macarena" except in utter silence. Their usual oldies dances were halted in 1996. The American Society of Composers, Authors & Publishers (ASCAP) notified camps and the organizations that sponsor camps (such as the Boy Scouts of America and the Girls Scouts of the USA) that they would be required to pay the licensing fees if they used any of the 4 million copyrighted songs written or published by any of the 68,000 members of ASCAP.

The fees for use of the songs have exceeded the budgets of many of the camps. One camp that operates only during the day charges its campers $44 per week. ASCAP wanted $591 for the season for the camp's use of songs such as "Edelweiss" (from *The Sound of Music*) and "This Land Is Your Land." ASCAP demanded fees for even singing the songs around the campfire. ASCAP's letters to the camps reminded the directors of the possible penalties of $5,000 and up to six days in jail and threatened lawsuits for any infringement of the rights of ASCAP members. Luckily, "Kumbaya" is not owned by an ASCAP member.

Several camp directors wrote and asked for a special program that would allow their camps a discount for the use of the songs. Many of the camps are not run as for-profit businesses but rather include camps such as those for children with cancer and AIDS. ASCAP now includes the following frequently asked question on its website (http://www.ascap.com):

> *Do I need permission to perform music as part of a presentation in class or at a training seminar?*
>
> *If the performance is part of face to face teaching activity at a non-profit educational institution, permission is not required. Permission is required when music is used as part of training seminars, conventions, or other commercial or business presentations.*

ASCAP has over 100 licensing fee arrangements. The fees range from $200 per $700 per year, but some organizations have negotiated lower fees. The Radio Music License Committee negotiated a $1.7 billion fee arrangement with ASCAP to cover its members through 2009.

In 1999, Congress passed the Fairness in Music Licensing Amendment [17 U.S.C. 110 (5)] to provide an exemption for restaurants (such as sports bars) that play radio music or television programs over speakers in their facilities. The law provides that because the radio and television rights have been acquired, restaurants and bars need not pay ASCAP additional fees. ASCAP opposed this change to the copyright laws and has proposed changes to it since 1999.

The issue of public use of popular songs and copyrights surfaced after the September 11, 2001, attacks, when Congress stood on the steps of the Capitol on the evening of September 11, 2001, and sang, "God Bless America." It was a spontaneous moment, and from that time the song became an integral part of all public functions, including the seventh-inning stretch during the World Series.

Irving Berlin wrote "God Bless America" in 1940. When he did, he pledged all the royalties from the song to benefit youth organizations in the United States, specifically the Girl Scouts and Boy Scouts.

Each time there is a performance of the song, royalties are paid to the trust fund Berlin established for the administration of the royalties for the Scouts. Since that time, just the groups in New York City have received over $6 million from song performances. The annual income from "God Bless America" public performances has been about $200,000. However, the song has become a sort of second national anthem since the time of the September 11, 2001, attacks, with royalties from public performances generating triple income in 2002.

Mr. Berlin died in 1989 at the age of 101, and his daughter, Mrs. Linda Emmett, administers the trust fund. Mrs. Emmett, who shares her father's commitment to the children of the United States, says that nothing would have pleased her father more than the song's newfound popularity and the resulting benefits to the Scouts.[58]

Discussion Questions

1. Why does ASCAP work so diligently to enforce its rights and collect the fees for its members' songs?

2. What risks does ASCAP run if the camps continue to use the songs without payment of the licensing fees?

3. What ethical and social responsibility issues do you see with respect to those camps that are strictly nonprofit operations?

4. Can you think of a compromise that would protect ASCAP members' rights but still offer the camps a reasonable chance to use the songs?

5. What would you do if you were an ASCAP member and owned the rights to a song a camp wished to use? Do you think Mr. Berlin's trust has the correct approach? Could his trust not simply donate the use of the song? What problems do you see with that practice?

Sources

Bumiller, Elisabeth, "ASCAP Asks Royalties from Girl Scouts and Regrets It," *New York Times,* December 17, 1996, p. B1.

Ringle, Ken, "Campfire Churls," *Washington Post,* August 24, 1996, p. B1; and August 28, 1996, p. C3.

Case 8.11

Microsoft vs. Google and "Snippets" of Books

Microsoft has undertaken a public campaign against Google for what Microsoft calls Google's "cavalier" approach to copyright protections on videos, books, and other materials that end up posted on the web. Microsoft is lending its support to the Authors Guild and the Association of American Publishers, two groups that have sued Google for making digital copies of copyrighted books without permission. Google copied the books from library copies. There are also several class-action suits by authors pending against Google.

---

[58]William Glaberson, "Irving Berlin Gave the Scouts a Gift of Song," *New York Times,* October 14, 2001, p. A21.

Google indicates that it only provides "snippets" from books and is acting legally and ethically in doing so.

Discussion Questions

1. Does Google's view of "snippets" translate to fair use protection?
2. Evaluate the issue of fairness in light of all of those who are affected by Google's decision.
3. Google also maintains that once someone has viewed a snippet of a book, he or she cannot return to that snippet. However, what would prevent students from simply using different computers to access snippets and then printing out and copying the pages for other students. The "snippets" often include full chapters and cases. Evaluate the conduct of the students who work together to avoid snippet limitations. Evaluate Google's role in facilitation of this conduct without the necessary controls or monitoring. How would you respond to students who say, "But the cost of textbooks is just too much. We have to find ways to reduce costs ourselves"?

Source

Gapper, John, "Microsoft Attacks Google on Copyright," *Financial Times*, March 6, 2006, p. 1.

Case 8.12

The Little Intermittent Windshield Wiper and Its Little Inventor

Robert W. Kearns, a Maryland inventor and former engineering professor at Wayne State University in Detroit, Michigan, obtained a patent for his first intermittent car windshield wiper system in 1967. *People* magazine described the genesis of Kearns's invention as follows:

When Robert Kearns popped open a champagne bottle on his wedding night in August 1953, he couldn't have seen that it might one day make him rich. At first he couldn't see much of anything; the cork hit him in the face, virtually blinding him in his right eye. But the accident got the homegrown inventor to thinking—about his eyes, the way they blink and, improbably, about how difficult it is to drive in a drizzling rain.

Kearns's musings led to a basement invention, a windshield wiper that automatically blinks on and off in light rain.[59]

He installed it in a 1962 Ford Galaxy, then demonstrated it for Ford. Ford installed the wiper system in its cars beginning in 1969 and did so under its own patents for such a system. During the 1970s, intermittent wiper systems began appearing on the cars of major U.S. and Japanese automakers. Kearns received no money for the use of these systems. The automakers maintained that the idea was an obvious one and it was only a matter of time before their engineers developed the same type of system. They also claimed that their systems differed from Kearns's in design and function.

Kearns led suit against Ford, General Motors, Chrysler, Fiat, Toyota, Ferrari, Volvo, Alfa-Romeo, Citroen, Honda, Isuzu, Mitsubishi, Nissan, Maserati, Peugeot, Renault, Rolls Royce, Saab, Toyota, and other Japanese auto manufacturers for a total of nineteen different defendants. He had planned to open his own firm to supply the intermittent windshield wiper systems to all automakers but was unable to do so after the companies

[59]Ken Gross, "Wiper Man Robert Kearns Won His Patent Fight with Ford, but That Didn't Mean He Was Out of the Wood," *People*, August 6, 1990.

manufactured the systems in-house. Dr. Kearns represented himself in the cases that ran through 1995 until final resolution or settlement. In fact, Kearns set up Kearns and Associates in a building across the street from the federal courthouse in Detroit in order to battle the auto manufacturers. His children worked for the company formed to litigate, and, at one point, Kearns was ordered to pay sanctions because his son had obtained confidential documents by dating a paralegal who worked at a law firm that was representing one of the auto manufacturers.[60]

In November 1990, Kearns settled his case with Ford Motor Company for $10.2 million, which amounted to 30 cents per car Ford sold with the intermittent wiper systems. He had turned down a $30 million offer from Ford and proceeded with litigation. In June 1992, a jury awarded Kearns $11.3 million in damages from Chrysler, or about 90 cents per car, for Chrysler's infringement of Kearns's patent. Chrysler had sold 12,564,107 vehicles with the device. Kearns had originally asked for damages ranging from $3 to $30 per car, or $37.7 to $377 million, based on the treble damage provisions of the patent infringement laws.[61] Chrysler appealed what it called the "unreasonable and excessive" verdict; however, the appeal was dismissed by the U.S. Supreme Court.[62] The amount Kearns received from Chrysler, $18.7 million, was far less than he had requested as damages.

Kearns continued to pursue his cases against the other car companies until the U.S. Supreme Court refused to reverse the dismissal of his case. He spent $4 million in legal fees in the Ford case and about $5.5 million on the case against Chrysler. He was represented by four law firms during the course of all the litigation. Dr. Kearns was a colorful figure who wrote an angry letter to the federal judge handling his first trial when the jury was unable to reach a verdict. After having the letter delivered to the judge, Dr. Kearns disappeared for several days. The jury could not reach a verdict, and the judge declared a mistrial. That case, the Ford case, was eventually settled.

Kearns said his success should be an inspiration for other inventors because it proves they can win against large corporations that have used others' ideas without reimbursement. Others say that Kearns's failed marriage and his near breakdown demonstrate that a refusal to negotiate can be harmful and that most of his money went to paying lawyers in the decades-long litigation.

Dr. Kearns died in February 2005, just after he appeared in *Forbes* magazine along with other inventors who had changed our daily lives by what they developed. Others in the group included Ray Tomlinson, the man who came up with using "@" for e-mail addresses, and Allen Gant Sr., the inventor of pantyhose.

Discussion Questions

1. Is it ethical to use an idea based on the risk analysis that the owner of that idea simply cannot afford to litigate the matter?
2. Why was the intermittent wiper system so important to the automakers?
3. Could Kearns have done anything further to protect himself?

4. If you were an executive with one of the companies still in litigation with Kearns, would you settle the case? Why or why not?
5. Why do you think the auto manufacturers fought Kearns so extensively? Is it possible that their engineers had been working simultaneously on the idea?

---

[60]Mike Hoffman, "Fighting Knockoff Artists Is Easy, If You've Got a Lifetime to Devote to It," *Inc.*, December 1997, http://www.inc.com/magazine/19971201/1374.html.

[61]*Kearns v Ford Motor Co.* 726 F.supp 159 (E.D. Mich. 1989); see also "Chrysler Told to Pay Inventor $11.3 Million," *New York Times*, June 12, 1992, p. C3.

[62]*Kearns v Ford Motor Corp.*, 62 F.3d 1430 (Ca.F.C. 1995), cert. denied, 516 U.S. 989 (1995).

Ethics and Government

The public trust. The fair shake. Government agencies should, respectively, hold and give both. But, if those agencies cross ethical lines, businesses are affected in their ability to operate in an open economy. Like a business, a government agency must also be diligent in honoring its ethical standards.

Government Employees

Reading 9.1

The Fish Bowl Existence of Government[1]

We in the public sector take a detached, perhaps even superior, attitude toward these [corporate] scandals because we are government employees. We feel secure knowing that we are not part of those evil corporate environments. We fancy ourselves immune to the bottom line pressures that led to these lapses in ethics and financial reporting. Such assumptions are dangerous. So long as human beings run organizations, whether profit, non-profit or government organizations, and those organizations have goals and tasks, there will be pressures and those pressures produce ethical lapses whether the accounting focuses on ROE or sources and uses.

For example, the August 2003 Columbia Accident Investigation Board Report provides a detailed look at the culture of NASA and what contributed to incidents such as the loss of the Challenger Space Shuttle following a launch that proceeded despite engineers' questions and doubts about the ability of the rocket booster o-rings to function at below-freezing temperatures, or the problems with the Hubble telescope and, finally, the causes of the recent Columbia crash. The NASA report reveals that this government agency and its employees felt the same types of pressures that employees at WorldCom and Enron felt as they struggled to make numbers. The struggle to meet the goal impaired their decision-making abilities. One employee quote from the report indicates his uncertainty about the impact of pressure, " . . . And I have to think that subconsciously that even though you don't want it to affect decision-making, it probably does."[2]

Another NASA employee reflected on the congressional budget issues and the time crunch of the deadlines and why safety problems may have been minimized or ignored: " . . . I don't know what Congress communicated to O'Keefe [the NASA administrator at the time]. I don't really understand the criticality of February 19th, that if we didn't make that date, did that mean the end of NASA? I don't know. . . . I would like to think that the technical issues and safety resolving technical issues can take priority over any budget or scheduling issue."[3]

Government employees experience different types of pressure, but pressure exists nonetheless to take ethical shortcuts in the performance of their duties. The pressure may be political. Or the pressure may come from the fear of losing one's position if the numbers fall short of a political expectation. The pressure may come from the fear of fallout if the real truth about financial issues emerges. But the fear and pressures for government employees, particularly those responsible for financial, budgeting and accountability issues, are as real as those felt in these former Fortune 500 companies.

---

[1]Excerpted from Marianne M. Jennings "Preventing Organizational Ethical Collapse," *Journal of Government Financial Management* 53(1): 12–21 (2004).

[2]August 2003 Columbia Accident Investigation Board Report, http://www.nasa.gov/columbia/home/index.html. Accessed July 1, 2010.

[3]*Id.*

Fundamentally, ethical collapses in any organization result in exploration of a paraphrase of Dr. Stanley Milgram's work on right, wrong and actions, "What is it about organizations that allows them to slip the restraints of human conscience?"[4]

A central goal of the Sarbanes–Oxley legislation and the ongoing reforms in corporate governance is not only to find ways to encourage employees to communicate their concerns about ethical lapses, but also to ensure that when employees do voice those concerns that there is a follow-up investigation and no retaliation against the employee. These two critical components of sound governance and an ethical culture were missing in the collapsed companies, and, as the NASA report bears out, can also be missing in government agencies. The application of Sarbanes–Oxley principles to government agencies can be found in this simple question of self-introspection, "Am I comfortable that employees in my agency have the means and ability to voice their concerns and raise issues?"

Answering that question requires an examination of the agency's culture. Studies of these collapsed corporations reveal that there are common threads that are predictors of ethical collapse. Watching for those traits and making changes to eliminate them provides a means for ensuring open and honest lines of communication between employees and managers.

Pressure

In a government agency, the pressure can be political. For example, in Arizona, public perception about the efficacy of its Child Protective Services resulted in audits and reports and a political battle that saw the agency respond to 355 requests for information from the legislature.[5] One audit report, using the figure of number of cases per case worker, concluded that case workers were overworked, a justification for more funds for the agency from the legislature. However, a follow-up analysis by an outsider found that the initial report included, in that per case number, cases that were actually closed. That initial number was deceptive, whether by accident or choice, and costs the agency credibility. The report was compiled during a period of intense public scrutiny and political pressure. Regardless of how anyone lands on the question of the agency, its efficacy and funding, the ethical issue of honesty transcends all: do the numbers depict fairly and accurately the current status of the organization?

That same question was at the heart of all the corporate scandals. The answer was that the numbers had some footnotes, some qualifiers and caveats that were not included in the financial statements, but the numbers were released to the public. The reason is the same, whether publicly-traded company or government agency: employees felt pressure to make the numbers do what they felt their superiors wanted them to do.

Conflicts

Conflicts from appointments and awards of contracts can develop through close connections between the board members and elected officials. For example, one city learned that one of the business people serving on it citizen's board for drug education was a partial owner, along with one of the city council members, of a drug education and rehab center that was awarded several city contracts through the board's approval. The

---

[4]Milgram said, "A substantial proportion of people do what they are told to do . . . irrespective of the content of that act and without limitations of conscience so long as they perceive that the command comes from a legitimate authority." Dr. Milgram found that 65 percent of his subjects would inflict pain on other human beings if told to do so by someone they perceived to be an authority figure. For a summary of his work, go to http://www.stanleymilgram .com. The figures were actually 61 percent in the United States and 66 percent in other countries.

[5]Laurie Roberts, "Bird Wings, Lips Flap, but CPS Remains Unrepaired," December 3, 2003. http://www.azcentral .com/arizonarepublic/news/articles/1203roberts03.html. (As originally accessed and researched.)

citizens are often the watchdogs of government actions and when their role becomes intertwined with those who appoint them, that objectivity and supervisory role is lost. Government agencies must step beyond statutory requirements and focus on creating a culture of virtue ethics. Doing so requires the following:

- Be sure those in the organization understand that goals, numbers, rankings, ratings and report results must be achieved within the parameters of pre-established an absolute values such as honesty, not giving false impressions, avoiding conflicts of interest, and fairness in application of rules and following procedures.
- Provide the means whereby employees can express their concerns and report unethical or illegal conduct. That means may be a hotline or employee concern line. It may be as simple as a suggestion box into which they can offer their questions, concerns and reports. Remember, however, to caution employees about the risk of paralyzing an organization with spiteful and petty complaints.
- Be sure that there is an effective mechanism to follow up on employee concerns and issues and that the organization is aware of that follow-up.
- Constantly review interconnections, conflicts and relationships on boards, particularly boards that award contracts and involve citizen representatives. Check company ownerships on sourcing and be certain conflicts rules are clear to those responsible for purchasing.
- Question even those who are competent, charismatic and compelling—those traits sometimes are a mask for underlying issues.
- Be certain that there is wisdom and experience in every unit so that the long-term perspective of the value of ethics is not lost.
- Make sure all employees are subject to the rules, that enforcement is uniform, that investigations are thorough and disciplinary action consistent.
- Question your own decisions: why am I structuring this report or this budget this way? what is on the line here and is my judgment clouded?
- Don't just comply with the law. The law was never intended to be the maximum standard of behavior; it is the minimum standard. Don't ask, "Could I do this?" Ask, "Should I do this?"
- Adopt and use absolute standards as a guide for decisions, not circumstances and not pressure.

These fixes create a culture of checks and balances, one in which questionable conduct is caught before it takes place and the public is left scratching its collective head, wondering, "Where were their minds and what were they thinking when they made these decisions?"

Discussion Questions

1. How are government agencies like corporations in terms of pressures that cause employees to engage in unethical conduct?

2. How do conflicts affect government employees' judgment?

3. Why is the ability to ask questions of leaders in any organization important?

Case 9.2

The Minerals Management Service: The Arms-Length Affairs with Oil Executives

The Role of MMS

The Minerals Management Service (MMS) is a division in the Department of Interior that is responsible for negotiating both onshore and offshore oil leases with oil companies and collecting the government's share of royalties from the drilling. However, MMS is also responsible for ensuring the safety of the oil companies' drilling operations, a job that some feel is inherently conflicted because the interest in maximizing royalties creates tension with the interest in curbing drilling activity or even requiring a shut-down when necessary. The often close relationships between government employees and the oil industry resulted in several investigations in MMS and the Department of the Interior.

Colorado MMS

The investigation at the Colorado MMS began when an employee made a phone call that indicated there were problems with the office's ethical culture. As a result of this anonymous and very general tip on "ethical culture," Earl Devaney, then–Inspector General for the Department of the Interior, conducted an investigation and issued a troubling report in April 2008.[6] The report indicates that MMS employees who were responsible for the negotiations of oil leases with oil company executives were engaged in behaviors that included rigging contracts, engaging in drug use and sexual relationships with oil company executives, and accepting golf trips, ski trips, and dinners from oil company employees.

In addition, Colorado MMS employees were using their positions for additional compensation and the development of potential employment relationships with oil companies. MMS employees were forming their own companies for purposes of being awarded oil company contracts for their consulting services to the companies. One employee earned $30,000 in consulting fees from oil companies that were not approved or disclosed because, in the employees' minds, there was no conflict since the fees from the oil companies were paid to a company created by the MMS employee. Employees shared information with certain companies about the key qualification criteria that MMS would be using in their decision processes. Between 2002 and 2006, one-third of the staff at the Colorado MMS accepted gifts from four oil companies on 135 occasions. On several occasions, some MMS employees who were attending industry meetings accepted lodging from industry members after meetings at local hotels where the meetings were held because they were too intoxicated to drive home

The MMS employees who were involved had created a special division, the Royalty in Kind (RIK) division that opted out of the ethics rules of the Department of Interior (DOI). RIK carried great weight in the DOI because it brought in $3.75 billion in royalties during a one-year period that was covered under the audit period. As a result of the power they wielded, the group was able to convince its superiors in Washington to allow them to opt out of reporting to their supervisor in the Colorado office and instead report directly to an individual in Washington, D.C., some 1,500 miles away.

When confronted with evidence of sexual relationships with industry contacts, RIK employees at Colorado MMS responded that "the sexual relationships were arms-length." Mr. Devaney explained in his report, "Sexual relationships with prohibited sources cannot, by definition, be arms-length."[7]

Ironically, one of the RIK employees who had a consulting company on the side circulated an e-mail to his staff members to remind them about the DOI ethics policy, "During this season of filing our annual disclosure reports and reviewing our ethics guidelines, it is important for us in the RIK office to pay especially close attention to the Federal ethics guidelines and to always have them in mind in conducting our everyday

---

[6]In early 2009, Mr. Devaney was appointed to serve as the auditor for the use of Reinvestment and Recovery Act funds.

[7]Memo of Earl Devaney to the Secretary of Interior, September 9, 2008. http://doi.bluewatermedia.com/pdf/Smith%20REDACTED%20FINAL_080708%20Final%20with%20transmittal%209_10%20date.pdf. Accessed July 1, 2010.

business. . . . Please pay close attention to the Ethics Guide distributed to all of you as it gives us a great and official template for our actions in this regard."[8]

Louisiana MMS and the Red-Jacket Symbolism

Prior to 1997, the Gulf Coast had been known as the "Dead Sea," a description coined by industry experts that reflected the lack of offshore drilling. Since the time of the 1969 oil spill near Santa Barbara, California, offshore drilling had been a dead industry. The days of what was known as the "red-jacket auctions" had ended. The red jacket was what the MMS official in charge of offshore minerals management wore to auction days when awarding oil rights to companies under the sealed-bid process the agency required. The red-jacket days had ended until drilling restrictions were eased on March 5, 1997. Shortly after, over 1,000 oil company bidders attended an MMS auction in New Orleans with some anticipation about a new direction by MMS. Chris Oynes, a portly fellow and the new Director for Offshore Energy and Minerals Management in MMS, was the new official placed in charge of the auction being held in New Orleans. Long-time industry members did not know what to think until Mr. Oynes pulled his size 46 red jacket from a brief case he had brought with him to the auction podium. Those present cheered because the jacket was symbolic of a new era of expanded drilling as well as a closer relationship between the oil industry and the government. Mr. Oynes has described the meaning of the moment as, "Let the good times roll."[9]

With this new expansion of offshore drilling, MMS experienced a new level of interconnection with the industry as well as political pressure from state and local politicians. Keeping and expanding the offshore oil rigs translated into jobs and revenues for the Gulf Coast states. The pressure from both federal and state governments was expansion for the royalties and the economic development the drilling presence of the industry brought. The Louisiana Division of MMS negotiated the oil-drilling agreement with BP for its Deepwater Horizon rig that was located off the coast of Louisiana and that exploded in April 2010, an explosion that resulted in the death of eleven rig workers, gushing oil after the explosion, and significant damage to the wildlife preserves and beaches along the Gulf Coast. (See Case 6.25.) Mr. Oynes became a powerful figure in MMS as well as in the Gulf and among the oil companies. The relationships were close.

No one realized how close until the BP Deepwater Horizon explosion and spill and the eerie simultaneous release of an inspector general's report on the conduct of government officials. When that report emerged in May 2010, immediately after the BP Deepwater Horizon explosion and spill, Mr. Oynes ended 21 years of service by stepping down from his position in response to the disturbing revelations of conflicts in the report.

Lake Charles, Louisiana MMS, and BP

In this division of MMS, located in Lake Charles, Louisiana, the Department of the Interior Inspector General (DOI IG) began an investigation in 2006 on the basis of yet another anonymous tip. Immediately following the investigation at that time, the regional director was fired for accepting gifts from companies working on oil drilling projects in the Gulf of Mexico, not disclosing the gifts, and then lying to investigators about accepting them. His termination led many in Washington to believe that the issues had been resolved. However, based on yet another anonymous letter sent in 2008 to the U.S. Attorney's Office in New Orleans, Louisiana, the DOI IG began another investigation. Because Mr. Devaney left the DOI in 2009 to become the auditor for the American

---

[8]*Id.*

[9]Jason DeParle, "Minerals Service Had a Mandate to Produce Results," *New York Times*, August 8, 2010, p. A1.

Recovery and Reinvestment Act funds, Acting IG Mary Kendall completed the investigation and issued the report on May 24, 2010.

The report concluded that Louisiana MMS employees were accepting hunting and fishing trips from oil industry executives, taking tickets to sporting events, using drugs while employed at the agency, and negotiating with oil companies for jobs using their government e-mail accounts. The IG found everything from pornography to inappropriate humor on the computers of the MMS employees.

The employees accepted private jet flights to games and were quite cavalier in their government e-mails about describing their activities. One MMS inspector sent the following e-mail around the office: "The 40 to 3 ass whipping LSU put on Miami was a lot more impressive in person. My daughter and I had a blast."

On the following day the same inspector sent another e-mail with pictures attached, including one with the oil company's plane on which he, and an oil and gas production company official, and others flew to Atlanta for the 2005 Peach Bowl game. The employees who participated in this event and others did not file the required gift disclosure forms. Only one employee in the Louisiana office filed a gift disclosure form between the years of 2005 and 2009.

When the Louisiana regional director, was asked about the gifts and trips, he responded, "Obviously, we're all oil industry." The local economies in states along the coast were dependent upon the continued drilling. Those in the MMS were rewarded for the revenue the offshore rigs produced for the government. The regional director also added,

> We're all from the same part of the country. Almost all of our inspectors have worked for oil companies out on these same platforms. They grew up in the same towns. Some of these people, they've been friends with all their life. They've been with these people since they were kids. They've hunted together. They fish together. They skeet shoot together. . . . They do this all the time."[10]

The report also brought out information about Mr. Oynes's conduct and relationship with the oil industry. The report revealed that Mr. Oynes's wife received a teaching award, one that was sponsored by the American Petroleum Industry.[11] But, Mr. Oynes was a valued federal employee. He won a Distinguished Service Award from the president, and his leases would bring in $824 million in royalties to the federal government.

Inspector Kendall indicated in her final report that she found the ease with which employees moved from government to industry and back created a fluid relationship that made it difficult for both sides to honor government policies and regulation. Some safety inspections (four during the audit period) were conducted by MMS employees who were in the process of accepting employment from the company whose rigs they were inspecting.

Other details in the report mirror the findings in the Colorado MMS report with pornography, meth use, and gifts being a part of the Louisiana MMS culture. There were also Casio watches as gifts and skeet-shooting outings with oil company executives.

The IG report notes that all of the employees were given ethics training each year that covered the following:

> Federal regulations and agency ethics rules prohibit employees from directly or indirectly soliciting or accepting gifts, including meals, over $20 at one time and $50 per year from a prohibited source. Federal employees are also prohibited from accepting

---

[10]Memo of Acting Inspector General Mary Kendall, May 24, 2010, to DOI Secretary Ken Salazar. http://www.eenews.net/public/25/15844/features/documents/2010/05/25/document_gw_02.pdf. Accessed July 1, 2010.

[11]Jason DeParle, "Minerals Service Had a Mandate to Produce Results," *New York Times,* August 8, 2010, p. A1.

gifts given in association with their official position. They are required to declare gifts and travel reimbursements aggregating over $335 during the reporting period, from any one source, as well as the identity of the source, in an annual financial disclosure report. For travel-related gifts in association with their official position, employees must document the travel itinerary, including dates, and the nature of the expenses.

Ironically, the report on misconduct at the Louisiana office also disclosed that BP had been recognized by the Louisiana MMS with a "safe award," given to companies that achieve the highest level of safety. However, the report also concluded that MMS inspectors often signed each other's reports on platform inspections and that the inspectors had missed a number of significant violations by oil companies in their rig operations. There was also an increase in the time between environmental and safety inspections and a decrease in the length of those reviews. However, the federal government recognized MMS for its focus on safety and the environment.

Discussion Questions

1. What is the purpose of a hotline?
2. Why was it necessary to terminate many of the employees singled out in the report?
3. At a staff meeting in 2006 for the Louisiana division, one of the environmental scientists questioned whether the drilling at deeper and deeper levels was safe. The regional director posed the question to the director for field operations. The response from the head of field operations was that the blowout preventers would stop explosions and spills. The blowout preventer at the BP Deepwater Horizon rig failed and resulted in the spill. The head of field operations was fired in 2007 for accepting gifts from oil companies and lying on his ethics form. What does this example illustrate? Describe what ethical issues are at the heart of the two audits at the MMS divisions. Why should we worry about these breaches of ethics by government employees?
4. List the rationalizations you can find in the case.
5. List the factors that contributed to the cultures of the agencies in Colorado and Louisiana.

Case 9.3

Kodak, the Appraiser, and the Assessor: Lots of Back Scratching on Valuation

This tale of a sort of sting operation required participation from business, government, and a professional. John Nicolo was a real property appraiser who did appraisal work for Eastman Kodak, Inc. (Kodak) at the request of one of Kodak's now-former employees, Mark Camarata, who served as Kodak's director of state and local taxes while employed there. Charles Schwab was the former assessor for the town of Greece, New York, an area that included Kodak headquarters. Kodak is both the largest employer and the largest property owner in the town of Greece.

According to the indictments in the case, Schwab made reductions in Kodak's real property tax assessment. Those reductions, according to calculations completed by Nicolo and Camarata, saved Kodak $31,527,168 in property taxes over a fifteen-year period. But, Schwab did not make those reductions as a matter of assessor policy, fond feelings for Kodak, or the goodness of his public servant heart. He made those reductions at the behest of the other two in exchange for payment. Nicolo's fee from Kodak, arranged according to a percentage of the amount he was able to save the company, was to be $7,881,798 (about 25 percent of Kodak's projected tax savings). After being paid over $4,000,000 of his fee from Kodak, Nicolo paid Camarata $1,553,300 for his role in hiring him and then paid Schwab $1,052,100. The essence of the arrangement was that the appraiser agreed to split the tax savings fee with the assessor in exchange for the reduction and with the Kodak employee in exchange for hiring him.

The group also managed to involve companies that were buying property from Kodak. For example, in 2004, ITT bought one of Kodak's buildings in its industrial park as Kodak was downsizing. Immediately upon its acquisition of the building, ITT got an assessment from Schwab that quadrupled the value of the building for purposes of tax assessment. Mr. Camarata referred the ITT officers to Mr. Nicolo, who then talked Mr. Schwab into reducing the assessment value. However, unbeknownst to ITT, the whole scenario had been set up by the group, according to trial testimony. Schwab reduced the assessment value and Nicolo split his fee with Camarata and Schwab.

Camarata entered a guilty plea to various federal fraud charges and agreed to cooperate with federal authorities in their prosecution of the other two of the property tax triumvirate who have been charged with fifty-six counts of fraud, money laundering, and other federal crimes. Mr. Camarata faced a possible penalty of twenty years but was sentenced in 2009 to two years because of what U.S. Federal District Judge David Latimer described as follows: "Your cooperation with the government was immediate and complete. Without your testimony, I think the verdict might have been much more difficult for the government to accomplish . . . your help was the linchpin for the government's case."[12]

Mr. Camarata was ordered to pay $10 million in restitution as part of his federal prosecution, but the total amount he will owe remains unclear because of federal income taxes owed, civil damages to Kodak and ITT, and taxes owed to the city based on the undervaluations.

When Kodak learned of the schemes, it immediately entered into discussions with the town of Greece for the reappraisal of its properties. Kodak also filed suit against Camarata and others seeking reimbursement from them for the fees that were paid as part of the scheme.

Discussion Questions

1. Was anyone really hurt by this? Didn't Kodak benefit?
2. Why do we worry about an agreement by an assessor to reduce the assessed value? Couldn't he have done that anyway, regardless of receiving payment?
3. Does the method for paying appraisers on a contingency basis encourage this type of involvement by government officials?
4. Why do you think the three (possibly five) decided to engage in the scheme? Are there any thoughts for your credo that come from your observations about what happened?

After his guilty plea and agreement to cooperate, Mr. Camarata's fellow defendants referred to him as a "liar and thief." What lesson do you learn from this reaction and interaction?

Source

Indictment, *U.S. v Camarata*, May 5, 2005, http://www.fbi.gov.

Case 9.4

The Governor and a Senate Seat Vacated by a President

Illinois governor Rod Blagojevich was arrested in the early hours of the morning at his Chicago home on January 9, 2009. He was arrested on the basis of wiretap transcripts of his conversations with various political operatives and officials about who should be

---

[12]Michael Zeigler, "Camarata Sentenced to Two Years for Role in Kickback Scheme," *Rochester Democrat*, July 7, 2009, p. A1.

appointed by him to fill the U.S. Senate seat vacated by President Barack Obama upon his election to the presidency. The conversations discuss whether the individuals would be willing to hold fundraisers for him and allude to the fact that there was a system of pay-to-play. Mr. Blagojevich stated on the tapes, "I want to make money . . . [the senate seat] is a valuable thing, you don't just give it away for nothing. . . . I've got this thing and it is f_____ golden, and, uh, uh, I'm just not giving it up for f_____ nothing. I'm not gonna do it. And I can always use it. I can parachute me there."[13]

There were also other tapes of Mr. Blagojevich's brother talking with Roland Burris, the man who would eventually be appointed to the seat, during which Robert Blagojevich asks Mr. Burris for checks, "You know if you guys could just write some checks, that'd be fine," to which Mr. Burris responds, "OK, OK, well, we, I, I will personally do something. I know I could give a check. Myself."[14]

After Mr. Blagojevich was indicted on sixteen felony counts of racketeering conspiracy, wire fraud, extortion conspiracy, attempted extortion, and making false statements to federal agents, he was impeached and thereby removed as governor. Indicted along with the impeached former governor were his brother, two former chiefs of staff, a campaign fundraiser, and a businessperson in what federal authorities referred to as an enterprise of corruption.

One former chief of staff for the former governor has been cooperating with the prosecutors in the case. Prosecutors allege that from the day he took office until he was arrested on January 9, 2009, the former governor was selling everything from signing bills to appointments to commissions. In one portion of the indictment, prosecutors allege that the former governor would simply agree to do something for someone in exchange for their holding a fundraiser for him. Prosecutors are calling the extensive efforts to gain from his political power the Blagojevich Enterprise.

Mrs. Blagojevich, who was heard speaking on some of the taped conversations, was not indicted. Mr. Blagojevich declared his innocence and carried through with his vow to fight the charges and clear his name as the trial began on June 1, 2010. He proclaimed, "I have done absolutely nothing wrong."[15]

The trial was off to a raucous start, with the judge ordering Mr. Blagojevich to stop tweeting during the trial and his defense lawyer offering the following insights in his opening statement, "That man is as honest as the day is long," (pointing to his client) and that Mr. Blagojevich has "good ethics" and "beautiful hair" even as he let the jurors know that "Rod has cheated on Patti."[16]

Assistant U.S. Attorney Carrie Hamilton offered the jurors a different perspective, "He corrupted the office of the governor of the state of Illinois for his own personal benefit. When you hear him say this senate seat is golden and he's not giving it up for nothing, you are going to know, that's how he viewed his power."[17]

Following a six-week trial, the jury deliberated for ten days and convicted Mr. Blagojevich on only one of the 24 felony counts, that of lying to the FBI during the course of the investigation. The jury was hung on the remaining counts and the judge declared a mistrial on those counts. The government has indicated it will seek a retrial.

---

[13]Douglas Belkin, Lauren Etter, and Timothy W. Martin, "Governor Jailed in Alleged Crime Spree," *Wall Street Journal,* December 8, 2008, p. A1; and Judy Keen and Mimi Hall, "Feds: Governor Tried to Sell Senate Seat," *USA Today,* December 10, 2008, p. 1A.

[14]AP, "On Tape, Burris Vows to Help Blagojevich," *USA Today,* May 27, 2009, p. 6A.

[15]Judy Keen, "Blagojevich, Five Associates Indicted," *USA Today,* April 3, 2009, p. 3A; and Monica Davey and Susan Saulny, "Blagojevich Indictment Lays Out Broad 'Enterprise' of Corruption," *New York Times,* April 3, 2009, p. A1.

[16]Ruth Rave, "Blago: 'Honest' with 'Beautiful Hair,'" June 8, 2010, http://liveshots.blogs.foxnews.com/2010/06/08/blago-honest-and-with-beautiful-hair. Accessed July 1, 2010.

[17]"Lawyers Give Openings in Blagojevich Trial," June 8, 2010, http://upi.com. Accessed July 1, 2010.

Discussion Questions

1. When the federal charges were announced, Chicago alderman Brian Doherty expressed his outrage over the former governor's conduct, "This is not like a guy taking $500 for a zoning change. This is selling a U.S. Senate seat."[18] Evaluate Mr. Doherty's statement for quality of its ethical reasoning.

2. What ethical category would the governor's conduct fall into?

3. How do you respond to Mr. Blagojevich's defense based on the notion that he was doing things that had always been done in Chicago?

4. List the stakeholders in this scenario and explain how they are affected.

Case 9.5

The Man Who Writes the Internal Revenue Code Has Tax Issues: The Rangel Round-Up

Former House Ways and Means Committee Chair, Charlie Rangel, has experienced a series of questions about his ethics as several practices, disclosures, and events emerged during the period from 2009 to 2010.

The Property Issues

In rent-controlled New York City, Mr. Rangel, who is the representative for the Harlem area, managed to wrangle several apartments from his landlord at the rock-bottom prices that characterize rent-control markets. Generally, New York residents are limited to one rent-controlled property.

Mr. Rangel received a homestead exemption for property he owned in Washington, D.C., even as he resided in the four rent-subsidized apartments in New York City. Rep. Rangel responded that where he lives is a "personal issue," and is not subject to a House ethics review.

The Income Tax Question

Mr. Rangel, as chair of Ways and Means, leads the group responsible for writing the tax code. However, he failed to report income he earned over two decades from renting his villa in the Dominican Republic. Mr. Rangel had a series of responses in sequence. The first was that he was confused because, "No hablo Español."[19] However, one constituent explained that Mr. Rangel had spoken to her in Spanish on a number of occasions. Mr. Rangel's second explanation was that he didn't understand the terms of his mortgage or that the rent had to be reported. The *New York Times* reported that Mr. Rangel also had an interest-free loan for the purchase of the property for a period of five years before paying off the loan. The loan was made to Mr. Rangel at an interest rate of 10.5% per annum but the interest was waived sometime during the first year of the loan, which was made by to Mr. Rangel by a group of investors who are also large donors to Mr. Rangel's campaigns for reelection.[20]

---

[18]*Id.*

[19]David Kocieniewski, "House Chairman Failed to Report $75,000 in Income," *New York Times*, September 5, 2008, p. A1.

[20]David Kocieniewski and David M. Halbfinger, "Interest Was Waived for Rangel on Loan for His Caribbean Villa," *New York Times*, September 6, 2008, p. A1.

The Quids, the Pros, and the Quos

The Charles Rangel School of Public Service at City College of New York received a $1 million donation from the CEO of an oil drilling firm at about the same time Chairman Rangel was ushering through the preservation of a lucrative tax loophole for the CEO's offshore company. Three years earlier, Mr. Rangel had proposed closing the offshore loophole in order to collect more taxes from offshore companies. Mr. Rangel said that there was no quid pro quo. Mr. Rangel disclosed that he had used House stationery to solicit donations to the college from executives and others, including the oil-drilling CEO.

Mr. Rangel paid $57,500 to his son's Web-design company over a two-year period. The funds came from a campaign account held by Mr. Rangel and were paid to Edisonian Innovative Works LLC, a company owned by Steven Charles Rangel and operated out of his Maryland home. Mr. Rangel lives with his son at the Maryland home (the same of homestead exemption fame) when the House is in session. The payments stopped when Steven Rangel was hired by the House Energy and Commerce Committee in January 2007. The payments were the largest spent on Web design by any member of the House. Rep. Rangel said he did nothing wrong, but will amend his disclosure statements to disclose that Edisonian is owned by his son. A source said of Steven Rangel's 2007 job at the House, "How does anyone get any gig on Capitol Hill? It's who you know."[21] Rep. Rangel has hired a forensic auditor to review his financial disclosure records. Rep. Rangel said that the auditors would find nothing wrong in his disclosures, that he is clean as a whistle.

Maurice Greenberg (former CEO of AIG) pledged $5 million to the City College of New York for the school of public service to be named in Rangel's honor. But, Mr. Rangel also met with AIG execs on April 21, 2008. City College's records indicate it had hopes of a $10 million donation from the company after the meeting. Shortly after the meeting, Mr. Rangel changed his position on a tax bill to include a provision favorable to AIG. Previously, Mr. Rangel was on record as opposing the AIG-beneficial provision. Mr. Rangel's staff has indicated he was persuaded to change his mind on the provision by fellow members of Congress. However, there was a post–April 21 letter from an AIG executive on the provision, a letter that urged Mr. Rangel to support the provision because it would save AIG millions.[22]

The law allows Mr. Rangel to seek donations from constituents for nonprofit institutions. However, House rules prohibit the use of House resources, including letterhead, for those solicitations because such donations should be voluntary and not "strong-armed" through the use of government position.

Speaker of the House Nancy Pelosi has expedited the Rangel ethics investigation on these issues.[23] Mr. Rangel stepped down as chair of Ways and Means pending the ethics investigation. Following two years of investigation, in July 2010, the ethics panel handed down thirteen charges against Mr. Rangel. Mr. Rangel attempted a negotiated deal with the panel but could not reach an agreement. Mr. Rangel's public hearings were scheduled to begin in September 2010. The hearings would be the first public hearings the House has held since Representative James Traficant of Ohio was tried for violations of House rules based on charges of bribery. Mr. Traficant was later convicted of criminal bribery charges and sentenced to prison.

---

[21]Christopher Cooper and John R. Wilke, "Rangel Paid Son $57,500 for Web Work," *Wall Street Journal*, December 6–7, 2008, p. A4.

[22]"Ethics Questions Still Hounding Rangel," *Washington Post*, December 2, 2008, p A1.

[23]Raymond Hernandez, "Rangel Inquiry to Move Swiftly, Pelosi Says," *New York Times*, November 27, 2008, p. A28.

Discussion Questions

1. Mr. Rangel is one of the most powerful members of Congress, in addition to having seniority through his forty years of service in the House. Do iconic leaders such as Mr. Rangel escape ethical scrutiny?

2. Do you see ethical breaches in what Mr. Rangel did?

3. Who is affected by Mr. Rangel's conduct in each of the areas?

4. Why do we worry about these types of behaviors in our elected officials?

5. Does the sequence of supposedly serendipitous events raise any concerns?

Case 9.6

"I Was Just Following Orders": The CIA, Interrogations, and the Role of Legal Opinions in the Conduct of Organizations

John Yoo, a professor of law at the University of California at Berkeley, worked in the Justice Department during the Bush 43 presidency. Mr. Yoo was the lawyer who was assigned the task of providing the executive branch with answers to three questions: (1) Were the detainees from terrorist group al Qaeda prisoners of war under the Geneva Convention? (2) Could they be detained without counsel and without a finding of criminal conduct? and (3) Were "enhanced interrogation techniques," including waterboarding, being used to obtain information from them about future terrorist attacks forms of torture under the Geneva Convention?

Mr. Yoo provided his responses to those questions in a memo to then–Attorney General Alberto Gonzalez on August 1, 2002.[24] The memo concluded that members of the al Qaeda terrorist network and Taliban soldiers were not prisoners of war because of a U.S. Supreme Court decision, *Ex parte Quirin*, 317 U.S. 1 (1942), in which the court held:

> The spy who secretly and without uniform passes the military lines of a belligerent in time of war, seeking to gather military information and communicate it to the enemy, or an enemy combatant who without uniform comes secretly through the lines for the purpose of waging war by destruction of life or property, are familiar examples of belligerents who are generally deemed to be entitled to the status of prisoners of war, but to be offenders against the law of war subject to trial and punishment by military tribunals.[25]

Further, those who were detained were not entitled to legal counsel and all of the protections afforded defendants under the U.S. Justice system:

> In modern conflicts, the practice of detaining enemy combatants and hostile civilians generally has been designed to balance the humanitarian purpose of sparing lives with the military necessity of defeating the enemy on the battlefield. The laws of war have thus long provided for the detention of enemy combatants until "the conclusion of peace." Hague Convention (IV) Respecting the Laws and Customs of War on Land, Oct. 18, 1907, art. 20, 36 Stat. 2277, 2301. . . . As Chief Executive and Commander in Chief, the President may order the detention of enemy combatants in order to prevent the individual from engaging in further hostilities against the United States, to deprive the enemy of that individual's service, and to collect information helpful to the United States' efforts to prosecute the armed conflict successfully.

---

[24]The memo is available at www.justice.gov. Accessed July 1, 2010.

[25]317 U.S., pp. 34–35

While enemy combatants may also be subject to criminal prosecution under United States or international law, no evidence of criminal liability is necessary for the U.S. Armed Forces to detain an enemy combatant. The Sixth Amendment right to counsel, which is expressly limited to "criminal proceeding[s]," has no bearing on the preventative detention of enemy combatants."[26]

On the question of enhanced interrogation, Professor Yoo concluded that there would probably be no prosecution of the United States for using these methods because they were self-enforcing and the jurisdiction of worldwide tribunals was voluntary, not mandatory.

In March 2002 at the request of Robert Hirshon, then president of the American Bar Association (ABA), the ABA Board of Governors established a Task Force on Treatment of Enemy Combatants. On August 8, 2002, the Task Force issued a Preliminary Report.[27] The report disagreed with Professor Yoo's response to the three questions and included the following contrasting views:

. . . we must be on constant guard against an excessive use of any power, military or otherwise, that results in the needless destruction of our rights and liberties. There must be a careful balancing of interests. And we must ever keep in mind that "The Constitution of the United States is a law for rulers and people, equally in war and in peace, and covers with the shield of its protection all classes of men, at all times, and under all circumstances."[28]

The ABA report also noted that in the *Quirin* case, the Nazi soldiers who had secreted themselves into the United States in 1942 and became the "enemy combatants" were still entitled to legal counsel before they were tried, convicted and sentenced to death.

On the question of enhanced interrogations, the ABA report noted that the Geneva Convention prohibits torture and provides that, when in doubt, assume someone is a prisoner of war and entitled to have such protections.

In addition to the legal opinions, there were significant pundit debates. The following is an exchange between Liz Cheney, the daughter of former vice president Dick Cheney, and Eugene Robinson, of the *Washington Post*, after Ms. Cheney argued that the enhanced interrogation program was effective in obtaining information to prevent terrorist attacks:

Robinson: But look, efficacy isn't the only thing we should be talking about here. We should also be talking about legality. We should be talking about whether what was done was legal. If I rob a bank and get away with it, there's a lot of efficacy there, but it's not legal.

Cheney: Yeah, but that's not a fair comparison. That's not fair. Because this program was very responsibly and carefully done. And if you look at the history of it, with the CIA coming to the NSC and saying, "We need to know what we can do legally." And the very legal opinions that the administration has released are in fact the documents that set out in great detail, this is what you can do, and this is what you can't do. If you cross this line, it becomes illegal. If you cross this line, it becomes torture. You have to look at the very specific and important legal restrictions that were put in place.

Robinson: I do not think that's the case. Torture is a war crime. It is a war crime.

[26]Supplemental memo of John Yoo to Alberto Gonzalez, February 7, 2003, at http://www.justice.gov/olc/docs/memo-aba-taskforce.pdf. Accessed July 1, 2020.

[27]http://www.abanet.org/leadership/enemy_combatants.pdf. Accessed July 1, 2010.

[28]Justice Frank Murphy, concurring in *Duncan v Kahanamoku*, 327 U.S. 304, 335 (1946).

Cheney:	That's right. And this wasn't torture. Those legal memos demonstrated where the line was, and where it would become torture.
Robinson:	Waterboarding was torture during the Spanish Inquisition, it was torture when Pol Pot did it, and I believe it was torture when we did it.[29]

In 2009, the Justice Department began investigations into the conduct of CIA officials in conducting the enhanced interrogations. Some expressed concern about the criminal prosecution of these government employees when they were simply following orders of a program that had been reviewed by legal counsel and given an imprimatur. In July 2010, the Department of Justice announced that it would not be prosecuting the officials.

Discussion Questions

1. List any rationalizations you see in the case.
2. Describe the legal versus the ethical confrontation in these facts. Be sure to focus on Professor Yoo's conclusion that the United States could not be prosecuted for use of the enhanced techniques. Is that the lawyer's role, to advise on legality? What are the risks of relying on such an opinion?
3. What is the difference between this case and other cases in this unit on government and other units on business? What is at risk here? Who is affected? Do our standards change because of the dire circumstances?
4. Suppose that you were hired by the CIA and directed to conduct enhanced interrogation of enemy combatants. What would be your thoughts, reactions, emotions, and analysis of the order? Is this a question of the lesser of two evils? Do I torture or shall I risk the loss of thousands of lives from a planned and pending terrorist plot? Who is affected by your decision to interrogate or not interrogate? To waterboard or not to waterboard?

Compare and Contrast

Refer back to the Goldman case (Case 2.11) and compare the company's approach to the law versus the compliance with the law in this case. Did both the government and Goldman follow the same approach to legality versus ethics? Is this the role of legal counsel in the management and administration of organizations?

Case 9.7

Paul Wolfowitz and the World Bank

Paul Wolfowitz was the head of the World Bank from June 1, 2005 until May 17, 2007. Mr. Wolfowitz was romantically involved with an executive at the bank, Shaza Riza. Mr. Wolfowitz went to the board with an ethics question about their relationship and her continuing employment. The bank board advised that Ms. Riza be relocated to a position beyond Mr. Wolfowitz's influence because of their relationship and also because their relationship would preclude her being promoted at the bank. On August 11, 2005, Mr. Wolfowitz wrote a memo to Xavier Coll, the bank's vice president of human resources, and suggested the following:

I now direct you to agree to a proposal which includes the following terms and conditions:

The terms and conditions included her future at the bank when Mr. Wolfowitz was no longer heading it as well as an obligation to find her other employment. Ms. Riza now earns $193,590 per year at a nonprofit organization, following a stint at the State

---

[29]Transcript, "Morning Joe," May 12, 2009, on http://msnbc.com.

Department at World Bank expense. She earned $132,000 at the World Bank (a salary that was tax-free because of diplomatic status).

In response to the questions raised about his relationship and the memo, Mr. Wolfowitz posted the following explanation on the World Bank website:

Let me just say a few words about the issue on everyone's mind. Two years ago, when I came to the Bank, I raised the issue of a potential conflict of interest and asked to be recused from the matter. I took the issue to the Ethics Committee and after extensive discussions with the Chairman, the Committee's advice was to promote and relocate Ms. Shaza Riza.

I made a good faith effort to implement my understanding of that advice, and it was done in order to take responsibility for settling an issue that I believed had potential to harm the institution. In hindsight, I wish I had trusted my original instincts and kept myself out of the negotiations. I made a mistake, for which I am sorry.

Not only was this a painful personal dilemma, but I also had to deal with it when I was new to this institution and I was trying to navigate in un-charted waters. The situation was unprecedented and exceptional. This was an involuntary reassignment and I believed there was a legal risk if this was not resolved by mutual agreement. I take full responsibility for the details. I did not attempt to hide my actions nor make anyone else responsible.

I proposed to the Board that they establish some mechanism to judge whether the agreement reached was a reasonable outcome. I will accept any remedies they propose.

In the larger scheme of things, we have much more important work to focus on. For those people who disagree with the things that they associate me with in my previous job, I'm not in my previous job. I'm not working for the U.S. government, I'm working for this institution and its 185 shareholders. I believe deeply in the mission of the institution and have a passion for it. I think the challenge of reducing poverty is of enormous importance.

Discussion Questions

1. What ethical issues do you see?
2. Did Mr. Wolfowitz act properly? Do you see any rationalizations?
3. What should the board have done?

Compare & Contrast

The overarching goal of Mr. Wolfowitz's tenure as head of the World Bank has been eliminating corruption in all countries that deal with the bank. In fact, Mr. Wolfowitz had been very effective in eliminating corruption by insisting that countries install online payment mechanisms for government fees and licenses. The result of these Internet transactions was that the in-person demand for additional fees by government officials was halted. The Internet transactions also provided a complete accounting system that could not be altered for purposes of siphoning funds. What effect does his personal conduct have on that goal?

Sources

Krishna Guha, "World Bank Staff Group Queries 'Misleading' Website Extracts," *Financial Times,* April 16, 2007, p. 3.

Krishna Guha, Javier Blas, Eoin Callan, and Scheherazade Daneshkhu, "Division Emerge as Wolfowitz Fights on," *Financial Times,* April 16, 2007, p. 1.

Greg Hitt, "Wolfowitz Digs in as Criticism Intensifies Within World Bank," *Wall Street Journal,* April 16, 2007, p. A3.

Greg Hitt, "Wolfowitz Memo, Dictating Raises Given to Friend, Now Haunts Him," *Wall Street Journal,* April 14, 2007, p. A1, A5.

Case 9.8

Hiding the Slip-Up on Oil Lease Accounting: Interior Motives

In 1998, the Department of the Interior began an incentive plan for oil companies that permitted the companies to waive the 12.5 percent royalty generally paid to the U.S. government for oil leases on federal land. The idea behind the waiver was that oil companies would then have additional cash for purposes of drilling for more oil. However, the waiver was to stop if oil rose above $34 per barrel. When the leases with the oil companies were signed, Department of the Interior officials had neglected to put in the $34 per barrel cap. The leases ran for ten to fifteen years. Officials at the department discovered the omission in 1999, but did not reveal their mistake and just let the leases run without the cap. When an Office of the Inspector General audit began looking at the leases, an employee within the department, who was later given a bonus, forged and backdated documents to try and dupe auditors into believing that the lease caps were in place. With oil topping $34 per barrel by 2002, and over 1,100 oil leases, the federal government lost billions in royalty fees by the time the *New York Times* discovered the misstep in the contracts.

Discussion Questions

1. Was the failure to collect the correct lease fees simply a mistake, an oversight?

2. Evaluate the conduct of the government official who developed the idea for forging and backdating documents to cover the oil lease oversight. Would a credo have helped? Why do employees believe that they can conceal information from an auditor or, in this case as well, the public?

3. Should the oil companies pay the amounts that would have been due had the clause been in the lease? Why or why not?

Sources

http://www.wrtg.com (as accessed in original research).

Edmund L. Andrews, "Interior Official Faults Agency over Its Ethics," *New York Times,* September 14, 2006, pp. C1, C4.

Case 9.9

Joe the Plumber, Child Support Records, and the Public Official's Disclosure

Samuel Joseph Wurzelbacher was, during 2008, a 34-year-old single father in Toledo, Ohio, who worked as a plumber. He rocketed to national fame when, during a visit to Wurzelbacher's neighborhood, from then–presidential candidate Barack Obama, Mr. Wurzelbacher asked Mr. Obama about his position on taxes, "I'm getting ready to buy a company that makes $250,000 to $280,000 a year. Your new tax plan is going to tax me more, isn't it?"[30] Because there were reporters and cameras along on the neighborhood sweep by the candidate, the exchange was filmed and then hit YouTube with a

---

[30]Charles Hurt, "Obama Fires a 'Robin Hood' Warning Shot," *New York Post,* October 15, 2008, http://www.nypost .com/p/news/politics/item_iQRtIQHjYPcEoMZ0lJX0hl;jsessionid=52E43BAABC23564016BD67E32F171DAA. Accessed July 1, 2010.

resulting negative reaction to Mr. Obama's response, "I think that when you spread the wealth around, it's good for everybody,"[31]

As a result of his fame, Mr. Wurzelbacher, who became known as "Joe the Plumber," also received some attention from Helen Jones-Kelley, director of the Department of Job and Family Services for the state of Ohio. A state investigation revealed that state child-support computers were tapped, in the days following the Obama–Wurzelbacher interchange, to check on child-support payments and whether Wurzelbacher was receiving welfare assistance or owed unemployment compensation taxes.

The investigation further disclosed that Ms. Jones-Kelley had contributed $2,500 to the Obama campaign, made the arrangements for an Ohio appearance by Mrs. Obama, and provided potential donor information to the national campaign office. Those offers and arrangements were made using her state e-mail account. Ms. Jones-Kelley was placed on paid leave pending the outcome of the investigations into possible misuse of state computers and e-mail. Jones-Kelley told state investigators that it was agency practice to check the backgrounds of someone "thrust quickly into the public spotlight," but Ohio Inspector General (OIG) Thomas P. Charles said there were "no policies or procedures to support her."[32] Mr. Charles also noted that the searches were done in the midst of a political campaign and concluded, "we determined that ODJFS Director Helen Jones-Kelley's authorization to search three confidential agency databases for information on Wurzelbacher was improper, and that her use of state email resources to engage in political activity was also improper."[33]

She was suspended for 30 days without pay by Ohio Governor Ted Strickland, but after political outcry that his penalty was too light, Ms. Jones-Kelley resigned from the $141,000 per year post that she had assumed in 2007.

Discussion Questions

1. What is the ethical issue involved in the searches authorized by Ms. Jones-Kelley?
2. Who is affected by the searches conducted?
3. What prevents government employees from searching records and releasing information about citizens? In the OIG's report, the conclusion includes the following:

> It is also our conclusion that the Deputy Director of Family Stability, Paul Fraunholtz and the Deputy Director of Unemployment Compensation, Judy Cicatiello played no direct role in the decision making process that led to the queries being run on Wurzelbacher. However, they are not without fault in this situation either—albeit to a lesser degree than Jones-Kelley. They oversee two of the confidential ODJFS database systems accessed to conduct queries on Wurzelbacher. We cannot accept as an excuse that they merely ran the query after receiving a request from senior management. They are responsible for ensuring that access to these databases is limited to the furtherance of the agency's functions or purposes. In this case, Fraunholtz and Cicatiello both failed to exercise independent judgment expected of senior management. At the very least they should have inquired how the requests related to legitimate agency operations.

What does this finding tell us about the importance of speaking up in an organization? Why do we resist speaking up when senior management makes the request? The OIG concludes with this statement, "Finally, we would like to commend employee Vanessa Niekamp for coming forward and bringing information to our attention under such difficult circumstances." Why do you think she disclosed what was going on with the searches? Did she do the ethical thing?

---

[31] *Id.*

[32] Report of Investigation, 2008299, http://watchdog.ohio.gov/investigations/2008299.pdf. Accessed July 1, 2010.

[33] *Id.*, p. ii.

Government Contracts

The existence of unlimited sources of funds often is used to justify behavior. In government contracts, the supply of funds seems endless, and the competition is stiff. These benefits and pressures often cause poor resolutions of ethical dilemmas. Pay particular attention to the impact of media coverage in the cases.

Case 9.10

Stanford University and Government Overhead Payments

Included in government research grants to universities are indirect cost payments designed to compensate for the researchers' use of the schools' facilities.

Stanford University received approximately $240 million in federal research funds annually. About $75 million went to actual research, while Stanford billed the federal government $85 million, or 20 percent of its operating budget, for its overhead.[34] The rest of the research funds went toward employee benefits. An audit of Stanford's research program in 1990 by U.S. Navy accountant Paul Biddle revealed that the school billed the government $3,000 for a cedar-lined closet in president Donald Kennedy's home (Hoover House), $2,000 for flowers, $2,500 for refurbishing a grand piano, $7,000 for bed sheets and table linens, $4,000 for a reception for trustees following Kennedy's 1987 wedding, and $184,000 for depreciation for a seventy-two-foot yacht as part of the indirect costs for federally funded research.[35]

In response to the audit, Stanford withdrew requests for reimbursement totaling $1.35 million as unallowable and inappropriate costs. Stanford's federal funds were cut by $18 million per year.[36]

Kennedy issued the following statements as the funding crisis evolved:

December 18, 1990: What was intended as government policy to build the capacity of universities through reimbursement of indirect costs leads to payments that are all too easily misunderstood.

Therefore, we will be reexamining our policies in an effort to avoid any confusion that might result.

At the same time, it is important to recognize that the items currently questioned, taken together, have an insignificant impact on Stanford's indirect-cost rate. . . .

Moreover, Stanford routinely charges the government less than our full indirect costs precisely to allow for errors and disallowances.

—*From a university statement*

---

[34]Colleen Cordes, "Universities Review Overhead Charges; Some Alter Policies on President's Home," *Chronicle of Higher Education,* April 3, 1991, p. A1.

[35]Maria Shao, "The Cracks in Stanford's Ivory Tower," *BusinessWeek,* March 11, 1991, 64–65.

[36]Gary McWilliams, "Less Gas for the Bunsen Burners," *Business Week,* May 20, 1991, 124–126; and Courtney Leatherman, "Stanford's Shift in Direction," *Chronicle of Higher Education,* September 7, 1994, p. A29.

January 14, 1991: We certainly ought to prune anything that isn't allowable—there isn't any question about that. But we're extending that examination to things that, although we believe are perfectly allowable, don't strike people as reasonable.

I don't care whether it's flowers, or dinners and receptions, or whether it's washing the table linen after it's been used, or buying an antique here or there, or refinishing a piano when its finish gets crappy, or repairing a closet and refinishing it—all those are investments in a university facility that serves a whole array of functions.

—From an interview with the Stanford Daily

January 23, 1991: Because acute public attention on these items threatens to overshadow the more important and fundamental issue of the support of federally sponsored research, Stanford is voluntarily withdrawing all general administration costs for operation of Hoover House claimed for the fiscal years since 1981. For those same years, we are also voluntarily withdrawing all such costs claimed for the operations of two other university-owned facilities.

—From a university statement

February 19, 1991: I am troubled by costs that are perfectly appropriate as university expenditures and lawful under the government rules but I believe ought not be charged to the taxpayer. I should have been more alert to this policy issue, and I should have insisted on more intensive review of these transactions.

—From remarks to alumni

March 23, 1991: Our obligation is not to do all the law permits, but to do what is right. Technical legality is not the guiding principle. Even in matters as arcane as government cost accounting, we must figure out what is appropriate and act accordingly. Over the years, we have not hesitated to reject numerous lawful and attractive business proposals, gifts, and even federal grants because they came with conditions we thought would be inappropriate for Stanford. Yet, with respect to indirect-cost recovery, we pursued what was permissible under the rules, without applying our customary standard of what is proper. . . .

The expenses for Hoover House—antique furniture, flowers, cedar closets—should have been excluded, and they weren't. That the amounts involved were relatively small is fortunate, but it doesn't excuse us. In our testimony before the subcommittee I did deal with this issue, but I obviously wasn't clear enough. I explained that we were removing Hoover House and some similar accounts from the cost pools that drew indirect-cost recovery because they plainly included inappropriate items. What came out in the papers was that Stanford removed the costs because it was forced to, not because it was wrong. . . . That is not so. To repeat, the allocation of these expenses to indirect-cost pools is inappropriate, regardless of its propriety under the law.

—From remarks to alumni[37]

By July 1991, Kennedy announced his resignation, effective August 1992, stating, "It is very difficult . . . for a person identified with a problem to be a spokesman for its solution."[38] Gerhard Casper, who was hired as Stanford's new president, said, "I just

---

[37]Karen Grassmuch, "What Happened at Stanford: Key Mistakes at Crucial Times in a Battle with the Government over Research Costs," *Chronicle of Higher Education*, May 15, 1991, p. A26.

[38]"Embattled Stanford President to Quit," *Mesa Tribune*, July 30, 1991, p. A6.

want this to remain one of the great universities in the world. I ask that we question what we are doing every day." Kennedy remains at Stanford, teaching biology.[39]

Stanford's donations declined that year; 1999 was the first time it saw an uptick in its donations since the time of this government overhead issue.[40]

Ultimately, Stanford settled with the federal government for $1.3 million, a small percentage of the $185 million of alleged overcharges that appeared in Biddle's report. The federal government also concluded that there was no fraud by Stanford. Biddle filed suit, seeking recovery of the statutory whistle-blower fee of 10 percent for finding the submitted costs that the government ultimately recovered from Stanford. His suit was dismissed.

Discussion Questions

1. Did Kennedy's ethics evolve during the crisis? Contrast his March 23, 1991, ethical posture with his December 18, 1990, assessment.
2. Is legal behavior always ethical behavior?
3. Do Casper's remarks reflect an ethical formula for Stanford's operations?
4. In a 2000 interview for an internal Stanford publication, Kennedy offered the following when asked about research and cost issues as he assumed the editorship of *Science*:

   One of the factors in the explosive growth of Stanford during the '60s and continuing into the '70s and '80s was the availability of federal funding for research. The policy behind that support was always that the government benefited from basic research because it eventually produced findings that could be converted to human service in one way or another and so the government continually built that capacity and built that capacity in universities. Its policy was that it would pay the full cost of research, including not only the direct cost that could be associated with particular programs but the indirect costs that had to be made by the university in order to stay in the business of doing sponsored research.

   Over time, the percentage of all research funding that was allocated to indirect cost grew. And it grew to a point in the late '80s and early '90s when it seemed to many people, some in Congress and some on this faculty, that it was an unacceptably large percentage and we recognized that though, probably not soon enough, made some

efforts to constrain it, but in fact it was high enough to trouble people and it was calculated, the indirect costs were calculated on the basis on a pool accounting mechanism no one in the public understood and indeed few people on the faculty understood. And when Congressman Dingell decided to make that the subject of a very high profile Congressional investigation and made Stanford the subject of it, we had a very, very bad time. We took a beating. It was sufficiently bad that after the hearings and during the summer of 1991, it became clear to me that there was so much faculty concern about the ruckus and whether Stanford would continue to be a target for this kind of thing that I decided that if you're part of a problem, you can't be part of a solution and so I resigned. I think that steadied things down considerably. It wasn't any fun to do that. It was not any fun to take a certain amount of newspaper abuse in connection with it. Stanford's recovered nicely. We're still not paid the indirect cost rate I think we are entitled to under articulated government policies, but the sequelae to the whole furor, I think, made it plain to everybody that Stanford hadn't engaged in any wrongdoing.

   I think there were a few people in other institutions who got caught up in the problem later when it was revealed that they had engaged in exactly the same practices we had who did a little finger pointing and said "Well, Stanford was pushing the

---

[39]Associated Press, "Stanford's Chief Resigns over Billing Controversy," *Arizona Republic*, July 30, 1991, p. A8.

[40]Leatherman, "Stanford's Shift in Direction," p. A29.

envelope." But in fact we weren't. Our indirect cost rate was high but it was in a cluster of other high rates, two or three or four other institutions which were comparable or within three or four percentage points.

So you can't make the case that we were doing stuff that others weren't also doing.[41]

List the rationalizations you see in this statement. Does he think Stanford did anything unethical?

Case 9.11

Yale University and the Compensation of Professors for Government Research: Double-Dipping or Confusion?

The U.S. Attorney for the District of Connecticut reached a settlement with Yale University on allegations that Yale violated federal regulations on grant administration and accounting. Without admitting guilt, Yale agreed to pay the federal government $7.6 million, half as damages and the other half as penalties. The investigation focused on the problem of funds left in federal grants. When the grant ends, the Feds get the funds back. The government alleged those at the university, however, transferred the funds to other unexpired grants for continuing use.

Also, the investigation focused on faculty summer salaries. Faculty members often serve under nine-month contracts. They are not paid in the summer unless they have summer school classes or have research dollars. However, to get those summer research dollars, faculty members must be devoted to research. Yale faculty, allegedly, did other things besides research during those summer periods but still billed the government for 100 percent of their salaries. They were compensated for those additional activities during the summer. The result is that the faculty have two sources of compensation. However, the activity reports faculty members must sign/certify that they have devoted 100 percent of their time to the lab and, because they are required by federal law, are signed under penalty of perjury.

Discussion Questions

1. Why is the university responsible for the conduct of the faculty members?
2. What advice would you offer to universities for the management of their grant funds?
3. Should this all matter if the faculty are indeed performing the required research under their grants?

Case 9.12

Minority-Owned Businesses and Reality

Federal, state, and local government agencies have special bidding priority and criteria for businesses that are owned by minorities or women when they are evaluating proposals for their contracts. As a result, many husbands have listed their wives as shareholders and/or officers in their companies even though their wives do not work in their businesses or invest any funds in their companies. Others have named their businesses in a way that gives the impression that they are minority-owned businesses.

---

[41]http://becoming.stanford.edu/interview/donaldkennedy.html. Accessed July 10, 2010.

Discussion Questions

1. Is this conduct legal? Is it ethical?
2. Explain who is affected by the use of these structure changes.
3. What was the purpose of the special bidding priority?
4. Why do you think the businesspeople find ways around the bidding priority rules?

Case 9.13

The My Tai Concession and the County Supervisor

Yvonne Atkinson Gates, the chairperson of the Clark County, Nevada, Commission, an elected office, also operated her own daiquiri business. Many of the new and expanding hotels in Clark County, where Las Vegas is located, have retail space available for shops and restaurants. Ms. Atkinson Gates, as a commissioner, makes decisions on whether proposed hotels and expansions will be approved.

Ms. Atkinson Gates was alleged to have approached executives from five casinos about leasing space for her daiquiri franchises. Ms. Atkinson Gates acknowledged the contacts but stated that they "were made in passing and cannot be considered solicitations."[42] She acknowledged actually seeking an arrangement with MGM Grand Resorts.

Sheldon Adelson, the chairperson of Las Vegas Sands, Inc. said, "I was shocked, absolutely shocked that Yvonne would come to me directly. I felt she was pressuring me to agree. And when I didn't, I think she went out of her way to vote against my project."[43] Adelson wanted to build a Sands Venetian Mall, but his proposal was not approved by the commission.

Upon its investigation of the matter, the Nevada State Ethics Commission found that Ms. Atkinson Gates had violated Nevada's rules of ethics for elected officials in her conduct with businesspeople regarding her daiquiri business. The Ethics Commission ruled by a 5-to-1 vote that she had used her position to obtain business concessions. She resigned as a Clark County Commissioner in early 2007; she did not complete her term that was slated to run until 2009. Despite the ethics reprimand, she had served as a commissioner for fourteen years. She was a superdelegate to the 2008 Democratic National Convention.

Discussion Questions

1. Is there a conflict in Ms. Atkinson Gates's solicitations?
2. How should she handle the business solicitations?
3. What conclusions did Mr. Adelson draw? Is he justified?
4. Ms. Atkinson Gates says she is a silent partner. Does this status help?

Case 9.14

Government Pricing and Finding a Way Around It

George Couto was a marketing manager with Bayer Corporation, the U.S. subsidiary of Bayer A.G., a German-based company. In 1995, Kaiser, the largest HMO in the United States, was demanding a discount for its bulk purchases of Cipro, an antibiotic manufactured

---

[42]Susan Green, "Official Defines Role in Venture," *Las Vegas Review Journal*, October 4, 1997, pp. 1A, 2A.

[43]Susan Green, "Official Sought Casino Leases," *Las Vegas Review Journal*, October 3, 1997, pp. 1A, 2A.

by Bayer. Bayer could grant the discount to Kaiser; however, that discount meant that it had to sell at that price to the federal government (under Medicaid regulations).[44]

To avoid having to give the federal government the discount, Couto oversaw the development and sale of a private-label Cipro for Kaiser. The drug was manufactured in Connecticut and sold to Kaiser under a private label at a 40 percent discount. Kaiser had indicated it would turn to Johnson & Johnson if it were not given a deep enough discount by Bayer.[45]

The plan was uncovered almost five years later, and Bayer agreed to pay $257 million to the federal government, at that time the largest Medicaid fraud settlement to date. Bayer also agreed to a $5.6 million criminal fine.

Couto was the person who led the federal government to Bayer and the plan, and such whistle-blowers are entitled to as much as 30 percent of the amount of the penalty. According to his testimony, Couto wrote a letter outlining the private label plan that had been in effect for almost five years after attending an ethics class in which Bayer's CEO indicated that employees should follow not just the letter of the law but also the spirit of the law.

Couto was deposed in the case and admitted his role, but three months after his deposition and five months before Bayer settled the case, Couto (age thirty-nine) died of pancreatic cancer. However, despite his misgivings about the private label plan, he did seek to obtain a President's Achievement Award from the CEO of Bayer for his retention of the Kaiser account.

Couto, divorced, was awarded 24 percent of the federal government's share of the fine Bayer paid. His three children are the primary beneficiaries of the $34 million award. Mr. Couto's brother, Mark, has organized an annual golf tournament in Brewster, Massachusetts, in his brother's name with the proceeds going to fight pancreatic cancer.

Discussion Questions

1. Should a participant in a scam to defraud the government be permitted to collect the whistle-blower fees?

2. Was what Bayer did a violation of the law or a creative interpretation of the statute?

3. How is this case similar to the Enron case (see Case 4.15)?

Case 9.15

Taser and Stunning Behavior

Taser began operations in Arizona in 1993 for the purpose of developing and manufacturing nonlethal self-defense devices. From 1993 through 1996, Taser focused on the development and sale of the AIR TASER, a self-defense weapon marketed to consumers. In December 1999, Taser introduced the ADVANCED TASER device, a product developed for sale to law enforcement agencies. The TASER X26 is sold to police and corrections agencies for $799.

The Taser technology uses compressed nitrogen to shoot two small, electrified probes up to a maximum distance of twenty-five feet. The probes and compressed nitrogen are stored in a replaceable cartridge attached to the Taser base.

Taser's focus from 1999 to 2001 was the development of a chain of distribution for the introduction of the product to law enforcement agencies (primarily in North America) as well as a national training program for the use of the ADVANCED TASER.

---

[44]*Bayer Corporation v Hoover Color Corporation*, 2000 WL 34014603 (U.S.).

[45]Peter Aronson, "A Rogue to Catch a Rogue," *National Law Journal*, August 18–25, 2003, p. A1.

Taser created a training board that consists of four active duty police officers and one representative from the airline industry as well as Taser's chief master instructor and king of the universe, Hans Marrero. Officers on active duty throughout the country serve as master and certified instructors for the company. They are paid $195 for each training session, and many of the officers, including those on the training board, have been awarded stock options by the company. Officers in Arizona, California, Canada, Texas, and Washington received stock options after recommending that their municipalities and agencies adopt Taser products for use by officers. The officers who received the options are now employed by Taser, Inc. The revelations about the officers and the option compensation came about because of suits filed by the *Arizona Republic* and *SEC Insight,* two publications seeking release of the company documents filed in lawsuits pending before Maricopa County Superior Court in Arizona. The court ruled against Taser and unsealed the documents. When asked by the *Arizona Republic* about the options, CEO Rick Smith responded via a company press release,

> The officers on our [training] board were involved in training operations at their respective departments—not the purchasing departments. They followed all relevant conflict-of-interest regulations at their departments, and the grant of stock options did not violate Taser's code of ethics nor industry norms.

Taser established the TASER Foundation for the families of fallen law enforcement officers in 2004. The TASER Foundation was funded with initial commitments for over $700,000 from TASER International, Inc., employees. The TASER Foundation's mission is to give back to the community by supporting the law enforcement community that helped with the development of distribution lines and training.

Discussion Questions

1. Evaluate Taser's actions in hiring the officers and using options as payment.
2. Evaluate the conduct of the officers in accepting the positions and the compensation from Taser.
3. What would you have done differently as an executive at Taser? As a police officer?
4. Are the connections among and between government agencies and Taser a necessary and inevitable part of Taser's type of product?

Case 9.16

Boeing and the Recruiting of the Government Purchasing Agent[46]

Darlene Druyun was a lifetime government employee, working her way up through the system to a position of Air Force acquisition officer. She had risen to the position of principal deputy assistant secretary in the U.S. Air Force. Known as the "Dragon Lady," Ms. Druyun had extensive knowledge about Defense Department policies and procedures and defense contractors and had honed tough negotiating skills. In the last quarter of 2002, Ms. Druyun, nearing her retirement, was interested in job opportunities after leaving government service.

Ms. Druyun's daughter, Heather McKee, was an employee at the St. Louis facilities for Boeing, Inc., a company that does a significant amount of business with the federal government. In court documents, Ms. Druyun indicated that Michael Sears, who was then Boeing's chief financial officer (CFO) and the man considered to be in line to be the next

---

[46]The author has done consulting work on ethics with Boeing to help with employee training on ethical issues. The facts in this case are drawn strictly from public accounts.

Boeing CEO, helped place her daughter in her job at Boeing. Ms. McKee's husband also worked for Boeing and was hired along with Ms. McKee when he was her fiancé. In September 2002, Ms. McKee sent an e-mail to Mr. Sears to let him know that her mother was planning to retire. Ms. McKee mentioned to Mr. Sears that her mother would probably end up working for Lockheed following her retirement from her government position, but that Ms. Druyun really wanted to work for Boeing.

As a result of this contact, Mr. Sears met with Ms. Druyun in October 2002, which was one month before Ms. Druyun recused herself from working on any contract decisions involving Boeing as a bidder. At the end of the meeting, Ms. Druyun has testified, Mr. Sears said, "This meeting never took place." When he returned to the offices, however, Mr. Sears sent out e-mails indicating that Ms. Druyun was receptive to employment. In a note sent to the chairman's office, Mr. Sears wrote, "Had a 'non-meeting' yesterday. Good reception to job, location, salary."

In October 2002, the two reached an employment arrangement. In January 2003, Ms. Druyun went to work for Boeing in its Chicago offices as a vice president, at a salary of $250,000 per year plus benefits. Pending before the Air Force at the time of the employment agreement was a bid by Boeing to supply the Air Force with 100 Boeing 767 refueling tankers. Also during this time, John Judy, a Boeing lawyer who was moving from Boeing offices in St. Louis to the Washington, D.C., area, purchased Ms. Druyun's home from her.[47]

During the summer of 2003, Boeing began an internal investigation of the circumstances surrounding Ms. Druyun's hiring. Ms. Druyun and Mr. Sears exchanged memos and e-mails with a timeline that they had reconstructed but one that did not reflect accurately what had really happened and what was easily traceable through meeting places and witnesses. Based on its internal investigation that revealed "compelling evidence" that the two had conspired to employ Ms. Druyun while she still had contracting authority and their subsequent attempts to cover up their conduct, Boeing dismissed both Ms. Druyun and Mr. Sears. Their dismissal for cause cost them any severance benefits.[48]

Ms. Druyun was charged by the federal government with violations of procurement statutes and conspiracy. She entered a guilty plea to conspiracy in April 2004 and told the court, "I deeply regret my actions and I want to apologize."[49] Ms. Druyun was originally scheduled to be sentenced to six months in prison, because she had agreed to cooperate with federal investigators. However, she was ultimately sentenced to nine months because federal investigators established that she had lied when asked whether she had ever showed favoritism to Boeing in awarding defense contracts. She initially stated that she had not shown such favoritism, but, after failing a lie detector test, she disclosed that she had given Boeing several contracts and pricing breaks in exchange for Boeing hiring her daughter and son-in-law. The supplemental factual statement for her second plea agreement also indicates that Ms. Druyun altered her notebook, the collection of contemporaneous notes she had given to prosecutors. After failing the lie detector test, she acknowledged changing entries and adding materials. She also indicated that she gave Boeing pricing breaks with the hope of helping her daughter and son-in-law with their careers at Boeing. She also indicated that she had approved a settlement with Boeing that was too high. Boeing and the Department of Defense renegotiated that settlement. Then–Boeing CEO Harry Stonecipher pledged that the company would address "any

---

[47]Leslie Wayne, "Boeing Dismisses 2 in Hiring of Official Who Left Pentagon," *New York Times*, November 25, 2003, pp. A1, C2.

[48]J. Lynn Lunsford and Andy Pasztor, "Boeing Dismisses Two Executives for Violating Ethical Standards," *Wall Street Journal*, November 25, 2003, pp. A1, A8.

[49]J. Lynn Lunsford and Andy Pasztor, "Former Boeing Official Pleads Guilty to Conspiracy," *Wall Street Journal*, April 21, 2004, pp. A1, A9.

inadequacies that need to be corrected." Ms. Druyun's daughter no longer works for Boeing.[50] Mr. Sears served a four-month sentence, and Ms. Druyun served a nine-month sentence. Ms. Druyun has also been ordered to pay restitution and contribute time to community service. Ms. Druyun was released from prison in October 2005.

Discussion Questions

1. What category of ethical dilemma is involved here?
2. What questions or models did Mr. Sears miss in choosing to recruit Ms. Druyun when he did? What was he hoping would happen? What do you think of his asking Ms. Druyun to cover up their meeting? What should the chairman of the board have done when he received Mr. Sears's e-mail about the "non-meeting"?
3. What were Ms. Druyun's motivations? What questions or models did she miss in making her decision to meet with Mr. Sears?
4. Evaluate the conduct of Ms. Druyun's daughter, Heather.

[50]Leslie Wayne, "Ex-Pentagon Official Gets 9 Months for Conspiring to Favor Boeing," *New York Times*, October 2, 2004, pp. B1, B13.

Government Responsibilities

How careful must government be with its power? The accountability of government employees for exercising authority is a critical area of focus in government ethics.

Case 9.17

The Prosecutors Who Withheld Evidence: The Senator's Trial

The U.S. Justice Department announced that it was dropping all charges against convicted former Alaska U.S. Senator Ted Stevens. U.S. Attorney General Eric Holder announced that his office had uncovered prosecutorial misconduct in that lawyers for the federal government had failed to disclose notes from a witness interview that included exculpatory evidence that would have cast doubt on Mr. Stevens' criminal intent.

Mr. Stevens had originally been convicted of making false statements on his federally mandated disclosure statements about gifts. The government alleged he failed to disclose significant gifts he received from federal contractors that were related to the remodeling of his home in Alaska. Mr. Holder's decision was the end of the case. Mr. Stevens was nearly reelected to the Senate despite having been convicted of criminal charges just a week before the November 2008 election. He lost the election by just over 3,000 votes. Following the loss, he returned to private life in Alaska. Mr. Holder made his announcement of the dismissal of charges in April 2009. Mr. Stevens died in a plane crash in the rugged mountain area 350 miles south of Anchorage, Alaska, on August 9, 2010.

Discussion Questions

1. What are the ethical duties of lawyers? Of prosecutors?
2. What are the rules of discovery for criminal and civil cases?
3. Mr. Nicholas Marsh, one of the prosecutors under investigation for the Stevens evidence issue, committed suicide in September 2010. Is there a credo moment for lawyers here?

Case 9.18

The Duke Lacrosse Team and the Prosecutor

In the wee hours of the morning (between March 13 and 14, 2006), two women who were hired as dancers went to a party being held by the Duke lacrosse team to perform. One of the women later (or early, depending on how one defines the wee hours) went to the police station in Durham to report being sexually assaulted by three of the Duke players.

By March 16, 2006, the police searched the house where the party was held and conducted with the accuser a photo ID session with pictures of the twenty-four lacrosse players. She was unable to identify her assailants but could identify several young men who were at the party. At a later photo lineup of twelve more team members, she was unable to identify any of them as either assailants or team members who were at the party.

On March 23, 2006, all forty-six members of the Duke team reported to the Durham police to give DNA samples. Within days, Mr. Michael B. Nifong, the district attorney for Durham, held the first of many press conferences on the case. Mr. Nifong said that the young men on the team were engaging in a "conspiracy of silence," but that the physical evidence in the case would be strong and conclusive.

The photo lineups continued, but the accuser had great difficulty, including identifying one of the young men on the team, but explained that whoever he was he had a moustache at the time of the assault. The officers knew that the young man who was identified had never had a moustache. Lawyers and police officers agree that the photo lineup process used by the Durham police for all of the sessions with the accuser violated not only Durham police rules but also standard procedures for such lineups. For example, one requirement is that the photos include photos of those who would not be associated with the crime scene, the alleged victim, or, in this case, the team. The photos shown consisted only of the Duke team members.

The response of the Duke community was swift and severe. Eighty-eight faculty members at Duke University took out a full-page newspaper ad condemning the white male, college athletics, and racism. Duke's president, on April 4, 2006, canceled the lacrosse team's season. Duke President Richard Brodhead called the events the team was involved in "sickening and repulsive."[51] The accuser was an African-American woman, and the players on the lacrosse team were white males. Reverend Jesse Jackson had taken a strong position in the case and offered the young woman a scholarship. Commentators referred to the case as a volatile one that was a mix of race, sex, and class.[52]

On April 10, 2006, the prosecutor's office (Mr. Nifong's office) received the results of the DNA analysis. None of the results linked any of the team members to the accuser. However, despite the difficulties with the lineups, Mr. Nifong stated at a public forum on April 11, 2006, that the accuser had identified at least one of the team members and that he was not concerned about the absence of DNA linkage.

On April 17, 2006, the grand jury returned indictments against Reade Seligmann and Collin Finnerty for rape, sexual assault, and kidnapping. Mr. Seligmann's lawyer was rebuffed when he offered evidence of his client's whereabouts at the time of the alleged assault, including time stamps from his use of an ATM, a credit card at a fast food restaurant, and his punch-in at his campus housing.

May 2, 2006, was the primary election in Durham, and Mr. Nifong emerged as the victor for the Democratic Party, winning the opportunity to run for re-election. Another team member, David F. Evans, was indicted on May 12, 2006, because there was a possible match between his DNA and some DNA found on the artificial fingernail of the victim that had been found under a trash can at the house where the party was held.

National attention on the case became a daily thing, with national news programs and talk shows focusing on the accuser, the team, and Duke. Mr. Seligmann, a graduating senior, had his job offer from Goldman Sachs revoked because of his indictment. As a result of the continuing news conferences and circus-like atmosphere, a judge ordered the parties to abide by a gag order as of July 17, 2006. As a result, a relative quiet settled over the case, with the exception of Mr. Nifong handily winning re-election on November 7, 2006.

At one of many pretrial hearings on various motions, Brian W. Meehan, a director of a DNA lab that performed the analysis of the players' DNA, admitted on December 6, 2006, that Mr. Nifong did not note in the documents turned over to defense lawyers that the DNA of a number of different men had been found on the accuser's clothing, body, and underwear. The accuser had been a stripper for a number of years. In fact, Reverend

[51]Eddie Timanus and Tim Peeler, "Duke Scraps Men's LaCrosse Season," *USA Today*, April 6, 2006, p. 1C.
[52]Duff Wilson, "Prosecutor in Duke Case Is Stripped of Law License," *New York Times*, June 17, 2007, p. A16.

Jackson's motto for the case, one in which he offered personal assistance for the young woman, had been "Don't strip. Scholarship." Mr. Meehan referred to the omission as an intentional one that he and Mr. Nifong had agreed to in advance of the report's release. On cross-examination at the hearing, Mr. Meehan admitted that he violated his own laboratory's processes and procedures in not turning over all of the exculpatory evidence.

By December 22, 2006, the accuser admitted that she could not be sure what had really happened, and as a result, Mr. Nifong dropped the rape charges, but continued with the prosecution of the kidnapping and assault charges.

National attention was back on the case, despite the gag order, and on December 26, 2006, the North Carolina State bar filed prosecutorial misconduct charges against Mr. Nifong. When the charges were filed, which included making "inflammatory remarks" about the case, Mr. Nifong withdrew from the case on January 13, 2007, and asked North Carolina's Attorney General's Office to assume responsibility for the case.

As the North Carolina attorney general began its review of the case, the North Carolina State bar added charges to its complaint against Mr. Nifong, including a charge that he withheld evidence from defense lawyers in the case.

On April 11, 2007, the North Carolina attorney general not only dropped all the remaining charges against the three young men, but also announced that the young men were innocent of any of the charges. The young men were issued an apology on behalf of the state. They have since settled a lawsuit they brought against Duke University for an amount that remains undisclosed.

On June 15, 2007, Mr. Nifong announced his resignation as district attorney for Durham at his state bar hearing on the charges. However, the ethics panel for the state bar hearing was unmoved and, forty minutes after the evidence was presented, issued its decision of disbarment. The panel noted that there was no other remedy that was appropriate because this was "a clear case of prosecutorial misconduct" that involved "dishonesty, fraud, deceit, and misrepresentation."[53]

On May 30, 2007, a Duke alum of the class of 1957 ran a full-page ad in several national newspapers, including *USA Today,* that had the following headline: "For a team very few people stood by, how about a standing ovation?"[54]

Discussion Questions

1. Why do you think a seasoned prosecutor and lawyer like Mr. Nifong was not more forthright with the evidence and findings in the lacrosse case? In referring to Nifong's conduct, a retired Durham police officer said, "It makes me think it's because of the upcoming election."[55] Are there some credo lessons in this conduct?

2. What insights can you offer about prosecutorial responsibility?

3. What insights can you offer for young people and college parties in the wee hours?

Compare & Contrast

What lessons are there for the Duke faculty, president, and university because of what happened here? Professor Lee D. Baker was one of the eighty-eight scholars who have since met to discuss a possible apology or retraction of their ad:

> *We had a long discussion about what the word "regret" means, and philosophy professors weighed in and we had a whole range of very detailed discussions in terms of*

---

[53]"The Mills of Justice Grind Slow," *National Review*, July 9, 2007, 10.

[54]*USA Today,* May 30, 2007, p. 5A.

[55]Oren Donnell, "Duke Case Prosecutor's Media Whirl Raises Eyebrows," *USA Today,* May 2, 2006, p. 2A.

the etymology of specific words. We were disappointed people did not understand the intention—it was never to rush to judgment, it was about listening to our students who have been trying to make their way in a not only racist and sexist campus, but country.[56]

Sources

David Barstow and Duff Wilson, "DNA Witness Jolted Dynamic of Duke Case," *New York Times*, December 24, 2006, pp. A1, A18.

"The Duke Case: A Timeline," *New York Times*, June 16, 2007, p. A11.

Sal Ruibal, "Lawyers Say DNA Tests Clear Players," *USA Today*, April 11, 2006, p. 1C.

Eddie Timanus and Tim Peeler, "Duke Scraps Men's LaCrosse Season," *USA Today*, April 6, 2006, p. 1C.

Duff Wilson, "Prosecutor in Duke Case Is Stripped of Law License," *New York Times*, June 17, 2007, p. A16.

Case 9.19

FEMA, Hurricane Katrina, and the Dilemmas of Regulation versus Human Life

On August 29, 2005, Hurricane Katrina was hitting the Gulf coastal states with a vengeance. Then-head of the Federal Emergency Management Agency (FEMA), Michael Brown, was interviewed by a number of news organizations about his agency's preparations and role. The following exchange of e-mails was later revealed in congressional hearings on the slowness of FEMA's response to the needs of the Gulf states' citizens:

> *An e-mail from a FEMA public relations officer to FEMA's then-director Brown calls the outfit he wore on a television appearance on August 29 "fabulous."*

> *Brown replied, "I got it at Nordstroms. Are you proud of me? Can I quit now? Can I go home?"*

> *Several hours later, with the New Orleans Superdome filling up quickly because of no other available shelter, Brown took the time to e-mail the PR officer again:*

> *"If you'll look at my lovely FEMA attire you'll really vomit. I am a [sic] fashion god."*[57]

Mr. Brown had additional difficulties. Many in New Orleans were stranded in their homes and apartments and the U.S. Coast Guard did not have enough of the right size boats to get to those who were stranded. Residents offered their boats and services to rescue their fellow citizens. FEMA refused to allow the private rescue because federal regulations require that the boat owners and those who would be helping have appropriate levels of liability insurance. Without that proof, FEMA would not give the go-ahead for the private rescuers.

Mr. Brown would resign his position shortly after the e-mails and the flurry of complaints that surrounded his handling of the rescue efforts.

---

[56]Christina Asquith, "Duke Professors Reject Calls to Apologize," *Diverse*, January 17, 2007, http://www.diverseeducation.com/artman/publish/article_6902.shtml. Accessed July 10, 2010.

[57]http://www.ushouse.gov/hearings/fema. Accessed July 10, 2010.

Discussion Questions

1. What cautions could you offer government officials about the use of e-mail?

2. What peculiar responsibilities do government officials have during emergencies? When are regulations trumped? Should they be disregarded in order to save lives?

3. What is the impact of the e-mails' disclosure on the reputation of government agencies and officials?

Ethics and Nonprofits

UNIT TEN

Good intentions are not necessarily the same as good ethics. In this final segment of the book, we take a look at good intentions gone amuck. These organizations had the goodwill and donations of others but abused that trust, with resulting consequences that had far-reaching effects. It is important to remember that the largest amount of money Charles Ponzi ever spent on anything from the funds he stole from others was to donate $100,000 to charity. Good intentions versus good ethics.

Nonprofits and Fraud

SECTION 10A

Sometimes the good intentions get the best of even the best-intentioned, and all the assumptions about goodness make for some easy marks, in terms of fraud. State attorneys general provide warnings on their websites about the risks of fraud clothed in goodness. Bennett M. Weiner, head of the Philanthropic Advisory Service of the Council of Better Business Bureaus, warns, "There's tremendous pressure on charities today to increase their revenues to meet expenses and growing public needs. Unfortunately, this can influence some organizations to take financial risks because of potential rewards."[1]

Case 10.1

New Era: If It Sounds Too Good to Be True, It Is Too Good to Be True

The Foundation for New Era Philanthropy was founded in 1989 by Mr. John G. Bennett Jr. New Era took in over $200 million between 1989 and May 1995 from 180 nonprofit organizations, when the Securities and Exchange Commission (SEC) brought suit against New Era and the foundation went into bankruptcy.

Mr. Bennett was, at that time, a charismatic individual who was able to bring in many individual and institutional investors (most of them nonprofit organizations that included many colleges and universities) with the promise of a double-your-money return.[2] The foundation began as a matching-gift program. Mr. Bennett would take the funds from the nonprofit, deposit them in a Prudential Insurance account that would earn interest at Treasury rates, and then work to find a matching donor. The intentions were good, and, initially, the funds were small. Mr. Bennett would later admit that there never were any matching donors. As word of his success spread, the size of the funds the nonprofits deposited increased and the greater the challenge became for finding a matching donor. And the pressure was growing. Mr. Bennett was receiving attention and accolades for his efforts. Former Philadelphia Mayor (now governor) Ed Rendell felt that Mr. Bennett's efforts had the potential for changing how people perceived Philadelphia both because of his success and also because the funds were helping nonprofits in their educational and community improvement efforts.[3]

Mr. Bennett often met personally with investors or their representatives and opened and closed his sessions with them with prayer.[4] Among the individual investors in New Era were Laurance Rockefeller, singer Pat Boone, then–President of Procter & Gamble John Pepper, John Whitehead, the former cohead of Goldman Sachs, and former Treasury Secretary William Simon. The institutional investors included Harvard, Princeton,

---

[1]William M. Bulkeley, "Charities' Coffers Easily Become Crooks' Booty," *Wall Street Journal*, June 5, 1995, pp. B1, B3.

[2]By the time of his sentencing, the issue of his mental competency was raised. In 2005, his lawyer requested an early release from prison for Mr. Bennett because of health issues.

[3]Robert Allen and Marshall Romney, "Lessons from New Era," *Internal Auditor*, October 1998, http://findarticles.com/p/articles/mi_m4153/is_5_55/ai_54250894/pg_8/?tag=content;col1. Accessed July 1, 2010.

[4]Steve Wulf, "Too Good to Be True," *Time*, May 29, 1995, p. 34.

University of Pennsylvania, the Nature Conservancy, and the National Museum of American Jewish History.[5]

In 1991, Melenie and Albert Meyer moved from their native South Africa to Michigan, where Mr. Meyer took a tenure-track position as an accounting professor at Spring Arbor College. Because there were only three accounting majors at the time he was hired, Mr. Meyer was also required to work part-time in the business office.[6]

During his first month in the business office, Mr. Meyer found that the college had transferred $294,000 to Heritage of Values Foundation, Inc. He connected the term *Heritage* with Reverend Jim Bakker and went to the library to research Heritage of Values Foundation, Inc. Although he found no connection to Jim Bakker, he could find no other information on the foundation. Mr. Meyer asked his supervisor, the vice president for business affairs, Ms. Janet M. Tjepkema, about Heritage of Values and the nature of the transfer. She explained that Heritage was the consultant that had found the New Era Foundation and had advised the college to invest in this "double your investment" fund.

Mr. Meyer attempted to research New Era but could find no registration for it in Pennsylvania, its headquarters location. He could not obtain information from New Era (there was no registration in Pennsylvania ever filed, and no tax returns were filed until 1993). Mr. Meyer continued to approach administrators of the college, but they seemed annoyed. He continued to collect information about New Era for the next two years. He gathered income tax returns and even spoke directly with Mr. Bennett. Mr. Meyer remained silent during the time that he gathered information because he was untenured and on a temporary work visa.[7] He also had a family to support, with three children. He was convinced that his concerns were justified when he discovered that New Era had reported only $34,000 in interest income for one year. With the portfolio it purported to hold, the interest income should have been about $1 million.

After he had collected files of information on New Era, which he labeled "Ponzi File," Mr. Meyer wrote a letter to the president of Spring Arbor as well as the chairman of the board of trustees for the college, warning them about his concerns regarding New Era. Mr. Meyer had also tried to talk with his colleagues about the information he had uncovered. He felt shunned by administrators and his colleagues, and, by April 1994, he and his wife were no longer attending any social functions held by the college. He was told by administrators that raising funds was tough enough without his meddling. He repeatedly tried to convince administrators not to place any additional funds with New Era. His advice was ignored, and Spring Arbor invested an additional $1.5 million in New Era in 1994. At that time, Spring Arbor College's total endowment was $6 million. The $1.5 million would later be lost as part of the New Era bankruptcy.

In March 1995, Mr. Meyer received tenure and began to try to help others by warning them about his concerns about New Era. He wrote to the SEC and detailed his information and concerns. The SEC then notified Prudential Securities, which was holding $73 million in New Era stock. Prudential began its own investigation and found resistance from New Era officers in releasing information. New Era began to unravel, and by June 1995 it was in bankruptcy. There were 300 creditors named, and net losses were $107 million. New Era was nothing but a Ponzi scheme. It was able to pay out double the investment, but only so long as it could recruit new participants. When it could no longer recruit participants, it was unable to pay on demands for withdrawal.

[5]Steve Secklow, "A New Era Consultant Lured Rich Donors over Pancakes, Prayer," *Wall Street Journal*, June 2, 1995, pp. A1, A4.

[6]Barbara Carton, "Unlikely Hero: A Persistent Accountant Brought New Era's Problems to Light," *Wall Street Journal*, May 19, 1995, pp. B1, B10.

[7]*Id.*

Mr. Bennett was indicted on eighty-two counts of fraud, money laundering, and tax code violations in March 1997.[8] Following his arraignment, he was released after posting his daughter's $115,000 house to cover his bond.[9] Mr. Bennett entered a no-contest plea in 1997 and was sentenced to twelve years in prison following six days of testimony during his sentencing hearing, including emotional pleas from Mr. Bennett. In ordering a reduced sentence, the judge departed from the 24.5 years dictated by the federal sentencing guidelines because Mr. Bennett had been "extraordinarily cooperative" in the investigation and because he had voluntarily turned over $1.5 million in assets to the bankruptcy court to be distributed to New Era participants.[10] The judge also noted what he felt was Mr. Bennett's diminished capacity.[11] The judge, in particularly harsh language, lectured Mr. Bennett on the egregious nature of his conduct: "It is possible for an ostensibly good and reverent person who is a true believer to engage in egregiously reprehensible and societally disruptive behavior."[12]

The nonprofit organizations that had invested in New Era recovered two-thirds of their investments and filed suit against Prudential Securities for recoupment of the remainder. That suit was settled without disclosure of its terms in 1996. The basis of the suit was that their funds were held in a single account at Prudential and that the funds were being used to repay New Era loans from Prudential instead of being invested as promised.

Mr. Meyer was still not embraced at his school for his efforts. Some still say that if Mr. Meyer had remained quiet, Mr. Bennett could have worked out the problems of New Era. Meyer was named a Michiganian of the Year for 1995.

Discussion Questions

1. Why did Mr. Meyer have so much difficulty convincing his college administrators that there was a problem with New Era?
2. Did Mr. Meyer follow the right steps in trying to bring New Era to the attention of the college officials?
3. What impact did Mr. Meyer's personal situation (visa and tenure issues) have on his desire to carry through with his concerns?
4. Why were administrators so reluctant to hear Mr. Meyer out? Mr. Bennett notified Spring Arbor College officials when Mr. Meyer called him and asked administrators to keep Mr. Meyer quiet. How would you read this kind of request? What would you do if you were an administrator?
5. About forty of the nonprofit organizations that had invested in New Era and withdrawn their funds and earnings prior to its collapse voluntarily agreed to return their money to the bankruptcy pool.[13] An administrator from Lancaster Bible College, in explaining the return of his college's funds to the trustee, quoted St. Paul's letter to the Philippians, "Let each of you look not only to his own interest, but also to the interests of others" (Phillipians 2:4). Hans Finzel, head of CB International, a missionary fund, said his organization would not be returning the money: "It's true that it's tainted money, but it's also true that we received it in good faith."[14] Compare and contrast the positions of the parties. Would you return the money?
6. Is this case an indication that nonprofits operate as businesses and are susceptible to the same business ethics issues? Should nonprofits have ethics programs and training for their staff and volunteers?

[8]Steve Secklow, "Retired Judge Will Sort Out New Era Mess," *Wall Street Journal,* June 29, 1995, pp. B1, B16.

[9]Steve Secklow, "How New Era's Boss Led Rich and Gullible into a Web of Deceit," *Wall Street Journal,* May 19, 1995, pp. A1, A5.

[10]Dinah Wisenberg Brin, "Philanthropy Scam Nets 12 Years," *USA Today,* September 23, 1997, p. 2A.

[11]Carton, "Unlikely Hero," pp. B1, B10.

[12]Joseph Slobodzian, "Bennett Gets 12 for New Era Scam," *National Law Journal,* October 6, 1997, p. A8.

[13]Andrea Gerlin, "Among the Few Given Money by New Era, Many See Blessings in Giving It Back," *Wall Street Journal,* June 20, 1995, pp. B1, B10.

[14]Michael A. Bloom, "Key in New Era Settlement," *National Law Journal,* July 15, 1996, p. A4.

Sources

Bloom, Michael A., "Key in New Era Settlement," *National Law Journal,* July 15, 1996, p. A4.

Davis, Ann, "Charity's Troubles Put Dechert in Bind," *National Law Journal,* May 29, 1995, p. A6.

Lambert, Wade, "Trustee in New Era Bankruptcy May Pursue 'Donations,'" *Wall Street Journal,* May 22, 1995, p. B3.

Secklow, Steve, "A New Era Consultant Lured Rich Donors over Pancakes, Prayers," *Wall Street Journal,* June 2, 1995, pp. A1, A4.

Secklow, Steve, "New Era's Bennett Gets 12-Year Sentence," *Wall Street Journal,* September 23,1997, p. B13.

Secklow, Steve, "Prudential Securities Agrees to Settle New Era Suits by Paying $18 Million," *Wall Street Journal,* November 18, 1996, p. A4.

Secklow, Steve, and Joseph Rebello, "IRS Is Studying Whether New Era's Donors Committed Fraud on Deductions," *Wall Street Journal,* May 24, 1995, p. A3.

Slobodzian, Joseph, "New Era Founder Says: God Made Him Do It," *National Law Journal,* March 17 1997, p. A9.

Case 10.2

The Baptist Foundation: Funds of the Faithful

Although founded in 1948, the Baptist Foundation of Arizona (BFA) took a dramatic strategic step in 1984 with a shift away from raising funds for starting up churches to a real estate investment nonprofit corporation. In its early days of the new strategy, the BFA did quite well because with a real estate boom, property values were increasing. In addition to a profitable real estate market, the BFA had a psychology going with its fund and with recruiting investors. Each year, at its annual convention, the BFA distributed its "Book of Reports," a financial compilation given to the convention attendees. However, the "Book of Reports" could be given to others as a means of recruiting new investors. The BFA used the term *stewardship investment* to describe the sort of higher calling that those who invested in BFA had. And for a good many years it looked as if Providence had had some hand in the BFA, for it was offering higher-than-market returns.[15]

However, by 1988 both the Arizona economy and its real estate market were sinking fast. Rather than disclose that the downturn had affected its holdings (as it had for all other real estate firms, for-profit and nonprofit alike), BFA opted not to write down its properties. The management team's compensation was tied to the performance of the fund. Arthur Andersen, the auditor for BFA, noted the presence of specific revenue targets set by management for each quarter, with compensation packages tied to those targets.

The nondisclosure was accomplished through the use of complex layers of transactions with related parties, accounts receivable, and a host of other accounting sleights of hand that allowed BFA to look as if it still had both the assets and income it had before the market downturn. BFA carried the properties at their full original values on its books, not at their true market values, figures that would have been significantly less and were driving many other real estate investment firms into bankruptcy. BFA's income doubled between 1996 and 1997, and had climbed from $350,000 in 1988 to $2.5 million in 1997. The numbers seemed quite nearly inexplicable given the downturn and the performance of all other real estate funds. BFA was selling its properties to board members and companies of board members at their book value or slightly higher in an effort to show gains, income, and cash flow for the BFA.

---

[15]This information can be found in the criminal information, cease and desist order, and bankruptcy filings all located at the Arizona Corporation Commission website, http://www.ccsd.cc.state.az.us.

Funds never really changed hands in these related parties' transactions. The transfers of funds and properties were like a large shell game among and between various non-profit entities. Some of the twenty-one individuals on the BFA board who decided against writing down the properties were also parties to the pseudo sales transactions of the properties to ALO and New Church Ventures. According to forensic auditors, a former director of BFA created ALO, Inc., and New Church Ventures, Inc., also nonprofit organizations. These corporations were shell corporations with no employees. However, significant amounts of BFA income were transferred to these two nonprofits as management fees, accounting fees, and marketing and administrative services fees. ALO purchased BFA's overvalued real estate holdings in exchange for promissory notes. Arizona Corporation Commission records show that for 1997, ALO reported that it owed BFA $70.3 million and New Church ventures $173.6 million.

BFA also created a web of other subsidiaries, including Christian Financial Partners, EVIG, and Select Trading Group. This tangled web made it difficult for potential investors to understand what BFA was doing or how it was earning its funds.

Because BFA's financial statements looked phenomenal, more investors joined, and the fraud lasted until 1999. In 1999, state officials issued a cease-and-desist order to stop the BFA from soliciting and bringing in new investors. In 1998, Andersen identified "earnings management" as a significant problem at BFA. However, Andersen did not see the earnings management as enough of a problem to halt its certification of BFA's financial statements. Andersen did question the significant transfers of fees to ALO and New Church Ventures. However, BFA officials never responded to auditors' requests for these two entities' records. Interestingly, the Arizona Corporation Commission records that showed the negative net worth of these two companies would have been available to anyone as a public record.

By the time the Baptist Foundation of Arizona collapsed in 1999, about 11,000 investors would lose $590 million.[16] The Arizona Attorney General's Office, which issued indictments and tried the fraud cases, called BFA the largest "affinity fraud" in U.S. history. Pastors and ministers had encouraged their parishioners to invest in BFA for their retirement even as the BFA used the funds to "do the Lord's work,"[17] including using the funds to build nursing homes for the aging and infirm, pay the salaries of pastors, and provide funding for Baptist ministries and missionary work. The fund was not a difficult sell because of the pledged noble efforts.

Andersen was charged with violations of Arizona securities laws for its failure to issue a qualified opinion on BFA when it became aware of the failure to write down properties as well as the earnings management strategies. Andersen settled with Arizona officials and agreed to pay $217 million in losses to investors, but, by the time of the settlement, Andersen was embroiled in the Enron and WorldCom settlements, and the ability to collect on the agreement was limited. Eight former BFA employees were indicted. Six entered guilty pleas and agreed to testify against Thomas Grabinski, the BFA's former general counsel, and William Crotts, the former BFA president. Following a trial that lasted ten months, Crotts was sentenced to six years and Grabinski to eight years for convictions on fraud and racketeering.[18]

The two men were also required to pay $159 million in restitution. Interestingly, the jury acquitted the two men of theft, and the trial reversed several of the convictions

---

[16]*Arizona v Crotts*, Az. App. June 2, 2009 (unpublished opinion). http://www.cofad1.state.az.us/memod/cr/cr060818 .pdf. Accessed July 1, 2010.

[17]Michael Kiefer, "2 Given Prison for Fraud Involving Baptist Group," *Arizona Republic*, September 30, 2006, pp. B1, B2.

[18]*Id.*

following a motion for post-judgment relief. The sentences were not imposed until September 2006, and the appeal on their cases was decided in 2009, with the appellate court affirming their convictions.[19] The appeal centered on an evidentiary question about a former officer who had entered into a plea agreement in exchange for his testimony. During the course of the trial, the former officer told prosecutors that he had lied in his earlier testimony. However, the appellate court concluded that defense lawyers were given additional time to recall witnesses and clear up the record and that there was no reversible error.

Discussion Questions

1. What similarities do you see between this nonprofit case and the cases of Enron, World-Com, and Tyco? Compare Andersen's conduct in Enron with Andersen's conduct in this case.

2. List the conflicts of interest you can see from the case.

3. Why do you think the board members thought they were immune from the economic cycle Arizona was experiencing?

Source

Criminal information, the cease and desist order, and bankruptcy filings are all located at the Arizona Corporation Commission website: http://www.ccsd.cc.state.az.us.

---

[19]*Arizona v Crotts*, Az. App. June 2, 2009 (unpublished opinion). http://www.cofad1.state.az.us/memod/cr/cr060818 .pdf. Accessed July 1, 2010.

Nonprofits and Management

Often with nonprofits, the problem is not fraud by the organization; it is fraud or misconduct or missteps within the organization. Whether because of inexperience, the need for flexibility in management, or, just as with companies, the drive for success and results, there have been some ethical issues that have proven costly for nonprofit organizations.

Case 10.3

ACORN: Community Organizers, Undercover Videos, and Advice

ACORN, the Association of Community Organizations for Reform Now, is an activist organization that works to obtain housing for low- to moderate-income individuals, assist with voter registration, and participate in community rallies on various issues such as public education and transit services. ACORN's mission statement includes the following:

> [ACORN] aims to organize a majority constituency of low- to moderate-income people across the United States. The members of ACORN take on issues of relevance to their communities, whether those issues are discrimination, affordable housing, a quality education, or better public services. ACORN believes that low- to moderate-income people are the best advocates for their communities, and so ACORN's low- to moderate-income members act as leaders, spokespeople, and decision-makers within the organization.[20]

James O'Keefe, 25, and Hannah Giles, 20, respectively a young reporter and an intern, had done research about ACORN and suspected that some of the organization's activities crossed legal and ethical lines. Mr. O'Keefe and Ms. Giles, posing, respectively, as a pimp and prostitute, went to ACORN offices in Baltimore, Brooklyn, Los Angeles, Philadelphia, and Washington, D.C. The two explained that they were looking for housing and that they were planning to bring in underage young women from other countries in order to establish a prostitution ring. They also had a undercover camera filming as they were interacting with the ACORN employees.

The ACORN employees did not caution the two about the legality of such activity or refuse to counsel them about obtaining housing. Rather, the ACORN employees advised the two not to bring up their occupations in their housing applications, "Honesty is not going to get you a house," and "You can't say what you do for a living."[21] Another ACORN counselor advised, "You know, what goes on in the house we don't care. We just help you with the mortgage."[22]

Following the release of the videos and substantial news coverage, ACORN's congressional funding was halted. Mr. O'Keefe and Ms. Giles were sued by ACORN employees for entrapment, violation of their privacy, and violation of state statutes that require

---

[20] http://www.acorn.org/about/mission. Accessed July 1, 2010.

[21] Jeremy Olshan, "'Pimp & Hooker' Catch B'lyn Staff," *New York Post*, September 14, 2009, http://www.nypost.com/p/news/local/brooklyn/item_Js4YPEcsCcxLZhAEehLhmL. Accessed July 1, 2010.

[22] Id.

565

permission prior to recording another on tape or video. Several attorneys general were reviewing the tapes to determine whether either Mr. O'Keefe or Ms. Giles or ACORN broke any laws.

Discussion Questions

1. A federal judge, in handling another case involving Mr. O'Keefe's alleged trespass at Senator Mary Landrieu's office said, in sentencing the young journalist to 100 hours of community service and a $1,500 fine, "Deception is alleged to have been used by the defendants to achieve their purposes which in and of itself is unconscionable. Perceived righteousness of a cause does not justify nefarious and potentially dangerous actions."[23] Is the judge correct? Or does the end justify the means? How do the issues of privacy and legality weigh in these circumstances?

2. If you were the national director of ACORN, what action would you take after viewing the videos of your employees on the national news?

Case 10.4

Giving and Spending the United Way

The United Way, which evolved from the local community chests of the 1920s, is a national organization that funnels funding to charities through a payroll deduction system.

Ninety percent of all charitable payroll deductions in 1991 were for the United Way. This system, however, has been criticized as coercive. Bonuses, for example, were offered for achieving 100 percent employee participation. Betty Beene, president of United Way of Tristate (New York, New Jersey, and Connecticut), commented, "If participation is 100 percent, it means someone has been coerced."[24] Tristate discontinued the bonuses and arm-twisting.

United Way's system of spending also came under fire through the actions of William Aramony, president of the United Way from 1970 to 1992. During his tenure, United Way receipts grew from $787 million in 1970 to $3 billion in 1990. But some of Aramony's effects on the organization were less positive.

In early 1992, the *Washington Post* reported that Aramony

- was paid $463,000 per year.
- flew first class on commercial airlines.
- spent $20,000 in one year for limousines.
- used the Concorde for trans-Atlantic flights.[25]

The article also revealed that one of the taxable spin-off companies Aramony had created to provide travel and bulk purchasing for United Way chapters had bought a $430,000 condominium in Manhattan and a $125,000 apartment in Coral Gables, Florida, for his use. Another spin-off had hired Aramony's son, Robert Aramony, as its president.

When Aramony's expenses and salary became public, Stanley C. Gault, chairman of Goodyear Tire & Rubber Company, asked, "Where was the board? The outside

---

[23]http://neworleans.fbi.gov/dojpressrel/pressrel10/no052610b.htm. Accessed July 1, 2010.

[24]Susan Garland, "Keeping a Sharper Eye on Those Who Pass the Hat," *BusinessWeek*, March 16, 1992, p. 39.

[25]As reported in "Ex-Executives of United Way Indicted," *(Phoenix) Arizona Republic*, September 14, 1994, p. A6.

auditors?"[26] Aramony resigned after fifteen chapters of the United Way threatened to withhold their annual dues to the national office.

Said Robert O. Bothwell, executive director of the National Committee for Responsive Philanthropy, "I think it is obscene that he is making that kind of salary and asking people who are making $10,000 a year to give 5 percent of their income."[27]

In August 1992, the United Way board of directors hired Elaine Chao, the Peace Corps director, to replace William Aramony at a salary of $195,000, with no perks.[28] She reduced staff from 275 to 185 and borrowed $1.5 million to compensate for a decline in donations. By 1995, United Way donations had still not returned to their 1991 level of $3.2 billion. Ms. Chao has since left the United Way and served as secretary of labor for the Bush administration from 2001–2009. Ms. Chao is married to Republican U.S. Senator Mitch McConnell of Kentucky.

In September 1994, William Aramony and two other United Way officers, including the chief financial officer, were indicted by a federal grand jury for conspiracy, mail fraud, and tax fraud. The indictment alleged the three officers diverted more than $2.74 million of United Way funds to purchase an apartment in New York City for $383,000, interior decorating for $72,000, a condominium, vacations, and a lifetime pass on American Airlines. In addition, $80,000 of United Way funds were paid to Aramony's girlfriend, a 1986 high school graduate, for consulting, even though she did no work.

On April 3, 1995, Aramony was found guilty of twenty-five counts of fraud, conspiracy, and money laundering. Two other United Way executives were also convicted. Mr. Aramony was sentenced to eighty-four months in prison (and fined $300,000) and was released in 2004. He lives in Alexandria, Virginia, and United Way executives continue to refer to his tenure and all the problems associated with it as "the great unpleasantness."

By April 1998, donation levels were still not completely reinstated, but did increase (up 4.7 percent) for the first time since the 1992 Aramony crisis. Relationships between local chapters and the national organization were often strained, and the recent Boy Scouts of America boycott has created additional tension. United Way's donations fell 11 percent since 1991 while overall charitable giving was up 9 percent.

In January 2000, a federal district court judge awarded Mr. Aramony the full value of his deferred compensation plan, or $4.2 million. Judge Shira Scheindlin ruled in favor of Mr. Aramony because she said there was no clause for forfeiting the money if Mr. Aramony committed a felony. Such a so-called bad boy clause had been discussed by the board when it was in the process of approving the deferred compensation plan for Mr. Aramony and other United Way executives. However, the bad-boy clause never made it into the final agreement.[29]

Judge Scheindlin also ruled that United Way could withhold $2.02 million of the amount due under the deferred compensation plan to cover salary, investigation costs, and interest on those amounts. She did not award Mr. Aramony attorneys' fees for having to bring the suit against United Way to collect his deferred compensation.

Many in the nonprofit field say that the shadow of William Aramony looms over the nonprofit world. However, when he was released from prison in 2002, the warden, guards, and inmates, who all called him "Mr. Aramony" spoke of him with fondness because of his work in prison in trying to provide educational opportunities for his

---

[26]Garland, "Keeping a Sharper Eye on Those Who Pass the Hat," p. 39.

[27]Felicity Barringer, "United Way Head Is Forced Out in a Furor over His Lavish Style," *New York Times*, February 28, 1992, p. A1.

[28]Desda Moss, "Peace Corps Director to Head United Way," *USA Today*, August 27, 1992, p. 6A; and Sabra Chartrand, "Head of Peace Corps Named United Way President," *New York Times*, August 27, 1992, p. A8.

[29]David Cay Johnston, "Ex-United Way Chief Owed $4.2 Million," *New York Times*, January 5, 2000, p. C4.

fellow inmates. They described him as being tireless in his efforts to teach everything from reading to math to, ironically, business operations.

Discussion Questions

1. Was there anything unethical about Aramony's expenditures?
2. Was the board responsible for the expenditures?
3. Is the perception as important as the acts themselves?
4. If Aramony were a CEO of a for-profit firm, would your answers change?
5. What obstacles did Chao face as she assumed the United Way helm?
6. Do you think Aramony should have asked for his deferred compensation funds? Why would the board pay him those funds? What could boards do to limit compensation paid to CEOs who resign following misconduct at the company?

Sources

Allen, Frank E., and Susan Pulliam, "United Way's Rivals Take Aim at Its Practices," *Wall Street Journal,* March 6, 1992, pp. B1, B6.

Barringer, Felicity, "Ex-Chief of United Way Vows to Fight Accusations," *New York Times,* April 10, 1992, p. A13.

Duffy, Michael, "Charity Begins at Home," *Time,* March 9, 1992, p. 48.

"Ex-Executives of United Way Indicted," *(Phoenix) Arizona Republic,* September 14, 1994, p. A6.

Kinsley, Michael, "Charity Begins with Government," *Time,* April 6, 1992, p. 74.

Moss, Desda, "Change Is Focus of United Way Meeting," *USA Today,* August 19, 1992, p. 7A.

Moss, Desda, "Former United Way Chief Charged with Looting Funds," *USA Today,* September 14, 1994, p. 1A.

Moss, Desda, "United Way's Ex-Chief Guilty of Using Funds," *USA Today,* April 14, 1995, p. 1A.

Case 10.5

The Red Cross, New York, and Ground Zero

Following the September 11, 2001, attacks on the World Trade Center and Washington, D.C., there were many who had lost loved ones, their homes or businesses, or both.

The outpouring of support from the American public was overwhelming. The public donated $543 million for the September 11 disaster relief fund.[30] However, the Red Cross indicated it would use the funds for infrastructure support and not necessarily all of it would go to victims and their families.

When the decision to use the funds in this manner was made, Dr. Bernadine Healy resigned as president of the Red Cross, giving up her $450,010 annual salary and position.

The American public was outraged and demanded that the funds go to the victims and their families. The Red Cross eventually relented, admitted an error in judgment, and agreed to the limited and intended use of the funds.

Discussion Questions

1. Did the Red Cross commit an ethical violation in its initial decision?
2. What do you think of Dr. Healy's decision? Is she a whistle-blower?
3. What policies should the Red Cross establish for the future in fundraising and fund disbursement?

[30]Marvin Olasky, "Charity Doesn't Have to Mean Bureaucracy," *Wall Street Journal,* November 21, 2001, p. A15.

Case 10.6

The Cornell Researchers Funded by the Foundation

Brilliant researchers at Cornell discovered a new imaging technique that can detect lung cancer early enough to allow removal of tumors. Weill Cornell Medical College researcher, Dr. Claudia Hensche, released her groundbreaking work on lung cancer in 2006 in the *New England Journal of Medicine*. A footnote in the article indicated that nearly all of the $3.6 million in funding for her research had come from The Foundation for Lung Cancer: Early Detection, Prevention, and Treatment. However, a 2008 *New York Times* story revealed that nearly all of the funding for the Foundation had come from The Vector Group, the parent of Liggett Group, a cigarette company.[31] A 2009 *Wall Street Journal* article disclosed that Dr. Hensche, whose research work and publication on treating lung cancer focused on the use of the tomography machine, was also receiving royalties from General Electric, one of the leading manufacturers of such machines.[32]

If the physician-researchers are correct in their work and findings, they have made a major breakthrough. However, cries of foul have emerged as the physician-researchers fret that valuable science is being discredited because of "tobacco taint." But another expert has countered, "the Cornell scientists promoting it are also trained professionals who have (conflict of interest disclosure infractions aside) successfully run the gauntlet of peer review. The top Cornell administrator who approved the tobacco payments is also a distinguished physician-scientist."[33]

Discussion Questions

1. Are there grades or levels of conflicts of interest? How are conflicts managed?
2. Who are the stakeholders in analyzing this question about the disclosure of funding for research and royalties related to research focus?
3. What guidelines should universities have for their researchers? What guidelines should companies have for their donations? What guidelines should editors have for publication of research results?

---

[31]Gardiner Harris, "Cigarette Company Paid for Lung Cancer Study," *New York Times*, March 26, 2008, p. A1.

[32]Keith J. Winstein, "Medical Journal Criticized Over Lack of Disclosure on Authors," *Wall Street Journal*, January 12, 2009, p. A9.

[33]David A Shaywitz and Thomas P. Stossel, "Attack of the Pharmascolds," *The Weekly Standard*, May 12, 2008, pp. 11–13.

Alphabetical Index

Aaron Feuerstein and Malden Mills (Case 6.4) — 356–358
ACORN: Community Organizers, Undercover Videos, and Advice (Case 10.3) — 565–566
Adam Smith: An Excerpt from The Theory of Moral Sentiments (Reading 8.4) — 505–506
Adelphia: Good Works via a Hand in the Till (Case 3.8) — 113–117
The Analyst Who Needed a Preschool (Case 6.9) — 367–370
Ann Hopkins and Price Waterhouse (Case 6.23) — 399–404
Appeasing Stakeholders with Public Relations (Reading 3.4) — 104–105
The Areas of Ethical Challenges in Business (Reading 2.9) — 71–72
Arizona Senate Bill 1070: Immigration Laws, Employers, Enforcement, and Emotion (Case 6.16) — 382–384
Arthur Andersen: A Fallen Giant (Case 4.16) — 246–253

Bank of America: The Merrill Takeover, the Disclosures, and the Board (Case 4.12) — 216–217
The Baptist Foundation: Funds of the Faithful (Case 10.2) — 562–564
Baseball and Steroids (Case 3.13) — 138–145
Bausch & Lomb and Krispy Kreme: Channel Stuffing and Cannibalism (Case 4.14) — 228–233
Beech-Nut and the No-Apple-Juice Apple Juice (Case 4.23) — 280–285
The Benefits of Diversity: Remarks of Doug Daft, Former CEO of Coca-Cola (Reading 6.13) — 376–380
Bernie Madoff: Just Stay Away from the 17th Floor (Case 4.28) — 311–312
Bhopal: When Safety Standards Differ (Case 5.7) — 333–334
Bloggers, Chat Rooms, and E-Mail: Your Employer Is Watching (Case 6.18) — 386–387
Boeing, Lockheed, and the Documents (Case 8.2) — 496–501
Boeing and the Recruiting of the Government Purchasing Agent (Case 9.16) — 548–550
BP: Pipeline, Refinery, and Offshore-Drilling Safety (Case 6.25) — 411–422
Business with a Soul: A Reexamination of What Counts in Business Ethics (Reading 3.3) — 101–104

Cheerios and Cholesterol and Rice Krispies and Immunity (Case 7.3) — 432–434
Chiquita Banana and Mercenary Protection (Case 5.2) — 319–322
Cintas and OSHA (Case 6.3) — 354–355
The Coke Employee Who Offered Inside Information to Pepsi (Case 8.5) — 506–508
The Compliance Officer Who Strayed (Case 8.6) — 508–510
Copyright, Songs, and Charities (Case 8.10) — 518–519
The Cornell Researchers Funded by the Foundation (Case 10.6) — 569
Craigslist and Ad Screening (Case 7.7) — 439–440

Dad, the Actuary, and the Stats Class (Case 1.13) — 39
Dayton-Hudson's Contributions to Planned Parenthood, and Target and the Bell Ringers (Case 3.15) — 146
The Death of the Great Disposable Diaper Debate (Case 3.18) — 153–155
Dennis Kozlowski: Tyco and the $6,000 Shower Curtain (Case 4.13) — 218–228
Do Cheaters Prosper? (Case 2.14) — 85
Docs, Pharmas, Medical Journals, Funded Research, and Pizza (Case 6.8) — 363–366
The Duke Lacrosse Team and the Prosecutors (Case 9.18) — 551–554

E. coli, Jack-in-the-Box, and Cooking Temperatures (Case 7.13) — 461–462
The Effects of Compensation Systems: Incentives, Bonuses, Pay, and Ethics (Reading 4.4) — 172–176
English-Only Employer Policies (Case 6.11) — 373–374
Enron: The CFO, Conflicts, and Cooking the Books with Natural Gas and Electricity (Case 4.15) — 233–246
The Ethics of Bankruptcy (Case 4.20) — 272–274
The Ethics of Confrontation (Reading 6.22) — 396–399
The Ethics of Responsibility (Reading 2.2) — 48–49
The Ethics of Walking Away: Buyers Have No Moral Duty to Lender (Case 4.21) — 275–278
The Ethics Officer and First Class for TSA (Case 1.16) — 41–42
Exxon and Alaska (Case 6.24) — 405–411

Facebook, MySpace, and YouTube Screening of Employees (Case 6.17) — 385–386
Fannie, Freddie, Wall Street, Main Street, and the Subprime Mortgage Market: Of Moral Hazards (Case 3.10) — 121–132
Fast Food Liability (Case 7.24) — 490–492

FEMA, Hurricane Katrina, and the Dilemmas of Regulation versus Human Life (Case 9.19) ... 554–555
FINOVA and the Loan Write-Off (Case 4.10) ... 206–211
The Fish Bowl Existence of Goverment (Reading 9.1) ... 525–527
Ford and Its Pinto and GM and Its Malibu: The Repeating Exploding Gas Tank Problem (Case 7.11) ... 452–458
The Former Soviet Union: A Study of Three Companies: PwC, Ikea, and AES (Case 5.4) ... 323
Frozen Coke and Burger King and the Richmond Rigging (Case 7.17) ... 468–471

Getting Information from Employees Who Know to Those Who Can and Will Respond (Reading 4.26) ... 289–293
Giving and Spending the United Way (Case 10.4) ... 566–568
The Glowing Recommendation (Reading 6.21) ... 395–396
Google, Yahoo, and Human Rights in China (Case 5.9) ... 337–339
Government Pricing and Finding a Way Around It (Case 9.14) ... 546–547
The Governor and a Senate Seat Vacated by a President (Case 9.4) ... 532–534

Hank Greenberg and AIG (Case 1.7) ... 27–28
HealthSouth: The Scrushy Way (Case 4.6) ... 183–192
Herman Miller and Its Rain Forest Chairs (Case 3.17) ... 151–153
Hiding the Slip-Up on Oil Lease Accounting: Interior Motives (Case 9.8) ... 540
Hollywood Ads (Case 7.5) ... 438
How Leaders Lose Their Way: What Price Hubris? (Reading 2.4) ... 59–61

"I Was Just Following Orders": The CIA, Interrogations, and the Role of Legal Opinions in the
   Conduct of Organizations (Case 9.6) ... 536–538
Ice-T, the *Body Count* Album, and Shareholder Uprising (Case 3.12) ... 133–138
If It's Legal, It's Ethical; and Besides, Everyone Does It (Reading 4.18) ... 257–262
Intel and the Chips: When You Have Made a Mistake (Case 7.19) ... 478–481
Is Business Bluffing Ethical? (Reading 2.3) ... 49–58
Is It None of Our Business? (Reading 6.20) ... 390–394

Jack Welch and the Harvard Interview (Case 6.19) ... 387–390
JCPenney and Its Wealthy Buyer (Case 6.6) ... 361–362
Jett and Kidder, Leeson and Barings, Kerviel and Société Générale: Compensation-Fueled Dishonesty (Case 4.7) ... 192–199
Joe Camel: The Cartoon Character Who Sold Cigarettes and Nearly Felled an Industry (Case 7.1) ... 425–430
Joe the Plumber, Child Support Records, and the Public Official's Disclosure (Case 9.9) ... 540–541
Jonathan Lebed: The Middle School Tycoon (Case 8.7) ... 510–511
Julie Roehm: The Walmart Ad Exec with Expensive Tastes (Case 6.10) ... 370–372

Kodak, the Appraiser, and the Assessor: Lots of Back Scratching on Valuation (Case 9.3) ... 531–532
Kraft, Barney Rubble, and Shrek (Case 7.6) ... 438–439

The Little Intermittent Windshield Wiper and Its Little Inventor (Case 8.12) ... 520–521
The Little Teacher Who Could: Piper, Kansas, and Term Papers (Case 1.10) ... 34–37

The Man Who Writes the Internal Revenue Code Has Tax Issues: The Rangel Round-Up (Case 9.5) ... 534–536
Marjorie Kelly and the Divine Right of Capital (Reading 3.6) ... 108–111
Martha Stewart: Not Such a Good Thing (Case 2.7) ... 63–69
Merck and Vioxx (Case 7.10) ... 447–452
The Mess at Marsh McLennan (Case 7.16) ... 465–468
Michael Novak on Capitalism and the Corporation (Reading 3.5) ... 105–108
Michael Vick, Dogs, Rush Limbaugh, and the NFL (Case 3.14) ... 145–146
Microsoft vs. Google and "Snippets" of Books (Case 8.11) ... 519–520
The Minerals Management Service: The Arms-Length Affairs with Oil Executives (Case 9.2) ... 527–531
Minority-Owned Businesses and Reality (Case 9.12) ... 545–546
The Mommy Doll (Case 7.21) ... 487
Moral Relativism and the Either/or Conundrum (Reading 2.5) ... 61–62
The Movie Ticket (Case 1.11) ... 37
The Moving Line (Reading 4.1) ... 159–160
The My Tai Concession and the County Supervisor (Case 9.13) ... 546

NASA and the Space Shuttle Booster Rockets (Case 4.24) ... 285–288
Nestlé: When Products Translate Differently (Case 5.8) ... 335–337
The New Environmentalism (Reading 3.16) ... 149–151
New Era: If It Sounds Too Good to Be True, It Is Too Good to be True (Case 10.1) ... 559
The New Shareholder: Taking Over to Change the Culture (Reading 4.17) ... 253–256
Not All Employees Are Equal When It Comes to Moral Development (Reading 4.2) ... 160–163

On Leaving to Spend More Time with Family (Case 2.8) ... 69–70
On Plagiarism (Reading 1.14) ... 40–41

On Rationalizing and Labeling: The Things We Do That Make Us Uncomfortable, but We
    Do Them Anyway (Reading 1.5) 22–26
On Sweatshops, Nike, and Kathie Lee (Case 5.6) 326–332
On-the-Job Fetal Injuries (Case 6.12) 374–376
The Options for Whistle-Blowers (Reading 4.22) 279

P=f(x) The Probability of an Ethical Outcome Is a Function of the Amount of Money Involved:
    Pressure (Reading 2.6) 62–63
The Pack of Gum (Case 1.18) 43
The Parable of the Sadhu, Pressure, Small Windows of Opportunity, and Temptation (Reading 1.2) 4–10
Paul Wolfowitz and the World Bank (Case 9.7) 538–540
Peanut Corporation of America and Salmonella (Case 7.14) 462–463
Pfizer and the $2.3 Billion Fine for Sales Tactics (Case 7.15) 464–465
Plant Closings, Downsizings, Company Closings, Government Takeovers, Bankruptcies, and
    Pensions (Case 6.5) 358–360
A Primer on Accounting Issues and Ethics and Earnings Management (Reading 4.19) 262–272
A Primer on Covenants Not to Compete: Are They Valid? (Reading 8.1) 495–496
A Primer on Product Liability (Case 7.8) 441–443
A Primer on Sarbanes–Oxley (Reading 4.11) 212–216
A Primer on the FCPA (Reading 5.10) 340–342
Product Dumping (Case 5.5) 325–326
The Prosecutors Who Withheld Evidence: The Senator's Trial (Case 9.17) 551
Puffing Your Resume (Case 1.12) 37–38

The Red Cross, New York, and Ground Zero (Case 10.5) 568
The Regulatory Cycle, Social Responsibility, Business Strategy, and Equilibrium (Reading 3.9) 117–121
The Rigged Election (Case 2.15) 86
Royal Dutch and the Reserves (Case 4.8) 199–200

Salt Lake City, the Olympics, and Bribery (Case 5.12) 344–350
School of Thought on Social Responsibility (Reading 3.7) 111–113
Sears and High-Cost Auto Repairs (Case 7.20) 481–486
Seinfeld in the Workplace (Case 6.14) 380–381
Siemens and Bribery, Everywhere (Case 5.11) 342–344
Simmons, Mervyn's, and the Private Equity Firms That Bankrupt Them (Case 8.8) 511–513
Sleeping on the Job and on the Way Home (Case 6.2) 353–354
The Slippery Slope, the Blurred Lines, and How We Never Do Just One Thing (Reading 1.6) 26–27
Slotting: Facilitation, Costs, or Bribery? (Case 7.18) 472–477
The Social Responsibility of Business Is to Increase Its Profits (Reading 3.1) 91–96
Some Simple Tests for Resolving Ethical Dilemmas (Reading 1.8) 29–34
Some Steps for Analyzing Ethical Dilemmas (Reading 1.9) 34
Speeding on the Job: Obeying the Rules: Why We Do and Don't (Case 1.17) 42–43
Spring Break, Beer, and Alcohol on Campus (Case 7.2) 430–432
A Stakeholder Theory of the Modern Corporation (Reading 3.2) 96–101
Stanford University and Government Overhead Payments (Case 9.10) 542–545
Starwood, Hilton, and the Suspiciously Similar New Hotel Designs (Case 8.3) 501–504
Stem-Cell Research (Case 7.22) 487–489
Stock Options, Backdating, and Disclosure Options: What Happened Here? (Reading 4.9) 200–206
A Structured Approach for Solving Ethical Dilemmas and Trying Out Your Ethical Skills on
    Some Business Cases (Reading 2.10) 72–73
Subprime Loans: The Under-the-Radar Loans That Felled a Market (Case 7.4) 434–437
The Subprime Saga: Bear Stearns, Lehman, Merrill, and CDOs (Reading 4.5) 176–183

Taser and Stunning Behavior (Case 9.15) 547–548
Tiffany, Louis Vuitton, eBay, Landlords, and Knock-Offs (Case 8.9) 514–518
Toro and Its Product Liability Program (Case 7.23) 489–490
Toyota, the CEO, the Assistant, and Inaction (Case 6.15) 381–382
Toyota: Sudden Acceleration or Bad Drivers or Pesky Floor Mats? (Case 7.12) 458–461
The Trading Desk, Perks, and "Dwarf Tossing" (Case 6.7) 362–363
Transnational Shipping and the Pirates (Case 5.3) 322–323
Travel Expenses: A Change for Extra Income (Case 2.13) 84–85
Two Sets of Books on Safety (Reading 6.1) 353
Tylenol: Decades of Dilemmas (Case 7.9) 444–447
The Types of Ethical Dilemmas: From Truth to Honesty to Conflicts (Reading 1.4) 17–22

West Virginia University and the Governor's Daughter (Case 2.16)   86–87
Westland/Hallmark Meat Packing Company and the Cattle Standers (Case 4.25)   288–289
What Are Ethics? From Line-Cutting to Kant (Reading 1.3)   10–17
What Happens in Boulder Stays in Boulder: Cell Phone Alibis (Case 2.12)   84
What Was Up with Wall Street? The Goldman Standard and Shades of Gray (Case 2.11)   73–84
What's Different about Business Ethics? (Reading 2.1)   47–48
Whole Foods, John Mackey, and Health Care Debates (Case 3.11)   132–133
Why an International Code of Ethics Would Be Good for Business (Reading 5.1)   315–319
Why Corporations Can't Control Chicanery (Reading 4.3)   164–172
Wi-Fi Piggybacking (Case 1.15)   41
WorldCom: The Little Company That Couldn't after All (Case 4.27)   293–310

Yale University and the Compensation of Professors for Goverment Research: Double-Dipping or
   Confusion? (Case 9.11)   545
You, Your Values, and Credo (Reading 1.1)   3–4

Business Discipline Index

Accounting

3.8	Adelphia: Good Works via a Hand in the Till	113
4.7	Jett and Kidder, Leeson and Barings, Kerviel and Société Générale: Compensation-Fueled Dishonesty	192
4.8	Royal Dutch and the Reserves	199
4.10	FINOVA and the Loan Write-Off	206
4.11	A Primer on Sarbanes–Oxley	212
4.13	Dennis Kozlowski: Tyco and the $6,000 Shower Curtain	218
4.14	Bausch & Lomb and Krispy Kreme: Channel Stuffing and Cannibalism	228
4.15	Enron: The CFO, Conflicts, and Cooking the Books with Natural Gas and Electricity	233
4.16	Arthur Andersen: A Fallen Giant	246
4.27	WorldCom: The Little Company That Couldn't After All	293
6.23	Ann Hopkins and Price Waterhouse	399
9.5	The Man Who Writes the Internal Revenue Code Has Tax Issues: The Rangel Round-Up	534
9.8	Hiding the Slip-Up on Oil Lease Accounting: Interior Motives	540
9.10	Stanford University and Government Overhead Payments	542
9.11	Yale University and the Compensation of Professors for Government Research: Double-Dipping or Confusion?	545
10.1	New Era: If It Sounds Too Good to Be True, It Is Too Good to Be True	559
10.2	The Baptist Foundation: Funds of the Faithful	562
10.4	Giving and Spending the United Way	566

Advertising

3.12	Ice-T, the *Body Count* Album, and Shareholder Uprisings	133
5.8	Nestlé: When Products Translate Differently	335
7.1	Joe Camel: The Cartoon Character Who Sold Cigarettes and Nearly Felled an Industry	425
7.2	Spring Break, Beer, and Alcohol on Campus	430
7.3	Cheerios and Cholesterol and Rice Krispies and Immunity	432
7.5	Hollywood Ads	438
7.6	Kraft, Barney Rubble, and *Shrek*	438
7.7	Craigslist and Ad Screening	439
7.13	E. coli, Jack-in-the-Box, and Cooking Temperatures	461

Business Communications

3.15	Dayton-Hudson's Contributions to Planned Parenthood, and Target and the Bell-Ringers	146
4.8	Royal Dutch and the Reserves	199
4.9	Stock Options, Backdating, and Disclosure Options: What Happened Here?	200
4.24	NASA and the Space Shuttle Booster Rockets	285
4.26	Getting Information from Employees Who Know to Those Who Can and Will Respond	289
6.21	The Glowing Recommendation	395
7.19	Intel and the Chips: When You Have Made a Mistake	478

Business Law

3.12	Ice-T, the *Body Count* Album, and Shareholder Uprisings	133
4.5	The Subprime Saga: Bear Stearns, Lehman, Merrill, and CDOs	176
4.18	If It's Legal, It's Ethical; and Besides, Everyone Does It	257
4.20	The Ethics of Bankruptcy	272
5.2	Chiquita Banana and Mercenary Protection	319
5.4	The Former Soviet Union: A Study of Three Companies: PwC, Ikea, and AES	323
5.10	A Primer on the FCPA	340
5.11	Siemens and Bribery, Everywhere	342
5.12	Salt Lake City, the Olympics, and Bribery	344
6.6	JCPenney and Its Wealthy Buyer	361
6.7	The Trading Desk, Perks, and "Dwarf Tossing"	362
6.11	English-Only Employer Policies	373
6.12	On-the-Job Fetal Injuries	374

6.13	The Benefits of Diversity: Remarks of Doug Daft, Former CEO of Coca-Cola	376
6.14	*Seinfeld* in the Workplace	380
6.16	Arizona Senate Bill 1070: Immigration Laws, Employers, Enforcement, and Emotion	382
6.18	Bloggers, Chat Rooms, and E-Mail: Your Employer Is Watching	386
6.21	The Glowing Recommendation	395
6.23	Ann Hopkins and Price Waterhouse	399
6.24	Exxon and Alaska	405
7.8	A Primer on Product Liability	441
7.9	Tylenol: Decades of Dilemmas	444
7.11	Ford and Its Pinto and GM and Its Malibu: The Repeating Exploding Gas Tank Problem	452
7.12	Toyota: Sudden Acceleration or Bad Drivers or Pesky Floor Mats?	458
7.16	The Mess at Marsh McLennan	465
7.18	Slotting: Facilitation, Costs, or Bribery?	472
7.19	Intel and the Chips: When You Have Made a Mistake	478
7.20	Sears and High-Cost Auto Repairs	481
8.1	A Primer on Covenants Not to Compete: Are They Valid?	495
8.5	The Coke Employee Who Offered Inside Information to Pepsi	506
8.6	The Compliance Officer Who Strayed	508
8.8	Simmons, Mervyn's, and the Private Equity Firms That Bankrupt Them	511
8.9	Tiffany, Louis Vuitton, eBay, Landlords, and Knock-Offs	514
8.10	Copyright, Songs, and Charities	518
8.11	Microsoft vs. Google and "Snippets" of Books	519
8.12	The Little Intermittent Windshield Wiper and Its Little Inventor	520

Compliance Programs

1.17	Speeding on the Job: Obeying the Rules: Why We Do and Don't	42
3.14	Michael Vick, Dogs, Rush Limbaugh, and the NFL	145
4.2	Not All Employees Are Equal When It Comes to Moral Development	160
4.11	A Primer on Sarbanes–Oxley	212
8.6	The Compliance Officer Who Strayed	508

Conflicts of Interest

2.11	What Was Up with Wall Street? The Goldman Standard and Shades of Gray	73
4.16	Arthur Andersen: A Fallen Giant	246
6.6	JCPenney and Its Wealthy Buyer	361
6.8	Docs, Pharmas, Medical Journals, Funded Research, and Pizza	363
6.9	The Analyst Who Needed a Preschool	367
6.10	Julie Roehm: The Walmart Ad Exec with Expensive Tastes	370
6.19	Jack Welch and the Harvard Interview	387
8.2	Boeing, Lockheed, and the Documents	496
8.3	Starwood, Hilton, and the Suspiciously Similar New Hotel Designs	501
9.3	Kodak, the Appraiser, and the Assessor: Lots of Back Scratching on Valuation	531
9.5	The Man Who Writes the Internal Revenue Code Has Tax Issues: The Rangel Round-Up	534
9.7	Paul Wolfowitz and the World Bank	538
9.13	The My Tai Concession and the County Supervisor	546
10.6	The Cornell Researchers Funded by the Foundation	569

Corporate Governance

4.2	Not All Employees Are Equal When It Comes to Moral Development	160
4.3	Why Corporations Can't Control Chicanery	164
4.4	The Effects of Compensation Systems: Incentives, Bonuses, Pay, and Ethics	172
4.7	Jett and Kidder, Leeson and Barings, Kerviel and Société Générale: Compensation-Fueled Dishonesty	192
4.9	Stock Options, Backdating, and Disclosure Options: What Happened Here?	200
4.10	FINOVA and the Loan Write-Off	206
4.11	A Primer on Sarbanes–Oxley	212
4.12	Bank of America: The Merrill Takeover, the Disclosures, and the Board	216
4.13	Dennis Kozlowski: Tyco and the $6,000 Shower Curtain	218
4.14	Bausch & Lomb and Krispy Kreme: Channel Stuffing and Cannibalism	228
4.15	Enron: The CFO, Conflicts, and Cooking the Books with Natural Gas and Electricity	233
4.17	The New Shareholder: Taking Over to Change the Culture	253
4.27	WorldCom: The Little Company That Couldn't After All	293
5.3	Transnational Shipping and the Pirates	322
6.1	Two Sets of Books on Safety	353
6.2	Sleeping on the Job and on the Way Home	353

6.3   Cintas and OSHA   354
6.25   BP: Pipeline, Refinery, and Offshore-Drilling Safety   411
8.2   Boeing, Lockheed, and the Documents   496
8.3   Starwood, Hilton, and the Suspiciously Similar New Hotel Designs   501
8.4   Adam Smith: An Excerpt from *The Theory of Moral Sentiments*   505
9.16   Boeing and the Recruiting of the Government Purchasing Agent   548

Cyberlaw
1.15   Wi-Fi Piggybacking   41
6.17   Facebook, MySpace, and YouTube Screening of Employers   385
6.18   Bloggers, Chat Rooms, and E-Mail: Your Employer Is Watching   386
8.9   Tiffany, Louis Vuitton, eBay, Landlords, and Knock-Offs   514

Economics
2.6   *P=f(x)* The Probability of an Ethical Outcome Is a Function of the Amount of Money Involved: Pressure   62
2.13   Travel Expenses: A Chance for Extra Income   84
3.1   The Social Responsibility of Business Is to Increase Its Profits   91
3.2   A Stakeholder Theory of the Modern Corporation   96
7.4   Subprime Loans—The Under-the-Radar Loans That Felled a Market   432
7.18   Slotting: Facilitation, Costs, or Bribery?   472
8.4   Adam Smith: An Excerpt from *The Theory of Moral Sentiments*   505
8.8   Simmons, Mervyn's, and the Private Equity Firms That Bankrupt Them   511

Finance
2.11   What Was Up with Wall Street? The Goldman Standard and Shades of Gray   73
3.10   Fannie, Freddie, Wall Street, Main Street, and the Subprime Mortgage Market: Of Moral Hazards   121
4.5   The Subprime Saga: Bear Stearns, Lehman, Merrill, and CDOs   176
4.7   Jett and Kidder, Leeson and Barings, Kerviel and Société Générale: Compensation-Fueled Dishonesty   192
4.10   FINOVA and the Loan Write-Off   206
4.15   Enron: The CFO, Conflicts, and Cooking the Books with Natural Gas and Electricity   233
4.17   The New Shareholder: Taking Over to Change the Culture   253
4.18   If It's Legal, It's Ethical; and Besides, Everyone Does It   257
4.19   A Primer on Accounting Issues and Ethics and Earnings Management   262
4.20   The Ethics of Bankruptcy   272
4.21   The Ethics of Walking Away   275
4.27   WorldCom: The Little Company That Couldn't After All   293
4.28   Bernie Madoff: Just Stay Away from the 17th Floor   311
6.7   The Trading Desk, Perks, and "Dwarf Tossing"   362
8.7   Jonathan Lebed: The Middle School Tycoon   510

Government
3.9   The Regulatory Cycle, Social Responsibility, Business Strategy, and Equilibrium   117
4.24   NASA and the Space Shuttle Booster Rockets   285
8.2   Boeing, Lockheed, and the Documents   496
9.1   The Fish Bowl Existence of Government   525
9.2   The Minerals Management Service: The Arms-Length Affairs with Oil Executives   527
9.3   Kodak, the Appraiser, and the Assessor: Lots of Back Scratching on Valuation   531
9.6   "I Was Just Following Orders": The CIA, Interrogations, and the Role of Legal Opinions in the
            Conduct of Organizations   536
9.8   Hiding the Slip-Up on Oil Lease Accounting: Interior Motives   540
9.9   Joe the Plumber, Child Support Records, and the Public Official's Disclosure   540
9.10   Stanford University and Government Overhead Payments   542
9.11   Yale University and the Compensation of Professors for Government Research: Double-Dipping or Confusion?   545
9.12   Minority-Owned Businesses and Reality   545
9.14   Government Pricing and Finding a Way Around It   546
9.15,   Taser and Stunning Behavior   547
9.17   The Prosecutors Who Withheld Evidence: The Senator's Trial   551
9.18   The Duke Lacrosse Team and the Prosecutor   551
9.19   FEMA, Hurricane Katrina, and the Dilemmas of Regulation versus Human Life   554

Health Care
3.11   Whole Foods, John Mackey, and Health Care Debates   132
4.6   HealthSouth: The Scrushy Way   183

5.7	Bhopal: When Safety Standards Differ	333
6.5	Plant Closings, Downsizings, Company Closings, Government Takeovers, Bankruptcies, and Pensions	358
6.8	Docs, Pharmas, Medical Journals, Funded Research, and Pizza	363
6.12	On-the-Job Fetal Injuries	374
7.9	Tylenol: Decades of Dilemmas	444
7.10	Merck and Vioxx	447
7.15	Pfizer and the $2.3 Billion Fine for Sales Tactics	464
7.22	Stem-Cell Research	487

International Operations
3.9	The Regulatory Cycle, Social Responsibility, Business Strategy, and Equilibrium	117
5.1	Why an International Code of Ethics Would Be Good for Business	315
5.2	Chiquita Banana and Mercenary Protection	319
5.3	Transnational Shipping and the Pirates	322
5.4	The Former Soviet Union: A Study of Three Companies: PwC, Ikea, and AES	323
5.5	Product Dumping	325
5.6	On Sweatshops, Nike, and Kathie Lee	326
5.7	Bhopal: When Safety Standards Differ	333
5.8	Nestlé: When Products Translate Differently	335
5.9	Google, Yahoo, and Human Rights in China	337
5.10	A Primer on the FCPA	340
5.11	Siemens and Bribery, Everywhere	342
5.12	Salt Lake City, the Olympics, and Bribery	344
6.13	The Benefits of Diversity: Remarks of Doug Daft, Former CEO of Coca-Cola	376
6.25	BP: Pipeline, Refinery, and Offshore-Drilling Safety	411
8.9	Tiffany, Louis Vuitton, eBay, Landlords, and Knock-Offs	514
9.7	Paul Wolfowitz and the World Bank	538

Labor Law
5.6	On Sweatshops, Nike, and Kathie Lee	326
5.7	Bhopal: When Safety Standards Differ	333
6.1	Two Sets of Books on Safety	353
6.3	Cintas and OSHA	354
6.4	Aaron Feuerstein and Malden Mills	356
6.11	English-Only Employer Policies	373
6.12	On-the-Job Fetal Injuries	374
6.13	The Benefits of Diversity: Remarks of Doug Daft, Former CEO of Coca-Cola	376
6.14	*Seinfeld* in the Workplace	380
6.16	Arizona Senate Bill 1070: Immigration Laws, Employers, Enforcement, and Emotion	382
6.23	Ann Hopkins and Price Waterhouse	399
6.25	BP: Pipeline, Refinery, and Offshore-Drilling Safety	411

Management
2.4	How Leaders Lose Their Way: What Price Hubris?	59
3.11	Whole Foods, John Mackey, and Health Care Debates	132
3.13	Baseball and Steroids	138
4.3	Why Corporations Can't Control Chicanery	164
4.26	Getting Information from Employees Who Know to Those Who Can and Will Respond	289
4.27	WorldCom: The Little Company That Couldn't After All	293
4.28	Bernie Madoff: Just Stay Away from the 17th Floor	311
6.4	Aaron Feuerstein and Malden Mills	356
6.9	The Analyst Who Needed a Preschool	367
6.10	Julie Roehm: The Walmart Ad Exec with Expensive Tastes	370
6.23	Ann Hopkins and Price Waterhouse	399
6.24	Exxon and Alaska	405
7.16	The Mess at Marsh McLennan	465
10.4	Giving and Spending the United Way	566

Marketing
3.3	Business with a Soul: A Reexamination of What Counts in Business Ethics	101
3.4	Appeasing Stakeholders with Public Relations	104
3.12	Ice-T, the *Body Count* Album, and Shareholder Uprisings	133
3.18	The Death of the Great Disposable Diaper Debate	153
5.5	Product Dumping	325
5.8	Nestlé: When Products Translate Differently	335

6.8   Docs, Pharmas, Medical Journals, Funded Research, and Pizza   363
6.24 Exxon and Alaska   405
7.1   Joe Camel: The Cartoon Character Who Sold Cigarettes and Nearly Felled an Industry   425
7.2   Spring Break, Beer, and Alcohol on Campus   430
7.3   Cheerios and Cholesterol and Rice Krispies and Immunity   432
7.4   Subprime Loans—The Under-the-Radar Loans That Felled a Market   432
7.15 Pfizer and the $2.3 Billion Fine for Sales Tactics   464
7.17 Frozen Coke and Burger King and the Richmond Rigging   468
7.19 Intel and the Chips: When You Have Made a Mistake   478
9.15 Taser and Stunning Behavior   547

Nonprofit Management
9.10 Stanford University and Government Overhead Payments   542
10.1 New Era: If It Sounds Too Good to Be True, It Is Too Good to Be True   559
10.2 The Baptist Foundation: Funds of the Faithful   562
10.3 ACORN: Community Organizers, Undercover Videos, and Advice   565
10.4 Giving and Spending the United Way   566
10.5 The Red Cross, New York, and Ground Zero   568
10.6 The Cornell Researchers Funded by the Foundation   569

Operations
1.13 Dad, the Actuary, and the Stats Class   39
4.8   Royal Dutch and the Reserves   199
4.23 Beech-Nut and the No-Apple-Juice Apple Juice   280
5.2   Chiquita Banana and Mercenary Protection   319
5.4   The Former Soviet Union: A Study of Three Companies: PwC, Ikea, and AES   323
6.21 The Glowing Recommendation   395
6.24 Exxon and Alaska   405
6.25 BP: Pipeline, Refinery, and Offshore-Drilling Safety   411
7.13 E. coli, Jack-in-the-Box, and Cooking Temperatures   461
7.14 Peanut Corporation of America and Salmonella   462
7.19 Intel and the Chips: When You Have Made a Mistake   478

Organizational Behavior
1.10 The Little Teacher Who Could: Piper, Kansas, and Term Papers   35
2.11 What Was Up with Wall Street? The Goldman Standard and Shades of Gray   73
3.10 Fannie, Freddie, Wall Street, Main Street, and the Subprime Mortgage Market: Of Moral Hazards 121
3.13 Baseball and Steroids   138
3.14 Michael Vick, Dogs, Rush Limbaugh, and the NFL   145
4.3   Why Corporations Can't Control Chicanery   164
4.4   The Effects of Compensation Systems: Incentives, Bonuses, Pay, and Ethics   172
4.5   The Subprime Saga: Bear Stearns, Lehman, Merrill, and CDOs   176
4.6   HealthSouth: The Scrushy Way   183
4.10 FINOVA and the Loan Write-Off   206
4.13 Dennis Kozlowski: Tyco and the $6,000 Shower Curtain   218
4.14 Bausch & Lomb and Krispy Kreme: Channel Stuffing and Cannibalism   228
4.15 Enron: The CFO, Conflicts, and Cooking the Books with Natural Gas and Electricity   233
4.18 If It's Legal, It's Ethical; and Besides, Everyone Does It   257
6.10 Julie Roehm: The Walmart Ad Exec with Expensive Tastes   370
6.14 Seinfeld in the Workplace   380
6.20 Is It None of Our Business?   390
6.23 Ann Hopkins and Price Waterhouse   399
9.7   Paul Wolfowitz and the World Bank   538
9.9   Joe the Plumber, Child Support Records, and the Public Official's Disclosure   540
10.3 ACORN: Community Organizers, Undercover Videos, and Advice   565

Purchasing
4.23 Beech-Nut and the No-Apple-Juice Apple Juice   280
5.6   On Sweatshops, Nike, and Kathie Lee   326
6.6   JCPenney and Its Wealthy Buyer   361
9.14 Government Pricing and Finding a Way Around It   546

Quality Management
4.23 Beech-Nut and the No-Apple-Juice Apple Juice   280
4.24 NASA and the Space Shuttle Booster Rockets   285

4.25   Westland/Hallmark Meat Packing Company and the Cattle Standers   288
5.5   Product Dumping   325
7.9   Tylenol: Decades of Dilemmas   444
7.11   Ford and Its Pinto and GM and Its Malibu: The Repeating Exploding Gas Tank Problem   452
7.12   Toyota: Sudden Acceleration or Bad Drivers or Pesky Floor Mats?   458
7.13   E. coli, Jack-in-the-Box, and Cooking Temperatures   461
7.14   Peanut Corporation of America and Salmonella   462
7.20   Sears and High-Cost Auto Repairs   481

Regulation

2.7   Martha Stewart: Not Such a Good Thing   63
4.4   The Effects of Compensation Systems: Incentives, Bonuses, Pay, and Ethics   172
4.6   HealthSouth: The Scrushy Way   183
4.9   Stock Options, Backdating, and Disclosure Options: What Happened Here?   200
4.14   Bausch & Lomb and Krispy Kreme: Channel Stuffing and Cannibalism   228
4.20   The Ethics of Bankruptcy   272
4.25   Westland/Hallmark Meat Packing Company and the Cattle Standers   288
5.2   Chiquita Banana and Mercenary Protection   319
5.5   Product Dumping   325
5.11   Siemens and Bribery, Everywhere   342
7.1   Joe Camel: The Cartoon Character Who Sold Cigarettes and Nearly Felled an Industry   425
7.3   Cheerios and Cholesterol and Rice Krispies and Immunity   432
7.5   Hollywood Ads   438
7.7   Craigslist and Ad Screening   439
8.7   Jonathan Lebed: The Middle School Tycoon   510
8.9   Tiffany, Louis Vuitton, eBay, Landlords, and Knock-Offs   514
9.13   The My Tai Concession and the County Supervisor   546

Social Responsibility

2.8   On Leaving to Spend More Time with Family   69
3.1   The Social Responsibility of Business Is to Increase Its Profits   86
3.2   A Stakeholder Theory of the Modern Corporation   96
3.3   Business with a Soul: A Reexamination of What Counts in Business Ethics   101
3.8   Adelphia: Good Works via a Hand in the Till   113
3.9   The Regulatory Cycle, Social Responsibility, Business Strategy, and Equilibrium   117
3.10   Fannie, Freddie, Wall Street, Main Street, and the Subprime Mortgage Market: Of Moral Hazards   121
3.11   Whole Foods, John Mackey, and Health Care Debates   132
3.12   Ice-T, the *Body Count* Album, and Shareholder Uprisings   133
3.14   Michael Vick, Dogs, Rush Limbaugh, and the NFL   145
3.15   Dayton-Hudson's Contributions to Planned Parenthood, and Target and the Bell-Ringers   146
3.16   The New Environmentalism   149
3.17   Herman Miller and Its Rain Forest Chairs   151
3.18   The Death of the Great Disposable Diaper Debate   153
4.17   The New Shareholder: Taking Over to Change the Culture   253
5.6   On Sweatshops, Nike, and Kathie Lee   326
5.7   Bhopal: When Safety Standards Differ   333
5.8   Nestlé: When Products Translate Differently   335
6.2   Sleeping on the Job and on the Way Home   353
6.4   Aaron Feuerstein and Malden Mills   356
6.5   Plant Closings, Downsizings, Company Closings, Government Takeovers, Bankruptcies, and Pensions   358
6.24   Exxon and Alaska   405
6.25   BP: Pipeline, Refinery, and Offshore-Drilling Safety   411
7.1   Joe Camel: The Cartoon Character Who Sold Cigarettes and Nearly Felled an Industry   425
7.2   Spring Break, Beer, and Alcohol on Campus   430
7.6   Kraft, Barney Rubble, and *Shrek*   438
7.7   Craigslist and Ad Screening   439
7.21   The Mommy Doll   487
7.22   Stem-Cell Research   487
7.23   Toro and Its Product Liability Program   489
7.24   Fast Food Liability   490
8.10   Copyright, Songs, and Charities   518
9.6   "I Was Just Following Orders": The CIA, Interrogations, and the Role of Legal Opinions in the
       Conduct of Organizations   536

Strategy

2.5	Moral Relativism and the Either/or Conundrum	61
2.15	The Rigged Election	86
3.12	Ice-T, the *Body Count* Album, and Shareholder Uprisings	133
3.15	Dayton-Hudson's Contributions to Planned Parenthood, and Target and the Bell-Ringers	146
3.17	Herman Miller and Its Rain Forest Chairs	151
3.18	The Death of the Great Disposable Diaper Debate	153
4.3	Why Corporations Can't Control Chicanery	164
6.24	Exxon and Alaska	405
7.1	Joe Camel: The Cartoon Character Who Sold Cigarettes and Nearly Felled an Industry	425
7.2	Spring Break, Beer, and Alcohol on Campus	430
7.9	Tylenol: Decades of Dilemmas	444
7.10	Merck and Vioxx	444
7.11	Ford and Its Pinto and GM and Its Malibu: The Repeating Exploding Gas Tank Problem	452
7.12	Toyota: Sudden Acceleration or Bad Drivers or Pesky Floor Mats?	458
7.17	Frozen Coke and Burger King and the Richmond Rigging	468
7.18	Slotting: Facilitation, Costs, or Bribery?	472
7.19	Intel and the Chips: When You Have Made a Mistake	478
8.3	Starwood, Hilton, and the Suspiciously Similar New Hotel Designs	501
8.5	The Coke Employee Who Offered Inside Information to Pepsi	506
8.12	The Little Intermittent Windshield Wiper and Its Little Inventor	520

Supply Chain Management

4.23	Beech-Nut and the No-Apple-Juice Apple Juice	280
5.5	Product Dumping	325
5.6	On Sweatshops, Nike, and Kathie Lee	326
6.6	JCPenney and Its Wealthy Buyer	361
7.13	E. coli, Jack-in-the-Box, and Cooking Temperatures	461
7.17	Frozen Coke and Burger King and the Richmond Rigging	468

Whistle-Blowing

4.22	The Options for Whistle-Blowers	279
4.23	Beech-Nut and the No-Apple-Juice Apple Juice	280
4.24	NASA and the Space Shuttle Booster Rockets	285
4.25	Westland/Hallmark Meat Packing Company and the Cattle Standers	288
4.26	Getting Information from Employees Who Know to Those Who Can and Will Respond	289
4.28	Bernie Madoff: Just Stay Away from the 17th Floor	311
6.15	Toyota, the CEO, the Assistant, and Inaction	381
6.19	Jack Welch and the Harvard Interview	387
7.15	Pfizer and the $2.3 Billion Fine for Sales Tactics	464
7.17	Frozen Coke and Burger King and the Richmond Rigging	468
9.2	The Minerals Management Service: The Arms-Length Affairs with Oil Executives	527
9.14	Government Pricing and Finding a Way Around It	546
10.1	New Era: If It Sounds Too Good to Be True, It Is Too Good to Be True	559

Product/Company/Individuals/ Subject Index

AAP (American Academy of Pediatrics)
5.8   Nestlé: When Products Translate Differently   336

ABA (American Bar Association)
9.6   "I Was Just Following Orders": The CIA, Interrogations, and the Role of Legal
          Opinions in the Conduct of Organizations   537

ACORN (Association of Community Organizations for Reform Now)
10.3   ACORN: Community Organizers, Undercover Videos, and Advice   565

Adelphia
3.8   Adelphia: Good Works via a Hand in the Till   113

AES Company
5.4   The Former Soviet Union: A Study of Three Companies: PwC, Ikea, and AES   324

Aguirre, Fernando
5.2   Chiquita Banana and Mercenary Protection   321

AICPA (American Institute of Certified Public Accountants)
4.19   A Primer on Accounting Issues and Ethics and Earnings Management   267

AIG (American International Group)
1.7   Hank Greenberg and AIG   27
4.4   The Effects of Compensation Systems: Incentives, Bonuses, Pay, and Ethics   172

Alderson, Sandy
3.13   Baseball and Steroids   138

AMA (American Medical Association)
6.8   Docs, Pharmas, Medical Journals, Funded Research, and Pizza   364
7.1   Joe Camel: The Cartoon Character Who Sold Cigarettes and Nearly Felled an Industry   426

American Academy of Pediatrics (AAP)
5.8   Nestlé: When Products Translate Differently   336

American Bar Association (ABA)
9.6   "I Was Just Following Orders": The CIA, Interrogations, and the Role of Legal Opinions
          in the Conduct of Organizations   537

American Institute of Certified Public Accountants (AICPA)
4.19   A Primer on Accounting Issues and Ethics and Earnings Management   267

American International Group (AIG)
1.7   Hank Greenberg and AIG   27
4.4   The Effects of Compensation Systems: Incentives, Bonuses, Pay, and Ethics   172

American Medical Association (AMA)
6.8   Docs, Pharmas, Medical Journals, Funded Research, and Pizza   364
7.1   Joe Camel: The Cartoon Character Who Sold Cigarettes and Nearly Felled an Industry   426

American Medical Students Association (AMSA)
6.8   Docs, Pharmas, Medical Journals, Funded Research, and Pizza   365

American Society of Composers, Authors & Publishers (ASCAP)
8.10   Copyright, Songs, and Charities   518

American Union Carbide Corporation
5.7   Bhopal: When Safety Standards Differ   333

AMSA (American Medical Students Association)
6.8   Docs, Pharmas, Medical Journals, Funded Research, and Pizza   365

Anheuser-Busch
7.2   Spring Break, Beer, and Alcohol on Campus   431

Aristotle
1.3   What Are Ethics?   15

Arthur Andersen
2.4   How Leaders Lose Their Way: What Price Hubris?   59
4.3   Why Corporations Can't Control Chicanery   165
4.16 Arthur Andersen: A Fallen Giant   246

ASCAP (American Society of Composers, Authors & Publishers)
8.10 Copyright, Songs, and Charities   518

Association of Community Organizations for Reform Now (ACORN)
10.3 ACORN: Community Organizers, Undercover Videos, and Advice   565

AT&T
6.9   The Analyst Who Needed a Preschool   367

Atkins Diet
4.14 Bausch & Lomb and Krispy Kreme: Channel Stuffing and Cannibalism   231

Bacanovic, Peter
2.7   Martha Stewart: Not Such a Good Thing   63

Bank of America
4.12 Bank of America: The Merrill Takeover, the Disclosures, and the Board   216
4.19 A Primer on Accounting Issues and Ethics and Earnings Management   263

Baptist Foundation of Arizona (BFA)
10.2 The Baptist Foundation: Funds of the Faithful   562

Baridis, Marisa
8.6   The Compliance Officer Who Strayed   508

Barings Bank
4.7   Jett and Kidder, Leeson and Barings, Kerviel and Société Générale: Compensation-Fueled Dishonesty   192

Barnes, Brenda C.
2.8   On Leaving to Spend More Time with Family   69

Barnes, Roger
3.10 Fannie, Freddie, Wall Street, Main Street, and the Subprime Mortgage Market: Of Moral Hazards   126

Bausch & Lomb
4.14 Bausch & Lomb and Krispy Kreme: Channel Stuffing and Cannibalism   228

Baxter, J. Clifford
4.15 Enron: The CFO, Conflicts, and Cooking the Books with Natural Gas and Electricity   241

Bayer
9.14 Government Pricing and Finding a Way Around It   546

Bear Stearns
4.18 If It's Legal, It's Ethical; and Besides, Everyone Does It   259
4.5   The Subprime Saga: Bear Stearns, Lehman, Merrill, and CDOs   176

Beech-Nut
4.23 Beech-Nut and the No-Apple-Juice Apple Juice   280

Ben & Jerry's
3.3   Business with a Soul: A Reexamination of What Counts in Business Ethics   103

Bennett, John G. Jr.
10.1   New Era: If It Sounds Too Good to Be True, It Is Too Good to Be True   559

Bentham, Jeremy
1.3   What Are Ethics?   13

Berkshire Hathaway Company
4.10   FINOVA and the Loan Write-Off   210

BFA (Baptist Foundation of Arizona)
10.2   The Baptist Foundation: Funds of the Faithful   562

Bilzerian, Paul A.
4.20   The Ethics of Bankruptcy   273

Blackstone Group
8.3   Starwood, Hilton, and the Suspiciously Similar New Hotel Designs   501

Blagojevich, Rod
9.4   The Governor and a Senate Seat Vacated by a President   532

Blanchard, Kenneth
1.8   Some Simple Tests for Resolving Ethical Dilemmas   31

Blankfein, Lloyd
2.11   What Was Up with Wall Street? The Goldman Standard and Shades of Gray   77

Blumenthal, Richard
1.5   On Rationalizing and Labeling   22

Body Shop International ("BSI")
3.3   Business with a Soul: A Reexamination of What Counts in Business Ethics   103

Boeing
6.5   Plant Closings, Downsizings, Company Closings, Government Takeovers, Bankruptcies, and Pensions   359
6.20   Is It None of Our Business?   390
8.2   Boeing, Lockheed, and the Documents   496
9.16   Boeing and the Recruiting of the Government Purchasing Agent   548

Boisjoly, Roger
4.24   NASA and the Space Shuttle Booster Rockets   286

Borden
7.18   Slotting: Facilitation, Costs, or Bribery?   475

BP
6.25   BP: Pipeline, Refinery, and Offshore-Drilling Safety   411
9.2   The Minerals Management Service: The Arms-Length Affairs with Oil Executives   529

Brabbs, Steven
4.27   WorldCom: The Little Company That Couldn't after All   300

Brennan, Edward A.
7.20   Sears and High-Cost Auto Repairs   482

Bresch, Heather
2.16   West Virginia University and the Governor's Daughter   86

Brewer, Jan
6.16   Arizona Senate Bill 1070: Immigration Laws, Employers, Enforcement, and Emotion   382

Brown, Michael
9.19   FEMA, Hurricane Katrina, and the Dilemmas of Regulation versus Human Life   554

Browne, John
6.25   BP: Pipeline, Refinery, and Offshore-Drilling Safety   412

"BSI" (Body Shop International)
3.3   Business with a Soul: A Reexamination of What Counts in Business Ethics   103

Bud Light
7.2   Spring Break, Beer, and Alcohol on Campus   431

Buffett, Warren
1.8   Some Simple Tests for Resolving Ethical Dilemmas   32

Bullock, Ken
5.12   Salt Lake City, the Olympics, and Bribery   346

Burberry
8.9   Tiffany, Louis Vuitton, eBay, Landlords, and Knock-Offs   517

Burger King
7.17   Frozen Coke and Burger King and the Richmond Rigging   468

Burke, Edmund
6.22   The Ethics of Confrontation   398

Burnham, Daniel P.
2.8   On Leaving to Spend More Time with Family   69

Canseco, Jose
3.13   Baseball and Steroids   138

Capellas, Michael D.
4.27   WorldCom: The Little Company That Couldn't after All   307

Carlin, Wayne
3.8   Adelphia: Good Works via a Hand in the Till   115

Carnation
5.8   Nestlé: When Products Translate Differently   336

Carr, Albert Z.
2.3   Is Business Bluffing Ethical?   49

Cartier
8.9   Tiffany, Louis Vuitton, eBay, Landlords, and Knock-Offs   514

Caterpillar
6.5   Plant Closings, Downsizings, Company Closings, Government Takeovers, Bankruptcies, and Pensions   359

Causey, Richard
4.15   Enron: The CFO, Conflicts, and Cooking the Books with Natural Gas and Electricity   243
4.16   Arthur Andersen: A Fallen Giant   247

CDOS (Collateralized Debt Obligations)
4.5   The Subprime Saga: Bear Stearns, Lehman, Merrill, and CDOs   176

Ceconi, Margaret
4.15   Enron: The CFO, Conflicts, and Cooking the Books with Natural Gas and Electricity   239

Cell Phones
2.12   What Happens in Boulder Stays in Boulder: Cell Phone Alibis   84

Chevrolet Malibu
7.11   Ford and Its Pinto and GM and Its Malibu: The Repeating Exploding Gas Tank Problem   457

China
5.9   Google, Yahoo, and Human Rights in China   337

Chiquita Banana
5.2   Chiquita Banana and Mercenary Protection   319

Chrysler
8.12   The Little Intermittent Windshield Wiper and Its Little Inventor   520

CIA
9.6   "I Was Just Following Orders": The CIA, Interrogations, and the Role of Legal Opinions
       in the Conduct of Organizations   536

Cintas
6.3   Cintas and OSHA   354

Cioffi, Ralph R.
4.18   If It's Legal, It's Ethical; and Besides, Everyone Does It   259

Cisco
6.18   Bloggers, Chat Rooms, and E-Mail: Your Employer Is Watching   386

Citigroup
4.5   The Subprime Saga: Bear Stearns, Lehman, Merrill, and CDOs   176
6.9   The Analyst Who Needed a Preschool   367

Clemens, Roger
1.5   On Rationalizing and Labeling   22

Coca-Cola, Inc.
6.13   The Benefits of Diversity: Remarks of Doug Daft, Former CEO of Coca-Cola   376
7.17   Frozen Coke and Burger King and the Richmond Rigging   468
8.5   The Coke Employee Who Offered Inside Information to Pepsi   506

Collateralized Debt Obligations (CDOs)
4.5   The Subprime Saga: Bear Stearns, Lehman, Merrill, and CDOs   176

Collins, Stephen
2.8   On Leaving to Spend More Time with Family   70

Conference Board
2.9   The Areas of Ethical Challenges in Business   71

Conran, Jim
7.20   Sears and High-Cost Auto Repairs   482

Consumer Product Safety Commission
5.5   Product Dumping   325

Coors Light
7.2   Spring Break, Beer, and Alcohol on Campus   431

Copyright
8.10   Copyright, Songs, and Charities   518

Cornell University
10.6   The Cornell Researchers Funded by the Foundation   569

Corporate and Criminal Fraud Accountability Act of 2002
4.11   A Primer on Sarbanes–Oxley   215

Corzine, Jon
2.11   What Was Up with Wall Street? The Goldman Standard and Shades of Gray   77

Countrywide
2.4   How Leaders Lose Their Way: What Price Hubris?   59
3.10   Fannie, Freddie, Wall Street, Main Street, and the Subprime Mortgage Market: Of Moral Hazards   129

COX-2 Inhibitors
7.10   Merck and Vioxx   448

Craigslist
7.7   Craigslist and Ad Screening   439

Cramer, Jim
2.11   What Was Up with Wall Street? The Goldman Standard and Shades of Gray   77

Cuneo, Dennis
6.15   Toyota, the CEO, the Assistant, and Inaction   381

Daft, Doug
6.13   The Benefits of Diversity: Remarks of Doug Daft, Former CEO of Coca-Cola   376

Dayton-Hudson Corporation
3.15   Dayton-Hudson's Contributions to Planned Parenthood, and Target and the Bell Ringers   146

de Tocqueville, Alexis
3.5   Michael Novak on Capitalism and the Corporation   108

Delainey, David
4.15   Enron: The CFO, Conflicts, and Cooking the Books with Natural Gas and Electricity   242

Delta
6.5   Plant Closings, Downsizings, Company Closings, Government Takeovers, Bankruptcies, and Pensions   359

Divine Command Theory
1.3   What Are Ethics?   12

Drexel Burnham
4.3   Why Corporations Can't Control Chicanery   165

Drucker, Peter
1.8   Some Simple Tests for Resolving Ethical Dilemmas   29
2.2   The Ethics of Responsibility   48

Duke Lacrosse Team
9.18   The Duke Lacrosse Team and the Prosecutor   551

Duncan, David
4.16   Arthur Andersen: A Fallen Giant   247

Ebay
8.9   Tiffany, Louis Vuitton, eBay, Landlords, and Knock-Offs   514

Ebbers, Bernard J.
4.27   WorldCom: The Little Company That Couldn't after All   293

EBIT (Earnings Before Interest and Taxes)
4.19   A Primer on Accounting Issues and Ethics and Earnings Management   267

EBITDA (Earnings before Interest Taxes, Depreciation, and Amortization)
4.19   A Primer on Accounting Issues and Ethics and Earnings Management   267

E. F. Hutton
4.3   Why Corporations Can't Control Chicanery   165

Employee Retirement Income Security Act (ERISA)
6.5   Plant Closings, Downsizings, Company Closings, Government Takeovers, Bankruptcies, and Pensions   358

Enron
4.9   Stock Options, Backdating, and Disclosure Options: What Happened Here?   201
4.15   Enron: The CFO, Conflicts, and Cooking the Books with Natural Gas and Electricity   233
6.20   Is It None of Our Business?   391

Entine, Jon
3.3   Business with a Soul: A Reexamination of What Counts in Business Ethics   101

Entitlement Theory (Rights Theory)
1.3   What Are Ethics?   14

Erisa (Employee Retirement Income Security Act)
6.5   Plant Closings, Downsizings, Company Closings, Government Takeovers, Bankruptcies, and Pensions   358

Esrey, William T.
4.27   WorldCom: The Little Company That Couldn't after All   295

Ethical Egoism Theory
1.3   What Are Ethics?   12

Exxon
3.16   The New Environmentalism   151
6.24   Exxon and Alaska   405

Fair Isaac Co. (FICO)
7.4   Subprime Loans—The Under-the-Radar Loans That Felled a Market   434

Faneuil, Douglas
2.7   Martha Stewart: Not Such a Good Thing   63

Fannie Mae
3.10   Fannie, Freddie, Wall Street, Main Street, and the Subprime Mortgage Market: Of Moral Hazards   121

FASB (Financial Accounting Standards Board)
4.15   Enron: The CFO, Conflicts, and Cooking the Books with Natural Gas and Electricity   234

Fastow, Andrew
1.3   What Are Ethics?   15
4.15   Enron: The CFO, Conflicts, and Cooking the Books with Natural Gas and Electricity   242

Fastow, Lea
4.15   Enron: The CFO, Conflicts, and Cooking the Books with Natural Gas and Electricity   242

FCPA (Foreign Corrupt Practices ACT)
5.10   A Primer on the FCPA   340

Fehr, Don
3.13   Baseball and Steroids   138

FEMA (Federal Emergency Management Agency)
9.19   FEMA, Hurricane Katrina, and the Dilemmas of Regulation versus Human Life   554

Feuerstein, Aaron
6.4   Aaron Feuerstein and Malden Mills   356

FICO (Fair Isaac Co.)
7.4   Subprime Loans—The Under-the-Radar Loans That Felled a Market   434

Fidelity Investments
6.7   The Trading Desk, Perks, and "Dwarf Tossing"   362

Financial Accounting Standards Board (FASB)
4.15   Enron: The CFO, Conflicts, and Cooking the Books with Natural Gas and Electricity   234

Finova Group, Inc.
4.10   FINOVA and the Loan Write-Off   206

Fiorina, Carly
2.8   On Leaving to Spend More Time with Family   70

Firestone
6.22   The Ethics of Confrontation   397

Fisher, George
3.9   The Regulatory Cycle, Social Responsibility, Business Strategy, and Equilibrium   117

Foley, Bill
3.17 Herman Miller and Its Rain Forest Chairs   151

Ford
6.22 The Ethics of Confrontation   397
7.11 Ford and Its Pinto and GM and Its Malibu: The Repeating Exploding Gas Tank Problem   452
8.12 The Little Intermittent Windshield Wiper and Its Little Inventor   520

Ford, John N.
2.8   On Leaving to Spend More Time with Family   69

Foreign Corrupt Practices Act (FCPA)
5.10 A Primer on the FCPA   340

Fox, Neal
3.12 Ice-T, the *Body Count* Album, and Shareholder Uprisings   134

Freeman, R. Edward
3.2   A Stakeholder Theory of the Modern Corporation   96

Friedman, Milton
3.1   The Social Responsibility of Business Is to Increase Its Profits   91

Frierson, James
3.9   The Regulatory Cycle, Social Responsibility, Business Strategy, and Equilibrium   117

Frito-Lay
7.18 Slotting: Facilitation, Costs, or Bribery?   472

GAAP (Generally Accepted Accounting Principles)
3.10 Fannie, Freddie, Wall Street, Main Street, and the Subprime Mortgage Market: Of Moral Hazards   125
4.19 A Primer on Accounting Issues and Ethics and Earnings Management   267

Galesi, Francesco
4.27 WorldCom: The Little Company That Couldn't after All   302

Galleon Group Hedge Fund
4.18 If It's Legal, It's Ethical; and Besides, Everyone Does It   260

Gandhi, Mahatma
1.8   Some Simple Tests for Resolving Ethical Dilemmas   32

Geffen, David
3.12 Ice-T, the *Body Count* Album, and Shareholder Uprisings   134

Gellerman, Saul
4.3   Why Corporations Can't Control Chicanery   164

General Mills
7.3   Cheerios and Cholesterol and Rice Krispies and Immunity   432

Generally Accepted Accounting Principles (GAAP)
3.10 Fannie, Freddie, Wall Street, Main Street, and the Subprime Mortgage Market: Of Moral Hazards   125
4.19 A Primer on Accounting Issues and Ethics and Earnings Management   267

GFC (Greyhound Financial Corporation)
4.10 FINOVA and the Loan Write-Off   206

Giambi, Jason
3.13 Baseball and Steroids   138

Glisan, Ben
4.15 Enron: The CFO, Conflicts, and Cooking the Books with Natural Gas and Electricity   243

GM (General Motors)
6.5   Plant Closings, Downsizings, Company Closings, Government Takeovers, Bankruptcies, and Pensions   358
7.11   Ford and Its Pinto and GM and Its Malibu: The Repeating Exploding Gas Tank Problem   452

Goldman Sachs
2.11   What Was Up with Wall Street? The Goldman Standard and Shades of Gray   73

Google
1.4   The Types of Ethical Dilemmas: From Truth to Honesty to Conflicts   21
5.9   Google, Yahoo, and Human Rights in China   337
8.11   Microsoft vs. Google and "Snippets" of Books   519

Gorelick, Jamie
3.10   Fannie, Freddie, Wall Street, Main Street, and the Subprime Mortgage Market: Of Moral Hazards   124

Green, Dianna
1.12   Puffing Your Résumé   38

Greenberg, Hank
1.7   Hank Greenberg and AIG   27

Greenfield, Jerry
3.12   Ice-T, the *Body Count* Album, and Shareholder Uprisings   134

Greenpeace
3.16   The New Environmentalism   149

Greyhound Financial Corporation (GFC)
4.10   FINOVA and the Loan Write-Off   206

Grubman, Jack
4.5   The Subprime Saga: Bear Stearns, Lehman, Merrill, and CDOs   179
6.9   The Analyst Who Needed a Preschool   367

Guardiola, Jose
5.6   On Sweatshops, Nike, and Kathie Lee   332

Gucci
8.9   Tiffany, Louis Vuitton, eBay, Landlords, and Knock-Offs   517

Gunty, Murry
2.15   The Rigged Election   86

Halfon, Robert
3.4   Appeasing Stakeholders with Public Relations   104

Hatsopoulos, John W.
3.12   Ice-T, the *Body Count* Album, and Shareholder Uprisings   134

Healthsouth
4.6   HealthSouth: The Scrushy Way   183
6.20   Is It None of Our Business?   391

Henze, Diana
4.6   HealthSouth: The Scrushy Way   185

Herman Miller, Inc.
3.17   Herman Miller and Its Rain Forest Chairs   151

Heston, Charlton
3.12   Ice-T, the *Body Count* Album, and Shareholder Uprisings   133

Hilton
8.3   Starwood, Hilton, and the Suspiciously Similar New Hotel Designs   501

Hopkins, Ann
6.23   Ann Hopkins and Price Waterhouse   399

Howard, J. Timothy
3.10   Fannie, Freddie, Wall Street, Main Street, and the Subprime Mortgage Market: Of Moral Hazards   124, 126

Hoyvald, Nils
4.23   Beech-Nut and the No-Apple-Juice Apple Juice   281

Hurricane Katrina
9.19   FEMA, Hurricane Katrina, and the Dilemmas of Regulation versus Human Life   554

IBM
7.19   Intel and the Chips: When You Have Made a Mistake   478

ICE-T
3.12   Ice-T, the *Body Count* Album, and Shareholder Uprisings   133

Ikea
5.4   The Former Soviet Union: A Study of Three Companies: PwC, Ikea, and AES   323

Intel
7.19   Intel and the Chips: When You Have Made a Mistake   478

Iroquois Brands, Ltd.
4.17   The New Shareholder: Taking Over to Change the Culture   253

IRS
2.13   Travel Expenses: A Chance for Extra Income   84

Jack-in-the-Box
7.13   E. coli, Jack-in-the-Box, and Cooking Temperatures   461

JCPenney
6.6   JCPenney and Its Wealthy Buyer   361

Jeffries & Co.
6.7   The Trading Desk, Perks, and "Dwarf Tossing"   362

Jennings, Marianne M.
3.16   The New Environmentalism   149
3.3   Business with a Soul: A Reexamination of What Counts in Business Ethics   101

Jett, Joseph
4.7   Jett and Kidder, Leeson and Barings, Kerviel and Société Générale: Compensation-Fueled Dishonesty   192

Johnson, David R.
5.12   Salt Lake City, the Olympics, and Bribery   345

Johnson, James A.
3.10   Fannie, Freddie, Wall Street, Main Street, and the Subprime Mortgage Market: Of Moral Hazards   124

Johnson & Johnson
7.9   Tylenol: Decades of Dilemmas   444

Johnson Controls, Inc.
6.12   On-the-Job Fetal Injuries   374

Jones, Charles
4.23   Beech-Nut and the No-Apple-Juice Apple Juice   281

Kant, Immanuel
1.3   What Are Ethics?   13

Kearns, Robert W.
8.12   The Little Intermittent Windshield Wiper and Its Little Inventor   520

Kellett, Stiles A. Jr.
4.27   WorldCom: The Little Company That Couldn't after All   302

Kellogg
7.3   Cheerios and Cholesterol and Rice Krispies and Immunity   433

Kelly, Marjorie
3.6   Marjorie Kelly and the Divine Right of Capital   108

KELP (Key Employee Corporate Loan Program), TYCO
4.13   Dennis Kozlowski: Tyco and the $6,000 Shower Curtain   222

Kerviel, Jérôme
4.7   Jett and Kidder, Leeson and Barings, Kerviel and Société Générale: Compensation-Fueled Dishonesty   192

Kessel, Richard
7.20   Sears and High-Cost Auto Repairs   482

Key Employee Corporate Loan Program (KELP), TYCO
4.13   Dennis Kozlowski: Tyco and the $6,000 Shower Curtain   222

Khan, Roomy
4.2   Not All Employees Are Equal When It Comes to Moral Development   160

Kidder Peabody
4.7   Jett and Kidder, Leeson and Barings, Kerviel and Société Générale: Compensation-Fueled Dishonesty   192

King, Martin Luther, Jr.
1.8   Some Simple Tests for Resolving Ethical Dilemmas   32

Kmart
7.18   Slotting: Facilitation, Costs, or Bribery?   477

Kobayashi, Sayaka
6.15   Toyota, the CEO, the Assistant, and Inaction   381

Kodak
9.3   Kodak, the Appraiser, and the Assessor: Lots of Back Scratching on Valuation   531

Koenig, Mark
4.15   Enron: The CFO, Conflicts, and Cooking the Books with Natural Gas and Electricity   243

Konheim, Bud
3.12   Ice-T, the *Body Count* Album, and Shareholder Uprisings   134

Kopchinski, John
7.15   Pfizer and the $2.3 Billion Fine for Sales Tactics   464

Kopper, Michael J.
4.15   Enron: The CFO, Conflicts, and Cooking the Books with Natural Gas and Electricity   243

Kozlowski, Dennis
4.13   Dennis Kozlowski: Tyco and the $6,000 Shower Curtain   218

Kraft
7.6   Kraft, Barney Rubble, and Shrek   438

Krispy Kreme
4.14   Bausch & Lomb and Krispy Kreme: Channel Stuffing and Cannibalism   228

Lavery, John
4.23   Beech-Nut and the No-Apple-Juice Apple Juice   280

Lay, Kenneth
4.15   Enron: The CFO, Conflicts, and Cooking the Books with Natural Gas and Electricity   234

LDDS (Long Distance Discount Service)
4.27   WorldCom: The Little Company That Couldn't after All   293

Lebed, Jonathan
8.7   Jonathan Lebed: The Middle School Tycoon   510

Lee, Kathie
5.6   On Sweatshops, Nike, and Kathie Lee   326

Lee, Matthew
4.26   Getting Information from Employees Who Know to Those Who Can and Will Respond   289

Leeson, Nick
4.7   Jett and Kidder, Leeson and Barings, Kerviel and Société Générale: Compensation-Fueled Dishonesty 192

Lefcoe, George
4.1   The Moving Line   159

Lehman Bros
4.5   The Subprime Saga: Bear Stearns, Lehman, Merrill, and CDOs   176

Lehman Brothers
4.26   Getting Information from Employees Who Know to Those Who Can and Will Respond   289

Leucadia National Corporation
4.10   FINOVA and the Loan Write-Off   210

Levin, Robert J.
3.10   Fannie, Freddie, Wall Street, Main Street, and the Subprime Mortgage Market: Of Moral Hazards   124

Levitt, Arthur
4.19   A Primer on Accounting Issues and Ethics and Earnings Management   262

Lewis, Kenneth D.
4.12   Bank of America: The Merrill Takeover, the Disclosures, and the Board   217

Licari, Jerome J.
4.23   Beech-Nut and the No-Apple-Juice Apple Juice   280

Lie, Erik
4.9   Stock Options, Backdating, and Disclosure Options: What Happened Here?   204

Locke, Charles S.
4.24   NASA and the Space Shuttle Booster Rockets   287

Locke, John
1.3   What Are Ethics?   14

Lockheed
8.2   Boeing, Lockheed, and the Documents   496

Locklear, Jim G.
6.6   JCPenney and Its Wealthy Buyer   361

Long Distance Discount Service (LDDS)
4.27   WorldCom: The Little Company That Couldn't after All   293

Louis Vuitton
8.9   Tiffany, Louis Vuitton, eBay, Landlords, and Knock-Offs   514

Lucent Technologies
6.5   Plant Closings, Downsizings, Company Closings, Government Takeovers, Bankruptcies, and Pensions   359

Mackey, John
3.11   Whole Foods, John Mackey, and Health Care Debates   132

Maclean, Richard
3.16   The New Environmentalism   149

Madoff, Bernie
4.28   Bernie Madoff: Just Stay Away from the 17th Floor   311

Malden Mills
6.4   Aaron Feuerstein and Malden Mills   356

Malibu
7.11   Ford and Its Pinto and GM and Its Malibu: The Repeating Exploding Gas Tank Problem   457

Managerial Capitalism
3.2   A Stakeholder Theory of the Modern Corporation   97

Manfred, Robert
3.13   Baseball and Steroids   138

Markoff, Philip H.
7.7   Craigslist and Ad Screening   440

Marks, Bruce
3.10   Fannie, Freddie, Wall Street, Main Street, and the Subprime Mortgage Market: Of Moral Hazards   129

Mark-to-Market Accounting
4.15   Enron: The CFO, Conflicts, and Cooking the Books with Natural Gas and Electricity   234

Marsh McLennan (MMC)
7.16   The Mess at Marsh McLennan   465

Mayopoulos, Timothy J.
4.12   Bank of America: The Merrill Takeover, the Disclosures, and the Board   216

McCoy, Bowen H. (BUZZ)
1.2   The Parable of the Sadhu   4
2.5   Moral Relativism and the Either/or Conundrum   61

McDonald, Allan
4.24   NASA and the Space Shuttle Booster Rockets   286

McDonald's
6.2   Sleeping on the Job and on the Way Home   353
7.24   Fast Food Liability   490

McGuire, William W.
4.9   Stock Options, Backdating, and Disclosure Options: What Happened Here?   202

McGwire, Mark
3.13   Baseball and Steroids   138

MCI
4.27   WorldCom: The Little Company That Couldn't after All   294

McNeil Consumer Products, Inc.
7.9   Tylenol: Decades of Dilemmas   444

Merck
7.10   Merck and Vioxx   447

Merrill Lynch
4.3   Why Corporations Can't Control Chicanery   170
4.5   The Subprime Saga: Bear Stearns, Lehman, Merrill, and CDOs   176
4.12   Bank of America: The Merrill Takeover, the Disclosures, and the Board   216
4.15   Enron: The CFO, Conflicts, and Cooking the Books with Natural Gas and Electricity   236
6.5   Plant Closings, Downsizings, Company Closings, Government Takeovers, Bankruptcies, and Pensions   359

Mervyn's
8.8   Simmons, Mervyn's, and the Private Equity Firms That Bankrupt Them   511

Microsoft
8.11   Microsoft vs. Google and "Snippets" of Books   519

Mill, John Stuart
1.3   What Are Ethics?   13

Miller Brewing Company
6.14   *Seinfeld* in the Workplace   380

Miller Lite
7.2   Spring Break, Beer, and Alcohol on Campus   431

Minerals Management Service (MMS)
9.2   The Minerals Management Service: The Arms-Length Affairs with Oil Executives   527

MMC (Marsh McLennan)
7.16   The Mess at Marsh McLennan   465

MMS (Minerals Management Service)
9.2   The Minerals Management Service: The Arms-Length Affairs with Oil Executives   527

Mohebbi, Afshin
2.8   On Leaving to Spend More Time with Family   69

Moore, Demi
7.5   Hollywood Ads   438

Morgan Stanley
4.5   The Subprime Saga: Bear Stearns, Lehman, Merrill, and CDOs   176
8.6   The Compliance Officer Who Strayed   508

Moynihan, Daniel Patrick
2.3   Is Business Bluffing Ethical?   53

Mozilo, Angelo
3.10   Fannie, Freddie, Wall Street, Main Street, and the Subprime Mortgage Market: Of Moral Hazards   129

Mudd, Daniel H.
3.10   Fannie, Freddie, Wall Street, Main Street, and the Subprime Mortgage Market: Of Moral Hazards   126

Myers, David
4.27   WorldCom: The Little Company That Couldn't after All   300

MySpace
6.17   Facebook, MySpace, and YouTube Screening of Employees   385

Nader, Ralph
7.8   A Primer on Product Liability   442

NADS (National Association of Diaper Services)
3.18   The Death of the Great Disposable Diaper Debate   154

NASA (National Aeronautics and Space Administration)
4.24   NASA and the Space Shuttle Booster Rockets   285

Nash, Laura
1.8   Some Simple Tests for Resolving Ethical Dilemmas   29

Nathanson, Marc B.
3.12   Ice-T, the *Body Count* Album, and Shareholder Uprisings   135

Neighborhood Assistance Corporation
3.10   Fannie, Freddie, Wall Street, Main Street, and the Subprime Mortgage Market: Of Moral Hazards   129

Nestlé
5.8   Nestlé: When Products Translate Differently   335

New Era Philanthropy
10.1   New Era: If It Sounds Too Good to Be True, It Is Too Good to Be True   559

NFL
3.14   Michael Vick, Dogs, Rush Limbaugh, and the NFL   145

Nifong, Michael B.
9.18   The Duke Lacrosse Team and the Prosecutor   552

Nike
5.6   On Sweatshops, Nike, and Kathie Lee   326

Non-GAAP Measures
4.19   A Primer on Accounting Issues and Ethics and Earnings Management   267

Novak, Michael
3.3   Business with a Soul: A Reexamination of What Counts in Business Ethics   103
3.5   Michael Novak on Capitalism and the Corporation   104

Nozick, Robert
1.3   What Are Ethics?   14

Oliver, Michael
1.12   Puffing Your Résumé   38

Olson, John
4.15   Enron: The CFO, Conflicts, and Cooking the Books with Natural Gas and Electricity   236

O'Neal, Stan
4.5   The Subprime Saga: Bear Stearns, Lehman, Merrill, and CDOs   179

OSHA
6.3   Cintas and OSHA   354

Otaka, Hideaki
6.15   Toyota, the CEO, the Assistant, and Inaction   381

Palm, Gregory K.
2.11   What Was Up with Wall Street? The Goldman Standard and Shades of Gray   82

Palmeiro, Rafael
3.13   Baseball and Steroids   138

Partow, Kourosh
7.4   Subprime Loans—The Under-the-Radar Loans That Felled a Market   434

Paulson, Henry
2.11   What Was Up with Wall Street? The Goldman Standard and Shades of Gray   77

PCAOB (Public Company Accounting Oversight Board)
4.11   A Primer on Sarbanes–Oxley   212

Peale, Norman Vincent
1.8   Some Simple Tests for Resolving Ethical Dilemmas   31

Peanut Corporation of America
7.14   Peanut Corporation of America and Salmonella   462

Pelton, Christine
1.10   The Little Teacher Who Could: Piper, Kansas, and Term Papers   34

Pepsi
8.5   The Coke Employee Who Offered Inside Information to Pepsi   506

Pfizer
7.15   Pfizer and the $2.3 Billion Fine for Sales Tactics ... 464

Philip Morris
7.1   Joe Camel: The Cartoon Character Who Sold Cigarettes and Nearly Felled an Industry ... 427

Pinto
7.11   Ford and Its Pinto and GM and Its Malibu: The Repeating Exploding Gas Tank Problem ... 452

Pirates
5.3   Transnational Shipping and the Pirates ... 322

PIW (Public Interest Watch)
3.16   The New Environmentalism ... 151

Planned Parenthood
3.15   Dayton-Hudson's Contributions to Planned Parenthood, and Target and the Bell Ringers ... 146

Plato
1.3   What Are Ethics? ... 15

Ponzi Scheme
4.28   Bernie Madoff: Just Stay Away from the 17th Floor ... 311

Poseley, Tara
2.8   On Leaving to Spend More Time with Family ... 69

Prada
8.9   Tiffany, Louis Vuitton, eBay, Landlords, and Knock-Offs ... 517

Price Waterhouse
6.23   Ann Hopkins and Price Waterhouse ... 399

PriceWaterhouseCoopers (PWC)
5.4   The Former Soviet Union: A Study of Three Companies: PwC, Ikea, and AES ... 323

Prince, Chuck
4.5   The Subprime Saga: Bear Stearns, Lehman, Merrill, and CDOs ... 179

Procter & Gamble
3.18   The Death of the Great Disposable Diaper Debate ... 153

Public Company Accounting Oversight Board (PCAOB)
4.11   A Primer on Sarbanes–Oxley ... 212

Public Interest Watch (PIW)
3.16   The New Environmentalism ... 151

Putnam Investments
7.16   The Mess at Marsh McLennan ... 466

PWC (PriceWaterhouseCoopers)
5.4   The Former Soviet Union: A Study of Three Companies: PwC, Ikea, and AES ... 323

Quattrone, Frank
4.18   If It's Legal, It's Ethical; and Besides, Everyone Does It ... 258

Raff, Beryl B.
2.8   On Leaving to Spend More Time with Family ... 69

Raines, Franklin D.
3.10   Fannie, Freddie, Wall Street, Main Street, and the Subprime Mortgage Market: Of Moral Hazards ... 124

Rainforest Alliance
5.2   Chiquita Banana and Mercenary Protection ... 319

Rajappa, Sampath
3.10 Fannie, Freddie, Wall Street, Main Street, and the Subprime Mortgage Market: Of Moral Hazards   123

Rajaratnam, Raj
4.18 If It's Legal, It's Ethical; and Besides, Everyone Does It   260

Rand, Ayn
1.3 What Are Ethics?   12

Rangel, Charlie
9.5 The Man Who Writes the Internal Revenue Code Has Tax Issues: The Rangel Round-Up   534

Rawls, John
1.3 What Are Ethics?   14

Red Cross
10.5 The Red Cross, New York, and Ground Zero   568

Reynolds, Burt
4.20 The Ethics of Bankruptcy   273

Rice, Kenneth D.
4.15 Enron: The CFO, Conflicts, and Cooking the Books with Natural Gas and Electricity   243

Rigas, John
3.8 Adelphia: Good Works via a Hand in the Till   113

Rights Theory (Entitlement Theory)
1.3 What Are Ethics?   14

RJR (R.J. Reynolds)
7.1 Joe Camel: The Cartoon Character Who Sold Cigarettes and Nearly Felled an Industry   425

Roehm, Julie
6.10 Julie Roehm: The Walmart Ad Exec with Expensive Tastes   370

Romney, Mitt
5.12 Salt Lake City, the Olympics, and Bribery   347

Royal Dutch/Shell Group
4.8 Royal Dutch and the Reserves   199

Rubin, Robert
2.11 What Was Up with Wall Street? The Goldman Standard and Shades of Gray   77
4.5 The Subprime Saga: Bear Stearns, Lehman, Merrill, and CDOs   182

Safeway
6.5 Plant Closings, Downsizings, Company Closings, Government Takeovers, Bankruptcies, and Pensions   359

Salomon Brothers/Salomon Smith Barney
4.27 WorldCom: The Little Company That Couldn't after All   295
6.9 The Analyst Who Needed a Preschool   367

Salquist, Roger
3.12 Ice-T, the *Body Count* Album, and Shareholder Uprisings   133

Sanborn, George
3.12 Ice-T, the *Body Count* Album, and Shareholder Uprisings   135

Sanders, Teresa
4.6 HealthSouth: The Scrushy Way   187

Sarbanes–Oxley Act (2002)
4.11 A Primer on Sarbanes–Oxley   212

Scally, Raouf
5.12   Salt Lake City, the Olympics, and Bribery   345

Schenkkan, Dick
7.20   Sears and High-Cost Auto Repairs   482

Schilling, Curt
3.13   Baseball and Steroids   138

Scrushy, Richard
1.4   The Types of Ethical Dilemmas: From Truth to Honesty to Conflicts   21
4.6   HealthSouth: The Scrushy Way   183

Sears
7.20   Sears and High-Cost Auto Repairs   481

Siemens
5.11   Siemens and Bribery, Everywhere   342

Simmons Mattress Company
8.8   Simmons, Mervyn's, and the Private Equity Firms That Bankrupt Them   511

Skilling, Jeffrey
2.8   On Leaving to Spend More Time with Family   69
4.15   Enron: The CFO, Conflicts, and Cooking the Books with Natural Gas and Electricity   236

Skyy Blue Malt Liquor
7.2   Spring Break, Beer, and Alcohol on Campus   431

Small, Lawrence M.
3.10   Fannie, Freddie, Wall Street, Main Street, and the Subprime Mortgage Market: Of Moral Hazards 124

Smith, Adam
1.3   What Are Ethics?   12
8.4   Adam Smith: An Excerpt from The Theory of Moral Sentiments   505

Social Contract (Theory of Justice)
1.3   What Are Ethics?   14

Société Générale
4.7   Jett and Kidder, Leeson and Barings, Kerviel and Société Générale: Compensation-Fueled Dishonesty 192

Solomon, Robert
1.3   What Are Ethics?   15

Sosa, Sammy
3.13   Baseball and Steroids   138

Southwest Airlines
6.5   Plant Closings, Downsizings, Company Closings, Government Takeovers, Bankruptcies, and Pensions 359

Spitzer, Eliot
7.16   The Mess at Marsh McLennan   466

Stanford University
9.10   Stanford University and Government Overhead Payments   542

Starwood
8.3   Starwood, Hilton, and the Suspiciously Similar New Hotel Designs   501

Steel, Robert
2.11   What Was Up with Wall Street? The Goldman Standard and Shades of Gray   77

Stem-Cell Research
7.22   Stem-Cell Research   487

Steroids
3.13   Baseball and Steroids   138

Stevens, Ted
9.17   The Prosecutors Who Withheld Evidence: The Senator's Trial   551

Stewart, Martha
2.7   Martha Stewart: Not Such a Good Thing   63

Stubbs, Stoney M. Jr.
3.12   Ice-T, the *Body Count* Album, and Shareholder Uprisings   135

Sullivan, Scott
4.27   WorldCom: The Little Company That Couldn't after All   298

Sunbeam, Inc.
4.19   A Primer on Accounting Issues and Ethics and Earnings Management   265

Swartz, Mark
4.13   Dennis Kozlowski: Tyco and the $6,000 Shower Curtain   226

Sysco
7.18   Slotting: Facilitation, Costs, or Bribery?   477

Tannin, Matthew M.
4.18   If It's Legal, It's Ethical; and Besides, Everyone Does It   259

Target
3.15   Dayton-Hudson's Contributions to Planned Parenthood, and Target and the Bell Ringers   146

Taser
9.15   Taser and Stunning Behavior   547

Taylor, Henry
2.3   Is Business Bluffing Ethical?   49

Tenneco
4.19   A Primer on Accounting Issues and Ethics and Earnings Management   263

Thain, John
2.11   What Was Up with Wall Street? The Goldman Standard and Shades of Gray   77

Theory of Justice (Social Contract)
1.3   What Are Ethics?   14

Thomas, Frank
3.13   Baseball and Steroids   138

Thomson, Todd S.
4.5   The Subprime Saga: Bear Stearns, Lehman, Merrill, and CDOs   179

Thornburgh, Richard
4.27   WorldCom: The Little Company That Couldn't after All   299

Tiffany
8.9   Tiffany, Louis Vuitton, eBay, Landlords, and Knock-Offs   514

Toro Company
7.23   Toro and Its Product Liability Program   489

Tourre, Fabrice
2.11   What Was Up with Wall Street? The Goldman Standard and Shades of Gray   79

Towers, Kevin
3.13   Baseball and Steroids   138

Toyota
6.15   Toyota, the CEO, the Assistant, and Inaction   381
7.12   Toyota: Sudden Acceleration or Bad Drivers or Pesky Floor Mats?   458

Transnational Shipping
5.3   Transnational Shipping and the Pirates   322

Tyco
4.9   Stock Options, Backdating, and Disclosure Options: What Happened Here?   201
6.20   Is It None of Our Business?   392

Tyco International
4.13   Dennis Kozlowski: Tyco and the $6,000 Shower Curtain   218

Tylenol
7.9   Tylenol: Decades of Dilemmas   444

United Airlines (UA)
3.9   The Regulatory Cycle, Social Responsibility, Business Strategy, and Equilibrium   119
6.5   Plant Closings, Downsizings, Company Closings, Government Takeovers, Bankruptcies, and Pensions   358

United Way
10.4   Giving and Spending the United Way   566

UnitedHealth Group
4.9   Stock Options, Backdating, and Disclosure Options: What Happened Here?   202

Van de Vijver, Walter
4.8   Royal Dutch and the Reserves   199

Vericon Resources, Inc.
1.12   Puffing Your Résumé   38

Verizon
6.5   Plant Closings, Downsizings, Company Closings, Government Takeovers, Bankruptcies, and Pensions   359

Vick, Michael
3.14   Michael Vick, Dogs, Rush Limbaugh, and the NFL   145

Villy Nielsen, APS
7.21   The Mommy Doll   487

Viniar, David
2.11   What Was Up with Wall Street? The Goldman Standard and Shades of Gray   79

Vinson, Betty
4.27   WorldCom: The Little Company That Couldn't after All   306

Vioxx
7.10   Merck and Vioxx   447

Waldron, John
5.6   On Sweatshops, Nike, and Kathie Lee   332

Walmart
6.10   Julie Roehm: The Walmart Ad Exec with Expensive Tastes   370

Watkins, Philip
4.6   HealthSouth: The Scrushy Way   189

Watkins, Sherron
4.15   Enron: The CFO, Conflicts, and Cooking the Books with Natural Gas and Electricity   239
4.16   Arthur Andersen: A Fallen Giant   248

Watts, Philip
4.8   Royal Dutch and the Reserves   199

Welch, Jack
6.19   Jack Welch and the Harvard Interview   387

Westland/Hallmark Meat Packing Company
2.1   What's Different about Business Ethics?   47
4.25   Westland/Hallmark Meat Packing Company and the Cattle Standers   288

Whistle-Blowers
4.22   The Options for Whistle-Blowers   279

White, Brent T.
4.21   The Ethics of Walking Away   275

White-Collar Crime Penalty Enhancement Act of 2002
4.11   A Primer on Sarbanes–Oxley   216

Whole Foods
3.11   Whole Foods, John Mackey, and Health Care Debates   132

Wilberforce, William
2.4   How Leaders Lose Their Way: What Price Hubris?   61

Winkelried, Jon
2.11   What Was Up with Wall Street? The Goldman Standard and Shades of Gray   82

Wolfowitz, Paul
9.7   Paul Wolfowitz and the World Bank   538

Woods, Tiger
1.4   The Types of Ethical Dilemmas: From Truth to Honesty to Conflicts   20

World Bank
9.7   Paul Wolfowitz and the World Bank   538

Worldcom
4.3   Why Corporations Can't Control Chicanery   165
4.9   Stock Options, Backdating, and Disclosure Options: What Happened Here?   201
4.27   WorldCom: The Little Company That Couldn't after All   293
6.20   Is It None of Our Business?   391
6.9   The Analyst Who Needed a Preschool   367

Wurzelbacher, Joseph
9.9   Joe the Plumber, Child Support Records, and the Public Official's Disclosure   540

Yahoo!
5.9   Google, Yahoo, and Human Rights in China   337

Yale University
9.11   Yale University and the Compensation of Professors for Government Research:
       Double-Dipping or Confusion?   545

Yoo, John
9.6   "I Was Just Following Orders": The CIA, Interrogations, and the Role of
       Legal Opinions in the Conduct of Organizations   536

Young, Frank
7.9   Tylenol: Decades of Dilemmas   444

YouTube
6.17   Facebook, MySpace, and YouTube Screening of Employees   385

Topic Index

Advertising
7.1   Joe Camel: The Cartoon Character Who Sold Cigarettes and Nearly Felled an Industry   425
7.2   Spring Break, Beer, and Alcohol on Campus   430
7.3   Cheerios and Cholesterol and Rice Krispies and Immunity   432
7.4   Subprime Loans–The Under-the-Radar Loans That Felled a Market   434
7.5   Hollywood Ads   438
7.6   Kraft, Barney Rubble, and Shrek   438
7.7   Craigslist and Ad Screening   439

Affirmative Action
6.12   On-the-Job Fetal Injuries   374
6.13   The Benefits of Diversity: Remarks of Doug Daft, Former CEO of Coca-Cola   376

Agency
6.6   JCPenney and Its Wealthy Buyer   361

Appropriation
8.12   The Little Intermittent Windshield Wiper and Its Little Inventor   520

Auditors
3.9   The Regulatory Cycle, Social Responsibility, Business Strategy, and Equilibrium   117
4.3   Why Corporations Can't Control Chicanery   164
4.16   Arthur Andersen: A Fallen Giant   246
4.27   WorldCom: The Little Company That Couldn't After All   293

Bankruptcy
4.15   Enron: The CFO, Conflicts, and Cooking the Books with Natural Gas and Electricity   233
4.20   The Ethics of Bankruptcy   272
4.27   WorldCom: The Little Company That Couldn't After All   293
8.8   Simmons, Mervyn's, and the Private Equity Firms That Bankrupt Them   511

Bribery
5.1   Why an International Code of Ethics Would Be Good for Business   315
5.3   Transnational Shipping and the Pirates   322
5.10   A Primer on the FCPA   340
5.11   Siemens and Bribery, Everywhere   342
5.12   Salt Lake City, the Olympics, and Bribery   344

Categorical Imperative
1.3   What Are Ethics? From Line-Cutting to Kant   10

Christian Consequentialism
5.6   On Sweatshops, Nike, and Kathie Lee   326
6.19   Jack Welch and the Harvard Interview   387

Compensation
4.4   The Effects of Compensation Systems: Incentives, Bonuses, Pay, and Ethics   172
4.7   Jett and Kidder, Leeson and Barings, Kerviel and Société Générale: Compensation-Fueled Dishonesty   192
4.10   FINOVA and the Loan Write-Off   206
4.13   Dennis Kozlowski: Tyco and the $6,000 Shower Curtain   218
6.5   Plant Closings, Downsizings, Company Closings, Government Takeovers, Bankruptcies, and Pensions   358

Competition
7.16   The Mess at Marsh McLennan   465
7.18   Slotting: Facilitation, Costs, or Bribery?   472

8.1 A Primer on Covenants Not to Compete: Are They Valid? 495
8.2 Boeing, Lockheed, and the Documents 496
8.3 Starwood, Hilton, and the Suspiciously Similar New Hotel Designs 501
8.4 Adam Smith: An Excerpt from *The Theory of Moral Sentiments* 505
8.5 The Coke Employee Who Offered Inside Information to Pepsi 506

Conflicts of Interest
6.6 JCPenney and Its Wealthy Buyer 361
6.10 Julie Roehm: The Walmart Ad Exec with Expensive Tastes 370
8.2 Boeing, Lockheed, and the Documents 496
9.16 Boeing and the Recruiting of the Government Purchasing Agent 548
10.6 The Cornell Researchers Funded by the Foundation 569

Contracts
4.21 The Ethics of Walking Away 275
7.19 Intel and the Chips: When You Have Made a Mistake 478
7.20 Sears and High-Cost Auto Repairs 481
8.1 A Primer on Covenants Not to Compete: Are They Valid? 495
8.3 Starwood, Hilton, and the Suspiciously Similar New Hotel Designs 501

Contributions
3.8 Adelphia: Good Works via a Hand in the Till 113
3.15 Dayton-Hudson's Contributions to Planned Parenthood, and Target and the Bell Ringers 146
10.1 New Era: If It Sounds Too Good to Be True, It Is Too Good to Be True 559
10.2 The Baptist Foundation: Funds of the Faithful 562
10.4 Giving and Spending the United Way 566
10.5 The Red Cross, New York, and Ground Zero 568

Cookie Jar Reserves
4.19 A Primer on Accounting Issues and Ethics and Earnings Management 262

Copyright Infringement
8.9 Tiffany, Louis Vuitton, eBay, Landlords, and Knock-Offs 514
8.10 Copyright, Songs, and Charities 518
8.11 Microsoft vs. Google and "Snippets" of Books 519
8.12 The Little Intermittent Windshield Wiper and Its Little Inventor 520

Corporate Governance
2.4 How Leaders Lose Their Way: What Price Hubris? 59
2.6 $P = f(x)$ The Probability of an Ethical Outcome Is a Function of the Amount of Money Involved: Pressure 62
4.3 Why Corporations Can't Control Chicanery 164
4.5 The Subprime Saga: Bear Stearns, Lehman, Merrill, and CDOs 176
4.9 Stock Options, Backdating, and Disclosure Options: What Happened Here? 200
4.11 A Primer on Sarbanes–Oxley 212
4.12 Bank of America: The Merrill Takeover, the Disclosures, and the Board 216
4.14 Bausch & Lomb and Krispy Kreme: Channel Stuffing and Cannibalism 228
4.17 The New Shareholder: Taking Over to Change the Culture 253
4.18 If It's Legal, It's Ethical; and Besides, Everyone Does It 257
4.26 Getting Information from Employees Who Know to Those Who Can and Will Respond 289
4.28 Bernie Madoff: Just Stay Away from the 17th Floor 311
5.4 The Former Soviet Union: A Study of Three Companies: PwC, Ikea, and AES 323
6.1 Two Sets of Books on Safety 353
6.3 Cintas and OSHA 354
6.16 Arizona Senate Bill 1070: Immigration Laws, Employers, Enforcement, and Emotion 382
8.4 Adam Smith: An Excerpt from *The Theory of Moral Sentiments* 505

Deontology
6.18 Bloggers, Chat Rooms, and E-Mail: Your Employer Is Watching 386
6.23 Ann Hopkins and Price Waterhouse 399

Discrimination
6.11 English-Only Employer Policies 370
6.12 On-the-Job Fetal Injuries 374
6.16 Arizona Senate Bill 1070: Immigration Laws, Employers, Enforcement, and Emotion 382
6.23 Ann Hopkins and Price Waterhouse 399

Divine Command
1.3   What Are Ethics? From Line-Cutting to Kant   10
1.8   Some Simple Tests for Resolving Ethical Dilemmas   29

Downsizing
6.4   Aaron Feuerstein and Malden Mills   356
6.5   Plant Closings, Downsizings, Company Closings, Government Takeovers, Bankruptcies, and Pensions   358

EBITA
4.19   A Primer on Accounting Issues and Ethics and Earnings Management   262
4.27   WorldCom: The Little Company That Couldn't After All   293

Egoism
1.3   What Are Ethics? From Line-Cutting to Kant   10
4.27   WorldCom: The Little Company That Couldn't After All   293

Environment
3.3   Business with a Soul: A Reexamination of What Counts in Business Ethics   101
3.16   The New Environmentalism   149
3.17   Herman Miller and Its Rain Forest Chairs   151
3.18   The Death of the Great Disposable Diaper Debate   153
6.24   Exxon and Alaska   405
6.25   BP: Pipeline, Refinery, and Offshore-Drilling Safety   411

Equity
4.15   Enron: The CFO, Conflicts, and Cooking the Books with Natural Gas and Electricity   233
4.20   The Ethics of Bankruptcy   272
8.8   Simmons, Mervyn's, and the Private Equity Firms That Bankrupt Them   511

Executive Compensation
2.11   What Was Up with Wall Street? The Goldman Standard and Shades of Gray   73
3.10   Fannie, Freddie, Wall Street, Main Street, and the Subprime Mortgage Market: Of Moral Standards   121
4.3   Why Corporations Can't Control Chicanery   164
4.4   The Effects of Compensation Systems: Incentives, Bonuses, Pay, and Ethics   172

Finance
2.11   What Was Up with Wall Street? The Goldman Standard and Shades of Gray   73
3.10   Fannie, Freddie, Wall Street, Main Street, and the Subprime Mortgage Market: Of Moral Standards   121
4.5   The Subprime Saga: Bear Stearns, Lehman, Merrill, and CDOs   176
4.11   A Primer on Sarbanes–Oxley   212
4.16   Arthur Andersen: A Fallen Giant   246
4.18   If It's Legal, It's Ethical; and Besides, Everyone Does It   257
4.21   The Ethics of Walking Away   275
4.27   WorldCom: The Little Company That Couldn't After All   293
4.28   Bernie Madoff: Just Stay Away from the 17th Floor   311
6.7   The Trading Desk, Perks, and "Dwarf Tossing"   362
6.9   The Analyst Who Needed a Preschool   367
7.4   Subprime Loans–The Under-the-Radar Loans That Felled a Market   434

Foreign Countries–Differing Business Practices
5.1   Why an International Code of Ethics Would Be Good for Business   315
5.2   Chiquita Bananas and Mercenary Protection   319
5.4   The Former Soviet Union: A Study of Three Companies: PwC, Ikea, and AES   323
5.5   Product Dumping   325
5.6   On Sweatshops, Nike, and Kathie Lee   326
5.7   Bhopal: When Safety Standards DIffer   333
5.9   Google, Yahoo, and Human Rights in China   337
5.12   Salt Lake City, the Olympics, and Bribery   344

Gifts
4.1   The Moving Line   159
5.12   Salt Lake City, the Olympics, and Bribery   344
6.7   The Trading Desk, Perks, and "Dwarf Tossing"   362
6.8   Docs, Pharmas, Medical Journals, Funded Research, and Pizza   363
9.2   The Minerals Management Service: The Arms-Length Affairs with Oil Executives   527

Government Contracts

4.11	A Primer on Sarbanes–Oxley	212
4.27	WorldCom: The Little Company That Couldn't After All	293
8.2	Boeing, Lockheed, and the Documents	496
9.10	Stanford University and Government Overhead Payments	542
9.11	Yale University and the Compensation of Professors for Government Research: Double-Dipping or Confusion?	545
9.12	Minority-Owned Businesses and Reality	545
9.13	The My Tai Concession and the County Supervisor	546
9.14	Government Pricing and Finding a Way Around It	546
9.15	Taser and Stunning Behavior	547
9.16	Boeing and the Recruiting of the Government Purchasing Agent	548

Government Employees

1.17	Speeding on the Job: Obeying the Rules: Why We Do and Don't	42
9.1	The Fish Bowl Existence of Government	525
9.2	The Minerals Management Service: The Arms-Length Affairs with Oil Executives	527
9.3	Kodak, the Appraiser, and the Assessor: Lots of Back Scratching on Valuation	531
9.4	The Governor and a Senate Seat Vacated by a President	532
9.5	The Man Who Writes the Internal Revenue Code Has Tax Issues: The Rangel Round-Up	534
9.6	"I Was Just Following Orders": The CIA, Interrogations, and the Role of Legal Opinions in the Conduct of Organizations	536
9.7	Paul Wolfowitz and the World Bank	538
9.8	Hiding the Slip-Up on Oil Lease Accounting: Interior Motives	538
9.9	Joe the Plumber, Child Support Records, and the Public Official's Disclosure	540

Government Responsibilities

9.6	"I Was Just Following Orders": The CIA, Interrogations, and the Role of Legal Opinions in the Conduct of Organizations	536
9.17	The Prosecutors Who Withheld Evidence: The Senator's Trial	551
9.18	The Duke Lacrosse Team and the Prosecutor	551
9.19	FEMA, Hurricane Katrina, and the Dilemmas of Regulation versus Human Life	554

Grease Payments

5.1	Why an International Code of Ethics Would Be Good for Business	315
5.10	A Primer on the FCPA	340
5.12	Salt Lake City, the Olympics, and Bribery	344

Health

3.11	Whole Foods, John Mackey, and Health Care Debates	132
3.13	Baseball and Steroids	138
4.6	HealthSouth: The Scrushy Way	183
5.8	Nestlé: When Products Translate Differently	335
6.8	Docs, Pharmas, Medical Journals, Funded Research, and Pizza	363
7.1	Joe Camel: The Cartoon Character Who Sold Cigarettes and Nearly Felled an Industry	425
7.2	Spring Break, Beer, and Alcohol on Campus	430
7.3	Cheerios and Cholesterol and Rice Krispies and Immunity	432
7.9	Tylenol: Decades of Dilemmas	444
7.10	Merck and Vioxx	447
7.13	E. coli, Jack-in-the-Box, and Cooking Temperatures	461
7.14	Peanut Corporation of America and Salmonella	462
7.15	Pfizer and the $2.3 Billion Fine for Sales Tactics	464
7.22	Stem-Cell Research	487
7.24	Fast Food Liability	490

Honesty

1.10	The Little Teacher Who Could: Piper, Kansas, and Term Papers	34
1.15	Wi-Fi Piggybacking	41
1.16	The Ethics Officer and First Class for TSA	41
2.2	The Ethics of Responsibility	48
2.3	Is Business Bluffing Ethical?	49
2.7	Martha Stewart: Not Such a Good Thing	63
2.13	Travel Expenses: A Chance for Extra Income	84
2.15	The Rigged Election	86
4.7	Jett and Kidder, Leeson and Barings, Kerviel and Société Générale: Compensation-Fueled Dishonesty	192

4.8	Royal Dutch and the Reserves	199
4.9	Stock Options, Backdating, and Disclosure Options: What Happened Here?	200
4.11	A Primer on Sarbanes–Oxley	212
4.20	The Ethics of Bankruptcy	272
6.6	JCPenney and Its Wealthy Buyer	361
6.21	The Glowing Recommendation	395
6.22	The Ethics of Confrontation	396

Inside Information

2.7	Martha Stewart: Not Such a Good Thing	63
2.11	What Was Up with Wall Street? The Goldman Standard and Shades of Gray	73
4.2	Not All Employees Are Equal When It Comes to Moral Development	160
4.18	If It's Legal, It's Ethical; and Besides, Everyone Does It	257
8.6	The Compliance Officer Who Strayed	508

Internal Audit/Controls

2.13	Travel Expenses: A Chance for Extra Income	84
4.10	FINOVA and the Loan Write-Off	206
4.13	Dennis Kozlowski: Tyco and the $6,000 Shower Curtain	218
4.14	Bausch & Lomb and Krispy Kreme: Channel Stuffing and Cannibalism	228
4.15	Enron: The CFO, Conflicts, and Cooking the Books with Natural Gas and Electricity	233

Mergers and Acquisitions

4.13	Dennis Kozlowski: Tyco and the $6,000 Shower Curtain	218
4.27	WorldCom: The Little Company That Couldn't After All	293
8.8	Simmons, Mervyn's, and the Private Equity Firms That Bankrupt Them	511

Misrepresentation

2.16	West Virginia University and the Governor's Daughter	86
7.20	Sears and High-Cost Auto Repairs	481

Moral Responsibility

1.13	Dad, the Actuary, and the Stats Class	39
4.21	The Ethics of Walking Away	275
6.20	Is It None of Our Business?	390
7.11	Ford and Its Pinto and GM and Its Malibu: The Repeating Exploding Gas Tank Problem	452
7.12	Toyota: Sudden Acceleration or Bad Drivers or Pesky Floor Mats?	458
7.13	E. coli, Jack-in-the-Box, and Cooking Temperatures	461
7.14	Peanut Corporation of America and Salmonella	462
9.6	"I Was Just Following Orders": The CIA, Interrogations, and the Role of Legal Opinions in the Conduct of Organizations	536

NGOs

3.16	The New Environmentalism	149

Nonprofit Organizations

10.1	New Era: If It Sounds Too Good to Be True, It Is Too Good to Be True	559
10.2	The Baptist Foundation: Funds of the Faithful	562
10.3	ACORN: Community Organizers, Undercover Videos, and Advice	565
10.4	Giving and Spending the United Way	566
10.5	The Red Cross, New York, and Ground Zero	568
10.6	The Cornell Researchers Funded by the Foundation	569

Options

4.9	Stock Options, Backdating, and Disclosure Options: What Happened Here?	200

Plant Closings

6.4	Aaron Feuerstein and Malden Mills	356
6.5	Plant Closings, Downsizings, Company Closings, Government Takeovers, Bankruptcies, and Pensions	358

Pricing

7.16	The Mess at Marsh McLennan	465

Privacy

5.9	Google, Yahoo, and Human Rights in China	337
6.18	Bloggers, Chat Rooms, and E-Mail: Your Employer Is Watching	386

6.20   Is It None of Our Business?   390
10.3   ACORN: Community Organizers, Undercover Videos, and Advice   565

Product Quality
4.23   Beech-Nut and the No-Apple-Juice Apple Juice   280
4.24   NASA and the Space Shuttle Booster Rockets   285
4.25   Westland/Hallmark Meat Packing Company and the Cattle Standers   288
5.5   Product Dumping   325
7.9   Tylenol: Decades of Dilemmas   444

Product Safety
7.8   A Primer on Product Liability   441
7.9   Tylenol: Decades of Dilemmas   444
7.10   Merck and Vioxx   447
7.11   Ford and Its Pinto and GM and Its Malibu: The Repeating Exploding Gas Tank Problem   452
7.12   Toyota: Sudden Acceleration or Bad Drivers or Pesky Floor Mats?   458
7.13   E. coli, Jack-in-the-Box, and Cooking Temperatures   461
7.14   Peanut Corporation of America and Salmonella   462

Property Rights
8.9   Tiffany, Louis Vuitton, eBay, Landlords, and Knock-Offs   514
8.12   The Little Intermittent Windshield Wiper and Its Little Inventor   520

Purchasing Agents
6.6   JCPenney and Its Wealthy Buyer   361
6.8   Docs, Pharmas, Medical Journals, Funded Research, and Pizza   363
6.9   The Analyst Who Needed a Preschool   367
7.17   Frozen Coke and Burger King and the Richmond Rigging   468
9.14   Government Pricing and Finding a Way Around It   546

Securities Fraud
2.7   Martha Stewart: Not Such a Good Thing   63
8.7   Jonathan Lebed: The Middle School Tycoon   510

Sexual Harassment
6.14   *Seinfeld* in the Workplace   380
6.15   Toyota, the CEO, the Assistant, and Inaction   381
6.21   The Glowing Recommendation   395

Shareholder Rights
2.11   What Was Up with Wall Street? The Goldman Standard and Shades of Gray   73
3.2   A Stakeholder Theory of the Modern Corporation   96
3.3   Business with a Soul: A Reexamination of What Counts in Business Ethics   101
3.4   Appeasing Stakeholders with Public Relations   104
3.5   Michael Novak on Capitalism and the Corporation   105
3.6   Marjorie Kelly and the Divine Right of Capital   108
3.7   Schools of Thought on Social Responsibility   111
3.8   Adelphia: Good Works via a Hand in the Till   113
3.10   Fannie, Freddie, Wall Street, Main Street, and the Subprime Mortgage Market: Of Moral Standards   121
3.12   Ice-T, the *Body Count* Album, and Shareholder Uprisings   133
4.17   The New Shareholder: Taking Over to Change the Culture   253

Social Responsibility
2.8   On Leaving to Spend More Time with Family   69
3.1   The Social Responsibility of Business Is to Increase Its Profits   91
3.2   A Stakeholder Theory of the Modern Corporation   96
3.3   Business with a Soul: A Reexamination of What Counts in Business Ethics   101
3.4   Appeasing Stakeholders with Public Relations   104
3.5   Michael Novak on Capitalism and the Corporation   105
3.6   Marjorie Kelly and the Divine Right of Capital   108
3.7   Schools of Thought on Social Responsibility   111
3.8   Adelphia: Good Works via a Hand in the Till   113
3.10   Fannie, Freddie, Wall Street, Main Street, and the Subprime Mortgage Market: Of Moral Standards   121
3.11   Whole Foods, John Mackey, and Health Care Debates   132
3.13   Baseball and Steroids   138